COLLEGE
SCHOLARSHIPS
AND FINANCIAL AID

ARCO

COLLEGE SCHOLARSHIPS

AND FINANCIAL AID

John Schwartz, Staff Writer, *Washington Post*

Wintergreen / Orchard House, Inc.

New Orleans, Louisiana • Brunswick, Maine

MACMILLAN • USA

Seventh Edition

Macmillan General Reference
A Simon & Schuster Macmillan Company
1633 Broadway
New York, NY 10019-6785

An Arco Book

MACMILLAN is a registered trademark of Macmillan, Inc.
ARCO is a registered trademark of Prentice-Hall, Inc.

Manufactured in the United States of America

10 9 8 7 6 5 4 3 2 1

ISBN: 0-02-861928-5

Contents

A Word of Thanks

This is the seventh edition of *College Scholarships and Financial Aid*. When I first approached the project, I was a newly-minted reporter for *Newsweek On Campus*, the famous newsweekly's five-year experiment in producing a magazine for the college market. College financial aid was an interesting, if abstract, subject. A lot has changed in the ensuing years—I now write about science and other topics for *The Washington Post*, have three kids, and have begun to worry in earnest about paying for their college educations. That's justice, I suppose.

A book like this would not be possible without the selfless work of professionals in the financial aid field whose job it is to get the word out and who don't seem to mind when guys like me recycle their labors for money. Madeleine McLean Longano, Associate Director of Communications for the National Association of Student Financial Aid Administrators, has been a consistent source of good stuff. So has Jerry S. Davis, Research Director for SALLIE MAE, the Student Loan Marketing Association, who in his previous incarnation at the Pennsylvania Higher Education Authority compiled an annual goldmine of state financial aid information. Mr. Davis has shown a geniality and grace under pressure that all of us could learn from. Thanks also to my editors at ARCO and the good folks at Wintergreen/Orchard House, who compile the databases and make this book work. This year, Judith Lewenthal again came to the rescue as researcher. Overqualified for all that she tackles, Judy nonetheless consented to lend her considerable skills to the effort.

As I write this, my family is asleep nearby, so rather than wake them I'll just thank them here. Jeanne, my wife, has suffered through my awful work hours and worse work habits. The kids, too, are a powerful incentive for me to learn as much as possible about paying for college: daughter Elizabeth, now almost ten, is a constant source of wonder; Sam Austin has charged toward the seven-year mark pretty much intact. And then there's Joey, the one-year-old newcomer who has come into my life late enough so that I will eventually be paying his tuition bills with my socal security checks. Without them, none of this would be necessary.

Introduction

The last time we published this book, we were two years into the first Democratic administration in more than a decade. The previous administration didn't spend a lot of time worrying about making college more affordable, but Bill Clinton made improving financial aid one of his top priorities. His campaign was focused on a single issue—"It's the economy, stupid" was the sign in the War Room in Little Rock—and paying for college was a perfect middle-class hot button. More important, it was one of the issues Clinton seemed actually to care deeply about. As he spoke of a program of national service that would encourage volunteerism and defray college costs, you could tell that it came from the heart. Arkansas, after all, is not a rich state. Clinton could see daily what needed to be done. And while promises of financial aid reform alone did not elect Bill Clinton, it's clear that it was part of the package of planned reforms that helped to put him over the top.

At this writing, a half year into his second term, Clinton has not made much headway against making college more affordable for all Americans—he has announced big programs, but has not been able to push bills that match that vision through Congress. Clinton passed a national service program and created a new "direct lending" system that bypasses commercial institutions and has called for megabucks in new financial aid. The Republican political leadership has targeted each of those programs for caps, cuts, or dismantling.

More on that later. For the purposes of this introduction, let me simply say that times really are changing. Read your newspaper: The news, now more than any time in the last two decades, could create new opportunities—or take them away—overnight.

The positive early response to Clinton's proposals underscores the basic point of this book: Financial aid is not just for the needy any more. Considering the high cost of college today, *everyone* is needy. Everybody could use a little help paying for the kids' college education—well, maybe not Ross Perot, but certainly the rest of us. Tuition has long had a habit of rising faster than the rate of inflation. The costliest schools demand some $26,000 in tuition and residential fees each year, and the College Board estimates that the average four-year private college costs nearly $12,823 annually. Public schools, while cheaper, top $3,500 annually, for in-state students.

The good news is that a college education is still not out of reach for just about anybody who really wants it. Things are not getting any easier, but it can be done. "For most Americans, the fact remains that college is still accessible, especially in light of financial aid currently available," said College Board president Donald M. Stewart said in September 1996. "Focusing too much on the highest-priced institutions overstates the problem and unduly alarms the public."

Schools know that they cost too darned much, and many of them are now struggling to find ways to provide value—or, at least, the *image* of value—to students. In a recent story on offbeat tuition plans, *Washington Post* staff writer Rene Sanchez wrote that "Colleges across the country have begun trying to recruit and keep students worried about soaring tuition costs with a brand-new sales pitch: Let's make a deal." While warning that some bargains could be exaggerated, Sanchez cited several innovative schemes:

• Michigan State has pledged to incoming freshmen that tuition won't rise any faster than inflation for the next four years.

• Indiana University promises that some students who can't take all of their required course work within a four-year program (since some required courses aren't available every semester) will get the fifth year for free.

• Middlebury College in Vermont, like several other small, expensive liberal arts colleges, has created a three-year degree program to help cut costs by as much as $18,000 overall.

Cost consciousness has put more pressure than ever on schools, David Warren, president of the National Association of Independent Colleges and Universities, told Sanchez, "creating a lot of experiments with tuition prices. I don't know a university president who is not engaged in strategic planning along these lines."

We put together this book to help you do a little strategic planning of your own, to help you get the money you need to pay for college. The aid maze is so complex that most of us could use a friendly guide. Yet so many of the guides to getting financial aid are not what computer types call "user-friendly." In fact, some seem almost user-hostile. Most could put Sominex out of business. They are dull, wordy, and overly complex. This book is intended to be different—lively, easy to read, and to the point. The book describes the many avenues to financial aid. It shows how you can plan to pay for your college education. And it even takes you by the hand in filling out cumbersome financial aid applications. We have tried to make this the most useful, readable guide to financial aid on the market today. But it is not a guide for everyone: In the first place, we have chosen principally to provide information pertaining to undergraduates looking for financial aid.

We've done some selecting for you already. Several scholarship guides we have come across fatten their pages with thousands of scholarships that are next to useless. They may apply to too few people, offering money to, say, blue-eyed virgins from Lourdes, Tennessee. If you qualify, you probably already know about that scholarship. And if you aren't a blue-eyed virgin from Lourdes, Tennessee, you can't get the money. So why include it? Other scholarships are a little, well, chintzy—some don't even cover the cost of textbooks. We decided to provide you with a realistic list. Most scholarship sources in this book provide an award of at least $1,000 annually.

At the same time, you need to keep in mind that more than 80 percent of all aid comes from federal and state programs, not the private scholarships listed here. So while we give you a healthy list of private scholarships, we encourage you to focus your attention on the sources of aid that matter—the government programs discussed here in the front of the book—before you spin your wheels applying to every program under the sun.

This guide is regularly updated. Financial aid programs aren't etched in stone; they change from year to year depending on factors ranging from the whims of Congress to losses incurred by the stock portfolios of the foundations behind their grants. Often factors affect higher education funding from directions no one could ever predict. Take for example the effects of fuel prices on the University of Texas. During the mid-1980s, the Organization of Oil Producing and Exporting Countries lost its self-discipline and flooded world markets with oil, dropping fuel prices and setting off a disastrous recession in oil-producing American states like Texas. The Texas recession spun out of control, dragging down with it the banking, real estate, and agriculture sectors of the economy. The Texas legislature, scrambling to make up for the lost tax revenues, raised college tuition across the board—without commensurately raising financial aid. Thus what was widely considered one of the best bargains in American higher education became a mere good deal. Using an up-to-date guide gives you the edge in calculating tuition dollars, shopping for aid money, and anticipating unpleasant surprises.

Before you go any further—Do you really want to go to college? Ask yourself that question. If you have bought this book, you probably have already decided that college is the way to go. But what if you're not planning to follow the standard business route? Maybe deep in your heart of hearts you know you're a plumber. You have loved pipes and joints since infancy. You have a plumber's soul. Though a degree in mechanical engineering might enhance your appreciation of the plumbing aesthetic, you don't need it to get started. Considering that a Manhattan plumber makes more than $50 an hour, college begins to look like a lot of time and money down the drain.

If you do decide to skip college, you'll be in good company. Among the noncollegiate, you will find such well-known authors as Ernest Hemingway and Rudyard Kipling, as well as Abraham Lincoln and Wee Kim Wee, president of Singapore. Other famous people, like Walter Cronkite and Apple Computer cofounder Steven Jobs, left college before graduating.

In all fairness to the colleges, it should be noted that many of the noncollege success stories decided not to go onto higher education at a time (or in a culture) in which a degree was less than essential. Uncle Sam democratized college after World War II by paying for the educations of millions of returning servicemen. That college-educated generation expected its kids to go to college, too. More and more Americans are going to college: According to the Bureau of Labor Statistics, nearly half of workers aged 25 to 64 in the U.S. have had some college experience, and 26 percent of workers in that group have had at least four years of college. So it's harder than before to buck the trend.

Besides—while there are a lot of college-educated taxicab drivers, there's also plenty of evidence that going to college pays. Studies regularly show that college graduates earn more than those who do not attend. Higher education simply gives you a leg up in the job market. The Bureau of Labor Statistics reports that nearly 90 percent of people with four or more years of college are in the labor force: that means that they are either working or looking for work. People with a high school degree alone don't fare so well: only 77 percent of that group is in the labor force. A January 1988 report entitled *The Forgotten Half: Non-College Youth in America* says, "The plight of the young person without advanced education, never easy, has become alarming in recent years." The report went on to say, "In a fast-changing economy that demands increasingly specialized skills, these young people are in danger of being left at the starting gate." The business world pays attention to credentials (maybe too much attention, but that's a subject for a different book), and a college degree is one of the basics. And the professions are getting more specialized, not less.

Ultimately, the value of a college education has to be measured in terms that go beyond the balance sheet. Something about dollar signs and decimal points flattens the wonder inherent in the college experience. It's about forming lifelong friendships, and more. I met my wife the week before classes started my freshman year; we first kissed in a dorm lounge while studying for a history exam. Friends from college days now work all over the world—as lawyers, political consultants, journalists, cartoonists and more. I'd be much poorer for not having known them.

Treated right, higher education is a four-year excursion into the life of the mind, with opportunities for gaining knowledge and personal growth. At its best, college teaches you how to learn, so that you can tackle any task set before you. With the right courses, you can heighten your appreciation of literature and the arts, making the acquisition of knowledge a lifelong pleasure. Yes, it's important to find the money to pay for school. But once the financial side is taken care of, enjoy! Take advantage of this unique opportunity to broaden your horizons and expand your powers of thought.

Anyone Can Pay for College

1. The Short Course: What This Section Will Tell You

In effect, this chapter serves as a short version of the book, with fundamental information about financial aid for people in a hurry. You'll find capsule descriptions of the basic kinds of financial aid, some tips here and there, and a few warnings to make sure you don't lose out. The chapter also includes a long-term and short-term view of trends in paying for college that could help you plan for the near and distant future.

2. There Are Right and Wrong Ways to Pay for College

In *Citizen Kane*, Charles Foster Kane tells an associate, "It ought to be easy to make money—if that's all you want to do." When he made that statement, Kane—like the man he was modeled on, publishing magnate William Randolph Hearst—was a millionaire many times over. You, the reader, are probably not a millionaire many times over. Even if Kane was right, college is not the time to make moneymaking your sole goal. When you're going to college, the last thing you want to do is to spend so much time trying to pay the bills that you can't enjoy the experience—or worse, can't keep up with your studies.

There are plenty of bad ways to pay your way through college. The most common is simple overwork: taking on two or more jobs to make ends meet. One friend of mine worked his way through law school with no less than three part-time jobs. He ended up spending a semester recuperating from hepatitis, and almost had to put off graduating. (Today he's a successful attorney—still overworked, but getting paid handsomely for it.) Other diseases, such as mononucleosis, commonly spring from exhaustion. Why ruin four great years of your life by keeping your nose so close to the grindstone that you can't even enjoy your studies, much less develop a social life? If you decide to work through your college days, choose your employment wisely. Later in this book, we give you some tips on creating your own small business in order to earn money, and direct you to guides that show schemes that have worked for students in the past.

Another way to pay college expenses that gets students into trouble is taking on an oversized debt burden. Taking on a certain amount of debt has become just about unavoidable, as loan money has replaced a lot of the grant money in the average financial aid package. But education funding experts have warned that taking on too heavy a burden of debts may cause students to look toward safer, higher-paying careers than they might otherwise be attracted to. The same experts also fear that the prospect of being in debt could be enough to scare many lower-income students away from college, or from majors they might find personally fulfilling (say, teaching or fine arts) but which they feel will never allow them to repay the loans. We lose a lot of good teachers to the ranks of lawyers and engineers that way. While student loans are an increasingly important part of financial aid packages, most schools still have some discretion as to how much of your aid package should be made up of loans and how much should be made up of outside grants. (It is sometimes possible to get a college financial aid officer to alter the makeup of a financial aid package.) Parents have to decide, when looking at financial aid packages, how much pain they can stand—and how much of the debt burden they can, in good conscience, shift to their kids. We'll return to these topics a little later.

Some ideas aren't just bad: they're illegal. Shady moneymaking schemes attract a number of students for the same reason that they attract criminals: quick money, and lots of it. However, the risk often outweighs the reward, and few students show the street smarts to escape the long arm of the law. In my college days, a few acquaintances tried to hustle up extra money by dealing drugs. None of them were arrested, but most found they lost money more often than made it. Their college education had not yet honed their business skills, and besides, they generally had trouble keeping out of the inventory. One friend was clubbed to death, apparently because of a deal gone sour. There have got to be better ways to raise a buck than that. (In case you were wondering, most of my college friends, like the overworked law student, were fine, upstanding young people who have terrific jobs today.)

The purpose of this book is to help you spend your time wisely and to get the maximum amount of financial aid funds from the most lucrative sources. That way, you'll be less likely to run yourself into the ground trying to make up for aid money you might otherwise have gotten.

3. Figuring Out What College Will Really Cost

The student is more than just a seeker of knowledge—he or she is also a consumer in the academic marketplace. And all good shoppers know the value of comparison shopping. Comparing colleges, while a complex task, pays off. The main areas of comparison are these: tuition and fees, books and supplies, room and board, transportation, and personal expenses. Most colleges publish a "consumer brochure"—a handy resource that sets out expenses. That brochure is a helpful starting point for any student or family.

Tuition and fees vary widely, but the most basic dividing line between institutions is public versus private. Private schools simply tend to be pricier. But before you strike all private schools from your list, consider this: Public schools are far from cheap—and out-of-state tuition at many of the most respected public universities rivals that of the average private school.

Books and supplies don't vary as much from school to school as do tuition and fees, but they can add hundreds of dollars each semester to the bill and must be counted in. These costs vary depending on the field of study, so it is important to find out typical figures from the academic department or from students within the major.

Room and board can make up a huge chunk of college costs. Room and board can be measured simply if the student is living in a dormitory: it's part of the total bill. According to the College Board, in 1996 the average cost of room and board at four-year private colleges was $5,166; at public schools, $4,152. Both had risen about five percent over the previous year's figure. But don't think living at home will simply clear that cost from the college budget. For one thing, you won't save as much money as you think on wholesome, home-cooked meals. Irregular class hours will force the student to buy at least one meal a day on or near campus. And if the student is going to live off campus, living expenses could run even higher, with variations from school to school. The differences between paying for an apartment in Athens, Georgia, and Cambridge, Massachusetts, are enough to skew comparisons of schools that might otherwise appear to be similarly priced.

Personal expenses may add up to more than parents expect. Although students have historically lived on the cheap, the Benetton generation is more prone to fancy accessories than its grubbier parents, for whom a year-old pair of (non-designer) blue jeans could be considered formal wear. Even the Seattle/Grunge look could be expensive if you went to fancy department stores for those fashionably worn-out lumberjack shirts. Again, geographic variation wreaks havoc on expense estimates. Travel expenses might include air fare for out-of-state students or simply gas and car repair for commuters. In any case, this easily overlooked category can add thousands to the college bundle of costs. Finally, don't forget to add in known medical costs, such as treatment and pharmaceuticals for an existing medical condition.

When you start to see the real cost of college, you might give serious consideration to getting a degree from one of those institutions that advertises on matchbook covers, or to exploring a career in auto repair. DON'T PANIC! Expensive institutions know that they cost more than most people can pay, and they often have the resources to help you. After all, if the students don't come, they have to shut their doors.

Once you know what different schools might cost, it's time to work out what you and your family can afford to pay. Taking the difference between what the college costs and what you can afford to pay gives you the amount of your need. This deceptively simple term, "need," doesn't necessarily mean what you think it ought to mean, or what you would like for it to mean. It's a specific, technical term for the amount you cannot pay on your own, and is the amount left after your Expected Family Contribution (EFC) is subtracted from your cost of education. Schools determine how much families should pay based on sets of formulas that each institution chooses. Some choose the federal formulas established by Congress, while others go by what's known as the Institutional Methodology. So it's important to make sure you know what each school you'll be applying to expects to know; one size does not fit all.

Financial assistance comes in three basic flavors: grants, loans, and work-study. Grants do not need to be repaid, while loans must be repaid some day. In 1996, according to the College Board, grants represented 42 percent, and loans 57 percent, of total federal, state, and institutional student aid. Work-study lets students work in order to gain the money to pay for school. You and the financial aid administrator at the college of your choice will negotiate a financial assistance package that will probably contain some combination of these three varieties of aid.

Your aid will come from a number of sources, from the most massive federal programs down to institutional funds unique to your school. Aid might come from the state, private foundations, the school, or even an employer. If the aid comes from a federal government program or a state agency, it is known as public aid; sources such as employers, donors, or foundations are known as private aid.

4. Financial Aid: What It Is

Federal Aid

Since the federal government is the largest source of student aid, it pays to know something about the major federal programs. The federal government, through the Department of Education, offers the best-known college financial aid programs. These are:

Pell Grants

In 1996, some 14 percent of American college students received Pell Grants. This program was once known as the Basic Educational Opportunity Grant program, and you might see it referred to as such in older materials. These grants are distributed based on family need and education costs at your school. The maximum available in the 1997–98 school year is $2,700 per year, though the maximum amount changes from year to year depending on how Congress funds the program. The average grant reported in a 1994 study by the census bureau was $1,375. Eligibility is determined by a standard formula which was passed into law by Congress; that calculates your Expected Family Contribution. If that EFC figure falls below a certain threshold, you'll be eligible for a Pell. Once you've applied for aid, you'll receive a Student Aid Report that gives your Expected Family Contribution number and tells you if you qualify. The amount of the grant you may receive is not standardized. Different schools, with their varying tuitions, disburse different amounts. Pell Grants are available until you get your undergraduate degree. While Pell Grants once went only to students who attend school at least half-time (another term with a strict definition—see the glossary for more details), part-time students are now eligible so long as their expected family contribution is in line with federal requirements. By the way—even if you think you will not qualify for a Pell Grant, you need to apply. Many schools won't consider you for aid until they see your Pell results.

Other Aid

■ There are two main kinds of low-interest loans for students and parents these days: the Federal Direct Student Loans (Direct Loan) Program and the Federal Family Education Loan (FFEL) Program. Direct Loans come directly from the federal government. The FFEL loans involve private lenders such as banks, credit unions, and savings and loans. Aside from that difference, the loans are pretty much the same; which program you get your money from depends on which program your school participates in. We'll get deeper into the details of these programs in the chapter entitled "The World of Available Aid—Public Channels."

■ Payment on some of these loans can be deferred, postponed, or even reduced, depending on your circumstances. Loans can be deferred while you continue your studies, or if you encounter economic hardship or are unable to find full-time employment for up to three years.

■ Parents who are applying for the financial aid go for what are called PLUS Loans. Like the Staffords, PLUS Loans are available from both the Direct Loan and the FFEL program. The interest rate varies from year to year, running as high as nine percent.

■ The Direct and FFEL programs also allow what are called "Consolidation Loans" to help borrowers combine different kinds of student loans into a simpler payment scheme.

■ Three of the federal programs are "campus-based": Federal Supplemental Educational Opportunity Grants (FSEOG), Federal Work-Study (FWS), and Federal Perkins Loans. "Campus-based" simply means that the programs are administered by financial aid officers at each school. As we mentioned above, these are not entitlement programs like the Pell Grant or the Stafford Loans. The government gives each school a set amount of cash; when it's gone, it is really gone—no more campus-based aid can be had until the next year's allotment comes through. The schools set their own deadlines for these programs, so ask at your school's financial aid office and apply as early as possible to catch some of the money before it runs out.

■ Federal Supplemental Educational Opportunity Grants (FSEOG) are administered by the schools. Not all schools participate in the program, and the grants are awarded based on financial need—"exceptional financial need" is the way the government brochures put it. Unlike the Pell Grants program, which provides some money to every eligible student, the FSEOG programs only get a certain amount of funds each year. That means that once the fund dries up, there's no more until next year.

■ Federal Work-Study (FWS): This is basically a part-time job, funded by the federal government and administered by your school. Most undergraduates are paid by the hour, and often at the minimum wage. Graduate students may be paid by the hour or may receive a salary. The jobs are awarded on the basis of need, the size of FWS funds at your school, and the size of your aid package.

■ Federal Perkins loans are low-interest loans for students with "exceptional" financial need. They're also an exceptionally good deal at just five percent interest. The program is administered by the school; undergraduates can borrow $3,000 a year up to a total of $15,000. Perkins loan payment can be deferred in case of unemployment, and reduced or even cancelled if you pursue certain much-needed professions, including teaching in designated low-income schools, or in certain child family service agencies, or in Head Start, VISTA, the Peace Corps, and other options.

The federal government has several other ways of helping students get through school. The government provides a tuition-free education for thousands of students. The only catch is that the schools are owned by Uncle Sam: They are the military academies. If you don't mind the haircut and want to serve your country through the military, the service academies are an excellent way to do so while getting your degree. If you don't get into these highly competitive academies, the service branches maintain ROTC units on many campuses. The ROTC is another rich lode of scholarships. The ROTC also has a number of scholarships geared toward helping minority students, and boosting the number of students entering important-but-strained career fields such as the health professions. There's more on those programs in the chapter, "The World of Available Aid—Public Channels."

State Aid

In 1995–96, states expected to award just under $3 billion in total grant aid to more than 2,000,000 postsecondary students. About 85 percent is in need-based aid to undergraduates—states collectively award nearly $2 billion in need-based grants to undergraduates, according to the most recent survey by the authoritative New York State Higher Education Services Corporation. It's part of a continuing trend among the states to increase their support for higher education. However, each state is different, and some states spend far more than others. Five states—California, Illinois, New Jersey, New York, and Pennsylvania,—awarded about 60 percent of the national total, $1.5 billion altogether in undergraduate need-based aid.

Also, states go through cycles of generosity and stinginess that are virtually impossible to predict. But look for programs that state legislatures have instituted in order to attract more students to certain career fields, such as teaching, and so-called "non-need-based" programs (usually academic scholarships), which are booming.

College Funds

This money includes everything from athletic to academic, or merit, scholarships. The last few years have also been building years for college and university endowments, with hundreds of millions of dollars flowing into schools as diverse as Harvard University and the University of Washington (thanks, Bill Gates!). Some, but certainly not all, of this endowment money has gone into scholarship funds. Other college funds might find their way to students in the form of tuition discounts for prepayment, aid in receiving loans, and other innovative programs. Most schools also keep funds on hand for short-term emergency loans for students.

Employers

Many employers help put students through college through the burgeoning field of cooperative education, in which students alternate semesters of school with semesters of work. Not only does this provide professional skills and a leg up in the employment game, it also puts money in the student's pocket. It is best developed at technical and engineering schools like Georgia Tech, which places hundreds of students into positions in a five-year degree program, but all kinds of institutions offer cooperative education programs—almost 1,000 schools boast such programs. (See page 49 for a table of cooperative programs.)

Many employers also pay their employees to go to school. Millions of employees have the right to go back to school on their company tab, though relatively few choose to take the time. Other programs pay for the dependents of employees to attend school.

Private Scholarships

This is a relatively small part of the financial aid picture, and many carry daunting eligibility requirements—the old "red-haired Methodist from Georgia" problem. There's a lot more money to be drawn from federal and state programs, but hundreds of millions of dollars are nonetheless available in private scholarships—not an amount to turn your nose up at. There really are scholarships for left-handed students; Juniata College in Huntington, Pennsylvania, has had one since 1978. Just remember to go after the big money first and early, and then look around for whatever private scholarships you might be able to pick up.

5. The Long-Term Trends in Paying for College

The long-term trends in paying for college have repercussions for every student and every family. Three main trends have shown up lately: Families are paying a larger share of college costs these days and will continue to do so; financial aid funding is shifting away from grants and toward loans; and the number of college-age students is decreasing. Let's look at each individually.

Students and parents are indeed paying an increasing share of college costs, because federal aid to education hasn't kept up with student need. During the Reagan years, the emphasis in federal aid shifted to the needs of the poorer students as funds dwindled. Between 1980 and 1988, the number of students overall who received federal aid plummeted, and Pell Grants went from being a program for middle- and low-income students to being almost exclusively a low-income program. In 1980, 31.5

percent of all freshmen received Pell Grants; in 1988 the percentage had dropped to just 15.6 percent—the lowest level in the history of the program, according to the Cooperative Institutional Research Program. Other federal aid programs showed similar declines. The percentage of freshmen receiving Supplemental Educational Opportunity Grants dropped from eight percent in 1980 to less than four percent in 1988. And fewer students than ever are entering the federally funded Federal Work-Study program, which, during the same time dropped to less than seven percent from 14.5 percent.

The dropoff in federal assistance has sent students to other sources to make up their college funds. "These trends suggest that the burden of paying for college is increasingly falling on students, their families, and the nation's colleges," said Alexander W. Astin, professor of higher education at UCLA's Graduate School, who directs the annual survey of freshmen that provides the information cited above for the American Council on Education. Family contribution, savings, loans, and institutional grants are on the rise. A 1985 study by the National Institute of Independent Colleges and Universities points out that between 1979–80 and 1983–84, the average family contribution toward paying the price of attending an independent college or university grew from $3,313 to $5,705 for recipients of federal aid—a jump from 53 to 62 percent. The rate of increase was largest for low-income families, soaring 97 percent from $329 to $648 for families with annual incomes of less than $20,000. Nearly 80 percent of freshmen depended on their families for meeting college costs in 1988—a record high, up from about 70 percent in 1980. The percentage of freshmen relying on college grants and scholarships jumped from about 13 percent in 1980 to 20 percent in 1988.

At the same time that families have been required to shoulder more of the burden of college costs, the nature of the remaining aid has changed radically. The past few years have seen a marked shift in aid away from grants, which do not need to be repaid, and toward loans, which must eventually be repaid. Today loans make up about half of the aid that goes to college students, which means that recent graduates go into the world with a debt burden that is nothing short of massive—especially for graduates of professional and medical schools.

One trend that shows an eventual silver lining is the sweep of demographics. The post-World War II baby boom is coming to an end. Demographic predictions indicated higher education enrollments would have already started to drop off in the 1980s as the baby boomers waned. The dropoff has not happened yet—largely because of a 15 percent growth in the enrollment of 22- to 34-year-olds between 1980 and 1988. Still, the 18-year-old population will continue to ebb into the 1990s, until a baby "boomlet" that is expected to push enrollments back to mid-70s levels by the year 2000. All this means a coming drop in the pool of college-age students. While the best-known and most prestigious public and private schools will continue to attract a steady stream of applicants, the nation's smaller private schools will suffer. In the last decade nearly 150 small liberal arts colleges shut down, as more students in a shrinking overall pool of college-age students opted for less expensive public education.

The reason that this news is good news for students is that it means many colleges are working harder to attract students. As a corollary to that trend of a diminishing pool of college-aged students, we can expect to see continued strong demand for students with high scholastic achievement. Such scholarships are not based on need, and will remain popular since bringing these students into a school helps the reputation and academic climate of a campus—and because such programs are the easiest student aid to sell to alumni and other sources of contributions.

Of course, the shrinking population of college-age students could also be bad news. The danger is that fewer students will mean less tuition for the schools. That could start a vicious cycle in which schools, pressed for money, will have to raise their tuition to bring in more bucks; that will in turn drive away more students, so the remaining students will have to pay even more, and so on. It makes sense, then, to think about the nature of a school's endowment in making your choice of a college. Schools that are largely dependent on tuition for their income will be more likely to raise tuition in this environment than those that have cushy endowments. Most schools publish a breakdown of the sources of their money; read it and choose wisely.

One final note on demographics: While minority enrollment has been growing over the past few years, it has not kept pace with the minority groups' greater representation within the larger population. At the same time, the portion of the school-age population that is made up of minority students is growing; minority students could make up almost a third of Americans between the ages of 18 and 24. The effects of such changes can only be guessed at so far, but there is a distinct possibility of a greater percentage of aid money being committed to providing educational opportunities for black and Hispanic students in coming years.

Financial Aid News Update

■ **Hold the presses!** In the days before this edition of *College Scholarships and Financial Aid* went to press, the U.S. Congress and President Bill Clinton worked out a budget and tax agreement. Most of the attention went to the tax credit for dependent children, but the package also offers a number of new breaks to college students and their parents. The tax implications for these new provisions will take a while to work out, but here's a rough outline of what Washington gift-wrapped for taxpayers:

*Under the new laws, $2,500 in interest on student loans will be tax deductible for the first five years of the loan. Because students just getting out of college don't generally make a lot of money, they aren't in the kind of tax bracket that would make this a huge break. But at the 15 percent taxation rate, the student would save $150 on $1,000 worth of interest.

*Parents would be able to tap the value of their IRAs for college costs without paying a tax penalty.

*New forms of IRAs will be available, including the Kidsave IRA for college costs.

(Because these changes occurred just days before the last files went out to the publisher, this is the only place in this book in which you'll see references to the new tax bill. So if you need more information on how your family could best take advantage of the changes in the tax code, sit down with a competent financial adiviser.)

The new laws let both Democrats and Republicans claim that they had worked to balance the federal budget and helped middle-class families as well. But the good news doesn't mask the fact that these are very unpredictable times when it comes to financing a college education. That means it's vitally important that people who receive or want to receive aid to be ready to act quickly if the environment changes. These are times of rapid change and uncertainty; the best advice is to read your newspaper and try to follow what's going on.

■ **Monies for financial aid: What was up, what was down:** Although money for Pell Grants has been on the rise since the mid-1980s, economists estimate that purchasing power of the Pell Grant has fallen 37 percent since 1980. The current maximum: $2,700 per year. But since Congress often appropriates less than the administration requests for grants, more students will be worried about getting money at all than getting the maximum. Other programs are each feeling the squeeze, too, as President Clinton and Congress look for ways to trim the

budget deficit. Today's programs are going to feel a lot of pain, whichever side ends up winning.

Since the amount of federal money allocated to higher education has not kept up with the overall rate of inflation, and since college tuition has risen at about twice the rate of overall inflation, it means that college will be harder than ever to pay for. No surprise there.

State aid has been trying to catch up with college costs and to make up for losses from federal shortfalls. In the 1995–96 academic year, the states awarded nearly $3 billion in all kinds of grant aid to more than two million students—an increase of 2.2 percent over the previous school year. Of that amount, 85 percent was need-based grant aid to undergraduate and graduate students, and the remaining 15 percent was non-need-based grant aid. State spending has increased 52.9 percent in the five years coming up to the 1995-96 school year, according to the New York State Higher Education Services Corporation.

At the same time, it's worth outlining the broad areas that are obviously important to Bill Clinton, because those are programs he will be working the hardest to enact. Those fall into two main areas: a program of national service and an attempt to take over a large portion of the student loan business.

■ **Putting kids to work:** Candidate Clinton spoke in glowing terms of programs like Vista and the Peace Corps, in which young people got a chance to do good for others for a couple of years before doing well for themselves in their careers. During the campaign, Clinton said that by 1996, he would double the amount of financial aid for higher education, spending billions on national service alone. He pledged to create a program of national service that would allow college students to pay off their loans by helping to rebuild America—to put "a new generation of Americans" to work, serving in hospitals, schools, and shelters. Its core would be college-age students, paid the minimum wage while in service, of which the feds would pick up 85 percent. For each year's service (up to two years) the student would also earn up to an additional $5,000 to be applied by the government toward a year of college or other advanced study.

It sounded great to many Americans. The media loved it. But conservatives looked at the plan and had a pronounced case of sticker shock: The maximum price tag per student, spread over four years, would be $22,580, plus health benefits, all paid by taxpayers. By 1997, some $3.4 billion would be needed to run the program and support 150,000 participants.

It wasn't just the Bob Dole crowd criticizing this one. Some critics noted that the $3.4 billion was more than a quarter of the $12.7 billion we were spending in 1993 on student financial aid—and reaching far fewer kids. Those lucky few would get nearly twice the money the average student on financial aid received in guaranteed student loans, and wouldn't have to pay anything back. The numbers looked scary—especially if it meant money for the new program might come at the expense of the old. Clinton's proposed 1994 budget cut $1.2 billion from student aid.

So Congress took a cleaver to the national service plan. What emerged was a smaller, $10 million pilot program begun with great fanfare in the summer of 1993. It allows 1,000 to 1,500 students to tutor and counsel youths and clean up neighborhoods in exchange for money for college or job training.

Sounds like small potatoes, right? But if it gets good reviews, the program could expand. If it gets anywhere near the dreams that Clinton proposed at first, National Service could end up as a revolutionary way to pay for college. Watch it closely. Whatever such a program might mean for the fiscal health of the country, it could be a fabulous deal for the individual students lucky enough to get in.

As of this writing, the Republican majority in Congress had targeted Clinton's pet project for even deeper cuts or elimination.

■ **Uncle Sam takes on SALLIE MAE:** The second broad initiative in the Clinton administration could turn out to be the biggest change to financial aid in decades. Known as the Direct Student Loan program, it is intended to take the business of taking student loans away from the businesses that have handled it in the past and giving the job to the federal government. The goal: to save more than $2 billion a year.

How? The flaws in the system are expensive, Clinton said. The amount of money that the U.S. loses because of students who don't pay their college loans is nothing short of astonishing—about $3 billion each year. At a 1993 speech to Illinois high schoolers, Clinton pointed out that part of the reason the default rate is so high is that "a lot of people. . . are making money out of the present system." Clinton went on to explain that the system was set up to make money for lenders whether students paid their loans or not. That's the "guaranteed" part of guaranteed student loans; many financial institutions are just as happy to get their payments from Uncle Sam as from students, who might have more trouble paying. The system, Clinton said, "is confusing and it's costly, and the more money that goes to other things, the less money that's available to provide low-cost loans to the students of America."

Clinton took special aim at SALLIE MAE, the Student Loan Marketing Association, which made $394 million of the total $1 billion profit that all lenders made on student loans in 1992. Clinton's blunt proposal: Get rid of the middlemen and take over the loan business. Students could then pay off the loans after graduation through a payroll deduction of a percentage of salary or through, yes, performing national service.

It's another interesting idea, but it's even more controversial than the national service plan. A trial run of the system is now in effect, right alongside the old student loan system of applying for loans through private lenders. Will it expand? Will it last? Stay tuned—and read those newspapers.

■ **Colleges feel the heat:** Schools hardly need to be reminded that they need to cut costs. While tuition continues to rise at an annual rate of seven percent—far higher than the inflation rate for the rest of the economy—schools are feeling the financial squeeze more than ever. Expensive research programs and physical costs are making schools reconsider their funding priorities. The Johns Hopkins University is in the middle of a five-year plan to cut costs—a plan that includes eliminating programs in its prestigious arts and sciences school. Washington University has shut down its dentistry school, and has announced plans gradually to close its department of sociology. And Columbia University has been phasing out such prestigious programs as its archival management program, geography, and linguistics departments, transferring some courses to other departments and dropping others entirely. These aren't podunk schools —these are high-powered, wealthy institutions. So you can imagine what this means for smaller schools without the prestige and fancy endowments. And you can bet that the impact on financial aid, already severe, will only get worse. With school costs increasing and with government funds decreasing—especially state budgets, which look sickly across the nation and which are causing legislators to eye state school tuition increases more hungrily than ever—colleges are looking for every way to make students pay more of their share of education.

Students, too, appear to be making college choices with more emphasis on affordability and financial aid. In a recent survey by the College Bound, a publication for admissions advisers, nearly 92 percent of colleges said economic factors are "casting an ominous shadow on college admissions and creating personal and institutional tensions." The newsletter quoted a Purdue University administrator who said "Most students who cancelled admissions at Purdue did so because of little or no financial aid or scholarships."

Some analysts say that the whole question of college costs has been miscast—that the skyrocketing price of college is at least partly an illusion, albeit one that drives away prospective students. The *New York Time* in 1991 that applications to many private institutions had declined between 5 and 15 percent in the past year, a combination of smaller student population and recessionary pressures on the families footing the bills. Applications were up at the better public institutions. Consultant Peter Drucker writes in the *Wall Street Journal*: "The market share of the prestige colleges has been falling steadily these past five years, perhaps by as much as one-fifth. . . There is only one reason for this decline in market share: 'sticker shock'." Drucker's point is that even though private college costs hit the $20,000 range, the average student in private schools pays closer to $11,000 after financial aid—not pocket change, but a lot closer to what the prestigious public schools charge for out-of-state tuition. Financial aid administrators recognize the coming crisis, too: in a recent edition of the administrator magazine, *Student Aid Transcript*, Robin Jenkins, Director of Financial Management Center of the National Association of College and University Business Officers, wrote that institutions need marketing strategies "based on cost containment and educational value (price/cost) rather than manipulating price (and calling it financial aid) if they are to successfully meet consumer demand and public policy expectations."

Will a price war ensue? Don't hold your breath: The colleges aren't really set up for deep discounts, especially at tuition-dependent private schools. But schools with less arrogant and self-destructive administrations will find that they can limit their budget increases; in late 1994, Michigan State President Peter McPherson guaranteed that new students arriving in 1995 would see their tuition rise no more than the rate of inflation for the next four years. It's not a cut, and it's not even a guarantee: McPherson said the promise was "contingent upon state appropriation increases for MSU's general fund of at least the rate of inflation. But it's the kind of promise students and parents are going to want to hear, more and more—and the kind of promise that they will examine carefully before signing on the dotted line.

Other Trends to Watch

If you've been accepted to a top school, you might find good news in a 1992 trial that declared the practices of an organization called the Overlap Group illegal. Since 1958, MIT and the eight Ivy League universities have met several times a year to set joint principles for awarding financial aid and to negotiate individual aid awards for students who applied to at least two of the institutions. The result of the overlap process was that a student's cost of attending any of the schools was approximately the same. In the world of business, such practices are called price fixing, and invoke the wrath of antitrust laws. The universities seemed to feel that they were above all that, since by conserving their precious endowments they were furthering the cause of education. Soon after the suit was filed in May 1991, the Ivies originally named as defendants—Harvard, Yale, Brown, Dartmouth, Columbia, Princeton, Cornell, and the University of Pennsylvania—signed a consent decree, admitting to no wrongdoing but agreeing to stop the overlap activities. MIT decided to fight—and lost.

What does all of this legal stuff mean for the average applicant? For one thing, it means that the schools can't collude to set the same amount of financial aid for all applicants; a strong negotiator can play one school against another and shop for the best deal. The schools also agreed to base financial aid solely on need, and not merit. Ultimately, of course, this high-minded legal action might mean that the schools have less money for financial aid altogether, and so fewer students will receive financial aid. But for now, it means it's time to play "Let's make a deal!" The Justice Department also is investigating a group of 14 smaller colleges that engaged in similar activities of meeting to discuss financial aid practices. These colleges include Williams, Amherst, Bowdoin, Wellesley, Vassar, Middlebury, and Tufts.

Colleges have been trying to fight their big-spender images with a variety of programs. Many of them can help students shave thousands of dollars from their higher education costs, while others have an almost hucksterish quality that seems more calculated to generate headlines and attract students than to help a large number of students pay for college. So when you hear about a program, ask yourself who will benefit from the program and how much it will do for them. Is it a continuing program, or a one-shot promotion? You'll find a full discussion of alternative financing methods in the chapter, "Getting the Most College for the Money."

Endnotes: Tips on Filling Out the Application

Here are a few tips on filling out your financial aid application for the filer who is in a hurry. The most important point for applicants to specific scholarships is: Don't apply if you're not eligible. Some students try a scattershot approach, submitting hundreds of letters for awards they couldn't possibly receive because of everything from academic standards to geographic requirements. The glut of these semifraudulent applications has caused many foundations actually to ask that their names be removed from the scholarship rolls—thus injuring deserving students who might not otherwise find out about the programs.

The second tip—and this is a deceptively obvious point—is to fill out the entire application properly. The late, great, legal educator Bernard Ward used to talk about judging essays for civic competitions. To weed out the flood of entries, the first thing he recalled doing was to measure the margins on each page. If the applicant's typing slopped over the prescribed margins, Ward would blithely chuck the essay without a thought as to its content. Heed Ward's example: fill out the forms letter-perfectly. Leave no blanks: where a question doesn't apply, simply write in "n/a" and move on. Some agencies return forms that have blanks, and the paper runaround can make you miss important deadlines. If you're having trouble making sense of the federal Financial Aid Application, you can call a toll-free hotline at the Department of Education. The number is 1-800-4-FED-AID. In numbers, that's 1-800-433-3243. The TTD number for the hearing-impaired is 301-369-0518.

A third tip, or warning: Use common sense if you pay an outsider to help you with your financial aid search. Most students still hear about financial aid opportunities through high school guidance counselors or college financial aid officers. While this is often a good route to take, sometimes such officials are overworked, or can't keep up with changes in the financial aid scene on top of their other duties. Thus families often can't get the high-quality, individual attention they desire from the usual free channels. At the same time, many families look for help simply in filling out financial aid forms and in managing the complex applications process—the same way families hire experts to help file their tax forms. That is why many families have turned to independent financial counselors, many of whom are former guidance counselors and financial planners. They also pay $40 or more for computerized scholarship searches. But some of these firms walk a fine line between what is acceptable, what is unethical—and what is illegal.

Independent financial aid-finding services might help find more money, but it might come at the expense of your conscience. While a college financial aid officer is likely to describe the world as it is, a paid financial planner is likelier to describe that world as it could be, going so far as to offer suggestions of ways for parents to hide income from disclosure requirements on financial aid forms. Advisers might recommend shifting assets into retirement accounts, annuities, or universal life insurance policies—none of which need to be listed on financial aid applications. Though not illegal, some college financial aid officers claim the practices are unethical at least, and that they take aid money away from truly needy students. Financial aid professionals don't look kindly on the "bend the rules" financial guys. SALLIE MAE executive Jerry Davis recalls sitting down with a financial adviser to talk about his investments when the young whiz kid started telling Davis about how he advises parents on how to hide their assets to escape their being accounted for in a needs analysis. Some of the advice was a little, shall we say, dishonest. Davis said nothing at the time, but did sit down and write a letter the next evening to the young man telling him that if he had indeed found a loophole, he could be sure that Davis would work to close it. Davis takes such things seriously—but so should you. The penalty for lying on federal aid forms is as much as ten years in jail; you can read that part right by where you sign your name.

Some for-profit financial aid services go over the line. A while back, officials at Canisius College, a small Buffalo, New York, school, noticed that 350 of the school's 3,000 financial aid requests had been put together by a local aid-search firm. (The official realized that many of the forms were filled out in the same handwriting.) Nothing wrong with that, but the school did more checking and discovered that the forms contained many interesting errors, from undervalued homes to claims of more children in college than were actually attending. According to the *Wall Street Journal*, if the misinformation had not been detected Canisius could have paid $400,000 more for aid than it should have—about five percent of its annual financial aid budget.

Beyond the familiarity with fancy footwork, many experts question whether these financial aid entrepreneurs provide much of a service. Orlow Austin, financial aid director for the University of Illinois–Urbana-Champaign, performed an informal check on such services. Austin asked students who were already receiving financial aid from his office to file with financial aid-finding services. He found that once the services had gotten their $40 or more from the students, they rarely uncovered more sources of financial aid than the students had already procured through the school's own financial aid office. Austin also points out that while many of these services offer a money-back guarantee, it is a rare student who actually takes the trouble to ask for a refund—largely because the aid process is so complex that students are unlikely to know when they have not been well served, and are also likely to blame themselves for not working hard enough to pursue financial aid avenues. The Federal Trade Commission has warned that a lot of the companies offering to hook students up with scholarships are little more than scams that take your money and either do nothing or print out information that's readily available for free.

Finally, many of these self-proclaimed financial "experts" know a lot less than you will after having read this book. They could be stockbrokers or financial wizards who have sniffed an opportunity in education costs, but many of them haven't done the necessary homework needed to serve the individual student. And like stockbrokers, many of them are just pushing the hot instrument of the moment—a tuition aid plan that has recently burst on the scene that will earn them a healthy commission if they can force it on you. The one-size-fits-all approach wasn't appreciated in Procrustes' day, and works no better today. If you do decide that you need to speak with a financial adviser, protect yourself. Anyone can call himself an investment adviser, so it's important to find someone with special expertise. Certified Financial Planners have at least three years of experience and have taken at least a two-year course in financial planning and a six-part certification exam. College finances make up a part of that training and testing. "That's one of the most-requested strategies—to set up a game plan for sending a kid through college," says Mark Tuttle of the Institute of Certified Financial Planners, the nonprofit organization that polices the profession. To track down a

CFP in your area, call the Institute at 1-800-282-PLAN (7526). They can even refer you to CFPs who specialize in college planning.

The lesson: It pays to establish a strong relationship with the financial aid officers at your school. They are most likely to know the field well and to have special knowledge about what is available at your school. And if you must go outside for help, remember Jiminy Cricket's credo: Let your conscience be your guide.

You and the Tax Laws: What the IRS Has Done to Higher Education

Tax-savings opportunities have been limited for parents or students trying to meet the high costs of higher education. However, things may be changing as Congress increasingly focuses on education as a top national priority and on tax incentives to ease the cost burden.

However, tax-saving opportunities remain, and there is talk in Washington of providing new tax breaks to help shoulder the cost burdens of college.

This chapter will give you the outlines, but of course you should sit down with your family's investment adviser to see how the tax laws apply directly to you. Let's look at each broad category individually.

Income Splitting Has All But Split, But Some Help Is on the Way

Once upon a time parents could spin off their income to their kids and their lower tax bracket, which would mean less taxes paid while keeping money all in the family. Tax shelters like the Clifford Trust proliferated. Nowadays the tax laws have gotten tough on kiddie tax shelters—though income splitting is still a good idea, if you do it right. If you give your child investments that produce income of $1,300 or less a year—and this amount changes annually with inflation—the first $650 (also changes annually) is tax free, and the next $650 is taxed to the child at the child's tax rate. However, if a child under age 14 has investment income exceeding $1,300 (as adjusted for inflation), the so-called "Kiddie-Tax" subjects the excess to tax at the parent's higher tax rate. Children who are at least age 14 at the end of the year are taxed on all of their investment income at their own tax bracket rate.

In order to shift any income to a child, you must acutally transfer ownership of the income-producing asset to the child. You cannot instruct the bank to credit the interest from your account to the child. You have to transfer ownership of the account itself.

When you transfer substantial assets to your child, there is a potential gift tax liability, but under the annual exclusion, you can give up to $10,000 per child, per year, without triggering the gift tax, and this amount is increased to $20,000 if you are married and your spouse agrees to split the gift.

Parents can accomplish a degree of income splitting by creating custodial accounts for their children through a bank, mutual fund, or brokerage firm.

In the case of a custodial account handled through a brokerage, for example, an adult—parent, grandparent, guardian, or any adult—opens a stock account at a broker's office in the child's name. The custodian then can buy and sell the securities, collect the income from sales and investment, and spend it on the child or plow it back into the account. The custodian need not be that adult—in fact, a bank or trust company can serve as custodian. When the child comes of age, he or she can take over the account and sell off the securities, or keep the ball rolling. But remember the caveat above: If the child is under 14 years of age and the income rises above $1,300 a year, the excess will be taxed at the parent's rate. Also, income from the account that is used to discharge a parent's support obligation is taxable to the parent. The rules governing custodial accounts vary from state to state, but those differences don't generally affect tax consequences of having the accounts.

What sort of properties make good gifts to minors? Gifts that require little attention; if you exercise too much control over the child's property, the IRS might not let you call it a gift for the purposes of shifting income. Some of these set-it-and-forget-it investments include bonds, which you can buy in the minor's name and which sit quietly until the date of maturity—the bond's, that is, not the child's. Many savvy investors are buying zero-coupon municipal bonds, which are tax-free and can be timed to reach maturity when your child is ready for college.

Buying mutual funds through a custodial account for your child provides professional management of your investment, although there are market risks to principal depending on the type of fund selected. Keep in mind that as far as income splitting is concerned, the Kiddie-Tax rules discussed earlier limit the amount of tax that can be saved through a mutual fund custodian account.

Even good old U.S. Savings Bonds can make an attractive gift investment when you consider that you don't have to report the interest income until the year the bond is cashed in or matures. That means you can buy bonds for an under-14-year-old and defer interest reporting until the child has reached 14 years of age, when the income will be taxed at the child's lower rate.

The tax law provides some families with a break that makes Series EE Savings Bonds even more attractive. If you use those bonds to pay tuition or other educational fees for yourself or your family, the accrued interest on the re-deemed bonds may be excluded from your reported in-come. There are a few requirements, of course. The new law only applies to EE bonds issued after 1989, and the purchaser has to be age 24 or older before the month of is-sue. So if you bought them in your child's name, or if you jointly own them with your child, you don't qualify. You must elect to defer the reporting of interest accrued on the bonds to the time when you redeem them, instead of re-porting the interest annually. Then, in the year you redeem a qualifying EE savings bond, the amount of excludable bond interest depends on a comparison of the bond re-demption proceeds to your tuition and related free pay-ments, as well as your income. You figure the exclusion on IRS Form 8815. If the education expenses exceed the amount you receive when redeeming your bonds (princi-pal and interest), all of the bond interest may be excluded from income if you qualify under the income-based phase-out rules. If the expenses are less than the redemption pro-ceeds, you divide the expenses by the redemption pro-ceeds and that resulting percentage of bond interest is tax free if permitted under the phaseout rules. Every year, the phaseout threshold is adjusted for inflation. For example, on 1997 federal tax returns, a full exlusion was available to single taxpayers and heads of households with modified adjusted gross income of up to $50,850, and to married couples filing jointly and qualified widow(ers) with up to $76,250. If income exceeds the phaseout threshold, the ex-clusion is phased out over the next $30,000 for joint return filers and qualified widow(ers). The phaseout is over the next $15,000 for singles and heads of households. A mar-ried person filing separately cannot claim the exclusion re-gardless of income or educational expenses.

Several states now offer a local version of this deal, commonly known as "Baccalaureate Bonds." They act like zero-coupon bonds, which is to say your kid gets no income until they mature.

A word to the investment-wise: Many investment ad-visers have taken a long look at the Savings Bond plan and have decided that they don't offer as sweet a deal as you might like. The income restrictions make them a difficult game to play—if your earnings power increases, you lose the tax benefit of all your scrimping. Besides—there are a lot of relatively safe investments out there, such as stock-based mutual funds, that tend to generate far more income than bonds do. The stock market may go up and down, but its general trend over the years has been a steady rise that beats almost any other investment you could name.

State Prepaid Tuition Plans and College Savings Plans

There is good news about those headline-grabbing state programs that let you prepay tuition years ahead of time or allow you to make annual contributions to a tax-deferred college savings plan. These plans were given a boost by 1996 changes in tax laws.

Until the student starts college, earnings on plan con-tributions accrue tax free; the earnings are not taxed to the parents, to the student, or to the state trust holding the con-tributions. When the tuition benefits are eventually dis-tributed from the account on the student's behalf, the stu-dent will pay tax on the benefit under annuity-type rules. If a refund is made to the parent or to other contributors, as in cases in which the child does not attend a college included in the program, the refund is taxable to the extent that it exceeds the original contribution.

The contributing parent (or other relative) is not sub-ject to gift tax at the time of the contribution. Even when tuition payments are distributed from the account, there is no gift tax provided that the state program issues a check for tuition that is endorsed by the student and then depos-ited in the college's bank account.

Scholarships and Grants

Students receive a tax break for scholarships and fellow-ship grants, but it is limited. Tax-free treatment is allowed only to degree candidates, and only to the part of the grant used to pay for tuition and course-related supplies. If you use the grant for room and board, it is taxable. Also taxable is a grant that pays for teaching or research services that are required as a condition of receiving the grant.

The Loan Ranger: Hi-Yo Silver, Away!

Under the tax law, not all mortgages are alike. Those mort-gages taken out on or before October 14, 1987, are simple: all of the interest on loans secured by your principal resi-dence or second home is deductible, regardless of how the proceeds are used.

The interest deduction rules for mortgages taken out after October 13, 1987 are not so simple. To fully deduct the interest on a mortgage loan that is partly or wholly used to pay college costs, the loans must be within the limits for home equity debt. Home equity debt refers to all loans in-curred after October 13, 1987 that are secured by a princi-pal residence or second home and *which are not* home ac-quisition loans. Home acquisition loans are those used to buy, build, or improve a principal residence or second home securing the loan.

There are separate loan limits for home acquisition debt and home equity debt. Interest on home acquisition debt is fully deductible if the total debt does not exceed $1,000,000 (or $500,000 if married filing separately), re-duced by any loans from before October 14, 1987.

The loan limits for home equity debt as well as home acquisition debt apply to the combined mortgage loans for your principal residence and second home. If the limits are exceeded, interest paid on the excess is not deductible as home mortgage interest, but if you use the loan for invest-ment or business purposes, the interest may be deductible.

Letting the Boss Pay

If an employer foots the bill for an employee's college tuition and related fees, part or all of the benefit may be tax free. A law allowing tax-free treatment for employer-financed undergraduate courses expired May 31, 1997, but Congress is likely to extend the tax break for at least a few years more, perhaps permanently. Without the up-to-$5,250 exclusion, an employer's payment for courses may still be tax free if an employee has met the employer's minimum educational standards and can prove that the courses are job related and do not lead to qualification for a new profession.

Keep an Eye on Congress

The Clinton Administration and the Republican opposition in Congress are both vowing to help out parents by enacting new tax breaks for education. Among the possibilities are a tax credit or deduction for tuition and tax-free distributions for college could be received. Any new tax breaks are likely to be hedged with restrictions on the amount of qualifying expenses and income limits for eligible taxpayers. Given the changeable nature of politics, it pays to keep up with the tax news or hire a tax-wise accountant who does so that you can be assured of taking advantage of all available tax breaks.

Intermission—The Loan Route

No other aspect of paying for college is as bewildering—or as frightening—as loans. Other forms of assistance make more sense. The concepts behind work-study and other forms of work are pretty familiar: you work, you get paid. As the lawyers say, quid pro quo—something for something. The concept of grants is pretty easy, too: Someone gives you money, you spend it. You don't give it back. In effect, you are getting something for nothing. (No wonder grants are so hard to get.)

Owing money is just plain unpleasant. Polonius told Hamlet, "Neither a borrower nor lender be," and most of us wish we could take his advice. We don't like being in someone's debt. But for a lot of middle-class families, borrowing is a fact of life. It is the leverage that got the folks their house, their car, and probably helped them along toward other major purchases on the way.

But there are differences between their time and yours. For many of our parents, loans have been a way of life—and a pathway to riches. Parents getting started in the 1950s and the 1960s took out loans with relatively low interest rates and bought homes, which appreciated greatly in value. The value of the homes ballooned through the 1970s and 1980s, exceeding the cost of the mortgage and making it possible to generate even more money through second mortgages and home equity loans. This isn't the way it worked out for everyone, of course, but it served as a pattern of success for a generation.

The succeeding generations haven't had it so lucky. Runaway inflation in the 1970s raised both the value of property and the cost of credit. Not only are homes out of the reach of many young people today, but also loans for college are beginning to look quite forbidding. When deciding how much they can afford to pay up front, parents who have benefitted from the real estate and interest rate ride might have to dig deeper than they'd like to, since the alternative means shifting the financial burden to a generation that looks like it will end up having less ability to pay those debts back, on the whole.

Perhaps the scariest result of the growth in borrowing to pay for higher education is that borrowing could be squeezing many people out of the world of financial aid—and thus college. A recent report sponsored by Congress and the College Board warned that the growing debt burden might represent a threat for society at large, perhaps burdening the current generation beyond its ability to pay. The report further speculated that borrowing was a tougher concept for the poor than for the middle class, and that these groups would have more trouble repaying their loans than better-off students. So the trend toward borrowing was most threatening to the poor, and especially to minorities. Some prospective students, uncertain of their ability to find a job lucrative enough to allow repaying a loan, might simply avoid loans, and college, altogether. Thus borrowing could be part of what's behind the fact that black and Hispanic students do not attend college in numbers commensurate with their percentage in the population as a whole.

The sad fact is that borrowing is here to stay; you will almost certainly have to borrow to complete your education. Even if Bill Clinton saves his Direct Loan program from the Republican budget knife, you'll still end up owing money—but the creditor will be Uncle Sam, the guy who brought you the Internal Revenue Service. But getting a loan is not a death knell. Many programs, especially the federal loan programs, have provisions to make your debt burden more manageable. For one thing, several of them (such as the Perkins Loan) give you a grace period of six months. And some of the programs even let you delay payment for other reasons, like joining the Peace Corps. More and more programs are allowing students to defer or reduce loan payments in return for working in much-needed professions such as nursing; the current administration in Washington wants to expand such options.

It's also important to keep in mind that those earlier generations had the right idea—that borrowing is still a smart way to make big-ticket expenses like an education more manageable. Karl E. Case, Professor of Economics at Wellesley College, has published a paper in the Journal of Student Financial Aid that looks at how different ways of meeting college costs affect the percentage of family income that the colleges get. While his basic point is that long-term saving and financial planning is the best way to reduce the burden of college costs, his comparisons of loans and burdens are nonetheless eye-opening. He writes:

"A household with a $40,000 income takes home about $2,150 a month after taxes. A yearly parental contribution of $5,430, if paid out of a year's income, would be $453 a month or 21% of take-home pay. Since the child is in school for four years, that would be $453 per month for four years. But...

"Using a parent loan with a 9% interest rate for 10 years the monthly payment would be cut to $174 per month or 8.1% of take-home pay.

"If parents had started saving six years prior to college earning 6% on their savings, the whole bill could have been paid for $150 per month over 10 years (6 years before and 4 years during college)—7.1% of income with no borrowing.

"If parents had started when the child was 8 years old and took out an 8-year parent loan, the whole thing could have been financed for $75 per month or 3.5% of income."

Case goes on in the paper to show that the same logic applies to families with higher or lower income.

Complex numbers aside, Case's basic principles apply to all debt burdens: paying over a longer period of time reduces the amount that you have to pay each year or each month. And since savings generate income for you in the form of interest, it is an even better way to prepare for any debt burden. Unfortunately, it is probably too late for you to do this kind of long-range planning for your education; most buyers of this book are headed for college within a year or so, but Case's advice can well apply to a younger family member. Look again at the difference between the effect on income of long-term borrowing as opposed to paying out tuition semester by semester, and you'll see that borrowing is a necessary evil—more necessary now than ever. That's why so many colleges, states, and private institutions are presenting innovative loan programs and programs to allow installment payment of tuition.

Of course, government programs are political footballs—you can expect everything from funding levels to entitlement rules to be tinkered and tampered with from year to year. So it's important to keep up with financial aid news to know what's coming your way.

Finding Financial Information On the Internet

It's only natural that you should expect to find gobs of college information online. The global network of computer networks known as the Internet was nurtured in academe. Today you can find a stunning range of information out there in the ether, including some of the most up-to-date data on financial aid and college finances available anywhere. (Besides, you know, this book.) You can get some of it even if your only access to the Internet is via electronic mail!

The easiest way to find information is through the World Wide Web (WWW), the part of the Internet that links far-flung computer systems effortlessly, and with lots of flashy multimedia enhancements. It's getting hard to find a college these days that doesn't have a "home page" on the WWW to advertise itself to prospective students; many of these pages have pointers to the school's financial aid information. Many financial aid offices also operate Gophers, which are systems on the Internet that make it easy to find information, but without the fancy bells and whistles of the Web. So if you have access to the Internet, surf over to your new school and check it out!

There are also plenty of online resources that provide general information on financial aid, available for free via the WWW. A great place to start looking into the nuts and bolts of student financial aid is the source of so much of it: the federal government. The Department of Education maintains a website that, while not a model of clarity, provides a great deal of reliable information. You can also download the software necessary to apply for federal financial aid directly from the site. Go to http://www.ed.gov/prog_info/SFA/StudentGuide/1997–8/index.html.

The College Board also maintains a site with lots of financial aid information and forms to be downloaded. You can find it at www.collegeboard.org.

And then there's Sallie Mae, the company that provides much of the money that goes into higher education loans. Sallie Mae's website has another introductory guide to financial aid, this one very well adapted to the multimedia enviroment with plenty of links, illustrations and other bells and whistles that make it as entertaining as it is informative: http://www.salliemae.com/home/content.html

These are official sources of information—but there's a great deal of excellent unofficial information out there as well. One of the best is the Financial Aid Information WWW Page, produced by Mark Kantrowitz, author of the *Prentice Hall Guide to Scholarships and Fellowships for Math and Science Students*, listed below. The WWW page is a gold mine: It includes access to scholarship and fellowship databases, information on grants and loans, an extensive bibliography, and links to school Web and Gopher systems. Like all good Web pages, this one contains links to most of the other important sources of financial aid information contained on other computer systems. So we won't go into a long list of Web page addresses here, since one leads to the other.

To find the Financial Aid Information Page, aim your Web browser toward this address, or URL: http://www.finaid.org/finaid.html

Kantrowitz also produces a FAQ—short for "Frequently Asked Questions"—list that covers a lot of the basic information about financial aid. You can find it through the WWW page. If you don't have WWW access but do have simple electronic mail access, you can send an email message to: mail-server@rtfm.mit.edu, containing only the words "help" and "index" on separate lines. You will receive instructions for retrieving the financial aid FAQ (and others on thousands of topics, by the way; rtfm is a massive FAQ repository).

Signet Bank has even put the full text online of the current edition of the popular book, *Don't Miss Out: The Ambitious Student's Guide to Financial Aid* by Robert and Anna Leider. (It's free, but contains many come-ons to buy other guides and services from their financial aid publishing house, Octameron Associates.) You can find it at the Signet Bank Student Loan Home Page: http://www.signet.com/collegemoney

A number of sites now offer to hook students up with scholarship money online. Some are excellent resources, others are scams, according to recent warnings by the Federal Trade Commission. How can you tell good from bad? The biggest tip-off is money: if somebody wants a lot of it in order to conduct a search for you, you're probably dealing with the wrong folks. The bills can quickly outstrip the value of scholarships discovered—and often, these folks aren't finding anything that you wouldn't come across with some smart online searching of your own.

The best search services turn out to be free! Take the increasingly popular Fastweb (www.fastweb.com), which scans 180,000 sources of financial aid once the user fills out the online profile—and sends updates to your e-mailbox as new sources become available. It's truly awesome. A few other sites offer similar services, and can be found at http://www.rams.com/srn/search.htm and http://www.collegeboard.org/fundfinder/bin/fundfind01.pl.

For a more activist page, wander over to Student Financial Aid Crisis in America!, maintained by the National Association of Graduate–Professional Students. It contains updates on legislation aimed at cutting financial aid programs and links to other political sites. You can find it at: http://nagps.varesearch.com/Student_Aid/more.html

A warning about Web sites: they change. The Internet is a very active place, and addresses can be ephemeral things. That's why it's important to familiarize yourself with the kinds of Internet search tools like Veronica (for gophering around) and WWW search engines like Lycos so that you can always find the kind of information you want without the hassles of following a rabbit trail in cyberspace. They can be remarkably easy to use. A few of the tried and true sites for finding things online include Yahoo! (www.yahoo.com), which organizes the Web in outline form so that you can track down information by category. You can get directly to Yahoo!'s financial aid resources by going to http://www.yahoo.com/Business _and_Economy/Companies/Education/Financial_Aid/. You can also search the entire World Wide Web for certain words or phrases by using such sites as Altavista (www. altavista.digital.com) and HotBot (www.hotbot.com.)

The World of Available Aid— Public Channels

What This Chapter Will Do

O.K.—let's get back to work. In this chapter we will go into greater detail about the publicly funded sources of financial aid. We will cover federal programs and state programs. The federal programs make up the bulk of all funding for financial aid. On the state side, we will compare state appropriations to show which states are the big spenders and which are the skinflints. We will describe the range of programs available from the states. We also include the state offices that oversee financial aid so that you can continue the hunt for specific state programs on your own.

Federal Government Programs

Pell Grants

Before we even describe Pell Grants and how tough it is to get money out of this need-based federal program, here's a point about them that we can't stress enough: EVEN IF YOU THINK YOU COULDN'T POSSIBLY BE ELIGIBLE FOR A PELL GRANT, YOU SHOULD APPLY. Many other aid programs require that you first apply for a Pell. If you bypass the Pell, you pass up a great deal of possible aid, including the Stafford Loan program. So if you're serious about applying for financial aid, APPLY FOR A PELL GRANT EVERY YEAR THAT YOU ARE IN COLLEGE.

What it is: Pell Grants are, as the name implies, grants—they need not be repaid. Though the funding for Pell Grants comes from the federal government, your school gives you the money—or, in some cases, merely credits your tuition account. Your school will tell you which forms you must fill out to apply for a Pell Grant; different schools require different forms. (We will go into more detail on the different financial aid forms in the chapter, "Putting Your Financial Aid Package Together.")

Prior to 1980, Pell Grants were called Basic Educational Opportunity Grants; older materials might refer to them as such. If you see terms like BEOG or Guaranteed Student Loan (until recently, the name for the FFEL Stafford Loan Program), you shouldn't use those outdated materials. Times change, and the old stuff can steer you wrong.

The budget for Pell Grants is not limited: There is no cap on the number of Pell Grants that will be handed out in a given year. Washington budgets according to its expectations and hopes for the best. However, if program budgets get tight, the maximum award can be shaved somewhat by the Secretary of Education. The important thing to remember with Pell Grants is that if you qualify and apply on time—no later than May 1—you will get your money. The early bird doesn't get a better worm when it comes to Pells, but missing your deadline means getting no money at all.

Pell Grants can be used for five years of undergraduate study, or six if the student is pursuing a course of study that requires more than four years. Factors that exempt students from the five- and six-year limits include death of a relative, personal illness or injury to the student, or the need to take remedial courses. Your school might have other rules for extending Pell support.

How to qualify: Students must be U.S. citizens and must be attending school at least half-time. (As you can imagine, "half-time" is a term with a very specific definition. The Department of Education defines that this way: "At schools measuring progress by credit hours and academic terms (semesters, trimesters, or quarters), 'half-time' means at least six semester hours or quarter hours per term. At schools measuring progress by credit hours but not using academic terms, 'half-time' means at least twelve semester hours or eighteen quarter hours per year. At schools measuring progress by clock hours, 'half-time' means at least twelve hours per week." If that isn't confusing enough, individual schools can set higher minimum requirements—which means you should check with your school to find out its definition.)

Whether or not you will get a Pell Grant depends on a formula, passed into law by Congress, that is applied to the information you provide in your financial aid application. The formula produces a Student Aid Index number. The lower the Student Aid Index number, the more money you can get in your grant. The maximum available for the 1997–98 school year is $2,700. These grants are distributed based on family need and education costs at your school. The formula that the Education Department uses to determine your Expected Family Contribution (EFC) is established by Congress; it shows up on the

Student Aid Report that comes back after you've applied. If you want to know everything there is to know about how that magic number comes about, the Department of Education publishes a booklet, "Expected Family Contribution (EFC) Formulas," which you can order from the Federal Student Aid Information Center, P.O. Box 84, Washington, D.C. 20044.

Federal Supplemental Equal Educational Opportunity Grants

What it is: FSEOG is another grant for undergraduates. As grants, FSEOG's do not need to be repaid. This is a campus-based program, which means it is administered by the schools—but not all schools participate, so check with your financial aid office. It provides up to $4,000 a year, depending on your need. Unlike Pell Grants, SEOG funds are "campus-based," which means they come to schools in a set amount. Once that fund is depleted, there's no more until next year. The lesson: Apply early (your school sets its own deadline for these grants).

How to qualify: They are earmarked by Congress for students with exceptional financial need, and first priority goes to Pell Grant recipients. Schools decide whether to give FSEOGs to students who do not attend more than half-time.

Federal Work-Study

What it is: FWS lets you earn while you learn in jobs either on- or off-campus, administered through the financial aid office. The amount you earn will be at least the federal minimum wage, but you can earn more depending on the kind of work that the school finds for you. The total amount you earn will be determined by the school; working more hours than those assigned will not get you more money.

The range of work-study jobs is limited only by the imagination of your school aid office, and many aid officers have surprisingly broad imaginations. Thus your school might have arranged myriad jobs on campus in each academic department, from cleaning out the baboon cages to helping run the projectors for college movies. Off-campus jobs abound, too, and often involve working for a private or public nonprofit organization or a local, state, or federal agency. And many schools have linked up with private employers near the campus to give you valuable real-world job experience. Some colleges even have large employment offices to help students sort out all their options. (College Work-Study is not the same as cooperative education, in which the school helps students divide their time between school and a career-oriented job. A description of cooperative education begins on page 48.)

How to qualify: Both undergraduates and graduate students are eligible for this campus-based program.

Financial aid administrators dole out work-study jobs based on your need. Part-time students may be eligible, depending on the school. Again, since work-study is campus based, the money is allocated to the school in a lump. Once it's gone, it's gone. Pay attention to the school's application deadlines.

Federal Perkins Loans (formerly National Direct Student Loans)

What it is: This is a broad program of federal loans—and loans have to be paid back, with interest. However, Perkins Loans offer extremely low interest—five percent—which is far better than you can get at a commercial lending institution. The school will either pay you directly or credit your tuition account.

Depending on how much money you need and how much money the school can give out, Perkins Loans can give you quite a bit of money. You can borrow up to $15,000 as an undergraduate—$3,000 for each year. Some schools that have extremely low default rates on their loans are allowed to give out even more Perkins Loan money; check to see if your school is one of the lucky few.

How to qualify: Of course, with money this cheap there's a catch. Perkins Loans are only available to students who demonstrate exceptional financial need. Though the loans go primarily to full-time students, some schools also give them to part-time and half-time students. These loans are made through your school's financial aid office. This is another campus-based program, which means that the amount of funds are limited by how much money your school got from Washington. So find out the application deadlines at your school and get the applications in early.

When to pay it back: If you are a "new borrower"— that is, if you enroll after July 1, 1987, and you have no other outstanding Perkins Loans or Federal Direct Student Loans or have paid off your own loans—then you have a grace period of nine months after you graduate, leave school, or drop below half-time attendance. Your school might have different rules concerning payback for students who drop below half-time, so check with your school's financial aid office before dropping too many classes. If you are not a new borrower, your grace period is six months. In either case, you will have as much as ten years to repay your loan.

You can stop the clock on your Perkins Loan so long as you continue your studies at least half-time. You can also hold off repayment for up to three years by working in the Peace Corps or VISTA Programs, or comparable full-time volunteer work for a qualified tax-exempt organization; active duty in the Armed Forces or in the commissioned corps of the U.S. Public Health Service; or serving in the National Oceanic and Atmospheric Administration Corps. Uncle Sam also now allows deferments if you work as a teacher in a federally-defined "teacher shortage area"; your school's education department should have information on which programs qualify you for that deferment. You can also hold off payments for as much as three years if you become temporarily totally disabled, or can't work because you're caring for a spouse or other dependent who becomes temporarily totally disabled. Certain internships can get you a two-year deferment, and mothers of preschool-aged children who are working at a salary that pays no more than a dollar above minimum wage get a one-year deferment. There's even a parental leave deferment of up to six months for pregnant borrowers, or borrowers who are caring for newborn or newly adopted children. If you become unemployed, your school may have programs to defer the principal of your loan during your period of unemployment. Being on your way to employment can also get you a deferment: under certain conditions, an internship or residency program that is required to begin professional practice or service. But none of these deferments is automatic; you have to apply for a deferment through your school, and you have to continue paying off your loans until the deferment goes through. Otherwise, you could be found in default. You can even get all or part of your loan forgiven altogether. Part of your loan will be wiped off the books if you become a teacher of handicapped children, or teach in a designated elementary or secondary school that serves low-income kids. In either case, your entire loan will be cancelled in the fifth straight year of full-time teaching. Your college can provide you with a list of designated schools that will help you do well for yourself by doing good. Working in certain Head Start programs will also cancel up to 100 percent of your loan; by your seventh Head Start year, the slate will be wiped clean for your entire loan. And as much as 70 percent of your loan can be cancelled if you volunteer for the Peace Corps or VISTA. Finally, the military often repays a portion of your loan as an incentive to sign up.

Direct and FFEL Program Loans

What it is: Life used to be much simpler when this program was just known as the Stafford Loan. In recent years, a number of new Federal loan programs have proliferated, thanks in part to the government's entry into the direct loan field. But before you wander into the maze of program titles, you need to know one thing: There are differences in benefits between Federal direct loans and the old-fashioned federally subsidized loans.

The two broad programs are now known as the Federal Direct Student Loan Program and the Federal Family Education Loan (FFEL) Program. Under the Direct Loan Program, Uncle Sam makes the loans directly to students and parents through the school. With FFELs, you get the money from banks, credit unions, or savings and loans.

Direct Loans and FFEL Program Loans come in two flavors: subsidized or unsubsidized. If your financial need is great enough that you qualify for a subsidized loan, the federal government will pay the interest on the loan until you begin paying the loan back—usually, after college. An unsubsidized loan is not awarded on the basis of need, but it's more expensive than the subsidized kind. If you qualify for an unsubsidized loan, your interest charges will begin from the time you first get the loan until you pay it in full.

If you're entering the FFEL program (getting the money from a financial institution like a bank), then the programs are either known as subsidized or unsubsidized Stafford Loans. If you sign up for a Direct Loan program (that is, the government is handing out the money through the school), the programs are known as the Direct Stafford Loans (the subsidized kind) or the Direct Unsubsidized Stafford Loan. You can mix and match subsidized and unsubsidized money, so long as both loans are from the same program—either FFEL or the Direct Loan Program.

Stafford Loans, like Federal Perkins Loans or any loans, have to be repaid with interest. If you get a Direct Loan, your lender is the U.S. Department of Education; the loan is processed by the school and you don't have to seek out a lender. If you get an FFEL loan, you'll be dealing with a private lender such as a bank, a credit union, or a savings and loan. Your school's financial aid officer or state guaranty agency can help you connect with a lender. Sometimes the school itself is the lender. (A list of state guaranty agencies begins on page 29 along with the list of state financial aid offices.) The federal government reinsures the loans that the lender has made, making them more amenable to the idea of lending to students. While the rate of interest isn't as low as with Perkins Loans, Stafford Loans are easier to obtain—and the rate is awfully good.

How good are they? The interest rate charged on all flavors of Stafford Loans has fluctuated over time, but has consistently remained below market value for loans—and, in fact, is a better deal than can be found anywhere this side of the five percent Perkins Loan. The rate fluctuates from year to year, but cannot exceed 8.25 percent, with a three percent origination fee and a one percent insurance fee. In 1995, the rate was 7.43 percent for the first four years of repayment. Depending on your need, Stafford Loans can add up to a total of $23,000 for a dependent undergraduate student or $46,000 as an independent undergraduate student, with no more than $23,000 of that amount in subsidized loans.

Dependent undergraduate students can borrow up to $2,625 if they are first-year students enrolled in a program of study that is at least a full academic year; $3,500 if they have completed the first year of study and the remainder of the program is at least a full academic year; and $5,500 a year for students who have completed two years of study and the remainder of the program is at least a full academic year.

The numbers add up a little differently for independent undergraduates of parents who do not qualify for PLUS. Those folks can borrow up to $6,625 for first-year students enrolled in a program of study that is at least a full academic year (only $2,625 of this amount may be in subsidized loans); $7,500 for those who have completed the first year of study and the remainder of the program is at least a full academic year (only $3,500 of this amount may be in subsidized loans); and $10,500 a year for those who have completed two years of study and the remainder of the program is at least a full academic year (only $5,500 of this amount may be in subsidized loans).

These loans cost some money up front: an "origination fee" of four percent, which is deducted from the loan in installments. The state guaranty agency might also take its cut—up to three percent—also to be taken out proportionately from each loan disbursement as an insurance premium. You could also be charged late fees and collection costs if you don't keep up with your payments.

How to qualify: Students must be attending school at least half-time. (For a definition of "half-time," see the entry under "Pell Grants" or turn to the glossary.) Both undergraduate and graduate students are eligible. Students must demonstrate need. But like the Pell Grant program, there is no cap on the number of students who can receive these loans.

When to pay it back: You have to dig into your pocket six months after you graduate, leave school, or drop below half-time status. You usually have five years to repay the debt, though some allow as much as 10 years. As with Perkins Loans, Uncle Sam has made provision for deferments: up to three years for students unable to find full-time employment, or who can show economic hardship.

As with Perkins Loans, you can even get all or part of your loan forgiven altogether. If you become totally and permanently disabled or file for bankrupcy (in some cases), or if you die, the loan will be forgiven. That's cold comfort.

PLUS Loans for Parents

What they are: Like Stafford Loans, PLUS Loans provide additional funds for educational expenses—but these are not need-based. PLUS loans go to parents. As with Stafford Loans, these low-interest loans can either come directly from the Federal government, or from a lender such as a bank, a credit union, or a savings and loan. The Direct Loan Program offers the Federal Direct PLUS Loan; the FFEL Program offers the Federal PLUS Loan. If you enter the FFEL program, your financial aid officer or state guaranty agency can help you connect with a lender.

Sometimes the school itself is the lender. (See the list of state guaranty agencies on page 29.) PLUS loan interest rates are variable, though they cannot rise higher than nine percent. During the 1996–97 award year the rate was set at 8.72 percent. Parents can borrow as much as is needed to meet the cost of attendance minus the student's other financial aid.

How to qualify: PLUS loans are open to parents who have a child who is enrolled at least half-time and is a dependent student. (See discussion of dependency, beginning on page 115.)

When to pay it back: Debtors usually must begin repaying interest on these loans within 60 days after first getting the money, with no grace period. Deferments are possible in times of economic hardship or unemployment, but only on the loan principal; interest continues to pile up during the deferment period. There are very few avenues for cancellation or reduction of these loans: They include death (but not disability) of the student, or if the school closes its doors before the student can complete the program of study.

A Note on Repayment

Loan consolidation: Until 1983, students could lump together all of their education loans into one loan with a low, federally subsidized interest rate under a program known as OPTIONS. Consolidation disappeared for a while while Congress tried to figure out how to make the program, which was convenient for students and their families, less costly for the government.

The government brought back consolidation with the Higher Education Amendments of 1986. Today's consolidation is more tightly controlled and costs the borrower more. Here are the details:

Consolidation loans can replace combinations of loans that you would normally pay individually into one payment each month. Like all of the other loan programs, consolidation loans can now come from lenders or directly from the Federal government.

There are three kinds of Direct Consolidation Loans: Direct Subsidized Consolidation Loans, Direct Unsubsidized Consolidation Loans and Direct PLUS Consolidation Loans. In the case of Direct Subsidized and Unsubsidized Consolidation Loans, you'll pay an interest rate that can't go higher than 8.25 percent. With Direct PLUS Consolidation Loans, the rate can't go higher than nine percent. The Direct Consolidation Loan programs offer a range of repayment options. The FFEL Consolidation Loans are similar to the Direct Program's loans, but come from financial institutions. The financial institution will charge an interest rate based on the weighted average of the original interest rate on the loans being pooled together. If you need more information on the consolidation process, call 1-800-557-7392.

Other Avenues to Federal Funds

The Military

How you feel about the military in general will determine whether you skip the next few paragraphs or not. The simple point is this: unless you have conscientious objections to serving in the Armed Forces, the military could be a way to help finance your college education. The military offers a number of ways to help students pay for college, though none of today's programs match the largesse of the GI Bill that educated the post-World War II generation. In return for the years of military service, you receive everything from a cheaper education to one that costs you no money at all. Service academies such as West Point offer a tuition-free college education. Each branch of the service has its own academy with its own character and traditions. These academically rigorous institutions are excellent, especially for the technical fields, and you can't beat the price.

If you'd rather not attend a service academy—or can't get in—chances are that your school will have a Reserve Officer Training Corps—and that organization, too, can help you pay for college. Standing scholarships are available that put $100 each month into your pocket for as much as five years, and ad hoc scholarships are announced all the time to attract students into areas the military feels a need to beef up—usually in the technical fields. Even without ROTC scholarships, students in the ROTC earn $100 each month in their junior and senior years (though they receive nothing as freshmen and sophomores). Once on active duty, students stand a good chance of being sent back to school and having all or part of their tuition picked up by Uncle Sam. The New GI Bill matches the soldier's contribution to a college fund; after emerging from the Armed Services, a student-to-be can amass a war chest of more than $10,000. There are also state programs to help members of the military, as well as funds from public and private sources for families of former military. Healthy benefits are also available to those who enlist in the National Guard.

Whether or not you care for the military, be sure that you have registered for the draft if you are male. Uncle Sam is now tying aid to draft registration: if you don't sign up, you can't sign up for aid.

Federal Programs Offered Through the Department of Health and Human Services

Other federal programs that do not come from the Education Department have millions of dollars to spread around. Many of them are directed toward influencing career choices—say, producing more medical professionals. Here are a few of the most prominent ones:

Several campus-based programs get their funding from the Department of Health and Human Services. As campus-based programs, they are administered by the school and funded in a lump sum from the federal government. Campus-based programs can run out of money, and so it is important to check your school's deadline and apply early in order to be sure to get all the money you can get.

■ Nursing Student Loan Program applies to nursing students attending certain nursing schools. Both full-time and half-time students are eligible, depending on the school. Students must demonstrate financial need. The student can then receive up to $2,500 each year (and $4,000 annually in the last two years of your program) for a maximum of $13,000. Repayment of the five percent loans begins nine months after the borrower leaves school and can stretch over ten years, with deferments for active duty in the Armed Forces, Coast Guard, National Oceanic and Atmospheric Administration, or the U.S. Public Health Service or as a Peace Corps volunteer.

■ Financial Assistance for Disadvantaged Health Professions Students provides up to $10,000 per year to full-time students in medicine, osteopathic medicine, and dentistry. Not only must students prove exceptional financial need, but they must also come from a disadvantaged background.

■ Undergraduates pursuing degrees in Pharmacy can also qualify for two programs that are otherwise restricted to graduate students. These are the Health Profession Student Loan (HPSL) and the Health Education Student Loan (HEAL). Your departmental financial aid advisor should be able to help you with information on these programs.

For More Information on Federal Financial Aid Programs

Write or call one of the regional offices of the U.S. Department of Education:

REGION I

Connecticut, Maine, Massachusetts, New Hampshire, Rhode Island, Vermont

U.S. Department of Education
Student Financial Assistance Programs
J.W. McCormack Post Office and Courthouse Building
Room 502
Boston, MA 02109
(617) 223-9338

REGION II

New Jersey, New York, Puerto Rico, Virgin Islands, Panama Canal Zone

U.S. Department of Education
Student Financial Assistance Programs
75 Park Place, Room 1206
New York, NY 10007
(212) 264-4022

REGION III

Delaware, District of Columbia, Maryland, Pennsylvania, Virginia, West Virginia

U.S. Department of Education
Student Financial Assistance Programs
3535 Market Street, Room 16200
Philadelphia, PA 19104
(215) 596-0247

REGION IV

Alabama, Florida, Georgia, Kentucky, Mississippi, North Carolina, South Carolina, Tennessee

U.S. Department of Education
Office of Student Financial Assistance
101 Marietta Tower, Suite 2203
Atlanta, GA 30323
(800) 433-3243

REGION V

Illinois, Indiana, Michigan, Minnesota, Ohio, Wisconsin

U.S. Department of Education
Office of Student Financial Assistance
111 North Canal Street, Room 830
Chicago, IL 60605
(800) 433-3243

REGION VI & VII

Arkansas, Iowa, Kansas, Louisiana, Missouri, Nebraska, New Mexico, Oklahoma, Texas

U.S. Department of Education
Student Financial Assistance Programs
1200 Main Tower, Room 2150
Dallas, TX 75202
(214) 767-3811

REGION VIII

Colorado, Montana, North Dakota, South Dakota, Utah, Wyoming

U.S. Department of Education
Office of Student Financial Assistance Programs
1391 North Speer Boulevard, Suite 800
Denver, CO 80204-2512
(303) 844-3676

REGION IX

Arizona, California, Hawaii, Nevada, American Samoa, Guam, Federated States of Micronesia, Marshall Islands, Republic of Palau, Wake Island

U.S. Department of Education
Office of Student Financial Assistance
50 United Nations Plaza
San Francisco, CA 94102
(415) 437-8293

REGION X

Alaska, Idaho, Oregon, Washington

U.S. Department of Education
Office of Student Financial Assistance Programs
1000 Second Avenue, Suite 1200
Seattle, WA 98104-1023
(206) 287-1770

Endnotes on Federal Aid

If reading about federal sources of aid makes your brain hurt and you still need answers, there is a Federal Student Aid Information Center. Its toll-free number is 1-800-433-3243. The people on the other end of the line can tell you if the school you're applying to participates in federal aid programs, help you file an application, explain student eligibility requirements, and more. They accept calls between the hours of 9:00 a.m. and 5:30 p.m. Eastern Standard Time, Monday through Friday. Usually, they are even pleasant—no small trick these days.

Getting Financial Aid from the States

The 50 states vary widely in the amount of aid that each gives to education, according to the authoritative new York State Higher Education Services Corporation, which keeps track of state financial aid expenditures. In 1995-96, states awarded nearly $3 billion in total grant aid to more than two million college-aid students—about 2.2 percent more than the previous years' spending. About 85 percent of that amount went to need-based aid. The New York group predicts the numbers will continue to rise.

Some states are haves, others are have-nots. Whether the states like it or not, some do spend more than others. A lot more. In the 1995–96 school year, five states (California, Illinois, New Jersey, New York, and Pennsylvania) awarded $1.5 billion in undergraduate need-based aid—a whopping 60 percent of the total for that category.

Don't pack the car and head for California yet. While there are plenty of ways to look at how much money states spend on their college students, it's hard to come by numbers that make sense. Less populous states argue that just citing raw dollar amounts spent overall is misleading, because they end up spending more per capita on their small number of students. Some also complain that the full extent of their aid doesn't show up in standard measures: for instance, several states argue that their schools are so inexpensive that students don't need much financial aid—so that the states are penalized in the rankings for having a strong economic climate and helping students out with low tuition.

The estimated top ten spenders of need-based grant aid per full-time undergraduate for 1993–94 were:

New York	$841
Illinois	$812
New Jersey	$788
Pennsylvania	$706
Minnesota	$685
Vermont	$569
Indiana	$410
Washington	$379
Iowa	$368
Virginia	$355

Source: *National Association of State Student Grant and Aid Programs.*

Types of Programs Administered by the States

The range of state aid is dizzyingly broad, and shows the political process at work. Along with the standard varieties of need-based aid, states are now moving heavily into non-need-based aid programs that reward, say, outstanding academic achievement. The state legislatures also try to influence future careers by offering money to students who pursue certain areas of study or professions, just as the federal government rewards students entering the health professions. Many states push math and science studies for students who intend to go into teaching, while others boost a kaleidescopic array of professions ranging from bilingual education to teaching.

Other state programs try to reward people less for what they do than who they are. Minority group programs and programs to aid the dependents of prisoners of war or police officers killed in active duty all fall under this broad heading. Many also offer low-interest loan programs that are similar to federal loan aid. And to make the state's private colleges more attractive, several states now offer "equalization" money to help the private colleges' tuition match that of the public institutions.

The best benefit a state offers is the protection it gives its own citizens in the form of in-state tuition at its public institutions. Resident status is also a requirement for eligibility for certain aid programs. If you plan to attend a public school out of state, some students find it worthwhile to take the time beforehand to establish residency in the state of choice—often by moving there early and getting a job. But since establishing residency takes two years in some states, many students feel they just don't have the time.

Attracted to an academic program offered in another state but don't want to give up possible aid from your own state? Many states have established agreements to allow you to take advantage of your home state's aid while studying elsewhere.

The No-Need Aid Trend: Some Information and a Little Advice

Remember that trend toward non-need-based aid? In all during the 1995–96 school year, 32 states had such programs, and they doled out some $411 million. Those programs have been growing, though over 90 percent of grant dollars that states award to undergraduates are need based, according to the National Association of State Scholarship and Grant Programs. Of the non-need pool, the biggest chunk of cash went into academic scholarships. So study up! It pays.

Non-need-based aid is usually broken down into three categories:

(1) Tuition equalization programs, which help reduce the difference in tuition costs between public and private schools;

(2) Scholarship programs or merit awards, which reward academic achievement and are largely aimed at charming academic talent into staying in state;

(3) Categorical aid programs, which encourage students to go into particular fields of study such as math and science, or which help special constituencies like veterans and police officers.

As with all state programs, some give a lot more money than others. In the 1993–94 school year, for example, most of the growth in non-need-based programs could be attributed to Florida and Georgia, which bumped up spending by more than $26 million.

As you've probably figured out from the list of states above, having a new program doesn't automatically mean that money will shower upon you. The spurt in no-need monies is still puny compared to the massive $2 billion that go to undergraduates based on need annually. Starting new programs makes legislators feel good; actually giving those programs enough money to make a difference makes state legislators feel decidedly less good. Thus when you exclude behemoth programs like New York's Part-Time Student Grant Program and Ohio's Student Choice Program, the average allotment for these programs drops off dramatically. That's why the 19th annual report from the National Association of State Scholarship and Grant Programs said that "adding new programs has contributed little to the growth of state grant aid." Of course, a million dollars is not pocket change; most of us would be very happy with just a fraction of that. Simply keep this advice in mind: Don't get so hung up on cashing in on the new that you ignore the larger sums that are available from more traditional programs.

State-Administered Aid Programs That Get Their Funding from the Federal Government

Several federally funded aid programs are administered by individual states. This gives a little more consistency to the crazy quilt of state aid programs, giving you some program names to look out for when going over state aid information.

■ State Student Incentive Grants: While the states administer the program and decide individually whether the grants apply to full- or half-time students, the program is partially funded by the federal government. Annual maximum: $2,500.

■ Robert C. Byrd Honors Scholarship Program: This program recognizes 10 students from each congressional district for outstanding academic achievement, providing $1,500 for the first year of higher education study.

■ Paul Douglas Teacher Scholarship Program: a merit-based, state-administered program intended to encourage students who graduate in the top 10 percent of their classes to enter the field of teaching. The states may give each student up to $5,000 a year for up to four years; the student is then obligated to teach for two years.

The State of the States

The entry for each state in the list below consists of addresses and phone numbers. These refer to the agencies that oversee most of the student aid. You should be able to get current information from counselors at your high school or at the college financial aid office, but sometimes the world does not work as well as we would like. If you can't get the facts from those sources and need more than what the list below provides, the state agencies have the most up-to-date and comprehensive information.

State Guaranty Agency

This heading refers to the state guarantying agency or nonprofit organization that administers the FFEL Stafford and PLUS loans. While the federal government sets the loan limits and interest rates for these programs, the states set their own limitations and conditions. You will want to contact them for the latest information on loan availability and repayment and deferment conditions; the guaranty agency can also put you in touch with willing lenders.

State Aid

This office is a central clearinghouse for the aid programs provided within the state. Since even programs that sound similar vary in their particulars from state to state, this office can help you sort out the differences.

Under the category of state aid, we list the different state programs administered by that state aid agency, and also list programs administered by other agencies.

Alabama

One agency for information on Stafford Loan/PLUS and state aid:

Alabama Commission on Higher Education
P.O. Box 302000
Montgomery, AL 36130-2000
(334) 242-1998

Alaska

State Guaranty Agency for Stafford Loan/PLUS:
U.S. Department of Education
Office of Student Financial Assistance
1000 Second Avenue, Suite 1200
Seattle, WA 98174-1023
(206) 287-1770

For information on state aid:
Alaska Commission on Postsecondary Education
3030 Vintage Boulevard
Juneau, AK 99801
(907) 465-2962

Arizona

United Student Aid Group
Arizona Education Loan Program
25 South Arizona Place, Suite 530
Chandler, AZ 85225
(602) 814-9988
(800) 551-1353

For information on state aid:
Contact the individual college/institution.

Arkansas

State Guaranty Agency for Stafford Loan/PLUS:
Student Loan Guaranty Foundation of Arkansas
219 South Victory
Little Rock, AR 72201
(501) 372-1491

For information on state aid:
Department of Higher Education
114 East Capitol
Little Rock, AR 72201-1884
(501) 371-2000

California

State Guaranty Agency:
California Student Aid Commission
P.O. Box 510845
Sacramento, CA 94245–0845
(916) 323-0435

Colorado

State Guaranty Agency for Stafford Loan/PLUS:
Colorado Student Loan Program
999 Eighteenth Street, Suite 425
Denver, CO 80202
(303) 294-5050

For information on state aid:
Colorado Commission on Higher Education
1300 Broadway, Second Floor
Denver, CO 80203
(303) 866-2723

Connecticut

State Guaranty Agency for Stafford Loan/PLUS:
Connecticut Student Loan Foundation
P.O. Box 1009
Rocky Hill, CT 06067
(860) 257-4001

For information on state aid:
Connecticut Department of Higher Education
61 Woodland Street
Hartford, CT 06105-2391
(860) 566-2618

Delaware

State Guaranty Agency for Stafford Loan/PLUS:
Delaware Education Loan Services
Carvel State Office Building
820 North French Street, Fourth Floor
Wilmington, DE 19801
(302) 577-6055

For information on state aid:
Delaware Higher Education Commission
Carvel State Office Building
820 North French Street, Fourth Floor
Wilmington, DE 19801
(302) 577-3240

District of Columbia

State Guaranty Agency for Stafford Loan/PLUS:
American Student Assitance Corporation
Attention: ASA Call Center
330 Stuart Street
Boston, MA 02116
(800) 999-9080

For information on state aid:
Office of Postsecondary Education
Research and Assistance
D.C. Department of Human Services
2100 Martin Luther King, Jr. Avenue SE, Suite 401
Washington, D.C. 20020
(202) 727-3688

Florida

State Guaranty Agency for Stafford Loan/PLUS:
Office of Student Financial Assistance
Department of Education
P.O. Box 7019
Tallahassee, FL 32314-7019
(800) 366-3475

For information on state aid:
Office of Student Financial Assistance
Department of Education
325 West Gaines Street, 255 Collins
Tallahassee, FL 32399-0400
(904) 487-0049

Georgia

One agency for information on Stafford Loan/PLUS and state aid:

Georgia Student Finance Commission
2082 East Exchange Place, Suite 200
Tucker, GA 30084
(770) 723-1029

Hawaii

State Guaranty Agency for Stafford Loan/PLUS:

Hawaii Education Loan Program
P.O. Box 22187
Honolulu, HI 96823
(808) 593-2262

For information on state aid:

State Postsecondary Education Commission
209 Bachman Hall
University of Hawaii
2444 Dole Street, Room 209
Honolulu, HI 96822
(808) 956-8213

Idaho

State Guaranty Agency for Stafford Loan/PLUS:

Student Loan Fund of Idaho, Inc.
P.O. Box 730
Fruitland, ID 83619–0730
(208) 452-4058

For information on state aid:
Office of State
Board of Education
P.O. Box 83720
Boise, ID 83720-0037
(208) 334-2270

Illinois

One agency for information on Stafford Loan/PLUS and state aid:

Illinois Student Assistance Commission
1755 Lake Cooke Road
Deerfield, IL 60015
(847) 948-8500

Indiana

One agency for information on Stafford Loan/PLUS and state aid:

State Student Assistance Commission of Indiana
150 West Market Street, Suite 500
Indianapolis, IN 46204
(317) 232-2350

Iowa

One agency for information on Stafford Loan/PLUS and state aid:

Iowa College Student Aid Commission
200 10th Street, Fourth Floor
Des Moines, IA 50309
(515) 281-4890

Kansas

State Guaranty Agency for Stafford Loan/PLUS:

USA Services, Incorporated
3 Townsite Plaza
Suite 220
120 S.E. Sixth Street
Topeka, KS 66603
(785) 234-0072

For information on state aid:

Kansas Board of Regents
Student Financial Aid Section
700 SW Harrison Street, Suite 1410
Topeka, KS 66603
(785) 296-3517

Kentucky

One agency for information on Stafford Loan/PLUS and state aid:

Kentucky Higher Education Assistance Authority
1050 U.S. 127 South
Suite 102
Frankfort, KY 40601
(502) 696-7200

Louisiana

One agency for information on Stafford Loan/PLUS and state aid:

Louisiana Office of Student Financial Assistance
P.O. Box 91202
Baton Rouge, LA 70821-9202
(504) 922-1011

Maine

One agency for information on Stafford Loan/PLUS and state aid:

Finance Authority of Maine
State House Station 119
1 Weston Court
Augusta, ME 04333
(207) 287-2183

Maryland

State Guaranty Agency for Stafford Loan/PLUS:
United Student Aid Group
555 Fairmont Avenue
Towson, MD 21218
(410) 337-0274

For information on state aid:
Maryland State Scholarship Administration
16 Francis Street
Annapolis, MD 21401
(410) 974-5370

Massachusetts

State Guaranty Agency for Stafford Loan/PLUS:
American Student Assistance
330 Stuart Street
Boston, MA 02116
(617) 426-9434

For information on state aid:
Office of Student Financial Assistance
330 Stuart Street
Boston, MA 02116
(617) 727-9420

Michigan

State Guaranty Agency for Stafford Loan/PLUS:
Michigan Guaranty Agency
P.O. Box 30047
Lansing, MI 48909-7547
(517) 373-0760
(800) MGA-LOAN

For information on state aid:
Michigan Higher Education Assistance Authority
Office of Scholarships and Grants
P.O. Box 30462
Lansing, MI 48909-7962
(517) 373-3394

Minnesota

State Guaranty Agency for Stafford Loan/PLUS:
Northstar Guaranty Inc./Great Lakes Higher Education Guaranty Corporation
P.O. Box 64102
St. Paul, MN 55164-0102
(612) 290-8795
(800) 366-0032

For information on state aid:
Minnesota Higher Education Services Office
Capitol Square, Suite 400
550 Cedar Street
St. Paul, MN 55101–2292
(612) 296-3974
(800) 657-3866

Mississippi

State Guaranty Agency for Stafford Loan/PLUS:
U.S.A. Funds
P.O. Box 618
Indianapolis, IN 46206
(800) 824-7044

For information on state aid:
Mississippi Postsecondary Education Financial Assistance Board
Student Financial Aid
3825 Ridgewood Road
Jackson, MS 39211-6453
(601) 982-6663

Missouri

One agency for information on Stafford Loan/PLUS and state aid:
Coordinating Board for Higher Education
CBHE/MSLP
P.O. Box 6730
Jefferson City, MO 65102
(573) 751-3940
(800) 473-6757

Montana

One agency for information on Stafford Loan/PLUS and state aid:
Montana Guaranteed Student Loan Program
2500 Broadway
Helena, MT 59620-3103
(406) 444-6594

Nebraska

Stafford Loan/PLUS:
Nebraska Higher Education Loan Program
Educational Planning Center
13 "O" Street
Lincoln, NE 68508
(402) 471-2847

For information on state aid:
Coordinating Commission for Postsecondary Education
P.O. Box 95005
Lincoln, NE 68509-5005
(402) 471-2847

Nevada

State Guaranty Agency for Stafford Loan/PLUS:
United Student Aid Group
P.O. Box 3028
Chandler, AZ 85244-3028
(800) 824-7044

For information on state aid:
University of Nevada–Reno
Student Financial Services
Mailstop 076
Reno, NV 89557
(702) 784-4666

New Hampshire

State Guaranty Agency for Stafford Loan/PLUS:
New Hampshire Higher Education Assistance Foundation
P.O. Box 877
Concord, NH 03302
(603) 225-6612

For information on state aid:
New Hampshire Postsecondary Education Commission
2 Industrial Park Drive
Concord, NH 03301-8512
(603) 271-2555

New Jersey

One agency for information on Stafford Loan/PLUS and state aid:
New Jersey Office of Student Assistance
P.O. Box 543
Trenton, NJ 08625
(609) 588-3200
(800) 792-8670

New Mexico

State Guaranty Agency for Stafford Loan/PLUS:
New Mexico Educational Assistance Foundation
P.O. Box 27020
Albuquerque, NM 87125
(505) 345-3371

For information on state aid:
Commission on Higher Education
1068 Cerrillos Road
Santa Fe, NM 87501-4295
(505) 827-7383

New York

State Guaranty Agency for Stafford Loan/PLUS:
New York State Higher Education Services Corporation
Loans Division
99 Washington Avenue
Albany, NY 12255
(518) 473-1574
(800) 642-6234

For information on state aid:
New York State Higher Education Services Corporation
Tuition Assistance
99 Washington Avenue
Albany, NY 12255
(518) 474-5642

North Carolina

State Guaranty Agency for Stafford Loan/PLUS:
College Foundation
P.O. Box 12100
Raleigh, NC 27605-2100
(919) 821-4771

For information on state aid:
North Carolina State Education Assistance Authority
P.O. Box 2688
Chapel Hill, NC 27515
(919) 549-8614

North Dakota

State Guaranty Agency for Stafford Loan/PLUS:

Bank of North Dakota
Student Loan Program
P.O. Box 5509
Bismarck, ND 58506-5509
(701) 328-5660
(800) 472-2166

For information on state aid:

North Dakota Student Financial Assistance Program
North Dakota University System
600 East Boulevard
Bismarck, ND 58505-0230
(701) 328-4114
(800) 537-5420

Ohio

State Guaranty Agency for Stafford Loan/PLUS:
Great Lakes Higher Education Corp.
P.O. Box 182174
Columbus, OH 43218-2174
(614) 755-7400

For information on state aid:
Ohio Board of Regents
State Grants and Scholarships
P.O. Box 182452
Columbus, OH 43218-2452
(614) 466-7420
(888) 833-1133

Oklahoma

One agency for information on Stafford Loan/PLUS and
state aid:
Oklahoma Guaranteed Student Loan Program
P.O. Box 3000
Oklahoma City, OK 73101-3000
(405) 858-4300

Oregon

One agency for information on Stafford Loan/PLUS and
state aid:
Oregon State Scholarship Commission
1500 Valley River Drive, Suite 100
Eugene, OR 97401
(503) 687-7400
(800) 452-8807

Pennsylvania

State Guaranty Agency for Stafford Loan/PLUS:
Pennsylvania Higher Education Assistance Agency
PHEAA Loan Division
1200 North Seventh Streeet
Harrisburg, PA 17102
(717) 720-2654
(800) 692-7392

For information on state aid:
Pennsylvania Higher Education Assistance Agency
1200 North Seventh Street
Harrisburg, PA 17102
(717) 720-2654

Rhode Island

One agency for information on Stafford Loan/PLUS and
state aid:
Rhode Island Higher Education Assistance Authority
560 Jefferson Boulevard
Warwick, RI 02886
(401) 736-1100
(800) 922-9855

South Carolina

State Guaranty Agency for Stafford Loan/PLUS:
South Carolina Student Loan Corporation
Interstate Center, Suite 210
P.O. Box 21487
Columbia, SC 29221
(803) 798-0916

For information on state aid:
Higher Education Tuition Grants Commission
Keenan Building, Room 811
P.O. Box 12159
Columbia, SC 29211
(803) 734-1200

South Dakota

State Guaranty Agency for Stafford Loan/PLUS:
Education Assistance Corporation
115 First Avenue, SW
Aberdeen, SD 57401
(605) 225-6423 or (800) 592-1802

For information on state aid:
Department of Education and Cultural Affairs
Office of the Secretary
700 Governor's Drive
Pierre, SD 57501
(605) 773-3134

Tennessee

One agency for information of Stafford Loan/PLUS, and state aid:
Tennessee Student Assistance Corporation
404 James Robertson Parkway
Parkway Towers, Suite 1950
Nashville, TN 37243-0820
(800) 257-6526 (out-of-state)
(615) 741-1346

Texas

State Guaranty Agency for Stafford Loan/PLUS:
Texas Guaranteed Student Loan Corporation
P.O. Box 201725
Austin, TX 78720-1725
(512) 219-5700

For information on state aid:
Texas Higher Education Coordinating Board
Student Services Division
P.O. Box 12788
Austin, TX 78711
(512) 483-6340

Utah

State Guaranty Agency for Stafford Loan/PLUS:
Utah System of Higher Education
P.O. Box 45202
Salt Lake City, UT 84145-0202
(801) 321-7100

For information on state aid:
Utah System of Higher Education
Student Loans
P.O. Box 45202
Salt Lake City, UT 84145-0202
(801) 321-7100

Vermont

One agency for information on Stafford Loan/PLUS and state aid:
Vermont Student Assistance Corporation
Champlain Mill
P.O. Box 2000
Winooski, VT 05404
(802) 655-9602, (800) 642-3177

Virginia

State Guaranty Agency for Stafford Loan/PLUS:
Educational Credit Management Corporation
411 East Franklin, Suite 300
Richmond, VA 23219
(804) 644-6400

For information on state aid:
State Council of Higher Education for Virginia
James Monroe Building
101 North 14th Street
Richmond, VA 23219
(804) 225-2624

Washington

State Guaranty Agency for Stafford Loan/PLUS:
Northwest Education Loan
500 Colman Building
811 First Avenue
Seattle, WA 98104
(206) 461-5470

For information on state aid:
Higher Education Coordinating Board
Financial Aid Office
P.O. Box 43430
Olympia, WA 98504-3430
(360) 753-7800

West Virginia

State Guaranty Agency for Stafford Loan/PLUS:
West Virginia Education Loan Services
P.O. Box 591
Charleston, WV 25301
(304) 345-7211

For information on state aid:
West Virginia Higher Education Grant Program
1018 Kanawaha Boulevard East, Suite 700
Charleston, WV 25301
(304) 588-4614

Wisconsin

State Guaranty Agency for Stafford Loan/PLUS:
Great Lakes Higher Education Corporation
2401 International Lane
Madison, WI 53704
(608) 246-1800

For information on state aid:
Wisconsin Higher Educational Aids Board
P.O. Box 7885
Madison, WI 53707-7885
(608) 267-2206

Wyoming

State Guaranty Agency for Stafford Loan/PLUS:
United Student Aid Group
1912 Capitol Avenue, Suite 320
Cheyenne, WY 82001
(307) 635-3259

For information on state aid:
Student Financial Aid Office
University of Wyoming
P. O. Box 3335
Laramie, WY 82071-3335
(307) 766-3886

Puerto Rico

State Guaranty Agency for Stafford Loan/PLUS:
University of Puerto Rico
Financial Aid Office
P.O. Box 364894
San Juan, PR 00936
(787) 764-3710

For information on state aid:
Council on Higher Education
P.O. Box 23305-UPR Station
Rio Piedras, PR 00931
(787) 764-3256

Intermission — Righting the Balance

Before we move from the governmental sources of aid into the private realm, we should discuss two broad categories of assistance that span both public and private assistance. The first is aid to certain minorities: If you are a member of a group that has suffered from discrimination past or present, there's a category of student aid that you should know about that doesn't fit into neat pigeonholes. These are broad areas that have contributions kicked in from all sources of aid—federal, state, the schools themselves, and private groups—and which attempt to correct past wrongs by providing new opportunities.

A second type of program attempts to correct a very different type of imbalance: the lack of students entering certain professions, such as teaching or the health professions. To get more students into these areas, government and private organizations are holding out the promise of cash. You can even find programs intended to promote these fields for minority students—an interesting twofer that students with the right qualifications can't afford to pass up.

We don't list every program offered at the federal, state, college, and local level here. We will concentrate on the federal level, where much of the money is. You can then write to the state aid agency (pages 29–36) for more detailed information. And of course, check in with your high school counselor or your college financial aid office for more information.

Minorities

Minorities students looking for financial aid will not find much of interest at the federal level; federal monies are concentrated in counseling for minority students. Still, many colleges have implemented minority recruitment and retention programs and can direct you to funds available at the schools you're most interested in. For a list of reference guides to the more prominent scholarships for minority students, see the bibliography on page 119.

To find money, students should look to the states, colleges, and private organizations. Several states have funded programs to enhance the opportunities of minority students, from the Cal Grant B program to the Florida Seminole-Miccosukee Indian Scholarship Program. Contact your state agency for information. (List, page 29.)

Colleges are trying to fulfill their federal commitment to affirmative action programs by working harder to recruit and retain qualified minority students. Even in these times of political attacks and reassessment of affirmative action guidelines, many schools still recruit vigorously and many have minority affairs officers on campus who, in conjunction with the financial aid office, can help you find your way to academic funding.

Think the days of minority scholarships are over? Try telling it to Anne Connolly, a college student from the Washington, D.C. area, who was flooded with scholarship offers as she neared high school graduation in 1994. In all, she had offers from 47 schools that totalled $1.2 million. Of course, she had a 4.0 grade point average and perfect attendance since kindergarten. According to a story in the Washington Post, another student, Patrice Arrington, got a similar bounty of offers based on her 3.4 grade point average; she was also an all-American volleyball player. They are unusual cases, sure—but they're for real. It happens.

Private organizations also do what they can to add to the numbers of minority students in higher education. One such program is the Wilkins Educational Scholarship Program, which is offered by the National Association for the Advancement of Colored People and funded by major corporations.

About a dozen of these $1,000 scholarships are awarded annually; contact:

Youth and College Division
NAACP
4805 Mount Hope
Baltimore, MD 21215
(410) 358-8900

For more programs, look up minority scholarships in the index to our own roster of scholarships, which begins on page 505. While some come from religious organizations and civic groups, many of these scholarships are supplied by professional associations. The best-known program aids minority students interested in engineering careers; the program is funded through the schools. For a list of schools that participate in the program, write:

National Action Council for Minorities in Engineering
The Empire State Building
350 Fifth Avenue, Suite 2212
New York, NY 10118-2299
(212) 279-2626

The federal government has also developed a number of programs to aid American Indians. The Bureau of Indian Affairs Higher Education Program provides need-based scholarships and loans to Indian tribal members who have at least one-fourth degree Indian blood. The school's financial aid office should have information on the different programs, or you can get applications from your home agency, tribe, or regional office. Or write:

Bureau of Indian Affairs Higher Education Program
Office on Indian Education
1849 C Street, NW
Washington, D.C. 20240
(202) 208-6156 or -3478

To find out if your chosen profession has a minority scholarship program, first look up the group in a reference work such as Gale's *Encyclopedia of Associations*. Contact the group and ask whether minority scholarships exist.

Women

The money for women in higher education comes almost exclusively from the colleges and private sources. College money most often takes the form of athletic scholarships; for an up-to-date listing of such awards, write for General Information to:

Women's Sports Foundation
Isenhower Park
East Meadow, NY 11554
(800) 227-3988

Another lode of scholarship and loan money for women is through professional organizations such as the Society of Women Engineers (United Engineering Center, 120 Wall Street New York, NY 10005; (212) 509-9577), and the Business and Professional Women's Foundation (2012 Massachusetts Avenue, NW, Washington DC 20036; (202) 293-1200).

If you are a female student with small children, you should find out whether your school offers day care for free or at low cost. Some schools do this now—often through their school of social work, which means enthusiastic, careful attention. In any case, the expenses associated with raising kids should be reflected in your financial need, which could get you more aid.

Handicapped Students

Along with the assorted state programs for blind students, the Qualls Memorial Scholarships provide ten to twenty scholarships for blind students each year that range in value from $1,000 to $2,500. Contact the Floyd Qualls Memorial Scholarship Committee, American Council of the Blind, 1155 15th Street, NW, Suite 720, Washington, D.C. 20005; (202) 467-5081.

Gallaudet University, the nation's leading institution of higher education for the deaf, has developed a vigorous financial aid program that combines government aid with its own funds. For more information write the Financial Aid Office, Gallaudet University, 800 Florida Avenue, NE, Washington, D.C. 20002; (202) 651-5290/TTD: same.

The Alexander Graham Bell Association for the Deaf, Inc. (3417 Volta Place, NW, Washington, D.C. 20007; (202) 337-5220) also provides many scholarships for deaf students attending higher education institutions for hearing students.

Attracting Students into Necessary Professions

Teaching

The federal government's most lucrative program to attract bright students into the field of teaching is now known as the Paul Douglas Teacher Scholarship Program. It was formerly known as the Carl D. Perkins Teacher Scholarship and the Congressional Teacher Scholarship. The program is administered by the states, and goes to students who rank in the top 10 percent of their graduating class (or who have GED scores recognized by the state to match that ranking). Washington allows the states to award each recipient up to $5,000 each year. Sound great? It is. But look out for the catch—each year that the student receives the scholarship has to be paid back with two years of teaching. If the student doesn't fulfill this requirement, the money has to be repaid, with interest. For more information, check with your state aid agency for specific eligibility criteria, which varies from state to state.

When contacting the state agency about the Douglas scholarships, be sure to ask about other teaching programs the state may offer—many promote teaching heavily. Private foundations also offer teaching scholarships; see the index of scholarships by major beginning on page 488.

Health Professions

On the federal level, there exist several well-funded programs intended to draw students into what the Department of Health and Human Services calls "shortage areas" in the health professions. Most of these are directed toward graduate study—fields such as medicine, osteopathy, dentistry, veterinary medicine, optometry, podiatry, pharmacy, chiropractic, and public health. Rest assured that when you finish your premed program, there are several federal programs to help students who can demonstrate need. Remember, too, that the military provides many scholarship opportunities within the health professions for students who join ROTC or who enlist in the Armed Forces. Programs that benefit undergraduates and which are sponsored by the Department of Health and Human Services include:

Health Professions Student Loan Program: Helps full-time students who can demonstrate need and who are pursuing Bachelor of Science degrees in pharmacy; it also applies to certain graduate studies. Students may receive a maximum of $2,500 on top of tuition each academic year; selection is made by the school. The nine percent loans have a ten-year payback time that begins a year after the student finishes full-time studies. Students can get deferments of three years while serving in the uniformed service or as a Peace Corps volunteer, or while pursuing advanced professional training.

Nursing Student Loan Program: Applies to nursing students attending certain nursing schools. Both full-time and half-time students are eligible, depending on the school. Students must demonstrate financial need. The student can then receive up to $2,500 each year for a maximum of $10,000. Selection is made by the individual school. Repayment of the six percent loans begins nine months after the borrower leaves school and can stretch over ten years, with deferments for active duty in the armed forces, Coast Guard, National Oceanic and Atmospheric Administration, U.S. Public Health Service, or as a Peace Corps volunteer.

For additional information on nursing aid, get the booklet, *Scholarships and Loans for Nursing Education,* by sending $16.95 plus $3.95 shipping and handling ($20.90 total) to:

National League for Nursing
350 Hudson Street
New York, NY 10014
(212) 989-9393

For information on state and private programs in the health professions, check with your college financial aid office, as well as the advising office within your academic department. Several private programs can be found through the index of scholarship sources by major that begins on page 488. Looking through a directory of associations, such as *Gale*'s *Encyclopedia of Associations*, can give you the addresses of the professional associations that represent your specialty within the health professions. These associations can be a good source of information on additional sources of financial aid.

Public Service

The Harry S Truman Scholarship is offered to more than 100 students each year who wish to pursue careers in public service. The foundation awards between 75 and 85 scholarships each year (paying tuition, fees, books, and room and board) each worth approximately $30,000. Your school must nominate you for this award. For more information, contact:

Harry S Truman Scholarship Foundation
712 Jackson Place, NW
Washington, D.C. 20006
(202) 395-7429

The World of Available Aid— Private Channels

In this chapter we discuss the many sources of financial aid outside of the government. The world of private aid is more complex than that of public aid—and the public aid, as we have already seen, is pretty complex. But the sources of public aid are limited to the federal government and the 50 states. Private sources of aid are not only more numerous, but are also tougher to track down—they range from the colleges themselves to private foundations, companies, and other programs such as the National Merit Scholarship Corporation. Trying to keep track of all of these sources on your own borders on the impossible. We list many of them here, and have provided an extensive scholarship directory later in this book.

Since the field of private financial aid is so dauntingly broad, we recommend that you not try to master it on your own. Find out who knows about sources of aid and pick their brains. Your search should take you to those people who know about the financial aid sources for your school and for your career area. High school counselors can provide the information you need on locally-available scholarships. For special programs available through your college, consult the school's financial aid office—America's colleges have about $5 billion in their own funds to help students. For corporate programs, ask your boss (or your parents' bosses) or the company officer in charge of employee benefit programs. This may mean a lot of telephone calls, personal visits, and letters. But this will be time well spent.

About the organization of this chapter: We have placed aid from the colleges' own funds in this chapter on "private sources." Of course, this broad heading nonetheless includes state-run, "public" institutions. But since many of these public schools have endowments that go to helping their students, we have put them in the same category as the private schools for the purposes of this section, if for no other reason than to simplify things.

A Warning about the True Value of Scholarships

There's a caveat that we should deal with before getting to the goods: Getting a scholarship may not help you pay for college. That's because the school will probably either count the award into what it was already going to give you, or add it to your ability to pay. Either way, you are left digging into your pocket for the same amount of money as before. The school is then able to divert the money that would have gone to you to another student who has not been as enterprising as yourself. Sound like a ripoff? Maybe. But it's one way schools have found to stretch their much-needed aid dollars. And remember: Getting the scholarship gives you plenty of what you might call "prestige points." These honors look good on your resume, which could help you in your later application to graduate school or job hunt. That warning behind us, let's look at the sources of funds.

The Schools Do Their Part: The $5 Billion Question

In days gone by, many schools held out a "need-blind" admissions policy. The phrase means that if a student is accepted at a college, that student will be able to attend; money will be found somewhere. A lofty concept, few schools have been able to preserve "need-blind" as anything more than a concept in these cash-tight days.

In fact, "need-blind" puts schools in an uncomfortable cycle: by guaranteeing to subsidize the costs for so many of their students, they often find themselves needing to raise tuition—creating even more need for the school to have to fill somehow. The result can be chilling: Smith College, facing 20 percent annual increases in its financial aid budget over the last five years, decided that enough is enough. Starting in 1991, the school decided it would rank students who have been accepted for admission and hand out the money from the top down. Students highest on the list will see all of their financial aid needs met; below the fateful line, students will be on their own unless Smith can find the money elsewhere.

So again, a little investigative work is in order on your part. You should check in with the college financial aid office to see if the school maintains a "need-blind" policy. You might be surprised—it's not just the Ivies. Smaller schools like Franklin and Marshall College in Pennsylvania have managed to hold on to need-blind values. Still, if a school tells you it has need-blind admissions, try to find out what that actually means in practice. Don't be afraid to ask tough questions; for the kind of money you'll be spending, you deserve answers.

Today we look to the colleges for supplements to our education funding that include endowed scholarships, scholarships for athletic or academic prowess, work-study, and even loans from the school's own funds. Some private schools even offer "tuition remission"—that is, a discount on the official cost of tuition. (For a look at other innovative ways that schools have used to make paying for college less burdensome, see the next chapter, "Getting the Most College for the Money.")

All of these college gambits cost money. As a practical matter, this means that it behooves you as an academic consumer to keep in mind the school's bottom line while you are trying to make your college choice. It may seem an obvious point, but a school with a bountiful endowment like billionaire Harvard is going to be in a better position to offer you financial aid than a less wealthy institution. And a school that is truly strapped financially could burden you with tuition increases once you enter—or even fold. It happens.

With that chilling thought behind us, let's look at each broad category of student aid from the colleges.

Grants and Scholarships

Academic scholarships: Just as the states have been providing increasing amounts of money for programs to attract academic stars, the individual schools have been hustling to gain the prestige of enrolling academically talented students. If you earn a certain grade point average, or score higher than a certain level on the SAT or ACT, most schools will offer enticements to attend. Some schools also provide special lures for valedictorians or students who have achieved other academic honors. Not every school promotes academic scholarships; the nation's most prestigious institutions attract a consistently high level of scholar, so many don't refer to academic scholarships as such. Academic scholarships are most important to schools on the make: those institutions that are trying to build an academically strong student body but don't have the academic traditions of the Ivy League schools as a draw.

Money comes to scholars in a number of ways. The school may offer the awards according to a formula or set of conditions, such as a set SAT score. In addition to the funds available under the standard formula, the school might hold money in reserve to offer to especially promising students in order to sweeten the pot. Instead of actually spending money on bright students, many private schools simply offer tuition remission.

Need is a factor in most academic scholarships. Most of them offer a no-need minimum of a small amount —often less than $300. Beyond that, demonstrated need can up the annual award into the thousands. It's worth asking your school whether there are special no-need scholarships above the need-based variety, and whether you can qualify.

Athletic scholarships: Don't laugh. Even if you're not going to win the Heisman Trophy, there could be athletic scholarships for you out there. (If you are going to win the

Heisman Trophy, you're not going to be reading this book, anyway.) Sure, the super-jocks have got football, basketball, baseball, and the like sewn up. But most colleges also have money to help students who show promise. The best jocks will be wooed by the biggest schools. But one of the smaller schools you are considering may have an ambitious sports program in a sport you might be pretty good at. Though your skills might not have gotten you far at Big State U, the other school might be happy to have you—and willing to supply a little money to entice you. And not just in football, basketball, or baseball. Many schools offer scholarships in sports you might never have thought of, including: archery, badminton, bowling, crew, fencing, gymnastics, lacrosse, sailing, skiing, synchronized swimming, and volleyball. Come on—if they're going to make curling an Olympic sport, can varsity tiddly-winks be far behind?

At the beginning of this chapter, we talked about contacting the people who know where the money is. In this case you need to talk not just with your high school guidance counselor but also with your coach. Together you can figure out which schools' athletic programs might want you. Numerous college guides break down athletic scholarships by sport to make your search easier. Contact the college coaches at the most likely schools with a letter detailing your athletic achievement and pointing out that you would need financial aid. Be ready to provide the coaches who respond to your letter with more information and letters of recommendation.

The college as bank: Many colleges now offer long-term or short-term emergency loans out of their own funds. Ask at your financial aid office to see if your school has such a program. Many of them help students who do not otherwise qualify for need-based aid, and offer lower interest than commercial banks. Fairleigh Dickinson University of New Jersey uses its foundation money to subsidize interest on parent loans to keep the interest rates low. Other schools such as Lafayette College in Pennsylvania pay the interest on student loans while the student is in college, taking the pressure off students and their families during the college years. The school must be paid back within twelve years of graduation.

Looking for more funding power, 30 of the most prestigious colleges in New England banded together to form a group known as The Consortium on Financing a Higher Education; together with private enterprises such as the New England Loan Marketing Corporation (NELLIE MAE) and the Educational Resources Institute, they have created a loan program that they dubbed SHARE. Parents can borrow up to $20,000 annually at a reasonable interest rate. (See a fuller description of NELLIE MAE's offerings in the chapter, "Getting the Most College for the Money.")

Other Private Sources of Funds

Student organizations: You can make your social life pay off. Many student organizations sponsor scholarships for deserving students. Many fraternities, sororities, honor societies, and campus professional groups, among others, have programs, which are almost always limited to their members. If you're a joiner, you might open up some financial aid opportunities. Your school's financial aid office should have the breakdown of programs by organization, as will the organizations themselves.

National Merit Scholarships

Just about everybody who intends to go on to college ends up taking the PSAT/NMSQT test in their junior year of high school. It's preparation for the SAT—and more important, it puts you into competition for financial awards that can put a good deal of money in your pocket. But the competition is stiff: a mere 13,500 of the million students who take the PSAT/NMSQT each year are eligible to compete for these awards. Some schools, like Texas A&M University, work extra hard to recruit National Merit finalists and scholars because of the prestige that winning the award brings to the institution. So even though the actual amount of money received by finalists is usually not that great, it can get you offers of more attractive financial aid packages as schools vie for you. The three types of awards are:

■ $2,000 National Merit Scholarship. There are about 1,800 of these awarded each year; they are one-time-only awards. Need is not considered in these awards.

■ College-sponsored scholarships. Schools offer finalists scholarships out of their own pockets. Fewer than 250 colleges offer about 2,100 scholarships to National Merit finalists each year, including institutions ranging from the University of Chicago to Texas A&M University. The scholarships range from an annual $500 non-need grant to a maximum of $2,000 annually. Beyond that $500 minimum, the award must make up half of the student's calculated need.

■ Corporate-sponsored scholarships. Like the school-sponsored awards, the roughly 1,700 corporate-sponsored awards are renewable and can be received for all four years of college. And like the school-sponsored awards, they range from a minimum of $500 to $2,000 per year, though some go higher. While some of these programs apply to students with no direct tie to the corporation—say, those who live in the vicinity of one of the sponsoring company's plants—very, very few of these awards go to students whose parents do not work for the sponsoring corporation. For the most up-to-date information available on the National Merit Scholarships program, call the organization directly at (847) 866-5100.

Some of the Schools that Sponsor National Merit Scholarships

American University
Arizona State University
Auburn University
Baylor University
Boston University
Bowling Green State University
Carleton College
Case Western Reserve University
College of the Holy Cross
College of William and Mary
DePauw University
Emory University
Florida State University
Furman University
George Washington University
Georgia Institute of Technology
Grinnell College
Harvey Mudd College
Iowa State University
Johns Hopkins University
Louisiana State University
Macalester College
Miami University
Michigan State University
Mississippi State University
New York University
Northwestern University
Oberlin College
Ohio State University (all campuses)
Rensselaer Polytechnic Institute
Rice University
Rose-Hulman Institute of Technology
Rutgers, The State University of New Jersey
     (all campuses)
Southern Methodist University
Texas A&M University (all campuses)
Trinity University
Tulane University
University of Alabama
University of Arizona
University of California at Davis
University of California at Los Angeles
University of California at San Diego
University of Chicago
University of Delaware

University of Florida
University of Georgia Foundation
University of Houston
University of Maryland (all campuses)
University of Miami
University of New Orleans
University of Missouri–Columbia
University of Nebraska–Lincoln
University of Oklahoma
University of Rochester
University of South Carolina (all campuses)
University of Southern California
University of Texas at Austin
University of Washington
Vanderbilt University
Virginia Polytechnic Institute and State University
Washington University
Wheaton College (Illinois)

Some of the Corporations that Provide National Merit Scholarships

These are some of the corporations listed in a recent Student Bulletin of the National Merit Scholarship Corporation. Since the American corporate landscape is changing rapidly due to mergers, acquisitions, and general belt-tightening, this list tends to shift a great deal from year to year. Check with your employer even if it is not mentioned on this list, and make sure your company still supports the program if it is on the list.

Abbott Laboratories
ADT Security Systems
Allied-Signal
American Cyanamid
American Home Products Corporation
Amoco
ARCO
Armstrong World Industries
Arthur Andersen
Avon Products
B & W Nuclear Technologies
BASF Corporation
Bechtel
Bell & Howell
BellSouth
BFGoodrich
BFI Corporation
Black & Decker
Blount

Boeing
Boston Edison
BP America
Bridgestone/Firestone
Bristol-Myers
Brown & Williamson Tobacco
Burroughs Wellcome
California Medical Education and Research
Capital Cities/ABC
CIBA-GEIGY
CIGNA Corporation
Collins & Aikman Corporation
ConAgra
CONSOL
Consolidated Papers
Continental Corporation
Cooper Industries
Crum and Forster
CSX Corporation
Data General
Deluxe Corporation
Digital Equipment Corporation
Dow Chemical Company
Dow Corning
Dow Jones
Dresser Industries
Dun & Bradstreet
Duracell
Eastman Kodak
Eaton Corporation
Equitable Life Assurance Society of the U. S.
Ethyl Corporation
Fisher-Price
Fleming Companies
FMC Corporation
GATX Corporation
General Mills
Georgia-Pacific Corporation
Gillette
Goodyear Tire & Rubber
Greyhound Lines
GTE Corporation
Harsco Corporation
Hoechst Celanese Corporation
Honeywell
ICI Americas
Ingersoll-Rand
Inland Steel-Ryerson
Interlake
International Paper

ITT Hartford Fire Insurance
K mart
Thomas J. Lipton
Litton Industries
Lockheed
Loews
LTV Corporation
Lucky Stores
MAXUS Energy Corporation
May Department Stores
Maytag
McDermott
McDonald's Corporation
McGraw-Hill
McKesson Corporation
Meredith Corporation
Metropolitan Life
Miles
Minnesota Mining and Manufacturing (3M)
Mobil
Monsanto
Motorola
National Distillers Distributors
National Medical Enterprises
Navistar
New Jersey Bell Telephone
New York Times Company
Norfolk Southern
Occidental Petroleum
Olin Corporation
Owens-Corning Fiberglas
Paramount Communications
Parker Hannifin Corporation
Penn Mutual
Pennsylvania Power & Light
PepsiCo
Pet
Pfizer
Phelps Dodge
Philadelphia Electric
Polaroid
PPG Industries
Prudential
Public Service Enterprise
Quaker Oats
Quantum Chemical
Raytheon
Rexham Corporation
RJR Nabisco

Rockwell International
Rohm and Haas
Santa Fe Pacific Corporation
Sara Lee
Schering-Plough Corporation
Shell Oil
Siemens
Sony Corporation of America
State Farm Companies
Sterling Winthrop
Stone & Webster
Sun Company
Tenneco
Textron
Times Mirror Company
Transamerica Corporation
Transco Energy Company
TRINOVA Corporation
Unilever United States
Union Electric
Union Pacific Corporation
United Airlines
United Services Automobile Association
United States Fidelity & Guaranty
United States Shoe Corporation
Upjohn
UPS
USG Corporation
Warner-Lambert
Weyerhaeuser Company
Robert W. Woodruff Foundation
Xerox

A number of other programs are looking for ways to give a hand to academically gifted students. By looking though the scholarship index, you will be able to find programs that provide such aid, like the National Honor Society, which provides about 250 scholarships worth $1,000 each year. (You apply through the chapter at your high school, but the main number is (202) 785-2255.) The famous Westinghouse Science Scholarships program distributes about $205,000 among 40 winners. (Write Science Service, 1719 N Street, NW, Washington, D.C. 20036.) The federal government has weighed in with programs like the Robert C. Byrd Honors Scholarship Program, a state-administered gold mine that recognizes outstanding academic achievement by giving 10 students from each congressional district a one-time, $1,500 scholarship for their first year of college study. Another program, the Presidential Scholars, rewards about 120 high scorers on standardized entrance exams with a free trip to Washington; the Dodge Foundation then gives each recipient $1,000. You don't apply for this one, though—

the program chooses you. And, of course, more and more states are trying to help bright students. Some of these programs are based on financial need, but a growing number are not. See the section on state aid for the non-need-based programs, or write the state aid agency for more detailed information. The list of agencies begins on page 29.

Letting the Boss Pay

Employer tuition plans: This is the great unclaimed area of financial aid, with billions of dollars available to millions of employees. Unfortunately, there's a Catch-22 involved: Many companies won't hire you for a good position until you have your college degree. But if you are willing to attend college part-time, and to start in a lowly position, you will find many companies that will pay for your higher education. Though guides to employers with such programs are commercially available, they also tend to be expensive; you can also find them in the public library or through your school library or guidance counselor.

The company wants to make sure it will get its money's worth, so plans generally come with a hitch or two. The most important hitch: you have to make the grade. In "reimbursement" plans, in which you have to put up the tuition money at first, you get the money back only when you have successfully completed the course—in some programs, that means with a grade of "B" or better. In other programs the company pays up front—but you will still have to repay the company if you drop out or flunk. Also, you might have to prove that the courses you are taking are somehow related to your work. Still, an understanding boss can help you to frame your educational needs in such a way that they fit in nicely with the company objectives.

The cooperative way: In co-op education, you combine your time in the classroom with practical experience on the job. It's something for everyone: You the student get a job and the employer gets a highly motivated work force. Co-op programs not only put money in your pocket—roughly $1 billion a year in co-op wages nationwide—they also provide you with job contacts for the future. You get to try out your chosen profession—kick the tires, drive it around the block—to see if it's really what you would like to do. If it is, you have another advantage: Often the firm you worked for is the one that hires you after graduation. Fully 40 percent continue working for their co-op employer after graduation. Another 40 percent find work in fields directly related to their co-op assignments, while about 15 percent enroll in law or other professional schools. Add up those percentages, and its pretty easy to see that co-oping it leads to jobs.

Roughly 1,000 colleges have cooperative programs of some kind or another—including some schools where virtually all of the students are in cooperative education programs, such as Antioch College in Yellow Springs, Ohio, Drexel University in Philadelphia, and Northeastern University in Boston. Some 50,000 employers hire on the co-op plan—including the largest provider of co-op jobs, the federal government, which hires nearly 12,000 students each year.

Co-oping takes time. Whether you alternate semesters of work and study or work part-time while attending school, the programs usually require five years. Still, 200,000 students each year seem to feel the time is worth spending. See pages 48 to 101 for information on co-op programs. You can get more data on all schools with co-op programs by writing:

National Commission for Cooperative Education
360 Huntington Avenue 384 CP
Boston, MA 02115-5096
(617) 373-3770

Getting help from your future colleagues: If you have made your career choice, you might be eligible for aid from the professional association, or associations, that serve the field. Of course, if you really want to get financial aid in your chosen career field and want to get a head start besides, you should consider attending a college that has a cooperative education program. (See co-op programs, page 48.) But if your school doesn't provide such programs, then you might be able to get help from the professional association. There is an industry group for every trade and profession, from dental hygienists to hotel management to wine experts. Of course, most of this money gravitates toward schools that have well-regarded programs in the field, such as journalism at Northwestern University or meat science at Sul Ross State University. For suggestions on the strongest schools in your career area, you should consult guides such as *Rugg's Recommendations on the Colleges*. Still, many professional groups offer "portable" scholarships that are not tied to a particular school.

We have listed many career-connected scholarships in the index of majors that begins on page 488; there you can find scholarships for diverse fields such as acting, aviation, entomology, and criminal justice. However, there are thousands of such associations, and we could not include all of them or their programs in our list. So it is worth your while to find out about any other opportunities offered by your professional group. Trade groups are easy enough to find: reference works like *Gale's Encyclopedia of Associations*, available at the library, can give you the addresses and telephone numbers. Once you have the addresses, write to request their scholarship information, including a stamped, self-addressed envelope.

Working for Uncle Sam through the Junior Fellowship Program

The Junior Fellowship Program resembles cooperative education, but with some important differences: for one thing, your boss is the federal government. Also, you join the Junior Fellowship Program in high school—though you don't begin working until college—and apply through your high school guidance counselor. Unlike cooperative education, which is only offered through certain schools, Junior Fellows can attend any school—you work during breaks in the college term. You also have to have very good grades and prove financial need. And here's the good part: though the program is limited to 5,000 participants at a time, it has historically had thousands of vacancies. If your high school guidance counselor doesn't have information on this program, you can write for it yourself:

Director, Office of Personnel Management
1900 E Street, NW
Washington, D.C. 20415

Other Private Sources of Aid

Many organizations provide scholarships, though the amount is usually small. If you have already gotten all you are going to get from the big-ticket sources of financial aid, like federal and state programs and your college resources, you may be able to get a little extra from sources you might not have considered. Here's a list to start you on your way:

Your local government: Your city, county, or even your school district might have scholarship money or other special programs. Though many of these only amount to a few hundred dollars, some offer funds in the thousands. Finding them involves investigative work on your part, since relatively few of these make their way into the big scholarship databases. But you can find them: your high school or college financial aid officer should have some information about these programs. The Chamber of Commerce and public library might have leads, too. Keep an eye out for scholarships in the local news section of your newspaper.

Unions: Despite the tough times that America's unions are going through, many still offer funds for the education of their members' children. Information about some of these programs can be found in the scholarship roster; for more specific information you should contact the secretary of your union local. Union programs are offered both by the national organization and by the local chapters. You can get some information from your local; to get the fullest amount of information, write for the comprehensive AFL-CIO guide, which is free to members: *AFL-CIO Guide to Union Sponsored Scholarships, Awards and Student Financial Aid.*

Department of Publication, AFL-CIO
815 16th Street, NW
Washington, D.C. 20006
(202) 637-5000

Foundations: Many private foundations and educational trusts provide funds for students. Organizations like the Hattie M. Strong Foundation provide Strong Foundation Loans from $2,500 per year, on average, to students who are a year away from college graduation. (1620 I Street, NW, Suite 105, Washington, D.C. 20006.) Some have rather odd restrictions: the Ernestine Matthews Trust Scholarships, for example, offers around $750 per year—but recipients must sign a statement that they will neither smoke nor use alcoholic beverages while receiving the scholarship. You can find others in the scholarship directory.

Community organizations in general: Don't forget to check into scholarship programs available as a multitude of awards, including a $2,000 scholarship at the national level for children of veterans called The American Legion Auxiliary National President's Scholarship. There's also a National High School Oratorical Contest with a grand prize of $16,000 and many $1,000 scholarships. More important, each state organization and its auxiliary offer scholarships. The Legion is most valuable to students who are the children of veterans, but not exclusively to them. For the most up-to-date listing of the Legion's programs and contests, you should send three dollars to get a copy of *Need a Lift?* Write to:

The American Legion
National Emblem Sales
P.O. Box 1050
Indianapolis, IN 46206
(317) 630-1200

Religious organizations: Churches and religious organizations also have money to give. Groups like the Aid Association for Lutherans host contests and offer scholarships and loans. Find these groups through your church, your campus Bible Chair, or in *Gale's Encyclopedia of Associations.* You might run into a number of restrictions, including a requirement of religious study or of attending a church-sponsored school.

Ethnic societies: Sure, you're proud to be an Armenian. But did you know that your Armenian ancestry could qualify you for scholarships? The Armenian Relief Society (80 Bigelow Ave, Watertown, MA 02172) has many available. So does the Armenian General Benevolent Union, which offers both scholarships and loans (31 West 52nd Street, New York, NY 10019 (212) 765-8260). Are you a woman of Greek descent? Perhaps you have a relative in the Daughters of Penelope. If so, you might qualify for one of that organization's awards, such as the Helen Karagianis Memorial Award or the Pota Sarastis Memorial Award. (Scholarship Committee,

Daughters of Penelope, Supreme Headquarters, 1422 K Street, NW, Washington, D.C. 20005; (202) 234-9741.)

We've only scratched the surface of ethnic funds available. Many national groups in the U.S. sponsor programs to help each new generation better itself through higher education. If you or your parents aren't members of such organizations, you can find their names and addresses in *Gale's Encyclopedia of Associations*, available in your library. Send them a request for information on college aid along with a stamped, self-addressed envelope.

Youth clubs and jobs: Think back to your childhood—or to more recent high school experience. You can find scholarships for former Boy Scouts, newspaper carriers, and even golf caddies. Really. The Western Golf Association maintains an Evans Scholars House, where lucky former caddies live for free, at 14 universities—Colorado, Illinois, Indiana, Marquette, Miami (Ohio), Michigan State, U of Michigan, Minnesota, Missouri, Northern Illinois State U at DeKalb, Northwestern, Ohio State, Purdue, and Wisconsin. The sponsoring organization also covers tuition. Students at state universities that do not have an Evans House can get their tuition and a housing allowance paid by the sponsoring organization. Caddies who served for more than two years and show financial need may apply to:

Western Golf Association, Evans Scholarship
One Briar Road
Golf, IL 60029
(847) 724-4600

As for your participation in high school activities, you might have made yourself eligible for scholarships if you were a member of 4-H, Future Homemakers of America, or distributive education programs. You might also want to check with your high school counselor for other awards that get overlooked.

The contest route: Many of the organizations alluded to above sponsor contests in essay writing and oratory. That's just the tip of the iceberg for competitions ranging from science competitions to beauty pageants. Many of them sponsor scholarships for prizes. Each summer, the National Association of Secondary School Principals puts its stamp of approval on a long roster of these programs in its Advisory List of National Contests and Activities. For a copy of this list, send a request for publication #210-9295, $8.00 plus $3.00 for shipping and handling to:

National Association of Secondary School Principals
Attention: Sales Office
1904 Association Drive
Reston, VA 22090
(703) 860-0220

Warning: Entering a lot of contests can be time-consuming—and you're going to need a lot of time to apply for the traditional channels of financial aid. Don't get lost on a rabbit trail—go after the big game first by applying for financial aid through your school's financial aid office. Once you've done that, and if you have a little extra time, you might give some of the contests listed by the principals a try—your odds of winning are no worse than those on getting many of the private foundation scholarships mentioned in this book.

If there's any lesson to take away from this chapter, it is simply this: Get to know your college financial aid officer. This is the person who can help you ferret out money, and who has some power, however limited, to ease your financial aid burden. The position of student aid administration is fast becoming a hardship post. Aid officers report that angry students have hit them and threatened their lives. And one tragic case a few years back ended in death. A student threw coffee on Willie Pappas, director of financial aid at Delgado Community College in Louisiana. When Pappas followed the student out into a parking lot, the student shot him.

Obviously, this is no way to get your financial aid package improved. Financial aid officers don't take the job to abuse students and pinch pennies; they are in the business of helping students. Unfortunately, they are also working within the school's budgetary limits—and the school is juggling the financial needs of students with its own priorities for research, faculty pay, physical improvements, and shiny new leather chairs for the trustees to sit on at their meetings. And so they are tough.

But not necessarily heartless. They will listen to reason and respond to real problems. With solid negotiation, you might be able to get your financial aid officer to adjust the formula for computing your need: The officer can adjust your family contribution down or the cost of education up to reduce your aid burden. The key is to deal with financial aid officers politely and responsibly. Don't try to con them—students sharper than you have tried, and failed. Have all your ducks in a row: Keep track of your financial records and be ready to back up your case with documentation.

Cooperative Education

Cooperative education lets you mix career-oriented jobs with your college education over the course of your degree program. Unlike internships, which tend to be nonpaying jobs that students work into their schedules as best they can, cooperative programs can pay the bills and are an integral part of the school's degree program and your career plans. About 40 percent of co-op students end up working for their co-op employer after graduation, and another 40 percent find employment in their co-op job field. Depending on the money you earn, a co-op job can cover a great deal of your college costs. And since co-op graduates tend to have higher starting salaries than non-co-op grads, you can pay off college debts earlier. That's why we have included this list of institutions that participate in cooperative education programs: to let you know where to apply if you decide that cooperative education is the route you want to take. Once you have used this chart to identify colleges with programs in your field of interest, contact the school's Cooperative Education department and ask for more information on the program.

For more information about cooperative education, see page 40, "Letting the Boss Pay."

The categories covered by this list are as follows:

1. **Agriculture (AG):** includes natural resources, animal and poultry sciences, livestock, plant and soil science
2. **Art (AR):** arts, including architecture, commercial art, communications, crafts, fine arts, and performing arts
3. **Business (BU)**
4. **Computer Science (CS)**
5. **Education (ED)**
6. **Engineering (EN)**
7. **Health Professions (HP)**
8. **Home Economics (HE)**
9. **Humanities (HU)**
10. **Natural Sciences (NS):** includes biology, mathematics, and physical sciences
11. **Social and Behavioral Science (SB)**
12. **Technologies (TE)**
13. **Vocational Arts (VA):** includes trade and industrial courses

Many schools offer more than one category.

Undergraduate Programs in Cooperative Education

State/Institution	AG	AR	BU	CS	ED	EN	HP	HE	HU	NS	SB	TE	VA
Alabama													
Alabama A&M U Normal, AL 35762	✓	✓	✓	✓		✓	✓	✓	✓	✓	✓	✓	✓
Alabama St U Montgomery, AL 36101–0271		✓	✓	✓	✓	✓			✓	✓	✓		
Alabama, U of Tuscaloosa, AL 35487–0132		✓	✓	✓	✓	✓	✓		✓	✓	✓		
Alabama, U of, Birmingham Birmingham, AL 35294–0104				✓		✓							
Alabama, U of, Huntsville Huntsville, AL 35899			✓	✓		✓			✓				
Auburn U Auburn University, AL 36849	✓	✓	✓	✓		✓			✓	✓			
Auburn U, Montgomery Montgomery, AL 36117–3596		✓	✓	✓	✓	✓	✓		✓	✓	✓		
Concordia Coll Selma, AL 36701				✓									
Jacksonville St U Jacksonville, AL 36265–9982			✓	✓								✓	✓
Miles Coll Fairfield, AL 35064						✓							
Mobile, U of Mobile, AL 36663–0220			✓	✓		✓	✓						
Montevallo, U of Montevallo, AL 35115–6000						✓							
Samford U Birmingham, AL 35229			✓	✓					✓				

State/Institution	AG	AR	BU	CS	ED	EN	HP	HE	HU	NS	SB	TE	VA
South Alabama, U of Mobile, AL 36688–0002		✔	✔	✔	✔	✔	✔		✔	✔	✔		
Stillman Coll Tuscaloosa, AL 35403						✔	✔						
Tuskegee U Tuskegee, AL 36088	✔		✔	✔	✔	✔	✔	✔		✔	✔		

Alaska

State/Institution	AG	AR	BU	CS	ED	EN	HP	HE	HU	NS	SB	TE	VA
Alaska Southeast, U of, Juneau Juneau, AK 99801			✔	✔					✔				
Alaska, U of, Anchorage Anchorage, AK 99508			✔	✔		✔						✔	✔
Alaska, U of, Fairbanks Fairbanks, AK 99775–7480							✔						
Sheldon Jackson Coll Sitka, AK 99835–7699			✔		✔						✔		

Arizona

State/Institution	AG	AR	BU	CS	ED	EN	HP	HE	HU	NS	SB	TE	VA
Arizona St U Tempe, AZ 85287–1203			✔			✔							
Arizona, U of Tucson, AZ 85721–0007	✔	✔	✔	✔	✔	✔	✔	✔	✔	✔	✔		
Embry-Riddle Aeronautical U Prescott, AZ 86301–3720			✔	✔		✔							
Northern Arizona U Flagstaff, AZ 86011			✔			✔	✔						

Arkansas

State/Institution	AG	AR	BU	CS	ED	EN	HP	HE	HU	NS	SB	TE	VA
Arkansas, U of, Fayetteville Fayetteville, AR 72701	✔	✔	✔	✔		✔		✔	✔	✔	✔		

State/Institution	AG	AR	BU	CS	ED	EN	HP	HE	HU	NS	SB	TE	VA
Arkansas, U of, Little Rock Little Rock, AR 72204–1099			✔	✔		✔			✔	✔		✔	
Arkansas, U of, Pine Bluff Pine Bluff, AR 71611–2799	✔		✔	✔		✔		✔	✔	✔	✔		✔
Harding U Searcy, AR 72149		✔	✔	✔	✔		✔	✔	✔	✔	✔		
Ouachita Baptist U Arkadelphia, AR 71998–0001			✔							✔	✔		

California

State/Institution	AG	AR	BU	CS	ED	EN	HP	HE	HU	NS	SB	TE	VA
Acad of Art Coll San Francisco, CA 94105		✔											
Biola U La Mirada, CA 90639	✔	✔	✔	✔	✔	✔	✔			✔	✔	✔	✔
California Lutheran U Thousand Oaks, CA 91360–2787		✔	✔	✔		✔			✔	✔	✔		
California Maritime Acad Vallejo, CA 94590–0644					✔								
California Polytechnic St U San Luis Obispo, CA 93407–0005	✔		✔	✔		✔							
California St Polytechnic U Pomona, CA 91768–4019	✔		✔	✔		✔					✔		
California St U, Bakersfield Bakersfield, CA 93311–1099		✔	✔	✔	✔				✔	✔	✔		
California St U, Fresno Fresno, CA 93740–0057	✔	✔	✔	✔	✔	✔	✔	✔	✔	✔	✔	✔	✔
California St U, Fullerton Fullerton, CA 92834–9480		✔	✔	✔	✔	✔	✔		✔	✔	✔		
California St U, Hayward Hayward, CA 94542		✔	✔	✔	✔		✔		✔	✔	✔		

State/Institution	AG	AR	BU	CS	ED	EN	HP	HE	HU	NS	SB	TE	VA
California St U, Long Beach Long Beach, CA 90840		✓	✓	✓	✓	✓	✓	✓	✓	✓	✓	✓	✓
California St U, Sacramento Sacramento, CA 95819		✓	✓	✓	✓	✓			✓	✓	✓		
California St U, San Bernardino San Bernardino, CA 92407–2397	✓	✓	✓			✓					✓		
California St U, Stanislaus Turlock, CA 95382	✓	✓	✓	✓		✓			✓	✓	✓		✓
California, U of, Berkeley Berkeley, CA 94720	✓	✓	✓	✓	✓	✓	✓	✓	✓	✓	✓	✓	✓
California, U of, Davis Davis, CA 95616–8678												✓	
California, U of, Riverside Riverside, CA 92521	✓	✓	✓		✓	✓	✓		✓	✓	✓	✓	
Chapman U Orange, CA 92866			✓	✓	✓					✓			
Concordia U Irvine, CA 92612–3299			✓		✓					✓			
Design Inst of San Diego San Diego, CA 92121		✓											
Golden Gate U San Francisco, CA 94105			✓	✓								✓	
Humboldt St U Arcata, CA 95521						✓				✓			
Humphreys Coll Stockton, CA 95207–3896			✓	✓								✓	✓
Loma Linda U Loma Linda, CA 92350						✓				✓	✓		
New Coll of California San Francisco, CA 94131				✓									

State/Institution	AG	AR	BU	CS	ED	EN	HP	HE	HU	NS	SB	TE	VA
Pacific Christian Coll Fullerton, CA 92831		✔		✔	✔	✔				✔	✔		
Pacific Union Coll Angwin, CA 94508			✔	✔								✔	
Patten Coll Oakland, CA 94601			✔										
Pepperdine U Malibu, CA 90263–4392						✔							
San Diego, U of San Diego, CA 92110–2492						✔							
San Francisco, U of San Francisco, CA 94117–1080		✔											
San Jose St U San Jose, CA 95192–0009	✔	✔			✔	✔	✔		✔	✔	✔		
Santa Clara U Santa Clara, CA 95053						✔							
Sonoma St U Rohnert Park, CA 94928										✔	✔		
Southern California, U of Los Angeles, CA 90089–0911						✔							
St. Mary's Coll Moraga, CA 94556						✔							
Western U of Health Sciences Pomona, CA 91766–1889							✔						
Whittier Coll Whittier, CA 90608						✔							

Canada

State/Institution	AG	AR	BU	CS	ED	EN	HP	HE	HU	NS	SB	TE	VA
Alberta, U of Edmonton, Alberta, CN T6G 2M7		✔	✔			✔							

State/Institution	AG	AR	BU	CS	ED	EN	HP	HE	HU	NS	SB	TE	VA
Calgary, U of Calgary, Alberta, CN T2N 1N4			✔	✔					✔	✔	✔		
Carleton U Ottawa, Ontario, CN K1S 5B6				✔		✔				✔	✔		
Concordia U Montreal, Quebec, CN H3G 1M8			✔	✔		✔				✔			
Ottawa, U of Ottawa, Ontario, CN K1N 6N5		✔	✔	✔		✔			✔	✔			
Waterloo, U of Waterloo, Ontario, CN N2L 3G1		✔	✔	✔	✔	✔	✔			✔	✔	✔	

Colorado

State/Institution	AG	AR	BU	CS	ED	EN	HP	HE	HU	NS	SB	TE	VA
Colorado Christian U Lakewood, CO 80226–7499		✔											
Colorado Coll Colorado Springs, CO 80903				✔		✔	✔					✔	
Colorado Sch of Mines Golden, CO 80401–9952				✔		✔							
Colorado St U Fort Collins, CO 80523–0015	✔												
Colorado Tech U Colorado Springs, CO 80907–3896				✔		✔						✔	
Colorado, U of, Boulder Boulder, CO 80309						✔							
Colorado, U of, Denver Denver, CO 80217–3364		✔	✔	✔		✔	✔			✔	✔		✔
Mesa St Coll Grand Junction, CO 81502–2647			✔							✔			✔
Metropolitan St Coll of Denver Denver, CO 80217–3362	✔	✔	✔	✔	✔	✔	✔		✔	✔	✔	✔	✔

State/Institution	AG	AR	BU	CS	ED	EN	HP	HE	HU	NS	SB	TE	VA
Southern Colorado, U of Pueblo, CO 81001						✔						✔	

Connecticut

State/Institution	AG	AR	BU	CS	ED	EN	HP	HE	HU	NS	SB	TE	VA
Bridgeport, U of Bridgeport, CT 06601		✔	✔	✔		✔			✔	✔	✔		
Central Connecticut St U New Britain, CT 06050		✔	✔	✔	✔				✔	✔	✔	✔	
Connecticut, U of Storrs, CT 06269	✔	✔	✔	✔	✔	✔	✔		✔	✔	✔		
Eastern Connecticut St U Willimantic, CT 06226			✔	✔					✔	✔	✔		
Fairfield U Fairfield, CT 06430–5195						✔							
Hartford, U of West Hartford, CT 06117		✔	✔	✔		✔				✔		✔	
New Haven, U of West Haven, CT 06516		✔	✔	✔		✔			✔	✔	✔		
Sacred Heart U Fairfield, CT 06432–1000		✔	✔	✔			✔		✔	✔	✔		
Southern Connecticut St U New Haven, CT 06515		✔	✔	✔	✔		✔		✔	✔	✔	✔	✔
Teikyo Post U Waterbury, CT 06723–2540			✔		✔				✔		✔		
Western Connecticut St U Danbury, CT 06810		✔	✔	✔					✔	✔	✔	✔	

Delaware

State/Institution	AG	AR	BU	CS	ED	EN	HP	HE	HU	NS	SB	TE	VA
Delaware St U Dover, DE 19901–2275			✔		✔		✔	✔				✔	

State/Institution	AG	AR	BU	CS	ED	EN	HP	HE	HU	NS	SB	TE	VA
Delaware, U of Newark, DE 19716			✓			✓							
Goldey-Beacom Coll Wilmington, DE 19808			✓	✓									
Wilmington Coll New Castle, DE 19720			✓		✓	✓							

District of Columbia

State/Institution	AG	AR	BU	CS	ED	EN	HP	HE	HU	NS	SB	TE	VA
American U Washington, DC 20016–8001	✓	✓	✓	✓		✓			✓	✓	✓		
Catholic U of America Washington, DC 20064					✓	✓							
District of Columbia, U of the Washington, DC 20008			✓	✓				✓				✓	
George Washington U Washington, DC 20052			✓	✓	✓	✓	✓		✓	✓	✓		
Howard U Washington, DC 20059			✓			✓							
Southeastern U Washington, DC 20024			✓			✓							
Strayer Coll Washington, DC 20005			✓	✓									

Florida

State/Institution	AG	AR	BU	CS	ED	EN	HP	HE	HU	NS	SB	TE	VA
Barry U Miami Shores, FL 33161–6695						✓							
Bethune-Cookman Coll Daytona Beach, FL 32114–3099			✓	✓	✓		✓		✓	✓	✓		
Central Florida, U of Orlando, FL 32816	✓	✓	✓	✓	✓	✓			✓	✓	✓	✓	

State/Institution	AG	AR	BU	CS	ED	EN	HP	HE	HU	NS	SB	TE	VA
Embry-Riddle Aeronautical U Daytona Beach, FL 32114–3900			✔	✔		✔						✔	
Florida Atlantic U Boca Raton, FL 33431–0991		✔	✔		✔	✔			✔	✔	✔		
Florida Inst of Tech Melbourne, FL 32901–6975		✔	✔	✔	✔				✔	✔	✔		
Florida International U Miami, FL 33199	✔	✔	✔	✔	✔	✔			✔	✔	✔	✔	✔
Florida Memorial Coll Miami, FL 33054			✔										
Florida, U of Gainesville, FL 32611	✔		✔	✔		✔			✔				
Jacksonville U Jacksonville, FL 32211		✔											
North Florida, U of Jacksonville, FL 32224–2645			✔	✔		✔	✔				✔	✔	
Nova Southeastern U Fort Lauderdale, FL 33314			✔	✔								✔	
Orlando Coll Orlando, FL 32810		✔		✔			✔						
South Florida, U of Tampa, FL 33620		✔	✔	✔		✔	✔			✔	✔		
Tampa, U of Tampa, FL 33606–1490				✔									
West Florida, U of Pensacola, FL 32514–5750			✔	✔									

Georgia

State/Institution	AG	AR	BU	CS	ED	EN	HP	HE	HU	NS	SB	TE	VA
Albany St U Albany, GA 31705		✔	✔				✔			✔	✔		

State/Institution	AG	AR	BU	CS	ED	EN	HP	HE	HU	NS	SB	TE	VA
Armstrong Atlantic St U Savannah, GA 31419				✓		✓							
Atlanta Coll of Art Atlanta, GA 30309		✓											
Augusta St U Augusta, GA 30904–2200			✓	✓				✓	✓	✓			
Berry Coll Mt. Berry, GA 30149			✓	✓				✓	✓	✓	✓		
Clark Atlanta U Atlanta, GA 30314						✓							
Clayton Coll & St U Morrow, GA 30260			✓	✓		✓						✓	
Columbus St U Columbus, GA 31907–5645	✓	✓	✓	✓	✓	✓		✓	✓	✓	✓	✓	
Georgia Coll & St U Milledgeville, GA 31061		✓	✓	✓				✓	✓	✓			
Georgia Inst of Tech Atlanta, GA 30332			✓	✓		✓						✓	
Georgia Southern U Statesboro, GA 30460–8024			✓			✓						✓	
Georgia Southwestern St U Americus, GA 31709–4693			✓	✓								✓	
Georgia St U Atlanta, GA 30303		✓	✓	✓	✓		✓		✓	✓	✓		
Georgia, U of Athens, GA 30602	✓	✓	✓	✓	✓			✓	✓	✓	✓	✓	✓
Kennesaw St U Kennesaw, GA 30144–5591		✓	✓	✓				✓	✓	✓			
Mercer U Macon, GA 31207			✓			✓							

State/Institution	AG	AR	BU	CS	ED	EN	HP	HE	HU	NS	SB	TE	VA
Morehouse Coll Atlanta, GA 30314			✔	✔		✔	✔				✔		
North Georgia Coll & St U Dahlonega, GA 30597			✔	✔					✔				
Oglethorpe U Atlanta, GA 30319–2797	✔	✔	✔	✔	✔	✔	✔		✔	✔	✔		
Paine Coll Augusta, GA 30901–3182			✔	✔						✔	✔		
Savannah St U Savannah, GA 31404			✔	✔		✔							
Southern Polytech St U Marietta, GA 30060–2896				✔								✔	
Thomas Coll Thomasville, GA 31792–7499					✔		✔						
Valdosta St U Valdosta, GA 31698	✔	✔	✔	✔	✔				✔	✔	✔		✔

Guam

State/Institution	AG	AR	BU	CS	ED	EN	HP	HE	HU	NS	SB	TE	VA
Guam, U of Mangilao, GU 96923	✔	✔	✔	✔	✔			✔	✔	✔	✔		

Hawaii

State/Institution	AG	AR	BU	CS	ED	EN	HP	HE	HU	NS	SB	TE	VA
Brigham Young U, Hawaii Laie, HI 96762–1294			✔								✔		
Hawaii Pacific U Honolulu, HI 96813			✔	✔					✔				
Hawaii, U of, Hilo Hilo, HI 96720–4091				✔									
Hawaii, U of, Manoa Honolulu, HI 96822	✔	✔	✔	✔	✔	✔	✔		✔	✔	✔	✔	

State/Institution	AG	AR	BU	CS	ED	EN	HP	HE	HU	NS	SB	TE	VA
Idaho													
Albertson Coll Caldwell, ID 83605					✔	✔							
Boise Bible Coll Boise, ID 83714					✔								
Boise St U Boise, ID 83725						✔							
Idaho, U of Moscow, ID 83844–3133	✔	✔	✔	✔	✔	✔		✔	✔	✔	✔		✔
Lewis-Clark St Coll Lewiston, ID 83501–2698		✔			✔			✔			✔	✔	✔
Northwest Nazarene Coll Nampa, ID 83686					✔	✔							
Illinois													
Art Inst of Chicago, Sch of the Chicago, IL 60603		✔											
Augustana Coll Rock Island, IL 61201					✔								
Benedictine U Lisle, IL 60532–0900						✔							
Bradley U Peoria, IL 61625		✔	✔	✔	✔	✔	✔	✔	✔	✔	✔		
Chicago St U Chicago, IL 60628					✔								
East-West U Chicago, IL 60605			✔	✔		✔						✔	
Elmhurst Coll Elmhurst, IL 60126–3296						✔							

State/Institution	AG	AR	BU	CS	ED	EN	HP	HE	HU	NS	SB	TE	VA
Greenville Coll Greenville, IL 62246–0159		✔	✔	✔					✔	✔	✔		
Illinois Inst of Tech Chicago, IL 60616				✔		✔	✔						
Illinois St U Normal, IL 61761–6901			✔	✔						✔	✔		
Illinois, U of, Chicago Chicago, IL 60680		✔	✔	✔		✔	✔		✔	✔	✔		
Illinois, U of, Urbana-Champaign Urbana, IL 61801						✔						✔	
Lincoln Christian Coll & Sem Lincoln, IL 62656–2111					✔								
MacMurray Coll Jacksonville, IL 62650						✔							
North Central Coll Naperville, IL 60566–7063						✔	✔						
Northern Illinois U DeKalb, IL 60115	✔	✔	✔	✔	✔	✔			✔	✔	✔	✔	
Northwestern U Evanston, IL 60204–3060				✔		✔							
Principia Coll Elsah, IL 62028						✔							
Southern Illinois U, Carbondale Carbondale, IL 62901	✔		✔		✔	✔						✔	
St. Francis, Coll of Joliet, IL 60435						✔							
Trinity Christian Coll Palos Heights, IL 60463													✔
Western Illinois U Macomb, IL 61455–1390	✔		✔	✔				✔	✔	✔	✔	✔	

State/Institution	AG	AR	BU	CS	ED	EN	HP	HE	HU	NS	SB	TE	VA
Indiana													
Ball St U Muncie, IN 47306	✔	✔	✔	✔			✔	✔		✔	✔	✔	
Calumet Coll of St. Joseph Whiting, IN 46394			✔										
Earlham Coll Richmond, IN 47374–4095			✔			✔							
Evansville, U of Evansville, IN 47722				✔		✔							
Franklin Coll Franklin, IN 46131						✔	✔						
Huntington Coll Huntington, IN 46750					✔								
Indiana Inst of Tech Fort Wayne, IN 46803		✔	✔										
Indiana St U Terre Haute, IN 47809	✔	✔	✔				✔	✔		✔	✔	✔	
Indiana U Bloomington Bloomington, IN 47405		✔	✔	✔			✔		✔	✔	✔		
Indiana U Northwest Gary, IN 46408		✔	✔										
Indiana U-Purdue U Fort Wayne Fort Wayne, IN 46805–1499				✔		✔						✔	
Indiana U-Purdue U, Indianapolis Indianapolis, IN 46202–5143	✔	✔	✔	✔	✔	✔	✔		✔	✔	✔	✔	
Indianapolis, U of Indianapolis, IN 46227–3697				✔	✔	✔		✔		✔	✔	✔	
Oakland City U Oakland City, IN 47660													✔

State/Institution	AG	AR	BU	CS	ED	EN	HP	HE	HU	NS	SB	TE	VA
Purdue U West Lafayette, IN 47907	✔		✔	✔		✔				✔		✔	
Purdue U, Calumet Hammond, IN 46323				✔		✔						✔	
Southern Indiana, U of Evansville, IN 47712			✔			✔							
Taylor U, Fort Wayne Fort Wayne, IN 46807			✔										
Tri-State U Angola, IN 46703–0307			✔	✔		✔				✔		✔	
Valparaiso U Valparaiso, IN 46383–6493			✔	✔		✔	✔		✔	✔	✔		

Iowa

State/Institution	AG	AR	BU	CS	ED	EN	HP	HE	HU	NS	SB	TE	VA
Coe Coll Cedar Rapids, IA 52402						✔							
Cornell Coll Mount Vernon, IA 52314						✔	✔						
Iowa St U Ames, IA 50011–2010	✔		✔	✔	✔	✔			✔	✔	✔	✔	
Iowa Wesleyan Coll Mount Pleasant, IA 52641						✔						✔	
Iowa, U of Iowa City, IA 52242–1396	✔	✔	✔	✔	✔	✔			✔	✔	✔	✔	
Maharishi U of Management Fairfield, IA 52557				✔									
Marycrest International U Davenport, IA 52804–4096	✔	✔	✔						✔	✔	✔		
Morningside Coll Sioux City, IA 51106						✔	✔						

State/Institution	AG	AR	BU	CS	ED	EN	HP	HE	HU	NS	SB	TE	VA
Northern Iowa, U of Cedar Falls, IA 50614–0033		✔	✔	✔	✔		✔	✔	✔	✔	✔	✔	
Northwestern Coll Orange City, IA 51041						✔							
Simpson Coll Indianola, IA 50125		✔	✔	✔	✔	✔	✔		✔	✔	✔		
St. Ambrose U Davenport, IA 52803–2898		✔	✔	✔	✔	✔	✔				✔	✔	

Kansas

State/Institution	AG	AR	BU	CS	ED	EN	HP	HE	HU	NS	SB	TE	VA
Bethany Coll Lindsborg, KS 67456–1897						✔							
Bethel Coll North Newton, KS 67117						✔							
Emporia St U Emporia, KS 66801		✔	✔	✔	✔	✔			✔	✔	✔		
Kansas Newman Coll Wichita, KS 67213		✔	✔	✔	✔		✔		✔	✔	✔	✔	
Kansas St U Manhattan, KS 66506	✔	✔	✔	✔	✔	✔		✔		✔	✔		
Kansas Wesleyan U Salina, KS 67401						✔	✔						
Kansas, U of Lawrence, KS 66045						✔							
Manhattan Christian Coll Manhattan, KS 66502	✔		✔	✔	✔			✔	✔			✔	
McPherson Coll McPherson, KS 67460			✔										
Pittsburg St U Pittsburg, KS 66762		✔	✔	✔	✔	✔	✔	✔		✔	✔	✔	✔

State/Institution	AG	AR	BU	CS	ED	EN	HP	HE	HU	NS	SB	TE	VA
Southwestern Coll Winfield, KS 67156						✔							
Washburn U of Topeka Topeka, KS 66621												✔	✔
Wichita St U Wichita, KS 67260–0113	✔	✔	✔	✔	✔	✔			✔	✔	✔	✔	

Kentucky

State/Institution	AG	AR	BU	CS	ED	EN	HP	HE	HU	NS	SB	TE	VA
Eastern Kentucky U Richmond, KY 40475–3101	✔	✔	✔	✔	✔	✔	✔	✔	✔	✔	✔	✔	✔
Georgetown Coll Georgetown, KY 40324–1696				✔						✔			
Kentucky, U of Lexington, KY 40506	✔		✔	✔		✔							
Lindsey Wilson Coll Columbia, KY 42728			✔							✔			
Louisville, U of Louisville, KY 40292			✔	✔	✔	✔							
Murray St U Murray, KY 42071	✔	✔	✔	✔	✔	✔	✔	✔	✔	✔	✔	✔	✔
Northern Kentucky U Highland Heights, KY 41099		✔	✔							✔	✔	✔	
Thomas More Coll Crestview Hills, KY 41017		✔	✔	✔			✔		✔	✔	✔		
Transylvania U Lexington, KY 40508–1797						✔							
Union Coll Barbourville, KY 40906			✔								✔		
Western Kentucky U Bowling Green, KY 42101	✔	✔	✔	✔	✔		✔	✔	✔	✔	✔	✔	✔

State/Institution	AG	AR	BU	CS	ED	EN	HP	HE	HU	NS	SB	TE	VA
Louisiana													
Grambling St U Grambling, LA 71245			✔	✔			✔	✔	✔	✔	✔	✔	
Louisiana St U & A&M Coll Baton Rouge, LA 70803–2750	✔		✔	✔		✔				✔	✔		
Louisiana St U, Shreveport Shreveport, LA 71115			✔										
Louisiana Tech U Ruston, LA 71272	✔					✔		✔					
Loyola U New Orleans New Orleans, LA 70118						✔							
McNeese St U Lake Charles, LA 70609–2495				✔		✔							
New Orleans, U of New Orleans, LA 70148	✔	✔	✔	✔	✔	✔	✔		✔	✔	✔		
Nicholls St U Thibodaux, LA 70310			✔										
Northeast Louisiana U Monroe, LA 71209			✔			✔							
Southeastern Louisiana U Hammond, LA 70402			✔									✔	
Southern U & A&M Coll Baton Rouge, LA 70813						✔							
Xavier U of Louisiana New Orleans, LA 70125	✔	✔	✔			✔	✔		✔	✔	✔		
Maine													
Husson Coll Bangor, ME 04401			✔	✔	✔	✔							

State/Institution	AG	AR	BU	CS	ED	EN	HP	HE	HU	NS	SB	TE	VA
Maine Coll of Art Portland, ME 04101		✔											
Maine Maritime Acad Castine, ME 04420			✔			✔							
Maine, U of Orono, ME 04469	✔		✔	✔	✔	✔	✔	✔	✔	✔	✔		
Maine, U of, Augusta Augusta, ME 04330–9410			✔										
Maine, U of, Machias Machias, ME 04654			✔		✔				✔		✔		
New England, U of Biddeford, ME 04005			✔		✔		✔		✔	✔			
Southern Maine, U of Gorham, ME 04038		✔	✔	✔	✔	✔	✔		✔	✔	✔	✔	✔
Thomas Coll Waterville, ME 04901–9986			✔										
Unity Coll Unity, ME 04988–0532		✔								✔			

Maryland

State/Institution	AG	AR	BU	CS	ED	EN	HP	HE	HU	NS	SB	TE	VA
Baltimore, U of Baltimore, MD 21201			✔	✔					✔		✔		
Bowie St U Bowie, MD 20715		✔	✔	✔	✔	✔				✔	✔		
Capitol Coll Laurel, MD 20708				✔		✔							✔
Columbia Union Coll Takoma Park, MD 20912			✔	✔	✔	✔	✔						
Coppin St Coll Baltimore, MD 21216					✔	✔	✔						

State/Institution	AG	AR	BU	CS	ED	EN	HP	HE	HU	NS	SB	TE	VA
Frostburg St U Frostburg, MD 21532			✔										
Johns Hopkins U Baltimore, MD 21218				✔	✔	✔							
Maryland, U of, Baltimore County Baltimore, MD 21250	✔	✔	✔			✔	✔		✔	✔	✔	✔	
Maryland, U of, College Park College Park, MD 20742		✔	✔			✔							
Maryland, U of, Eastern Shore Princess Anne, MD 21853	✔	✔		✔	✔					✔		✔	
Maryland, U of, University Coll College Park, MD 20742–1600	✔	✔	✔						✔	✔	✔		
Morgan St U Baltimore, MD 21251			✔		✔	✔						✔	
Mt St. Mary's Coll Emmitsburg, MD 21727		✔	✔	✔		✔			✔	✔	✔		
Salisbury St U Salisbury, MD 21801			✔										
Towson St U Towson, MD 21252–7097	✔	✔	✔			✔			✔	✔	✔		
Villa Julie Coll Stevenson, MD 21153			✔	✔		✔			✔	✔	✔	✔	
Western Maryland Coll Westminster, MD 21157					✔	✔					✔		

Massachusetts

State/Institution	AG	AR	BU	CS	ED	EN	HP	HE	HU	NS	SB	TE	VA
Atlantic Union Coll South Lancaster, MA 01561	✔	✔	✔	✔		✔			✔			✔	
Bay Path Coll Longmeadow, MA 01106			✔		✔		✔						

State/Institution	AG	AR	BU	CS	ED	EN	HP	HE	HU	NS	SB	TE	VA
Boston U Boston, MA 02215						✔							
Gordon Coll Wenham, MA 01984		✔	✔	✔	✔	✔	✔		✔	✔	✔		
Massachusetts Inst of Tech Cambridge, MA 02139						✔							
Massachusetts Maritime Acad Buzzards Bay, MA 02532–1803						✔						✔	
Massachusetts, U of, Amherst Amherst, MA 01003	✔	✔	✔	✔	✔	✔	✔	✔	✔	✔		✔	
Massachusetts, U of, Boston Boston, MA 02125–3393	✔	✔	✔	✔		✔			✔	✔	✔		
Massachusetts, U of, Dartmouth North Dartmouth, MA 02747–2300						✔							
Massachusetts, U of, Lowell Lowell, MA 01854		✔				✔							
Merrimack Coll North Andover, MA 01845		✔	✔				✔	✔	✔	✔	✔		
Museum of Fine Arts, Sch of the Boston, MA 02115		✔											
Northeastern U Boston, MA 02115		✔	✔	✔	✔	✔	✔		✔	✔	✔	✔	
Springfield Coll Springfield, MA 01109–3797		✔	✔	✔	✔		✔		✔	✔	✔		
Suffolk U Boston, MA 02108		✔	✔	✔	✔	✔	✔		✔	✔	✔	✔	
Wentworth Inst of Tech Boston, MA 02115		✔	✔		✔							✔	
Westfield St Coll Westfield, MA 01086		✔	✔	✔	✔					✔	✔		

State/Institution	AG	AR	BU	CS	ED	EN	HP	HE	HU	NS	SB	TE	VA
Worcester Polytechnic Inst Worcester, MA 01609			✔			✔			✔	✔			

Mexico

State/Institution	AG	AR	BU	CS	ED	EN	HP	HE	HU	NS	SB	TE	VA
ITESM, Irapuato Irapuato, Guanajuato, MX 36660			✔										
ITESM, Leon Leon, Guanajuato, MX 37190			✔	✔	✔	✔							
ITESM, Mexico City 14380 Mexico City, D.F., MX			✔	✔		✔							
ITESM, Mexico State Estado de Mexico, MX			✔	✔		✔							
ITESM, Tampico Altamira, Tamaulipas, MX 89120			✔			✔							

Michigan

State/Institution	AG	AR	BU	CS	ED	EN	HP	HE	HU	NS	SB	TE	VA
Aquinas Coll Grand Rapids, MI 49506–1799	✔	✔	✔	✔		✔			✔	✔	✔		
Baker Coll, Auburn Hills Auburn Hills, MI 48326–2642			✔			✔							
Baker Coll, Cadillac Cadillac, MI 49601–9169			✔										
Baker Coll, Flint Flint, MI 48507						✔							
Baker Coll, Jackson Jackson, MI 49202–1290			✔			✔							
Baker Coll, Mt Clemens Clinton Township, MI 48035–4701			✔			✔							
Baker Coll, Muskegon Muskegon, MI 49442		✔	✔			✔							✔

State/Institution	AG	AR	BU	CS	ED	EN	HP	HE	HU	NS	SB	TE	VA
Baker Coll, Owosso Owosso, MI 48867–4400			✓				✓						
Baker Coll, Port Huron Port Huron, MI 48060–2597			✓				✓						
Calvin Coll Grand Rapids, MI 49546			✓		✓								
Central Michigan U Mount Pleasant, MI 48859												✓	✓
Cleary Coll Ypsilanti, MI 48197			✓										
Cornerstone Coll Grand Rapids, MI 49505					✓								
Detroit Coll of Business Dearborn, MI 48126			✓				✓						
Detroit Mercy, U of Detroit, MI 48221			✓	✓	✓	✓	✓		✓	✓	✓	✓	
Eastern Michigan U Ypsilanti, MI 48197		✓	✓	✓		✓	✓	✓	✓	✓	✓	✓	✓
Ferris St U Big Rapids, MI 49307–2251			✓	✓	✓		✓				✓	✓	✓
GMI Engineering & Management Inst Flint, MI 48504–4898			✓	✓	✓								
Grand Valley St U Allendale, MI 49401					✓	✓	✓						
Kendall Coll of Art & Design Grand Rapids, MI 49503–3194		✓											
Lake Superior St U Sault Sainte Marie, MI 49783						✓							✓

State/Institution	AG	AR	BU	CS	ED	EN	HP	HE	HU	NS	SB	TE	VA
Lawrence Tech U Southfield, MI 48075						✔							
Madonna U Livonia, MI 48150	✔	✔	✔				✔	✔	✔	✔	✔		
Marygrove Coll Detroit, MI 48221–2599	✔	✔	✔	✔									✔
Michigan Christian Coll Rochester Hills, MI 48307					✔								
Michigan St U East Lansing, MI 48824–0590				✔		✔							
Michigan Tech U Houghton, MI 49931–1295		✔	✔			✔	✔			✔	✔	✔	
Michigan, U of, Ann Arbor Ann Arbor, MI 48109						✔							
Michigan, U of, Dearborn Dearborn, MI 48128–1491	✔	✔	✔	✔	✔	✔			✔	✔	✔		
Michigan, U of, Flint Flint, MI 48502–2186		✔	✔	✔	✔	✔			✔	✔	✔	✔	
Oakland U Rochester, MI 48309–4401		✔	✔	✔	✔	✔			✔	✔	✔		
Olivet Coll Olivet, MI 49076	✔	✔	✔	✔					✔	✔	✔		
Siena Heights Coll Adrian, MI 49221	✔	✔	✔	✔		✔			✔	✔	✔		
St. Mary's Coll Orchard Lake, MI 48324		✔	✔	✔		✔				✔	✔		
Wayne St U Detroit, MI 48202				✔	✔	✔					✔		
Western Michigan U Kalamazoo, MI 49008		✔	✔		✔							✔	

State/Institution	AG	AR	BU	CS	ED	EN	HP	HE	HU	NS	SB	TE	VA

Minnesota

State/Institution	AG	AR	BU	CS	ED	EN	HP	HE	HU	NS	SB	TE	VA
Augsburg Coll Minneapolis, MN 55454		✔	✔	✔	✔	✔	✔		✔	✔	✔	✔	
Concordia Coll, Moorhead Moorhead, MN 56562		✔	✔	✔			✔	✔	✔	✔	✔		
Hamline U St. Paul, MN 55104–1284						✔	✔						
Minneapolis Coll of Art & Design Minneapolis, MN 55404		✔											
Minnesota, U of, Morris Morris, MN 56267			✔	✔	✔				✔	✔	✔		
Moorhead St U Moorhead, MN 56563	✔					✔	✔	✔					
North Central Bible Coll Minneapolis, MN 55404				✔			✔						
Northwestern Coll St. Paul, MN 55113	✔					✔							
St. Catherine, Coll of St. Paul, MN 55105						✔	✔			✔			
St. Cloud St U St. Cloud, MN 56301							✔					✔	
St. Mary's U of Minnesota Winona, MN 55987–1399						✔	✔						

Mississippi

State/Institution	AG	AR	BU	CS	ED	EN	HP	HE	HU	NS	SB	TE	VA
Alcorn St U Lorman, MS 39096	✔		✔	✔	✔	✔	✔	✔		✔	✔	✔	
Belhaven Coll Jackson, MS 39202							✔						

State/Institution	AG	AR	BU	CS	ED	EN	HP	HE	HU	NS	SB	TE	VA
Jackson St U Jackson, MS 39217			✔	✔						✔			
Mississippi St U Mississippi State, MS 39762	✔	✔	✔	✔	✔	✔		✔			✔	✔	
Mississippi Valley St U Itta Bena, MS 38941			✔	✔						✔	✔	✔	
Rust Coll Holly Springs, MS 38635			✔	✔					✔	✔	✔		
Southern Mississippi, U of Hattiesburg, MS 39406	✔	✔	✔	✔	✔	✔	✔	✔	✔	✔	✔	✔	
Tougaloo Coll Tougaloo, MS 39174			✔		✔	✔				✔	✔		

Missouri

State/Institution	AG	AR	BU	CS	ED	EN	HP	HE	HU	NS	SB	TE	VA
Central Missouri St U Warrensburg, MO 64093						✔							
Columbia Coll Columbia, MO 65216						✔							
Culver-Stockton Coll Canton, MO 63435–1299			✔			✔	✔					✔	
Drury Coll Springfield, MO 65802			✔			✔	✔						
Evangel Coll Springfield, MO 65802						✔							
Fontbonne Coll St. Louis, MO 63105		✔	✔	✔	✔	✔	✔	✔			✔	✔	✔
Lincoln U Jefferson City, MO 65102–0029	✔												
Lindenwood Coll St. Charles, MO 63301			✔	✔									

State/Institution	AG	AR	BU	CS	ED	EN	HP	HE	HU	NS	SB	TE	VA
Maryville U of St. Louis St. Louis, MO 63141–7299		✔	✔	✔	✔		✔		✔	✔	✔		
Missouri, U of, Columbia Columbia, MO 65211	✔	✔				✔			✔	✔	✔		
Missouri, U of, Kansas City Kansas City, MO 64110			✔	✔		✔				✔	✔		
Missouri, U of, Rolla Rolla, MO 65409–0910			✔	✔		✔			✔	✔	✔		
Missouri, U of, St. Louis St. Louis, MO 63121–4499			✔				✔				✔		
Northwest Missouri St U Maryville, MO 64468	✔												
Ozark Christian Coll Joplin, MO 64801					✔								
Ozarks, Coll of the Point Lookout, MO 65726	✔	✔	✔	✔	✔	✔	✔	✔	✔	✔	✔	✔	
Rockhurst Coll Kansas City, MO 64110–2561			✔	✔					✔	✔	✔		
Southeast Missouri St U Cape Girardeau, MO 63701			✔										
Southwest Baptist U Bolivar, MO 65613–2496						✔	✔						
Southwest Missouri St U Springfield, MO 65804	✔	✔	✔	✔	✔		✔	✔	✔	✔	✔	✔	✔
Stephens Coll Columbia, MO 65215						✔							
Washington U St. Louis, MO 63130–4899			✔			✔							
Webster U St. Louis, MO 63119–3194		✔	✔	✔	✔		✔		✔	✔	✔		

State/Institution	AG	AR	BU	CS	ED	EN	HP	HE	HU	NS	SB	TE	VA
Montana													
Carroll Coll Helena, MT 59625			✓										
Great Falls, U of Great Falls, MT 59405			✓	✓					✓		✓		
Montana St U, Northern Havre, MT 59501	✓		✓	✓					✓	✓	✓	✓	✓
Montana Tech, U of Montana Butte, MT 59701–8997			✓	✓		✓			✓				
Montana, U of Missoula, MT 59812		✓	✓	✓			✓		✓		✓		
Rocky Mountain Coll Billings, MT 59102–1796	✓	✓	✓	✓	✓	✓			✓	✓	✓	✓	
Salish Kootenai Coll Pablo, MT 59855			✓				✓						✓
Nebraska													
Chadron St Coll Chadron, NE 69337	✓	✓	✓	✓	✓		✓	✓	✓	✓	✓	✓	
Grace U Omaha, NE 68108	✓	✓	✓	✓	✓		✓				✓	✓	
Hastings Coll Hastings, NE 68902–0269					✓	✓							
Nebraska Christian Coll Norfolk, NE 68701	✓	✓	✓	✓	✓	✓	✓	✓	✓	✓	✓	✓	✓
Nebraska, U of, Lincoln Lincoln, NE 68588	✓	✓	✓	✓	✓	✓	✓	✓	✓	✓	✓	✓	✓
Nebraska, U of, Omaha Omaha, NE 68182–0005			✓			✓							

State/Institution	AG	AR	BU	CS	ED	EN	HP	HE	HU	NS	SB	TE	VA
Peru St Coll Peru, NE 68421–0010		✔	✔	✔	✔				✔	✔	✔	✔	
Wayne St Coll Wayne, NE 68787	✔	✔	✔	✔	✔			✔	✔	✔	✔	✔	✔

Nevada

State/Institution	AG	AR	BU	CS	ED	EN	HP	HE	HU	NS	SB	TE	VA
Nevada, U of, Reno Reno, NV 89557–0002	✔		✔		✔	✔							

New Hampshire

State/Institution	AG	AR	BU	CS	ED	EN	HP	HE	HU	NS	SB	TE	VA
Keene St Coll Keene, NH 03435–2604		✔	✔	✔	✔	✔	✔	✔		✔	✔	✔	✔
New Hampshire Coll Manchester, NH 03106–1045			✔	✔	✔				✔		✔		

New Jersey

State/Institution	AG	AR	BU	CS	ED	EN	HP	HE	HU	NS	SB	TE	VA
Caldwell Coll Caldwell, NJ 07006		✔	✔	✔		✔			✔	✔	✔		
Drew U Madison, NJ 07940						✔							
Fairleigh Dickinson U Teaneck, NJ 07666		✔	✔	✔	✔				✔	✔	✔	✔	
Georgian Court Coll Lakewood, NJ 08701–2697		✔	✔				✔			✔	✔		
Jersey City St Coll Jersey City, NJ 07305		✔	✔	✔			✔		✔	✔	✔		
Kean Coll of New Jersey Union, NJ 07083–0411			✔	✔								✔	✔
Medicine & Dentistry of N.J., U of Newark, NJ 07107			✔	✔		✔				✔			

State/Institution	AG	AR	BU	CS	ED	EN	HP	HE	HU	NS	SB	TE	VA
Montclair St U Upper Montclair, NJ 07043–1624		✔	✔	✔			✔	✔	✔	✔	✔	✔	✔
Ramapo Coll of New Jersey Mahwah, NJ 07430		✔	✔	✔					✔	✔	✔		
Richard Stockton Coll of New Jersey Pomona, NJ 08240		✔	✔	✔	✔		✔		✔	✔	✔		
Rowan U Glassboro, NJ 08028			✔		✔								
Seton Hall U South Orange, NJ 07079–2689			✔	✔		✔	✔			✔	✔		
Westminster Choir Coll of Rider U Princeton, NJ 08540								✔			✔		

New Mexico

Eastern New Mexico U Portales, NM 88130		✔	✔	✔	✔			✔		✔			
New Mexico Highlands U Las Vegas, NM 87701			✔	✔		✔	✔			✔	✔	✔	
New Mexico St U Las Cruces, NM 88003–8001	✔		✔	✔	✔	✔		✔	✔	✔	✔	✔	
New Mexico, U of Albuquerque, NM 87131			✔			✔							
Western New Mexico U Silver City, NM 88062			✔		✔								✔

New York

Alfred U Alfred, NY 14802–1205			✔			✔							
Audrey Cohen Coll New York, NY 10013			✔		✔		✔		✔		✔		

State/Institution	AG	AR	BU	CS	ED	EN	HP	HE	HU	NS	SB	TE	VA
Concordia Coll Bronxville, NY 10708			✔										
Cornell U Ithaca, NY 14853	✔					✔							
CUNY, City Coll New York, NY 10031						✔			✔		✔		
CUNY, York Coll Jamaica, NY 11451			✔	✔		✔							
Daemen Coll Amherst, NY 14226	✔	✔							✔		✔		
Dominican Coll of Blauvelt Orangeburg, NY 10962			✔	✔	✔		✔		✔		✔		
Dowling Coll Oakdale, NY 11769			✔	✔	✔		✔		✔	✔	✔	✔	
Fashion Inst of Tech New York, NY 10001–5992	✔	✔											
Five Towns Coll Dix Hills, NY 11746–6055			✔		✔							✔	✔
Insurance, Coll of New York, NY 10007			✔										
Iona Coll New Rochelle, NY 10801			✔	✔	✔				✔	✔	✔		
Keuka Coll Keuka Park, NY 14478						✔							
Long Island U, Brooklyn Brooklyn, NY 11201	✔	✔	✔									✔	
Long Island U, CW Post Brookville, NY 11548–1300	✔	✔	✔	✔		✔			✔	✔	✔		
Long Island U, Southampton Coll Southampton, NY 11968	✔	✔			✔		✔		✔	✔	✔		

State/Institution	AG	AR	BU	CS	ED	EN	HP	HE	HU	NS	SB	TE	VA
Manhattan Coll Riverdale, NY 10471		✓	✓	✓	✓	✓			✓	✓	✓	✓	
Marist Coll Poughkeepsie, NY 12601		✓	✓	✓	✓				✓	✓	✓	✓	
Marymount Manhattan Coll New York, NY 10021			✓										
Mercy Coll Dobbs Ferry, NY 10522					✓						✓		
Mt St. Mary Coll Newburgh, NY 12550–3598		✓	✓	✓			✓		✓	✓	✓	✓	
Nazareth Coll of Rochester Rochester, NY 14618										✓			
New Rochelle, Coll of New Rochelle, NY 10805	✓	✓							✓	✓	✓		
New York St Coll of Ceramics, Alfred U Alfred, NY 14802	✓					✓							
Polytechnic U Brooklyn, NY 11201				✓		✓			✓	✓	✓		
Rensselaer Polytechnic Inst Troy, NY 12180		✓	✓			✓			✓	✓	✓		
Roberts Wesleyan Coll Rochester, NY 14624–1997						✓							
Rochester Inst of Tech Rochester, NY 14623			✓	✓		✓	✓			✓	✓	✓	
Russell Sage Coll Troy, NY 12180		✓	✓	✓	✓		✓		✓	✓	✓		
St. Thomas Aquinas Coll Sparkill, NY 10976–1050						✓	✓						
SUNY Coll, Cortland Cortland, NY 13045		✓	✓	✓	✓		✓		✓	✓	✓		

State/Institution	AG	AR	BU	CS	ED	EN	HP	HE	HU	NS	SB	TE	VA
SUNY Coll, Fredonia Fredonia, NY 14063	✔				✔	✔							
SUNY Coll, Oneonta Oneonta, NY 13820		✔				✔	✔	✔					
SUNY Coll, Plattsburgh Plattsburgh, NY 12901		✔	✔	✔	✔		✔		✔	✔	✔		
SUNY Coll, Potsdam Potsdam, NY 13676–2294		✔	✔	✔		✔	✔		✔				
SUNY Health Science Ctr, Syracuse Syracuse, NY 13210						✔							
SUNY Inst of Tech, Utica/Rome Utica, NY 13504–3050			✔	✔			✔		✔			✔	✔
SUNY Maritime Coll Throggs Neck, NY 10465						✔							
SUNY New Paltz New Paltz, NY 12561–2499			✔	✔		✔					✔		
SUNY, Buffalo State Coll Buffalo, NY 14222		✔	✔	✔	✔				✔		✔	✔	✔
SUNY, Purchase Coll Purchase, NY 10577					✔								
Syracuse U Syracuse, NY 13244						✔							
U.S. Merchant Marine Acad Kings Point, NY 11024–1699						✔							
Utica Coll of Syracuse U Utica, NY 13502–4892			✔	✔									
Webb Inst Glen Cove, NY 11542						✔							

State/Institution	AG	AR	BU	CS	ED	EN	HP	HE	HU	NS	SB	TE	VA
North Carolina													
Campbell U Buies Creek, NC 27506					✔							✔	
East Carolina U Greenville, NC 27858–4353	✔	✔	✔	✔			✔	✔	✔	✔	✔	✔	✔
Elizabeth City St U Elizabeth City, NC 27909	✔	✔	✔				✔			✔	✔	✔	
Elon Coll Elon College, NC 27244			✔	✔			✔		✔				
Fayetteville St U Fayetteville, NC 28301		✔											
John Wesley Coll High Point, NC 27265				✔									
Johnson C Smith U Charlotte, NC 28216	✔	✔	✔	✔			✔		✔				
Livingstone Coll Salisbury, NC 28144		✔	✔	✔					✔	✔	✔		
Mars Hill Coll Mars Hill, NC 28754							✔						
Methodist Coll Fayetteville, NC 28311			✔		✔								
Mt Olive Coll Mount Olive, NC 28365	✔	✔	✔						✔	✔	✔		
North Carolina A&T St U Greensboro, NC 27411		✔				✔							
North Carolina St U Raleigh, NC 27695–7103	✔	✔	✔	✔	✔	✔			✔	✔	✔	✔	
North Carolina Wesleyan Coll Rocky Mount, NC 27804		✔	✔						✔	✔	✔		

State/Institution	AG	AR	BU	CS	ED	EN	HP	HE	HU	NS	SB	TE	VA
North Carolina, U of, Charlotte Charlotte, NC 28223–0001		✓	✓	✓	✓				✓	✓	✓	✓	
Pfeiffer U Misenheimer, NC 28109		✓	✓	✓					✓	✓	✓		
Piedmont Bible Coll Winston–Salem, NC 27101–5197					✓								
St. Augustine's Coll Raleigh, NC 27610			✓		✓					✓			
Wake Forest U Winston–Salem, NC 27109						✓	✓						
Warren Wilson Coll Asheville, NC 28815	✓	✓	✓		✓				✓	✓	✓		
Western Carolina U Cullowhee, NC 28723		✓	✓	✓	✓	✓	✓	✓	✓	✓	✓		
Winston-Salem St U Winston–Salem, NC 27110			✓	✓					✓	✓			

North Dakota

State/Institution	AG	AR	BU	CS	ED	EN	HP	HE	HU	NS	SB	TE	VA
Jamestown Coll Jamestown, ND 58405			✓										
Mary, U of Bismarck, ND 58504–9652			✓	✓	✓		✓						
Mayville St U Mayville, ND 58257–1299			✓	✓	✓							✓	
North Dakota St U Fargo, ND 58105	✓	✓	✓	✓	✓	✓	✓	✓	✓	✓	✓	✓	
North Dakota, U of Grand Forks, ND 58202–8172	✓	✓	✓	✓	✓	✓	✓	✓	✓	✓	✓	✓	✓
Valley City St U Valley City, ND 58072–4098		✓	✓		✓					✓	✓	✓	

State/Institution	AG	AR	BU	CS	ED	EN	HP	HE	HU	NS	SB	TE	VA
Ohio													
Akron, U of Akron, OH 44325	✔	✔	✔		✔			✔	✔	✔		✔	
Art Acad of Cincinnati Cincinnati, OH 45202		✔											
Bowling Green St U Bowling Green, OH 43403	✔	✔	✔	✔		✔		✔	✔	✔	✔	✔	
Case Western Reserve U Cleveland, OH 44106			✔	✔		✔				✔			
Central St U Wilberforce, OH 45384			✔	✔									
Cincinnati Bible Coll & Sem Cincinnati, OH 45204–3200					✔								
Cincinnati, U of Cincinnati, OH 45221–0091			✔	✔		✔			✔				
Cleveland St U Cleveland, OH 44115	✔	✔	✔	✔	✔				✔	✔	✔	✔	
David Myers Coll Cleveland, OH 44115–1096			✔				✔					✔	
Dayton, U of Dayton, OH 45469			✔	✔		✔				✔		✔	
Defiance Coll Defiance, OH 43512		✔	✔	✔		✔			✔	✔	✔		
Findlay, U of Findlay, OH 45840–3695										✔			
Franciscan U of Steubenville Steubenville, OH 43952–6701					✔								
Heidelberg Coll Tiffin, OH 44883					✔	✔							

State/Institution	AG	AR	BU	CS	ED	EN	HP	HE	HU	NS	SB	TE	VA
Kent St U Kent, OH 44242–0001												✓	
Lourdes Coll Sylvania, OH 43560			✓										
Malone Coll Canton, OH 44709			✓	✓	✓		✓		✓	✓	✓		
Miami U Oxford, OH 45056				✓		✓						✓	
Mt St. Joseph, Coll of Cincinnati, OH 45233–1672	✓	✓	✓	✓			✓		✓	✓	✓		
Mt Union Coll Alliance, OH 44601			✓	✓	✓		✓		✓	✓	✓		
Notre Dame Coll of Ohio South Euclid, OH 44121	✓	✓					✓		✓	✓	✓		
Ohio Northern U Ada, OH 45810						✓							✓
Ohio St U, Columbus Columbus, OH 43210–1200	✓		✓	✓		✓			✓	✓	✓		
Ohio St U, Newark Newark, OH 43055			✓			✓							
Ohio U Athens, OH 45701–2979				✓		✓							
Rio Grande, U of Rio Grande, OH 45674	✓	✓		✓		✓			✓	✓	✓	✓	
Toledo, U of Toledo, OH 43606			✓	✓	✓	✓	✓		✓	✓	✓	✓	✓
Ursuline Coll Pepper Pike, OH 44124	✓	✓	✓	✓			✓		✓	✓	✓		
Walsh U North Canton, OH 44720			✓	✓		✓							

State/Institution	AG	AR	BU	CS	ED	EN	HP	HE	HU	NS	SB	TE	VA
Wilberforce U Wilberforce, OH 45384		✔	✔	✔		✔			✔	✔	✔		
Wooster, Coll of Wooster, OH 44691						✔	✔			✔			
Wright St U Dayton, OH 45435			✔	✔		✔			✔	✔			
Youngstown St U Youngstown, OH 44555–0001			✔			✔							

Oklahoma

State/Institution	AG	AR	BU	CS	ED	EN	HP	HE	HU	NS	SB	TE	VA
Langston U Langston, OK 73050	✔		✔		✔		✔						
Northeastern St U Tahlequah, OK 74464			✔		✔							✔	
Oklahoma Baptist U Shawnee, OK 74801		✔	✔	✔						✔	✔		
Oklahoma Panhandle St U Goodwell, OK 73939	✔												
Oklahoma St U Stillwater, OK 74078						✔							
Oklahoma, U of Norman, OK 73019			✔			✔							
Oral Roberts U Tulsa, OK 74171							✔				✔		

Oregon

State/Institution	AG	AR	BU	CS	ED	EN	HP	HE	HU	NS	SB	TE	VA
Bassist Coll Portland, OR 97201													✔
Eastern Oregon U LaGrande, OR 97850	✔	✔	✔		✔								

State/Institution	AG	AR	BU	CS	ED	EN	HP	HE	HU	NS	SB	TE	VA
George Fox U Newberg, OR 97132						✔							
Linfield Coll McMinnville, OR 97128–6894						✔							
Northwest Christian Coll Eugene, OR 97401–3727				✔		✔			✔	✔	✔		
Oregon Inst of Tech Klamath Falls, OR 97601–8801		✔	✔			✔						✔	
Oregon St U Corvallis, OR 97331	✔	✔	✔	✔	✔	✔	✔	✔	✔	✔	✔		✔
Pacific U Forest Grove, OR 97116				✔		✔	✔						
Portland St U Portland, OR 97207–0751		✔	✔	✔	✔	✔			✔	✔	✔		
Reed Coll Portland, OR 97202–8199		✔	✔	✔		✔							

Pennsylvania

State/Institution	AG	AR	BU	CS	ED	EN	HP	HE	HU	NS	SB	TE	VA
Albright Coll Reading, PA 19612–5234									✔				
Beaver Coll Glenside, PA 19038–3295		✔	✔	✔					✔	✔	✔		
Bryn Athyn Coll of the New Church Bryn Athyn, PA 19009	✔	✔	✔	✔	✔					✔	✔		
Cabrini Coll Radnor, PA 19087–3698	✔	✔	✔	✔			✔		✔	✔	✔		
California U of Pennsylvania California, PA 15419	✔	✔	✔	✔	✔	✔			✔	✔	✔	✔	✔
Chatham Coll Pittsburgh, PA 15232				✔	✔	✔							

State/Institution	AG	AR	BU	CS	ED	EN	HP	HE	HU	NS	SB	TE	VA
Chestnut Hill Coll Philadelphia, PA 19118–2693		✔	✔	✔	✔		✔		✔	✔	✔		
Cheyney U of Pennsylvania Cheyney, PA 19319		✔	✔	✔	✔		✔	✔	✔	✔	✔		
Clarion U of Pennsylvania Clarion, PA 16214						✔							
Delaware Valley Coll Doylestown, PA 18901	✔		✔	✔	✔								
Drexel U Philadelphia, PA 19104		✔	✔	✔			✔	✔	✔	✔	✔	✔	
Duquesne U Pittsburgh, PA 15282							✔						
Eastern Coll St. Davids, PA 19087–3696							✔						
Edinboro U of Pennsylvania Edinboro, PA 16444						✔							
Elizabethtown Coll Elizabethtown, PA 17022						✔							
Gannon U Erie, PA 16541			✔			✔							
Geneva Coll Beaver Falls, PA 15010		✔					✔						
Gettysburg Coll Gettysburg, PA 17325–1484					✔	✔	✔						
Gwynedd-Mercy Coll Gwynedd Valley, PA 19437				✔									
Holy Family Coll Philadelphia, PA 19114			✔	✔	✔		✔		✔	✔	✔		
Immaculata Coll Immaculata, PA 19345		✔	✔	✔	✔		✔	✔	✔	✔	✔		

State/Institution	AG	AR	BU	CS	ED	EN	HP	HE	HU	NS	SB	TE	VA
Juniata Coll Huntingdon, PA 16652–2119						✔	✔			✔			
King's Coll Wilkes–Barre, PA 18711		✔	✔	✔					✔	✔	✔		
LaSalle U Philadelphia, PA 19141–1199		✔	✔	✔			✔		✔	✔	✔		
Lebanon Valley Coll of Pennsylvania Annville, PA 17003						✔	✔						
Lehigh U Bethlehem, PA 18015–3035						✔							
Lincoln U Lincoln University, PA 19352		✔	✔	✔			✔		✔	✔	✔		
Lock Haven U of Pennsylvania Lock Haven, PA 17745						✔							
Lycoming Coll Williamsport, PA 17701–5192						✔	✔			✔			
Mercyhurst Coll Erie, PA 16546	✔	✔	✔	✔			✔	✔	✔	✔	✔		
Messiah Coll Grantham, PA 17027–0800	✔	✔	✔	✔	✔	✔			✔	✔	✔		
Millersville U of Pennsylvania Millersville, PA 17551–0302	✔	✔	✔	✔	✔	✔			✔	✔	✔	✔	
Moore Coll of Art & Design Philadelphia, PA 19103	✔				✔								
Moravian Coll Bethlehem, PA 18018						✔	✔						
Mt Aloysius Coll Cresson, PA 16630							✔						✔
Muhlenberg Coll Allentown, PA 18104–5586						✔	✔						

State/Institution	AG	AR	BU	CS	ED	EN	HP	HE	HU	NS	SB	TE	VA
Neumann Coll Aston, PA 19014–1298		✔	✔	✔	✔				✔	✔	✔		
Pennsylvania Coll of Tech Williamsport, PA 17701–5799	✔	✔	✔	✔	✔	✔	✔		✔	✔		✔	✔
Pennsylvania St U University Park, PA 16802						✔							
Pennsylvania St U, Harrisburg Middletown, PA 17057												✔	
Philadelphia Coll of Bible Langhorne, PA 19047–2990			✔	✔									
Philadelphia Coll of Pharm & Sci Philadelphia, PA 19104–4495					✔		✔		✔				
Philadelphia Coll of Textiles & Science Philadelphia, PA 19144	✔	✔	✔			✔			✔	✔		✔	✔
Pittsburgh, U of, Bradford Bradford, PA 16701–2898						✔							
Pittsburgh, U of, Johnstown Johnstown, PA 15904						✔							
Pittsburgh, U of, Pittsburgh Pittsburgh, PA 15260						✔							
Point Park Coll Pittsburgh, PA 15222		✔											
Robert Morris Coll Moon Township, PA 15108–1189			✔	✔	✔		✔		✔				
St. Vincent Coll Latrobe, PA 15650–2690			✔	✔	✔		✔	✔	✔	✔	✔		
Temple U Philadelphia, PA 19122–1803			✔	✔		✔				✔			
Thiel Coll Greenville, PA 16125		✔	✔	✔	✔	✔	✔		✔	✔	✔		

State/Institution	AG	AR	BU	CS	ED	EN	HP	HE	HU	NS	SB	TE	VA
Valley Forge Christian Coll Phoenixville, PA 19460					✓								
Villanova U Villanova, PA 19085						✓							
Widener U Chester, PA 19013			✓			✓							
Wilkes U Wilkes–Barre, PA 18766	✓	✓	✓	✓	✓				✓	✓	✓	✓	
York Coll of Pennsylvania York, PA 17403–3426						✓							

Puerto Rico

State/Institution	AG	AR	BU	CS	ED	EN	HP	HE	HU	NS	SB	TE	VA
Polytechnic U of Puerto Rico Hato Rey, PR 00919						✓							
Puerto Rico, U of, Bayamon Tech U Coll Bayamon, PR 00959–1919		✓	✓									✓	
Puerto Rico, U of, Humacao U Coll Humacao, PR 00791					✓	✓			✓	✓			
Puerto Rico, U of, Mayaguez Mayaguez, PR 00681–5000	✓					✓					✓		
Sacred Heart, U of the Santurce, PR 00914		✓	✓	✓			✓		✓	✓	✓		

Rhode Island

State/Institution	AG	AR	BU	CS	ED	EN	HP	HE	HU	NS	SB	TE	VA
Johnson & Wales U Providence, RI 02903–3703			✓										
Rhode Island Coll Providence, RI 02908	✓	✓	✓	✓		✓			✓	✓	✓	✓	✓
Rhode Island, U of Kingston, RI 02881	✓	✓				✓	✓						

State/Institution	AG	AR	BU	CS	ED	EN	HP	HE	HU	NS	SB	TE	VA
South Carolina													
Benedict Coll Columbia, SC 29204						✓							
Charleston, Coll of Charleston, SC 29424			✓										
Clemson U Clemson, SC 29634–5124	✓		✓	✓	✓	✓			✓	✓	✓		
Coker Coll Hartsville, SC 29550		✓	✓		✓		✓		✓	✓	✓		
Columbia Coll Columbia, SC 29203						✓							
Erskine Coll Due West, SC 29639						✓	✓						
Francis Marion U Florence, SC 29501–0547						✓						✓	
Lander U Greenwood, SC 29649			✓	✓									
Medical U of South Carolina Charleston, SC 29425–2970							✓						
Morris Coll Sumter, SC 29150–3599			✓	✓	✓		✓		✓	✓	✓		
Presbyterian Coll Clinton, SC 29325						✓							
South Carolina St U Orangeburg, SC 29117–7127			✓			✓							
South Carolina, U of Columbia, SC 29208		✓	✓	✓		✓			✓	✓	✓		
South Carolina, U of, Aiken Aiken, SC 29801		✓	✓	✓	✓				✓	✓			

State/Institution	AG	AR	BU	CS	ED	EN	HP	HE	HU	NS	SB	TE	VA
Southern Wesleyan U Central, SC 29630							✔						
Voorhees Coll Denmark, SC 29042			✔	✔	✔				✔	✔	✔		
Winthrop U Rock Hill, SC 29733		✔	✔	✔			✔		✔	✔	✔	✔	

South Dakota

State/Institution	AG	AR	BU	CS	ED	EN	HP	HE	HU	NS	SB	TE	VA
Dakota St U Madison, SD 57042		✔	✔	✔			✔			✔			
National Coll Rapid City, SD 57701			✔	✔			✔						
Oglala Lakota Coll Kyle, SD 57752													✔
South Dakota Sch of Mines & Tech Rapid City, SD 57701–3995				✔		✔				✔			
South Dakota St U Brookings, SD 57007	✔		✔	✔	✔	✔		✔					

Tennessee

State/Institution	AG	AR	BU	CS	ED	EN	HP	HE	HU	NS	SB	TE	VA
Austin Peay St U Clarksville, TN 37044	✔		✔			✔							
Bryan Coll Dayton, TN 37321–7000							✔						
Carson-Newman Coll Jefferson City, TN 37760			✔	✔									
Cumberland U Lebanon, TN 37087			✔										
East Tennessee St U Johnson City, TN 37614–0731		✔	✔	✔					✔	✔	✔	✔	

State/Institution	AG	AR	BU	CS	ED	EN	HP	HE	HU	NS	SB	TE	VA
Freed-Hardeman U Henderson, TN 38340				✔							✔		
King Coll Bristol, TN 37620		✔	✔	✔					✔		✔		
Knoxville Coll Knoxville, TN 37921						✔							
Lane Coll Jackson, TN 38301						✔							
LeMoyne-Owen Coll Memphis, TN 38126		✔	✔	✔	✔	✔			✔	✔	✔	✔	
Memphis Coll of Art Memphis, TN 38104		✔											
Memphis, U of Memphis, TN 38152							✔						
Middle Tennessee St U Murfreesboro, TN 37132	✔	✔	✔	✔	✔		✔	✔	✔	✔	✔	✔	
Milligan Coll Milligan College, TN 37682						✔							
Tennessee St U Nashville, TN 37209–1561	✔		✔	✔		✔				✔			
Tennessee Tech U Cookeville, TN 38505	✔	✔	✔	✔	✔	✔	✔	✔		✔	✔	✔	✔
Tennessee, U of, Chattanooga Chattanooga, TN 37403			✔			✔	✔				✔	✔	
Tennessee, U of, Knoxville Knoxville, TN 37996–0230	✔	✔	✔	✔		✔					✔		
Tennessee, U of, Martin Martin, TN 38238	✔		✔			✔		✔			✔		
Union U Jackson, TN 38305–3697			✔										

State/Institution	AG	AR	BU	CS	ED	EN	HP	HE	HU	NS	SB	TE	VA
Texas													
Abilene Christian U Abilene, TX 79699–9100	✔					✔	✔						
Houston, U of Houston, TX 77004			✔	✔		✔			✔	✔	✔	✔	✔
Houston, U of, Clear Lake Houston, TX 77058–1098			✔	✔					✔	✔			
Houston, U of, Downtown Houston, TX 77002			✔										
Howard Payne U Brownwood, TX 76801							✔						
Huston-Tillotson Coll Austin, TX 78702			✔	✔	✔				✔	✔	✔		
Incarnate Word, U of the San Antonio, TX 78209–6397	✔	✔	✔	✔		✔			✔	✔	✔		
Jarvis Christian Coll Hawkins, TX 75765			✔	✔	✔				✔	✔	✔		
Lamar U Beaumont, TX 77710	✔					✔	✔						
McMurry U Abilene, TX 79697							✔						
North Texas, U of Denton, TX 76203–3797	✔	✔	✔			✔	✔		✔	✔	✔	✔	✔
Northwood U, Texas Campus Cedar Hill, TX 75104–0058			✔										
Prairie View A&M U Prairie View, TX 77446	✔		✔	✔		✔						✔	
Southern Methodist U Dallas, TX 75275						✔							

96   Programs in Cooperative Education

State/Institution	AG	AR	BU	CS	ED	EN	HP	HE	HU	NS	SB	TE	VA
Southwestern Adventist U Keene, TX 76059			✔	✔						✔	✔	✔	
St. Edward's U Austin, TX 78704			✔	✔									
St. Thomas, U of Houston, TX 77006			✔										
Sul Ross St U Alpine, TX 79832												✔	
Tarleton St U Stephenville, TX 76402	✔	✔	✔		✔			✔			✔		
Texas A&M U, College Station College Station, TX 77843–1265	✔		✔	✔		✔	✔		✔	✔	✔	✔	✔
Texas A&M U, Corpus Christi Corpus Christi, TX 78412			✔	✔					✔	✔	✔	✔	✔
Texas A&M U, Kingsville Kingsville, TX 78363	✔					✔		✔			✔		
Texas Southern U Houston, TX 77004												✔	
Texas Woman's U Denton, TX 76204–5589		✔	✔	✔									
Texas, U of, Arlington Arlington, TX 76019			✔			✔							
Texas, U of, Austin Austin, TX 78712–1157						✔				✔			
Wayland Baptist U Plainview, TX 79072						✔							
West Texas A&M U Canyon, TX 79016	✔	✔	✔	✔	✔				✔	✔	✔	✔	

State/Institution	AG	AR	BU	CS	ED	EN	HP	HE	HU	NS	SB	TE	VA
Utah													
Brigham Young U Provo, UT 84602	✔	✔	✔	✔	✔	✔	✔	✔	✔	✔	✔	✔	✔
Utah St U Logan, UT 84322–1600	✔	✔	✔	✔	✔	✔	✔	✔	✔	✔	✔	✔	✔
Utah, U of Salt Lake City, UT 84112		✔			✔				✔		✔		
Vermont													
Castleton St Coll Castleton, VT 05735	✔	✔	✔	✔	✔				✔	✔	✔		
Champlain Coll Burlington, VT 05402–0670			✔	✔			✔						
Goddard Coll Plainfield, VT 05667		✔			✔				✔		✔		
Lyndon St Coll Lyndonville, VT 05851–0919			✔		✔		✔		✔	✔	✔		
Marlboro Coll Marlboro, VT 05344				✔									
Norwich U Northfield, VT 05663			✔			✔				✔		✔	
Southern Vermont Coll Bennington, VT 05201			✔			✔			✔		✔		
St. Michael's Coll Colchester, VT 05439			✔			✔							
Vermont, U of Burlington, VT 05401–0160			✔			✔							

State/Institution	AG	AR	BU	CS	ED	EN	HP	HE	HU	NS	SB	TE	VA

Virginia

State/Institution	AG	AR	BU	CS	ED	EN	HP	HE	HU	NS	SB	TE	VA
George Mason U Fairfax, VA 22030		✔	✔	✔	✔	✔	✔		✔	✔	✔		✔
Hampton U Hampton, VA 23368		✔	✔	✔	✔	✔					✔		
James Madison U Harrisonburg, VA 22807			✔										
Mary Washington Coll Fredericksburg, VA 22401–5358				✔									
Norfolk St U Norfolk, VA 23504	✔	✔	✔	✔	✔	✔	✔	✔	✔	✔	✔	✔	✔
Old Dominion U Norfolk, VA 23529–0030	✔	✔	✔	✔	✔	✔	✔		✔	✔	✔	✔	
Randolph-Macon Coll Ashland, VA 23005–5505					✔	✔	✔						
Randolph-Macon Woman's Coll Lynchburg, VA 24503						✔							
Shenandoah U Winchester, VA 22601					✔	✔							
St. Paul's Coll Lawrenceville, VA 23868			✔		✔					✔	✔		
Virginia Commonwealth U Richmond, VA 23284–9005	✔	✔	✔	✔			✔		✔	✔	✔		
Virginia Polytechnic Inst & St U Blacksburg, VA 24061–0202	✔	✔	✔	✔		✔		✔	✔	✔	✔		
Virginia Union U Richmond, VA 23220			✔			✔			✔	✔	✔		
Virginia, U of Charlottesville, VA 22906						✔							

State/Institution	AG	AR	BU	CS	ED	EN	HP	HE	HU	NS	SB	TE	VA

Washington

State/Institution	AG	AR	BU	CS	ED	EN	HP	HE	HU	NS	SB	TE	VA
Central Washington U Ellensburg, WA 98926–7463		✔	✔	✔	✔			✔	✔	✔	✔	✔	
City U Bellevue, WA 98004			✔	✔	✔		✔						
Evergreen St Coll Olympia, WA 98505	✔	✔	✔	✔					✔	✔	✔		
Pacific Lutheran U Tacoma, WA 98447		✔	✔	✔	✔	✔	✔		✔	✔	✔		
Puget Sound, U of Tacoma, WA 98416		✔	✔	✔	✔		✔		✔	✔	✔		
Seattle Pacific U Seattle, WA 98119	✔	✔	✔		✔		✔		✔	✔	✔		
Walla Walla Coll College Place, WA 99324–3000			✔	✔	✔								
Washington, U of Seattle, WA 98195			✔			✔							
Whitman Coll Walla Walla, WA 99362			✔		✔	✔							
Whitworth Coll Spokane, WA 99251			✔	✔						✔			

West Virginia

State/Institution	AG	AR	BU	CS	ED	EN	HP	HE	HU	NS	SB	TE	VA
Charleston, U of Charleston, WV 25304	✔	✔					✔						
Davis & Elkins Coll Elkins, WV 26241			✔										
Marshall U Huntington, WV 25755			✔										✔

State/Institution	AG	AR	BU	CS	ED	EN	HP	HE	HU	NS	SB	TE	VA
Ohio Valley Coll Parkersburg, WV 26101			✔		✔								
Shepherd Coll Shepherdstown, WV 25443	✔	✔	✔					✔	✔	✔	✔		
West Virginia St Coll Institute, WV 25112–1000	✔	✔	✔	✔	✔								
West Virginia U Morgantown, WV 26506–6009						✔							
West Virginia U Inst of Tech Montgomery, WV 25136			✔	✔		✔						✔	
West Virginia U, Parkersburg Parkersburg, WV 26101	✔	✔	✔	✔	✔	✔			✔	✔	✔	✔	
West Virginia, Coll of Beckley, WV 25801			✔										

Wisconsin

State/Institution	AG	AR	BU	CS	ED	EN	HP	HE	HU	NS	SB	TE	VA
Cardinal Stritch U Milwaukee, WI 53217	✔	✔	✔	✔		✔					✔		
Concordia U Wisconsin Mequon, WI 53097	✔												
Marian Coll of Fond du Lac Fond du Lac, WI 54935	✔	✔			✔		✔		✔	✔	✔		
Marquette U Milwaukee, WI 53201–1881			✔	✔		✔				✔			
Milwaukee Inst of Art & Design Milwaukee, WI 53202		✔											
Mt Senario Coll Ladysmith, WI 54848			✔		✔						✔		
Northland Coll Ashland, WI 54806	✔		✔	✔	✔					✔	✔		

State/Institution	AG	AR	BU	CS	ED	EN	HP	HE	HU	NS	SB	TE	VA
St. Norbert Coll DePere, WI 54115						✔							
Viterbo Coll LaCrosse, WI 54601–8802		✔		✔		✔							
Wisconsin, U of, Eau Claire Eau Claire, WI 54701				✔			✔		✔	✔	✔		
Wisconsin, U of, LaCrosse LaCrosse, WI 54601		✔	✔	✔			✔		✔				
Wisconsin, U of, Madison Madison, WI 53706	✔		✔		✔	✔		✔					
Wisconsin, U of, Milwaukee Milwaukee, WI 53201–0749						✔							
Wisconsin, U of, Platteville Platteville, WI 53818	✔		✔			✔						✔	
Wisconsin, U of, River Falls River Falls, WI 54022	✔												
Wisconsin, U of, Stout Menomonie, WI 54751		✔	✔	✔	✔	✔		✔	✔	✔	✔	✔	✔
Wisconsin, U of, Superior Superior, WI 54880		✔	✔			✔							

Wyoming

State/Institution	AG	AR	BU	CS	ED	EN	HP	HE	HU	NS	SB	TE	VA
Wyoming, U of Laramie, WY 82071		✔	✔	✔	✔	✔	✔	✔	✔	✔	✔	✔	

Getting the Most College for the Money: Cash Savers and Cash Makers

While the previous chapter told several ways that schools can provide more money for you to go to college, or even give you a discount on the price, this chapter is about ways to stretch your college dollars. It deals with innovative programs that the colleges are coming up with to help you meet their ever-increasing tuition. It also looks at ways you can save or even make money while getting your degree. But before we jump in, a word of warning: No program is set in stone. Schools change course. A program mentioned in this chapter, or elsewhere in this book, may no longer be in place when you check into it. At the same time, new programs are springing up all the time. So check out the full range of programs and payment options available at your school, or at the schools you're thinking of attending. The more you know, the better you'll do.

Innovative Tuition Plans

More and more colleges and universities are looking for ways to take the sting out of paying college tuition. For many of them, this means offering plans that make it possible to get around paying for college all in one formidable annual chunk. Many colleges now offer a range of payment plans. Washington University in St. Louis, a trailblazer in providing innovative payment programs, was early in offering a Tuition Stabilization Plan in 1979. That program freezes the cost of tuition for students who paid tuition up front; the school offered a loan program to make the huge payment possible. The vast majority of families involved in the program exercise the loan option, but the school keeps its default rate very low. Washington University has a broader loan program called the Cost Stabilization Program, which offers protection for tuition, room, and board. CSP offers parents a fixed-rate, low-interest, monthly pay-back plan that stretches out over 10 years. Washington University requires no collateral on these loans.

Another school with a lot of payment plans to offer is the University of Pennsylvania. Its Penn Plan is a veritable smorgasbord of payment options that allow students to freeze their tuition by making hefty payments up front, or simply to pay tuition on a monthly basis instead of once a year. The school even offers a revolving line of credit (Visa card-style) for nontuition expenses.

There are as many programs as there are colleges, and programs at different schools that sound similar may have significant differences between them. There's no substitute for getting the full description of all of your school's program from the school itself. However, if you would like a broad survey of programs available at different schools, you can order a chart-filled paperback, *College Check Mate* from Octameron Associates (P.O. Box 2748, Alexandria, VA 22301).

Colleges are also getting smarter about giving students and their families more ways to pay for college. Many schools now allow tuition to be paid through regular electronic funds transfers from bank accounts or through credit cards. But look out for that interest rate on those credit cards! Some of the rates charged by banks on their cards would make a loan shark blush.

Paying on the Installment Plan

More schools are starting to allow families to pay tuition on the installment plan, or using their own endowments to make tuition loans that the families repay in installments. Schools ranging from the University of Michigan to Muskingum College in New Concord, Ohio, provide such plans, often with lower-than-commercial interest rates. The installments might run monthly, or as little as two per semester; they can be stretched out over several years. Check with your school for more details.

Banks and private companies are also working with colleges to create installment-plan tuition programs. Sometimes the colleges run the plans, and sometimes the private companies run them on their own.

Many private companies are willing to make a little money by acting as go-between for you and your school. Academic Management Services, Inc. of Pawtucket, R.I., makes the lump payment to the college for you; you then work out a schedule of repayment to the company, paying a $45 fee to the company that includes insurance on the life of the parent for the balance of the debt. Another is the Student Loan Marketing Association, SALLIE MAE, through its Family Education Financing program (1050 Thomas Jefferson Street, NW, Washington, D.C. 20007; (202) 333-8000). The NELLIE MAE, an organization focused in the Northeast, provides a range of loans (NELLIE MAE, 50 Braintree Hill Park, Suite 300, Braintree, MA 02184; (617) 849-1325). One such supplemental college loan which is available at many colleges, EXCEL, ranges from $2,000 to $20,000 annually with a cumulative maximum of $80,000 per student. The interest rates run between two and four percent higher than the prime rate, as published in the *Wall Street Journal.* NELLIE MAE also works with a group of 30 schools that make up the Consortium on Financing Higher Education to provide SHARE loans. The loan amounts are the same as EXCEL loans, as is the interest rate. Students who attend one of the consortium schools are eligible for SHARE loans; contact your financial aid office to see if your school is one of them. The Consortium schools read like a Who's Who of American Higher Education:

Amherst College

Barnard College

Brown University

Bryn Mawr College

Carleton College

Columbia University

Cornell University

Georgetown University

Harvard University

The Johns Hopkins University

Massachusetts Institute of Technology

Mount Holyoke College

Northwestern University

Oberlin College

Pomona College

Princeton University

Radcliffe College

Rice University

Smith College

Stanford University

Swarthmore College

Trinity College

The University of Chicago

University of Pennsylvania

The University of Rochester

Washington University

Wellesley College

Wesleyan University

Williams College

Yale University

You can get a list of other nationally available programs, along with local financial institutions that offer student loans, from your college financial aid office or state aid guaranty agency (see list on page 29).

Putting the Money Up Front

Schools like having money in the bank, and the sooner the better. They can earn interest on it, invest it, and otherwise have fun with it. That's why they are willing to make attractive offers in return for getting money quickly that you would eventually pay them anyway.

Prepayment discounts and bonuses: A number of schools offer discounts on tuition for students who pay their entire semester's worth (or year's worth) in a single up-front chunk. Kendall College in Illinois will give students a 10 percent discount. Other schools, like Cedarville College in Ohio and George Washington University in Washington, D.C., will give students a bonus for paying in advance. Again, check with your school to see if it offers such programs.

Getting a big head start: Tuition "futures": A few years ago, financial and education writers began singing the praises of a promising development for parents with young children: the pay now, learn later plan that was pioneered by Duquesne University. The program was part investment, part promise: if parents would prepay a certain amount many years before their child was to attend college, then the school would guarantee that the student's tuition would be paid in full by the time he or she arrived. The school would invest the cash. It also planned to make a little more money out of a tricky provision in Duquesne's plan. If the student couldn't get into the school or didn't want to attend, the parents would only get back the money they had originally invested—not the earned interest over those years. Despite the drawbacks, the innovative idea was widely hailed, and some states began looking into versions of the program that they could institute.

Now the future of the pay now, learn later plans seems less rosy. In 1987, less than three years after the plan was announced, Duquesne suspended its program until the world of investments looked more lucrative. But parent interest had been dropping off anyway, because the plan didn't make it easy to choose a school other than Duquesne—so tough luck if little Timmy has his heart set on Notre Dame. Critics of the Duquesne plan charge that the school jumped into the game with unrealistic pricing. About a dozen other private schools still have such plans in place, with varying degrees of success at keeping them going.

While the private sector seems to be reassessing its role in the education futures market, the states have been looking at ways to jump in. After all, tuition costs have become a hot issue politically as well as financially, and states have greater resources to help them weather future shocks. Many states have already enacted legislation to help give parents tuition guarantees or tax breaks. Several states now offer a local version of so-called "Baccalaureate Bonds." They act like zero-coupon bonds, which is to say your kids get no income—and pay no tax—until they mature. Illinois has created special tax-exempt savings bonds that pay extra interest if they are redeemed to pay educational expenses—a grant of up to $400 is added to the regular interest for each $5,000 of bonds. North Carolina has passed a similar program.

The federal government has stepped in, too. Series EE Savings Bonds are a stable, long-term college investment with some tax advantages. If you use those bonds to pay tuition or other educational fees for yourself or your family, the accrued interest on the redeemed bonds may be excluded from your reported income. There are a few requirements, of course. The law only applies to EE bonds issued after 1989, and the purchaser has to be older than 24. There are stringent income restrictions on these bonds: if your family income tops $60,000, the tax deduction fades away.

A handful of states have tuition guarantee plans so far. Most of the programs work pretty much like the Duquesne plan, except that students can use the tuition payments to attend any public school in the state. Michigan, Wyoming, Florida, Indiana, Maine, and Tennessee have such programs. Missouri passed its own savings plan, but with no guarantee that it would cover all of the costs of tuition when the bill came due, simply allowing parents to put away money without having to pay state income taxes on the interest. Illinois staked its hopes for the future on selling parents bonds that are exempt from federal taxes. Here's how it works: the families buy what are known as zero–coupon bonds. The state uses the money to do whatever states do; if the family holds on to the bond for five years and then cashes it in to pay college tuition, the state kicks in a supplemental interest payment over and above the interest that the state would normally pay. Illinois has sold a lot of bonds since starting the program in 1987, and many other states have adopted that approach.

One of the more interesting pay now, learn later options has been offered by a private bank, the College Savings Bank of Princeton, N.J. They call their idea the College Sure CD and it works this way: parents buy certificates of deposit, just like the CDs that people have been using as savings investments for years. But the rate on the College Sure CD is pegged to the average rate of inflation for tuition and other college costs. Unlike the Duquesne plan and its copies, the College Sure CD can be used at any college. However, the earnings rate is not as sexy as some of the higher-flying plans: to buy four years at Yale for one of today's second graders, parents would have to pay more than $90,000. The bank expects people to make regular payments into a CD account over time as a buffer against rising college costs, not to plunk down $90,000. And it promises stability: The instrument is a CD, fully insured by the Federal Deposit Insurance Board for up to $100,000. Right now the College Sure CD is sold through the bank and through PaineWebber.

Innovative Come-Ons

As we have already said, students are in rather short supply, especially where the smaller private colleges are concerned. Many of them have tried to find eye-catching ways to cut the cost of attendance. Some of the methods are almost hucksterish in nature, but if you already like the school, why not take advantage? Below we list a few that have been offered here and there; see if your school uses any of them:

Profiting by leadership: Some schools offer a tuition break for taking a leadership role in student organizations, from the school newspaper to the student government.

A legacy: Some schools reduce tuition for children of alumni/ae.

Lotteries: A few schools (or their student organizations) sponsor tuition lotteries: if your number comes up, your year is free. This is only for students who are already attending, of course.

Volume, volume, volume: Many schools now offer discounts for bringing other family members along. Fairleigh-Dickinson University in New Jersey gives a discount, while Lake Erie College in Ohio accepts twins for the price of one—a higher-ed twofer.

Bring a buddy: Several schools will give you a tuition discount for convincing a friend to attend.

Test the waters: Schools are letting prospective students try their first credits at a discount. Some, like John Brown University in Arkansas, even let high school juniors and seniors attend classes for free! They count as real courses, and are later transferable. Other come-ons are just as ingenious: Marian College of Fond du Lac, Wisconsin, offers its first part-time course for just $100.

Anniversary specials: A few years ago, Goucher College celebrated its centennial by offering one student a year's tuition at the same rate as students paid the year the school was founded.

Tuition matching: Some private schools now match tuition with public schools to stay competitive; Bard offers to charge students in the top 10 percent of their high school graduating class anywhere in the U.S. the same tuition as they could get from a public school in their home state. (Remember, too, that many states now offer scholarship programs to equalize tuition rates between public and private schools.)

"Adopt-a-student" programs: In these programs, the school gets local companies to contribute. The companies participate to give something back to the community and to raise their public relations profile—but many of them get something more out of the deal. Sometimes these programs require the recipient to work at the company after graduation. This could be a back-door way for enterprising students to get the job they want and to make extra money while attending college. Check with your financial aid office or student employment office for details.

"Differential pricing": Schools are offering discounts for any number of odd reasons. Some give students a price break on less desirable housing—that could mean anything from teensy rooms to no air conditioning. Other schools let new students study for less than upper-classmen. Still other schools charge students less for some majors than for others. Options like these give you a little more control over how much your college education will cost. Your college financial aid office will be able to tell you if any of these benefits apply to you; you might also check with your campus housing and food service offices to see if any discounts are offered.

"Moral obligation scholarships": These are a gift from the school to you—granted with a "moral obligation" to pay the money back after graduation. Along with their feelgood charm, these programs pack a potent tax benefit: Since the payback is technically construed to be a gift to the school, the student gets a tax deduction. Bethel College in Indiana and Rice University in Texas are among a growing number of schools jumping on the moral obligation bandwagon.

Colleges are constantly thinking up new, headline-grabbing alternatives; keep an eye on the media for programs that pop up unexpectedly. A favorite we've run across lately is the Woz scholarship at the University of Colorado at Boulder, kicked off with a $100,000 grant from Apple Computer cofounder Steve Wozniack. It is intended to provide support for "hackers"—computer users who love to learn through exploring computer systems and programs—even those they're not supposed to get into. Wozniak calls these "mild social deviants" important because of the tremendous learning that comes from hacking forays. Deserving hackers get a tuition grant and a job in the computer science department, as well as extra computer time—on a computer system dedicated to their use, not the school's main computers.

A Warning: All Good Things Must Come to an End

It's a fact of life: Many of the great college tuition plans end up running afoul of the IRS sooner or later. One previously popular method of saving for college, shifting assets to the children in order to take advantage of their lower taxation rate, has been all but eliminated by changes in the tax laws. And we have seen that the IRS is already taking a long look at the long-term tuition prepayment plans. We can expect the "moral obligation scholarships" to get the same kind of scrutiny. In fact, any program that promises to help people save money for college at low tax rates will attract the attention of the IRS. So it's important to check with the school to see if the IRS has ruled that the school's "too-good-to-be-true" program really is too good to be true.

Other Ways to Cut College Costs: Nontraditional Courses of Study

Cramming a Degree into a Shorter Time

A number of schools have found ways to cram the four-year college experience into three years. Middlebury College in Vermont, Albertus Magnus College in Connecticut, Valparaiso University in Indiana and Upper Iowa University all say you can do it in three years and save big. Some medical and law schools will allow you to enroll without having obtained an undergraduate degree. Most of these grad schools work together with their own campus' undergraduate schools to create a single compressed degree. Others simply require a certain list of courses; you can be accepted to the school upon completion of those courses, which fit into a three-year plan. Compressed degree plans aren't for the faint of heart: the pressure to pack it all in can be brutal. Also, the gains could be illusory if they are gotten at the price of studying through the summer and having to forego summer job income.

Credit and Degrees by Exam

The College Board has agreements with more than half of the nation's colleges to honor the program's AP exams and give credit or advanced placement. More than 150,000 students annually take AP exams, and two-thirds of them score high enough to place out. Needless to say, if you place out of a course, that is tuition saved. More than 10,000 students were eligible last year to place out of all freshman year courses. More than 20 tests are offered by AP, including English, calculus, American history, European history, biology, chemistry, physics, computer science, art, music, and many languages. Take the tests through your school for about $50 apiece, or contact the College Board, 45 Columbus Avenue, New York, NY 10023.

In addition, many schools offer some form of credit by examination: Opportunities range from selected courses to the entire course catalogue. Check the school's academic catalogue, or ask at individual departments.

Saving Money

Once a student gets to college, many ways to save money present themselves that may not have been apparent at home. Students are famous for living in near-poverty;

unless you have joined a class-conscious clique, you find that near-poverty can be quite genteel. Buying used books not only saves money, it also can give you a head start on underlining your texts. Living in alternative housing like off-campus cooperative houses costs much less than dorms or apartments, and can build strong friendships as well—though your diet might suffer at the hands of housemates whose cooking leaves something to be desired. Buying food from organizations like food co-ops also saves a dollar here and there. Well-worn clothes and classy Goodwill castoffs can give a certain cachet and save money that would otherwise be spent on a costlier wardrobe. In other words, living poor pays.

A more upscale way to save money in college is to play the real estate game. Rather than giving money to a landlord, why not buy a campus-area condo or house? You can supplement your mortgage by renting out extra rooms, and can pay off a substantial amount of your college expenses if the property appreciates in value when you sell it. But the last point is a big "if." Despite the promises of real estate brokers, property values sometimes drop. There's no such thing as a no-risk deal. Still, if you have the money, owning your college home can be a very attractive option.

Some families try to save money by having the student live at home. This option saves dorm or apartment rental costs and looks very attractive on the surface. Yet there are a number of hidden costs to staying at home—not the least of which is losing out on a major part of the college social experience by not being at the center of things. Commuting costs can cut away at the money that living at home saves. Another reason why staying at home is more expensive than it looks: food. The student who stays at home won't be able to eat all meals at home; the odd hours that students keep will keep them away from home at mealtimes. So commuter students tend to spend a lot of money in campus-area eateries, while students in dorms buy a relatively inexpensive meal plan. Meal plans may be available for non-dormers and are worth looking into. Also, most parents won't stand for the poverty chic that can make student dollars stretch so far, and so will spend more money on clothing than the student would spend on his or her own.

Tapping into Family Resources

There are a few other sources of funds that you might not have considered for college financing—quiet assets that don't present themselves as obvious cash cows. But they are there. These include:

Home equity loans: These allow parents to draw on the increased value of their homes. The rates and repayment schedules can be more favorable then those offered on student loans from private sources and schools.

Company funds: Many employee pension funds and savings plans allow withdrawals for tuition. These withdrawals are often subject to rigid restrictions and stiff penalties, though some companies make the process easier—or even let parents borrow against the value of their savings plans. Check with your personnel office for details.

Barter and service deals: Some schools will make a deal with parents to exchange a wide range of gifts for tuition. Almost any type of property can be swapped under such a program. Even if the college can't use what you have to offer, it might resell it; this occurs often when corporations make odd gifts to schools, such as yachts, for tax purposes. Ask if the college has a barter program.

Making Money: The Job World Beyond Work-Study

Instead of relying on your college for a moderate-to-low-paying work-study job, why not strike out on your own? If you have an entrepreneurial flair, you might find that a little investment of time and effort can provide you with a comfortable living while you are in school—and after. Michael Dell began selling computers while he was in college—now his company sells millions of dollars worth of IBM-compatible computers each year under the Dell Computer logo. On a smaller scale, you might find plenty of opportunity among your fellow students. Students know students; once you have identified an item that you need, you can buy it in bulk and offer it to others who share your needs. This explains the proliferation of student-run services that offer discounts on everything from computer diskettes to lecture notes. One enterprising group of students even offered speedy delivery of birth control devices.

The clearinghouse for information on entrepreneurship in college is the Association of College Entrepreneurs, a group founded by college students in 1983 and which now numbers more than 4,500 members. It's based in Wichita, Kansas, but has local chapters nationwide. And your own campus business department might have people who can give you pointers: More than 600 schools across the nation have entrepreneurship courses.

For students interested in the entrepreneurial route, one book could serve as a wellspring of ideas: *How to Pay Your Way Through College (The Smart Way)* by John J. Lyons ($7.95, Banbury Books). This lively book presents more than 50 money-making opportunities for college students, ranging from resume writing to delivering birthday cakes and final exam "care packages." (The author's credentials are solid: as a college student he started a car-cleaning business aimed at luxury models. By the time he graduated he had opened franchises in Florida, Delaware, and California—and was making $50,000 a year.) Each plan is based on actual student experience, and Lyons even puts the reader on the way to forming a business plan by projecting the startup costs and materials needed.

Books like Lyons' can give you ideas on businesses you could start that won't require so much work that you'll flunk out—less of your time, at least, than nonpaying extracurricular activities such as working for the school newspaper or student government. Though these extracurriculars look good on your resume, working your way through college is an attractive resume item, too. And you might even be able to make your career interest pay. If your school doesn't have an established cooperative education program, you might be able to work something out on your own. Do you want to be a journalist? Write freelance articles. If your interest is politics, why not see if there are part-time positions in a nearby politician's office, or working with political consultants? You'll be lining your pocket and picking up real-life experience at the same time.

For another extreme version of college jobs, you might check out Heidi Mattson's 1995 memoir, *Ivy League Stripper*. Mattson said she turned to stripping when her financial aid fell through and her work-study professor made sexual advances. It's not the kind of part-time work that I'd ever recommend anyone engage in, but Mattson insists that without lucrative nights of topless dancing at the Foxy Lady, she could not have afforded her days pursuing a degree at Brown University.

A warning about entrepreneurship: Before you decide that starting your own business is the answer to all your financial needs, watch a few reruns of *The Honeymooners* or *Dobie Gillis*. Get-rich-quick schemes have long been the stock in trade of situation comedies because of their tendency to get the schemer into hot water—and into debt. It's time for a personal story to illustrate the point.

When I was in college, one roommate was always looking for the fast train to riches, like the time he went prospecting for gold in the American West. None of the schemes panned out, but he had fun—until he decided to make money on the historic rivalry between the University of Texas and Texas A&M. (Typical UT joke against an A&M student, known as an "Aggie": "How do you know when an Aggie has been using your word processor? There's Liquid Paper all over the screen.") My friend decided to sell a newspaper parody that made fun of UT on one side and made fun of A&M on the other, and distribute the publication at the big Thanksgiving football game between the two schools.

The idea sounded good, but it was a disaster. My buddy put in countless hours of writing and editing, and spent hundreds of dollars in printing costs. (These were the days before easy desktop publishing). But the paper bombed. The conservative alumni attending the game didn't know what to make of it; many who did buy it were offended by the jokes against their alma mater. Some of the jokes were funny, though, if you'd like to see a copy. I think my buddy still has a few thousand in a closet somewhere. But don't worry too much about him. He and a successful publishing executive met and fell in love, and these days he's living in a Manhattan penthouse. So things work out.

Putting Your Financial Aid PackageTogether

The Three Commandments of Applying for Financial Aid:

Before getting down to the nuts and bolts of applying for financial aid, it's worth keeping three "commandments" in mind. Without them, a hundred pages of instruction are useless. The three commandments are:

1: Be Prompt!

Read the deadlines below. Meet each deadline. Since many programs work from a fund of limited size, wasting time can waste money. Start applying for financial aid right after January 1—as soon after you receive your W-2 forms as possible. (No, you can't apply before then.) That's when you can begin filling out your IRS forms, too. That will make filling out the financial aid forms easier. Besides, if you have a refund coming you'll get it faster.

2: Be Accurate!

Fill in all of the blanks on every form, and fill them out accurately and legibly. Read the instructions fully. Any blank spaces or mistakes can cause the overworked aid agencies to send your form back to you to be filled in again. You'll not only have to do more work, but you'll delay the processing of your financial aid application—and that delay could keep you from receiving as much aid as you could have gotten.

3: Be Organized!

If there was ever a reason to get organized, this is it. You have to keep track of all of your applications to different colleges and the financial aid applications to those colleges. Make copies of every piece of correspondence you send out, keeping all of it in a fanfold organizer or file box, organized by school. Many financial aid guides go so far as to recommend sending all aid correspondence via certified mail so that you will have a record of having sent items and of their being received. The College Board, on the other hand, says registered mail is a bother and slows the application process. We say: If you are applying well in advance, spend the money for a little security.

Another reason for all this organization: By getting organized from the start, you will find it easier to fill out your forms again next year—and remember, you have to apply for aid every year.

The Timetable: Your Most Important Financial Aid Dates

Junior Year of High School

October: Take the PSAT exam. This important test will not only give you a taste of what's in store on the SAT; it will also qualify you for the National Merit Scholarship. A good score on the exam can really boost your chances of getting scholarships, and since there are fewer questions on the PSAT than on the SAT, a little preparation beforehand can make a big impact on your score. Some financial aid experts go so far as to recommend that high schoolers take one of the prep courses offered for the PSAT; you should at least consider working through one of the review books available in bookstores, high schools, and libraries.

If you have not already begun to consider your college choices, you should be sending off for college brochures and financial aid information. Talk to friends from high school who have attended the colleges, and to alumni. It's a good time to begin touring the campuses that seem the most promising to you. While on campus, be sure to check out the financial aid office. Does it appear to be efficiently run? Does it look like the sort of place where you will get personalized service? If possible, schedule an interview with a financial aid adviser at the school to determine the school's resources and how much of your college costs your family will be expected to provide.

Senior Year of High School/Year Before Going to College

Fall: Begin narrowing down your college choices to the ones that interest you the most. Ask those schools for admissions applications and financial aid forms. Send in your applications for admission to your favorites well before the deadlines that each school lists. Be sure to take your time writing any essays the school requires; you want to stand out as a lucid thinker and a clear writer, not as someone who doesn't care enough to do a good job on an application.

January 1: You can't apply for financial aid before January 1 of the year you intend to go to college. But you should apply as soon as the ball drops in Times Square. People who file at the time of the deadline risk losing out on the college's own aid and those funds from campus-based federal financial aid programs. When you hear "Auld Lang Syne," think about your financial aid forms.

April 15: If you haven't done your financial aid forms yet because your IRS forms weren't done, you've probably just lost that excuse. Time's a-wastin'. A lot of students and their families have already turned in financial aid forms—and their tax forms besides. And they've probably already gotten their IRS refunds back, too.

June 30: Whether you apply electronically or by mail, your aid application must be received by the processing agency listed on the form by June 30 for the coming school year. It's really very late by now – and the processing agency is still going to take weeks to run your forms through, so it's later than you think. Still, better late than never. Before you buy the hot dogs and hit the beach, make sure you've got the forms in the mail.

June 30: Your school's financial aid office must receive your application and your student aid report—the forms you get back from the processing agency—by this deadline. If you are already in college, your deadline is the last day of enrollment for that year. Again, this is the absolute deadline. It's much better to get this in far ahead of time, and beginning January 1.

Freshman Year, Sophomore Year, Etc.

January 1: Apply for financial aid all over again. You need to do this every year.

Applying for Financial Aid: The Nuts and Bolts

Applying for financial aid begins with your applications at the federal level; other aid providers look to the information you provide to the federal government. Your school will tell you which forms to fill out, but the basics of applying for federal aid are the same for whatever form you use.

Are You Eligible for Financial Aid?

There are eligibility requirements for financial aid. You must be enrolled at least half-time to receive aid from the Direct or FFEL Program loan programs. Half-time enroll-

ment is not required for the campus-based student aid programs such as Federal Supplemental Educational Opportunity Grants (FSEOG), Federal Work-Study (FWS), and Federal Perkins Loans. Individual schools have various qualifications for the campus-based programs. You must be what the government calls a "regular student," which means you are enrolled in an institution to get a degree or certificate, or are completing course work that enables you to qualify for admission.

Eligibility also depends on citizenship: You must be a citizen or an eligible noncitizen. If you are not a citizen, you must be a U.S. national or a U.S. permanent resident with an Alien Registration Receipt Card—or you must fall into one of the arcane categories listed in the glossary under "Citizen/Eligible Noncitizen." (For example, those whom the Immigration and Naturalization Service has designated "Cuban-Haitian entrant, status pending" are eligible for aid, while students on an F-1 or F-2 student visa are not.)

You can be knocked out of eligibility for any more federal student aid if you are in default. Uncle Sam will do his best to get his money back, too: You may find the government deducting payments from your paycheck, or your U.S. Internal Revenue Service refund might be redirected to the Treasury.

And to clinch your eligibility, you will have to sign several pieces of paper: You must sign a "statement of educational purpose" that promises you will use your federal student aid funds for school-related expenses only. You must also sign a "statement of registration status" that states you have registered for the draft, if you are required to do so. If you don't register, you can't get aid. (If you say you registered but you really didn't, there could be repercussions: The Education Department has begun to turn the list of liars over to the Justice Department.) The financial aid form has a check-off that allows you to register automatically when you file for aid, but make sure you get confirmation back from the Selective Service that you did, in fact, successfully register. The Selective Service has been known to lose or misplace the occasional form. (A guy I know from Texas, Rob Addy, was initially denied a prestigious White House internship because the government said he hadn't registered. Only after a friendly newspaper reporter, Steve Twomey, proved that he had in fact registered on his financial aid form did the White House relent and reinstate him.)

After you have applied for aid and received your Student Aid Report (see page 111), you will have to add a "statement of updated information" to your aid request that certifies that the items listed in your Student Aid Report are still correct.

Dependent or Independent?

Few financial aid questions are as important as whether you will be considered a dependent or independent student. If you are considered a dependent student, your parents must report their income and assets along with yours (and with your spouse's, if you are married). If you are classified as an independent student, you report only your own income and assets (along with your spouse's, if you are married). Unless you are a rock star, you probably make less money than your parents, and you will be eligible for more aid if you can be certified as an independent student. You should answer these questions to see if you can make the independent classification:

Are you 24 years old or older? You will be automatically considered an independent student if you are 24 years old by December 31 of the year you receive the financial aid award.

Are you a vet? A veteran of the U.S. Armed Forces is also automatically considered an independent student. This doesn't apply to former National Guardsmen, Reservists, or to former members of the Armed Forces who received a dishonorable discharge.

Are both of your parents dead, or are you a ward of the court? Wards of the court are also independent, as are students whose parents are dead and who don't have an adoptive parent or legal guardian.

Do you have legal dependents other than a spouse? That includes your child, so long as the child gets at least half its support from you, or any other legal dependents who get more than half their support from you and who will continue to get that support through the award year.

Do your parents claim you as a tax exemption? If you are a SINGLE undergraduate student with no dependents and if your parents or guardian didn't claim you as a dependent on the previous two tax returns, you might qualify as an independent student. You must also prove that you had annual total resources, other than what the folks have kicked in, of more than $4,000 in those years. This includes wages, salaries, tips, student financial aid, personal loans for educational purposes, interest income, dividend income, and other income or benefits such as fellowships.

If you are MARRIED and can say that your parents or guardian won't claim you as a dependent on their next tax return, you will also be considered independent.

Living with your parents, by the way, does not automatically make you a dependent. But the school aid administrator can nonetheless take a hard look at the situation and can factor in the cost of room and board at home—among other support—to determine whether to increase the amount of parental contribution, the student contribution, or otherwise to fiddle with your financial aid package.

Your school's aid administrator can change your status from dependent to independent if he or she thinks circumstances warrant the switch. Though the financial aid officer has every reason to want to look to your parents to shoulder the burden of your financial aid, the switch to in-

dependent status occurs from time to time. See the passage below on dealing with financial aid officers.

Special Circumstances

If you don't qualify as an independent student by the basic rules outlined above but feel that special circumstances dictate that you should be considered as an independent student anyway, you will be happy to know that the school aid administrator has the power to reclassify you as he or she sees fit. The aid administrator has the power to adjust your family contribution, or some element of your cost of education, such as tuition at private schools. However, you shouldn't assume that just because that person has the power that you will get your status changed—far from it. So it would be especially foolish for you to fill out your aid application as an independent if you don't automatically qualify unless you have gotten specific instructions from your aid administrator. The procedure for making the change will depend on the aid applications used and the individual school's rules, so you definitely need to follow the lead of the aid administrator.

A radical change in your life will change the way the aid administrator sees you and your plea for aid. If one of your parents dies, you should list only the income of the surviving parent. If the parent dies after you have filed, you should contact the school's financial aid office, since the loss in family income certainly should be reflected in your aid package. If one of your parents becomes unemployed, that can also change your status. Losing benefits such as child support or Social Security can sway an administrator. Anything that makes you substantially poorer affects your chances to receive aid.

Other family issues that come up when filling out the forms include the following:

■ If you are a single student with dependent children and you provide more than half the support for the children, independent status is automatic. But if you and your dependent children live with your parents and they provide more than half the support, you probably won't be classified as independent.

■ If you are separated or divorced, give the aid administrator information that applies directly to you— report only your own share of the joint asssets and liabilities.

■ If your parents are divorced, the aid administrator wants the information from the parent you have lived with for the most time over the year before you file. That parent should fill out the form as a single head of household, and only list his or her income and his or her portion of the joint assets and debts. If you didn't live with either parent, or you lived with each an equal amount of time, you should list the parent who gave you the most financial support in the year before you file. If you got no support from either parent or if you got equal support from each in that time, list the parent who gave the most in a previous, uneven year.

■ If you have a stepparent who has married the parent who supports you, you should provide that person's financial information along with that of your natural parent's.

Applying for Aid

The forms you need to fill out in order to apply for aid vary from state to state and from institution to institution, depending on the "need analysis service" used by the state or institution. Your school will let you know which forms you must complete and will provide them to you. The most common forms are:

■ The U.S. Department of Education's Free Application for Federal Student Aid (FAFSA), which is the main application for the Pell Grant. Some schools offer this grant application in electronic form, so you don't have to worry about your eraser rubbing through the paper;

■ The College Scholarship Service's CSS Financial Aid PROFILE;

■ The Pennsylvania Higher Education Assistance Agency's Application for Pennsylvania State Grant and Federal Student Aid (PHEAA);

■ The Student Aid Application for California (SAAC);

■ The Illinois State Scholarship Commission's Application for Federal and State Student Aid (AFSSA).

The forms, while not easy, are not impossible to fill out on your own.

The state forms tend to be shorter and easier to complete than the nationally distributed forms. You don't have to fill out the FAFSA if you are filling out one of the other forms; those forms let you apply for Pell Grants and other federal aid at the same time. Checking a box on the forms tells the state to send your financial information along to a federal processing center.

Your school's application instructions will give you the information you need about applying for other forms of aid—several states, for instance, require that you fill out still more forms to apply for their own aid programs. The school's own application, and the state applications, might have separate deadlines that you will have to pay heed to.

Once you have applied, the processing agency will take between four and six weeks to turn your application around. You may be asked to confirm information or to correct the forms and then return them to be processed again. (You didn't listen to the second commandment!) The reprocessing will add another two or three weeks to your wait.

After processing your data, you will begin to receive a lot of paper. Your application for federal aid through the FAFSA or the other forms will be used to generate a Student Aid Report, or SAR. The SAR puts your data into a financial aid Cuisinart and figures out whether you qualify

for federal student aid. It generates a Student Aid Index number, which lets you know whether you qualify for a Pell Grant, and a Family Contribution number, which will be used to see whether you qualify for campus-based programs such as FSEOG, Federal Work-Study, Federal Perkins Loans, and the Stafford programs.

If you qualify for a Pell Grant, your SAR will arrive in three parts. The Information Summary, Part 1, will tell you how to check the SAR for errors. You use Part 2, the Information Review Form, to correct any errors in the SAR. Your school will use Part 3, Pell Grant Payment Document, to decide how much money you will receive. Immediately make copies of Part 1 and send one to the financial aid office of each school you are applying to. You'll submit all three parts of the SAR to the school you ultimately decide to attend.

Didn't get the Pell? Don't worry—very few applicants do. But now you have something very important: your family contribution number. Send that information to your financial aid administrator, who will use it to figure out whether you qualify for other federal student aid.

If you are very unlucky, the Department of Education or your school might decide that you need to submit to "verification." This is like an IRS audit. You may have to verify everything from income to household size to federal taxes paid. You may have a long one-on-one with your aid administrator, and have to produce documents or fill out a verification worksheet. If you don't comply, kiss your aid goodbye. Some schools require verification from every financial aid applicant.

How Need Analysis Works

How was it determined that you would or would not receive a Pell Grant?

By strict exercise of the Pell Grant Methodology. If you want to look it up, the Education Department publishes it each year in the Federal Register. But if you do look it up, you might be disappointed; it does not even purport to be an accurate look at your family's financial ability. It's just the numerical filter that the Education Department uses to ration the amount of Pell Grant money it has decided that it needs. As far as the Pell Grant Methodology goes, your school is only interested in whether your Student Aid Index qualifies you for a Pell, and pays little attention to what it purports to say about your financial status.

To figure out the family's financial strength, most schools now rely on what is known as the Uniform Methodology—or, in its latest form, the Congressional Methodology. Congress has mandated through the Higher Education Amendments of 1986 that schools will use the Congressional Methodology to determine the expected family contribution for campus-based and Stafford programs. Many schools are making the switch; get the lowdown from your school and familiarize yourself with the ins and outs of the evaluation process. So even though the next few paragraphs promise to be slow going, it's worth slogging through to understand how your school will judge your ability to pay.

For DEPENDENT STUDENTS, the expected family contribution (EFC) is broken down into four parts:

■   contribution from parental income
■   contribution from parental assets
■   contribution from student income
■   contribution from student assets

For INDEPENDENT STUDENTS, EFC boils down to:

■   contribution from student (and spouse, if any) income
■   contribution from student (and spouse, if any) assets

When families earn $15,000 or less, the need analysis excludes any consideration of assets. While the Pell Grant and Congressional methods both take into account required expenses such as taxes and unusual medical expenses, and while both let the family set aside a certain amount for retirement or emergencies, the two methodologies part ways when figuring out how that income and those assets can be sheltered, and how much. Also, both methodologies make allowances for the expected family contribution whenever another member of the family heads off to college.

Getting the Award Letter

Once the school has all the information it needs, it can put together an aid package that will probably include a combination of grants (precious few), loans (too many), and work-study employment. You will get your notification of what your aid package contains in an award letter. This document gives you an idea of your probable cost of attendance, how your need was determined, what your need turned out to be, and the composition of that aid package. If you are satisfied with the aid package, you sign the documents that come with the form and send them back to the school.

Even if you haven't decided which school to attend, you should move quickly to accept the aid package from each school that offers one. That's the only way to keep your options open. Schools set response deadlines: If you don't respond to your aid letter within that time, you could miss out on the funds that have been offered to you. Accepting the aid package does not obligate you to attend the school. This isn't to say you should keep a number of colleges on a string—choose your college as quickly as possible so that the schools you don't choose can distribute the money to other students.

But before you leap to accept that award letter, evaluate your offers with a cold eye. Don't be fooled by big numbers; pay special attention to how much of the offer is made up of grants and how much is made up of loans. Which schools are tossing in special awards for academic or athletic merit? If scholarships are offered, are they renewable or are they one-shot wonders that will leave you high and dry next year? Break out your calculator and compare the loan interest rates offered by different institutions, and check out whether the payback requirements for those loans are especially onerous. And as for work-study offers, keep in mind the study load before you and ask yourself whether you will be able to juggle work and school right off the bat. You may accept part of the award and reserve the right to appeal any objectionable parts.

Getting More: Appealing to the Financial Aid Officer

Say you want to attend a certain school, but the award letter was a major disappointment. Is there anything you can do to change the school's mind? As we have already seen, the aid officers have a degree of latitude within which to change their estimate of a student's need, especially in cases of hardship. If you are dissatisfied with your award, you might want to put together your case for more aid and present it to the school's financial aid officer. The sooner the better: As matriculation day approaches, the aid officer's discretionary power dries up with his or her funds.

Try for a face-to-face meeting, so long as (1) the travel expenses aren't prohibitive or (2) the school is not too big to provide that kind of personal service. If you get your foot in the door, politely present youself in the best possible light to the financial aid officer—make the school want you. Push your abilities and accomplishments and the reasons that you and the school make a good match.

You'll do best if you remember the old adage: It's nice to be nice. Financial aid officers suffer a lot of abuse. You do not want to add to the stress in your financial aid officer's life. Read your Dale Carnegie to polish those people skills, and take a look at a remarkably handy guide: "Financial Aid Officers: What They Do—To You and For You." Written by a financial aid officer, the booklet outlines a winning strategy for helping a harried financial aid officer see your side of things. (Octameron Associates, P.O. Box 2748, Alexandria, VA 22301. They also require $2.00 for postage and handling chages.)

Glossary of Financial Aid Terms

Ability to Benefit: Applies to most students who are admitted to a postsecondary institution but who do not have a high school diploma or a GED high school diploma equivalency. To receive federal student aid, a student admitted on the basis of ability to benefit must fulfill one of the following conditions:

1.) Pass a standardized admissions test that measures the student's aptitude successfully to complete the course of study. If the student fails the test, he or she must complete step #2 to qualify for aid.

2.) Enroll in and successfully complete a remedial program that is required by the school and that does not exceed one academic year. If the student fails the admissions test mentioned in step #1, or if the student is admitted on the basis of counseling given by the school, he or she would be required to enroll in the remedial program.

3.) Receive a GED before graduating from the course of study or by the end of the first year of the course of study—whichever comes first.

Local financial aid administrators will have more information as to the specifics at your school.

Academic Year: The Federal government defines this as "A period of time during which a full-time student is expected to complete at least 24 semester or trimester hours at an institution that measures program length in credit hours." The official definition notes that "Academic years vary from school to school, and even from educational program to educational program at the same school."

Assets: Savings and checking accounts, home or business value, stocks, bonds, money market funds, mutual funds, real estate, trust funds, etc. Cars are not considered assets, nor are possessions such as stamp collections or musical instruments.

Campus-Based Programs: Federal Supplemental Educational Opportunity Grants (FSEOG's), Federal Work-Study (FWS), and Federal Perkins Loan Program. These federal programs are called campus-based because they're administered by the financial aid administrator at the school. Your financial aid package may contain aid from one or more of these programs.

Citizen/Eligible Noncitizen: You must be one of the following to receive federal student aid:

1.) U.S. citizen

2.) U.S. national (which includes natives of American Samoa or Swain's Island)

3.) U.S. permanent resident who has an I-151 or I-551 or I-551-C (Alien Registration Receipt Card)

If you're not in one of these categories, you must have a Departure Record (I-94) from the U.S. Immigration and Naturalization Service (INS) showing one of the following designations:

1.) "Refugee"
2.) "Asylum Granted"
3.) "Indefinite Parole" and/or "Humanitarian Parole"
4.) "Cuban-Haitian Entrant, Status Pending"
5.) "Conditional Entrant" (valid only if issued before April 1, 1980)
6.) Other eligible noncitizen with a Temporary Resident Card (I-688)

The Federal government says you can also be eligible based on the Family Unity Status category with an approved I-797 (Voluntary Departure and Immigrant Petition.)

Also, you're eligible for federal student aid if you have a suspension of deportation case pending before Congress.

You are NOT eligible for student financial aid if you only have a Notice of Approval to Apply for Permanent Residence (I-171 or I-464). If you are in the United States on an FI or F2 student visa only, or on a J1 or J2 exchange visitor visa only, you can't get federal student aid. Also, persons with G series visas (pertaining to international organizations) are not eligible for federal student aid.

Citizens and eligible noncitizens may also receive loans from the FFEL and Direct Loan Programs at participating foreign schools.

Residents of Palau, the Federated States of Micronesia, and the Marshall Islands are only eligible for Pell Grants, Federal Supplemental Educational Opportunity Grants (FSEOG's), or Federal Work-Study only. These residents should check with their financial aid administrators for more information.

CSS/Financial Aid PROFILE: A centralized financial aid application service operated by the College Scholarship Service of the College Board. You can register for the service by completing the PROFILE registration form, which is available online at www.collegeboard.org. You can even complete it online. Following the registration step, CSS prepares a customized financial aid application that contains information required by the participating schools and sponsors and mails the application to the student. You complete the PROFILE application and mail it to CSS, which prepares Financial Need Analysis Reports for schools and programs that you designated.

Consolidation Loan/Direct Consolidation Loan: You can get two kinds of consolidation loans: FFEL Consolidation Loans and Direct Consolidation Loans. Both allow you to bring together your different loans under one umbrella to simplify repayment. Loan payout can take from 10 to 30 years.

Cost of Education (or Cost of Attendance): The total amount it will cost a student to go to school. It is usually expressed as a yearly figure. It includes tuition and fees; on-campus room and board (or a housing and food allowance for off-campus students); and allowances for books, supplies, transportation, child care, costs related to a handicap, and miscellaneous expenses. It also includes reasonable costs for study abroad programs. An allowance, determined by the school, is also included for reasonable costs connected with a student's employment as part of a cooperative education program. For students attending school less than half-time, the COA includes only tuition and fees and an allowance for books, supplies, transportation, and dependent-care expenses. Talk to the financial aid administrator at the school you're planning to attend if you have any unusual expenses that may affect your cost of education or your ability to pay that cost.

Default: Failure to repay a student loan according to the terms agreed to when you signed a promissory note. Default may also result from failure to submit requests for deferment or cancellation on time. If you default on a student loan, your school, lender, state government, and the federal government all can take action to recover the money. Default may affect your future credit rating for years to come, making it harder to secure loans for things like cars or a home. You also won't be able to receive additional federal aid or a deferment of your loan repayments if you decide to return to school. Also, you may be liable for expenses incurred in collecting the loan. The lender you have defaulted against could ask your employer after you leave school to deduct payments toward the debt from your paycheck. Finally, U.S. Department of Education may ask the Internal Revenue Service to withhold your income tax refund and apply it to your debt.

Dislocated Worker: A person so classified by the appropriate state agency (such as the state employment service or job service). Generally, a dislocated worker is unemployed because 1.) He or she has been terminated or laid off; 2.) The plant or other facility where he or she worked has closed; 3.) He or she was self-employed, but is not now because of poor economic conditions in the community or because a natural disaster has occurred.

If one of these conditions applies to you, to your spouse, or to your parents, your (and/or their) financial circumstances will be specially considered in determining the ability to pay for your education.

To find out if you, your spouse, or one of your parents qualifies as a dislocated worker, contact your local state employment service or local Job Training Partnership Act (JTPA) service (listed under state agencies in the telephone book). Or contact your city or county employment and training program (listed under city or county agencies). If you have any trouble finding these offices, your financial aid administrator should have a list of Employment and Training offices you can contact.

Displaced Homemaker: Someone who—

1.) Has not worked in the labor force for a substantial number of years (for example, approximately five years or more), but during those years has worked in the home providing unpaid services for family members;

2.) Has depended on public assistance or on the income of another family member, but is no longer receiving that income, or who has been receiving public assistance because of dependent children in the home;

3.) Is unemployed or underemployed and is having trouble obtaining or upgrading employment. "Unemployed" means not working this week but being available for work and having made specific efforts to get a job sometime during the last four weeks. "Underemployed" means working part-time (even though full-time employment is desired), because work is slack or because only part-time work is available.

If all of these conditions apply to you, to your spouse, or to your parents, your (and/or their) financial circumstances will be specially considered in determining the ability to pay for your education.

Eligible Program: A course of study that leads to a degree or certificate at a school that takes part in one or more of the Federal student aid programs. To get federal aid, you must be enrolled in an eligible program, with two exceptions:

1.) If your school has told you that you must take certain course work to qualify for admission into one of its eligible programs, you can get a Direct Loan or an FFEL Program Loan (or parents can get a PLUS Loan) for up to 12 months while you're completing that course work, as long as you're attending at least half-time. You must also meet the usual student aid eligibility requirements;

2.) If you're enrolled at least half-time in a program for a professional credential or certification required by a state for employment as an elementary or secondary school teacher, you can get a Federal Perkins Loan, Federal Work-Study, an FFEL Stafford Loan, a Direct Loan (or your parents can get a PLUS Loan) while you are enrolled in that program.

Exit Interview: A counseling session you must attend before you leave your school, if you have any of the federal loans described in this book. At this session, your school will give you information on the average amount borrowers owe, the amount of your monthly repayment, and about deferment, refinancing, and loan consolidation options.

Expected Family Contribution (EFC): This figure is determined by a formula established by Congress. It indicates how much of your family's financial resources should be available to help pay for school. This amount is used to determine your eligibility for aid from the campus-based programs. This number is important because your financial aid administrator will subtract it from your cost of education to find out how much you can't pay. To determine your contribution, the information you fill in on an aid application is evaluated. Factors such as your (and your family's) taxable and nontaxable income, as well as assets such as savings or the net worth of a home, are considered in determining your family's financial strength. Certain allowances are subtracted from both income and assets to protect part of them for future needs. A portion of the remaining amount is considered available to help pay for postsecondary educational costs.

If you have any unusual expenses that may affect your family contribution, make sure that you notify your financial aid administrator.

Family Financial Statement (FFS): An American College Testing Program form to assess the student's need for monetary aid. If requested by the student, the need assessment will be sent to a college's financial aid office.

Financial Aid Form (FAF): Form provided by the College Board College Scholarship Service for assessing and informing some colleges of a student's family's financial situtation. This once-ubiquitous form is now being phased out in favor of the College Board's CSS/Financial Aid PROFILE.

Financial Aid Package: The total amount of financial aid a student receives. Federal and nonfederal aid such as loans, grants, or work-study are combined in a "package" to help meet the student's need. Using available resources to give each student the best possible package of aid is one of the major responsibilities of a school's financial aid administrator.

Financial Aid Transcript: A record of the Department of Education student aid you've received. If you've received federal student aid and you transfer, you must request that your old school(s) send your financial aid transcript to the school you'll be attending. If your new school doesn't receive a financial aid transcript from the old one(s), you won't receive aid from Department of Education programs.

Part 1 of the 1997–98 Student Aid Report contains a statement of registration status. You must sign either that one or a similar one prepared by your school. (Some schools require all students to sign a statement, indicating either that the student has registered or is not required to do so.)

NOTE: If you already have a statement on file with your school, you do not have to sign another one unless your registration status has changed.

Free Application for Federal Student Aid (FAFSA): The form used to apply for federal aid. You can apply electronically, through your school, or by using the same software on your computer at home, or at high schools, postsecondary schools, many public libraries, or Educational Opportunity Centers. You can get FAFSA software (it runs on computers that have the Windows operating system) by downloading it at www.ed.gov/offices/OPE/express.html or by phoning 1-800-801-0576.

Guaranty Agency: The organization that administers FFEL Programs for your school. The federal government sets loan limits and interest rates, but each state is free to set its own additional limitations, within federal guidelines. This agency is the best source of information on FFELs in your state. The name, address, and telephone number of your state agency can be found in this book or by calling the Federal Student Aid Information Center at 1-800-433-3243.

Half-time: You must be attending school at least half-time to be eligible to receive a Federal Pell Grant, a Federal Supplemental Educational Opportunity Grant (FSEOG), Federal Work-Study (FWS), and Federal Perkins Loan Programs. Half-time enrollment is not a requirement to receive aid from the campus-based programs.

At schools measuring progress by credit hours and academic terms (semesters, trimesters, or quarters), "half-time" means at least six semester hours or quarter hours per term. At schools measuring progress by credit hours but not using academic terms, "half-time" means at least 12 semester hours or 18 quarter hours per year. At schools measuring progress by clock hours, "half-time" means at least 12 hours per week. Note that schools may choose to set higher minimums than these.

Internship Deferment: A period during which loan payments can be deferred if a borrower is participating in a program of supervised practical training required to begin professional practice or service. For a new borrower, an internship also means a degree or certificate program offered by a postsecondary school, hospital, or health care facility with postgraduate training. If you're enrolled in an internship program, you may defer repayment of some loans for up to two years.

Parental Leave Deferment: A period of up to six months during which loan payments can be postponed if a borrower is pregnant, or if he or she is taking care of a newborn or newly adopted child. The borrower must be unemployed and not attending school. To get this deferment, you must apply within six months after you leave school or drop below half-time status.

Promissory Note: The binding legal document you sign when you get a student loan. It lists the conditions under which you're borrowing and the terms under which you agree to pay back the loan.

Regular Student: One who is enrolled in an institution to obtain a degree or certificate. Generally, federal aid is only available to regular students. There are exceptions for some programs: See "Eligible Program."

Satisfactory Progress: To be eligible to receive Federal student aid, you must maintain satisfactory academic progress. If you're enrolled in a program that is no longer than two years, the following definition of satisfactory progress applies to you: you must be maintaining a "C" average by the end of your second academic year of study or have an academic standing consistent with your institution's graduation requirements. You must continue to maintain satisfactory progress for the rest of your course of study.

If you're enrolled in a program that is shorter than two years, you must meet your school's written standard of satisfactory progress. Check with your school to find out what that standard is.

Selective Service Registration: If required by law, you must register or arrange to register with the Selective Service to receive federal student aid. A statement appears on the 1997–98 Student Aid Report (SAR) that lets you state that you have registered or to explain why you are not required to register. This requirement applies to males born on or after January 1, 1960 who are citizens or eligible noncitizens who are not currently on active duty in the armed forces. Citizens of the Federated States of Micronesia, the Marshall Islands, or Palau are exempt.

Statement of Educational Purpose/Certification Statement on Refunds and Default: You must sign this statement in order to receive federal student aid. By signing it, you agree to use your student aid only for educa-

tion-related expenses. Part 1 of the 1997–98 Student Aid Report (SAR) contains such a statement. You must sign either this one or a similar one prepared by your school.

Statement of Updated Information: You must sign a statement certifying that the following Student Aid Report (SAR) items are still correct at the time you submit your SAR to your school: your status as a dependent/independent student, the number of your family members, and the number of those members enrolled in postsecondary education at least half-time. If information for any items changes after you submit your application, you must update the information so that it is correct as of the date you sign your SAR. Otherwise, you will not be able to receive Federal student aid. The only exception to the requirement to update is when changes occur because your marital status changes. In that case, you need not update.

Student Aid Index (SAI): The number that appears on your Student Aid Report (SAR), telling you about your Pell Grant eligibility. The SAI is the result of a series of calculations based on the information you reported when you applied for federal student aid.

At-A-Glance Financial Aid Calendar

When	What To Do

Junior Year of High School

- **October**
  - ☞ Take PSAT
  - ☞ Send for college brochures and financial aid information
  - ☞ Begin campus tours; talk to financial aid advisers at colleges

Senior Year of High School

- **September to December**
  - ☞ Narrow down your college choices
  - ☞ Ask schools for admission applications and financial aid forms
  - ☞ Send in applications for admission

- **January 1**
  - ☞ Send in financial aid applications

- **April 1**
  - ☞ Most college acceptances and rejections have been sent out

- **June 30**
  - ☞ Your financial aid application must be received by the processing agency listed on the form
  - ☞ Your school's financial aid office must have received your application and student aid report

Financial Aid Forms Update

There are a number of ways to apply for federal financial aid—but it all starts with the Free Application for Federal Student Aid (FAFSA). You can apply electronically through your school, or you can use the Department of Education's FAFSA Express software. It runs on computers that use the Windows operating system and which have a modem. Computers with the program set up and running can be found at many high schools, public libraries, and Educational Opportunity Centers. Or you can download a copy yourself from the Education Department's website by going to this address: www.ed.gov/office/OPE/express.html. Or you can order the software on diskette by calling 1-800-801-0576. Or you can forego technology altogether and ask for the version of the form that comes on old fashioned paper by writing to the

> Federal Student Aid Information Center
> P.O. Box 84
> Washington, D.C. 20044

More information about the form, which is to be used for applying for federal aid and public funds like Pell Grants, Stafford Loans, or Perkins Loans, is available through a toll-free number: 1-800-4 FEDAID.

The federal forms are required for anyone applying for federal funds—and many institutions use them as well. But some schools require other forms as well, and you should check with your school to determine exactly which forms they'll be looking for from you.

A number of changes have been announced by organizations supplying application forms for privately administered funds. The FFS, the Family Financial Statement, put out by the ACT, has been discontinued. The FAF, issued by the College Board, will also be discontinued as of Fall 1995. The FAF will be replaced by a new form, the CSS/PROFILE. Colleges and universities began to register with the College Board in the Spring of 1995 if they wanted their applicants to use the new form. Colleges will be responsible for notifying applicants if the new forms are required. It is a good idea for students applying for private or institutional funds to check with the schools they are interested in to see if additional forms are required or if other procedures must be followed.

Bibliography

Helpful Materials: General Guides

Books and pamphlets

When a book is not generally available from bookstores or libraries, we have included the address to write for it directly. Since the cost of books rises as fast as the cost of tuition, it's worth writing or calling a publisher to confirm the price—and that the book is still in print. DON'T JUST SEND THEM MONEY IN AN ENVELOPE!! Then they get angry and write letters to ME.

Octameron Associates

P.O. Box 2748, Alexandria, VA 22301

This company publishes 17 booklets in all to help you plan out your college financial aid strategy and make yourself a more attractive college candidate. They are the brainchild of Robert and Anna Leider. If you want a shorter, quicker way into the financial aid process than you'll get from a large book, the Octameron booklets are as zippy as it gets. The best booklets aimed at the college financial aid process are:

Don't Miss Out: The Ambitious Student's Guide to Financial Aid/$8.00

The As and Bs of Academic Scholarships/$7.50

Financial Aid Officers: What They Do—To You and For You/$5.00

Other Publishers

How to Pay for Your Children's College Education/$12.95
Gerald Krefetz
College Board Publications
P.O. Box 886
New York, NY 10101

The College Cost Book/$16.00
College Board Publications
P.O. Box 886
New York, NY 10101
(Costs of more than 3,000 schools, and more ways to stretch your education dollar.)

The College Board Guide to Going to College While Working: Strategies for Success/$9.95
Gene Hawes
College Board Publications
P.O. Box 886
New York, NY 10101

Need a Lift?/$3.00
American Legion Education Program
P.O. Box 1050
Indianapolis, IN 46206

The Student Loan Handbook: All About the Guaranteed Student Loan and Other Forms of Financial Aid
Betterway Publications
White Hall, VA 22987

The Right College/$22.00
(Arco)
Macmillan Publishing
201 West 103rd Street
Indianapolis, IN 46290

Princeton Review Student Access Guide: Paying for College/$14.00
Chany, Kalman
Random House

How to Put Your Kids Through College/$15.95
Consumer Reports Books Editors
Edelstein, Scott
Consumer Reports

College Costs Today/free
New York Life Insurance Company
51 Madison Avenue
New York, NY 10010
(College costs at most American schools.)

The Public Ivys: A Guide to America's Best State Colleges & Universities/$19.95
Richard Moll
Penguin
120 Woodbine Street
Bergenfield, NJ 07621
(Essays on public schools whose quality rivals or exceeds that of the best private schools.)

The College Money Book: How to Get a High-Quality Education at the Lowest Possible Cost/(price not available)
David M. Brownstone, Gene R. Hawes
Macmillan

**The Great American National Scholarships &
Grants Guide**/$12.95
Anthony Darby
DClaren Publishing
P.O. Box 250963
W. Bloomfield, MI 48325

Specific Areas of Interest

**AFL–CIO Guide to Union Sponsored
Scholarships; Awards and Student
Financial Aid**
Department of Publication, AFL–CIO
815 16th Street, NW
Washington, DC 20006
(202) 637-5000
(The best guide to union sponsored scholarships, with a
good bibliography of financial aid sources.)

Army College Fund
U.S. Army Department of Defense
620 Central Avenue
Federal Center Building R
Alameda, CA 95401

Army ROTC Scholarships
Army ROTC/Department of Military Science
74 D Harmon Gym
UC Berkeley
Berkeley, CA 94720

Directory for the Arts/$6.00
Center for Arts Information
152 West 42nd Street
New York, NY 10036

**Prentice Hall Guide to Scholarships & Fellow-
ships for Math & Science Students: A Resource
Guide for Students Pursuing Careers in Mathe-
matics, Science, & Engineering**/$29.95
Kantrowitz, Mark
Prentice-Hall
Englewood Cliffs, NJ

Directory of Athletic Scholarships/$29.95
Alan Green
Facts on File
460 Park Avenue South
New York, NY 10016

**Federal Benefits for Veterans and
Dependents**/$3.75
Superintendent of Documents
P.O. Box 371954
Pittsburgh, PA 15250

Financial Aid for College Students/free
American Chemical Society/Education Department
1155 16th Street, NW
Washington, DC 20036

**Grants, Fellowships and Prizes of Interest
to Historians**/$8.00 for members, $10.00 for non-
members
American Historical Association
400 A Street, SE
Washington, DC 20003

National Directory of Internships
National Society for Experiential Education
3509 Haworth Drive, Suite 207
Raleigh, NC 27609

The Journalist's Road to Success
The Newspaper Fund
P.O. Box 300
Princeton, NJ 08543-0300

Publications Catalog (many titles)/free
National League of Nursing
30 Hudson Street
New York, NY 10014

Programs in Cooperative Education/free
The National Commission for Cooperative Education
300 Huntington Avenue
Boston, MA 02115

Student Financial Aid/free
American Speech, Language, and Hearing Association
Department of Public Information and Publications
Careers and Information Services Section
10801 Rockville Pike
Rockville, MD 20852

**Financial Aid for the Disabled and their
Families, 6th ed.**/$38.00
Reference Services Pr.

**How to Find Money for College: The Disabled
Student**/$21.20
Schwartz, Saryl Z.
Path-College Affordable Prod.

Financial Aid for Minority Students

Garrett Park Press
P.O. Box 190, Garrett Park, MD 20896
(301) 946-2553
This company produces a number of guides to help minor-
ity students track down aid money. The titles cost $5.95.
Titles include:

Financial Aid for Minorities in Business & Law

Financial Aid for Minorities in Education

Financial Aid for Minorities in Engineering and Sciences

Financial Aid for Minorities in Health Fields

Financial Aid for Minorities in Journalism/Mass Communications

Scholarship Listings

Free Money for College: A Guide to More than 1,000 Grants & Scholarships for Undergraduate Study, 3rd Ed./$24.95
Laura Blum
Facts on File

Financial Aids for Higher Education: A Catalog for Undergraduates
Oreon Keeslar
William C. Brown Publishers
2460 Kerper Boulevard
Dubuque, IA 52001

Keys to Financing a College Education/$4.95
Marguerite Dennis
Barron

The Scholarship Book: The Comprehensive Guide to Private-Sector Scholarships, Grants, and Loans for Undergraduates/$19.95
Daniel Cassidy, President, National Scholarship
Research Service, and Michael J. Alves
Prentice-Hall, Inc.
P.O. Box 11074
Des Moines, IA 50336

Chronicle Student Aid Annual/$19.95
Chronicle Guidance Publications, Inc.
66 Aurora Street
Moravia, NY 13118

Scholarships, Fellowships, & Loans/$80.00
S. Norman Feingold/Marie Feingold
Bellman
P.O. Box 34937
Bethesda, MD 20817

Directory of Scholarships and Grants

How to Use the Scholarship Listings

In the following section, scholarships have been placed in categories by majors/fields of interest. A list of the group titles into which the categories are placed follows; the reader is also encouraged to review both the Category List (pages 125-126) that identifies which categories are included in each group, and the Index of Majors at the back of the book.

> Agriculture/Animal Science
> Allied Health
> Business
> Communications
> Creative/Performing Arts
> Education
> Engineering/Technology
> Language/Literature/Humanities
> Medicine/Nursing
> Science/Mathematics
> Social Science/Political Science/Law
> Other/Miscellaneous

Each scholarship may include the following information; if an item of data does not appear, the sponsoring organization has not supplied it.

> **Name of award**
> **Address** of sponsoring organization to be contacted
> **Telephone number** of sponsoring organization
> **Average award** and/or **Amount of award, Maximum award, Minimum award**: the average or set dollar amount, or range of dollar amounts within which the award falls
> **Number of awards** given annually
> **Deadline**: date by which applications for the award must be filed
> **College level**: level in college or university student must have attained in order to be eligible for award
> **Majors/Fields**: the majors or fields of interest for which the awards are given
> **Criteria**: describes general information and requirements for the particular award, e.g., ethnic group, test scores, residency, renewability, etc.
> **Contact**: name and/or title of person to contact for additional information, and address and/or telephone number if different from that of sponsoring organization

The following is a sample listing:

---

706 **Judith Resnik Memorial Scholarship**

Society of Women Engineers (SWE)
120 Wall Street, 11th Floor
New York, NY 10005-3902
(212) 509-9577, (212) 509-0224 (fax)
Average award: $2,000
Number of awards: 1
Deadline: February 1
College level: Senior
Majors/Fields: Aeronautical engineering, aerospace engineering
Criteria: Applicant must be a woman, have a minimum 3.5 GPA, be a SWE member, be studying in an engineering field with a space-related major, and be planning a career in the space industry. Awarded every year.
Contact: Scholarships.

Indexes

The **Index of Majors** (page 488) lists majors alphabetically. After each major is a list of the numbers of scholarships that list that major as a criterion for eligibility.

The **Index of Criteria** (page 495) lists other criteria required for scholarship eligibility. These may include academic record or National Merit status; parents' place of employment or involvement in an alumni/ae association, club, or union; handicap; gender; military affiliation; state, county, or city of residence; race or ethnic background; religion; or sport. The numbers of scholarships that require a particular criterion are listed after entry.

The **Index of Scholarships** (page 505) lists all awards alphabetically by the name of the award.

Category List

The following is a list of the major areas of study in which specific scholarships have been categorized. All scholarships with miscellaneous majors or which are categorized by criteria other than the major or field of interest have been placed in the **Other** category.

Agriculture/ Animal Science

Agribusiness
Agriculture
Agronomy/Land Management
Animal Science/Veterinary Medicine
Forestry
Horticulture/Plant Sciences
Wildlife Resources/Management

Allied Health

Allied Health
Dental/Medical Assistance
Dietetics/Food Science/Nutrition
Medical Technology
Pharmacy
Physical/Occupational Therapy
Respiratory Therapy

Business

Accounting
Business Administration/Management
Hospitality/Hospitality Administration
Human Resources Management
Insurance
Marketing/Sales/Retailing
Real Estate
Secretarial Studies
Transportation/Traffic Management

Communications

Communications
Communications Disorders
Journalism
Library Science
Photojournalism
Radio/TV Broadcasting
Speech/Forensics

Creative/Performing Arts

Architecture/Landscape Architecture
Art History
Creative/Performing Arts–General
Drama/Theatre
Fashion Design/Interior Decorating
Film/Photography
Fine Arts
Graphic Arts
Instrumental Music
Music–General
Voice

Education

Education–General
Elementary/Secondary Education
Special Education

Engineering/Technology

Aerospace/Aeronautical Engineering
Chemical Engineering
Civil/Environmental Engineering
Computer Science
Electrical/Electronic Engineering
Engineering–General
Industrial/Manufacturing Engineering
Mechanical Engineering
Mining/Metallurgical/Materials
   Engineering
Nuclear Engineering

Language/Literature/Humanities

Classical Studies
Cultural Studies
English/Literature/Writing
Foreign Languages
History
Humanities
Religion/Theology/Philosophy

Medicine/Nursing

Dentistry
Medicine
Nursing

Science/Mathematics

Atmospheric Sciences/Meteorology
Biology
Chemistry
Earth Science
Environmental Science
Life Sciences–General

Marine Science
Mathematics
Physical Sciences
Physics
Sciences–General

Social Science/Political Science/Law

Home Economics
Law
Military Science/ROTC
Political Science
Social Sciences–General
Sociology/Social Work
Urban Planning

Other/Miscellaneous

Academic/Leadership Ability
Athletic Ability
Automotive Studies
City/County of Residence
Club Affiliation
Corporate Affiliation
Culinary Arts/Baking
Ethnic/Race-Specific
Gender-Specific
Military Affiliation
Multiple Majors
National Merit
Other
Physically Handicapped
Religious Affiliation
State/Country of Residence
Textile Science
Union Affiliation
Vocational/Technical

Agriculture/Animal Science

Agribusiness

1   Jacob Van Namen/Vans Marketing Scholarship

Bedding Plants Foundation, Inc.
P.O. Box 27241
Lansing, MI 48909
Average award: $1,250
Deadline: April 1
College level: Junior, Senior, Graduate
Majors/Fields: Agribusiness
Criteria: Applicant must must be involved in agribusiness marketing and distribution of floral products, and submit letters of recommendation, transcript, and statement of intent. Citizens of any country may apply.

2   L.E. Mathers Memorial Scholarship

New Mexico State University
Box 30001
Department 5100
Las Cruces, NM 88003-0001
(505) 646-4105
Average award: Full tuition
Deadline: March 1
College level: Junior
Majors/Fields: Agricultural business, agricultural economics
Criteria: Applicant must have at least half of the required credits for a major in the department of agricultural economics and agricultural business, have a minimum 2.8 GPA, demonstrate financial need, and be a U.S. citizen. Selection is based upon academic promise, character, and leadership. Preference is given to New Mexico residents. Awarded every year. Award may be used only at sponsoring institution.
Contact: College of Agriculture and Home Economics, (505) 646-1807.

3   NCFC Education Foundation Scholarship

National Council of Farmer Cooperatives (NCFC)
50 F Street, NW
Suite 900
Washington, DC 20001
(202) 626-8700
http://access.digex.net/~ncfc
Average award: $1,000
Number of awards: 2
Deadline: March 1
College level: Sophomore, Junior, Senior
Criteria: Applicant must be enrolled in an accredited four-year college or university in the U.S., have completed the equivalent of at least one full academic year of course work, and rank in the top quarter of the class or have at least a 3.0 GPA.
Contact: Undergraduate Scholarships, NCFC Education Foundation.

Agriculture

4   AACC Undergraduate Scholarships
American Association of Cereal Chemists (AACC)
3340 Pilot Knob Road
St. Paul, MN 55121-2097
Maximum award: $2,000
Number of awards: 15
Deadline: April 1; must be endorsed by academic department head by March 15
College level: Sophomore, Junior, Senior
Majors/Fields: Cereal science
Criteria: Applicant must be a full-time student with a minimum 3.0 GPA, enrolled in a program emphasizing cereal science/technology, and recommended by department head or faculty advisor. Selection is based upon academic record, career interest, courses taken, jobs held (part- or full-time), active participation in student science club, and grades in science classes. Recipient must reapply on same basis as new applicants for renewal. Awarded every year.
Contact: Dr. Elwood F. Caldwell, Chairman, AACC Scholarship Jury.

5   Arch E. McClanahan Agricultural Memorial Scholarship
University of Tennessee, Knoxville
Financial Aid Office
115 Student Services Building
Knoxville, TN 37994
(615) 974-3131
Average award: $3,000
Number of awards: 6
Deadline: December 1
College level: Freshman
Majors/Fields: Agriculture
Criteria: Applicant must be a Tennessee resident, have a minimum 3.5 GPA, minimum composite ACT score of 25 (combined SAT I score of 980), and demonstrate outstanding performance in school and community activities that support professional career development. Acceptable academic and leadership performance is required to retain scholarship. Awarded every year. Award may be used only at sponsoring institution.
Contact: Agricultural Sciences and Natural Resources, 310 Agricultural Engineering Building, Knoxville, TN 37996, (615) 974-7506.

6   California Farm Bureau Scholarship
California Farm Bureau Scholarship Foundation
1601 Exposition Boulevard – FB 13
Sacramento, CA 95815
(916) 924-4052
Average award: $1,250
Maximum award: $2,000
Minimum award: $1,000
Number of awards: 33
Deadline: March 1
College level: Unspecified undergraduate
Majors/Fields: Agriculture
Criteria: Selection is based upon scholastic achievement, career goals, leadership skills, and determination. Scholarship must be used at a four-year college or university in California. Recipient must reapply for renewal. Awarded every year.
Contact: Nina M. Danner, Scholarship Coordinator, ndanner@cfbf.com.

7   Daughters of the American Revolution Scholarship

Texas A&M University–Kingsville
Scholarships
Box 116
Kingsville, TX 78363
(512) 593-3907, (512) 593-2991 (fax)
http://www.tamuk.edu
Average award: $1,200
Number of awards: No limit
Deadline: March 10
College level: Freshman, Sophomore, Junior, Senior
Majors/Fields: Agriculture.
Criteria: Applicant must have a minimum 3.0 GPA and minimum combined SAT I score of 970 (ACT score of 21). Renewable if recipient maintains a minimum 3.0 GPA. Award may be used only at sponsoring institution.
Contact: Your department, College of Agriculture and Human Sciences.

8   Farm Credit Scholarship

Clemson University
G-01 Sikes Hall
Clemson, SC 29634-5123
(803) 656-2280
Average award: $1,600
Number of awards: 3
Deadline: March 1
College level: Junior, Senior
Majors/Fields: Agricultural/applied economics
Criteria: Applicant must have a minimum 2.5 GPA and be a resident of Florida, Georgia, North Carolina, or South Carolina. Awarded every year. Award may be used only at sponsoring institution.
Contact: Marvin Carmichael, Director of Financial Aid.

9   Future Farmers of America Sweepstakes Award

New Mexico State University
Box 30001
Department 5100
Las Cruces, NM 88003-0001
(505) 646-4105
Average award: Full tuition
Number of awards: 1
Deadline: March 1
College level: Freshman
Majors/Fields: Agriculture
Criteria: Applicant must have participated on one of the high school teams that won the sweepstakes award. Awarded every year. Award may be used only at sponsoring institution.
Contact: Greeley W. Myers, Director of Financial Aid.

10   George E. and Leila Giles Singleton Scholarship

Clemson University
G-01 Sikes Hall
Clemson, SC 29634-5123
(803) 656-2280
Average award: $1,100
Number of awards: 1
Deadline: March 1
College level: Freshman
Majors/Fields: Agricultural education, agricultural engineering, agricultural mechanization/business, agricultural/applied economics, agronomy, animal industries
Criteria: Applicant must be a South Carolina resident, have a minimum 2.5 GPA, and demonstrate financial need. Satisfactory GPA and completion of at least 12 credit hours per semester are required to retain scholarship. Awarded every year. Award may be used only at sponsoring institution.
Contact: Marvin Carmichael, Director of Financial Aid.

11   Houston Livestock Show and Rodeo Scholarship

Southwest Texas State University
J.C. Kellam Building
San Marcos, TX 78666
(512) 245-2340
Maximum award: $1,500
Number of awards: 20
Deadline: March 15
College level: Sophomore, Junior, Senior
Majors/Fields: Agriculture
Criteria: Applicant must major in agriculture and demonstrate leadership, academic ability, and financial need. Scholarship is primarily for students with 30 or more semester hours. Awarded every year. Award may be used only at sponsoring institution.
Contact: Scholarship Committee, Department of Agriculture, (512) 245-2315.

12   J.W. Jones Endowed Agricultural Scholarship

Clemson University
G-01 Sikes Hall
Clemson, SC 29634-5123
(803) 656-2280
Average award: $4,000
Number of awards: 1
Deadline: March 1
College level: Freshman, Sophomore, Junior, Senior
Majors/Fields: Agricultural education, agricultural engineering, agricultural/applied economics, agricultural mechanization/business, agronomy, animal industries
Criteria: Applicant must have a minimum 2.5 GPA. Satisfactory GPA and completion of at least 12 credit hours per semester are required to retain scholarship. Awarded every year. Award may be used only at sponsoring institution.
Contact: Marvin Carmichael, Director of Financial Aid.

13   Jack Wright Memorial Scholarship

University of Tennessee, Knoxville
Financial Aid Office
115 Student Services Building
Knoxville, TN 37994
(615) 974-3131
Maximum award: $1,200
Maximum number of awards: 6
Minimum number of awards: 5
Deadline: February 1
College level: Freshman
Majors/Fields: Agriculture
Criteria: Selection is based upon academic performance, leadership ability, and financial need. Award is for four years. Awarded every year. Award may be used only at sponsoring institution.
Contact: Agricultural Sciences and Natural Resources, 310 Agricultural Engineering Building, Knoxville, TN 37996, (615) 974-7506.

14   Lehman M. Bauknight Scholarship

Clemson University
G-01 Sikes Hall
Clemson, SC 29634-5123
(803) 656-2280
Maximum award: $1,250
Number of awards: 1
Deadline: March 1
College level: Freshman, Sophomore, Junior, Senior
Criteria: Applicant must have a minimum 2.5 GPA and be enrolled in the College of Agricultural Sciences, the College of Forest and Recreation Resources, or the Dept of Agricultural Education. Satisfactory GPA and completion of at least 12 credits per semester are required to retain scholarship. Awarded every year. Award may be used only at sponsoring institution.
Contact: Marvin Carmichael, Director of Financial Aid.

15 M.C. McKenzie Memorial Scholarship

Clemson University
G-01 Sikes Hall
Clemson, SC 29634-5123
(803) 656-2280
Average award: $1,500
Number of awards: 1
Deadline: March 1
College level: Freshman, Sophomore
Majors/Fields: Agricultural engineering, agricultural mechanization/business
Criteria: Applicant must have a minimum 2.5 GPA. Minimum 2.5 GPA and completion of at least 12 credit hours per semester are required to retain scholarship. Awarded every year. Award may be used only at sponsoring institution.
Contact: Marvin Carmichael, Director of Financial Aid.

16 Marlboro County Farm Bureau Scholarship in Agriculture

Clemson University
G-01 Sikes Hall
Clemson, SC 29634-5123
(803) 656-2280
Average award: $2,000
Number of awards: 1
Deadline: March 1
College level: Sophomore
Majors/Fields: Agricultural sciences
Criteria: Applicant must be a resident of Marlboro County, S.C., have a minimum 2.0 GPA, and be enrolled in the College of Agricultural Sciences. Awarded every year. Award may be used only at sponsoring institution.
Contact: Marvin Carmichael, Director of Financial Aid.

17 New Mexico Agricultural Chemical and Plant Food Association Scholarship

New Mexico State University
Box 30001
Department 5100
Las Cruces, NM 88003-0001
(505) 646-4105
Average award: Full tuition
Number of awards: 3
Deadline: March 1
College level: Freshman, Sophomore, Junior, Senior
Majors/Fields: Agriculture, agricultural economics, agricultural education, agronomy, entomology, extension education, home economics, horticulture, plant pathology, preforestry
Criteria: Selection is based upon financial need, scholarship potential, moral character, and leadership qualities. Recommendation of the scholarship committee is required to retain scholarship. Awarded every year. Award may be used only at sponsoring institution.
Contact: Greeley W. Myers, Director of Financial Aid.

18 Starkey-Ritchie Endowed Agricultural Scholarship

Clemson University
G-01 Sikes Hall
Clemson, SC 29634-5123
(803) 656-2280
Average award: $1,800
Number of awards: 1
Deadline: March 1
College level: Freshman, Sophomore, Junior, Senior
Majors/Fields: Agricultural education, agricultural engineering, agricultural mechanization/business, agricultural/applied economics, agronomy, animal industries
Criteria: Applicant must have a minimum 2.5 GPA. Award may be used only at sponsoring institution.
Contact: Scholarships.

19 Thomas Stephen Buie Memorial Scholarship

Clemson University
G-01 Sikes Hall
Clemson, SC 29634-5123
(803) 656-2280
Maximum award: $1,300
Number of awards: 1
Deadline: March 1
College level: Junior, Senior
Majors/Fields: Agricultural sciences, agronomy
Criteria: Applicant must have a minimum 2.5 GPA and be enrolled in the College of Agricultural Sciences. Preference is given to student in agronomy. Awarded every year. Award may be used only at sponsoring institution.
Contact: Marvin Carmichael, Director of Financial Aid.

20 UAL Scholarship

United Agribusiness League (UAL) Scholarship Program
54 Corporate Park
Irvine, CA 92714
(714) 975-1424
Average award: $2,500
Maximum award: $6,000
Minimum award: $1,000
Number of awards: 7
Deadline: April 15
College level: Freshman, Sophomore, Junior, Senior, college seniors
Majors/Fields: Agriculture
Criteria: Applicant must be a member of UAL, an employee of a member of UAL, the child of a member of UAL, or the child of an employee of a member of UAL. Recipient must reapply for renewal. Awarded every year.
Contact: Sandy Hamilton, Director of Member Services.

21 W.L. Abernathy Jr. Scholarship

Clemson University
G-01 Sikes Hall
Clemson, SC 29634-5123
(803) 656-2280
Maximum award: $1,500
Number of awards: 4
Deadline: March 1
College level: Freshman, Sophomore, Junior, Senior
Criteria: Applicant must be a South Carolina resident enrolled in the College of Agricultural, Forestry and Life Sciences. At least two recipients are entering freshmen. Awarded every year. Award may be used only at sponsoring institution.
Contact: Marvin Carmichael, Director of Financial Aid.

22 W.N. McAdams Memorial Scholarship

Clemson University
G-01 Sikes Hall
Clemson, SC 29634-5123
(803) 656-2280
Average award: $1,200
Number of awards: 1
Deadline: March 1
College level: Freshman, Sophomore
Majors/Fields: Agricultural engineering
Criteria: Applicant must have a minimum 2.5 GPA. Minimum 2.5 GPA and completion of at least 12 credit hours per semester are required to retain scholarship. Awarded every year. Award may be used only at sponsoring institution.
Contact: Marvin Carmichael, Director of Financial Aid.

23   William J. Oates Endowed Scholarship

Clemson University
G-01 Sikes Hall
Clemson, SC 29634-5123
(803) 656-2280
Average award: $1,500
Number of awards: 5
Deadline: March 1
College level: Freshman, Sophomore, Junior, Senior
Majors/Fields: Agricultural engineering
Criteria: Applicant must have a minimum 2.5 GPA. Satisfactory GPA and completion of at least 12 credit hours per semester are required to retain scholarship. Awarded every year. Award may be used only at sponsoring institution.
Contact: Marvin Carmichael, Director of Financial Aid.

Agronomy/Land Management

24   Crop and Weed Science Annual Scholarship

Clemson University
G-01 Sikes Hall
Clemson, SC 29634-5123
(803) 656-2280
Maximum award: $1,000
Number of awards: 1
Deadline: March 1
College level: Freshman, Sophomore, Junior, Senior
Majors/Fields: Agronomy
Criteria: Applicant must have a minimum 2.0 GPA. Preference is given to student concentrating in agronomic systems or weed science. Minimum 2.5 GPA and completion of at least 12 credits per semester are required to retain scholarship. Awarded every year. Award may be used only at sponsoring institution.
Contact: Marvin Carmichael, Director of Financial Aid.

25   Dr. and Mrs. H.P. Cooper Agronomy Scholarship

Clemson University
G-01 Sikes Hall
Clemson, SC 29634-5123
(803) 656-2280
Maximum award: $1,100
Number of awards: 2
Deadline: March 1
College level: Freshman, Sophomore, Junior, Senior
Majors/Fields: Agronomy
Criteria: Applicant must have a minimum 2.5 GPA. Awarded every year. Award may be used only at sponsoring institution.
Contact: Marvin Carmichael, Director of Financial Aid.

26   Joe B. Douthit Memorial Soil and Water Conservation Scholarship

Clemson University
G-01 Sikes Hall
Clemson, SC 29634-5123
(803) 656-2280
Maximum award: $1,000
Number of awards: 4
Deadline: March 1
College level: Freshman, Sophomore, Junior, Senior
Majors/Fields: Agronomy, agricultural engineering
Criteria: Applicant must have a minimum 2.5 GPA and be interested in soil and water conservation. Satisfactory GPA and completion of at least 12 credits per semester are required to retain scholarship. Awarded every year. Award may be used only at sponsoring institution.
Contact: Marvin Carmichael, Director of Financial Aid.

Animal Science/Veterinary Medicine

27   American Veterinary Medical Foundation Scholarship

AVMA Foundation
1931 North Meacham Road, Suite 100
Schaumburg, IL 60173
(847) 925-8070, (847) 925-1329 (fax)
74232.1722@compuserve.com
Maximum award: $2,000
College level: Sophomore, Junior, Senior
Majors/Fields: Veterinary
Criteria: Award may be used at AVMA accredited schools only.
Contact: Ellen Siciliano, Program Manager, 74232.1722@compuserve.com.

28   Beville Hal Reagan Scholarship in Animal Science

University of Tennessee, Knoxville
Financial Aid Office
115 Student Services Building
Knoxville, TN 37994
(615) 974-3131
Average award: $2,000
Number of awards: 1
Deadline: February 1
College level: Freshman
Majors/Fields: Animal science
Criteria: Applicant must have actively participated in 4-H, FFA, or other youth agricultural programs and have a minimum composite ACT score of 24. Minimum 2.75 cumulative GPA and 3.25 GPA in animal science major is required to retain scholarship for third and fourth years. Applicant must participate in Animal Science Department's clubs and activities. Awarded every year. Award may be used only at sponsoring institution.
Contact: Agricultural Sciences and Natural Resources, 310 Agricultural Engineering Building, Knoxville, TN 37996, (615) 974-7506.

29   Council of Milk Producers League of South Carolina Endowed Scholarship

Clemson University
G-01 Sikes Hall
Clemson, SC 29634-5123
(803) 656-2280
Maximum award: $1,500
Number of awards: 1
Deadline: March 1
College level: Freshman
Majors/Fields: Animal/dairy/veterinary science
Criteria: Applicant must be a South Carolina resident and have a minimum 2.5 GPA. Awarded every year. Award may be used only at sponsoring institution.
Contact: Marvin Carmichael, Director of Financial Aid.

30   Equestrian Science Scholarship

William Woods University
200 West Twelfth Street
Fulton, MO 65251-1098
(573) 592-4232, (573) 592-1146 (fax)
http://www.wmwoods.edu
Maximum award: $2,000
Deadline: June 1
College level: Freshman, Sophomore, Junior, Senior
Majors/Fields: Equestrian science
Criteria: Recommendation from trainer and videotape of riding recommended. Recipient must have a minimum 3.0 GPA in equestrian science major (minimum 2.75 GPA overall), complete one applied and one lecture equestrian class, perform at horse shows, and have recommendation to retain scholarship. Awarded every year. Award may be used only at sponsoring institution.
Contact: Laura L. Archuleta, Director for Student Financial Aid, larchule@iris.wmwoods.edu.

31   Harness Horse Youth Foundation

Harness Horse Youth Foundation
14950 Greyhound Court
Carmel, IN 45032
(317) 848-5132, (317) 848-5132 (fax)
http://www.hhyf.org
Average award: $3,500
Minimum award: $1,000
Number of awards: 10
Deadline: April 30
College level: Sophomore, Junior, Senior, Graduate
Majors/Fields: Equine-related field
Criteria: Selection is based upon experience with horses (especially harness horses), financial need, and scholastic achievements. Reapplication is required to retain scholarship.
Contact: Ellen Taylor, Executive Director.

Forestry————————————

32   Edward S. Moore Foundation Scholarship

Clemson University
G-01 Sikes Hall
Clemson, SC 29634-5123
(803) 656-2280
Maximum award: $2,500
Number of awards: 1
Deadline: December 31
College level: Freshman
Majors/Fields: Forestry
Criteria: Applicant must be a South Carolina resident. Minimum 2.5 GPA and completion of at least 12 credits per semester are required to retain scholarship. Awarded every year. Award may be used only at sponsoring institution.
Contact: Marvin Carmichael, Director of Financial Aid.

33   James William Byrd Endowed Memorial Scholarship

Clemson University
G-01 Sikes Hall
Clemson, SC 29634-5123
(803) 656-2280
Maximum award: $1,500
Number of awards: 3
Deadline: March 1
College level: Freshman
Majors/Fields: Forestry
Criteria: Applicant must have a minimum 2.0 GPA. Satisfactory GPA and completion of at least 12 credits per semester are required to retain scholarship. Awarded every year. Award may be used only at sponsoring institution.
Contact: Marvin Carmichael, Director of Financial Aid.

34   Ottis and Calista Causey Endowed Scholarship

Clemson University
G-01 Sikes Hall
Clemson, SC 29634-5123
(803) 656-2280
Maximum award: $2,400
Number of awards: 1
Deadline: March 1
College level: Freshman, Sophomore, Junior, Senior
Majors/Fields: Forestry
Criteria: Applicant must have a minimum 2.5 GPA. Satisfactory GPA and completion of at least 12 credits per semester are required to retain scholarship. Awarded every year. Award may be used only at sponsoring institution.
Contact: Marvin Carmichael, Director of Financial Aid.

35   Sharp Academic Merit Scholarship

Mississippi State University
Department of Student Financial Aid
P.O. Box 6238
Mississippi State, MS 39762
(601) 325-7430
Average award: $3,000
Deadline: February 1
College level: Freshman
Majors/Fields: Forestry
Criteria: Applicant must have a minimum composite ACT score of 31. Selection is based upon ACT scores and high school academic record. Minimum 3.0 GPA in required forestry courses is required to retain scholarship. Awarded every year. Award may be used only at sponsoring institution.
Contact: Audrey S. Lambert, Director of Student Financial Aid.

36   Virginia Forestry Association Scholarship

Virginia Forestry Association
1205 East Main Street
Richmond, VA 23219
(804) 644-8462
Average award: $1,000
Maximum award: $1,500
Number of awards: 8
Deadline: March 31
College level: Freshman, Sophomore, Junior, Senior
Majors/Fields: Forestry
Criteria: Applicant must major in forestry or any curriculum in the School of Forestry at Virginia Polytech Inst and State U. Selection is based upon, in order of importance: academic standing, motivation, apparent ability to contribute to the forestry profession, extracurricular activities, evidence of leadership, and financial need. Awarded every year.
Contact: Charles F. Finley Jr., Executive Vice President.

Horticulture/Plant Sciences————

37   Achievement and Recognition Project Scholarship

National Junior Horticultural Association (NJHA)
401 North Fourth Street
Durant, OK 74701
(405) 924-0771
Maximum award: $500
Number of awards: 4
Deadline: October 15
Criteria: Applicant must be between the ages of 15 and 22 and have participated previously in NJHA projects and conventions. Applicant must provide a resume listing occupation, future plans, activities and awards with NJHA and elsewhere, and a narrative detailing how a travel/study scholarship would be of use. An interiew at the NJHA convention is also required.
Contact: Dr. Joe Maxson, Executive Secretary.

38   Carl F. Dietz Memorial Scholarship

Bedding Plants Foundation, Inc.
P.O. Box 27241
Lansing, MI 48909
Average award: $1,000
Number of awards: 1
Deadline: April 1
College level: Sophomore, Junior, Senior
Majors/Fields: Horticulture
Criteria: Applicant must have a special interest in bedding plants, submit letters of recommendation, transcript, and statement of intent. Citizens of any country may apply. Awarded every year.

39   Earl J. Small Growers Scholarship

Bedding Plants Foundation, Inc.
P.O. Box 27241
Lansing, MI 48909
Average award: $2,000
Number of awards: 2
Deadline: April 1
College level: Sophomore, Junior, Senior
Majors/Fields: Horticulture
Criteria: Applicant must intend to pursue a career in greenhouse production, be a U.S. or Canadian citizen, submit letters of recommendation, transcript, and statement of intent. Awarded every year.

40   GSCAA Scholars

Golf Course Superintendents Association of America
Foundation
1421 Research Park Drive
Lawrence, KS 66049
(913) 832-4445, (913) 832-4433 (fax)
fundmail@gcsaa.org
http://www.gcsaa.org
Average award: $2,500
Maximum award: $3,500
Minimum award: $500
Number of awards: 10
Deadline: June 1
College level: Sophomore, Junior, Senior
Majors/Fields: Botany, chemistry, forestry, golf course managment, horticulture, plant science, turfgrass science
Criteria: Applicant must have completed at least the first year of a collegiate turfgrass management program and be planning a career as a golf course superintendent. Selection is based upon academic excellence, extracurricular activities, and recommendations from college advisors and golf course superintendents or other employers. International students attending a US institution may also apply. Awarded every year.
Contact: Jack Schwartz, Director of Development, (913) 841-2240.

41   Gus Cunningham Wofford Memorial Scholarship

Clemson University
G-01 Sikes Hall
Clemson, SC 29634-5123
(803) 656-2280
Average award: $2,000
Number of awards: 1
Deadline: March 1
College level: Sophomore, Junior, Senior
Majors/Fields: Horticulture
Criteria: Applicant must have a minimum 2.5 GPA and be a resident of Lourens County, S.C. Satisfactory GPA and completion of at least 12 credit hours per semester are required to retain scholarship. Awarded every year. Award may be used only at sponsoring institution.
Contact: Marvin Carmichael, Director of Financial Aid.

42   Harold Bettinger Memorial Scholarship

Bedding Plants Foundation, Inc.
P.O. Box 27241
Lansing, MI 48909
Average award: $1,000
Number of awards: 1
Deadline: April 1
College level: Sophomore, Junior, Senior, Graduate, Doctoral
Majors/Fields: Horticulture
Criteria: Applicant must submit letters of recommendation, transcript, and statement of intent. Citizens from any country may apply Awarded every year.

43   Herbert Wardle, Jr. Fund

Maine Community Foundation
210 Main Street
P.O. Box 148
Ellsworth, ME 04605
(207) 667-9735
Average award: $2,000
Deadline: May 1
College level: Freshman
Majors/Fields: Botany, horticulture, orchids, related fields
Criteria: Applicant must be a Maine resident and a graduate of Mount Desert High School in Maine. Recipient must reapply for renewal. Awarded every year.
Contact: Scholarship Coordinator.

44   Jerry Baker College Freshmen Scholarship

Bedding Plants Foundation, Inc.
P.O. Box 27241
Lansing, MI 48909
Average award: $2,000
Deadline: April 1
College level: Freshman
Majors/Fields: Gardening, horticulture, landscaping
Criteria: Applicant must submit letters of recommendation, transcript, and statement of intent. Citizens of any country may apply. Awarded every year. Award may be used at U.S. or Canadian schools only.

45   Jerry Wilmot Scholarship

Bedding Plants Foundation, Inc.
P.O. Box 27241
Lansing, MI 48909
Average award: $2,000
Deadline: April 1
College level: Sophomore, Junior, Senior
Majors/Fields: Business, finance, horticulture
Criteria: Applicant must intend to pursue a career in garden center management, submit letters of recommendation, transcript, and statement of intent. Citizens of any country may apply.

46   John Andrew Stephenson Endowed Scholarship

Clemson University
G-01 Sikes Hall
Clemson, SC 29634-5123
(803) 656-2280
Average award: $2,000
Number of awards: 2
Deadline: March 1
College level: Freshman, Sophomore, Junior, Senior
Majors/Fields: Horticulture
Criteria: Applicant must have a minimum 2.5 GPA. Renewable if recipient maintains satisfactory GPA and completes at least 12 credits per semester. Award may be used only at sponsoring institution.
Contact: Scholarships.

47   National Council of State Garden Clubs Scholarship

New Mexico State University
Box 30001
Department 5100
Las Cruces, NM 88003-0001
(505) 646-4105
Average award: $4,000
Number of awards: 20
Deadline: November 1
College level: Freshman, Sophomore, Junior, Senior
Majors/Fields: Horticulture
Criteria: Applicant must have a minimum 3.0 GPA and be a resident of the state from which he or she is applying. Only one applicant may be submitted by each state annually. Awarded every year. Award may be used only at sponsoring institution.
Contact: College of Agricultural and Home Economics, (505) 646-1807.

48   National Council of State Garden Clubs Scholarship

National Council of State Garden Clubs
4401 Magnolia Avenue
St. Louis, MO 63110
(314) 776-7574, (314) 776-5108 (fax)
nesgc.franm@worlonet.att.net
Average award: $3,500
Number of awards: 32
Deadline: March 1
College level: Junior, Senior, Graduate
Majors/Fields: Horticulture, floriculture, land management, landscape design, urban planning, forestry, agronomy, and related subjects
Criteria: Applicant must be a U.S. citizen, and have the endorsement of the State Garden Club from the state in which he or she is a permanent resident. Recipient must reapply for renewal. Awarded every year.
Contact: Scholarship Chairman.

49   Procter-Chanin Scholarship

Worcester County Horticultural Society
Tower Hill Botanic Garden
P.O. Box 598
Boylston, MA 01505-0598
(508) 869-6111, (508) 869-0314 (fax)
thbg@towerhillbg.org
Average award: $1,500
Maximum award: $2,000
Minimum award: $500
Number of awards: 3
Deadline: May 1
College level: Sophomore, Junior, Senior, Graduate, Doctoral
Majors/Fields: Horticulture
Criteria: Applicant must be a New England resident or be attending a New England college. Selection is based upon interest in horticulture, sincerity of purpose, academic performance, and financial need. Recipient must reapply for renewal. Awarded every year.
Contact: Jeanne Survell, Scholarship Committee.

50   Scottish Gardening Scholarship

National Junior Horticultural Association (NJHA)
401 North Fourth Street
Durant, OK 74701
(405) 924-0771
Average award: Round trip transportation, food, lodging, tuition, $100 monthly stipend
Deadline: December 31
College level: Horticultural students
Criteria: Applicant must be a U.S. citizen at least 18 years of age with limited experience studying horticulture (one summer's employment or the equivalent). Award is to study horticulture at the Threave School of Gardening in Scotland for a period of one year starting the second week in August. Applicant must have a high school diploma and good academic standing. An interview, preferably at the NJHA convention, is required.
Contact: Dr. Joe Maxson, Executive Secretary.

51   Scotts Company Scholars

Golf Course Superintendents Association of America Foundation
1421 Research Park Drive
Lawrence, KS 66049
(913) 832-4445, (913) 832-4433 (fax)
fundmail@gcsaa.org
http://www.gcsaa.org
Average award: $2,500
Number of awards: 2
Deadline: March 8
College level: Freshman, Sophomore, Junior, Senior
Criteria: Applicant must be interested in a career in the green industry. Preference is given to students from diverse socio-economic and cultural backgrounds. Awarded every year.
Contact: Jack Schwartz, Director of Development.

52   Student Essay Contest

Golf Course Superintendents Association of America Foundation
1421 Research Park Drive
Lawrence, KS 66049
(913) 832-4445, (913) 832-4433 (fax)
fundmail@gcsaa.org
http://www.gcsaa.org
Average award: $600
Maximum award: $1,000
Minimum award: $400
Number of awards: 3
Deadline: March 31
College level: Sophomore, Junior, Senior, Graduate, Doctoral
Majors/Fields: Agronomy, turfgrass science, golf course management
Criteria: Applicant must submit essay focusing on the relationship between golf courses and the environment. Awarded every year.
Contact: Jack Schwartz, Director of Development.

53   Timothy Bigelow Scholarship

Horticultural Research Institute, Inc.
1250 Eye Street, NW
Suite 500
Washington, DC 20005
(202) 789-2900, (202) 789-1893 (fax)
Maximum award: $2,500
Number of awards: 2
Deadline: May 15
College level: Junior, Senior, Graduate
Majors/Fields: Landscape, horticulture, or related major
Criteria: Applicant must be a resident of Connecticut, Maine, Massachusetts, New Hampshire, Rhode Island, or Vermont, with a minimum 2.25 GPA (3.0 for graduate students), who is enrolled full-time in an accredited program at a two- or four-year institution. Awarded every year.
Contact: Mrs. Ashby Ruden, Director of Horticultural Research.

54   Vocational Scholarship

Bedding Plants Foundation, Inc.
P.O. Box 27241
Lansing, MI 48909
Average award: $2,000
Deadline: April 1
College level: Any student accepted into a one-or-two year program who will be enrolled for the entire next year
Majors/Fields: Horticulture
Criteria: Applicant must have intentions of becoming a floriculture plant producer and/or operations manager upon completion of studies. Applicant must include transcript, and statement of intent. Selection will be based upon financial need and scholastic record. Awarded every year.

Wildlife Resources/Management——

55   Rockefeller State Wildlife Scholarship

Louisiana Office of Student Financial Assistance
P.O. Box 91202
Baton Rouge, LA 70821-9202
(504) 922-1012, (504) 922-1089 (fax)
Average award: $1,000
Number of awards: 60
Deadline: April 1
College level: Freshman, Sophomore, Junior, Senior, Graduate, Doctoral
Majors/Fields: Forestry, wildlife, marine science
Criteria: Applicant must be a U.S. citizen or eligible noncitizen, be a resident of Louisiana, enroll full-time in a Louisiana public college or university, and have a minimum 2.5 GPA. FAFSA must be postmarked by March 15. Minimum 2.5 GPA required for renewal. Awarded every year.
Contact: Winona Kahao, Director of Scholarship/Grant Division, (504) 922-1038.

Allied Health

Allied Health

56   Allied Health/Lettie Pate Whitehead Scholarship

Georgia State University
P.O. Box 4040
Atlanta, GA 30302
(404) 651-2227, (404) 651-3418 (fax)
http://www.gsu.edu
Average award: $300
Maximum award: $1,500
Number of awards: 80
Deadline: None
College level: Freshman, Sophomore, Junior, Senior, Graduate
Majors/Fields: Allied health
Criteria: Applicant must be a resident of one of nine southern states and demonstrate financial need. Selection is based upon academics. Awarded every year. Award may be used only at sponsoring institution.
Contact: Gwyn Francis, Director of Financial Aid.

57   Annual Scholarship Program

Physician Assistant Foundation of the American Academy of Physician Assistants
950 N. Washington Street
Alexandria, VA 22314
(703) 836-2272, extension 3113
http://www.aapa.org
Maximum award: $5,000
Maximum number of awards: 50
Minimum number of awards: 40
Deadline: February 1
College level: Students enrolled in CAHEA/CAPHEP-accredited PA Program
Majors/Fields: Physician assistant
Criteria: Applicant must be enrolled in a CAHEA-accredited physician assistant program, and be a member of the American Academy of Physician Assistants. Selection is based upon financial need, commitment/involvement to the profession, and academic record. Awarded every year.
Contact: Barbara Taylor, Program Coordinator, (703) 836-2272, ext. 3113.

58   Constance L. Lloyd/ACMPE Scholarship

American College of Medical Practice Executives (ACMPE)
104 Inverness Terrace East
Englewood, CO 80112-5306
(303) 799-1111
Average award: $1,000
Deadline: June 1
College level: Freshman, Sophomore, Junior, Senior, Graduate, Doctoral
Majors/Fields: Heath care
Criteria: Applicant must be a woman enrolled at an accredited college or university in Georgia. Applicant must submit a letter stating career goals and objectives, a resume showing employment history with a brief narrative describing specific employment responsibilities in health care field, and three letters of recommendation. Reference letters should address performance, character, potential to succeed, and need for scholarship support. Awarded every year.
Contact: Laurie Draizen, Executive Assistant, (303) 799-1111, extension 206.

59   Dean's Scholarship

Thomas Jefferson University, College of Allied Health Sciences
130 South Ninth Street
Philadelphia, PA 19107
(215) 955-6531
Average award: $5,000
Number of awards: 18
Deadline: None
College level: Junior
Majors/Fields: Diagnostic imaging, laboratory sciences, nursing, occupational therapy, physical therapy
Criteria: Selection is based upon academic record. Minimum 3.0 GPA is required to retain scholarship. Awarded every year. Award may be used only at sponsoring institution.
Contact: Bonnie Lee Behm, Director of Financial Aid, (215) 955-1957.

60   FORE Undergraduate Scholarship

Foundation of Record Education (FORE) of American Health Information Management Association (AHIMA)
919 North Michigan Avenue
Suite 1400
Chicago, IL 60611-1683
(312) 787-2672
Average award: $1,500
Number of awards: 2
Deadline: July 1
College level: Sophomore, Junior, Senior
Majors/Fields: Health information management, health information technology
Criteria: Applicant must have been accepted for admission into a CAHEA-approved program. Awarded every year.
Contact: Scholarship Committee, (312) 787-2672, extension 302.

61   Health Careers Scholarship

International Order of the King's Daughters and Sons
P.O. Box 1310
Brookhaven, MS 39601
(601) 883-5418
Maximum award: $1,000
Number of awards: 50
Deadline: April 1
College level: Junior
Majors/Fields: Dentistry, medical technology, medicine, nursing, occupational therapy, pharmacy, physical therapy
Criteria: Applicant must be a U.S. or Canadian citizen enrolled in an accredited school of study in the U.S. or Canada. Pre-med students are not eligible. Enclose a stamped, self-addressed, business-sized envelope with inquiry. Updated application, financial statement, and transcript are required to retain scholarship. Awarded every year.
Contact: Mrs. Fred Cannon, Health Careers Director.

62 Home for Aged Women Scholarship

Shawnee State University
940 Second Street
Portsmouth, OH 45662-4344
(614) 355-2237
Maximum award: $2,000
Number of awards: 24
Deadline: April 15
College level: Freshman, Sophomore
Majors/Fields: Health sciences
Criteria: Applicant must be a woman, be pursuing an associate degree, be studious, and demonstrate financial need. Early application is recommended. Two awards are for $2,000 each, two for $1,000 each, 20 for $500 each. Awarded every year. Award may be used only at sponsoring institution.
Contact: Financial Aid Office, (614) 355-2485.

63 J.D. Archbold Memorial Hospital Scholarship

J. D. Archbold Memorial Hospital
Department of Education
P.O. Box 1018
Thomasville, GA 31799
(912) 228-2795
Average award: $2,000
Number of awards: 25
Deadline: None
College level: Junior, Senior
Majors/Fields: Health care
Criteria: Applicant must be in the last two years of an undergraduate program in a health care field utilized by the hospital and must commit to three years full-time employment at Archbold Medical Center after graduation. Awarded every year.
Contact: Donna C. McMillan, Assistant to the Director of Education.

64 Marcelle Dodson Estes Scholarship

University of West Florida
11000 University Parkway
Pensacola, FL 32514-5750
(904) 474-2400
Maximum award: $1,100
Deadline: None
College level: Sophomore, Junior, Senior, graduate students
Majors/Fields: Health-related discipline
Criteria: Preference is given to nursing major. Scholarship is renewable. Awarded every year. Award may be used only at sponsoring institution.
Contact: Nursing Department, (904) 474-2881.

65 Maxine Williams Scholarship Program

American Association of Medical Assistants' Endowment
20 North Wacker Drive
Suite 1575
Chicago, IL 60606
(312) 899-1500
Maximum award: $1,000
Number of awards: 6
Deadline: February 1; June 1
College level: Freshman, Sophomore
Majors/Fields: Medical assisting
Criteria: Selection is based upon interest in and a commitment to a career in medical assisting, financial need, and aptitude. Award is limited to individuals enrolled or soon to be enrolled in a post-secondary program accredited by the Commission on Accreditation of Allied Health Education Programs (CAAHEP). Students studying other allied health professions or planning to enter medical school are not eligible. Awarded every year.
Contact: Deborah Murphy, Director of Operations.

66 National AMBUCS Scholarship for Therapists

AMBUCS
P.O. Box 5127
High Point, NC 27262
(910) 888-6052
Maximum award: $1,500
Deadline: April 15
College level: Junior, Senior, Graduate, Doctoral
Majors/Fields: Hearing audiology, music therapy, occupational therapy, physical therapy, recreational therapy, speech language pathology
Criteria: Applicant must be U.S. citizen, have a minimum 3.0 GPA, and be accepted into an accredited program. Assistant programs are not eligible. Selection is based upon financial need, academic record, motivation, application form, and IRS Form 1040. Send self-addressed, stamped envelope for application. Awarded every year.
Contact: Scholarships.

67 Professional Scholarship

Maryland Higher Education Commission
State Scholarship Administration
16 Francis Street
Annapolis, MD 21401-1781
(410) 974-5370, (410) 974-5994 (fax)
http://www.ubalt.edu/www/mhec
Average award: $625
Maximum award: $1,000
Minimum award: $200
Number of awards: 240
Deadline: March 1
College level: Freshman, Sophomore, Junior, Senior, Graduate, Doctoral
Majors/Fields: Dentistry, law, medicine, nursing, pharmacy
Criteria: Scholarship is renewable. Awarded every year. Award may be used at eligible Maryland schools only.
Contact: Lula Caldwell, Program Administrator.

68 Rehabilitation Training Program

U.S. Department of Education Rehabilitation Services Administration (RSA)
Division of Resource Development
Washington, DC 20202-2649
(202) 205-9400
Average award: $4,000
College level: Junior, Senior, Graduate, Doctoral
Majors/Fields: Rehabilitation
Criteria: Awards are granted to institutions of higher education, which in turn, award scholarships directly to students. Applicant should contact colleges directly to learn the availability and requirements for awards and contact RSA to obtain a list of colleges with RSA grants. All scholars must meet a work-or-repay requirement by working for a specified period after completing education in a state rehabilitation agency or related program. Scholarship is renewable.
Contact: Dr. Richard P. Melia, Director of Division of Resource Development, U.S. Department of Education, Mail Stop 2649, Washington, DC 20202.

69 Smart Corporation Scholarship

Foundation of Record Education (FORE) of American Health Information Management Association (AHIMA)
919 North Michigan Avenue
Suite 1400
Chicago, IL 60611-1683
(312) 787-2672
Average award: $1,100
Number of awards: 1
Deadline: July 1
College level: Sophomore, Junior, Senior
Majors/Fields: Health information management, health information technology
Criteria: Applicant must have been accepted for admission into a CAHEA-approved program. Awarded every year.
Contact: (312) 787-2672, extension 302.

70   Suburban Hospital Scholarship

Suburban Hospital Scholarship Program
Office of Personnel
8600 Old Georgetown Road
Bethesda, MD 20814
(301) 530-3850
Maximum award: $5,000
Number of awards: 8
Deadline: April 30
College level: Junior, Senior, Graduate
Majors/Fields: Medical technology, nursing, occupational therapy, physical therapy, physician assistant, radiology technology, respiratory therapy
Criteria: Applicant must reside in the metropolitan Washington, D.C. area, have a minimum 2.5 GPA, and be within four semesters of graduation from a nursing, radiology technology, respiratory therapy, medical technology, physical therapy, occupational therapy, or physician assistant program. Minimum 2.5 GPA is required to retain scholarship. Awarded every year.
Contact: Beth Murphy, Employment Manager.

71   Transcriptions, Ltd. Scholarship

Foundation of Record Education (FORE) of American Health Information Management Association (AHIMA)
919 North Michigan Avenue
Suite 1400
Chicago, IL 60611-1683
(312) 787-2672
Maximum award: $3,000
Number of awards: 2
Deadline: July 1
College level: Sophomore, Junior, Senior, Graduate, Doctoral
Majors/Fields: Health information management (undergraduate or graduate), health information technology (undergraduate)
Criteria: Applicant must be enrolled in a CAHEA-approved program. Awarded every year.
Contact: Scholarship Committee, (312) 787-2672, extension 302.

Dental/Medical Assistancy

72   ADHA Certificate/Associate Degree Scholarship

American Dental Hygienists' Association (ADHA)
444 North Michigan Avenue
Suite 3400
Chicago, IL 60611
(312) 440-8900
Maximum award: $1,000
Number of awards: 25
Deadline: June 15
College level: Freshman
Majors/Fields: Dental hygiene
Criteria: Applicant must be enrolled full time in a certificate or associate degree program leading to licensure as a dental hygienist, demonstrate community service, leadership, and extracurricular involvement, and have a minimum cumulative 3.0 GPA (minimum 3.0 GPA in secondary school natural science courses or pre-dental hygiene college courses).
Contact: Scholarships.

73   ADHA Scholarship

American Dental Hygienists' Association (ADHA)
444 North Michigan Avenue
Suite 3400
Chicago, IL 60611
(312) 440-8900
Average award: $1,250
Maximum award: $1,500
Minimum award: $1,000
Number of awards: 34
Deadline: April 1
College level: Sophomore, Junior, Senior, Graduate, Doctoral
Majors/Fields: Dental hygiene
Criteria: Applicant must document financial need of at least $1,500, be enrolled in a full-time dental hygiene program in the U.S., have completed a minimum of one year of dental hygiene curriculum, and have a minimum 3.0 GPA. Selection for some awards is based upon minority status, academic performance, or degree status. Awarded every year.
Contact: Cyndi Weingard, Associate Administrator, (312) 440-8944.

74   Dental Assisting Scholarship

American Dental Association (ADA) Endowment and Assistance Fund, Inc.
211 East Chicago Avenue
17th Floor
Chicago, IL 60611-2678
(312) 440-2567
Average award: $1,000
Number of awards: 25
Deadline: September 15
College level: Freshman
Majors/Fields: Dental assisting
Criteria: Applicant must be a U.S. citizen entering a full-time, ADA-accredited program and have a minimum 2.8 GPA. Selection is based upon financial need, academic achievement, and personal and professional goals. Awarded every year.
Contact: Marsha Mountz, ADA Endowment Fund.

75   Dental Hygiene Scholarship

American Dental Association (ADA) Endowment and Assistance Fund, Inc.
211 East Chicago Avenue
17th Floor
Chicago, IL 60611-2678
(312) 440-2567
Average award: $1,000
Number of awards: 25
Deadline: August 15
College level: Second-year dental hygiene students
Majors/Fields: Dental hygiene
Criteria: Applicant must be a U.S. citizen enrolled full-time as a second-year student at an ADA-accredited dental hygiene school and have a minimum 2.8 GPA. Selection is based upon financial need, academic achievement, and personal and professional goals. Scholarship is renewable. Awarded every year.
Contact: Marsha Mountz, ADA Endowment Fund.

76   Dental Lab Tech Scholarship

American Dental Association (ADA) Endowment and Assistance Fund, Inc.
211 East Chicago Avenue
17th Floor
Chicago, IL 60611-2678
(312) 440-2567
Average award: $1,000
Number of awards: 25
Deadline: August 15
College level: Freshman, Sophomore
Majors/Fields: Dental laboratory technology
Criteria: Applicant must be a U.S. citizen, an entering or first-year student at an ADA-accredited dental laboratory technology school, and have a minimum 2.8 GPA. Selection is based upon financial need, academic achievement, and personal and professional goals. Scholarship is renewable. Awarded every year.
Contact: Marsha Mountz, ADA Endowment Fund.

77   Juliette A. Southard Dental Assistant Teacher Education Scholarship

American Dental Assistants Association (ADAA)
203 North LaSalle Street
Suite 1320
Chicago, IL 60601-1550
(312) 664-3327
Maximum award: $2,000
Deadline: July 15
Majors/Fields: Dental assistant
Criteria: Applicant must be a U.S. citizen and an ADAA member currently certified or qualified for certification as a dental assistant. Scholarship is renewable if satisfactory progress is maintained.
Contact: Scholarships, 919 North Michigan Avenue, Chicago, IL 60611.

Dietetics/Food Science/Nutrition———————

78   ADA Scholarship

American Dietetic Association Foundation
216 West Jackson
Chicago, IL 60606
(312) 899-0040
Average award: $1,000
Maximum award: $3,000
Minimum award: $350
Number of awards: 150
Deadline: February 15
College level: Senior, Graduate, Doctoral
Majors/Fields: Dietetics
Criteria: Selection is based upon financial need, academic standing, and professional potential. Awarded every year.
Contact: Linda Maraba, ADA Foundation Team.

79   IFT Freshman/Sophomore Scholarship

Institute of Food Technologists (IFT)
Scholarship Department
221 North LaSalle Street
Chicago, IL 60601
(312) 782-8424, (312) 782-8348 (fax)
Maximum award: $1,000
Number of awards: 30
Deadline: February 15 (freshman); March 1 (sophomore)
College level: Freshman, Sophomore
Majors/Fields: Food science, food technology
Criteria: Applicant must be pursuing an approved program in food science/technology. Freshman applicant must be a scholastically outstanding high school graduate or senior entering college for the first time. Sophomore applicant must have a minimum 2.5 GPA and recommendations from the department head and another faculty member. Reapplication is required to retain scholarship. Awarded every year. Award may be used at approved schools only.
Contact: Patti Pagliuco, Fellowship/Scholarship Program Administrator.

80   IFT Junior/Senior Scholarship

Institute of Food Technologists (IFT)
Scholarship Department
221 North LaSalle Street
Chicago, IL 60601
(312) 782-8424, (312) 782-8348 (fax)
Maximum award: $2,000
Number of awards: 64
Deadline: February 1
College level: Junior, Senior
Majors/Fields: Food engineering, food science, food technology, quality assurance
Criteria: Applicant must be a scholastically outstanding sophomore or junior enrolled in an approved food science/technology program, or a sophomore transfer into such a program. The IFT Food Engineering Division scholarship encourages the pursuit of activities in food engineering in an ABET-accredited engineering major or an IFT-approved program. Reapplication is required to retain scholarship. Awarded every year. Approved schools only.
Contact: Patti Pagliuco, Scholarship Program Administrator.

81   Nestle Frozen Food Company Scholarship

Clemson University
G-01 Sikes Hall
Clemson, SC 29634-5123
(803) 656-2280
Average award: $1,500
Number of awards: 1
Deadline: March 1
College level: Freshman, Sophomore, Junior, Senior
Majors/Fields: Food science
Criteria: Applicant must have a minimum 2.5 GPA. Award may be used only at sponsoring institution.
Contact: Scholarships.

Medical Technology———————

82   AMT Student Scholarship

American Medical Technologists (AMT)
710 Higgins Road
Park Ridge, IL 60068
(847) 823-5169
Average award: $250
Number of awards: 5
Deadline: April 1
College level: Freshman
Majors/Fields: Dental assisting, medical technology, medical assisting, phlebotomy
Criteria: Applicant must demonstrate academic qualifications and financial need and be a U.S. resident. Awarded every year.
Contact: Lillian Peska, Scholarship Coordinator.

83   ASCP/AMS Scholarship

American Society of Clinical Pathologists (ASCP)
2100 West Harrison Street
Chicago, IL 60612-3798
Maximum award: $1,000
Number of awards: 50
Deadline: October 31
College level: Students in final clinical year of study
Majors/Fields: Cytotechnology, histologic technician/histotechnologist, medical laboratory technician, medical technologist
Criteria: Applicant must be a U.S. citizen or permanent resident alien enrolled in an accredited program, demonstrate financial need and academic qualifications, and submit three recommendations. Awarded every year.
Contact: Jennifer Joos, Scholarship Coordinator, (312) 738-1336, jenniferj@ascp.org.

84   Medical Technology Scholarship

Daemen College
4380 Main Street
Amherst, NY 14226
(716) 839-8254, (716) 839-8516 (fax)
http://www.daemen.edu
Average award: $2,000
Deadline: None
College level: Freshman, Sophomore, Junior, Senior, Graduate
Majors/Fields: Medical technology
Criteria: Scholarship is renewable. Awarded every year. Award may be used only at sponsoring institution.
Contact: Laura Worley, Director of Financial Aid.

Pharmacy

85   American Drug Stores Scholarship

University of Utah
Financial Aid and Scholarships Office
105 Student Services Building
Salt Lake City, UT 84112
(801) 581-6211
Average award: $1,250
Number of awards: 4
Deadline: February 1
College level: Junior, Senior
Majors/Fields: Pharmacy
Criteria: Applicant must be in the last two years of a B.S. pharmacy program, enroll for a minimum of 12 credit hours per quarter, and be interested in the community practice of pharmacy. Reapplication is required to retain scholarship. Awarded every year. Award may be used only at sponsoring institution.
Contact: Dr. Jan Bair, A050 University Hospital, Salt Lake City, UT 84112, (801) 581-2147.

86   Eckerd Pharmacy Student Financial Assistance Scholarship

Eckerd Pharmacy Assistance Program
P.O. Box 4689
Clearwater, FL 34618
(813) 399-6821, (813) 399-7637 (fax)
http://www.eckerd.com
Maximum award: $2,000
Number of awards: 120
Deadline: May 1
College level: College students accepted into an accredited school of pharmacy
Majors/Fields: Pharmacy
Criteria: Reapplication is required to retain scholarship. Awarded every year.
Contact: Karen Hutchins, Pharmacy Recruiting Manager, 8333 Bryan Dairy Road, Clearwater, FL 34618, 71111.1511@compuserve.com.

87   Ewart A. Swinyard Scholarship

University of Utah
Financial Aid and Scholarships Office
105 Student Services Building
Salt Lake City, UT 84112
(801) 581-6211
Maximum award: $1,500
Number of awards: 7
Deadline: February 1
College level: Sophomore, Junior, Senior, Graduate, Doctoral
Majors/Fields: Pharmacy
Criteria: Applicant must enroll in the pharmacy program for at least 12 credit hours per quarter. Reapplication is required to retain scholarship. Awarded every year. Award may be used only at sponsoring institution.
Contact: Dr. Jan Bair, A050 University Hospital, Salt Lake City, UT 84112, (801) 581-2147.

88   Grace P. Swinyard Memorial Scholarship

University of Utah
Financial Aid and Scholarships Office
105 Student Services Building
Salt Lake City, UT 84112
(801) 581-6211
Maximum award: $1,500
Number of awards: 7
Deadline: February 1
College level: Sophomore, Junior, Senior, Graduate, Doctoral
Majors/Fields: Pharmacy
Criteria: Applicant must enroll in the pharmacy program for at least 12 credit hours per quarter. Preference is given to female applicants. Reapplication is required to retain scholarship. Awarded every year. Award may be used only at sponsoring institution.
Contact: Dr. Jan Bair, A050 University Hospital, Salt Lake City, UT 84112, (801) 581-2147.

89   Pay Less Drugs Scholarship

University of Utah
Financial Aid and Scholarships Office
105 Student Services Building
Salt Lake City, UT 84112
(801) 581-6211
Average award: $3,000
Number of awards: 3
Deadline: February 1
College level: Junior, Senior
Majors/Fields: Pharmacy
Criteria: Applicant must be in the last two years of a B.S. pharmacy program, enroll for at least 12 credit hours per quarter, and be interested in the community practice of pharmacy. Reapplication is required to retain scholarship. Awarded every year. Award may be used only at sponsoring institution.
Contact: Dr. Jan Bair, A050 University Hospital, Salt Lake City, UT 84112, (801) 581-2147.

90   Presidential Scholarship

NARD Foundation
205 Daingerfield Road
Alexandria, VA 22314-6973
(703) 683-8200, (703) 683-3619 (fax)
http://www.ncpanet.org
Average award: $2,000
Number of awards: 14
Deadline: Spring
Majors/Fields: Pharmacy
Criteria: Applicant must be a full-time student. Selection is based upon academic achievement, leadership qualities, career objectives, and extracurricular accomplishments. Awarded every year. Award may be used at U.S. schools only
Contact: Debbie Tankersely, Scholarships.

91   Smith's Food and Drug Center Scholarship

University of Utah
Financial Aid and Scholarships Office
105 Student Services Building
Salt Lake City, UT 84112
(801) 581-6211
Average award: $2,500
Number of awards: 2
Deadline: February 1
College level: Junior, Senior
Majors/Fields: Pharmacy
Criteria: Applicant must be in the last two years of a B.S. Pharmacy program, enroll for at least 12 credit hours per quarter, and be interested in the community practice of pharmacy. Reapplication is required to retain scholarship. Awarded every year. Award may be used only at sponsoring institution.
Contact: Dr. Jan Bair, A050 University Hospital, Salt Lake City, UT 84112, (801) 581-2147.

92 Undergraduate Research Fellowship in Pharmaceutics

Pharmaceutical Research and Manufacturers of America Foundation, Inc.
1100 15th Street, NW
Washington, DC 20005
(202) 835-3470
Average award: $5,000
Number of awards: 10
Deadline: October 1
College level: Pharmacy school students
Majors/Fields: Biology, chemistry, pharmacy
Criteria: Award is to stimulate undergraduate students to pursue advanced degrees in pharmaceutics. Awarded every year.
Contact: Donna Moore, Director of Programs.

Physical/Occupational Therapy——————

93 NSDAR Occupational Therapy Scholarships

National Society of the Daughters of the American Revolution (NSDAR)
NSDAR Administration Building, Office of the Committees
1776 D Street, NW
Washington, DC 20006-5392
(202) 879-3292
Average award: $500
Number of awards: 10
Deadline: February 15, August 15
College level: Freshman, Sophomore, Junior, Senior, Graduate, Doctoral
Majors/Fields: Occupational therapy, physical therapy
Criteria: Applicant must be a U.S. citizen and submit a letter of sponsorship from a local DAR chapter. All inquiries must include a self-addressed, stamped envelope. Awarded every year.
Contact: Administrative Assistant, Office of the Committees/Scholarships.

94 Occupational Therapist and Physical Therapist Scholarship/Loan

Florida Department of Education
Office of Student Financial Assistance
255 Collins
Tallahassee, FL 32399-0400
(904) 487-0049
Maximum award: $4,000
Deadline: April 15
College level: Sophomore, Junior, Senior, Graduate
Majors/Fields: Occupational therapy, physical therapy
Criteria: Applicant must be enrolled full time in a therapist assistant or therapist program at an eligible Florida institution, meet the registration requirements of the Selective Service System, have participated in the college-level communication and computation skills testing (CLAST) program, and declare intent to be employed for a minimum of three years as a licensed therapist in Florida public schools. Failure to fulfill employment obligation will convert scholarship to a loan. Renewable if undergraduate recipient maintains a minimum 2.0 GPA and earns a minimum 12 credit hours per term; graduate recipient must maintain a minimum 3.0 GPA and earn a minimum of nine credit hours per term. Awarded every year.
Contact: Dr. Cynthia Burton, BSSEE.

95 Physical and Occupational Therapists and Assistants Grant

Maryland Higher Education Commission
State Scholarship Administration
16 Francis Street
Annapolis, MD 21401-1781
(410) 974-5370, (410) 974-5994 (fax)
http://www.ubalt.edu/www/mhec
Average award: $1,583
Maximum award: $2,000
Number of awards: 12
Deadline: July 1
College level: Freshman, Sophomore, Junior, Senior
Majors/Fields: Occupational therapy, occupational therapy assistant, physical therapy, physical therapy assistant
Criteria: Applicant must be a Maryland resident, full-time student, and agree to serve as a therapist or assistant to handicapped children in Maryland public schools for one year for each year of the award. Scholarship is renewable. Awarded every year. Award may be used at eligible Maryland schools only.
Contact: Margaret Riley, Program Administrator.

96 Physical Therapy Scholarship

Ordean Foundation
501 Ordean Building
Duluth, MN 55802
(218) 726-4785
Maximum award: $2,000
Number of awards: 20
Deadline: April 1
College level: Junior, Senior
Majors/Fields: Physical therapy
Criteria: Applicant must have a minimum 2.8 GPA, and be a resident of Duluth, Minn., or surrounding government entity in St. Louis County, Minn. Selection is based upon financial need. Renewal is based upon continuing financial need. Awarded every year. Award may be used at College of St. Scholastica only.
Contact: Julie Ledermann, Financial Aid Coordinator, College of Saint Scholastica, 1200 Kenwood Avenue, Duluth, MN 55811, (218) 723-6656.

Respiratory Therapy——————

97 ARCF Scholarship

American Respiratory Care Foundation (ARCF)
11030 Ables Lane
Dallas, TX 75229
(972) 243-2272
Average award: $1,250
Number of awards: 1
Deadline: June 30
College level: Sophomore
Majors/Fields: Respiratory therapy
Criteria: Applicant must be a first- or second-year student, a U.S. citizen, enrolled in an AMA-approved respiratory care training program, have a minimum 3.0 GPA, have written an original reference paper on respiratory care, and submit recommendations from the program director and medical director. Awarded every year.
Contact: Joy Rea, Administrator.

98   ARCF Scholarship

American Association for Respiratory Care
11030 Ables Lane
Dallas, TX 75229-4593
(972) 243-2272
Average award: $1,250
Number of awards: 1
Deadline: June 30
College level: Sophomore
Majors/Fields: Respiratory therapy
Criteria: Applicant must be enrolled full-time at a CAAHEP-approved school of respiratory therapy, have a minimum 3.0 GPA, and must submit an original essay on some facet of respiratory care. This essay is the major basis for selection. Awarded every year.
Contact: Scholarships.

99   Jimmy A. Young Memorial Scholarship

American Association for Respiratory Care
11030 Ables Lane
Dallas, TX 75229-4593
(972) 243-2272
Average award: $1,000
Number of awards: 1
Deadline: June 30
College level: Sophomore, Junior, Senior
Majors/Fields: Respiratory therapy
Criteria: Applicant must be a minority student enrolled full-time at a CAAHEP-approved school of respiratory therapy and must submit an original essay on some facet of respiratory care. This essay is the major basis for selection. Awarded every year.
Contact: Scholarships.

100   Jimmy A. Young Memorial Scholarship

American Respiratory Care Foundation (ARCF)
11030 Ables Lane
Dallas, TX 75229
(972) 243-2272
Average award: $1,000
Number of awards: 1
Deadline: June 30
College level: Sophomore
Majors/Fields: Respiratory therapy
Criteria: Applicant must be a U.S. citizen of minority origin, be enrolled in an AMA-approved respiratory care training program, have a minimum 3.0 GPA, submit an original reference paper on respiratory care, and submit letters of recommendation from the program director and medical director. Awarded every year.
Contact: Joy Rea, Administrator.

101   Robert M. Lawrence Scholarship

American Association for Respiratory Care
11030 Ables Lane
Dallas, TX 75229-4593
(972) 243-2272
Average award: $2,500
Number of awards: 1
Deadline: June 30
College level: Junior, Senior
Majors/Fields: Respiratory therapy
Criteria: Applicant must be enrolled full-time at a CAAHEP-approved school of respiratory therapy and must submit an original referenced paper and an essay describing how the award will assist the applicant. Awarded every year.
Contact: Scholarships.

102   William W. Burgin Scholarship

American Association for Respiratory Care
11030 Ables Lane
Dallas, TX 75229-4593
(972) 243-2272
Average award: $2,500
Number of awards: 1
Deadline: June 30
College level: Sophomore
Majors/Fields: Respiratory therapy
Criteria: Applicant must be enrolled full-time in an associate degree program at a CAAHEP-accredited school of respiratory therapy and must submit an original referenced paper and an essay describing how the award will assist the applicant. Awarded every year.
Contact: Scholarships.

Business

Accounting

103 Accounting Alumni Scholarship
The University of Alabama
Box 870162
Tuscaloosa, AL 35487-0162
(205) 348-6756
Average award: $2,470
Number of awards: 1
Deadline: January
College level: Sophomore, Junior, Senior
Majors/Fields: Accounting
Criteria: Awarded every year. Award may be used only at sponsoring institution.
Contact: Culverhouse School of Accountancy, Box 870220, Tuscaloosa, AL 35487-0220.

104 AICPA Minority Scholarship
The University of Alabama
Box 870162
Tuscaloosa, AL 35487-0162
(205) 348-6756
Average award: $2,470
Number of awards: 1
Deadline: December 1 (spring); July 1 (fall)
College level: Sophomore, Junior, Senior
Majors/Fields: Accounting
Criteria: Applicant must be member of a minority. Awarded twice each year. Award may be used only at sponsoring institution.
Contact: AICPA, 1211 Avenue of the Americas, New York, NY 10036-8775.

105 Alumni Association of Coopers & Lybrand Scholarship
University of Calgary
Department of Financial Aid
2500 University Drive, NW
Calgary, Alberta, CN T2N 1N4
(403) 220-7872, (403) 282-2999 (fax)
Average award: $1,250
Number of awards: 2
Deadline: June 15
College level: Senior
Majors/Fields: Accounting, management
Criteria: Applicant must be interested in a career as a chartered accountant. Both awards are based upon academic merit; one also considers Applicant's demonstration of leadership abilities through extracurricular activities. Awarded every year. Award may be used only at sponsoring institution.
Contact: J. Van Housen, Director of Student Awards/Financial Aid.

106 Artesia Data Systems, Inc. Scholarship
New Mexico State University
Box 30001
Department 5100
Las Cruces, NM 88003-0001
(505) 646-4105
Average award: Full tuition
Number of awards: 2
Deadline: March 1
College level: Sophomore, Junior, Senior
Majors/Fields: Accounting, business computer systems
Criteria: Selection by the faculty is based upon academic performance and financial need. Awarded every year. Award may be used only at sponsoring institution.
Contact: Advising Center, College of Business Administration and Economics, (505) 646-4084.

107 Arthur H. Carter Scholarship
American Accounting Association (AAA)
5717 Bessie Drive
Sarasota, FL 34233
(941) 921-7747, (941) 923-4093 (fax)
Average award: $2,500
Maximum number of awards: 50
Minimum number of awards: 40
Deadline: April 1
College level: Junior, Senior, Graduate
Majors/Fields: Accounting
Criteria: Applicant must be a U.S. citizen, be enrolled for at least 12 semester hours in a school that is an member of the AACSB or ACBSP, and take at least two accounting-related courses. Applicant must submit letters of recommendation and transcripts. Awarded every year.
Contact: Mary Cole, Office Manager.

108 Arthur H. Carter Scholarship
The University of Alabama
Box 870162
Tuscaloosa, AL 35487-0162
(205) 348-6756
Average award: $2,500
Number of awards: 1
Deadline: April 1
College level: Junior, Senior, Graduate
Majors/Fields: Accounting
Criteria: Reapplication is required for renewal. Awarded every year. Award may be used only at sponsoring institution.
Contact: Paige Cooper, Scholarship Coordinator.

109 ASWA Scholarship
American Society of Women Accountants (ASWA)
1255 Lynnfield
Suite 257
Memphis, TN 38119-7235
(901) 680-0470
Average award: $2,000
Minimum award: $1,000
Number of awards: 3
Deadline: January 31
College level: Junior, Senior
Majors/Fields: Accounting
Criteria: Applicant must be a female accounting major with a minimum 3.0 GPA, have completed at least 60 semester hours, and demonstrate financial need. Awarded every year.
Contact: Scholarships.

110 Deloitte & Touche Scholarship
Georgia State University
P.O. Box 4040
Atlanta, GA 30302
(404) 651-2227, (404) 651-3418 (fax)
http://www.gsu.edu
Average award: $2,100
Number of awards: 1
Deadline: November 15
College level: Junior
Majors/Fields: Accounting
Criteria: Applicant must demonstrate the academic and leadership skills required to succeed in public accounting. Renewable for one year if recipient maintains satisfactory progress. Awarded every year. Award may be used only at sponsoring institution.
Contact: School of Accountancy, (404) 651-2611.

111   Ernst and Whinney Foundation Scholarship

Ernst and Whinney Foundation Scholarship
2000 National City Center
Cleveland, OH 44114
(216) 861-5000
Average award: $18,000
Maximum number of awards: 6
Minimum number of awards: 5
Deadline: June 1
Criteria: Applicant must plan to teach after completing studies. Accounting applicants must have had three years of accounting work experience in the U.S. Awarded every year.
Contact: Scholarship.

112   IAIEF Scholarship

Independent Accountants International Educational Foundation (IAIEF), Inc.
9200 South Dadeland Boulevard Suite 510
Miami, FL 33156
(305) 670-0580, (305) 670-3818 (fax)
iaintl@accountants.org
http://www.accountants.org
Maximum award: $2,500
Maximum number of awards: 30
Minimum number of awards: 14
Deadline: February 28
College level: Junior, Senior, Graduate, Doctoral
Majors/Fields: Accounting
Criteria: Awarded every year.
Contact: Pat Marsh, General Assistant.

113   IMA/Stuart Cameron and Margaret McLeod Scholarship

Institute of Management Accountants (IMA)
10 Paragon Drive
Montvale, NJ 07645-1760
(800) 638-4427, (201) 573-0559 (fax)
Maximum award: $3,000
Number of awards: 18
Deadline: February 15
College level: Junior, Senior, Graduate
Majors/Fields: Financial management, management accounting
Criteria: Awarded every year.
Contact: Carl S. Basso, CMA, Regional Executive.

114   John T. Steed Accounting Scholarship

University of Oklahoma
University Affairs
900 Asp Avenue, Room 236
Norman, OK 73019-0401
(405) 325-1701
Average award: $2,500
Number of awards: 1
Deadline: February 8
College level: Freshman
Majors/Fields: Accounting
Criteria: Selection is based upon GPA, class rank, test scores, and commitment to accounting. Award is for four years. Awarded every year. Award may be used only at sponsoring institution.
Contact: School of Accounting, 200 Adams Hall, (405) 325-4221.

115   Kerr McGee Corporation Student Scholarship

University of Oklahoma
University Affairs
900 Asp Avenue, Room 236
Norman, OK 73019-0401
(405) 325-1701
Average award: $4,000
Number of awards: 1
Deadline: February 7
College level: Junior
Majors/Fields: Accounting
Criteria: Applicant must be an Oklahoma resident. Scholarship is renewable. Awarded every year. Award may be used only at sponsoring institution.
Contact: School of Accounting, 200 Adams Hall, (405) 325-4221.

116   Ledger & Quill Scholarship

DePaul University
1 East Jackson Boulevard
Chicago, IL 60604
(312) 362-8704, (312) 362-5749 (fax)
Average award: Full tuition
Number of awards: 2
Deadline: None
College level: Freshman
Majors/Fields: Accounting
Criteria: Applicant must rank in the top tenth of class, have a minimum composite ACT score of 27 (combined SAT I score of 1220) and demonstrate strong leadership and extracurricular involvement. Minimum 3.4 GPA as a full-time student in the School of Accountancy is required to retain scholarship. Awarded every year. Award may be used only at sponsoring institution.
Contact: Jennifer Sparrow, Scholarship Coordinator, jsparrow@wppost.depaul.edu.

117   Melvoin and Strobel Scholarships

DePaul University
1 East Jackson Boulevard
Chicago, IL 60604
(312) 362-8704, (312) 362-5749 (fax)
Average award: Half tuition
Number of awards: 2
Deadline: None
College level: Freshman
Majors/Fields: Accounting
Criteria: Applicant must have a minimum composite ACT score of 27 or combined SAT I score of 1220 and rank in the top tenth of class. Scholarship is renewable. Awarded every year. Award may be used only at sponsoring institution.
Contact: Jennifer Sparrow, Scholarship Coordinator, jsparrow@wppost.depaul.edu.

118   Michael J. McBride Scholarship

University of Northern Iowa
Financial Aid Office
Cedar Falls, IA 50613-0024
(319) 273-2700 or (800) 772-2736
Average award: Comprehensive tuition
Number of awards: 1
Deadline: Spring
College level: Freshman, Sophomore, Junior, Senior
Majors/Fields: Accounting
Criteria: Selection is based upon financial need, strong academic credentials, and strong leadership and citizenship qualities. Satisfactory scholastic achievement is required to retain scholarship. Awarded whenever current recipient graduates. Award may be used only at sponsoring institution.
Contact: Evelyn Waack, Scholarship Coordinator, Financial Aid, Cedar Falls, IA 50613-0024, (319) 273-2700 or (800) 772-2736.

119   NSPA Scholarship Award

National Society of Public Accountants (NSPA) Scholarship Foundation
1010 North Fairfax Street
Alexandria, VA 22314-1574
(703) 549-6400
Average award: $1,000
Minimum award: $500
Number of awards: 26
Deadline: March 10
College level: Sophomore, Junior, Senior
Majors/Fields: Accounting
Criteria: Applicant must be a U.S. or Canadian citizen majoring in accounting with a minimumgrade average of "B" in a full-time degree program at an accredited U.S. college or university. Awarded every year.
Contact: Susan E. Noell, Foundation Director.

120   Paul Garner/Arthur Andersen Scholarship

The University of Alabama
Box 870162
Tuscaloosa, AL 35487-0162
(205) 348-6756
Average award: $1,100
Number of awards: 1
Deadline: January
College level: Sophomore, Junior, Senior
Majors/Fields: Accounting
Criteria: Awarded every year. Award may be used only at sponsoring institution.
Contact: Culverhouse School of Accountancy, Box 870220, Tuscaloosa, AL 35487-0220.

121   Robert Kaufman Memorial Scholarship Fund

Independent Accountants International Educational Foundation (IAIEF), Inc.
9200 South Dadeland Boulevard
Suite 510
Miami, FL 33156
(305) 670-0580, (305) 670-3818 (fax)
iaintl@accountants.org
http://www.accountants.org
Maximum award: $1,500
Maximum number of awards: 30
Minimum number of awards: 12
Deadline: February 28
College level: Junior, Senior, Graduate, Doctoral
Majors/Fields: Accounting
Criteria: Awarded every year.
Contact: Pat Marsh, General Assistant.

122   Scholarships for Minority Accounting Students

American Institute of Certified Public Accountants
1211 Avenue of the Americas
New York, NY 10036-8775
(212) 596-6200
Maximum award: $5,000
Deadline: July 1
College level: Sophomore, Junior, Senior, Graduate, Doctoral
Majors/Fields: Accounting
Criteria: Applicant must be a U.S. citizen, have a minimum 3.0 GPA, and be either African-American, Hispanic, Native American, or Pacific Islander. Selection is based upon merit and academic achievement. Financial need is considered. Recipient must reapply for renewal. Awarded every year.
Contact: Scholarships.

123   William R. Bryden Memorial Scholarship

Northwood University – Midland Campus
3225 Cook Road
Midland, MI 48640-2398
(515) 837-4160
Average award: $1,500
Number of awards: 2
Majors/Fields: Accounting
Criteria: Applicant must be a U.S. citizen and demonstrate academic merit and financial need. Award may be used only at sponsoring institution.
Contact: Dixie Dee Maxwell.

Business Administration/ Management

124   ABWA Severn River Chapter Scholarship

American Business Women's Association (ABWA) Severn River Chapter
P.O. Box 6337
Annapolis, MD 21401-0337
Average award: $1,000
Maximum number of awards: 2
Minimum number of awards: 1
Deadline: February 1
College level: Freshman, Sophomore, Junior, Senior
Majors/Fields: Business
Criteria: Applicant must be a woman who is a U.S. citizen and a resident of Anne Arundel County, Md. Applicant must be seeking a business or professional career, have a minimum 3.0 GPA, and demonstrate financial need. Selection is based upon scholastic standing and number of applicants. Awarded every year.
Contact: Education Chairman, P.O. Box 119, Severna Park, MD 21147.

125   Arthur and Genevieve Roth Scholarship

Kosciuszko Foundation
15 East 65th Street
New York, NY 10021
(212) 734-2130
Average award: $1,000
Deadline: January 15
Majors/Fields: Banking, business administration, finance
Criteria: Awarded to U.S. citizens of Polish descent. Preference is given to those who plan to attend the Arthur T. Roth Sch of Business Administration of Long Island U. Awarded every year.
Contact: Scholarships.

126   Barber Dairies Scholarship

The University of Alabama
Box 870162
Tuscaloosa, AL 35487-0162
(205) 348-6756
Average award: $2,500
Number of awards: 1
Deadline: March 1
College level: Junior, Senior
Criteria: Applicant must demonstrate financial need, enterprise, and campus leadership. Written application is required. Awarded every year. Award may be used only at sponsoring institution.
Contact: Scholarships, College of Commerce and Business Administration, Box 870223, Tuscaloosa, AL 35487-0223, (800) 828-2622.

127 Barber Dairies Scholarship

Jacksonville State University
Jacksonville, AL 36265-9982
(205) 782-5006
Average award: $2,500
Deadline: March 15
College level: Junior, Senior
Majors/Fields: Commerce/business
Criteria: Selection is based upon academic record, entrepreneurship, and leadership. Awarded every year. Award may be used only at sponsoring institution.
Contact: Student Financial Aid Office.

128 Bellingham Rotary Club Scholarship

Western Washington University
516 High Street
Bellingham, WA 98226-9006
(206) 650-3471
Average award: Tuition, books, and fees
Number of awards: 2
Deadline: March 31
College level: Junior, Senior
Majors/Fields: Business, economics
Criteria: Selection is based upon academic performance and extracurricular activities. Satisfactory progress is required to retain scholarship for an additional year. Awarded every year. Award may be used only at sponsoring institution.
Contact: College of Business and Economics, 419 Parks Hall, Bellingham, WA 98225, (206) 650-3896.

129 Business Educators Award

Five Towns College
305 North Service Road
Dix Hills, NY 11746-6055
(516) 424-7000
Average award: $1,000
Maximum award: $1,500
Number of awards: 18
Deadline: Early application is recommended
College level: Freshman, Sophomore, Junior, Senior
Majors/Fields: Business
Criteria: Applicant must be accepted for admission as a full-time student. Selection is based upon academic potential, financial need, and service to school. Awarded every year. Award may be used only at sponsoring institution.
Contact: Financial Aid Office.

130 Business Scholarship

Milwaukee School of Engineering
1025 North Broadway
Milwaukee, WI 53202-3109
(800) 332-6763, (414) 277-7475 (fax)
goran@admin.msoe.edu
www.msoe.edu
Average award: Half tuition
Number of awards: 2
Deadline: February 1
College level: Freshman
Criteria: Applicant must have a minimum 3.0 GPA. Recommendation is suggested. Application is required. Recipient must maintain a minimum 3.0 GPA to retain scholarship for four years. Awarded every year. Award may be used only at sponsoring institution.
Contact: Sue Minzlaff, Financial Aid Office, (414) 277-7222, minzlaff@admin.msoe.edu.

131 Carthy Foundation Scholarship in Management

University of Calgary
Department of Financial Aid
2500 University Drive, NW
Calgary, Alberta, CN T2N 1N4
(403) 220-7872, (403) 282-2999 (fax)
Average award: $3,800
Number of awards: 1
Deadline: June 15
College level: Senior
Majors/Fields: Management
Criteria: Selection is based upon academic merit. Awarded every year. Award may be used only at sponsoring institution.
Contact: J. Van Housen, Director of Student Awards/Financial Aid.

132 Daniel Webster Scholarship

Webster University
470 East Lockwood
St. Louis, MO 63119-3194
(314) 968-7004
www.websteruniv.edu
Award: Full tuition, room and board, book stipend
Number of awards: 5
Deadline: February 1
College level: Freshman
Majors/Fields: International business
Criteria: Applicant must be a first-time, traditional freshman and have a minimum 3.6 GPA, rank in top tenth of class, and a minimum composite ACT score of 29 (combined SAT score of 1300). Applicant must demonstrate leadership and community activities, submit two letters of recommendation (one each from teacher or school counselor and community leader), and write essay on a required topic. Interviews are required for finalists. Award is for four years. Renewable if recipient maintains full-time enrollment and minimum 3.5 cumulative GPA. Awarded every year. Award may be used only at sponsoring institution.
Contact: Shannon Frank, Coordinator of University Scholarships.

133 Dean's Business Scholarship

DePaul University
1 East Jackson Boulevard
Chicago, IL 60604
(312) 362-8704, (312) 362-5749 (fax)
Average award: $4,000
Maximum award: $8,000
Minimum award: $2,000
Number of awards: 62
Deadline: None
College level: Freshman
Majors/Fields: Business, commerce
Criteria: Applicant must rank in the top tenth of secondary school class, have a minimum composite ACT score of 27 (combined SAT I score of 1220), and demonstrate leadership and a strong commitment to the study of business. Minimum 3.0 GPA as a full-time College of Commerce student is required to retain scholarship. Awarded every year. Award may be used only at sponsoring institution.
Contact: Jennifer Sparrow, Scholarship Coordinator, jsparrow@wppost.depaul.edu.

134 Dean's Business Transfer Scholarship

DePaul University
1 East Jackson Boulevard
Chicago, IL 60604
(312) 362-8704, (312) 362-5749 (fax)
Average award: $3,000
Maximum award: $4,000
Minimum award: $1,500
Number of awards: 45
Deadline: None
College level: Transfer
Majors/Fields: Commerce
Criteria: Applicant must be a transfer from an Illinois community college and have at least 30 semester or 45 quarter hours of transferred credit and a minimum 3.5 GPA. Scholarship is renewable. Awarded every year. Award may be used only at sponsoring institution.
Contact: Jennifer Sparrow, Scholarship Coordinator, jsparrow@wppost.depaul.edu.

135 Detroit Fad Annual Scholarship Fund

Northwood University – Midland Campus
3225 Cook Road
Midland, MI 48640-2398
(515) 837-4160
Average award: $2,000
Majors/Fields: Business
Criteria: Applicant must be a U.S. citizen having demonstrated academic merit and financial need. Applicants from the counties of Detroit, will be given top priority. Awarded every year. Award may be used only at sponsoring institution.
Contact: Dixie Dee Maxwell.

136 Donald W. Fogarty International Student Paper Competition

American Production & Inventory Control Society (APICS), Inc./Education & Research (E&R) Foundation, Inc.
500 West Annandale Road
Falls Church, VA 22046-4274
(703) 237-8344, (800) 444-2742, (703) 237-8450 (fax)
m_lythgoe@apics-hq.org
http://www.apics.org
Maximum award: $1,750
Number of awards: 162
Deadline: May 15
College level: Freshman, Sophomore, Junior, Senior, Graduate, Doctoral
Majors/Fields: Production and operations management
Criteria: Applicant must be enrolled as either a part- or full-time graduate or undergraduate student. Prospective applicants are encouraged to use the 800 number to request a manual (item #01002) and the name of local APICS chapter. Recipient must submit a new paper to retain scholarship. Awarded every year.
Contact: Michael H. Lythgoe/Wendy Whittaker, Director/E&R Foundation Associate, (703) 237-8585, extension 202.

137 Faculty Scholars Program

The University of Alabama
Box 870162
Tuscaloosa, AL 35487-0162
(205) 348-6756
Average award: $1,250
Number of awards: 10
Deadline: March 1
College level: Sophomore
Criteria: Awarded to full-time, highly qualified, motivated students in College of Commerce and Business Administration. Recipients must work 10 hours per week with faculty mentor in research and/or teaching activities. Renewable for two years. Awarded every year. Award may be used only at sponsoring institution.
Contact: Student Services Office, College of Commerce & Business Administration, Box 870223, Tuscaloosa, AL 35487-0223, (800) 828-2622.

138 Fleming Companies, Inc. Scholarship

University of Oklahoma
University Affairs
900 Asp Avenue, Room 236
Norman, OK 73019-0401
(405) 325-1701
Average award: $2,500
Number of awards: 2
Deadline: February 8
College level: Junior
Majors/Fields: Accounting, management information systems, marketing
Criteria: Applicant must have a minimum 3.0 GPA. Preference is given to women and minorities. Awarded every year. Award may be used only at sponsoring institution.
Contact: College of Business Administration, 208 Adams Hall, Norman, OK 73019-0450, (405) 325-6021.

139 Fukunaga Foundation Scholarship

Trustees of Fukunaga Foundation Scholarship
P.O. Box 2788
Honolulu, HI 96803
(808) 521-6511, (808) 533-1369 (fax)
Maximum award: $2,000
Maximum number of awards: 16
Minimum number of awards: 10
Deadline: April 15
College level: Graduate, unspecified undergraduate
Majors/Fields: Business administration
Criteria: Applicant must be a permanent resident of Hawaii (at least one year), rank in top quarter of class, have a minimum 3.0 GPA, and demonstrate financial need. He or she must also demonstrate the ability, industriousness, dependability, and determination needed to succeed in business within the Pacific Basin area. Applicant must maintain a minimum 3.0 GPA and full-time status to retain award. Awarded every year.
Contact: Evie Kobayashi, Fukunaga Foundation Scholarship Committee.

140 General Mills Accounting Award

General Mills, Incorporated
Division of Employment
9200 Wayzata
Minneapolis, MN 55440
Average award: $1,000
Number of awards: 1
Deadline: March 1
Criteria: Applicant's career goal should be industrial accounting or financial management. Awarded every year.

141   General Motors (GM) Scholarship
New Mexico State University
Box 30001
Department 5100
Las Cruces, NM 88003-0001
(505) 646-4105
Average award: Tuition, books, stipend, and summer internship
Deadline: March 1
College level: Sophomore, Junior, Senior
Majors/Fields: Business
Criteria: Applicant must be a U.S. citizen and have a minimum 3.2 GPA. Selection by GM personnel is based upon academic record, extracurricular activities, and long-term interest in the auto industry. Awarded every year. Award may be used only at sponsoring institution.
Contact: Advising Center, College of Business Administration and Economics, (505) 646-4084.

142   Golden State Minority Foundation Scholarship
Golden State Minority Foundation
1055 Wilshire Boulevard
Los Angeles, CA 90017
(800) 666-4763
Average award: $2,000
Number of awards: 100
*Deadline:*November 1 (Northern California, Houston); April 1 (Southern California); March 1 (Michigan)
College level: Junior, Senior, Graduate, Doctoral
Majors/Fields: Business administration, economics
Criteria: Applicant must attend school in or be a resident of California, Michigan, or Houston, Tex., be black, Latino, or Native American, and be a U.S. citizen or permanent legal resident. Applicant must be enrolled full-time, employed no more than 25 hours per week, have a minimum 3.0 GPA, and be majoring in business administration, economics, or a related field at a four-year college or university. Awarded every year.
Contact: Ivan A. Houston, President.

143   Gordon Davis Palmer Memorial Scholarship
The University of Alabama
Box 870162
Tuscaloosa, AL 35487-0162
(205) 348-6756
Average award: $2,206
Number of awards: 1
Deadline: March 1
College level: Sophomore, Junior, Senior
Criteria: Applicant must be Alabama resident and student in College of Commerce and Business Administration. Preference is given to resident of Tuscaloosa County with minimum 3.0 GPA. Award is for four years. Awarded as funds are available. Award may be used only at sponsoring institution.
Contact: Office of Student Financial Services.

144   H. Gordon Martin Scholarship
Northern Kentucky University
Administrative Center 416
Nunn Drive
Highland Heights, KY 41099-7101
(606) 572-5144
Average award: In-state tuition
Deadline: February 1
College level: Freshman
Majors/Fields: Business
Criteria: Applicant must be a graduate of Ludlow, Ky., high school with a minimum composite ACT score of 18. Awarded every year. Award may be used only at sponsoring institution.
Contact: Robert E. Sprague, Director of Financial Aid.

145   John M. Olin School of Business Dean's Scholarship
Washington University
One Brookings Drive
Campus Box 1089
St. Louis, MO 63130
(314) 935-6000 or (800) 638-0700
Average award: Full tuition
Number of awards: 1
College level: Freshman
Majors/Fields: Business
Criteria: Selection is based upon academic merit; financial need is not considered. Satisfactory academic progress is required to retain scholarship. Awarded every year. Award may be used only at sponsoring institution.
Contact: Office of Undergraduate Admission.

146   Junior Achievement Scholarship in Applied Economics
Alfred University
Alumni Hall
26 North Main Street
Alfred, NY 14802
(607) 871-2159
Average award: $4,000
Deadline: May 1
College level: Freshman
Majors/Fields: Business
Criteria: Applicant must have successfully completed or be taking applied economics, have completed 16 academic units including algebra I, algebra II, and geometry, have successfully completed or will be completing a college-preparatory program, and meet admissions requirements. Applicant must submit written recommendations from a Junior Achievement representative and an applied economics teacher. Award is for eight consecutive semesters. Recipient must maintain minimum 2.0 GPA, full-time status, and good citizenship. Awarded every year. Award may be used only at sponsoring institution.
Contact: Scholarships.

147   Kemper Scholar Internship and Grant
James S. Kemper Foundation
1 Kemper Drive
Long Grove, IL 60049-0001
(847) 320-2847
Maximum award: $7,000
Maximum number of awards: 70
Minimum number of awards: 60
Deadline: Deadline varies by school
College level: Sophomore, Junior, Senior
Majors/Fields: Business
Criteria: Recipients participate in summer internships for all years of college. Applicants must demonstrate maturity, curiosity, imagination, and a desire to relate positively to society through a business career. Awarded every year. Award may be used at one of the following schools: Beloit Coll, Brigham Young U, Drake U, Howard U, Illinois State U, Lake Forest Coll, LaSalle U, Loyola U, Millikin U, Northern Illinois U, U of the Pacific, Valparaiso U, Wake Forest U, Washington and Lee U, Washington U, U of Wisconsin–Whitewater.
Contact: James R. Connor, Executive Director.

148   Kerr McGee Scholarship
University of Oklahoma
University Affairs
900 Asp Avenue, Room 236
Norman, OK 73019-0401
(405) 325-1701
Average award: $4,000
Number of awards: 1
Deadline: February 7
College level: Junior
Majors/Fields: Management information systems
Criteria: Selection is based upon merit and financial need. Awarded every year. Award may be used only at sponsoring institution.
*Contact:*Coordinator of MIS Program, 206 Adams Hall, Norman, OK 73019, (405) 352-2651.

149   LeRoy Bacon Memorial Scholarship

Mesa State College
Financial Aid Department
P.O. Box 2647
Grand Junction, CO 81502
(970) 248-1396
Maximum award: Tuition and fees
Number of awards: 1
College level: Senior
Majors/Fields: Business finance
Criteria: Applicant must be enrolled full time and have a minimum 3.5 GPA. Awarded every year. Award may be used only at sponsoring institution.
Contact: School of Professional Studies/Business Area.

150   Marting's Department Store Scholarship

Shawnee State University
940 Second Street
Portsmouth, OH 45662-4344
(614) 355-2237
Average award: $1,500
Number of awards: 1
Deadline: April 1
College level: Freshman, Sophomore, Junior, Senior
Majors/Fields: Business, retailing
Criteria: Applicant must be a recent high school graduate or current student from the Portsmouth, Ohio, area. Award includes offer of employment. Awarded every year. Award may be used only at sponsoring institution.
Contact: Kathy Sly, Marting's Department Store, 515 Chillicothe Street, Portsmouth, OH 45662.

151   Michael and Francesca Marinelli Scholarships

National Italian American Foundation (NIAF)
Educational Scholarship Program
1860 19th Street, NW
Washington, DC 20009-5599
(202) 530-5315
Maximum award: $2,000
Maximum number of awards: 3
Minimum number of awards: 1
Deadline: May 31
College level: Freshman, Sophomore, Junior, Senior
Criteria: Applicant must be Italian-American, submit transcript, and demonstrate financial need. Awarded every year. Award may be used only at American U in Rome, or Nova U.
Contact: Dr. Maria Lombardo, Education Director.

152   Michigan Business School Association Scholarship

Baker College of Jackson
2800 Springport Road
Jackson, MI 49202
(517) 788-7800
Average award: $1,200
Number of awards: 12
Deadline: February 28
College level: Freshman
Criteria: Applicant must have a minimum 2.5 GPA. Selection is based upon academic record. Renewable for up to four years if recipient maintains enrollment. Awarded every year. Award may be used only at sponsoring institution.
Contact: Valerie Heldt, Director of Admissions.

153   Phi Chi Theta Scholarship

Phi Chi Theta Foundation
8656 Totempole Drive
Cincinnati, OH 45249
Maximum award: $1,000
Maximum number of awards: 3
Minimum number of awards: 1
Deadline: May 1
College level: Sophomore, Junior, Senior, Graduate, Doctoral
Majors/Fields: Business, economics
Criteria: Applicant must be a woman who demonstrates leadership, motivation, scholastic achievement, and financial need. Send a stamped, self-addressed envelope for the application. Transcript and recommendations are required. Awarded every year.
Contact: Scholarship Chairman.

154   Quality Cup Scholarship

Rochester Institute of Technology
One Lomb Memorial Drive
Rochester, NY 14623
(716) 475-2186
Average award: $5,000
Number of awards: 10
Deadline: January 1
College level: Freshman
Majors/Fields: Business, engineering
Criteria: Applicant must be selected as an RIT/*USA Today* Quality Cup Medal Winner by a participating high school and participate in a scholarship competition on campus. Scholarship is renewable. Awarded every year. Award may be used only at sponsoring institution.
Contact: Verna Hazen, Director of Financial Aid.

155   Samuel D. Southern Scholarship

University of Calgary
Department of Financial Aid
2500 University Drive, NW
Calgary, Alberta, CN T2N 1N4
(403) 220-7872, (403) 282-2999 (fax)
Average award: $1,250
Number of awards: 2
Deadline: June 15
College level: Senior
Majors/Fields: Finance, management
Criteria: Selection is based upon academic merit. Applicant must have been a resident of Alberta for at least five years. Awarded every year. Award may be used only at sponsoring institution.
Contact: J. Van Housen, Director of Student Awards/Financial Aid.

156   School of Business Scholarship

Colorado Christian University
180 South Garrison Street
Lakewood, CO 80226
(303) 202-0100, extension 117, (303) 274-7560 (fax)
drwilliams@ccu.edu
http://www.ccu.edu
Average award: $1,021
Maximum award: $2,500
Minimum award: $400
Number of awards: 19
Deadline: March 21
College level: Junior, Senior, Graduate
Criteria: Applicant must be enrolled full time in the School of Business. Awarded every year. Award may be used only at sponsoring institution.
Contact: Kent McGowan, Director of Financial Aid.

157   Texas Business Hall of Fame Foundation Scholarship

University of Texas at San Antonio
Office of Student Financial Aid
6900 North Loop 1604 West
San Antonio, TX 78249-0687
(210) 691-44855
Average award: $2,500
Number of awards: 1
Deadline: March 1
College level: Senior, Graduate
Majors/Fields: Business
Criteria: Applicant must be a U.S. citizen who is a graduating senior or a first-year M.B.A. student. Award is for four semesters. Awarded every year. Award may be used only at sponsoring institution.
Contact: Office of the Dean, College of Business, HB 4.01.23.

158   Walter D. Hershey Memorial Scholarship

Portland State University
Financial Aid Department
P.O. Box 751
Portland, OR 97207-0751
(503) 725-5270
Maximum award: $1,200
Number of awards: 4
Deadline: In February
College level: Junior
Majors/Fields: Business
Criteria: Awarded every year. Award may be used only at sponsoring institution.
Contact: Scholarships, School of Business Administration – Student Services.

Hospitality/Hospitality Administration——

159   AHF Scholarship

American Hotel Foundation (AHF)
1201 New York Avenue, NW, Suite 600
Washington, DC 20005-3931
(202) 289-3181, (202) 289-3199 (fax)
ahf@ahma.com
Maximum award: $1,000
Number of awards: 150
College level: Junior, Senior
Majors/Fields: Hospitality, lodging program
Criteria: Applicant must be enrolled full time at an AHF-approved two- or four-year college or university. Application and selection process is completed through the individual institution. Scholarship is renewable. Awarded every year. Award may be used at participating schools only.
Contact: Head of Hospitality Program.

160   Alice Banks Award/Charles FitzSimmons/ Frances Tally Award

International Association of Hospitality Accountants (IAHA), Inc.
P.O. Box 203008
Austin, TX 78720-3008
(512) 346-5680
Average award: $1,500
Number of awards: 3
Deadline: March 31
College level: Sophomore, Junior, Senior
Majors/Fields: Accounting, hospitality management, management information systems
Criteria: Applicant must have a minimum 3.0 GPA. Selection is based upon resume, transcript, essay, references, and community involvement. Awarded every year.
Contact: Awards.

161   American Express Card Scholarship

American Hotel Foundation (AHF)
1201 New York Avenue, NW, Suite 600
Washington, DC 20005-3931
(202) 289-3181, (202) 289-3199 (fax)
ahf@ahma.com
Maximum award: $2,000
Deadline: March 1
College level: Freshman, Sophomore, Junior, Senior
Majors/Fields: Hospitality, lodging program
Criteria: Applicant must have held a full-time position (minimum 20 hours per week) in a hotel or motel that is a member of AH&MA for a minimum of 12 months. Dependents of AH&MA member hotel or motel employees are also eligible. Scholarship is renewable. Awarded every year.
Contact: Michelle Poinelli, Scholarships Program Coordinator, ahf@ahma.com.

162   Capstone Hotel Scholarship

The University of Alabama
Box 870162
Tuscaloosa, AL 35487-0162
(205) 348-6756
Average award: $2,000
Deadline: March 15
College level: Junior, Senior
Majors/Fields: Hospitality management, restaurant management
Criteria: One award is for a junior and one for a senior. Awarded every year. Award may be used only at sponsoring institution.
Contact: Dean, College of Human Environmental Sciences, Box 870158, Tuscaloosa, AL 35487-0158, (205) 348-6250.

163   David L. and Lorna L. Cole Memorial Scholarship

New Mexico State University
Box 30001
Department 5100
Las Cruces, NM 88003-0001
(505) 646-4105
Average award: $1,700
Maximum award: Tuition and fees
Number of awards: 1
Deadline: March 1
College level: Freshman, Sophomore, Junior, Senior
Majors/Fields: Hotel management, restaurant management, hospitality, tourism
Criteria: Applicant must have a minimum 2.5 GPA. Financial need is not considered. Awarded every year. Award may be used only at sponsoring institution.
Contact: Greeley W. Myers, Director of Financial Aid.

164   IAHA Scholarship

International Association of Hospitality Accountants (IAHA), Inc.
P.O. Box 203008
Austin, TX 78720-3008
(512) 346-5680
Average award: $1,000
Number of awards: 4
Deadline: March 31
College level: Sophomore, Junior, Senior
Majors/Fields: Accounting, hospitality management, management information systems
Criteria: Applicant must have a minimum 3.0 GPA. Selection is based upon resume, transcript, essay, references, and community involvement. Awarded every year.
Contact: Scholarship.

165 IFEC Foodservice Communicators Scholarship

International Foodservice Editorial Council (IFEC)
P.O. Box 491
Hyde Park, NY 12538
(914) 452-4345, (914) 452-0532 (fax)
ifec@aol.com
Average award: $1,500
Maximum award: $2,000
Minimum award: $1,000
Number of awards: 4
Deadline: March 15
College level: Sophomore, Junior, Senior, Graduate, Doctoral
Majors/Fields: Communications arts, food service, hospitality
Criteria: Applicant must demonstrate financial need. Selection is based upon essay. Awarded every year.
Contact: Carol Metz, Executive Director.

166 Maine Inkeepers Association Scholarship

Maine Innkeepers Association
305 Commercial Street
Portland, ME 04101
(207) 773-7670
Maximum award: $1,000
Maximum number of awards: 10
Minimum number of awards: 6
Deadline: May
College level: Freshman, Sophomore, Junior, Senior
Majors/Fields: Culinary arts, hotel/motel management
Criteria: Awarded every year.
Contact: Scholarships.

167 Undergradute Scholarship Program

Educational Foundation of the National Restaurant Association
250 South Wacker Drive
Suite 1400
Chicago, IL 60606-5834
(800) 765-2122
Maximum award: $5,000
Deadline: March 1
College level: Sophomore, Junior, Senior
Majors/Fields: Food service, hospitality
Criteria: Applicant must have a minimum 3.0 GPA and 1,000 hours of work experience in the food service/hospitality industry. Awarded every year.
Contact: Scholarship Program Coordinator.

Human Resources Management———————

168 Intercultural Training Scholarship

School for International Training (SIT)
P.O. Box 676
Kipling Road
Brattleboro, VT 05302
(802) 257-7751, (802) 258-3500 (fax)
admissions.sit@worldlearning.org
http://www.worldlearning/sit.html
Average award: $1,000
Number of awards: 4
Deadline: April 1
College level: Master's degree candidate
Majors/Fields: Intercultural management
Criteria: Applicant must be employed for a minimum of one year as a trainer or human resource professional. Financial need may be considered. Applicant must be enrolled in a degree program. Awarded every year. Award may be used only at sponsoring institution.
Contact: Mary Henderson, Financial Aid Officer, (802) 258-3280.

Information Management——————

169 FORE Undergraduate Scholarships

American Health Information Management Association
919 North Michigan Avenue
Suite 1400
Chicago, IL 60611-1683
Average award: $1,500
Number of awards: 2
Deadline: July 1
Majors/Fields: Health information management, health information technology
Criteria: Applicant must have been accepted into a program for health information management or technology. Selection is based upon educational achievement, financial need, statement of objectives, and references.
Contact: Scholarships, Attn: FORE Library.

Insurance——————————

170 Actuarial Scholarships for Minority Students

Society of Actuaries/Casualty Actuarial Society
475 North Martingale Road
Suite 800
Schaumburg, IL 60173
(847) 706-3500, (847) 706-3599 (fax)
Average award: $1,200
Maximum award: $1,800
Minimum award: $1,000
Number of awards: 20
Deadline: May 1
College level: Freshman, Sophomore, Junior, Senior
Majors/Fields: Actuarial science
Criteria: Selection is based upon racial/ethnic background, financial need, and academic merit. Recipient must reapply for renewal. Awarded every year.
Contact: Susan Martz, Minority Recruiting Coordinator, (847) 706-3543, smartz@soa.org.

171 Calgary Life Underwriters Scholarship in Insurance and Risk Management

University of Calgary
Department of Financial Aid
2500 University Drive, NW
Calgary, Alberta, CN T2N 1N4
(403) 220-7872, (403) 282-2999 (fax)
Average award: $3,000
Number of awards: 1
Deadline: June 15
College level: Senior
Majors/Fields: Insurance, risk management
Criteria: Applicant must have a minimum 3.0 GPA. Selection is based upon academic merit, extracurricular activities, and interest in the life insurance industry. Awarded every year. Award may be used only at sponsoring institution.
Contact: J. Van Housen, Director of Student Awards/Financial Aid.

172 Encon Scholarship

University of Calgary
Department of Financial Aid
2500 University Drive, NW
Calgary, Alberta, CN T2N 1N4
(403) 220-7872, (403) 282-2999 (fax)
Average award: $3,000
Number of awards: 1
Deadline: June 15
College level: Senior
Majors/Fields: Insurance, risk management
Criteria: Selection is based upon academic merit. Awarded every year. Award may be used only at sponsoring institution.
Contact: J. Van Housen, Director of Student Awards/Financial Aid.

173   Jack L. McKewen Scholarship

The University of Alabama
Box 870162
Tuscaloosa, AL 35487-0162
(205) 348-6756
Average award: $2,470
Number of awards: 1
Deadline: March 15
College level: Sophomore, Junior, Senior
Majors/Fields: Insurance, marketing
Criteria: Awarded every year. Award may be used only at sponsoring institution.
Contact: Student Services Office, College of Commerce and Business Administration, Box 870223, Tuscaloosa, AL 35487-0223.

174   Jarvis W. Palmer Scholarship

The University of Alabama
Box 870162
Tuscaloosa, AL 35487-0162
(205) 348-6756
Average award: $1,778
Number of awards: 1
Deadline: March 15
College level: Sophomore, Junior, Senior
Majors/Fields: Insurance
Criteria: Applicant must be an Alabama resident. Awarded every year. Award may be used only at sponsoring institution.
Contact: Scholarships – Department of Economics, Finance, and Legal Studies, College of Commerce and Business Administration, Box 870224, Tuscaloosa, AL 35487-0224.

175   Robert S. Spencer Memorial Foundation Scholarship

Georgia State University
P.O. Box 4040
Atlanta, GA 30302
(404) 651-2227, (404) 651-3418 (fax)
http://www.gsu.edu
Average award: $10,000
Number of awards: 1
Deadline: December 1
College level: Sophomore, Junior, Senior, Graduate, Doctoral
Majors/Fields: Insurance, risk management
Criteria: Applicant must plan to pursue a career in risk management. Awarded every year. Award may be used only at sponsoring institution.
Contact: Department of Risk Management and Insurance, (404) 651-2725.

Marketing/Sales/Retailing

176   Harry A. Applegate Memorial Scholarship

Distributive Education Clubs of America (DECA)
1908 Association Drive
Reston, VA 22091
(703) 860-5000
Average award: $1,000
Maximum award: $1,500
Maximum number of awards: 20
Minimum number of awards: 15
Deadline: Second Monday in March
College level: Freshman, Sophomore, Junior, Senior, Graduate
Majors/Fields: Marketing, marketing education, merchandising
Criteria: Applicant must be a DECA member. Selection is based upon academic record, SAT I or ACT scores, leadership, and financial need. Reapplication is required to retain scholarship. Awarded every year.
Contact: Tim Coffey, Director of Corporate Marketing.

Real Estate

177   Appraisal Institute Education Trust Scholarship

Appraisal Institute
875 North Michigan Avenue
Suite 2400
Chicago, IL 60611-1980
(312) 335-4100, (312) 335-4200 (fax)
Maximum award: $3,000
Number of awards: 50
Deadline: March 15
College level: Sophomore, Junior, Senior, Graduate, Doctoral
Majors/Fields: Land economics, real estate, real estate appraisal
Criteria: Applicant must be a U.S. citizen and full-time undergraduate or graduate student. Applicant must submit recommendations, statement, transcripts, and proposed study program. Selection is based upon academic excellence. Financial need is not considered. Awarded every year.
Contact: Charlotte Timms, Project Coordinator, (312) 335-4136.

Secretarial Studies

178   NCRA Scholarship Fund

National Court Reporters Association
8224 Old Courthouse Road
Vienna, VA 22182-3808
(703) 556-6272
Maximum award: $1,500
Number of awards: 3
Deadline: April 1
College level: Sophomore
Majors/Fields: Court reporting
Criteria: Selection is based upon essay and academic record. Awarded every year.
Contact: Penny Compher, Assistant Director for Education.

Transportation/Traffic Management

179   Air Travel Card Grant

American Society of Travel Agents (ASTA) Scholarship Foundation, Inc.
1101 King Street
Alexandria, VA 22314
(703) 739-2782, (703) 684-8319 (fax)
http://www.astanet.com
Average award: $3,000
Number of awards: 1
Deadline: in June or July
College level: Freshman, Sophomore, Junior, Senior
Majors/Fields: Business travel management, tourism, travel
Criteria: Applicant must submit a 500-word essay. Recipient must reapply for renewal. Awarded every year.
Contact: Scholarships.

180   A.J. (Andy) Spielman Scholarship

American Society of Travel Agents (ASTA) Scholarship Foundation, Inc.
1101 King Street
Alexandria, VA 22314
(703) 739-2782, (703) 684-8319 (fax)
http://www.astanet.com
Average award: $3,000
Number of awards: 2
Deadline: in summer and fall
College level: Proprietary travel school
Majors/Fields: Travel
Criteria: Applicant must be re-entering the work force in the field of travel and submit a 500-word essay. Reapplication is required for renewal. Awarded every year.
Contact: Scholarships.

181 Alaska Airlines Scholarship

American Society of Travel Agents (ASTA) Scholarship Foundation, Inc.
1101 King Street
Alexandria, VA 22314
(703) 739-2782, (703) 684-8319 (fax)
http://www.astanet.com
Average award: $2,000
Number of awards: 1
Deadline: in June or July
College level: Sophomore, Junior, Senior
Majors/Fields: Travel, tourism
Criteria: Applicant must submit a 500-word essay. Reapplication is required for renewal. Awarded every year.
Contact: Scholarships.

182 American Express Travel Scholarship

American Society of Travel Agents (ASTA) Scholarship Foundation, Inc.
1101 King Street
Alexandria, VA 22314
(703) 739-2782, (703) 684-8319 (fax)
http://www.astanet.com
Average award: $2,500
Number of awards: 1
Deadline: in June or July
College level: Freshman, Sophomore, Junior, Senior, Proprietary travel school
Majors/Fields: Tourism, travel
Criteria: Applicant must submit a 500-word essay on the future of the travel industry. Reapplication is required for renewal. Awarded every year.
Contact: Scholarships.

183 Arizona Chapter Dependent/Employee Membership Scholarship

American Society of Travel Agents (ASTA) Scholarship Foundation, Inc.
1101 King Street
Alexandria, VA 22314
(703) 739-2782, (703) 684-8319 (fax)
http://www.astanet.com
Average award: $1,500
Number of awards: 1
Deadline: in June or July
College level: Freshman, Sophomore, Junior, Senior, Final year of junior college
Criteria: Applicant must be the dependent of an active ASTA Arizona Chapter agency member or associate member, or be an employee or the dependent of an employee of an Arizona ASTA member agency. Applicant must be enrolled in a school in Arizona. Reapplication is required to retain scholarship. Awarded every year.
Contact: Scholarships.

184 Arizona Chapter Gold

American Society of Travel Agents (ASTA) Scholarship Foundation, Inc.
1101 King Street
Alexandria, VA 22314
(703) 739-2782, (703) 684-8319 (fax)
http://www.astanet.com
Average award: $3,000
Number of awards: 1
Deadline: in June or July
College level: Sophomore, Junior, Senior
Majors/Fields: Travel, tourism
Criteria: Applicant must be enrolled at an accredited four-year college in the state of Arizona and submit a 500-word essay. Reapplication is required for renewal. Awarded every year.
Contact: Scholarships.

185 Avis Rent-a-Car Scholarship

American Society of Travel Agents (ASTA) Scholarship Foundation, Inc.
1101 King Street
Alexandria, VA 22314
(703) 739-2782, (703) 684-8319 (fax)
http://www.astanet.com
Average award: $2,000
Number of awards: 1
Deadline: in June or July
College level: Sophomore, Junior, Senior, Graduate, Doctoral
Majors/Fields: Travel, tourism
Criteria: Applicant must have worked part-time in the travel industry and submit a 500-word essay. Reapplication is required for renewal. Awarded every year.
Contact: Scholarships.

186 Fred & Ginger Deines Scholarships

Transportation Clubs International (TCI) Scholarship
P.O. Box 52
Arabi, LA 70032
(504) 278-1107, (504) 278-1110 (fax)
Maximum award: $1,000
Maximum number of awards: 4
Minimum number of awards: 2
Deadline: April 30
College level: Sophomore, Junior, Senior, Graduate, Doctoral
Majors/Fields: Transportation, traffic management
Criteria: Applicant must be a Canadian citizen and be enrolled at a college or university in Canada or the U.S., or be a Mexican citizen and be enrolled at a college or university in the U.S. or Mexico. Selection is based upon scholastic ability, potential, professional interest, character, and financial need. Awarded every year.
Contact: Gay Fielding.

187 George Reinke Scholarship

American Society of Travel Agents (ASTA) Scholarship Foundation, Inc.
1101 King Street
Alexandria, VA 22314
(703) 739-2782, (703) 684-8319 (fax)
http://www.astanet.com
Average award: $2,000
Number of awards: 4
Deadline: In summer and fall
College level: Proprietary travel school, junior college
Majors/Fields: Travel, tourism
Criteria: Applicant must demonstrate financial need and submit a 500-word essay. Reapplication is required for renewal.
Contact: Scholarships.

188 Healy Scholarship

American Society of Travel Agents (ASTA) Scholarship Foundation, Inc.
1101 King Street
Alexandria, VA 22314
(703) 739-2782, (703) 684-8319 (fax)
http://www.astanet.com
Average award: $2,000
Number of awards: 1
Deadline: In June or July
College level: Sophomore, Junior, Senior, Graduate
Majors/Fields: Travel, tourism
Criteria: Applicant must have a minimum 3.0 GPA and submit a 500-word essay. Write for application. Reapplication is required for renewal. Awarded every year.
Contact: Scholarships.

189   Holland-America Line Westours, Inc. Scholarship

American Society of Travel Agents (ASTA) Scholarship Foundation, Inc.
1101 King Street
Alexandria, VA 22314
(703) 739-2782, (703) 684-8319 (fax)
http://www.astanet.com
Average award: $2,000
Number of awards: 2
Deadline: In June or July
College level: Freshman, Sophomore, Junior, Senior, Graduate, Doctoral, proprietary travel schools
Majors/Fields: Tourism, travel
Criteria: Applicant must submit a 500-word essay on the future of the cruise industry. Reapplication is required for renewal. Awarded every year.
Contact: Scholarships.

190   J. Desmond Slattery Marketing Award

Travel & Tourism Research Association (TTRA)
Box 516
Pittsford, NY 14534
(716) 475-6061
Maximum award: $1,000
Number of awards: 1
Deadline: March 1
College level: Sophomore, Junior, Senior, Graduate, Doctoral
Majors/Fields: Travel research
Criteria: Applicant must submit either a paper or project.

191   Joseph R. Stone Scholarships

American Society of Travel Agents (ASTA) Scholarship Foundation, Inc.
1101 King Street
Alexandria, VA 22314
(703) 739-2782, (703) 684-8319 (fax)
http://www.astanet.com
Average award: $2,400
Number of awards: 3
Deadline: in June or July
College level: Freshman, Sophomore, Junior, Senior
Majors/Fields: Travel, tourism
Criteria: Applicant must be the child of a travel industry employee and submit a 500-word essay. Reapplication is required for renewal. Awarded every year.
Contact: Scholarships.

192   Logistics Education Foundation Scholarship

SOLE–The International Society of Logistics
8100 Professional Place
Suite 211
Hyattsville, MD 20785
(301) 459-8446, (301) 459-1522 (fax)
hq@sole.org
http://www.sole.org
Average award: $1,000
Number of awards: 8
Deadline: April 15
College level: Freshman, Sophomore, Junior, Senior, Graduate, Doctoral
Majors/Fields: Logistics or related field
Criteria: Awarded every year.
Contact: Katherine O'Dea, Director of Professional Development, hq@sole.org.

193   Northern California/Richard Epping Scholarship

American Society of Travel Agents (ASTA) Scholarship Foundation, Inc.
1101 King Street
Alexandria, VA 22314
(703) 739-2782, (703) 684-8319 (fax)
http://www.astanet.com
Average award: $2,000
Number of awards: 1
Deadline: in June or July
College level: Freshman, Sophomore, Junior, Senior, proprietary travel school
Majors/Fields: Travel, tourism
Criteria: Applicant must apply to a school located in California or northern Nevada, be a permanent resident of either northern California or northern Nevada, and submit a 500-word essay. Reapplication is required for renewal. Awarded every year.
Contact: Scholarships.

194   Pollard Scholarship

American Society of Travel Agents (ASTA) Scholarship Foundation, Inc.
1101 King Street
Alexandria, VA 22314
(703) 739-2782, (703) 684-8319 (fax)
http://www.astanet.com
Average award: $2,000
Number of awards: 2
Deadline: in summer and fall
College level: Proprietary travel school, junior college
Majors/Fields: Travel, tourism
Criteria: Applicant must be re-entering the job market and submit a 500-word essay. Reapplication is required for renewal. Awarded every year.
Contact: Scholarships.

195   Princess Cruises and Princess Tours Scholarships

American Society of Travel Agents (ASTA) Scholarship Foundation, Inc.
1101 King Street
Alexandria, VA 22314
(703) 739-2782, (703) 684-8319 (fax)
http://www.astanet.com
Average award: $2,000
Number of awards: 2
Deadline: in June or July
College level: Freshman, Sophomore, Junior, Senior, proprietary travel school
Majors/Fields: Travel, tourism
Criteria: Applicant must submit a 300-word essay on two features that cruise ships will need to offer passengers in the next ten years. Reapplication is required for renewal. Awarded every year.
Contact: Scholarships.

196   Southern California Chapter/Pleasant Hawaiian Holidays Scholarship

American Society of Travel Agents (ASTA) Scholarship Foundation, Inc.
1101 King Street
Alexandria, VA 22314
(703) 739-2782, (703) 684-8319 (fax)
http://www.astanet.com
Average award: $2,000
Number of awards: 1
Deadline: in June or July
College level: Freshman, Sophomore, Junior, Senior
Majors/Fields: Travel, tourism
Criteria: Applicant must submit a 500-word essay and attend school in southern California. Reapplication is required for renewal. Awarded every year.
Contact: Scholarships.

Communications

Communications Disorders——————

197   Graduate Student Scholarship

American Speech-Language-Hearing Foundation
10801 Rockville Pike
Rockville, MD 20852
(301) 897-5700, (301) 571-0457 (fax)
Maximum award: $4,000
Number of awards: 7
Deadline: June 6
College level: Graduate, Doctoral
Majors/Fields: Communication disorders, communication sciences
Criteria: Applicant must be a full-time graduate student. Selection is based upon academic promise and outstanding academic achievement. One scholarship gives priority to foreign or minority students studying in the continental U.S.; one scholarship gives priority to disabled students. Awarded every year.
Contact: Graduate Student Scholarship Competition.

198   Sertoma Communicative Disorders Scholarship

Sertoma International
1912 East Meyer Boulevard
Kansas City, MO 64132
(816) 333-8300, (816) 333-4320 (fax)
infosertoma@sertoma.org
http://www.sertoma.org
Average award: $2,500
Number of awards: 30
Deadline: in the spring
College level: Graduate
Majors/Fields: Audiology, communicative disorders, speech/language pathology
Criteria: Applicant must have a minimum 3.2 GPA, be a citizen or permanent resident of the U.S., Canada, or Mexico, and be accepted into a master's degree program at a school in North America. U.S. institution must be accredited by the Education Standards Board of the American Speech-Language-Hearing Association. Send self-addressed stamped envelope for further information. Recipient must reapply for renewal. Awarded every year.
Contact: $2500 Scholars.

199   Young Scholars Award for Minority Students

American Speech-Language-Hearing Foundation
10801 Rockville Pike
Rockville, MD 20852
(301) 897-5700, (301) 571-0457 (fax)
Average award: $2,000
Number of awards: 1
Deadline: June 6
College level: Graduate
Majors/Fields: Speech-language pathology, audiology
Criteria: Applicant must be a U.S. citizen, a minority, and be accepted for full-time study in a graduate program. Applicant must submit a formal paper. Awarded every year.
Contact: Graduate Student Scholarship Competition.

Communications——————

200   Albert M. Becker Memorial Scholarship

New York State Legion Press Association
P.O. Box 1239
Syracuse, NY 13201-1239
Average award: $1,000
Number of awards: 1
Deadline: June 1
College level: Freshman
Majors/Fields: Communications
Criteria: Applicant must be the child of a member of the New York American Legion or Auxiliary, member of American Legion Juniors, or graduate of Boys State or Girls State. Applicant must be entering or attending an accredited four-year college. Awarded every year.
Contact: Scholarship Chairman.

201   Art Edgerton/Northwest Ohio Black Media Association Scholarship

University of Toledo
Financial Aid Office
Toledo, OH 43606-3390
(419) 537-2056
Average award: $2,000
Number of awards: 1
Deadline: January 28
College level: Freshman, Sophomore, Junior, Senior
Majors/Fields: Communication
Criteria: Applicant must be African-American. Selection is based upon essay, interview, and demonstration of leadership. Awarded every year. Award may be used only at sponsoring institution.
Contact: Clyde Hughes, P.O. Box 9232, Toledo, OH 43697-9232, (419) 245-6000.

202   Communications Scholarship

Liberty University
1971 University Boulevard
Lynchburg, VA 24502-2269
(800) 543-5317
Average award: $1,959
Number of awards: 44
Deadline: Three months prior to start of semester
College level: Freshman, Sophomore, Junior, Senior
Criteria: Applicant must have experience in debate, yearbook, or school newspaper. Scholarship is renewable. Awarded every year. Award may be used only at sponsoring institution.
Contact: School of Communications, (800) 522-6225, extension 2777.

203   Florence Herz Stone Scholarship

Florence Herz Stone Scholarship
P.O. Box 1343
Indianapolis, IN 46206
Maximum award: $1,000
Number of awards: 1
Deadline: March 1
College level: Senior
Majors/Fields: Communications
Criteria: Awarded every year. Award may be used only in Indiana.

204   Frank Wright Scholarship

Northwood University – Midland Campus
3225 Cook Road
Midland, MI 48640-2398
(515) 837-4160
Average award: $1,875
Majors/Fields: Communications
Criteria: Applicant must be a U.S. citizen and demonstrate financial need. Award may be used only at sponsoring institution.
Contact: Dixie Dee Maxwell.

205   Gladys Brown Edwards Memorial Scholarship

Arabian Horse Trust
12000 Zuni Street
Westminster, CO 80234-2300
(303) 450-4710, (303) 450-4707 (fax)
Average award: $1,000
Number of awards: 1
Deadline: March 1
College level: Junior, Senior
Majors/Fields: Media Communications
Criteria: Applicant must have an ongoing interest in and commitment to horses. Awarded every year.
Contact: Scholarship Committee.

206   Helen Miller Malloch Scholarship

National Federation of Press Women (NFPW), Inc.
4510 West 89th Street
Suite 110
Prairie Village, KS 66207-2282
Average award: $1,000
Number of awards: 1
Deadline: May 1
College level: Junior, Senior, Graduate, Doctoral
Majors/Fields: Communications
Criteria: Selection is based upon academic performance, career potential, and financial need. Awarded every year.
Contact: Scholarships, P.O. Box 99, Blue Springs, MO 64013.

207   Leonard M. Perryman Communications Scholarship for Ethnic Minority Students

United Methodist Communications
Public Media Division
P.O. Box 320
Nashville, TN 37202-0320
(615) 742-5405, (615) 742-5404 (fax)
Maximum award: $2,500
Number of awards: 1
Deadline: February 15
College level: Junior, Senior
Majors/Fields: Journalism, mass communications, religious communication
Criteria: Applicant must be an ethnic minority student intending to pursue a career in religious communication, including audiovisual media, and electronic and print journalism. Awarded every year.
Contact: Jackie Vaughan, Scholarship Committee, scholarships@umcom.umc.org.

208   Mel Allen Endowed Scholarship

The University of Alabama
Box 870162
Tuscaloosa, AL 35487-0162
(205) 348-6756
Average award: $2,500
Number of awards: 1
Deadline: February 15
College level: Freshman
Majors/Fields: Communication
Criteria: Applicant must be enrolled full time in College of Communication. Minimum 3.0 GPA is required to retain scholarship. Awarded every year. Award may be used only at sponsoring institution.
Contact: Scholarship Committee, College of Communication, Box 870172, Tuscaloosa, AL 35487-0172.

209   Minority Media Scholarship

Sacramento Bee
P.O. Box 15779
Sacramento, CA 96852
(916) 321-1790, (916) 321-1783 (fax)
rvandiest@sacbee.com
http://www.sacbee.com
Average award: $2,500
Maximum award: $5,000
Minimum award: $1,000
Number of awards: 10
Deadline: March 14
College level: Freshman, Sophomore, Junior, Senior, Graduate
Majors/Fields: Mass communication
Criteria: Applicant must be a member of a minority group living in the Sacramento, Calif. three-county area. Awarded every year.
Contact: Robbi Van Diest, Scholarship Coordinator, (916) 321-1794.

210   "Pap" Dunnavant Endowed Scholarship

The University of Alabama
Box 870162
Tuscaloosa, AL 35487-0162
(205) 348-6756
Average award: $2,282
Number of awards: 1
Deadline: February 15
College level: Junior
Majors/Fields: Telecommunication
Criteria: Applicant must be an outstanding full-time student. Preference to applicants from Tennessee Valley in northern Alabama. Awarded every year. Award may be used only at sponsoring institution.
Contact: Scholarship Committee, College of Communication, Box 870172, Tuscaloosa, AL 35487-0172.

211   Stan Wallace Journalism Scholarship

PanEnergy Corportation
P.O. Box 1642
Houston, TX 77251-1642
(713) 627-4608
Average award: $1,250
Number of awards: 1
Deadline: April 1
College level: Freshman, Sophomore, Junior, Senior
Majors/Fields: Communications
Criteria: Applicant must be a senior attending a Texas Region IV high school (public or private) and be nominated by his or her principal or journalism teacher. Each school may nomimate one candidate. Minimum 3.0 GPA per semester is required to retain scholarship. Awarded every year.
Contact: Dianne Wilson, Scholarship Coordinator.

212   STC Scholarship

Society for Technical Communication (STC)
901 North Stuart Street
Suite 904
Arlington, VA 22203-1854
(703) 522-4114
Average award: $2,000
Number of awards: 14
Deadline: February 15
College level: Sophomore, Junior, Senior, Graduate, Doctoral
Majors/Fields: Technical communication
Criteria: Applicant must be a full-time student in a technical communication program. Selection is based upon academic record and potential for contributing to the profession of technical communication. Awarded every year.
Contact: STC Office.

213 Washington Scholarship

SDX Foundation of Washington
U.S. News & World Report
2400 North Street, NW, Room 610
Washington, DC 20037
(202) 955-2330
Average award: $2,000
Maximum number of awards: 8
Minimum number of awards: 6
Deadline: March 1
College level: Sophomore, Junior
Criteria: Applicant must be a member of Sigma Delta Chi and be a full-time sophomore or junior at a college or university in metropolitan Washington, D.C. Demonstration of financial need is required. Scholarship is renewable. Awarded every year.
Contact: Scholarships.

214 Whittle Communications Minority Scholarship

University of Tennessee, Knoxville
Financial Aid Office
115 Student Services Building
Knoxville, TN 37994
(615) 974-3131
Average award: Comprehensive tuition
Number of awards: 20
Deadline: February 1
College level: Freshman, Sophomore, Junior, Senior
Majors/Fields: Communications
Criteria: Applicant must be a minority Tennessee resident from an accredited Tennessee high school with a minimum 3.0 GPA and a minimum ACT English score of 24. Applicant will be able to intern at Whittle Communications while attending the university. Scholarship is renewable. Awarded every year. Award may be used only at sponsoring institution.
Contact: College of Communications, 302 Communications and Extension Building, Knoxville, TN 37996, (615) 974-3031.

Journalism———————

215 AAJA Internship Grant

Asian American Journalists Association (AAJA)
1765 Sutter Street
San Francisco, CA 94115
(415) 346-2051, (415) 346-6343 (fax)
aaja1@aol.com
http://www.aaja.org
Average award: $1,000
Deadline: April 15
Criteria: Applicant must work as an intern for a news organization. Selection is based upon a commitment to the field of journalism, a sensitivity to Asian-American issues (as demonstrated by community involvement), journalistic and scholastic ability, and financial need.
Contact: Hien Nguyen, Program Coordinator.

216 AAJA General Scholarships

Asian American Journalists Association (AAJA)
1765 Sutter Street
San Francisco, CA 94115
(415) 346-2051, (415) 346-6343 (fax)
aaja1@aol.com
http://www.aaja.org
Maximum award: $2,000
Number of awards: 14
Deadline: April 15
College level: Freshman, Sophomore, Junior, Senior, Graduate
Criteria: Applicant must be enrolled full time. Selection is based upon a commitment to the field of journalism, a sensitivity to Asian-American issues as demonstrated by community involvement, journalistic ability, scholastic ability, and financial need.
Contact: Hien Nguyen, Program Coordinator.

217 AEJ Minority Summer Internship Program

Association for Education in Journalism (AEJ)
NYU Institute of Afro-American Affairs
269 Mercer Street, Suite 601
New York, NY 10003
(212) 998-2130
Average award: $2,000
Number of awards: 15
Deadline: September 18
College level: Sophomore, Junior, Senior, Graduate
Majors/Fields: Journalism
Criteria: Applicant must be enrolled full-time, be a member of a minority group (African-American, Asian, Hispanic, Native American, Pacific Islander), and demonstrate a commitment to journalism by a staff postion in campus media, or a previous internship. Preference is given to juniors.
Contact: Glenda Noel-Doyle, Program Coordinator.

218 Albert Spiezny Journalism Scholarship/ John Kierzkowski Scholarship

Kosciuszko Foundation
15 East 65th Street
New York, NY 10021
(212) 734-2130
Average award: $5,000
Number of awards: 3
Deadline: January 15
Majors/Fields: Journalism
Criteria: Awarded on a competitive basis to U.S. citizens of Polish descent. Scholarships are connected with the possibility of apprentice editorship on the staff of *New Horizons* magazine, an English-language monthly devoted to Polish and Polish-American affairs. Award pays funds toward tuition expenses at the Graduate School of Journalism of Columbia U. Awarded every year.
Contact: Scholarships.

219 Art Peters Copy Editing Internship

Philadelphia Inquirer Minority Intern Program
P.O. Box 8263
Philadelphia, PA 19101
(215) 854-2419, (215) 854-2771
Average award: $493 per week
Number of awards: 4
Deadline: December 15
College level: Sophomore, Junior, Senior
Majors/Fields: Print journalism
Criteria: Applicant must be black and have a strong interest in a career in copy editing. Work experience in college newspaper is preferred. Renewable if performance in first year of internship is satisfactory. Awarded every year.
Contact: Arlene Morgan, Senior Editor/Development, 400 North Broad Street, Philadelphia, PA 19101, (215) 854-2419.

220 Asbury Park Press Scholarships in the Media for Local Minority Students

Asbury Park Press
3601 Highway 66
P.O. Box 1550
Neptune, NJ 07754
(932) 922-6000 (932) 922-4818 (fax)
Average award: $2,000
Number of awards: 3
Deadline: March 1, last Friday in April
College level: Freshman
Majors/Fields: Journalism, media
Criteria: Applicant must be a minority student (African-American, Hispanic-American, Asian-American, or Native American) and demonstrate interest in journalism. Preference given to residents of New Jersey and to applicants attending college in New Jersey. Minimum 2.5 GPA and satisfactory progress are required to retain scholarship for one additional year. Awarded every year.
Contact: Lawrence Benjamin, Staff Development Editor.

221   Baltimore Sun Scholarship for Minority Journalists

Baltimore Sun
501 North Calvert Street
Baltimore, MD 21278
(301) 332-6268
Average award: $5,000
Number of awards: 1
College level: Freshman
Majors/Fields: Journalism
Criteria: Applicant must be a member of a minority group who is planning to attend the U of Maryland, College Park. Selection is based upon academic excellence, writing skills, participation in extracurricular activities, and the student's commitment to a career in journalism. Awarded every year.
Contact: Scholarships.

222   Barbara L. Frye Scholarship

Capital Press Club of Florida
336 East College Avenue
Tallahassee, FL 32301
(904) 222-3095, (904) 222-9891 (fax)
Maximum award: $2,000
Deadline: June 15
College level: Freshman, Sophomore, Junior, Senior
Criteria: Applicant must be the graduate of a Florida high school or be attending or planning to attend a Florida college or university, and must demonstrate dedication to a journalism career and aptitude for print or broadcast journalism. Submission of essay and work samples required. Race and financial need may be considered. Recipient must reapply for renewal.
Contact: Florida Press Center.

223   Battle Creek Enquirer Memorial Scholarship

Battle Creek Enquirer
155 West Van Buren Street
Battle Creek, MI 49016
(616) 964-7161
Average award: $1,000
Number of awards: 1
Majors/Fields: Journalism
Criteria: Applicant must live within the area served by the *Battle Creek Enquirer.* Awarded every year.
Contact: Sharon Samfilippo, Director of Human Resources.

224   Bob Eddy Scholarship/Richard Peck Scholarship

Society of Professional Journalists
25 South Street
Fairfield, CT 06430
Maximum award: $2,000
Number of awards: 6
Deadline: April 15
College level: Junior, Senior
Majors/Fields: Journalism
Criteria: Applicant must be a Connecticut resident attending any college or a nonresident enrolled at a Connecticut college. Work samples (stories or tapes), essay about career goals in journalism, and college transcript are required. Awarded every year.
Contact: Cindy Simoneau, Former Chapter President, (203) 330-6391.

225   Buffalo News Scholarship

State University of New York at Buffalo
Buffalo, NY 14260
(716) 831-2000, (716) 829-2022 (fax)
Average award: $3,000
College level: Junior, Senior
Criteria: Applicant must submit an essay describing interest and goal in journalism, demonstrate journalistic ability, and file FAFSA. Preference is given to an underrepresented minority who is willing and able to accept a paid summer intership at the *Buffalo News.* Award may be used only at sponsoring institution.
Contact: Scholarships.

226   Buford Boone Memorial Endowed Scholarship

The University of Alabama
Box 870162
Tuscaloosa, AL 35487-0162
(205) 348-6756
Average award: $1,000
Number of awards: 4
Deadline: February 15
College level: Junior, Senior
Criteria: Applicant must plan a career in print journalism and have a minimum 3.0 GPA. Priority is given to students who work part-time during school. Application is available from College of Communication. Minimum 3.0 GPA is required to retain scholarship. Awarded every year. Award may be used only at sponsoring institution.
Contact: Scholarship Committee, College of Communication, Box 870172, Tuscaloosa, AL 35487-0172.

227   Chevron Journalism Economics Scholarship

The University of Alabama
Box 870162
Tuscaloosa, AL 35487-0162
(205) 348-6756
Average award: $1,500
Number of awards: 2
Deadline: February 15
College level: Sophomore, Junior
Majors/Fields: Journalism
Criteria: Applicant must be a journalism major minoring in economics. Awarded every year. Award may be used only at sponsoring institution.
Contact: Scholarship Committee, College of Communication, Box 870172, Tuscaloosa, AL 35487-0172, (205) 348-5520.

228   Dow Jones Newspaper Fund Editing Intern Programs

Dow Jones Newspaper Fund
P.O. Box 300
Princeton, NJ 08543-0300
(609) 452-2820, (609) 520-5804 (fax)
newsfund@wsj.dowjones.com
http://www.dowjones.com/newsfund
Average award: $1,000
Number of awards: 65
Deadline: November 15
College level: Senior, Graduate
Criteria: Applicant must be a U.S. citizen and must work the full summer at a copy desk of a daily newspaper, online newspaper, or real-time financial news service (identified by DJNF). Recipient will receive a $1,000 scholarship to apply toward his or her following year in college as well as regular wages from the news media for which he or she works. Recipient must attend a two-week training seminar before beginning the internship; seminar is paid for by the Newspaper Fund. Request application between August 15 and November 1. Applicant must take editing test as part of the application by November 15. For a list of campus test monitors and an application, contact the Newspaper Fund. Awarded every year.
Contact: Newspaper Editing Program.

229   Edward J. Nell Memorial Journalism Scholarships

Quill & Scroll Foundation
School of Journalism and Mass Communication
University of Iowa
Iowa City, IA 52242-1528
Maximum number of awards: 10
Minimum number of awards: 8
Deadline: November 1 (yearbook contest); February 5 (writing/photo contest)
College level: Freshman
Majors/Fields: Journalism
Criteria: Applicant must be the winner of either the Yearbook Excellence Contest or the Writing/Photo Contest. Awarded every year.
Contact: Scholarships, quill-scroll@uiowa.edu.

230 Express News Paul Thompson Scholarship
Texas Professional Communicators
P.O. Box 173
Denison, TX 75021-0173
(903) 465-8567
kcasey@tenet.edu
Average award: $1,000
Number of awards: 1
Deadline: March 20
College level: Sophomore, Junior, Senior, Graduate, Doctoral
Majors/Fields: Print journalism
Criteria: Applicant must be enrolled in an accredited journalism program and live in the circulation area of the *San Antonio Express News'* in Central/South Texas. Awarded every year.
Contact: Julia Kearney, Scholarship Director.

231 F. Ward Just Scholarship
F. Ward Just Scholarship Foundation
c/o Kennedy
805 Baldwin Ave, Apt. 308
Waukegan, IL 60085-2359
(312) 680-7002
Average award: $4,000
Minimum award: $2,000
Number of awards: 2
Deadline: March 1
College level: Freshman
Majors/Fields: Journalism
Criteria: Applicant must demonstrate financial need, rank in top half of graduating class, have outstanding character and promise, and show interest in a career in the newspaper business or broadcasting. Renewable if a minimum "C" grade average is maintained. Awarded every year.
Contact: Richard F. Kennedy, Vice President, 5844 Heather Ridge Drive, Gurnee, IL 60031.

232 Fred Russell/Grantland Rice TRA Scholarship
Thoroughbred Racing Associations (TRA)
420 Fair Hill Drive
Suite 1
Elkton, MD 21921
Average award: $10,000
Deadline: January 1
College level: Freshman
Criteria: Applicant must demonstrate a special interest and demonstrate potential in the field of sportswriting. Awarded every year.
Contact: Vanderbilt University, Coordinator of Special Scholarships, 2305 West End Avenue, Nashville, TN 37203, (615) 322-2561.

233 Golf Writers Association of America Scholarship
California State University, Fullerton
P.O. Box 34080
Fullerton, CA 92634-9480
(714) 773-3128
Average award: $3,000
Number of awards: 1
Deadline: January
College level: Junior
Majors/Fields: Communications, print journalism
Criteria: Selection is based upon academic achievement and financial need. Awarded every year. Award may be used only at sponsoring institution.
Contact: Vickey Takeuchi, Scholarship Coordinator.

234 GPEF Scholarship
Georgia Press Educational Foundation (GPEF)
3066 Mercer University Drive
Suite 200
Atlanta, GA 30341-4137
(770) 454-6776, (770) 454-6778 (fax)
gapress@aol.com
Maximum award: $1,500
Maximum number of awards: 7
Minimum number of awards: 4
Deadline: February 1
College level: Freshman, Sophomore, Junior, Senior
Majors/Fields: Print journalism
Criteria: Applicant must be a Georgia resident and attend a state school in Georgia. Recipient must reapply for renewal. Awarded every year.
Contact: GPEF Coordinator, Scholarships.

235 Hugh Sparrow Memorial Endowed Scholarship
The University of Alabama
Box 870162
Tuscaloosa, AL 35487-0162
(205) 348-6756
Maximum award: $1,542
Number of awards: 3
Deadline: February 15
College level: Sophomore, Junior
Criteria: Applicant must be enrolled full time and be planning a career in print journalism. Priority is given to student who combines academic excellence with professional promise. Minimum 3.0 GPA is required to retain scholarship. Awarded every year. Award may be used only at sponsoring institution.
Contact: Scholarship Committee, College of Communication, Box 870172, Tuscaloosa, AL 35487-0172.

236 I.F. Stone Award for Student Journalism
The Nation Institute
72 Fifth Avenue
New York, NY 10011
(212) 242-8400, (212) 463-9712 (fax)
institute@thenation.com
Average award: $1,000
Number of awards: 1
Deadline: June 29
College level: Sophomore, Junior, Senior, Graduate
Criteria: Applicant must be enrolled at a U.S. college or university and submit an article which was written between June 30 and June 29 of the previous academic year. Awarded every year.
Contact: Peter Meyer/Sandy Wood, Executive Director.

237 Jack Kassewitz/Garth Reeves Jr. Memorial Scholarships
Society of Professional Journalists South Florida Pro Chapter
c/o *The Miami Herald*
One Herald Plaza
Miami, FL 33132-1693
(305) 376-3564
Average award: $1,000
Minimum award: $500
Number of awards: 2
Deadline: March 1
College level: Freshman, Sophomore, Junior, Senior, Graduate
Majors/Fields: Journalism
Criteria: Applicant must be preparing for a career in journalism and be a resident of South Florida. Selection is based upon need, grades, participation in student publication, general character, and potential. Reapplication is required to retain scholarship. Awarded every year.
Contact: John D. Hopkins, Scholarship Chairman, SPJ.

238   John M. Will Memorial Scholarship

John M. Will Scholarship Foundation
P.O. Box 290
Mobile, AL 36601
(334) 405-1300
Maximum award: $5,000
Number of awards: 1
Deadline: March 1
College level: Freshman, Sophomore, Junior, Senior, Graduate, Doctoral
Majors/Fields: Journalism
Criteria: Applicant must be a resident of Baldwin, Clarke, Conecuh, Escambia, Mobile, Monroe, or Washington counties in Alabama, Escambia or Santa Rosa counties in Florida, or George or Jackson counties in Mississippi. Applicant must submit cover letter, transcript, and recommendation. Recipient must reapply for renewal. Awarded every year.
Contact: Steele Holman II, Secretary of the Foundation.

239   John S. Knight Scholar Award

John S. Knight Memorial Journalism Fund Corp.
c/o David B. Cooper
44 East Exchange Street
Akron, OH 44309
(330) 996-3510, (330) 996-3520 (fax)
Average award: $2,500
Number of awards: 5
Deadline: March 1
College level: Sophomore, Junior, Senior, Graduate, Doctoral
Majors/Fields: Journalism, mass communications, public relations
Criteria: Selection is based upon academic performance, career goals, financial need, and professional activities. Preference is given to applicants who are residents of or attending college in the Ohio counties of Medina, Portage, Stark, Summit, or Wayne. Continued academic achievement is required to retain scholarship. Awarded every year.
Contact: Katie Byard, Chair of Scholarship Nominating Committee, *Akron Beacon Journal,* 44 East Exchange Street, Akron, OH 44309, (330) 722-3271.

240   Knight-Ridder Inc. Minority Scholarship

Detroit Free Press
321 West Lafayette
Detroit, MI 48226
(313) 222-6873
Maximum award: $5,000
Maximum number of awards: 4
Minimum number of awards: 3
Deadline: January 15
College level: Freshman
Majors/Fields: Journalism, communications
Criteria: Applicant must be a minority (Asian, black, Hispanic, or Native American) with a minimum 3.0 GPA.
Contact: Scholarships.

241   McMahon Memorial Scholarship

University of Oklahoma
University Affairs
900 Asp Avenue, Room 236
Norman, OK 73019-0401
(405) 325-1701
Average award: $5,000
Number of awards: 5
Deadline: February 15
College level: Freshman
Majors/Fields: Journalism, mass communication
Criteria: Selection is based upon test scores, GPA, and personal interview. Awarded every year. Award may be used only at sponsoring institution.
Contact: Director of School of Journalism and Mass Communication, 860 Van Vleet Oval, Norman, OK 73019, (405) 325-2721.

242   *Modesto Bee* Internship

Modesto Bee Minority Intern Program
P.O. Box 5256
Modesto, CA 95352
(209) 578-2351, (209) 578-2207 (fax)
editor@modbee.com
Average award: $3,500
Number of awards: 10
Deadline: December 31
College level: Sophomore, Junior, Senior, Graduate
Majors/Fields: Journalism
Criteria: Applicant must submit a cover letter, a resume, three references, and five work samples. Awarded every year.
Contact: Internships.

243   NAHJ Scholarship

National Association of Hispanic Journalists (NAHJ)
1193 National Press Building
Washington, DC 20045
(202) 662-7145, (202) 662-7144 (fax)
Average award: $1,000
Maximum award: $2,000
Deadline: February 28
College level: Freshman, Sophomore, Junior, Senior, Graduate, Doctoral
Majors/Fields: Journalism, mass communication
Criteria: Applicant must submit a sample of best work, resume, recommendations, essay, transcript, and application. For application, send a self-addressed, stamped envelope with request. Awarded every year.
Contact: Rebecca K. Finley, Scholarships.

244   National High School Journalist of the Year Sister Rita Jeanne Scholarship

Journalism Education Association
Kedzie Hall, Room 103
Kansas State University
Manhattan, KS 66506
(913) 532-5532, (913) 532-5563 or 913 532-7309 (fax)
jea@spub.ksu.edu
http://www.jea.org/
Maximum award: $2,000
Number of awards: 3
Deadline: February 15
College level: Freshman
Majors/Fields: Journalism
Criteria: Applicant must be planning to study journalism in college, be planning a career in journalism, have a minimum 3.0 GPA, and have participated in high school journalism for at least two years. Awarded every year.
Contact: Your State's Contest Coordinator.

245   Nebraska Press Association Scholarship

Nebraska Press Association Foundation, Inc.
1120 K Street
Lincoln, NE 68508
(402) 476-2851, 800 369-2850
Average award: $1,000
Number of awards: No limit
Deadline: February 28
College level: Freshman, Sophomore, Junior, Senior
Majors/Fields: Print journalism
Criteria: Applicants must have graduated from a Nebraska high school. Applicant must enroll (or have already enrolled) in a Nebraska college/university that offers a curriculum which will qualify a graduating student for at least an entry level position in print journalism. Preference is given to applicants with an interest in news, editorial, photography, circulation, production, or advertising careers on a weekly, semi-weekly, or daily newspaper. Selection is based upon scholastic ability, financial ability, and good citizenship in school and community. Applicant must submit a statement regarding career plans in the field of print journalism. Award may be used at Nebraska schools only.
Contact: Allen Beermann.

246 New York Financial Writers Association Scholarship
New York Financial Writers Association
P.O. Box 20281 Greeley Square Station
New York, NY 10001-0003
(800) 533-7551, (800) 533-7560 (fax)
Average award: $2,000
Number of awards: 10
Deadline: end of February
College level: Junior, Senior, Graduate, Doctoral
Majors/Fields: Financial/business journalism
Criteria: Applicant must be attending a school in the New York metropolitan area. Awarded every year. New York City schools only.
Contact: Sally Heinemann, Scholarship Chairperson, (212) 504-7701.

247 Newhouse Scholarship Program
National Association of Hispanic Journalists (NAHJ)
1193 National Press Building
Washington, DC 20045
(202) 662-7145, (202) 662-7144 (fax)
Average award: $5,000
Deadline: February 28
College level: Junior, Senior
Majors/Fields: Journalism, mass communication
Criteria: Applicant must be enrolled full time. Award is given for two years. Recipient receives funding to attend the NAHJ convention as well as an internship during the summer between junior and senior year. Awarded every year.
Contact: Rebecca K. Finley, Scholarships.

248 NJPA Internship/Scholarship Program
New Jersey Press Association
840 Bear Tavern Road
Suite 305
West Trenton, NJ 08628-1019
njpress@aol.com
http://members.aol.com/teengleman/njcpa/contests.html
Average award: $2,000
Number of awards: 5
Deadline: January 15
College level: Junior, Senior
Criteria: Applicant must be interested in a newspaper career. Recipient of scholarship will receive paid internship at a New Jersey newspaper in addition to scholarship. Awarded every year.

249 Press Club of Dallas Foundation Scholarships
Press Club of Dallas Foundation
400 North Olive, LB 218
Dallas, TX 75201
(214) 740-9988, (214) 740-9989 (fax)
dallaspc@aol.com
Average award: $1,000
Maximum award: $3,000
Number of awards: 10
Deadline: May 1
College level: Junior, Senior, Graduate
Majors/Fields: Journalism, mass communications, public relations
Criteria: Applicant must be a Texas resident, provide samples of work, and demonstrate financial need. Recipient must reapply each year. Awarded every year.
Contact: Carol Wortham, Executive Director.

250 San Antonio Express News Elaine Noll Scholarship
Texas Professional Communicators
P.O. Box 173
Denison, TX 75021-0173
(903) 465-8567
kcasey@tenet.edu
Average award: $1,000
Number of awards: 1
Deadline: March 20
College level: Sophomore, Junior, Senior, Graduate, Doctoral
Majors/Fields: Journalism
Criteria: Applicant must be a woman pursuing a career in sportswriting. Awarded every year.
Contact: Kay Casey, Scholarship Director, kcasey2tenet.edu.

251 South Carolina Press Association Foundation Newspaper Scholarship
South Carolina Press Association Foundation
P.O. Box 11429
Columbia, SC 29211
(803) 750-9561, (803) 551-0903 (fax)
SCPress@cyberspace.infi.net
Average award: $2,000
Maximum award: $2,500
Number of awards: 3
Deadline: June 1
College level: Junior, Senior
Criteria: Applicant must attend a South Carolina college and be interested in a career in newspapers. Selection is based upon grades, participation in journalistic activities in college, and recommendations of faculty members. Financial need may be considered. If applicant does not work in newspapers within five years after graduation, scholarship becomes a loan and must be repaid. Satisfactory progress is required for renewal. Awarded every year. South Carolina colleges or universities only.
Contact: Jennifer Roberts, Assistant Director.

Library Science ────────────

252 Harold Lancour Scholarship for Foreign Study
Beta Phi Mu
School of Library and Information Studies
Florida State University
Tallahassee, FL 32306-2048
(904) 644-3907, (904) 644-6253 (fax)
beta_phi_mu@lis.fsu.edu
http://www.fsu.edu/~lis/beta/
Maximum award: $1,000
Number of awards: 1
Deadline: March 15
College level: Graduate, Doctoral, librarians or library school students for foreign research or study
Majors/Fields: Library science
Criteria: Applicant must demonstrate relevance of proposed foreign study to work or school. Awarded every year.
Contact: Dr. F. William Summers, Executive Secretary.

Photojournalism

253   Bob East Scholarship

National Press Photographers (NPP) Foundation
3200 Croasdaile Drive
Suite 306
Durham, NC 27705
(800) 289-6772
Average award: $1,000
Number of awards: 1
Deadline: March 1
College level: Sophomore, Junior, Senior, Graduate
Majors/Fields: Photojournalism
Criteria: Applicant must submit a portfolio of at least five single images and a picture story. Awarded every year.
Contact: Chuck Fadely, *The Miami Herald*, One Herald Plaza, Miami, FL 33132, (305) 376-3750.

254   Joseph Ehrenreich Scholarship

National Press Photographers (NPP) Foundation
3200 Croasdaile Drive
Suite 306
Durham, NC 27705
(800) 289-6772
Average award: $1,000
Number of awards: 5
Deadline: March 1
College level: Sophomore, Junior, Senior
Majors/Fields: Photojournalism
Criteria: Applicant must have journalism potential, great financial need, photo aptitude, and academic ability. Portfolio is required. Applicant must be in a bachelor's degree program at a recognized four-year college or university with courses in photojournalism. Awarded every year.
Contact: Mike Smith, 321 West Lafayette Boulevard, Detroit, MI 48231, (313) 646-7286.

255   NPP Foundation Still Scholarship

National Press Photographers (NPP) Foundation
3200 Croasdaile Drive
Suite 306
Durham, NC 27705
(800) 289-6772
Average award: $1,000
Number of awards: 1
Deadline: March 1
College level: Sophomore, Junior, Senior
Criteria: Applicant must have had courses in photojournalism in a program leading to a bachelor's degree. Award is aimed at an applicant with journalism potential, but with little opportunity and great need. Awarded every year.
Contact: Bill Sanders, 640 N.W. 100th Way, Coral Springs, FL 33071.

256   Reid Blackburn Scholarship

National Press Photographers (NPP) Foundation
3200 Croasdaile Drive
Suite 306
Durham, NC 27705
(800) 289-6772
Average award: $1,000
Number of awards: 1
Deadline: March 1
College level: Sophomore, Junior, Senior
Majors/Fields: Photojournalism
Criteria: Applicant must be a high school graduate and be pursuing a career in photojournalism, either currently in college or in the working world. Selection is based upon the philosophy and goals statement in the application. Awarded every year.
Contact: Steve Small, *Saint Petersburg Times*, 490 First Avenue South, Saint Petersburg, FL 33701, (813) 893-8231.

Radio/TV Broadcasting

257   Alabama Cable Television Association/ Otto Miller Scholarship

The University of Alabama
Box 870162
Tuscaloosa, AL 35487-0162
(205) 348-6756
Average award: $2,000
Number of awards: 1
Deadline: February 15
College level: Junior
Majors/Fields: Telecommunication
Criteria: Preference is given to applicants interested in a career in cable television. Awarded every year. Award may be used only at sponsoring institution.
Contact: Scholarship Committee, College of Communication, Box 870172, Tuscaloosa, AL 35487-0172, (205) 348-5520.

258   BEA Scholarships

Broadcast Education Association (BEA)
1771 N Street, NW
Washington, DC 20036-2891
(202) 429-5354
Average award: $5,000
Minimum award: $1,250
Number of awards: 7
Deadline: January 15
College level: Junior, Senior, Graduate, Doctoral
Majors/Fields: Broadcasting, radio, radio/TV broadcasting, media law
Criteria: Applicant must be enrolled at a BEA-member institution. Selection is based upon substantial evidence of superior academic performance and potential to be an outstanding contributor to radio. Applicant must demonstratete interest in the radio industry, high integrity, and personal and professional responsibility. Awarded every year.
Contact: Lara Sulimenko, Membership Services Assistant.

259   Broadcast Communications Scholarship

William Woods University
200 West Twelfth Street
Fulton, MO 65251-1098
(573) 592-4232, (573) 592-1146 (fax)
http://www.wmwoods.edu
Maximum award: $2,000
Deadline: June 1
College level: Freshman, Sophomore, Junior, Senior
Majors/Fields: Broadcast communications
Criteria: Audition is required. Recipient must maintain full-time enrollment and a minimum 3.0 GPA in broadcast communications major (minimum 2.75 GPA overall), and audition for at least one theatre production to retain scholarship. Awarded every year. Award may be used only at sponsoring institution.
Contact: Laura L. Archuleta, Director for Student Financial Aid, larchule@iris.wmwoods.edu.

260   Carole Simpson Scholarship

Radio and Television News Directors Foundation (RTNDF), Inc.
1000 Connecticut Avenue, NW
Suite 615
Washington, DC 20036
(202) 467-5212, (202) 223-4007 (fax)
gwenl@rtndf.org
http://www.rtndf.org
Average award: $2,000
Number of awards: 1
Deadline: March 1
College level: Sophomore, Junior, Senior, Graduate, Doctoral
Majors/Fields: Broadcast journalism
Criteria: Applicant must be a minority student enrolled in an electronic journalism sequence at an accredited or nationally recognized college or university. Awarded every year.
Contact: Gwen Lyda, Development Coordinator, gwenl@rtndf.org.

261 Charles Clark Cordle Memorial Scholarship

The ARRL Foundation, Inc.
225 Main Street
Newington, CT 06111
(860) 594-0230
foundation@arrl.org
http://www.arrl.org/arrlf/scholgen
Maximum award: $1,000
Number of awards: 1
Deadline: February 1
College level: Unspecified undergraduate and graduate students
Criteria: Applicant must have a radio license. Preference is given to residents of Georgia or Alabama studying in either state, with a minimum 2.5 GPA.
Contact: Scholarships.

262 Charles N. Fisher Memorial Scholarship

The ARRL Foundation, Inc.
225 Main Street
Newington, CT 06111
(860) 594-0230
foundation@arrl.org
http://www.arrl.org/arrlf/scholgen
Maximum award: $1,000
Number of awards: 1
Deadline: February 1
Majors/Fields: Communications, electronics, or related field
Criteria: Applicant must have a radio license. Preference is given to residents of the Southwestern Division (Arizona and Los Angeles, Orange County, San Diego, and Santa Barbara, Calif.).
Contact: Scholarships.

263 Ed Bradley Scholarship

Radio and Television News Directors Foundation (RTNDF), Inc.
1000 Connecticut Avenue, NW
Suite 615
Washington, DC 20036
(202) 467-5212, (202) 223-4007 (fax)
gwenl@rtndf.org
http://www.rtndf.org
Maximum award: $5,000
Number of awards: 1
Deadline: March 1
College level: Sophomore, Junior, Senior, Graduate, Doctoral
Majors/Fields: Broadcast journalism
Criteria: Applicant must be a minority student who desires a career in broadcast or cable news. Awarded every year.
Contact: Gwen Lyda, Development Coordinator.

264 F. Charles Ruling, N6FR Memorial Scholarship

The ARRL Foundation, Inc.
225 Main Street
Newington, CT 06111
(860) 594-0230
foundation@arrl.org
http://www.arrl.org/arrlf/scholgen
Maximum award: $1,000
Number of awards: 1
Deadline: February 1
College level: Unspecified undergraduate and graduate students
Majors/Fields: Communications, electronics, or related field
Criteria: Applicant must have a general class radio license.
Contact: Scholarships.

265 Harold E. Ennes Scholarship

Society of Broadcast Engineers (SBE)
8445 Keystone Crossing
Suite 140
Indianapolis, IN 46240
(317) 253-1640, (317) 253-0418 (fax)
http://www.sbe.org
Average award: $1,000
Maximum number of awards: 2
Minimum number of awards: 1
Deadline: July 1
College level: Freshman, Sophomore, Junior, Senior, Graduate
Majors/Fields: Broadcast engineering
Criteria: Applicant must have a career interest in the technical aspects of broadcasting and must be recommended by two members of the SBE. Preference is given to SBE members. Awarded every year.
Contact: Linda Godby, Certification Director.

266 Harold E. Fellows Scholarship

Broadcast Education Association (BEA)
1771 N Street, NW
Washington, DC 20036-2891
(202) 429-5354
Average award: $1,250
Number of awards: 4
Deadline: January 15
College level: Junior, Senior, Graduate, Doctoral
Majors/Fields: Broadcasting
Criteria: Applicant must be enrolled at a BEA-member institution. Selection is based upon substantial evidence of superior academic performance and potential to be an outstanding contributor to the field. Applicant should demonstrate interest in the general field of broadcasting and provide evidence of a high order of integrity and sense of responsibility. Applicant must provide proof of employment or internship at a National Association of Broadcasters station. Awarded every year.
Contact: Lara Sulimenko, Membership Services Assistant.

267 Irving W. Cook, WA0CGS Scholarship

The ARRL Foundation, Inc.
225 Main Street
Newington, CT 06111
(860) 594-0230
foundation@arrl.org
http://www.arrl.org/arrlf/scholgen
Maximum award: $1,000
Number of awards: 1
Deadline: February 1
College level: Unspecified undergraduate and graduate students
Majors/Fields: Communications, electronics, or related field
Criteria: Applicant must have a radio license. Preference is given to Kansas residents.
Contact: Scholarships.

268 K2TEO Martin J. Green, Sr. Memorial Scholarship

The ARRL Foundation, Inc.
225 Main Street
Newington, CT 06111
(860) 594-0230
foundation@arrl.org
http://www.arrl.org/arrlf/scholgen
Maximum award: $1,000
Number of awards: 1
Deadline: February 1
Criteria: Applicant must have a general class radio license. Preference is given to students who come from a Ham family (parents, grandparents, brothers, sisters).
Contact: Scholarships.

269   L. Phil Wicker Scholarship

The ARRL Foundation, Inc.
225 Main Street
Newington, CT 06111
(860) 594-0230
foundation@arrl.org
http://www.arrl.org/arrlf/scholgen
Maximum award: $1,000
Number of awards: 1
Deadline: February 1
Majors/Fields: Communications, electronics, or related field
Criteria: Applicant must have a general class radio license. Preference is given to residents of Roanoke Division (North Carolina, South Carolina, Virginia, West Virginia).
Contact: Scholarships.

270   Len Allen Award of Merit

Radio and Television News Directors Foundation (RTNDF), Inc.
1000 Connecticut Avenue, NW
Suite 615
Washington, DC 20036
(202) 467-5212, (202) 223-4007 (fax)
gwenl@rtndf.org
http://www.rtndf.org
Average award: $1,000
Number of awards: 1
Deadline: March 1
College level: Sophomore, Junior, Senior, Graduate, Doctoral
Majors/Fields: Broadcast journalism
Criteria: Applicant must desire a career in radio news or news management. Awarded every year.
Contact: Gwen Lyda, Development Coordinator.

271   Mary Lou Brown Scholarship

The ARRL Foundation, Inc.
225 Main Street
Newington, CT 06111
(860) 594-0230
foundation@arrl.org
http://www.arrl.org/arrlf/scholgen
Maximum award: $2,500
Deadline: February 1
College level: Unspecified undergraduate and graduate students
Criteria: Applicant must have a general class radio license. Preference is given to residents of Arkansas, Idaho, Montana, Oregon, or Washington attending school in one of those states, with a minimum 3.0 GPA and demonstrated interest in promoting the Amateur Radio Service.
Contact: Scholarships.

272   Minoru Yasui Memorial Scholarship for Broadcast

Asian American Journalists Association (AAJA)
1765 Sutter Street
San Francisco, CA 94115
(415) 346-2051, (415) 346-6343 (fax)
aaja1@aol.com
http://www.aaja.org
Average award: $1,000
Deadline: April 15
College level: Freshman, Sophomore, Junior, Senior, Graduate
Majors/Fields: Broadcast journalism
Criteria: Scholarship seeks to encourage Asian men to pursue on-air careers in broadcast journalism. Selection is based upon a commitment to the field of journalism, a sensitivity to Asian-American issues as demonstrated by community involvement, journalistic ability, scholastic ability, and financial need.
Contact: Hien Nguyen, Program Coordinator.

273   NPP Foundation Television News Scholarship

National Press Photographers (NPP) Foundation
3200 Croasdaile Drive
Suite 306
Durham, NC 27705
(800) 289-6772
Average award: $1,000
Number of awards: 1
Deadline: March 1
College level: Junior, Senior
Majors/Fields: Broadcasting
Criteria: Applicant must have courses in TV news photojournalism in a program leading to a bachelor's degree and must submit a video tape with examples of work. Award is aimed at applicant with television news potential but with little opportunity and great need. Awarded every year.
Contact: Ned Hockman, Professor Emeritus, School of Journalism, University of Oklahoma, 800 Hoover, Norman, OK 73072-6151.

274   Paul and Helen L. Grauer Scholarship

The ARRL Foundation, Inc.
225 Main Street
Newington, CT 06111
(860) 594-0230
foundation@arrl.org
http://www.arrl.org/arrlf/scholgen
Maximum award: $1,000
Number of awards: 1
Deadline: February 1
College level: Sophomore, Junior, Senior, Graduate, Doctoral
Majors/Fields: Communications, electronics, or related field
Criteria: Applicant must have a novice class radio license. Preference is given to residents of Midwest Division (Iowa, Kansas, Missouri, Nebraska) who attend school within the division.
Contact: Scholarships.

275   Perry F. Hadlock Memorial Scholarship

The ARRL Foundation, Inc.
225 Main Street
Newington, CT 06111
(860) 594-0230
foundation@arrl.org
http://www.arrl.org/arrlf/scholgen
Maximum award: $1,000
Number of awards: 1
Deadline: February 1
College level: Sophomore, Junior, Senior, Graduate, Doctoral
Majors/Fields: Electronic engineering
Criteria: Applicant must have a general class radio license. Preference is given to students attending Clarkson U.
Contact: Scholarships.

276   PHD ARA Scholarship

The ARRL Foundation, Inc.
225 Main Street
Newington, CT 06111
(860) 594-0230
foundation@arrl.org
http://www.arrl.org/arrlf/scholgen
Maximum award: $1,000
Number of awards: 1
Deadline: February 1
Majors/Fields: Computer science, electronic engineering, journalism
Criteria: Applicant must have a radio license. Preference is given to residents of Iowa, Kansas, Missouri, or Nebraska who are children of deceased radio amateurs.
Contact: Scholarships.

277 Quarton McElroy Broadcast Scholarship

Iowa Broadcasters Association
P.O. Box 71186
Des Moines, IA 50325
(515) 224-7237
Average award: $2,500
Number of awards: 4
Deadline: April 15
College level: Freshman
Majors/Fields: Broadcast journalism, broadcasting
Criteria: Applicant must be a senior graduating from an Iowa high school who will attend an Iowa college or university. Awarded every year.
Contact: Scholarships.

278 RTNDF Undergraduate Scholarship

Radio and Television News Directors Foundation (RTNDF), Inc.
1000 Connecticut Avenue, NW
Suite 615
Washington, DC 20036
(202) 467-5212, (202) 223-4007 (fax)
gwenl@rtndf.org
http://www.rtndf.org
Average award: $1,000
Number of awards: 10
Deadline: March 1
College level: Sophomore, Junior, Senior
Majors/Fields: Broadcast journalism
Criteria: Applicant must be planning a career in broadcast or cable news. Awarded every year.
Contact: Gwen Lyda, Development Coordinator.

279 Senator Barry Goldwater (K7UGA) Scholarship

The ARRL Foundation, Inc.
225 Main Street
Newington, CT 06111
(860) 594-0230
foundation@arrl.org
http://www.arrl.org/arrlf/scholgen
Maximum award: $5,000
Number of awards: 1
Deadline: February 1
College level: Unspecified undergraduate and graduate students
Criteria: Applicant must have at least a novice class radio license and be attending a regionally accredited institution.
Contact: Scholarships.

280 Summer Fellowship

International Radio and Television Society Foundation (IRTS)
420 Lexington Avenue
Suite 1714
New York, NY 10170-0101
(212) 867-6650, (212) 867-6653 (fax)
http://www.irts.org
Average award: Travel and housing costs, stipend for expenses
Number of awards: 19
Deadline: November 20
College level: College juniors and seniors
Criteria: Applicant must be enrolled full time, be a communications major or have participated in communications-related extracurricular activities, and be able to participate in the nine-week program. Awarded every year.
Contact: Maria De Leon-Fisher, Senior Director of Program Adminin-stration, (212) 867-6650, extension 304.

281 WTOL-TV Broadcast and Communications Scholarship

University of Toledo
Financial Aid Office
Toledo, OH 43606-3390
(419) 537-2056
Average award: $3,000
Number of awards: 1
College level: Junior
Majors/Fields: Broadcast communications
Criteria: Applicant must be black or Hispanic. Minimum 3.0 GPA is recommended. Award is for two years. Awarded every year. Award may be used only at sponsoring institution.
Contact: J.C. Caldwell, 50 Men and Women of Toledo, Inc., P.O. Box 3557, Toledo, OH 43608, (419) 729-4654.

282 "You've Got a Friend in Pennsylvania" Scholarship

The ARRL Foundation, Inc.
225 Main Street
Newington, CT 06111
(860) 594-0230
foundation@arrl.org
http://www.arrl.org/arrlf/scholgen
Maximum award: $1,000
Number of awards: 1
Deadline: February 1
Criteria: Applicant must have a general class radio license and be a member of the ARRL. Preference is given to Pennsylvania residents.
Contact: Scholarships.

Speech/Forensics———

283 Alabama Forensics Council Scholarship

The University of Alabama
Box 870162
Tuscaloosa, AL 35487-0162
(205) 348-6756
Average award: Full tuition
Number of awards: 20
Deadline: March 1
College level: Freshman, Sophomore, Junior, Senior
Criteria: Applicant must be interested in and show aptitude for forensics program. Apply to Department of Speech Communication. Minimum 3.0 GPA is required to retain scholarship. Awarded every year. Award may be used only at sponsoring institution.
Contact: Scholarship Committee, College of Communication, Box 870172, Tuscaloosa, AL 35487-0172.

284 Alben W. Barkely Debate Scholarship

Emory University
1380 Oxford Road, NE
Atlanta, GA 30322
(404) 727-6039
Average award: Full tuition
Number of awards: 2
Deadline: Early application is recommended
College level: Freshman
Criteria: Applicant must have had outstanding debating experience. Renewable for four years of undergraduate study. Awarded every year. Award may be used only at sponsoring institution.
Contact: Melissa Wade, Director of Barkley Forum, Drawer U.

285   Debate Scholarship

DePaul University
1 East Jackson Boulevard
Chicago, IL 60604
(312) 362-8704, (312) 362-5749 (fax)
Average award: $3,500
Maximum award: $6,000
Minimum award: $1,000
Number of awards: 10
Deadline: February 1
College level: Freshman
Criteria: Applicant must participate on the debate team and practice policy-style debate. Scholarship is renewable. Awarded every year. Award may be used only at sponsoring institution.
Contact: Jennifer Sparrow, Scholarship Coordinator, jsparrow@wppost.depaul.edu.

286   Forensics Scholarship

Ripon College
300 Seward Street
P.O. Box 248
Ripon, WI 54971
(800) 94-RIPON, (414) 748-7243 (fax)
adminfo@mac.ripon.edu
http://www.ripon.edu
Maximum award: $3,000
Number of awards: 5
Deadline: December 1 (early decision), March 1
College level: Freshman, Transfer
Criteria: Selection is based upon honors and recognition received for high school activity. Applicant must interview with Ripon College forensics coach and be accepted for admission at Ripon College. Renewable if good academic standing is maintained and recipient participates in forensics. Awarded every year. Award may be used only at sponsoring institution.
Contact: Paul J. Weeks, Vice President and Dean of Admission.

287   Marion Fletcher Scholarship

Mesa State College
Financial Aid Department
P.O. Box 2647
Grand Junction, CO 81502
(970) 248-1396
Maximum award: Tuition and fees
Number of awards: 1
College level: Sophomore, Junior, Senior
Majors/Fields: Speech, theatre
Criteria: Applicant must be enrolled full time and have a minimum 3.0 GPA. Awarded every year. Award may be used only at sponsoring institution.
Contact: School of Humanities and Social Sciences.

288   National Oratorical Contest Scholarship

The American Legion
Education and Scholarships Program
P.O. Box 1055
Indianapolis, IN 46206
(317) 630-1212
http://www.legion.org
Maximum award: $19,000
Number of awards: 74
Deadline: in December
College level: Freshman
Criteria: Applicant must be under 20 years of age, attending high school or junior high, and must compete in the American Legion oratorical contest at the national level. Scholarship must be used at a college or university in the U.S. for actual school costs, including tuition, room and board, fees, and books. Scholarship can be used over a period of eight years until the funds are exhausted. Awarded every year.
Contact: Mike Buss, Assistant Director, Americanism & Children & Youth, P.O. Box 1055, Indianapolis, IN 46206.

289   Oratorical Contest Scholarship

American Legion – Alabama
P.O. Box 1069
120 North Jackson Street
Montgomery, AL 36101-1069
(202) 262-6638
Maximum award: $5,000
Number of awards: 3
Deadline: State Finals in March
College level: Freshman
Criteria: Scholarship is awarded to the top three winners of the State Oratorical Contest. Awarded every year.
Contact: Department Adjutant.

290   Oratorical Contest Scholarship

American Legion – California
Department Adjutant
117 Veterans War Memorial Building
San Francisco, CA 94102
Maximum award: $1,000
Number of awards: 6
College level: Freshman
Criteria: Scholarship is for the winners of the state oratorical contest; applicants are selected by schools and participate in district contests, followed by area and departmental finals. Applicant should see his or her local high school counselor for further information. Awarded every year.
Contact: Department Adjutant.

291   Oratorical Contest Scholarship

American Legion – Florida
Department Headquarters
P.O. Box 547936
Orlando, FL 32854-7936
(407) 295-2631, (407) 299-0901 (fax)
fllegion@orl.mindspring.com
http://www.floridalegion.org
Average award: $1,333
Maximum award: $2,500
Minimum award: $1,000
Number of awards: 6
Deadline: October 1
College level: Freshman
Criteria: Applicant must be enrolled in any public, private, or parochial high school in the state of Florida. Award is for the first through sixth winners in the Oratorical Contest, a speaking contest based upon the U.S. Constitution. Awarded every year.
Contact: Larry Leudenburg, Scholarships.

292   Oratorical Contest Scholarship

American Legion – Illinois
P.O. Box 2910
Bloomington, IL 61702
(309) 663-0361
Maximum award: $1,600
Maximum number of awards: 10
Minimum number of awards: 5
Deadline: in January
College level: Freshman
Criteria: Applicant must be a student at any accredited high school in Illinois and compete in the state oratorical contest. Awarded every year.
Contact: Department Headquarters.

293 Oratorical Contest Scholarship

American Legion – Indiana
Americanism Office
777 North Meridian Street
Indianapolis, IN 46204
(317) 630-1264, (317) 237-9891 (fax)
Average award: $650
Maximum award: $1,250
Minimum award: $250
Number of awards: 8
Deadline: Early December
College level: Freshman
Criteria: Applicant must participate in local contests and must attend an Indiana high school. Speech must be on some aspect of the U.S. Constitution. Awarded every year.
Contact: Sheri Mitchell, Americanism Office.

294 Oratorical Contest Scholarship

American Legion – Iowa
Department Headquarters
720 Lyon Street
Des Moines, IA 50309
Maximum award: $2,000
Number of awards: 3
Deadline: September
College level: Freshman
Criteria: Applicant must attend an accredited high school in Iowa, enter the contest at the local level, and must plan to attend a college or university in Iowa. Awarded every year.
Contact: Department Headquarters.

295 Oratorical Contest Scholarship

American Legion – Kansas
1314 Topeka Avenue
Topeka, KS 66612
(913) 232-9315
Maximum award: $1,000
Number of awards: 4
College level: Freshman
Criteria: Awarded every year.
Contact: Scholarships.

296 Oratorical Contest Scholarship

American Legion – Maryland
War Memorial Building
101 North Gay Street
Baltimore, MD 21202
(410) 752-3104, (410) 752-3822 (fax)
Maximum award: $2,500
Number of awards: 7
Deadline: October 1
College level: Freshman
Criteria: Applicant must be between the ages of 16 and 19. Awarded every year.
Contact: Thomas L. Davis, Adjutant.

297 Oratorical Contest Scholarship

American Legion – Massachusetts
Room 546-2
State House
Boston, MA 02133
(617) 727-2966, (617) 727-2969 (fax)
Average award: $833
Maximum award: $1,000
Minimum award: $400
Number of awards: 4
Deadline: December 15
College level: Freshman
Criteria: Applicant must be a student under age 20 and enrolled in junior or senior high school at time of contest. Awarded every year.
Contact: James Conway, Oratorical Chairman, 7 Belmont Street, Charlestown, MA 02129, (617) 242-6187.

298 Oratorical Contest Scholarship

American Legion – Michigan
212 North Verlinden
Lansing, MI 48915
(517) 371-4720, (517) 371-2401 (fax)
info@michiganlegion.org
http://www.michiganlegion.org
Maximum award: $1,000
Number of awards: 5
Deadline: February
College level: Freshman
Criteria: Applicant must be a finalist in the oratorical contest. Awarded every year.
Contact: Department Adjutant, info@michiganlegion.org.

299 Oratorical Contest Scholarship

American Legion – Minnesota
Education Committee
State Veterans Service Building
St. Paul, MN 55155
Maximum award: $1,200
Number of awards: 8
Deadline: April 1
College level: Freshman
Criteria: Applicant must be a winner in the annual oratorical contest. Awarded every year.
Contact: Department Oratorical Chairman.

300 Oratorical Contest Scholarship

American Legion – Missouri
Department Adjutant
P.O. Box 179
Jefferson City, MO 65102
(314) 893-2353
Maximum award: $1,000
Number of awards: 4
College level: Freshman
Criteria: Applicant must be a winner in the Missouri annual oratorical contest. Awarded every year.
Contact: Department Adjutant.

301 Oratorical Contest Scholarship

American Legion – Nebraska
Department Headquarters
P.O. Box 5205
Lincoln, NE 68505
(402) 464-6338
Maximum award: $1,000
Number of awards: 4
College level: Freshman
Criteria: Applicant must be a winner of the Nebraska Department Oratorical Contest. Awarded every year.
Contact: Robert Craig, Department Adjutant.

302 Oratorical Contest Scholarship

American Legion – New Jersey
Legion 146
Route 130
Bordertown, NJ 08505-2226
(609) 695-5418
Maximum award: $4,000
Number of awards: 5
College level: Freshman
Criteria: Applicant must be a winner in the New Jersey Department Oratorical Contest. Awarded every year.
Contact: Department Adjutant, War Memorial Building, Trenton, NJ 08608.

303   Oratorical Contest Scholarship

American Legion – New York
Department Adjutant
112 State Street, Suite 400
Albany, NY 12207
(518) 463-2215
Maximum award: $6,000
Number of awards: 5
College level: Freshman
Criteria: Applicant must compete at local, county, district, and zone levels before the five finalists may compete for this award. Awarded every year.
Contact: Richard M. Pedro, Department Adjutant.

304   Oratorical Contest Scholarship

American Legion – South Carolina
P.O. Box 11355
Columbia, SC 29211
(803) 799-1992, (803) 771-9831 (fax)
Maximum award: $1,600
Number of awards: 5
Deadline: None
College level: Freshman
Criteria: Applicant must compete in and win the High School Oratorical Contest. Scholarship is renewable. Awarded every year.
Contact: Jim Hawk, Department Adjutant.

305   Oratorical Contest Scholarship

American Legion – Tennessee
State Headquarters
215 Eighth Avenue, North
Nashville, TN 37203
(615) 254-0568, (615) 255-1551 (fax)
Average award: $2,500
Maximum award: $5,000
Minimum award: $1,500
Number of awards: 3
Deadline: January
College level: Freshman
Criteria: Applicant must attend high school in Tennessee and be a winner in the state oratorical contest. Contestant must speak 8 to 10 minutes on some phase of the U.S. Constitution, emphasizing the attendant duties and obligations of a citizen to our government. Awarded every year.
Contact: A. Mike Hammer, Department Adjutant.

306   Oratorical Contest Scholarship

American Legion – Texas
Department of Texas
P.O. Box 789
Austin, TX 78767
(512) 472-4138
Maximum award: $1,000
Maximum number of awards: 4
Minimum number of awards: 4
Deadline: November
College level: Freshman
Criteria: Applicant must be a Texas resident, current high school student, be sponsored by an American Legion post, and be a winner in the state oratorical contest. Awarded every year.
Contact: Department Oratorical Chairman.

307   Oratorical Contest Scholarship

American Legion – Virginia
Department Adjutant
1805 Chantilly Street
Richmond, VA 23230
(804) 353-6606, (804) 358-1940 (fax)
valeg@aol.com
http://members.aol.com/valeg/valegion.htm
Average award: $767
Maximum award: $1,100
Minimum award: $600
Maximum number of awards: 3
Minimum number of awards: 1
Deadline: December 1
College level: Freshman
Criteria: Applicant must be a winner of the Virginia Department oratorical contest and attend high school in Virginia. Awarded every year.
Contact: Cornelius T. O'Neill, Department Adjutant, P.O. Box 11025, Richmond, VA 23230, valeg@aol.com.

308   Oratorical Contest Scholarship

American Legion – Wisconsin
Department Headquarters
812 East State Street
Milwaukee, WI 53202
Maximum award: $1,000
Number of awards: 12
College level: Freshman
Criteria: Applicant must be a winner of the state or regional high school oratorical contests. Awarded every year.
Contact: Scholarships.

309   Voice of Democracy Audio-Essay Competition

Veterans of Foreign Wars (VFW)
406 West 34th Street
Kansas City, MO 64111
(816) 968-1117
Maximum award: $20,000
Number of awards: 55
Deadline: November 1
College level: Freshman
Criteria: Applicant must be a 10th-, 11th-, or 12th-grade high school student or the dependent of a U.S. military or civilian service person in an overseas school. Awarded every year.
Contact: Gordon R. Thorson, National Director, Voice of Democracy.

310   W.T. Goodloe Rutland Endowed Scholarship

The University of Alabama
Box 870162
Tuscaloosa, AL 35487-0162
(205) 348-6756
Average award: $1,500
Number of awards: 1
Deadline: March 1
College level: Freshman
Criteria: Priority is given to full-time freshmen with demonstrated potential in debate/forensics whose academic and leadership records, standardized test scores, and recommendations indicate interest in studying human communication. Apply to Department of Speech Communication. Awarded every year. Award may be used only at sponsoring institution.
Contact: Scholarship Committee, College of Communication, Box 870172, Tuscaloosa, AL 35487-0172.

Creative/Performing Arts

Architecture/Landscape Architecture————

311   AIA Minority/Disadvantaged Scholarship

American Architectural Foundation
1735 New York Avenue, NW
Washington, DC 20006
Maximum award: $2,500
Number of awards: 20
Deadline: January 15
College level: Freshman, Sophomore
Majors/Fields: Architecture
Criteria: Applicant must be a minority or disadvantaged U.S. resident nominated by an individual architect or firm, an AIA chapter, a community design center, a guidance counselor, a teacher, a dean or administrative head of an accredited school of architecture, or a director of a community, civic, or religious organization. Scholarship is renewable. Awarded every year. Award may be used only at schools accredited by NAAB (National Architecture Accrediting Board).
Contact: Mary Fellier, Scholarships.

312   AILA/Yamagami/Hope Fellowship

Landscape Architecture Foundation
4401 Connecticut Avenue, NW #500
Washington, DC 20008
(202) 686-0068, (202) 686-1001 (fax)
Average award: $1,000
Deadline: August 2
College level: Landscape architects who have been in practice for three years and wish to continue their education.
Majors/Fields: Landscape architecture
Criteria: Applicant must submit a summary (500 word maximum), statement of intent (100 word maximum), and two letters of recommendation.
Contact: Scholarships.

313   Edith H. Henderson Scholarship

Landscape Architecture Foundation
4401 Connecticut Avenue, NW #500
Washington, DC 20008
(202) 686-0068, (202) 686-1001 (fax)
Average award: $1,000
Deadline: March 31
Majors/Fields: Landscape architecture
Criteria: Applicant must submit typewritten essay (200-400 words) in review of Edith H. Henderson's book entitled "Edith Henderson's Home Landscape Companion," and have participated in a class in public speaking or creative writing.
Contact: Scholarships.

314   Edward D. Stone Jr. and Associates Minority Scholarship

Landscape Architecture Foundation
4401 Connecticut Avenue, NW #500
Washington, DC 20008
(202) 686-0068, (202) 686-1001 (fax)
Average award: $1,000
Number of awards: 2
Deadline: March 31
Majors/Fields: Landscape architecture
Criteria: Applicant must be a minority student and must submit essay, color slides of best work, and two letters of recommendation. Awarded every year.
Contact: Scholarships.

315   Harriet Barnhart Wimmer Scholarship

Landscape Architecture Foundation
4401 Connecticut Avenue, NW #500
Washington, DC 20008
(202) 686-0068, (202) 686-1001 (fax)
Average award: $1,000
Number of awards: 1
Deadline: March 31
College level: Junior, Senior
Majors/Fields: Landscape architecture
Criteria: Applicant must be a woman who has demonstrated excellence in design ability and sensitivity to the environment. Applicant must submit typed, double-spaced autobiography of personal and professional goals (500 word maximum), one letter or recommendation, and samples of graphics work.
Contact: Scholarships.

316   James W. Fitzgibbon Scholarship

Washington University
One Brookings Drive
Campus Box 1089
St. Louis, MO 63130
(314) 935-6000 or (800) 638-0700
Average award: Full tuition plus $1,000 stipend
Number of awards: 1
Deadline: January 15
College level: Freshman
Majors/Fields: Architecture
Criteria: Applicant must submit portfolio. Selection is based upon academic merit; financial need is not considered. Satisfactory academic performance is required to retain scholarship. Awarded every year. Award may be used only at sponsoring institution.
Contact: Office of Undergraduate Admission.

317   King and Johnson Scholarship

University of Tennessee, Knoxville
Financial Aid Office
115 Student Services Building
Knoxville, TN 37994
(615) 974-3131
Average award: $2,500
Number of awards: 1
Deadline: February 1
College level: Junior, Senior
Majors/Fields: Architecture
Criteria: Applicant must be a high school graduate and resident of Tennessee, show promise in architecture, and demonstrate financial need. Applicant also receives internship employment with King and Johnson Architects, Inc. Scholarship is renewable. Awarded every year. Award may be used only at sponsoring institution.
Contact: College of Architecture and Planning, 19 Art and Architecture Building, Knoxville, TN 37996, (615) 974-5265.

318   LAF/CLASS Fund Scholarships and Internships

Landscape Architecture Foundation
4401 Connecticut Avenue, NW #500
Washington, DC 20008
(202) 686-0068, (202) 686-1001 (fax)
Maximum award: $2,000
Number of awards: 16
Deadline: March 31
College level: Senior, Graduate
Majors/Fields: Landscape architecture
Criteria: Applicant must submit a 300 word (maximum) statement on landscape architecture, a 100 word (maximum) statement indicating intended use of funds, and letters of recommendation, and have academic, community, and professional involvement. Award may be used only at California Polytechnic St U at San Luis Obispo, California St Polytechnic U at Pomona, UC Davis, UC Irvine, and UC Los Angeles.
Contact: Scholarships.

319   Mark Kaminski Summer Internship

Smithsonian Institution Cooper-Hewitt Museum Internships
2 East 91st Street
New York, NY 10128
Average award: $2,500
Number of awards: 1
Deadline: March 31
College level: Sophomore, Junior, Senior, Graduate
Majors/Fields: Architecture, architectural history, design/criticism, museum education, museum studies
Criteria: Internship encourages promising young students to explore careers in the museum profession. Internship runs annually from the second week of June through the second week of August. Housing is not provided.
Contact: Intern Coordinator, Cooper-Hewitt, National Museum of Design.

320   Minority/Disadvantaged Scholarship

American Institute of Architects (AIA)
1735 New York Avenue, NW
Washington, DC 20006
(202) 626-7300, (202) 626-7511
Maximum award: $2,500
Number of awards: 20
Deadline: January 16
College level: Freshman, Sophomore, Transfer
Majors/Fields: Architecture
Criteria: Applicant must be a minority or disadvantaged U.S. resident and be nominated by an architect, local AIA chapter, a community design center, guidance counselor or teacher, faculty member from an accredited architecture school, or director of a community or religious organization by December 3. Applicant must be entering a degree program at a school of architecture approved by the National Architectural Accrediting Board. Good academic standing in an accredited school of architecture and financial need is required to retain scholarship. Awarded every year.
Contact: AIA/AAF Scholarship Program Director, (202) 626-7511.

321   NSA/ASLA Student Competition in Landscape Architecture

National Stone Association (NSA)
1415 Elliot Place, NW
Washington, DC 20007
(800) 342-1415, (202) 342-1100 (fax)
Maximum award: $2,000
Number of awards: 3
Deadline: May 15
College level: Sophomore, Junior, Senior, Graduate
Majors/Fields: Landscape architecture
Criteria: Selection is based upon overall excellence in design, creativity, and sensitivity to community needs. Awarded every year.
Contact: Robert S. Brown, Jr., Director of Public Affairs.

322   Rain Bird Scholarship

Landscape Architecture Foundation
4401 Connecticut Avenue, NW #500
Washington, DC 20008
(202) 686-0068, (202) 686-1001 (fax)
Average award: $1,000
Number of awards: 1
Deadline: March 31
College level: Junior, Senior
Majors/Fields: Landscape architecture
Criteria: Applicant must submit essay and demonstrate commitment to the profession through participation in extracurricular activities and exemplary scholastic achievements. Financial need is considered.
Contact: Scholarships.

323   Raymond E. Page Scholarship

Landscape Architecture Foundation
4401 Connecticut Avenue, NW #500
Washington, DC 20008
(202) 686-0068, (202) 686-1001 (fax)
Average award: $1,000
Number of awards: 1
Deadline: March 31
College level: Junior, Senior
Majors/Fields: Landscape architecture
Criteria: Applicant must submit a double-spaced, two-page essay describing the applicant's need for financial assistance and how the award is to be used and a letter of recommendation.
Contact: Scholarships.

324   RTKL Traveling Fellowship

American Institute of Architects (AIA)
1735 New York Avenue, NW
Washington, DC 20006
(202) 626-7300, (202) 626-7511
Average award: $2,500
Number of awards: 1
Deadline: February 14
College level: Senior
Majors/Fields: Architecture
Criteria: Applicant must be in the second-to-last year of a bachelor or master of architecture program and planning to travel outside the United States or be accepted in a professional degree program and planning foreign travel that will have a beneficial and direct relationship to educational goals. Selection is based upon statement of purpose, relevance of the travel plans to the educational goals, academic performance, and recommendations. Awarded every year.
Contact: Scholarships, (202) 626-7511.

325   Scholarship Program for Professional Degree Candidates

American Institute of Architects (AIA)
1735 New York Avenue, NW
Washington, DC 20006
(202) 626-7300, (202) 626-7511
Average award: $1,000
Maximum award: $2,500
Minimum award: $500
Number of awards: 230
Deadline: February 1
College level: Senior, Graduate, Fourth-year B.Arch. students
Majors/Fields: Architecture
Criteria: Applicant must attend a school accredited by the National Architectural Accrediting Board or recognized by the Royal Architectural Institute of Canada. Selection is based upon statement of goals, academic performance, recommendations, and financial need. Awarded every year.
Contact: Mary Felber, Scholarships, (202) 626-7511.

326 Thomas P. Papandrew Scholarship

Landscape Architecture Foundation
4401 Connecticut Avenue, NW #500
Washington, DC 20008
(202) 686-0068, (202) 686-1001 (fax)
Average award: $1,000
Deadline: March 31
Majors/Fields: Landscape architecture
Criteria: Applicant must be an Arizona resident, submit transcript and letter of reference, be a full-time student, and a member of an ethnic group underrepresented in the College of Architecture and Environmental Design. Renewable if recipient continues to demonstrate financial need. Award may be used only at Arizona St U.
Contact: Scholarships.

327 William J. Locklin Scholarship

Landscape Architecture Foundation
4401 Connecticut Avenue, NW #500
Washington, DC 20008
(202) 686-0068, (202) 686-1001 (fax)
Average award: $1,000
Deadline: March 31
Majors/Fields: Lighting design
Criteria: Applicant must submit essay, visual samples, and letter of recommendation.
Contact: Scholarships.

Art History

328 Cloisters College Internship

Metropolitan Museum of Art
Attn: Internship Programs
1000 Fifth Avenue
New York, NY 10028-0198
(212) 879-5500, extension 3710
Average award: $2,000
Number of awards: 8
Deadline: February 5
College level: Sophomore, Junior, Senior
Majors/Fields: Art history
Criteria: Recipient will conduct gallery workshops for groups of New York City day campers at the Cloisters, a medieval European branch museum. The nine-week internship runs from June to August and also includes intensive training in The Cloisters Collection and museum teaching techniques. Special consideration is given to first- and second-year students. Awarded every year.
Contact: College Internship Program, The Cloisters, Fort Tryon Park, New York, NY 10040, (212) 795-3640.

329 Metropolitan Museum of Art Summer Internship

Metropolitan Museum of Art
Attn: Internship Programs
1000 Fifth Avenue
New York, NY 10028-0198
(212) 879-5500, extension 3710
Average award: $2,500
Number of awards: 14
Deadline: In January
College level: Senior, Graduate, Doctoral
Majors/Fields: Art history
Criteria: Applicant should have a strong background in art history. Undergraduate interns work on departmental projects, give gallery talks, and work at the Visitor Information Center. Graduate assistant is appointed to a specific department, participating in various projects and gaining practical, first-hand experience. Program runs ten weeks, from June through August. Graduate applicant should have completed one year of graduate school. Scholarship is renewable. Awarded every year.
Contact: Coordinator for Internships, (212) 570-3710.

330 Peter Krueger Summer Internship

Smithsonian Institution Cooper-Hewitt Museum Internships
2 East 91st Street
New York, NY 10128
Average award: $2,500
Number of awards: 6
Deadline: March 31
College level: Sophomore, Junior, Senior, Graduate
Majors/Fields: Art history, design, museum education, museum studies
Criteria: Internship encourages promising young students to explore careers in the museum profession. Internship runs annually from the second week of June through the second week of August. Housing is not provided.
Contact: Intern Coordinator, Cooper-Hewitt, National Museum of Design, 2 East 91st Street, New York, NY 10128.

331 Smithsonian Institution Internships and Fellowships

Smithsonian Institution Conservation Analytical Laboratory Interns
Museum Support Center
MRC 534
Washington, DC 20560
(301) 238-3700
Maximum award: $27,000
Number of awards: 9
Deadline: February 15
College level: Freshman, Sophomore, Junior, Senior, Graduate, Doctoral, Post-doctoral research
Majors/Fields: Art conservation, archaeology, natural history, preservation science
Criteria: Awarded every year.
Contact: Carol Grissom, Coordinator of Training, (301) 238-3732.

Creative/Performing Arts–General

332 Abby Weed Grey Scholarship

Minneapolis College of Art and Design
2501 Stevens Avenue South
Minneapolis, MN 55404
(612) 874-3782
Average award: $6,000
Number of awards: 1
Deadline: March 15
College level: Freshman
Criteria: Applicant must be a new student entering in fall semester, admitted by March 15. Portfolio and application are required. Financial need is not considered. Renewable for eight semesters based upon full-time attendance and academic performance. Awarded every year. Award may be used only at sponsoring institution.
Contact: Leann Winkelaar, Director of Financial Aid, (612) 874-3783.

333 Admissions Scholarship

Minneapolis College of Art and Design
2501 Stevens Avenue South
Minneapolis, MN 55404
(612) 874-3782
Average award: $2,000
Number of awards: 20
Deadline: March 15
College level: Freshman
Criteria: Applicant must be a new student entering in fall semester, admitted by March 15. Portfolio and application are required. Financial need is not considered. Renewable for eight semesters based upon full-time attendance and academic performance. Awarded every year. Award may be used only at sponsoring institution.
Contact: Leann Winkelaar, Director of Financial Aid, (612) 874-3783.

334   Art Department Scholarship

College of Notre Dame of Maryland
4701 North Charles Street
Baltimore, MD 21210
(410) 532-5369
Maximum award: $3,000
Deadline: December 31
College level: Freshman
*Criteria:*Applicant must be a woman, meet admissions requirements, and demonstrate artistic ability in the art competition. Renewable for up to four years. Awarded every year. Award may be used only at sponsoring institution.
Contact: Financial Aid Office.

335   Arts Recognition and Talent Search (ARTS)

National Foundation for Advancement in the Arts
800 Brickell Avenue, Suite 500
Miami, FL 33131
(305) 377-1147 or 800 970-ARTS, (305) 377-1149 (fax)
nfaa@nfaa.org
http://www.nfaa.org
Maximum award: $3,000
Number of awards: 400
Deadline: October 1; June 1 (early application)
College level: Freshman
*Criteria:*Applicant must be a U.S. citizen or permanent resident (unless applying in jazz), a high school senior or age 17 or 18 on December 1, and talented in dance, classical, jazz, vocal music, theatre, visual arts, photography, or creative writing. Awarded every year.
Contact: Wendy Paige Wheeler, Programs Associate.

336   ARTS Scholarship

Minneapolis College of Art and Design
2501 Stevens Avenue South
Minneapolis, MN 55404
(612) 874-3782
Average award: $1,000
Number of awards: 1
Deadline: March 15
College level: Freshman
Criteria: Awarded to applicant selected by the Art Recognition and Talent Search (ARTS) Competition. Applicant must be admitted to school and must participate in competition. Financial need is considered. Awarded every year. Award may be used only at sponsoring institution.
*Contact:*Leann Winkelaar, Director of Financial Aid, (612) 874-3783.

337   Associates Scholarship

Minneapolis College of Art and Design
2501 Stevens Avenue South
Minneapolis, MN 55404
(612) 874-3782
Average award: $2,000
Number of awards: 15
Deadline: March 15
College level: Freshman
Criteria: Applicant must be a new student entering in fall semester, admitted by March 15. Portfolio and application are required. Financial need is not considered. Awarded every year. Award may be used only at sponsoring institution.
*Contact:*Leann Winkelaar, Director of Financial Aid, (612) 874-3783.

338   Creative and Performing Arts Scholarship

Indiana State University
217 North Sixth Street
Terre Haute, IN 47809
(812) 237-2121, (812) 237-8023 (fax)
admisu@amber.indstate.edu
http://www.isu.indstate.edu
Average award: $1,100
Number of awards: 25
Deadline: February 1
College level: Freshman
*Criteria:*Applicant must excel in art, creative writing, dance, music, or theatre. Audition or portfolio is required. Satisfactory GPA and full-time enrollment are required to retain scholarship. Awarded every year. Award may be used only at sponsoring institution.
Contact: Steve Manuel, Scholarships, Office of Admissions, (800) 742-0891.

339   Creative and Performing Arts Scholarship

Colorado State University
Financial Aid Office
103 Administration Annex Building
Fort Collins, CO 80523-8024
(970) 491-6321, (970) 491-5010 (fax)
Average award: $1,000
Maximum award: $1,500
Minimum award: $500
Number of awards: 250
Deadline: February 14
College level: Freshman, Sophomore, Junior, Senior
*Majors/Fields:*Art, creative writing, dance, forensics, music, theatre
Criteria: Applicant must have outstanding talent in art, creative writing, dance, forensics, music, or theatre. Audition may be required. Contact the awarding department for application information. Minimum 2.4 GPA, continued talent, and reapplication required for renewal. Awarded every year. Award may be used only at sponsoring institution.
Contact: Department of Major.

340   Creative Arts Award

Kent State University
P.O. Box 5190
Kent, OH 44242-0001
(216) 672-2972
Maximum award: $1,800
Deadline: October 31
College level: Freshman
Majors/Fields: Art, dance, fashion design, interior design, music, theatre
*Criteria:*Selection is based upon academic and artistic performance. Minimum 2.0 GPA is required to retain scholarship. Awarded every year. Award may be used only at sponsoring institution.
Contact: Theodore Hallenbeck, Director of Financial Aid, 103 Michael Schwartz Center, P.O. Box 5190, Kent, OH 44242-0001.

341   Dean's Special Talent Scholarship

Ohio University
Office of Student Financial Aid and Scholarships
Athens, OH 45701
(614) 593-4141, (614) 593-4140 (fax)
Average award: $1,250
Maximum award: $1,500
Minimum award: $750
Number of awards: 80
Deadline: March 1
College level: Sophomore, Junior, Senior
Majors/Fields: Art, dance, music, theatre, visual communications
*Criteria:*Selection is based upon talent and academic qualifications. Awarded every year. Award may be used only at sponsoring institution.
Contact: Mrs. Yang-Hi Kim, Associate Director of Scholarships and Grants.

342   Distinguished Artist Award

Hope College
P.O. Box 9000
Holland, MI 49422-9000
(616) 395-7850, (616) 395-7130 (fax)
admissions@hope.edu
http://www.hope.edu
Average award: $2,500
Deadline: February 15
College level: Freshman, Sophomore, Junior, Senior
Majors/Fields: Art, dance, music, theatre
Criteria: Applicant must demonstrate talent and have at least a minor in the field in which the scholarship is awarded. Renewable if recipient maintains a minimum 2.6 GPA. Awarded every year. Award may be used only at sponsoring institution.
Contact: James R. Bekkering, Vice President for Admissions.

343   Distinguished Student Award for Visual and Performing Arts

University of Maine
Orono, ME 04469
(207) 581-1324
Maximum award: $2,000
Maximum number of awards: 20
Minimum number of awards: 7
Deadline: February 1
College level: Freshman
Majors/Fields: Art, music, theatre/dance
Criteria: Some scholarships are renewable. Awarded every year. Award may be used only at sponsoring institution.
Contact: Office of Enrollment Management, 5713 Chadbourne Hall, Orono, ME 04469-5713, (207) 581-1826.

344   Fine Arts and Performing Arts Scholarship

Molloy College
1000 Hempstead Avenue
P.O. Box 5002
Rockville Centre, NY 11571-5002
(516) 678-5000
Maximum award: Full tuition
Deadline: late February (recommended); April 15
College level: Freshman
Majors/Fields: Art, communication arts, music
Criteria: Applicant must be a first-time, full-time student, demonstrate ability through audition, portfolio, or other documented experience, and file FAFSA. Recipient must maintain a minimum 3.0 GPA, complete at least 12 credit hours per semester, major in the field for which award was given, and reapply to retain scholarship. Awarded every year. Award may be used only at sponsoring institution.
Contact: Kathleen Bonnici, Director of Financial Aid.

345   Friends of Fine Arts Scholarship

Northern Kentucky University
Administrative Center 416
Nunn Drive
Highland Heights, KY 41099-7101
(606) 572-5144
Award: In-state tuition
Deadline: February 1
College level: Freshman, Sophomore, Junior, Senior
Majors/Fields: Art, music, theatre
Criteria: Awarded every year. Award may be used only at sponsoring institution.
Contact: Robert E. Sprague, Director of Financial Aid.

346   In-School Players Scholarship

Southwest Missouri State University
Student Financial Aid
901 South National Avenue
Springfield, MO 65804-0095
(417) 836-5000 or (800) 492-7900
Average award: $1,000
Number of awards: 6
Deadline: March 31
College level: Freshman, Sophomore, Junior, Senior
Criteria: Applicant must have performance experience in acting and/or music. Reapplication and audition are required to retain scholarship. Awarded every year. Award may be used only at sponsoring institution.
Contact: Scholarship Committee, (417) 836-5262, (800) 492-7900.

347   Junior and Community College Performing Arts Scholarship

Alabama Commission on Higher Education
P.O. Box 302000
Montgomery, AL 36130-2000
(334) 242-1998, (334) 242-0268 (fax)
Award: In-state tuition
College level: Freshman, Sophomore
Criteria: Applicant must attend a public junior or community college in Alabama on a full-time basis. Selection is based upon demonstrated talent determined through competitive auditions. Financial need is not considered. Awarded every year.
Contact: Dr. William H. Wall, Director of Grants and Scholarships, (334) 242-2274.

348   NLAPW Grant

National League of American Pen Women, Inc. (NLAPW)
1300 Seventeenth Street, NW
Washington, DC 20036
(717) 225-3023
Average award: $1,000
Number of awards: 3
Deadline: January 15
Majors/Fields: Art, letters, music
Criteria: Applicant must be a woman at least age 35 and must submit a description of her background and her idea for creative use of the money. Send self-addressed, stamped envelope by August 1 of odd-numbered year to receive current information. Awarded in even-numbered years.
Contact: Shirley Holden Helberg, National Scholarship Chair.

349   Partnership Scholarship

The University of the Arts
320 South Broad Street
Philadelphia, PA 19102
(800) 616-2787, or 215 732-4832, (215) 875-5458 (fax)
http://www.uarts.edu
Average award: Half tuition
Number of awards: 3
Deadline: March 15
College level: Freshman
Majors/Fields: Multimedia, performing arts, visual arts, writing.
Criteria: Applicant must be a graduate of Philadelphia Comprehensive High School who is nominated by the high school access coordinator and the high school visual or performing arts faculty. Renewable if recipient maintains full-time status and good academic standing. Awarded every year. Award may be used only at sponsoring institution.
Contact: Director of Admission.

350   Performance Scholarship

The College of Wooster
Office of Admissions
Wooster, OH 44691
(330) 263-2270, (330) 263-2621 (fax)
admissions@acs.wooster.edu
http://www.wooster.edu
Maximum award: $6,000
Deadline: February 15
College level: Freshman
Criteria: Awarded to applicants who demonstrate accomplishment and promise in music, theatre, or Scottish arts. Selection is based upon achievement, audition, and potential. Recipient must maintain academic progress toward degree to retain scholarship. Renewable for four years. Awarded every year. Award may be used only at sponsoring institution.
Contact: Office of Admissions.

351   Performance Scholarship

Muskingum College
163 Stormont Drive
New Concord, OH 43762
(614) 826-8139
Average award: $1,250
Maximum award: $3,000
Minimum award: $300
Number of awards: 160
Deadline: April 1
College level: Freshman, Sophomore, Junior, Senior
Criteria: Selection is based upon talent and potential in art, broadcasting, forensics, music, or theatre. Some majors have minimum academic requirements. Amount of award may vary by field of study. Scholarship is renewable. Awarded every year. Award may be used only at sponsoring institution.
Contact: Doug Kellar, Director of Admission.

352   Performing and Creative Arts Scholarship

State University of New York at Buffalo
Buffalo, NY 14260
(716) 831-2000, (716) 829-2022 (fax)
Average award: $2,000
College level: Freshman, Sophomore, Junior, Senior
Majors/Fields: Arts
Criteria: Applicant must have a minimum combined SAT I score of 1150, maintain a minimum 90 unweighted grade average, and complete the audition process. Scholarship is renewable. Awarded every year. Award may be used only at sponsoring institution.
Contact: Josephine Capuana, Administrative Director, 214 Talbert Hall, Buffalo, NY 14260, (716) 645-3020.

353   Portfolio Scholarship

Cleveland Institute of Art
11141 East Boulevard
Cleveland, OH 44106
(216) 421-7425, (216) 421-7438 (fax)
http://www.cia.edu
Maximum award: Full tuition
Minimum award: $2,000
Number of awards: 237
Deadline: May 1
College level: Incoming freshmen
Criteria: Applicant must submit portfolio of slides or pieces of work. Renewable for up to four years. Awarded every year. Award may be used only at sponsoring institution.
Contact: Catherine Redhead, Director of Admissions, (216) 421-7418.

354   Portfolio Scholarship

Minneapolis College of Art and Design
2501 Stevens Avenue South
Minneapolis, MN 55404
(612) 874-3782
Average award: $6,000
Number of awards: 1
Deadline: March 15
College level: Freshman
Criteria: Applicant must be a new student entering in fall semester, admitted by March 15. Portfolio and application are required. Financial need is not considered. Renewable for eight semesters based upon full-time attendance and academic performance. Awarded every year. Award may be used only at sponsoring institution.
Contact: Leann Winkelaar, Director of Financial Aid, (612) 874-3783.

355   Proficiency Award

Mount Union College
1972 Clark Avenue
Alliance, OH 44601
(216) 821-5320
Maximum award: $3,000
Deadline: None
College level: Freshman
Criteria: Awarded to applicants who demonstrate talent in art, communications, music, or theatre arts. Audition (music and theatre arts) or portfolio (art and communications) is required. Awarded every year. Award may be used only at sponsoring institution.
Contact: Office of Admissions.

356   Provost's Special Talent Scholarship

Ohio University
Office of Student Financial Aid and Scholarships
Athens, OH 45701
(614) 593-4141, (614) 593-4140 (fax)
Average award: $1,250
Maximum award: $1,500
Minimum award: $1,000
Number of awards: 50
Deadline: February 15
College level: Freshman
Majors/Fields: Art, music, theatre, visual communication, dance
Criteria: Applicant must be a student in the College of Fine Arts. Selection is based upon talent and academic qualifications. Awarded every year. Award may be used only at sponsoring institution.
Contact: Mrs. Yang-Hi Kim, Associate Director of Scholarships and Grants.

357   Shirly and Miles Fitterman Scholarship, Virginia M. Binger Scholarship, Wanda Gag Scholarship

Minneapolis College of Art and Design
2501 Stevens Avenue South
Minneapolis, MN 55404
(612) 874-3782
Award: Full tuition
Number of awards: 1
Deadline: March 15
College level: Senior
Criteria: Applicant must have a minimum 3.0 GPA. Selection is competitive. Awarded every year. Award may be used only at sponsoring institution.
Contact: Leann Winkelaar, Director of Financial Aid, (612) 874-3783.

358 Talent Scholarship

Wright State University
Coordinator of Scholarships
Dayton, OH 45435
(513) 873-5721
Average award: $1,000
Maximum award: $1,200
Minimum award: $500
Number of awards: 35
College level: Freshman
Majors/Fields: Music, theatre, dance
Criteria: Audition is required. Awarded every year. Award may be used only at sponsoring institution.
Contact: Judy Rose, Assistant Director of Financial Aid, (513) 873-2321.

359 Talent/Service Award

Chapman University
333 North Glassell Street
Orange, CA 92866
(714) 997-6741, (714) 997-6743 (fax)
http://www.chapman.edu
Maximum award: 80% of tuition
Minimum award: 20% of tuition
Deadline: None
College level: Freshman, Sophomore, Junior, Senior
Criteria: Applicant must be a full-time undergraduate who has demonstrated talent and skill in art, dance, theatre, film/TV, oral communications, music, or creative writing. Selection is based upon GPA, performance criteria (audition, portfolio), and recommendation from faculty. FAFSA required. Scholarship is renewable. Awarded every year. Award may be used only at sponsoring institution.
Contact: Scholarships.

360 Visual and Performing Arts Scholarship

Washington State University
Office of Scholarship Services
Pullman, WA 99164-1728
(509) 335-1059
Average award: $900
Maximum award: $1,500
Minimum award: $200
Number of awards: 50
Deadline: February 15
College level: Freshman, Transfer
Criteria: Applicant must have talent or skill in the visual or performing arts. Audition or portfolio may be required. Awarded every year. Award may be used only at sponsoring institution.
Contact: Johanna H. Davis, Assistant Director.

361 Vivien B. Head Scholarship

New Mexico State University
Box 30001
Department 5100
Las Cruces, NM 88003-0001
(505) 646-4105
Maximum award: $1,300
Deadline: March 1
College level: Sophomore, Junior, Senior
Majors/Fields: Art, music, theatre arts
Criteria: Applicant must be a U.S. citizen, have a minimum 3.0 GPA, demonstrate financial need, be of good moral attitude and character, and demonstrate ability and aptitude in chosen field. Essay on career goals and support for the free enterprise system is required. Interview may be requested. Renewable for up to eight semesters. Awarded every year. Award may be used only at sponsoring institution.
Contact: College of Arts and Sciences, (505) 646-2001.

Drama/Theatre——————

362 Dean's Theatre Performance Scholarship

DePaul University
1 East Jackson Boulevard
Chicago, IL 60604
(312) 362-8704, (312) 362-5749 (fax)
Average award: $4,000
Maximum award: $8,000
Minimum award: $2,000
Number of awards: 8
Deadline: None
College level: Freshman
Majors/Fields: Drama
Criteria: Applicant must posess strong academic credentials, demonstrate a strong interest in the theatre, and be admitted to the theatre studies program. Selection is based upon performance. Minimum 2.5 GPA as a full-time student in theatre studies is required to retain scholarship. Awarded every year. Award may be used only at sponsoring institution.
Contact: Jennifer Sparrow, Scholarship Coordinator, jsparrow@wppost.depaul.edu.

363 Dean's Theatre Studies and Theatre Design and Technology Scholarships

DePaul University
1 East Jackson Boulevard
Chicago, IL 60604
(312) 362-8704, (312) 362-5749 (fax)
Average award: $4,000
Maximum award: $8,000
Minimum award: $2,000
Number of awards: 24
Deadline: None
College level: Freshman, Transfer
Majors/Fields: Costume construction, costume design, lighting design, production management, scene design, theatre studies, theatre technology
Criteria: Applicant must submit a portfolio of theatre-related projects, have strong academic credentials, and demonstrate a strong interest in theatre. Transfer applicant must have minimum 3.0 GPA. Minimum 2.5 GPA as a full-time theatre student in the conservatory program is required to retain scholarship. Awarded every year. Award may be used only at sponsoring institution.
Contact: Jennifer Sparrow, Scholarship Coordinator, jsparrow@wppost.depaul.edu.

364 Drama Scholarship

California Baptist College
8432 Magnolia Avenue
Riverside, CA 92504
(909) 689-5771
Maximum award: $3,000
Number of awards: 20
Deadline: None
College level: Freshman, Sophomore, Junior, Senior
Criteria: Selection is based upon merit and performance. Scholarship is renewable. Awarded every year. Award may be used only at sponsoring institution.
Contact: Phillip Martinez, Director of Admissions/Financial Aid.

365   Drama Scholarship

Colorado Christian University
180 South Garrison Street
Lakewood, CO 80226
(303) 202-0100, extension 117, (303) 274-7560 (fax)
drwilliams@ccu.edu
http://www.ccu.edu
Average award: $586
Maximum award: $1,500
Minimum award: $250
Number of awards: 27
Deadline: None
College level: Freshman, Sophomore, Junior, Senior
Criteria: Applicant must be enrolled full time and appear in theatre productions. Audition required. Awarded every year. Award may be used only at sponsoring institution.
Contact: Kent McGowan, Director of Financial Aid.

366   Eve Yoquelet Scholarship for Theatre Arts

New Mexico State University
Box 30001
Department 5100
Las Cruces, NM 88003-0001
(505) 646-4105
Maximum award: $1,750
Maximum number of awards: 2
Minimum number of awards: 1
Deadline: March 1
College level: Sophomore, Junior, Senior
Majors/Fields: Theatre arts
Criteria: Applicant must be enrolled full time and have a minimum 3.0 GPA. Scholarship is renewable. Awarded every year. Award may be used only at sponsoring institution.
Contact: Head of Department of Theatre Arts.

367   Mark Medoff Scholarship

New Mexico State University
Box 30001
Department 5100
Las Cruces, NM 88003-0001
(505) 646-4105
Maximum award: Tuition and fees
Deadline: March 1
College level: Sophomore, Junior, Senior
Majors/Fields: Theatre arts
Criteria: Applicant must be enrolled full time, excel in theatre arts, and have a minimum 3.0 GPA. Preference is given to applicants with the greatest financial need. Scholarship is renewable. Awarded every year. Award may be used only at sponsoring institution.
Contact: Head of Department of Theatre Arts.

368   Theatre Scholarship

William Woods University
200 West Twelfth Street
Fulton, MO 65251-1098
(573) 592-4232, (573) 592-1146 (fax)
http://www.wmwoods.edu
Average award: $1,500
Maximum award: $2,000
Minimum award: $500
Number of awards: 2
Deadline: June 1
College level: Freshman, Sophomore, Junior, Senior
Majors/Fields: Theatre
Criteria: Audition is required. Recipient must maintain a minimum 2.75 GPA overall (3.0 GPA in major) and participate in theatre productions to retain scholarship. Awarded every year. Award may be used only at sponsoring institution.
Contact: Laura L. Archuleta, Director for Student Financial Aid, larchule@iris.wmwoods.edu.

369   Theatre Scholarship

Elon College
2700 Campus Box
Elon College, NC 27244
(800) 334-8448 extension 1
Maximum award: $2,000
College level: Freshman
Majors/Fields: Music theatre, theatre arts
Criteria: Selection is based upon application, recommendations, and audition/interview. Renewable for up to four years. Awarded every year. Award may be used only at sponsoring institution.
Contact: Division of Fine Arts, (910) 584-2440.

370   Theatre Scholarship

Ripon College
300 Seward Street
P.O. Box 248
Ripon, WI 54971
(800) 94-RIPON, (414) 748-7243 (fax)
adminfo@mac.ripon.edu
http://www.ripon.edu
Maximum award: $3,000
Number of awards: 5
College level: Freshman, transfers
Criteria: Applicant must interview with theatre department and be accepted for admission to Ripon College. Renewable if recipient participates in theatre department. Awarded every year. Award may be used only at sponsoring institution.
Contact: Paul J. Weeks, Vice President & Dean of Admission.

371   Theatre Talent Scholarship

Wilmington College
Pyle Center Box 1325
Wilmington, OH 45177
(800) 341-9318, (513) 382-7077 (fax)
admission@wilmington.edu
http://www.wilmington.edu
Maximum award: $5,000
Deadline: May 1
College level: Freshman
Majors/Fields: Theatre
Criteria: Applicant must have a minimum 2.8 GPA, major or minor in theatre, and must audition. Awarded every year. Award may be used only at sponsoring institution.
Contact: Financial Aid Office, Pyle Center Box 1184, Wilington, OH 45177.

372   Thomas A. Erhard Playwright's Scholarship

New Mexico State University
Box 30001
Department 5100
Las Cruces, NM 88003-0001
(505) 646-4105
Maximum award: Tuition and fees
Deadline: March 1
College level: Sophomore, Junior, Senior
Majors/Fields: Theatre arts
Criteria: Applicant must have a minimum 3.0 GPA, demonstrate promise as a playwright, and submit a play for consideration. Awarded every year. Award may be used only at sponsoring institution.
Contact: Head of Department of Theatre Arts.

Fashion Design/Interior Decorating———

373   Erlaine Pitts Scholarship

Art Institute of Fort Lauderdale
1799 S.E. 17th Street
Fort Lauderdale, FL 33316-3000
(800) 275-7603
Average award: $2,980
Number of awards: 1
College level: Freshman
Majors/Fields: Interior design
Criteria: Selection is based upon service to the school, academic progress, attendance, and professionalism. Awarded every year. Award may be used only at sponsoring institution.
Contact: Laura Waterman, Director of Student Financial Services, (305) 463-3000, extension 471.

374   IFDA Educational Foundation Student Scholarship

International Furnishings and Design Association (IFDA)
1200 19th Street, NW #300
Washington, DC 20036-2422
(202) 857-1897, (202) 223-4579 (fax)
Average award: $1,000
Maximum number of awards: 2
Minimum number of awards: 1
Deadline: October 15
College level: Sophomore, Junior, Senior, Graduate, Doctoral
Majors/Fields: Design, art, graphics, and related majors.
Criteria: Applicant must be an IFDA member enrolled in a furnishing and design-related program. Recipient must reapply to retain scholarship. Awarded every year.
Contact: IFDA Executive Office.

375   S. Harris Memorial Scholarship

American Society of Interior Designers Educational Foundation, Inc.
608 Massachusetts Avenue, NE
Washington, DC 20002-6006
(202) 546-3480, (202) 546-3240 (fax)
Average award: $1,500
Number of awards: 2
Deadline: March 4
College level: Junior, Senior, Graduate
Majors/Fields: Interior design
Criteria: Applicant must submit transcript and recommendations. Selection is based upon financial need and academic and creative accomplishments. Awarded every year.
Contact: Educational Foundation Manager.

Film/Photography———

376   Carole Fielding Student Grants

University Film and Video Association
University of Baltimore School of Communications Design
1420 N. Charles Street
Baltimore, MD 21201
(410) 837-6061
Maximum award: $4,000
Deadline: January 1
College level: Sophomore, Junior, Senior, Graduate, Doctoral
Criteria: Applicant must be sponsored by a faculty member who is an active member of the University Film and Video Association.
Contact: Julie Simon, UFVA Scholarship/Grants Chairperson, jsimon@ubmail.ubalt.edu.

Fine Arts———

377   Alumni and Friends Scholarship

Pacific Northwest College of Art
1219 Southwest Park
Portland, OR 97205
(503) 266-4391
Average award: $1,500
Maximum award: $3,000
Minimum award: $1,000
Number of awards: 2
Deadline: April 30
College level: Sophomore, Junior, Senior
Criteria: Selection is based upon merit. Awarded every year. Award may be used only at sponsoring institution.
Contact: Jennifer Satalino, Financial Aid Director, (503) 226-4391, extension 266.

378   Art Institute of Fort Lauderdale Scholarship

Art Institute of Fort Lauderdale
1799 South 17th Street
Fort Lauderdale, FL 33316-3000
(800) 275-7603
Average award: $2,980
Number of awards: 1
College level: Freshman
Criteria: Selection is based upon academic consideration, talent, and professionalism. Awarded every year. Award may be used only at sponsoring institution.
Contact: Laura Waterman, Director of Student Financial Services, 1799 SE 17th Street, Fort Lauderdale, FL 33316, (305) 463-3000, extension 417.

379   Art Portfolio Review Scholarship

Alfred University
Alumni Hall
26 North Main Street
Alfred, NY 14802
(607) 871-2159
Maximum award: $3,600
Deadline: February 15
College level: Artists enrolling at School of Art and Design of New York State College of Ceramics
Majors/Fields: School of Art/Design of New York State College of Ceramics
Criteria: Applicant must provide a portfolio. Renewable following annual review of art course work. Awarded every year. Award may be used only at sponsoring institution.
Contact: Scholarships.

380   Art Scholarship

Cedar Crest College
100 College Drive
Allentown, PA 18104
(610) 740-3785, (610) 606-4647 (fax)
cccadmis@cedarcrest.edu
www.cedarcrest.edu
Average award: $1,500
Number of awards: 3
Deadline: Rolling
College level: Freshman
Majors/Fields: Art
Criteria: Portfolio review is required. Renewable if recipient maintains good academic standing. Awarded every year. Award may be used only at sponsoring institution.
Contact: Judith Neyhart, Vice President for Enrollment Management, Financial Aid Office.

381   Art Scholarship

Jacksonville State University
Jacksonville, AL 36265-9982
(205) 782-5006
Average award: Full tuition
College level: Freshman, Sophomore, Junior, Senior
Majors/Fields: Art
Criteria: Awarded every year. Award may be used only at sponsoring institution.
Contact: Art Department.

382   Art Scholarship

William Woods University
200 West Twelfth Street
Fulton, MO 65251-1098
(573) 592-4232, (573) 592-1146 (fax)
http://www.wmwoods.edu
Maximum award: $2,000
Deadline: June 1
College level: Freshman, Sophomore, Junior, Senior
Majors/Fields: Art
Criteria: Portfolio is required. Recipient must continue in major, participate in departmental activities, and maintain full-time enrollment and a minimum 2.75 GPA (3.0 GPA in major) to retain scholarship. Awarded every year. Award may be used only at sponsoring institution.
Contact: Laura L. Archuleta, Director for Student Financial Aid, larchule@iris.wmwoods.edu.

383   Art Scholarship for Mature Women

National League of American Pen Women, Inc. (NLAPW)
1300 Seventeenth Street, NW
Washington, DC 20036
(717) 225-3023
Average award: $1,000
Number of awards: 1
Deadline: January 15
Majors/Fields: Art
Criteria: Applicant must be a woman, at least age 35, and must submit description of background, proposal for use of money, and three prints (5x7, 4x6, or bigger) of work in any medium: oil, water color, original works on paper, sculpture, or photography. Photographs should be submited as 8x10 prints. Awarded in even-numbered years.
Contact: Scholarships.

384   Arts Scholarship

Bradford College
320 South Main Street
Haverhill, MA 01835
(508) 372-7161, (508) 372-5240 (fax)
bradcoll@aol.com
http://bradford.edu
Average award: $4,000
Maximum award: $5,000
Minimum award: $1,000
Number of awards: 5
Deadline: None
College level: Freshman, Sophomore, Junior, Senior
Criteria: Applicant must demonstrate talent in art and creative writing. Scholarship is renewable. Awarded every year. Award may be used only at sponsoring institution.
Contact: Scholarships.

385   Bertha Langhorst Werner Scholarship

Art Academy of Cincinnati
1125 Saint Gregory Street
Cincinnati, OH 45202-1700
(513) 721-5205, (800) 323-5692, (513) 562-8778 (fax)
Average award: $1,500
Maximum award: $2,000
Minimum award: $500
Number of awards: 13
Deadline: May 1
College level: Sophomore, Junior, Senior
Criteria: Award may be used only at sponsoring institution.
Contact: Karen Geiger, Director of Financial Aid, (513) 562-8751.

386   Bible Quiz Scholarship and Fine Arts Achievement Scholarship

Valley Forge Christian College
1401 Charlestown Road
Phoenixville, PA 19460
(610) 935-0450, (610) 935-9353 (fax)
Average award: $1,000
Maximum award: Full tuition
Number of awards: 4
Deadline: None
College level: Freshman
Criteria: Awarded to applicant who reaches national level in fine arts competition. Awarded every year. Award may be used only at sponsoring institution.
Contact: Tim Burns, Director of Admissions.

387   Bradley Endowed Art Scholarship

The University of Alabama
Box 870162
Tuscaloosa, AL 35487-0162
(205) 348-6756
Average award: $2,170
Number of awards: 1
Deadline: Fall
College level: Sophomore, Junior, Senior
Majors/Fields: Art
Criteria: Selection is based upon competitive exhibition of work. Awarded each year as funds are available. Award may be used only at sponsoring institution.
Contact: Department of Art, Box 870270, Tuscaloosa, AL 35487-0270.

388   Conway and Proetz Scholarships

Washington University
One Brookings Drive
Campus Box 1089
St. Louis, MO 63130
(314) 935-6000 or (800) 638-0700
Average award: Full tuition
Number of awards: 1
Deadline: None
College level: Freshman
Majors/Fields: Fine arts
Criteria: Awarded to an applicant to the School of Art who includes portfolio. Selection is based upon academic/artistic merit without regard to financial need. Satisfactory academic performance is required to retain scholarship. Awarded every year. Award may be used only at sponsoring institution.
Contact: Office of Undergraduate Admissions.

389 Dean's Art Scholarship

DePaul University
1 East Jackson Boulevard
Chicago, IL 60604
(312) 362-8704, (312) 362-5749 (fax)
Average award: $4,000
Maximum award: $8,000
Minimum award: $2,000
Deadline: None
College level: Freshman, Transfer
Majors/Fields: Art advertising, art history, design, studio art
Criteria: Applicant must demonstrate strong academic credentials and strong interest in the study of art. Transfer applicant must have minimum 3.0 GPA. Portfolio is required of design and studio majors; essay on an artist or period of art is required of art history majors. Minimum 2.5 GPA as a full-time art major is required to retain scholarship. Awarded every year. Award may be used only at sponsoring institution.
Contact: Jennifer Sparrow, Scholarship Coordinator, jsparrow@wppost.depaul.edu.

390 Elizabeth Greenshields Foundation Award

Elizabeth Greenshields Foundation
1814 Sherbrooke Street West, Suite #1
Montreal, Quebec, Canada, H3H 1E4
(514) 937-9225
Average award: $10,000 (Canadian)
Number of awards: 50
Deadline: None
College level: Sophomore, Junior, Senior, Graduate, Doctoral, practicing artists who have completed their formal art training
Majors/Fields: Drawing, painting, printmaking, sculpture
Criteria: Applicant must present work which is representational or figurative, have already started or completed training in an established school of art, and demonstrate through past work and future plans a commitment to making art a lifetime career. Applicant must reapply and submit new work for renewal. Awarded every year.
Contact: Micheline Leduc, Administrator and Secretary.

391 Fine and Performing Arts Scholarship

Birmingham-Southern College
Arkadelphia Road
Birmingham, AL 35254
(205) 226-4688
Maximum award: $4,000
Deadline: February 1
College level: Freshman
Majors/Fields: Art, dance, music, theatre
Criteria: Applicant must participate in Fine Arts Scholarship Day on campus and must audition or submit portfolio. Scholarship is renewable. Awarded every year. Award may be used only at sponsoring institution.
Contact: Forrest Stuart, Interim Director of Financial Aid Services.

392 Fine and Performing Arts Workshop

Shawnee State University
940 Second Street
Portsmouth, OH 45662-4344
(614) 355-2237
Average award: $2,750
Deadline: May 15; early application is recommended
College level: Freshman, Sophomore, Junior, Senior, Transfer
Majors/Fields: Visual arts
Criteria: Applicant must be a full-time student and maintain a minimum 3.0 GPA in visual arts courses. FAFSA is required. Recipient must work at least 10 hours per week in lab. Awarded every year. Award may be used only at sponsoring institution.
Contact: Financial Aid Office, (614) 355-2485.

393 Fine Arts Award

Rhodes College
2000 North Parkway
Memphis, TN 38112
(901) 843-3700, (901) 843-3719 (fax)
adminfo@rhodes.edu
http://www.rhodes.edu
Maximum award: $12,300
Number of awards: 8
Deadline: Early application is recommended
College level: Freshman
Majors/Fields: Fine arts
Criteria: Applicant must demonstrate achievement in art, music, or theatre, and must submit portfolio for art or audition for music and theatre. Competition takes place in February. Financial need is considered. Renewal is based upon continued achievement. Awarded every year. Award may be used only at sponsoring institution.
Contact: David J. Wottle, Dean of Admissions and Financial Aid, (800) 844-5969.

394 Fine Arts Performance Scholarship

Houghton College
1 Willard Avenue
Houghton, NY 14744
(716) 567-9328
Average award: $2,000
Maximum award: $5,000
Minimum award: $500
Number of awards: 14
Deadline: March 15
College level: Freshman
Majors/Fields: Art, music
Criteria: Applicant must participate in art or music. Recipient must continue to participate in art or music to retain scholarship. Awarded every year. Award may be used only at sponsoring institution.
Contact: Troy Martin, Director of Financial Aid.

395 Fine Arts Scholarship

Piedmont College
165 Central Avenue
Demorest, GA 30535
(706) 778-3000
Average award: $1,000
Maximum award: $5,000
Minimum award: $500
Number of awards: 30
Deadline: May 1
College level: Freshman, Sophomore, Junior, Senior
Majors/Fields: Art, music, theatre
Criteria: Applicant must demonstrate talent in art, music, or theatre. Audition or portfolio is required. Renewal is based upon continued interest and participation in art, music, or theatre. Awarded every year. Award may be used only at sponsoring institution.
Contact: Kenneth L. Owen, Director of Financial Aid.

396 Frances Hook Scholarship Fund Art Awards Contest

Frances Hook Scholarship Fund
P.O. Box 597346
Chicago, IL 60659-7346
(708) 673-ARTS, (708) 673-2782 (fax)
Maximum award: $3,000
Number of awards: 170
Deadline: March 1
College level: Freshman, Sophomore, Junior, Senior, students in grades 1-12
Majors/Fields: Two-dimensional-art-related curriculum
Criteria: Applicant must be age 24 or under, be represented to the Fund by an art teacher or school administrator, and submit portfolio of original work. Recipient has up to five years to use award for supplies or tuition. Awarded every year.
Contact: Mr. W.L. Volchenboum, Executive Director.

397   Howard D. Goodson Scholarship

The University of Alabama
Box 870162
Tuscaloosa, AL 35487-0162
(205) 348-6756
Award: In-state tuition for half a year
Deadline: Fall
College level: Sophomore, Junior, Senior
Majors/Fields: Art
Criteria: Selection is based upon competitive exhibition of work. Awarded each year as funds are available. Award may be used only at sponsoring institution.
Contact: Department of Art, Box 870270, Tuscaloosa, AL 35487-0270.

398   Le Maxie Glover Scholarship

University of Toledo
Financial Aid Office
Toledo, OH 43606-3390
(419) 537-2056
Average award: $3,000
Number of awards: 1
Deadline: January 28
College level: Freshman
Majors/Fields: Art, art education, art history
Criteria: Applicant must be an African-American student enrolling in the art department at the Toledo Museum of Art. Award is for four years. Awarded every year. Award may be used only at sponsoring institution.
Contact: J.C. Caldwell, 50 Men and Women of Toledo, Inc., P.O. Box 3557, Toledo, OH 43608, (419) 729-4654.

399   Leta Kennedy Scholarship

Pacific Northwest College of Art
1219 Southwest Park
Portland, OR 97205
(503) 266-4391
Average award: $2,000
Number of awards: 3
Deadline: April 1
College level: Freshman
Criteria: Applicant must have a minimum 3.25 GPA and submit portfolio. Applicants for foundation program also are eligible. Awarded every year. Award may be used only at sponsoring institution.
Contact: Jennifer Satalino, Financial Aid Director, (503) 226-4391, extension 266.

400   Mary M. Morgan Scholarship

The University of Alabama
Box 870162
Tuscaloosa, AL 35487-0162
(205) 348-6756
Average award: $2,113
Number of awards: 1
Deadline: Fall
College level: Sophomore, Junior, Senior
Majors/Fields: Art
Criteria: Selection is based upon competitive exhibition of work. Awarded each year as funds are available. Award may be used only at sponsoring institution.
Contact: Department of Art, Box 870270.

401   Nancy Tonkin Scholarship

Pacific Northwest College of Art
1219 Southwest Park
Portland, OR 97205
(503) 266-4391
Average award: $2,000
Number of awards: 3
Deadline: April 24
College level: Sophomore, Junior, Senior
Criteria: Selection is based upon portfolio. Reapplication is required to retain scholarship. Awarded every year. Award may be used only at sponsoring institution.
Contact: Jennifer Satalino, Financial Aid Director, (503) 226-4391, extension 266.

402   NSS Scholarship

National Sculpture Society (NSS)
1177 Avenue of the Americas
New York, NY 10036
(212) 764-5645, (212) 764-5651 (fax)
Maximum award: $1,000
Deadline: May 31
College level: Freshman, Sophomore, Junior, Senior, Graduate, Doctoral
Majors/Fields: Figurative sculpture, realist sculpture
Criteria: Applicant must submit a brief biography and explanation of sculpture background, two recommendations, and black and white 8"x10" photos of at least three works, and demonstrate financial need. Recipient must reapply and provide proof of successful completion of course work to retain scholarship. Awarded every year.
Contact: Scholarships.

403   Presidential Merit Scholarship

The University of the Arts
320 South Broad Street
Philadelphia, PA 19102
(800) 616-2787, or 215 732-4832, (215) 875-5458 (fax)
http://www.uarts.edu
Maximum award: $6,500
Deadline: March 15
College level: Freshman, Sophomore, Junior, Senior
Majors/Fields: Multimedia, performing arts, visual arts, writing
Criteria: Selection is based upon academic merit and talent. Recipient must maintain full-time enrollment and minimum 3.0 GPA to retain scholarship. Awarded every year. Award may be used only at sponsoring institution.
Contact: Office of Admission.

404   Rachel Griffin Scholarship

Pacific Northwest College of Art
1219 Southwest Park
Portland, OR 97205
(503) 266-4391
Average award: $1,000
Maximum award: $3,000
Minimum award: $500
Number of awards: 3
Deadline: April 30
College level: Sophomore, Junior, Senior
Criteria: Selection is based upon merit. Awarded every year. Award may be used only at sponsoring institution.
Contact: Jennifer Satalino, Financial Aid Director, (503) 226-4391, extension 266.

405   Robert C. Lee Printmaking Scholarship

Pacific Northwest College of Art
1219 Southwest Park
Portland, OR 97205
(503) 266-4391
Average award: $1,000
Maximum award: $1,500
Minimum award: $600
Number of awards: 3
Deadline: None
College level: Sophomore, Junior, Senior
Majors/Fields: Printmaking
Criteria: Selection is based upon portfolio. Reapplication is required to retain scholarship. Awarded every year. Award may be used only at sponsoring institution.
Contact: Jennifer Satalino, Financial Aid Director, (503) 226-4391, extension 266.

406   Society for the Fine Arts Scholarship

The University of Alabama
Box 870162
Tuscaloosa, AL 35487-0162
(205) 348-6756
Award: In-state tuition for half a year
Deadline: Fall
College level: Sophomore, Junior, Senior
Majors/Fields: Art
Criteria: Selection is based upon competitive exhibition of work. Awarded each year as funds are available. Award may be used only at sponsoring institution.
Contact: Department of Art, Box 870270, Tuscaloosa, AL 35487-0270.

407   Stacey Scholarship Fund

John F. and Anna Lee Stacey Scholarship Fund for
Art Education
National Cowboy Hall of Fame
1700 Northeast 63rd
Oklahoma City, OK 73111
(405) 478-2250
Average award: $3,000
Minimum award: $1,000
Number of awards: 2
Deadline: February 1
College level: Art students age 18 to 35
Majors/Fields: Drawing, painting
Criteria: Applicant must be a U.S. citizen and artist who is skilled in and devoted to the classical or conservative tradition of painting or drawing. Applications are accepted after October 1, and should include 35mm slide portfolio. Reapplication is required for renewal. Awarded every year.
Contact: Ed Muno, Art Director.

408   Talent Scholarship in Fine Arts

Marietta College
Fifth Street
Marietta, OH 45750
(614) 376-4712
Average award: $3,500
Number of awards: 6
Deadline: March 1
College level: Freshman
Criteria: Renewable if minimum 2.0 GPA, continuous full-time enrollment, and involvement in arts are maintained. Awarded every year. Award may be used only at sponsoring institution.
Contact: James M. Bauer, Associate Dean/Director of Financial Aid.

409   The Nordan Fine Arts Program

Texas Christian University
2800 South University Drive
Fort Worth, TX 76129
(817) 921-7858, (817) 921-7462 (fax)
frogaid@tcu.edu
Maximum award: $4,000
Number of awards: 34
Deadline: May 1
College level: Freshman, Sophomore, Junior, Senior
Criteria: Awarded to applicant with exceptional talent in art, ballet or modern dance, music, or theatre. Renewable for up to four years if recipient continues to meet requirements. Awarded every year. Award may be used only at sponsoring institution.
Contact: Dean of College of Fine Arts & Communication, Box 30793.

410   Virginia Museum of Fine Arts Fellowships

Virginia Museum of Fine Arts
Education and Outreach Division
2800 Grove Avenue
Richmond, VA 23221-2466
(804) 367-0824
Average award: $5,000
Maximum award: $8,000
Minimum award: $4,000
Number of awards: 9
Deadline: March 1
College level: Freshman, Sophomore, Junior, Senior, Graduate, Doctoral, Professional artists
Majors/Fields: Crafts, drawing, film, mixed media, painting, photography, printmaking, sculpture, video, graduate art history
Criteria: Applicant must be a legal resident of Virginia for one year prior to the deadline. Students must be enrolled full time at an accredited college, university, or school of the arts. Selection is based upon submission of three films, research papers, or published articles or of slides of ten works. Undergraduate and graduate applicants can reapply annually to retain scholarship. Professional applicant must wait five years to reapply. Awarded every year.
Contact: Fellowship Program.

411   Walter and Michael Lantz Prize

National Sculpture Society (NSS)
1177 Avenue of the Americas
New York, NY 10036
(212) 764-5645, (212) 764-5651 (fax)
Average award: $1,000
Number of awards: 1
Deadline: Early April
College level: Emerging sculptors
Majors/Fields: Sculpture
Criteria: Applicant must demonstrate ability in the use of form and composition, and in comprehension of technique, with an emphasis on figurative or realist work, and be a U.S. resident. Letter of application, including a brief biography and explanation of background in sculpture, $10 entry fee, 10-20 slides of work, and a self-addressed, stamped envelope for slide return are required. Awarded every year.
Contact: National Sculpture Competition for Emerging Sculptors.

412   Young American Creative Patriotic Art Contest

Ladies Auxiliary to the Veterans of Foreign Wars
406 West 34th Street
Kansas City, MO 64111
(816) 561-8655, (816) 931-4753 (fax)
Maximum award: $3,000
Number of awards: 5
Deadline: April 1
College level: Freshman
Majors/Fields: Art
Criteria: Applicant must attend school in the same state as the sponsoring Auxiliary and submit artwork for creative, patriotic art competition. Awarded every year.
Contact: Judy Millick, Administrator of Programs.

Graphic Arts

413   Angelo Divencenzo Scholarship

Art Institute of Fort Lauderdale
1799 S.E. 17th Street
Fort Lauderdale, FL 33316-3000
(800) 275-7603
Average award: $2,980
Number of awards: 1
College level: Freshman
Majors/Fields: Visual communications
Criteria: Selection is based upon academic excellence, attitude, and professionalism. Awarded every year. Award may be used only at sponsoring institution.
Contact: Laura Waterman, Director of Student Financial Services, (305) 463-3000, extension 471.

414   Colorado Institute of Art Scholarship

Colorado Institute of Art
200 East Ninth Avenue
Denver, CO 80203
(303) 837-0825, (303) 860-8560 (fax)
Average award: Full tuition
Maximum award: $26,000
Number of awards: 8
Deadline: March 15
College level: Freshman
Majors/Fields: Computer animation, culinary arts, fashion design, industrial design, interior design, multimedia, photography, video production, graphic design, web site administration
Criteria: Applicant must submit slides of original artwork, actual photographs, or written projects (depending on major). Selection is based upon merit, talent, and academic background. Minimum 2.5 GPA is required to retain scholarship. Awarded every year.
Contact: Barbara H. Browning, Director of Admissions.

415   CPIA Scholarship Trust Fund

Canadian Printing Industry Association (CPIA)
Fuller Building, Suite 906
75 Albert Street
Ottawa, Ontario, CN K1P 5E7
(613) 236-7208, (613) 236-8169 (fax)
Average award: $1,000
Number of awards: 50
Deadline: June 30
College level: Freshman
Majors/Fields: Graphic communications, graphic technician
Criteria: Applicant must attend school in Canada and be planning a career in graphic communications. Renewable if minimum grade average of "B" is maintained. Awarded every year.
Contact: Michael Makin, Administrator/President.

416   Jessie E. and Jay D. Rudolph Scholarship

State University of New York College at Oswego
King Hall/Alumni and University Development
Oswego, NY 13126
(315) 341-3003/3281, (315) 341-5570 (fax)
Average award: $1,500
College level: Senior
Majors/Fields: Graphic arts
Criteria: Applicant must have a minimum 3.0 GPA and a demonstrated commitment to graphic arts. Awarded every year. Award may be used only at sponsoring institution.
Contact: Scholarship Coordinator.

417   Printing and Publishing Industry National Scholarship Program

National Scholarship Trust Fund
4615 Forbes Avenue
Pittsburgh, PA 15213-3796
(412) 621-6941, (412) 621-3049 (fax)
Maximum award: $1,000
Maximum number of awards: 100
Minimum number of awards: 80
Deadline: January 15 (entering freshmen); March 15 (other students)
College level: Freshman, Sophomore, Junior, Senior
Majors/Fields: Graphic communications
Criteria: Selection is based upon test scores and recommendations; minimum 3.0 GPA is required. Minimum 3.0 GPA is required to retain scholarship. Awarded every year.
Contact: Ann Mayhew, Administrative Assistant.

418   Robert P. Scripps Graphic Arts Grant

Scripps Howard Foundation
P.O. Box 5380
Cincinnati, OH 45201-5380
(513) 977-3035, (513) 977-3800 (fax)
cottingham@scripps.com
http://www.scripps.com/foundation/
Maximum award: $3,000
Deadline: February 25
College level: Junior, Senior
Majors/Fields: Graphic arts
Criteria: Applicant must be a U.S. citizen, have good scholastic standing, demonstrate interest in the field of journalism, major in graphic arts as applied to the newspaper industry, and have the potential to become an administrator in newspaper production. Renewable if recipient maintains good academic standing. Awarded every year.
Contact: Patty Cottingham, Executive Director.

Instrumental Music

419   Band Scholarship

Mississippi Valley State University
14000 Highway 82 West
Itta Bena, MS 38941
(601) 254-3335, (601) 254-7900 (fax)
Maximum award: $7,270
Number of awards: 80
Deadline: None
College level: Freshman, Sophomore, Junior, Senior
Criteria: Minimum 2.0 GPA required to retain scholarship. Awarded every year. Award may be used only at sponsoring institution.
Contact: Leonard Tramiel, Band Director, (601) 254-3490.

420   Brass and Woodwind Players Award

Five Towns College
305 North Service Road
Dix Hills, NY 11746-6055
(516) 424-7000
Average award: $4,500
Maximum award: $6,000
Number of awards: 3
Deadline: Early application is recommended
College level: Freshman, Sophomore, Junior, Senior
Criteria: Applicant must be a brass or woodwind player accepted for admission as a full-time student. Selection is based upon service to school. Awarded every year. Award may be used only at sponsoring institution.
Contact: Financial Aid Office.

421 Chopin Piano Scholarship

Kosciuszko Foundation
15 East 65th Street
New York, NY 10021
(212) 734-2130
Maximum award: $2,500
Number of awards: 3
Deadline: March 31
Majors/Fields: Piano
Criteria: Award is designed to encourage highly talented American students of piano to study and play the works of Chopin. Competition is open to U.S. citizens and legal residents, regardless of ethnic background, who have demonstrated unusual musical ability but have not yet made extensive professional appearances. Contestant must be between age 15 and age 21 as of the opening date of the competition. Awarded every year.
Contact: Scholarships.

422 Isabel Rutter Endowment Scholarship

New Mexico State University
Box 30001
Department 5100
Las Cruces, NM 88003-0001
(505) 646-4105
Average award: Full tuition
Number of awards: 1
Deadline: March 1
College level: Sophomore, Junior, Senior
Majors/Fields: Violin
Criteria: Applicant must be a student of violin selected by the director of the Las Cruces Symphony. Awarded every year. Award may be used only at sponsoring institution.
Contact: College of Arts and Sciences, (505) 646-2001.

423 Michael Twarowski Scholarship

Kosciuszko Foundation
15 East 65th Street
New York, NY 10021
(212) 734-2130
Average award: $1,500
Number of awards: 1
Deadline: January 15
Majors/Fields: Piano, violin
Criteria: Applicant must be a U.S. citizen of Polish descent. Awarded every year.
Contact: Scholarships.

424 Music Assistance Fund Scholarship

American Symphony Orchestra League
1156 15th Street, NW, Suite 800
Washington, DC 20005-1704
(202) 776-0212, (202) 776-0224 (fax)
league@symphony.org
Maximum award: $3,500
Number of awards: 55
Deadline: December 15
College level: Unspecified graduate, unspecified undergraduate
Majors/Fields: Music
Criteria: Applicant must be an African-American U.S. citizen who is currently attending or planning to attend a U.S. conservatory or school of music, and be a student of orchestral instruments majoring in music (peformance concentration desired). Piano, composition, conducting, saxophone, or vocal majors are not eligible. Award allows recipient to attend a recognized summer program of music study and/or academic institution. Applicant should plan to pursue a career with a symphony orchestra. Selection is based upon financial need, recommendation, and talent. Audition is required. Renewal is based upon audition and continued financial need. Awarded when sufficient funds are available.
Contact: Lorri Ward, Special Assistant to the President, MAF@symphony.org.

425 National Young Artists Competition in Organ Performance

American Guild of Organists
475 Riverside Drive, Suite 1260
New York, NY 10115
(212) 870-2310, (212) 870-2163 (fax)
Maximum award: $2,000
Deadline: May 1
Majors/Fields: Organ
Criteria: Applicant must be an organist age 22 to age 32, a member of the American Guild of Organists, and seriously interested in pursuing a recital career. Selection is based upon a comprehensive application procedure and three rounds of playing competition. Competition is held every other year.
Contact: Awards.

426 Regional Competitions for Young Organists

American Guild of Organists
475 Riverside Drive, Suite 1260
New York, NY 10115
(212) 870-2310, (212) 870-2163 (fax)
Maximum award: $1,000
Majors/Fields: Organ
Criteria: Applicant may compete only in region of residence or school and must be age 23 or under. Applicant need not be a member of the American Guild of Organists.
Contact: Awards.

427 Sau-Wing Lam Scholarship

Beloit College
700 College Street
Beloit, WI 53511
(608) 363-2663
Average award: $2,500
Number of awards: 2
Deadline: January 31
College level: Freshman
Criteria: Applicant must demonstrate talent with bowed string instruments. Selection is based upon audition and instructor recommendations. Minimum 2.5 GPA is required to retain scholarship. Awarded every year. Award may be used only at sponsoring institution.
Contact: Thomas Kreiser, Coordinator of Freshman Financial Aid, (608) 363-2500.

428 Tiny Grimes Memorial Scholarship

Five Towns College
305 North Service Road
Dix Hills, NY 11746-6055
(516) 424-7000
Maximum award: $3,000
Deadline: Early application is recommended
College level: Senior
Criteria: Applicant must be a guitar student enrolled full time. Selection is based upon ability, academic achievement, and financial need. Awarded every year. Award may be used only at sponsoring institution.
Contact: Financial Aid Office.

429 William Kapell Piano Competition

Maryland Summer Institute for the Creative and Performing Arts/Rossborough Festival
4321 Hartwick Road, #220
College Park, MD 20740
(301) 403-8370, (301) 403-8375 (fax)
Maximum award: $20,000 plus New York recital and other engagements
Deadline: March 15
College level: Advanced pianists
Majors/Fields: Piano
Criteria: Major biennial international music competition for the most advanced pianists only. Competition rounds examine solo repertoire and performance with symphony orchestra. Applicant must be age 18 to age 33. Competitions will be held in 1998 and 2000.
Contact: Donald Reinhold, Assistant Director, intlcomp@umdacc.umd.edu.

Music Composition

430   "Citta di Trieste" Music Award

International Competition for Symphonic Composition
Piazza dell'Unita d'Italia, 4-Palazzo
Municipale 34121 Trieste, IT
Award: 10,000,000 lire, plus the winner's work will be performed by the "G. Verdi" Municipal Theatre of Trieste
Number of awards: 1
Deadline: April 30
College level: Any composer of any nationality and age, excluding those who have won first prize in previous editions
Majors/Fields: Music composition
Criteria: Applicant must submit an original composition for a large orchestra (choir, vocal, and instrumental soloists are excluded) with the length of the work specified on the score. The score must be unpublished and never have been performed. Applicant must sign the score and supply full name, nationality, date and place of birth, address and telephone number, curriculum vitae (covering studies and musical experience), two passport-size photographs, and declaration stating that the composition is unpublished and never has been performed.
Contact: Secretariat, "Citta di Trieste" Music Award, Palazzo Municipale.

431   Music Scholarship for Mature Women

National League of American Pen Women, Inc. (NLAPW)
1300 Seventeenth Street, NW
Washington, DC 20036
(717) 225-3023
Average award: $1,000
Number of awards: 1
Deadline: January 15
Majors/Fields: Music
Criteria: Applicant must be a woman age 35 or over and must submit background and one or two scores of musical composition. Each score should have a minimum performance time of 10 minutes and a maximum time of 18 minutes. Compositions should not have previously won an award. Awarded in even-numbered years.
Contact: Scholarships.

432   Young Composers Award

National Guild of Community Schools of the Arts
Young Composers Awards
40 North Van Brunt Street, Suite 32
Englewood, NY 07631
(201) 871-3337
Maximum award: $1,000
Number of awards: 4
Deadline: May 1
College level: Secondary school students, music students in private study or recognized musical institution
Criteria: Applicant must be a U.S. or Canadian citizen, age 13 to age 18. Four copies of manuscript, entry fee of $5, official entry form, and certification by teacher required. Awarded to first, second, third, and fourth place prize winners. Awarded every year.
Contact: Kate Brackett, Executive Assistant.

Music–General

433   Anne Gannett Scholarship

Maine Federation of Music Clubs (MFMC)
c/o Joyce Chaplin
92 Raymond Road
Brunswick, ME 04011
(207) 725-1125
Average award: $1,000
Maximum award: $1,250
Number of awards: 1
Deadline: May 9
College level: Freshman, Sophomore
Majors/Fields: Music
Criteria: Applicant must be a resident of Maine and a member of MFMC and be enrolled as a music major in an accredited institution. Selection is based upon audition and academic standing. Awarded in odd-numbered years.
Contact: Joyce Chaplin, Scholarship Committee Chair.

434   ASCAP Foundation Grants to Young Composers

American Society of Composers, Authors, and Publishers (ASCAP)
ASCAP Building, One Lincoln Plaza
New York, NY 10023
(212) 621-6327
Maximum award: $2,500
Number of awards: 27
Deadline: March 15
College level: Freshman, Sophomore, Junior, Senior, Graduate, Doctoral
Criteria: Applicant must be a U.S. resident under age 30. Awarded every year.
Contact: Frances Richard, Director, Symphony & Concert Department.

435   Choir Scholarship

Mississippi Valley State University
14000 Highway 82 West
Itta Bena, MS 38941
(601) 254-3335, (601) 254-7900 (fax)
Maximum award: $7,270
Number of awards: 50
Deadline: April 1
College level: Freshman, Sophomore, Junior, Senior
Criteria: Minimum 2.0 GPA required to retain scholarship. Awarded every year. Award may be used only at sponsoring institution.
Contact: Dr. Sandra Scott, Chairperson, Department of Fine Arts, (601) 254-3485.

436   Choral Scholars Award

University of San Diego
Alcala Park
San Diego, CA 92110-2492
(619) 260-4514
Average award: Half tuition
College level: Freshman
Majors/Fields: Music program, Choral Scholars
Criteria: Selection is based upon audition. Renewable for up to four years if recipient maintains a minimum 3.0 GPA and involvement in Choral Scholars singing group, and participates in specific program curriculum. Awarded every year. Award may be used only at sponsoring institution.
Contact: Department of Fine Arts.

437   Christian Gregor Scholarship

Salem College
P.O. Box 10548
Winston-Salem, NC 27108
(910) 721-2808
Average award: $5,000
College level: Freshman
Majors/Fields: Music
Criteria: Applicant must be a woman, must audition during Scholarship Weekend, and must submit reference from music teacher. Selection is based upon general musicianship, technical proficiency, level of repertoire, academic achievement, and citizenship. Recipient must maintain a minimum 2.0 GPA (3.0 GPA in music courses) to retain scholarship. Awarded every year. Award may be used only at sponsoring institution.
Contact: Bruce Blackman, Director of Financial Aid.

438 Conservatory Performance Award

Lawrence University
P.O. Box 599
Appleton, WI 54912-0599
(414) 832-6500, (414) 832-6782 (fax)
excel@lawrence.edu
http://www.lawrence.edu
Average award: $4,000
Maximum award: $10,000
Minimum award: $3,000
Number of awards: 25
Deadline: February 1
College level: Freshman
Majors/Fields: Music
Criteria: Selection is based upon musical talent and audition with faculty. Recipient must continue to show exemplary performance skills to retain scholarship. Awarded every year. Award may be used only at sponsoring institution.
Contact: Director of Admissions.

439 Dunford Music Scholarship

Salem College
P.O. Box 10548
Winston-Salem, NC 27108
(910) 721-2808
Average award: $2,500
College level: Freshman
Majors/Fields: Music
Criteria: Applicant must be a woman, must audition during Scholarship Weekend, and must submit reference from music teacher. Selection is based upon general musicianship, technical proficiency, level of repertoire, academic achievement, and citizenship. Recipient must maintain a minimum 2.0 GPA (3.0 GPA in music courses) to retain scholarship. Awarded every year. Award may be used only at sponsoring institution.
Contact: Bruce Blackman, Director of Financial Aid.

440 Eileen Phillips Cohen Music Scholarship

University of Wisconsin–Eau Claire
105 Garfield Avenue
Eau Claire, WI 54701
(715) 836-3373
Average award: $2,034
Number of awards: 3
Deadline: July 28
College level: Sophomore, Junior, Senior
Majors/Fields: Music
Criteria: Selection is based upon musical talent and good citizenship. Financial need may be considered. Audition is required. Awarded every year. Award may be used only at sponsoring institution.
Contact: Melissa Vogler, Financial Aid Counselor.

441 Emily K. Rand Scholarship

Rand Memorial Trust Fund
c/o Joyce Chaplin
92 Raymond Road
Brunswick, ME 04011
(207) 725-1125
Average award: $1,000
Maximum award: $2,000
Minimum award: $500
Number of awards: 4
Deadline: May 6
College level: Freshman, Sophomore, Junior, Senior, Graduate, Doctoral
Majors/Fields: Music
Criteria: Applicant must be a resident of Cumberland, Oxford, or York county, Maine, between age 17 and age 25 at time of audition. Audition should draw primarily from classical idiom and be 10-minutes long. Applicant must have outstanding musical ability and good scholastic rating. Scholarship is renewable. Awarded every year.
Contact: Joyce Chaplin, Chairman.

442 F.L. Fenwick Scholarship in Music

University of Calgary
Department of Financial Aid
2500 University Drive, NW
Calgary, Alberta, CN T2N 1N4
(403) 220-7872, (403) 282-2999 (fax)
Average award: $2,500
Number of awards: 1
College level: Freshman, Sophomore, Junior, Senior
Majors/Fields: Music, pipe organ
Criteria: Awarded on the recommendation of the audition jury or the spring jury to a student studying the pipe organ. If no organist qualifies, students studying harpsichord will become eligible. Awarded every year. Award may be used only at sponsoring institution.
Contact: J. Van Housen, Director of Student Awards/Financial Aid.

443 Filene Music Scholarship

Skidmore College
815 North Broadway
Saratoga Springs, NY 12866-1632
(518) 584-5000, (518) 581-7462 (fax)
admissions@scott.skidmore.edu
http://www.skidmore.edu
Average award: $6,000
Number of awards: 16
Deadline: February 1
College level: Freshman, Sophomore, Junior, Senior
Criteria: Awarded on basis of competition. Four awards given for each class. Registration forms available from Admissions Office. Recipient must meet departmental requirements to retain scholarship. Awarded every year. Award may be used only at sponsoring institution.
Contact: Mary Lou W. Bates, Director of Admissions, (518) 584-5000, extension 2213, mbates@skidmore.edu.

444 Fletcher Foundation Scholarship

Salem College
P.O. Box 10548
Winston-Salem, NC 27108
(910) 721-2808
Average award: $7,500
Number of awards: 1
College level: Freshman
Majors/Fields: Music
Criteria: Applicant must be a woman, must audition during Scholarship Weekend, and must submit reference from music teacher. Selection is based upon general musicianship, technical proficiency, level of repertoire, academic achievement, and citizenship. Recipient must maintain a minimum 2.0 GPA (3.0 GPA in music courses) to retain scholarship. Awarded every year. Award may be used only at sponsoring institution.
Contact: Bruce Blackman, Director of Financial Aid.

445 Gabriel Burda Scholarship

Saint Vincent College
Admissions and Financial Aid
300 Fraser Purchase Road
Latrobe, PA 15650-2690
(412) 537-4540, (412) 537-4554 (fax)
info@stvincent.edu
http://www.stvincent.edu
Average award: $2,000
Number of awards: 1
Deadline: November 1; early application is recommended
College level: Freshman
Majors/Fields: Music
Criteria: Applicant must be a high school senior planning to major in music. Selection is based upon audition, including one Baroque or Classical piece and one Romantic or Contemporary piece, and upon exam held in fall. Application is required. Recipient must maintain major and GPA to retain scholarship. Awarded every year. Award may be used only at sponsoring institution.
Contact: Rev. Earl Henry, Dean of Admission and Financial Aid.

446 George David Weiss Award

Five Towns College
305 North Service Road
Dix Hills, NY 11746-6055
(516) 424-7000
Average award: $2,000
Number of awards: 1
Deadline: Early application is recommended
College level: Freshman
Majors/Fields: Music
Criteria: Awarded to the applicant who best exemplifies the qualities of composer/songwriter George David Weiss. Applicant must be enrolled as a full-time student. Awarded every year. Award may be used only at sponsoring institution.
Contact: Financial Aid Office.

447 Glenn Miller Scholarship

Glenn Miller Birthplace Society
711 North 14th Street
Clarinda, IA 51632
(712) 542-4439
Maximum award: $1,500
Number of awards: 4
Deadline: March 15
College level: Freshman, Sophomore
Majors/Fields: Instrumental music, vocal music
Criteria: Applicant must intend to make music a central part of life. Awarded every year.
Contact: Scholarships.

448 Herbert and Golden Fitch Memorial Scholarship

Fort Collins Symphony Association
P.O. Box 1963
Fort Collins, CO 80522-1963
(970) 482-4823, (970) 482-4858 (fax)
http://www.fcsymphony.org
Average award: $1,000
Number of awards: 1
Deadline: None
College level: Freshman, Sophomore, Junior, Senior
Majors/Fields: Music
Criteria: Applicant must be a music student at Colorado St U who is available to play in the orchestra and is recommended by Maestro Will Schwartz. Scholarship is renewable. Awarded every other year.
Contact: Maestro Will Schwartz, Music Director.

449 Joseph H. Bearns Prize in Music

Bearns Prize Committee
Columbia University Department of Music
2960 Broadway, MC#1813
New York, NY 10027
Maximum award: $3,000
Deadline: February 15
Criteria: Applicant must be a U.S. citizen between age 18 and age 25 as of January 1 of the award year. Awarded every year.
Contact: Bearns Prize Committee, Administrative Aide, (212) 854-3825.

450 Lawrence M. and Louise Kresge Isaacs Endowment for Music Scholarship

Susquehanna University
Selinsgrove, PA 17870
(717) 372-4450
Maximum award: $7,500
Deadline: None
College level: Freshman, Sophomore, Junior, Senior
Majors/Fields: Music
Criteria: Applicant must demonstrate academic achievement and must audition with music faculty. Awarded every year. Award may be used only at sponsoring institution.
Contact: Office of Financial Aid.

451 Marjorie Brown Leff Scholarship

Beloit College
700 College Street
Beloit, WI 53511
(608) 363-2663
Average award: $2,500
Number of awards: 7
Deadline: January 31
College level: Freshman
Criteria: Applicant must demonstrate talent in vocal or instrumental music, keyboard performance, or music composition. Selection is based upon competitive audition and recommendations by music instructors. Minimum 2.5 GPA is required to retain scholarship. Awarded every year. Award may be used only at sponsoring institution.
Contact: Thomas Kreiser, Coordinator of Freshman Financial Aid, (608) 363-2500.

452 Music Department Scholarship

University of Tennessee, Knoxville
Financial Aid Office
115 Student Services Building
Knoxville, TN 37994
(615) 974-3131
Average award: $1,500
Deadline: February 1
College level: Freshman, Sophomore, Junior, Senior
Majors/Fields: Music
Criteria: Length of awards varies. Awarded every year. Award may be used only at sponsoring institution.
Contact: Scholarship Coordinator, College of Liberal Arts, 220 Ayres Hall, Knoxville, TN 37996, (615) 974-4481.

453 Music Department Tuition Remission Scholarship

Portland State University
Financial Aid Department
P.O. Box 751
Portland, OR 97207-0751
(503) 725-5270
Average award: $2,500
Deadline: In May
College level: Sophomore, Junior, Senior
Majors/Fields: Music
Criteria: Applicant must demonstrate outstanding musical skill. Renewable if minimum 3.0 GPA is maintained. Awarded every year. Award may be used only at sponsoring institution.
Contact: Scholarships, Music Department, (503) 725-3011.

454 Music Ensemble Scholarship

Lynchburg College
Lynchburg, VA 24501
(804) 522-8228
Average award: $2,000
Number of awards: 4
Deadline: February 15
College level: Freshman
Criteria: Selection is based upon audition and performance. Two awards are for Wind Ensemble, and two are for new members of Concert Choir. Renewable for up to four years. Awarded every year. Award may be used only at sponsoring institution.
Contact: Scholarships.

455 Music Grant

University of Indianapolis
1400 East Hanna Avenue
Indianapolis, IN 46227-3697
(317) 788-3217
Average award: $1,909
Maximum award: $5,000
Minimum award: $500
Number of awards: 51
Deadline: None
College level: Freshman
Majors/Fields: Music
Criteria: Applicant must audition before music faculty and participate in various musical organizations. Recipient must continue in music to retain scholarship. Awarded every year. Award may be used only at sponsoring institution.
Contact: Music Department, (317) 788-3255.

456 Music Major Academic Scholarship

Emmanuel College
212 Spring Street
P.O. Box 129
Franklin Springs, GA 30639-0129
(706) 245-7226
Average award: $2,200
Maximum award: $4,600
Minimum award: $1,000
Number of awards: 4
Deadline: April 1
College level: Freshman
Majors/Fields: Music
Criteria: Applicant must have a minimum combined SAT I score of 1150 and demonstrate performance ability. Awarded every year. Award may be used only at sponsoring institution.
Contact: Glenn A. Bailey, Director of Financial Aid.

457 Music Performance Award

Capital University
2199 East Main Street
Columbus, OH 43209-2394
(614) 236-6511
Maximum award: $3,500
Number of awards: 50
Deadline: August 1
College level: Freshman, Transfer
Majors/Fields: Music
Criteria: Selection is based upon audition. Renewable for up to eight semesters if minimum 2.0 GPA and musical proficiency are maintained. Awarded every year. Award may be used only at sponsoring institution.
Contact: Steve Crawford, Assistant Director of Admission.

458 Music Performance Grant

Campbellsville University
Office of Financial Aid
200 West College Street
Campbellsville, KY 42718
(502) 465-8158
Maximum award: $2,000
Number of awards: 25
Deadline: April 1 (priority)
College level: Freshman, Sophomore, Junior, Senior
Criteria: Applicant must be offered a music performance grant contract by the music department, be approved by the chairperson of the Fine Arts division, have a minimum 2.0 GPA, and be a full-time student. FAFSA is required. Scholarship is renewable. Awarded every year. Award may be used only at sponsoring institution.
Contact: Music Department.

459 Music Performance Scholarship

Eckerd College
4200 54th Avenue South
St. Petersburg, FL 33711
(813) 864-8331, 800 456-9009, (813) 866-2304 (fax)
admissions@eckerd.edu
http://www.eckerd.edu
Average award: $3,500
Maximum award: $5,000
Minimum award: $1,000
Number of awards: 15
Deadline: None
College level: Freshman, Transfer
Criteria: Applicant must have outstanding performance skills in instrumental, keyboard, or vocal music. Renewable if recipient maintains a minimum 2.0 GPA. Awarded every year. Award may be used only at sponsoring institution.
Contact: Dr. Richard Hallin, Dean of Admissions.

460 Music Program Scholarship

Five Towns College
305 North Service Road
Dix Hills, NY 11746-6055
(516) 424-7000
Maximum award: $1,500
Number of awards: 15
Deadline: Early application is recommended
College level: Freshman, Sophomore, Junior, Senior
Majors/Fields: Music program
Criteria: Applicant must be accepted for admission as a full-time student. Selection is based upon performance ability, service to school, and financial need. Awarded every year. Award may be used only at sponsoring institution.
Contact: Financial Aid Office.

461 Music Scholarship

American Legion–Kansas
1314 Topeka Avenue
Topeka, KS 66612
(913) 232-9315
Average award: $1,000
Number of awards: 1
Deadline: Febuary 15
College level: Freshman, Sophomore, Junior
Majors/Fields: Music
Criteria: Scholarship must be used at an approved Kansas college or university. Awarded every year.
Contact: Scholarships.

462 Music Scholarship

California Baptist College
8432 Magnolia Avenue
Riverside, CA 92504
(909) 689-5771
Maximum award: $5,000
Deadline: None
College level: Freshman, Sophomore, Junior, Senior
Criteria: Selection is based upon merit and performance. Scholarship is renewable. Awarded every year. Award may be used only at sponsoring institution.
Contact: Phillip Martinez, Director of Admissions/Financial Aid.

463 Music Scholarship

Bluffton College
280 West College Avenue
Bluffton, OH 45817
(419) 358-3257, (419) 358-3232 (fax)
admissions@bluffton.edu
http://www.bluffton.edu
Average award: $1,200
Number of awards: 8
Deadline: May 1
College level: Freshman
Majors/Fields: Music
Criteria: Audition is required. Scholarship is renewable. Awarded every year. Award may be used only at sponsoring institution.
Contact: Dan Parent, Admissions Counselor, (419) 358-3250.

464 Music Scholarship

Colorado Christian University
180 South Garrison Street
Lakewood, CO 80226
(303) 202-0100, extension 117, (303) 274-7560 (fax)
drwilliams@ccu.edu
http://www.ccu.edu
Average award: $907
Maximum award: $3,080
Minimum award: $100
Number of awards: 70
Deadline: None
College level: Freshman, Sophomore, Junior, Senior
Criteria: Applicant must be enrolled full time and involved in a music ensemble. Preference is given to music majors. Awarded every year. Award may be used only at sponsoring institution.
Contact: Kent McGowan, Director of Finacial Aid.

465 Music Scholarship

Elon College
2700 Campus Box
Elon College, NC 27244
(800) 334-8448 extension 1
Maximum award: $7,500
Majors/Fields: Music, music education, music performance
Criteria: Selection is based upon audition and interview. Band and choral scholarships are available to music and non-music majors. Renewable for up to four years. Awarded every year. Award may be used only at sponsoring institution.
Contact: Department of Music, (910) 582-2440.

466 Music Scholarship

Liberty University
1971 University Boulevard
Lynchburg, VA 24502-2269
(800) 543-5317
Average award: $1,197
Maximum award: $3,000
Minimum award: $200
Number of awards: 203
Deadline: April 15
College level: Freshman, Sophomore, Junior, Senior
Criteria: Applicant must have experience and ability in vocal and/or instrumental music. Scholarship is renewable. Awarded every year. Award may be used only at sponsoring institution.
Contact: Department of Fine Arts, (800) 522-6225, extension 2318.

467 Music Scholarship

Philadelphia College of Bible
200 Manor Avenue
Langhorne, PA 19047-2992
(215) 752-5800
Average award: $5,000
Maximum award: $8,000
Minimum award: $3,000
Number of awards: 3
Deadline: None
College level: Freshman
Majors/Fields: Music
Criteria: Selection is based upon competition in categories of brass, strings, and woodwind instruments, organ, piano, and voice. Audition is required. Awarded every year. Award may be used only at sponsoring institution.
Contact: Travis S. Roy, Financial Aid Administrator.

468 Music Scholarship

Queens College
1900 Selwyn Avenue
Charlotte, NC 28274
(704) 337-2212, 800 849-0202, (704) 337-2403 (fax)
cas@rex.queens.edu
http://www.queens.edu
Maximum award: $2,000
Deadline: None
College level: Freshman, Sophomore, Junior, Senior
Majors/Fields: Music
Criteria: Selection is based upon application and audition. Renewable for up to four years. Awarded every year. Award may be used only at sponsoring institution.
Contact: Music Department.

469 Music Scholarship

Ripon College
300 Seward Street
P.O. Box 248
Ripon, WI 54971
(800) 94-RIPON, (414) 748-7243 (fax)
adminfo@mac.ripon.edu
http://www.ripon.edu
Average award: $3,000
Number of awards: No limit
Deadline: December 1 (early decision), March 1
College level: Freshman, Transfer
Criteria: Applicant must be accepted for admission and must audition. Recipient must participate in musical group to retain scholarship. Awarded every year. Award may be used only at sponsoring institution.
Contact: Paul J. Weeks, Vice President and Dean of Admission.

470 Music Scholarship

Seton Hill College
Greensburg, PA 15601
(412) 838-4293, (412) 830-4611 (fax)
Average award: $1,000
Maximum award: $2,000
Minimum award: $250
College level: Freshman, Sophomore, Junior, Senior
Majors/Fields: Music
Criteria: Audition is required. Scholarship is renewable. Awarded every year. Award may be used only at sponsoring institution.
Contact: Director of Financial Aid.

471 Music Scholarship

Susquehanna University
Selinsgrove, PA 17870
(717) 372-4450
Maximum award: $3,000
Deadline: None
College level: Freshman, Transfer
Majors/Fields: Music
Criteria: Awards are given to music majors and selected non-music majors for band/orchestral instruments, keyboard, and voice. Selection is based upon competitive audition. Scholarship is renewable. Awarded every year. Award may be used only at sponsoring institution.
Contact: Office of Financial Aid.

472 Music Scholarship

Valley Forge Christian College
1401 Charlestown Road
Phoenixville, PA 19460
(610) 935-0450, (610) 935-9353 (fax)
Average award: $1,000
Maximum award: $2,000
Minimum award: $500
Number of awards: 15
Deadline: August 1
College level: Freshman
Majors/Fields: Music
Criteria: Selection is based upon formal audition and written application. Audition is required for renewal. Awarded every year. Award may be used only at sponsoring institution.
Contact: Tim Burns, Director of Admissions.

473 Music Scholarship

Wingate University
Wingate, NC 28174-0157
(800) 755-5550, (704) 233-8110 (fax)
admit@wingate.edu
http://www.wingate.edu
Average award: $1,500
Maximum award: $3,000
Minimum award: $500
Number of awards: 35
Deadline: April 1
College level: Freshman, Sophomore, Junior
Majors/Fields: Music
Criteria: Audition is required. Scholarship is renewable. Awarded every year. Award may be used only at sponsoring institution.
Contact: Walt Crutchfield, Dean of Admissions, Office of Admissions, Campus Box 3059, Wingate, NC 28174.

474 National Orchestral Institute

Maryland Summer Institute for the Creative and Performing Arts/Rossborough Festival
4321 Hartwick Road, #220
College Park, MD 20740
(301) 403-8370, (301) 403-8375 (fax)
Award: Full tuition, room, and board for three-week program
Deadline: February and March
Majors/Fields: Music
Criteria: Applicant must be a talented musician age 18 to age 30 on the threshold of professional career. Awards are for participation in a three-week orchestral training program held each June at the University of Maryland College Park. Recipient must re-audition for renewal. Awarded every year.
Contact: Donald Reinhold, Director, National Orchestra Institute, noi@umdacc.umd.edu.

475 Presser Foundation Scholarship

Western Washington University
516 High Street
Bellingham, WA 98226-9006
(206) 650-3471
Average award: $2,250
Number of awards: 1
College level: Senior
Majors/Fields: Music
Criteria: Applicant must be nominated by the music department faculty. Awarded every year. Award may be used only at sponsoring institution.
Contact: Music Department, 273 Performing Arts Center, Bellingham, WA 98225, (206) 650-3130.

476 San Francisco Conservatory of Music Scholarship

San Francisco Conservatory of Music
1201 Ortega Street
San Francisco, CA 94122
(415) 759-3422, (415) 759-3499 (fax)
http://www.sfcm.edu
Average award: $7,000
Maximum award: $16,300
Minimum award: $300
Number of awards: 190
Deadline: March 1
College level: Freshman, Sophomore, Junior, Senior, Graduate, Doctoral
Criteria: Applicant must be enrolled full time. Recipient must maintain a minimum 2.0 GPA, complete at least 24 credit hours per year, and pass performance exam to retain scholarship. Awarded every year. Award may be used only at sponsoring institution.
Contact: Colleen Katzowitz, Director of Student Services.

477 Sorantin Young Artist Award

San Angelo Symphony Orchestra
P.O. Box 5922
San Angelo, TX 76902
(915) 658-5877, (915) 653-1045 (fax)
Maximum award: $2,000
Number of awards: 6
Deadline: October 23
College level: Freshman, Sophomore, Junior, Senior, Graduate, Doctoral
Majors/Fields: Piano, vocal, instrumental
Criteria: Applicant must be a vocalist under age 31 as of November 22, or an instrumentalist or pianist under age 28 as of November 22. Awarded every year.
Contact: Awards Manager.

478 Theodore Pressor Scholarship

The University of Alabama
Box 870162
Tuscaloosa, AL 35487-0162
(205) 348-6756
Average award: $1,800
Number of awards: 1
Deadline: March 1
College level: Senior
Criteria: Applicant must demonstrate great potential in music. Awarded every year. Award may be used only at sponsoring institution.
Contact: School of Music, Box 870366, Tuscaloosa, AL 35487-0366.

479   WAMSO Young Artist Competition Scholarship

Women's Association of the Minnesota Orchestra (WAMSO)
Orchestra Hall
1111 Nicollet Mall
Minneapolis, MN 55403
(612) 371-5654, (612) 371-7176 (fax)
Maximum award: $3,750
Number of awards: 7
Deadline: October 17
Criteria: Awarded every year. Award may be used only at Augsburg College, Hamline University, University of Iowa, Macalester College, University of Minnesota, College of St. Catherine, St. Cloud State University, University of St. Thomas, University of Wisconson-Eau Claire.
Contact: Shirley Taradash or Connie Sommers, Co-chairpersons.

Voice

480   Altamura-Enrico Caruso Voice Competition, USA

Enrico Caruso Voice Competition, USA
Inter-Cities Performing Arts, Inc.
4000 Bergenline Avenue
Union City, NJ 07087
(201) 863-4211
Maximum award: $10,000
Deadline: May 31
Majors/Fields: Operatic studies
Criteria: Applicant must be a young professional majoring in operatic studies, currently performing in opera, and wishing to advance to the next level. Awarded every year.
Contact: Inter-Cities Performing Arts, Inc.

481   Bi-Annual Operatic Vocal Competition for North American Artists

Baltimore Opera Company
1202 Maryland Avenue
Baltimore, MD 21201
(410) 625-1600, (410) 727-7854 (fax)
Maximum award: $10,000
Number of awards: 8
Deadline: May 1
College level: Freshman, Sophomore, Junior, Senior, Graduate, Doctoral
Majors/Fields: Opera, voice
Criteria: Applicant must be between age 20 and age 35. Prizes are awarded with the understanding that they will be used to further voice training, learn operatic roles, develop dramatic ability, or perfect foreign languages. Scholarship is renewable. Scholarship is awarded every other year.
Contact: James Harp, Competition Coordinator.

482   Marcella Sembrich Voice Scholarship

Kosciuszko Foundation
15 East 65th Street
New York, NY 10021
(212) 734-2130
Average award: $1,000
Number of awards: 1
Deadline: January 15
Majors/Fields: Vocal music
Criteria: Award is to encourage highly talented students of voice to study the works of Polish composers. Scholarship is awarded to U.S. citizens or legal residents, regardless of ethnic background, who have demonstrated unusual musical ability but have not yet made extensive professional appearances. Applicant must be between age 19 and age 25. In addition to an application, a tape of at least 20 minutes in length, including at least one song by a Polish composer, must be submitted. Awarded every year.
Contact: Scholarships.

483   Marian Anderson Vocal Arts Competition

Maryland Summer Institute for the Creative and Performing Arts/Rossborough Festival
4321 Hartwick Road, #220
College Park, MD 20740
(301) 403-8370, (301) 403-8375 (fax)
Maximum award: $20,000 plus New York recital and other engagements
Deadline: March 15
College level: Advanced vocalists
Majors/Fields: Voice
Criteria: Major quadrennial international music competition for the most advanced vocalists only. Competition rounds examine solo repertoire and performance with symphony orchestra. Applicant must be age 21 to age 39. Competition is held in 1999 and 2003.
Contact: Donald Reinhold, Assistant Director, intlcomp@umdacc.umd.edu.

484   Metropolitan Opera National Council Regional Award

Metropolitan Opera
National Council Auditions
Lincoln Center
New York, NY 10023
(212) 799-3100
Maximum award: $10,000
Maximum number of awards: 5
Minimum number of awards: 1
Deadline: Varies
Majors/Fields: Music, voice
Criteria: Applicant must have a voice with operatic potential, have musical training, should be able to sing in more than one language, and be a U.S. citizen or resident for at least one year. Applicants must compete in the district and regional levels before advancing to the nationals. Selection is based upon audition. Scholarship is renewable. Awarded every year.
Contact: Awards, Lincoln Center, New York, NY 10023, (212) 870-4515.

485   Robert Knauf Vocal Music Scholarship

Northern Kentucky University
Administrative Center 416
Nunn Drive
Highland Heights, KY 41099-7101
(606) 572-5144
Award: In-state tuition
Deadline: February 1
College level: Freshman, Sophomore, Junior, Senior
Majors/Fields: Vocal music
Criteria: Applicant must major in vocal music and submit two reference letters from former and/or present vocal instructors. Award is renewable for up to three years. Awarded every year. Award may be used only at sponsoring institution.
Contact: Robert E. Sprague, Director of Financial Aid.

Education

Education–General

486 A. Martin and Ruth Zucker Memorial Scholarship

University of Toledo
Financial Aid Office
Toledo, OH 43606-3390
(419) 537-2056
Maximum award: $2,000
Maximum number of awards: 7
Minimum number of awards: 1
College level: Freshman, Sophomore, Junior, Senior
Majors/Fields: Education
Criteria: Awarded every year. Award may be used only at sponsoring institution.
Contact: Dean, College of Education and Allied Professions, (419) 537-2025.

487 AASA Educational Administration Scholarship

American Association of School Administrators (AASA)
1801 North Moore Street
Arlington, VA 22209
(703) 528-0700, (703) 528-2146 (fax)
dpierce@assa.org
http://www.aasa.org
Average award: $2,000
Number of awards: 6
Deadline: September 1
College level: Graduate students
Majors/Fields: Education, administration, educational leadership
Criteria: Applicant must be a graduate student currently enrolled in an educational administration program with plans to make public school superintendency a life career. Applicant is recommended by department chair at the individual's institution. Awarded every year.
Contact: Darlene S. Pierce, Director of Grants and Awards, dpierce@aasa.org.

488 Bertie Taylor Rogers Memorial Scholarship

Texas A&M University–Kingsville
Scholarships
Box 116
Kingsville, TX 78363
(512) 593-3907, (512) 593-2991 (fax)
http://www.tamuk.edu
Maximum award: $1,000
Number of awards: No limit
Deadline: March 24
College level: Freshman
Majors/Fields: Education
Criteria: Applicant must rank in the top 15% of graduating class and have a minimum combined SAT I score of 970 (ACT score of 21). Award may be used only at sponsoring institution.
Contact: School Relations.

489 Carroll Donovan Memorial Scholarship

Texas A&M University–Kingsville
Scholarships
Box 116
Kingsville, TX 78363
(512) 593-3907, (512) 593-2991 (fax)
http://www.tamuk.edu
Average award: $500
Number of awards: No limit
Deadline: March 24
College level: Freshman, Sophomore, Junior, Senior
Majors/Fields: Education
Criteria: Applicant must have a minimum 3.0 GPA and combined SAT I score of 970 (ACT score of 21). Recipient must maintain a minimum 3.0 GPA to retain scholarship. Award may be used only at sponsoring institution.
Contact: School Relations.

490 Challenge Scholars Program

North Carolina Department of Public Instruction
301 North Wilmington Street
Raleigh, NC 27601-2825
(919) 715-1000, (919) 715-1094 (fax)
Number of awards: 50
Deadline: in February
College level: High school freshman, sophomore, or junior students
Majors/Fields: Teaching
Criteria: Applicants must maintain a minimum 3.0 GPA throughout their remaining high school career and must pursue a program of study throughout high school to prepare them for admission to an institute of higher education. Applicant must also achieve a score of 900 or greater on the SAT (or the established minimum for the PTSL) and pursue a course of study leading to licensure to teach in the public schools of North Carolina. Awarded every year.

491 Child Care Provider Scholarship

Maryland Higher Education Commission
State Scholarship Administration
16 Francis Street
Annapolis, MD 21401-1781
(410) 974-5370, (410) 974-5994 (fax)
http://www.ubalt.edu/www/mhec
Maximum award: $2,000
Number of awards: 90
Deadline: June 30
College level: Freshman, Sophomore, Junior, Senior
Majors/Fields: Child development, early childhood education
Criteria: Applicant must be a Maryland resident with a minimum 2.0 GPA, file a completed Child Care Provider application, and be enrolled in a program leading to an associate or bachelor's degree or a Child Development Associate Credential. Applicant must agree to work one year in a Maryland childcare center as a day care provider or staff member for each year of the award. Reapplication is required to retain scholarship for three additional years. Awarded every year.
Contact: Michael Smith, Program Administrator.

492   Christa McAuliffe Teacher Scholarship Loan

Delaware Higher Education Commission
820 North French Street
Fourth Floor
Wilmington, DE 19801
(302) 577-3240, (302) 577-6765 (fax)
mlaffey@state.de.us
http://www.state.de.us/high-ed/commiss/webpage.htm
Average award: $3,620
Maximum award: $9,020
Minimum award: $1,000
Number of awards: 18
Deadline: March 31
College level: Freshman, Sophomore, Junior
Majors/Fields: Education
Criteria: Applicant must be a Delaware resident and agree to teach in Delaware one year for each year the award was received or pay back the loan. Renewable if recipient maintains a minimum 2.75 GPA. Awarded every year. Award may be used at Delaware schools only.
Contact: Maureen Laffey, Associate Director.

493   Congressional Teacher Scholarship (NC)

Congressional Teacher Scholarship Program
Respective Schools of North Carolina
Average award: $5,000
Number of awards: 50
Majors/Fields: Education
Criteria: Applicant must be enrolled in good standing in an approved teacher education program, have ranked in top tenth of high school graduating class, and have interest in teaching in North Carolina. Applicants are nominated by deans of education at the 44 public and private schools in North Carolina with teacher education programs. Renewable if academic performance is maintained. Awarded every year. Award may be used at North Carolina schools with teacher education programs only.
Contact: Dean of Education.

494   Courtney Erin Todt Memorial Scholarship

Shawnee State University
940 Second Street
Portsmouth, OH 45662-4344
(614) 355-2237
Average award: $1,300
Deadline: April 15
College level: Sophomore
Criteria: Applicant must be a full-time student, be pursuing bachelor's degree, have a minimum 3.0 GPA, be involved in community activities, and must indicate on application a goal of positively impacting children. FAFSA is required. Early application is recommended. Awarded every year. Award may be used only at sponsoring institution.
Contact: Financial Aid Office, (614) 355-2485.

495   David A. DeBolt Teacher Shortage Scholarship

Illinois Student Assistance Commission/Client Support Services
1755 Lake Cook Road
Deerfield, IL 60015-5209
(800) 899-ISAC, (708) 948-8500
Maximum award: $3,000
Deadline: May 1
College level: Sophomore, Junior, Senior, Graduate, Doctoral
Majors/Fields: Education
Criteria: Applicant must be a U.S. citizen or eligible noncitizen and a legal resident of Illinois. Applicant must be enrolled or accepted for enrollment on at least a half-time basis as an undergraduate in a qualified teacher education program at an approved Illinois institution in a teacher shortage discipline. Preference is given to minority applicants. Recipient must sign a contract promising to teach one year for each year of scholarship assistance or repay the money plus interest. Scholarship is renewable. Awarded every year.
Contact: Manager of Scholarships and Specialized Grants.

496   David G. Besco Memorial Scholarship

Shawnee State University
940 Second Street
Portsmouth, OH 45662-4344
(614) 355-2237
Average award: $2,750
Deadline: April 15
College level: Sophomore, Junior, Senior
Majors/Fields: Teacher education/mathematics
Criteria: Applicant must be a resident of Ohio and have a minimum cumulative 3.5 GPA and minimum 3.0 GPA in major and education courses. Early application is recommended. Awarded every year. Award may be used only at sponsoring institution.
Contact: Financial Aid Office, (614) 355-2485.

497   Dean William H. Washington and Miriam Betts Washington Scholarship

Clemson University
G-01 Sikes Hall
Clemson, SC 29634-5123
(803) 656-2280
Average award: $1,800
Number of awards: 3
Deadline: March 1
College level: Freshman, Sophomore, Junior, Senior
Majors/Fields: Education
Criteria: Applicant must have a minimum 2.5 GPA. Awarded every year. Award may be used only at sponsoring institution.
Contact: Marvin Carmichael, Director of Financial Aid.

498   Dean's Education Scholarship

DePaul University
1 East Jackson Boulevard
Chicago, IL 60604
(312) 362-8704, (312) 362-5749 (fax)
Average award: $4,000
Maximum award: $8,000
Minimum award: $2,000
Deadline: None
College level: Freshman, Transfers
Majors/Fields: Early childhood education, elementary education, secondary education
Criteria: Applicant must present strong academic credentials and a strong interest in teaching. Transfer applicant must have a minimum 3.0 GPA. Minimum 2.75 GPA freshman year (minimum 3.0 GPA thereafter) as a full-time education major is required to retain scholarship. Awarded every year. Award may be used only at sponsoring institution.
Contact: Jennifer Sparrow, Scholarship Coordinator.

499   Distinguished Scholar Teacher Education

Maryland Higher Education Commission
State Scholarship Administration
16 Francis Street
Annapolis, MD 21401-1781
(410) 974-5370, (410) 974-5994 (fax)
http://www.ubalt.edu/www/mhec
Average award: $3,000
Number of awards: 52
Deadline: July 1
College level: Freshman, Sophomore, Junior, Senior, Graduate
Majors/Fields: Education
Criteria: Applicant must be a Distinguished Scholar award recipient and must teach in a Maryland public school one year for each year of award. Minimum 3.0 GPA is required to retain scholarship. Awarded every year.
Contact: Margaret Riley, Program Administrator.

500 Doris Ledbetter Memorial Scholarship

Jacksonville State University
Jacksonville, AL 36265-9982
(205) 782-5006
Average award: $1,000
Deadline: March 15
College level: Unspecified undergraduate
Majors/Fields: Education, nursing
Criteria: Financial need is considered. Awarded every year. Award may be used only at sponsoring institution.
Contact: Student Financial Aid Office.

501 Education Scholarship

Cedar Crest College
100 College Drive
Allentown, PA 18104
(610) 740-3785, (610) 606-4647 (fax)
cccadmis@cedarcrest.edu
www.cedarcrest.edu
Average award: $1,500
Number of awards: 2
Deadline: Rolling
College level: Freshman
Majors/Fields: Education
Criteria: Renewable if recipient maintains good academic standing. Awarded every year. Award may be used only at sponsoring institution.
Contact: Judith Neyhart, Vice President for Enrollment Management, Financial Aid Office.

502 Ellis and Hilda McCune Scholarship

California State University, Hayward
Office of Finanical Aid
WA545
Hayward, CA 94542-3028
(510) 885-3616, (510) 885-4627 (fax)
http://www.csuhayward.edu/
Average award: $1,000
Number of awards: 1
Deadline: May 1
College level: Junior, transfer student entering junior year
Majors/Fields: Teacher education
Criteria: Applicant must be a have a minimum 3.25 GPA, be enrolled full time, and submit letters of recommendation, summary of educational and career goals, official transcript from junior college, and FAFSA. Financial need is considered. Awarded every year. Award may be used only at sponsoring institution.
Contact: Scholarship Coordinator.

503 Emergency Secondary Education Award

University of West Alabama
Station Four
Livingston, AL 35470
(205) 652-3400, (205) 652-3522 (fax)
http://www.westal.edu
Average award: $3,996
Deadline: April 15
College level: Junior, Senior
Majors/Fields: Math education, science education
Criteria: Applicant must be a resident of Alabama. Scholarship is renewable. Awarded every year. Award may be used only at sponsoring institution.
Contact: Richard Hester, Director of Admissions, (205) 652-3400, extension 3578, rth@uwamail.westal.edu.

504 Flora Rogge College Scholarship

Minnesota Federation of Teachers
Scholarship Committee
168 Aurora Avenue
St. Paul, MN 55103
(612) 227-8583 or (800) 652-9710
Average award: $1,000
Number of awards: 1
Deadline: First Friday in March
College level: Freshman
Majors/Fields: Education
Criteria: Applicant must be a Minnesota high school senior planning to pursue a teacher training program in college. Selection is based upon financial need, academic achievement, promise of leadership ability, and good character. Awarded every year.
Contact: LuAnn Schmaus, Director of Publications.

505 Future Teachers Conditional Scholarship

Western Washington University
516 High Street
Bellingham, WA 98226-9006
(206) 650-3471
Average award: $3,000
Deadline: April 15
College level: Freshman, Sophomore, Junior, Senior
Majors/Fields: Education
Criteria: Applicant must be a Washington State resident, have a minimum cumulative 3.3 high school GPA or minimum 3.0 college GPA, and have declared intent to complete a program leading to initial teacher certification or additional teaching endorsements. Recipient must teach for ten years in a Washington public school or will be required to repay the scholarship. Selection is based upon academic excellence, commitment to teaching, leadership ability, community service involvement, and ability to act as a role model for children including targeted ethnic minorities. Satisfactory academic progress is required to retain scholarship for up to five years. Awarded every year. Award may be used only at sponsoring institution.
Contact: Francine E. Titus, Scholarship Coordinator.

506 Galen S. Besco Memorial Scholarship

Shawnee State University
940 Second Street
Portsmouth, OH 45662-4344
(614) 355-2237
Average award: $2,750
Deadline: April 15
College level: Sophomore, Junior, Senior
Majors/Fields: Teacher education/English
Criteria: Applicant must be a resident of Ohio and have a minimum cumulative 3.5 GPA and minimum 3.0 GPA in major and education courses. Early application is recommended. Awarded every year. Award may be used only at sponsoring institution.
Contact: Financial Aid Office, (614) 355-2485.

507 Gottschall-Rex Memorial Scholarship

University of Toledo
Financial Aid Office
Toledo, OH 43606-3390
(419) 537-2056
Maximum award: $1,600
Maximum number of awards: 5
Minimum number of awards: 1
College level: Freshman, Sophomore, Junior, Senior
Majors/Fields: Health education, physical education
Criteria: Applicant must be a Toledo woman enrolled full time. Selection is based upon financial need and academic achievement. Awarded every year. Award may be used only at sponsoring institution.
Contact: Dean, College of Education and Allied Professions, Toledo, OH 43606, (419) 537-2025.

508   **Harold Shamblin Scholarship**

Jacksonville State University
Jacksonville, AL 36265-9982
(205) 782-5006
Average award: $1,000
Deadline: March 15
College level: Freshman, Sophomore, Junior, Senior
Majors/Fields: Education
Criteria: Awarded every year. Award may be used only at sponsoring institution.
Contact: Student Financial Aid Office.

509   **Homer W. Heathman, Jr. Memorial Scholarship**

New Mexico State University
Box 30001
Department 5100
Las Cruces, NM 88003-0001
(505) 646-4105
Average award: Full tuition and fees
Deadline: March 1
College level: Sophomore, Junior, Senior
Majors/Fields: Education
Criteria: Applicant must be a graduate of a New Mexico high school. Selection is based upon character, scholarship, and financial need. Awarded every year. Award may be used only at sponsoring institution.
Contact: College of Education, (505) 646-2119.

510   **Howard M. Soule Graduate Fellowship**

Phi Delta Kappa
Eighth Street and Union Avenue
P.O. Box 789
Bloomington, IN 47402
(812) 339-1156, (812) 339-0018 (fax)
Average award: $950
Maximum award: $1,500
Minimum award: $500
Number of awards: 5
Deadline: May 1
College level: Unspecified graduate
Majors/Fields: Education
Criteria: Applicant must be a full-time graduate student in any field of education and a member in good standing of Phi Delta Kappa. Awarded every year.
Contact: Howard D. Hill, Director of Chapter Programs, hhill@pdkintl.org.

511   **Indiana Minority Teacher Scholarship**

State Student Assistance Commission of Indiana
150 West Market Street
Suite 500
Indianapolis, IN 46204-2811
(317) 232-2350
Maximum award: $4,000
Maximum number of awards: 500
Minimum number of awards: 300
Deadline: Varies with college attended
College level: Freshman, Sophomore, Junior, Senior
Majors/Fields: Education
Criteria: Applicant must be a black or Hispanic Indiana resident with a minimum 2.0 GPA who agrees to teach in Indiana upon certification. Reapplication, minimum 2.0 GPA, and full-time enrollment are required to retain scholarship. Awarded every year.
Contact: Yvonne Heflin, Director of Special Programs.

512   **International Education Scholarship**

School for International Training (SIT)
P.O. Box 676
Kipling Road
Brattleboro, VT 05302
(802) 257-7751, (802) 258-3500 (fax)
admissions.sit@worldlearning.org
http://www.worldlearning/sit.html
Average award: $1,000
Number of awards: 5
Deadline: April 1
College level: Master's degree candidate
Majors/Fields: Intercultural management
Criteria: Applicant must be employed for a minimum of two years as an international education professional. Financial need may be considered. Applicant must be enrolled in a degree program. Awarded when there are qualified applicants. Award may be used only at sponsoring institution.
Contact: Mary Henderson, Financial Aid Officer, (802) 258-3280.

513   **J. Lloyd Rogers Family Scholarship**

Southwest Texas State University
J.C. Kellam Building
San Marcos, TX 78666
(512) 245-2340
Average award: $1,000
Number of awards: 3
Deadline: March 1
College level: Junior, Senior
Majors/Fields: Education
Criteria: Applicant must be a man who has completed 60 credit hours of college-level work. Awarded every year. Award may be used only at sponsoring institution.
Contact: Elementary and Secondary Education Office, (512) 245-2315.

514   **J.C.U. Johnson Memorial Scholarship**

Jacksonville State University
Jacksonville, AL 36265-9982
(205) 782-5006
Average award: $1,950
Deadline: March 15
Majors/Fields: Education
Criteria: Applicant must be a resident of Calhoun County, Ala. Awarded every year. Award may be used only at sponsoring institution.
Contact: Student Financial Aid Office.

515   **James C. Inzer Jr.-Alabama Power Endowed Scholarship**

The University of Alabama
Box 870162
Tuscaloosa, AL 35487-0162
(205) 348-6756
Average award: $1,800
Number of awards: 1
Deadline: March 15
College level: Freshman, Sophomore, Junior, Senior
Majors/Fields: College of Education
Criteria: Applicant must be enrolled full time, demonstrate financial need, and be an Alabama resident. Satisfactory academic progress is required to retain scholarship. Awarded every year. Award may be used only at sponsoring institution.
Contact: Coordinator, Capstone College of Education Society, Box 870231, Tuscaloosa, AL 35487-0231.

516   James Harris Fitts Scholarship

The University of Alabama
Box 870162
Tuscaloosa, AL 35487-0162
(205) 348-6756
Average award: $1,000
Number of awards: 1
Deadline: March 15
College level: Freshman, Sophomore, Junior, Senior
Majors/Fields: College of Education
Criteria: Applicant must be under age 23 and planning a teaching career in Alabama. Awarded every year. Award may be used only at sponsoring institution.
Contact: Coordinator, Capstone College of Education Society, Box 870231, Tuscaloosa, AL 35487-0231.

517   Julia Victor and Leslie Carlisle McDonald Scholarship

Southwest Texas State University
J.C. Kellam Building
San Marcos, TX 78666
(512) 245-2340
Average award: $1,250
Number of awards: 2
Deadline: March 1
College level: Freshman, Sophomore, Junior, Senior
Majors/Fields: Education
Criteria: Applicant must have a minimum 3.0 GPA, be enrolled in the teacher education program for at least 12 credit hours, and be a member of at least one professional organization related to education. Awarded yearly as funds are available. Award may be used only at sponsoring institution.
Contact: Elementary and Secondary Education Office, (512) 245-2315.

518   LBJ Achievement Scholarship in Education

Southwest Texas State University
J.C. Kellam Building
San Marcos, TX 78666
(512) 245-2340
Average award: $1,000
Number of awards: 10
Deadline: November 15, March 15
College level: Junior, Senior
Majors/Fields: Education
Criteria: Applicant must be a black or Hispanic Texas resident enrolled full time with a minimum 3.0 GPA. Minimum 3.0 GPA is required to retain scholarship. Awarded every year. Award may be used only at sponsoring institution.
Contact: Coordinator of Scholarships, Office of Student Financial Aid, 601 University Drive, San Marcos, TX 78666-4602, (512) 245-2315.

519   Lillian E. Glover Scholarship

Illinois Congress of Parents and Teachers
901 South Spring Street
Springfield, IL 62704
(217) 528-9617
Maximum award: $1,000
Number of awards: 50
Deadline: March 1
College level: Freshman
Majors/Fields: Education, education-related degree program
Criteria: Applicant must have graduated from an Illinois public high school and have ranked in top fifth of class. Awarded every year.
Contact: Virginia Brown, Scholarship Chairman, 9012 Knoxville Road, Milan, IL 61264.

520   Margy Ann Pollard Memorial Scholarship

Texas A&M University–Kingsville
Scholarships
Box 116
Kingsville, TX 78363
(512) 593-3907, (512) 593-2991 (fax)
http://www.tamuk.edu
Average award: $500
Number of awards: 2
Deadline: March 24
College level: Freshman, Sophomore, Junior, Senior
Majors/Fields: Education
Criteria: Applicant must have a minimum 3.0 GPA and combined SAT I score of 970 (ACT score of 21). Award may be used only at sponsoring institution.
Contact: School Relations.

521   Mark and Marian Berkin Physical Education Endowed Scholarship

The University of Alabama
Box 870162
Tuscaloosa, AL 35487-0162
(205) 348-6756
Average award: $1,000
Number of awards: 1
Deadline: March 15
College level: Junior, Senior
Majors/Fields: Human performance program
Criteria: Applicant must have completed at least 60 credit hours with a minimum 2.5 GPA (passing grades in all courses) and demonstrate financial need. Satisfactory academic progress and reapplication are required for renewal. Awarded every year. Award may be used only at sponsoring institution.
Contact: Coordinator, Capstone College of Education Society, Box 870231, Tuscaloosa, AL 35487-0231.

522   Mary Esther Lily Avis Bursary/Scholarship

University of Calgary
Department of Financial Aid
2500 University Drive, NW
Calgary, Alberta, CN T2N 1N4
(403) 220-7872, (403) 282-2999 (fax)
Average award: $2,000
Number of awards: 16
Deadline: June 15
College level: Sophomore, Junior, Senior
Majors/Fields: Education
Criteria: Selection is based upon academic merit and financial need. Awarded every year. Award may be used only at sponsoring institution.
Contact: J. Van Housen, Director of Student Awards/Financial Aid.

523   Mildred Sheppard Scholarship

Jacksonville State University
Jacksonville, AL 36265-9982
(205) 782-5006
Average award: $1,000
Deadline: March 15
Majors/Fields: Education
Criteria: Applicant must commit in writing to major in education and teach K-12 for at least two years. Awarded every year. Award may be used only at sponsoring institution.
Contact: Student Financial Aid Office.

524   Missouri Teacher Education Scholarship

Missouri Department of Elementary and Secondary Education
P.O. Box 480
Jefferson City, MO 65102
(573) 751-1668
Average award: $2,000
Number of awards: 230
Deadline: February 15
College level: Freshman, Sophomore, Junior, non-traditional students
Majors/Fields: Education
Criteria: Applicant must be a resident of Missouri, rank in the top 15 percent of high school class, or score in the top 15 percent on the SAT I, ACT, or SCAT exams. Applicant must agree to teach in the Missouri public schools (PreK-12) for five years after graduation. Awarded every year.
Contact: Janet Goeller, Director of Teacher Recruitment & Retention, jgoeller@mailidese.state.mo.us.

525   New Mexico Space Grant Teacher Fellowship

New Mexico State University
Box 30001
Department 5100
Las Cruces, NM 88003-0001
(505) 646-4105
Maximum award: $10,000
Number of awards: 3
Deadline: March 1
College level: Freshman, Sophomore, Junior, Senior
Majors/Fields: Education, elementary education, math, science
Criteria: Applicant must be enrolled in a teacher certification program, have a minimum 3.25 GPA, be a U.S. citizen, and agree to work in the educational program at the Space Center in Alamogordo, N.Mex. Preference is given to women and minority students. Awarded every year. Award may be used only at sponsoring institution.
Contact: Greeley W. Myers, Director of Financial Aid.

526   Onderdonk Family Memorial Scholarship

University of Texas at San Antonio
Office of Student Financial Aid
6900 North Loop 1604 West
San Antonio, TX 78249-0687
(210) 691-44855
Average award: Tuition and fees for six credits
Number of awards: 2
College level: Student teachers
Criteria: Applicant must have a minimum 3.0 GPA, be a U.S. citizen or permanent resident, and be a student teacher. Awarded every year. Award may be used only at sponsoring institution.
Contact: Office of the Dean, College of Business, Division of Education, 6900 North Loop 1604 West, San Antonio, TX 78249.

527   Paul Douglas Conditional Scholarship

Western Washington University
516 High Street
Bellingham, WA 98226-9006
(206) 650-3471
Maximum award: $5,000
Deadline: Mid-January
College level: Freshman, Sophomore, Junior, Senior
Majors/Fields: Education
Criteria: Applicant must be a Washington State resident, rank in top tenth of high school class, and agree to teach for two years for each year the scholarship is received. Scholarship is renewable. Awarded every year. Award may be used only at sponsoring institution.
Contact: Francine E. Titus, Scholarship Coordinator.

528   Paul Douglas Teacher Scholarship

California State Polytechnic University, Pomona
3801 West Temple Avenue
Pomona, CA 917684019
(909) 869-3700
Average award: $5,000
Number of awards: 6
Criteria: Award may be used only at sponsoring institution.
Contact: Crystal Steele, Financial Aid Counselor.

529   Paul Douglas Teacher Scholarship

District of Columbia Office of Postsecondary Education, Research, and Assistance
2100 Martin Luther King Jr. Avenue, SE
Suite 401
Washington, DC 20020
(202) 727-3685
Average award: $5,000
Number of awards: 6
Deadline: Last Friday of June
College level: Freshman, Sophomore, Junior, Senior
Majors/Fields: Education
Criteria: Applicant must be a District of Columbia resident enrolled full time with good academic standing, rank in the top tenth of graduating class, express an interest in teaching, demonstrate financial need, submit a recommendation, have a minimum cumulative 2.5 GPA, and have a minimum 3.0 GPA in math, science, and foreign languages. Reapplication is required to retain scholarship. Awarded every year.
Contact: Laurencia O. Henderson, Student Financial Assistance Specialist.

530   Paul Douglas Teacher Scholarship

Illinois Student Assistance Commission/Client Support Services
1755 Lake Cook Road
Deerfield, IL 60015-5209
(800) 899-ISAC, (708) 948-8500
Average award: $4,536
Maximum award: $5,000
Minimum award: $2,459
Number of awards: 160
Deadline: August 1
College level: Freshman, Sophomore, Junior, Senior
Majors/Fields: Education
Criteria: Applicant must be a U.S. citizen or eligible noncitizen and a legal resident of Illinois. Applicant must rank in top tenth of high school class and be enrolled full time or accepted for full-time enrollment as an undergraduate in a qualified teacher education program at an approved Illinois institution. Recipient must sign a contract promising to teach two years for each year of scholarship assistance or repay the money plus interest. Scholarship is renewable. Awarded every year.
Contact: Manager of Scholarships and Specialized Grants.

531   Paul Douglas Teachers Scholarship

The Master's College
21726 Placerita Canyon Road
Santa Clarita, CA 91321-1200
(805) 259-3540, (805) 288-1037 (fax)
Maximum award: $5,000
College level: Sophomore, Junior, Senior, Graduate
Majors/Fields: Education
Criteria: Applicant must demonstrate commitment to a teaching career in preschool, elementary, or secondary school level. Recipient must teach full-time for two years for each year of award, or repay money with interest. Scholarship is renewable. Awarded every year. Award may be used only at sponsoring institution.
Contact: Timothy C. Wiegert, Associate Director of Enrollment, (800) 568-6248 extension 450.

532 Paul Douglas Teacher Scholarship

Montana Commission on Higher Education
University of Montana
33 South Last Chance Gulch
Helena, MT 59620
(406) 444-6594
Average award: $5,000
Maximum number of awards: 10
Minimum number of awards: 5
College level: Unspecified undergraduate
Majors/Fields: Education
Criteria: Applicant must be a U.S. citizen, a resident of Montana, and must attend a program leading to the teaching profession in grades K-12. Rank in top tenth of secondary school class is required. Scholarship is renewable. Awarded every year.
Contact: Bill Lannan, Director of Montana Guaranteed Student Loan Program, (406) 444-6954.

533 Paul Douglas Teacher Scholarship

North Carolina State Department of Public Instruction
301 North Wilmington Street
Raleigh, NC 27601-2825
(919) 715-1120
Maximum award: $5,000
Maximum number of awards: 40
Minimum number of awards: 20
Deadline: in April
College level: Freshman, Sophomore, Junior, Senior
Majors/Fields: Education
Criteria: Applicant must be a U.S. citizen, a North Carolina resident, and rank in the top tenth of class. Selection is based upon academic standing, leadership, service, and interest in teaching. Preference is given to applicants who intend to teach disabled children, those with limited English proficiency, or preschool-age children, or who teach in an inner-city, rural, or geographically isolated school. Scholarship is renewable. Awarded every year.
Contact: Scholarships, North Carolina State Education Assistance Authority, P.O. Box 2688, Chapel Hill, NC 27515.

534 Paul Douglas Teacher Scholarship

Ohio Board of Regents, State Grants and Scholarships Department
309 South Fourth Street
P.O. Box 182452
Columbus, OH 43218-2452
(614) 466-1190, (614) 752-5903 (fax)
Average award: $5,000
Number of awards: 40
Deadline: Second Friday in March
College level: Freshman, Sophomore, Junior, Senior, Graduate, Doctoral
Majors/Fields: Education
Criteria: Applicant must be a U.S. citizen or eligible noncitizen, an Ohio resident attending an Ohio postsecondary school, must rank in top tenth of classm be pursuing teacher certification, and attend school full time. Applicant must not default on any student loan or owe a refund on any federal aid. Satisfactory academic progress is required to retain scholarship. Awarded every year. Ohio schools only.
Contact: Barbara Closser, Paul Douglas Teacher Scholarship Administrator, (614) 644-6629.

535 Paul Douglas Teacher Scholarship

State Council of Higher Education for Virginia
James Monroe Building, 10th Floor
101 North 14th Street
Richmond, VA 23219
(804) 786-1690, (804) 225-2604 (fax)
Maximum award: $5,000
College level: Freshman, Sophomore, Junior, Senior
Majors/Fields: Education
Criteria: Applicant must be a Virginia resident, attend a college or university in Virginia, and rank in the top tenth of class. Recipients must teach two years for each year the scholarship is received. Scholarship is renewable. Awarded every year.
Contact: Scholarships.

536 Paul Douglas Scholarship

University of Texas at San Antonio
Office of Student Financial Aid
6900 North Loop 1604 West
San Antonio, TX 78249-0687
(210) 691-44855
Average award: $5,000
Deadline: July 1
College level: Freshman, Sophomore, Junior, Senior
Majors/Fields: Education
Criteria: Applicant must be a Texas resident enrolled full time, a U.S. citizen, rank in the top tenth of class, have a minimum 3.0 GPA, demonstrate financial need, and make a commitment to teach after graduation. Minimum 3.0 GPA is required to retain scholarship for two additional years. Awarded every year. Award may be used only at sponsoring institution.
Contact: Scholarship Office.

537 Paul Douglas Teacher Scholarship

Trinity Bible College
50 Sixth Avenue South
Ellendale, ND 58436-7150
Maximum award: $5,000
Deadline: April 15
College level: Freshman
Majors/Fields: Elementary/teacher education
Criteria: Applicant must be a resident of North Dakota, rank in top tenth of class, and submit application. Scholarship is renewable. Awarded every year.
Contact: North Dakota University System, 600 East Boulevard, Bismarck, ND 58505-0230.

538 Paul Douglas Teacher Scholarship

University of Utah
Financial Aid and Scholarships Office
105 Student Services Building
Salt Lake City, UT 84112
(801) 581-6211
Maximum award: $5,000
Deadline: March 30
College level: Freshman
Majors/Fields: Education
Criteria: Applicant must be a Utah resident and rank in the top tenth of class. Preference is given to applicants planning to major in Utah-designated teacher shortage areas including math, science, and special education. Applicant must obtain teacher certification and teach full time for at least two years for each year of scholarship assistance received. Good academic standing and full-time enrollment are required to retain scholarship. Awarded every year. Award may be used only at sponsoring institution.
Contact: Dr. Mark Spencer, Utah System of Higher Education, 3 Triad Center, Suite 550, 355 West North Temple, Salt Lake City, UT 84180.

539 Phi Delta Kappa Scholarship Grants for Prospective Educators

Phi Delta Kappa
Eighth Street and Union Avenue
P.O. Box 789
Bloomington, IN 47402
(812) 339-1156, (812) 339-0018 (fax)
Average award: $1,100
Maximum award: $5,000
Minimum award: $1,000
Number of awards: 47
Deadline: January 31
College level: Freshman
Majors/Fields: Education
Criteria: Applicant must rank in top third of graduating class. Selection is based upon scholarship, recommendations, written expression, interest in teaching as a career, and school and community activities. Awarded every year.
Contact: Howard D. Hill, Director of Chapter Programs, hhill@pdkintl.org.

540   Project HELP Scholarship

Spalding University
851 South Fourth Street
Louisville, KY 40203
(502) 585-9911
Average award: Full tuition
Number of awards: 30
Deadline: March 1 (priority)
College level: Freshman, Sophomore, Junior, Senior, Transfers
Majors/Fields: Interdisciplinary early childhood education
Criteria: Awarded every year. Award may be used only at sponsoring institution.
Contact: Dean of the College of Education.

541   Promise–Prospective Teacher Scholarship Loan

North Carolina Department of Public Instruction
301 North Wilmington Street
Raleigh, NC 27601-2825
(919) 715-1000, (919) 715-1094 (fax)
Average award: $900
Maximum award: $2,500
Number of awards: 200
Deadline: in February
College level: Freshman, Sophomore, Junior, Senior, Graduate
Majors/Fields: Teaching or audiology, library/media services, school psychology/counseling, speech/language impaired
Criteria: Applicant must pursue a full-time program at either a North Carolina college or university with an approved teacher education program or a technical institute or community college with a program transferable to an approved teacher education program. Scholarship recipients are obligated to teach one year in a North Carolina public school for each year of assistance they receive. Minimum 2.5 GPA during freshman year and 3.0 GPA each year thereafter (up to four years) to retain scholarship. Awarded every year. Award may be used at North Carolina Schools only.

542   PROMISE Teacher Scholarship

Georgia Student Finance Commission
2082 East Exchange Place
Suite 200
Tucker, GA 30084
(770) 414-3000, (912) 757-3626, (800) 776-6878
Average award: $3,000
College level: Freshman, Sophomore, Junior, Senior
Majors/Fields: Education
Criteria: Applicant does not have to be a Georgia resident; financial need is not considered. Award may be used at eligible Georgia schools only.
Contact: Scholarships.

543   Public School Teacher Scholarship

School for International Training (SIT)
P.O. Box 676
Kipling Road
Brattleboro, VT 05302
(802) 257-7751, (802) 258-3500 (fax)
admissions.sit@worldlearning.org
http://www.worldlearning/sit.html
Average award: $500
Number of awards: 8
Deadline: April 1
College level: Master's degree candidate
Majors/Fields: Teaching
Criteria: Applicant must be a teacher of ESL, French, or Spanish in a U.S. public school who has made exceptional contributions to his or her school in work as a language teacher. Financial need may be considered. Applicant must be enrolled in a degree program. Awarded every year. Award may be used only at sponsoring institution.
Contact: Mary Henderson, Financial Aid Officer, (802) 258-3280.

544   Robert C. Byrd Honors Scholarship

State Student Assistance Commission of Indiana
150 West Market Street
Suite 500
Indianapolis, IN 46204-2811
(317) 232-2350
Number of awards: 283
Deadline: April 24
College level: Freshman
Criteria: Applicant must be an Indiana resident. Satisfactory academic progress is required to retain scholarship. Awarded every year.
Contact: Yvonne Heflin, Director of Special Programs, 150 West Market Street, Suite 500, Indianapolis, IN 46204-2811.

545   Robert C. Byrd Honors Scholarship

Illinois Student Assistance Commission/Client Support Services
1755 Lake Cook Road
Deerfield, IL 60015-5209
(800) 899-ISAC, (708) 948-8500
Average award: $1,500
Deadline: January 13
College level: Freshman, Sophomore, Junior, Senior
Majors/Fields: Education
Criteria: Applicant must be a U.S. citizen or eligible noncitizen, a legal resident of Illinois, rank in top two percent of class, have a minimum 3.8 GPA, and/or a minimum combined SAT I score of 1100 (composite ACT score of 27), and attend an Illinois institution. Recipient must sign a contract promising to teach two years for each year of scholarship assistance or repay the money plus interest. Renewable for up to four years. Awarded every year.
Contact: Manager of Scholarships and Specialized Grants.

546   Robert C. Byrd Honors Scholarship

North Carolina State Department of Public Instruction
301 North Wilmington Street
Raleigh, NC 27601-2825
(919) 715-1120
Maximum award: $1,500
Number of awards: 150
Deadline: in February
College level: Freshman
Majors/Fields: Education
Criteria: Applicant must be a North Carolina resident, have a minimum 3.0 GPA and minimum combined SAT I score of 850, demonstrate outstanding academic achievement, and show promise of continued academic excellence. Priority is given to applicants who wish to teach in public schools, particularly in the areas of math and science. Renewable for up to four years if satisfactory academic progress and full-time enrollment are maintained. Awarded every year.
Contact: Scholarships.

547   Sally Booth Eisenhower Endowed Scholarship

The University of Alabama
Box 870162
Tuscaloosa, AL 35487-0162
(205) 348-6756
Average award: $1,000
Number of awards: 1
Deadline: March 15
College level: Freshman, Sophomore, Junior, Senior
Majors/Fields: College of Education
Criteria: Awarded to degree-seeking student with demonstrated financial need. Satisfactory academic progress and reapplication are required for renewal. Awarded every year. Award may be used only at sponsoring institution.
Contact: Coordinator, Capstone College of Education Society, Box 870231, Tuscaloosa, AL 35487-0231.

548   Sanford and Irene Loef Scholarship

Clemson University
G-01 Sikes Hall
Clemson, SC 29634-5123
(803) 656-2280
Average award: $2,500
Number of awards: 1
Deadline: March 1
College level: Sophomore, Junior, Senior
Majors/Fields: Industrial education
Criteria: Applicant must have a minimum 2.5 GPA. Satisfactory GPA and completion of at least 12 credit hours per semester are required to retain scholarship. Awarded every year. Award may be used only at sponsoring institution.
Contact: Marvin Carmichael, Director of Financial Aid.

549   Sharon Christa McAuliffe Memorial Teacher Education Award

Maryland Higher Education Commission
State Scholarship Administration
16 Francis Street
Annapolis, MD 21401-1781
(410) 974-5370, (410) 974-5994 (fax)
http://www.ubalt.edu/www/mhec
Maximum award: $9,600
Number of awards: 44
Deadline: December 31
College level: Junior, Senior, Graduate, Doctoral
Majors/Fields: Education
Criteria: Applicant must be a full-time undergraduate student, public school teacher, or part-time degree-holding, nonteacher at a Maryland degree-granting institution with an approved teacher education program. Applicant must be a Maryland resident, have a minimum 3.0 GPA, and have completed at least 60 credit hours. Applicant must agree to teach one year in a Maryland public school in a critical shortage area for each year of the award. Minimum 3.0 GPA is required to retain scholarship for one additional year. Awarded every year.
Contact: Michael Smith, Program Administrator.

550   Steffensen Cannon Scholarship

University of Utah
Financial Aid and Scholarships Office
105 Student Services Building
Salt Lake City, UT 84112
(801) 581-6211
Maximum award: $8,500
Deadline: January 15
College level: Freshman, Sophomore, Junior, Senior, Graduate
Majors/Fields: Education
Criteria: Applicant must be enrolled in the College of Humanities or Graduate School of Education or intend to go into teacher education. Freshman applicant must rank in top quarter of class, undergraduate applicant must have a minimum 2.75 GPA, and graduate applicant must have a minimum 3.0 GPA. Priority is given to descendents of Ellen Christina Steffensen Cannon. Good academic standing is required to retain scholarship for an additional year. Awarded every year. Award may be used only at sponsoring institution.
Contact: Education Advising Center, 226 Milton Bennion Hall, Salt Lake City, UT 84112, (801) 581-7780.

551   Teacher Assistant Scholarship Loan

North Carolina Department of Public Instruction
301 North Wilmington Street
Raleigh, NC 27601-2825
(919) 715-1000, (919) 715-1094 (fax)
Maximum award: $1,200
Deadline: in January
Majors/Fields: Teaching or audiology, library/media services, school psychology/counseling, speech/language impaired.
Criteria: Applicant must be a legal North Carolina resident who does not already hold teacher licensure. Applicant must either hold a bachelor's degree or have already completed the general college courses prerequisites to admission to a degree program at a four-year institute. Applicant must have the endorsement of the superintendent of the employing local school system. Scholarship recipients are obligated to teach one year in a North Carolina public school for each year of assistance they receive. Renewable up to four years if recipient maintains a minimum 2.5 GPA and completion of 12 semester hours from September 1–August 31. Awarded every year. Award may be used at North Carolina schools only.

552   Teaching Fellows Program

Elon College
2700 Campus Box
Elon College, NC 27244
(800) 334-8448 extension 1
Average award: Full tuition, room, and board
Number of awards: 20
College level: Freshman
Majors/Fields: Education
Criteria: Applicant must be a North Carolina resident and be chosen by Public School Forum of North Carolina. Grant is forgiven if recipient teaches in North Carolina public school system for four years after graduation. Apply to Public School Forum of North Carolina. Award is for four years. Awarded every year. Award may be used only at sponsoring institution.
Contact: Office of Admissions and Financial Planning.

553   Teaching Scholars Program

Tennessee Student Assistance Corporation
Parkway Towers, Suite 1950
404 James Robertson Parkway
Nashville, TN 37243-0820
(615) 741-1346, (615) 741-6101 (fax)
Average award: $3,000
Number of awards: 50
Deadline: April 15
College level: Junior, Senior, Graduate, Doctoral
Majors/Fields: Education
Criteria: Applicant must attend school in Tennessee. Recipient must maintain a minimum 2.75 GPA for renewal. Awarded every year. Award may be used at Tennessee schools only.
Contact: Stella Flynn, Program Coordinator.

554   Technology Scholarship Program for Alabama Teachers

Alabama Commission on Higher Education
P.O. Box 302000
Montgomery, AL 36130-2000
(334) 242-1998, (334) 242-0268 (fax)
Average award: $848
Maximum award: $2,505
Minimum award: $279
College level: Doctoral, teachers taking technology courses for credit or non-credit
Majors/Fields: Technology courses
Criteria: Applicant must be a full-time, regularly certified, Alabama public school teacher. Scholarship is renewable. Awarded every year.
Contact: Dr. William H. Wall, Director of Grants and Scholarship, (334) 242-2274.

555   Underwood-Smith Teacher Scholarship

State College and University Systems of West Virginia
Central Office
1018 Kanawha Boulevard, Suite 700
Charleston, WV 25301-2827
(304) 558-4618, (304) 558-4622 (fax)
crocket@scusco.wvnet.edu
http://www.scusco.wvnet.edu/
Average award: $4,503
Maximum award: $5,000
Minimum award: $1,373
Number of awards: 45
Deadline: April 1
College level: Freshman, Sophomore, Junior, Senior, Graduate, Doctoral
Majors/Fields: Education
Criteria: Applicant must be a West Virginia resident who will attend a West Virginia institution of higher education full time, seeking teacher certification at the preschool, elementary, or secondary level. Undergraduate applicant must rank in the top tenth of class, score in the top tenth statewide of those taking the ACT, or have a cumulative 3.25 GPA after successfully completing two years of course work at an approved institution. Graduate applicant must have graduated in the top tenth of college class. Minimum 3.0 GPA is required for freshmen and sophomores and 3.25 GPA for juniors for renewal. Awarded every year.
Contact: Tammy Jenkins, Scholarship Programs Coordinator, jenkins@scusco.wvnet.edu.

556   Wallace and Ersel Webb Sharples Memorial Scholarship

Western Montana College of the University of Montana
Dillon, MT 59725
(406) 683-7511
Average award: $1,000
Number of awards: 2
Deadline: February 15
College level: Freshman
Majors/Fields: Teacher education
Criteria: Awarded every year. Award may be used only at sponsoring institution.
Contact: Scholarships.

557   William Winter Teacher Scholar Program

Mississippi Board of Trustees of State Institutions of Higher Learning
Student Financial Aid Office
3825 Ridgewood Road
Jackson, MS 39211-6453
(601) 982-6663, (601) 982-6527 (fax)
Maximum award: $3,000
College level: Freshman, Junior, Senior
Majors/Fields: Education
Criteria: Applicant must be a Mississippi resident. Minimum 2.5 GPA is required for renewal. Awarded every year.
Contact: Mississippi Postsecondary Education Financial Assistance Board.

558   Woodring Scholarship

Western Washington University
516 High Street
Bellingham, WA 98226-9006
(206) 650-3471
Average award: $2,250
Number of awards: 10
Deadline: April 15
College level: Junior, Senior, Graduate, Doctoral
Majors/Fields: Education, elementary education, secondary education
Criteria: Applicant must have precollege test scores in the top ten percent, have at least 30 college credits, and be preparing for a career in public school teaching at the elementary or secondary school level. Awarded every year. Award may be used only at sponsoring institution.
Contact: Jill Clark, Scholarship Assistant.

Elementary/Secondary Education

559   Celia Koontz Findlay Scholarship in Elementary Education

University of Toledo
Financial Aid Office
Toledo, OH 43606-3390
(419) 537-2056
Maximum award: $1,400
Number of awards: 2
College level: Sophomore, Junior, Senior
Majors/Fields: Elementary education
Criteria: Applicant must be a U.S. citizen and demonstrate academic achievement and financial need. Awarded every year. Award may be used only at sponsoring institution.
Contact: Dean, College of Education and Allied Professions, Toledo, OH 43606, (419) 537-2025.

560   Council on Public Higher Education Scholarship

Southwest Missouri State University
Student Financial Aid
901 South National Avenue
Springfield, MO 65804-0095
(417) 836-5000 or (800) 492-7900
Average award: $1,000
Number of awards: 10
Deadline: March 31
College level: Junior, Senior
Majors/Fields: Biology, chemistry, education, foreign language, mathematics, physics
Criteria: Applicant must have completed a minimum of 75 credit hours and be preparing for a career as a math, biology, chemistry, physics, or foreign language teacher at the elementary or secondary level. Financial need is not considered. Awarded every year. Award may be used only at sponsoring institution.
Contact: Scholarship Committee, (417) 836-5262.

561   Florence C. Painter Memorial Scholarship

Southwest Missouri State University
Student Financial Aid
901 South National Avenue
Springfield, MO 65804-0095
(417) 836-5000 or (800) 492-7900
Average award: $1,600
Number of awards: 2
Deadline: March 31
College level: Junior, Senior
Majors/Fields: Secondary education
Criteria: Applicant must have a minimum 3.0 GPA and demonstrate financial need. Preference is given to those planning to teach Spanish. Reapplication is required to retain scholarship. Awarded every year. Award may be used only at sponsoring institution.
Contact: Scholarship Committee, (417) 836-5262.

562   Hewlett-Packard Scholarship

Society of Women Engineers (SWE)
120 Wall Street
11th Floor
New York, NY 10005-3902
(212) 509-9577, (212) 509-0224 (fax)
Average award: $1,000
Number of awards: 7
Deadline: May 15
College level: Junior, Senior
Majors/Fields: Computer science, electrical engineering
Criteria: Applicant must be a woman, have a minimum 3.5 GPA, and be an active supporter and contributor to SWE. Awarded every year.
Contact: Scholarships.

563   Mary Emma Key McKinley Scholarship

The University of Alabama
Box 870162
Tuscaloosa, AL 35487-0162
(205) 348-6756
Average award: $1,000
Number of awards: 4
Deadline: March 15
College level: Freshman, Sophomore, Junior, Senior
Majors/Fields: Early childhood education
Criteria: Applicant must be enrolled full time and demonstrate an aptitude for and commitment to a career in early childhood education. Scholarship committee sets specific academic requirements. Awarded every year. Award may be used only at sponsoring institution.
Contact: Coordinator, Capstone College of Education Society, Box 870231, Tuscaloosa, AL 35487-0231, (205) 348-6881.

564   Math/Science/Foreign Language Scholarship

University of Utah
Financial Aid and Scholarships Office
105 Student Services Building
Salt Lake City, UT 84112
(801) 581-6211
Average award: $1,500
Maximum number of awards: 9
Minimum number of awards: 3
Deadline: March 1
College level: Sophomore, Junior, Senior, Graduate
Majors/Fields: Secondary education with major/minor in mathematics, biology, chemistry, computer science, geology, physics, French, German, Spanish
Criteria: Applicant must be pursuing teacher certification in Utah and have a minimum 3.0 cumulative GPA. Minimum 3.0 GPA and 12 credits per quarter are required to retain undergraduate scholarship. At least nine credit hours per quarter are required to retain graduate scholarship. Awarded every year. Award may be used only at sponsoring institution.
Contact: Education Advising Center, 226 Milton Bennion Hall, Salt Lake City, UT 84112, (801) 581-7780.

565   Ruth Eshelman Althouse Scholarship

Elizabethtown College
One Alpha Drive
Elizabethtown, PA 17022
(717) 361-1404, (717) 361-1485 (fax)
College level: Junior, Senior
Majors/Fields: Elementary education, secondary education.
Criteria: Applicant must be a full-time student who has completed two years of study and anticipates a career in elementary or secondary education. Award may be used only at sponsoring institution.
Contact: M. Clarke Paine, Director of Financial Aid, painemc@acad.etown.edu.

Special Education ────────

566   Child Welfare Scholarship

American Legion–Wisconsin Auxiliary
Department Executive Secretary
812 East State Street
Milwaukee, WI 53202-3493
(414) 271-0124
Average award: $1,000
Number of awards: 1
Deadline: March 15
College level: Graduate, Doctoral
Majors/Fields: Special education
Criteria: Applicant must be a Wisconsin resident, have a minimum 3.2 GPA, demonstrate financial need, attend an accredited school, and be the child, wife, or widow of a veteran. Granddaughters and great-granddaughters of veterans are eligible if they are American Legion Auxiliary members. Awarded every year.
Contact: Scholarships.

567   Emily Nelson Moseley Memorial Scholarship

Southwest Missouri State University
Student Financial Aid
901 South National Avenue
Springfield, MO 65804-0095
(417) 836-5000 or (800) 492-7900
Average award: $2,400
Number of awards: 3
Deadline: March 31
College level: Junior, Senior
Majors/Fields: Special education
Criteria: Selection is based upon academic performance. Satisfactory academic progress is required to retain scholarship. Awarded every year. Award may be used only at sponsoring institution.
Contact: Scholarship Committee, (417) 836-5262.

568   NCEA-CDA Special Education Scholarship

Catholic Daughters of the Americas
National Headquarters
10 West 71st Street
New York, NY 10023
Average award: $500
Number of awards: 4
Deadline: May 1
College level: Unspecified undergraduate
Majors/Fields: Special education
Criteria: Applicant must be a teacher in a Catholic school, have a letter of endorsement from the school principal or religious authority, and earn a minimum of four hours of course credit. Awarded every year.
Contact: Helen Johnson, National Scholarship Chairman, 1111 S. Garrison #204, Lakewood, CO 80232.

569   Special Education Services Scholarship

State Student Assistance Commission of Indiana
150 West Market Street
Suite 500
Indianapolis, IN 46204-2811
(317) 232-2350
Maximum award: $1,000
Number of awards: 75
Deadline: Determined by college or university
College level: Freshman, Sophomore, Junior, Senior
Majors/Fields: Occupational therapy, physical therapy, special education
Criteria: Applicant must be an Indiana resident with a minimum 2.0 GPA who agrees to teach in Indiana upon certification. Reapplication and satisfactory academic progress are required to retain scholarship. Awarded every year.
Contact: Yvonne D. Heflin, Director of Special Programs.

570   UCT Scholarship for Teachers of the Mentally Handicapped

Order of United Commercial Travelers of America (UCT)
632 North Park Street
P.O. Box 159019
Columbus, OH 43215-8619
(614) 228-3276
Average award: $500
Maximum award: $750
Minimum award: $100
Number of awards: 350
Deadline: None
College level: Senior, Graduate, Doctoral
Majors/Fields: Mental retardation
Criteria: Applicant must plan to be of service to the mentally handicapped in the U.S. or Canada. Preference is given to UCT members. Scholarship is renewable. Awarded every year.
Contact: Sally Lambert, Scholarship Coordinator, (800) 848-0123.

Engineering/Technology

Aerospace/Aeronautical Engineering

571   AAAA Scholarship Grant Program

AAAA Scholarship Foundation, Inc.
49 Richmondville Avenue
Westport, CT 06880-2000
Maximum award: $12,000
Deadline: June 15
College level: Freshman
Criteria: Selection is based upon academic merit and personal achievement. Applicant planning to attend St. Louis U is eligible for a $3,000 award. Applicant pursuing a four-year B.S. degree in an aeronautical-related science is eligible for a $4,000 award. Awarded every year.
Contact: Scholarships.

572   AIAA Graduate Scholarship

American Institute of Aeronautics and Astronautics (AIAA)
Student Programs Department, 1801 Alexander Bell Drive
Suite 500
Reston, VA 22091
(703) 264-7500, (703) 264-7551 (fax)
custserv@aiaa.org
http://www.aiaa.org
Average award: $5,000
Number of awards: 8
Deadline: January 31
College level: Doctoral
Majors/Fields: Aeronautical engineering, aerospace engineering, engineering
*Criteria:*Applicant must be a U.S. citizen or permanent resident, have a minimum 3.0 GPA, and major in some field of science or engineering encompassed by the technical activities of AIAA. Awarded every year.
*Contact:*Student Programs Department, 1801 Alexander Bell Drive, Suite 500, Reston, VA 22091.

573   AIAA Undergraduate Scholarship

American Institute of Aeronautics and Astronautics (AIAA)
Student Programs Department, 1801 Alexander Bell Drive
Suite 500
Reston, VA 22091
(703) 264-7500, (703) 264-7551 (fax)
custserv@aiaa.org
http://www.aiaa.org
Average award: $2,000
Number of awards: 30
Deadline: January 31
College level: Sophomore, Junior, Senior
Majors/Fields: Aeronautical engineering, aerospace engineering, engineering
*Criteria:*Selection is based upon academic credentials, career goals, recommendations, and extracurricular activities. Applicant must be a U.S. citizen or permanent resident, have a minimum 3.0 GPA, and major in some field of science or engineering encompassed by the technical activities of the AIAA. Reapplication and minimum 3.0 GPA required to retain scholarship. Awarded every year.
Contact: Student Programs Department.

574   Air Traffic Control Association Scholarship

Air Traffic Control Association, Inc.
2300 Clarendon Boulevard
Suite 711
Arlington, VA 22201
(703) 522-5717, (703) 527-7251 (fax)
atca@worldnet.att.net
Average award: $2,000
Maximum award: $2,500
Minimum award: $1,500
Number of awards: 5
Deadline: May 1
College level: Freshman, Sophomore, Junior, Senior, Graduate, Doctoral, aviation career professional for part-time study
Majors/Fields: Aviation
Criteria: Applicant must be enrolled in an aviation-related course of study. Selection is based upon academic performance and financial need. Awarded every year.
Contact: Gabriel A. Hartl, President.

575   Burnside Memorial Scholarship/McAllister Memorial Scholarship

AOPA Air Safety Foundation
421 Aviation Way
Frederick, MD 21701
(301) 695-2000
Average award: $1,000
Number of awards: 2
Deadline: March 31
College level: Junior, Senior
Majors/Fields: Aviation
*Criteria:*Applicant must have a minimum 3.25 GPA and submit a transcript and 250-word essay. Self-addressed, stamped envelope required to receive application. Awarded every year.
Contact: Robin Sharitz, Scholarship Coordinator.

576   Fellowship in Aerospace History (NASA)

American Historical Association
400 A Street, SE
Washington, DC 20003
(202) 544-2422, (202) 544-8307 (fax)
aha@theaha.org
http://chnm.gmu.edu/chnm/aha
Maximum award: $30,000
Minimum award: $21,000
Number of awards: 1
Deadline: February 1
College level: Doctoral, Ph.D. in history or related field
Majors/Fields: Aerospace history
Criteria: Applicants must be U.S. citizens, and possess a doctorate degree in history or a closely related field or be enrolled in a doctoral degree-granting program. Fellowship is to research a project related to aerospace history. Awarded every year.
Contact: Awards Coordinator.

577   Judith Resnik Memorial Scholarship

Society of Women Engineers (SWE)
120 Wall Street, 11th Floor
New York, NY 10005-3902
(212) 509-9577, (212) 509-0224 (fax)
Average award: $2,000
Number of awards: 1
Deadline: February 1
College level: Senior
Majors/Fields: Aeronautical engineering, aerospace engineering
Criteria: Applicant must be a woman, have a minimum 3.5 GPA, be a SWE member, be studying in an engineering field with a space-related major, and be planning a career in the space industry. Awarded every year.
Contact: Scholarships.

578   National Air and Space Museum Internship Program

Smithsonian Institution National Air and Space Museum
MRC 305
Educational Services Department
Washington, DC 20560
Average award: $3,500
Deadline: February 15
College level: Sophomore, Junior, Senior, Graduate, Doctoral
Criteria: Applicant must have a strong academic performance and currently be enrolled in a degree-granting program at an accredited school. Application, letters of academic recommendation, and transcripts are required. Awarded every year.
Contact: Coordinator of Student Services.

579   Tuskegee Airmen Scholarship

Tuskegee Airmen
East Coast Chapter
P.O. Box 62404
Washington, DC 20029-2404
Number of awards: 10
Deadline: January-February
College level: Freshman
Majors/Fields: Aerospace, aeronautics
Criteria: Applicant must be a graduate of a high school in the Maryland, Washington, D.C., and Virginia area, and demonstrate financial need. Minimum 3.0 GPA is required. Awarded every year.
Contact: Scholarships.

580   Vertical Flight Foundation Engineering Scholarships

American Helicopter Society
217 North Washington Street
Alexandria, VA 22314
(703) 684-6777, (703) 739-9279 (fax)
ahs703@aol.com
http://www.vtol.org
Average award: $2,000
Number of awards: 10
Deadline: February 1
College level: Junior, Senior, Graduate, Doctoral
Majors/Fields: Aeronautical, aerospace, vertical flight technology, vertical flight design
Criteria: Award is available to those interested in helicopter and vertical flight technology. Applicant must submit a current, official grade transcript, academic and character endorsements with application. Piloting students are not eligible for the award. Awarded every year.
Contact: Enid A. Nichols, Scholarship Coordinator.

Chemical Engineering——

581   Charles Edward Littlejohn Jr. Memorial Scholarship

Clemson University
G-01 Sikes Hall
Clemson, SC 29634-5123
(803) 656-2280
Average award: $1,000
Number of awards: 6
Deadline: March 1
College level: Freshman, Sophomore, Junior, Senior
Majors/Fields: Chemical engineering
Criteria: Applicant must have a minimum 2.5 GPA. Satisfactory GPA and completion of at least 12 credit hours per semester are required to retain scholarship. Awarded every year. Award may be used only at sponsoring institution.
Contact: Marvin Carmichael, Director of Financial Aid.

582   Chemical/Natural Gas Engineering Scholarship

Texas A&M University–Kingsville
Scholarships
Box 116
Kingsville, TX 78363
(512) 593-3907, (512) 593-2991 (fax)
http://www.tamuk.edu
Maximum award: $1,500
Number of awards: 7
Deadline: March 31 and November 15
College level: Freshman, Sophomore, Junior, Senior
Majors/Fields: Chemical/natural gas engineering
Criteria: Applicant must have a minimum 2.7 GPA and combined SAT I score of 1010 (composite ACT score of 22), with a minimum SAT I math score of 530 (ACT math score of 25). Recipient must maintain a minimum 2.7 GPA to retain scholarship. Award may be used only at sponsoring institution.
Contact: School Relations.

583   Department of Energy Summer Fellowship

Electrochemical Society
10 South Main Street
Pennington, NJ 08534-2896
(609) 737-1902, (609) 737-2743 (fax)
ecs@electrochem.org
http://www.electrochem.org
Average award: $3,000
Number of awards: 5
Deadline: January 1
College level: Doctoral
Majors/Fields: Electrochemical science/engineering, energy research, solid state science/engineering
Criteria: Applicant must be enrolled in a recognized college or university in the U.S. or Canada. Selection is based upon academic record, letter of recommendation, and personal statement. Award is for summer study and/or research. Recipient may not hold other appointments or fellowships. Recipient must reapply for renewal. Awarded every year.
Contact: Dr. Johna Leddy, Department of Chemistry, University of Iowa, Iowa City, IA 52242, (319) 335-1720, johna_leddy@uiowa.edu.

584   Diamond Shamrock Corporation Scholarship

Texas A&M University–Kingsville
Scholarships
Box 116
Kingsville, TX 78363
(512) 593-3907, (512) 593-2991 (fax)
http://www.tamuk.edu
Average award: $1,000
Number of awards: 1
Deadline: March 31 and November 15
College level: Freshman, Sophomore, Junior, Senior
Majors/Fields: Chemical/natural gas engineering
Criteria: Applicant must have a minimum 2.7 GPA and combined SAT I score of 1010 (composite ACT score of 22), with a minimum SAT I math score of 530 (ACT math score of 25). Renewable if recipient maintains a minimum 2.7 GPA. Award may be used only at sponsoring institution.
Contact: School Relations.

585   Dow Outstanding Junior Scholarship

Clemson University
G-01 Sikes Hall
Clemson, SC 29634-5123
(803) 656-2280
Average award: $1,000
Number of awards: 1
Deadline: March 1
College level: Senior
Majors/Fields: Chemical engineering
Criteria: Applicant must rank in the top fifth of class. Awarded every year. Award may be used only at sponsoring institution.
Contact: Marvin Carmichael, Director of Financial Aid.

586   Dr. Edward Groth Jr. Memorial Scholarship

New Mexico State University
Box 30001
Department 5100
Las Cruces, NM 88003-0001
(505) 646-4105
Average award: Full tuition
Deadline: March 1
College level: Junior, Senior
Majors/Fields: Chemical engineering
Criteria: Applicant must have a minimum 3.2 GPA, be involved in community organizations, and be an active member of the American Institute of Chemical Engineers. Awarded every year. Award may be used only at sponsoring institution.
Contact: College of Engineering, (505) 646-3547.

587   Electrochemical Society Summer Fellowship

Electrochemical Society
10 South Main Street
Pennington, NJ 08534-2896
(609) 737-1902, (609) 737-2743 (fax)
ecs@electrochem.org
http://www.electrochem.org
Maximum award: $9,000
Number of awards: 3
Deadline: January 1
College level: Graduate, Doctoral
Majors/Fields: Field of interest to The Electrochemical Society
Criteria: Applicant must be enrolled in a recognized college or university in the U.S. or Canada. Selection is based upon academic record, letter of recommendation, and personal statement. Award is for summer study and/or research. Recipient may not hold other appointments or fellowships. Recipient must reapply for renewal. Awarded every year.
Contact: Dr. Johna Leddy, Department of Chemistry, University of Iowa, Iowa City, IA 52242, (319) 335-1720, johna_leddy@uiowa.edu.

588   F.M. Becket Memorial Award

Electrochemical Society
10 South Main Street
Pennington, NJ 08534-2896
(609) 737-1902, (609) 737-2743 (fax)
ecs@electrochem.org
http://www.electrochem.org
Average award: $3,500
Number of awards: 1
Deadline: January 1
College level: Graduate, Doctoral
Majors/Fields: Electrochemical science/technology, solid science/technology
Criteria: Applicant must be enrolled in a recognized college, university, or institute of technology in the continental U.S. or Canada. Selection is based upon academic record, letter of recommendation, and personal statement. Award is for at least two months research and study overseas at an approved institution. Recipient must reapply for renewal. Awarded every other year. Award may be used only at Chemnitz U of Tech (Chemnitz, Germany), Max-Planck-Institut fur Festkorperforschung (Stuggart, Germany), U of New South Wales (Sydney, Australia), U of Sheffield (Sheffield, England), U of Stockholm (Stockholm, Sweden), other approved overseas institutions.
Contact: Marc Cahay, Committee Chairman, ECECS Department, 832 Rhodes Hall, ML 30, University of Cincinnati, Cincinnati, OH 45221-0030, (513) 556-4754, mcahay@ucunix.san.uc.edu.

589   James Hay and Mary Lu Black Memorial Endowed Scholarship

The University of Alabama
Box 870162
Tuscaloosa, AL 35487-0162
(205) 348-6756
Average award: $1,000
Number of awards: 1
Deadline: January 15
College level: Freshman, Sophomore, Junior, Senior
Majors/Fields: Chemical engineering
Criteria: Applicant must be a full-time student. Satisfactory academic progress is required to retain scholarship. Awarded every year. Award may be used only at sponsoring institution.
Contact: Engineering Student Services, 112 Mineral Industries Building, Box 870200, Tuscaloosa, AL 35487-0200, (205) 348-6408.

590   Plastics/Chemical Scholarship

Shawnee State University
940 Second Street
Portsmouth, OH 45662-4344
(614) 355-2237
Average award: $2,750
Deadline: May 15
College level: Freshman
Majors/Fields: Plastics/chemical engineering technology
Criteria: Awarded to outstanding applicant from high school in Lawrence, Pike, or Scioto County. Applicant must rank in top third of class and have taken algebra and chemistry. FAFSA is required. Early application is recommended. Award may be for two or four years. Awarded every year. Award may be used only at sponsoring institution.
Contact: Financial Aid Office, (614) 355-2485.

591   Robert Davis Scholarship

New Mexico State University
Box 30001
Department 5100
Las Cruces, NM 88003-0001
(505) 646-4105
Average award: $1,000
Number of awards: 4
Deadline: March 1
College level: Freshman
Majors/Fields: Chemical engineering
Criteria: Selection is based upon academic standing, extracurricular activities, honors, career goals, and recommendations. Awarded every year. Award may be used only at sponsoring institution.
Contact: Greeley W. Myers, Director of Financial Aid.

592   Texas Eastman Kodak Scholarship

New Mexico State University
Box 30001
Department 5100
Las Cruces, NM 88003-0001
(505) 646-4105
Average award: Full tuition
Deadline: March 1
College level: Sophomore
Majors/Fields: Chemical engineering
Criteria: Applicant must have a minimum 3.0 GPA and agree to work the summer between junior and senior years. Awarded every year. Award may be used only at sponsoring institution.
Contact: College of Engineering, (505) 646-3547.

Civil/Environmental Engineering

593   Abel Wolman Fellowship

American Water Works Association
6666 West Quincy Avenue
Denver, CO 80235
(303) 347-6210, (303) 794-8915 (fax)
bmurphy@awwa.org
Average award: $20,000
Number of awards: 1
Deadline: January 15
College level: Doctoral
Majors/Fields: Water supply, water treatment
Criteria: Applicant must be pursuing doctoral study and research related to the field of water supply and treatment. Applicant must have citizenship or permanent resident status in the U.S., Canada, or Mexico. Satisfactory progress required to retain scholarship. Awarded every year.
Contact: Scholarship Coordinator.

594   AGC Education and Research Foundation Graduate Award

Associated General Contractors (AGC) Education and Research Foundation
1957 E Street, NW
Washington, DC 20006
(202) 393-2040
Average award: $7,500
Deadline: November 15
College level: Graduate, Doctoral
Majors/Fields: Civil engineering, construction engineering
Criteria: Applicant must pursue a graduate degree full time and be a U.S. citizen or permanent resident. Selection is based upon grades, extracurricular activities, employment experience, financial need, and a demonstrated desire to pursue a construction career. Awarded every year.
Contact: Director of Programs.

595   AGC Education and Research Foundation Undergraduate Scholarship Program

Associated General Contractors (AGC) Education and Research Foundation
1957 E Street, NW
Washington, DC 20006
(202) 393-2040
Average award: $1,500
Deadline: November 1
College level: Sophomore, Junior, Senior
Majors/Fields: Civil engineering, construction
Criteria: Applicant must plan to pursue a career in the construction industry, enroll in a four- or five-year program, and be a U.S. citizen or permanent resident alien. Selection is based upon grades, extracurricular activities, employment experience, financial need, and desire for a construction career. Renewable for up to four years if recipient maintains satisfactory GPA. Awarded every year.
Contact: Director of Programs.

596   American Society of Civil Engineers (ASCE), Orange County Branch Scholarship

California State University, Fullerton
P.O. Box 34080
Fullerton, CA 92634-9480
(714) 773-3128
Maximum award: $2,000
Number of awards: 2
Deadline: December 1
College level: Junior, Senior
Majors/Fields: Civil engineering
Criteria: Applicant must be a continuing upper-division student who has been an ASCE member for at least one year. Selection is based upon ASCE participation, academic achievement, and applicant's personal statement. Awarded every year. Award may be used only at sponsoring institution.
Contact: Vickey Takeuchi, Scholarship Coordinator.

597   Arthur S. Tuttle Memorial National Scholarship Fund

American Society of Civil Engineers (ASCE)
1801 Alexander Bell Drive
Reston, VA 20191-9743
(800) 548-2723
jmarilley@asce.org
Maximum award: $5,000
Deadline: March 1
College level: Doctoral
Majors/Fields: Civil engineering
Criteria: Applicant must be a member in good standing of the National ASCE. Awarded every year.
Contact: Student Services.

598   ASCE Construction Engineering Scholarship and Student Prize

American Society of Civil Engineers (ASCE)
1801 Alexander Bell Drive
Reston, VA 20191-9743
(800) 548-2723
jmarilley@asce.org
Average award: $1,000
Number of awards: 1
Deadline: March 1
College level: Sophomore, Junior, Senior
Majors/Fields: Engineering
Criteria: Applicant must be a member of an ASCE Student Chapter and also a National Student Member in good standing. The scholarship essay must deal with construction engineering. Scholarship is renewable. Awarded every year.
Contact: Student Services.

599   ASDSO Scholarship

Association of State Dam Safety Officials (ASDSO)
450 Old East Vine Street
2nd Floor
Lexington, KY 40507-1544
(606) 257-5140, (606) 323-1958 (fax)
damsafety@juno.com
http://ourworld.compuserve.com/homepages/ASDSO
Average award: $2,500
Maximum award: $5,000
Minimum award: $500
Number of awards: 2
Deadline: February 15
College level: Junior, Senior
Majors/Fields: Civil engineering or other field of study relating to dam safety
Criteria: Scholarship is renewable. Awarded every year.
Contact: Lori Spragens, Executive Director.

600   BCM Scholarship

The University of Alabama
Box 870162
Tuscaloosa, AL 35487-0162
(205) 348-6756
Average award: $1,500
Number of awards: 1
Deadline: January 15
College level: Freshman, Sophomore, Junior, Senior
Majors/Fields: Civil engineering
*Criteria:*Applicant must be black. Awarded every year. Award may be used only at sponsoring institution.
*Contact:*Engineering Student Services, 112 Mineral Industries Building, Box 870200, Tuscaloosa, AL 35487-0200, (205) 348-6408.

601   California Council of Civil Engineers and Land Surveyors Scholarship

California State Polytechnic University, Pomona
3801 West Temple Avenue
Pomona, CA 91768-4019
(909) 869-3700
Average award: $1,000
Number of awards: 2
Criteria: Award may be used only at sponsoring institution.
Contact: Crystal Steele, Financial Aid Counselor.

602   Carolina Air Pollution Control Association Annual Scholarship

Clemson University
G-01 Sikes Hall
Clemson, SC 29634-5123
(803) 656-2280
Maximum award: $1,000
Number of awards: 1
Deadline: March 1
College level: Sophomore, Junior, Senior
Majors/Fields: Environmental engineering, environmental science
Criteria: Applicant must have a minimum 3.0 GPA in the College of Engineering and Science. Awarded every year. Award may be used only at sponsoring institution.
Contact: Scholarships.

603   Civil Engineering Scholarship

Clemson University
G-01 Sikes Hall
Clemson, SC 29634-5123
(803) 656-2280
Average award: $900
Maximum award: $2,100
Number of awards: 5
Deadline: March 1
College level: Freshman, Sophomore, Junior, Senior
Majors/Fields: Civil engineering
Criteria: Applicant must have a minimum 2.5 GPA. Awarded every year. Award may be used only at sponsoring institution.
Contact: Marvin Carmichael, Director of Financial Aid.

604   Cohos Evamy Partners Design Competition

University of Calgary
Department of Financial Aid
2500 University Drive, NW
Calgary, Alberta, CN T2N 1N4
(403) 220-7872, (403) 282-2999 (fax)
Maximum award: $5,000
Deadline: June 15
College level: Junior, Senior
Majors/Fields: Civil engineering, structural engineering
*Criteria:*Applicant must be a Canadian citizen or permanent resident, have a minimum 3.0 GPA, and plan a career in structural engineering. Selection is based upon performance in the annual structural design competition. Awarded every year. Award may be used only at sponsoring institution.
Contact: J. Van Housen, Director of Financial Aid.

605   Dollar Rent-A-Car Scholarship

New Mexico State University
Box 30001
Department 5100
Las Cruces, NM 88003-0001
(505) 646-4105
Average award: $1,000
Number of awards: 5
Deadline: March 1
College level: Sophomore, Junior
Majors/Fields: Civil engineering
Criteria: Applicant must have a minimum 3.0 GPA and demonstrate financial need. Awarded every year. Award may be used only at sponsoring institution.
Contact: College of Engineering, (505) 646-3547.

606   Freeman Fellowship

American Society of Civil Engineers (ASCE)
1801 Alexander Bell Drive
Reston, VA 20191-9743
(800) 548-2723
jmarilley@asce.org
Maximum award: $5,000
Deadline: February 1
College level: Doctoral
Majors/Fields: Hydraulic construction
*Criteria:*Applicant must be a National ASCE member in good standing and under age 45. Stipend will be awarded based on funds available from the endowment.
Contact: Student Services.

607   George H. and Wilhelmina Q. Echols Endowed Civil Engineering Scholarship

The University of Alabama
Box 870162
Tuscaloosa, AL 35487-0162
(205) 348-6756
Average award: $1,000
Number of awards: 1
Deadline: January 15
College level: Freshman, Sophomore, Junior, Senior
Majors/Fields: Civil engineering
Criteria: Applicant must be from Tuscaloosa County or state of Alabama. Awarded every year. Award may be used only at sponsoring institution.
*Contact:*Engineering Student Services, 112 Mineral Industries Building, Box 870200, Tuscaloosa, AL 35487-0200, (205) 348-6408.

608   Graduate Scholarship Programs

Associated General Contractors Education and Research Foundation
1957 E Street, NW
Washington, DC 20006
(202) 393-2040, (202) 347-4004 (fax)
Average award: $7,500
Number of awards: 2
Deadline: November 1
College level: Graduate, Doctoral
Majors/Fields: Civil engineering, construction
*Criteria:*Selection is based upon academic performance, extracurricular activities, employment experience, financial status, and a demonstrated interest in a construction industry career. Awarded every year.
Contact: Director of Programs.

609   Helen Meeks McKerley Memorial Scholarship/ Polly H. and Walter L. Lowry Memorial Scholarship

Clemson University
G-01 Sikes Hall
Clemson, SC 29634-5123
(803) 656-2280
Average award: $1,000
Number of awards: 3
Deadline: March 1
College level: Sophomore, Junior, Senior
Majors/Fields: Civil engineering
Criteria: Applicant must have a minimum 2.5 GPA. Minimum 3.0 GPA and completion of at least 12 credit hours per semester are required to retain scholarship. Awarded every year. Award may be used only at sponsoring institution.
Contact: Marvin Carmichael, Director of Financial Aid.

610   John C. Robbins Scholarship

American Water Works Association New York Section
Department of Civil Engineering
University at Buffalo
Buffalo, NY 14260
(716) 645-2409
Average award: $1,000
Number of awards: 1
Deadline: November 30
College level: Junior, Senior
Criteria: Applicant must have a major that is considered beneficial to the New York State water works. Selection is based upon academic achievement and extracurricular activities. Awarded every year.
Contact: John E. Van Benschoten, Associate Professor.

611   NAWIC Founders' Scholarship Foundation

National Association of Women in Construction (NAWIC)
327 Adams Street
Fort Worth, TX 76104
(817) 877-5551, 800 552-3506, (817) 877-0324 (fax)
nawic@ohramp.net
Maximum award: $2,000
Number of awards: 35
Deadline: February 1
College level: Sophomore, Junior, Senior
Majors/Fields: Construction
Criteria: Selection is based upon applicant's grades, extracurricular activities, employment experience, interest in construction, evaluations, and financial need. Recipient must reapply for renewal. Awarded every year.
Contact: Maria Lopez, Scholarships.

612   NRF/Chicago Roofing Contractors Association Scholarship

National Roofing Foundation (NRF)
10255 West Higgins Road
Suite 600
Rosemont, IL 60018-5607
(847) 299-9070
Average award: $2,000
Deadline: April 1
College level: Freshman, Sophomore, Junior, Senior
Criteria: Applicant must live in Cook, Lake, DuPage, Kane, Kendall, DeKalb, McHenry, or Will counties in Illinois. Scholarship is renewable.
Contact: Scholarship Coordinator, (847) 299-1183.

613   O.H. Ammann Research Fellowship in Structural Engineering

American Society of Civil Engineers (ASCE)
1801 Alexander Bell Drive
Reston, VA 20191-9743
(800) 548-2723
jmarilley@asce.org
Average award: $5,000
Number of awards: 1
Deadline: February 15
College level: Graduate, Doctoral
Majors/Fields: Structural engineering
Criteria: Applicant must be a National ASCE member in good standing. Award is to encourage the creation of new knowledge in the field of structural design and construction. Committee on Society Honors determines if scholarship may be retained. Awarded every year.
Contact: Student Services.

614   Peter D. Courtois Concrete Construction Scholarship

American Concrete Institute/CONREF
P.O. Box 19150
Farmington Hills, MI 48333
(810) 848-3713
Average award: $1,000
Number of awards: 2
Deadline: February 1
College level: Senior
Majors/Fields: Concrete construction, engineering, technology
Criteria: Applicant must demonstrate interest and ability in the field of concrete construction and be a U.S. or Canadian citizen. Applicant must submit transcripts, recommendations, and essay. Awarded every year.
Contact: Dot Lepping, Scholarship Coordinator, P.O. Box 9094, Farminton Hills, MI 48333, (313) 532-2600.

615   Roofing Industry Scholarship/Grant

National Roofing Foundation (NRF)
10255 West Higgins Road
Suite 600
Rosemont, IL 60018-5607
(847) 299-9070
Average award: $1,000
Number of awards: 2
Deadline: January 9
College level: Freshman, Sophomore, Junior, Senior
Criteria: Applicant must be an immediate family member of a regular contractor member of National Roofing Contractors Association. Renewable if recipient maintains minimum "C+" grade average. Awarded every year.
Contact: Scholarship Coordinator.

616   Russel L. Sutphen Scholarship

American Water Works Association New York Section
Department of Civil Engineering
University at Buffalo
Buffalo, NY 14260
(716) 645-2409
Average award: $1,000
Number of awards: 1
Deadline: Novemeber 30
College level: Graduate, Doctoral
Criteria: Applicant must have a major that is considered beneficial to water works in New York State. Selection is based upon academic achievement and extracurricular activities. Awarded every year.
Contact: John E. Van Benschoten, Associate Professor.

617   Samuel Fletcher Tapman ASCE Student Chapter Scholarship

American Society of Civil Engineers (ASCE)
1801 Alexander Bell Drive
Reston, VA 20191-9743
(800) 548-2723
jmarilley@asce.org
Average award: $1,500
Number of awards: 3
Deadline: March 1
College level: Sophomore, Junior, Senior
Majors/Fields: Civil engineering
Criteria: Applicant must be an ASCE National Student Member; only one application per student chapter may be submitted. Selection is based upon the appraisal of the applicant's justification of the award, educational plans, academic performance, potential for development, leadership capacity, and financial need. Previous recipients are eligible to reapply. Awarded every year.
Contact: Student Services.

618   Trent R. Dames & William W. Moore Fellowship

American Society of Civil Engineers (ASCE)
1801 Alexander Bell Drive
Reston, VA 20191-9743
(800) 548-2723
jmarilley@asce.org
Maximum award: $10,000
Maximum number of awards: 2
Minimum number of awards: 1
Deadline: December 1
Majors/Fields: Engineering, earth science
Criteria: Awarded on a competitive basis for a proposed research project. Applicant must be an ASCE member and have completed his or her doctoral degree within the last three years or have several years of industrial or postdoctoral experience and be within first two years as a full-time faculty member. Letter of reference required. Awarded every year.
Contact: Student Services.

619   Undergraduate Scholarship Programs

Associated General Contractors Education and Research Foundation
1957 E Street, NW
Washington, DC 20006
(202) 393-2040, (202) 347-4004 (fax)
Average award: $1,500
Number of awards: 70
Deadline: November 1
College level: Sophomore, Junior, Senior, Doctoral
Majors/Fields: Civil engineering, construction
Criteria: Applicant must be a U.S. citizen or permanent resident alien. Renewable if satisfactory GPA and summer employment are maintained. Awarded every year.
Contact: Director of Programs.

Computer Science

620   El Paso Natural Gas Company Scholarship

New Mexico State University
Box 30001
Department 5100
Las Cruces, NM 88003-0001
(505) 646-4105
Average award: $2,000
Number of awards: 1
Deadline: March 1
College level: Sophomore, Junior, Senior
Majors/Fields: Computer science
Criteria: Applicant must have a minimum 3.2 GPA. Selection is based upon scholastic ability and academic potential. Awarded every year. Award may be used only at sponsoring institution.
Contact: College of Arts and Sciences, (505) 646-2001.

621   IEEE Computer Society Richard E. Merwin Scholarship

Institute for Electrical and Electronics Engineers, Inc. (IEEE)
445 Hoes Lane
P.O. Box 1331
Piscataway, NJ 08855-1331
(908) 562-3840, (908) 981-9019 (fax)
Average award: $3,000
Number of awards: 4
Deadline: May 15
College level: Graduate
Majors/Fields: Computer engineering
Criteria: Applicant must be active in the IEEE Computer Branch Chapter.
Contact: Computer Society of the IEEE, 1730 Massachusetts Avenue, NW, Washington, DC 20036-1903, (202) 371-0101.

622   John E. Aloha Annual Memorial Scholarship

Clemson University
G-01 Sikes Hall
Clemson, SC 29634-5123
(803) 656-2280
Average award: $1,000
Number of awards: 2
Deadline: March 1
College level: Freshman, Sophomore, Junior, Senior
Majors/Fields: Computer science/engineering
Criteria: Applicant must be a computer science/engineering major and a graduate of Ben Lippen School or Swansea High School or a resident of Lexington County, South Carolina. Applicant must have a minimum 2.5 GPA. Award may be used only at sponsoring institution.
Contact: Scholarships.

623   Microsoft Corp. Scholarships

Society of Women Engineers (SWE)
120 Wall Street, 11th Floor
New York, NY 10005-3902
(212) 509-9577, (212) 509-0224 (fax)
Number of awards: 10
Deadline: February 1
College level: Sophomore, Junior, Senior, Graduate
Majors/Fields: Computer engineering, computer science
Criteria: Applicant must be a woman, have a minimum 3.5 GPA, and have a career interest in the field of microcomputer software. Awarded every year.
Contact: Scholarships.

624   Robert H. Kahn Jr. Foundation Scholarship

University of West Florida
11000 University Parkway
Pensacola, FL 32514-5750
(904) 474-2400
Maximum award: $1,500
Number of awards: 2
Deadline: None
College level: Freshman
Majors/Fields: Computer science
Criteria: Applicant must have a minimum 3.0 GPA, be enrolled full-time, be pursuing a degree program, and demonstrate financial need. Satisfactory academic progress is required to retain scholarship. Awarded every year. Award may be used only at sponsoring institution.
Contact: Georganne E. Major, Senior Financial Aid Officer.

625   Ronne and Donald Hess Scholarship in Computer Science

Birmingham-Southern College
Arkadelphia Road
Birmingham, AL 35254
(205) 226-4688
Maximum award: $5,000
Number of awards: 2
Deadline: January 5
College level: Freshman
Majors/Fields: Computer science
Criteria: Applicant should rank in top fifth of class, have a minimum composite ACT score of 26 (combined SAT I score of 1050), and have leadership ability. Awarded to winner of Computer Programming Competition sponsored by Division of Science and Mathematics. Minimum 3.0 GPA is required to retain scholarship. Awarded every year. Award may be used only at sponsoring institution.
Contact: Forrest Stuart, Interim Director of Financial Aid Services.

626   Texaco Data Processing Scholarship

Texas A&M University–Kingsville
Scholarships
Box 116
Kingsville, TX 78363
(512) 593-3907, (512) 593-2991 (fax)
http://www.tamuk.edu
Average award: $1,000
Number of awards: No limit
Deadline: April 2
College level: Sophomore, Junior, Senior
Majors/Fields: Computer information systems
Criteria: Applicant must have a minimum 2.75 GPA and a minimum 60 credit hours (plus nine credit hours of computer information systems) completed. Renewable if recipient maintains a minimum 3.0 GPA. Award may be used only at sponsoring institution.
Contact: Your department, College of Business Administration.

Electrical/Electronic Engineering

627   Alan McCrary Johnstone Scholarship

Clemson University
G-01 Sikes Hall
Clemson, SC 29634-5123
(803) 656-2280
Average award: $800
Number of awards: 4
Deadline: March 1
College level: Junior, Senior
Majors/Fields: Electrical engineering
Criteria: Applicant must be a South Carolina resident and have a minimum 2.5 GPA. Awarded every year. Award may be used only at sponsoring institution.
Contact: Marvin Carmichael, Director of Financial Aid.

628   Alcoa Electrical Engineering Scholarship

Texas A&M University–Kingsville
Scholarships
Box 116
Kingsville, TX 78363
(512) 593-3907, (512) 593-2991 (fax)
http://www.tamuk.edu
Average award: $1,000
Number of awards: 1
Deadline: April 15 and November 15
College level: Sophomore, Junior, Senior
Majors/Fields: Electrical engineering
Criteria: Applicant must have a minimum 2.7 GPA, minimum combined SAT I score of 1010 (composite ACT score of 22) and 60 completed credit hours. Renewable if recipient maintains a minimum 2.7 GPA. Award may be used only at sponsoring institution.
Contact: Your department, College of Engineering.

629   Aristech Scholarship

Shawnee State University
940 Second Street
Portsmouth, OH 45662-4344
(614) 355-2237
Average award: $500
Number of awards: 5
Deadline: April 15
College level: Freshman
Majors/Fields: Electrical/computer engineering technology
Criteria: Applicant must be a high school graduate or GED recipient, have good academic standing and good character, and be enrolled in a four-year program. Early application is recommended. Awarded every year. Award may be used only at sponsoring institution.
Contact: Financial Aid Office, (614) 355-2485.

630   Billy Mitchell Chapter Association of Old Crows Scholarship

University of Texas at San Antonio
Office of Student Financial Aid
6900 North Loop 1604 West
San Antonio, TX 78249-0687
(210) 691-44855
Average award: $1,000
Number of awards: 7
Deadline: None
College level: Junior, Senior
Majors/Fields: Electrical engineering
Criteria: Applicant must have a minimum 3.0 GPA. Reapplication and minimum 3.0 GPA are required to retain scholarship. Awarded every year. Award may be used only at sponsoring institution.
Contact: Office of the Director, Division of Engineering, 6900 North Loop 1604 West, San Antonio, TX 78249, (210) 691-4490.

631   Central Power & Light Electrical Engineering Scholarship

Texas A&M University–Kingsville
Scholarships
Box 116
Kingsville, TX 78363
(512) 593-3907, (512) 593-2991 (fax)
http://www.tamuk.edu
Average award: $1,000
Number of awards: 2
Deadline: March 31
College level: Freshman
Majors/Fields: Electrical engineering
Criteria: Applicant must have a minimum 3.0 GPA, rank in the top quarter of graduating class, and have a minimum combined SAT I score of 1170 (composite ACT score of 26) with a minimum SAT I math score of 550 (ACT math score of 26). Renewable if recipient maintains a minimum 3.0 GPA. Award may be used only at sponsoring institution.
Contact: School Relations.

632   Charles Legeyt Fortescue Fellowship

Institute for Electrical and Electronics Engineers, Inc. (IEEE)
445 Hoes Lane
P.O. Box 1331
Piscataway, NJ 08855-1331
(908) 562-3840, (908) 981-9019 (fax)
Average award: $24,000 stipend
Number of awards: 1
Deadline: January 15
College level: Graduate
Majors/Fields: Electrical engineering
Criteria: Applicant must provide GRE scores. Awarded every other year.
Contact: Secretary of the Fellowship Committee, (732) 562-3480, awards@ieee.org.

633   John Mark Williams Scholarship

Clemson University
G-01 Sikes Hall
Clemson, SC 29634-5123
(803) 656-2280
Average award: $900
Number of awards: 2
Deadline: March 1
College level: Sophomore
Majors/Fields: Electical engineering
Criteria: Applicant must have a minimum 3.2 GPA. Awarded every year. Award may be used only at sponsoring institution.
Contact: Scholarships.

634   Julia Kiene Fellowship in Electrical Energy

Electrical Women's Round Table, Inc.
P.O. Box 292793
Nashville, TN 37229-2793
(615) 890-1272, (615) 890-1272 (fax)
Average award: $2,000
Number of awards: 1
Deadline: March 1
College level: Graduate, Doctoral
Majors/Fields: Communications, education, electrical engineering, journalism, marketing, radio/TV broadcasting
Criteria: Applicant must be a woman pursuing graduate work toward an advanced degree in any phase of electrical energy. Selection is based upon academic aptitude, vocational promise, character, financial need, and willingness to continue a career in a field related to electrical energy. These fields include communications, education, electrical engineering, electric utilities, extension work, housing and home furnishings, journalism, manufacturers of electrical household equipment, marketing, radio, research, and television. Recipient must reapply to retain scholarship. Awarded every year.
Contact: Ann Cox, Executive Director.

635   Lyle Mamer Fellowship

Electrical Women's Round Table, Inc.
P.O. Box 292793
Nashville, TN 37229-2793
(615) 890-1272, (615) 890-1272 (fax)
Average award: $1,000
Number of awards: 1
Deadline: March 1
College level: Graduate, Doctoral
Majors/Fields: Communications, education, electrical engineering, journalism, marketing, radio/TV broadcasting
Criteria: Applicant must be a woman pursuing graduate work toward an advanced degree in any phase of electrical energy. Selection is based upon academic aptitude, vocational promise, character, financial need, and willingness to continue a career in a field related to electrical energy. These fields include communications, education, electrical engineering, electric utilities, extension work, housing and home furnishings, journalism, manufacturers of electrical household equipment, marketing, radio, research, and television. Recipient must reapply to retain scholarship. Awarded every year.
Contact: Ann Cox, Executive Director.

636   Red Crawford Kiwanis Scholarship

Mesa State College
Financial Aid Department
P.O. Box 2647
Grand Junction, CO 81502
(970) 248-1396
Average award: $1,250
College level: Junior
Majors/Fields: Electronics technology
Criteria: Applicant must be a Colorado resident. Priority is given to electronics majors. Awarded every year. Award may be used only at sponsoring institution.
Contact: Unified Technical Education Center.

637   Robert W. Thunen Memorial Scholarship

Illuminating Engineering Society of North America
IES Golden Gate Section
460 Brannen Street, P.O. Box 77527
San Francisco, CA 94107-1527
Average award: $2,500
Minimum award: $1,000
Number of awards: 2
Deadline: March 27
College level: Junior, Senior, Graduate, Doctoral
Majors/Fields: Lighting, lighting application, lighting design
Criteria: Applicant must be a student at an accredited institution in northern California, Nevada, Oregon, or Washington and must submit a statement of purpose and three recommendations. Reapplication and continuation in previously approved program is required to retain scholarship. Awarded every year.
Contact: Linda M. Esselstein, Chairman of Thunen Fund, (415) 854-6924.

638   Schlumberger Collegiate Award Scholarship

Clemson University
G-01 Sikes Hall
Clemson, SC 29634-5123
(803) 656-2280
Average award: $3,000
Number of awards: 1
Deadline: March 1
College level: Junior, Senior
Majors/Fields: Electrical engineering
Criteria: Applicant must have a minimum 2.5 GPA. Awarded every year. Award may be used only at sponsoring institution.
Contact: Marvin Carmichael, Director of Financial Aid.

639   William G. Hill Memorial Scholarship

Clemson University
G-01 Sikes Hall
Clemson, SC 29634-5123
(803) 656-2280
Average award: $3,000
Number of awards: 2
Deadline: March 1
College level: Sophomore, Junior, Senior
Majors/Fields: Electrical engineering
Criteria: Applicant must have a minimum 2.5 GPA and participate in Army or Air Force ROTC. Awarded every year. Award may be used only at sponsoring institution.
Contact: Marvin Carmichael, Director of Financial Aid.

Engineering–General

640   3M Corp. Annual Scholarship

Clemson University
G-01 Sikes Hall
Clemson, SC 29634-5123
(803) 656-2280
Average award: $3,000
Number of awards: 1
Deadline: March 1
College level: Sophomore, Junior, Senior
Majors/Fields: Engineering
Criteria: Applicant must have a minimum 2.0 GPA. Awarded every year. Award may be used only at sponsoring institution.
Contact: Marvin Carmichael, Director of Financial Aid.

641 Adams Scholarship Fund

American Society of Agricultural Engineers (ASAE)
2950 Niles Road
St. Joseph, MI 49085-9659
(616) 429-0300, (616) 429-3852 (fax)
hq@asae.org
Deadline: April 15
College level: Junior, Senior
Majors/Fields: Agricultural engineering, biological engineering
Criteria: Applicant must be an undergraduate student member of ASAE in at least the second year of study in an ABET or CEAB accredited program, have a minimum 2.5 GPA, have a special interest in design and development of agricultural machinery products, demonstrate financial need and have dean or department chair must submit corroborating statement.
Contact: Linda J. Fritsch, Administrator.

642 Air and Waste Management Association Scholarship Endowment Trust Fund

Air and Waste Management Association
One Gateway Center
Third Floor
Pittsburgh, PA 15222
(412) 232-3444
Average award: $3,000
Maximum award: $5,000
Minimum award: $1,000
Maximum number of awards: 6
Minimum number of awards: 4
Deadline: First week of December
College level: Doctoral
Majors/Fields: Air pollution control, waste management
Criteria: Applicant must be enrolled full time. Awarded every year.
Contact: International Headquarters.

643 Alex C. and Margaret Page Hood and Rotary Club of Las Cruces Scholarship

New Mexico State University
Box 30001
Department 5100
Las Cruces, NM 88003-0001
(505) 646-4105
Average award: Full tuition
Number of awards: 2
Deadline: March 1
College level: Freshman, Sophomore, Junior, Senior
Majors/Fields: Engineering
Criteria: Applicant must demonstrate financial need, have a minimum 3.0 GPA, and have been a resident of New Mexico for at least one year. One applicant is selected by the Rotary Club and one by the College of Engineering. Reapplication is required for renewal. Awarded every year. Award may be used only at sponsoring institution.
Contact: Greeley W. Myers, Director of Financial Aid.

644 Alex R. Cummings Bursary

University of Calgary
Department of Financial Aid
2500 University Drive, NW
Calgary, Alberta, CN T2N 1N4
(403) 220-7872, (403) 282-2999 (fax)
Average award: $2,500
Number of awards: 1
Deadline: July 15
College level: Freshman
Majors/Fields: Engineering
Criteria: Selection is based upon financial need and academic merit. Awarded every year. Award may be used only at sponsoring institution.
Contact: J. Van Housen, Director of Student Awards/Financial Aid.

645 Alexander S. Langsdorf Fellowship

Washington University
One Brookings Drive
Campus Box 1089
St. Louis, MO 63130
(314) 935-6000 or (800) 638-0700
Average award: Full tuition plus a $2,500 stipend.
Number of awards: 4
Deadline: January 15
College level: Freshman
Majors/Fields: Applied science, engineering
Criteria: Selection is based upon academic merit without regard to financial need. Application is required. Satisfactory academic performance is required to retain scholarship. Awarded every year. Award may be used only at sponsoring institution.
Contact: Office of Undergraduate Admissions, (800) 638-0700 or (314) 935-6000.

646 Ambassador Franklin H. Williams Scholarship

Stevens Institute of Technology
Castle Point on Hudson
Hoboken, NJ 07030
(201) 216-5201, (201) 216-8348 (fax)
sheridan_d@stmisb.adm.stevens-tech.edu
http://www.stevens-tech.edu
Average award: Comprehensive tuition
Number of awards: 2
College level: Freshman
Majors/Fields: Chemical engineering, mechanical engineering, civil engineering
Criteria: Applicant must be a U.S. citizen or permanent citizen, African-American, Latino, or Native American and have a minimum combined SAT I score of 1250 or composite ACT score of 28, minimum 3.5 GPA, and rank in the top 15% of class. Minimum 3.0 GPA and summer internship at Exxon are required to retain scholarship. Awarded every year. Award may be used only at sponsoring institution.
Contact: David Sheridan, Director of Financial Aid.

647 Andersen Consulting Engineering Scholarship

University of Tennessee, Knoxville
Financial Aid Office
115 Student Services Building
Knoxville, TN 37994
(615) 974-3131
Average award: $1,500
Deadline: February 1
College level: Junior
Majors/Fields: Engineering
Criteria: Applicant must have demonstrated academic achievement and service to fellow man through participation in extracurricular activities, community projects or the Co-op program. Preference is given to applicants who are U.S. citizens, have a minimum 3.25 GPA, and demonstrate leadership and ambition to achieve a college education. Scholarship is renewable. Awarded every year. Award may be used only at sponsoring institution.
Contact: College of Engineering, 118 Perkins Hall, Knoxville, TN 37996, (615) 974-2454.

648 Anne Maureen Whitney Barrow Memorial Scholarship

Society of Women Engineers (SWE)
120 Wall Street, 11th Floor
New York, NY 10005-3902
(212) 509-9577, (212) 509-0224 (fax)
Average award: $4,000
Number of awards: 1
Deadline: May 15
College level: Freshman
Majors/Fields: Engineering, engineering technology
Criteria: Applicant must be a woman and have a minimum 3.5 GPA. Scholarship is renewable.
Contact: Scholarships.

649   ASAE Student Engineer of the Year Scholarship
American Society of Agricultural Engineers (ASAE)
2950 Niles Road
St. Joseph, MI 49085-9659
(616) 429-0300, (616) 429-3852 (fax)
hq@asae.org
Maximum award: $1,000
Deadline: January 30
College level: Sophomore, Junior, Senior
Majors/Fields: Agricultural engineering, biological engineering
Criteria: Applicant must be an undergraduate student member of ASAE and an active participant in a student ASAE branch organization or a comparable student professional organization. Applicant must have a minimum 3.0 GPA and must have been enrolled for at least one year in an ABET or CEAB-accredited agricultural or biological engineering program in the U.S. or Canada. Selection is based upon character, service, leadership, participation in school activities, level of financial self-support, and essay. Awarded every year.
Contact: ASAE Headquarters.

650   ASHRAE Graduate Grant-in-Aid
American Society of Heating, Refrigerating, and Air Conditioning Engineers (ASHRAE)
1791 Tullie Circle, NE
Atlanta, GA 30329
(404) 636-8400, (404) 321-5478 (fax)
http://www.ashrae.org
Number of awards: 15
Deadline: December 15
College level: Graduate, Doctoral
Majors/Fields: Engineering
Criteria: Grant is intended to encourage the applicant to continue his or her preparation for service in the HVAC&R industry. Applicant must be a member of ASHRAE student chapter. The faculty advisor must submit application form. Thesis for master's or doctoral degree must be in the field of heating, air conditioning, ventilation, refrigeration, or allied fields; relevance of the proposed research is a consideration for awarding the grant. Awarded every year.
Contact: William Seaton, Manager of Research.

651   ASHRAE Scholarship
American Society of Heating, Refrigerating, and Air Conditioning Engineers (ASHRAE)
1791 Tullie Circle, NE
Atlanta, GA 30329
(404) 636-8400, (404) 321-5478 (fax)
http://www.ashrae.org
Average award: $3,000
Maximum award: $5,000
Minimum award: $2,000
Number of awards: 5
Deadline: December 1
College level: Sophomore, Junior, Senior
Majors/Fields: Engineering. Program must be ABET accredited
Criteria: Selection is based upon financial need, minimum 3.0 GPA, faculty recommendations, leadership ability, and potential service to the HVAC and/or refrigeration profession. Consideration is given to participation of the student and advisor in ASHRAE. Reapplication is required to retain scholarship. Awarded every year.
Contact: Lois Benedict, Staff Liaison, Scholarship Fund Trustees.

652   ASNE Scholarship
American Society of Naval Engineers (ASNE)
1452 Duke Street
Alexandria, VA 22314-3458
(703) 836-6727, (703) 836-7491 (fax)
asnehq.asne@mcimail.com
http://www.jhuapl.edu/asne
Average award: $2,000
Number of awards: 15
Deadline: February 15
College level: Senior, Graduate
Majors/Fields: Aeronautical engineering, electrical/electronic engineering, marine engineering, naval architecture, ocean engineering, physical sciences
Criteria: Applicant must be enrolled in a full-time, undergraduate or master's degree program or be a co-op student at an accredited college or university. Applicant must demonstrate or express a genuine interest in a career in naval engineering and be a U.S. citizen. Selection is based upon academic record, work history, professional promise, extracurricular activities, and recommendations. Financial need may be considered. Awarded every year.
Contact: Captain Dennis Pignotti, USN (Ret), Scholarships.

653   ASSE Student Paper Awards
American Society of Safety Engineers (ASSE)
1800 East Oakton Street
Des Plaines, IL 60018-2187
Maximum award: $1,000
Number of awards: 3
Deadline: January 31
Majors/Fields: Safety engineering
Criteria: Applicant must be a full-time undergraduate student in a safety/health degree program. Selection is based upon the paper's relevance to important safety issues, persuasiveness, impact, quality of writing, technical accuracy, and feasibility. Awarded every year.
Contact: Awards.

654   AWU Student Research Fellowship Program
Associated Western Universities, Inc. (AWU)
4190 South Highland Drive, Suite 211
Salt Lake City, UT 84124
(801) 273-8900, (801) 277-5632 (fax)
info@sl.awu.org
http://www.awu.org
Average award: $4,000
Number of awards: 500
Deadline: February 1 (priority)
College level: Junior, Senior, Graduate, Doctoral
Majors/Fields: Engineering, mathematics, science
Criteria: Institutional affiliation and citizen restrictions may apply for some awards or facilities. Award may be used by graduate applicants for non-thesis research. Recipient must reapply for renewal. Awarded every year.
Contact: Attn:Student Research Fellowship Program.

655   B&W Nuclear Technologies' Aid-to-Education Annual Scholarship
Clemson University
G-01 Sikes Hall
Clemson, SC 29634-5123
(803) 656-2280
Maximum award: $1,000
Number of awards: 1
Deadline: March 1
College level: Senior
Majors/Fields: Engineering
Criteria: Applicant must have a minimum 3.0 GPA. Awarded every year. Award may be used only at sponsoring institution.
Contact: Marvin Carmichael, Director of Financial Aid.

656   Blount Presidential Scholarship

Auburn University
Auburn University, AL 36849
(334) 844-4723
Average award: $5,000
Deadline: December 15
College level: Freshman
Majors/Fields: Building science, civil engineering, mechanical engineering
Criteria: Applicant must have a minimum 3.5 GPA and minimum combined SAT I score of 1210 (composite ACT score of 29). Renewable for up to three years if minimum "B" grade average is maintained. Awarded every year. Award may be used only at sponsoring institution.
Contact: Mary Lynn Saidla, Assistant Director for Scholarships.

657   B. Charles Tiney Memorial ASCE Student Chapter Scholarship

American Society of Civil Engineers (ASCE)
1801 Alexander Bell Drive
Reston, VA 20191-9743
(800) 548-2723
jmarilley@asce.org
Average award: $2,000
Maximum award: $3,000
Deadline: March 1
College level: Sophomore, Junior, Senior
Majors/Fields: Engineering
Criteria: Applicant must be an ASCE National Student Member in good standing and demonstrate financial need. Only one application per student chapter may be submitted. Awarded every year.
Contact: Student Services.

658   BMW/SAE Engineering Scholarship

Society of Automotive Engineers (SAE)
400 Commonwealth Drive
Warrendale, PA 15096-0001
(412) 772-8534, (412) 776-1615 (fax)
lorile@sae.org
http://www.sae.org
Average award: $1,500
Number of awards: 1
Deadline: December 1
College level: Freshman
Majors/Fields: Engineering
Criteria: Applicant must be a U.S. citizen, have a minimum 3.75 GPA, and rank in the 90th percentile in both verbal and math on the SAT I or ACT. Applicant must attend a program accredited by ABET. Minimum 3.0 GPA is required to retain scholarship. Awarded every year.
Contact: Lori Pail, Scholarship Coordinator.

659   Boeing Defense and Space Group Engineering Scholarship

The University of Alabama
Box 870162
Tuscaloosa, AL 35487-0162
(205) 348-6756
Average award: $2,000
Number of awards: 1
Deadline: January 15
College level: Junior
Majors/Fields: Engineering
Criteria: Applicant must have high scholastic merit and excellent leadership skills, be approved to work in the U.S., and be willing to accept a summer internship with Boeing. Awarded every year. Award may be used only at sponsoring institution.
Contact: Engineering Student Services, 112 Mineral Industries Building, Box 870200, Tuscaloosa, AL 35487-0200, (205) 348-6408.

660   Brigadier General William Mackentyre Thames Jr. Engineering Scholarship

Clemson University
G-01 Sikes Hall
Clemson, SC 29634-5123
(803) 656-2280
Average award: $1,250
Number of awards: 1
Deadline: March 1
College level: Freshman, Sophomore, Junior, Senior
Majors/Fields: Engineering
Criteria: Applicant must have a minimum 2.5 GPA. Renewable if recipient maintains satisfactory GPA and completes at least 12 credits per semester. Award may be used only at sponsoring institution.
Contact: Scholarships.

661   Calvin M. Woodward Fellowship

Washington University
One Brookings Drive
Campus Box 1089
St. Louis, MO 63130
(314) 935-6000 or (800) 638-0700
Average award: Half tuition
Number of awards: 27
Deadline: January 15
College level: Freshman
Majors/Fields: Applied science, engineering
Criteria: Selection is based upon academic merit without regard to financial need. Application is required. Satisfactory academic performance is required to retain scholarship. Awarded every year. Award may be used only at sponsoring institution.
Contact: Office of Undergraduate Admissions.

662   Campbell Scholarship

Alfred University
Alumni Hall
26 North Main Street
Alfred, NY 14802
(607) 871-2159
Average award: $1,000
Deadline: Fall
College level: Freshman
Majors/Fields: Ceramic, electrical, or mechanical engineering
Criteria: Selection is based upon campus exam competition. Renewable if minimum 3.0 GPA and full-time enrollment are maintained. Awarded every year. Award may be used only at sponsoring institution.
Contact: Scholarships.

663   Carolina Power & Light Annual Scholarship

Clemson University
G-01 Sikes Hall
Clemson, SC 29634-5123
(803) 656-2280
Maximum award: $2,000
Number of awards: 1
Deadline: March 1
College level: Freshman
Majors/Fields: Engineering
Criteria: Applicant must be a minority student, have a minimum 2.0 GPA, and be a resident of a South Carolina county served by Carolina Power & Light Co. Satisfactory GPA and completion of at least 12 credits per semester are required to retain scholarship. Awarded every year. Award may be used only at sponsoring institution.
Contact: Marvin Carmichael, Director of Financial Aid.

664   Carolina Section of the National Association of Corrosion Engineers Scholarship

Clemson University
G-01 Sikes Hall
Clemson, SC 29634-5123
(803) 656-2280
Average award: $1,000
Number of awards: 1
Deadline: March 1
College level: Junior, Senior
Majors/Fields: Engineering
Criteria: Applicant must be a South Carolina resident and have a minimum 2.5 GPA. Awarded every year. Award may be used only at sponsoring institution.
Contact: Marvin Carmichael, Director of Financial Aid.

665   Cecil C. Humphreys/Herff Engineering Scholarship

University of Memphis
Scates Hall 204
Memphis, TN 38152
(901) 678-3213, (901) 678-5621 (fax)
katkinsn@cc.memphis.edu
http://www.memphis.edu/
Maximum award: $4,420
Deadline: January 15
College level: Freshman
Majors/Fields: Engineering
Criteria: Applicant must have a minimum composite ACT score of 30 or combined SAT I score of 1320. Selection is based upon test scores, academic record, interview, excellence of performance in area of interest, and quantity and quality of extracurricular activities. Minimum 3.0 GPA for the first year (3.25 GPA thereafter) and 10 service hours per year are required for renewal. Awarded every year. Award may be used only at sponsoring institution.
Contact: Katherine Atkinson, Scholarship Coordinator.

666   Chevron Canada Resources Limited Scholarship in Engineering

University of Calgary
Department of Financial Aid
2500 University Drive, NW
Calgary, Alberta, CN T2N 1N4
(403) 220-7872, (403) 282-2999 (fax)
Average award: $1,500
Number of awards: 3
Deadline: June 15
College level: Senior
Majors/Fields: Chemical engineering, civil engineering, mechanical engineering
Criteria: Selection is based upon outstanding academic merit. Preference is given to Canadian citizens interested in oil production, drilling, design and construction, gas processing, or reservoir engineering. Awarded every year. Award may be used only at sponsoring institution.
Contact: J. Van Housen, Director of Student Awards/Financial Aid.

667   Chevron Scholarship

Society of Women Engineers (SWE)
120 Wall Street, 11th Floor
New York, NY 10005-3902
(212) 509-9577, (212) 509-0224 (fax)
Average award: $2,000
Number of awards: 2
Deadline: February 1
College level: Sophomore, Junior
Majors/Fields: Chemical engineering, mechanical engineering, petroleum engineering
Criteria: Applicant must be a U.S. citizen, a woman, and be enrolled at a school, college or university with an accredited engineering program. Awarded every year.
Contact: Scholarships.

668   Christenson Engineering Corporation Scholarship

Western Washington University
516 High Street
Bellingham, WA 98226-9006
(206) 650-3471
Average award: $2,000
Number of awards: 1
Deadline: April 15
College level: Sophomore, Junior, Senior
Majors/Fields: Technology
Criteria: Applicant must be a full-time student with a declared major in a technical program of studies of the Technology Dept. GPA is considered. Awarded every year. Award may be used only at sponsoring institution.
Contact: Technology Department, 204 Ross Engineering Technology, Bellingham, WA 98225, (206) 650-3380.

669   Chrysler Corporation Scholarship

Society of Women Engineers (SWE)
120 Wall Street, 11th Floor
New York, NY 10005-3902
(212) 509-9577, (212) 509-0224 (fax)
Average award: $1,750
Number of awards: 1
Deadline: February 1
College level: Sophomore, Junior, Senior
Majors/Fields: Computer science, engineering
Criteria: Applicant must be a woman and have a minimum 3.5 GPA. Applicant must be a minority or other member of an underrepresented group. Awarded every year.

670   CIBA-GEIGY Scholarship

University of South Alabama
260 Administration Building
Mobile, AL 36688-0002
(334) 460-6231
Average award: $2,500
Deadline: Early application is recommended
College level: Freshman
Majors/Fields: Engineering
Criteria: Applicant must be a resident of Washington County. Renewable for up to four years. Awarded every year. Award may be used only at sponsoring institution.
Contact: Catherine P. King, Director of Admissions.

671   Cincinnati Milacron Scholarship

Clemson University
G-01 Sikes Hall
Clemson, SC 29634-5123
(803) 656-2280
Maximum award: $1,000
Number of awards: 1
Deadline: March 1
College level: Freshman, Sophomore, Junior, Senior
Majors/Fields: Computer engineering , electrical engineering, industrial engineering, mechanical engineering
Criteria: Applicant must have a minimum 2.0 GPA. Preference is given to participant in cooperative education program. Satisfactory GPA and completion of at least 12 credits per semester are required to retain scholarship. Awarded every year. Award may be used only at sponsoring institution.
Contact: Marvin Carmichael, Director of Financial Aid.

672 Clemson/Sonoco Scholars Program

Clemson University
G-01 Sikes Hall
Clemson, SC 29634-5123
(803) 656-2280
Maximum award: $1,250
Number of awards: 5
Deadline: March 1
College level: Freshman, Sophomore, Junior, Senior
Majors/Fields: Chemical engineering, electrical engineering, industrial engineering, management, mechanical engineering
Criteria: Applicant must have a minimum 2.5 GPA. Scholarship is rotated among the departments of chemical engineering, electrical engineering, industrial engineering, management, and mechanical engineering. Awarded every year. Award may be used only at sponsoring institution.
Contact: Marvin Carmichael, Director of Financial Aid.

673 College of Engineering Scholarship

Texas A&M University–Kingsville
Scholarships
Box 116
Kingsville, TX 78363
(512) 593-3907, (512) 593-2991 (fax)
http://www.tamuk.edu
Maximum award: $2,000
Number of awards: 2
Deadline: March 31
College level: Freshman
Majors/Fields: Engineering
Criteria: Applicant must rank in the top quarter of graduating class and have a minimum combined SAT I score of 1170 (composite ACT score of 26). Award may be used only at sponsoring institution.
Contact: School Relations.

674 CR Resources Limited Entrance Scholarship

University of Calgary
Department of Financial Aid
2500 University Drive, NW
Calgary, Alberta, CN T2N 1N4
(403) 220-7872, (403) 282-2999 (fax)
Average award: $3,000
Number of awards: 1
Deadline: March 15
College level: Freshman
Majors/Fields: Engineering
Criteria: Applicant must be a Canadian citizen or permanent resident. Selection is based upon academic merit, contribution to school and community life, and academic promise. Awarded every year. Award may be used only at sponsoring institution.
Contact: J. Van Housen, Director of Student Awards/Financial Aid.

675 Cryovac Endowed Engineering Scholarship

Clemson University
G-01 Sikes Hall
Clemson, SC 29634-5123
(803) 656-2280
Maximum award: $1,500
Number of awards: 2
Deadline: March 1
College level: Freshman, Sophomore, Junior, Senior
Majors/Fields: Chemical, computer, electrical, mechanical engineering
Criteria: Applicant must have a minimum 2.5 GPA. Satisfactory GPA and completion of at least 12 credits per semester are required to retain scholarship. Awarded every year. Award may be used only at sponsoring institution.
Contact: Marvin Carmichael, Director of Financial Aid.

676 Cryovac Scholarship

Clemson University
G-01 Sikes Hall
Clemson, SC 29634-5123
(803) 656-2280
Average award: $1,000
Number of awards: 1
Deadline: March 1
College level: Junior, Senior
Majors/Fields: Chemical, computer, electrical, mechanical engineering
Criteria: Applicant must have a minimum 2.5 GPA. Awarded every year. Award may be used only at sponsoring institution.
Contact: Marvin Carmichael, Director of Financial Aid.

677 Digital Equipment Corp. Scholarship

New Mexico State University
Box 30001
Department 5100
Las Cruces, NM 88003-0001
(505) 646-4105
Average award: $1,500
Number of awards: 2
Deadline: March 1
College level: Sophomore, Junior, Senior
Majors/Fields: Electrical engineering, mechanical engineering, industrial engineering
Criteria: Applicant must be American Indian or Hispanic. Awarded every year. Award may be used only at sponsoring institution.
Contact: College of Engineering, (505) 646-3547.

678 Dorothy Lemke Howarth Scholarship

Society of Women Engineers (SWE)
120 Wall Street, 11th Floor
New York, NY 10005-3902
(212) 509-9577, (212) 509-0224 (fax)
Average award: $2,000
Number of awards: 3
Deadline: February 1
College level: Junior
Majors/Fields: Engineering
Criteria: Applicant must be a U.S. citizen, a woman, and have a minimum 3.5 GPA. Awarded every year.
Contact: Scholarships.

679 Dotterweich Memorial Engineering Scholarship

Texas A&M University–Kingsville
Scholarships
Box 116
Kingsville, TX 78363
(512) 593-3907, (512) 593-2991 (fax)
http://www.tamuk.edu
Average award: $2,000
Number of awards: 1
Deadline: March 31
College level: Freshman, Sophomore, Junior, Senior
Majors/Fields: Natural gas engineering
Criteria: Applicant must rank in the top tenth of his or her class and have a minimum combined SAT I score of 1130 (composite ACT score of 25). Renewable if recipient maintains a minimum 3.25 GPA. Award may be used only at sponsoring institution.
Contact: School Relations.

680   Dow Black Scholars Award

Mississippi State University
Department of Student Financial Aid
P.O. Box 6238
Mississippi State, MS 39762
(601) 325-7430
Average award: $2,500
Number of awards: 2
Deadline: February 1
College level: Freshman
Majors/Fields: Chemical engineering, mechanical engineering
Criteria: Applicant must be black and have a minimum composite ACT score of 21 (combined SAT I score of 860). Minimum 3.0 GPA is required to retain scholarship. Awarded every year. Award may be used only at sponsoring institution.
Contact: Audrey S. Lambert, Director of Student Financial Aid.

681   Dual Degree Scholarship Program/ Undergraduate Scholarship Program

AT&T Bell Laboratories
University Relations
101 Crawfords Corner Road, Room 1E-213, P.O. Box 3030
Holmdel, NJ 07733-3030
(908) 949-4301
Average award: Full-tuition, fees, room, board, book allowance, and summer employment (including travel expenses and housing)
Number of awards: 3
Deadline: June 10
College level: Freshman
Majors/Fields: Computer engineering, computer science, electrical engineering, mathematics, mechanical engineering, physics, systems engineering
Criteria: Applicant must be a U.S. citizen or permanent resident who is black, Hispanic, Native American, female Asian/Pacific Islander, or female Caucasian. Selection is based upon scholastic aptitude, academic performance, class rank, strength of high school curriculum, leadership, motivation, and ability. Applicant must attend Atlanta U, Clark U, Morehouse Coll, Morris Brown Coll, or Spelman Coll for three years or U of Alabama, Auburn U, Boston U, Georgia Inst of Tech, Rensselaer Polytech Inst, or Rochester Inst of Tech for two years. Scholarship is renewable. Awarded every year.
Contact: Scholarship Administrator, 101 Crawfords Corner Road, Holmdel, NJ 07733-3030.

682   Eastman Kodak Scholarship

New Mexico State University
Box 30001, Department 5100
Las Cruces, NM 88003-0001
(505) 646-4105
Average award: Tuition and fees
Deadline: March 1
College level: Sophomore
Majors/Fields: Chemical engineering, electrical engineering, mechanical engineering
Criteria: Applicant must be enrolled full time with a minimum 3.0 GPA. Recipient must maintain a minimum 3.0 GPA and accept summer employment to retain scholarship. Awarded every year. Award may be used only at sponsoring institution.
Contact: College of Engineering, (505) 646-3547.

683   Edward D. Hendrickson/SAE Engineering Scholarship

Society of Automotive Engineers (SAE)
400 Commonwealth Drive
Warrendale, PA 15096-0001
(412) 772-8534, (412) 776-1615 (fax)
lorile@sae.org
http://www.sae.org
Average award: $1,000
Number of awards: 1
Deadline: December 1
College level: Freshman
Majors/Fields: Engineering
Criteria: Applicant must be a U.S. citizen, have a minimum 3.75 GPA, and rank in the 90th percentile in both verbal and math on the SAT I or ACT. Applicant must attend a progam accredited by ABET. Minimum 3.0 GPA is required to retain scholarship. Awarded every year.
Contact: Lori Pail, Scholarship Coordinator.

684   El Paso Natural Gas Co. (Engineering)

New Mexico State University
Box 30001, Department 5100
Las Cruces, NM 88003-0001
(505) 646-4105
Average award: $2,000
Number of awards: 2
Deadline: March 1
College level: Junior
Majors/Fields: Chemical engineering, mechanical engineering
Criteria: Applicant must have a minimum 3.0 GPA. Selection is based upon scholastic ability and academic potential with preference given to minority students. Awarded every year. Award may be used only at sponsoring institution.
Contact: College of Engineering, (505) 646-3547.

685   Employees of Duke Power Scholars Program

Clemson University
G-01 Sikes Hall
Clemson, SC 29634-5123
(803) 656-2280
Average award: $2,000
Number of awards: 8
Deadline: March 1
College level: Junior, Senior
Criteria: Preference is given in the following order to applicants majoring in electrical engineering, mechanical engineering, civil engineering, accounting, and computer science. Applicant must have a minimum 2.5 GPA. Minimum 3.0 GPA with at least 12 credits per semester is required to retain scholarship. Awarded every year. Award may be used only at sponsoring institution.
Contact: Marvin Carmichael, Director of Financial Aid.

686   Engineering Scholarship Program/ Undergraduate Scholarship Programs

AT&T Bell Laboratories
University Relations
101 Crawfords Corner Road, Room 1E-213, P.O. Box 3030
Holmdel, NJ 07733-3030
(908) 949-4301
Average award: Full tuition, fees, room, board, book allowance, and summer employment (includes travel expenses and housing)
Number of awards: 15
Deadline: January 15
College level: Freshman
Majors/Fields: Computer engineering, computer science, electrical engineering, mechanical engineering, systems engineering
Criteria: Applicant must be a U.S. citizen or permanent resident who is black, Hispanic, Native American, female Asian/Pacific Islander, or female Caucasian. Selection is based upon scholastic aptitude, academic performance, class rank, strength of high school curriculum, leadership, motivation, and ability. Program is specifically intended for women and those ethnic groups that are underrepresented at AT&T; however, anyone may apply. Minimum "B" average and satisfactory performance during summer employment is required to retain scholarship. Awarded every year.
Contact: ESP Administrator.

687   Engineering Technology Scholarship

American Society of Heating, Refrigerating, and Air Conditioning Engineers (ASHRAE)
1791 Tullie Circle, NE
Atlanta, GA 30329
(404) 636-8400, (404) 321-5478 (fax)
http://www.ashrae.org
Maximum award: $3,000
Number of awards: 1
College level: First-year student enrolled in a two-year program
*Majors/Fields:*Engineering in relation to the HVAC&R field. Program must lead to an associate degree in engineering technology and must be ABET accredited
Criteria: Selection is based upon financial need, minimum 3.0 GPA, faculty recommendations, leadership ability, and potential service to the HVAC&R profession. Awarded every year.
Contact: Lois K. Benedict, Staff Liason, Scholarship Trustees.

688   Faculty of Engineering Associates Scholarship

University of Calgary
Department of Financial Aid
2500 University Drive, NW
Calgary, Alberta, CN T2N 1N4
(403) 220-7872, (403) 282-2999 (fax)
Average award: $3,000
Number of awards: 1
Deadline: March 15
College level: Freshman
Majors/Fields: Engineering
*Criteria:*Applicant must be a Canadian citizen or permanent resident. Selection is based upon academic merit, contribution to school and community life, and academic promise. Awarded every year. Award may be used only at sponsoring institution.
Contact: J. Van Housen, Director of Student Awards/Financial Aid.

689   Florida Engineering Foundation Scholarships

Florida Engineering Society
P.O. Box 750
Tallahassee, FL 32302
(904) 224-0177
fes@fleng.org
http://www.asksam.com/fes/
Average award: $1,000
Maximum award: $5,000
Number of awards: 15
Deadline: January 15
College level: Freshman, Junior, Senior, Junior transfer
Majors/Fields: Engineering
Criteria: Applicant must have minimum 3.0 GPA and minimum 600 math and 500 verbal SAT scores and be enrolled at one of four ABET accredited institutions in Florida. Award may be used at four selected Florida schools only.
Contact: Win Bolton, Scholarship Coordinator.

690   Florida Rock Industries, Inc. Scholarship

Southern College of Technology
1100 South Marietta Parkway
Marietta, GA 30060-2896
(800) 869-1102, 404 528-7290
Average award: $1,500
College level: Sophomore, Junior, Senior
Criteria: Applicant must be a full-time co-op student (minimum 12 credit hours per quarter). Preference is given to applicants in construction industry-related field. Co-op employment is available but not required. Financial need is considered. Minimum 2.8 GPA is required to retain scholarship. Awarded every year. Award may be used only at sponsoring institution.
Contact: Director of Scholarships and Financial Aid.

691   Fluor Daniel Canada, Inc. Scholarship

University of Calgary
Department of Financial Aid
2500 University Drive, NW
Calgary, Alberta, CN T2N 1N4
(403) 220-7872, (403) 282-2999 (fax)
Average award: $2,000
Number of awards: 3
College level: Junior, Senior
*Majors/Fields:*Chemical engineering, civil engineering, electrical engineering, mechanical engineering
*Criteria:*Applicant must be a Canadian citizen or permanent resident and be enrolled full time. Selection is based upon academic merit. Awarded every year. Award may be used only at sponsoring institution.
Contact: J. Van Housen, Director of Student Awards/Financial Aid.

692   Fred M. Young Sr./SAE Engineering Scholarship

Society of Automotive Engineers (SAE)
400 Commonwealth Drive
Warrendale, PA 15096-0001
(412) 772-8534, (412) 776-1615 (fax)
lorile@sae.org
http://www.sae.org
Average award: $1,000
Number of awards: 1
Deadline: December 1
College level: Freshman
Majors/Fields: Engineering
*Criteria:*Applicant must be a U.S. citizen, have a minimum 3.75 GPA, and rank in the 90th percentile in verbal and math on the SAT I or ACT. Minimum 3.0 GPA is required to retain scholarship. Awarded every year.
Contact: Lori Pail, Scholarship Coordinator.

693   Gas Producers Association Mike Baker Memorial Scholarship

Texas A&M University–Kingsville
Scholarships
Box 116
Kingsville, TX 78363
(512) 593-3907, (512) 593-2991 (fax)
http://www.tamuk.edu
Average award: $1,000
Number of awards: 1
Deadline: March 31 and November 15
College level: Freshman, Sophomore, Junior, Senior
Majors/Fields: Natural gas engineering
*Criteria:*Applicant must have a minimum 3.0 GPA and minimum combined SAT I score of 1130 (composite ACT score of 25) with a minimum SAT I math score of 530 (ACT math score of 25). Renewable if recipient maintains a minimum 3.0 GPA. Award may be used only at sponsoring institution.
Contact: School Relations.

694   General Electric Foundation Scholarship

Society of Women Engineers (SWE)
120 Wall Street, 11th Floor
New York, NY 10005-3902
(212) 509-9577, (212) 509-0224 (fax)
Average award: $1,000 scholarship plus $500 to attend the National Convention/Student Conference
Number of awards: 3
Deadline: May 15
College level: Freshman
Majors/Fields: Engineering
*Criteria:*Applicant must be a U.S. citizen, a woman, and have a minimum 3.5 GPA. Continued academic achievement is required to retain scholarship for up to three additional years. Awarded every year.
Contact: Louise Bacon, Executive Assistant.

695   General Motors Foundation Scholarship

Society of Women Engineers (SWE)
120 Wall Street, 11th Floor
New York, NY 10005-3902
(212) 509-9577, (212) 509-0224 (fax)
Average award: $1,000
Number of awards: 2
Deadline: February 1
College level: Junior
Majors/Fields: Automotive engineering, chemical engineering, electrical engineering, engineering technology, industrial engineering, manufacturing engineering, materials engineering, mechanical engineering
Criteria: Applicant must be a woman, have a minimum 3.2 GPA, demonstrate leadership with a position of responsibility in a student organization, and have a career interest in the automotive industry and/or manufacturing environment. Scholarship is renewable. Awarded every year.
Contact: Scholarships.

696   General Motors Scholarship (Engineering)

New Mexico State University
Box 30001
Department 5100
Las Cruces, NM 88003-0001
(505) 646-4105
Average award: Tuition, book allowance, and stipend
Deadline: March 1
College level: Sophomore
Majors/Fields: Electrical engineering, industrial engineering, mechanical engineering
Criteria: Applicant must be a U.S. citizen and have a minimum 3.2 GPA. Scholarship is renewable. Awarded every year. Award may be used only at sponsoring institution.
Contact: College of Engineering, (505) 646-3547.

697   George Swygert and Wilfred P. Tiencken Endowed Scholarship

Clemson University
G-01 Sikes Hall
Clemson, SC 29634-5123
(803) 656-2280
Average award: $1,000
Number of awards: 2
Deadline: March 1
College level: Freshman, Sophomore, Junior, Senior
Majors/Fields: Engineering
Criteria: Applicant must have a minimum 2.5 GPA. Satisfactory GPA and completion of at least 12 credit hours per semester are required to retain scholarship. Awarded every year. Award may be used only at sponsoring institution.
Contact: Marvin Carmichael, Director of Financial Aid.

698   Glynn A. Lindsey Scholarship

Clemson University
G-01 Sikes Hall
Clemson, SC 29634-5123
(803) 656-2280
Average award: $1,000
Number of awards: 1
Deadline: March 1
College level: Freshman, Sophomore, Junior, Senior
Majors/Fields: Construction science/management
Criteria: Applicant must have a minimum 2.0 GPA. Preference is given to resident of Greenville or Pickens county, S.C. Awarded every year. Award may be used only at sponsoring institution.
Contact: Marvin Carmichael, Director of Financial Aid.

699   Graduate Research Program for Women/ Cooperative Research Fellowship Program/Ph.D. Fellowship Program

AT&T Bell Laboratories
University Relations
101 Crawfords Corner Road, Room 1E-213, P.O. Box 3030
Holmdel, NJ 07733-3030
(908) 949-4301
Average award: Full-tuition, fees, $13,200 annual stipend, book allowance, and summer employment (including travel expenses and housing)
Number of awards: 44
Deadline: January 15 ; January 20 for Ph.D. program
College level: Doctoral, graduate
Majors/Fields: Chemistry, chemical engineering, communications science, computer engineering, computer science, electrical engineering, information science, mathematics, mechanical engineering, physics, statistics
Criteria: Applicant must be a U.S. citizen or permanent resident who is black, Hispanic, Native American, female Asian/Pacific Islander or female Caucasian. Selection is based upon scholastic aptitude, academic performance, class rank, leadership, motivation, and ability. Ph.D. program is by invitation only. Scholarship is renewable. Awarded every year.
Contact: University Relations, 101 Crawfords Corner Road, Holmdel, NJ 07733-3030, (908) 949-2943.

700   GTE Foundation Scholarship

Society of Women Engineers (SWE)
120 Wall Street, 11th Floor
New York, NY 10005-3902
(212) 509-9577, (212) 509-0224 (fax)
Average award: $1,000
Number of awards: 9
Deadline: February 1
College level: Sophomore, Junior
Majors/Fields: Computer science, electrical engineering
Criteria: Applicant must be a U.S. citizen, a woman, and have a minimum 3.5 GPA. Awarded every year.

701   H. Buford Goff Jr. Endowed Scholarship

Clemson University
G-01 Sikes Hall
Clemson, SC 29634-5123
(803) 656-2280
Maximum award: $1,500
Number of awards: 2
Deadline: March 1
College level: Freshman, Sophomore, Junior, Senior
Majors/Fields: Electrical engineering, mechanical engineering
Criteria: Applicant must have a minimum 2.5 GPA. Awarded every year. Award may be used only at sponsoring institution.
Contact: Marvin Carmichael, Director of Financial Aid.

702   Hardaway Foundation Scholarship

The University of Alabama
Box 870162
Tuscaloosa, AL 35487-0162
(205) 348-6756
Average award: $1,000
Number of awards: 1
Deadline: January 15
College level: Freshman, Sophomore, Junior, Senior
Majors/Fields: Engineering
Criteria: Preference is given to residents of Georgia, Alabama, Virginia, Mississippi, and Florida (in that order). Awarded every year. Award may be used only at sponsoring institution.
Contact: Engineering Student Services, 112 Mineral Industries Building, Box 870200, Tuscaloosa, AL 35487-0200, (205) 348-6408.

703   Hearin-Hess Engineering Scholarship

Mississippi State University
Department of Student Financial Aid
P.O. Box 6238
Mississippi State, MS 39762
(601) 325-7430
Average award: $4,000
Number of awards: 7
Deadline: February 1
College level: Freshman
Majors/Fields: Engineering
Criteria: Applicant must have a minimum composite ACT score of 30 (combined SAT I score of 1240). Minimum 3.0 GPA in required engineering courses and enrollment in the College of Engineering are required to retain scholarship. Awarded every year. Award may be used only at sponsoring institution.
Contact: Audrey S. Lambert, Director of Student Financial Aid, P.O. Box 6238, Mississippi State, MS 39762.

704   Houston Chapter of A.P.I. Scholarship

Texas A&M University–Kingsville
Scholarships
Box 116
Kingsville, TX 78363
(512) 593-3907, (512) 593-2991 (fax)
http://www.tamuk.edu
Maximum award: $1,500
Number of awards: 3
Deadline: March 31 and November 15
College level: Freshman, Sophomore, Junior, Senior
Majors/Fields: Natural gas engineering
Criteria: Applicant must have a minimum 3.0 GPA and minimum combined SAT I score of 1130 (composite ACT score of 25) with a minimum SAT I math score of 530 (ACT math score of 25). Scholarship is renewable. Award may be used only at sponsoring institution.
Contact: School Relations.

705   Howard Eugene Hord Endowed Scholarship

Clemson University
G-01 Sikes Hall
Clemson, SC 29634-5123
(803) 656-2280
Maximum award: $1,400
Number of awards: 1
Deadline: March 1
College level: Sophomore, Junior, Senior
Majors/Fields: Engineering
Criteria: Applicant must have a minimum 2.5 GPA. Awarded every year. Award may be used only at sponsoring institution.
Contact: Marvin Carmichael, Director of Financial Aid.

706   Hughes Bachelor of Science Scholarship

California State University, Fullerton
P.O. Box 34080
Fullerton, CA 92634-9480
(714) 773-3128
Average award: Salary, benefits and educational expenses
Deadline: March 15
College level: Junior, Senior
Majors/Fields: Aeronautical engineering, applied mathematics, computer science, electrical engineering, mechanical engineering, physics, systems engineering
Criteria: Applicant must have a minimum 3.0 GPA, be a U.S. citizen, and demonstrate academic achievement and professional promise. Scholarship program allows qualified applicants to complete their B.S. degree while beginning a technical career at Hughes Aircraft Company. Scholarship is renewable. Awarded every year. Award may be used only at sponsoring institution.
Contact: Vickey Takeuchi, Scholarship Coordinator.

707   Ivy Parker Memorial Scholarship

Society of Women Engineers (SWE)
120 Wall Street, 11th Floor
New York, NY 10005-3902
(212) 509-9577, (212) 509-0224 (fax)
Average award: $2,000
Number of awards: 1
Deadline: February 1
College level: Junior, Senior
Majors/Fields: Engineering
Criteria: Applicant must be a woman, have a minimum 3.5 GPA, and demonstrate financial need. Junior recipients may reapply for continued support for following year. Awarded every year.
Contact: Louise Bacon, Executive Assistant.

708   J. Wesley Davis Scholarship

Clemson University
G-01 Sikes Hall
Clemson, SC 29634-5123
(803) 656-2280
Average award: $1,000
Number of awards: 1
Deadline: March 1
College level: Freshman, Sophomore, Junior, Senior
Majors/Fields: Engineering
Criteria: Applicant must have a minimum 2.5 GPA and be enrolled in College of Engineering. Awarded every year. Award may be used only at sponsoring institution.
Contact: Marvin Carmichael, Director of Financial Aid.

709   J.E. Sirrine Company Engineering Scholarship

Clemson University
G-01 Sikes Hall
Clemson, SC 29634-5123
(803) 656-2280
Average award: $1,000
Number of awards: 2
Deadline: March 1
College level: Freshman
Majors/Fields: Engineering
Criteria: Applicant must have a minimum 2.5 GPA. Awarded every year. Award may be used only at sponsoring institution.
Contact: Marvin Carmichael, Director of Financial Aid.

710   James A. "Shine" Milling Presidential Scholarship

Clemson University
G-01 Sikes Hall
Clemson, SC 29634-5123
(803) 656-2280
Maximum award: $5,500
Number of awards: 2
Deadline: March 1
College level: Freshman
Majors/Fields: Engineering, industrial management
Criteria: Two awards are renewable for one additional year. Awarded every year. Award may be used only at sponsoring institution.
Contact: Marvin Carmichael, Director of Financial Aid.

711   Judith Resnik Challenger Scholarship for Women

Carnegie Mellon University
5000 Forbes Avenue
Pittsburgh, PA 15213
(412) 268-2068
Average award: Half tuition
Number of awards: 20
Deadline: February 15
College level: Freshman
Majors/Fields: Computer science, engineering, science
Criteria: Applicant must be a woman. Scholarship is renewable. Awarded every year. Award may be used only at sponsoring institution.
Contact: Linda M. Anderson, Director of Financial Aid.

712   Kelvin Lane Morris Memorial Scholarship

Clemson University
G-01 Sikes Hall
Clemson, SC 29634-5123
(803) 656-2280
Average award: $1,600
Number of awards: 1
Deadline: March 1
College level: Freshman, Sophomore, Junior, Senior
Majors/Fields: Engineering
Criteria: Applicant must have a minimum 2.5 GPA. Awarded every year. Award may be used only at sponsoring institution.
Contact: Marvin Carmichael, Director of Financial Aid.

713   Kodak Scholarship

Clemson University
G-01 Sikes Hall
Clemson, SC 29634-5123
(803) 656-2280
Average award: Full tuition
Number of awards: 1
Deadline: March 1
College level: Freshman, Sophomore
Majors/Fields: Chemical engineering, mechanical engineering
Criteria: Applicant must rank in top quarter of class, have a minimum 2.0 GPA, and have three years remaining in curricula. Recipient may not concurrently hold a scholarship sponsored by another industry. Renewable if recipient remains in original discipline of study and maintains a minimum 3.0 GPA. Awarded every year. Award may be used only at sponsoring institution.
Contact: Marvin Carmichael, Director of Financial Aid.

714   L. Irvin Sanders Endowed Scholarship

Clemson University
G-01 Sikes Hall
Clemson, SC 29634-5123
(803) 656-2280
Average award: $1,350
Number of awards: 1
Deadline: March 1
College level: Freshman, Sophomore, Junior, Senior
Majors/Fields: Agricultural engineering
Criteria: Applicant must have a minimum 2.5 GPA. Award may be used only at sponsoring institution.
Contact: Scholarships.

715   Lillian Moller Gilbreth Scholarship

Society of Women Engineers (SWE)
120 Wall Street, 11th Floor
New York, NY 10005-3902
(212) 509-9577, (212) 509-0224 (fax)
Average award: $5,000
Number of awards: 1
Deadline: February 1
College level: Junior, Senior
Majors/Fields: Engineering
Criteria: Applicant must be a woman with a minimum 3.5 GPA who demonstrates outstanding potential and achievement. Awarded every year.
Contact: Louise Bacon, Executive Assistant.

716   Management of the Industrial Associates Minority Engineering Scholarship

Clemson University
G-01 Sikes Hall
Clemson, SC 29634-5123
(803) 656-2280
Maximum award: $1,000
Deadline: None
College level: Freshman, Sophomore, Junior, Senior
Majors/Fields: Engineering
Criteria: Awarded every year. Award may be used only at sponsoring institution.
Contact: Marvin Carmichael, Director of Financial Aid.

717   Marion Killian Arthur Memorial Scholarship

Clemson University
G-01 Sikes Hall
Clemson, SC 29634-5123
(803) 656-2280
Average award: $1,600
Number of awards: 1
Deadline: March 1
College level: Freshman, Sophomore, Junior, Senior
Majors/Fields: Engineering
Criteria: Applicant must have a minimum 2.5 GPA. Financial need is considered. Satisfactory GPA and completion of at least 12 credits per semester are required to retain scholarship. Awarded every year. Award may be used only at sponsoring institution.
Contact: Marvin Carmichael, Director of Financial Aid.

718   Martin Marietta Corp. Scholarship

University of Tennessee, Knoxville
Financial Aid Office
115 Student Services Building
Knoxville, TN 37994
(615) 974-3131
Average award: $1,500
Deadline: February 1
College level: Freshman, Sophomore, Junior, Senior
Majors/Fields: Engineering
Criteria: Awarded every year. Award may be used only at sponsoring institution.
Contact: College of Engineering, 118 Perkins Hall, Knoxville, TN 37996, (615) 974-2454.

719   Men's Auxiliary of the SWE Memorial Scholarship

Society of Women Engineers (SWE)
120 Wall Street, 11th Floor
New York, NY 10005-3902
(212) 509-9577, (212) 509-0224 (fax)
Average award: $2,000
Number of awards: 2
Deadline: February 1
College level: Sophomore, Junior, Senior, Graduate
Majors/Fields: Engineering
Criteria: Applicant must be a woman and have a minimum 3.5 GPA. Selection is based upon scholarship and financial need. Awarded every year.
Contact: Scholarships.

720   MidCon Corp. Scholarship

New Mexico State University
Box 30001
Department 5100
Las Cruces, NM 88003-0001
(505) 646-4105
Average award: $2,000
Deadline: March 1
College level: Junior
Majors/Fields: Civil engineering, electrical engineering, mechanical engineering
Criteria: Applicant must have a minimum 2.5 GPA and accept a summer internship in the year the scholarship is granted. Awarded every year. Award may be used only at sponsoring institution.
Contact: College of Engineering, (505) 646-3547.

721 Minority Engineering and Sciences Scholarship

General Motors Corporation (GMC)
3044 West Grand Boulevard
Detroit, MI 48202
Maximum award: $5,000
Number of awards: 104
College level: Sophomore, Junior, Senior
Majors/Fields: Engineering, science
Criteria: Applicant must be a member of one of the following minority groups: Alaskan Native, American Indian, Asian-American, African-American, Mexican-American/Chicano, Hispanic, or Puerto Rican. Contact the engineering department to ask if the university participates in the scholarship program.

722 Minority Engineering Program Scholarship

University of Utah
Financial Aid and Scholarships Office
105 Student Services Building
Salt Lake City, UT 84112
(801) 581-6211
Maximum award: $1,500
Maximum number of awards: 6
Minimum number of awards: 4
Deadline: February 1
College level: Freshman, Sophomore, Junior, Senior
Majors/Fields: Engineering
Criteria: Applicant must be a U.S. citizen who is a member of an underrepresented ethnic or gender group. Reapplication is required to retain scholarship. Awarded every year. Award may be used only at sponsoring institution.
Contact: Kate Rhodes, MEP Director, 2220 Merrill Engineering Building, Salt Lake City, UT 84112, (801) 581-8954.

723 Natural Gas Engineering Scholarship

Texas A&M University–Kingsville
Scholarships
Box 116
Kingsville, TX 78363
(512) 593-3907, (512) 593-2991 (fax)
http://www.tamuk.edu
Maximum award: $1,500
Number of awards: 1
Deadline: March 31 and November 15
College level: Freshman, Sophomore, Junior, Senior
Majors/Fields: Natural gas engineering
Criteria: Applicant must have a minimum 3.0 GPA and minimum combined SAT I score of 1130 (composite ACT score of 25) with a minimum SAT I math score of 530 (ACT math score of 25). Renewable if recipient maintains a minimum 3.0 GPA. Award may be used only at sponsoring institution.
Contact: School Relations.

724 Norcen Energy Canadian Scholarship Series in Engineering

University of Calgary
Department of Financial Aid
2500 University Drive, NW
Calgary, Alberta, CN T2N 1N4
(403) 220-7872, (403) 282-2999 (fax)
Average award: $1,500
Number of awards: 6
Deadline: June 15
College level: Junior, Senior
Majors/Fields: Chemical engineering, mechanical engineering
Criteria: Applicant must be a Canadian citizen or permanent resident. Special consideration is given to applicants interested in a career in the oil and gas industry. Selection is based primarily upon academic merit. Financial need and extracurricular activities are considered. Awarded every year. Award may be used only at sponsoring institution.
Contact: J. Van Housen, Director of Student Awards/Financial Aid.

725 Northrop Corp. Founders Scholarship

Society of Women Engineers (SWE)
120 Wall Street, 11th Floor
New York, NY 10005-3902
(212) 509-9577, (212) 509-0224 (fax)
Average award: $1,000
Number of awards: 1
Deadline: May 15
College level: Sophomore
Majors/Fields: Engineering
Criteria: Applicant must be a woman, have a minimum 3.5 GPA, and be a student member of SWE. U.S. citizenship is preferred. Awarded every year.
Contact: Louise Bacon, Executive Assistant.

726 NRF/North East Roofing Contractors Association Scholarship

National Roofing Foundation (NRF)
10255 West Higgins Road
Suite 600
Rosemont, IL 60018-5607
(847) 299-9070
Average award: $1,000
Number of awards: 1
Deadline: January 9
College level: Freshman, Sophomore, Junior, Senior
Majors/Fields: Architecture, construction, engineering
Criteria: Applicant must major in a roofing industry-related field and reside in Connecticut, Maine, Massachusetts, New Hampshire, New Jersey, New York, Pennsylvania, Rhode Island, or Vermont. Renewable if recipient maintains minimum "C+" grade average. Awarded every year.
Contact: Scholarship Coordinator.

727 O.S. Wyly Endowed Scholarship

Clemson University
G-01 Sikes Hall
Clemson, SC 29634-5123
(803) 656-2280
Average award: $3,200
Number of awards: 1
Deadline: March 1
College level: Freshman
Majors/Fields: Electrical engineering, ceramic engineering, chemical engineering, civil engineering, mechanical engineering, physics
Criteria: Applicant must have a minimum 2.5 GPA and be a graduate of Walhalla High School. Financial need is considered. Renewable if recipient maintains satisfactory GPA and completes at least 12 credits per semester. Award may be used only at sponsoring institution.
Contact: Scholarships.

728 Olive Lynn Salembier Scholarship

Society of Women Engineers (SWE)
120 Wall Street, 11th Floor
New York, NY 10005-3902
(212) 509-9577, (212) 509-0224 (fax)
Average award: $2,000
Number of awards: 1
Deadline: May 15
College level: Sophomore, Junior, Senior, Graduate, Doctoral
Majors/Fields: Engineering
Criteria: Applicant must be a woman who has been out of the engineering job market for a minimum of two years. Scholarship is to aid in obtaining the credentials necessary to re-enter the job market as an engineer. Awarded every year.
Contact: Louise Bacon, Executive Assistant.

729   Peter Peterson/UT/EFO Scholarship

University of Toledo
Financial Aid Office
Toledo, OH 43606-3390
(419) 537-2056
Average award: $1,200
Number of awards: 4
Deadline: January 28
College level: Freshman
Majors/Fields: Engineering
Criteria: Applicant must be an outstanding graduate of an Ohio high school and demonstrate great potential in engineering. Scholarship is renewable. Awarded every year. Award may be used only at sponsoring institution.
Contact: Dean, College of Engineering.

730   Petroleum Society of CIM (Calgary Section) Scholarship

University of Calgary
Department of Financial Aid
2500 University Drive, NW
Calgary, Alberta, CN T2N 1N4
(403) 220-7872, (403) 282-2999 (fax)
Average award: $1,500
Number of awards: 4
Deadline: June 15
College level: Junior, Senior
Majors/Fields: Engineering
Criteria: Selection is based upon academic merit and extracurricular activities. Awarded every year. Award may be used only at sponsoring institution.
Contact: J. Van Housen, Director of Student Awards/Financial Aid.

731   Piedmont Chapter of the South Carolina SPE Endowed Scholarship

Clemson University
G-01 Sikes Hall
Clemson, SC 29634-5123
(803) 656-2280
Average award: $2,000
Number of awards: 1
Deadline: March 1
College level: Sophomore, Junior, Senior
Majors/Fields: Engineering
Criteria: Applicant must be a South Carolina resident and have a minimum 2.5 GPA. Financial need is considered; minimum GPA requirement may be waived in case of need. Satisfactory GPA and completion of at least 12 credit hours per semester are required to retain scholarship. Awarded every year. Award may be used only at sponsoring institution.
Contact: Marvin Carmichael, Director of Financial Aid.

732   Piedmont Chapter of the South Carolina SPE Engineering Scholarship

Clemson University
G-01 Sikes Hall
Clemson, SC 29634-5123
(803) 656-2280
Average award: $2,000
Number of awards: 1
Deadline: March 1
College level: Sophomore, Junior, Senior
Majors/Fields: Engineering
Criteria: Applicant must be a South Carolina resident and have a minimum 2.5 GPA. Satisfactory GPA and completion of at least 12 credit hours per semester are required to retain scholarship. Awarded every year. Award may be used only at sponsoring institution.
Contact: Marvin Carmichael, Director of Financial Aid.

733   Quarry Engineering Scholarship

National Stone Association (NSA)
1415 Elliot Place, NW
Washington, DC 20007
(800) 342-1415, (202) 342-1100 (fax)
Maximum award: $2,500
Number of awards: 8
Deadline: May 1
College level: Sophomore, Junior, Senior, Graduate
Majors/Fields: Civil engineering, geology, mining engineering
Criteria: Preference is given to applicants who have held summer employment in aggregates industry. Scholarship is renewable. Awarded every year.
Contact: Robert S. Brown, Jr., Director of Public Affairs.

734   Randall K. Nutt Engineering Scholarship

University of Tennessee, Knoxville
Financial Aid Office
115 Student Services Building
Knoxville, TN 37994
(615) 974-3131
Maximum award: Tuition and Fees
Number of awards: 1
Deadline: February 1
College level: Freshman
Majors/Fields: Computer engineering, engineering
Criteria: Applicant must have a minimum 3.0 GPA and minimum composite ACT score of 23. Primary consideration is given to graduates of Farragut High School, Ooltewah High School, or Hohenwald High School, with other Tennessee residents secondary. Priority is given to applicants with financial need, without other aid, and those interested in electrical or computer engineering. Award is for four years. Awarded every year. Award may be used only at sponsoring institution.
Contact: College of Engineering, 118 Perkins Hall, Knoxville, TN 37996, (615) 974-2454.

735   Robert W. Cotton Memorial Scholarship Competition

Consulting Engineers Council of Metropolitan Washington, DC
8811 Colesville Road, Suite G106
Silver Spring, MD 20910
(301) 588-6616
Maximum award: $5,000
Number of awards: 10
Deadline: February 15
College level: Junior, Senior
Majors/Fields: Consulting engineering
Criteria: Applicant must be a U.S. citizen, rank in top half of class, and reside or study in the metropolitan Washington, D.C., area. Selection is based upon academic record, extracurricular activities, engineering-related job experience, and recommendations. Awarded every year.
Contact: Alpha Moore, Scholarship Coordinator.

736   S.J. Cerny Engineering Scholarship

University of Oklahoma
University Affairs
900 Asp Avenue, Room 236
Norman, OK 73019-0401
(405) 325-1701
Average award: $3,000
Number of awards: 1
Deadline: April 1
College level: Freshman, Sophomore, Junior, Senior, Graduate, Doctoral
Majors/Fields: Engineering
Criteria: Applicant must be an Oklahoma resident, demonstrate financial need, have a minimum 3.0 GPA, and be a full-time engineering student. Preference is given to petroleum and geological engineering majors. Awarded every year. Award may be used only at sponsoring institution.
Contact: Associate Dean for Academic Programs, College of Engineering, Room 107, CEC, Norman, OK 73019, (405) 325-2621.

737 Safety Equipment Distributors Association Scholarship

American Society of Safety Engineers (ASSE)
1800 East Oakton Street
Des Plaines, IL 60018-2187
Number of awards: 2
Deadline: January 31
Majors/Fields: Safety engineering
Criteria: Applicant must be a full-time student, member of ASSE with at least one semester of studies left after announcement of results in May, and a minimum 2.75 GPA. Selection is based upon academic performance, career goals, extracurricular activities, and quality and scope of endorsement by nominee's faculty adviser, faculty member, and/or chapter officer. Awarded every year.
Contact: Scholarships.

738 Schwing America Inc. Concrete Scholarship

American Concrete Institute/CONREF
P.O. Box 19150
Farmington Hills, MI 48333
(810) 848-3713
Average award: $2,000
Number of awards: 15
Deadline: February 1
College level: Senior
Majors/Fields: Architecture, construction, engineering, technology
Criteria: Applicant must be a full-time student and be planning a career in a conrete-related field. Selection is based upon academic record and career potential. Essay, recommendation, and transcripts are required. Award may be used only at the following schools: Arizona St U, Brown U, Clemson U, Colorado Sch of Mines, Cornell U, Georgia Tech, The Johns Hopkins U, U of Houston, Iberoamericana U, Iowa St U, U of Kansas, U of Minnesota, Norwich U, U of Southern California at Los Angeles, Tulane U, Villanova U, and Waterloo U.
Contact: Dot Lepping, Scholarships, P.O. Box 9094, Farmington Hills, MI 48333.

739 Sherwood E. Liles Engineering Scholarship

Clemson University
G-01 Sikes Hall
Clemson, SC 29634-5123
(803) 656-2280
Average award: $1,600
Number of awards: 2
Deadline: March 1
College level: Freshman
Criteria: Applicant must be a South Carolina resident, have a minimum 2.5 GPA, and be enrolled in the College of Engineering and Science. Minimum 3.0 GPA and completion of at least 12 credit hours are required to retain scholarship. Awarded every year. Award may be used only at sponsoring institution.
Contact: Marvin Carmichael, Director of Financial Aid.

740 SHPE Foundation Educational Grant

Society of Hispanic Professional Engineers (SHPE) Foundation
5400 East Olympic Boulevard
Suite 210
Los Angeles, CA 90022
(213) 888-2080
Maximum award: $7,000
Number of awards: 250
Deadline: April 15
College level: Freshman, Sophomore, Junior, Senior, Graduate, Doctoral
Majors/Fields: Engineering, science
Criteria: Reapplication is required to retain scholarship. Awarded every year.
Contact: Kathy Borunda, Manager of Corporate Development.

741 Sister Kathleen Feeley/BG&E Scholarship in Engineering

College of Notre Dame of Maryland
4701 North Charles Street
Baltimore, MD 21210
(410) 532-5369
Average award: $5,000
Deadline: December 31
College level: Freshman
Majors/Fields: Engineering
Criteria: Applicant must be a woman, have a minimum 3.0 GPA and minimum combined SAT I score of 1100, have strong achievement in math and science, and live in Baltimore Gas & Electric service areas. BG&E provides summer employment and textbook reimbursement. Award is for three years. Awarded every year. Award may be used only at sponsoring institution.
Contact: Financial Aid Office.

742 SNAME Scholarship

Society of Naval Architects and Marine Engineers (SNAME)
601 Pavonia Avenue
Jersey City, NJ 07306
(201) 798-4800, (201) 798-4975 (fax)
Maximum award: $10,000
Number of awards: 5
Deadline: February 1
College level: Freshman, Sophomore, Junior, Senior, Doctoral
Majors/Fields: Marine engineering, naval architecture, ocean engineering
Criteria: Applicant must be a U.S. or Canadian citizen and an SNAME member in good standing for at least one year. Undergraduate grant-in-aid is available directly through UC Berkeley, Florida Atlantic U, Maine Maritime Acad, Massachusetts Inst of Tech, U of Michigan, SUNY Maritime Coll, U of New Orleans, U of Newfoundland, Texas A&M U-College Station, or Virginia Tech. Awarded every year.
Contact: Francis M. Cagliari, Executive Director.

743 Society for the Advancement of Material and Process Engineering (SAMPE), Orange County Chapter Scholarship

California State University, Fullerton
P.O. Box 34080
Fullerton, CA 92634-9480
(714) 773-3128
Maximum award: $2,000
Deadline: April
Majors/Fields: Engineering, science
Criteria: Applicant must be a student member of SAMPE, or the child of a SAMPE member, enrolled full time. Selection is based upon academic achievement, recommendations, extracurricular activities, personal statement, and interest in materials and process engineering. Awarded every year. Award may be used only at sponsoring institution.
Contact: Vickey Takeuchi, Scholarship Coordinator.

744 Society of Women Engineers (SWE) Orange County Chapter Scholarship

California State University, Fullerton
P.O. Box 34080
Fullerton, CA 92634-9480
(714) 773-3128
Maximum award: $2,000
Number of awards: 2
Deadline: April
College level: Sophomore, Junior, Senior
Majors/Fields: Engineering
Criteria: Applicant must be a full-time, female engineering student. Selection is based upon academic achievement, leadership, professional activities, financial need, work experience, and recommendations. Awarded every year. Award may be used only at sponsoring institution.
Contact: Vickey Takeuchi, Scholarship Coordinator.

745   SPE Foundation Scholarship

The Society of Plastics Engineers (SPE) Foundation
14 Fairfield Drive
Brookfield, CT 06804
(203) 740-5434, (203) 775-8490 (fax)
Average award: $3,500
Maximum award: $4,000
Minimum award: $3,000
Number of awards: 7
Deadline: December 15
College level: Freshman, Sophomore, Junior, Senior
Majors/Fields: Plastics engineering, polymer science
Criteria: Applicant must demonstrate financial need and academic qualifications. Recipient must maintain required GPA in major and reapply for renewal. Awarded every year.
Contact: Gail R. Bristol, Development Director.

746   Stanley C. Pace Fellowship

Washington University
One Brookings Drive
Campus Box 1089
St. Louis, MO 63130
(314) 935-6000 or (800) 638-0700
Average award: Full tuition plus $2,500 stipend
Number of awards: 1
College level: Freshman
Majors/Fields: Engineering, applied science
Criteria: Selection is based upon academic merit without regard to financial need. Application is required. Satisfactory academic performance is required to retain scholarship. Awarded every year. Award may be used only at sponsoring institution.
Contact: Office of Undergraduate Admissions, (800) 638-0700 or (314) 935-6000.

747   Talisman Energy Bursary

University of Calgary
Department of Financial Aid
2500 University Drive, NW
Calgary, Alberta, CN T2N 1N4
(403) 220-7872, (403) 282-2999 (fax)
Average award: $1,000
Number of awards: 1
Deadline: June 15
College level: Sophomore, Junior, Senior
Majors/Fields: Economics, engineering, geology, geophysics, management
Criteria: Selection is based upon academic merit and financial need. Awarded every year. Award may be used only at sponsoring institution.
Contact: J. Van Housen, Director of Student Awards/Financial Aid, 2500 University Drive, NW, Calgary, Alberta, CN T2N 1N4.

748   Technical Minority Scholarship Program

Technical Minority Scholarship Program
Xerox Square-026
Rochester, NY 14644
Maximum award: $5,000
Number of awards: 30
Deadline: September 1
College level: Sophomore, Junior, Senior, Doctoral
Majors/Fields: Computer science, engineering, mathematics, optics, physics, science
Criteria: Applicant must be a minority student. Reapplication is required for renewal. Awarded every year.
Contact: Scholarships.

749   Technology Regents Scholarship

Southwest Missouri State University
Student Financial Aid
901 South National Avenue
Springfield, MO 65804-0095
(417) 836-5000 or (800) 492-7900
Average award: $1,000
Number of awards: 5
Deadline: March 31
College level: Freshman
Majors/Fields: Technology
Criteria: Awarded every year. Award may be used only at sponsoring institution.
Contact: Scholarship Committee, (417) 836-5262.

750   Texaco Foundation Scholarship

Society of Women Engineers (SWE)
120 Wall Street, 11th Floor
New York, NY 10005-3902
(212) 509-9577, (212) 509-0224 (fax)
Average award: $2,000 plus a $500 travel grant to attend the National Convention/Student Conference
Number of awards: 2
Deadline: February 1
College level: Junior
Majors/Fields: Chemical engineering, mechanical engineering
Criteria: Applicant must be a U.S. citizen or authorized to work in the U.S., a woman, a SWE member, rank in the top fifth of class, and have a minimum 3.5 GPA. Reapplication and rank in top fifth of class are required to retain scholarship. Awarded every year.
Contact: Scholarships.

751   Texas–Yes! Scholarships

Texas Society of Professional Engineers
P.O. Box 2145
Austin, TX 78768
(512) 472-9286, (512) 472-2934 (fax)
mickie@tspe.org
http://www.tspe.org
Maximum award: $2,000
Number of awards: 7
Deadline: March 29
College level: Freshman
Majors/Fields: Engineering
Criteria: Applicant must be enrolled in an ABET accredited program at a Texas school, and have participated in at least one TSPE-sponsored education program. Awarded every year. Texas schools only.
Contact: Mickie McElroy, Education Director.

752   Thomas M. Hunter Endowed Scholars Program

Clemson University
G-01 Sikes Hall
Clemson, SC 29634-5123
(803) 656-2280
Maximum award: $2,500
Number of awards: 2
Deadline: None
College level: Freshman
Majors/Fields: Engineering
Criteria: Selection is based upon admissions application. Renewable for up to three years if recipient maintains minimum 3.0 GPA and completes at least 12 credits each semester. Awarded every year. Award may be used only at sponsoring institution.
Contact: Marvin Carmichael, Director of Financial Aid.

753 Thomas R. Camp Scholarship

American Water Works Association
6666 West Quincy Avenue
Denver, CO 80235
(303) 347-6210, (303) 794-8915 (fax)
bmurphy@awwa.org
Average award: $5,000
Number of awards: 1
Deadline: January 15
College level: Graduate, Doctoral
Majors/Fields: Water supply, water treatment
Criteria: Applicant must be doing applied research in the drinking water field at an institution of higher learning in the U.S., Canada, Guam, Puerto Rico, or Mexico. Selection is based upon academic record and leadership potential. Awarded when applications are received from clearly outstanding candidates.
Contact: Scholarship Coordinator.

754 TMC/SAE Donald D. Dawson Technical Scholarship

Society of Automotive Engineers (SAE)
400 Commonwealth Drive
Warrendale, PA 15096-0001
(412) 772-8534, (412) 776-1615 (fax)
lorile@sae.org
http://www.sae.org
Average award: $1,500
Number of awards: 1
Deadline: December 1
College level: Freshman
Majors/Fields: Engineering
Criteria: Applicant must be a U.S. citizen and have a minimum 3.25 GPA and minimum SAT I scores of 550 verbal and 600 math (composite ACT score of 27). Minimum 3.0 GPA is required to retain scholarship. Awarded every year.
Contact: Lori Pail, Scholarship Coordinator.

755 Tony Neidermayer Memorial Bursary

University of Calgary
Department of Financial Aid
2500 University Drive, NW
Calgary, Alberta, CN T2N 1N4
(403) 220-7872, (403) 282-2999 (fax)
Average award: $1,500
Number of awards: 4
Deadline: June 15
College level: Sophomore, Junior, Senior
Majors/Fields: Engineering
Criteria: Selection is based upon academic merit and financial need. Awarded every year. Award may be used only at sponsoring institution.
Contact: J. Van Housen, Director of Student Awards/Financial Aid.

756 TSPE Regional Scholarships

Texas Society of Professional Engineers
P.O. Box 2145
Austin, TX 78768
(512) 472-9286, (512) 472-2934 (fax)
mickie@tspe.org
http://www.tspe.org
Number of awards: 5
Deadline: December 1
College level: Freshman
Majors/Fields: Engineering
Criteria: Applicant must be enrolled in an ABET-accredited program in a Texas institution. Awarded every year. Award may be used at Texas schools only.
Contact: Mickie McElroy, Education Director.

757 UMA Group Scholarship

University of Calgary
Department of Financial Aid
2500 University Drive, NW
Calgary, Alberta, CN T2N 1N4
(403) 220-7872, (403) 282-2999 (fax)
Average award: $1,800
Number of awards: 1
Deadline: June 15
College level: Sophomore
Majors/Fields: Engineering
Criteria: Selection is based upon academic merit. Awarded every year. Award may be used only at sponsoring institution.
Contact: J. Van Housen, Director of Student Awards/Financial Aid.

758 United Negro College Fund Scholarship

General Motors Corporation (GMC)
3044 West Grand Boulevard
Detroit, MI 48202
Maximum award: $5,000
Number of awards: 8
College level: Sophomore, Junior, Senior
Majors/Fields: Engineering
Criteria: Applicant must be a member of one of the following minority groups: Alaskan Native, American Indian, Asian-American, African-American/black, Mexican-American/Chicano, Hispanic, or Puerto Rican. Contact the engineering department to ask if the university participates in the scholarship program.
Contact: L.J. Wicker, Manager, Education Relations, (313) 556-3509.

759 V. Mohan Malhotra Fellowship

American Concrete Institute/CONREF
P.O. Box 19150
Farmington Hills, MI 48333
(810) 848-3713
Deadline: February 1
College level: Graduate
Majors/Fields: Concrete materials science research
Criteria: Applicant must be proficient in English (or French as required in Province of Quebec or Spanish in Puerto Rico). Awarded every year.
Contact: Dot Lepping, Scholarship Coordinator.

760 V.B. Higgins Engineering Fund Scholarship

Clemson University
G-01 Sikes Hall
Clemson, SC 29634-5123
(803) 656-2280
Average award: $1,000
Number of awards: 14
Deadline: March 1
College level: Sophomore, Junior, Senior
Majors/Fields: Engineering
Criteria: Applicant must have a minimum 2.5 GPA. Awarded every year. Award may be used only at sponsoring institution.
Contact: Marvin Carmichael, Director of Financial Aid.

761   VSPE Educational Fund Scholarship

Virginia Society of Professional Engineers
9291 Laurel Grove Road, Suite 10
Mechanicsville, VA 23116-2969
(804) 780-6883, (804) 730-6850 (fax)
vspe@aol.com
Average award: $1,000
Number of awards: 1
Deadline: March 1
College level: Freshman
Majors/Fields: Engineering
Criteria: Applicant must have a minimum 3.0 GPA and a minimum 600 math and 500 verbal SAT scores, and have applied for admission to one of the participating institutions. Selection is based upon applicant's activities, honors, essay, and courses. Award may be used at the following schools only: George Mason U, Hampton U, Old Dominion U, U of Virginia, Virginia Commonwealth U, Virginia Military Inst, or Virginia Polytechnic and State U.
Contact: Leigh M. Dicks, Executive Director.

762   W. Glenn Hawkins Scholarship

Clemson University
G-01 Sikes Hall
Clemson, SC 29634-5123
(803) 656-2280
Average award: $1,000
Number of awards: 1
Deadline: March 1
College level: Sophomore, Junior, Senior
Majors/Fields: Construction science/management
Criteria: Applicant must have a minimum 2.0 GPA. Preference is given to resident of Greenville or Pickens county, S.C. Awarded every year. Award may be used only at sponsoring institution.
Contact: Marvin Carmichael, Director of Financial Aid.

763   WERC Fellowship

New Mexico State University
Box 30001
Department 5100
Las Cruces, NM 88003-0001
(505) 646-4105
Maximum award: $1,500
Number of awards: 13
Deadline: March 15
College level: Sophomore, Junior, Senior
Majors/Fields: Engineering
Criteria: Applicant must be enrolled full time in the College of Engineering, have a minimum 2.5 GPA, be a U.S. citizen or permanent resident, and agree to participate in and document results of a research project. Awarded every year. Award may be used only at sponsoring institution.
Contact: Dr. Ron Bhada, College of Engineering, (505) 646-3547.

764   Westinghouse Bertha Lamme Scholarship

Society of Women Engineers (SWE)
120 Wall Street, 11th Floor
New York, NY 10005-3902
(212) 509-9577, (212) 509-0224 (fax)
Average award: $1,000
Number of awards: 3
Deadline: May 15
College level: Freshman
Majors/Fields: Engineering
Criteria: Applicant must be a U.S. citizen, a woman, and have a minimum 3.5 GPA. Continued academic achievement is required to retain scholarship for up to three additional years. Awarded every year.
Contact: Louise Bacon, Executive Assistant.

765   Weyerhaeuser Black Scholars Award

Mississippi State University
Department of Student Financial Aid
P.O. Box 6238
Mississippi State, MS 39762
(601) 325-7430
Average award: $3,000
Number of awards: 1
Deadline: February 1
College level: Freshman
Majors/Fields: Chemical engineering, electrical engineering, mechanical engineering
Criteria: Applicant must be black and have a minimum composite ACT score of 21 (combined SAT I score of 860). Minimum 3.0 GPA is required to retain scholarship. Awarded every year. Award may be used only at sponsoring institution.
Contact: Audrey S. Lambert, Director of Student Financial Aid.

766   William A. McCalla Memorial Scholarship

The University of Alabama
Box 870162
Tuscaloosa, AL 35487-0162
(205) 348-6756
Average award: $1,000
Number of awards: 1
Deadline: January 15
College level: Freshman
Majors/Fields: Engineering
Criteria: Renewable for up to three years of undergraduate study if satisfactory academic progress is maintained. Awarded every year. Award may be used only at sponsoring institution.
Contact: Engineering Student Services, 112 Mineral Industries Building, Box 870200, Tuscaloosa, AL 35487-0200, (205) 348-6408.

767   William E. Jackson Award

RTCA, Inc. William E. Jackson Award
1140 Connecticut Avenue, NW, Suite 1020
Washington, DC 20036
(202) 833-9339, (202) 833-9434 (fax)
http://www.rtca.org
Average award: $2,000
Number of awards: 1
Deadline: June 30
College level: Doctoral
Majors/Fields: Aviation electronics, telecommunication systems
Criteria: Applicants must submit two copies each of a one-to two-page summary of their paper, a biographical sketch of the candidate, and a recommendation from the candidate's instructor, professor, or department head. Selection is based upon thesis, project report, or technical journal paper. Awarded every year.
Contact: Harold Moses, Program Director, hmoses@rtca.org.

768   William E. Weisel Scholarship

Society of Manufacturing Engineers (SME) Education Foundation
One SME Drive, P.O. Box 930
Dearborn, MI 48121
(313) 271-1500, extension 512, (313) 240-6095 (fax)
murrdor@sme.org
Average award: $1,000
Number of awards: 1
Deadline: March 1
College level: Sophomore, Junior, Senior
Majors/Fields: Automated systems, engineering, robotics, technology
Criteria: Applicant must be a U.S. or canadian citizen, enrolled full time in a degree program, have completed at least 30 credit hours, and maintain a minimum 3.5 GPA. Recipient will be asked to contribute $1,000 in the future to the fund, as his/her career becomes successful, to guarantee to same educational opportunity to other worthy students. Financial need is not a consideration. Students may apply in succeeding years. Awarded every year.
Contact: Grants Coordinator, (313) 271-1500.

769 William Lemond Hamilton Bursary

University of Calgary
Department of Financial Aid
2500 University Drive, NW
Calgary, Alberta, CN T2N 1N4
(403) 220-7872, (403) 282-2999 (fax)
Average award: $2,000
Number of awards: 6
Deadline: June 15
College level: Freshman, Sophomore, Junior, Senior
Majors/Fields: Engineering, geology, geophysics, management
Criteria: Applicant must be a Canadian citizen planning a career in the resource industry. Selection is based upon financial need, extra-curricular activities, and academic merit. Awarded every year. Award may be used only at sponsoring institution.
Contact: J. Van Housen, Director of Student Awards/Financial Aid.

770 Wisconsin Space Grant Consortium Scholarship

Milwaukee School of Engineering
1025 North Broadway
Milwaukee, WI 53202-3109
(800) 332-6763, (414) 277-7475 (fax)
goran@admin.msoe.edu
www.msoe.edu
Average award: $5,500
Number of awards: 2
Deadline: February 1
College level: Freshman
Majors/Fields: Computer engineering, electrical engineering, mechanical engineering
Criteria: Applicant must have a minimum 3.5 GPA and a minimum composite ACT score of 25 (combined SAT I score of 1060), and be planning an aerospace-oriented career. Application required. Recipient must maintain a minimum 3.0 GPA to retain scholarship for four years. Awarded every year. Award may be used only at sponsoring institution.
Contact: Sue Minzlaff, Financial Aid Office, (414) 277-7222, minzlaff@admin.msoe.edu.

771 Wyn Molded Plastics Inc. Scholarship

Shawnee State University
940 Second Street
Portsmouth, OH 45662-4344
(614) 355-2237
Average award: $1,000
Number of awards: 4
Deadline: April 15
College level: Freshman
Majors/Fields: Plastics engineering technology
Criteria: Applicant must be a resident of Pickaway or Ross County. Award includes summer employment. Early application is recommended. Awarded every year. Award may be used only at sponsoring institution.
Contact: E. Wayne Miller, C.E.O., Wyn Molded Plastics, Inc., 30627 Orr Road, Circleville, OH 43113, (614) 474-7546.

Industrial/Manufacturing Engineering

772 Applied Power Scholarship Award

Society of Manufacturing Engineers (SME) Education Foundation
One SME Drive, P.O. Box 930
Dearborn, MI 48121
(313) 271-1500, extension 512, (313) 240-6095 (fax)
murrdor@sme.org
Average award: $1,000
Number of awards: 2
Deadline: March 1
College level: Sophomore, Junior, Senior
Majors/Fields: Manufacturing engineering
Criteria: Applicant must be enrolled full time in a degree program, have completed at least 30 credit hours, and maintain a minimum 3.5 GPA. Financial need is not a consideration.
Contact: Grandt Coordinator, (313) 271-1500, murrdor@sme.org.

773 Caterpillar Scholars Award Fund

Society of Manufacturing Engineers (SME) Education Foundation
One SME Drive, P.O. Box 930
Dearborn, MI 48121
(313) 271-1500, extension 512, (313) 240-6095 (fax)
murrdor@sme.org
Average award: $2,000
Number of awards: 5
Deadline: March 1
College level: Sophomore, Junior, Senior
Majors/Fields: Manufacturing engineering technology, manufacturing technology
Criteria: Applicant must be enrolled full time in a degree program, have completed at least 30 credit hours, and maintain a minimum 3.0 GPA. Financial need is not a consideration. Awarded every year.
Contact: Grants Coordinator.

774 Clinton Helton Scholarship

Society of Manufacturing Engineers (SME) Education Foundation
One SME Drive, P.O. Box 930
Dearborn, MI 48121
(313) 271-1500, extension 512, (313) 240-6095 (fax)
murrdor@sme.org
Average award: $830
Number of awards: 3
Deadline: March 1
College level: Sophomore, Junior, Senior
Majors/Fields: Manufacturing engineering, manufacturing engineering technology
Criteria: Applicant must be enrolled full time in a degree program, have completed at least 30 credit hours, and maintain a minimum 3.3 GPA. Financial need is not a consideration. Recipients may apply in succeeding years. Awarded every year. Colorado Sch of Mines, Colorado St U, U of Colorado.
Contact: Grants Coordiantor.

775   Dwight D. Gardner Scholarship

Institute of Industrial Engineers (IIE)
25 Technology Park/Atlanta
Norcross, GA 30092
(770) 449-0460, (770) 263-8532 (fax)
www.iienet.org
Average award: $1,500
Number of awards: 5
Deadline: November 15
College level: Sophomore, Junior, Senior
Majors/Fields: Industrial engineering
Criteria: Applicant must be an active IIE member, be enrolled full time, and have a minimum 3.4 GPA. Selection is based upon scholastic ability, character, leadership, potential service to the profession, and financial need. Awarded every year.
Contact: Heather Gilbert, University Operations Coordinator, (770) 449-0461 extension 140, hgilbert@www.iienet.org.

776   Gianninoto Scholarship Fund

Industrial Designers Society of America
1142-E Walker Road
Great Falls, VA 22066
(703) 759-0100, (703) 759-7679 (fax)
isda@erols.com
http://www.idsa.org
Average award: $2,000
Number of awards: 1
Deadline: April 30
College level: Doctoral
Majors/Fields: Industrial design
Criteria: Applicant must submit slide portfolio and letters of support. Awarded every year.
Contact: Celia Weinstein, Director of Internal Affairs.

777   Gilbreth Memorial Followship

Institute of Industrial Engineers (IIE)
25 Technology Park/Atlanta
Norcross, GA 30092
(770) 449-0460, (770) 263-8532 (fax)
www.iienet.org
Average award: $2,500
Number of awards: 5
Deadline: November 15
College level: Graduate, Doctoral
Majors/Fields: Industrial engineering
Criteria: Applicant must be an active IIE member, be enrolled full time, and have a minimum 3.4 GPA. Selection is based upon scholastic ability, character, leadership, potential service to the profession, and financial need. Awarded every year.
Contact: Heather Gilbert, University Operations Coordinator, (770) 449-0461 extension 140, hgilbert@www.iienet.org.

778   Kalamazoo Chapter No. 116–Roscoe Douglas Scholarship Award

Society of Manufacturing Engineers (SME) Education Foundation
One SME Drive, P.O. Box 930
Dearborn, MI 48121
(313) 271-1500, extension 512, (313) 240-6095 (fax)
murrdor@sme.org
Average award: $1,500
Number of awards: 1
Deadline: March 1
College level: Sophomore, Junior, Senior
Majors/Fields: Manufacturing engineering, manufacturing engineering technology
Criteria: Applicant must be enrolled full time in a degree program, have completed at least 30 credit hours, and maintain a minimum 3.0 GPA. Financial need is not a consideration. Recipients may apply in succeeding years. Awarded every year. Award may be used at the following schools only: Glen Oaks Comm Coll, Jackson Comm Coll, Kalamazoo Valley Comm Coll, Kellogg Comm Coll, Lake Michigan Coll, Southwestern Michigan Coll, Western Michigan U.
Contact: Grants Coordinator.

779   Myrtle and Earl Walker Scholarship

Society of Manufacturing Engineers (SME) Education Foundation
One SME Drive, P.O. Box 930
Dearborn, MI 48121
(313) 271-1500, extension 512, (313) 240-6095 (fax)
murrdor@sme.org
Average award: $500
Number of awards: 20
Deadline: March 1
College level: Sophomore, Junior, Senior
Majors/Fields: Manufacturing engineering, manufacturing engineering technology
Criteria: Applicant must be enrolled full time in a degree program, have completed at least 30 credit hours, and maintain a minimum 3.5 GPA. Financial need is not a consideration. Awarded every year.
Contact: Grants Coorinator.

780   Pulp and Paper Merit Award

Pulp & Paper Foundation, Inc.
North Carolina State University
Box 8005
Raleigh, NC 27695-8005
(919) 515-5661, (919) 515-6302 (fax)
http://www2.ncsu.edu/ncsu/forest_resources/cfr/scholar.html
Maximum award: $3,700
Maximum number of awards: 100
Minimum number of awards: 80
Deadline: January 15
College level: Freshman, Sophomore, Junior, Senior
Majors/Fields: Wood/paper science
Criteria: Applicant must be a U.S. citizen. Minimum 2.90 GPA is required to retain scholarship. Awarded every year. Award may be used only at North Carolina State University.
Contact: J. Ben Chilton, Executive Director.

781   St. Louis Chapter No.17 Scholarship

Society of Manufacturing Engineers (SME) Education
Foundation
One SME Drive, P.O. Box 930
Dearborn, MI 48121
(313) 271-1500, extension 512, (313) 240-6095 (fax)
murrdor@sme.org
Average award: $900
Number of awards: 4
Deadline: March 1
College level: Sophomore, Junior
Majors/Fields: Manufacturing engineering, industrial technology
Criteria: Applicant must be enrolled full time in a degree program, and maintain a minimum 3.5 GPA. Financial need is a consideration. not a consideration. Recipients may apply in succeeding years. Awarded every year. Award may be used at the following schools only: Jefferson Coll, Mineral Area Coll, St. Louis Comm Coll at Florissant Valley, U of Missouri-Rolla, Southeast Missouri St U-Cape Girardeau Southern Illinois U-Carbondale, Washington U
Contact: Grants Coordinator.

782   U.S. Department of Energy Predoctoral Fellowships in Integrated Manufacturing

National Research Council
2101 Constitution Avenue
Washington, DC 20418
(202) 334-2872
Number of awards: 12
Deadline: Early November
College level: Doctoral
Majors/Fields: Integrated manufacturing
Criteria: Fellowship is awarded for three years. Awarded every year.
Contact: Fellowship Office.

783   Undergraduate Scholarship

Industrial Designers Society of America
1142-E Walker Road
Great Falls, VA 22066
(703) 759-0100, (703) 759-7679 (fax)
isda@erols.com
http://www.idsa.org
Average award: $2,000
Number of awards: 1
Deadline: May 3
College level: Senior
Majors/Fields: Industrial design
Criteria: Awarded every year.
Contact: Celia Weinstein.

784   United Parcel Services Scholarship for Female Students

Institute of Industrial Engineers (IIE)
25 Technology Park/Atlanta
Norcross, GA 30092
(770) 449-0460, (770) 263-8532 (fax)
www.iienet.org
Average award: $2,500
Number of awards: 1
Deadline: November 15
College level: Sophomore, Junior, Senior
Majors/Fields: Industrial engineering
Criteria: Applicant must be a woman, an active IIE member, be enrolled full time, and have a minimum 3.4 GPA. Selection is based upon scholastic ability, character, leadership, potential service to the profession, and financial need. Awarded every year.
Contact: Heather Gilbert, University Operations Coordinator, (770) 449-0461, extension 140, hgilbert@www.iienet.org.

785   United Parcel Services Scholarship for Minority Students

Institute of Industrial Engineers (IIE)
25 Technology Park/Atlanta
Norcross, GA 30092
(770) 449-0460, (770) 263-8532 (fax)
www.iienet.org
Average award: $2,500
Number of awards: 1
Deadline: November 15
College level: Sophomore, Junior, Senior
Majors/Fields: Industrial engineering
Criteria: Applicant must be a member of an minority group, an active IIE member, be enrolled full time, and have a minimum 3.4 GPA. Selection is based upon scholastic ability, character, leadership, potential service to the profession, and financial need. Awarded every year.
Contact: Heather Gilbert, University Operations Coordinator, (770) 449-0461 extension 140, hgilbert@www.iienet.org.

786   Wayne Kay Graduate Fellowship

Society of Manufacturing Engineers (SME) Education
Foundation
One SME Drive, P.O. Box 930
Dearborn, MI 48121
(313) 271-1500, extension 512, (313) 240-6095 (fax)
murrdor@sme.org
Average award: $5,000
Number of awards: 10
Deadline: March 1
College level: Graduate, Doctoral
Majors/Fields: Industrial engineering, manufacturing engineering
Criteria: Applicant must be enrolled full time in a graduate degree program, and maintain a minimum 3.5 GPA. Applicant must have proven scholastic ability, exemplary character and leadership, and demonstrated potential for future leadership in the profession. Financial need is not a consideration. Awarded every year.
Contact: Grants Coordinator.

Mechanical Engineering———

787   Amoco Scholarship

The University of Alabama
Box 870162
Tuscaloosa, AL 35487-0162
(205) 348-6756
Average award: $1,300
Number of awards: 1
Deadline: January 15
College level: Junior, Senior
Majors/Fields: Mechanical engineering
Criteria: Awarded every year. Award may be used only at sponsoring institution.
Contact: Engineering Student Services, 112 Mineral Industries Building, Box 870200, Tuscaloosa, AL 35487-0200, (205) 348-6408.

788   ASME Graduate Teaching Fellowship

American Society of Mechanical Engineers (ASME)
Education Services Department
345 East 47th Street
New York, NY 10017-2392
(212) 705-8131, (212) 705-7143 (fax)
malaven@asme.org
http://www.asme.org
Average award: $5,000
Number of awards: 2
Deadline: October 7
College level: Doctoral
Majors/Fields: Mechanical engineering
Criteria: Applicant must be pursuing a doctorate in mechanical engineering as a terminal degree, desire engineering education for a career, hold a teaching assistantship at a university, be a U.S. citizen or permanent resident, be a student member of ASME, and have an undergraduate degree from an ABET-accredited program. Women and minorities are encouraged to apply. Award is for a maximum of three years. Awarded every year.
Contact: Nellie Malave, Education Services Department.

789   Babcock & Wilcox Annual Scholarship

Clemson University
G-01 Sikes Hall
Clemson, SC 29634-5123
(803) 656-2280
Maximum award: $1,000
Number of awards: 1
Deadline: March 1
College level: Senior
Majors/Fields: Mechanical engineering
Criteria: Applicant must have a minimum 2.5 GPA. Scholarship is renewable. Awarded every year. Award may be used only at sponsoring institution.
Contact: Marvin Carmichael, Director of Financial Aid.

790   Elisabeth M. and Winchell M. Parsons Scholarship

American Society of Mechanical Engineers (ASME)
Education Services Department
345 East 47th Street
New York, NY 10017-2392
(212) 705-8131, (212) 705-7143 (fax)
malaven@asme.org
http://www.asme.org
Average award: $1,500
Number of awards: 1
Deadline: February 15
College level: Doctoral
Majors/Fields: Mechanical engineering
Criteria: Awarded every year.
Contact: ASME Auxiliary, (212) 705-7375.

791   F.W. "Beich" Beichley Scholarship

American Society of Mechanical Engineers (ASME)
Education Services Department
345 East 47th Street
New York, NY 10017-2392
(212) 705-8131, (212) 705-7143 (fax)
malaven@asme.org
http://www.asme.org
Average award: $1,500
Number of awards: 1
Deadline: April 15
College level: Junior, Senior
Majors/Fields: Mechanical engineering or related program
Criteria: Applicant must be a member of ASME. Selection based upon leadership, potential contribution to the mechanical engineering profession, and scholastic ability. Financial need is considered. Awarded every year.
Contact: Nellie Malave, Administrative Assistant.

792   Frank William & Dorothy Given Miller ASME Auxiliary Scholarship

American Society of Mechanical Engineers (ASME)
Education Services Department
345 East 47th Street
New York, NY 10017-2392
(212) 705-8131, (212) 705-7143 (fax)
malaven@asme.org
http://www.asme.org
Maximum award: $1,500
Maximum number of awards: 2
Minimum number of awards: 2
Deadline: April 15
College level: Junior, Senior
Majors/Fields: Mechanical engineering or related program
Criteria: Applicant must be a member of ASME. Selection is based upon leadership, potential contribution to the mechanical engineering profession, and scholastic ability. Financial need is considered. Awarded every year.
Contact: Nellie Malave, Scholarships, 345 East 47th Street, Mail Stop 5T, New York, NY 10017-2392, mamaven@asme.org.

793   Garland Duncan Scholarship

American Society of Mechanical Engineers (ASME)
Education Services Department
345 East 47th Street
New York, NY 10017-2392
(212) 705-8131, (212) 705-7143 (fax)
malaven@asme.org
http://www.asme.org
Maximum award: $2,500
Number of awards: 2
Deadline: April 15
College level: Junior, Senior
Majors/Fields: Mechanical engineering or related program
Criteria: Applicant must be a member of ASME. Selestion based upon character, integrity, leadership, potential contribution to the mechanical engineering profession, and scholastic ability. Financial need is considered. Awarded every year.
Contact: Nellie Malave, Administrative Assistant, 345 East 47th Street, Mail Stop 5T, New York, NY 10017, malaven@asme.org.

794   Grothus-Pi Tau Sigma Award

New Mexico State University
Box 30001
Department 5100
Las Cruces, NM 88003-0001
(505) 646-4105
Average award: Full tuition
College level: Sophomore
Majors/Fields: Mechanical engineering
Criteria: Awarded for spring semester. Selection is made by department head and Pi Tau Sigma faculty advisers. Awarded every year. Award may be used only at sponsoring institution.
Contact: College of Engineering, (505) 646-3547.

795   International Gas Turbine Institute Scholarship

Texas A&M University–Kingsville
Scholarships
Box 116
Kingsville, TX 78363
(512) 593-3907, (512) 593-2991 (fax)
http://www.tamuk.edu
Average award: $1,000
Number of awards: No limit
Deadline: April 15 and November 15
College level: Sophomore, Junior, Senior
Majors/Fields: Mechanical engineering
Criteria: Applicant must have a competitive class rank. Award may be used only at sponsoring institution.
Contact: Your department, College of Engineering.

796 International Gas Turbine Institute Scholarship

American Society of Mechanical Engineers (ASME)
Education Services Department
345 East 47th Street
New York, NY 10017-2392
(212) 705-8131, (212) 705-7143 (fax)
malaven@asme.org
http://www.asme.org
Average award: $1,000
Number of awards: 80
Majors/Fields: Mechanical engineering
Criteria: Applicant's school must apply and qualify; recipient is selected by ASME Student Section. Awarded every year.
Contact: Scholarships.

797 John and Elsa Gracik Scholarship

American Society of Mechanical Engineers (ASME)
Education Services Department
345 East 47th Street
New York, NY 10017-2392
(212) 705-8131, (212) 705-7143 (fax)
malaven@asme.org
http://www.asme.org
Maximum award: $1,500
Number of awards: 4
Deadline: April 15
College level: Freshman, Sophomore, Junior, Senior
Majors/Fields: Mechanical engineering or related program
Criteria: Applicant must be a member of ASME. Selection is based upon leadership, potential contribution to the mechanical engineering profession, and scholastic ability. Financial need is considered. Awarded every year.
Contact: Nellie Malave, Scholarships, 345 East 47th Street, Mail Stop 5T, New York, NY 1001.

798 Kenneth Andrew Roe Scholarship

American Society of Mechanical Engineers (ASME)
Education Services Department
345 East 47th Street
New York, NY 10017-2392
(212) 705-8131, (212) 705-7143 (fax)
malaven@asme.org
http://www.asme.org
Maximum award: $5,000
Number of awards: 1
Deadline: April 15
College level: Junior, Senior
Majors/Fields: Mechanical engineering or related program
Criteria: Applicant must be a member of ASME. Selection is based upon leadership, potential contribution to the mechanical engineering profession, and scholastic ability. Financial need is considered. Awarded every year.
Contact: Nellie Malave, Scholarships, 345 East 47th Street, Mail Stop 5T, New York, NY 10017.

799 Marjorie Roy Rothermel Scholarship

American Society of Mechanical Engineers (ASME)
Education Services Department
345 East 47th Street
New York, NY 10017-2392
(212) 705-8131, (212) 705-7143 (fax)
malaven@asme.org
http://www.asme.org
Average award: $1,500
Number of awards: 1
Deadline: February 15
College level: Graduate
Majors/Fields: Mechanical engineering
Criteria: Awarded every year.
Contact: ASME Auxiliary, (212) 705-7733.

800 Pellette & Associates Scholarship

New Mexico State University
Box 30001
Department 5100
Las Cruces, NM 88003-0001
(505) 646-4105
Average award: Full tuition
Deadline: March 1
College level: Sophomore, Junior, Senior
Majors/Fields: Mechanical engineering
Criteria: Applicant must be enrolled full time, have a minimum 2.5 GPA, be a New Mexico resident, and be a U.S. citizen. Awarded every year. Award may be used only at sponsoring institution.
Contact: College of Engineering, (505) 646-3547.

801 Rice-Cullimore Scholarship

American Society of Mechanical Engineers (ASME)
Education Services Department
345 East 47th Street
New York, NY 10017-2392
(212) 705-8131, (212) 705-7143 (fax)
malaven@asme.org
http://www.asme.org
Average award: $2,000
Number of awards: 2
Deadline: February 15
College level: Graduate, Doctoral
Majors/Fields: Mechanical engineering
Criteria: Applicant must be a foreign student who qualifies in his or her home country and through the Institute of International Education. Awarded every year.
Contact: ASME Auxiliary, (212) 705-7375.

802 Solid Waste Processing Division Scholarship

American Society of Mechanical Engineers (ASME)
Education Services Department
345 East 47th Street
New York, NY 10017-2392
(212) 705-8131, (212) 705-7143 (fax)
malaven@asme.org
http://www.asme.org
Maximum award: $2,000
Number of awards: 5
Deadline: February 1
College level: Freshman, Sophomore, Junior, Senior, Graduate, Doctoral
Majors/Fields: Solid waste management
Criteria: Applicant must attend a North American college or university with an established program in solid waste management. Awarded every year.
Contact: Scholarships, (212) 705-7375.

803 Sylvia W. Farny Scholarship

American Society of Mechanical Engineers (ASME)
Education Services Department
345 East 47th Street
New York, NY 10017-2392
(212) 705-8131, (212) 705-7143 (fax)
malaven@asme.org
http://www.asme.org
Average award: $1,500
Maximum award: $2,000
Number of awards: 8
Deadline: February 15
College level: Senior
Majors/Fields: Mechanical engineering
Criteria: Selection is based upon academic achievement, financial need, and character. Awarded every year.
Contact: ASME Auxiliary, (212) 705-7375.

804   William J. and Mary Jane E. Adams, Jr. Scholarship

American Society of Mechanical Engineers (ASME)
Education Services Department
345 East 47th Street
New York, NY 10017-2392
(212) 705-8131, (212) 705-7143 (fax)
malaven@asme.org
http://www.asme.org
Average award: $1,000
Number of awards: 1
Deadline: April 15
College level: Freshman, Sophomore, Junior, Senior, Graduate, Doctoral
Majors/Fields: Mechanical engineering or related program
Criteria: Applicant must be an ASME student member attending a college in ASME Region IX (California, Hawaii, or Nevada). Awarded every year.
Contact: Nellie Malave, Scholarships, (212) 705-7234.

Mining/Metallurgical/ Materials Engineering

805   Amoco Foundation Scholarship

The University of Alabama
Box 870162
Tuscaloosa, AL 35487-0162
(205) 348-6756
Average award: $1,000
Number of awards: 1
Deadline: January 15
College level: Freshman, Sophomore, Junior, Senior
Majors/Fields: Mineral engineering
Criteria: Preference is given to applicant with petroleum specialization. Awarded every year. Award may be used only at sponsoring institution.
Contact: Engineering Student Services, 112 Mineral Industries Building, Box 870200, Tuscaloosa, AL 35487-0200, (205) 348-6408.

806   ASM Foundation Undergraduate Scholarship

American Society for Metals (ASM) Foundation for Education and Research
Materials Park, OH 44073
(216) 338-5151, (216) 338-4634 (fax)
ASMFER@po.asm-intl.org
http://www.asm-intl.org
Maximum award: $5,000
Number of awards: 41
Deadline: June 15
College level: Sophomore, Junior, Senior
Majors/Fields: Materials science and engineering, metallurgy
Criteria: Applicants must be citizens of the U.S., Canada, or Mexico. For some awards, applicant must be an ASM member and demonstrate financial need. Awarded every year.
Contact: Kristi Foster, Administrator, Student/University Relations.

807   ASM Undergraduate Scholarship

ASM Foundation for Education and Research
Materials Park, OH 44073
(216) 338-5151, (216) 338-4634 (fax)
asmfer@po.asm-intl.org
http://www.asm-intl.org
Average award: Full tuition
Number of awards: 40
Deadline: June 15
College level: Sophomore, Junior, Senior
Majors/Fields: Materials science and engineering, metallurgy
Criteria: Applicant must be a U.S., Canadian, or Mexican citizen and be a member of the ASM. Selection is based upon interest in metallurgy and materials science, motivation, achievement, scholarship, and potential. Some awards require demonstration of financial need. Recipient must reapply for renewal. Awarded every year.
Contact: Kristi Foster, Administrator of Student/University Relations.

808   Desk and Derrick Educational Trust Scholarship

Desk and Derrick Educational Trust
4823 S. Sheridan Road
Suite 308A
Tulsa, OK 74145-5717
(918) 622-1675, (918) 622-1675 (fax)
Maximum award: $1,000
Number of awards: 12
Deadline: April 1
College level: Junior, Senior, Graduate
Majors/Fields: Chemical engineering, geology, petroleum engineering
Criteria: Applicant must be a U.S. or Canadian citizen and demonstrate financial need. Minimum 3.0 GPA is required to retain scholarship. Awarded every year.
Contact: Janice J. Davis, Chairman, 8140 Walnut Hill Lane, Suite 601, Dallas, TX 75231, (214) 363-5005.

809   Geneva Steel Scholarship

University of Utah
Financial Aid and Scholarships Office
105 Student Services Building
Salt Lake City, UT 84112
(801) 581-6211
Maximum award: $2,200
Number of awards: 2
Deadline: May 1
College level: Sophomore, Junior, Senior
Majors/Fields: Metallurgical engineering
Criteria: Awarded every year. Award may be used only at sponsoring institution.
Contact: Department of Metallurgical Engineering, 412 William C. Browning Building, Salt Lake City, UT 84112, (801) 581-5158.

810   Gordon L. Roberts Scholarship/James R. Cudworth Memorial Scholarship

The University of Alabama
Box 870162
Tuscaloosa, AL 35487-0162
(205) 348-6756
Average award: $1,000
Number of awards: 2
Deadline: January 15
College level: Freshman, Sophomore, Junior, Senior
Majors/Fields: Mineral engineering
Criteria: Awarded every year. Award may be used only at sponsoring institution.
Contact: Engineering Student Services, 112 Mineral Industries Building, Box 870200, Tuscaloosa, AL 35487-0200, (205) 348-6408.

811   H.E. "Eddie" Chiles Centennial Scholarship

University of Oklahoma
University Affairs
900 Asp Avenue, Room 236
Norman, OK 73019-0401
(405) 325-1701
Average award: $5,000
Number of awards: 1
Deadline: March 1
College level: Junior, Senior
Majors/Fields: Petroleum engineering
Criteria: Applicant must have a minimum 3.0 GPA and be enrolled full time. Awarded every year. Award may be used only at sponsoring institution.
Contact: Scholarship Coordinator for Petroleum and Geological Engineering, T301 Energy Center, Norman, OK 73019-0628, (405) 325-2921.

812   James F. Schumar Scholarship

American Nuclear Society (ANS)
555 North Kensington Avenue
LaGrange Park, IL 60526
(708) 352-6611
Maximum award: $3,500
Number of awards: 1
Deadline: March 1
College level: Graduate, Doctoral
Majors/Fields: Material science
Criteria: Applicant must be a U.S. citizen or permanent resident pursuing graduate studies in material science and technology for nuclear applications at a U.S. institution. Applicant must be sponsored by an ANS local section, division, student branch, committee member, or organization member. Include self-addressed stamped envelope with request. Awarded every year.
Contact: Scholarship Coordinator.

813   Jim Walter Resources Mining Scholarship

The University of Alabama
Box 870162
Tuscaloosa, AL 35487-0162
(205) 348-6756
Average award: $1,000
Number of awards: 1
Deadline: January 15
College level: Freshman, Sophomore, Junior, Senior
Majors/Fields: Mineral engineering
Criteria: Applicant must be a dependent of employee of Jim Walter Resources. Awarded every year. Award may be used only at sponsoring institution.
Contact: Engineering Student Services, 112 Mineral Industries Building, Box 870200, Tuscaloosa, AL 35487-0200, (205) 348-6408.

814   Milton H. Ward Scholarship

The University of Alabama
Box 870162
Tuscaloosa, AL 35487-0162
(205) 348-6756
Average award: $2,400
Number of awards: 1
Deadline: January 15
College level: Sophomore, Junior, Senior
Majors/Fields: Mineral engineering
Criteria: Applicant must have a mining specialization. Awarded every year. Award may be used only at sponsoring institution.
Contact: Engineering Student Services, 112 Mineral Industries Building, Box 870200, Tuscaloosa, AL 35487-0200, (205) 348-6408.

815   Petroleum and Geological Engineering Distinguished Scholarship

University of Oklahoma
University Affairs
900 Asp Avenue, Room 236
Norman, OK 73019-0401
(405) 325-1701
Maximum award: $1,000
Maximum number of awards: 3
Minimum number of awards: 1
Deadline: March 1
College level: Freshman, Sophomore, Junior, Senior
Majors/Fields: Petroleum engineering, geological engineering
Criteria: Applicant must be a U.S. citizen or permanent resident. Selection is based upon merit. Awarded every year. Award may be used only at sponsoring institution.
Contact: Director of Petroleum and Geological Engineering, College of Engineering, Room F301, Energy Center, Norman, OK 73019, (405) 325-2921.

816   PGE Excellence in Engineering Distinguished Scholarship

University of Oklahoma
University Affairs
900 Asp Avenue, Room 236
Norman, OK 73019-0401
(405) 325-1701
Average award: $3,000
Maximum number of awards: 20
Minimum number of awards: 15
Deadline: March 1
College level: Freshman
Majors/Fields: Geological engineering, petroleum engineering
Criteria: Applicant must have a minimum 3.0 GPA, rank in top quarter of graduating class, and have a minimum composite ACT score of 25. Selection is based upon extracurricular participation, leadership, recommendations, and essay. Awarded every year. Award may be used only at sponsoring institution.
Contact: Scholarship Coordinator for Petroleum and Geological Engineering, T301 Energy Center, Norman, OK 73019-0628, (405) 325-2921.

817   Scholarship Loan Fund

Woman's Auxiliary to the AIME, Inc. Scholarship
345 East 47th Street, 14th Floor
New York, NY 10017
(212) 705-7692, (212) 705-8024 (fax)
Average award: $4,085
Maximum award: $10,000
Minimum award: $1,700
Deadline: March 15
College level: Junior, Senior, Graduate, Doctoral
Majors/Fields: Geology, materials science, metallurgy, mineral sciences, mining, mining economics, petroleum, related fields
Criteria: Recipient is expected to repay 50% of the money that is received from the fund, with no interest charge. Repayment begins within six months of graduation and must be completed within a six year period. Reapplication is required to retain scholarship. Awarded every year.
Contact: Chairman of the Scholarship Loan Fund.

818   Scholarships in Mineral Engineering

The University of Alabama
Box 870162
Tuscaloosa, AL 35487-0162
(205) 348-6756
Average award: $1,000
Deadline: January 15
Number of awards: 5
College level: Freshman, Sophomore, Junior, Senior
Majors/Fields: Mineral engineering
Criteria: Applicant must have mining specialization. Awarded every year. Award may be used only at sponsoring institution.
Contact: Engineering Student Services, 112 Mineral Industries Building, Box 870200, Tuscaloosa, AL 35487-0200, (205) 348-6408.

819   SME Coal Division Scholarship

The University of Alabama
Box 870162
Tuscaloosa, AL 35487-0162
(205) 348-6756
Average award: $1,000
Number of awards: 1
Deadline: January 15
College level: Freshman, Sophomore, Junior, Senior
Majors/Fields: Mineral engineering
Criteria: Applicant must be SME member. Awarded every year. Award may be used only at sponsoring institution.
Contact: Engineering Student Services, 112 Mineral Industries Building, Box 870200, Tuscaloosa, AL 35487-0200, (205) 348-6408.

820 **Soceity of Petroleum Engineers-Southeastern Section Scholarship**

The University of Alabama
Box 870162
Tuscaloosa, AL 35487-0162
(205) 348-6756
Average award: $2,000
Number of awards: 1
Deadline: January 15
College level: Freshman, Sophomore, Junior, Senior
Majors/Fields: Mineral engineering
Criteria: Applicant must have petroleum specialization. Awarded every year. Award may be used only at sponsoring institution.
Contact: Engineering Student Services, 112 Mineral Industries Building, Box 870200, Tuscaloosa, AL 35487-0200, (205) 348-6408.

821 **Society of Petroleum Engineers-Warrior Basin Section Scholarship**

The University of Alabama
Box 870162
Tuscaloosa, AL 35487-0162
(205) 348-6756
Average award: $1,000
Number of awards: 1
Deadline: January 15
College level: Junior
Majors/Fields: Mineral engineering
Criteria: Applicant must have petroleum specialization. Awarded every year. Award may be used only at sponsoring institution.
Contact: Engineering Student Services, 112 Mineral Industries Building, Box 870200, Tuscaloosa, AL 35487-0200, (205) 348-6408.

822 **Warrior Basin Chapter American Petroleum Institue Endowed Petroleum Engineering Scholarship**

The University of Alabama
Box 870162
Tuscaloosa, AL 35487-0162
(205) 348-6756
Average award: $1,000
Number of awards: 1
Deadline: January 15
College level: Freshman, Sophomore, Junior, Senior, Graduate
Majors/Fields: Petroleum engineering
Criteria: Preference is given to dependent of member of API's Warrior Basin chapter. Renewable for course of undergraduate and graduate study if satisfactory academic progress is maintained. Awarded every year. Award may be used only at sponsoring institution.
Contact: Engineering Student Services, 112 Mineral Industries Building, Box 870200, Tuscaloosa, AL 35487-0200, (205) 348-6408.

823 **William C. Browning Scholarship**

University of Utah
Financial Aid and Scholarships Office
105 Student Services Building
Salt Lake City, UT 84112
(801) 581-6211
Maximum award: $3,039
Number of awards: 20
Deadline: February 15
College level: Freshman, Sophomore, Junior, Senior
Majors/Fields: Mining engineering
Criteria: Applicant must be a U.S. citizen, have a minimum 3.0 GPA, and show a strong background in mathematics, physics, and chemistry. Selection is based upon GPA, ACT scores, and academic performance in math and science. Scholarship is renewable. Awarded every year. Award may be used only at sponsoring institution.
Contact: Dr. M. K. McCarter, 313 William C. Browning Building, Salt Lake City, UT 84112, (801) 581-8603.

Nuclear Engineering────────────

824 **ANS Delayed Education for Women Scholarship**

American Nuclear Society (ANS)
555 North Kensington Avenue
LaGrange Park, IL 60526
(708) 352-6611
Maximum award: $3,500
Number of awards: 1
Deadline: March 1
College level: Sophomore, Junior, Senior, Graduate, students entering four-year curriculum
Majors/Fields: Nuclear engineering, nuclear science
Criteria: Applicant must be a woman, must have experienced at least a one-year delay or interruption in undergraduate studies, be entering a four-year curriculum at a U.S. institution, be a U.S. citizen or permanent resident, have proven academic ability, must demonstrate financial need, and must be sponsored by an ANS local section, division, student branch, committee, member, or organization member. Include a self-addressed, stamped envelope with request. Awarded every year.
Contact: Scholarship Coordinator.

825 **ANS Division Scholarship**

American Nuclear Society (ANS)
555 North Kensington Avenue
LaGrange Park, IL 60526
(708) 352-6611
Maximum award: $3,500
Number of awards: 11
Deadline: March 1
College level: Junior, Senior, Graduate, Doctoral
Majors/Fields: Nuclear engineering, nuclear science
Criteria: Applicant must be a U.S. citizen or permanent resident enrolled in a U.S. institution and must be sponsored by an ANS local section, division, student branch, committee member, or organization member. Include self-addressed stamped envelope with request. Awarded every year.
Contact: Scholarship Coordinator, (312) 352-6611.

826 **James R. Vogt Memorial Scholarship**

American Nuclear Society (ANS)
555 North Kensington Avenue
LaGrange Park, IL 60526
(708) 352-6611
Maximum award: $3,500
Number of awards: 1
Deadline: March 1
College level: Junior, Senior, Graduate
Majors/Fields: Nuclear science, radio-analytical chemistry
Criteria: Applicant must be a U.S. citizen or permanent resident, be enrolled in a U.S. institution, be an undergraduate or first-year graduate student doing or proposing research in radio-analytical chemistry or analytical applications of nuclear science, and must be sponsored by an ANS local section, division, student branch, committee member, or organization member. Include a self-addressed, stamped envelope with request. Awarded every year.
Contact: Scholarship Coordinator.

827 John and Muriel Landis Scholarship

American Nuclear Society (ANS)
555 North Kensington Avenue
LaGrange Park, IL 60526
(708) 352-6611
Maximum award: $3,500
Number of awards: 8
Deadline: March 1
College level: Freshman, Sophomore, Junior, Senior, Graduate, Doctoral
Majors/Fields: Nuclear engineering, nuclear science
Criteria: Applicant must be a U.S. citizen or permanent resident with greater than average financial need enrolled in a U.S. institution. Minority and female applicants are encouraged to apply; however, selection is without regard to race, creed, or sex. Applicant must be sponsored by an ANS local section, division, student branch, committee member, or organization member. Include a self-addressed, stamped envelope with request. Awarded every year.
Contact: Scholarship Coordinator.

828 Paul A. Greebler Memorial Scholarship

American Nuclear Society (ANS)
555 North Kensington Avenue
LaGrange Park, IL 60526
(708) 352-6611
Maximum award: $3,500
Number of awards: 1
Deadline: March 1
College level: Graduate, Doctoral
Majors/Fields: Nuclear engineering, nuclear science, reactor physics
Criteria: Applicant must be a U.S. citizen or permanent resident enrolled in a U.S. institution pursuing graduate studies in reactor physics. Applicant must be sponsored by an ANS local section, division, student branch, committee member, or organization member. Include a self-addressed, stamped envelope with request. Awarded every year.
Contact: Scholarship Coordinator.

829 Robert A. Dannels Memorial Scholarship

American Nuclear Society (ANS)
555 North Kensington Avenue
LaGrange Park, IL 60526
(708) 352-6611
Maximum award: $3,500
Number of awards: 1
Deadline: March 1
College level: Graduate, Doctoral
Majors/Fields: Nuclear engineering, nuclear science
Criteria: Handicapped persons are encouraged to apply. Applicant must be a U.S. citizen or permanent resident enrolled in a U.S. institution and must be sponsored by an ANS local section, division, student branch, committee member, or organization member. Include a self-addressed stamped envelope with request. Awarded every year.
Contact: Scholarship Coordinator.

830 Robert T. Liner Scholarship

American Nuclear Society (ANS)
555 North Kensington Avenue
LaGrange Park, IL 60526
(708) 352-6611
Maximum award: $3,500
Deadline: March 1
College level: Junior, Senior
Majors/Fields: Nuclear engineering, nuclear science
Criteria: Applicant must be a U.S. citizen or permanent resident who has completed one year of study leading to a degree in nuclear science or nuclear engineering. Include a self-addressed stamped envelope with request.
Contact: Scholarship Coordinator.

Language/Literature/Humanities

Classical Studies

831   ACL/NJCL National Latin Examination Scholarship

ACL/NJCL National Latin Examination
P.O. Box 95
Mount Vernon, VA 22121
(800) 459-9847, (703) 455-6799 (call first) (fax)
Average award: $1,000
Maximum number of awards: 60
Minimum number of awards: 15
Deadline: May 15
College level: Freshman
Majors/Fields: Latin, Greek
Criteria: Applicant must take the ACL/NJCL National Latin Exam. Applications will automatically be mailed to the gold medal winners who qualify from the exam. Recipient must agree to take at least one year of Latin or classical Greek in college. Recipient must continue to take Latin or Greek to retain scholarship. Awarded every year.
Contact: Jane H. Hall, Chairman, (703) 360-4354.

832   Darius and Nathan Flinchum Scholarship

Georgia State University
P.O. Box 4040
Atlanta, GA 30302
(404) 651-2227, (404) 651-3418 (fax)
http://www.gsu.edu
Average award: Full tuition
Number of awards: 1
Deadline: None
College level: Junior
Majors/Fields: Classics
Criteria: Applicant must have a minimum "B" grade average and excellent character. Awarded every year. Award may be used only at sponsoring institution.
Contact: College of Arts and Sciences, (404) 651-2291.

833   Fellowship in Roman Studies

American Numismatic Society
Broadway at 155th Street
New York, NY 10032
(212) 234-3130
Maximum award: $5,000
Deadline: March 1
Criteria: Fellowship is for support of a substantive research project concerning the Roman world, allowing for an extended residence in New York, work in the Society's cabinet and library, and consultation with relevant staff. Applicant must be a U.S. citizen affiliated with a North American institution of higher learning, demonstrate academic competence, and submit a detailed proposal for project.
Contact: Fellowships.

834   NJCL Scholarship

American Classical League (ACL)
National Junior Classical League (NJCL) Scholarships
Miami University
Oxford, OH 45056
(513) 529-7741
Maximum award: $1,000
Number of awards: 6
Deadline: May 1
College level: Freshman
Majors/Fields: Classics
Criteria: Applicant must be a NJCL member who will enter college in upcoming academic year and plans to continue the study of the classics. Special consideration is given to applicants who plan to teach Greek, Latin, or classical humanities. Selection is based upon application, recommendations, grades, and service in the NJCL.
Contact: Scholarships, Miami University, Oxford, OH 45056.

Cultural Studies

835   Bradley/Gamble Fellows Program in Population Studies

School for International Training (SIT)
P.O. Box 676
Kipling Road
Brattleboro, VT 05302
(802) 257-7751, (802) 258-3500 (fax)
admissions.sit@worldlearning.org
http://www.worldlearning/sit.html
Average award: $5,000
Maximum award: $10,000
Minimum award: $2,500
Number of awards: 1
Deadline: April 1
College level: Bachelor's and master's degree candidates
Criteria: Applicant must be a candidate for a Bachelor of International Studies or a Master of International Administration. Financial need may be considered. Applicant must maintain satisfactory academic progress and continue to demonstrate financial need to retain scholarship. Awarded every year. Award may be used only at sponsoring institution.
Contact: Mary Henderson, Financial Aid Officer, (802) 258-3280.

836   Community College International Studies Scholarship

School for International Training (SIT)
P.O. Box 676
Kipling Road
Brattleboro, VT 05302
(802) 257-7751, (802) 258-3500 (fax)
admissions.sit@worldlearning.org
http://www.worldlearning/sit.html
Average award: $1,000
Maximum award: $1,500
Minimum award: $750
Number of awards: 4
Deadline: April 1
College level: Bachelor's degree candidate, Tranfer
Criteria: Applicant must be transferring from a community or junior college into the Bachelor of International Studies program. Financial need may be considered. Recipient must maintain satisfactory academic progress and continue to demonstrate financial need to retain scholarship. Awarded every year. Award may be used only at sponsoring institution.
Contact: Mary Henderson, Financial Aid Officer, (802) 258-3280.

837   Dr. Casimir Kierzkowski Scholarship

Kosciuszko Foundation
15 East 65th Street
New York, NY 10021
(212) 734-2130
Average award: $1,000
Number of awards: 1
Deadline: January 15
Majors/Fields: Polish studies
Criteria: Applicant must be a U.S. citizen of Polish descent. In the application or request for application, the name of the award being applied for should not be specified; this determination is made by the scholarship committee. Awarded every year.
Contact: Scholarships.

838   E. Catherine Barclay Scholarship

University of Calgary
Department of Financial Aid
2500 University Drive, NW
Calgary, Alberta, CN T2N 1N4
(403) 220-7872, (403) 282-2999 (fax)
Average award: $3,000
Number of awards: 1
Deadline: February 15
College level: Sophomore, Junior, Senior
Criteria: Award is for a U of Calgary student to pursue studies by enrolling full time at the U de Bourgogne in Dijon, France. Selection is based upon academic merit, ability in oral French, and extracurricular activities demonstrating good citizenship. Awarded every year. Award may be used only at sponsoring institution.
Contact: J. Van Housen, Director of Student Awards/Financial Aid.

839   Endowment for Biblical Research (Boston) and ASOR Summer Research Grants and Travel Scholarships

American Schools of Oriental Research (ASOR)
656 Beacon Street
Fifth Floor
Boston, MA 02215-2010
Maximum award: $1,500
Maximum number of awards: 9
Minimum number of awards: 9
Deadline: February 1
College level: Freshman, Sophomore, Junior, Senior, Graduate, Doctoral, Post-doctoral
Majors/Fields: Archaeology, anthropology, linguistics, natural sciences
Criteria: Award is for travel or research to the Holy Land on archaeological or excavation projects, textual or linguistic study, anthropology or natural sciences studies, or interpretation or analysis of excavated material and manuscripts. Research in biblical periods is encouraged. Awarded every year.
Contact: Pamela Turner, Administrative Assistant.

840   Fellowships for the Bosphorus Summer Language Program in Advanced Turkish

American Research Institute in Turkey (ARIT)
c/o University Museum
33rd and Spruce Streets
Philadelphia, PA 19104-6324
(215) 898-3474, (215) 898-0657 (fax)
leinwand@sas.upenn.edu
Award: Travel expenses, fees, and stipend
Maximum number of awards: 12
Minimum number of awards: 10
Deadline: February 15
College level: Junior, Senior, Graduate, Doctoral
Criteria: Applicant must be a U.S. citizen or permanent resident, currently enrolled in a degree program with a minimum "B" grade average and at least two years of Turkish language study or equivalent, and must pass proficiency exam. Awarded every year.
Contact: Sheila Andrew, Washington University, Campus Box 1230, One Brookings Drive, St. Louis, MO 63130-4899, (314) 935-5166, sandrew@artsci.wustl.edu.

841   Irish Way Scholarship

Irish American Cultural Institute
Irish Way
433 Raymond Boulevard
Newark, NJ 07105
Maximum award: $1,000
Number of awards: 50
College level: Freshman, Sophomore
Majors/Fields: Irish studies
Criteria: Selection is based upon application information, recommendation from teacher(s)/counselor, and grades.
Contact: Scholarships.

842   Jennifer C. Groot Fellowship in the Archaeology of Jordan

American Schools of Oriental Research (ASOR)
656 Beacon Street
Fifth Floor
Boston, MA 02215-2010
Maximum award: $1,500
Number of awards: 2
Deadline: February 1
College level: Junior, Senior, Graduate, Doctoral
Criteria: Applicant must be a U.S. or Canadian citizen with a desire to participate in an archaeological excavation in Jordan. Awarded every year.
Contact: Carrie S. Nee, ASOR U.S. Representative.

843   King Olav V Norwegian-American Heritage Fund

Sons of Norway Foundation
1455 West Lake Street
Minneapolis, MN 55408
(612) 827-3611, (612) 827-0658 (fax)
Average award: $580
Maximum award: $1,500
Minimum award: $250
Number of awards: 15
Deadline: March 1
College level: Freshman, Sophomore, Junior, Senior, Graduate, Doctoral
Majors/Fields: Norwegian studies
Criteria: Applicant must be an American, age 18 or older, who demonstrates a sincere interest in the Norwegian heritage or a Norwegian who demonstrates an interest in American heritage. Applicant must further the study of these heritages at a recognized educational institution. Selection is based upon GPA, participation in school and community activities, work experience, education and career goals, and personal and school references. Awarded every year.
Contact: Liv Dahl, Administrative Director, Heritage Programs.

844   National Welsh-American Foundation Exchange Scholarship

National Welsh-American Foundation
24 Essex Road
Scotch Plains, NJ 07076
Maximum award: $5,000
Number of awards: 1
Deadline: March 1
Majors/Fields: Welsh studies
Contact: Scholarships.

845   Scholarship for Study in Japan

The Japan-America Society of Washington
1020 19th Street, NW, LL #40
Washington, DC 20036
(202) 833-2210, (202) 833-2456 (fax)
Maximum award: $6,000
Deadline: March 1
Criteria: Applicant must have completed at least one year of college study in the U.S., started studying the Japanese language and culture, and mobilized substantial financial support. Selection is based upon scholastic achievement, motivation, and financial need. Awarded every year.
Contact: Scholarships.

846   SIT Fund

School for International Training (SIT)
P.O. Box 676
Kipling Road
Brattleboro, VT 05302
(802) 257-7751, (802) 258-3500 (fax)
admissions.sit@worldlearning.org
http://www.worldlearning/sit.html
Average award: $2,000
Maximum award: $4,000
Minimum award: $500
Number of awards: 62
Deadline: April 30 (fall semester); October 15 (spring semester)
College level: Undergraduate
Criteria: Applicant must be a participant in the semester-abroad program. Financial need is considered. Awarded every year. Award may be used only at sponsoring institution.
Contact: Mary Henderson, Financial Aid Officer, (802) 258-3280.

847   Student Diversity Scholarship

School for International Training (SIT)
P.O. Box 676
Kipling Road
Brattleboro, VT 05302
(802) 257-7751, (802) 258-3500 (fax)
admissions.sit@worldlearning.org
http://www.worldlearning/sit.html
Average award: $1,000
Maximum award: $2,000
Minimum award: $500
Number of awards: 19
Deadline: April 1
College level: Degree candidate
Criteria: Applicant must have a world view or life experience which can enhance the diversity of the school's learning community and must be enrolled in a degree program. Financial need may be considered. Recipient must maintain satisfactory academic progress and continue to demonstrate financial need to retain award. Awarded every year. Award may be used only at sponsoring institution.
Contact: Mary Henderson, Financial Aid Officer, (802) 258-3280.

848   Study Abroad Scholarship

University of Utah
Financial Aid and Scholarships Office
105 Student Services Building
Salt Lake City, UT 84112
(801) 581-6211
Maximum award: $1,500
Deadline: March 7 (summer and fall quarters); November 21 (winter and spring quarters)
College level: Sophomore, Junior, Senior
Criteria: Applicant must be a matriculated, full-time student with at least 36 credit hours and a minimum 3.0 GPA. Award is for study abroad. Preference is given to applicants who will be sophomores or juniors during the time abroad and to applicants who have not previously received the scholarship. Awarded every year. Award may be used only at sponsoring institution.
Contact: International Center, 159 Olpin Union, Salt Lake City, UT 84112, (801) 581-5849.

849   Year Abroad Program at Universities in Poland

Kosciuszko Foundation
15 East 65th Street
New York, NY 10021
(212) 734-2130
Award: Tuition, housing and monthly stipend for living expenses
Deadline: January 15
College level: Junior, Senior, Graduate, Doctoral
Majors/Fields: Polish studies
Criteria: Applicant must be an American student wishing to pursue an undergraduate course of Polish language, literature, history, and culture at a university in Poland. Students enrolled in an M.A. or Ph.D. program may apply if they are not at the dissertation level. Selection is based upon academic performance and motivation for pursuing studies in Poland. Awarded every year.
Contact: Scholarships.

English/Literature/Writing—

850   Americanism Essay Scholarship

American Legion–California Auxiliary
Auxiliary Department Headquarters
401 Van Ness #113
San Francisco, CA 94102-4586
Average award: $1,000
Number of awards: 1
Criteria: First prize class 3 (grades 10-12) Americanism essay contest. Awarded every year.
Contact: Essay Scholarships.

851   Anthem Essay Contest

Ayn Rand Institute
Essay Contest Information
P.O. Box 6004 EF
Inglewood, CA 90312
(310) 306-9232
Maximum award: $1,000
Number of awards: 31
Deadline: March 30
College level: High school freshmen and sophomores
Criteria: Applicant must enter essay contest. The winning essay must demonstrate an outstanding grasp of the philosophic meaning of Ayn Rand's novelette *Anthem*. Awarded every year.
Contact: David Bomardier, Essay Contest Coordinator.

852   Art or Writing Award

Scholastic Inc.
555 Broadway
New York, NY 10012
(212) 343-6493
Maximum award: $5,000
Number of awards: 500
Deadline: January 1
College level: Students in grades 7-12
Criteria: Selection is based upon accomplishment in art, creative writing, or photography. Awarded every year.
Contact: Scholastic Art or Writing Awards.

853 A.T.J. Cairns Memorial Undergraduate Scholarship
University of Calgary
Department of Financial Aid
2500 University Drive, NW
Calgary, Alberta, CN T2N 1N4
(403) 220-7872, (403) 282-2999 (fax)
Average award: $2,000
Number of awards: 4
Deadline: June 15
College level: Freshman, Sophomore, Junior, Senior
Majors/Fields: Creative writing, English literature
Criteria: Applicant must be registered full time with a major or minor in English. Two awards are for men and two for women. Selection is based upon academic merit in creative writing and English literature. Awarded every year. Award may be used only at sponsoring institution.
Contact: J. Van Housen, Director of Student Awards/Financial Aid.

854 Buford Boone Memorial Scholarship
The University of Alabama
Box 870162
Tuscaloosa, AL 35487-0162
(205) 348-6756
Maximum award: $1,300
Number of awards: 1
Deadline: January 25
College level: Junior, Senior
Majors/Fields: English
Criteria: Applicant must have completed at least nine credit hours of English courses with a minimum 3.2 GPA and have a minimum 3.0 GPA overall. Awarded every year. Award may be used only at sponsoring institution.
Contact: Department of English, Box 870244, Tuscaloosa, AL 35487-0244.

855 Dr. William Calvert Memorial Scholarship
Jacksonville State University
Jacksonville, AL 36265-9982
(205) 782-5006
Average award: Full tuition
College level: Junior, Senior
Majors/Fields: English
Criteria: Awarded every year. Award may be used only at sponsoring institution.
Contact: Head of English Department.

856 Dog Writers' Educational Trust Scholarship
Dog Writers' Educational Trust
c/o Mary Ellen Tarman
P.O. Box E
Hummelstown, PA 17036-0199
(717) 566-7030
Average award: $1,000
Number of awards: 4
Deadline: December 31
College level: Freshman, Sophomore, Junior, Senior, Graduate, Doctoral
Criteria: Applicant must demonstrate involvement in dog-related activities. Selection is based upon dog-related activities (40%), academic performance (25%), financial need (20%), and future plans (15%). A $25 application fee is required. Awarded every year.
Contact: Mary Ellen Tarman, Executive Secretary.

857 Fountainhead College Scholarship Essay Contest
Ayn Rand Institute
Essay Contest Information
P.O. Box 6004 EF
Inglewood, CA 90312
(310) 306-9232
Maximum award: $5,000
Number of awards: 16
Deadline: April 15
College level: High school juniors and seniors
Criteria: Applicant must enter essay contest. The winning essay must demonstrate an outstanding grasp of the philosophical and psychological meaning of Ayn Rand's novel *The Fountainhead.* Awarded every year.
Contact: David Bombardier, Essay Contest Coordinator.

858 Frank V. Cosby Memorial English Scholarship
The University of Alabama
Box 870162
Tuscaloosa, AL 35487-0162
(205) 348-6756
Maximum award: $1,500
Number of awards: 1
Deadline: January 25
College level: Junior, Senior
Majors/Fields: English
Criteria: Applicant must have completed at least nine credit hours of English courses with a minimum 3.2 GPA and have a minimum 3.0 GPA overall. Awarded every or every other year. Award may be used only at sponsoring institution.
Contact: Department of English, Box 870244, Tuscaloosa, AL 35487-0244.

859 Guideposts Young Writer's Contest
Guideposts
16 East 34th Street
New York, NY 10016
(212) 251-8100, (212) 684-0689 (fax)
Maximum award: $6,000
Number of awards: 8
Deadline: Late November
College level: Freshman
Criteria: Applicant must be a high school junior or senior who submits an original first-person story of a memorable or moving actual experience. Selection is based upon the sincerity, writing ability, and story value of the manuscript. Recipients must plan to attend college after high school, and awards are to be used within a five-year period as college scholarships only. Write for official contest rules in September. Awarded every year.
Contact: Surujnie Pooran, Secretary.

860 Houk Scholarship
Hamline University
1536 Hewitt Avenue
St. Paul, MN 55104
(612) 641-2207
Average award: $2,000
Number of awards: 1
Deadline: January 20
College level: Freshman
Criteria: Applicant must rank in top tenth of class and have a minimum ACT English score of 25 (SAT I verbal score of 560). Awarded to applicant with exceptional writing ability and potential for a writing career. Major in English is not required but is strongly recommended. Renewable for up to three years. Awarded every year. Award may be used only at sponsoring institution.
Contact: Brian Peterson, Senior Associate Director of Undergraduate Admission.

861   Languages and Literature Award

University of West Alabama
Station Four
Livingston, AL 35470
(205) 652-3400, (205) 652-3522 (fax)
http://www.westal.edu
Maximum award: $1,500
Deadline: April 15
College level: Junior, Senior, Graduate
Majors/Fields: English
Criteria: Renewable for recipient who has completed 96 quarter hours. Awarded every year. Award may be used only at sponsoring institution.
Contact: Richard Hester, Director of Admissions, (205) 652-3400, extension 3578, rth@uwamail.westmail.edu.

862   Lee David Black and Florence Weinberg Black Memorial Scholarship

The University of Alabama
Box 870162
Tuscaloosa, AL 35487-0162
(205) 348-6756
Maximum award: $1,500
Maximum number of awards: 3
Minimum number of awards: 1
Deadline: January 25
College level: Junior, Senior
Majors/Fields: English
Criteria: Applicant must have completed at least nine credit hours of English courses with a minimum 3.2 GPA and have a minimum 3.0 GPA overall. Awarded every year. Award may be used only at sponsoring institution.
Contact: Department of English, Box 870244, Tuscaloosa, AL 35487-0244.

863   Letters Scholarship for Mature Women

National League of American Pen Women, Inc. (NLAPW)
1300 Seventeenth Street, NW
Washington, DC 20036
(717) 225-3023
Average award: $1,000
Number of awards: 1
Deadline: January 15
Criteria: Applicant must be a woman age 35 or over and must submit background. Award is given on a rotating basis for novel; short story, essay, or drama; and poetry. Awarded in even-numbered years.
Contact: Scholarships.

864   National Peace Essay Contest

United States Institute of Peace
1550 M Street, NW
Suite 700
Washington, DC 20005-1708
(202) 457-1700, (202) 429-6063 (fax)
heather_kerr@usip.org
http://www.usip.org
Maximum award: $5,000
Number of awards: 53
Deadline: Varies
College level: Freshman
Criteria: Applicant must write a 1,500-word essay on a topic dealing with international conflict resolution. Specific topic changes yearly.
Contact: Heather Kerr-Stewart, Education Specialist, heather_kerr@usip.org.

865   O.B. Emerson Endowed Scholarship

The University of Alabama
Box 870162
Tuscaloosa, AL 35487-0162
(205) 348-6756
Maximum award: $1,500
Maximum number of awards: 2
Minimum number of awards: 1
Deadline: January 25
College level: Junior, Senior
Majors/Fields: English
Criteria: Applicant must have completed at least nine credit hours of English courses with a minimum 3.2 GPA and have a minimum 3.0 GPA overall. Awarded every year. Award may be used only at sponsoring institution.
Contact: Department of English, Box 870244, Tuscaloosa, AL 35487-0244.

866   Pablo Neruda Prize for Poetry

NIMROD International
600 South College Ave
Tulsa, OK 74104-3126
(918) 584-3333, (918) 582-2787 (fax)
Maximum award: $1,000
Number of awards: 4
Deadline: April 17
Criteria: Awarded every year.
Contact: Awards, 2210 South Main Street, Tulsa, OK 74110-1190.

867   Shelley Hoffman Scholarship

Maharishi University of Management
1000 North 4th Street, DB 1132
Fairfield, IA 52557-1132
(515) 472-1156
Average award: $2,000
Maximum award: $4,000
Minimum award: $1,000
Number of awards: 2
Deadline: April 1
College level: Sophomore, Junior, Senior
Majors/Fields: Creative writing
Criteria: Awarded to applicant who has cerebral palsy (major in creative writing not required) or to applicant on the basis of a portfolio of recent work. Recipient must maintain high GPA and have literature department approval to retain scholarship. Awarded every year. Award may be used only at sponsoring institution.
Contact: Tom Rowe, Director of Financial Aid, (515) 472-1133.

868   Weber English Scholarship

Holy Names College
3500 Mountain Boulevard
Oakland, CA 94619-1699
(510) 436-1327
Average award: $2,000
Number of awards: 1
Deadline: March 2
College level: Freshman
Majors/Fields: English
Criteria: Applicant must submit essay for competition. Awarded every year. Award may be used only at sponsoring institution.
Contact: Paula J. Lehrberger, Director of Financial Aid.

869   Webster's New World Writing Competition

Webster's New World Dictionaries
1633 Broadway-Sixth Floor
New York, NY 10019
(212) 654-8212, (212) 654-4711 (fax)
Claire-Smith@Prenhall.com
Average award: $1,000
Number of awards: 2
Deadline: March 1
College level: High school juniors and seniors
Criteria: Applicant must be a resident of the U.S. or Canada and submit an original essay on competition's subject. Awarded every year.
Contact: Claire Smith, Associate Marketing Manager.

870   William March Memorial Scholarship

The University of Alabama
Box 870162
Tuscaloosa, AL 35487-0162
(205) 348-6756
Maximum award: $1,500
Maximum number of awards: 3
Minimum number of awards: 1
Deadline: January 25
College level: Junior, Senior
Majors/Fields: English
Criteria: Applicant must have completed at least nine credit hours of English courses with a minimum 3.2 GPA and have a minimum 3.0 GPA overall. Awarded every year. Award may be used only at sponsoring institution.
Contact: Department of English, Box 870244, Tuscaloosa, AL 35487-0244.

871   Wright Bryan Memorial Fund Scholarship

Clemson University
G-01 Sikes Hall
Clemson, SC 29634-5123
(803) 656-2280
Maximum award: $1,500
Number of awards: 1
Deadline: March 1
College level: Freshman, Sophomore, Junior, Senior
Majors/Fields: English
Criteria: Applicant must have a minimum 2.5 GPA. Renewable if recipient maintains satisfactory GPA and completes at least 12 credits per semester. Awarded every year. Award may be used only at sponsoring institution.
Contact: Scholarships.

872   Writing Scholarship

Jacksonville State University
Jacksonville, AL 36265-9982
(205) 782-5006
Average award: Full tuition
College level: Freshman, Sophomore, Junior, Senior
Criteria: Awarded every year. Award may be used only at sponsoring institution.
Contact: Head of English Department.

873   Yvonne Duffy Fund Scholarship

Texas A&M University–Kingsville
Scholarships
Box 116
Kingsville, TX 78363
(512) 593-3907, (512) 593-2991 (fax)
http://www.tamuk.edu
Average award: $2,000
Number of awards: No limit
Deadline: July 15 and March 17
College level: Freshman, Sophomore, Junior, Senior
Majors/Fields: English
Criteria: Applicant must rank in top quarter of graduating class and have a minimum combined SAT I score of 970 (composite ACT score of 21). Financial need is considered. Renewable if recipient maintains a minimum 2.8 GPA. Award may be used only at sponsoring institution.
Contact: School Relations.

Foreign Languages——————

874   American Association of Teachers of German Testing and Awards Program

American Association of Teachers of German, Inc.
112 Haddontowne Court #104
Cherry Hill, NJ 08034
(609) 795-5553
Award: All-expenses-paid study trip to Germany
Number of awards: 54
Deadline: February 26
Majors/Fields: German
Criteria: Applicant must score above the 90th percentile to be eligibile for a one-month study trip to Germany. Selection is based upon application, interview, and essay competition. Awarded every year.
Contact: Awards Program.

875   Eurocentres Scholarships

Foundation for European Language and Education
Centres Schools
Eurocentres
Seestrasse 247
Ch-8038 Zurich, SW
(41)1 485 52 51, (41)1 482 50 54 (fax)
100632.136@compuserve.com
http://www.clark.net/pub/eurocent/home.htm
Average award: $1,500
Maximum award: $2,000
Minimum award: $500
Majors/Fields: Foreign languages
Criteria: Applicant must be between ages 18 and 30, have a good previous knowlege of the foreign language to be studied, and be enrolled in a Eurocentres program. Award may be used only at Eurocentres' European Language and Educational Centres.
Contact: Eric Steenbergen, Scholarship Department.

876   Prizes for Best Syllabi in German Studies

German Academic Exchange Service (DAAD)
950 Third Avenue, 19th Floor
New York, NY 10022
(212) 758-3223, (212) 755-5780 (fax)
daadny@daad.org
http://www.daad.org
Average award: $1,000
Deadline: March 1
Majors/Fields: German studies
Criteria: Prizes are given for innovative interdisciplinary or comparative approaches to the teaching of German studies, including language, politics, history, literature, cinema, anthropology, culture, art, music, women's studies, and Jewish studies.
Contact: Prof. Sander L. Gilman, Department of German Studies, 194 Goldwin Smith Hall, Cornell University, Ithaca, NY 14853, (202) 332-9312, aicgsdoc@jhunix.hcf.jhu.edu.

877   Summer Language Courses Grant

German Academic Exchange Service (DAAD)
950 Third Avenue
19th Floor
New York, NY 10022
(212) 758-3223, (212) 755-5780 (fax)
daadny@daad.org
http://www.daad.org
Maximum award: Tuition, fees, living expenses
Minimum award: Partial tuition, fees, living expenses
Deadline: January 31
College level: Junior, Senior, Graduate, Faculty
Criteria: Applicant must have a minimum of two years of college-level German or equivalent. There are five programs of study; specific requirements vary for each. Programs range in duration from three to eight weeks, and consist of intensive language courses at various sites in Germany.
Contact: Barbara Motyka, Program Officer, daadny@daad.org.

History

878   DAR American History Scholarship

National Society of the Daughters of the American Revolution (NSDAR)
NSDAR Administration Building, Office of the Committees
1776 D Street, NW
Washington, DC 20006-5392
(202) 879-3292
Average award: $1,000
Maximum award: $2,000
Number of awards: 3
Deadline: February 1
College level: Freshman
Majors/Fields: American history
Criteria: Applicant must be a U.S. citizen and submit a letter of sponsorship from a local DAR chapter. Selection is based upon academic excellence, commitment to the field of American history, and financial need. All inquiries must include a self-addressed, stamped envelope. Annual transcript review and approval are required to retain scholarship. Awarded every year.
Contact: Administrative Assistant, Scholarships.

879   Frederick Jackson Turner Award

Organization of American Historians
112 North Bryan Street
Bloomington, IN 47408-4199
(812) 855-9852, (812) 855-0696 (fax)
oah@oah.indiana.edu
http://www.indiana.edu/~
Average award: $1,000
Deadline: September 1
Criteria: Award is for an author's first book on some significant phase of American history. Awarded every year.
Contact: Kara Hamm, Award and Prize Committee Coordinator, kara@oah.indiana.edu.

880   Hazel Butler Garms U.S. History Scholarship

Mesa State College
Financial Aid Department
P.O. Box 2647
Grand Junction, CO 81502
(970) 248-1396
Average award: $1,500
Number of awards: 1
College level: Junior, Senior
Majors/Fields: History
Criteria: Applicant must have a minimum 3.0 GPA. Awarded every year. Award may be used only at sponsoring institution.
Contact: School of Humanities and Social Sciences.

881   Merle Curti Award

Organization of American Historians
112 North Bryan Street
Bloomington, IN 47408-4199
(812) 855-9852, (812) 855-0696 (fax)
oah@oah.indiana.edu
http://www.indiana.edu/~
Average award: $1,000
Deadline: October 1
Majors/Fields: American History
Criteria: Award recognizes books in the field of American social and intellectual history. Awarded every year.
Contact: Kara Hamm, Award and Prize Committee Coordinator, kara@oah.indiana.edu.

882   Opal R. and Opal A. Lovett Scholarship

Jacksonville State University
Jacksonville, AL 36265-9982
(205) 782-5006
Average award: $1,320
Deadline: March 15
College level: Sophomore, Junior, Senior
Majors/Fields: Art, English, history
Criteria: Applicant must have a minimum 2.5 GPA. Awarded every year. Award may be used only at sponsoring institution.
Contact: Student Financial Aid Office.

883   Presidio La Bahia Award

Sons of the Republic of Texas
1717 8th Street
Bay City, TX 77414
(409) 245-6644, (409) 245-6644 (fax)
srttexas@tgn.net
http://www.tgn.net/~srttexas
Average award: $1,200
Number of awards: 3
Deadline: September 1
College level: Freshman, Sophomore, Junior, Senior, Graduate, Doctoral
Criteria: Applicant must have published within the last calender year a piece related to any aspect of the Spanish colonial period in Texas. Awarded every year.
Contact: Melinda Williams, Administrative Assistant, srttexas@tgn.net.

884   Ray Allen Billington Prize

Organization of American Historians
112 North Bryan Street
Bloomington, IN 47408-4199
(812) 855-9852, (812) 855-0696 (fax)
oah@oah.indiana.edu
http://www.indiana.edu/~
Average award: $1,000
Deadline: October 1
Majors/Fields: American History
Criteria: Awarded for the best book in American frontier history. Awarded in even-numbered years.
Contact: Kara Hamm, Award and Prize Committee Coordinator, kara@oah.indiana.edu.

885 Richard W. Leopold Prize

Organization of American Historians
112 North Bryan Street
Bloomington, IN 47408-4199
(812) 855-9852, (812) 855-0696 (fax)
oah@oah.indiana.edu
http://www.indiana.edu/~
Average award: $1,500
Deadline: September 1
Majors/Fields: American history
Criteria: Prize is given for the best book written by a historian connected with federal, state, or municipal government, in the areas of foreign policy, military affairs broadly construed, the historical activities of the federal government, or biography in one of the above areas. Awarded in odd-numbered years.
Contact: Kara Hamm, Award and Prize Committee Coordinator, kara@oah.indiana.edu.

886 Summerfield G. Roberts Award

Sons of the Republic of Texas
1717 8th Street
Bay City, TX 77414
(409) 245-6644, (409) 245-6644 (fax)
srttexas@tgn.net
http://www.tgn.net/~srttexas
Average award: $2,500
Number of awards: 1
Deadline: January 15
College level: Freshman, Sophomore, Junior, Senior, Graduate, Doctoral
Criteria: Award is to encourage literary effort and research about historical events and personalities during the days of the Republic of Texas, 1836-1846, and to stimulate interest in this period. Manuscript must be written or published during the calendar year for which the award is given; it may be either fiction or nonfiction, poetry, essay, play, short story, novel, or biography. Competition is open to all writers everywhere. Awarded every year.
Contact: Melinda Williams, Administrative Assistant.

887 Texas History Essay Contest

Sons of the Republic of Texas
1717 8th Street
Bay City, TX 77414
(409) 245-6644, (409) 245-6644 (fax)
srttexas@tgn.net
http://www.tgn.net/~srttexas
Maximum award: $3,000
Number of awards: 3
Deadline: February 3
College level: Freshman
Criteria: Applicant must submit a 1,500- to 2,000-word essay on Texas history. Selection is based upon depth of research into Texas history, originality of thought and expression, and organization. Awarded every year.
Contact: Melinda Williams, Administrative Assistant.

888 Woodruff Traveling Fellowship

Archaeological Institute of America
656 Beacon Street
4th Floor
Boston, MA 02215-2010
(617) 353-9361, (617) 353-6550 (fax)
aia@bu.edu
http://csaws.brynmawr.edu:443/aia.html
Average award: $5,000
Number of awards: 1
Deadline: November 1
College level: Doctoral
Majors/Fields: Archaeology
Criteria: Award is for the support of dissertation research in Italy and the western Mediterranean. Applicant must have completed all Ph.D. requirements except for the dissertation prior to application. Awarded every year.
Contact: Fellowships, 656 Beacon Street, 4th floor, Boston, MA 02215-2010, aia@bu.edu.

Humanities————————————————

889 Clara and Arleigh B. Williamson Scholarship

City University of New York, The College of Staten Island
2800 Victory Boulevard
Staten Island, NY 10314-9881
(718) 982-2259
Average award: Full tuition
Deadline: None
College level: Freshman
Majors/Fields: Humanities
Criteria: Applicant must be a graduate of a Staten Island high school, be enrolled full time, have a minimum 3.5 GPA, and be involved in community/school service. Transcript and two letters of recommendation from teachers are required. Financial need is not a major consideration. Awarded every year. Award may be used only at sponsoring institution.
Contact: Office of Student Recruitment and Scholarships.

890 DAAD-ACLS Grants for the Humanities and Social Sciences

German Academic Exchange Service (DAAD)
950 Third Avenue, 19th Floor
New York, NY 10022
(212) 758-3223, (212) 755-5780 (fax)
daadny@daad.org
http://www.daad.org
Award: Tuition and living expenses
College level: Scholars from U.S. universities
Majors/Fields: Humanities, social sciences
Criteria: Award is for joint research projects with German researchers. Awarded every year.
Contact: Steven Wheatley, American Council of Learned Societies, 228 East 45th Street, New York, NY 10017-3398, (212) 697-1505, colette@acls.org.

891 Dr. Stanislas Chylinski Scholarship

Kosciuszko Foundation
15 East 65th Street
New York, NY 10021
(212) 734-2130
Average award: $1,000
Number of awards: 1
Deadline: January 15
Majors/Fields: Humanities, Social Sciences
Criteria: Applicant must be a U.S. citizen of Polish descent. In the application or request for application, the name of the award being applied for should not be specified; this determination is made by the scholarship committee. Awarded every year.
Contact: Scholarships.

892 Dunbar Scholarship

Denison University
Box H
Granville, OH 43023
(614) 587-6276, 800-DENISON, (614) 587-6306 (fax)
admissions@denison.edu
http://www.denison.edu
Average award: Full tuition
Number of awards: 1
Deadline: January 1
College level: Freshman
Criteria: Applicant must be an outstanding student in the humanities and must meet criteria for Honors Program. Essay, teacher recommendations, and interview or campus visitation program are required. Minimum GPA is required for renewal. Awarded every year. Award may be used only at sponsoring institution.
Contact: Kevin Freeman, Scholarships, (614) 587-6791.

893   George E. Mylonas Scholarship

Washington University
One Brookings Drive
Campus Box 1089
St. Louis, MO 63130
(314) 935-6000 or (800) 638-0700
Average award: Full tuition plus $1,000 stipend
Number of awards: 3
Deadline: January 15
College level: Freshman
Majors/Fields: Humanities
Criteria: Selection is based upon academic merit without regard to financial need. Application is required. Satisfactory academic performance is required to retain scholarship. Awarded every year. Award may be used only at sponsoring institution.
Contact: Office of Undergraduate Admissions.

894   International Exchange, Study, or Work Abroad Scholarship

School for International Training (SIT)
P.O. Box 676
Kipling Road
Brattleboro, VT 05302
(802) 257-7751, (802) 258-3500 (fax)
admissions.sit@worldlearning.org
http://www.worldlearning/sit.html
Average award: $1,000
Maximum award: $2,000
Number of awards: 6
Deadline: April 1
College level: Bachelor's degree candidate
Majors/Fields: World issues
Criteria: Applicant must have been a participant in an international exchange, study, or work abroad program. Financial need may be considered. Applicant must be enrolled in a degree program. Applicant must maintain satisfactory academic progress and continue to demonstrate financial need. Awarded every year. Award may be used only at sponsoring institution.
Contact: Mary Henderson, Financial Aid Officer, (802) 258-3280.

895   Kosciuszko Foundation New York Scholarship

Kosciuszko Foundation
15 East 65th Street
New York, NY 10021
(212) 734-2130
Average award: $1,000
Deadline: January 15
Criteria: Applicant must be a member or the dependent of a member of the Brooklyn Polish National Alliance. Awarded every year.
Contact: Scholarships.

896   Larry Temple Scholarship

University of Texas at Austin
P.O. Box 7758
UT Station
Austin, TX 78713-7758
(512) 475-6200, (512) 475-6296 (fax)
finaid@www.utexas.edu
http://www.utexas.edu/student/finaid
Average award: $7,000
Number of awards: 5
Deadline: December 1
College level: Freshman, Sophomore, Junior, Senior
Criteria: Preference is given to applicant majoring in liberal arts, fine arts, or social work and to Texas residents. Awarded every year. Award may be used only at sponsoring institution.
Contact: Joe Wilcox, Scholarship Coordinator, (512) 475-6282.

897   Rex Howell Memorial Fund

Mesa State College
Financial Aid Department
P.O. Box 2647
Grand Junction, CO 81502
(970) 248-1396
Maximum award: Full tuition, fees, book allowance, living allowance
College level: Junior, Senior
Majors/Fields: Humanities/fine arts
Criteria: Applicant must have a minimum 3.0 GPA and demonstrate financial need. Awarded every year. Award may be used only at sponsoring institution.
Contact: School of Humanities and Social Sciences.

898   Sidney Hillman Prize

Sidney Hillman Foundation Incorporated
15 Union Square
New York, NY 10003
(212) 242-0700
Average award: $1,000
Number of awards: 6
Deadline: January 16
Criteria: Award is given for outstanding contributions dealing with the themes of individual civil liberties, improved race relations, a strengthened labor movement, the advancement of social welfare and economic security, greater world understanding, and related problems. Contributions may be in the fields of daily or periodical journalism, non-fiction, radio, and television. Only work appearing in the year prior to the deadline is eligible for consideration. Unpublished manuscripts of any kind are not eligible.
Contact: Sidney Hillman Foundation.

Religion/Theology/ Philosophy

899   International Fellowship in Jewish Studies

Memorial Foundation for Jewish Culture
15 East 26th Street
New York, NY 10010
(212) 679-4074
Average award: $2,500
Maximum award: $4,000
Minimum award: $1,000
Deadline: October 31
College level: Any qualified scholar, researcher, or artist proposing a project in a field of Jewish specialization
Majors/Fields: Jewish studies
Criteria: Award is to assist well-qualified individuals in carrying out an independent scholarly, literary, or art project in a field of Jewish specialization which makes a significant contribution to the understanding, preservation, enhancement, or transmission of Jewish culture. Recipient must request renewal in writing. Ordinarily, no more than two grants are made to one individual. Awarded every year.
Contact: Fellowships.

900 International Scholarship for Community Service

Memorial Foundation for Jewish Culture
15 East 26th Street
New York, NY 10010
(212) 679-4074
Average award: $2,000
Minimum award: $1,000
Number of awards: 50
Deadline: November 30
College level: Senior, Graduate, Doctoral
Majors/Fields: Jewish studies
Criteria: Award is to assist well-qualified individuals train for careers in the rabbinate, Jewish education, and social work, and as religious functionaries in Diaspora Jewish communities in need of such personnel. Applicant must undertake training in chosen field in a recognized yeshiva, teacher training seminary, school of social work, university, or other educational institution, and commit to serve in a community of need for two or three years. Students planning to serve in the U.S., Canada, or Israel are not eligible. Reapplication is required to retain scholarship. Awarded every year.
Contact: Dr. Jerry Hochbaum, Executive Vice President.

901 Light Ministries Scholarship

Liberty University
1971 University Boulevard
Lynchburg, VA 24502-2269
(800) 543-5317
Average award: $6,575
Number of awards: 21
Deadline: March 31
College level: Freshman, Sophomore, Junior, Senior
Criteria: Applicant must have an interest in outreach ministries. Scholarship is renewable. Awarded every year. Award may be used only at sponsoring institution.
Contact: Director, Light Ministries, (800) 522-6225, extension 2641.

902 Samuel Robinson Award

Presbyterian Church USA
Office of Financial Aid for Studies
100 Witherspoon Street
Louisville, KY 40202-1396
(502) 569-5776, (502) 569-8766 (fax)
Average award: $1,000
Deadline: April 1
College level: Junior, Senior
Criteria: Applicant must be a full-time junior or senior at a Presbyterian-related college or university. Applicant must successfully recite the answers of the Westminster Shorter Catechism and write a 2,000-word original essay on a related assigned topic. Awarded every year. Award may be used only at Presbyterian schools.
Contact: Scholarship.

903 Word of Life Scholarship

Liberty University
1971 University Boulevard
Lynchburg, VA 24502-2269
(800) 543-5317
Average award: $6,000
Number of awards: 411
Deadline: June 1
College level: Sophomore, Junior
Criteria: Applicant must be a graduate of the Word of Life Bible Inst in New York. Satisfactory academic progress is required to retain scholarship. Awarded every year. Award may be used only at sponsoring institution.
Contact: Admissions Representative.

904 Youth Scholarship

Liberty University
1971 University Boulevard
Lynchburg, VA 24502-2269
(800) 543-5317
Average award: $5,563
Number of awards: 67
Deadline: May 1
College level: Freshman, Sophomore, Junior, Senior
Criteria: Applicant must demonstrate leadership ability and/or participate on a youth ministry team. Scholarship is renewable. Awarded every year. Award may be used only at sponsoring institution.
Contact: Center for Youth Ministries, (800) 522-6225, extension 2310.

Medicine/Nursing

Dentistry

905   Dental Student Scholarship and Minority Dental Student Scholarship

American Dental Association (ADA) Endowment and Assistance Fund, Inc.
211 East Chicago Avenue, 17th Floor
Chicago, IL 60611-2678
(312) 440-2567
Average award: $2,500
Number of awards: 50
Deadline: June 15, July 1 (minority scholarship)
College level: Second-year dental students
Majors/Fields: Dentistry
Criteria: Applicant must be a U.S. citizen and have a minimum 3.0 GPA. Minority applicant must be African-American, Hispanic, or Native American and have a minimum 2.5 GPA. Selection is based upon financial need, academic achievement, and personal and professional goals. Recipient must reapply for renewal. Awarded every year.
Contact: Marsha Mountz, ADA Endowment Fund.

906   Dr. Charles A. Vernale Student Loan Award

Connecticut State Dental Association
62-64 Rush Street
Hartford, CT 06106
(203) 278-5550
Average award: $2,000
Number of awards: 1
Deadline: June 30
College level: Dental students
Majors/Fields: Dentistry
Criteria: Applicant must be a Connecticut resident with a predoctoral degree in dental medicine. Awarded every year.
Contact: Noel Bishop, Executive Director.

907   Dr. Glayton Wilson Grier Scholarship

Dr. G. Wilson Grier Scholarship
c/o Peter K. Schaeffer, DDS
1071 South Governors Avenue
Dover, DE 19904
(302) 674-1080, (302) 674-1046 (fax)
Average award: $1,000
Number of awards: 3
Deadline: March 15
College level: Dental school
Majors/Fields: Dentistry
Criteria: Applicant must be a Delaware resident; first-year dental students are not eligible, but postdoctoral students may apply. Selection is based upon grades. Financial need is considered. Reapplication required to retain scholarship. Awarded every year.
Contact: Margaret Novak, Secretary, Delaware State Dental Society, 1925 Lovering Ave, Wilmington, DE 19806, (302) 654-4335.

908   William L. Tucker Scholarship

State University of New York at Buffalo
Buffalo, NY 14260
(716) 831-2000, (716) 829-2022 (fax)
Average award: $1,150
College level: Sophomore, Junior, Senior
Majors/Fields: Dentistry
Criteria: Selection is based upon class rank. Award may be used only at sponsoring institution.
Contact: Scholarships.

Medicine

909   AAOA Scholarship Award

Auxiliary to the American Osteopathic Association (AAOA)
142 East Ontario Street
Chicago, IL 60611
(312) 280-5800
Average award: $3,000
Deadline: April 15
College level: Sophomore
Majors/Fields: Osteopathic medicine
Criteria: Selection is based upon high scholastic standing (rank in top fifth of class), financial need, good moral character, good motivation, and aptitude for a career in osteopathic medicine. Recipient must not have a full tuition scholarship received from another source. Award is paid directly to the osteopathic college to be applied toward tuition, books, and equipment. Awarded every year.
Contact: Mrs. Judie Colwell, AAOA Scholarship Chairman, 4376 Shire Cove Road, Hilliard, OH 43026, (614) 876-2293.

910   ACMPE Presidential Scholarship

American College of Medical Practice Executives (ACMPE)
104 Inverness Terrace East
Englewood, CO 80112-5306
(303) 799-1111
Maximum award: $1,000
Deadline: June 1
Majors/Fields: Medical group practice, medical practice management
Criteria: Selection is based upon an individual profile with key personal, academic and professional background information, including an explanation of the applicant's particular need for professional development and statement of goals. Applicant must be an ACMPE member. Awarded every year.
Contact: Laurie Draizen, Executive Assistant, (303) 799-1111, extension 206.

911   AKC Veterinary Scholarship

American Kennel Clubs (AKC)
51 Madison Avenue
New York, NY 10010
Average award: $2,500
Maximum award: $5,000
Minimum award: $1,000
Number of awards: 25
Deadline: May 1
College level: Veterinary students matriculating at accredited U.S. institutions
Majors/Fields: Veterinary medicine
Criteria: Selection is based upon participation in the sport of pure-bred dogs, financial need, and scholastic achievement. Application must be made through the school's financial aid office. No school may submit more than four applications in any year. Reapplication is required to retain scholarship. Awarded every year.
Contact: Scholarships, (212) 696-8234.

912   Alman H. Cooke Scholarship

State University of New York at Buffalo
Buffalo, NY 14260
(716) 831-2000, (716) 829-2022 (fax)
Average award: $1,500
College level: Medicial students
Majors/Fields: Medicine
Criteria: Scholarship is renewable. Awarded every year. Award may be used only at sponsoring institution.
Contact: Scholarships.

913 Dr. Walter Freund Memorial Scholarship

State University of New York College at Oswego
King Hall/Alumni and University Development
Oswego, NY 13126
(315) 341-3003, (315) 341-3281, (315) 341-5570 (fax)
Average award: $3,000
Number of awards: 2
Deadline: January 31
College level: Senior
Majors/Fields: Pre-medical
Criteria: Applicant must submit scores from Medical College Admissions Test (MCAT). Application is required. Awarded every year. Award may be used only at sponsoring institution.
Contact: Chair of Pre-Med Advisory Committee or Office of Dean of Arts and Sciences, (315) 341-2290 or (315) 341-2767.

914 Edgar J. Saux/FACMPE Scholarship

American College of Medical Practice Executives (ACMPE)
104 Inverness Terrace East
Englewood, CO 80112-5306
(303) 799-1111
Maximum award: $1,000
Deadline: June 1
College level: Freshman, Sophomore, Junior, Senior
Majors/Fields: Health care administration, medical group management
Criteria: Applicant must submit a letter stating career goals and objectices, an explantion of the individual's need for professional development such as gaps in formal education or changing health care environment, and a resume showing employment history with a brief narrative describing specific employment responsibilities in health care field. Awarded every year.
Contact: Laurie Draizen, Executive Assistant, (303) 799-1111, extension 206.

915 Fresno-Madera Medical Society Scholarship

Fresno-Madera Medical Society Scholarship Foundation
P.O. Box 31
Fresno, CA 93707
(209) 224-4224, extension 12, (209) 224-0276 (fax)
Average award: $1,000
Maximum award: $1,500
Number of awards: 12
Deadline: May 15
College level: Medical school students
Majors/Fields: Medicine
Criteria: Applicant must have been a resident of either Fresno or Madera counties for at least one year and be approved for matriculation in a medical school. Award will be sent to the school of matriculation to be administered toward tuition, lab fees, books, and any other valid educational expenses. Scholarship is renewable. Awarded every year.
Contact: Ellen Burton, Administrative Secretary.

916 Harry J. Harwick Scholarship

American College of Medical Practice Executives (ACMPE)
104 Inverness Terrace East
Englewood, CO 80112-5306
(303) 799-1111
Average award: $2,000
Number of awards: 1
Deadline: June 1
College level: Freshman, Sophomore, Junior, Senior, Graduate, Doctoral
Majors/Fields: Health care administration, medical group practice
Criteria: Applicant must submit a letter stating career goals and objectives, a resume showing employment history with a brief narrative describing specific employment responsibilities in health care field, and three letters of recommendation. Reference letters should address performance, character, potential to succeed, and need for scholarship support. Awarded every year.
Contact: Laurie Draizen, Executive Assistant, (303) 799-1111, extension 206.

917 Helen N. and Harold B. Shapira Scholarship

Shapira Scholarship Awards Fund
American Heart Association, Minnesota Affiliate
4701 West 77th Street
Minneapolis, MN 55435
(612) 835-3300
Average award: $1,000
Number of awards: 2
Deadline: April 1
College level: Unspecified graduate, unspecified undergraduate
Majors/Fields: Medically related curriculum with application to the heart and blood vessel system
Criteria: Applicant must be attending a four-year college or university or a medical school in the state of Minnesota. Renewable if recipient maintains satisfactory scholastic progress. Awarded every year.
Contact: Joyce C. Lampion, Research Administrator.

918 Henry Viets Fellowship

Myasthenia Gravis Foundation of America, Inc.
222 South Riverside Plaza
Suite 1540
Chicago, IL 60606
(312) 258-0522, (800) 541-5454, (312) 258-0461 (fax)
MGFA@aol.com
http://www.med.unc.edu/mgfa/
Average award: $3,000
Number of awards: 4
Deadline: March 15
College level: Premedical and medical students
Criteria: Applicant must be planning to study in the area of myasthenia gravis. Awarded every year.
Contact: Fellowships, (800) 541-5454.

919 Irene and Daisy MacGregor Memorial Scholarship

National Society of the Daughters of the American Revolution (NSDAR)
NSDAR Administration Building, Office of the Committees
1776 D Street, NW
Washington, DC 20006-5392
(202) 879-3292
Average award: $5,000
Number of awards: 2
Deadline: April 15
College level: Medical school
Majors/Fields: Medicine
Criteria: Applicant must be a U.S. citizen pursuing an M.D. to become a medical doctor and be sponsored by a local DAR chapter. Selection is based upon academic excellence, commitment to the field of medicine, and financial need. All inquiries must include a self-addressed, stamped envelope. Applicant may be male or female. Annual transcript review required to retain scholarship. Awarded every year.
Contact: Administrative Assistant, Scholarships.

920 James H. Cummings Scholarship

State University of New York at Buffalo
Buffalo, NY 14260
(716) 831-2000, (716) 829-2022 (fax)
Average award: $1,100
College level: Medical students
Majors/Fields: Medicine
Criteria: Scholarship is renewable. Awarded every year. Award may be used only at sponsoring institution.
Contact: Scholarships.

921 Lawrence W. Mills Award

Auxiliary to the American Osteopathic Association (AAOA)
142 East Ontario Street
Chicago, IL 60611
(312) 280-5800
Average award: $5,000
Number of awards: 1
Deadline: April 15
College level: Sophomore
Majors/Fields: Osteopathic medicine
Criteria: Selection is based upon high scholastic standing (rank in top fifth of class), financial need, good moral character, good motivation, and aptitude for a career in osteopathic medicine. Recipient must not have a full tuition scholarship from another source. Award is given to the winner of the AAOA scholarship competition and is paid directly to the osteopathic college to be applied toward tuition, books, and equipment. Awarded every year.
Contact: Mrs. Judie Colwell, AAOA Scholarship Chairman, 4376 Shire Cove Road, Hilliard, OH 43026, (614) 876-2293.

922 M.A. Cartland Shackford Medical Fellowship

Wellesley College
Center for Work & Service
Wellesley, MA 02181
(617) 283-3525, (617) 283-3674 (fax)
fellowships@bulletin.wellesley.edu
Maximum award: $3,500
Number of awards: 2
Deadline: December 16
College level: College senior/other for medical degree study
Majors/Fields: Dentistry (D.M.D.), medicine (M.D.), veterinary medicine
Criteria: Applicant must be a woman and a graduate of an American institution and be planning a career in medicine, preferably in general practice, not psychiatry. Scholarship is renewable. Awarded every year.
Contact: Secretary to the Committee on Graduate Fellowships, (617) 283-2347.

923 Massachusetts Federation of Polish Women's Clubs Scholarship

Kosciuszko Foundation
15 East 65th Street
New York, NY 10021
(212) 734-2130
Average award: $1,000
Number of awards: 1
Deadline: January 15
Majors/Fields: Medicine
Criteria: Applicant must be a young woman of Polish descent. In the application or request for application, the name of the award being applied for should not be specified; this determination is made by the scholarship committee. Awarded every year.
Contact: Scholarships.

924 Medical Laboratory Scholarship

Shawnee State University
940 Second Street
Portsmouth, OH 45662-4344
(614) 355-2237
Average award: $2,750
Deadline: May 15
College level: Freshman
Majors/Fields: Medical laboratory
Criteria: Applicant must be a U.S. citizen, a resident of Ohio, have a minimum 3.0 GPA, rank in top third of class, be between age 17 and age 22, and have completed high school algebra and chemistry. FAFSA is required. Early application is recommended. Award is for two years. Awarded every year. Award may be used only at sponsoring institution.
Contact: Financial Aid Office, (614) 355-2485.

925 Midwest Section Scholarship

American College of Medical Practice Executives (ACMPE)
104 Inverness Terrace East
Englewood, CO 80112-5306
(303) 799-1111
Average award: $2,000
Maximum number of awards: 3
Minimum number of awards: 1
Deadline: June 1
College level: Freshman, Sophomore, Junior, Senior, Graduate, Doctoral
Majors/Fields: Health care administration, medical group management, medical practice management
Criteria: Applicant must reside in the Midwest section and submit a letter stating career goals and objectives, a resume showing employment history with a brief narrative describing specific employment responsibilities in health care field, and three letters of recommendation. Reference letters should address performance, character, potential to succeed, and need for scholarship support. Awarded every year.
Contact: Laurie Draizen, Executive Assistant, (303) 799-1111, extension 206.

926 Ramsay and Elaine O'Neal Scholarship

Mississippi State University
Department of Student Financial Aid
P.O. Box 6238
Mississippi State, MS 39762
(601) 325-7430
Average award: $3,000
Number of awards: 1
Deadline: February 1
College level: Freshman
Criteria: Applicant must have a minimum composite ACT score of 28 (combined SAT I score of 1160), plan to enter medical or dental school, and participate in Scholarship Day. Minimum 3.5 GPA and completion of at least 32 semester hours per year are required to retain scholarship. Awarded every year. Award may be used only at sponsoring institution.
Contact: Audrey S. Lambert, Director of Student Financial Aid.

927 Richard L. Davis Managers' Scholarship

American College of Medical Practice Executives (ACMPE)
104 Inverness Terrace East
Englewood, CO 80112-5306
(303) 799-1111
Maximum award: $1,000
Maximum number of awards: 2
Minimum number of awards: 1
Deadline: June 1
College level: Sophomore, Junior, Senior, Graduate, Doctoral
Majors/Fields: Medical group management
Criteria: Applicant must submit a letter stating career goals and objectives, with an explanation of the individual's need for professional development such as gaps in formal education or changing health care environment, a resume showing employment history with a brief narrative describing specific employment responsibilities in health care field, and three letters of recommendation. Reference letters should address performance, character, potential to succeed, and need for scholarship support. Awarded every year.
Contact: Laurie Draizen, Executive Assistant, (303) 799-1111, extension 206.

928 Richard L. Davis National Scholarship

American College of Medical Practice Executives (ACMPE)
104 Inverness Terrace East
Englewood, CO 80112-5306
(303) 799-1111
Maximum award: $1,000
Number of awards: 5
Deadline: June 1
College level: Freshman, Sophomore, Junior, Senior, Graduate, Doctoral
Majors/Fields: Medical group management, medical practice management
Criteria: Applicant must submit a letter stating career goals and objectives, a resume showing employment history with a brief narrative describing specific employment responsibilities in health care field, and three letters of recommendation. Reference letters should address performance, character, potential to succeed, and need for scholarship support. Awarded every year.
Contact: Laurie J. Draizen, Executive Assistant, (303) 799-1111, extension 206.

929 Rock Sleyster Memorial Scholarship

American Medical Association
515 North State Street
Chicago, IL 60610
(312) 464-4691, (312) 464-5830 (fax)
Average award: $2,500
Number of awards: 20
Deadline: May 1
College level: Rising senior in medical school
Majors/Fields: Psychiatry
Criteria: Applicant must be a U.S. citizen enrolled in an accredited U.S. or Canadian medical school and demonstrate financial need and an interest in psychiatry. Applicant must be nominated by the psychiatry department and dean's office and submit an application, recommendations, financial statement, and transcript. Awarded every year.
Contact: Harry S. Jonas, M.D., Assistant Vice President, Division of Undergraduate Medical Education, (312) 464-4657.

930 Sarah Perry Wood Medical Fellowship

Wellesley College
Center for Work & Service
Wellesley, MA 02181
(617) 283-3525, (617) 283-3674 (fax)
fellowships@bulletin.wellesley.edu
Maximum award: $24,000
Deadline: December 16
College level: Medical students
Majors/Fields: Medicine
Criteria: Applicant must be a woman and a graduate of Wellesley College. Selection is based upon merit and need. Awarded every year.
Contact: Secretary to the Committee on Graduate Fellowships, (617) 283-2347.

931 Tinsley Randolph Harrison Scholarship

Birmingham-Southern College
Arkadelphia Road
Birmingham, AL 35254
(205) 226-4688
Average award: Full tuition
Number of awards: 1
Deadline: January 5
College level: Freshman
Majors/Fields: Pre-medicine
Criteria: Applicant should rank in top 5% of class, have a composite ACT score of 28-36 (combined SAT I score of 1150-1400), have leadership ability, and be planning a career in medicine. Selection is based upon academic qualifications. Minimum 3.0 GPA is required to retain scholarship. Awarded every year. Award may be used only at sponsoring institution.
Contact: Forrest Stuart, Interim Director of Financial Aid Services.

932 Western Section Scholarship

American College of Medical Practice Executives (ACMPE)
104 Inverness Terrace East
Englewood, CO 80112-5306
(303) 799-1111
Average award: $2,000
Maximum number of awards: 2
Minimum number of awards: 1
Deadline: June 1
College level: Sophomore, Junior, Senior, Graduate, Doctoral
Majors/Fields: Medical practice management
Criteria: Applicant must have been an MGMA Western section member for two years. Applicant must submit a letter stating goals and objectives, a resume showing employment history with a brief narrative describing specific employment responsibilities in health care field, and three letters of recommendation. Reference letters should address performance, character, potential to succeed, and need for scholarship support. Awarded every year.
Contact: Laurie Draizen, Executive Assistant, (303) 799-1111, extension 206.

Nursing

933 Ailene C. Ewell Scholarship Award

Chi Eta Phi Sorority, Inc.
3029 Thirteenth Street, NW
Washington, DC 20009
(202) 232-3460 (fax)
Average award: $1,000
Maximum award: $2,000
Minimum award: $500
Maximum number of awards: 25
Minimum number of awards: 20
Deadline: February 28
College level: Senior
Majors/Fields: Nursing
Criteria: Applicant must be referred by a chapter of Chi Eta Phi Sorority. Selection is based upon financial need, scholastic ability, interest in nursing, and leadership potential. Satisfactory academic progress is required to retain scholarship. Awarded every year.
Contact: Scholarships.

934 Cannon Memorial Hospital Annual Nursing Scholarship

Clemson University
G-01 Sikes Hall
Clemson, SC 29634-5123
(803) 656-2280
Maximum award: $1,250
Number of awards: 1
Deadline: March 1
College level: Freshman, Sophomore, Junior, Senior
Majors/Fields: Nursing
Criteria: Applicant must have a minimum 2.5 GPA and be a resident of Pickens County, S.C. Satisfactory GPA and completion of at least 12 credits per semester are required to retain scholarship. Awarded every year. Award may be used only at sponsoring institution.
Contact: Marvin Carmichael, Director of Financial Aid.

935   D.C. Nurses Training Corps Grant

District of Columbia Office of Postsecondary Education, Research, and Assistance
2100 Martin Luther King Jr. Avenue, SE, Suite 401
Washington, DC 20020
(202) 727-3685
Average award: $13,700
Maximum award: $22,000
Minimum award: $8,631
Number of awards: 16
Deadline: Last Friday in April
College level: Freshman, Sophomore, Junior, Senior
Majors/Fields: Nursing
Criteria: Applicant must be a District of Columbia resident, demonstrate financial need, have a minimum 2.5 GPA, be in good academic standing, and be accepted for or enrolled in a full-time nursing program at a District of Columbia institution. Reapplication, financial need, and good academic standing are required to retain scholarship. Awarded every year.
Contact: Laurencia O. Henderson, Student Financial Assistance Specialist.

936   Delaware Nursing Incentive Scholarship Loan

Delaware Higher Education Commission
820 North French Street, Fourth Floor
Wilmington, DE 19801
(302) 577-3240, (302) 577-6765 (fax)
mlaffey@state.de.us
http://www.state.de.us/high-ed/commiss/webpage.htm
Average award: $2,360
Maximum award: $3,000
Number of awards: 12
Deadline: March 31
College level: Freshman, Delaware state employees enrolled part-time
Majors/Fields: Nursing
Criteria: Applicant must be a Delaware resident enrolled in a RN, LPN or AN program. Renewable if recipient maintains a minimum 2.75 GPA. Awarded every year. Award may be used only at Delaware schools.
Contact: Maureen Laffey, Associate Director.

937   Dr. Else T. Marcus Scholarship

City University of New York, The College of Staten Island
2800 Victory Boulevard
Staten Island, NY 10314-9881
(718) 982-2259
Average award: Full tuition
Number of awards: 4
Deadline: None
College level: Graduates of associate degree program with R.N. certification who are entering bachelor's degree program, licensed R.N.'s entering bachelor's degree program
Majors/Fields: Nursing
Criteria: Applicant must be a Staten Island resident. Awarded every year. Award may be used only at sponsoring institution.
Contact: Office of Student Recruitment and Scholarships.

938   Eight & Forty Nursing Scholarship

Eight & Forty Scholarship Program
P.O. Box 1055
Indianapolis, IN 46206
(317) 630-1212
Average award: $2,500
Number of awards: 22
Deadline: May 15
College level: R.N.
Majors/Fields: Nursing
Criteria: Applicant must be a U.S. citizen and a R.N. studying nursing with a lung and respiratory disease emphasis. Awarded every year.
Contact: William A. Pease, Program Manager.

939   Elaine Potter Benfer Scholarship

New Mexico State University
Box 30001
Department 5100
Las Cruces, NM 88003-0001
(505) 646-4105
Maximum award: $2,400
Number of awards: 1
Deadline: March 1
College level: Sophomore, Junior, Senior
Majors/Fields: Nursing
Criteria: Applicant must be willing to volunteer with the Red Cross. Awarded every year. Award may be used only at sponsoring institution.
Contact: Greeley W. Myers, Director of Financial Aid.

940   Frances Tompkins Scholarship

Foundation of the National Student Nurses' Association, Inc.
555 West 57th Street, Suite 1327
New York, NY 10019
(212) 581-2215, (212) 581-2368 (fax)
nsna@nsna.org
http://www.nsna.org
Maximum award: $2,000
Number of awards: 55
Deadline: January 30
College level: Sophomore, Junior, Senior, Graduate, Doctoral
Majors/Fields: Nursing
Criteria: Applicant must be enrolled at a state-approved school of nursing or pre-nursing in an associate degree, baccalaureate, diploma, generic doctorate, or generic master's program. Selection is based upon academic achievement, financial need, and involvement in student nursing organizations and community service related to health care. Applicant will automatically be considered for any specialty scholarships for which he or she is eligible. Awarded every year.
Contact: Scholarships.

941   George W. Nunn, Richard W. Stuhr, and Joseph Wallace Nursing Scholarship

The University of Alabama
Box 870162
Tuscaloosa, AL 35487-0162
(205) 348-6756
Average award: $2,000
Number of awards: 1
Deadline: March 15
College level: Freshman, Sophomore, Junior, Senior
Majors/Fields: Nursing
Criteria: Applicant must be enrolled full time in the Capstone College of Nursing. Awarded every year. Award may be used only at sponsoring institution.
Contact: Capstone College of Nursing, Box 870358, Tuscaloosa, AL 35487-0358.

942   Immunex Bachelors Scholarship

Oncology Nursing Foundation
501 Holiday Drive
Pittsburgh, PA 15220-2749
(412) 921-7373, (412) 921-6565 (fax)
Maximum award: $2,000
Number of awards: 2
Deadline: February 1
College level: Sophomore, Junior, Senior
Majors/Fields: Oncology nursing
Criteria: Applicant must be an R.N. with an interest in and a commitment to oncology nursing. Awarded every year.
Contact: Celia A. Hindes, Development Associate, (412) 921-7373, extension 242.

943 Maymi Walker Chandler Scholarship
Georgia State University
P.O. Box 4040
Atlanta, GA 30302
(404) 651-2227, (404) 651-3418 (fax)
http://www.gsu.edu
Average award: $3,333
Number of awards: 3
Deadline: None
College level: Freshman, Sophomore, Junior, Senior, Graduate, Doctoral
Majors/Fields: Nursing
Criteria: Selection is based upon GPA, leadership, and finanacial need. Awarded every year. Award may be used only at sponsoring institution.
Contact: School of Nursing, (404) 651-3040.

944 McFarland Charitable Foundation Scholarship
Havana National Bank
112 South Orange Street
Havana, IL 62644
(309) 543-3361
Average award: $7,000
Maximum award: $12,000
Minimum award: $1,000
Number of awards: 5
Deadline: May 1
College level: Freshman, Sophomore, Junior, Senior
Majors/Fields: Registered nursing
Criteria: Applicant must contractually agree to practice registered nursing in the Havana, Ill., area for one year for each year of financing. Repayment is required for nonfulfillment of contractual obligation. Co-signers are required. Award is for several years. Awarded every year.
Contact: Linda M. Butler, Vice President and Senior Trust Officer.

945 New York State Primary Care Service Corps Scholarship
Higher Education Services Corporation
99 Washington Avenue
Albany, NY 12255
(518) 473-7087, (518) 474-2839 (fax)
http://www.hesc.com
Maximum award: $15,000
Deadline: April 8
Majors/Fields: Midwifery, nurse practitioner, physician assistant
Criteria: Applicant must be within two years (four years if studying part time) of being eligible to apply for licensure. Applicant must agree to practice in a designated, state-operated, or non-profit facility for 18 months for each year of aid received (full-time); nine months for each year of aid received (part-time). Scholarship is renewable. Awarded every year.
Contact: New York State Department of Health, Corning Tower, Room 1602, Empire State Plaza, Albany, NY 12237, (518) 473-7019.

946 Nurse Training Scholarship
American Legion–Oregon Auxiliary
P.O. Box 1730
Wilsonville, OR 97070-1730
(503) 682-3162
Average award: $1,500
Number of awards: 1
Deadline: June 1
College level: Freshman
Majors/Fields: Nursing
Criteria: Applicant must be the child or widow of a deceased veteran or the wife of a disabled veteran who has been accepted by an accredited hospital or university school of nursing. Selection is based upon ability, aptitude, character, determination, seriousness of purpose, and financial need. Awarded every year.
Contact: Chairman of Education.

947 Nurses' MGF Research Fellowship
Myasthenia Gravis Foundation of America, Inc.
222 South Riverside Plaza
Suite 1540
Chicago, IL 60606
(312) 258-0522, (800) 541-5454, (312) 258-0461 (fax)
MGFA@aol.com
http://www.med.unc.edu/mgfa/
Maximum award: $2,000
Deadline: February 1
College level: R.N.s
Criteria: Applicant must be planning research in the area of myasthenia gravis. Awarded every year.
Contact: Fellowships, (800) 541-5454.

948 Nursing Alumni Endowed Scholarship (Class of May 1989)
Clemson University
G-01 Sikes Hall
Clemson, SC 29634-5123
(803) 656-2280
Average award: $1,250
Number of awards: 1
Deadline: March 1
College level: Freshman, Sophomore, Junior, Senior
Majors/Fields: Nursing
Criteria: Applicant must have a minimum 2.5 GPA. Satisfactory GPA and completion of at least 12 credit hours per semester are required to retain scholarship. Awarded every year. Award may be used only at sponsoring institution.
Contact: Marvin Carmichael, Director of Financial Aid.

949 Nursing Education Loan/Scholarship Program
Mississippi Board of Trustees of State Institutions of Higher Learning
Student Financial Aid Office
3825 Ridgewood Road
Jackson, MS 39211-6453
(601) 982-6663, (601) 982-6527 (fax)
Maximum award: $2,000
College level: Junior, Senior, Graduate
Majors/Fields: Nursing
Criteria: Applicant must be a Mississippi resident pursuing a B.S.Nurs., M.S.Nurs., or D.S.Nurs. Renewable if 2.5 GPA is maintained. Awarded every year.
Contact: Mississippi Postsecondary Education Financial Assistance Board.

950 Nursing Education Scholarship
Baptist Hospital
1000 West Moreno Street
Pensacola, FL 32501
(904) 434-4911
Average award: $1,500
Number of awards: 20
Deadline: November 30, April 30
College level: Unspecified undergraduate
Majors/Fields: Nursing
Criteria: Recipient must sign contractual agreement with Baptist Hospital agreeing to work one year as a nurse employed at the prevailing wage for each year the student is in the scholarship program. Should the graduate nurse decline to accept employment with Baptist Hospital upon graduation or be unable to pass the State Board Exam, the scholarship loan must be repaid with seven percent interest. Scholarship is renewable. Scholarship is awarded twice a year.
Contact: Pat Williams, Director of Nursing, Division II.

951   Nursing Fund Scholarship

State Student Assistance Commission of Indiana
150 West Market Street
Suite 500
Indianapolis, IN 46204-2811
(317) 232-2350
Average award: $500
Maximum award: $5,000
Maximum number of awards: 400
Minimum number of awards: 200
College level: Freshman, Sophomore, Junior, Senior
Majors/Fields: Nursing
Criteria: Applicant must be an Indiana resident and demonstrate financial need. Reapplication and satisfactory academic progress are required to retain scholarship. Awarded every year.
Contact: Yvonne D. Heflin, Director of Special Programs.

952   Nursing Grant Program for Persons of Color

Minnesota Higher Education Services Office Division of Student Financial Aid
Suite 400, Capitol Square
550 Cedar Street
St. Paul, MN 55101
(800) 657-3866, (612) 296-3974
http://www.heso.state.mn.us
Maximum award: $4,000
Number of awards: 65
College level: Freshman, Sophomore, Junior, Senior, Graduate, Doctoral
Majors/Fields: Nursing
Criteria: Applicant must be a U.S. citizen, meet state residency requirements, be Asian-/Pacific-American, African-American, American Indian, or Hispanic-American, be enrolled at least half-time, must not be in default on a student loan, demonstrate financial need, and be willing to serve in Minnesota for three years upon receipt of R.N. Applicant must reapply for renewal. Awarded every year.
Contact: Financial Aid Division Staff, (800) 657-3866, larter@heso.state.mn.us.

953   Nursing Scholarship

Cedar Crest College
100 College Drive
Allentown, PA 18104
(610) 740-3785, (610) 606-4647 (fax)
cccadmis@cedarcrest.edu
www.cedarcrest.edu
Average award: $1,500
Number of awards: 2
Deadline: Rolling
College level: Freshman
Majors/Fields: Nursing
Criteria: Interview strongly recommended. Renewable if recipient maintains good academic standing. Awarded every year. Award may be used only at sponsoring institution.
Contact: Judith Neyhart, Vice President for Enrollment Management, Financial Aid Office.

954   Nursing Scholarship

Milwaukee School of Engineering
1025 North Broadway
Milwaukee, WI 53202-3109
(800) 332-6763, (414) 277-7475 (fax)
goran@admin.msoe.edu
www.msoe.edu
Average award: Half tuition
Number of awards: 1
Deadline: February 1
College level: Freshman
Criteria: Applicant must have minimum 3.0 GPA. recommendation is suggested. Renewable up to four years if recipient maintains minimum 3.0 GPA. Awarded every year. Award may be used only at sponsoring institution.
Contact: Sue Minzlaff, Financial Aid Office, (414) 277-7222, minzlaff@admin.msoe.edu.

955   Oncology Nursing Certification Corporation Bachelor's Scholarship and Oncology Nursing Foundation Ethnic Minority Bachelor's Scholarship

Oncology Nursing Foundation
501 Holiday Drive
Pittsburgh, PA 15220-2749
(412) 921-7373, (412) 921-6565 (fax)
Maximum award: $2,000
Number of awards: 13
Deadline: February 1
College level: Sophomore, Junior, Senior
Majors/Fields: Oncology Nursing
Criteria: Applicant must be an R.N. with an interest in and a commitment to oncology nursing. Three awards are reserved for applicants who are members of a racial/ethnic minority. Awarded every year.
Contact: Celia A. Hindes, Development Associate, (412) 921-7373, extension 242.

956   Peggy Gardner Deane Endowed Nursing Scholarship

Clemson University
G-01 Sikes Hall
Clemson, SC 29634-5123
(803) 656-2280
Maximum award: $1,250
Number of awards: 2
Deadline: March 1
College level: Junior, Senior
Majors/Fields: Nursing
Criteria: Applicant must have a minimum 3.0 GPA and be a resident of Anderson County, S.C. Renewable if recipient maintains satisfactory GPA and completes at least 12 credits per semester. Award may be used only at sponsoring institution.
Contact: Scholarships.

957   Primary Care Service Corps Scholarship

New York State Primary Care Service Corps
Room 1602, Corning Tower
Empire State Plaza
Albany, NY 12237
(518) 473-7019, (518) 473-8434 (fax)
Maximum award: $15,000
Number of awards: 80
Deadline: Early April
College level: Junior, Senior, Graduate
Majors/Fields: Midwife, nurse practitioner, physician assistant
Criteria: Applicant must submit evidence of enrollment in or acceptance for full- or part-time study in a professional program at an institution approved by the New York State Board of Regents, be within 24 months of completing the program for full-time and 48 months for part-time study, and becoming eligible to apply for a license, certificate, or registration in the profession of study, and meet the character and moral standards required for licensure. Applicant must be prepared to fulfill a service obligation in an underserved area or facility. Recipient must maintain full- or part-time attendance in approved program of study. Awarded every year. Award may be used only at approved schools.
Contact: Philip Passero, Assistant Director.

958   Roberta Pierce Scofield Bachelor's Scholarship

Oncology Nursing Foundation
501 Holiday Drive
Pittsburgh, PA 15220-2749
(412) 921-7373, (412) 921-6565 (fax)
Maximum award: $2,000
Number of awards: 3
Deadline: February 1
College level: Sophomore, Junior, Senior
Majors/Fields: Oncology nursing
Criteria: Applicant must be an R.N. with an interest in and commitment to oncology nursing. Awarded every year.
Contact: Celia A. Hindes, Development Associate, (412) 921-7373, extension 242.

959 Scholarship for L.V.N.s Becoming Professional Nurses

Texas Higher Education Coordinating Board
Student Financial Assistance
P.O. Box 12788, Capitol Station
Austin, TX 78711-2788
(512) 427-6340
Average award: $1,908
Maximum award: $2,500
Minimum award: $1,500
Number of awards: 50
Deadline: July 15
College level: Freshman, Sophomore, Junior, Senior, Graduate, Doctoral
Majors/Fields: Nursing
Criteria: Applicant must be a Texas resident enrolled at least half time in a program leading to an associate, bachelor's, or graduate degree in professional nursing at a Texas public or independent nonprofit institution. Applicant may have been previously licensed to practice as a vocational nurse. Recipient must reapply to retain scholarship. No preference is given to renewals. Awarded every year.
Contact: Jane Caldwell, Director of Grants and Special Programs, (512) 427-6455.

960 Scholarship for Rural B.S.N. or Graduate Nursing Students

Texas Higher Education Coordinating Board
Student Financial Assistance
P.O. Box 12788, Capitol Station
Austin, TX 78711-2788
(512) 427-6340
Average award: $2,266
Maximum award: $2,500
Number of awards: 17
Deadline: July 15
College level: Freshman, Sophomore, Junior, Senior, Graduate, Doctoral
Majors/Fields: Nursing
Criteria: Applicant must be a Texas resident from a rural county enrolled at least half time in a program leading to a B.S.N. or graduate degree in professional nursing at any nonprofit public or independent institution in Texas. Recipient must reapply to retain scholarship. No preference is given to renewals. Awarded every year.
Contact: Jane Caldwell, Director of Grants and Special Programs, (512) 427-6455.

961 State Nursing Scholarship and Living Expenses Grant

Maryland Higher Education Commission
State Scholarship Administration
16 Francis Street
Annapolis, MD 21401-1781
(410) 974-5370, (410) 974-5994 (fax)
http://www.ubalt.edu/www/mhec
Maximum award: $2,400
Number of awards: 285
Deadline: March 1 (FAFSA), June 30 (SSA)
College level: Freshman, Sophomore, Junior, Senior, Doctoral
Majors/Fields: Nursing
Criteria: Applicant must be a Maryland resident and agree to serve as a full-time nurse in a shortage area of Maryland for one year for each year of award. Applicant must file separate application to be considered for a living expenses grant. Minimum 3.0 GPA, satisfactory academic progress, and reapplication are required to retain scholarship. Awarded every year. Award may be used only at Maryland schools.
Contact: Lula Caldwell, Program Administrator.

962 Thomas S. Dobson Scholarship

University of Calgary
Department of Financial Aid
2500 University Drive, NW
Calgary, Alberta, CN T2N 1N4
(403) 220-7872, (403) 282-2999 (fax)
Average award: $2,500
Number of awards: 1
Deadline: July 15
College level: Freshman
Majors/Fields: Nursing
Criteria: Selection is based upon academic merit and extracurricular activities. Awarded every year. Award may be used only at sponsoring institution.
Contact: J. Van Housen, Director of Student Awards/Financial Aid.

963 Tuscaloosa Clinic Nursing Scholarship

The University of Alabama
Box 870162
Tuscaloosa, AL 35487-0162
(205) 348-6756
Average award: $1,900
Number of awards: 1
Deadline: March 15
College level: Sophomore, Junior, Senior
Majors/Fields: Nursing
Criteria: Applicant must be enrolled full time. Award may be used only at sponsoring institution.
Contact: Capstone College of Nursing, Box 870358, Tuscaloosa, AL 35487-0358.

964 Willie Johnson Annual Scholarship

Clemson University
G-01 Sikes Hall
Clemson, SC 29634-5123
(803) 656-2280
Average award: $1,200
Number of awards: 2
Deadline: March 1
College level: Freshman, Sophomore, Junior, Senior
Majors/Fields: Nursing
Criteria: Applicant must be a resident of Anderson, Cherokee, Greenville, Laurens, Oconee, Pickens, or Spartanburg county, S.C., and have a minimum 2.5 GPA. Minimum 3.0 GPA and completion of at least 12 credit hours per semester are required to retain scholarship. Awarded every year. Award may be used only at sponsoring institution.
Contact: Marvin Carmichael, Director of Financial Aid.

965 Willie Johnson Scholarship

Clemson University
G-01 Sikes Hall
Clemson, SC 29634-5123
(803) 656-2280
Average award: $1,250
Number of awards: 2
Deadline: March 1
College level: Freshman, Sophomore, Junior, Senior
Majors/Fields: Nursing
Criteria: Applicant must have a minimum 3.0 GPA. Financial need is considered. Satisfactory GPA and completion of at least 12 credit hours per semester are required to retain scholarship. Awarded every year. Award may be used only at sponsoring institution.
Contact: Marvin Carmichael, Director of Financial Aid.

Science/Mathematics

Atmospheric Sciences/Meteorology

966 **AMS 75th Anniversary Campaign Scholarship and Dr. Pedro Grau Undergraduate Scholarship**
American Meteorological Society (AMS)
45 Beacon Street
Boston, MA 02108-3693
(617) 227-2426, extension 235
Average award: $2,500
Number of awards: 1 each
Deadline: June 17
College level: Senior
Majors/Fields: Atmospheric science, hydrologic science, meteorology, oceanic science
Criteria: Applicant must be a U.S. citizen or permanent resident enrolled in an accredited U.S. institution and show clear intent to make atmospheric science a career. Selection is based upon academic excellece and achievement. Awarded every year.
Contact: Stephanie Kehoe, Fellowship/Scholarship Coordinator.

967 **AMS/Industry Undergraduate Scholarship**
American Meteorological Society (AMS)
45 Beacon Street
Boston, MA 02108-3693
(617) 227-2426, extension 235
Average award: $2,000
Deadline: February 15
College level: Junior, Senior
Majors/Fields: Atmospheric science, hydrologic science, meteorology, oceanic science
Criteria: Applicant must be a U.S. citizen or permanent resident, have a minimum 3.0 GPA, and demonstrate a clear intent to pursue a career in the atmospheric or related oceanic or hydrologic sciences after graduation or graduate school. Satisfactory academic progress, full-time enrollment, and preparation for a career in the atmospheric or related sciences are required to retain scholarship. Awarded every year.
Contact: Stephanie Kehoe, Fellowship/Scholarship Coordinator.

968 **Howard T. Orville Scholarship in Meteorology**
American Meteorological Society (AMS)
45 Beacon Street
Boston, MA 02108-3693
(617) 227-2426, extension 235
Average award: $2,000
Number of awards: 1
Deadline: June 15
College level: Senior
Majors/Fields: Meteorology, atmospheric science, oceanic science, hydrologic science
Criteria: Applicant must have a minimum 3.0 GPA, be a U.S. citizen or permanent resident, be enrolled full-time in an accredited U.S. institution, and intend to make atmospheric science a career. Selection is based upon academic excellence and achievement. Awarded every year.
Contact: Stephanie Kehoe, Fellowship/Scholarship Coordinator, (617) 227-2426, ext. 235.

969 **Paul H. Kutschenreuter Scholarship**
American Meteorological Society (AMS)
45 Beacon Street
Boston, MA 02108-3693
(617) 227-2426, extension 235
Average award: $5,000
Number of awards: 1
Deadline: June 15
College level: Senior
Majors/Fields: Atmospheric science, hydrologic science, meteorology, oceanic science
Criteria: Applicant must be a U.S. citizen or permanent resident attending an accredited U.S. institution, have a minimum 3.0 GPA, and show clear intent to make the atmospheric or related sciences a career. Selection is based upon academic excellence, achievement, and financial need. Awarded every year.
Contact: Stephanie Kehoe, Fellowship/Scholarship Coordinator.

Biology

970 **Biology Research Scholarship**
University of Utah
Financial Aid and Scholarships Office
105 Student Services Building
Salt Lake City, UT 84112
(801) 581-6211
Maximum award: $1,500
Number of awards: 20
Deadline: February 1
College level: Freshman, Sophomore, Junior, Senior
Majors/Fields: Biology
Criteria: Applicant must be interested in pursuing laboratory research experience leading to a career in biological research. Scholarship is renewable. Awarded every year. Award may be used only at sponsoring institution.
Contact: Biology Department, Hughes Biological Research Program, Salt Lake City, UT 84112, (801) 581-8921.

971 **Biology Scholarship**
Cedar Crest College
100 College Drive
Allentown, PA 18104
(610) 740-3785, (610) 606-4647 (fax)
cccadmis@cedarcrest.edu
www.cedarcrest.edu
Average award: $1,500
Number of awards: 25
Deadline: Rolling
College level: Freshman
Majors/Fields: Biology
Criteria: Interview strongly recommended. Renewable if recipient maintains good academic standing. Awarded every year. Award may be used only at sponsoring institution.
Contact: Judith Neyhart, Vice President for Enrollment Management, Financial Aid Office.

972   Fr. Maximillian Duman Biology Scholarship

Saint Vincent College
Admissions and Financial Aid
Latrobe, PA 15650-2690
(412) 537-4540, (412) 537-4554 (fax)
info@stvincent.edu
http://www.stvincent.edu
Average award: $1,500
Number of awards: 1
Deadline: March 1
College level: Freshman
Criteria: Pre-registration is required. Selection is based upon performance on a competitive biology exam. Renewable if recipient maintains GPA and completes specified biology courses. Award may be used only at sponsoring institution.
Contact: Rev. Earl Henry O.S.B., Director of Admission, 300 Fraser Purchase Road, Latrobe, PA 15650.

973   HHMI Traineeship Program

University of Texas at San Antonio
Office of Student Financial Aid
6900 North Loop 1604 West
San Antonio, TX 78249-0687
(210) 458-4154
Average award: $5,000
Number of awards: 6
Deadline: Rolling
College level: Freshman, Sophomore, Junior, Senior
Majors/Fields: Biology
Criteria: Applicant must be a U.S. citizen, have a minimum 3.0 GPA, and commit to a career in biomedical research. Minimum 3.0 GPA is required to retain scholarship. Awarded every year. Award may be used only at sponsoring institution.
Contact: Division of Life Sciences, MARC Office, Room 4.02.46 SB.

974   John L. Gill Scholarship in Memory of Grace E. Gill and John E. Gill, M.D.

New Mexico State University
Box 30001
Department 5100
Las Cruces, NM 88003-0001
(505) 646-4105
Average award: Full tuition
Deadline: March 1
College level: Sophomore, Junior, Senior
Majors/Fields: Biology, health science, premedicine
Criteria: Applicant must be studying a medically related field. Preference is given to premedical students who are graduates of a Las Cruces high school. Award is for up to three semesters. Awarded every year. Award may be used only at sponsoring institution.
Contact: College of Arts and Sciences, (505) 646-2001.

975   Kenyon Scholarship

Hamline University
1536 Hewitt Avenue
St. Paul, MN 55104
(612) 641-2207
Average award: $2,500
Number of awards: 3
Deadline: January 20
College level: Freshman
Majors/Fields: Biology
Criteria: Applicant must rank in top tenth of class, have three years of mathematics and lab science courses, and demonstrate excellence in biological sciences and interest in the field beyond class requirements. Renewable for up to three years if recipient maintains a minimum 3.25 GPA in math and science courses and a minimum 3.5 GPA in biology courses. Awarded every year. Award may be used only at sponsoring institution.
Contact: Brian Peterson, Senior Associate Director of Undergraduate Admission.

976   Minorities' Access to Research Careers Program Scholarship

New Mexico State University
Box 30001, Department 5100
Las Cruces, NM 88003-0001
(505) 646-4105
Award: Tuition, travel to one scientific meeting, and $3,000 stipend
Deadline: March 1
College level: Junior, Senior
Majors/Fields: Biology, biomedical science
Criteria: Applicant must be a minority student, have a minimum 3.0 GPA, and demonstrate a strong commitment to a career in biomedical science. Awarded every year. Award may be used only at sponsoring institution.
Contact: College of Arts and Sciences, (505) 646-2001.

977   Minority Undergraduate Research Fellowship

American Society for Microbiology (ASM)
Office of Education and Training
1325 Massachusetts Avenue, NW
Washington, DC 20005
(202) 942-9295
http://www.asmusa.org/edusrc/edu23a.htm
Average award: $2,000 stipend plus travel and housing
Deadline: February 1
College level: Junior, Senior
Majors/Fields: Biological sciences with emphasis in the microbiological sciences
Criteria: Applicant must be a U.S. citizen or permanent resident and minority student planning to attend graduate school. Fellowship begins on June 1 and lasts two to three months.
Contact: Irene Hulede, Office of Education and Training.

978   Undergraduate Research Fellowship

American Society for Microbiology (ASM)
Office of Education and Training
1325 Massachusetts Avenue, NW
Washington, DC 20005
(202) 942-9295
http://www.asmusa.org/edusrc/edu23a.htm
Maximum award: $4,000
Deadline: February 1
College level: Sophomore, Junior
Majors/Fields: Microbiological sciences
Criteria: Applicant must be a U.S. citizen or permanent resident and a second- or third-year undergraduate planning to attend graduate school. Fellowship begins June 1 and lasts three to six months. Awarded every year.
Contact: Irene V. Hulede, Office of Education and Training.

Chemistry————————————

979   ACS Scholars Program

American Chemical Society (ACS)
1155 16th Street, NW
Washington, DC 20036
Maximum award: $5,000
Number of awards: 150
Deadline: February 28
College level: Freshman, Sophomore, Junior, Senior
Majors/Fields: Chemistry, chemical-related science
Criteria: Applicant must be an African-American, Hispanic/Latino, or Native American (including Native Hawaiian and Alaskan Native) with a minimum 3.0 GPA. Scholarship is renewable. Awarded every year.
Contact: Dorothy Rodmann, Scholarship Administrator, (202) 872-6250 or 800 227-5558.

980   Annual Chemistry Scholarship

Clemson University
G-01 Sikes Hall
Clemson, SC 29634-5123
(803) 656-2280
Maximum award: $2,400
Number of awards: 1
Deadline: None
College level: Freshman
Majors/Fields: Chemistry
Criteria: Selection is based upon admissions application. Minimum 3.0 GPA and completion of at least 12 credits are required to retain scholarship. Awarded every year. Award may be used only at sponsoring institution.
Contact: Marvin Carmichael, Director of Financial Aid.

981   Chemistry Scholarship

Cedar Crest College
100 College Drive
Allentown, PA 18104
(610) 740-3785, (610) 606-4647 (fax)
cccadmis@cedarcrest.edu
www.cedarcrest.edu
Average award: $1,500
Number of awards: 1
Deadline: Rolling
College level: Freshman
Majors/Fields: Chemistry
Criteria: Interview strongly recommended. Renewable if recipient maintains good academic standing. Awarded every year. Award may be used only at sponsoring institution.
Contact: Judith Neyhart, Vice President of Enrollment Management, Financial Aid Office.

982   CIBA/Geigy Annual Prestige Scholarship in Chemistry

Clemson University
G-01 Sikes Hall
Clemson, SC 29634-5123
(803) 656-2280
Maximum award: $6,000
Number of awards: 1
Deadline: None
College level: Freshman
Majors/Fields: Chemistry
Criteria: Selection is based upon admissions application. Minimum 3.0 GPA and completion of at least 12 credits per semester are required to retain scholarship. Awarded every year. Award may be used only at sponsoring institution.
Contact: Marvin Carmichael, Director of Financial Aid.

983   Dow Scholarship in Chemistry

Southwest Texas State University
J.C. Kellam Building
San Marcos, TX 78666
(512) 245-2340
Average award: $2,000
Number of awards: 2
Deadline: March 15
College level: Freshman
Majors/Fields: Chemistry
Criteria: Applicant must have good ACT or SAT I scores and a strong high school record in science and mathematics, and show ability and potential for advanced study in chemistry. Personal interview may be required. Minimum GPA and course load are required to retain scholarship. Awarded every year. Award may be used only at sponsoring institution.
Contact: Department of Chemistry, (512) 245-2315.

984   E.G. Coombe Family Bursary in Chemistry

University of Calgary
Department of Financial Aid
2500 University Drive, NW
Calgary, Alberta, CN T2N 1N4
(403) 220-7872, (403) 282-2999 (fax)
Average award: $1,500
Number of awards: 2
Deadline: June 15
College level: Sophomore, Junior, Senior
Majors/Fields: Chemistry
Criteria: Applicant must be a Canadian citizen or permanent resident. Selection is based primarily upon financial need. Academic merit and extracurricular activities are considered. Awarded every year. Award may be used only at sponsoring institution.
Contact: J. Van Housen, Director of Student Awards/Financial Aid.

985   Eugene T. Scafe Memorial Scholarship

Southwest Missouri State University
Student Financial Aid
901 South National Avenue
Springfield, MO 65804-0095
(417) 836-5000 or (800) 492-7900
Average award: $1,100
Number of awards: 3
Deadline: March 31
College level: Junior, Senior
Majors/Fields: Chemistry
Criteria: Applicant must have a minimum 3.0 cumulative GPA and have completed at least 18 credit hours in chemistry with a minimum 3.0 GPA in those classes. Minimum 3.0 GPA is required to retain scholarship. Awarded every year. Award may be used only at sponsoring institution.
Contact: Scholarship Committee, (417) 836-5262 or (800) 492-7900.

986   Fr. Bertin Emling Chemistry Scholarship

Saint Vincent College
Admissions and Financial Aid
Latrobe, PA 15650-2690
(412) 537-4540, (412) 537-4554 (fax)
info@stvincent.edu
http://www.stvincent.edu
Average award: $1,500
Number of awards: 1
Deadline: March 1
College level: Freshman
Criteria: Pre-registration required. Selection is based upon performance on a competitive chemistry exam. Renewable if recipient maintains GPA and completes specified chemistry courses. Awarded every year. Award may be used only at sponsoring institution.
Contact: Rev. Earl Henry O.S.B., Dean of Admission and Financial Aid, 300 Fraser Purchase Road, Latrobe, PA 15650.

987   Welch Research Fellowship

Texas A&M University–Kingsville
Scholarships
Box 116
Kingsville, TX 78363
(512) 593-3907, (512) 593-2991 (fax)
http://www.tamuk.edu
Maximum award: $1,800
Number of awards: No limit
Deadline: April 15
College level: Sophomore, Junior, Senior
Majors/Fields: Chemistry
Criteria: Applicant must have a minimum 2.3 GPA. Award may be used only at sponsoring institution.
Contact: Your department, College of Arts and Sciences.

Earth Science————————————————

988   AGI Minority Geoscience Undergraduate Scholarship

American Geological Institute
4220 King Street
Alexandria, VA 22302-1507
(703) 379-2480
Maximum award: $10,000
Number of awards: 30
Deadline: February 1
College level: Freshman, Sophomore, Junior, Senior
*Majors/Fields:*Earth science education, geochemistry, geology, geophysics, hydrology, meteorology, physical oceanography, planetary geology
Criteria: Applicant must be a U.S. citizen who is black, Hispanic, or Native American (American Indian, Eskimo, Hawaiian, or Samoan) with a minimum 2.8 GPA (minimum 3.0 GPA in science and mathematics). Selection is based upon academic excellence, financial need, and potential for professional success. Minimum 3.0 GPA and three letters of recommendation are required to retain scholarship. Awarded every year.
Contact: Director of Education and Human Resources.

989   Conoco Scholarship Award

University of Oklahoma
University Affairs
900 Asp Avenue, Room 236
Norman, OK 73019-0401
(405) 325-1701
Maximum award: $2,000
Deadline: March 1
College level: Freshman, Sophomore, Junior, Senior, Graduate, Doctoral
Majors/Fields: Geology, geophysics
*Criteria:*Applicant must have a minimum 3.0 GPA. Selection is based upon merit and financial need. Awarded every year. Award may be used only at sponsoring institution.
Contact: Director of School of Geology and Geophysics, 100 East Boyd Street, Room G-114, EC, Norman, OK 73019, (405) 325-3253.

990   Geophysics Special Fund Scholarship

University of Utah
Financial Aid and Scholarships Office
105 Student Services Building
Salt Lake City, UT 84112
(801) 581-6211
Average award: $1,500
Number of awards: 5
Deadline: February 1
College level: Freshman, Sophomore, Junior, Senior, Graduate, Doctoral
Majors/Fields: Geophysics
Criteria: Applicant must be a matriculated geophysics major. Awarded every year. Award may be used only at sponsoring institution.
Contact: Dr. Allan A. Ekdale, 602 William C. Browning Building, Salt Lake City, UT 84112-1183, (801) 581-7162.

Environmental Science————

991   EPA Tribal Lands Environmental Science Scholarship

American Indian Science and Engineering Society
Scholarship Coordinator
5661 Airport Boulevard
Boulder, CO 80301
(303) 939-0023, (303) 939-8150 (fax)
ascholar@spot.colorado.edu
http://www.colorado.edu/aises
Average award: $4,000
Number of awards: 68
Deadline: June 15
College level: Junior, Senior, Graduate, Doctoral
*Majors/Fields:*Biochemistry, biology, chemistry, chemical engineering, entomology, environmental economics, environmental science, hydrology, toxicology, related environmental sciences
*Criteria:*Applicant must have a minimum 2.5 GPA and be enrolled full time. Summer employment at an EPA facility and/or on an Indian reservation is also offered if resources are available. Recipient must reapply for renewal. Awarded every year.
Contact: Scholarship Coordinator.

992   Holbrook Island Sanctuary Corp. Scholarship

Maine Community Foundation
210 Main Street, P.O. Box 148
Ellsworth, ME 04605
(207) 667-9735
Average award: $1,000
Deadline: April 15
College level: Freshman
Majors/Fields: Botany, ecology, environmental education, geology, interpretation, marine biology, natural history, ornithology, park management, teaching, zoology
Criteria: Applicant must be a graduating senior from a Hancock County, Maine, high school, planning to continue an education in a field relevant to Holbrook Island Sanctuary and its programs. Applicant must submit a project proposal to be completed at the sanctuary during the summer, a teacher recommendation, and essay. Recipient must reapply for renewal.
Contact: Scholarship Coordinator.

993   Laurie Ircandia Memorial Scholarship

University of Calgary
Department of Financial Aid
2500 University Drive, NW
Calgary, Alberta, CN T2N 1N4
(403) 220-7872, (403) 282-2999 (fax)
Average award: $3,500
Number of awards: 1
Deadline: June 15
College level: Junior, Senior
Majors/Fields: Ecology, environmental protection, marine biology, zoology
*Criteria:*Applicant must intend to pursue graduate study. Selection is based upon academic merit and extracurricular activities in the fields of study. Awarded every year. Award may be used only at sponsoring institution.
Contact: J. Van Housen, Director of Student Awards/Financial Aid.

994   Student Paper Competition

Water Environment Federation (WEF)
601 Wythe Street
Alexandria, VA 22314-1994
(703) 684-2400, extension 7795
http://www.wef.org
Maximum award: $1,000
Number of awards: 12
Deadline: February 1
College level: Sophomore, Junior, Senior, Graduate, Doctoral
Majors/Fields: Water environment
Criteria: Selection is based upon relevancy of subject matter and originality of thoughts, concepts, and solutions presented. Papers may deal with any aspect of water pollution control, water quality problems, water-related concerns, or hazardous wastes. To enter, submit a 500- to 1,000-word abstract with a completed application.
Contact: Program Specialist, MA/Technical Programs, lclark@wef.org.

995   Toro Industry Advancement Award

Landscape Architecture Foundation
4401 Connecticut Avenue, NW #500
Washington, DC 20008
(202) 686-0068, (202) 686-1001 (fax)
Average award: $2,000
Number of awards: 1
Deadline: March 31
Criteria: Award was established to recognize exemplary design projects that display effective use of irrigation techniques in creating quality environments. Awarded every year.
Contact: Scholarships.

Life Sciences–General

996   American Foundation for Aging Research Scholarship

American Foundation for Aging Research
North Carolina State University
Box 7622
Raleigh, NC 27695
(919) 515-5679, (919) 515-2047 (fax)
Average award: $1,000
Minimum award: $500
Number of awards: 6
Deadline: None
College level: Junior, Senior, Doctoral
Majors/Fields: Biology, cell biology, immunology, molecular biology, neurobiology, virology
Criteria: Applicant must be enrolled in a U.S. degree-granting program. Selection is based upon research proposals. Award is for aging research, such as cancer research. $3.00 handling and processing fee should accompany request for application. Recipient must make progress towards degree and research to retain scholarship. Awarded every year.
Contact: Executive Secretary.

997   ESA Undergraduate Scholarship

Entomological Society of America (ESA)
9301 Annapolis Road
Lanham, MD 20706-3115
Average award: $1,500
Number of awards: 4
Deadline: May 31
College level: Junior, Senior
Majors/Fields: Biology, entomology, zoology or related fields
Criteria: Applicant must be an undergraduate at a recognized university or college in the U.S., Mexico, or Canada and have completed a minimum of 30 credit hours by the time the award is presented. Selection is based upon demonstrated enthusiasm, interest and achievement in biology, and academic achievements. Special consideration may be given to applicants demonstrating financial need. Awarded every year.
Contact: ESA Undergraduate Scholarships.

998   National Zoological Park Minority Traineeships

Friends of the National Zoo
National Zoological Park
Washington, DC 20008
Maximum award: $2,400
Number of awards: 4
Deadline: February 21
Majors/Fields: Animal behavior, ecology, education, exhibit evaluation, exhibit planning, exotic animal medicine, facilities design, genetics, horticulture, husbandry, nutrition, public affairs, reproduction, veterinary pathology, zoo graphics
Criteria: Applicant must be a minority. Selection is based upon statement of interest, scholastic achievement, relevant experience, and letters of reference.
Contact: Traineeships.

999   National Zoological Park Research Traineeships

Friends of the National Zoo
National Zoological Park
Washington, DC 20008
Maximum award: $2,400
Number of awards: 10
Deadline: February 21
Majors/Fields: Animal behavior, ecology, exotic animal medicine, reproduction, veterinary pathology
Criteria: Selection is based upon statement of interest, scholarship achievement, relevant experience, and letters of reference.
Contact: Traineeships.

1000   Terminix Scholarship

Clemson University
G-01 Sikes Hall
Clemson, SC 29634-5123
(803) 656-2280
Average award: $1,600
Number of awards: 3
Deadline: March 1
College level: Freshman, Sophomore, Junior, Senior
Majors/Fields: Entomology
Criteria: Applicant must have a minimum 2.5 GPA. Preference is given to entering freshmen. Satisfactory GPA and completion of at least 12 credit hours per semester are required to retain scholarship. Awarded every year. Award may be used only at sponsoring institution.
Contact: Marvin Carmichael, Director of Financial Aid.

Marine Science

1001   Olin Fellowship

Atlantic Salmon Federation
P.O. Box 807
Calais, ME 04619
(506) 529-4581, (506) 529-4985 (fax)
atsal@nbnet.nb.ca
Average award: $1,500
Maximum award: $3,000
Minimum award: $1,000
Number of awards: 4
Deadline: March 15
College level: Sophomore, Junior, Senior, Graduate, Doctoral
Majors/Fields: Atlantic salmon management
Criteria: Awarded every year.

1002 Our World Underwater Scholarship

Our World Underwater Scholarship Society
P.O. Box 4428
Chicago, IL 60680
(312) 666-6525, (312) 666-6846 (fax)
103502,3724@compuserve.com
http://www.owu.ycq.org
Maximum award: $13,000
Number of awards: 1
Deadline: November 30
Criteria: Applicant must be a certified SCUBA diver between age 21 and 24 (as of March 1), have a good academic record, and pass a medical/physical exam. Applicant should be interested in a career in marine science or a closely related underwater field. Award is for a year of intensive travel. Awarded every year.
Contact: Scholarship Application Coordinator.

1003 Robert Dean Stethem Memorial Scholarship

Charles County Board of Education School Commitee
Box D
La Plata, MD 20646
(301) 932-6610
Average award: $1,000
Number of awards: 1
Deadline: May 15
Majors/Fields: Marine science
Criteria: Applicant must be a U.S. citizen and demonstrate financial need. Scholarship is renewable. Awarded every year.
Contact: Scholarships.

1004 Seaspace Scholarship

Seaspace, Inc.
P.O. Box 3753
Houston, TX 77253-3753
(713) 467-6675
Average award: $1,000
Number of awards: 19
Deadline: March 1
College level: Junior, Senior, Graduate, Doctoral
Majors/Fields: Marine science
Criteria: Applicant must have a minimum 3.5 undergraduate GPA or 3.0 graduate GPA. Financial need is considered. Awarded every year.
Contact: Mr. Jesse Cancelmo, Scholarship Coordinator, huc@huc.ycg.org.

Mathematics——————————

1005 Andree Memorial Scholarship

University of Oklahoma
University Affairs
900 Asp Avenue, Room 236
Norman, OK 73019-0401
(405) 325-1701
Maximum award: $2,000
Maximum number of awards: 5
Minimum number of awards: 3
Deadline: February 14
College level: Freshman, Sophomore, Junior, Senior
Majors/Fields: Mathematics
Criteria: Applicant must be interested in computer-related mathematics. Selection is based upon academic record, financial need, and leadership as expressed through participation in the U of Oklahoma chapter of Pi Mu Epsilon. Awarded every year. Award may be used only at sponsoring institution.
Contact: Mathematics Department Graduate Advisor, 601 Elm, Norman, OK 73019, (405) 325-6711.

1006 Bruce Dixson Scholar and Mentor Award

Mesa State College
Financial Aid Department
P.O. Box 2647
Grand Junction, CO 81502
(970) 248-1396
Average award: $2,000
Number of awards: 1
College level: Sophomore, Junior, Senior
Majors/Fields: Mathematics, natural sciences
Criteria: Applicant must be enrolled full time and demonstrate financial need, academic performance, and potential to contribute to chosen profession. Awarded every year. Award may be used only at sponsoring institution.
Contact: School of Natural Sciences and Mathematics.

1007 Eastman Scholarship in Mathematics

University of Nebraska, Lincoln
14th and R Streets
Lincoln, NE 68588
(402) 472-2030, (402) 472-9826 (fax)
http://www.unl.edu/scholfa/cover.html
Average award: $3,000
Maximum award: $4,000
Minimum award: $500
Number of awards: 12
Deadline: January 15
College level: Freshman, Sophomore, Junior, Senior
Majors/Fields: Mathematics
Criteria: Applicant must be a Nebraska high school graduate. Minimum 3.5 GPA, full-time enrollment, and satisfactory progress toward degree in math are required to retain scholarship. Awarded every year. Award may be used only at sponsoring institution.
Contact: Debre Angustyn, Assistant Director of Scholarships.

1008 Goodwin Foundation Scholarship

Mesa State College
Financial Aid Department
P.O. Box 2647
Grand Junction, CO 81502
(970) 248-1396
Maximum award: Tuition and fees
College level: Junior, Senior
Majors/Fields: Mathematics, natural science
Criteria: Applicant must have a minimum 3.5 GPA and demonstrate financial need. Awarded every year. Award may be used only at sponsoring institution.
Contact: School of Natural Science and Mathematics.

1009 Mathematics Scholarship

Saint Vincent College
Admissions and Financial Aid
Latrobe, PA 15650-2690
(412) 537-4540, (412) 537-4554 (fax)
info@stvincent.edu
http://www.stvincent.edu
Average award: $1,500
Number of awards: 1
Deadline: March 1
College level: Freshman
Criteria: Pre-registration is required. Selection is based upon performance on a competitive math exam. Renewable if recipient maintains GPA and completes specified math courses. Awarded every year. Award may be used only at sponsoring institution.
Contact: Rev. Earl Henry, O.S.B., Dean of Admission and Financial Aid, 300 Fraser Purchase Road, Latrobe, PA 15650.

1010   Mathematics Workship

Shawnee State University
940 Second Street
Portsmouth, OH 45662-4344
(614) 355-2237
Average award: $2,750
Deadline: May 15; early application is recommended
College level: Freshman, Sophomore, Junior, Senior, Transfer
Majors/Fields: Mathematics, science
Criteria: Applicant must be a full-time student and be willing to work 10 hours per week in mathematics lab. FAFSA is required. Recipient must maintain a minimum 3.0 GPA in math courses to retain scholarship. Awarded every year. Award may be used only at sponsoring institution.
Contact: Financial Aid Office, (614) 355-2485.

1011   Newbern Bush Memorial Scholarship

Jacksonville State University
Jacksonville, AL 36265-9982
(205) 782-5006
Average award: $1,250
Deadline: March 15
Majors/Fields: Math
Criteria: Applicant must be a native-born Alabama resident. Awarded every year. Award may be used only at sponsoring institution.
Contact: Student Financial Aid Office.

Physical Sciences

1012   EOSAT Award for Application of Digital Landsat TM Data

American Society for Photogrammetry and Remote Sensing (ASPRS)
ASPRS Awards Program, Suite 210
5410 Grosvenor Lane
Bethesda, MD 20814-2160
(301) 493-0290, (301) 493-0208 (fax)
scholarships@asprs.org
www.asprs.org/asprs
Maximum award: $4,000
Number of awards: 1
Deadline: December 1
College level: Sophomore, Senior, Doctoral
Majors/Fields: Remote sensing
Criteria: Applicant must be enrolled full-time at a college or university with image processing facilities. Awarded every year.
Contact: Meredith Zimmerman, Executive Secretary.

1013   Jerome and Mary Straka Scholarship

Kosciuszko Foundation
15 East 65th Street
New York, NY 10021
(212) 734-2130
Average award: $1,000
Number of awards: 1
Deadline: January 15
Majors/Fields: Chemistry, science
Criteria: Applicant must be a U.S. citizen of Polish descent. In the application or request for application, the name of the award being applied for should not be specified; this determination is made by the scholarship committee. Awarded every year.
Contact: Scholarships.

1014   Margaret M. Patterson Scholarship

Kosciuszko Foundation
15 East 65th Street
New York, NY 10021
(212) 734-2130
Average award: $1,000
Deadline: January 15
Majors/Fields: Engineering, science
Criteria: Applicant must be a U.S. citizen of Polish descent. In the application or request for application, the name of the award being applied for should not be specified; this determination is made by the scholarship committee. Awarded every year.
Contact: Scholarships.

1015   Norcen Energy Canadian Scholarship Series in Geology and Geophysics

University of Calgary
Department of Financial Aid
2500 University Drive, NW
Calgary, Alberta, CN T2N 1N4
(403) 220-7872, (403) 282-2999 (fax)
Average award: $1,500
Number of awards: 2
Deadline: June 15
College level: Junior, Senior
Majors/Fields: Geology, geophysics
Criteria: Applicant must be a Canadian citizen or permanent resident. Special consideration is given to applicants expressing interest in the oil and gas industry. Selection is based upon academic merit, financial need, and extracurricular activities. Awarded every year. Award may be used only at sponsoring institution.
Contact: J. Van Housen, Director of Student Awards/Financial Aid.

1016   NSPS Scholarship

American Congress on Surveying and Mapping (ACSM)
Awards Director
5410 Grosvenor Lane
Bethesda, MD 20814-2122
(301) 493-0200
Average award: $1,000
Number of awards: 2
Deadline: January 1
College level: Freshman, Sophomore, Junior, Senior
Majors/Fields: Surveying
Criteria: Applicant must be enrolled in a four-year degree program. Awarded every year.
Contact: ACSM Awards Director.

1017   SEG Foundation Scholarship

Society of Exploration Geophysicists (SEG) Foundation
P.O. Box 702740
Tulsa, OK 74170-2740
(918) 497-5530, (918) 497-5558 (fax)
Average award: $1,200
Maximum award: $3,000
Minimum award: $500
Number of awards: 81
Deadline: March 1
College level: Freshman, Sophomore, Junior, Senior, Graduate, Doctoral
Majors/Fields: Geophysics
Criteria: Applicant must intend to pursue a college course directed toward a career in exploration geophysics and have an interest in and aptitude for physics, mathematics, and geology. Applicant must be one of the following: a high school student with above-average grades planning to enter college the next fall; an undergraduate college student whose grades are above average; a graduate student whose studies are directed toward a career in exploration geophysics in operations, teaching, or research. Financial need is considered, but the competence of the student as indicated by the application is most important. Satisfactory scholastic standing, availability of funds, and a course of study leading to a career in exploration geophysics are required to retain scholarship. Awarded every year.
Contact: Marge Gerhart, Scholarship Coordinator, (918) 497-5500.

Physics

1018 Henry E. and Barbara G. Vogel Scholarship

Clemson University
G-01 Sikes Hall
Clemson, SC 29634-5123
(803) 656-2280
Average award: $1,400
Number of awards: 1
Deadline: March 1
College level: Freshman, Sophomore, Junior, Senior
Majors/Fields: Physics
Criteria: Applicant must have a minimum 2.5 GPA. Renewable if recipient maintains satisfactory GPA and completes at least 12 credits per semester. Awarded every year. Award may be used only at sponsoring institution.
Contact: Scholarships.

Sciences–General

1019 AAAS Mass Media Science and Engineering Fellows Program

American Association for the Advancement of Science (AAAS)
1333 H Street, NW
Washington, DC 20005
(202) 326-6670, (202) 371-9849 (fax)
Maximum award: $4,000
Number of awards: 15
Deadline: January 15
College level: Junior, Senior, Graduate
Majors/Fields: Engineering, natural sciences, social sciences
Criteria: Applicant must be an advanced student (graduate or outstanding junior or senior undergraduate) in the natural sciences, social sciences, or engineering. Program places students as reporters, researchers, and production assistants for a ten-week period during the summer at radio stations, television stations, networks, newspapers, and magazines.
Contact: Amie E. Hubbard, Coordinator.

1020 American Cartographic Association Scholarship

American Congress on Surveying and Mapping (ACSM)
Awards Director
5410 Grosvenor Lane
Bethesda, MD 20814-2122
(301) 493-0200
Average award: $1,000
Deadline: January 1
College level: Junior, Senior
Majors/Fields: Cartography
Criteria: Applicant must be enrolled in a mapping-science curriculum in a four-year degree program. Awarded every year.
Contact: ACSM Awards Director.

1021 American Society of Crime Laboratory Directors' Scholarship

American Society of Crime Laboratory Scholarship Award
Execusuites, Suite 350
15200 Shady Grove Road
Rockville, MD 20850
http://www.shadow.net/~datachem
Average award: $1,000
Number of awards: 2
Deadline: February 1
College level: Sophomore, Junior, Senior, Graduate, Doctoral
Majors/Fields: Forensic science
Criteria: Awarded at the discretion of the ASCLD Board of Directors.
Contact: Dr. Michael J. Camp, Laboratory Director, State Crime Lab, 1578 South 11th Street, Milwaukee, WI 53204, (414) 382-7500.

1022 Arthur Holly Compton Fellowship

Washington University
One Brookings Drive, Campus Box 1089
St. Louis, MO 63130
(314) 935-6000 or (800) 638-0700
Average award: Full tuition plus $1,000 stipend
Number of awards: 6
Deadline: January 15
College level: Freshman
Majors/Fields: Mathematics, natural science
Criteria: Selection is based upon academic merit without regard to financial need. Application is required. Satisfactory academic performance is required to retain scholarship. Awarded every year. Award may be used only at sponsoring institution.
Contact: Office of Undergraduate Admissions.

1023 Barry M. Goldwater Scholarship

Portland State University
Financial Aid Department
P.O. Box 751
Portland, OR 97207-0751
(503) 725-5270
Maximum award: $7,000
Majors/Fields: Engineering, mathematics, natural science
Criteria: Applicant must have a minimum 3.0 GPA. Top quarter of class candidates are nominated by the university. Awarded every year. Award may be used only at sponsoring institution.
Contact: Scholarships, Mathematical Sciences Department, (503) 725-3432.

1024 Berntsen International Scholarship in Surveying

American Congress on Surveying and Mapping (ACSM)
Awards Director
5410 Grosvenor Lane
Bethesda, MD 20814-2122
(301) 493-0200
Average award: $1,500
Number of awards: 2
Deadline: January 1
College level: Freshman, Sophomore, Junior, Senior
Majors/Fields: Surveying
Criteria: Applicant must be enrolled in a four-year degree program. Awarded every year.
Contact: ACSM Awards Director.

1025 Berntsen International Scholarship in Surveying Technology

American Congress on Surveying and Mapping (ACSM)
Awards Director
5410 Grosvenor Lane
Bethesda, MD 20814-2122
(301) 493-0200
Average award: $1,500
Number of awards: 1
Deadline: January 1
College level: Junior college/technical college
Majors/Fields: Surveying technology
Criteria: Applicant must be enrolled in a two-year program. Awarded every year.
Contact: ACSM Awards Director.

1026   C. Louis and Thelma Ferrell Van Buren Scholarship

Southwest Missouri State University
Student Financial Aid
901 South National Avenue
Springfield, MO 65804-0095
(417) 836-5000 or (800) 492-7900
Average award: $1,300
Number of awards: 2
Deadline: March 31
College level: Junior, Senior
Majors/Fields: Mathematics, science
Criteria: Applicant must have a minimum 3.0 GPA. Participation in extracurricular activities is also considered. Reapplication is required to retain scholarship. Awarded every year. Award may be used only at sponsoring institution.
Contact: Scholarship Committee, (417) 836-5262 or (800) 492-7900.

1027   Daniel Swarovski & Co. Scholarship

Gemological Institute of America (GIA)
Financial Aid Office
5345 Armada Drive
Carlsbad, CA 92008-4698
(619) 603-4004, 619 603-4005
Average award: $1,625
Number of awards: 6
Deadline: November 1
College level: Gemology students
Majors/Fields: Gemology
Criteria: Applicant must have at least three years prior employment in the jewelry industry, demonstrate financial need, and submit three letters of recommendation. Awarded every year.
Contact: Financial Aid Office.

1028   Dean's Science Scholarship

DePaul University
1 East Jackson Boulevard
Chicago, IL 60604
(312) 362-8704, (312) 362-5749 (fax)
Average award: $4,000
Maximum award: $8,000
Minimum award: $2,000
Deadline: None
College level: Freshman
Majors/Fields: Science
Criteria: Applicant must rank in the top tenth of class, have a minimum composite ACT score of 27 (combined SAT I score of 1200), and have a strong interest in the study of science. Minimum 2.75 GPA during first year (3.0 GPA thereafter) is required to retain scholarship. Awarded every year. Award may be used only at sponsoring institution.
Contact: Jennifer Sparrow, Scholarship Coordinator, jsparrow@wppost.depaul.edu.

1029   DMI/Dairy Shrine Milk Marketing Scholarship

Dairy Shrine
100 MBC Drive
Shawano, WI 54166
(715) 526-2141, (715) 526-3219 (fax)
Maximum award: $1,000
Number of awards: 3
Deadline: March 15
College level: Sophomore, Junior, Senior
Majors/Fields: Dairy science, home economics, journalism, milk marketing
Criteria: Awarded every year.
Contact: James Leuenberger, Secretary/Treasurer.

1030   Dr. Robert H. Goddard Scholarship

National Space Club
655 15th Street, NW
Suite 300
Washington, DC 20005
Maximum award: $10,000
Number of awards: 1
Deadline: January 10
College level: Senior, Graduate, Doctoral
Majors/Fields: Aeronautics, engineering, science
Criteria: Applicant must be a U.S. citizen intending to pursue undergraduate or graduate studies in science or engineering. Selection is based upon college record, recommendations, accomplishments demonstrating creativity and leadership, scholastic plans for the aerospace sciences and technology, and proven past research in space-related science and engineering. Applicant may be eligible to compete for a second year. Awarded every year.
Contact: Chairman of the Scholarship Committee.

1031   Dupont Challenge/Science Essay Award

General Learning Communications
900 Skokie Boulevard
Northbrook, IL 60062
(847) 205-3000
Maximum award: $1,500
Number of awards: 54
Deadline: January 31
College level: Freshman
Majors/Fields: Science
Criteria: Applicant must be currently enrolled in a public or nonpublic school in the U.S., U.S. territories, or Canada in grades 7 through 12. A 700- to 1,000-word essay and official entry form are required. Awarded every year.
Contact: General Learning Communications.

1032   Duracell/National Science Teachers' Association Scholarship Competition

National Science Teachers' Association (NSTA)
1840 Wilson Boulevard
Arlington, VA 22201-3000
(703) 312-9258, (703) 522-6193 (fax)
ecrossley@nsta.org
Maximum award: $20,000
Number of awards: 100
Deadline: Mid-January
College level: Freshman
Criteria: Applicant must be a student in grades 9-12, reside in the U.S. or its territories, and must create and build a working device powered by batteries that can perform a practical function. The top 100 finalists will send their actual devices in for judging. Awarded every year.
Contact: Eric Crossley, National Science Teachers' Association.

1033   FFS Student Fellowships

Fight for Sight/The Research Division of Prevent Blindness America
500 East Remington Road
Schaumburg, IL 60173
(847) 843-2020
Maximum award: $1,500
Number of awards: 20
Deadline: March 1
College level: Graduate, Medical, Unspecified undergraduate
Majors/Fields: Ophthalmology, visual sciences
Criteria: Applicant must be a U.S. or Canadian resident demonstrating interest in eye research and visual sciences. Applicant must identify own sponsoring institution. Recipient must reapply for renewal.
Contact: Program Coordinator.

1034 Gina Finzi Memorial Student Summer Fellowship

Lupus Foundation of America
4 Research Place, Suite 180
Rockville, MD 20850-3226
(301) 670-9292
Average award: $2,000
Number of awards: 10
Deadline: February 1
College level: Senior, Graduate, Doctoral
Majors/Fields: Biology, chemistry, life science, psychosocial science, science
Criteria: Fellowship is given to foster interest in lupus erythematosus in the areas of basic, clinical, or psychological research under the supervision of an established investigator. Awarded every year.
Contact: Patricia S. Leisy, Director of Education Services.

1035 Gorgas Foundation Inc. Scholarship

Birmingham-Southern College
Arkadelphia Road
Birmingham, AL 35254
(205) 226-4688
Award: Full tuition
Number of awards: 1
Deadline: None
College level: Freshman
Criteria: Awarded to the winner of the Alabama Science Competition. Awarded every year. Award may be used only at sponsoring institution.
Contact: Admissions Office, (800) 523-5793, extension 4696.

1036 HBCU/MI Environmental Consortium Scholarship

Texas A&M University–Kingsville
Scholarships
Box 116
Kingsville, TX 78363
(512) 593-3907, (512) 593-2991 (fax)
http://www.tamuk.edu
Maximum award: $1,500
Number of awards: No limit
Deadline: July 26
College level: Sophomore, Junior, Senior
Majors/Fields: Environmental/physical sciences
Criteria: Applicant must have a minimum 3.0 GPA, a minimum GRE score of 1100, and at least 60 completed credit hours. Award may be used only at sponsoring institution.
Contact: Your department, College of Engineering.

1037 Joseph F. Dracup Scholarship

American Congress on Surveying and Mapping (ACSM)
Awards Director
5410 Grosvenor Lane
Bethesda, MD 20814-2122
(301) 493-0200
Average award: $2,000
Number of awards: 1
Deadline: January 1
College level: Freshman, Sophomore, Junior, Senior
Majors/Fields: Geodetic surveying
Criteria: Applicant must be committed to a career in geodetic surveying. Awarded every year.
Contact: ACSM Awards Director.

1038 Leica Inc. Surveying Scholarship

American Congress on Surveying and Mapping (ACSM)
Awards Director
5410 Grosvenor Lane
Bethesda, MD 20814-2122
(301) 493-0200
Average award: $1,000
Number of awards: 2
Deadline: January 1
College level: Freshman, Sophomore, Junior, Senior
Majors/Fields: Surveying
Criteria: Applicant must be enrolled in a four-year degree program. Recipient also earns a $2,000 credit for his or her school for the purchase of Leica equipment and $500 credit to a graduating senior for the purchase of Leica equipment. Awarded every year.
Contact: ACSM Awards Director.

1039 Margaret Bush Wilson Scholarship

University of Missouri–St. Louis
8001 Natural Bridge Road
St. Louis, MO 63121
(314) 553-6396
Average award: $3,000
Number of awards: 15
Deadline: April 1
College level: Freshman
Majors/Fields: Biology, chemistry, computer science, mathematics, physics
Criteria: Applicant must have been heavily involved in the Bridge Program. Satisfactory academic progress and completion of at least 24 hours per year are required to retain scholarship. Awarded every year. Award may be used only at sponsoring institution.
Contact: James D. Reed, Financial Aid Adviser.

1040 Mastin Foundation Scholarship

Heidelberg College
310 East Market Street
Tiffin, OH 44883
(419) 448-2293, (414) 448-2124 (fax)
jweing@mail.heidelberg.edu
Average award: $10,000
Number of awards: 1
Deadline: March 1
College level: Freshman
Majors/Fields: Natural sciences, mathematics
Criteria: Applicant must be a National Merit finalist or semifinalist, or have a minimum composite ACT score of 27. Minimum 3.0 GPA and natural science major are required to retain scholarship. Awarded every year. Award may be used only at sponsoring institution.
Contact: Juli Weininger, Director of Financial Aid.

1041 Minority Access for Research Careers (MARC) Scholarship

University of Texas at San Antonio
Office of Student Financial Aid
6900 North Loop 1604 West
San Antonio, TX 78249-0687
(210) 458-4154
Average award: Tuition, fees, and travel allowance
Number of awards: 10
Deadline: None
College level: Junior, Senior
Majors/Fields: Engineering, sciences
Criteria: Applicant must be a minority U.S. citizen or have a permanent visa, have a minimum 3.0 GPA, and make a commitment to graduate school and a career in biomedical research. Minimum 3.0 GPA is required to retain scholarship. Awarded every year. Award may be used only at sponsoring institution.
Contact: Division of Life Sciences, MARC Office, Room 4.02.46 SB.

1042 Monsanto Scholarship

Denison University
Box H
Granville, OH 43023
(614) 587-6276, 800-DENISON, (614) 587-6306 (fax)
admissions@denison.edu
http://www.denison.edu
Average award: Half tuition
Number of awards: 1
Deadline: January 1
College level: Freshman
Majors/Fields: Science
Criteria: Applicant must be African-American or Hispanic and from the St. Louis, Mo., area. Selection is based upon academic excellence, extracurricular achievements, and personal interview. Minimum GPA is required for renewal. Awarded every year. Award may be used only at sponsoring institution.
Contact: Mary Early, Scholarships, (614) 587-6621.

1043 NASA/Wisconsin Space Grant Consortium Scholarship

Lawrence University
P.O. Box 599
Appleton, WI 54912-0599
(414) 832-6500, (414) 832-6782 (fax)
excel@lawrence.edu
http://www.lawrence.edu
Average award: $5,000
Maximum number of awards: 5
Minimum number of awards: 2
Deadline: February 1
College level: Freshman
Majors/Fields: Biology, chemistry, economics, government, mathematics, physics
Criteria: Applicant must submit essay on interest in space. Application is available from admissions office. Minimum 3.0 GPA required to retain scholarship. Awarded every year. Award may be used only at sponsoring institution.
Contact: Director of Admissions.

1044 New Mexico Space Grant Undergraduate Scholarship

New Mexico State University
Box 30001, Department 5100
Las Cruces, NM 88003-0001
(505) 646-4105
Maximum award: $3,000
Number of awards: 5
Deadline: March 1
College level: Freshman, Sophomore, Junior, Senior
Majors/Fields: Astronomy, biology, chemistry, computer science, earth science, mathematics, physics
Criteria: Applicant must be a U.S. citizen, enroll in the College of Engineering or College of Arts and Sciences, and have a minimum 3.25 GPA. Preference is given to women and minority students. Awarded every year. Award may be used only at sponsoring institution.
Contact: Greeley W. Myers, Director of Financial Aid.

1045 Pearl and Burritt Hiatt Scholarship

Wilmington College
Pyle Center Box 1325
Wilmington, OH 45177
(800) 341-9318, (513) 382-7077 (fax)
admission@wilmington.edu
http://www.wilmington.edu
Average award: $5,000
Deadline: May 1
College level: Freshman
Majors/Fields: Sciences
Criteria: Applicant must have a minimum 3.0 GPA and either rank in top two-tenths of class or have a minimum composite ACT score of 25 (combined SAT I score of 1050). Selection is based upon academic record. Renewable if recipient maintains a minimum 3.3 GPA. Awarded every year. Award may be used only at sponsoring institution.
Contact: Financial Aid Office.

1046 Porter McDonnell Memorial Award

American Congress on Surveying and Mapping (ACSM)
Awards Director
5410 Grosvenor Lane
Bethesda, MD 20814-2122
(301) 493-0200
Average award: $1,000
Number of awards: 1
Deadline: January 1
College level: Sophomore, Junior, Senior
Majors/Fields: Surveying, mapping
Criteria: Applicant must be a woman with the potential for leadership in the surveying and mapping profession. Awarded every year.
Contact: ACSM Awards Director.

1047 Robert E. Altenhofen Memorial Scholarship

American Society for Photogrammetry and Remote Sensing (ASPRS)
ASPRS Awards Program, Suite 210
5410 Grosvenor Lane
Bethesda, MD 20814-2160
(301) 493-0290, (301) 493-0208 (fax)
scholarships@asprs.org
www.asprs.org/asprs
Maximum award: $1,000
Number of awards: 1
Deadline: December 1
College level: Sophomore, Junior, Senior, Graduate
Majors/Fields: Photogrammetry
Criteria: Applicant must be a student or an active member of ASPRS. Awarded when sufficient funds are available and qualified applicants apply.
Contact: Meredith Zimmerman, Executive Secretary.

1048 Scholarship for Distinguished Achievement in Science and Mathematics

Susquehanna University
Selinsgrove, PA 17870
(717) 372-4450
Maximum award: $7,500
Deadline: None
College level: Freshman
Majors/Fields: Computer science, mathematics, sciences
Criteria: Selection is based upon outstanding academic achievement. Awarded every year. Award may be used only at sponsoring institution.
Contact: Office of Financial Aid.

1049 Science and Engineering Research Semester

Argonne National Laboratory
Argonne, IL 60439-4845
(708) 252-3371
http://www.dep.anl.gov
Award: $225 per week stipend, housing, and certain travel expenses
Deadline: March 15 (fall); October 20 (spring)
College level: Unspecified undergraduates
Majors/Fields: Engineering, science
Criteria: Applicant must be a U.S. citizen or permanent resident alien and have a minimum 3.0 GPA. Selection is based upon academic record, statement of interests, and faculty recommendations. Renewable for up to twelve months upon mutual consent of sponsoring laboratory scientist and the Division of Educational Programs.
Contact: Division of Educational Programs.

1050 Science and Mathematics Scholarship

The College of Wooster
Office of Admissions
Wooster, OH 44691
(330) 263-2270, (330) 263-2621 (fax)
admissions@acs.wooster.edu
http://www.wooster.edu
Maximum award: $10,000
Deadline: February 15
College level: Freshman
Criteria: Applicant must have a minimum 3.0 GPA, rank in top tenth of class, and be nominated by a counselor or teacher. Selection is based upon achievement and interest in computer, mathematical, natural, or physical sciences. Recipient must maintain academic progress toward degree to retain scholarship. Renewable for four years. Awarded every year. Award may be used only at sponsoring institution.
Contact: Office of Admissions.

1051 Science Fair Scholarship

Mount Union College
1972 Clark Avenue
Alliance, OH 44601
(216) 821-5320
Average award: $1,500
Deadline: None
College level: Freshman
Criteria: Applicant must have achieved superior rating at regional and/or state Ohio Academy of Science Fairs in senior year. Awarded every year. Award may be used only at sponsoring institution.
Contact: Office of Admissions.

1052 Science Fellows Scholarship

Elon College
2700 Campus Box
Elon College, NC 27244
(800) 334-8448 extension 1
Average award: $2,000
College level: Freshman
Majors/Fields: Biology, chemistry, computer science, mathematics, physics
Criteria: Eligible applicants are nominated through admissions office and invited to participate in scholarship competition. Recipients must participate in Honors Program and must progress toward presenting research results during final year. Renewable for up to four years if recipient maintains satisfactory academic progress and participation in Honors Program. Awarded every year. Award may be used only at sponsoring institution.
Contact: Office of Admission and Financial Planning.

1053 Seiko Youth Challenge

Seiko Corporation of America
c/o DRB Communications
1234 Summer Street
Stamford, CT 06905
(800) 323-1550
Average award: $9,375
Maximum award: $25,000
Minimum award: $5,000
Number of awards: 5
Deadline: Februry 28
College level: Freshman
Criteria: Applicant must identify, research, analyze, and propose a solution to a local environmental problem. Selection is based upon imagination and originality of approach, depth of research, methodology, practicality of implementation, and magnitude of local environmental impact. Projects may be up to 10 pages in length with up to a 10-page appendix. Applicants must be in grades 9 through 12 working in teams of 2 to 4 people with the guidance of a faculty advisor. Awarded every year.
Contact: Robert Bigda, Program Administrator.

1054 Sonoco Annual Scholarship

Clemson University
G-01 Sikes Hall
Clemson, SC 29634-5123
(803) 656-2280
Average award: $1,250
Number of awards: 2
Deadline: March 1
College level: Freshman, Sophomore, Junior, Senior
Majors/Fields: Packaging science
Criteria: Applicant must have a minimum 2.5 GPA. Awarded every year. Award may be used only at sponsoring institution.
Contact: Marvin Carmichael, Director of Financial Aid.

1055 Southwestern Bell Scholarship

University of Missouri–St. Louis
8001 Natural Bridge Road
St. Louis, MO 63121
(314) 553-6396
Average award: $2,500
Number of awards: 2
Deadline: April 1
College level: Freshman
Criteria: Applicant must have a minimum cumulative 3.0 GPA and have participated in the Engelmann Math and Science Institute or the Bridge Program. Minimum 3.2 cumulative GPA is required to retain scholarship. Awarded every year. Award may be used only at sponsoring institution.
Contact: James D. Reed, Financial Aid Advisor.

1056 SPIE Educational Grants and Scholarships in Optical Engineering

International Society for Optical Engineering (SPIE)
SPIE Scholarship Committee
P.O. Box 10
Bellingham, WA 98227-0010
(360) 676-3290, (360) 647-1445 (fax)
Maximum award: $7,000
Number of awards: 23
Deadline: April 4
College level: Freshman, Sophomore, Junior, Senior, Graduate, Doctoral
Majors/Fields: Optical/opto-electronic applied science, optical/opto-electronic engineering
Criteria: Selection is based upon the long-range contribution the applicant could make to optics and optical engineering. Financial need is not a factor. Awarded every year.
Contact: Alson E. Hathaway, Scholarship Committee.

1057 Summer Research Participation Program

Argonne National Laboratory
Argonne, IL 60439-4845
(708) 252-3371
http://www.dep.anl.gov
Award: $225 per week stipend, housing, certain travel expenses
Deadline: February 1
College level: Junior, Senior, Graduate
Majors/Fields: Engineering, science
Criteria: Applicant must be a U.S. citizen or permanent resident alien and have a minimum 3.0 GPA. Selection is based upon academic record, statement of interests, and faculty recommendations.
Contact: Division of Educational Programs.

1058 TAPPI Technical Division Scholarships

Technical Association of the Pulp & Paper Industry (TAPPI)
Technology Park/Atlanta
P.O. Box 105113
Atlanta, GA 30348-5113
(770) 446-1400, (770) 446-6947 (fax)
techdiv@tappi.org
http://www.tappi.org
Maximum award: $3,000
Number of awards: 20
Deadline: January 31
College level: Sophomore, Junior, Senior, Graduate, Doctoral
Majors/Fields: Engineering, forest resources, nonwovens, packaging, paper, pulp, science
Criteria: Awarded every year.
Contact: Marilyn Cooper, Technical Services Department, (770) 209-7410.

1059 Thomas Edison/Max McGraw Scholarship

National Science Education Leadership Association (NSELA)
Edison/McGraw Scholarship
P.O. Box 5556
Arlington, VA 22205
(703) 524-8646, (703) 524-3929 (fax)
http://science.coe.uwf.edu/nsela/scholar.htm
Average award: $3,000
Maximum award: $5,000
Minimum award: $1,500
Number of awards: 10
Deadline: December 15
College level: Freshman, high school students in grades 9 through 12
Criteria: Please contact web page for more information. Reapplication with project is required for renewal. Awarded every year.
Contact: Patricia J. McWethy, NSELA Executive Director.

1060 Tiger Pack Annual Scholarship

Clemson University
G-01 Sikes Hall
Clemson, SC 29634-5123
(803) 656-2280
Average award: $1,500
Number of awards: 1
Deadline: March 1
College level: Freshman, Sophomore, Junior, Senior
Majors/Fields: Packaging science
Criteria: Applicant must have a minimum 2.5 GPA. Awarded every year. Award may be used only at sponsoring institution.
Contact: Scholarships.

1061 Traineeships in Exhibit Interpretation, Public Affairs, Education, Horticulture, Facilities Design, and Photography

Friends of the National Zoo
National Zoological Park
Washington, DC 20008
Maximum award: $2,400
Majors/Fields: Education, facilities design, horticulture, photography, public affairs, zoo graphics
Criteria: Selection is based upon statement of interest, scholastic achievement, relevant experience, and letters of reference.
Contact: Traineeships.

1062 University DOE Laboratory Cooperative Program

U.S. Department of Energy Lab Co-op Programs
P.O. Box 117
Oak Ridge, TN 37831-0117
(423) 576-3192, (423) 421-5220 (fax)
Award: $250 per week
Number of awards: 1,000
Deadline: In January
College level: Sophomore, Junior, Senior, Graduate, Doctoral
Majors/Fields: Computer science, engineering, mathematics, science
Criteria: Applicant must be a U.S. citizen or permanent resident, age 18 or older, and enrolled in an accredited U.S. institution. Awards are summer or semester appointments to DOE labs or research centers. Awarded every year.
Contact: Linda Holmes, Group Manager, holmesl@orau.gov.

1063 Wells Scholarship

Denison University
Box H
Granville, OH 43023
(614) 587-6276, 800-DENISON, (614) 587-6306 (fax)
admissions@denison.edu
http://www.denison.edu
Average award: Full tuition
Number of awards: 1
Deadline: January 1
College level: Freshman
Majors/Fields: Science, mathematics
Criteria: Applicant must be an outstanding student in science or mathematics and must meet criteria for Honors Program. Essay, teacher recommendations, and interview or campus visitation program are required. Minimum GPA is required for renewal. Awarded every year. Award may be used only at sponsoring institution.
Contact: Janet Schultz, Scholarships, (614) 587-6625.

1064 Westinghouse Science Talent Search

Science Service Inc.
1719 N Street, NW
Washington, DC 20036
(202) 785-2255
http://www.tss-inc.com/sciserv/
Maximum award: $40,000
Number of awards: 40
Deadline: Late November/early December (varies every year)
College level: Freshman
Criteria: Applicant must complete a science research project and submit a written report and an entry form. Awarded every year.
Contact: Yvonne V. Tilghman, Deputy Director of Youth Programs.

1065 William H. Greaves Undergraduate Scholarship

Northern Kentucky University
Administrative Center 416
Nunn Drive
Highland Heights, KY 41099-7101
(606) 572-5144
Award: In-state tuition and books
Deadline: February 1
College level: Freshman, Sophomore, Junior, Senior
Majors/Fields: Computer science, electrical engineering technology, engineering, manufacturing technology, mathematics, science
Criteria: Freshman applicant must rank in top quarter of class and have a minimum composite ACT score of 25; upperclass applicant must have a minimum cumulative GPA of 3.0. Award is renewable for two or three years. Awarded every year. Award may be used only at sponsoring institution.
Contact: Robert E. Sprague, Director of Financial Aid.

Social Science/Political Science/Law

Home Economics————————

1066   Ann Lane Homemaker Scholarship

Texas Electric Cooperatives, Inc.
Ann Lane Homemaker Scholarship
P.O. Box 9589
Austin, TX 78766
(512) 454-0311 extension 212, (512) 454-3587 (fax)
Maximum award: $1,000
Number of awards: 1
Deadline: March 1
College level: Freshman
Criteria: Applicant must be a Texas resident, attend an accredited Texas university, college, or technical school and be an active member of Future Homemakers of America. Selection is based upon FHA high school/community activities and financial need. Essay on "The Role of the Homemaker" is required. Awarded every year.
Contact: Dennis Engelke, Director of Member Services, P.O. Box 9589, Austin, TX 78766-9589.

1067   Candle Fellowship

Phi Upsilon Omicron
171 Mount Hall, 1050 Carmack Road
The Ohio State University
Columbus, OH 43210
(614) 421-7860
Average award: $1,000
Number of awards: 2
Deadline: February 1
College level: Graduate
Majors/Fields: Home economics
*Criteria:*Applicant must be a Phi Upsilon Omicron member. Selection is based upon scholastic record, honors, extracurricular activities, scholarly work, and statement of professional goals. Awarded every year.
Contact: National Office.

1068   Diamond Anniversary Fellowships

Phi Upsilon Omicron
171 Mount Hall, 1050 Carmack Road
The Ohio State University
Columbus, OH 43210
(614) 421-7860
Average award: $1,000
Number of awards: 2
Deadline: March 1
College level: Graduate, Doctoral
Majors/Fields: Home economics
*Criteria:*Applicant must be a Phi Upsilon Omicron member. Selection is based upon scholastic record, honors, extracurricular activities, scholarly work, and statement of professional goals. Awarded every year.
Contact: National Office.

1069   Founders Fellowship

Phi Upsilon Omicron
171 Mount Hall, 1050 Carmack Road
The Ohio State University
Columbus, OH 43210
(614) 421-7860
Average award: $1,500
Number of awards: 1
Deadline: March 1
College level: Doctoral
Majors/Fields: Home economics
Criteria: Applicant must be a Phi Upsilon Omicron member, have completed at least half the credit hour requirements toward a Ph.D. in home economics, and have had several years of successful employment in home economics. Awarded every year.
Contact: National Office.

1070   Hazel Putnam Roach Fellowship

American Association of Family and Consumer Sciences
1555 King Street
Alexandria, VA 22314
(703) 706-4600
Average award: $3,000
Number of awards: 1
Deadline: January 16
College level: Graduate
Majors/Fields: Home economics
Criteria: Applicant must be a U.S. citizen. Awarded every year.
Contact: Fellowships.

1071   Jewell L. Taylor Fellowship

American Association of Family and Consumer Sciences
1555 King Street
Alexandria, VA 22314
(703) 706-4600
Average award: $5,000
Number of awards: 1
Deadline: January 16
College level: Graduate, Doctoral
Majors/Fields: Home economics
Criteria: Applicant must be a U.S. citizen. Awarded every year.
Contact: Foundation Associate.

1072   Lillian P. Schoephoerster Scholarship

Phi Upsilon Omicron
171 Mount Hall, 1050 Carmack Road
The Ohio State University
Columbus, OH 43210
(614) 421-7860
Average award: $1,000
Number of awards: 1
Deadline: March 1
College level: Non-traditional undergraduate student
Majors/Fields: Home economics
Criteria: Applicant must be a Phi Upsilon Omicron member and a nontraditional student. Awarded every year.
Contact: National Office, phiu@magnus.acs.ohio-state.edu.

1073 Presidents Research Fellowship

Phi Upsilon Omicron
171 Mount Hall, 1050 Carmack Road
The Ohio State University
Columbus, OH 43210
(614) 421-7860
Average award: $1,000
Number of awards: 1
Deadline: March 1
College level: Graduate, Doctoral
Majors/Fields: Home economics
Criteria: Applicant must be a member of Phi Upsilon Omicron and submit research prospectus that demonstrates the need for the research. Awarded every year.
Contact: National Office, phiu@magnus.acs.ohio-state.edu.

Law

1074 Alberta Law Foundation Scholarship

University of Calgary
Department of Financial Aid
2500 University Drive, NW
Calgary, Alberta, CN T2N 1N4
(403) 220-7872, (403) 282-2999 (fax)
Maximum award: $5,000
Deadline: May 1
College level: Junior, Senior
Majors/Fields: Law
Criteria: Selection is based upon academic record, LSAT score, maturity, extracurricular activities, work experience, and community involvement. If possible, one award will be given to an Aboriginal Canadian. High academic standing is required to retain scholarship for two additional years. Awarded every year. Award may be used only at sponsoring institution.
Contact: J. Van Housen, Director of Student Awards/Financial Aid.

1075 CLEO Scholarship

Council on Legal Education Opportunity
1420 N Street, NW
Suite T-1
Washington, DC 20005
(202) 785-4840, (202) 223-5633 (fax)
Average award: $7,000
Number of awards: 470
Deadline: February 1
College level: Doctoral
Majors/Fields: Law
Criteria: Applicant must be financially and educationally disadvantaged. Scholarship is renewable. Awarded every year.
Contact: Gretchen Wessel, Admissions Analyst.

1076 Community College Scholarship

Western State University College of Law–San Diego
2121 San Diego Avenue
San Diego, CA 92100
(619) 297-9700
Maximum award: $2,000
Number of awards: 18
Deadline: July 15 (fall); December 15 (spring)
College level: Entering law students
Majors/Fields: Law
Criteria: Applicant must be a graduate of a California community college with an associate degree and be first-time student. Selection is based upon academic accomplishment and potential for law study. Three awards ($500, $1,000, $2,000) are given at each campus for students entering in fall and spring. Application, college and graduate school transcripts, current resume, personal statement, and two letters of recommendation are required. Awarded every year. Award may be used only at sponsoring institution.
Contact: Kathy Kordis or Jennifer Keller, Associate Directors of Financial Aid.

1077 Community Service/Pro Bono Scholarship

Western State University College of Law–San Diego
2121 San Diego Avenue
San Diego, CA 92100
(619) 297-9700
Maximum award: $2,000
Number of awards: 18
Deadline: July 15 (fall); December 15 (spring)
College level: Entering law students
Majors/Fields: Law
Criteria: Selection is based upon record of community service or volunteer work for the good of the public and potential for law study. Three awards ($500, $1,000, $2,000) are given at each campus for students entering in fall and spring. Application, college and graduate school transcripts, current resume, details and verification of community service, personal statement, and two letters of recommendation are required. Awarded every year. Award may be used only at sponsoring institution.
Contact: Kathy Kordis or Jennifer Keller, Associate Directors of Financial Aid.

1078 Directors' Scholarship

Western State University College of Law–San Diego
2121 San Diego Avenue
San Diego, CA 92100
(619) 297-9700
Maximum award: $5,300
Deadline: None
College level: Continuing law students who have completed one full year of study with a minimum 19 units
Majors/Fields: Law
Criteria: Awarded automatically to top three-tenths of eligible students. Amount of award is based upon rank/GPA and number of units per semester. Financial need is not considered. Awarded every year. Award may be used only at sponsoring institution.
Contact: Kathy Kordis or Jennifer Keller, Associate Directors of Financial Aid.

1079 Holland & Hart Minority Scholarship

University of Colorado at Boulder
Campus Box 106
Boulder, CO 80309-0106
(303) 492-5091
Average award: $5,000
Number of awards: 2
Deadline: As soon as possible after January 1
College level: Freshman, Sophomore, Junior, Senior, Graduate
Majors/Fields: Law
Criteria: Applicant must be a minority student whose achievements show promise of success in law school and the legal profession. Financial need is considered. Awarded every year. Award may be used only at sponsoring institution.
Contact: Office of Financial Aid.

1080 John W. Green Scholarship

University of Tennessee, Knoxville
Financial Aid Office
115 Student Services Building
Knoxville, TN 37994
(615) 974-3131
Average award: In-state tuition and fees
Deadline: February 1
College level: Law students
Majors/Fields: Law
Criteria: Selection is based upon merit of members of the three law classes who have unusual ability in the general development of character, ambition to excel, and interest in the general development and advancement of the ethical standards of the legal profession. Awarded every year. Award may be used only at sponsoring institution.
Contact: College of Law, 1505 West Cumberland Avenue, Knoxville, TN 37996, (615) 974-4131.

1081 Law Enforcement Career Scholarship

Association of Former Agents of the United States Secret Service, Inc.
P.O. Box 848
Annandale, VA 22003-0848
Average award: $1,000
Maximum award: $1,500
Minimum award: $500
Number of awards: 3
Deadline: April 1
College level: Junior, Senior, Graduate, Doctoral
Majors/Fields: Law enforcement, police administration
Criteria: Applicant must have completed at least one year of study in law enforcement prior to applying and must be a U.S. citizen. Selection is based upon academic standing. Awarded every year.
Contact: P. Hamilton Brown, Executive Secretary.

1082 Law Enforcement Personnel Scholarship

Western State University College of Law–San Diego
2121 San Diego Avenue
San Diego, CA 92100
(619) 297-9700
Maximum award: $2,000
Number of awards: 18
Deadline: July 15 (fall); December 15 (spring)
College level: Entering law students
Majors/Fields: Law
Criteria: Applicant must be an active duty, safety-sworn law enforcement officer. Selection is based upon accomplishment in law enforcement and potential for law study. Three awards ($500, $1,000, $2,000) are given at each campus for students entering in fall and spring. Application, college and graduate school transcripts, current resume, verification of safety-sworn status, personal statement, and two letters of recommendation are required. Awarded every year. Award may be used only at sponsoring institution.
Contact: Kathy Kordis or Jennifer Keller, Associate Directors of Financial Aid.

1083 Law School Scholarship for Library School Graduates

American Association of Law Libraries
Scholarships and Grants Committee
53 West Jackson Boulevard, Suite 940
Chicago, IL 60604
(312) 939-4764
Average award: $1,800
Number of awards: 6
Deadline: March 17
College level: Graduate
Majors/Fields: Law
Criteria: Applicant must be a library school graduate who is working toward a law degree at an accredited law school, has no more than 36 semester credit hours of study remaining, and who has meaningful law library experience. Awarded every year.
Contact: Ronda Bedrook, Scholarships and Grants Committee, 53 West Jackson Boulevard, Suite 940, Chicago, IL 60604.

1084 Legal Secretary, Assistant, and Paralegal Scholarship

Western State University College of Law–San Diego
2121 San Diego Avenue
San Diego, CA 92100
(619) 297-9700
Maximum award: $2,000
Number of awards: 18
Deadline: July 15 (fall); December 15 (spring)
College level: Entering law students
Majors/Fields: Law
Criteria: Applicant must be currently employed, have at least two years of full-time work experience, and be a first-time student. Selection is based upon accomplishment in legal profession and potential for law study. Three awards ($500, $1,000, $2,000) are given at each campus for students entering in fall and spring. Application, college and graduate school transcripts, current resume, verification of employment, personal statement, and two letters of recommendation are required. Awarded every year. Award may be used only at sponsoring institution.
Contact: Kathy Kordis or Jennifer Keller, Associate Directors of Financial Aid.

1085 Littleton-Griswold Research Grant

American Historical Association
400 A Street, SE
Washington, DC 20003
(202) 544-2422, (202) 544-8307 (fax)
aha@theaha.org
http://chnm.gmu.edu/chnm/aha
Maximum award: $1,000
Deadline: February 1
College level: Doctoral
Majors/Fields: American legal history, law and society
Criteria: Applicant must be a member of the American Historical Association. Preference will be given to Ph.D. candidates and junior scholars. Scholarship is renewable. Awarded every year.
Contact: Awards Coordinator.

1086 LSAT Scholarship

Western State University College of Law–San Diego
2121 San Diego Avenue
San Diego, CA 92100
(619) 297-9700
Maximum award: $15,000
Deadline: None
College level: Entering law students
Majors/Fields: Law
Criteria: Awarded automatically based upon applicant's highest single score on LSAT (Law School Admission Test), for first two semesters (at rate of 40% of award per semester) plus summer session (20% of award). Amount of award depends on score. Awarded every year. Award may be used only at sponsoring institution.
Contact: Kathy Kordis or Jennifer Keller, Associate Directors of Financial Aid.

1087 May M. Walker Scholarship

University of Oklahoma
University Affairs
900 Asp Avenue, Room 236
Norman, OK 73019-0401
(405) 325-1701
Maximum award: $1,000
Number of awards: 5
Deadline: September 1
College level: Sophomore, Junior, Senior, Graduate
Majors/Fields: Law
Criteria: Applicant must have a minimum 3.0 GPA, be a full-time student, and demonstrate financial need and ability to succeed. Awarded every year. Award may be used only at sponsoring institution.
Contact: Admissions and Records, Law Center, Room 221, 300 Timberdell Road, Norman, OK 73019, (405) 325-4729.

1088   Merv Leitch, Q.C. Scholarship

University of Calgary
Department of Financial Aid
2500 University Drive, NW
Calgary, Alberta, CN T2N 1N4
(403) 220-7872, (403) 282-2999 (fax)
Average award: $3,500
Number of awards: 2
Deadline: May 1
College level: Senior, Graduate
Majors/Fields: Constitutional law, law, natural resources law
Criteria: Selection is based upon academic merit and extracurricular activities. One award is for second-year constitutional law student, and the other is for third-year natural resources law student. Awarded every year. Award may be used only at sponsoring institution.
Contact: J. Van Housen, Director of Student Awards/Financial Aid.

1089   National Association of Black Woman Attorneys Writing Scholarship

National Association of Black Woman Attorneys
724 Ninth Street, NW
Suite 206
Washington, DC 20001
(202) 637-3570, (202) 637-4892 (fax)
Maximum award: $5,000
Number of awards: 4
Deadline: September 15
College level: Graduate
Majors/Fields: Law
Criteria: Applicant must be a black female law student. Essay is required. The subject of the essay changes each year but always focuses on an issue of contemporary concern. Scholarship is renewable. Awarded every year.
Contact: Mabel D. Haden, Esq., President, 724 9th Street, NW, Suite 206, Washington, DC 20001.

1090   Richard S. Nelson Scholarship

Northern Kentucky University
Administrative Center 416
Nunn Drive
Highland Heights, KY 41099-7101
(606) 572-5144
Average award: $2,500
Deadline: February 1
College level: Graduate
Majors/Fields: Law
Criteria: Applicant must be a resident of northern Kentucky. Scholarship is renewable. Awarded every year. Award may be used only at sponsoring institution.
Contact: Assistant Dean, Chase College of Law, Highland Heights, KY 41099.

1091   Young Lawyers Program

German Academic Exchange Service (DAAD)
950 Third Avenue
19th Floor
New York, NY 10022
(212) 758-3223, (212) 755-5780 (fax)
daadny@daad.org
http://www.daad.org
Average award: Tuition, fees, monthly allowance, travel subsidy, health insurance
Deadline: March 15
College level: Lawyers holding a J.D. or LL.B. degree, who have passed the bar exam
Majors/Fields: Law
Criteria: Applicant must be a lawyer under 32 years of age, with an excellent command of the German language. Award is for 10-month program in Germany to study the country's legal structure. Awarded every year.
Contact: Antje Wiessmann, Program Officer.

Military Science/ROTC

1092   AFROTC High School Scholarship

The University of Alabama
Box 870162
Tuscaloosa, AL 35487-0162
(205) 348-6756
Average award: $3,080
Number of awards: 1
Deadline: December 1
College level: Freshman
Criteria: Applicant must have a minimum 2.5 GPA, rank in top quarter of class, and have a minimum composite ACT score of 24 (minimum score of 21 in math and English). Extracurricular activities and interview are considered. Most awards go to students majoring in technical fields (computer science, engineering, math, nursing, physics); some go to students in accounting, business, or finance. Recipient must complete AFROTC academic courses and lab and serve four years as commissioned officer in U.S. Air Force. Awards are for three and four years. Awarded every year. Award may be used only at sponsoring institution.
Contact: Unit Enrollment Officer, AFROTC, Box 870258, Tuscaloosa, AL 35487-0258, (205) 348-5900.

1093   AFROTC Nurse Scholarship

The University of Alabama
Box 870162
Tuscaloosa, AL 35487-0162
(205) 348-6756
Average award: $3,080
Number of awards: 1
Deadline: late May
College level: Freshman, Sophomore, Junior, Senior
Criteria: Selection is based upon ACT/SAT I score, GPA, recommendations, and interview. Recipient must complete AFROTC courses and lab and serve four years as commissioned officer in U.S. Air Force. Awarded for two or three years. Awarded every year. Award may be used only at sponsoring institution.
Contact: Unit Enrollment Officer, AFROTC, Box 870258, Tuscaloosa, AL 35487-0258, (205) 348-5900.

1094   Air Force ROTC Airman Scholarship and Commissioning Program (ASCP)

U.S. Air Force ROTC–HQ AFROTC/RROO
551 East Maxwell Boulevard
Maxwell AFB, AL 36112-6106
(334) 953-2091
kitchen@falcon.rotc.af.mil
Average award: Tuition, books, fees, and $100 per month allowance
College level: Active duty enlisted personnel
Majors/Fields: Engineering, pharmacy, physical therapy, pre-health, science
Criteria: Scholarship offers active duty enlisted personnel the opportunity to earn a commission while completing requirements for an undergraduate degree as an Air Force ROTC cadet. Applicant must be a U.S. citizen, under 25 years of age as of June 30 in year of graduation and commission, have letter of recommendation from immediate commander, have letter of acceptance and institutional evaluation of prior college credits from a school offering the AFROTC Four-Year Program, have a letter of academic eligibility from the AFROTC Commander at the college or university, have a minimum 2.0 GPA, be admitted to a school offering Air Force ROTC and the academic major of school, and be of good moral character. Scholarship is renewable. Awarded every year.
Contact: HQ AFROTC/RROO.

1095 Air Force ROTC Nursing Scholarships

U.S. Air Force ROTC–HQ AFROTC/RROO
551 East Maxwell Boulevard
Maxwell AFB, AL 36112-6106
(334) 953-2091
kitchen@falcon.rotc.af.mil
Average award: Tuition, books, fees, and $100 per month allowance
College level: Freshman
Majors/Fields: Nursing
Criteria: Air Force nursing scholarship program helps interested students pursue a nursing degree and earn an Air Force officer commission through Air Force ROTC. Applicant must gain acceptance to a school of nursing accredited by the National League of Nursing and submit a personal statement of interest and reasons for pursuing a nursing degree and an Air Force commission. Scholarship is renewable. Awarded every year.
Contact: HQ AFROTC, Scholarship Actions Sections.

1096 Air Force ROTC Scholarship

Southwest Texas State University
J.C. Kellam Building
San Marcos, TX 78666
(512) 245-2340
Average award: Tuition, books, fees, and $100 per month allowance
Deadline: March 15
College level: Freshman, Sophomore, Junior, Senior
Criteria: Selection is based upon scholarship, merit, and potential as a cadet corps member and future officer. Renewable for two to three-and-a-half years. Awarded every year. Award may be used only at sponsoring institution.
Contact: AFROTC Detachment 840, San Marcos, TX 78666, (512) 245-2182.

1097 Air Force ROTC Scholarship

The University of Alabama
Box 870162
Tuscaloosa, AL 35487-0162
(205) 348-6756
Maximum award: $8,228
Deadline: December 1 (four year scholarship)
College level: Freshman, Sophomore, Junior
Criteria: Applicant must be enrolled full time. Selection is based upon ACT/SAT I scores, GPA, Air Force Officer Qualifying Test score, personal interview, leadership ability, and cadet corps involvement. Awards are for two, two-and-a-half, three, three-and-a-half, and four years. Awarded every year. Award may be used only at sponsoring institution.
Contact: Unit Enrollment Officer, AFROTC, Box 870258, Tuscaloosa, AL 35487-0258, (205) 348-5900.

1098 Air Force ROTC Scholarship

University of Southern Mississippi
Office of Recruitment and Orientation
Box 5166
Hattiesburg, MS 39406-5166
(601) 266-5000
Average award: Tuition, books, fees, and $100 per month allowance
College level: Freshman, Sophomore, Junior
Criteria: Selection is competitive. Award is available for two to four years. Awarded every year. Award may be used only at sponsoring institution.
Contact: Professor of Aerospace Studies, Box 5145, Hattiesburg, MS 39406-5145.

1099 Air Force ROTC Scholarship

University of Texas at San Antonio
Office of Student Financial Aid
6900 North Loop 1604 West
San Antonio, TX 78249-0687
(210) 691-44855
Average award: Tuition, books, fees, and $100 per month allowance
Deadline: December 1 (entering freshmen)
College level: Freshman, Sophomore, Junior
Criteria: Applicant must be a U.S. citizen, rank in the top quarter of class, and have a minimum composite ACT score of 24 or combined SAT I score of 1000. Award is for two to four years. Minimum 2.5 GPA is required to retain scholarship. Awarded every year. Award may be used only at sponsoring institution.
Contact: Air Force ROTC, 6900 North Loop 1604 West, San Antonio, TX 78249, (210) 691-4624.

1100 Air Force ROTC Scholarship

University of Oklahoma
University Affairs
900 Asp Avenue, Room 236
Norman, OK 73019-0401
(405) 325-1701
Average award: Tuition, books, fees, and $100 per month allowance
Deadline: December 1 (entering freshman); January of sophomore year for others
College level: Freshman, Junior
Criteria: Applicant must be a U.S. citizen, meet medical and physical qualifications, and be under age 25 at college graduation. High school applicant must have a minimum 2.5 GPA, rank in the top quarter of class, and have a minimum composite ACT score of 24. College applicant must have a minimum 2.5 GPA. Most scholarships are in engineering, nursing, and meteorology. Scholarship is renewable. Awarded every year. Award may be used only at sponsoring institution.
Contact: Professor of Aerospace Studies, 171 Felgar Street, Norman, OK 73019-0604, (405) 325-3211.

1101 Air Force ROTC Scholarship

New Mexico State University
Box 30001
Department 5100
Las Cruces, NM 88003-0001
(505) 646-4105
Average award: Tuition, books, fees, and $100 per month allowance
Deadline: December 15
College level: Freshman, Sophomore, Junior
Criteria: Applicant must agree to enroll in the Air Force ROTC program and serve as an Air Force officer for four years active duty upon graduation. Awards are for two, two-and-a-half, three, three-and-a-half, and four years. Awarded every year. Award may be used only at sponsoring institution.
Contact: Department of Aerospace Studies, Las Cruces, NM 88003.

1102 Air Force ROTC Science/Engineering Scholarship

University of Utah
Financial Aid and Scholarships Office
105 Student Services Building
Salt Lake City, UT 84112
(801) 581-6211
Average award: Tuition, books, fees, and $100 per month allowance
Deadline: December 1
College level: Freshman, Sophomore, Junior
Majors/Fields: Architecture, civil engineering, computer science, electrical engineering, mathematics, mechanical engineering, meteorology, metallurgical engineering, nuclear engineering, physics
Criteria: Applicant must commit to being an Air Force officer after graduation and major in science or engineering. Award is for two to four years. Awarded every year. Award may be used only at sponsoring institution.
Contact: Capt. Cristen DeYoung, Air Force ROTC, 2009 Annex Building, Salt Lake City, UT 84112-1107, (801) 581-6236.

1103 Air Force ROTC/Villanova Scholars Award

Villanova University
Villanova, PA 19085
(215) 645-4010
Average award: $5,870
Number of awards: 2
Deadline: January 15
College level: Freshman
Criteria: Applicant must be receiving level II AFROTC scholarship as designated by the Air Force. Academic eligibility must be maintained to retain scholarship. Awarded every year. Award may be used only at sponsoring institution.
Contact: George J. Walter, Director of Financial Aid.

1104 Air Force Scholarship

University of Arkansas, Fayetteville
Office of Scholarships and Financial Aid
114 Hunt Hall
Fayetteville, AR 72701
(501) 575-3806
Average award: Tuition, books, fees, and $100 per month allowance
Deadline: December 1
College level: Freshman
Criteria: Selection is based upon test scores and GPA. Interview is required. Award is for two to four years. Awarded every year. Award may be used only at sponsoring institution.
Contact: Professor for Aerospace Studies, (501) 575-3651.

1105 Army Reserve Officer Training Corps 2 and 3 Year Green to Gold Scholarship

University of Oklahoma
University Affairs
900 Asp Avenue, Room 236
Norman, OK 73019-0401
(405) 325-1701
Average award: Tuition, books, fees, and $100 per month allowance
Deadline: March 15
College level: Sophomore, Junior
Criteria: Applicant must be enlisted on active duty with a minimum of two years on active duty as of date of discharge, and meet medical and administrative requirements. Selection is based upon academic performance and leadership potential. Award is for two or three years. Awarded every year. Award may be used only at sponsoring institution.
Contact: Professor of Military Science, 290 West Brooks, Armory Room 1, Norman, OK 73019, (405) 325-2011.

1106 Army ROTC 2 Year Camp Challenge Scholarship

University of Oklahoma
University Affairs
900 Asp Avenue, Room 236
Norman, OK 73019-0401
(405) 325-1701
Average award: Tuition, books, fees, and $100 per month allowance
Deadline: April 30
College level: Junior
Criteria: Applicant must meet medical and administrative requirements, attend a six-week summer camp, and have a minimum of 55 undergraduate credit hours with no formal military training. Award is for two years. Awarded every year. Award may be used only at sponsoring institution.
Contact: Professor of Military Science, 290 West Brooks, Armory Room 1, Norman, OK 73019-0220, (405) 325-2011.

1107 Army ROTC Four-Year Scholarship

The University of Alabama
Box 870162
Tuscaloosa, AL 35487-0162
(205) 348-6756
Maximum award: $8,228
Deadline: December 1
College level: Freshman, Sophomore, Junior
Criteria: Selection is based upon ACT/SAT I scores, GPA, leadership and athletic achievements, and interview performance. Award is for four years. Awarded every year. Award may be used only at sponsoring institution.
Contact: Army ROTC, Box 870260, Tuscaloosa, AL 35487-0260, (205) 348-5917.

1108 Army ROTC Program

Molloy College
1000 Hempstead Avenue
P.O. Box 5002
Rockville Centre, NY 11571-5002
(516) 678-5000
Average award: Tuition, books, fees, and $100 per month allowance
College level: Sophomore, Junior, Senior
Criteria: Applicant must be enrolled full time and meet qualifications. Recipient will participate in ROTC through Hofstra U or St. John's U. Award may be for two, three, or four years. Awarded every year. Award may be used only at sponsoring institution.
Contact: Kathleen Bonnici, Director of Financial Aid.

1109 Army ROTC Scholarship

Pacific Lutheran University
Tacoma, WA 98447
(206) 535-7161
Average award: Tuition, books, fees, and $100 per month allowance
College level: Sophomore, Junior, Senior
Criteria: Awarded every year. Award may be used only at sponsoring institution.
Contact: ROTC Office, (206) 535-8740.

1110 Army ROTC Scholarship

Texas A&M University–Kingsville
Scholarships
Box 116
Kingsville, TX 78363
(512) 593-3907, (512) 593-2991 (fax)
http://www.tamuk.edu
Average award: Comprehensive tuition
Number of awards: No limit
Deadline: March 1
College level: Freshman, Sophomore, Junior, Senior
Criteria: Applicant must have a minimum 2.5 GPA, rank in top quarter of graduating class, and have a minimum combined SAT I score of 970 (ACT score of 21). Renewable if recipient maintains a minimum 2.0 GPA. Award may be used only at sponsoring institution.
Contact: ROTC Department.

1111 Army ROTC Scholarship

John Carroll University
20700 North Park Boulevard
Cleveland, OH 44118
(216) 397-4248
Average award: Tuition, books, fees, and $100 per month allowance
College level: Applicants selected by U.S. Army
Criteria: Applicant must meet U.S. Army ROTC requirements. FAFSA is recommended. Award is for three or four years. Awarded every year. Award may be used only at sponsoring institution.
Contact: Military Science Department.

1112 Army ROTC Scholarship

U.S. Army ROTC
Gold QUEST Center
P.O. Box 3279
Warminster, PA 18974-0128
Average award: Tuition, books, fees, and $100 per month allowance
Deadline: April 15
College level: Freshman, Sophomore, Junior, Senior
Criteria: Applicant must be a U.S. citizen, meet physical standards, and agree to accept commission and serve for four years. Selection is based upon standardized test scores, class rank, extracurricular activities, and personal interview. Award is for two, three, or four years. Awarded every year.
Contact: Army ROTC Scholarships (AD).

1113 Army ROTC Scholarship

Mount Union College
1972 Clark Avenue
Alliance, OH 44601
(216) 821-5320
Average award: Tuition and $100 per month allowance
College level: Unspecified undergraduate
Criteria: Applicant must meet program requirements. Award may be for two, three, or four years. Awarded every year. Award may be used only at sponsoring institution.
Contact: Office of Admissions.

1114 Army ROTC Scholarship

Hofstra University
126 Memorial Hall
Hempstead, NY 11550
(516) 463-6677
Maximum award: $8,000 or 80% of tuition, whichever is greater, plus monthly subsistence allowance
College level: Freshman, Sophomore, Junior, Senior
Criteria: Applicant must be a U.S. citizen, at least 17 years old, who is a high school graduate or has an equivalency certificate. Scholarship is renewable. Awarded every year. Award may be used only at sponsoring institution.
Contact: Army ROTC, 130 Hofstra University, Hempstead, NY 11550-1090, (516) 463-5648.

1115 Army ROTC Scholarship

University of Texas at San Antonio
Office of Student Financial Aid
6900 North Loop 1604 West
San Antonio, TX 78249-0687
(210) 691-44855
Average award: Tuition, books, fees, and $100 per month allowance
Deadline: December 1 (incoming freshmen)
College level: Freshman, Sophomore, Junior
Criteria: Applicant must be a U.S. citizen, have a minimum 2.5 GPA, and have a minimum combined SAT I score of 850 or composite ACT score of 17. Award is for two to four years. Minimum 2.0 GPA is required to retain scholarship. Awarded every year. Award may be used only at sponsoring institution.
Contact: Army ROTC, 6900 North Loop 1604 West, San Antonio, TX 78249-0687, (210) 691-4622.

1116 Army ROTC Scholarship

University of Utah
Financial Aid and Scholarships Office
105 Student Services Building
Salt Lake City, UT 84112
(801) 581-6211
Average award: Tuition, books, fees, and $100 per month allowance
Maximum award: $22,500
Deadline: December 1 (incoming freshman), February 15 (continuing student)
College level: Freshman, Sophomore, Junior
Criteria: Applicant must be a U.S. citizen, demonstrate academic excellence, and meet established medical, physical, moral, and age criteria. Preference is given to technical and nursing majors. Applicant must agree to serve four years as a commissioned officer in the U.S. Army. Some two-year awards are available for Reserve Forces Duty only. Awards are for two, three, or four years. Awarded every year. Award may be used only at sponsoring institution.
Contact: Major Caryl Buford, Military Science Building, Salt Lake City, UT 84112, (801) 581-6716 or 801 581-6717.

1117 Army ROTC Scholarship

New Mexico State University
Box 30001
Department 5100
Las Cruces, NM 88003-0001
(505) 646-4105
Average award: Tuition, books, fees, and $100 per month allowance
Deadline: December 1 (entering freshman)
College level: Freshman, Sophomore, Junior, Senior
Criteria: Applicant must serve as a commissioned officer in the active army upon graduation. Awards are for one, two, three, or four years. Awarded every year. Award may be used only at sponsoring institution.
Contact: Department of Military Science, Las Cruces, NM 88003.

1118 Army ROTC Scholarship

University of Southern Mississippi
Office of Recruitment and Orientation
Box 5166
Hattiesburg, MS 39406-5166
(601) 266-5000
Average award: Tuition, books, fees, and $100 per month allowance
College level: Freshman, Sophomore, Junior
Criteria: Selection is competitive. Awards are for two, three, or four years. Awarded every year. Award may be used only at sponsoring institution.
Contact: Professor of Military Science, Box 5042, Hattiesburg, MS 39406-5042.

1119 Army ROTC Scholarship

University of Oklahoma
University Affairs
900 Asp Avenue, Room 236
Norman, OK 73019-0401
(405) 325-1701
Average award: Tuition, books, fees, and $100 per month allowance
Deadline: March 1
College level: Freshman, Sophomore, Junior
Criteria: Applicant must meet medical and administrative requirements. Selection is based upon academic performance and leadership potential. Scholarship is available in engineering, nursing, and general studies. Award is for two, three, or four years. Awarded every year. Award may be used only at sponsoring institution.
Contact: Professor of Military Science, 290 West Brooks, Armory Room 1, Norman, OK 73019-0220, (405) 325-2011.

1120   Army ROTC Simultaneous Membership Program

New Mexico State University
Box 30001
Department 5100
Las Cruces, NM 88003-0001
(505) 646-4105
Average award: $3,000
Deadline: Prior to start of semester
College level: Freshman, Sophomore, Junior, Graduate, Doctoral
Criteria: Applicant must agree to accept a commission in the active Army, Army Reserve, or National Guard upon graduation and to participate in upper-division Army ROTC courses and National Guard or Reserve monthly drill meetings. Applicant must have a minimum 2.0 GPA, be between age 17 and 28, be enrolled full time, and have at least two years of academic work remaining. Scholarship is renewable. Awarded every year. Award may be used only at sponsoring institution.
Contact: Greeley W. Myers, Director of Financial Aid.

1121   Army ROTC Two and Three-Year Scholarship

The University of Alabama
Box 870162
Tuscaloosa, AL 35487-0162
(205) 348-6756
Average award: $3,080
Number of awards: 1
Deadline: January 31
College level: Sophomore, Junior
Criteria: Selection is based upon competitive ACT/SAT I score, college GPA, leadership and athletic achievements, and interview performance. Awarded for two or three years. Awarded every year. Award may be used only at sponsoring institution.
Contact: Army ROTC, Box 870260, Tuscaloosa, AL 35487-0260, (205) 348-5917.

1122   Army ROTC Two-Year Nurse Scholarship

The University of Alabama
Box 870162
Tuscaloosa, AL 35487-0162
(205) 348-6756
Average award: $3,080
Number of awards: 1
Deadline: January 31
College level: Junior
Criteria: Selection is based upon competitive ACT/SAT I score, college GPA, leadership and athletic achievements, and interview performance. Award is for two years. Awarded every year. Award may be used only at sponsoring institution.
Contact: Army ROTC, Box 870260, Tuscaloosa, AL 35487-0260, (205) 348-5917.

1123   Army ROTC/Villanova Scholars Award

Villanova University
Villanova, PA 19085
(215) 645-4010
Average award: $2,707
Maximum award: $2,774
Minimum award: $2,640
Number of awards: 2
Deadline: January 15
College level: Freshman
Criteria: Applicant must be selected by the Army for an 80-percent tuition scholarship. Minimum 3.25 GPA is required to retain scholarship. Awarded every year. Award may be used only at sponsoring institution.
Contact: George J. Walter, Director of Financial Aid.

1124   Loan Repayment Program

U.S. Army
P.O. Box 3219
Warminster, PA 18974-9844
(800) USA Army
http://www.goarmy.com
Maximum award: $65,000
Deadline: Continually accepting applications
College level: Junior, Senior, Graduate, Doctoral
Criteria: Applicant must enlist in the Army for three years. Awarded every year.
Contact: U.S. Army.

1125   Marquette ROTC Scholarship Enhancement

Marquette University
P.O. Box 1881
Milwaukee, WI 53201-1881
(414) 288-7302, (414) 288-3764 (fax)
go2marquette@vms.csd.mu.edu
http://www.mu.edu
Maximum award: $12,000
Deadline: None
College level: Freshman, Transfer
Criteria: Four-year ROTC scholarship winners receive a $24,000 enhancement at $6,000 per year. Three-year ROTC scholarship winners receive a $24,000 enhancement at $12,000 the first year and $4,000 for each of the following three years. Both replace any other Marquette scholarship offer. Renewable if recipient remains in ROTC. Awarded every year. Award may be used only at sponsoring institution.
Contact: Carlos Garces, Senior Assistant Director of Admissions.

1126   Naval ROTC Scholarship

University of Oklahoma
University Affairs
900 Asp Avenue, Room 236
Norman, OK 73019-0401
(405) 325-1701
Average award: Tuition, books, fees, and $1000 per year
Deadline: January 1
College level: Freshman, Sophomore, Junior, Senior
Criteria: Applicant must have a good academic record, be physically qualified, and have leadership potential. College students must have completed one year of calculus by the end of sophomore year. Award is for two, three or four years. Awarded every year. Award may be used only at sponsoring institution.
Contact: Professor of Naval Science, 290 West Brooks, Norman, OK 73019-0001, (405) 325-2021.

1127   Naval ROTC Tweeddale Scholarship

University of Oklahoma
University Affairs
900 Asp Avenue, Room 236
Norman, OK 73019-0401
(405) 325-1701
Average award: Tuition, books, fees, and $1000 per year
Deadline: None
College level: Sophomore, Junior
Majors/Fields: Nursing
Criteria: Applicant must have completed at least one term of college course work with a minimum grade of "C" in all courses including one college-level math, must meet physical qualifications, and must demonstrate leadership potential. Awarded every year. Award may be used only at sponsoring institution.
Contact: Professor of Naval Science, 290 West Brooks, Norman, OK 73019-0220, (405) 325-2021.

1128 ROTC Room and Board Scholarship

Texas A&M University–Kingsville
Scholarships
Box 116
Kingsville, TX 78363
(512) 593-3907, (512) 593-2991 (fax)
http://www.tamuk.edu
Average award: Full room and board
Number of awards: 12
Deadline: None
College level: Freshman, Sophomore, Junior, Senior, Graduate
Criteria: Applicant must have a minimum 2.5 GPA, minimum combined SAT I score of 970 (ACT score of 21) and be enrolled in ROTC. Renewable if recipient maintains a minimum 2.5 GPA. Award may be used only at sponsoring institution.
Contact: ROTC Department.

1129 ROTC Scholarship

Elon College
2700 Campus Box
Elon College, NC 27244
(800) 334-8448 extension 1
Average award: Tuition, books, fees, and $100 per month allowance
College level: Freshman
Criteria: Selection is based upon merit. Financial need is not considered. Award is for two, three, or four years. Awarded every year. Award may be used only at sponsoring institution.
Contact: Department of Military Science, (910) 584-2554, (910) 584-2555.

1130 ROTC Scholarship

Rhodes College
2000 North Parkway
Memphis, TN 38112
(901) 843-3700, (901) 843-3719 (fax)
adminfo@rhodes.edu
http://www.rhodes.edu
Average award: Tuition, books, fees, and $100 per month allowance
College level: Sophomore, Junior, Senior
Criteria: Applicant must meet requirements of Crosstown ROTC program through U of Memphis. Recipients are eligible to receive Rhodes grants of $2,000–$5,000, renewable for three years if recipient keeps ROTC scholarship. Award is for more than one year. Awarded every year. Award may be used only at sponsoring institution.
Contact: ROTC, University of Memphis, Memphis, TN 38152, (901) 678-2933 (Army), (901) 678-2681 (Air Force).

1131 Two Year Army National Guard/Army Reserve Force Duty Scholarship

University of Oklahoma
University Affairs
900 Asp Avenue, Room 236
Norman, OK 73019-0401
(405) 325-1701
Average award: Tuition, books, fees, and $100 per month allowance
Deadline: March 1
College level: Junior
Criteria: Applicant must be a National Guard or Army Reserve student and meet medical and administrative requirements. Selection is based upon academic performance and leadership potential. Award is for two years. Awarded every year. Award may be used only at sponsoring institution.
Contact: Professor of Military Science, 290 West Brooks, Armory Room 1, Norman, OK 73019-0220, (405) 325-2011.

1132 U.S. Air Force ROTC

U.S. Air Force ROTC–HQ AFROTC/RROO
551 East Maxwell Boulevard
Maxwell AFB, AL 36112-6106
(334) 953-2091
kitchen@falcon.rotc.af.mil
Maximum award: Tuition, books, fees, and $100 per month allowance
Deadline: December 2
College level: Freshman
Majors/Fields: Architecture, computer science, engineering, mathematics, meteorology, nursing, physics
Criteria: Applicant must be a U.S. citizen, have a minimum 2.5 GPA, rank in the top quarter of class, have a minimum composite ACT score of 24 or combined SAT I score of 1100, be a high school graduate, have never enrolled full time at a college (except for joint high school/college programs), and be at least 17 years of age by October 31 of first college year and under 25 years of age by June 30 in the year of college graduation and Air Force commission. Awarded every year.
Contact: HQ AFROTC/RROO.

1133 U.S. Army Scholarship

University of Arkansas, Fayetteville
Office of Scholarships and Financial Aid
114 Hunt Hall
Fayetteville, AR 72701
(501) 575-3806
Average award: Full tuition, books, fees, room, board, and $100 monthly allowance
Deadline: December 1
College level: Freshman
Criteria: Selection is based upon test scores and GPA. Interview is required. Award is for two to four years. Awarded every year. Award may be used only at sponsoring institution.
Contact: Professor of Military Science, (501) 575-4251.

Political Science————————

1134 Cortez A.M. Ewing Public Service Fellowship

University of Oklahoma
University Affairs
900 Asp Avenue, Room 236
Norman, OK 73019-0401
(405) 325-1701
Maximum award: $4,000
Maximum number of awards: 6
Minimum number of awards: 4
Deadline: December 15
College level: Sophomore, Junior, Senior
Majors/Fields: Political science
Criteria: Preference is given to students expecting to return to the U of Oklahoma campus in the fall following the summer congressional internship. Awarded every year. Award may be used only at sponsoring institution.
Contact: Political Science Department, 455 West Lindsey, Norman, OK 73019, (405) 325-2061.

1135 Gary Merrill Memorial Scholarship Program

Maine Community Foundation
210 Main Street
P.O. Box 148
Ellsworth, ME 04605
(207) 667-9735
Average award: $650
Maximum award: $1,500
Minimum award: $500
Number of awards: 1
Deadline: April 1
College level: Sophomore, Junior, Senior
Majors/Fields: Government studies, political science
Criteria: Applicant must be a Maine resident enrolled in a Maine college or university. Recipient must reapply for renewal. Awarded every year.
Contact: Scholarship Coordinator.

1136   Harry S Truman Scholarship

Harry S Truman Scholarship Foundation
712 Jackson Place, NW
Washington, DC 20006
(202) 395-4831, (202) 395-6995 (fax)
http://www.truman.gov
Maximum award: $13,500
Number of awards: 85
Deadline: January 27
College level: Senior, Graduate, Doctoral
Majors/Fields: Public service
Criteria: Applicant must be a U.S. citizen or U.S. national from American Samoa or the Commonwealth of the Northern Mariana Islands, rank in top quarter of class, have outstanding leadership potential, and be planning to pursue graduate school study to prepare for a career in public service. Minimum "B" grade average and continued preparation for a career in public service are required to retain scholarship. Awarded every year.
Contact: Scholarships.

1137   Vida Dutton Scudder Fellowship

Wellesley College
Center for Work & Service
Wellesley, MA 02181
(617) 283-3525, (617) 283-3674 (fax)
fellowships@bulletin.wellesley.edu
Maximum award: $2,000
Deadline: December 16
College level: College seniors/others for graduate study
Majors/Fields: Literature, political science, social science
Criteria: Applicant must be a woman and a graduate of Wellesley Coll who plans further study. Preference is given to those who have not previously held the award. Selection is based upon merit and need. Scholarship is renewable. Awarded every year.
Contact: Secretary to the Committee on Graduate Fellowships, (617) 283-2347.

Psychology

1138   Psychology Scholarship

Ordean Foundation
501 Ordean Building
Duluth, MN 55802
(218) 726-4785
Maximum award: $2,000
Number of awards: 20
Deadline: April 1
College level: Junior, Senior
Majors/Fields: Psychology
Criteria: Applicant must have a minimum 2.8 GPA, and be a resident of Duluth, Minn., or surrounding government entity in St. Louis County, Minn. Selection is based upon financial need. Renewal is based upon continuing financial need. Awarded every year. Award may be used only at Coll of St. Scholastica.
Contact: Julie Ledermann, Financial Aid Coordinator, College of St. Scholastica, 1200 Kenwood Avenue, Duluth, MN 55811, (218) 723-6656.

1139   Ralph A. Tesseneer Scholarship

Northern Kentucky University
Administrative Center 416
Nunn Drive
Highland Heights, KY 41099-7101
(606) 572-5144
Average award: In-state tuition
Deadline: February 1
College level: Junior, Senior
Majors/Fields: Psychology
Criteria: Applicant must have a minimum 3.0 GPA. Awarded every year. Award may be used only at sponsoring institution.
Contact: Robert E. Sprague, Director of Financial Aid.

Social Sciences–General

1140   Anna C. and Oliver C. Colburn Fellowship

Archaeological Institute of America
656 Beacon Street
4th Floor
Boston, MA 02215-2010
(617) 353-9361, (617) 353-6550 (fax)
aia@bu.edu
http://csaws.brynmawr.edu:443/aia.html
Average award: $11,000
Number of awards: 1
Deadline: February 1
College level: Doctoral, received Ph.D. within the last five years
Majors/Fields: Archaeology
Criteria: Fellowship is awarded contingent upon applicant's acceptance as an incoming associate member or student associate member of the American School of Classical Studies at Athens. Fellowship applicants must also apply to the American School. Applicant must be a U.S. or Canadian citizen or permanent resident and may not be a member of the American School during the year of application. Awarded in even-numbered years. American Sch of Classical Studies at Athens
Contact: Fellowships.

1141   Arnold J. Lien Scholarship

Washington University
One Brookings Drive
Campus Box 1089
St. Louis, MO 63130
(314) 935-6000 or (800) 638-0700
Average award: Full tuition plus $1,000 stipend
Number of awards: 3
Deadline: January 15
College level: Freshman
Majors/Fields: Social sciences
Criteria: Selection is based upon academic merit without regard to financial need. Application is required. Satisfactory academic performance is required to retain scholarship. Awarded every year. Award may be used only at sponsoring institution.
Contact: Office of Undergraduate Admission.

1142   Aspinall Foundation Award

Mesa State College
Financial Aid Department
P.O. Box 2647
Grand Junction, CO 81502
(970) 248-1396
Maximum award: $2,000
College level: Junior, Senior
Majors/Fields: Social science
Criteria: Applicant must be enrolled full time and have a minimum 3.0 GPA. Awarded every year. Award may be used only at sponsoring institution.
Contact: School of Humanities and Social Sciences.

1143   Aspinall-Paraho Award

Mesa State College
Financial Aid Department
P.O. Box 2647
Grand Junction, CO 81502
(970) 248-1396
Average award: $2,500
College level: Junior, Senior
Majors/Fields: Science, social science
Criteria: Applicant must be enrolled full time and have a minimum 3.0 GPA. Awarded every year. Award may be used only at sponsoring institution.
Contact: School of Humanities and Social Sciences.

1144   DAAD-NSF Grants for the Natural, Engineering, and Social Sciences

German Academic Exchange Service (DAAD)
950 Third Avenue
19th Floor
New York, NY 10022
(212) 758-3223, (212) 755-5780 (fax)
daadny@daad.org
http://www.daad.org
Average award: Travel and living expenses
Deadline: April 1
College level: Scholars and scientists from U.S. universities and research institutes
Majors/Fields: Engineering, natural, and social sciences
Criteria: Award is for joint research projects with colleagues at German universities. Awarded every year.
Contact: Christine French, National Science Foundation, 4201 Wilson Boulevard, Arlington, VA 22230, (703) 306-1702, cfrench@nsf.gov.

1145   Enid Hall Griswold Memorial Scholarship

National Society of the Daughters of the American Revolution
NSDAR Administration Building, Office of the Committees
1776 D Street, NW
Washington, DC 20006-5392
(202) 879-3292
Average award: $1,000
Number of awards: 2
Deadline: February 15
College level: Junior, Senior
Majors/Fields: Economics, government, history, political science
Criteria: Applicant must be a U.S. citizen and submit a letter of sponsorship from a local DAR chapter. Selection is based upon academic excellence, commitment to field of study, and financial need. All inquiries must include a self-addressed, stamped envelope. Awarded every year.
Contact: Administrative Assistant.

1146   Harriet and Leon Pomerance Fellowship

Archaeological Institute of America
656 Beacon Street
4th Floor
Boston, MA 02215-2010
(617) 353-9361, (617) 353-6550 (fax)
aia@bu.edu
http://csaws.brynmawr.edu:443/aia.html
Average award: $3,000
Number of awards: 1
Deadline: November 1
College level: Doctoral, received Ph.D. with the last five years
Majors/Fields: Archaeology
Criteria: Applicant must be a resident of the U.S. or Canada. Preference given to an applicant whose project requires travel to the Mediterranean for an individual project of scholarly nature related to Aegean Bronze Age archaeology. Awarded every year.
Contact: Fellowships.

1147   Kenan T. Erim Award

Archaeological Institute of America
656 Beacon Street
4th Floor
Boston, MA 02215-2010
(617) 353-9361, (617) 353-6550 (fax)
aia@bu.edu
http://csaws.brynmawr.edu:443/aia.html
Average award: $4,000
Number of awards: 1
Deadline: November 1
College level: Doctoral
Majors/Fields: Archaeology
Criteria: Applicant must be an American or international research and/or excavating scholar working on Aphrodisias material. Awarded every year.
Contact: Awards.

1148   Olivia James Traveling Fellowship

Archaeological Institute of America
656 Beacon Street
4th Floor
Boston, MA 02215-2010
(617) 353-9361, (617) 353-6550 (fax)
aia@bu.edu
http://csaws.brynmawr.edu:443/aia.html
Average award: $15,000
Number of awards: 1
Deadline: November 1
College level: Doctoral, received Ph.D. within the last five years
Majors/Fields: Archaeology, architecture, classics, history, sculpture
Criteria: Applicant must be a U.S. citizen or permanent resident. Award is for travel and study in Greece, the Aegean Islands, Sicily, southern Italy, Asia Minor, or Mesopotamia. Preference is given to projects of at least a half year's duration. Award is not intended to support field excavation projects. Awarded every year.
Contact: Fellowships.

1149   Wayne N. Aspinall Award

Mesa State College
Financial Aid Department
P.O. Box 2647
Grand Junction, CO 81502
(970) 248-1396
Average award: $4,000
Number of awards: 1
College level: Junior, Senior
Majors/Fields: Social science
Criteria: Applicant must be enrolled full time and have a minimum 3.0 GPA. Awarded every year. Award may be used only at sponsoring institution.
Contact: School of Humanities and Social Sciences.

Sociology/Social Work————

1150   Christie School Scholarship

Portland State University
Financial Aid Department
P.O. Box 751
Portland, OR 97207-0751
(503) 725-5270
Average award: $3,000
Number of awards: 1
Deadline: June 1
Majors/Fields: Social work
Criteria: Appliant must serve a three-term, two-day-a-week internship at Christie School. Awarded every year. Award may be used only at sponsoring institution.
Contact: Scholarships, Graduate School of Social Work, (503) 725-4712.

1151   Kerr Youth and Family Center Scholarship

Portland State University
Financial Aid Department
P.O. Box 751
Portland, OR 97207-0751
(503) 725-5270
Average award: $7,000
Number of awards: 1
Deadline: June 1
Majors/Fields: Social Work
Criteria: Applicant must have a demonstrated interest in child and family mental health. Award involves a three-term, two-day-a-week field assignment at Kerr Center. Awarded every year. Award may be used only at sponsoring institution.
Contact: Scholarships, Graduate School of Social Work, P.O. Box 751, Portland, OR 97207-0751, (503) 725-4712.

1152   Mt. Hood Community Mental Health Center Scholarship

Portland State University
Financial Aid Department
P.O. Box 751
Portland, OR 97207-0751
(503) 725-5270
Maximum award: $10,000
Number of awards: 1
Deadline: June 1
Majors/Fields: Social work
Criteria: Applicant must fulfill a three-term, two-day-a-week field instruction at Mt. Hood Community Mental Health Center. Scholarship is renewable. Awarded every year. Award may be used only at sponsoring institution.
Contact: Scholarships, Graduate School of Social Work, (503) 725-4712.

1153   Richard Klutznick Scholarship

B'nai B'rith Youth Organization
1640 Rhode Island Avenue, NW
Washington, DC 20036
(202) 857-6633
Average award: $2,500
Number of awards: 2
Deadline: April/May
College level: Graduate
Majors/Fields: Social work
Criteria: Applicant must be interested in working for Jewish agencies, have a positive attitude toward Jewish programs, demonstrate good scholarship, and attend an accredited school of social work majoring in group work. Applicant must accept employment with B'nai B'rith, if offered, and work for at least two years after graduation. Satisfactory GPA and reapplication are required to retain scholarship. Awarded every year.
Contact: Joseph Wittenstein, Assistant International Director.

1154   Social Work Scholarship

Ordean Foundation
501 Ordean Building
Duluth, MN 55802
(218) 726-4785
Maximum award: $2,000
Number of awards: 20
Deadline: April 1
College level: Junior, Senior
Majors/Fields: Social work
Criteria: Applicant must have a minimum 2.8 GPA, and be a resident of Duluth, Minn., or surrounding government entity in St. Louis County, Minn. Selection is based upon financial need. Renewal is based upon continuing financial need. Awarded every year. Award may be used only at Coll of St. Scholastica.
Contact: Julie Ledermann, Financial Aid Coordinator, College of St. Scholastica, 1200 Kenwood Avenue, Duluth, MN 55811, (218) 723-6656.

1155   Social Work Scholarship

Portland State University
Financial Aid Department
P.O. Box 751
Portland, OR 97207-0751
(503) 725-5270
Average award: $6,000
Number of awards: 1
Deadline: May 1
Majors/Fields: Social work
Criteria: Applicant must be a minority student who is interested in a career in child welfare services. Awarded every year. Award may be used only at sponsoring institution.
Contact: Scholarships, Graduate School of Social Work, (503) 725-4712.

Urban Planning

1156   American Planning Association Planning Fellowship

American Planning Association
122 South Michigan Avenue
Suite 1600
Chicago, IL 60605
(312) 431-9100, (312) 431-9985 (fax)
mmorrison@planning.org
Average award: $2,000
Maximum award: $3,500
Minimum award: $1,000
Maximum number of awards: 10
Minimum number of awards: 8
Deadline: May 15
College level: Graduate
Majors/Fields: Urban planning, regional planning
Criteria: Applicant must be a U.S. or Canadian citizen, demonstrate financial need, be enrolled in a graduate planning program that is accredited by the Planning Accreditation Board, and be African-American, Hispanic, or Native American. Awarded every year.
Contact: Margaret Morrison, Member Services Department.

1157   Charles Abrams Scholarship

American Planning Association
122 South Michigan Avenue
Suite 1600
Chicago, IL 60605
(312) 431-9100, (312) 431-9985 (fax)
mmorrison@planning.org
Average award: $2,000
Number of awards: 1
Deadline: April 30
College level: Graduate, Doctoral
Majors/Fields: Regional planning, urban planning
Criteria: Applicant must be a U.S. citizen, demonstrate financial need, and be accepted into a graduate planning program. Awarded every year. Award may be used only at the following schools: The New School for Social Research (New York), Harvard U, Massachusetts Institute of Technology (M.I.T.), U of Pennsylvania, Columbia U.
Contact: Margaret Morrison, Member Services Department.

1158   Patrick L. Monahan Memorial Scholarship

Western Washington University
516 High Street
Bellingham, WA 98226-9006
(206) 650-3471
Average award: $3,000
Deadline: April 15
College level: Freshman, Sophomore, Junior, Senior, Graduate, Doctoral
Majors/Fields: Geography, regional planning
Criteria: Applicant must demonstrate promise of significant professional contributions. Awarded every year. Award may be used only at sponsoring institution.
Contact: Geography Department, 217 Arntzen Hall, Bellingham, WA 98225, (206) 650-3284.

1159   Planning and Black Community Division Undergraduate Minority Scholarship Program

American Planning Association
122 South Michigan Avenue
Suite 1600
Chicago, IL 60605
(312) 431-9100, (312) 431-9985 (fax)
mmorrison@planning.org
Average award: $2,500
Number of awards: 1
Deadline: May 15
College level: Junior, Senior
Majors/Fields: Urban planning, regional planning
Criteria: Applicant must demonstrate financial need and be African-American, Hispanic, or Native American. Awarded every year.
Contact: Margaret Morrison, Member Services Department.

Other/Miscellaneous

Academic/Leadership Ability

1160 Academic Achievement Award

Texas A&M University, College Station
College Station, TX 77843-4233
(409) 845-1957
Average award: $2,500
Number of awards: 135
Deadline: December 5
College level: Freshman
Criteria: Applicant must have a minimum combined SAT I score of 1200-1850. Academic achievement, rigor of curriculum, extracurricular activities, prizes and awards, leadership, and school recommendations are considered. Minimum cumulative GPA of 2.5 is required to retain scholarship. Awarded every year. Award may be used only at sponsoring institution.
Contact: Susanna Finnell, Executive Director of Honors Programs and Academic Scholarships.

1161 Academic Achievement Award

Pacific Lutheran University
Tacoma, WA 98447
(206) 535-7161
Maximum award: $4,000
Deadline: January 31 (priority)
College level: Freshman
Criteria: Applicant must have a minimum 3.25 GPA and be accepted for admission by March 1. Renewable for up to six semesters if minimum 3.3 GPA is maintained. Awarded every year. Award may be used only at sponsoring institution.
Contact: Office of Financial Aid and Scholarships.

1162 Academic Achievement Awards

Cabrini College
610 King of Prussia Road
Radnor, PA 19087-3699
(610) 902-8420
Maximum award: $9,000
Number of awards: 50
Deadline: None
College level: Freshman, Transfers
Criteria: Minimum 2.5 GPA is required to retain scholarship. Awarded every year. Award may be used only at sponsoring institution.
Contact: Laurie Turns, Director of Admissions, (610) 902-8552.

1163 Academic Achievement Scholarship

Michigan Christian College
800 West Avon Road
Rochester Hills, MI 48307
(810) 650-6018, (810) 650-6060 (fax)
Maximum award: $3,000
Deadline: May 1 (priority)
College level: Freshman
Criteria: Applicant must have a minimum 3.0 GPA and a composite ACT score of 26-27 (combined SAT I score of 1140-1180), a composite ACT score of 28-29 (combined SAT I score of 1220-1260), a composite ACT score of 30-31 (combined SAT I score of 1300-1340), or a composite ACT score of 32-36 (combined SAT I score of 1380-1540). Amount of award varies by scores. Minimum GPA required to retain scholarship varies from 3.3 to 3.6, depending upon amount of award. Awarded every year. Award may be used only at sponsoring institution.
Contact: Admissions Office.

1164 Academic Achievement Scholarships and Talent Awards

College of Notre Dame of Maryland
4701 North Charles Street
Baltimore, MD 21210
(410) 532-5369
Average award: Partial tuition
Deadline: December 31
College level: Freshman
Criteria: Applicant must be a woman, have a 3.0 to 3.5 GPA and minimum combined SAT I score of 1000, demonstrate strong co-curricular activities and class rank, and have special talent, achievement, or leadership in such areas as art, creative writing, dance, drama, forensics, and music. Scholarship is renewable. Awarded every year. Award may be used only at sponsoring institution.
Contact: Financial Aid Office.

1165 Academic and Tuition Scholarship

Milwaukee School of Engineering
1025 North Broadway
Milwaukee, WI 53202-3109
(800) 332-6763, (414) 277-7475 (fax)
goran@admin.msoe.edu
http://www.msoe.edu
Maximum award: $5,400
Number of awards: 1100
Deadline: February 1
College level: Freshman
Criteria: Applicant must have a minimum 3.0 GPA. Recommendation and interview are suggested. Recipient must maintain a minimum 3.0 GPA to retain scholarship for four years. Awarded every year. Award may be used only at sponsoring institution.
Contact: Sue Minzlaff, Financial Aid Office, (414) 277-7222, minzlaff@admin.msoe.edu.

1166 Academic Award

Long Island University, C.W. Post Campus
Route 25A
Brookville, NY 11548
(516) 299-2338, (516) 299-2137 (fax)
admissions@collegehall.liunet.edu
http://www.liunet.edu
Maximum award: $2,500
Deadline: May 15
College level: Freshman
Criteria: Applicant must be enrolled full time. Selection is based upon academic record and financial need. Awarded every year. Award may be used only at sponsoring institution.
Contact: Financial Aid Office, 720 Northern Boulevard, Brookville, NY 11548.

1167 Academic Award

Webster University
470 East Lockwood
St. Louis, MO 63119-3194
(314) 968-7004
http://www.websteruniv.edu
Average award: $3,000
Maximum award: Full tuition
Minimum award: $1,000
Number of awards: 200
Deadline: April 1
College level: Freshman, Sophomore, Junior, Senior
Criteria: Minimum GPA (varies according to amount of award) and continuous full-time enrollment are required to retain scholarship. Awarded every year. Award may be used only at sponsoring institution.
Contact: Shannon Frank, Coordinator of University Scholarships.

1168 Academic Distinction Scholarship

Campbellsville University
Office of Financial Aid
200 West College Street
Campbellsville, KY 42718
(502) 465-8158
Maximum award: Full tuition
Deadline: April 1 (priority)
College level: Freshman
Criteria: Applicant must be a first-time, full-time freshman, have a minimum 3.25 GPA, and have a minimum composite ACT score of 30 (combined SAT I score of 1200). FAFSA is required. Awarded every year. Award may be used only at sponsoring institution.
Contact: Director of Financial Aid.

1169 Academic Excellence Award

Thiel College
75 College Avenue
Greenville, PA 16125
(412) 589-2250
Average award: $15,000
Number of awards: 2
Deadline: January 1
College level: Freshman
Criteria: Selection is based upon GPA, standardized test scores, essay, and on-campus interview. Scholarship is renewable. Awarded every year. Award may be used only at sponsoring institution.
Contact: Director of Financial Aid.

1170 Academic Excellence Award (AEA)

Long Island University, C.W. Post Campus
Route 25A
Brookville, NY 11548
(516) 299-2338, (516) 299-2137 (fax)
admissions@collegehall.liunet.edu
http://www.liunet.edu
Maximum award: Half tuition
Deadline: March 1
College level: Freshman
Criteria: Applicant must be a first-time, full-time student, have a minimum grade average of 88, and have a minimum SAT I verbal score of 500 and a minimum combined SAT I score of 1200 (composite ACT score of 27). Applicant must participate in Honors Program and Merit Fellowship. Renewable for up to four years if minimum 3.4 GPA (3.2 GPA after freshman year) and full-time enrollment (at least 12 credit hours per semester) are maintained. Awarded every year. Award may be used only at sponsoring institution.
Contact: Admissions Office, 720 Northern Boulevard, Brookville, NY 11548-1300. (516) 299-2413.

1171 Academic Excellence Scholarship

Shawnee State University
940 Second Street
Portsmouth, OH 45662-4344
(614) 355-2237
Maximum award: $11,000
Number of awards: 8
Deadline: April 15
College level: Freshman
Criteria: Applicant must have a minimum 3.5 GPA. Awarded to two of the top seniors from each school in Adams, Lawrence, Pike, and Scioto Counties. Both two-year and four-year awards are given. FAFSA is required. Early application is recommended. Awarded every year. Award may be used only at sponsoring institution.
Contact: Financial Aid Office, (614) 355-2485.

1172 Academic Excellence Scholarship

Doane College
1014 Boswell Avenue
Crete, NE 68333
(800) 333-6263, (402) 826-8600 (fax)
http://www.doane.edu
Average award: $4,000
Number of awards: 12
Deadline: None
College level: Freshman
Criteria: Selection is based upon standardized test scores and/or class rank. Renewable for up to four years (eight semesters) if minimum 3.5 GPA is maintained. Awarded every year. Award may be used only at sponsoring institution.
Contact: Janet Dodson, Director of Financial Aid, (402) 826-8260, jdodson@doane.edu.

1173 Academic Excellence Scholarship

University of Memphis
Scates Hall 204
Memphis, TN 38152
(901) 678-3213, (901) 678-5621 (fax)
katkinsn@cc.memphis.edu
http://www.memphis.edu/
Maximum award: $3,000
Deadline: January 15
College level: Freshman
Criteria: Applicant must have a minimum 3.25 GPA, and a minimum composite ACT score of 30 or combined SAT I score of 1320. Minimum 3.0 GPA after first year, (3.25 GPA thereafter), and service requirement of 20 hours per year are required to retain scholarship. Awarded every year. Award may be used only at sponsoring institution.
Contact: Katherine Atkinson, Scholarship Coordinator.

1174 Academic Excellence Scholarship

University of Mississippi
University, MS 38677
(601) 232-7175
Minimum award: $1,500
Maximum award: $3,460
Number of awards: 100
Deadline: July 1
College level: Freshman
Criteria: Applicant must have a minimum 3.0 GPA and minimum composite ACT score of 30 or minimum combined SAT I score of 1240. Minimum 3.0 GPA required to retain scholarship. Awarded every year. Award may be used only at sponsoring institution.
Contact: Betty Upton Magee, Scholarship Coordinator.

1175 Academic Excellence Scholarship

Mesa State College
Financial Aid Department
P.O. Box 2647
Grand Junction, CO 81502
(970) 248-1396
Maximum award: Tuition and fees
Deadline: March 12
College level: Freshman
Criteria: Applicant must be graduating from a Colorado District 51 high school, have a minimum 3.5 GPA, and be enrolled for at least 12 credit hours per semester. Recipient must maintain full-time enrollment and a minimum 3.5 GPA to retain scholarship. Awarded every year. Award may be used only at sponsoring institution.
Contact: Mesa State College Foundation, P.O. Box 3692, Grand Junction, CO 81502, (970) 248-1376.

1176 Academic Excellence Scholarship

University of Alberta
Edmonton, Alberta, CN T6G 2M7
(403) 492-3111
Maximum award: $2,500
Number of awards: 900
Deadline: June 15
College level: High school juniors for freshman year
Criteria: Award may be used only at sponsoring institution.
Contact: Student Awards Office, 103 Administration Building, Edmonton, AB T6G 2M7, (403) 492-3221.

1177 Academic General Scholarship

Saint Paul's College
406 Windsor Avenue
Lawrenceville, VA 23868
(804) 848-4505
Average award: $1,798
Maximum award: $2,400
Minimum award: $1,000
Number of awards: 20
Deadline: None
College level: Freshman, Sophomore, Junior, Senior, Graduate
Criteria: First-year applicants must have a minimum 2.7 GPA and a minimum combined SAT I score of 750. Minimum 2.7 GPA is required to retain scholarship. Awarded every year. Award may be used only at sponsoring institution.
Contact: Samuel L. Wade, J.D., Director of Financial Aid.

1178 Academic Grant and Scholarship

Viterbo College
815 South Ninth Street
LaCrosse, WI 54601-4797
(608) 791-0487
Average award: $3,500
Maximum award: $6,000
Minimum award: $2,000
Deadline: March 1
College level: Freshman, Sophomore, Junior, Senior
Criteria: Selection is based upon GPA and ACT score. Minimum 3.0 GPA is required to retain scholarship; minimum 2.0 GPA is required to retain grant. Awarded every year. Award may be used only at sponsoring institution.
Contact: Roland W. Nelson, Ph.D., Director of Admission, (608) 791-0420.

1179 Academic Honor Scholarship

Drury College
900 North Benton Avenue
Springfield, MO 65802
(417) 873-7319
Maximum award: $3,500
Deadline: March 1 (priority)
College level: Freshman
Criteria: Applicant must be accepted for full-time enrollment. Selection and amount of award is based upon ACT/SAT I scores and GPA. Renewable for up to four years if recipient maintains a minimum 2.75 GPA after first year (3.0 GPA thereafter). Awarded every year. Award may be used only at sponsoring institution.
Contact: Financial Aid Office.

1180 Academic Honor Scholarship

Ohio Northern University
525 South Main Street
Ada, OH 45810
(419) 772-2272, (419) 772-2313 (fax)
admissions-ug@onu.edu
http://www.onu.edu
Average award: $15,000
Number of awards: 6
Deadline: December 15
College level: Freshman
Criteria: Selection is by invitation upon admission. Renewable if recipient maintains a minimum 3.0 GPA (freshman year), and a minimum 3.30 GPA thereafter. Awarded every year. Award may be used only at sponsoring institution.
Contact: Wendell A. Schick, Director of Financial Aid.

1181 Academic Honor Scholarship

Campbellsville University
Office of Financial Aid
200 West College Street
Campbellsville, KY 42718
(502) 465-8158
Maximum award: Half tuition
Deadline: April 1 (priority)
College level: Freshman
Criteria: Applicant must be a first-time, full-time freshman, have a minimum 3.25 GPA, and have a minimum composite ACT score of 25 (combined SAT I score of 970). FAFSA is required. Awarded every year. Award may be used only at sponsoring institution.
Contact: Director of Financial Aid.

1182 Academic Honors Program

East Tennessee State University
P.O. Box 70722
Johnson City, TN 37614-0722
(615) 929-4300
Average award: Comprehensive tuition
Number of awards: 20
Deadline: None
College level: Freshman
Majors/Fields: Honors curriculum, Senior Honors Thesis
Criteria: Applicant must have a minimum 3.5 GPA and minimum composite ACT score of 29 (combined SAT I score of 1150) to be considered for admission into the Honors Program. Renewable for up to four years if minimum GPA is maintained. Minimum 2.75 GPA is required for up to 30 credit hours, 3.0 GPA for 30-45 credit hours, 3.15 GPA for 45-60 credit hours, 3.25 GPA or more than 60 credit hours. Awarded every year. Award may be used only at sponsoring institution.
Contact: Scholarships.

1183   Academic Incentive Award

Long Island University, C.W. Post Campus
Route 25A
Brookville, NY 11548
(516) 299-2338, (516) 299-2137 (fax)
admissions@collegehall.liunet.edu
http://www.liunet.edu
Average award: $3,000
Deadline: March 1
College level: First-time students
Criteria: Applicant must be a first-time, full-time student, have a minimum grade average of 85, and have a minimum combined SAT I score of 1100. Renewable for up to four years if minimum 3.2 GPA (3.0 GPA after freshman year) and full-time enrollment (at least 12 credit hours per semester) are maintained. Awarded every year. Award may be used only at sponsoring institution.
Contact: Admissions Office, 720 Northern Boulevard, Brookville, NY 11548, (516) 299-2414, admissions@collegehall.liunet.edu.

1184   Academic Major Award

Spalding University
851 South Fourth Street
Louisville, KY 40203
(502) 585-9911
Average Award: One-fourth tuition
Deadline: March 1 (priority)
College level: Freshman
Majors/Fields: Art, business, communication, computer science, English, history, math, science
Criteria: Applicant must demonstrate outstanding achievement in area of major (specific criteria set by departmental faculty), have three letters of recommendation, and be accepted for full-time enrollment. Scholarship is renewable. Awarded every year. Award may be used only at sponsoring institution.
Contact: Janice White Russell, Assistant Director of Financial Aid and Scholarship Coordinator, (502) 585-9911, extension 242.

1185   Academic Merit Awards

Mount Union College
1972 Clark Avenue
Alliance, OH 44601
(216) 821-5320
Maximum award: $5,000
Deadline: None
College level: Freshman
Criteria: Applicant must be a first-time, full-time freshman and have achieved one or more of the following: minimum 3.5 GPA, rank in top two-tenths of class, and minimum composite ACT score of 25 (combined SAT I score of 1050). Amount of award depends on number of criteria met. Renewable for four years if minimum 3.0 GPA is maintained. Awarded every year. Award may be used only at sponsoring institution.
Contact: Office of Admissions.

1186   Academic Merit Grant

Our Lady of the Lake University
411 S.W. 24th Street
San Antonio, TX 78207-4666
(512) 434-6711
Average award: $2,550
Deadline: Early application is recommended
College level: Freshman
Criteria: Applicant must have a 2.75-2.99 GPA and a minimum composite ACT score of 21 (combined SAT I score of 870). Renewable for up to seven semesters or completion of bachelor's degree (whichever comes first) if recipient maintains a minimum 3.0 GPA and completes at least 12 credit hours per semester. Awarded every year. Award may be used only at sponsoring institution.
Contact: Jeff R. Scofield, Director of Financial Aid.

1187   Academic Merit Scholarship

Saint Vincent College
Admissions and Financial Aid
Latrobe, PA 15650-2690
(412) 537-4540, (412) 537-4554 (fax)
info@stvincent.edu
http://www.stvincent.edu
Maximum award: Two-thirds tuition
Number of awards: 72
Deadline: None
College level: Freshman
Criteria: Applicant must rank in top tenth of class, have a minimum combined SAT I score of 1240, and be accepted for admission as a full-time student. Recipient must maintain a minimum 3.25 GPA as a full-time student to retain scholarship. Awarded every year. Award may be used only at sponsoring institution.
Contact: Rev. Earl Henry, Dean of Admission and Financial Aid, 300 Fraser Purchase Road, Latrobe, PA 15650.

1188   Academic Presidential Scholarship

Saint Paul's College
406 Windsor Avenue
Lawrenceville, VA 23868
(804) 848-4505
Average award: $3,500
Maximum award: $9,700
Minimum award: $1,000
Number of awards: 8
Deadline: None
College level: Freshman, Sophomore, Junior, Senior, Graduate
Criteria: First-year applicants must have a minimum 3.0 GPA and a minimum combined SAT I score of 900. Minimum 3.0 GPA is required to retain scholarship. Awarded every year. Award may be used only at sponsoring institution.
Contact: Samuel L. Wade, J.D., Director of Financial Aid.

1189   Academic Recognition Award

Lynchburg College
Lynchburg, VA 24501
(804) 522-8228
Maximum award: $6,000
Deadline: February 15
College level: Freshman
Criteria: Applicant must have a minimum "B" grade average and minimum combined SAT I score of 1100 (composite ACT score of 24). Awarded every year. Award may be used only at sponsoring institution.
Contact: Scholarships.

1190   Academic Recognition Scholarship

North Adams State College
Church Street
North Adams, MA 01247
(413) 662-5410, 800 292-6632, (413) 662-5179 (fax)
admissions@nasc.mass.edu
http://www.nasc.mass.edu
Average award: $1,750
Maximum award: $3,000
Minimum award: $500
Number of awards: 20
College level: Freshman, Sophomore, Junior
Criteria: Applicant must rank in top half of class and have a minimum combined SAT I score of 1000. Transfer applicants must have a minimum 2.75 GPA. Minimum 3.0 GPA is required to retain scholarship. Awarded every year. Award may be used only at sponsoring institution.
Contact: Denise Richardello, Dean of Enrollment Management, Admissions Office.

1191 Academic Recognition Scholarship

Lebanon Valley College
101 North College Avenue
Annville, PA 17003
(800) 445-6181, (717) 867-6026 (fax)
admiss@luc.edu
http://www.luc.edu
Average award: Half tuition
Number of awards: 10
Deadline: None
College level: Transfers
Criteria: Applicant must be a member of Phi Theta Kappa and be transferring from a junior or community college. Minimum 3.0 GPA is required to retain scholarship. Awarded every year. Award may be used only at sponsoring institution.
Contact: Bill Brown, Dean of Admission/Financial Aid.

1192 Academic Scholarship

University of Idaho
Moscow, ID 83843
(208) 885-6312, (208) 885-5592 (fax)
finaid@uidaho.edu
http://www.uidaho/edu
Average award: $1,200
Maximum award: $5,000
Minimum award: $1,000
Number of awards: 120
Deadline: February 15
College level: Freshman, Sophomore, Junior, Senior
Criteria: Individual scholarships have different requirements. Satisfactory academic progress is required to retain scholarship. Awarded every year. Award may be used only at sponsoring institution.
Contact: Dan Davenport, Director of Financial Aid.

1193 Academic Scholarship

William Woods University
200 West 12th Street
Fulton, MO 65251-1098
(573) 592-4232, (573) 592-1146 (fax)
http://www.wmwoods.edu
Maximum award: $5,000
Deadline: June 1
College level: Freshman, Sophomore, Junior, Senior
Criteria: Selection is based upon GPA and standardized test scores. Minimum GPA required to retain scholarship varies from 3.4 to 3.5 depending upon amount of award. Awarded every year. Award may be used only at sponsoring institution.
Contact: Laura L. Archuleta, Director for Student Financial Aid, larchule@iris.wmwoods.edu.

1194 Academic Scholarship

Emmanuel College
212 Spring Street
P.O. Box 129
Franklin Springs, GA 30639-0129
(706) 245-7226
Average award: $4,000
Maximum award: $4,600
Minimum award: $2,300
Number of awards: 12
Deadline: April 1
College level: Freshman
Criteria: Selection is based upon GPA and standardized test scores. Awarded every year. Award may be used only at sponsoring institution.
Contact: Glenn A. Bailey, Director of Financial Aid.

1195 Academic Scholarship

Hardin-Simmons University
Box 16075
2200 Hickory Street
Abilene, TX 79698-6075
(915) 670-1331
Average award: $3,000
Maximum award: $4,000
Minimum award: $2,000
Deadline: May 1
College level: Freshman
Criteria: Selection is based upon standardized test scores. Renewable if minimum 3.0 GPA and continuous full-time enrollment (at least 12 credit hours per semester) are maintained. Awarded every year. Award may be used only at sponsoring institution.
Contact: Fran Strange, Financial Aid Director.

1196 Academic Scholarship

Principia College
Elsah, IL 62028
(800) 277-4648, (800) 347-4000 (fax)
collegeadmissions@prin.edu
http://www.prin.edu
Average award: $2,500
Number of awards: 12
Deadline: None
College level: Freshman
Criteria: Recipient must maintain a minimum 3.2 GPA and support community standards to retain scholarship. Awarded every year. Award may be used only at sponsoring institution.
Contact: Martha Green Quirk, Director of Admissions and Enrollment, (618) 374-5180, mgq@prin.edu.

1197 Academic Scholarship

Queens College
1900 Selwyn Avenue
Charlotte, NC 28274
(704) 337-2212, (800) 849-0202, (704) 337-2403 (fax)
cas@rex.queens.edu
http://www.queens.edu
Maximum award: Full tuition
Deadline: None
College level: Freshman
Criteria: Renewable for up to four years. Awarded every year. Award may be used only at sponsoring institution.
Contact: Admissions Office.

1198 Academic Scholarship

California Baptist College
8432 Magnolia Avenue
Riverside, CA 92504
(909) 689-5771
Maximum award: $2,100
Deadline: None
College level: Freshman, Transfers
Criteria: Applicant must have a minimum 3.5 GPA and minimum combined SAT I score of 900 (composite ACT score of 21). Scholarship is renewable. Awarded every year. Award may be used only at sponsoring institution.
Contact: Phillip Martinez, Director of Admissions/Financial Aid.

1199 Academic Scholarship

Benedictine College
1020 North Second Street
Atchison, KS 66002
(913) 367-5340
Maximum award: $5,000
Deadline: None
College level: Freshman
Criteria: Applicant must be a first-time, full-time freshman and meet one of the following criteria: have a composite ACT score of 24-28 (combined SAT I score of 940-1140), rank in top 15% of class and have a minimum composite ACT score of 18 (combined SAT I score of 780), or have a 3.50-3.99 GPA and minimum composite ACT score of 18 (combined SAT I score of 780). FAFSA is required. Applicants who qualify for the Presidential, Director's, or Dean's Scholarships are ineligible. Renewable for up to four years if minimum 3.0 GPA is maintained. Awarded every year. Award may be used only at sponsoring institution.
Contact: Diane Adams, Associate Director of Admissions.

1200 Academic Scholarship

Bryan College
P.O. Box 7000
Bryan Hill Drive
Dayton, TN 37321-7000
(423) 775-2041, (423) 775-7330 (fax)
admiss@bryannet.bryan.edu
Maximum award: $2,500
Maximum number of awards: 86
Minimum number of awards: 51
Deadline: May 1
College level: Freshman, Sophomore, Junior, Senior, Transfers
Criteria: For $1,500 award, secondary school applicant must have a minimum 3.4 GPA and minimum composite ACT score of 24 (combined SAT I score of 1000). Other applicants must have a minimum 3.25 GPA. For $2,500 award, secondary school applicant must have a minimum 3.6 GPA and minimum composite ACT score of 26 (combined SAT I score of 1100). Other applicants must have a minimum 3.5 GPA. Scholarship is renewable. Awarded every year. Award may be used only at sponsoring institution.
Contact: Anne Rader, Director of Financial Aid, (423) 775-7224.

1201 Academic Scholarship

Caldwell College
9 Ryerson Avenue
Caldwell, NJ 07006
(201) 228-4424
Average award: $5,289
Minimum award: $3,000
Number of awards: 25
Deadline: March 1
College level: Freshman
Criteria: Minimum 3.0 GPA is required to retain scholarship. Awarded every year. Award may be used only at sponsoring institution.
Contact: Margaret T. Murnane, Director of Financial Aid, (201) 228-4424, extension 221.

1202 Academic Scholarship

College of New Rochelle
29 Castle Place
New Rochelle, NY 10805
(914) 654-5224
Average award: $5,000
Number of awards: 10
Deadline: None
College level: Freshman
Criteria: Applicant must have a minimum 90 grade average, rank in top two-tenths of class, or have a minimum combined SAT I score of 1100, and be accepted for admission. Scholarship is renewable. Awarded every year. Award may be used only at sponsoring institution.
Contact: Annette Gonzalez, Financial Aid Counselor.

1203 Academic Scholarship

Christian Heritage College
2100 Greenfield Drive
El Cajon, CA 92019
(619) 441-2200
Maximum award: $3,000
Deadline: Early application is recommended
College level: Freshman, Sophomore, Junior, Senior, Transfers
Criteria: Applicant must have a minimum 3.0 GPA (freshman or transfer) and a minimum combined SAT I score of 950 (composite ACT score of 23). Award is applied toward tuition only. Renewable for up to four years if minimum 3.4 GPA and continuous full-time enrollment are maintained. Awarded every year. Award may be used only at sponsoring institution.
Contact: Anna K. Manley, Director of Financial Aid.

1204 Academic Scholarship

Muskingum College
163 Stormont Drive
New Concord, OH 43762
(614) 826-8139
Average award: Full tuition
Number of awards: 400
College level: Freshman
Criteria: Selection is based upon academic ability and performance. Minimum 3.0 GPA is required to retain scholarship. Awarded every year. Award may be used only at sponsoring institution.
Contact: Doug Kellar, Director of Admission.

1205 Academic Scholarship

Lynn University
3601 North Military Trail
Boca Raton, FL 33431-5598
(561) 994-0770, (561) 247-3552 (fax)
admission@lynn.edu
http://www.lynn.edu
Maximum award: $5,000
Number of awards: 15
Deadline: None
College level: Freshman
Criteria: Applicants must meet two of three criteria: Rank in top third of class, have a minimum 3.0 GPA, have a minimum combined SAT I score of 1000. Minimum 3.0 GPA is required to retain scholarship. Awarded every year. Award may be used only at sponsoring institution.
Contact: James Sullivan, Director of Admissions.

1206 Academic Scholarship

Wisconsin Lutheran College
8800 West Bluemound Road
Milwaukee, WI 53226
(414) 443-8842, (414) 443-8514 (fax)
Average award: $5,000
Number of awards: 22
Deadline: May 1
College level: Freshman
Criteria: Applicant must have a minimum composite ACT score of 24 and either a minimum 3.3 GPA or rank in top quarter of class. Minimum 3.1 GPA is required to retain scholarship. Awarded every year. Award may be used only at sponsoring institution.
Contact: Donna Johnejack, Assistant Director of Financial Aid.

1207 Academic Scholarship

Southern Illinois University at Carbondale
Carbondale, IL 62901
(618) 453-5351
Average award: $1,664
Maximum award: $2,400
Minimum award: $927
Number of awards: 175
Deadline: Early application is recommended
College level: Freshman, Transfers who are graduates of Illinois Comm Coll
Criteria: Applicant must rank in top tenth of secondary school class and have a composite ACT score in 90th percentile nationwide. Transfer applicant must have a minimum 3.5 GPA as calculated by Southern Illinois U at Carbondale. Awarded every year. Award may be used only at sponsoring institution.
Contact: Tammy Cavaretta, Assistant Director, New Student Admission Services, (618) 536-4405.

1208 Academic Scholarship

Salem College
P.O. Box 10548
Winston-Salem, NC 27108
(910) 721-2808
Average award: $6,000
College level: Freshman
Criteria: Selection is based upon academic achievement. Minimum 3.0 GPA required to retain scholarship. Awarded every year. Award may be used only at sponsoring institution.
Contact: Bruce Blackman, Director of Financial Aid.

1209 Academic Scholarship

South Dakota State University
Box 2201
Brookings, SD 57007
(605) 688-4695, (605) 688-6384 (fax)
http://www.sdstate.edu
Average award: $800
Maximum award: $6,000
Minimum award: $500
Number of awards: 450
Deadline: Varies
College level: Sophomore, Junior, Senior, Graduate
Criteria: Applicants should contact their academic department for scholarship information. Awarded every year. Award may be used only at sponsoring institution.
Contact: Jay Larsen, Financial Aid Director, AD 106, Brookings, SD 57007, larsenj@adm.sdstate.edu.

1210 Academic Scholarship

Carleton University
202 Robertson Hall
1125 Colonel By Drive
Ottawa, Ontario, CN K1S 5B6
(613) 778-7400
Maximum award: $3,200
College level: Freshman
Criteria: Applicant must rank in the top 15% of class. Renewable if recipient maintains good academic standing. Award may be used only at sponsoring institution.
Contact: Awards Office, (613) 520-3600.

1211 Academic Scholarship

Loyola Marymount University
7900 Loyola Boulevard
Los Angeles, CA 90045-8350
(310) 338-2753, (310) 338-2793 (fax)
http://www.lmu.edu
Average award: $5,000
College level: Freshman
Criteria: Applicant must have a minimum 3.6 GPA and minimum SAT I math and verbal scores of 650 (combined SAT I score of 1300, composite ACT score of 29). Scholarship is renewable. Award may be used only at sponsoring institution.
Contact: Financial Aid Office.

1212 Academic Scholarship

Gwynedd-Mercy College
Sumneytown Pike
Gwynedd Valley, PA 19437
(215) 641-5570
Minimum award: Half tuition
Maximum award: Full tuition
Number of awards: 23
Deadline: January 15
College level: Freshman, Transfers
Criteria: Applicant must have a minimum 3.3 GPA (transfer applicant) or rank in top 15 % of class and have a minimum combined SAT I score of 1100 (high school applicant). Minimum 3.3 GPA is required to retain scholarship. Awarded every year. Award may be used only at sponsoring institution.
Contact: Kristine Weber, Associate Dean of Admissions, (215) 641-5510.

1213 Academic Scholarship

Mississippi Valley State University
14000 Highway 82 West
Itta Bena, MS 38941
(601) 254-3335, (601) 254-7900 (fax)
Maximum award: $7,270
Number of awards: 125
Deadline: March 1
College level: Freshman
Criteria: Minimum 3.2 GPA required to retain scholarship. Awarded every year. Award may be used only at sponsoring institution.
Contact: Maxcine Rush, Director of Admissions, (601) 254-3347.

1214 Academic Special Presidential Scholarship

Saint Paul's College
406 Windsor Avenue
Lawrenceville, VA 23868
(804) 848-4505
Average award: $6,951
Maximum award: $9,700
Minimum award: $1,000
Number of awards: 4
Deadline: None
College level: Freshman, Sophomore, Junior, Senior, Graduate
Criteria: Applicant must have a minimum 3.0 GPA. First-year applicants also must have a minimum combined SAT I score of 1200. Minimum 3.0 GPA is required to retain scholarship. Awarded every year. Award may be used only at sponsoring institution.
Contact: Samuel L. Wade, J.D., Director of Financial Aid.

1215 Academic Tuition Scholarship

Calumet College of St. Joseph
2400 New York Avenue
Whiting, IN 46394
(219) 473-4213
Average award: $2,859
Maximum award: $4,650
Minimum award: $1,450
Number of awards: 8
Deadline: March 1
College level: Freshman
Criteria: Minimum 3.0 GPA is required for renewal. Awarded every year. Award may be used only at sponsoring institution.
Contact: Katrina Foster, Technical Assistant to the Office of Financial Aid, (219) 473-4219.

1216 ACE 10 Scholarship (Achievement in a Community of Excellence)

Bridgewater College
East College Street
Bridgewater, VA 22812
(540) 828-2501
Average award: $6,255
Number of awards: 118
Deadline: None
College level: Freshman, Sophomore, Junior, Senior, Transfers
Criteria: Applicant must rank in top tenth of class. Transfer applicants must transfer a minimum of 26 credits and have a minimum 3.5 GPA. Renewable for up to three years if minimum 2.8 GPA is maintained. Awarded every year. Award may be used only at sponsoring institution.
Contact: J. Vern Fairchilds, Jr., Director of Financial Aid, (540) 828-5376, vfairchi@bridgewater.edu.

1217 ACE 20 Scholarship (Achievement in a Community of Excellence)

Bridgewater College
East College Street
Bridgewater, VA 22812
(540) 828-2501
Average award: $4,170
Number of awards: 81
Deadline: None
College level: Freshman, Sophomore, Junior, Senior
Criteria: Applicant must rank in second tenth of class. Transfer applicants must transfer a minimum of 26 credits and have a minimum 3.2 GPA. Renewable for up to three years if minimum 2.5 GPA is maintained. Awarded every year. Award may be used only at sponsoring institution.
Contact: J. Vern Fairchilds, Jr., Director of Financial Aid, (540) 828-5376, vfairchi@bridgewater.edu.

1218 ACE 30 Scholarship (Achievement in a Community of Excellence)

Bridgewater College
East College Street
Bridgewater, VA 22812
(540) 828-2501
Average award: $3,129
Number of awards: 86
Deadline: None
College level: Freshman
Criteria: Applicant must rank in third tenth of class. Transfer applicants must transfer a minimum of 26 credits and have a minimum 3.0 GPA. Renewable for up to three years if minimum 2.2 GPA is maintained. Awarded every year. Award may be used only at sponsoring institution.
Contact: J. Vern Fairchilds, Jr., Director of Financial Aid, (540) 828-5376, vfairchi@bridgewater.edu.

1219 Achievement Award

Beaver College
450 South Easton Road
Glenside, PA 19038-3295
(215) 572-2910, (215) 572-4049 (fax)
admiss@beaver.edu
http://www.beaver.edu
Average award: $1,815
Maximum award: $6,000
Minimum award: $1,000
Number of awards: 320
Deadline: None
College level: Freshman, Transfers
Criteria: Awarded to applicants for full-time admission who have demonstrated exceptional achievement in community service, leadership, school activities, or special talent. Recipient must maintain good academic standing to retain scholarship. Awarded every year. Award may be used only at sponsoring institution.
Contact: Melissa McCurdy, Scholarship Coordinator, mccurdy@beaver.edu.

1220 Achievement Award

Lebanon Valley College
101 North College Avenue
Annville, PA 17003
(800) 445-6181, (717) 867-6026 (fax)
admiss@luc.edu
http://www.luc.edu
Minimum award: One-fourth tuition
Number of awards: 38
Deadline: None
College level: Freshman
Criteria: Applicant must rank in top three-tenths of class. Minimum 2.5 GPA is required to retain scholarship. Awarded every year. Award may be used only at sponsoring institution.
Contact: Bill Brown, Dean of Admission/Financial Aid.

1221 Achievement Award

William Woods University
200 West 12th Street
Fulton, MO 65251-1098
(573) 592-4232, (573) 592-1146 (fax)
http://www.wmwoods.edu
Maximum award: $3,000
Deadline: June 1
College level: Freshman
Criteria: Selection is based upon GPA and standardized test scores. Recipient must reapply and maintain a minimum 3.4 GPA to retain scholarship. Awarded every year. Award may be used only at sponsoring institution.
Contact: Laura L. Archuleta, Director for Student Financial Aid, larchule@iris.wmwoods.edu.

1222 Achievement Class Award

University of Oklahoma
University Affairs
900 Asp Avenue, Room 236
Norman, OK 73019-0401
(405) 325-1701
Maximum award: $3,000
Number of awards: 76
Deadline: February 15
College level: Freshman
Criteria: Selection is based upon merit and leadership. Ethnic minorities are encouraged to apply. Awarded every year. Award may be used only at sponsoring institution.
Contact: Prospective Student Services, (405) 325-2151.

1223 Achievement Scholarship

Ohio Northern University
525 South Main Street
Ada, OH 45810
(419) 772-2272, (419) 772-2313 (fax)
admissions-ug@onu.edu
http://www.onu.edu
Average award: $12,500
Number of awards: 10
Deadline: December 15
College level: Freshman
Criteria: Selection is by invitation upon admission. Renewable if recipient maintains minimum 3.0 GPA. Awarded every year. Award may be used only at sponsoring institution.
Contact: Wendell A. Schick, Director of Financial Aid, admissions-ug@onu.edu.

1224 Achievement Scholarship

Syracuse University
201 Administration Building
Syracuse, NY 13244
(315) 443-1870
orange@suadmin.syr.edu
http://ww.syr.edu
Average award: $3,000
College level: Transfers
Criteria: Selection is based upon academic credentials, standardized tests, class rank, extracurricular and community involvement, and overall citizenship and character. Renewable if recipient maintains a minimum 2.5 GPA. Award may be used only at sponsoring institution.
Contact: Scholarships.

1225 Adelphi Scholarship

Adelphi University
South Avenue
Garden City, NY 11530
(516) 877-3050
Average award: $3,500
Maximum award: $4,000
Minimum award: $2,000
Number of awards: 300
Deadline: None
College level: Freshman
Criteria: Renewable for up to three years if recipient maintains a minimum 3.0 GPA. Awarded every year. Award may be used only at sponsoring institution.
Contact: Scholarships.

1226 Admission Scholarship

Saint Augustine's College
1315 Oakwood Avenue
Raleigh, NC 27610
(919) 516-4130
Average award: $2,500
Maximum award: $5,000
Minimum award: $1,000
Number of awards: 11
Deadline: May 15
College level: Freshman
Criteria: Applicant must have a minimum 90 grade average and a minimum combined SAT I score of 850 (composite ACT score of 18). Minimum 3.0 GPA is required to retain scholarship. Awarded every year. Award may be used only at sponsoring institution.
Contact: Mr. Wanzo Hendrix, Director of Admission, (919) 516-4012.

1227 Adult Education Scholarship

Baker College of Jackson
2800 Springport Road
Jackson, MI 49202
(517) 788-7800
Average award: $3,000
Number of awards: 6
Deadline: June 1
Criteria: Applicant must be an adult student and high school graduate, demonstrate a high level of academic success and be recommended by counselor or teacher. Minimum 2.5 GPA is required to retain scholarship. Awarded every year. Award may be used only at sponsoring institution.
Contact: Valerie Heldt, Director of Admissions.

1228 Adult Scholarship

University of Memphis
Scates Hall 204
Memphis, TN 38152
(901) 678-3213, (901) 678-5621 (fax)
katkinsn@cc.memphis.edu
http://www.memphis.edu/
Maximum award: $2,180
Deadline: April 15
Criteria: Applicant must have academic potential evidenced by job achievement and community involvement. Minimum 2.5 GPA and 30 service hours per semester (15 hours for part-time recipients) are required to retain scholarship. Awarded every year. Award may be used only at sponsoring institution.
Contact: Katherine Atkinson, Scholarship Coordinator.

1229 Advanced Study Tuition Grant (ASTG)

Long Island University, C.W. Post Campus
Route 25A
Brookville, NY 11548
(516) 299-2338, (516) 299-2137 (fax)
admissions@collegehall.liunet.edu
http://www.liunet.edu
Average award: $3,000
Deadline: July 1
College level: Transfers
Criteria: Applicant must have a minimum 3.25 GPA, have completed at least 32 credit hours before transferring, and be enrolled full time. Scholarship is renewable. Awarded every year. Award may be used only at sponsoring institution.
Contact: Admissions Office, 720 Northern Boulevard, Brookville, NY 11548-1300, (516) 299-2413.

1230 ALANA Leadership Merit Award

Dominican College of San Rafael
50 Acacia Avenue
San Rafael, CA 94901-2298
(415) 485-3204, (415) 485-3205 (fax)
enroll@dominican.edu
http://www.dominican.edu
Average award: $10,648
Maximum award: $10,685
Minimum award: $10,311
Number of awards: 10
Deadline: March 1
College level: Freshman
Criteria: Applicant must have a minimum 3.0 GPA in academic subjects from grades 9-12, demonstrate leadership and participation in community and school activities, express commitment to multicultural educational environment, and be African-American, Asian-American, Latin American, or Native American. Application is required. Renewable for up to four years if recipient maintains a minimum 2.5 GPA. Awarded every year. Award may be used only at sponsoring institution.
Contact: Susan Gutierrez, Director of Financial Aid.

1231   Alex G. McKenna Economic and Policy Scholarship

Saint Vincent College
Admissions and Financial Aid
Latrobe, PA 15650-2690
(412) 537-4540, (412) 537-4554 (fax)
info@stvincent.edu
http://www.stvincent.edu
Average award: $2,500
Number of awards: 1
Deadline: Early application is recommended
College level: Freshman
Majors/Fields: Minor in economics
Criteria: Applicant must be a high school junior or senior. Selection is based upon essay (specified topic addressing a current economic policy issue), extracurricular participation, standardized test scores, and transcript. Competition is held in fall. Registration is required. Renewable if recipient maintains minimum 3.25 GPA and completes a minor in economics. Awarded every year. Award may be used only at sponsoring institution.
Contact: Rev. Earl Henry, Dean of Admissions and Financial Aid, 300 Fraser Purchase Road, Latrobe, PA 15650.

1232   Allen Scholarship

Cedar Crest College
100 College Drive
Allentown, PA 18104
(610) 740-3785, (610) 606-4647 (fax)
cccadmis@cedarcrest.edu
www.cedarcrest.edu
Maximum award: $5,000
Number of awards: 4
Deadline: Rolling
College level: Freshman
Criteria: Applicant must demonstrate merit, leadership, and outstanding service to school and community. Scholarship is renewable. Awarded every year. Award may be used only at sponsoring institution.
Contact: Judith Neyhart, Vice President for Enrollment Management, Financial Aid Office.

1233   Alternative High School Scholarship

Baker College of Jackson
2800 Springport Road
Jackson, MI 49202
(517) 788-7800
Average award: Half tuition
Number of awards: 5
Deadline: June 1
College level: Freshman
Criteria: Applicant must be recommended by counselor or teacher. Minimum 2.5 GPA is required to retain scholarship. Awarded every year. Award may be used only at sponsoring institution.
Contact: Valerie Heldt, Director of Admissions.

1234   Alumni Academic Scholarships

Auburn University
Auburn University, AL 36849
(334) 844-4723
Average award: $2,100
Deadline: December 15
College level: Freshman
Criteria: Applicant must have a minimum 3.5 GPA and minimum combined SAT I score of 1210 (composite ACT score of 29). Awarded every year. Award may be used only at sponsoring institution.
Contact: Mary Lynn Saidla, Assistant Director for Scholarships.

1235   Alumni Achievement Scholarship

University of Southern California
University Park
Los Angeles, CA 90089-5012
(213) 740-1111
Average award: $9,800
Number of awards: 100
Deadline: December 15
College level: Freshman
Criteria: Applicant must rank in the top two percent of class, and have received national recognition for PSAT score. Selection is based upon academic performance and demonstrated leadership in school and in community. Consideration is given to National Hispanic and National Merit Scholars. Interview is required. Scholarship is renewable. Awarded every year. Award may be used only at sponsoring institution.
Contact: Office of Admission, University Park Campus, Los Angeles, CA 90089-0911.

1236   Alumni Association Scholarship

Louisiana State University and Agricultural and Mechanical College
Baton Rouge, LA 70803-2750
(504) 388-3103
Maximum award: $7,995
Number of awards: 100
Deadline: February 1
College level: Freshman
Criteria: Applicant must have excellent standardized test scores and high school academic record. Minimum 3.0 cumulative GPA and fulltime enrollment are required to retain scholarship. Awarded every year. Award may be used only at sponsoring institution.
Contact: Kathleen Sciacchetano, Director of Financial Aid.

1237   Alumni Award for Leadership and Talent

Denison University
Box H
Granville, OH 43023
(614) 587-6276, 800-DENISON, (614) 587-6306 (fax)
admissions@denison.edu
http://www.denison.edu
Maximum Award: One-Third tuition
Deadline: February 1
College level: Freshman
Majors/Fields: Behavioral sciences, English, foreign languages, mathematics, natural sciences, social sciences
Criteria: Applicant must rank in top half of class or have a successful record in college-preparatory courses, have a minimum combined SAT I score of 1010 (composite ACT score of 22), and demonstrate leadership, special talent, or commitment to community service. Selection is based upon academic record and achievement or talent in academic areas, in creative arts, or in church, community, or school organizations. Minimum GPA is required for renewal. Awarded every year. Award may be used only at sponsoring institution.
Contact: Scholarships.

1238 Alumni Club Scholarship

University of Southern California
University Park
Los Angeles, CA 90089-5012
(213) 740-1111
Maximum award: $4,000
Maximum number of awards: 120
Minimum number of awards: 100
Deadline: December 15
College level: Freshman
Criteria: Applicant must have a minimum 3.6 GPA and have a minimum combined SAT I score of 1200 (composite ACT score of 27), and demonstrate leadership ability. Interview is required. Scholarship is renewable. Awarded every year. Award may be used only at sponsoring institution.
Contact: Office of Admission, University Park Campus, Los Angeles, CA 98009-0911.

1239 Alumni Freshman Scholarship

University of Tennessee, Knoxville
Financial Aid Office
115 Student Services Building
Knoxville, TN 37994
(615) 974-3131
Maximum award: $2,500
Number of awards: 135
Deadline: February 1
College level: Freshman
Criteria: Applicant must have a minimum 3.0 GPA and minimum composite ACT score of 23. Financial need may be considered. Awarded every year. Award may be used only at sponsoring institution.
Contact: Office of Alumni Affairs, 600 Andy Holt Tower, Knoxville, TN 37996-0210, (615) 974-3011.

1240 Alumni Honors Scholarship

Hope College
P.O. Box 9000
Holland, MI 49422-9000
(616) 395-7850, (616) 395-7130 (fax)
admissions@hope.edu
http://www.hope.edu
Average award: $3,000
Deadline: February 15
College level: Freshman, Sophomore, Junior, Senior
Criteria: Applicant must have a minimum 3.75 GPA or a minimum 3.5 GPA and either rank in top fifth of class or have a minimum composite ACT score of 25 (combined SAT I score of 1040). Renewable if recipient maintains a minimum 2.75 GPA. Awarded every year. Award may be used only at sponsoring institution.
Contact: James R. Bekkering, Vice President for Admissions.

1241 Alumni Honors Scholarship

Texas A&M University–Kingsville
Scholarships
Box 116
Kingsville, TX 78363
(512) 593-3907, (512) 593-2991 (fax)
http://www.tamuk.edu
Maximum award: $5,000
Number of awards: 1
Deadline: March 3
College level: Freshman
Criteria: Applicant must have a minimum 3.0 GPA, rank in the top tenth of graduating class, and have minimum combined SAT I score of 1280 (ACT score of 29). Renewable if recipient maintains a minimum 3.5 GPA. Award may be used only at sponsoring institution.
Contact: Laura Knipper, Counselor.

1242 Alumni Memorial Scholarship

Oakland University
101 North Foundation Hall
Rochester, MI 48309-4401
(810) 370-3360, (810) 370-4462 (fax)
Average award: $2,500
Number of awards: 1
Deadline: February 1
College level: Freshman
Criteria: Minimum 3.25 GPA is required to retain scholarship. Awarded every year. Award may be used only at sponsoring institution.
Contact: Stacy M. Penkala, Assistant Director of Admissions.

1243 Alumni Scholarship

Cabrini College
610 King of Prussia Road
Radnor, PA 19087-3699
(610) 902-8420
Average award: $12,000
Number of awards: 1
Deadline: None
College level: Freshman
Criteria: Minimum 3.3 GPA is required to retain scholarship. Awarded every year. Award may be used only at sponsoring institution.
Contact: Laurie Turns, Director of Admissions, (610) 902-8552.

1244 Alumni Scholarship

Indiana State University
217 North Sixth Street
Terre Haute, IN 47809
(812) 237-2121, (812) 237-8023 (fax)
admisu@amber.indstate.edu
http://www.isu.indstate.edu
Average award: Full tuition
Number of awards: 25
Deadline: February 1
College level: Freshman
Criteria: Applicant must rank in the top tenth of graduating class. Satisfactory GPA and full-time enrollment are required to retain scholarship. Awarded every year. Award may be used only at sponsoring institution.
Contact: Steve Manuel, Scholarships, Office of Admissions, Terre Haute, IN 47809, (800) 742-0891.

1245 Alumni Scholarship

University of Indianapolis
1400 East Hanna Avenue
Indianapolis, IN 46227-3697
(317) 788-3217
Maximum award: $3,897
Number of awards: 30
Deadline: None
College level: Freshman
Criteria: Applicant must rank in top 15% of class, have a minimum combined SAT I score of 1100 (composite ACT score of 24), and demonstrate leadership potential. Recipient must maintain a minimum 2.7 GPA and full-time enrollment to retain scholarship. Awarded every year. Award may be used only at sponsoring institution.
Contact: Admissions Office, (317) 788-3216.

1246   Alumni Scholarship

Lawrence University
P.O. Box 599
Appleton, WI 54912-0599
(414) 832-6500, (414) 832-6782 (fax)
excel@lawrence.edu
http://www.lawrence.edu
Average award: $5,000
Number of awards: 50
Deadline: February 1
College level: Freshman
Criteria: Applicant must rank in top tenth of secondary school class and have a minimum 3.7 GPA; minimum combined SAT I score of 1100 (composite ACT score of 24) is recommended. Scholarships are competitive. Renewable if recipient maintains minimum 3.0 GPA. Awarded every year. Award may be used only at sponsoring institution.
Contact: Director of Admissions, excel@lawrence.edu.

1247   Alumni Scholarship

University of Miami
P.O. Box 248187
Coral Gables, FL 33124-5241
(305) 284-5212
Average award: $6,380
Number of awards: 136
College level: Freshman
Criteria: Selection is based upon academic achievement. Typically, applicant should rank in the top fifth of his or her class and have a minimum combined SAT I score of 1180 (composite ACT score of 26). Recipient must maintain minimum 3.0 GPA and 24 credit hours per year to retain scholarship. Awarded every year. Award may be used only at sponsoring institution.
Contact: Martin J. Carney, Director of Office of Financial Assistance Services, P.O. Box 248178, Coral Gables, FL 33124-5240, (305) 284-2270.

1248   Alumni Scholarship

University of South Carolina
Office of Admissions
Columbia, SC 29208
(803) 777-4067
Average award: $3,500
Number of awards: 30
Deadline: Early November
College level: Freshman
Criteria: Selection is based upon outstanding academic achievement. Minimum 3.0 GPA is required to retain scholarship. Awarded every year. Award may be used only at sponsoring institution.
Contact: Michael Jinnette, Scholarship Coordinator.

1249   Ambassador Scholarship

Mesa State College
Financial Aid Department
P.O. Box 2647
Grand Junction, CO 81502
(970) 248-1396
Maximum award: Tuition and fees
College level: Freshman
Criteria: Applicant must demonstrate leadership skills. Renewable for up to four years if recipient maintains a minimum 2.7 GPA and completes at least 12 credit hours per semester. Awarded every year. Award may be used only at sponsoring institution.
Contact: Office of Admission, (970) 248-1376.

1250   American Values Scholarship

John Carroll University
20700 North Park Boulevard
Cleveland, OH 44118
(216) 397-4248
Maximum award: $3,000
Deadline: April 1
College level: Freshman
Criteria: Applicant must have a minimum 3.5 GPA ("B+" grade average) and strong SAT I/ACT scores. Application is required; FAFSA is recommended. Selection is based upon evidence of exceptional academic and non-academic achievement and promise. Minimum 3.0 GPA and full-time enrollment are required to retain scholarship. Awarded every year. Award may be used only at sponsoring institution.
Contact: Office of Admission.

1251   Amigo Scholarship

University of New Mexico
Mesa Vista Hall
3rd Floor, Room 3020
Albuquerque, NM 87131
(505) 277-6090
Maximum award: In-state tuition plus $200
Deadline: None
College level: Freshman, Transfers
Criteria: Applicant must have a minimum 3.5 GPA with minimum composite ACT score of 23 or have a minimum 3.0 GPA with a minimum composite ACT score of 26 and cannot be a New Mexico resident. Minimum 3.0 GPA with 30 credit hours per year is required to retain scholarship. Awarded every year. Award may be used only at sponsoring institution.
Contact: Rita M. Padilla, Associate Director of Scholarships.

1252   Amy Shelton McNutt Scholarship

William Woods University
200 West 12th Street
Fulton, MO 65251-1098
(573) 592-4232, (573) 592-1146 (fax)
http://www.wmwoods.edu
Average award: 75% of tuition, room, and board
Number of awards: 1
Deadline: February 1
College level: Freshman
Criteria: Applicant must rank in top three tenths of graduating class, and have a minimum composite ACT score of 26 (combined SAT I score of 1180), submit essay, and have on-campus interview. Reapplication, a minimum 3.5 GPA, and involvement in campus activities are required for renewal. Awarded every year. Award may be used only at sponsoring institution.
Contact: Laura L. Archuleta, Director for Student Financial Aid, larchule@iris.wmwoods.edu.

1253   Andrew Carnegie Scholarship

Carnegie Mellon University
5000 Forbes Avenue
Pittsburgh, PA 15213
(412) 268-2068
Average award: Half tuition
Number of awards: 75
Deadline: February 15
College level: Freshman
Criteria: Minimum 3.25 Quality Point Average (QPA) on a 4.00 scale is required for renewal. Awarded every year. Award may be used only at sponsoring institution.
Contact: Linda M. Anderson, Director of Financial Aid.

1254 Andrew D. Holt Scholarship

University of Tennessee, Knoxville
Financial Aid Office
115 Student Services Building
Knoxville, TN 37994
(615) 974-3131
Average award: $2,500
Number of awards: 8
Deadline: February 1
College level: Freshman
Criteria: Applicant typically should have a minimum 3.9 GPA and a minimum composite ACT score of 30. Selection is based upon academic and leadership abilities. Award is for four years. Awarded every year. Award may be used only at sponsoring institution.
Contact: University Honors Program, F-101 Melrose Hall, Knoxville, TN 37916, (615) 974-7875.

1255 Angier B. Duke Scholarship

Duke University
P.O. Box 90397
Durham, NC 27706
(919) 684-6225, (919) 660-9811 (fax)
Average award: $18,400
Maximum award: $20,280
Number of awards: 15
Deadline: January 15
College level: Freshman
Criteria: Applicant must have high academic qualifications as determined by the A.B. Duke Selection Committee. A separate application is not required. Scholarship is renewable. Awarded every year. Award may be used only at sponsoring institution.
Contact: Christoph Guttentag, Director of Admissions, P.O. Box 90587, Durham, NC 27708-0587, (919) 684-3214.

1256 Anibal Excellence Scholarship

Oakland University
101 North Foundation Hall
Rochester, MI 48309-4401
(810) 370-3360, (810) 370-4462 (fax)
Average award: $2,500
Number of awards: 5
Deadline: February 1
College level: Freshman
Criteria: Minimum 3.25 GPA is required to retain scholarship. Awarded every year. Award may be used only at sponsoring institution.
Contact: Stacy M. Penkala, Assistant Director of Admissions.

1257 Ann P. Neupauer Scholarship

Stevens Institute of Technology
Castle Point on Hudson
Hoboken, NJ 07030
(201) 216-5201, (201) 216-8348 (fax)
sheridan_d@stmisb.adm.stevens-tech.edu
http://www.stevens-tech.edu
Average award: Full tuition
Number of awards: 10
College level: Freshman
Criteria: Applicant must be a U.S. citizen or permanent resident and have a minimum combined SAT I score of 1400. Minimum 3.2 GPA is required to retain scholarship. Awarded every year. Award may be used only at sponsoring institution.
Contact: David Sheridan, Director of Financial Aid, sheridan_d@stmisb.adm.stevens-tech.edu.

1258 Art Academy of Cincinnati Entrance Scholarship

Art Academy of Cincinnati
1125 Saint Gregory Street
Cincinnati, OH 45202-1700
(513) 721-5205, (800) 323-5692, (513) 562-8778 (fax)
Average award: $3,500
Maximum award: $8,000
Minimum award: $1,000
Number of awards: 12
Deadline: March 15
College level: Freshman, Sophomore, Junior
Criteria: Selection is based upon talent, letters of recommendation, and artist's statement. Portfolio is required. Renewable if 3.0 GPA and full-time status are maintained. Awarded every year. Award may be used only at sponsoring institution.
Contact: Douglas Dobbins, Director of Admissions, (513) 562-8757.

1259 Arthur J. Schmitt Scholarship

DePaul University
1 East Jackson Boulevard
Chicago, IL 60604
(312) 362-8704, (312) 362-5749 (fax)
Average award: $9,000
Number of awards: 25
Deadline: None
College level: Freshman
Criteria: Applicant must rank in the top tenth of class, have a minimum composite ACT score of 27 or combined SAT I score of 1220, and demonstrate strong leadership and extracurricular involvements. Minimum 3.3 GPA and full-time enrollment required to retain scholarship. Awarded every year. Award may be used only at sponsoring institution.
Contact: Jennifer Sparrow, Scholarship Coordinator, jsparrow@wppost.depaul.edu.

1260 Award of Excellence

Western Kentucky University
Cravens Library 101
Bowling Green, KY 42101
(502) 745-2551
Average award: $3,104
Number of awards: 106
Deadline: February 15
College level: Freshman
Criteria: Selection is based upon standardized test scores, cumulative GPA, and rank in class. Minimum 3.2 cumulative GPA is required to retain scholarship. Awarded every year. Award may be used only at sponsoring institution.
Contact: Dennis M. Smith, Assistant Director of Admissions.

1261 Badger Boy/Girl Scholarship

Ripon College
300 Seward Street
P.O. Box 248
Ripon, WI 54971
(800) 94-RIPON, (414) 748-7243 (fax)
adminfo@mac.ripon.edu
http://www.ripon.edu
Average award: $3,000
Number of awards: No limit
Deadline: December 1 (early decision) March 1
College level: Freshman, Transfers
Criteria: Applicant must have participated in Wisconsin's Badger State Program and be accepted for admission. Renewable if good academic standing is maintained. Awarded every year. Award may be used only at sponsoring institution.
Contact: Paul J. Weeks, Vice President and Dean of Admission.

1262   Baily Scholarship

Mary Baldwin College
Staunton, VA 24401
(540) 887-7022
Average award: $3,000
Number of awards: 20
Deadline: None
College level: Freshman
Criteria: Applicant must be enrolled full time in traditional degree program. Selection is based upon academic record and an on-campus interview. Scholarship is renewable. Awarded every year. Award may be used only at sponsoring institution.
Contact: Patricia LeDonne, Dean of Admissions and Financial Aid, (540) 887-7019.

1263   Baker Award

Baker University
P.O. Box 61
Baldwin City, KS 66006
(913) 594-4595
Maximum award: $2,250
Deadline: None
College level: Freshman, Transfers
Criteria: Applicant must have a minimum 2.7 GPA. Amount of award is based upon GPA, standardized test scores, and financial need. FAFSA is required. Minimum 2.5 GPA is required to retain scholarship. Awarded every year. Award may be used only at sponsoring institution.
Contact: Scholarships.

1264   Baldwin Scholarship

Mary Baldwin College
Staunton, VA 24401
(540) 887-7022
Average award: $3,000
Maximum award: $5,000
Minimum award: $2,000
Deadline: None
College level: Freshman
Criteria: Selection is based upon GPA and class rank. Applicant must be enrolled full time in traditional degree program. Scholarship is renewable. Awarded every year. Award may be used only at sponsoring institution.
Contact: Patricia LeDonne, Dean of Admissions and Financial Aid, (540) 887-7019.

1265   Bank One Scholarship

Indiana University Northwest
3400 Broadway
Gary, IN 46408
(219) 980-6777, (219) 981-4219 (fax)
wlee@iunhawl.iun.indiana.edu
Maximum award: Full tuition
Number of awards: 1
Deadline: March 15
College level: Freshman
Criteria: Selection is based upon academic achievement and potential for college success. Scholarship is renewable. Awarded every year. Award may be used only at sponsoring institution.
Contact: William D. Lee, Director of Admissions and Financial Aid, (219) 980-6991.

1266   Barry M. Goldwater Scholarship and Excellence in Education Program

Barry M. Goldwater Scholarship and Excellence in Education Foundation
6225 Brandon Avenue
Suite 315
Springfield, VA 22150-2519
(703) 756-6012, (703) 756-6015 (fax)
goldh2o@erols.com
http://www.act.org/goldwater
Maximum award: $7,000
Number of awards: 250
Deadline: mid-January
College level: Junior, Senior
Majors/Fields: Engineering, mathematics, natural sciences
Criteria: Applicant must be a U.S. citizen, permanent resident, or resident alien who submits letter of intent to obtain U.S. citizenship, with a minimum "B" grade average and rank in top quarter of class. Selection is based upon merit, outstanding potential, and intent to pursue career in mathematics, natural sciences, or engineering. Automatically renewed for sophomores. Awarded every year.
Contact: Goldwater Faculty Representative on campus.

1267   Baruch Scholarship

City University of New York, Baruch College
Undergraduate Admissions Office
Box 279, 17 Lexington Avenue
New York, NY 10010
(212) 447-3750
Average award: $2,600
Number of awards: 6
Deadline: February 15
College level: Freshman
Criteria: Applicant must have a minimum combined SAT I score of 1100, minimum high school average of 87, be interviewed, and submit an essay and two letters of recommendation. Renewable if a minimum 3.0 GPA after freshman year and 3.25 GPA thereafter is maintained. Awarded every year. Award may be used only at sponsoring institution.
Contact: Hugo Morales, Scholarship Coordinator, (212) 447-3753.

1268   Belk Scholarship

Wingate University
Wingate, NC 28174-0157
(800) 755-5550, (704) 233-8110 (fax)
admit@wingate.edu
http://www.wingate.edu
Average award: $6,230
Maximum award: $7,000
Minimum award: $5,000
Number of awards: 20
Deadline: April 15
College level: Freshman
Criteria: Minimum 3.2 GPA is required to retain scholarship. Awarded every year. Award may be used only at sponsoring institution.
Contact: Walt Crutchfield, Dean of Admissions, Campus Box 3059, Wingate, NC 28174.

1269   Bellarmine Scholarships

Bellarmine College
Newburg Road
Louisville, KY 40205
(502) 452-8131, (502) 452-8002 (fax)
http://www.bellarmine.edu
Maximum award: $10,850
Number of awards: 3
Deadline: January 15
College level: Freshman
Majors/Fields: Honors program
Criteria: Applicant must have a minimum 3.9 GPA, rank in the top 5% of graduating class, and have a minimum combined SAT I score of 1300 (composite ACT score of 30). Renewable if recipient maintains a minimum 3.5 GPA. Awarded every year. Award may be used only at sponsoring institution.
Contact: Timothy A. Sturgeon, Associate Dean of Admissions.

1270 Ben T. Huiet Endowment Fund Scholarship

Clemson University
G-01 Sikes Hall
Clemson, SC 29634-5123
(803) 656-2280
Average award: $2,500
Number of awards: 1
Deadline: March 1
College level: Freshman
Criteria: Selection is based upon admissions application. Renewable for up to three years if recipient maintains minimum 3.0 GPA and completes at least 12 credits each semester. Awarded every year. Award may be used only at sponsoring institution.
Contact: Marvin Carmichael, Director of Financial Aid.

1271 Benjamin Titus Roberts Scholarship

Roberts Wesleyan College
2301 Westside Drive
Rochester, NY 14624-1997
(716) 594-6422
Average award: $5,000
Number of awards: 25
Deadline: None
College level: Freshman, Transfers
Criteria: Freshman applicant must rank in top 15% of class, have a minimum combined SAT I score of 1200 (composite ACT score of 27), have character consistent with goals of college, and participate in Invitational Scholarship Competition. Transfer applicant must be a Phi Theta Kappa Scholar and have character consisent with goals of college. Applicant must be a full-time student. Competition participants not selected for this award will receive the Presidential Scholarship. Minimum 3.4 GPA is required to retain scholarship. Awarded every year. Award may be used only at sponsoring institution.
Contact: Brian P. Madden, Assistant Director of Financial Aid, (716) 594-6150.

1272 Birkett-Williams Scholarship

Ouachita Baptist University
410 Ouachita Street
Arkadelphia, AR 71998-0001
(501) 245-5570
Maximum award: $7,070
Number of awards: 7
Deadline: February 15
College level: Freshman, Sophomore, Junior, Senior
Majors/Fields: Business, education, humanities, music, natural science, religion, social science
Criteria: One award is given for each educational division. Minimum 3.5 GPA required to retain scholarship. Awarded every year. Award may be used only at sponsoring institution.
Contact: Susan Hurst, Director of Financial Aid.

1273 Bishop Maher Catholic Leadership Scholarship

University of San Diego
Alcala Park
San Diego, CA 92110-2492
(619) 260-4514
Maximum award: $3,000
College level: Freshman
Criteria: Applicant must be a Catholic who has demonstrated leadership in community, parish, or school. Amount of award is based upon academic performance, demonstrated leadership, and financial need. Application (available from Office of Financial Aid), letter from applicant, letter of recommendation from applicant's parish priest, and FAFSA are required. Scholarship is renewable. Awarded every year. Award may be used only at sponsoring institution.
Contact: Office of Financial Aid.

1274 Board of Control Scholarship

Grand Valley State University
Allendale, MI 49401
(616) 895-3234
Average award: $6,320
Maximum award: $6,638
Minimum award: $4,000
Number of awards: 12
Deadline: February 1
College level: Freshman
Criteria: Minimum 3.5 GPA is required to retain scholarship. Awarded every year. Award may be used only at sponsoring institution.
Contact: Ken Fridsma, Director of Financial Aid.

1275 Board of Directors Scholarship

Valparaiso University
Valparaiso, IN 46383-6493
(219) 464-5011, (219) 464-6898 (fax)
undergrad_admissions@valpo.edu
http:www.valpo.edu
Maximum award: $11,820
Deadline: May 1
College level: Freshman
Criteria: Selection is based upon academic accomplishments. Renewable for up to three years if minimum 3.0 GPA is maintained. Awarded every year. Award may be used only at sponsoring institution.
Contact: Office of Admissions and Financial Aid, Kretzman Hall, (888) GO VALPO.

1276 Board of Regents Scholarship

Baker College of Jackson
2800 Springport Road
Jackson, MI 49202
(517) 788-7800
Average award: Half tuition
Number of awards: 5
Deadline: May 1
College level: Freshman
Criteria: Applicant must have a minimum 3.5 GPA. Minimum 3.0 GPA is required to retain scholarship. Awarded every year. Award may be used only at sponsoring institution.
Contact: Valerie Heldt, Director of Admissions.

1277 Board of Regents Scholarship

Baker College of Owosso
Scholarships
1020 South Washington Street
Owosso, MI 48867
(800) 879-3797, 517 723-5251, (517) 729-6527 (fax)
Average award: $3,000
Number of awards: No limit
Deadline: May 15
College level: Freshman
Criteria: Applicant must have minimum 3.5 GPA. Renewable if recipient maintains minimum 3.0 GPA. Awarded every year. Award may be used only at sponsoring institution.
Contact: Bruce A. Lundeen, Vice President for Admissions, (517) 723-5251, extension 454, lundee_b@owosso.baker.edu.

1278　Board of Regents Scholarship

Concordia College
800 North Columbia Avenue
Seward, NE 68434
(402) 643-7270
Maximum award: Full tuition
Deadline: None
College level: Freshman
Criteria: Applicant must be a first-time, full-time freshman with a minimum 3.0 GPA and minimum composite ACT score of 24 (combined SAT I score of 1070) for minimum award. National Merit finalists may receive maximum award. Renewable for up to 10 consecutive undergraduate semesters if minimum 3.0 GPA is maintained. Awarded every year. Award may be used only at sponsoring institution.
Contact: Scholarships.

1279　Bonners Scholarship

Waynesburg College
51 West College Street
Waynesburg, PA 15370
(800) 225-7393, (412) 627-6416 (fax)
admission@waynesburg.edu
http://waynesburg.edu
Maximum award: $3,050
Number of awards: 20
Deadline: March 1
College level: Freshman
Criteria: Applicant must rank in top three-fifths of class, demonstrate commitment to community service, and meet specific academic and financial need criteria. Recipient must participate in enrichment activities, in community service activities for an average 10 hours per week, and in a summer service program for six to eight weeks. Fulfillment of program requirements is required to retain scholarship. Awarded every year. Award may be used only at sponsoring institution.
Contact: Robin Moore, Dean of Admissions, (412) 852-3248, 800 225-7393, admission@waynesburg.edu.

1280　Bookcliff Scholarship

Mesa State College
Financial Aid Department
P.O. Box 2647
Grand Junction, CO 81502
(970) 248-1396
Average award: Full tuition
College level: Freshman
Criteria: Applicant must demonstrate strong academic and/or leadership background. Selection is based upon GPA, class rank, and standardized test scores. A minimum index of 100 is recommended. Renewable for up to four years if recipient maintains a minimum 3.0 GPA, completes at least 15 credit hours per semester, and completes 50 hours of community service per year. Awarded every year. Award may be used only at sponsoring institution.
Contact: Office of Admission, (970) 248-1376.

1281　Boston College Scholarship/Grant

Boston College
Lyons Hall 210
140 Commonwealth Avenue
Chestnut Hill, MA 02167
(617) 552-3320
Average award: $6,600
Maximum award: $14,580
Minimum award: $200
Number of awards: 2,027
Deadline: April 21
College level: Sophomore, Junior, Senior
Criteria: Selection is based upon financial need and GPA. Reapplication, satisfactory GPA, and financial need required to retain scholarship. Awarded every year. Award may be used only at sponsoring institution.
Contact: Kerry Giza, Program Director of Undergraduate Financial Aid.

1282　Boston College Scholarship/Grant for Incoming Freshmen

Boston College
Lyons Hall 210
140 Commonwealth Avenue
Chestnut Hill, MA 02167
(617) 552-3320
Average award: $8,600
Maximum award: $14,580
Minimum award: $200
Number of awards: 78
Deadline: February 1
College level: Freshman
Criteria: Selection is based upon financial need and GPA. Reapplication, satisfactory GPA, and financial need required to retain scholarship. Awarded every year. Award may be used only at sponsoring institution.
Contact: Joyce M. Lezberg, Program Director, Incoming Student Financial Aid Office, (617) 552-4946.

1283　Bowman Foster Ashe Scholarship

University of Miami
P.O. Box 248187
Coral Gables, FL 33124-5241
(305) 284-5212
Average award: $14,355
Number of awards: 96
Deadline: None
College level: Freshman
Criteria: Applicant must rank in the top one percent of class and have minimum combined SAT I score of 1360 or composite ACT score of 31. Minimum 3.0 GPA and 24 credit hours per year required to maintain scholarship. Awarded every year. Award may be used only at sponsoring institution.
Contact: Martin J. Carney, Director of Office of Financial Assistance Services, (305) 284-2270.

1284　Bowman Scholarship

Kent State University
P.O. Box 5190
Kent, OH 44242-0001
(216) 672-2972
Average award: $3,500
Deadline: April 1
College level: Senior, Graduate, Doctoral
Criteria: Applicant must have a minimum 3.2 cumulative GPA. Minimum 2.0 GPA is required to retain scholarship. Awarded every year. Award may be used only at sponsoring institution.
Contact: Theodore Hallenbeck, Director of Financial Aid, 103 Michael Schwartz Center.

1285　Boys' and Girls' State Awards

Columbia College
1001 Rogers Street
Columbia, MO 65216
(800) 231-2391
Maximum award: $3,000
Number of awards: 5
Deadline: None
College level: Freshman
Criteria: Applicant must be an elected delegate to Boys' or Girls' State Convention ($1,000), governor or lt. governor ($2,000), or president or vice president of Boys' or Girls' nation ($3,000). Awarded every year. Award may be used only at sponsoring institution.
Contact: Financial Aid Office, (800) 231-2391, extension 7361.

1286 Bradford Scholar Program

Bradford College
320 South Main Street
Haverhill, MA 01835
(508) 372-7161, (508) 372-5240 (fax)
bradcoll@aol.com
http://bradford.edu
Average award: $15,380
Maximum award: Full tuition
Number of awards: 4
Deadline: None
College level: Freshman, Sophomore, Junior, Senior
Criteria: Selection is based upon academic achievement, class rank, campus visit, and extracurricular activities. Scholarship is renewable. Awarded every year. Award may be used only at sponsoring institution.
Contact: Scholarships.

1287 Brandel Presidential Scholarship

Auburn University
Auburn University, AL 36849
(334) 844-4723
Average award: $8,000
Number of awards: 1
Deadline: December 15
College level: Freshman
Majors/Fields: Mechanical engineering
Criteria: Applicant must have a minimum 3.5 GPA and minimum combined SAT I score of 1210 (composite ACT score of 29). Preference is given to residents of Orange County, Fla., Florida, and Alabama, in that order. Minimum "B" grade average is required for renewal. Awarded every year. Award may be used only at sponsoring institution.
Contact: Mary Lynn Saidla, Assistant Director for Scholarships.

1288 Briggs/May Scholarship

South Dakota State University
Box 2201
Brookings, SD 57007
(605) 688-4695, (605) 688-6384 (fax)
http://www.sdstate.edu
Maximum award: $5,000
Number of awards: 18
Deadline: January 25
College level: Freshman
Criteria: Applicant must have a minimum 3.9 GPA and a minimum composite ACT score of 29 and have participated in activities. Scholarship is renewable. Awarded every year. Award may be used only at sponsoring institution.
Contact: Jay Larsen, Financial Aid Director, AD 106, Brookings, SD 57007, larsenj@adm.sdstate.edu.

1289 Brookshire Foundation Honors Scholarship

Texas A&M University–Kingsville
Scholarships
Box 116
Kingsville, TX 78363
(512) 593-3907, (512) 593-2991 (fax)
http://www.tamuk.edu
Maximum award: $5,000
Number of awards: 1
Deadline: March 3
College level: Freshman
Criteria: Applicant must be a graduate of Kingsville or Kaufer high schools, have a minimum 3.0 GPA, rank in the top tenth of his or her graduating class, and have a minimum combined SAT I score of 1280 (ACT score of 29). Renewable if recipient maintains a minimum 3.5 GPA. Award may be used only at sponsoring institution.
Contact: Laura Knipper, Counselor.

1290 Brownson Memorial Leadership Scholarship

Mesa State College
Financial Aid Department
P.O. Box 2647
Grand Junction, CO 81502
(970) 248-1396
Average awards: Full tuition and fees
Number of awards: 8
College level: Sophomore, Junior, Senior
Majors/Fields: Business, music, vocational
Criteria: Applicant must have a minimum 2.5 GPA. Awarded to four athletes enrolled in the School of Business (baseball, basketball, football), one minority student, and one each for business, music, and vocational majors. Awarded every year. Award may be used only at sponsoring institution.
Contact: Office of Admission, (970) 248-1376.

1291 Buell Scholarship

Lawrence Technological University
21000 West Ten Mile Road
Southfield, MI 48075
(810) 204-2120
Average award: Full tuition plus a $1,000 stipend.
Number of awards: 6
Deadline: March 1
College level: Freshman
Criteria: Applicant must have a minimum 3.8 GPA, rank in top 5% of class, and have a minimum composite ACT score of 29. Minimum 3.0 GPA is required to retain scholarship. Awarded every year. Award may be used only at sponsoring institution.
Contact: Paul F. Kinder, Director of Financial Aid.

1292 Build the Bridge Scholarship

Elizabethtown College
One Alpha Drive
Elizabethtown, PA 17022
(717) 361-1404, (717) 361-1485 (fax)
Maximum award: Full tuition
Minimum award: $9,000
Number of awards: 8
Deadline: March 1
Criteria: Applicant must be a minority student demonstrating academic merit and financial need. Renewable if recipient has minimum 2.75 GPA at end of freshman year and 3.0 GPA at end of sophomore and junior years. Award may be used only at sponsoring institution.
Contact: M. Clarke Paine, Director of Financial Aid, painemc@acad.etown.edu.

1293 Cambridge Scholarship

Rhodes College
2000 North Parkway
Memphis, TN 38112
(901) 843-3700, (901) 843-3719 (fax)
adminfo@rhodes.edu
http://www.rhodes.edu
Average award: $12,300
Number of awards: 17
Deadline: February 1 (priority)
College level: Freshman
Criteria: Selection is based upon merit. Renewable if recipient maintains a minimum 3.25 GPA. Awarded every year. Award may be used only at sponsoring institution.
Contact: David J. Wottle, Dean of Admissions and Financial Aid, (800) 844-5969.

1294   Capstone Presidential Scholarship

Columbia College
1001 Rogers Street
Columbia, MO 65216
(800) 231-2391
Average award: Full tuition
Number of awards: 6
Deadline: March 15 (priority)
College level: Senior
Criteria: Applicant must have a minimum 3.85 GPA, have completed 90 credit hours (must have been enrolled at Columbia Coll for previous three years), and submit school's financial aid form. Previous Capstone Scholarship recipients are not eligible. Financial need is not considered. Awarded every year. Award may be used only at sponsoring institution.
Contact: Financial Aid Office, (800) 231-2391, extension 7361.

1295   Capstone Scholarship

Columbia College
1001 Rogers Street
Columbia, MO 65216
(800) 231-2391
Average award: Half tuition
Number of awards: 43
Deadline: March 15 (priority)
College level: Senior
Criteria: Applicant must have a minimum 3.4 GPA, have completed 90 credit hours (with the most recent 30 credits earned at Columbia Coll and not including ENG 100 or 104 or MATH 105), and submit school's financial aid form. Financial need is not considered. Awarded every year. Award may be used only at sponsoring institution.
Contact: Financial Aid Office.

1296   Carl L. and David M. Kahn Scholarship

Indiana University Northwest
3400 Broadway
Gary, IN 46408
(219) 980-6777, (219) 981-4219 (fax)
wlee@iunhawl.iun.indiana.edu
Maximum award: $2,500
Number of awards: 1
Deadline: March 15
College level: Freshman
Criteria: Selection is based upon academic achievement and potential for college success. Scholarship is renewable. Awarded every year. Award may be used only at sponsoring institution.
Contact: William D. Lee, Director of Admissions and Financial Aid, (219) 980-6991.

1297   Carl S. Ell Scholarship

Northeastern University
360 Huntington Avenue
150 Richards Hall
Boston, MA 02115
(617) 373-2000
Average award: $23,895
Number of awards: 50
Deadline: March 1
College level: Freshman
Criteria: Applicant must have a minimum combined SAT I score of 1250 and rank in the top five percent of class. Minimum 3.25 GPA and participation in the Honors program are required to retain scholarship. Awarded every year. Award may be used only at sponsoring institution.
Contact: Alan Kines, Director of Admissions, (617) 373-2200.

1298   Carol G. Belk Leadership Scholarship

Queens College
1900 Selwyn Avenue
Charlotte, NC 28274
(704) 337-2212, 800 849-0202, (704) 337-2403 (fax)
cas@rex.queens.edu
http://www.queens.edu
Maximum award: $6,000
Deadline: None
College level: Freshman
Criteria: Applicant must have a record of outstanding leadership in community and school and have potential for leadership in college. Financial need is considered. Scholarship is renewable. Awarded every year. Award may be used only at sponsoring institution.
Contact: Eileen T. Dills, Director of Financial Aid.

1299   Cecil C. Humphreys Merit Scholarship

University of Memphis
Scates Hall 204
Memphis, TN 38152
(901) 678-3213, (901) 678-5621 (fax)
katkinsn@cc.memphis.edu
http://www.memphis.edu/
Maximum award: $6,500
Deadline: January 15
College level: Freshman
Criteria: Applicant must be selected as a college-sponsored merit finalist and indicate the U of Memphis as first choice college with National Merit Scholarship Corporation. Scholarship is renewable. Awarded every year. Award may be used only at sponsoring institution.
Contact: Katherine Atkinson, Scholarship Coordinator.

1300   Cecil C. Humphreys Presidential Scholarship

University of Memphis
Scates Hall 204
Memphis, TN 38152
(901) 678-3213, (901) 678-5621 (fax)
katkinsn@cc.memphis.edu
http://www.memphis.edu/
Maximum award: $4,420
Deadline: January 15
College level: Freshman
Criteria: Applicant must have a minimum composite ACT score of 30 or combined SAT score of 1320. Selection is based upon test scores, high school transcript, interview, excellence of performance in an area of interest, and quantity and quality of extracurricular activities and is competitive. Minimum 3.0 GPA for first year (3.25 GPA thereafter), and service requirement of 10 hours per year are required to retain scholarship. Awarded every year. Award may be used only at sponsoring institution.
Contact: Katherine Atkinson, Scholarship Coordinator.

1301   Centenary Academic Scholarship

Centenary College of Louisiana
2911 Centenary Boulevard
Shreveport, LA 71104
(318) 869-5137, (318) 869-5005 (fax)
Maximum award: $8,000
Number of awards: 118
Deadline: March 15
College level: Freshman, Sophomore, Junior, Senior
Criteria: Applicant must have a minimum 3.0 GPA and a minimum composite ACT score of 24 (combined SAT I score of 1050). Minimum 3.0 GPA is required for renewal. Awarded every year. Award may be used only at sponsoring institution.
Contact: Mary Sue Rix, Director of Financial Aid, msrix@beta.centenary.edu.

1302 Centenary Scholarship

College of Notre Dame of Maryland
4701 North Charles Street
Baltimore, MD 21210
(410) 532-5369
*Average award:*Tuition reduced to $1,996 for four years.
Deadline: December 31
College level: Freshman
*Criteria:*Applicant must be a woman and be nominated by an alumna, a guidance counselor, or a high school principal. Selection is based upon academic ability, community and school involvement, and leadership qualities. Scholarship is renewable. Awarded every year. Award may be used only at sponsoring institution.
Contact: Financial Aid Office.

1303 Centennial Scholarship

Lee University
P.O. Box 3450
Cleveland, TN 37320-3450
(423) 614-8000
Average award: $5,232
Number of awards: 44
Deadline: September 1
College level: Freshman
*Criteria:*Applicant must have a minimum composite ACT score of 31 (combined SAT I score of 1350) and must enroll for academic year immediately following graduation. Award is equal to standard tuition each year and is for four years. Awarded every year. Award may be used only at sponsoring institution.
Contact: Gary Ray, Director of Admissions, (423) 614-8500.

1304 Centennial Scholarship

Mississippi University for Women
Columbus, MS 39701
(601) 329-7114, (601) 241-7481 (fax)
admissions@muw.edu
http://www.muw.edu/admissions
Maximum award: $7,600
Maximum number of awards: 10
Minimum number of awards: 8
Deadline: December 1
College level: Freshman, Sophomore, Junior, Senior
Criteria: Applicant must have minimum ACT score of 28. Minimum 3.3 GPA is required to retain scholarship. Awarded every year. Award may be used only at sponsoring institution.
*Contact:*Melanie Freeman, Director of Admissions, (601) 329-7105.

1305 Centennial Scholarship

Wingate University
Wingate, NC 28174-0157
(800) 755-5550, (704) 233-8110 (fax)
admit@wingate.edu
http://www.wingate.edu
Average award: $1,574
Maximum award: $2,500
Minimum award: $1,000
Number of awards: 105
Deadline: April 15
College level: Freshman
*Criteria:*Minimum 2.5 GPA is required to retain scholarship. Awarded every year. Award may be used only at sponsoring institution.
Contact: Walt Crutchfield, Dean of Admissions, Campus Box 3059, Wingate, NC 28174.

1306 Century III Leaders Program

National Association of Secondary School Principals
1904 Association Drive
Reston, VA 22091
Maximum award: $11,500
Number of awards: 520
Deadline: October 17
College level: Freshman
Criteria: Applicant must be nominated by a high school principal or guidance counselor. Participation begins at local school level and progresses to statewide competition among all local school winners. Two winners from each state and the District of Columbia receive $1,500 scholarships and all-expense-paid trips to national Century III leaders meeting, and have the opportunity to win additional $10,000 scholarship. State alternates receive $500 scholarships. Selection is based upon leadership skills, school and community involvement, and innovative thinking about America's future. Awarded every year.
Contact: Awards.

1307 Chancellor Scholarship

University of Pittsburgh, Pittsburgh Campus
4200 Fifth Avenue
Pittsburgh, PA 15260
(412) 624-4141
http://www.pitt.edu/-oafa/oafa.html
Maximum award: $19,558
Number of awards: 10
Deadline: January 15
College level: Freshman
Criteria: Selection is based upon high school performance, SAT I or ACT scores, essay, and interview. Minimum 3.0 GPA is required to retain scholarship. Awarded every year. Award may be used only at sponsoring institution.
Contact: Betsy A. Porter, Director of Admissions and Financial Aid, Office of Admissions & Financial Aid, Bruce Hall, Pittsburgh, PA 15260, (412) 624-7164.

1308 Chancellor Scholarship

Texas Christian University
2800 South University Drive
Fort Worth, TX 76129
(817) 921-7858, (817) 921-7462 (fax)
frogaid@tcu.edu
Maximum award: Full tuition up to 16 credit hours per semester
Number of awards: 44
Deadline: January 15
College level: Freshman
*Criteria:*Applicant must rank in top 15% of class and have a minimum combined SAT I score of 1180 (composite ACT score of 27). Renewable for up to eight semesters or 128 credit hours if recipient maintains a minimum 3.0 GPA after freshman year (3.25 GPA thereafter) and successfully completes at least 27 credit hours per year. Awarded every year. Award may be used only at sponsoring institution.
Contact: Office of Student Financial Aid, TCU Box 297012, Fort Worth, TX 76129.

1309 Chancellor's Alumni Scholarship

Louisiana State University and Agricultural and Mechanical College
Baton Rouge, LA 70803-2750
(504) 388-3103
Maximum award: $9,595
Number of awards: 10
Deadline: February 1
College level: Freshman
Criteria: Applicant must have an overall "A" grade average in high school English, math, social studies, and natural sciences. Interview and essay are required. Applicant must have a composite ACT score of 33, combined SAT I score of 1350, or a National Merit selection index score of at least 200. Minimum cumulative 3.0 GPA and full-time enrollment are required to retain scholarship. Awarded every year. Award may be used only at sponsoring institution.
Contact: Kathleen Sciacchetano, Director of Financial Aid.

1310   Chancellor's Scholarship

Appalachian State University
Boone, NC 28608
(704) 262-2000, (704) 262-3296 (fax)
http://www.appstate.edu
Average award: $4,000
Number of awards: 25
Deadline: December 13
Criteria: Renewable if recipient maintains minimum 3.4 GPA. Four-year award. Awarded every year. Award may be used only at sponsoring institution.
Contact: Dr. Donald B. Saunders, Coordinator, University Honors Programs, Appalachian State University, Boone, NC 28608, (704) 262-6013, saundersdb@appstate.edu.

1311   Chancellor's Scholarship

University of Arkansas, Fayetteville
Office of Scholarships and Financial Aid
114 Hunt Hall
Fayetteville, AR 72701
(501) 575-3806
Average award: Tuition, fees, $500 cash award, board and room
Deadline: February 15
College level: Freshman
Criteria: Applicant must have a minimum 3.5 GPA and one of the following: minimum composite ACT score of 33, minimum combined SAT I score of 1400, National Merit finalist or semifinalist, National Achievement finalist or semifinalist. Applicant must not have enrolled in any other postsecondary institution the fall or spring semester following high school graduation. Minimum 3.2 cumulative GPA and 30 hours per year are required to retain scholarship. Awarded every year. Award may be used only at sponsoring institution.
Contact: Office of Admissions, 200 Silas H. Hunt Hall, Fayetteville, AR 72701.

1312   Chancellor's Scholarship

Carleton University
202 Robertson Hall
1125 Colonel By Drive
Ottawa, Ontario, CN K1S 5B6
(613) 778-7400
Average award: $5,000
Number of awards: 8
Deadline: May 14
College level: Freshman
Criteria: Selection is based upon academic performance, interests, and activites. Renewable for three years if recipient maintains "A-" average. Awarded every year. Award may be used only at sponsoring institution.
Contact: Awards Office, (613) 520-3600.

1313   Chancellor's Scholarship

East Carolina University
East Fifth Street
Greenville, NC 27858
http://www.ecu.edu
Average award: $5,000
Number of awards: 5
Deadline: January 31
College level: Freshman
Criteria: Applicant must have a strong high school academic record and a record of extracurricular activities and leadership. Minimum cumulative 3.0 GPA and full-time enrollment are required to retain scholarship. Awarded every year. Award may be used only at sponsoring institution.
Contact: Gerry Clayton, Assistant Director of Admissions, (919) 757-6640.

1314   Chancellor's Scholarship

Indiana University-Purdue University Fort Wayne
2101 Coliseum Boulevard East
Fort Wayne, IN 46805-1499
(219) 481-6820
Average award: Half tuition
Number of awards: 25
Deadline: March 1 (fall)
College level: Freshman
Criteria: Applicant must rank in top 5% of class and have a minimum combined SAT I score of 1000, or rank in top tenth of class and have a minimum combined SAT I score of 1100. Preference is given to applicant who is accepted for admission by March 1. Renewable for up to three years if minimum 3.5 GPA and full-time enrollment are maintained. Awarded every year. Award may be used only at sponsoring institution.
Contact: Vickie E. Dahl, Financial Aid Administrator.

1315   Chancellor's Scholarship

University of Missouri–St. Louis
8001 Natural Bridge Road
St. Louis, MO 63121
(314) 553-6396
Average award: Full tuition
Number of awards: 29
Deadline: April 1
College level: Freshman
Criteria: Applicant must rank in top quarter of class, score in a high percentile on a college entrance test, and enroll full time. Awarded every year. Award may be used only at sponsoring institution.
Contact: James D. Reed, Financial Aid Adviser.

1316   Chancellor's Scholarship

Saint Martin's College
5300 Pacific Avenue, SE
Lacey, WA 98503
(360) 438-4397
Maximum award: $6,000
Number of awards: 19
Deadline: March 1
College level: Freshman, Sophomore, Junior, Senior
Criteria: Minimum 3.0 GPA is required to retain scholarship. Awarded every year. Award may be used only at sponsoring institution.
Contact: Ron Noborikawa, Director of Financial Aid.

1317   Chancellor's Scholarship

University of South Carolina at Aiken
171 University Parkway
Aiken, SC 29801
(803) 648-6851
Average award: $2,500
Maximum award: Full tuition
Number of awards: 15
Deadline: February 15
College level: Freshman
Criteria: Applicant must rank in top tenth of class and have a minimum combined SAT I score of 1000 (composite ACT score of 24). Recipient must maintain a minimum 3.0 GPA and full-time enrollment to retain scholarship. Awarded every year. Award may be used only at sponsoring institution.
Contact: A. Glenn Shumpert, Director of Financial Aid.

1318 Chancellor's Scholarship

Syracuse University
201 Administration Building
Syracuse, NY 13244
(315) 443-1870
orange@suadmin.syr.edu
http://ww.syr.edu
Average award: $6,000
College level: Freshman
Criteria: Selection is based upon academic credentials, standardized tests, class rank, extracurricular and community involvement, and overall citizenship and character. Renewable if recipient maintains a minimum 2.5 GPA. Award may be used only at sponsoring institution.
Contact: Scholarships.

1319 Chancellor's Scholarship

Western Baptist College
5000 Deer Park Drive, SE
Salem, OR 97301-9392
(503) 375-7006, (503) 585-4316 (fax)
http://www.wbc.edu
Average award: $2,500
Deadline: August 1
College level: Freshman
Criteria: Applicant must have a minimum 3.3 GPA, a combined SAT I score of 1100-1190 (composite ACT score of 24-26), and be an enrolled student. Minimum 3.3 GPA is required to retain scholarship. Awarded every year. Award may be used only at sponsoring institution.
Contact: Jennifer Cosens, Senior Financial Aid Officer.

1320 Chancellor's Scholarship

University of Wisconsin–Eau Claire
105 Garfield Avenue
Eau Claire, WI 54701
(715) 836-3373
Average award: $2,034
Number of awards: 5
Deadline: April 1
College level: Freshman
Criteria: Selection is based upon academic achievement, school and community leadership, and service. Applicant must have minimum composite ACT score of 29 or combined SAT I score of 1350. Awarded every year. Award may be used only at sponsoring institution.
Contact: Melissa Vogler, Financial Aid Counselor.

1321 Charles and Anne Duncan Scholarship

Emory University
1380 Oxford Road, NE
Atlanta, GA 30322
(404) 727-6039
Average award: Full tuition
Number of awards: 1
Deadline: November 15
College level: Freshman
Criteria: Applicant must be a student of outstanding merit and reside west of the Mississippi River. Priority is given to residents of Texas and the Southwest. Nomination by school or Emory Admission Committee is required. Renewable for four years of undergraduate study. Awarded every year. Award may be used only at sponsoring institution.
Contact: Office of Admissions, 200 Boisfeuillet Jones Center, Atlanta, GA 30322-1950, (404) 727-6036, (800) 727-6036.

1322 Charles Kirkland Dunlap Presidential Scholarship

Clemson University
G-01 Sikes Hall
Clemson, SC 29634-5123
(803) 656-2280
Maximum award: $6,000
Number of awards: 1
Deadline: None
College level: Freshman
Criteria: Selection is based upon admissions application. Minimum 3.0 GPA and completion of at least 12 credits per semester are required to retain scholarship. Awarded every year. Award may be used only at sponsoring institution.
Contact: Marvin Carmichael, Director of Financial Aid.

1323 Chet Jordan Leadership Award

Maine Community Foundation
210 Main Street
P.O. Box 148
Ellsworth, ME 04605
(207) 667-9735
Average award: $2,500
Number of awards: 1
Deadline: May 1
College level: Freshman, Sophomore, Junior, Senior
Criteria: Applicant must be a Maine resident, a graduate of a Maine high school, exhibit family values and community service, demonstrate academic or athletic excellence, and plan to attend college or technical school. Recipient must reapply for renewal. Awarded every year.
Contact: Joanne Foster, Jordan's Meats, Leadership Award, P.O. Box 574, Portland, ME 04112.

1324 Chris A. Yannopoulos Scholarship

Emory University
1380 Oxford Road, NE
Atlanta, GA 30322
(404) 727-6039
Average award: Full tuition
Deadline: November 15
College level: Freshman
Criteria: Applicant must have interest in classical studies or represent strengths brought to the U.S. by immigrants. Nomination by school or Emory Admission Committee is required. Renewable for four years of undergraduate study. Awarded every year. Award may be used only at sponsoring institution.
Contact: Office of Admissions, 200 Boisfeuillet Jones Center, Atlanta, GA 30322-1950, (404) 727-6036, (800) 727-6036.

1325 Christ College Diversity Scholarship

Valparaiso University
Valparaiso, IN 46383-6493
(219) 464-5011, (219) 464-6898 (fax)
undergrad_admissions@valpo.edu
http:www.valpo.edu
Maximum award: Full tuition
Deadline: January 15
College level: Freshman
Criteria: Applicant must be an American minority student who has been accepted into Valparaiso U Christ College. Selection is based upon academic accomplishments and leadership. Renewable for up to three years if minimum 3.0 GPA is maintained. Awarded every year. Award may be used only at sponsoring institution.
Contact: Office of Admissions and Financial Aid, Kretzman Hall, (888) GO VALPO.

1326   Citadel Scholarship

The Citadel
171 Moultrie Street
Charleston, SC 29409
(803) 953-5187
Average award: Comprehensive tuition
Number of awards: 20
Deadline: January 15
College level: Freshman
Criteria: Selection is based upon merit. Minimum 3.0 GPA is required to retain scholarship. Awarded every year. Award may be used only at sponsoring institution.
Contact: Hank Fuller, Director of Financial Aid.

1327   Clarence Beecher Allen Scholarship

The College of Wooster
Office of Admissions
Wooster, OH 44691
(330) 263-2270, (330) 263-2621 (fax)
admissions@acs.wooster.edu
http://www.wooster.edu
Maximum award: $15,000
Deadline: February 15
College level: Freshman
Criteria: Applicant must be African-American, have a minimum 3.0 GPA, rank in top 15% of class, and be nominated by a teacher, counselor, minister, business or community leader, or another person in position to identify outstanding candidates. Applicant must demonstrate academic achievement and potential for continued success in college. Recipient must maintain academic progress toward degree to retain scholarship. Renewable for four years. Awarded every year. Award may be used only at sponsoring institution.
Contact: Office of Admissions.

1328   Class of '38 Golden Anniversary Scholarship

Clemson University
G-01 Sikes Hall
Clemson, SC 29634-5123
(803) 656-2280
Maximum award: $2,500
Number of awards: 5
Deadline: March 1
College level: Freshman, Sophomore, Junior, Senior
Criteria: Applicant must have a minimum 2.5 GPA. Satisfactory GPA and completion of at least 12 credits per semester are required to retain scholarship. Awarded every year. Award may be used only at sponsoring institution.
Contact: Marvin Carmichael, Director of Financial Aid.

1329   Class of '39 Scholarship

Clemson University
G-01 Sikes Hall
Clemson, SC 29634-5123
(803) 656-2280
Maximum award: $3,500
Number of awards: 3
Deadline: March 1
College level: Freshman, Sophomore, Junior, Senior
Criteria: Applicant must have a minimum 2.0 GPA. Scholarships are rotated so that all of the university's colleges benefit in proportion to their total enrollment. Satisfactory GPA and completion of at least 12 credits per semester are required to retain scholarship. Awarded every year. Award may be used only at sponsoring institution.
Contact: Marvin Carmichael, Director of Financial Aid.

1330   Class of '41 Award

Clemson University
G-01 Sikes Hall
Clemson, SC 29634-5123
(803) 656-2280
Maximum award: $7,000
Number of awards: 3
College level: Freshman
Criteria: Selection is based upon applicant's admissions application. Renewable for up to three years if recipient maintains minimum 3.0 GPA and completes at least 12 credit hours per semester. Award may be used only at sponsoring institution.
Contact: Scholarships.

1331   Class of '49 Alumni Scholars Endowment

Clemson University
G-01 Sikes Hall
Clemson, SC 29634-5123
(803) 656-2280
Maximum award: $4,500
Number of awards: 1
Deadline: March 1
College level: Freshman
Criteria: Applicant must have a minimum 2.0 GPA. Renewable for up to three years if recipient maintains minimum 3.0 GPA and completes minimum of 12 credit hours each semester. Awarded every year. Award may be used only at sponsoring institution.
Contact: Marvin Carmichael, Director of Financial Aid.

1332   Class of 1936 Golden Anniversary Scholarship

Clemson University
G-01 Sikes Hall
Clemson, SC 29634-5123
(803) 656-2280
Maximum award: $3,500
Number of awards: 2
Deadline: None
College level: Freshman
Criteria: Selection is based upon admissions application. Minimum 3.0 GPA and completion of at least 12 credits per semester are required to retain scholarship. Awarded every year. Award may be used only at sponsoring institution.
Contact: Marvin Carmichael, Director of Financial Aid.

1333   Class Salutatorian Scholarship

The Master's College
21726 Placerita Canyon Road
Santa Clarita, CA 91321-1200
(805) 259-3540, (805) 288-1037 (fax)
Average award: $2,250
College level: Freshman
Criteria: Applicant must be salutatorian, have a minimum 3.75 GPA, and have a minimum combined SAT I score of 1150 (composite ACT score of 27). Awarded every year. Award may be used only at sponsoring institution.
Contact: Timothy C. Wiegert, Associate Director of Enrollment, (800) 568-6248, extension 450.

1334   Class Valedictorian Scholarship

The Master's College
21726 Placerita Canyon Road
Santa Clarita, CA 91321-1200
(805) 259-3540, (805) 288-1037 (fax)
Average award: $3,000
College level: Freshman
Criteria: Applicant must be valedictorian, have a minimum 3.85 GPA, and have a minimum combined SAT I score of 1150 (composite ACT score of 27). Awarded every year. Award may be used only at sponsoring institution.
Contact: Timothy C. Wiegert, Associate Director of Enrollment, (800) 568-6248, extension 450.

1335 Claude S. Lawson Memorial Scholarship

Birmingham-Southern College
Arkadelphia Road
Birmingham, AL 35254
(205) 226-4688
Maximum award: Full tuition
Number of awards: 5
Deadline: January 5
College level: Freshman
Majors/Fields: Health-related field
Criteria: Applicant should rank in top 5% of class, have a composite ACT score of 28-36 (combined SAT I score of 1150-1400), and have leadership ability. Selection is based upon academic qualifications. Minimum 3.0 GPA is required to retain scholarship. Awarded every year. Award may be used only at sponsoring institution.
Contact: Forrest Stuart, Interim Director of Financial Aid Services.

1336 College Scholar Award

The College of Wooster
Office of Admissions
Wooster, OH 44691
(330) 263-2270, (330) 263-2621 (fax)
admissions@acs.wooster.edu
http://www.wooster.edu
Maximum award: $15,000
Deadline: February 15
College level: Freshman
Criteria: Applicant must have a minimum 3.2 GPA and minimum SAT I verbal score of 600 or combined SAT I score of 1150 (composite ACT score of 28). Selection is based upon essay competition and faculty interview. Recipient must maintain academic progress toward degree to retain scholarship. Renewable for four years. Awarded every year. Award may be used only at sponsoring institution.
Contact: Office of Admissions.

1337 CollegeNET Scholarship

CollegeNET
Universal Algorithms, Inc.
One S.W. Columbia, Suite 100
Portland, OR 97258
(503) 973-5200, (503) 973-5252 (fax)
http://www.collegenet.com
Maximum award: $5,000
Number of awards: 5
Deadline: March 31
College level: Freshman
Criteria: Applicant must submit application for admission via College-NET and be accepted for full-time enrollment at one of the selected schools (list of schools can be found at http://www.collegenet.com). Awarded every year. Award may be used at elected schools only.
Contact: Betty Chapman, Administration Manager, Universal Algorithms.

1338 Collegiate Fellowship

Capital University
2199 East Main Street
Columbus, OH 43209-2394
(614) 236-6511
Maximum award: Full tuition
Number of awards: 16
Deadline: February 1
College level: Freshman
Criteria: Applicant must be accepted for admission by February 1. Selection is based upon campus competition (interview with faculty and written essay) held in March. Applicant is invited to compete based upon ACT/SAT I scores and school record. Renewable for up to eight semesters if minimum 3.0 GPA is maintained. Awarded every year. Award may be used only at sponsoring institution.
Contact: Kim Ebbrecht, Associate Director of Admissions.

1339 Collegiate Scholarship

Northwestern College
101 College Lane
Orange City, IA 51041
(800) 747-4757, (712) 737-7130, (712) 737-7164 (fax)
markb@nwciowa.edu
http://www.nwciowa.edu
Maximum award: $3,850
Deadline: None
College level: Freshman
Criteria: Applicant must rank in top tenth of class, have a minimum composite ACT score of 26, and submit recommendation and transcript. Minimum 3.0 GPA is required to retain scholarship. Awarded every year. Award may be used only at sponsoring institution.
Contact: Ron DeJong, Director of Admission, rondj@nwciowa.edu.

1340 Colonel Scholarship

Centre College
600 West Walnut Street
Danville, KY 40422
(606) 238-5350, (606) 238-5373 (fax)
admission@centre.edu
http://www.centre.edu
Average award: $5,000
Number of awards: 25
Deadline: February 1
College level: Freshman
Criteria: Interview is required. Renewable if recipient maintains good academic standing and a minimum 2.5 GPA. Awarded every year. Award may be used only at sponsoring institution.
Contact: Thomas B. Martin, Dean of Enrollment Management.

1341 Colonel William James and Elizabeth Perry Rushton Scholarship

Birmingham-Southern College
Arkadelphia Road
Birmingham, AL 35254
(205) 226-4688
Maximum award: Full tuition
Number of awards: 1
Deadline: January 5
College level: Freshman
Criteria: Applicant should rank in top 5% of class, have a composite ACT score of 28-36 (combined SAT I score of 1150-1400), and have leadership ability. Selection is based upon academic qualifications. Financial need is considered. Minimum 3.4 GPA is required to retain scholarship. Awarded every year. Award may be used only at sponsoring institution.
Contact: Forrest Stuart, Interim Director of Financial Aid Services.

1342 Columbia College Scholar Award

Columbia College
1001 Rogers Street
Columbia, MO 65216
(800) 231-2391
Average award: $11,998
Number of awards: 7
Deadline: February 14
College level: Freshman
Criteria: Applicant must have a minimum 3.6 GPA and minimum composite ACT score of 27 (combined SAT I score of 1200), must demonstrate leadership abilities, and provide four recommendations. Campus interview may be required. Financial need is not considered. Recipients with 30-90 credit hours must have a minimum 3.7 GPA for renewal. Awarded every year. Award may be used only at sponsoring institution.
Contact: Financial Aid Office, (800) 231-2391, extension 7361.

1343   Community College Presidential Scholarship

University of Memphis
Scates Hall 204
Memphis, TN 38152
(901) 678-3213, (901) 678-5621 (fax)
katkinsn@cc.memphis.edu
http://www.memphis.edu/
Average award: $2,180
Deadline: April 1
College level: Junior
Criteria: Applicant must be recommended by the president of a Tennessee community college. Minimum 2.8 GPA is required to retain scholarship. Awarded every year. Award may be used only at sponsoring institution.
Contact: Katherine Atkinson, Scholarship Coordinator, 204 Scates Hall, Memphis, TN 38152.

1344   Community College Scholarship

Columbia College
1001 Rogers Street
Columbia, MO 65216
(800) 231-2391
Average award: Half tuition
Number of awards: 2
Deadline: March 15 (priority)
College level: Transfers
Criteria: Applicant must have a minimum 3.4 GPA, have transferred from an accredited two-year school within one year of receiving degree with at least 60 transferable credits, have not attended another college since receiving degree, and submit school's financial aid form. Renewable as a Capstone Scholarship. Awarded every year. Award may be used only at sponsoring institution.
Contact: Financial Aid Office, (800) 231-2391, extension 7361.

1345   Community College Scholarship

Wayne State College
1111 Main Street
Wayne, NE 68787
(402) 375-7230, (800) 228-9972
Average award: Full tuition
Number of awards: 4
Deadline: None
College level: Transfers
Criteria: Awarded to a limited number of applicants transferring from Central Community Coll/Platte Campus, McCook Community Coll, Nebraska Indian Community Coll, and Northeast Community Coll. Awarded every year. Award may be used only at sponsoring institution.
Contact: Financial Aid Office.

1346   Community College Transfer Scholarship

University of Memphis
Scates Hall 204
Memphis, TN 38152
(901) 678-3213, (901) 678-5621 (fax)
katkinsn@cc.memphis.edu
http://www.memphis.edu/
Average award: $2,580
Deadline: April 1
College level: Junior
Criteria: Applicant must have an associate degree with a minimum 3.5 GPA. Minimum 2.8 GPA and a service requirement of 30 hours per year are required to retain scholarship. Awarded every year. Award may be used only at sponsoring institution.
Contact: Katherine Atkinson, Scholarship Coordinator.

1347   Commuting Scholars Award

Villanova University
Villanova, PA 19085
(215) 645-4010
Average award: $5,550
Number of awards: 38
Deadline: January 15
College level: Freshman
Criteria: Applicant must commute from parents' home, have a minimum combined SAT I score of 1200, and rank in the top tenth of class at the end of eleventh grade. Minimum 3.25 GPA and full-time enrollment are required to retain scholarship. Awarded every year. Award may be used only at sponsoring institution.
Contact: George J. Walter, Director of Financial Aid.

1348   Comp-Younts Scholarship

Piedmont College
165 Central Avenue
Demorest, GA 30535
(706) 778-3000
Average award: $9,260
Maximum award: Full tuition, room, and board
Number of awards: 2
Deadline: February 15
College level: Freshman
Criteria: Applicant must have a minimum GPA, a minimum combined SAT I score of 1100, and letters of recommendation. Recipient must participate in Piedmont Scholars Program and at least one other campus organization and live in college housing. Renewable for up to four years if minimum 3.5 GPA is maintained. Awarded every year. Award may be used only at sponsoring institution.
Contact: Kenneth L. Owen, Director of Financial Aid.

1349   Competitive Scholarship

Wheeling Jesuit University
316 Washington Avenue
Wheeling, WV 26003
(304) 243-2304
http://www.wju.edu/
Maximum award: $4,000
Deadline: early February
College level: Freshman
Majors/Fields: Biology, business, chemistry, clinical science (nuclear medicine or respiratory therapy), computer science, criminal justice, English literature, innovation/technology, mathematics, nursing, philosophy, physics, pre-engineering, pre-law, pre-medicine, psychology, secondary education, theology.
Criteria: Competitive scholarships are offered for the following extracurricular activities ($2,000 award): leadership of community service organization, choral, music (chapel music activities), writing (newspaper/yearbook). Maximum award is given for academic competitive scholarships. Recipient must continue to major or participate in appropriate field or activity and make satisfactory academic progress to retain scholarship. Awarded every year. Award may be used only at sponsoring institution.
Contact: Admissions Office.

1350   Compton Scholarship

The College of Wooster
Office of Admissions
Wooster, OH 44691
(330) 263-2270, (330) 263-2621 (fax)
admissions@acs.wooster.edu
http://www.wooster.edu
Maximum award: $14,000
Deadline: February 15
College level: Freshman
Criteria: Applicant must have a minimum 3.2 GPA, rank in top tenth of class, and be nominated by a counselor or teacher. Applicant must demonstrate independence, intellectual curiosity, and resourcefulness in scholarship interview. Recipient must maintain academic progress toward degree to retain scholarship. Renewable for four years. Awarded every year. Award may be used only at sponsoring institution.
Contact: Office of Admissions.

1351 Computer Based Honors Scholarship

The University of Alabama
Box 870162
Tuscaloosa, AL 35487-0162
(205) 348-6756
Average award: $2,000
Maximum award: $2,500
Deadline: December 20
College level: Freshman
*Criteria:*Applicant must have a minimum 3.8 GPA and minimum composite ACT score of 32 (combined SAT I score of 1350). Top 20 finalists visit the campus for interviews. Recipient will be able to work with the university computer facilities in course of study without majoring in computer science. Superior performance at the university and in the computer-based honors program is required to retain scholarship. Awarded every year. Award may be used only at sponsoring institution.
Contact: Helen Leathers, Scholarship Coordinator, Box 870132, Tuscaloosa, AL 35487-0132.

1352 Continuing Student Departmental Scholarship

University of Utah
Financial Aid and Scholarships Office
105 Student Services Building
Salt Lake City, UT 84112
(801) 581-6211
Average award: Resident tuition
Deadline: February 1 to March 30 (each department sets its own deadline)
College level: Sophomore, Junior, Senior
Criteria: Applicant must be a continuing undergraduate student who has declared a major and is nominated by the department. Awarded every year. Award may be used only at sponsoring institution.
Contact: Financial Aid and Scholarships Office.

1353 Cooperating School Scholarship

Wayne State College
1111 Main Street
Wayne, NE 68787
(402) 375-7230, (800) 228-9972
Average award: Half tuition
Deadline: None
College level: Freshman
Criteria: Applicant must rank in top half of class and attend a school that sponsors Wayne State Coll student teachers. Award is for four years. Scholarship is renewable. Awarded every year. Award may be used only at sponsoring institution.
Contact: Financial Aid Office.

1354 Cornerstone Scholarship

Columbia College
1001 Rogers Street
Columbia, MO 65216
(800) 231-2391
Average award: Half tuition
Number of awards: 26
Deadline: March 15 (priority)
College level: Sophomore
Criteria: Applicant must have a minimum 3.4 GPA, have completed 30-59.9 credit hours (with the most recent 30 credits earned at Columbia Coll and not including ENG 100 or 104 or MATH 105), and submit school's financial aid form. Financial need is not considered. Renewable as a Keystone Scholarship. Awarded every year. Award may be used only at sponsoring institution.
Contact: Financial Aid Office, (800) 231-2391, extension 7361.

1355 Corporate Scholarship

Jersey City State College
2039 Kennedy Boulevard
Jersey City, NJ 07305
(800) 441-JCSC, (201) 200-2044 (fax)
admissions@js51.jcstate.edu
Average award: $2,000
Maximum award: $3,000
Minimum award: $1,000
Number of awards: 20
Deadline: April 1
College level: Freshman, Sophomore, Junior, Senior, Transfers
Criteria: Selection is based upon GPA, class rank, and standardized test scores, or academic achievement. Minimum 3.3 GPA after each semester required to retain scholarship. Awarded every year. Award may be used only at sponsoring institution.
Contact: Bernice Hornchak, Director of Recruitment, 2309 Kennedy Boulevard, Jersey City, NJ 07305.

1356 CSU System-Wide Trustees' Award

California State University, Hayward
Office of Finanical Aid
WA545
Hayward, CA 94542-3028
(510) 885-3616, (510) 885-4627 (fax)
http://www.csuhayward.edu/
Average award: $2,500
Number of awards: 3
Deadline: April 21
College level: Freshman, Sophomore, Junior, Senior
Criteria: Applicant must be a full-time student. Two letters of recommendation, official transcript, and FAFSA are required. GPA and financial need are considered. Awarded every year. Award may be used only at sponsoring institution.
Contact: Scholarship Coordinator.

1357 Cuneo Foundation Scholarship

DePaul University
1 East Jackson Boulevard
Chicago, IL 60604
(312) 362-8704, (312) 362-5749 (fax)
Average award: $12,000
Number of awards: 1
Deadline: None
College level: Freshman
Majors/Fields: Preprofessional program
Criteria: Selection is based upon academic excellence. Scholarship is renewable. Awarded once every four years. Award may be used only at sponsoring institution.
Contact: Jennifer Sparrow, Scholarship Coordinator, jsparrow@wppost.depaul.edu.

1358 Currie and Kay Spivey Endowed Scholarship

Clemson University
G-01 Sikes Hall
Clemson, SC 29634-5123
(803) 656-2280
Average award: $3,000
Number of awards: 2
Deadline: None
College level: Freshman
*Criteria:*Selection is based upon admissions application. Renewable for up to three years if recipient maintains minimum 3.0 GPA and completes at least 12 credits per semester. Award may be used only at sponsoring institution.
Contact: Scholarships.

1359 D. Abbott Turner Scholarship

Emory University
1380 Oxford Road, NE
Atlanta, GA 30322
(404) 727-6039
Average award: Full tuition
Number of awards: 1
Deadline: November 15
College level: Freshman
Criteria: Applicant must be a graduate of a Georgia school, with preference given first to graduates of Brookstone School in Columbus and then to natives of the Chattahoochee Valley. Selection is based upon achievement, character, and service. Nomination by school or Emory Admission Committee is required. Renewable for four years of undergraduate study. Awarded every year. Award may be used only at sponsoring institution.
Contact: Office of Admissions, 200 Boisfeuillet Jones Center, Atlanta, GA 30322-1950, (404) 727-6036, (800) 727-6036.

1360 David M. Gardner Memorial/Academic Excellence Scholarship

Mesa State College
Financial Aid Department
P.O. Box 2647
Grand Junction, CO 81502
(970) 248-1396
Maximum award: Tuition and fees
Number of awards: 1
College level: Freshman
Criteria: Applicant must be a graduate of Central High School, Grand Junction, Colo., be enrolled full time, and have a minimum 3.5 GPA. Renewable for up to four years if recipient maintains a minimum 3.5 GPA and full-time enrollment. Awarded every year. Award may be used only at sponsoring institution.
Contact: Guidance Department, Central High School, Grand Junction, CO.

1361 Dean Scholars Award

Spelman College
350 Spelman Lane, SW
Atlanta, GA 30314
(404) 681-3643
Average award: $3,500
Maximum award: $7,000
Minimum award: $1,750
Number of awards: 81
Deadline: May 30
College level: Freshman, Sophomore, Junior, Senior
Criteria: Scholarship is renewable. Awarded every year. Award may be used only at sponsoring institution.
Contact: Dr. Freddye L. Hill, Academic Dean.

1362 Dean's Award

Ohio Wesleyan University
Office of Admissions
Delaware, OH 43015
(614) 368-3020, (614) 368-3314 (fax)
owuadmit@cc.owu.edu
http://www.owu.edu
Average award: $5,500
Maximum award: $7,000
Minimum award: $5,000
Number of awards: 350
Deadline: None
College level: Freshman, Sophomore, Junior, Senior
Criteria: Applicant must have a minimum 3.5 GPA, a minimum combined SAT I score of 1130 (composite ACT score of 23), or rank in the top fifth of class. Renewable if recipient maintains a minimum 2.75 GPA. Awarded every year. Award may be used only at sponsoring institution.
Contact: Douglas C. Thompson, Dean of Admission.

1363 Dean's Award

Washington and Jefferson College
Washington, PA 15301
(412) 223-6019
Maximum award: $3,000
Number of awards: 2
College level: Freshman
Criteria: Selection is based upon academic promise, extracurricular activities, and good citizenship. Renewable if recipient maintains a minimum 2.8 GPA. Awarded every year. Award may be used only at sponsoring institution.
Contact: Richard H. Soudan, Director of Financial Aid.

1364 Dean's Honors Scholarship

DePaul University
1 East Jackson Boulevard
Chicago, IL 60604
(312) 362-8704, (312) 362-5749 (fax)
Average award: $4,000
Maximum award: $8,000
Minimum award: $2,000
Number of awards: 65
Deadline: None
College level: Freshman
Majors/Fields: Liberal arts, sciences
Criteria: Applicant must rank in the top tenth of class, have a minimum composite ACT score of 27 or combined SAT I score of 1220, possess a strong interest in the study of liberal arts, and be willing to participate in the honors program. Minimum 2.75 GPA during first year, 3.0 GPA thereafter, as a full-time student in the Honors program is required to retain scholarship. Awarded every year. Award may be used only at sponsoring institution.
Contact: Jennifer Sparrow, Scholarship Coordinator, jsparrow@wppost.depaul.edu.

1365 Dean's Honor Scholarship

Tulane University
6823 St. Charles Avenue
New Orleans, LA 70118
(504) 865-5723
Average award: $16,925
Number of awards: 144
Deadline: December 15
College level: Freshman
Criteria: Minimum 3.0 GPA and full-time enrollment are required to retain scholarship. Awarded every year. Award may be used only at sponsoring institution.
Contact: Thomas P. Lovett, Director of Financial Aid.

1366 Dean's Scholars Award

Chapman University
333 North Glassell Street
Orange, CA 92866
(714) 997-6741, (714) 997-6743 (fax)
http://www.chapman.edu
Maximum award: $5,400
Deadline: None
College level: Freshman, Sophomore, Junior, Senior, Transfers
Criteria: Applicant must be an entering full-time student with a 3.25-3.49 GPA. Scholarship is renewable. Awarded every year. Award may be used only at sponsoring institution.
Contact: Scholarships.

1367 Dean's Scholarship

Boston University
Office of Financial Assistance
881 Commonwealth Avenue
Boston, MA 02215
(617) 353-4175
Average award: $6,000
Number of awards: 130
Deadline: February 1 (freshmen); May 15 (continuing students)
College level: Freshman, Sophomore, Junior, Senior
Criteria: Applicant is selected by the Deans of each School and College within the university on the basis of outstanding academic performance and potential. Award is for applicants who demonstrate low or no calculated financial need. Minimum 3.0 GPA and completion of at least 12 credit hours per semester are required to retain scholarship. Awarded every year. Award may be used only at sponsoring institution.
Contact: Maria B. DelSignore, Assistant Director, Special Programs.

1368 Dean's Scholarship

Centre College
600 West Walnut Street
Danville, KY 40422
(606) 238-5350, (606) 238-5373 (fax)
admission@centre.edu
http://www.centre.edu
Average award: $9,000
Deadline: February 1
College level: Freshman
Criteria: Interview is required. Renewable if recipient maintains good academic standing and a minumum 3.0 GPA (GPA requirement increases for subsequent years). Awarded every year. Award may be used only at sponsoring institution.
Contact: Thomas B. Martin, Dean of Enrollment Management.

1369 Dean's Scholarship

Dominican College of San Rafael
50 Acacia Avenue
San Rafael, CA 94901-2298
(415) 485-3204, (415) 485-3205 (fax)
enroll@dominican.edu
http://www.dominican.edu
Average award: $5,867
Maximum award: $7,123
Minimum award: $2,445
Number of awards: 34
Deadline: March 1
College level: Freshman, Transfers with fewer than 24 credit hours
Criteria: Applicant must have a minimum 3.3 GPA and strong SAT I scores, demonstrate leadership and service in community and school, and express commitment to liberal arts education. Application is required. Renewable for up to four years if recipient maintains a minimum 3.0 GPA. Awarded every year. Award may be used only at sponsoring institution.
Contact: Susan Gutierrez, Director of Financial Aid.

1370 Dean's Scholarship

Emmanuel College
400 The Fenway
Boston, MA 02115
(617) 735-9725
Average award: $6,000
Deadline: February 15
College level: Freshman
Criteria: Applicant must be a woman and have a minimum 3.4 GPA and minimum combined SAT I score of 1000 (composite ACT score of 23). Application, recommendations, transcript, standardized test scores, essay/portfolio, interview, and FAFSA required. Minimum 3.0 GPA required to retain scholarship. Awarded every year. Award may be used only at sponsoring institution.
Contact: Patricia K. Harden, Director of Financial Aid.

1371 Dean's Scholarship

Eureka College
300 East College
Eureka, IL 61530
(309) 467-6310
Average award: $5,000
Deadline: March 1
College level: Freshman
Criteria: Applicant must have a minimum 3.25 GPA. Scholarship is renewable. Awarded every year. Award may be used only at sponsoring institution.
Contact: Ellen M. Rigsby, Associate Director of Financial Aid.

1372 Dean's Scholarship

Ferris State University
901 South State Street
Big Rapids, MI 49307
(616) 592-2110
Average award: $2,500
Number of awards: 30
Deadline: January 10
College level: Freshman
Criteria: Applicant must have a minimum 3.5 GPA and minimum composite ACT score of 27. Recipient must maintain a minimum 3.25 GPA and full-time enrollment to retain scholarship for up to four years. Awarded every year. Award may be used only at sponsoring institution.
Contact: Dennis Batt, Interim Director of Scholarships and Financial Aid, Office of Scholarships and Financial Aid, 420 Oak Street, Prakken 104, Big Rapids, MI 49307-2020.

1373 Dean's Scholarship

University of Indianapolis
1400 East Hanna Avenue
Indianapolis, IN 46227-3697
(317) 788-3217
Maximum award: $6,495
Number of awards: 167
Deadline: None
College level: Freshman
Criteria: Applicant must rank in top 5%-7% of class, have a minimum combined SAT I score of 1270 (composite ACT score of 29), have academic record of college-preparatory courses, and demonstrate leadership. Recipient must maintain a minimum 3.0 GPA and full-time enrollment to retain scholarship. Awarded every year. Award may be used only at sponsoring institution.
Contact: Admissions Office, (317) 788-3216.

1374 Dean's Scholarship

Kansas Newman College
3100 McCormick Avenue
Wichita, KS 67213
(316) 942-4291
Average award: $2,500
College level: Freshman
Criteria: Applicant must have 3.0 GPA and minimum composite ACT score of 21 (combined SAT 1 score of 1100). Renewable if recipient maintains a minimum 3.25 GPA and full-time enrollment. Award may be used only at sponsoring institution.
Contact: Marla McClure, Director of Financial Aid, (316) 942-4291, extension 103, mcclurem@ksnewman.edu.

1375   Dean's Scholarship

Lee University
P.O. Box 3450
Cleveland, TN 37320-3450
(423) 614-8000
Average award: $2,616
Number of awards: 117
Deadline: None
College level: Freshman
Criteria: Applicant must have a composite ACT score of 24-26 (combined SAT I score of 1030-1140) and must enroll for academic year immediately following graduation. Award is equal to half of standard tuition. Awarded every year. Award may be used only at sponsoring institution.
Contact: Gary Ray, Director of Admissions, (423) 614 8500.

1376   Dean's Scholarship

Lynn University
3601 North Military Trail
Boca Raton, FL 33431-5598
(561) 994-0770, (561) 247-3552 (fax)
admission@lynn.edu
http://www.lynn.edu
Maximum award: $10,000
Number of awards: 15
College level: Freshman
Criteria: Applicant must meet two of three criteria: rank in the top fifth of class, minimum 3.25 GPA, or minimum combined SAT I score of 1100. Minimum 3.0 GPA required to retain scholarship. Awarded every year. Award may be used only at sponsoring institution.
Contact: James Sullivan, Director of Admissions.

1377   Dean's Scholarship

Marietta College
Fifth Street
Marietta, OH 45750
(614) 376-4712
Average award: $3,500
Deadline: March 1
College level: Freshman
Criteria: Renewable if minimum 3.0 GPA and continuous full-time enrollment are maintained. Awarded every year. Award may be used only at sponsoring institution.
Contact: James M. Bauer, Associate Dean/Director of Financial Aid.

1378   Dean's Scholarship

Messiah College
Grantham, PA 17027-0800
(717) 766-2511, (717) 691-6025 (fax)
http://www.messiah.edu
Average award: $2,000
Maximum award: $3,500
Minimum award: $1,000
Number of awards: 462
Deadline: None
College level: Freshman
Criteria: Applicant must graduate in top 15% of secondary school class or have a minimum combined SAT I score of 1100 (composite ACT score of 24). Minimum 3.0 GPA required to retain scholarship. Awarded every year. Award may be used only at sponsoring institution.
Contact: William G. Strausbaugh, Vice President for Enrollment Services, (717) 691-6000, strausba@messiah.edu.

1379   Dean's Scholarship

Milwaukee School of Engineering
1025 North Broadway
Milwaukee, WI 53202-3109
(800) 332-6763, (414) 277-7475 (fax)
goran@admin.msoe.edu
www.msoe.edu
Average award: $5,500
Number of awards: 144
Deadline: February 1
College level: Freshman
Criteria: Applicant must have a minimum 3.0 GPA and have completed four years of English, four years of math, and three years of science. Recommendation is suggested. Interview, extracurricular information, and personal statement required. Recipient must maintain a minimum 3.0 GPA to retain scholarship for four years. Awarded every year. Award may be used only at sponsoring institution.
Contact: Sue Minzlaff, Financial Aid Office, (414) 277-7222, minzlaff@admin.msoe.edu.

1380   Dean's Scholarship

Northern Kentucky University
Administrative Center 416
Nunn Drive
Highland Heights, KY 41099-7101
(606) 572-5144
Average award: In-state tuition
Deadline: February 1
College level: Junior, Senior
Criteria: Applicant must have a declared major and a minimum 3.5 GPA. Awarded every year. Award may be used only at sponsoring institution.
Contact: Robert E. Sprague, Director of Financial Aid.

1381   Dean's Scholarship

Ohio Northern University
525 South Main Street
Ada, OH 45810
(419) 772-2272, (419) 772-2313 (fax)
admissions-ug@onu.edu
http://www.onu.edu
Average award: $5,800
Maximum award: $9,000
Minimum award: $4,500
Number of awards: 361
Deadline: April 15
College level: Freshman
Criteria: Applicant must have a minimum 3.3 GPA, rank in top tenth of class, and have a minimum composite ACT score of 25 (combined SAT I score of 1150). Renewable if recipient maintains 3.0 GPA (freshman year), and 3.3 thereafter. Awarded every year. Award may be used only at sponsoring institution.
Contact: Wendell A. Schick, Director of Financial Aid.

1382   Dean's Scholarship

Principia College
Elsah, IL 62028
(800) 277-4648, (800) 347-4000 (fax)
collegeadmissions@prin.edu
http://www.prin.edu
Average award: $5,000
Number of awards: 3
Deadline: January 15
College level: Freshman
Criteria: Renewable if recipient maintains a minimum 3.5 GPA and continues to support community values. Awarded every year. Award may be used only at sponsoring institution.
Contact: Martha Green Quirk, Director of Admissions and Enrollment, (618) 374-5180, mgq@prin.edu.

1383 Dean's Scholarship

Rhodes College
2000 North Parkway
Memphis, TN 38112
(901) 843-3700, (901) 843-3719 (fax)
adminfo@rhodes.edu
http://www.rhodes.edu
Maximum award: $13,000
Number of awards: 5
Deadline: February 1 (priority)
College level: Freshman
Criteria: Applicant must be African-American. Selection is based upon merit. Renewable if recipient maintains a minimum 2.50 GPA. Awarded every year. Award may be used only at sponsoring institution.
Contact: David J. Wottle, Dean of Admissions and Financial Aid, (901) 843-3700, (800) 844-5969.

1384 Dean's Scholarship

Saint Joseph's College
Highway 231 South, P.O. Box 890
Rensselaer, IN 47978
(219) 866-6170, (219) 866-6100 (fax)
Maximum award: $4,500
Deadline: March 1 (priority)
College level: Freshman
Criteria: Selection is based upon academic achievements. Minimum 3.25 GPA is required to retain scholarship. Awarded every year. Award may be used only at sponsoring institution.
Contact: Frank Bevec, Director of Admission, P.O. Box 890, admissions@saintjoe.edu.

1385 Dean's Scholarship

Saint Martin's College
5300 Pacific Avenue, SE
Lacey, WA 98503
(360) 438-4397
Average award: $3,000
Number of awards: 40
Deadline: August 1
College level: Freshman
Criteria: Applicant must have a minimum 3.5 GPA and minimum combined SAT I score of 1000. Minimum 3.0 GPA is required to retain scholarship. Awarded every year. Award may be used only at sponsoring institution.
Contact: Ron Noborikawa, Director of Financial Aid.

1386 Dean's Scholarship

College of Saint Mary
1901 South 72nd Street
Omaha, NE 68124
(402) 399-2405
Maximum award: $6,000
Deadline: None
College level: Freshman
Criteria: Applicant must be a woman and rank first or second in class. Renewable for up to four years. Awarded every year. Award may be used only at sponsoring institution.
Contact: Enrollment Services.

1387 Dean's Scholarship

University of Southern California
University Park
Los Angeles, CA 90089-5012
(213) 740-1111
Maximum award: $6,000
Minimum award: $4,000
Maximum number of awards: 350
Minimum number of awards: 300
Deadline: December 15
College level: Freshman, Transfers
Criteria: Freshman applicant should rank in the top tenth of class and have standardized test scores above the 95th percentile. Transfer applicant should have a minimum 3.5 GPA and have completed at least 30 transferable credits. Scholarship is renewable. Awarded every year. Award may be used only at sponsoring institution.
Contact: Office of Admission, University Park Campus, Los Angeles, CA 90089-0911.

1388 Dean's Scholarship

Susquehanna University
Selinsgrove, PA 17870
(717) 372-4450
Maximum award: $3,500
Deadline: None
College level: Freshman, Sophomore, Junior, Senior, Transfers
Criteria: Awarded to applicants who have demonstrated strong academic achievement and outstanding extracurricular achievement, leadership, or volunteer service. Scholarship is renewable. Awarded every year. Award may be used only at sponsoring institution.
Contact: Office of Financial Aid.

1389 Dean's Scholarship

Syracuse University
201 Administration Building
Syracuse, NY 13244
(315) 443-1870
orange@suadmin.syr.edu
http://ww.syr.edu
Average award: $4,000
College level: Freshman
Criteria: Selection is based upon academic credentials, standardized tests, class rank, extracurricular and community involvement, and overall citizenship and character. Renewable if recipient maintains a minimum 2.5 GPA. Award may be used only at sponsoring institution.
Contact: Scholarships.

1390 Dean's Scholarship

Texas Christian University
2800 South University Drive
Fort Worth, TX 76129
(817) 921-7858, (817) 921-7462 (fax)
frogaid@tcu.edu
Maximum award: $4,750
Number of awards: 548
Deadline: January 15
College level: Freshman
Criteria: Applicant must rank in top 15% of class and have a minimum combined SAT I score of 1180 (composite ACT score of 27). Renewable for up to eight semesters or 128 credit hours if recipient maintains a minimum 3.0 GPA after freshman year (3.25 GPA thereafter) and successfully completes at least 27 credit hours per year. Awarded every year. Award may be used only at sponsoring institution.
Contact: Office of Student Financial Aid, TCU Box 297012, Fort Worth, TX 76129.

1391 Dean's Scholarship

Tri-State University
Angola, IN 46703-0307
(219) 665-4175
Maximum award: $6,000
Deadline: None
College level: Freshman
Criteria: Selection is based upon class rank and standardized test scores. Minimum 3.0 GPA is required to retain scholarship. Awarded every year. Award may be used only at sponsoring institution.
Contact: Financial Aid Office.

1392 Dean's Scholarship

Wilson College
1015 Philadelphia Avenue
Chambersburg, PA 17201-1285
(717) 264-4141, (717) 264-1578 (fax)
http://www.wilson.edu
Average award: One-fourth tuition
Number of awards: 10
Deadline: March 1
College level: Freshman, Transfers
Criteria: Applicant must be a woman, rank in top quarter of class, have a minimum combined SAT I score of 1100, and be enrolled full time. Transfer applicant must have a minimum 3.0 GPA in college work. Minimum 3.0 GPA is required to retain scholarship. Awarded every year. Award may be used only at sponsoring institution.
Contact: Jeffrey Stock, Associate Director of Admissions, (717) 262-2002.

1393 Dedman Distinguished Scholars Award

University of Texas at Austin
P.O. Box 7758
UT Station
Austin, TX 78713-7758
(512) 475-6200, (512) 475-6296 (fax)
finaid@www.utexas.edu
http://www.utexas.edu/student/finaid
Average award: $3,000
Maximum award: $7,000
Minimum award: $1,000
Number of awards: 6
Deadline: December 1
College level: Freshman
Majors/Fields: Liberal arts
Criteria: Applicant must rank in the top 5% of class and be enrolled in the College of Liberal Arts. Satisfactory academic progress is required to retain scholarship. Awarded every year. Award may be used only at sponsoring institution.
Contact: Liberal Arts Interdisciplinary Programs, Office of the Dean, College of Liberal Arts, Austin, TX 78703.

1394 Degenstein Scholarship

Susquehanna University
Selinsgrove, PA 17870
(717) 372-4450
Maximum award: $7,500
Deadline: None
College level: Freshman
Criteria: Selection and amount of award are based upon academic credentials. Preference is given to applicants intending to major or minor in programs in Sigmund Weis School of Business. Scholarship is renewable. Awarded every year. Award may be used only at sponsoring institution.
Contact: Office of Financial Aid.

1395 DeNobili Scholarship

Wheeling Jesuit University
316 Washington Avenue
Wheeling, WV 26003
(304) 243-2304
http://www.wju.edu/
Maximum award: $4,000
Deadline: None
College level: Freshman
Criteria: Applicant must be a graduate of a U.S. Jesuit school and have a minimum 2.5 GPA. Preference is given to those nominated by school principal. Academic merit determines amount of award. FAFSA is required. Satisfactory academic progress is required to retain scholarship. Awarded every year. Award may be used only at sponsoring institution.
Contact: Admissions Office.

1396 DeVry Bachelor's Degree Scholarship

DeVry Inc.
One Tower Lane
Oakbrook Terrace, IL 60181
Average award: Half tuition
Number of awards: 36
Deadline: May 1 (summer); August 1 (fall)
College level: Community college graduates with associate degree
Criteria: Applicant must have earned an associate degree with a minimum 3.3 GPA from an accredited community or junior college, be a U.S. citizen or permanent resident, and submit essay and two recommendations from community college faculty. DeVry employees and their immediate families are not eligible. Minimum 2.5 GPA is required for renewal. Awarded every year.
Contact: Director of Admissions, DeVry Institute which applicant wishes to attend.

1397 DeVry Scholarship

DeVry Inc.
One Tower Lane
Oakbrook Terrace, IL 60181
Maximum award: Full tuition
Minimum award: Half tuition
Number of awards: 120
Deadline: March 20
College level: Freshman
Criteria: Applicant must have minimum SAT I scores of 530 math and 470 verbal (ACT scores of 22 in both English and math) and must submit academic records, summary of extracurricular activities, and essay. Standardized test scores must be sent to the DeVry Inst applicant wishes to attend. Minimum 2.5 GPA is required for renewal. Awarded every year.
Contact: Director of Admissions, DeVry Institute which applicant wishes to attend.

1398 DeVry Scholarship

DeVry Institute of Technology (Addison)
1221 North Swift Road
Addison, IL 60101
(708) 953-1300
Maximum award: $2,970
Number of awards: 45
Deadline: March
College level: Freshman
Criteria: Selection is based upon essay, school record including activities, and standardized test scores. Renewable if minimum 2.5 GPA is maintained. Awarded every year. Award may be used only at sponsoring institution.
Contact: William Edwards, Dean of Students.

1399 Dewitt Wallace Scholarship

Spelman College
350 Spelman Lane, SW
Atlanta, GA 30314
(404) 681-3643
Average award: $3,500
Maximum award: $7,000
Minimum award: $1,750
Number of awards: 86
Deadline: May 30
College level: Freshman, Sophomore, Junior, Senior
Criteria: Scholarship is renewable. Awarded every year. Award may be used only at sponsoring institution.
Contact: Dr. Freddye L. Hill, Academic Dean.

1400 Director's Scholarship

Benedictine College
1020 North Second Street
Atchison, KS 66002
(913) 367-5340
Average award: $7,000
Number of awards: 20
Deadline: January 15
College level: Freshman
Criteria: Applicant must have a minimum 3.0 GPA and a minimum composite ACT score of 27 (combined SAT I score of 1060), or have a minimum 3.9 GPA. Applicant must have been accepted for admission as a first-time, full-time freshman. FAFSA is required. Renewable for up to four years if minimum 3.3 GPA is maintained. Awarded every year. Award may be used only at sponsoring institution.
Contact: Diane Adams, Associate Director of Admissions.

1401 Distinguished Academic Scholar Program

Hofstra University
126 Memorial Hall
Hempstead, NY 11550
(516) 463-6677
Average award: Full tuition
Deadline: February 15
College level: Freshman
Criteria: Applicant must have a minimum combined SAT I score of 1300 or composite ACT score of 29. Minimum 3.0 GPA at end of freshman year, 3.1 GPA at end of sophomore year, and 3.2 GPA at end of junior year are required to retain scholarship. Awarded every year. Award may be used only at sponsoring institution.
Contact: Joan Warren, Director of Financial and Academic Records.

1402 Distinguished Honor Scholarship

Ripon College
300 Seward Street
P.O. Box 248
Ripon, WI 54971
(800) 94-RIPON, (414) 748-7243 (fax)
adminfo@mac.ripon.edu
http://www.ripon.edu
Average award: $4,000
Maximum award: $7,000
Minimum award: $1,500
Number of awards: No limit
Deadline: December 1 (early decision) March 1
College level: Freshman, Transfers
Criteria: Applicant must have a minimum 3.3 GPA, rank in top quarter of class, have a minimum composite ACT score of 26, demonstrate leadership and community activities, and be accepted for admission. Renewable if recipient maintains minimum 2.5 GPA for first year, minimum 2.7 GPA for subsequent years. Awarded every year. Award may be used only at sponsoring institution.
Contact: Paul J. Weeks, Vice President and Dean of Admission.

1403 Distinguished Honors Scholarship

State University of New York at Buffalo
Buffalo, NY 14260
(716) 831-2000, (716) 829-2022 (fax)
Maximum award: $10,000
Number of awards: 20
College level: Freshman, Sophomore, Junior, Senior
Criteria: Applicant must rank in the top seven percent of class, have an unweighted grade average of 93, and have a minimum combined SAT I score of 1300. Scholarship is renewable. Awarded every year. Award may be used only at sponsoring institution.
Contact: Josephine Capuana, Administrative Director, 214 Talbert Hall, Box 601700, Buffalo, NY 14260-1700, (716) 645-3020.

1404 Distinguished Presidential Scholarship

Our Lady of the Lake University
411 S.W. 24th Street
San Antonio, TX 78207-4666
(512) 434-6711
Average award: Full tuition
Deadline: Early application is recommended
College level: Freshman
Criteria: Applicant must have a minimum 3.75 GPA and composite ACT score of 29-32 (combined SAT I score of 1200-1410), or a minimum 3.6 GPA and composite ACT score of 33-36 (combined SAT I score of 1420-1600). Financial need is not considered. Renewable for up to seven semesters or completion of bachelor's degree (whichever comes first) if recipient maintains a minimum 3.25 GPA and completes at least 12 credit hours per semester. Awarded every year. Award may be used only at sponsoring institution.
Contact: Jeff R. Scofield, Director of Financial Aid.

1405 Distinguished Scholar Award

Hope College
P.O. Box 9000
Holland, MI 49422-9000
(616) 395-7850, (616) 395-7130 (fax)
admissions@hope.edu
http://www.hope.edu
Average award: $5,000
Deadline: February 15
College level: Freshman, Sophomore, Junior, Senior
Criteria: Selection is based upon GPA, course selection, class rank, and standardized test scores. Renewable if recipient maintains a minimum 2.75 GPA. Awarded every year. Award may be used only at sponsoring institution.
Contact: James R. Bekkering, Vice President for Admissions.

1406 Distinguished Scholar Award

Central Missouri State University
Office of Admissions
Administration 104
Warrensburg, MO 64093
(816) 543-4541, (816) 543-8517 (fax)
Maximum award: $25,000
Average award: Tuition , room, board, and $150 book allowance per semester
Number of awards: 25
Deadline: February 15
College level: Freshman
Criteria: Applicant must have a minimum composite ACT score of 28, and either rank in the top five percent of class or have a minimum cumulative GPA of 3.75 at the end of sixth or seventh high school semester. Renewable if minimum 2.0 GPA after first semester, minimum 3.5 GPA after second semester, or minimum 3.75 GPA after fourth semester is maintained and thereafter at least 12 hours per semester are taken. Awarded every year. Award may be used only at sponsoring institution.
Contact: Scholarships and Awards Officer.

1407   Distinguished Scholar Award

University of Missouri–St. Louis
8001 Natural Bridge Road
St. Louis, MO 63121
(314) 553-6396
*Average award:*Full fees and $4,000 stipend
Number of awards: 2
Deadline: April 1
College level: Freshman
Criteria: Applicant must have rank in the top one percent in the state for PSAT scores and have an outstanding high school record. Minimum 3.2 cumulative GPA and 24 credithours per year are required to retain scholarship. Awarded every year. Award may be used only at sponsoring institution.
Contact: James D. Reed, Financial Aid Advisor.

1408   Distinguished Scholarship

Beaver College
450 South Easton Road
Glenside, PA 19038-3295
(215) 572-2910, (215) 572-4049 (fax)
admiss@beaver.edu
http://www.beaver.edu
Average award: $5,112
Maximum award: $14,590
Minimum award: $2,000
Number of awards: 506
Deadline: None
College level: Freshman, Transfers
Criteria: Selection is based upon academic criteria. Freshman applicants should rank in top two-tenths to top 5% of class and have combined SAT I scores of 1030-1400. Transfer applicants should have completed at least 30 credit hours and have a minimum 3.0 GPA. Full-time enrollment is required. Recipient must maintain good academic standing to retain scholarship. Awarded every year. Award may be used only at sponsoring institution.
Contact: Melissa McCurdy, Scholarship Coordinator,
mccurdy@beaver.edu.

1409   Diversity Appreciation Award

Colorado State University
Financial Aid Office
103 Administration Annex Building
Fort Collins, CO 80523-8024
(970) 491-6321, (970) 491-5010 (fax)
Maximum award: $5,000
Deadline: in December
College level: Freshman
Criteria: Applicant must demonstrate academic achievement and the ability to contribute to an appreciation of diversity. Limited funding may make it necessary to consider financial need as part of selection criteria. Renewable if recipient maintains minimum 2.0 cumulative GPA, continuous enrollment at Colorado State University, and satisfactory progress. Awarded every year. Award may be used only at sponsoring institution.
Contact: Eileen Giego, Financial Aid Counselor.

1410   Dr. Guy E. Snavely Scholarship

Birmingham-Southern College
Arkadelphia Road
Birmingham, AL 35254
(205) 226-4688
Maximum award: $6,000
Number of awards: 97
Deadline: January 5
College level: Freshman
Criteria: Applicant should rank in top 5% of class, have a composite ACT score of 28-36 (combined SAT I score of 1150-1400), and have leadership ability. Selection is based upon academic qualifications. Minimum 3.0 GPA is required to retain scholarship. Awarded every year. Award may be used only at sponsoring institution.
Contact: Forrest Stuart, Interim Director of Financial Aid Services.

1411   Dominican Academic Scholarship

Molloy College
1000 Hempstead Avenue
P.O. Box 5002
Rockville Centre, NY 11571-5002
(516) 678-5000
Maximum award: $5,000
Deadline: late February (recommended); April 15
College level: Freshman
Criteria: Applicant must be a first-time, full-time student and file FAFSA. Selection is based upon academic achievement. Recipient must maintain a minimum 3.0 GPA, complete at least 12 credit hours per semester, and reapply to retain scholarship. Awarded every year. Award may be used only at sponsoring institution.
Contact: Kathleen Bonnici, Director of Financial Aid.

1412   Dominican Need-Based Grant

Dominican College of San Rafael
50 Acacia Avenue
San Rafael, CA 94901-2298
(415) 485-3204, (415) 485-3205 (fax)
enroll@dominican.edu
http://www.dominican.edu
Average award: $4,564
Maximum award: $14,380
Minimum award: $133
Number of awards: 559
Deadline: None
College level: Freshman, Sophomore, Junior, Senior
Criteria: First-time freshman applicant must have a minimum 2.5 GPA; transfer applicant must have a minimum 2.0 GPA. Selection is based upon financial need. Application, FAFSA, and supporting documentation required. Minimum 2.0 GPA and completion of at least 12 credit hours per semester are required to retain scholarship. Awarded every year. Award may be used only at sponsoring institution.
Contact: Susan Gutierrez, Director of Financial Aid.

1413   Dudley Academic Scholarship

Auburn University
Auburn University, AL 36849
(334) 844-4723
Average award: $2,100
Deadline: December 15
College level: Freshman
Criteria: Applicant must have a minimum 3.5 GPA and minimum combined SAT I score of 1210 (composite ACT score of 29). Awarded every year. Award may be used only at sponsoring institution.
Contact: Mary Lynn Saidla, Assistant Director for Scholarships.

1414   Early Scholars Award

University of Memphis
Scates Hall 204
Memphis, TN 38152
(901) 678-3213, (901) 678-5621 (fax)
katkinsn@cc.memphis.edu
http://www.memphis.edu/
Maximum award: $2,442
Deadline: January 15
College level: Freshman
Criteria: Award is guaranteed to applicants with a minimum 3.5 high school GPA and a minimum composite ACT score of 27 or combined SAT I score of 1200. Minimum 3.0 GPA and a service requirement of 30 hours per year are required to retain scholarship. Awarded every year. Award may be used only at sponsoring institution.
Contact: Katherine Arkinson, Scholarship Coordinator.

1415 Edward D. Smith Scholarship

Emory University
1380 Oxford Road, NE
Atlanta, GA 30322
(404) 727-6039
Average award: Full tuition
Number of awards: 1
Deadline: November 15
College level: Freshman
Criteria: Awarded to applicant who demonstrates effective, unselfish service to others, outstanding academic achievement, and strong moral character. Priority is given to a graduate of the Westminster Schools in Atlanta. Nomination by school or Emory Admission Committee is required. Renewable for four years of undergraduate study. Awarded every year. Award may be used only at sponsoring institution.
Contact: Office of Admissions, 200 Boisfeuillet Jones Center, Atlanta, GA 30322-1950, (404) 727-6036, (800) 727-6036.

1416 Edwin A. Stevens Scholarship

Stevens Institute of Technology
Castle Point on Hudson
Hoboken, NJ 07030
(201) 216-5201, (201) 216-8348 (fax)
sheridan_d@stmisb.adm.stevens-tech.edu
http://www.stevens-tech.edu
Average award: $6,000
Maximum award: $12,000
Minimum award: $3,000
Number of awards: 500
Deadline: February 1
College level: Freshman, Transfers
Criteria: Applicant must be a U.S. citizen or permanent resident. Minimum GPA required to retain scholarship varies with amount of award. Awarded every year. Award may be used only at sponsoring institution.
Contact: David Sheridan, Director of Financial Aid, sheridan_d@stmisb.adm.stevens-tech.edu.

1417 Edwin L. and Ruth Kennedy Distinguished Professor Scholarship

Ohio University
Office of Student Financial Aid and Scholarships
Athens, OH 45701
(614) 593-4141, (614) 593-4140 (fax)
Average award: Full tuition
Number of awards: 18
Deadline: None
College level: Freshman, Sophomore, Junior, Senior
Criteria: Selection is based upon academic qualifications. Each Distinguished Professor personally selects recipient and determines specific major and academic program. Distinguished professor determines if scholarship is renewable. Awarded every year. Award may be used only at sponsoring institution.
Contact: Mrs. Yang-Hi Kim, Associate Director of Scholarships and Grants.

1418 Eisenhower Scholarship

Kansas Wesleyan University
100 East Claflin
Salina, KS 67401
(913) 827-5541
Average award: $2,000
Maximum award: $2,500
Minimum award: $1,500
Number of awards: 66
Deadline: None
College level: Freshman, Sophomore, Junior, Senior
Criteria: Applicant must have a minimum 3.5 GPA and minimum composite ACT score of 22. Minimum 3.25 GPA is required to retain scholarship. Awarded every year. Award may be used only at sponsoring institution.
Contact: Glenna Alexander, Director of Financial Assistance.

1419 Elizabeth Rose Hayes Scholarship

Birmingham-Southern College
Arkadelphia Road
Birmingham, AL 35254
(205) 226-4688
Maximum award: $11,160
Number of awards: 8
Deadline: January 5
College level: Freshman
Majors/Fields: Health-related field
Criteria: Applicant should rank in top two-tenths of class, have a minimum composite ACT score of 26 (combined SAT I score of 1050), and have leadership ability. Selection is based upon academic qualifications. Financial need is considered. Satisfactory academic progress is required to retain scholarship. Awarded every year. Award may be used only at sponsoring institution.
Contact: Forrest Stuart, Interim Director of Financial Aid Services.

1420 Elizabethtown Area School District Merit Scholarship

Elizabethtown College
One Alpha Drive
Elizabethtown, PA 17022
(717) 361-1404, (717) 361-1485 (fax)
Average award: $5,000
Number of awards: 3
College level: Freshman
Criteria: Applicant must be from Elizabethtown Area School District, be in top tenth of class, and have a minimum combined SAT score of 1150. Award may be used only at sponsoring institution.
Contact: M. Clarke Paine, Director of Financial Aid, painemc@acad.etown.edu.

1421 Elks National Foundation Most Valuable Student Award

Elks National Foundation
http://www.elks.org
Average award: $1,000
Maximum award: $5,000
Number of awards: 500
Deadline: Mid-January
College level: Freshman
Criteria: Applicant must be a U.S. citizen, reside within the jurisdiction of the B.P.O. Elks of the U.S.A., have scholarship rating of 90%, and rank in top five percent of his or her class. Selection is based upon scholarship, leadership, and financial need. Applications are available through local lodges in mid-November. Awarded every year.
Contact: Scholarship Chairman of local lodge.

1422 Emerging Leaders Scholarship

University of Memphis
Scates Hall 204
Memphis, TN 38152
(901) 678-3213, (901) 678-5621 (fax)
katkinsn@cc.memphis.edu
http://www.memphis.edu/
Maximum award: $2,580
Deadline: April 15
College level: Freshman, Sophomore, Junior, Senior
Criteria: Applicant must have a minimum 2.5 GPA, minimum composite ACT score of 20, demonstrate leadership qualities and participation in school activities. Recommendations and interview are required. Minimum 2.25 GPA for the first year (2.5 GPA thereafter), full-time status, and enrollment in certain classes are required for renewal. Awarded every year. Award may be used only at sponsoring institution.
Contact: Katherine Atkinson, Scholarship Coordinator.

1423   Emory College Scholarship

Emory University
1380 Oxford Road, NE
Atlanta, GA 30322
(404) 727-6039
*Average award:*Half tuition
Deadline: April 15
College level: Freshman
Criteria: Selection is based upon merit and financial need. Renewable for up to four years if minimum 3.2 GPA is maintained. Awarded every year. Award may be used only at sponsoring institution.
*Contact:*Office of Financial Aid, 300 Boisfeuillet Jones Center, Atlanta, GA 30322-1960, (404) 727-6039, (800) 727-6039.

1424   Endowed Scholarship

Hope College
P.O. Box 9000
Holland, MI 49422-9000
(616) 395-7850, (616) 395-7130 (fax)
admissions@hope.edu
http://www.hope.edu
Average award: $6,000
Deadline: February 15
College level: Freshman, Sophomore, Junior, Senior
*Criteria:*Applicant must have a minimum 3.6 GPA (90 grade average) and a minimum composite ACT score of 28 (combined SAT I score of 1240). Selection is based upon GPA, course selection, class rank, and standardized test scores. Recipients of National Merit, Presidential, or Trustee scholarships are not eligible for this award. Renewable if recipient maintains a minimum 3.0 GPA. Awarded every year. Award may be used only at sponsoring institution.
Contact: James R. Bekkering, Vice President for Admissions.

1425   Endowed Scholarships

University of California, Los Angeles
A129 Murphy Hall
Box 951435
Los Angeles, CA 90095-1435
(310) 206-0404
Maximum award: $3,000
Number of awards: 800
College level: Freshman, Sophomore, Junior, Senior
Criteria: Applicant with fewer than 20 units of university work must have a minimum 3.5 GPA; applicant with 20 or more units of work must have a minimum 3.3 GPA. Most scholarships are based upon financial need and some have specific qualifications established by the donors. Awarded every year. Award may be used only at sponsoring institution.
Contact: Beverly LeMay, Assistant Director of Scholarships, (310) 206-0417.

1426   Entrance Academic Competition Awards

University of Alberta
Edmonton, Alberta, CN T6G 2M7
(403) 492-3111
Maximum award: $3,000
Number of awards: 150
College level: Freshman
*Criteria:*Selection is based upon superior academic achievement in grade 12. Award may be used only at sponsoring institution.
*Contact:*Office of Student Awards, 103 Administration Building, Edmonton, AB T6G 2M7, (403) 492-3221.

1427   Evelyn Andres Whittaker Scholarship

Moore College of Art and Design
20th and the Parkway
Philadelphia, PA 19103
(215) 568-4515
Average award: $14,097
Number of awards: 1
Deadline: April 1
College level: Freshman
*Criteria:*Scholarship is renewable. Awarded every year. Award may be used only at sponsoring institution.
Contact: Karina Dayich, Associate Director of Admissions.

1428   Excellence Award

City University of New York, Baruch College
Undergraduate Admissions Office
Box 279, 17 Lexington Avenue
New York, NY 10010
(212) 447-3750
Average award: $3,300
Deadline: February 15
College level: Freshman
Criteria: Applicant must have a minimum high school grade average of 90, minimum combined SAT I score of 1300, be interviewed, and submit an essay and two letters of recommendation. Renewable if minimum 3.0 GPA for freshman year (3.25 GPA thereafter) is maintained. Awarded every year. Award may be used only at sponsoring institution.
Contact: Hugo Morales, Scholarship Coordinator.

1429   Excellence Scholarship

Gwynedd-Mercy College
Sumneytown Pike
Gwynedd Valley, PA 19437
(215) 641-5570
Average award: $3,250
Maximum award: $4,000
Minimum award: $2,500
Number of awards: 30
Deadline: None
College level: Freshman, Transfers
Criteria: Transfer applicant must have a minimum 3.3 GPA and at least 30 earned credits; high school applicant must rank in top quarter of class and have a minimum combined SAT I score of 1150. Minimum 3.0 GPA after first semester (minimum 3.3 GPA thereafter) required to retain scholarship. Awarded every year. Award may be used only at sponsoring institution.
Contact: Kristine Weber, Associate Dean of Admissions, (215) 641-5510.

1430   Excellence Scholarship

Houghton College
1 Willard Avenue
Houghton, NY 14744
(716) 567-9328
Average award: $2,000
Maximum award: $5,000
Minimum award: $1,000
Number of awards: 143
Deadline: March 15
College level: Freshman
Criteria: Minimum 2.75 GPA is required to retain scholarship. Awarded every year. Award may be used only at sponsoring institution.
Contact: Troy Martin, Director of Financial Aid.

1431   Excellence Scholarship

Syracuse University
201 Administration Building
Syracuse, NY 13244
(315) 443-1870
orange@suadmin.syr.edu
http://ww.syr.edu
Average award: $5,000
College level: Transfers
*Criteria:*Selection is based upon academic credentials, standardized tests, class rank, extracurricular and community involvement, and overall citizenship and character. Renewable if recipient maintains a minimum 2.5 GPA. Award may be used only at sponsoring institution.
Contact: Scholarships.

1432 Executive Women International Scholarship

Executive Women International
515 South, 700 East
Suite 2E
Salt Lake City, UT 84102
(801) 355-2800, (801) 355-2852 (fax)
Average award: $2,000
Maximum award: $10,000
Minimum award: $500
Number of awards: 6
Deadline: Varies by chapter (around March 15)
College level: High school juniors
Majors/Fields: Business, professional fields
Criteria: Applicant must be a secondary school junior attending a school located within the boundaries of a participating U.S. chapter. Selection is based upon academic achievement, leadership, and work experience. Send a self-addressed, stamped envelope. Awarded every year.
Contact: Debra G. Tucker, Staff Accountant.

1433 Faculty Merit Scholarship

University of West Florida
11000 University Parkway
Pensacola, FL 32514-5750
(904) 474-2400
Average award: Full in-state tuition
Number of awards: 2
Deadline: None
College level: Junior Transfers
Criteria: Applicant must have a minimum 3.5 GPA, be enrolled full time, and be pursuing a degree program. Awarded by academic department on rotating basis. Award is for up to 66 credit hours within two calendar years or until graduation, whichever comes first. Awarded every year. Award may be used only at sponsoring institution.
Contact: Georganne E. Major, Senior Financial Aid Officer.

1434 Faculty Scholarship

Centre College
600 West Walnut Street
Danville, KY 40422
(606) 238-5350, (606) 238-5373 (fax)
admission@centre.edu
http://www.centre.edu
Average award: $6,000
Deadline: February 1
College level: Freshman
Criteria: Interview is required. Renewable if recipient maintains good academic standing and minimum 2.8 GPA (GPA requirement increases for subsequent years). Awarded every year. Award may be used only at sponsoring institution.
Contact: Thomas B. Martin, Dean of Enrollment Management.

1435 Faculty Scholarship

Ohio Wesleyan University
Office of Admissions
Delaware, OH 43015
(614) 368-3020, (614) 368-3314 (fax)
owuadmit@cc.owu.edu
http://www.owu.edu
Average award: $9,570
Number of awards: 150
Deadline: March 1
College level: Freshman, Sophomore, Junior, Senior
Criteria: Applicant must rank in top tenth of class, have a minimum composite ACT score of 27 (combined SAT I score of 1270). Interview with faculty member is strongly recommended. Selection is based upon curriculum, extracurricular involvement, GPA, standardized test scores, and writing skills. Minimum 3.35 GPA by end of sophomore year is required to retain scholarship. Awarded every year. Award may be used only at sponsoring institution.
Contact: Douglas C. Thompson, Dean of Admission.

1436 Faculty Scholarship

Texas Christian University
2800 South University Drive
Fort Worth, TX 76129
(817) 921-7858, (817) 921-7462 (fax)
frogaid@tcu.edu
Maximum award: $3,200
Number of awards: 209
Deadline: January 15
College level: Freshman
Criteria: Applicant must rank in top 15% of class and have a minimum combined SAT I score of 1180 (composite ACT score of 27). Renewable for up to eight semesters or 128 credit hours is recipient maintains a minimum 3.0 GPA after freshman year (3.25 GPA thereafter) and successfully completes at least 27 credit hours per year. Awarded every year. Award may be used only at sponsoring institution.
Contact: Office of Scholarships and Financial Aid, TCU Box 297012, Fort Worth, TX 76129.

1437 Faculty Scholarship for Achievement

Denison University
Box H
Granville, OH 43023
(614) 587-6276, 800-DENISON, (614) 587-6306 (fax)
admissions@denison.edu
http://www.denison.edu
Average award: Full tuition
Number of awards: 35
Deadline: January 1
College level: Freshman
Criteria: Applicant must rank first or second in class and must meet criteria for Honors Program. Selection is based upon academic record, essay, extracurricular achievements, and counselor and teacher recommendations. Interview or campus visitation program is required. Finalist must submit special essay. Minimum GPA is required for renewal. Awarded every year. Award may be used only at sponsoring institution.
Contact: Janet Schultz, Scholarships, (614) 587-6625.

1438 Fanny Bullock Workman Fellowship

Wellesley College
Center for Work & Service
Wellesley, MA 02181
(617) 283-3525, (617) 283-3674 (fax)
fellowships@bulletin.wellesley.edu
Maximum award: $3,000
Deadline: December 16
College level: College seniors/others for graduate study
Criteria: Applicant must be a woman and a graduate of Wellesley Coll who plans further study. Preference is given to those who have not previously held the award. Selection is based upon merit and need. Scholarship is renewable. Awarded every year.
Contact: Secretary to the Committee on Graduate Fellowships, (617) 283-2347.

1439 Fellows Scholarship

High Point University
University Station
Montlieu Avenue
High Point, NC 27262-3598
(910) 841-9128, (910) 841-4599 (fax)
http://www.highpoint.edu
Average award: $2,500
Number of awards: 38
Deadline: February 1
College level: Freshman
Criteria: Applicant must be invited to attend Presidential Scholarship Interview Day. Competitive selection. Minimum 3.0 GPA is required to retain scholarship. Awarded every year. Award may be used only at sponsoring institution.
Contact: Jim Schlimmer, Dean of Admissions, Montlieu Avenue, High Point, NC 27262, (910) 841-9245.

1440   Flora Glenn Candler Scholarship

Emory University
1380 Oxford Road, NE
Atlanta, GA 30322
(404) 727-6039
Maximum award: Full tuition
Deadline: None
College level: Freshman
Criteria: Awarded to applicant who pursues excellence in academics and the performing arts. Nomination by school or Emory Admission Committee is required. Renewable for up to four years of undergraduate study. Awarded every year. Award may be used only at sponsoring institution.
Contact: Office of Admissions, 200 Boisfeuillet Jones Center, Atlanta, GA 30322-1950, (404) 727-6036, (800) 727-6036.

1441   Foster Scholarship

Cincinnati Bible College & Seminary
2700 Glenway Avenue
Cincinnati, OH 45204-3200
(800) 949-4CBC, (513) 244-8141, (513) 244-8140 (fax)
admission@cincybible.edu
http://www.cincybible.edu/home.html.
Average award: $5,600
Number of awards: 2
Deadline: May 1
College level: Freshman, Sophomore, Junior, Senior
Criteria: Applicant must have a minimum 3.8 GPA and minimum composite ACT score of 30 (combined SAT 1 score of 1340). Recipient must maintain minimum 3.67 GPA and full-time enrollment and complete FAFSA to retain scholarship. Awarded every year. Award may be used only at sponsoring institution.
Contact: Dick Hess, Director of Enrollment Services.

1442   Foundation Fellowship

University of Georgia
212 Terrell Hall
Athens, GA 30602
(706) 542-1466 (fax)
undergrad@admissions.uga.edu
http://www.uga.edu
Average award: Comprehensive tuition
Number of awards: 11
Deadline: December
College level: Freshman
Criteria: Applicant must have minimum 3.7 GPA and minimum combined SAT I score of 1300 (composite ACT score of 31). Selection is based upon extracurricular activities, leadership, work and volunteer experience, essay, personal statement, and recommendations. Renewable if recipient maintains 3.3 GPA and meets additional requirements. Awarded every year. Award may be used only at sponsoring institution.
Contact: Shelagh V. Reitman, Assistant Director of Admissions, (706) 542-8776.

1443   Foundation Scholarship

The Evergreen State College
Olympia, WA 98505
(360) 866-6000
Average award: $2,256
Number of awards: 40
Deadline: March 1
College level: Freshman, Transfers
Criteria: Applicant must be a first-time, full-time undergraduate and demonstrate academic achievement, leadership in community service, or talent in a particular area. Awarded every year. Award may be used only at sponsoring institution.
Contact: Arnaldo Rodriguez, Dean of Enrollment Services, Library 1221, Olympia, WA 98505, (360) 866-6000, extension 6310.

1444   Foundation Scholarship

Oakland University
101 North Foundation Hall
Rochester, MI 48309-4401
(810) 370-3360, (810) 370-4462 (fax)
Average award: $5,000
Number of awards: 5
Deadline: February 1
College level: Freshman
Criteria: Minimum 3.25 GPA is required to retain scholarship. Awarded every year. Award may be used only at sponsoring institution.
Contact: Stacy M. Penkala, Assistant Director of Admissions.

1445   Founder Scholarship

Elmira College
One Park Place
Elmira, NY 14901
(607) 735-1724, (607) 735-1718 (fax)
admissions@elmira.edu
www.elmira.edu
Average award: $5,000
Number of awards: 50
College level: Freshman
Criteria: Awarded to student demonstrating outstanding ability in one of six academic divisions: creative arts, economics/business administration, humanities, professional programs, social/behavioral sciences, mathematics/natural sciences. Applicant must be accepted for full-time enrollment. Selection is based upon academic record and standardized test scores. Minimum 3.0 GPA required for renewal. Awarded every year. Award may be used only at sponsoring institution.
Contact: Dean of Admissions, admissions@elmira.edu.

1446   Founder's Scholarship

Culver-Stockton College
One College Hill
Canton, MO 63435-1299
(314) 288-5221
Average award: $5,575
Number of awards: 100
Deadline: April 1
College level: Freshman
Criteria: Applicant must have a minimum 3.2 GPA or rank in top tenth of class, and a minimum composite ACT score of 22 (combined SAT I score of 920). Minimum 3.0 GPA is required to retain scholarship. Awarded every year. Award may be used only at sponsoring institution.
Contact: Diane Bozarth, Director of Student Financial Planning, (217) 231-6306.

1447   Founder's Scholarship

Ferris State University
901 South State Street
Big Rapids, MI 49307
(616) 592-2110
Average award: $6,000
Number of awards: 5
Deadline: January 10
College level: Freshman
Criteria: Applicant must have a minimum 3.9 GPA and minimum composite ACT score of 31. Recipient must maintain a minimum 3.25 GPA and full-time enrollment to retain scholarship for up to four years. Awarded every year. Award may be used only at sponsoring institution.
Contact: Dennis Batt, Interim Director of Scholarships and Financial Aid, Office of Scholarships and Financial Aid, 420 Oak Street, Prakken 104, Big Rapids, MI 49307-2020.

1448 Founder's Scholarship

Messiah College
Grantham, PA 17027-0800
(717) 766-2511, (717) 691-6025 (fax)
http://www.messiah.edu
Maximum award: $3,000
Number of awards: 10
Deadline: None
College level: Freshman
Criteria: Applicants must meet requirements for the President's or the Dean's scholarships. Renewable if recipient maintains a minimum 3.0 GPA and exhibits a continuing leadership role. Awarded every year. Award may be used only at sponsoring institution.
Contact: William Strausbaugh, Vice President for Enrollment Management, (717) 691-6000, strausba@messiah.edu.

1449 Founders, Award

Heidelberg College
310 East Market Street
Tiffin, OH 44883
(419) 448-2293, (414) 448-2124 (fax)
jweing@mail.heidelberg.edu
Average award: $10,000
Number of awards: 3
Deadline: December 15
College level: Freshman
Criteria: Selection is based upon an invitation-only competition held in February. Renewable if recipient maintains a minimum 3.0 GPA. Awarded every year. Award may be used only at sponsoring institution.
Contact: Juli Weininger, Director of Financial Aid.

1450 Founders' Scholarship

Tulane University
6823 St. Charles Avenue
New Orleans, LA 70118
(504) 865-5723
Average award: $6,000
Number of awards: 38
Deadline: March 1
College level: Freshman
Criteria: Minimum 2.7 GPA and full-time enrollment are required to retain scholarship. Awarded every year. Award may be used only at sponsoring institution.
Contact: Thomas P. Lovett, Director of Financial Aid.

1451 Founders Scholarship

Valparaiso University
Valparaiso, IN 46383-6493
(219) 464-5011, (219) 464-6898 (fax)
undergrad_admissions@valpo.edu
http:www.valpo.edu
Average award: Full tuition
Deadline: January 15
College level: Freshman
Criteria: Selection is based upon academic accomplishments. Renewable for up to three years if minimum 3.0 GPA is maintained. Awarded every year. Award may be used only at sponsoring institution.
Contact: Office of Admissions and Financial Aid, Kretzman Hall, (888) GO VALPO.

1452 Four-Year Honors Scholarship

Coppin State College
2500 West North Avenue
Baltimore, MD 21216
(410) 383-5520, (410) 462-4192 (fax)
Maximum award: $6,872
Number of awards: 25
Deadline: August 15
College level: Freshman
Criteria: Applicant must have a minimum 3.0 GPA and minimum combined SAT I score of 950, complete placement exam, and interview with Honors and Scholarship Committee. Minimum 2.5 GPA after first semester, minimum 2.8 GPA after first year, and minimum 3.0 GPA thereafter required to retain scholarship. Awarded every year. Award may be used only at sponsoring institution.
Contact: Traci D. Northcutt, Assistant Dean of the Honors Division, Honors Division, tnorthcutt@coe.coppin.und.edu.

1453 Frank A. Burtner Scholarship

Clemson University
G-01 Sikes Hall
Clemson, SC 29634-5123
(803) 656-2280
Maximum award: $3,500
Number of awards: 1
Deadline: March 1
College level: Junior, Senior
Criteria: Applicant must have a minimum 2.5 GPA and demonstrate excellent leadership qualities. Awarded every year. Award may be used only at sponsoring institution.
Contact: Marvin Carmichael, Director of Financial Aid.

1454 Frank J. Jervey Alumni Scholarship

Clemson University
G-01 Sikes Hall
Clemson, SC 29634-5123
(803) 656-2280
Maximum award: $2,500
Number of awards: 2
Deadline: None
College level: Freshman
Criteria: Selection is based upon admissions application. Minimum 3.0 GPA and completion of at least 12 credits per semester are required to retain scholarship. Awarded every year. Award may be used only at sponsoring institution.
Contact: Marvin Carmichael, Director of Financial Aid.

1455 Fred M. Roddy Merit Scholarship

University of Tennessee, Knoxville
Financial Aid Office
115 Student Services Building
Knoxville, TN 37994
(615) 974-3131
Average award: $2,500
Number of awards: 4
Deadline: February 1
College level: Freshman
Criteria: Selection is based upon academic merit and leadership. Applicant typically should have a 4.0 GPA and minimum composite ACT score of 33. Award is for four years. Awarded every year. Award may be used only at sponsoring institution.
Contact: University Honors Program, F-101 Melrose Hall, Knoxville, TN 37916, (615) 974-7875.

1456   Frederick T. Bonham Scholarship

University of Tennessee, Knoxville
Financial Aid Office
115 Student Services Building
Knoxville, TN 37994
(615) 974-3131
Average award: $2,500
Number of awards: 4
Deadline: February 1
College level: Freshman
Criteria: Selection is based upon academic merit, GPA, test scores, leadership, and extracurricular activities. Award is for four years. Awarded every year. Award may be used only at sponsoring institution.
Contact: University Honors Program, F-101 Melrose Hall, Knoxville, TN 37916, (615) 974-7875.

1457   Freshman Excellence Scholarship

Northern Kentucky University
Administrative Center 416
Nunn Drive
Highland Heights, KY 41099-7101
(606) 572-5144
Average award: In-state tuition
Deadline: February 1
College level: Freshman
Criteria: Applicant must rank in the top fifth of class and have a minimum composite ACT score of 20. Awarded every year. Award may be used only at sponsoring institution.
Contact: Robert E. Sprague, Director of Financial Aid.

1458   Freshman Grant

Grand View College
1200 Grandview Avenue
Des Moines, IA 50316
(515) 263-2820
Average award: $3,200
Maximum award: $5,000
Minimum award: $2,000
Number of awards: 120
Deadline: None
College level: Freshman
Criteria: Minimum 2.0 GPA is required to retain scholarship. Awarded every year. Award may be used only at sponsoring institution.
Contact: Lori S. Hanson, Director of Admissions, (515) 263-2800.

1459   Freshman Honors Scholarship

Kent State University
P.O. Box 5190
Kent, OH 44242-0001
(216) 672-2972
Maximum award: Full tuition
Deadline: None
College level: Freshman
Criteria: Selection is based upon academic record and test scores. Specific GPA in honors course work and full-time enrollment are required to retain scholarship. Awarded every year. Award may be used only at sponsoring institution.
Contact: Theodore Hallenbeck, Director of Financial Aid, 103 Michael Schwartz Center.

1460   Freshman Honors Scholarship I

Southern Nazarene University
6729 N.W. 39th Expressway
Bethany, OK 73008
(405) 491-6310, (405) 491-6320 (fax)
dlee@snu.edu
Average award: $4,800
Deadline: None
College level: Freshman
Criteria: Applicant must be enrolled full time and rank either first or second in class of at least 25 with a minimum composite ACT score of 27 (combined SAT I score of 1200) or have a minimum composite ACT of 32 (combined SAT I score of 1400). Minimum 3.85 GPA is required to retain scholarship. Awarded every year. Award may be used only at sponsoring institution.
Contact: Diana Lee, Director, Financial Assistance, dlee@snu.edu.

1461   Freshman Honors Scholarship II

Southern Nazarene University
6729 N.W. 39th Expressway
Bethany, OK 73008
(405) 491-6310, (405) 491-6320 (fax)
dlee@snu.edu
Average award: Full tuition, fees, room, and board
Deadline: None
College level: Freshman
Criteria: Applicant must be enrolled full time and either be a National Merit Finalist or have a minimum composite ACT score of 34 (or combined SAT I score of 1500). Minimum 3.85 GPA is required to retain scholarship. Awarded every year. Award may be used only at sponsoring institution.
Contact: Diana Lee, Director, Financial Assistance, dlee@snu.edu.

1462   Freshman Scholar Award

Trevecca Nazarene University
333 Murfreesboro Road
Nashville, TN 37210
(615) 248-1242
Average award: $8,064
Deadline: None
College level: Freshman
Criteria: Applicant must have a minimum standard composite score of 32 on the Enhanced ACT. Renewable as a Dean's Scholarship if recipient maintains a minimum 3.75 GPA. Awarded every year. Award may be used only at sponsoring institution.
Contact: Joanie Hall, Senior Assistant for Undergraduate Studies.

1463   Freshman Scholarship

Grand View College
1200 Grandview Avenue
Des Moines, IA 50316
(515) 263-2820
Average award: $4,700
Maximum award: $5,000
Minimum award: $4,500
Number of awards: 25
Deadline: None
College level: Freshman
Criteria: Minimum 3.0 GPA is required to retain scholarship. Awarded every year. Award may be used only at sponsoring institution.
Contact: Lori S. Hanson, Director of Admissions, (515) 263-2800.

1464 Fritz A. Bauer Scholarship

DePaul University
1 East Jackson Boulevard
Chicago, IL 60604
(312) 362-8704, (312) 362-5749 (fax)
Average award: $9,000
Number of awards: 25
Deadline: None
College level: Freshman
Majors/Fields: Commerce
Criteria: Applicant must rank in the top tenth of class, have a minimum composite ACT score of 27 or combined SAT I score of 1200, be enrolled in the College of Commerce, and demonstrate leadership and extracurricular involvement. Minimum 3.3 GPA with full-time enrollment is required to retain scholarship. Awarded every year. Award may be used only at sponsoring institution.
Contact: Jennifer Sparrow, Scholarship Coordinator, jsparrow@wppost.depaul.edu.

1465 General Academic Scholarship

University of Idaho
Moscow, ID 83843
(208) 885-6312, (208) 885-5592 (fax)
finaid@uidaho.edu
http://www.uidaho/edu
Average award: $800
Maximum award: $5,000
Minimum award: $500
Number of awards: 3100
Deadline: February 15
College level: Freshman, Sophomore, Junior, Senior
Criteria: Selection is based upon academic ability and activities. Awarded every year. Award may be used only at sponsoring institution.
Contact: Shawna Lindquist, Scholarship Advisor, Financiall Aid Office.

1466 General Academic Scholarships

University of North Texas
P.O. Box 13525
Denton, TX 76203
(817) 565-2302, (817) 565-2738 (fax)
http://www.unt.edu
Average award: $1,000
Maximum award: $8,700
Minimum award: $200
Number of awards: 600
Deadline: March 31
College level: Freshman, Sophomore, Junior, Senior, Graduate, Doctoral
Criteria: Applicant must be a full-time student with a minimum 3.0 GPA. Entering freshman applicants must also rank in top quarter of secondary school class and have a minimum combined SAT I score of 1100 (composite ACT score of 24). Renewable if recipient maintains a minimum 3.0 GPA and full-time enrollment. Awarded every year. Award may be used only at sponsoring institution.
Contact: Financial Aid and Scholarships.

1467 General John J. Pershing Scholarship

Truman State University
Office of Admission
McClain Hall 205
Kirksville, MO 63501
(816) 785-4114, (816) 785-7456 (fax)
admissions@truman.edu
http://www.truman.edu
Average award: Full tuition, room, board, $4,000 study-abroad stipend
Number of awards: 12
Deadline: January 15
College level: Freshman
Criteria: Applicant must graduate from high school in the year prior to award, have an excellent record of participation and leadership in school and community activities, and demonstrate preeminent intellectual capability. Scholarship is renewable. Awarded every year. Award may be used only at sponsoring institution.
Contact: Brad Chambers, Co-Director of Admission.

1468 General Scholarship

University of Oregon
1242 University of Oregon
Eugene, OR 97403-1242
(541) 346-3044, (541) 346-2537 (fax)
http://www.uoregon.edu/
Average award: $2,100
Maximum award: $2,900
Minimum award: $1,800
Number of awards: 870
Deadline: February 1
College level: Freshman, Sophomore, Junior, Senior, Graduate, Doctoral
Criteria: Selection is based upon academic standing, extracurricular activities, essay, and faculty recommendations. Awarded every year. Award may be used only at sponsoring institution.
Contact: Jim Gilmour, Associate Director of Financial Aid, (541) 346-1187, jgilmour@oregon.uoregon.edu.

1469 General Scholarship

San Jose State University
Office of Financial Aid, WS 275
One Washington Square
San Jose, CA 95192-0036
(408) 924-6100, (408) 924-6089 (fax)
Average award: $750
Maximum award: $5,000
Minimum award: $100
Number of awards: 350
Deadline: March 2
College level: Sophomore, Junior, Senior, Graduate
Criteria: Selection is based upon financial need, academic qualifications, community or school involvement, and employment history. Reapplication and satisfactory academic progress are required for renewal. Awarded every year. Award may be used only at sponsoring institution.
Contact: Janet M. Elliott, Scholarship Coordinator.

1470 Generation Excellence Scholarship

Lane College
545 Lane Avenue
Jackson, TN 38301
(901) 426-7537
Average award: $6,058
Maximum award: $8,398
Minimum award: $2,000
Deadline: None
College level: Freshman
Criteria: Minimum 3.0 GPA required to retain scholarship. Awarded every year. Award may be used only at sponsoring institution.
Contact: Ruth Maddox, Director of Admissions, (901) 426-7500.

1471 George E. Merrick Scholarship

University of Miami
P.O. Box 248187
Coral Gables, FL 33124-5241
(305) 284-5212
Average award: $6,380
Number of awards: 180
College level: Freshman
Criteria: Selection is based upon academic achievement. Applicant must rank in the top fifth of his or her class, have a minimum combined SAT I score of 1180 or a composite ACT score of 26. Recipient must maintain minimum 3.0 GPA and 24 credit hours per year. Awarded every year. Award may be used only at sponsoring institution.
Contact: Martin J. Carney, Director of Office of Financial Assistance Services, (305) 284-2270.

1472   Georgetown University Grant

Georgetown University
37th and O Streets, NW
Washington, DC 20057
(202) 687-4547, (202) 687-6542 (fax)
Average award: $10,000
Maximum award: $23,000
Minimum award: $500
Number of awards: 2134
Deadline: January 15 (entering freshmen); April 15 (continuing students)
College level: Freshman, Sophomore, Junior, Senior, Graduate, Doctoral
Criteria: Applicant must demonstrate financial need. Renewable if financial need is still demonstrated. Awarded every year. Award may be used only at sponsoring institution.
Contact: Patricia McWade, Dean of Student Financial Services, G-19 Healy Hall.

1473   Gramley Leadership and Service Scholarship

Salem College
P.O. Box 10548
Winston-Salem, NC 27108
(910) 721-2808
Average award: $6,000
College level: Freshman
Criteria: Selection is based upon academic record, leadership, and service. Recipient is expected to participate in campus and community activities. Minimum 2.5 GPA required to retain scholarship. Awarded every year. Award may be used only at sponsoring institution.
Contact: Bruce Blackman, Director of Financial Aid.

1474   Grand Mesa Scholarship

Mesa State College
Financial Aid Department
P.O. Box 2647
Grand Junction, CO 81502
(970) 248-1396
Maximum award: Tuition, fees, and $500.
College level: Freshman
Criteria: Applicant must have an outstanding academic background. Selection is based upon GPA, class rank, and standardized test scores. A minimum index of 125 is recommended. Renewable for up to four years if recipient maintains a minimum 3.5 GPA, completes at least 15 credit hours per semester, and completes 50 hours of community service per year. Awarded every year. Award may be used only at sponsoring institution.
Contact: Office of Admission.

1475   Harry S Truman Scholarship

University of Oklahoma
University Affairs
900 Asp Avenue, Room 236
Norman, OK 73019-0401
(405) 325-1701
Maximum award: $27,000
Number of awards: 3
Deadline: December 1
College level: Senior
Criteria: Applicant must rank in the top quarter of class. University selects three applicants to submit to the national office for this highly competitive national program. Awarded every year. Award may be used only at sponsoring institution.
Contact: Honors Program, Honors House, 347 Cate Center Drive, Norman, OK 73019, (405) 325-5291.

1476   Heidelberg Award

Heidelberg College
310 East Market Street
Tiffin, OH 44883
(419) 448-2293, (414) 448-2124 (fax)
jweing@mail.heidelberg.edu
Average award: $18,000
Number of awards: 2
Deadline: December 15
College level: Freshman
Criteria: Selection is based upon an invitation-only competition held in February. Renewable if recipient maintains a minimum 3.0 GPA. Awarded every year. Award may be used only at sponsoring institution.
Contact: Juli Weininger, Director of Financial Aid.

1477   Henry C. Goodrich Scholarship

Birmingham-Southern College
Arkadelphia Road
Birmingham, AL 35254
(205) 226-4688
Average award: Full tuition
Number of awards: 1
Deadline: January 5
College level: Freshman
Majors/Fields: Business-related field
Criteria: Applicant should rank in top 5% of class, have a composite ACT score of 28-36 (combined SAT I score of 1150-1400), have leadership ability, and be planning a career in business or a related field. Selection is based upon academic qualifications. Financial need is considered. Minimum 3.4 GPA is required to retain scholarship. Awarded every year. Award may be used only at sponsoring institution.
Contact: Forrest Stuart, Interim Director of Financial Aid Services.

1478   Henry King Stanford Scholarship

University of Miami
P.O. Box 248187
Coral Gables, FL 33124-5241
(305) 284-5212
Average award: $9,570
Number of awards: 360
Deadline: None
College level: Freshman, Transfers
Criteria: Applicant must rank in the top tenth of class, have a minimum 3.75 GPA, and have a minimum combined SAT I score of 1270 or composite ACT score of 28. Minimum 3.0 cumulative GPA and 24 credit hours per year are required to retain scholarship. Awarded every year. Award may be used only at sponsoring institution.
Contact: Martin J. Carney, Director of Office of Financial Assistance Services, (305) 284-2270, mcarney@umiamivm.ir.miami.edu.

1479   Henry L. Bowden Scholarship

Emory University
1380 Oxford Road, NE
Atlanta, GA 30322
(404) 727-6039
Average award: Full tuition
Deadline: November 15
College level: Freshman
Criteria: Awarded to applicant with outstanding academic achievement, character, and leadership who will make significant contributions at school. Georgia residents are given priority. Other residents of the Southeast are considered. Nomination by school or Emory Admission Committee is required. Renewable for four years of undergraduate study. Awarded every year. Award may be used only at sponsoring institution.
Contact: Office of Admissions, 200 Boisfeuillet Jones Center, Atlanta, GA 30322-1950, (404) 727-6036, (800) 727-6036.

1480 Henry Wells Scholarship

Wells College
Aurora, NY 13026
(315) 364-3264, (315) 364-3227 (fax)
admissions@wells.edu
http://www.wells.edu
Average award: Full tuition
Number of awards: 5
Deadline: November 1
College level: Freshman
Criteria: Applicant must have a minimum 3.0 GPA and rank in the top tenth of his or her class. Scholarship is renewable. Awarded every year. Award may be used only at sponsoring institution.
Contact: Susan Raith Sloan, Director of Admissions.

1481 Heritage Scholarship

Brigham Young University
Scholarship Office, A-41 ASB
P.O. Box 21009
Provo, UT 84602-1009
(801) 378-4104
scholarships@byu.edu
http://adm5.byu.edu/ar/dept_scholarships/scholar.html
Maximum award: $3,800
Number of awards: 400
Deadline: January 15
College level: Freshman
Criteria: Applicant must have a minimum 3.85 GPA and combined SAT I score of 1330 or composite ACT score of 31. Selection is based upon high academic qualifications, leadership skills, and service. Minimum 3.5 GPA and fulfillment of attendance requirements are required to retain scholarship. Awarded every year. Award may be used only at sponsoring institution.
Contact: Duane L. Bartle, Associate Director of Scholarships.

1482 Heritage Scholarship

Denison University
Box H
Granville, OH 43023
(614) 587-6276, 800-DENISON, (614) 587-6306 (fax)
admissions@denison.edu
http://www.denison.edu
Average award: Half tuition
Number of awards: No limit
Deadline: January 1
College level: Freshman
Criteria: Applicant must meet criteria for Honors Program. Selection is based upon academic record, essay, extracurricular achievements, and counselor and teacher recommendations. Interview or campus visitation program is required. Minimum GPA is required for renewal. Awarded every year. Award may be used only at sponsoring institution.
Contact: Scholarships.

1483 Heritage Scholarship

Salem College
P.O. Box 10548
Winston-Salem, NC 27108
(910) 721-2808
Average award: $7,000
College level: Freshman
Criteria: Applicant must be a woman. Selection is based upon excellent academic achievement and significant extracurricular involvement in high school, with preference given to minority students. Recipient must maintain a minimum 2.5 GPA and remain a full-time resident student to retain scholarship. Awarded every year. Award may be used only at sponsoring institution.
Contact: Bruce Blackman, Director of Financial Aid.

1484 High School Achievement Award

Cedar Crest College
100 College Drive
Allentown, PA 18104
(610) 740-3785, (610) 606-4647 (fax)
cccadmis@cedarcrest.edu
www.cedarcrest.edu
Maximum award: $3,000
Number of awards: 11
College level: Freshman
Criteria: Applicants must have a minimum SAT score of 1150 and rank in the top fifth of his or her class. Scholarship is renewable. Awarded every year. Award may be used only at sponsoring institution.
Contact: Judith Neyhart, Vice President for Enrollment Management, Financial Aid Office.

1485 High School Valedictorian Scholarship

Texas A&M University–Kingsville
Scholarships
Box 116
Kingsville, TX 78363
(512) 593-3907, (512) 593-2991 (fax)
http://www.tamuk.edu
Average award: Full tuition
Number of awards: No limit
Deadline: None
College level: Freshman
Criteria: Applicant must be the valedictorian of his or her high school graduating class. Award may be used only at sponsoring institution.
Contact: Registrar.

1486 Hofstra Recognition Scholarship

Hofstra University
126 Memorial Hall
Hempstead, NY 11550
(516) 463-6677
Maximum award: $4,500
Deadline: February 15
College level: Freshman
Criteria: Applicant must rank in the top tenth of class and have a minimum composite ACT score of 23 or combined SAT I score of 1070. Minimum 3.0 GPA by end of freshman year, 3.1 GPA by end of sophomore year, and 3.2 GPA by end of junior year are required to retain scholarship. Awarded every year. Award may be used only at sponsoring institution.
Contact: Joan Warren, Director of Financial and Academic Records.

1487 Honor and Challenge Scholarship

New York Institute of Technology
Old Westbury, NY 11568
(516) 686-7680
Average award: $2,800
Maximum award: $3,000
Minimum award: $2,600
Deadline: None
College level: Freshman
Criteria: Applicant must have a minimum "B" grade average and minimum combined SAT I score of 1100. Recipient must maintain a minimum 2.7 GPA and full-time enrollment to retain scholarship. Awarded every year. Award may be used only at sponsoring institution.
Contact: Beverly Tota, Director of Admissions, P.O. Box 8000, Old Westbury, NY 11568, (516) 686-7520.

1488 Honor Scholarship

Centre College
600 West Walnut Street
Danville, KY 40422
(606) 238-5350, (606) 238-5373 (fax)
admission@centre.edu
http://www.centre.edu
Maximum award: $5,000
Deadline: February 1
College level: Freshman
Criteria: Interview is required. Renewable if recipient maintains good academic standing and a minimum 2.5 GPA. Awarded every year. Award may be used only at sponsoring institution.
Contact: Thomas B. Martin, Dean of Enrollment Management.

1489 Honor Scholarship

Lee University
P.O. Box 3450
Cleveland, TN 37320-3450
(423) 614-8000
Average award: $2,616
Number of awards: 248
Deadline: None
College level: Sophomore, Junior, Senior
Criteria: Applicant must have a minimum 3.7 GPA and be enrolled for at least 12 credit hours per semester. Award equals one-half of tuition. Scholarship is renewable. Awarded every year. Award may be used only at sponsoring institution.
Contact: Phil Barber, Registrar, (423) 614-8500.

1490 Honor Scholarship

Louisiana State University and Agricultural and Mechanical College
Baton Rouge, LA 70803-2750
(504) 388-3103
Average award: $3,945
Number of awards: 500
Deadline: February 1
College level: Freshman
Criteria: Applicant must have high standardized test scores and an excellent academic record, especially in English and math. Minimum 3.0 cumulative GPA and full-time enrollment are required to retain scholarship. Awarded every year. Award may be used only at sponsoring institution.
Contact: Kathleen Sciacchetano, Director of Financial Aid.

1491 Honor Scholarship

Multnomah Bible College and Biblical Seminary
8435 Northeast Glisan Street
Portland, OR 97220
(503) 255-0332
Average award: $3,550
Number of awards: 10
College level: Freshman
Criteria: Scholarship is renewable. Awarded every year. Award may be used only at sponsoring institution.
Contact: Denys Fessenden, Dean of Students, (503) 251-5335.

1492 Honor Scholarship

College of Saint Mary
1901 South 72nd Street
Omaha, NE 68124
(402) 399-2405
Maximum award: $5,000
Deadline: None
College level: Freshman
Criteria: Selection is based upon academic excellence, class rank, GPA, and standardized test scores. Renewable for up to four years. Awarded every year. Award may be used only at sponsoring institution.
Contact: Enrollment Services.

1493 Honor Scholarship

Spalding University
851 South Fourth Street
Louisville, KY 40203
(502) 585-9911
Maximum award: $4,000
Deadline: March 1 (priority)
College level: Freshman, Sophomore, Junior, Senior, Transfers
Criteria: Applicant must have a minimum 3.4 GPA, minimum composite ACT score of 23, and three letters of recommendation and be accepted for full-time enrollment. Scholarship is renewable. Awarded every year. Award may be used only at sponsoring institution.
Contact: Janice White Russell, Assistant Director of Financial Aid and Scholarship Coordinator, (502) 585-9911, extension 242.

1494 Honor Scholarship

Warren Wilson College
P.O. Box 9000
Asheville, NC 28815
(704) 298-3325, (704) 298-1440 (fax)
admissions@warren-wilson.edu
http://www.warren-wilson.edu
Average award: $2,000
Maximum award: $4,000
Minimum award: $1,000
Number of awards: 11
Deadline: March 15
College level: Freshman
Criteria: Applicant must have a minimum 3.3 GPA and a minimum combined SAT score of 1200. A 250-word typed essay must be submitted with application. Scholarship is renewable. Awarded every year. Award may be used only at sponsoring institution.
Contact: Richard Blomgren, Dean of Admission.

1495 Honored Scholars Program

National Alliance for Excellence, Inc.
20 Thomas Avenue
Shrewsbury, NJ 07702
(908) 747-0028, (908) 842-2962 (fax)
sfaexcel@aol.com
http://www.excellence.org
Average award: $1,500
Maximum award: $5,000
Minimum award: $1,000
Number of awards: 50
Deadline: rolling
College level: Freshman, Sophomore, Junior, Senior, Graduate, Doctoral, Returning students
Criteria: Applicant must be a U.S. citizen, have taken the SAT I and received written results prior to application (minimum combined SAT I score of 1200), have a minimum 3.7 GPA, demonstrate outstanding academic achievement or excel in the visual/performing arts, and pursue full-time study at an accredited U.S. institution or participate in an approved foreign exchange program. Financial need is not considered. SAT I scores are not considered in visual/performing arts categories. Send self-addressed stamped envelope with application request. Awarded every year.
Contact: Linda Paras, President, 55 Highway 35, Suite 5, Red Bank, NJ 07701.

1496 Honors at Entrance Scholarship/Early Admission

University of Utah
Financial Aid and Scholarships Office
105 Student Services Building
Salt Lake City, UT 84112
(801) 581-6211
Average award: Resident tuition
Maximum number of awards: 2
Deadline: July 1
College level: Freshman
Criteria: Applicant must be admitted to the university under early admission and have an Admissions Index of at least 126. Minimum cumulative GPA of 3.7 and 36 hours of course work every three quarters are required to retain scholarship. Awarded every year. Award may be used only at sponsoring institution.
Contact: Financial Aid and Scholarships Office.

1497 Honors Award

Mount Olive College
634 Henderson Street
Mount Olive, NC 28365
(919) 658-2502
Maximum award: $5,000
Deadline: None
College level: Freshman
Criteria: Applicant must have a minimum 3.2 GPA, rank in top quarter of class, have a minimum combined SAT I score of 900 (composite ACT score of 20), and be accepted for admission. Recipient must participate in Honors Program. Nominees for Honors Program will receive $1,000 Presidential Award. Renewable for up to four years if recipient completes at least 30 semester hours per year, maintains a minimum 3.2 GPA, and satisfies the requirements of the Honors Program. Awarded every year. Award may be used only at sponsoring institution.
Contact: Tim Woodard, Director of Admissions.

1498 Honors College Presidential Scholarship

Pittsburg State University
1701 South Broadway
Pittsburg, KS 66762-7534
(316) 235-4240
Average award: $5,364
Number of awards: 12
Deadline: March 1
College level: Freshman
Criteria: Applicant must have a minimum 3.7 GPA and minimum composite ACT score of 28. Recipient must maintain a minimum 3.2 GPA to retain scholarship. Awarded every year. Award may be used only at sponsoring institution.
Contact: Dr. Robert Hilt, Director of the Honors College, Room 320 Russ Hall, (316) 235-4329.

1499 Honors Division Scholarship

Indiana University Bloomington
University Honors Division
324 North Jordan
Bloomington, IN 47405
(812) 855-3555, (812) 855-5416 (fax)
http://www.honors.indiana.edu
Maximum award: $5,000
Number of awards: 150
Deadline: January 25 (priority)
College level: Freshman
Criteria: Applicant must have a minimum combined SAT I score of 1270 (composite ACT score of 30) and rank in the top tenth of class. Selection is based upon test scores, high school performance, quality of writing in the essay on the application, participation in extracurricular activities, and work experience. Minimum cumulative 3.4 GPA, completion of three approved honors courses during first four semesters on campus, and attendance at one approved extracurricular activity each year are required to retain scholarship. Awarded every year. Award may be used only at sponsoring institution.
Contact: Rebecca Steele, Coordinator, Honors Division Scholarships, rsteele@indiana.edu.

1500 Honors Program Scholarship

Elon College
2700 Campus Box
Elon College, NC 27244
(800) 334-8448, extension 1
Maximum award: $8,000
Maximum number of awards: 80
Minimum number of awards: 60
College level: Freshman
Criteria: Eligible applicants are nominated through admissions office and invited to participate in scholarship competition. All nominees recieve $1,000 Presidential Scholarship. Recipients must participate in Honors Program. Selection is based upon GPA, class rank, standardized test scores, and course selection. Renewable for up to four years if recipient maintains satisfactory academic progress and participation in Honors Program. Awarded every year. Award may be used only at sponsoring institution.
Contact: Office of Admissions and Financial Planning.

1501 Honors Program Scholarship

Liberty University
1971 University Boulevard
Lynchburg, VA 24502-2269
(800) 543-5317
Maximum award: $5,400
Number of awards: 97
Deadline: April 1
College level: Freshman
Criteria: Applicant must have a minimum 3.5 GPA, rank in the top tenth of graduating class, and have minimum combined SAT I score of 1200 (composite ACT score of 28). Selection is based upon personal and academic recommendations and essay. Renewable if recipient maintains the minimum required GPA. Awarded every year. Award may be used only at sponsoring institution.
Contact: Dr. James Hunter, Director of Honors Program.

1502 Honors Recognition Award

Heidelberg College
310 East Market Street
Tiffin, OH 44883
(419) 448-2293, (414) 448-2124 (fax)
jweing@mail.heidelberg.edu
Maximum award: $3,000
Maximum number of awards: 30
Minimum number of awards: 5
Deadline: None
College level: Freshman
Majors/Fields: Honors program
Criteria: Selection is based upon competition held in February. Applicant must participate in community service and be invited into the Honors Program. Minimum 3.3 GPA is required for renewal. Awarded every year. Award may be used only at sponsoring institution.
Contact: Juli Weininger, Director of Financial Aid.

1503 Honors Scholarship

Eckerd College
4200 54th Avenue South
St. Petersburg, FL 33711
(813) 864-8331, 800 456-9009, (813) 866-2304 (fax)
admissions@eckerd.edu
http://www.eckerd.edu
Average award: $5,000
Maximum award: $7,000
Minimum award: $1,000
Number of awards: 50
Deadline: None
College level: Freshman, Transfers
Criteria: Awarded to most outstanding applicants. Financial need is considered. Renewable if recipient maintains a minimum 3.0 GPA. Awarded every year. Award may be used only at sponsoring institution.
Contact: Dr. Richard Hallin, Dean of Admissions.

1504 Honors Scholarship

College of New Rochelle
29 Castle Place
New Rochelle, NY 10805
(914) 654-5224
Average award: $7,500
Number of awards: 5
Deadline: None
College level: Freshman
Criteria: Applicant must have a minimum 91 grade average, rank in top tenth of class, have a minimum combined SAT I score of 1200, and be accepted for admission. Scholarship is renewable. Awarded every year. Award may be used only at sponsoring institution.
Contact: Annette Gonzalez, Financial Aid Counselor.

1505 Honors Scholarship

Principia College
Elsah, IL 62028
(800) 277-4648, (800) 347-4000 (fax)
collegeadmissions@prin.edu
http://www.prin.edu
Average award: $2,500
Number of awards: 30
Deadline: None
College level: Freshman
Criteria: Awarded every year. Award may be used only at sponsoring institution.
Contact: Martha Green Quirk, Director of Admissions and Enrollment, (618) 374-5180, mgq@prin.edu.

1506 Honors Scholarship

Saint Joseph's College
Highway 231 South
P.O. Box 890
Rensselaer, IN 47978
(219) 866-6170, (219) 866-6100 (fax)
Maximum award: $6,000
Deadline: March 1 (priority)
College level: Freshman
Criteria: Selection is based upon academic achievements. Minimum 3.25 GPA is required to retain scholarship. Awarded every year. Award may be used only at sponsoring institution.
Contact: Frank Bevec, Director of Admission.

1507 Honors Scholarship

University of Sioux Falls
1101 West 22nd Street
Sioux Falls, SC 57105-1699
(605) 331-6623
Average award: $4,700
Maximum award: $9,500
Minimum award: $2,400
Deadline: March 1
College level: Freshman
Criteria: Applicant must have a minimum composite ACT score of 26. Minimum 3.4 GPA is required to retain scholarship. Awarded every year. Award may be used only at sponsoring institution.
Contact: David Vikander, Director of Financial Aid.

1508 Honors Scholarship

State University of New York at Stony Brook
Stony Brook, NY 11794
(516) 632-6840
Average award: $2,000
Maximum award: $3,400
Number of awards: 40
Deadline: Mid-January
College level: Freshman
Criteria: Selection is based upon academic and extracurricular experiences. Minimum 3.0 GPA is required to retain scholarship. Awarded every year. Award may be used only at sponsoring institution.
Contact: Ana Maria Torres, Director of Financial Aid and Student Employment.

1509 Honors Scholarship

Valparaiso University
Valparaiso, IN 46383-6493
(219) 464-5011, (219) 464-6898 (fax)
undergrad_admissions@valpo.edu
http:www.valpo.edu
Maximum award: $3,940
Deadline: May 1
College level: Freshman
Criteria: Selection is based upon academic accomplishments. Renewable for three years if recipient maintains minimum 3.0 GPA. Awarded every year. Award may be used only at sponsoring institution.
Contact: Office of Admissions and Financial Aid, Kretzmann Hall, (888) GO VALPO.

1510 Houghton College Grant

Houghton College
1 Willard Avenue
Houghton, NY 14744
(716) 567-9328
Average award: $2,400
Maximum award: $3,500
Minimum award: $1,000
Number of awards: 215
Deadline: March 15
College level: Freshman
Criteria: Recipient must demonstrate continued financial need to retain scholarship. Awarded every year. Award may be used only at sponsoring institution.
Contact: Troy Martin, Director of Financial Aid.

1511 Howard Rock Scholarship

Alaska Village Initiatives, Inc.
1577 C Street, Suite 304
Anchorage, AK 99501
(907) 274-5400
avi@anc.ak.net
Maximum award: $5,000
Deadline: March 14
College level: Freshman, Sophomore, Junior, Senior, Graduate, Doctoral
Criteria: Applicant must be an Alaska native. Awarded every year.
Contact: Sharon Anderson, Scholarships.

1512 Hunter College Scholar Award

City University of New York, Hunter College
695 Park Avenue
New York, NY 10021
(212) 772-4820
Maximum award: $3,650
Number of awards: 20
Deadline: February 15
College level: Freshman
Criteria: Applicant must be a U.S. citizen or permanent resident. Recipient must maintain full-time enrollment and a minimum 3.0 GPA after freshman year (3.2 GPA after second year, 3.5 GPA thereafter) to retain scholarship. Awarded every year. Award may be used only at sponsoring institution.
Contact: Joseph A. Fantozzi, Associate Director of Admissions, (212) 772-4486.

1513 I.A. Rader/President's Scholarship

Milwaukee School of Engineering
1025 North Broadway
Milwaukee, WI 53202-3109
(800) 332-6763, (414) 277-7475 (fax)
goran@admin.msoe.edu
www.msoe.edu
Average award: Full tuition
Number of awards: 8
Deadline: February 1
College level: Freshman
Criteria: Applicant must have a minimum 3.2 GPA and minimum composite ACT score of 25 (combined SAT I score of 1060), have completed four years of English, four years of math, and three years of science including chemistry and physics, and provide extracurricular information, personal statement, and recommendation. Interview is required. Recipient must maintain continuous enrollment and a minimum 3.2 GPA and must conform to standards of behavior expected of all students to retain scholarship. Awarded every year. Award may be used only at sponsoring institution.
Contact: Sue Minzlaff, Financial Aid Office, (417) 277-7222, minzlaff@admin.msoe.edu.

1514 Ignatius Scholarship

Marquette University
P.O. Box 1881
Milwaukee, WI 53201-1881
(414) 288-7302, (414) 288-3764 (fax)
go2marquette@vms.csd.mu.edu
http://www.mu.edu
Average award: $7,000
Deadline: February 1
College level: Freshman, Transfers
Criteria: Selection is based upon academic achievement, class rank, standardized tests, and extracurricular activities. Minimum 3.0 GPA and full-time enrollment are required to retain scholarship. Awarded every year. Award may be used only at sponsoring institution.
Contact: Carlos Garces, Senior Assistant Director of Admissions.

1515 Incentive Grant/Scholarship

Chowan College
P.O. Box 1848
Murfreesboro, NC 27855
(800) 488-4101, (919) 398-1190 (fax)
admissions@micah.chowan.edu
http://www.chowan.edu
Average award: $2,875
Maximum award: $6,500
Minimum award: $1,500
Number of awards: 262
Deadline: August 1
College level: Freshman, Sophomore, Junior, Senior
Criteria: Selection is based upon SAT I scores and GPA. Minimum 2.0 GPA is required to retain grant. Minimum 3.0 GPA is required to retain scholarship. Awarded every year. Award may be used only at sponsoring institution.
Contact: Austine Evans, Vice President for Enrollment Management.

1516 Institute Scholarship

Monterrey Institute of Technology and Higher Education–
Chiapas Campus
Carr. a Tapanatepec Km. 149+746
Tuxtla Gutierrez, Chiapas, MX 29009
(961) 5-02-32
Average award: $1,506
Maximum award: $3,254
Minimum award: $480
Deadline: April 28 (fall); November 15 (spring)
College level: Freshman, Sophomore, Junior, Senior, Graduate, Doctoral
Criteria: Applicant must have a minimum 1,276 points for college (1,049 for secondary school) on admissions test and a minimum 90 grade average and demonstrate financial need. Minimum 85 grade average required to retain scholarship. Scholarship is awarded every semester. Award may be used only at sponsoring institution.
Contact: Lic. Jorge Arturo Gutierrez Mota, Student Affairs Director, (961) 502-00, (961) 502-41.

1517 Institutional Scholarship/Grant

Salem College
P.O. Box 10548
Winston-Salem, NC 27108
(910) 721-2808
Average award: $4,530
Maximum award: $15,995
Number of awards: 518
Deadline: None
College level: Freshman, Sophomore, Junior, Senior
Criteria: Financial need is considered. Satisfactory academic progress and continued financial need required to retain scholarship. Awarded every year. Award may be used only at sponsoring institution.
Contact: Bruce Blackman, Director of Financial Aid.

1518 International Freshman Academic Scholarship

University of Southern California
University Park
Los Angeles, CA 90089-5012
(213) 740-1111
Average award: $9,500
Number of awards: 15
College level: Freshman
Criteria: Scholarship is renewable. Awarded every year. Award may be used only at sponsoring institution.
Contact: Office of Admission.

1519 Involving Leaders Scholarship

Lynchburg College
Lynchburg, VA 24501
(804) 522-8228
Average award: $5,000
Deadline: February 15
College level: Freshman
Criteria: Applicant must have a minimum "B" grade average, have a minimum combined SAT I score of 950 (composite ACT score of 21), and demonstrate leadership skills in community or school life. Selection is competitive. Scholarship is renewable. Awarded every year. Award may be used only at sponsoring institution.
Contact: Scholarships.

1520   IPTAY Academic Scholarship Fund

Clemson University
G-01 Sikes Hall
Clemson, SC 29634-5123
(803) 656-2280
Average award: $2,500
Deadline: March 1
College level: Freshman
Criteria: Awarded to applicant who does not participate in intercollegiate athletics. Renewable for up to three years if recipient maintains minimum 3.0 GPA and completes at least 12 credits each semester. Awarded every year. Award may be used only at sponsoring institution.
Contact: Marvin Carmichael, Director of Financial Aid.

1521   Iris Leadership Award

Elmira College
One Park Place
Elmira, NY 14901
(607) 735-1724, (607) 735-1718 (fax)
admissions@elmira.edu
www.elmira.edu
Average award: $2,500
Number of awards: 100
College level: Freshman
Criteria: Awarded to outstanding school activity leaders as determined by Dean of Admissions. Applicant must be accepted for full-time enrollment. Minimum 2.5 GPA required for renewal. Awarded every year. Award may be used only at sponsoring institution.
Contact: Dean of Admissions, admissions@elmira.edu.

1522   Isaac Bashevis Singer Scholarship

University of Miami
P.O. Box 248187
Coral Gables, FL 33124-5241
(305) 284-5212
Average award: $19,140
Number of awards: 8
Deadline: None
College level: Freshman
Criteria: Applicant must rank in the top one percent of class, have a minimum 4.0 GPA, and have a minimum combined SAT I score of 1360 or composite ACT score of 31. Minimum 3.0 cumulative GPA and 24 credit hours per year are required to retain scholarship. Awarded every year. Award may be used only at sponsoring institution.
Contact: Martin J. Carney, Director of Office of Financial Assistance Services, (305) 284-2270, mcarney@umiamivm.ir.miami.edu.

1523   J. Glenn and Gladys Harris Scholarship

Indiana University Northwest
3400 Broadway
Gary, IN 46408
(219) 980-6777, (219) 981-4219 (fax)
wlee@iunhawl.iun.indiana.edu
Maximum award: Full tuition, fees, books
Number of awards: 1
Deadline: March 15
College level: Freshman
Criteria: Selection is based upon academic achievement and potential for college succes. Scholarship is renewable. Awarded every year. Award may be used only at sponsoring institution.
Contact: William D. Lee, Director of Admissions and Financial Aid, (219) 980-6991.

1524   J.R. Hyde Scholarship

Rhodes College
2000 North Parkway
Memphis, TN 38112
(901) 843-3700, (901) 843-3719 (fax)
adminfo@rhodes.edu
http://www.rhodes.edu
Average award: $21,668
Number of awards: 2
Deadline: January 15
College level: Freshman
Criteria: Awarded to outstanding first-year student. Applicant must be nominated by counselor, principal, headmaster, minister of the Presbyterian Church (USA), or alumnus. Special nomination form is required. Renewable if recipient maintains a minimum 3.25 GPA. Awarded every year. Award may be used only at sponsoring institution.
Contact: David J. Wottle, Dean of Admission and Financial Aid, (800) 844-5969.

1525   James Beasley Monroe Memorial Scholarship

Clemson University
G-01 Sikes Hall
Clemson, SC 29634-5123
(803) 656-2280
Average award: $3,500
Number of awards: 1
Deadline: March 1
College level: Freshman
Criteria: Applicant must have a minimum 2.0 GPA. Renewable for up to three years if recipient maintians minimum 3.0 GPA and completes at least 12 credits per semester. Awarded every year. Award may be used only at sponsoring institution.
Contact: Marvin Carmichael, Director of Financial Aid.

1526   James E. Scripps Scholarship

Scripps College
1030 Columbia Avenue
Claremont, CA 91711
(800) 770-1333
Average award: $7,500
Number of awards: 8
Deadline: December 1
College level: Freshman
Criteria: Selection is based upon academic performance, personal achievement, standardized test scores, recommendations, and involvement in community or school activities. Minimum "B" grade average in academic courses required to retain scholarship. Awarded every year. Award may be used only at sponsoring institution.
Contact: Patricia F. Goldsmith, Dean of Admission and Financial Aid.

1527   James Porter Merit Academic Scholarship

Albany State University
504 College Drive
Albany, GA 31705
(912) 430-4650, (912) 430-3936 (fax)
kcaldwell@rams.alsnet.peachnet.edu
Maximum award: $3,000
Number of awards: 10
Deadline: February 1
College level: Freshman, Graduate
Criteria: Renewable if recipient maintains a minimum "B" average as a full-time student. Awarded every year. Award may be used only at sponsoring institution.
Contact: Kathleen J. Caldwell, Director of Admissions and Financial Aid.

1528 Jay F.W. Pearson Scholarship

University of Miami
P.O. Box 248187
Coral Gables, FL 33124-5241
(305) 284-5212
Average award: $5,200
Number of awards: 15
College level: Freshman, Transfers
Criteria: Selection is based upon academic achievement. Typically, applicant should rank in the top fifth of class, have a minimum 3.5 GPA, and have a minimum combined SAT I score of 1180 or a composite ACT score of 26. Minimum 3.0 GPA and 24 credit hours per year are required to retain scholarship. Awarded every year. Award may be used only at sponsoring institution.
Contact: Martin J. Carney, Director of Office of Financial Assistance Services, (305) 284-2270.

1529 Jeff Parker Scholarship

Jacksonville State University
Jacksonville, AL 36265-9982
(205) 782-5006
Average award: Full tuition
Deadline: March 15
Majors/Fields: Commerce, business administration
Criteria: Applicant must have earned at least 90 semester hours. Selection is based upon GPA, university involvement, and financial need. Awarded every year. Award may be used only at sponsoring institution.
Contact: Student Financial Aid Office.

1530 Jefferson Caffery Scholarship

University of Southwestern Louisiana
East University Avenue
P.O. Box 44548
Lafayette, LA 70504
(318) 231-6515
Average award: $2,800
Deadline: January 5
College level: Freshman
Criteria: Applicant must have a minimum composite ACT score of 30 or be a National Merit semifinalist. Minimum 3.2 GPA is required to retain scholarship. Awarded every year. Award may be used only at sponsoring institution.
Contact: Adele Bulliard, Director of Scholarships.

1531 Jim and DeeGee Bannon Scholarship

Clemson University
G-01 Sikes Hall
Clemson, SC 29634-5123
(803) 656-2280
Average award: $5,800
Number of awards: 1
Deadline: March 1
College level: Freshman, Sophomore, Junior, Senior
Criteria: Applicant must have a minimum 2.5 GPA. Satisfactory GPA and completion of at least 12 credits per semester are required to retain scholarship. Awarded every year. Award may be used only at sponsoring institution.
Contact: Marvin Carmichael, Director of Financial Aid.

1532 Jo Nell Usrey Stephens Endowed Honors Scholarship

The University of Alabama
Box 870162
Tuscaloosa, AL 35487-0162
(205) 348-6756
Average award: $2,400
Number of awards: 1
Deadline: May
College level: Freshman
Criteria: Awarded to entering freshman in University Honors Program who is receiving no other scholarship aid from U of Alabama. Minimum 3.3 GPA is required to retain scholarship. Awarded every year. Award may be used only at sponsoring institution.
Contact: University Honors Program, Box 870169, Tuscaloosa, AL 35487-0169.

1533 John and Marjory Culver Scholarship

Southern Oregon University
Ashland, OR 97520
(503) 552-6161
Average award: Full tuition
Number of awards: 2
Deadline: None
College level: Junior, Senior, Graduate
Criteria: Applicant must be a graduate of a Jackson County, Oreg., high school, be enrolled full time, have a minimum 3.0 GPA, demonstrate commitment to community service, leadership ability, and/or exceptional non-scholastic achievements, and show financial need. Awarded every year. Award may be used only at sponsoring institution.
Contact: Barbara Sabol, Scholarship Coordinator, (503) 552-6163.

1534 John C. Pace Jr. Scholarship (Freshmen)

University of West Florida
11000 University Parkway
Pensacola, FL 32514-5750
(904) 474-2400
Maximum award: $4,000
Number of awards: 18
Deadline: March 1
College level: Freshman
Criteria: Maximum award is given to applicants who rank in top tenth of class, with priority given first to graduates from Escambia, Okaloosa, Santa Rosa, and Walton counties. Second priority is given to graduates from other schools in West Florida, and third priority to graduates from other Florida schools. Application is required. Ten minimum awards are given to applicants who meet other criteria. Satisfactory academic progress and/or minimum 3.0 GPA are required to retain scholarship. Renewable for up to four years. Awarded every year. Award may be used only at sponsoring institution.
Contact: Kathy Goggans, Office of Undergraduate Admissions, (904) 474-2230.

1535 John Cardinal Newman Scholarship

DePaul University
1 East Jackson Boulevard
Chicago, IL 60604
(312) 362-8704, (312) 362-5749 (fax)
Average award: $4,500
Maximum award: $9,000
Minimum award: $2,000
Number of awards: 30
Deadline: None
College level: Freshman
Criteria: Applicant must rank first in graduating class and demonstrate strong academics, leadership, and extracurricular involvements. Minimum 3.3 GPA with full-time enrollment is required to retain scholarship. Awarded every year. Award may be used only at sponsoring institution.
Contact: Jennifer Sparrow, Scholarship Coordinator, jsparrow@wppost.depaul.edu.

1536   John Carroll Grant

John Carroll University
20700 North Park Boulevard
Cleveland, OH 44118
(216) 397-4248
Maximum award: $5,000
Deadline: March 1
College level: Applicants accepted for admission
Criteria: Selection is based upon financial need. FAFSA is required. Minimum 2.0 GPA and full-time enrollment are required to retain scholarship. Awarded every year. Award may be used only at sponsoring institution.
Contact: Office of Admissions.

1537   John Carroll Scholarship

John Carroll University
20700 North Park Boulevard
Cleveland, OH 44118
(216) 397-4248
Maximum award: $5,000
Deadline: March 1
College level: Freshman, Transfers
Criteria: Applicant must have a minimum 3.0 GPA. Selection is based upon academic merit and financial need. FAFSA is required. Minimum 2.5 GPA and full-time enrollment are required to retain scholarship. Awarded every year. Award may be used only at sponsoring institution.
Contact: Office of Admission.

1538   John Henry Cardinal Newman Scholarship

Kansas Newman College
3100 McCormick Avenue
Wichita, KS 67213
(316) 942-4291
Average award: Full tuition
Number of awards: 3
Deadline: March 1
College level: Freshman
Criteria: Applicant must have a minimum 3.8 GPA (or minimum combined SAT 1 score of 1370), essay, community involvement, and letter of recommendation. Finalists must have on-campus interview. Renewable if recipient maintains 3.4 GPA. Awarded every year. Award may be used only at sponsoring institution.
Contact: Marla McClure, Director of Financial Aid, (316) 942-4291, extension 103, mcclurem@ksnewman.edu.

1539   Josephine C. Connelly Scholarship

Gwynedd-Mercy College
Sumneytown Pike
Gwynedd Valley, PA 19437
(215) 641-5570
Average award: $4,000
Maximum award: $9,000
Minimum award: $1,000
Number of awards: 73
Deadline: March 15
College level: Freshman, Transfers
Criteria: Applicant must be enrolled full time in degree-seeking program and be highly motivated. Selection is based upon academic achievement and participation in community or school activities. Scholarship is renewable. Awarded every year. Award may be used only at sponsoring institution.
Contact: Sr. Barbara A. Kaufman, Director of Student Financial Aid.

1540   Junior College Honors Scholarship

The University of Alabama
Box 870162
Tuscaloosa, AL 35487-0162
(205) 348-6756
Average award: $2,470
Number of awards: 5
Deadline: March
College level: Junior
Criteria: Applicant must be a transfer student from a junior college in Alabama with a minimum 3.5 GPA. Minimum 3.0 GPA is required to retain scholarship. Awarded every year. Award may be used only at sponsoring institution.
Contact: Molly Lawrence, Director of Financial Aid.

1541   Junior College Scholarship

Birmingham-Southern College
Arkadelphia Road
Birmingham, AL 35254
(205) 226-4688
Average award: $6,000
Deadline: February 24
College level: Junior Transfers
Criteria: Selection is based upon academic record, available standardized test scores, and recommendations. Renewable for senior year. Awarded every year. Award may be used only at sponsoring institution.
Contact: Admissions Office, (800) 523-5793, extension 4696.

1542   Junior College Transfer Scholarship

Jacksonville State University
Jacksonville, AL 36265-9982
(205) 782-5006
Average award: Full tuition
Deadline: May 15
College level: Transfers
Criteria: Selection is made by the presidents of junior colleges in Alabama. Awarded every year. Award may be used only at sponsoring institution.
Contact: Student Financial Aid Office.

1543   KARE Scholarship

Kent State University
P.O. Box 5190
Kent, OH 44242-0001
(216) 672-2972
Average award: Comprehensive tuition
Deadline: April 1
College level: Freshman, Sophomore, Junior, Senior
Criteria: Applicant must have a minimum cumulative GPA of 3.0. Selection is based upon strong academic credentials, exemplary leadership qualities, and school and community involvement. Minimum 2.0 GPA is required to retain scholarship. Awarded every year. Award may be used only at sponsoring institution.
Contact: Theodore Hallenbeck, Director of Financial Aid, 103 Michael Schwartz Center.

1544 Kelso-Battle Scholarship

Ferris State University
901 South State Street
Big Rapids, MI 49307
(616) 592-2110
Average award: $4,000
Number of awards: 5
Deadline: March 1
College level: Freshman
Majors/Fields: Actuarial science, applied mathematics, biotechnology, computer information systems, engineering, engineering technology, industrial chemistry, industrial environmental health management, pre-engineering, technology
Criteria: Applicant must have a minimum 3.5 GPA and a minimum composite ACT score of 26 and demonstrate financial need. FAFSA is required. Recipient must maintain a minimum 3.25 GPA and full-time enrollment to retain scholarship for up to four years. Awarded every year. Award may be used only at sponsoring institution.
Contact: Dennis Batt, Interim Director of Scholarships and Financial Aid, Office of Scholarships and Financial Aid, 420 Oak Street, Prakken 104, Big Rapids, MI 49307-2020.

1545 Kentucky Young Woman of the Year Scholarship

Campbellsville University
Office of Financial Aid
200 West College Street
Campbellsville, KY 42718
(502) 465-8158
Maximum award: Full tuition
Deadline: April 1 (priority)
College level: Freshman
Criteria: Applicant must be a first-time, full-time freshman, have a minimum 3.0 GPA, and be one of the following: winner, first runner-up, second runner-up, or scholastic winner in a county, regional, or state Young Woman of the Year competition. FAFSA is required. Awarded every year. Award may be used only at sponsoring institution.
Contact: Director of Financial Aid.

1546 Key Award

Elmira College
One Park Place
Elmira, NY 14901
(607) 735-1724, (607) 735-1718 (fax)
admissions@elmira.edu
www.elmira.edu
Average award: $5,000
Number of awards: 10
Deadline: March 1
College level: High school junior
Criteria: Applicant must rank in top tenth of secondary or prep school junior class, demonstrate school and community leadership, and be accepted for full-time enrollment. Renewable if recipient maintains minimum 3.0 GPA. Awarded every year. Award may be used only at sponsoring institution.
Contact: Dean of Admissions, admissions@elmira.edu.

1547 Keystone Scholarship

Columbia College
1001 Rogers Street
Columbia, MO 65216
(800) 231-2391
Average award: Half tuition
Number of awards: 24
Deadline: March 15 (priority)
College level: Junior
Criteria: Applicant must have a minimum 3.4 GPA, have completed 60-89.9 credit hours (with the most recent 30 credits earned at Columbia Coll and not including ENG 100 or 104 or MATH 105), and submit school's financial aid form. Financial need is not considered. Renewable as a Capstone Scholarship. Awarded every year. Award may be used only at sponsoring institution.
Contact: Financial Aid, (800) 231-2391, extension 7361.

1548 Kleberg First National Bank Honors Scholarship

Texas A&M University–Kingsville
Scholarships
Box 116
Kingsville, TX 78363
(512) 593-3907, (512) 593-2991 (fax)
http://www.tamuk.edu
Maximum award: $5,000
Number of awards: 1
Deadline: March 3
College level: Freshman
Criteria: Selection is based upon academic record. Financial need is not considered. Minimum 3.5 GPA is required to retain scholarship. Awarded every year. Award may be used only at sponsoring institution.
Contact: Laura Knippers, Counselor.

1549 Laut Scholarship

Wheeling Jesuit University
316 Washington Avenue
Wheeling, WV 26003
(304) 243-2304
http://www.wju.edu/
Average award: Half tuition
Maximum award: Full tuition
Number of awards: 8
Deadline: February
College level: Freshman
Criteria: Selection is based upon competition which includes essay and group interview. Participation is by invitation. Six minimum awards and two maximum awards are given. Satisfactory academic progress is required to retain scholarship. Awarded every year. Award may be used only at sponsoring institution.
Contact: Admissions Office.

1550 Lawrence Tech Scholarship

Lawrence Technological University
21000 West Ten Mile Road
Southfield, MI 48075
(810) 204-2120
Average award: Full tuition and fees
Number of awards: 45
Deadline: March 1
College level: Freshman
Criteria: Applicant must have a minimum 3.5 GPA, rank in top 20% of class, and have a minimum composite ACT score of 25. Minimum 3.0 GPA is required to retain scholarship. Awarded every year. Award may be used only at sponsoring institution.
Contact: Paul F. Kinder, Director of Financial Aid.

1551 Leader Honor Scholarship

Wilmington College
Pyle Center Box 1325
Wilmington, OH 45177
(800) 341-9318, (513) 382-7077 (fax)
admission@wilmington.edu
http://www.wilmington.edu
Average award: $7,000
Number of awards: 25
Deadline: February 1
College level: Freshman
Criteria: Applicant must have a minimum 3.0 GPA and either rank in top two-tenths of class or have a minimum composite ACT score of 25 (combined SAT I score of 1050). Selection is based upon academic record, leadership ability, and on-campus testing. Recipient must maintain a minimum 3.3 GPA and participate in campus organizations to retain scholarship. Awarded every year. Award may be used only at sponsoring institution.
Contact: Financial Aid Office, Pyle Center Box 1184.

1552   Leadership Award

Bradford College
320 South Main Street
Haverhill, MA 01835
(508) 372-7161, (508) 372-5240 (fax)
bradcoll@aol.com
http://bradford.edu
Average award: $4,000
Maximum award: $5,000
Minimum award: $1,000
Number of awards: 25
Deadline: None
College level: Freshman, Sophomore, Junior, Senior
Criteria: Selection is based upon personal character and leadership in school/community activities. Scholarship is renewable. Awarded every year. Award may be used only at sponsoring institution.
Contact: Scholarships.

1553   Leadership Award

Lebanon Valley College
101 North College Avenue
Annville, PA 17003
(800) 445-6181, (717) 867-6026 (fax)
admiss@lvc.edu
http://www.lvc.edu
Minimum award: One-third tuition
Number of awards: 83
Deadline: None
College level: Freshman
Criteria: Applicant must rank in top fifth of class. Minimum 2.75 GPA is required to retain scholarship. Awarded every year. Award may be used only at sponsoring institution.
Contact: Bill Brown, Dean of Admissions/Financial Aid.

1554   Leadership Award

Mount Olive College
634 Henderson Street
Mount Olive, NC 28365
(919) 658-2502
Maximum award: $3,000
Deadline: None
College level: Freshman
Criteria: Applicant must have a minimum 2.5 GPA, have a minimum combined SAT I score of 800 (composite ACT score of 18), and be accepted for admission. Applicant must have participated in at least four extra-curricular activities, with a leadership role in at least one. Renewable for up to four years if recipient completes at least 30 semester hours per year, maintains a minimum 2.3 GPA, and satisfies requirements of leadership program. Awarded every year. Award may be used only at sponsoring institution.
Contact: Tim Woodard, Director of Admissions.

1555   Leadership Award

Spalding University
851 South Fourth Street
Louisville, KY 40203
(502) 585-9911
Maximum award: Half tuition
Deadline: March 1 (priority)
College level: Freshman, Sophomore, Junior, Senior, Transfers
Criteria: Applicant must have a minimum 3.0 GPA and a composite ACT score of 20-26, list of leadership activities, personal essay, three letters of recommendation, and be accepted for full-time enrollment. Scholarship is renewable. Awarded every year. Award may be used only at sponsoring institution.
Contact: Janice White Russell, Assistant Director of Financial Aid and Scholarship Coordinator, (502) 585-9911, extension 242.

1556   Leadership Award

William Woods University
200 West 12th Street
Fulton, MO 65251-1098
(573) 592-4232, (573) 592-1146 (fax)
http://www.wmwoods.edu
Maximum award: $2,500
Deadline: February 1
College level: Freshman
Criteria: Applicant must rank in top half of graduating class. Selection is based upon academic acheivement, community involvement, leadership skills, honors, and awards. On-campus interview required. Recipient must reapply, maintain a minimum 2.75 GPA, and participate in campus activities to retain scholarship. Awarded every year. Award may be used only at sponsoring institution.
Contact: Laura L. Archuleta, Director for Student Financial Aid, larchule@iris.wmwoods.edu.

1557   Leadership Awards

University of Alberta
Edmonton, Alberta, CN T6G 2M7
(403) 492-3111
Maximum award: $5,000
Number of awards: 80
Deadline: March 15
College level: Freshman, Transfers
Criteria: Applicant must be involved in extracurricular or community activities in which leadership skills are demonstrated and have achieved superior academic standing. Award may be used only at sponsoring institution.
Contact: Student Awards Office, 103 Administration Building, Edmonton, AB T6G 2M7, (403) 492-3221.

1558   Leadership Merit Grant

Saint Vincent College
Admissions and Financial Aid
Latrobe, PA 15650-2690
(412) 537-4540, (412) 537-4554 (fax)
info@stvincent.edu
http://www.stvincent.edu
Maximum award: $2,500
Number of awards: 72
Deadline: March 1
College level: Freshman
Criteria: Applicant must submit resume of extracurricular activities and three recommendations from community leaders, counselors, or teachers and be accepted for admission as a full-time student. Renewable if recipient reapplies and maintains GPA. Awarded every year. Award may be used only at sponsoring institution.
Contact: Rev. Earl Henry, Dean of Admission and Financial Aid, 300 Fraser Purchase Road, Latrobe, PA 15650.

1559   Leadership Scholarship

Jacksonville State University
Jacksonville, AL 36265-9982
(205) 782-5006
Average award: Full tuition
Deadline: March 15
College level: Freshman, Sophomore, Junior, Senior
Criteria: Selection is based upon academic record and extracurricular activities. Awarded every year. Award may be used only at sponsoring institution.
Contact: Student Financial Aid Office.

1560 Leadership Scholarship

University of Judaism
15600 Mulholland Drive
Los Angeles, CA 90077
(310) 476-9777
Average award: Three-quarters tuition
Deadline: March 1
College level: Freshman, Transfers
Criteria: Applicant must have a minimum unweighted 3.2 GPA and demonstrate a commitment to academic achievement and community service through leadership in camp, community, congregation, school, or youth group. Scholarship application and two recommendations are required. Recipient must maintain a minimum 3.0 GPA and continue leadership activities to retain scholarship. Awarded every year. Award may be used only at sponsoring institution.
Contact: Tamara Greenebaum, Dean of Admissions.

1561 Leadership Scholarship

Loyola Marymount University
7900 Loyola Boulevard
Los Angeles, CA 90045-8350
(310) 338-2753, (310) 338-2793 (fax)
http://www.lmu.edu
Average award: $6,000
Number of awards: 20
College level: Freshman
Criteria: Applicant must have an excellent academic record and demonstrate exceptional leadership. Preference is given to applicants from disadvantaged backgrounds. Renewable for four years. Awarded every year. Award may be used only at sponsoring institution.
Contact: Financial Aid Office.

1562 Leadership Service Grant

Bluffton College
280 West College Avenue
Bluffton, OH 45817
(419) 358-3257, (419) 358-3232 (fax)
admissions@bluffton.edu
http://www.bluffton.edu
Maximum award: $3,000
Number of awards: 40
Deadline: None
College level: Freshman
Criteria: Applicant must rank in top half of class and have made contributions in co-curricular and service activities. Scholarship is renewable. Awarded every year. Award may be used only at sponsoring institution.
Contact: Dan Parent, Admissions Counselor, (419) 358-3250, parentd@bluffton.edu.

1563 Leadership/Special Achievement Scholarship

Queens College
1900 Selwyn Avenue
Charlotte, NC 28274
(704) 337-2212, 800 849-0202, (704) 337-2403 (fax)
cas@rex.queens.edu
http://www.queens.edu
Maximum award: $5,000
Deadline: None
College level: Freshman
Criteria: Renewable for up to four years. Awarded every year. Award may be used only at sponsoring institution.
Contact: Admissions Office.

1564 License to Learn Scholarship

Auburn University
Auburn University, AL 36849
(334) 844-4723
Average award: $2,100
Deadline: December 15
College level: Freshman
Criteria: Applican must be an Alabama resident. Applicant must have a minimum 3.5 GPA and minimum combined SAT I score of 1210 (composite ACT score of 29). Minimum "B" grade average is required for renewal. Awarded every year. Award may be used only at sponsoring institution.
Contact: Mary Lynn Saidla, Assistant Director for Scholarships.

1565 Lions Club, Grand Junction Scholarship

Mesa State College
Financial Aid Department
P.O. Box 2647
Grand Junction, CO 81502
(970) 248-1396
Maximum Award: Tuition and fees
College level: Freshman
Criteria: Applicant must be a graduate of a Mesa County high school, have a minimum 3.0 GPA, be degree-seeking, demonstrate financial need, and must not receive more than $1,000 in scholarships per year in addition to this award. Award is for four years. Awarded only when previous recipient no longer attends school or does not requalify. Award may be used only at sponsoring institution.
Contact: Office of Financial Aid, (970) 248-1376.

1566 Local Young Woman of the Year Scholarship

University of West Alabama
Station Four
Livingston, AL 35470
(205) 652-3400, (205) 652-3522 (fax)
http://www.westal.edu
Average award: Full tuition
Deadline: April 15
College level: Freshman
Criteria: Applicant must have won local Young Woman of the Year competiton. Renewable for up to four years if minimum 3.0 GPA is maintained. Awarded every year. Award may be used only at sponsoring institution.
Contact: Richard Hester, Director of Admissions, (205) 652-9661, extension 352.

1567 Loretta M. Antl Scholarship

Kent State University
P.O. Box 5190
Kent, OH 44242-0001
(216) 672-2972
Average award: $2,500
Deadline: April 1
College level: Freshman, Sophomore, Junior, Senior
Criteria: Applicant must have minimum cumulative GPA of 2.5. Minimum 2.0 GPA is required to retain scholarship. Awarded every year. Award may be used only at sponsoring institution.
Contact: Theodore Hallenbeck, Director of Financial Aid, 103 Michael Schwartz Center.

1568 Louisiana State Board of Trustees Academic Scholarship

Nicholls State University
P.O. Box 2005 NSU
Thibodaux, LA 70310
(504) 448-4048
Average award: $4,497
Number of awards: 25
Deadline: January 1
College level: Freshman
Criteria: Applicant must have a minimum 3.0 GPA and a minimum composite ACT score of 25, be graduating from an accredited Louisiana school, and be a resident of Louisiana. Recipient must maintain a minimum 3.0 GPA and full-time enrollment to retain scholarship. Awarded every year. Award may be used only at sponsoring institution.
Contact: Tania Johnson, University Scholarship Coordinator, (504) 448-4411.

1569 Lucy Hanes Chatham Scholarship

Salem College
P.O. Box 10548
Winston-Salem, NC 27108
(910) 721-2808
Average award: $10,000
Number of awards: 2
College level: Freshman
Criteria: Applicant must be a woman, have a superior academic record, and demonstrate leadership, responsibility, and concern for others. Selection is also based upon creativity, initiative, motivation, resourcefulness, and vigor. Finalists are invited for competition during Scholarship Weekend. Recipient must maintain a minimum 3.0 GPA and remain a full-time resident student to retain scholarship. Awarded every year. Award may be used only at sponsoring institution.
Contact: Bruce Blackman, Director of Financial Aid.

1570 Manley Menard Scholarship

Indiana University Northwest
3400 Broadway
Gary, IN 46408
(219) 980-6777, (219) 981-4219 (fax)
wlee@iunhawl.iun.indiana.edu
Maximum award: $2,500
Number of awards: 1
Deadline: March 15
College level: Freshman
Criteria: Selection is based upon academic achievement and potential for college success. Scholarship is renewable. Awarded every year. Award may be used only at sponsoring institution.
Contact: William D. Lee, Director of Admissions and Financial Aids, (219) 980-6991.

1571 Marquette Distinguished Scholars

Marquette University
P.O. Box 1881
Milwaukee, WI 53201-1881
(414) 288-7302, (414) 288-3764 (fax)
go2marquette@vms.csd.mu.edu
http://www.mu.edu
Average award: Full tuition
Number of awards: 5
Deadline: February 1
College level: Freshman
Criteria: Applicant must rank in the top 5% of class and have a minimum composite ACT score of 30 or combined SAT I score of 1300. Semifinalists are interviewed by a selection committee. Minimum 3.0 GPA and full-time enrollment are required to retain scholarship. Awarded every year. Award may be used only at sponsoring institution.
Contact: Carlos Garces, Senior Assistant Director of Admissions.

1572 Marquis Scholarship

Lafayette College
Easton, PA 18042-1770
(610) 250-5055, (610) 250-5355 (fax)
mccartyb@lafayette.edu
http://www.lafayette.edu/info/finaid
Maximum award: $27,150
Maximum number of awards: 55
Minimum number of awards: 45
Deadline: January 1 (admissions); February 15 (financial aid)
College level: Freshman
Criteria: Selection is based upon academic record, GPA, class rank, standardized test scores, and involvement in school, community, or fine arts programs. Renewable for up to four years of undergraduate study. Awarded every year. Award may be used only at sponsoring institution.
Contact: Barry McCarty, Director of Student Financial Aid, 107 Markle Hall, Easton, PA 18042-1777, mccartyb@lafayette.edu.

1573 Martin L. King Scholarship

Saint Paul's College
406 Windsor Avenue
Lawrenceville, VA 23868
(804) 848-4505
Average award: $5,000
Number of awards: 1
Deadline: None
College level: Sophomore, Junior, Senior, Graduate
Criteria: Applicant must be involved in college and community and demonstrate financial need. Minimum 3.0 GPA is required to retain scholarship. Award may be used only at sponsoring institution.
Contact: Samuel L. Wade, J.D., Director of Financial Aid.

1574 Martin Luther King Jr. Grant

Long Island University, C.W. Post Campus
Route 25A
Brookville, NY 11548
(516) 299-2338, (516) 299-2137 (fax)
admissions@collegehall.liunet.edu
http://www.liunet.edu
Maximum award: $3,700
Deadline: May 15
College level: Freshman, Sophomore, Junior, Senior
Criteria: Applicant must be economically disadvantaged and enrolled full time. Freshman applicant must have a minimum 85 grade average and minimum combined SAT I score of 900. Upperclass applicant must have a minimum 3.0 GPA. Two awarded every year. Award may be used only at sponsoring institution.
Contact: Financial Aid Office, 720 Northern Boulevard, Brookville, NY 11548.

1575 Martin Luther King Jr. Scholarship

Emory University
1380 Oxford Road, NE
Atlanta, GA 30322
(404) 727-6039
Average award: Full tuition, fees, room, board, and any additional need
Deadline: November 15
College level: Freshman
Criteria: Applicant must be a graduate of an Atlanta public school and be nominated by the principal. Awarded to applicant whose qualities of mind and spirit promise outstanding contributions to society. PROFILE is recommended. Awarded every year. Award may be used only at sponsoring institution.
Contact: Office of Admissions, 200 Boisfeuillet Jones Center, Atlanta, GA 30322-1950, (404) 727-6036, (800) 727-6036.

1576 Master's Scholar Award

The Master's College
21726 Placerita Canyon Road
Santa Clarita, CA 91321-1200
(805) 259-3540, (805) 288-1037 (fax)
Average award: Half tuition
Number of awards: 10
College level: Sophomore, Junior, Senior
Criteria: Applicant must have a minimum 3.75 GPA. Selection is based upon excellence in academics, character, integrity, and leadership abilities. Financial need is not considered. Minimum 3.75 GPA and reapplication required for renewal. Awarded every year. Award may be used only at sponsoring institution.
Contact: Timothy C. Wiegert, Associate Director of Enrollment, (800) 568-6248, extension 450.

1577 Maytag Scholarship Program

Maytag Corporation Foundation
403 West 4th Street N
Newton, IA 50208
(515) 791-6357, (515) 791-8376 (fax)
Maximum award: $2,000
Maximum number of awards: 30
Minimum number of awards: 25
Deadline: January 2
College level: Freshman
Criteria: Applicant must be a child of a Maytag Corportation employee and take the PSAT/NMSQT in the fall of his or her junior year in high school. Renewable if recipient maintains good grades. Awarded every year.
Contact: Janis C. Cooper, Director, Foundation Programs, (515) 791-8357.

1578 McGill University Scholarship

McGill University
845 Sherbrooke Street West
Montreal, Quebec, CN H3A 2T5
(514) 398-4455
Maximum award: $7,000
Deadline: January 15 (international students); March 15 (Canadian students)
College level: Freshman, Sophomore, Junior, Senior, Graduate
Criteria: Applicants do not apply for individual awards. One application for all awards is submitted with the admissions application. Continuing students are automatically considered based upon high academic achievement. Applicant should rank in the top five percent of class. Scholarship is renewable. Awarded every year. Award may be used only at sponsoring institution.
Contact: Scholarships, Office of Admissions, 847 Sherbrooke Street West, Montreal, Quebec, CN H3A 3N6.

1579 McWane Foundation Scholarship

Auburn University
Auburn University, AL 36849
(334) 844-4723
Average award: $6,000
Number of awards: 1
Deadline: December 15
College level: Freshman
Criteria: Applicant must have a minimum 3.5 GPA and minimum combined SAT I score of 1210 (composite ACT score of 29). Minimum "B" grade average is required for renewal. Awarded every year. Award may be used only at sponsoring institution.
Contact: Mary Lynn Saidla, Assistant Director for Scholarships.

1580 McWane Honors Award

Birmingham-Southern College
Arkadelphia Road
Birmingham, AL 35254
(205) 226-4688
Average award: Full tuition plus $10,000 stipend
Number of awards: 1
Deadline: January 5
College level: Freshman
Criteria: Applicant should rank in top 5% of class, have a composite ACT score of 28-36 (combined SAT I score of 1150-1400), and have leadership ability. Selection is based upon academic qualifications. Minimum 3.4 GPA is required to retain scholarship. Awarded every year. Award may be used only at sponsoring institution.
Contact: Forrest Stuart, Interim Director of Financial Aid Services.

1581 Mecklenburg Scholarship

Queens College
1900 Selwyn Avenue
Charlotte, NC 28274
(704) 337-2212, 800 849-0202, (704) 337-2403 (fax)
cas@rex.queens.edu
http://www.queens.edu
Average award: Full tuition
Number of awards: 3
Deadline: January 15
College level: Freshman
Criteria: Applicant must be a graduate of Charlotte-Mecklenburg public or private school. Selection is based upon academic achievement, leadership in school activities and organizations, and service to community and school. Application is required. Awarded every year. Award may be used only at sponsoring institution.
Contact: Admissions Office.

1582 Medalist Scholarship

Ohio State University–Columbus
Third Floor Lincoln Tower
1800 Cannon Drive
Columbus, OH 43210-1200
(614) 292-3980
Average award: Full in-state tuition
Deadline: January 15
College level: Freshman
Criteria: Applicant must rank in the top three percent of class and have a minimum composite ACT score of 29 or combined SAT I score of 1250. Competitive selection process begins in March of applicant's senior year. Applicant must not be a National Merit or National Achievment Scholar. Minimum 3.2 GPA and satisfactory academic progress are required to retain scholarship. Awarded every year. Award may be used only at sponsoring institution.
Contact: Mary Haldane, Director of Financial Aid.

1583 Medallion Scholarship

Western Michigan University
Kalamazoo, MI 49008
(616) 387-6012, (616) 387-6012 (fax)
http://www.wmich.edu
Maximum award: $6,250
Deadline: January 10
College level: Freshman
Criteria: Applicant must have a minimum 3.7 GPA, or a minimum 3.5 GPA and a minimum composite ACT score of 30. Minimum 3.25 GPA and at least 24 credits per year are required to retain scholarship. Awarded every year. Award may be used only at sponsoring institution.
Contact: Christopher Trembley, Assistant Director of Admissions, (616) 387-2000, ask-wmu@wmich.edu.

1584 Memorial Honors Scholarship

Hofstra University
126 Memorial Hall
Hempstead, NY 11550
(516) 463-6677
Maximum award: $7,500
Deadline: February 15
College level: Freshman
Criteria: Applicant must rank in the top 30% of class and have a minimum combined SAT I score of 1380 or composite ACT score of 31. Minimum 3.0 GPA by end of freshman year, 3.1 GPA by end of sophomore year, and 3.2 GPA by end of junior year are required to retain scholarship. Awarded every year. Award may be used only at sponsoring institution.
Contact: Joan Warren, Director of Financial and Academic Records.

1585 Merit and Chancellors Scholarships

Seton Hall University
400 South Orange Avenue
South Orange, NJ 07079-2689
(201) 761-9339
Average award: $7,000
Maximum award: Full tuition and fees
Minimum award: $4,500
Number of awards: 115
Deadline: February 15
College level: Freshman, Sophomore, Junior, Senior
Criteria: Awarded every year. Award may be used only at sponsoring institution.
Contact: Brian T. Lane, Assistant Director of Admissions.

1586 Merit Scholarship

Anna Maria College
Office of Admission
Paxton, MA 01612-1198
(508) 849-3360, (508) 849-3362 (fax)
admission@amc.anna-maria.edu
http://www.anna-maria.edu
Maximum award: $5,000
Deadline: March 1
College level: Freshman, Transfers
Criteria: Applicant must have a minimum combined SAT I score of 1000. Transfer applicant must have a minimum 3.25 GPA. Renewable if recipient maintains a minimum 3.25 GPA and full-time status. Awarded every year. Award may be used only at sponsoring institution.
Contact: Christine L. Soverow, Director of Admission.

1587 Merit Scholarship

Elms College (College of Our Lady of the Elms)
291 Springfield Street
Chicopee, MA 01013
(413) 592-3189, 800 255-ELMS, (413) 594-2781 (fax)
admissions@elms.edu
http://www.crocker.com/nelmscol/
Maximum award: Full tuition
Number of awards: 50
Deadline: None
College level: Freshman
Criteria: Applicant must be a woman, be accepted as a full-time, first-year undergraduate, and have a superior academic record. Applicant must complete the financial aid process. Satisfactory academic progress and full-time status required for renewal. Awarded every year. Award may be used only at sponsoring institution.
Contact: Janet DaSilva, Director, Financial Aid, dasilva@elms.edu.

1588 Merit Scholarship

Hillsdale College
33 East College Street
Hillsdale, MI 49242
(517) 437-7341
Average award: $3,500
Maximum award: Full tuition
Minimum award: $1,000
Number of awards: 50
Deadline: January 15
College level: Freshman
Criteria: Minimum 3.0 GPA and good citizenship required to retain scholarship. Awarded every year. Award may be used only at sponsoring institution.
Contact: Jeffrey S. Lantis, Director of Admissions, (517) 437-7341, extension 2327.

1589 Merit Scholarship

University of Judaism
15600 Mulholland Drive
Los Angeles, CA 90077
(310) 476-9777
Average award: Full tuition
Deadline: March 1
College level: Freshman, Transfers
Criteria: Applicant must have a minimum unweighted 3.6 GPA or a minimum unweighted 3.2 GPA and a minimum combined SAT I score of 1200. Preference is given to first-time freshmen. Minimum 3.2 GPA is required to retain scholarship. Awarded every year. Award may be used only at sponsoring institution.
Contact: Tamara Greenebaum, Dean of Admissions.

1590 Merit Scholarship

Rockford College
5050 East State Street
Rockford, IL 61108-2393
(815) 226-4050
Average award: $4,945
Maximum award: $7,400
Minimum award: $1,500
Number of awards: 105
Deadline: June 1 (recommended)
College level: Freshman, Sophomore, Junior, Senior
Criteria: Minimum 3.0 GPA required to retain scholarship. Awarded every year. Award may be used only at sponsoring institution.
Contact: Chris Moderson, Vice President, Enrollment Management.

1591 Missouri Valley College Scholarship

Missouri Valley College
500 East College
Marshall, MO 65340
(816) 886-6924
Average award: $5,000
Maximum award: $10,000
Minimum award: $1,000
Number of awards: 1,200
Deadline: September 1
College level: Freshman, Sophomore, Junior, Senior
Criteria: Minimum 2.0 GPA is required to retain scholarship. Awarded every year. Award may be used only at sponsoring institution.
Contact: Admissions Office.

1592 Molloy Scholar's Program

Molloy College
1000 Hempstead Avenue, P.O. Box 5002
Rockville Centre, NY 11571-5002
(516) 678-5000
Average award: Full tuition
Deadline: late February (recommended); April 15
College level: Freshman
Criteria: Applicant must be enrolled full-time, have a minimum 93 grade average and minimum combined SAT I score of 1100 (composite ACT score of 27), and file FAFSA. Recipient must maintain a minimum 3.5 GPA, complete at least 12 credit hours per semester, and reapply to retain scholarship. Awarded every year. Award may be used only at sponsoring institution.
Contact: Kathleen Bonnici, Director of Financial Aid.

1593 Monarch Merit Scholarship

Old Dominion University
Hampton Boulevard
Norfolk, VA 23529-0050
(804) 683-3683
Maximum award: $2,500
Number of awards: 45
Deadline: February 15
College level: Freshman
Criteria: Selection is based upon academic achievement and high school participation. Scholarship is renewable. Awarded every year. Award may be used only at sponsoring institution.
Contact: March A. Schutz, Assistant Director of Scholarships.

1594 Monsignor Horigan Scholarship

Bellarmine College
Newburg Road
Louisville, KY 40205
(502) 452-8131, (502) 452-8002 (fax)
http://www.bellarmine.edu
Average award: $3,610
Maximum award: $7,000
Minimum award: $1,500
Number of awards: 170
Deadline: January 15
College level: Freshman
Criteria: Applicant must have a minimum 3.4 GPA, rank in top quarter of class, and have a minimum composite ACT score of 24. Renewable for three years if minimum 3.0 GPA is maintained. Awarded every year. Award may be used only at sponsoring institution.
Contact: Timothy A. Sturgeon, Associate Dean of Admission.

1595 Monsignor McNeill Scholarship

Kansas Newman College
3100 McCormick Avenue
Wichita, KS 67213
(316) 942-4291
Average award: $6,000
Number of awards: 5
Deadline: March 1
College level: Freshman
Criteria: Applicant must have a minimum 3.8 GPA or minimum combined SAT 1 score of 1370, and submit essay, evidence of community involvement, and letter of recommendation. Finalists must have on-campus interview. Renewable if recipient maintains 3.4 GPA. Awarded every year. Award may be used only at sponsoring institution.
Contact: Marla McClure, Director of Financial Aid, (316) 942-4291, extension 103, mcclurem@ksnewman.edu.

1596 Monument Scholarship

Mesa State College
Financial Aid Department
P.O. Box 2647
Grand Junction, CO 81502
(970) 248-1396
Maximum award: Tuition and fees
College level: Freshman
Criteria: Applicant must have an outstanding academic background. Selection is based upon GPA, class rank, and standardized test scores. A minimum index of 120 is recommended. Renewable for up to four years if recipient maintains a minimum 3.2 GPA, completes at least 15 credit hours per semester, and completes 50 hours of community service per year. Awarded every year. Award may be used only at sponsoring institution.
Contact: Office of Admission, P.O. Box 2647, Grand Junction, CO 81502, (970) 248-1376.

1597 Morris Tuition Scholarship

Calumet College of St. Joseph
2400 New York Avenue
Whiting, IN 46394
(219) 473-4213
Average award: $1,475
Maximum award: $4,650
Minimum award: $388
Number of awards: 40
Deadline: March 1
College level: GED recipient
Criteria: Applicant must have a minimum average GED score of 50. Minimum 3.0 GPA is required for renewal. Awarded every year. Award may be used only at sponsoring institution.
Contact: Katrina Foster, Technical Assistant to the Office of Financial Aid, (219) 473-4219.

1598 Morse Scholarship

Rhodes College
2000 North Parkway
Memphis, TN 38112
(901) 843-3700, (901) 843-3719 (fax)
adminfo@rhodes.edu
http://www.rhodes.edu
Average award: $16,400
Number of awards: 5
Deadline: February 1 (priority)
College level: Freshman
Criteria: Selection is based upon merit. Renewable if recipient maintains a minimum 3.25 GPA. Awarded every year. Award may be used only at sponsoring institution.
Contact: David J. Wottle, Dean of Admissions and Financial Aid, (800) 844-5969.

1599 Mount Honors Scholarship

Mount Saint Mary's College
Emmitsburg, MD 21727
(301) 447-5207
Average award: $8,000
Number of awards: 42
Deadline: March 1
College level: Freshman
Criteria: Applicant must rank in top fifth of class and have a minimum combined SAT I score of 1100. Scholarship is renewable. Awarded every year. Award may be used only at sponsoring institution.
Contact: Lawrence J. Riordan, Chairperson of Scholarship Committee, (301) 447-5214.

1600   Mount Merit Grant

Mount Saint Mary's College
Emmitsburg, MD 21727
(301) 447-5207
Average award: $4,300
Maximum award: $5,000
Minimum award: $3,000
Number of awards: 75
Deadline: March 1
College level: Freshman
Criteria: Applicant must rank in top two-fifths of class and have a minimum combined SAT I score of 900. Scholarship is renewable. Awarded every year. Award may be used only at sponsoring institution.
Contact: Lawrence J. Riordan, Chairperson of Scholarship Committee, (301) 447-5214.

1601   Mount Scholarship

Mount Saint Mary's College
Emmitsburg, MD 21727
(301) 447-5207
Average award: $5,400
Maximum award: $7,000
Minimum award: $4,000
Number of awards: 55
Deadline: March 1
College level: Freshman
Criteria: Applicant must rank in top two-fifths of class and have a minimum combined SAT I score of 1000. Scholarship is renewable. Awarded every year. Award may be used only at sponsoring institution.
Contact: Lawrence J. Riordan, Chairperson of Scholarship Committee, (301) 447-5214.

1602   Mount Vernon College Grant and Scholarship

Mount Vernon College
2100 Foxhall Road, NW
Washington, DC 20007
(202) 625-4682
Average award: $6,000
Maximum award: $10,500
Minimum award: $1,500
Number of awards: 175
Deadline: June 1
College level: Freshman, Transfers
Criteria: Minimum 2.0 GPA is required to retain grant. Minimum 3.0 GPA is required to retain scholarship. Awarded every year. Award may be used only at sponsoring institution.
Contact: Anne R. Patrinicola, Director of Student Finance.

1603   Mountaineer Scholarship

West Virginia University
P.O. Box 6004
Morgantown, WV 26506-6004
(800) 344-9881, (304) 293-8763 (fax)
wvuinfo@wvu.edu
http://www.wvu.edu
Maximum award: $7,124
Deadline: January 15
College level: Freshman
Criteria: Applicant must have minimum 2.75 GPA. Renewable if recipient maintains 3.0 GPA. Awarded every year. Award may be used only at sponsoring institution.
Contact: Mary Ward, Scholars Program Coordinator.

1604   Music Scholarship

University of Miami
P.O. Box 248187
Coral Gables, FL 33124-5241
(305) 284-5212
Average award: $8,100
Maximum award: $18,220
Minimum award: $1,500
Number of awards: 207
Deadline: March 1
College level: Freshman, Sophomore, Junior
Majors/Fields: Music
Criteria: Scholarships are based upon entrance audition. Recipient must maintain 2.7 GPA (3.0 in major), and participate in music ensembles. Awarded every year. Award may be used only at sponsoring institution.
Contact: Jo Faulmann, Assistant Dean, School of Music, P.O. Box 248165, Coral Gables, FL 33124, (305) 284-2241, jfalman@umiamivm.ir.miami.edu.

1605   National Achievement Scholarship

University of South Carolina
Office of Admissions
Columbia, SC 29208
(803) 777-4067
Maximum award: $6,000
Number of awards: 5
College level: Freshman
Criteria: Applicant must be named a National Achievement Finalist by the National Merit Scholarship Corporation. Minimum 3.0 GPA required to retain scholarship. Awarded every year. Award may be used only at sponsoring institution.
Contact: Michael Jinnette, Scholarship Coordinator.

1606   National Alumni Association Honors Scholarship

The University of Alabama
Box 870162
Tuscaloosa, AL 35487-0162
(205) 348-6756
Average award: $4,470
Number of awards: 30
Deadline: December 3
College level: Freshman
Criteria: Applicant must have a minimum "B" grade average and minimum composite ACT score of 30 (combined SAT I score of 1240). Minimum 3.0 GPA is required to retain scholarship for four years. Awarded every year. Award may be used only at sponsoring institution.
Contact: Jeanetta Allen, Director of Financial Aid.

1607   National Alumni Association Leadership Award

The University of Alabama
Box 870162
Tuscaloosa, AL 35487-0162
(205) 348-6756
Average award: $2,470
Number of awards: 60
Deadline: December 3
College level: Freshman
Criteria: Applicant must have a minimum "B" grade average, minimum composite ACT score of 24 (combined SAT I score of 980), and demonstrate strong leadership in elected or volunteer positions in school organizations or in activities benefiting community, school, or state. Awarded every year. Award may be used only at sponsoring institution.
Contact: Jeanetta Allen, Director of Financial Aid.

1608 National Alumni Association Past Presidents Crimson Scholarship

The University of Alabama
Box 870162
Tuscaloosa, AL 35487-0162
(205) 348-6756
Maximum award: $7,470
Deadline: December 3
College level: Freshman
Criteria: Applicant must have a minimum 3.9 GPA, rank in top two percent of class, and have a minimum composite ACT score of 32 (combined SAT I score of 1350). Minimum 3.0 GPA is required to retain scholarship for four years. Awarded as funds are available. Award may be used only at sponsoring institution.
Contact: Jeanetta Allen, Director of Financial Aid.

1609 National Alumni Association Sesquicentennial Alumni Honors Scholarship

The University of Alabama
Box 870162
Tuscaloosa, AL 35487-0162
(205) 348-6756
Average award: $2,470
Number of awards: 10
Deadline: December 3
College level: Freshman
Criteria: Applicant must have a minimum "B" grade average and a minimum composite ACT score of 30 (combined SAT I score of 1240). Renewable for up to eight semesters if minimum 3.0 GPA is maintained. Awarded every year. Award may be used only at sponsoring institution.
Contact: National Alumni Association, P.O. Box 1928, Tuscaloosa, AL 35486-1928.

1610 National and Arbor Scholarships

University of Toronto
315 Bloor Street West
Toronto, Ontario, CN M5S 1A3
(416) 978-2190
Maximum award: $5,000
College level: Freshman
Criteria: Applicant must be a Canadian citizen and a winner of the National Book Award. Selection is based upon written application and academic results and references. 20 finalists are invited to selection interviews held in spring. Scholarship is renewable. Awarded every year. Award may be used only at sponsoring institution.
Contact: Admissions and Awards, (416) 978-2771.

1611 National Merit Finalist and SemiFinalist Award

Kansas Newman College
3100 McCormick Avenue
Wichita, KS 67213
(316) 942-4291
Average award: Full tuition
College level: Freshman, Transfers.
Criteria: Applicant must be a National Merit finalist or semifinalist. Transfer applicant must have a minimum 3.6 GPA. Renewable if recipient maintains 3.5 GPA and full-time enrollment. Award may be used only at sponsoring institution.
Contact: Marla McClure, Director of Financial Aid, (316) 942-4291, extension 103, mcclurem@ksnewman.edu.

1612 National Merit Finalist Scholarship

University of Kentucky
100 W.D. Funkhouser Building
Lexington, KY 40506
(606) 257-2000
Maximum award: $6,326
Number of awards: 70-75
Deadline: April 1
College level: Freshman
Criteria: Applicant must be named a National Merit finalist by the NMSC and list University of Kentucky as college choice by deadline. Renewable if recipient maintains minimum 3.3 cumulative GPA and carries minimum 12 credit hours each semester for letter grade. Awarded every year. Award may be used only at sponsoring institution.
Contact: Merit Scholarship Office, 211 Funkhouser Building, Lexington, KY 40506, (606) 257-4198.

1613 National Merit Finalists and Semifinalists Scholarship

University of West Alabama
Station Four
Livingston, AL 35470
(205) 652-3400, (205) 652-3522 (fax)
http://www.westal.edu
Average award: Full tuition
Deadline: April 15
College level: Freshman
Criteria: Applicant must be a National Merit finalist or semifinalist. Renewable for up to four years if minimum 3.0 GPA is maintained. Awarded every year. Award may be used only at sponsoring institution.
Contact: Richard Hester, Director of Admissions, (205) 652-9661, extension 352.

1614 National Merit Scholars Award

Colorado Christian University
180 South Garrison Street
Lakewood, CO 80226
(303) 202-0100, extension 117, (303) 274-7560 (fax)
drwilliams@ccu.edu
http://www.ccu.edu
Average award: $8,160
Number of awards: 1
Deadline: None
College level: Freshman, Sophomore, Junior, Senior
Criteria: Applicant must be enrolled full time. Renewable if recipient maintains minimum 3.85 GPA. Awarded every year. Award may be used only at sponsoring institution.
Contact: Kent McGowan, Director of Financial Aid.

1615 National Merit Scholarship

University of South Carolina
Office of Admissions
Columbia, SC 29208
(803) 777-4067
Maximum award: $6,000
Number of awards: 30
College level: Freshman
Criteria: Applicant must be named a National Merit finalist by the National Merit Scholarship Corporation. Minimum 3.0 GPA required to retain scholarship. Awarded every year. Award may be used only at sponsoring institution.
Contact: Michael Jinnette, Scholarship Coordinator.

1616   National Scholars Program

Eastern Michigan University
Office of Financial Aid
403 Pierce Hall
Ypsilanti, MI 48197
(313) 487-0455, (313) 487-1484 (fax)
financial.aid@mich.edu
http://www.emich.edu
Average award: $4,200
Number of awards: 100
Deadline: February 15
College level: Freshman
Criteria: Applicant must not be a resident of Michigan or Ohio and must have a minimum 3.5 GPA and a combined SAT I score of 1150 or composite ACT score of 25. Minimum 3.3 GPA and 15 credit hours per semester are required to retain scholarship. Awarded every year. Award may be used only at sponsoring institution.
Contact: Cynthia Van Pelt, Assistant Director of Scholarships, Office of Financial Aid.

1617   National Scholarship

Marquette University
P.O. Box 1881
Milwaukee, WI 53201-1881
(414) 288-7302, (414) 288-3764 (fax)
go2marquette@vms.csd.mu.edu
http://www.mu.edu
Average award: $4,000
Deadline: February 1
College level: Freshman, Transfers
Criteria: Selection is based upon academic achievement, class rank, standardized tests, and extracurricular activities. Minimum 2.0 GPA and full-time enrollment are required to retain scholarship. Awarded every year. Award may be used only at sponsoring institution.
Contact: Carlos Garces, Senior Assistant Director of Admissions.

1618   Navy League Scholarship

Navy League of the United States
Scholarship Program
2300 Wilson Boulevard
Arlington, VA 22201-3308
Maximum award: $2,500
Number of awards: 11
Deadline: April 1
Criteria: Aapplicant must be a U.S. citizen and under age 25. Selection is based upon academic performance, extracurricular activities, and financial need. Applicant must be a direct descendant of current, former, retired or deceased Coast Guard, Navy, Marine Corps, or Merchant Marine personnel. Preference is given to applicants planning to major in engineering or science. SASE required. Awarded every year.
Contact: Scholarships, 2300 Wilson Boulevard, Arlington, VA 22201-3308.

1619   NBD Fellows Award

Indiana University Northwest
3400 Broadway
Gary, IN 46408
(219) 980-6777, (219) 981-4219 (fax)
wlee@iunhawl.iun.indiana.edu
Maximum award: Full tuition
Number of awards: 2
Deadline: March 15
College level: Freshman
Criteria: Selection is based upon academic achievement and potential for college succes. Scholarship is renewable. Awarded every year. Award may be used only at sponsoring institution.
Contact: William D. Lee, Director of Admissions and Financial Aids, (219) 980-6991.

1620   Neal and Anne Berte Honors Scholarship

Birmingham-Southern College
Arkadelphia Road
Birmingham, AL 35254
(205) 226-4688
Maximum award: Full tuition
Number of awards: 1
Deadline: January 5
College level: Freshman
Criteria: Applicant should rank in top 5% of class, have a composite ACT score of 28-36 (combined SAT I score of 1150-1400), and have leadership ability. Selection is based upon academic qualifications and financial need. Minimum 3.0 GPA is required to retain scholarship. Awarded every year. Award may be used only at sponsoring institution.
Contact: Forrest Stuart, Interim Director of Financial Aid Services.

1621   Neihardt Scholars Program

Wayne State College
1111 Main Street
Wayne, NE 68787
(402) 375-7230, (800) 228-9972
Average award: Full tuition plus $500 stipend
Deadline: February 15
College level: Freshman, Transfers
Criteria: Applicant must have a minimum 3.3 GPA for six semesters or rank in top quarter of class and have a minimum composite ACT score of 25. Transfer applicant must have a minimum 3.5 GPA and have completed fewer than 40 credit hours. Application is required. Scholarship is renewable. Awarded every year. Award may be used only at sponsoring institution.
Contact: Financial Aid Office.

1622   Non-Resident Academic Scholarship

University of Memphis
Scates Hall 204
Memphis, TN 38152
(901) 678-3213, (901) 678-5621 (fax)
katkinsn@cc.memphis.edu
http://www.memphis.edu/
Average award: Registration fees, out-of-state tuition, and $300 book stipend
Deadline: January 15
College level: Freshman
Criteria: Applicant must have a minimum 3.25 GPA and a minimum composite ACT score of 30 (27 for minority applicant) or combined SAT I score of 1320 (1200 for minority applicant). Minimum 3.0 GPA and a service requirement of 30 hours per year are required to retain scholarship. Awarded every year. Award may be used only at sponsoring institution.
Contact: Katherine Atkinson, Scholarship Coordinator.

1623   Non-Traditional Student Award

Bradford College
320 South Main Street
Haverhill, MA 01835
(508) 372-7161, (508) 372-5240 (fax)
bradcoll@aol.com
http://bradford.edu
Minimum award: Half-tuition
Deadline: None
College level: Students resuming education
Criteria: Selection is based upon achievement and potential. Scholarship is renewable. Awarded every year. Award may be used only at sponsoring institution.
Contact: Scholarships.

1624 Norman V. Peale Scholarship

Northwestern College
101 College Lane
Orange City, IA 51041
(800) 747-4757, 712 737-7130, (712) 737-7164 (fax)
markb@nwciowa.edu
http://www.nwciowa.edu
Average award: $6,000
Number of awards: 8
Deadline: January
College level: Freshman
Criteria: Applicant must have a minimum 3.5 GPA and minimum composite ACT score of 25. Selection is based upon scholarship competition. Minimum 3.0 GPA is required to retain scholarship. Awarded every year. Award may be used only at sponsoring institution.
Contact: Ron DeJong, Director of Admission, rondj@nwciowa.edu.

1625 Northwestern Grant

Northwestern College
101 College Lane
Orange City, IA 51041
(800) 747-4757, 712 737-7130, (712) 737-7164 (fax)
markb@nwciowa.edu
http://www.nwciowa.edu
Maximum award: $2,500
Deadline: None
College level: Freshman, Sophomore, Junior, Senior
Criteria: Awarded to applicant who shows evidence of good character, leadership ability, and financial need. Awarded every year. Award may be used only at sponsoring institution.
Contact: Ron DeJong, Director of Admission, rondj@nwciowa.edu.

1626 Oakland University Merit Scholarship

Oakland University
101 North Foundation Hall
Rochester, MI 48309-4401
(810) 370-3360, (810) 370-4462 (fax)
Average award: $1,766
Maximum award: $2,534
Minimum award: $998
Deadline: February 1
College level: Freshman
Criteria: Minimum 3.25 GPA is required to retain scholarship. Awarded every year. Award may be used only at sponsoring institution.
Contact: Stacy M. Penkala, Assistant Director of Admissions.

1627 Oklahoma State Regents for Higher Education Academic Scholarship/Academic Scholars Award

Oklahoma State University
260 Student Union
Stillwater, OK 74078
(405) 744-7541
Average award: $7,000
Maximum award: $8,500
Minimum award: $6,000
Number of awards: 38
Deadline: July 1
College level: Freshman
Criteria: Applicant must be a National Merit, National Achievement, or National Hispanic scholar designating OSU as school of choice if not a resident of Oklahoma. Oklahoma resident may qualify by scoring in top 99.5 percentile of ACT/SAT I within various identified groups. Award may be used at any Oklahoma post-secondary school. Satisfactory GPA and minimum semester hours are required to retain scholarship. Awarded every year.
Contact: Bob Graalman, Director of University Scholarships.

1628 Oldham Scholars Award

University of Richmond
Richmond, VA 23173
(804) 289-8438
Average award: Full tuition, room and board, travel/study abroad stipend
Number of awards: 5
Deadline: January 1
College level: Freshman, Sophomore, Junior, Senior
Criteria: Applicant must have outstanding character, motivation, and scholarship. Award is highly competitive. Application must be made to Oldham Scholars Committee. Reapplication is required for renewal. Awarded every year. Award may be used only at sponsoring institution.
Contact: Scholars Office, (804) 289-8916.

1629 Opportunity Grant

Grand View College
1200 Grandview Avenue
Des Moines, IA 50316
(515) 263-2820
Average award: $1,350
Maximum award: $2,500
Minimum award: $200
Number of awards: 122
College level: Freshman
Criteria: Applicant must be enrolled full time and demonstrate financial need. Continued financial need is required to retain scholarship. Awarded every year. Award may be used only at sponsoring institution.
Contact: Lori S. Hanson, Director of Admissions, (515) 263-2800.

1630 Opportunity Scholarship

Coppin State College
2500 West North Avenue
Baltimore, MD 21216
(410) 383-5520, (410) 462-4192 (fax)
Maximum award: $3,436
Number of awards: 10
Deadline: August 15
College level: Freshman
Criteria: Applicant must have a minimum combined SAT I score of 1000. Awarded every year. Award may be used only at sponsoring institution.
Contact: Traci D. Northcutt, Assistant Dean of the Honors Division, Honors Division, tnorthcutt@coe.coppin.und.edu.

1631 Oregon Laurels Scholarship

Portland State University
Financial Aid Department
P.O. Box 751
Portland, OR 97207-0751
(503) 725-5270
Average award: $1,800
Maximum award: $2,175
Minimum award: $1,200
Number of awards: 15
Deadline: March 1
College level: Freshman, Sophomore, Junior, Senior
Criteria: Applicant must have a minimum 3.25 GPA. Preference is given to Oregon residents. Minimum 3.0 GPA is required to retain scholarship. Awarded every year. Award may be used only at sponsoring institution.
Contact: Virginia McElroy, Scholarship Coordinator.

1632   Otis A. Singletary Scholarship

University of Kentucky
100 W.D. Funkhouser Building
Lexington, KY 40506
(606) 257-2000
Maximum award: $11,506
Number of awards: 20
Deadline: the first Friday in January
College level: Freshman
Criteria: Applicant must have minimum 3.75 GPA and minimum composite ACT score of 31 (combined SAT score of 1360). Renewable if recipient maintains minimum 3.3 cumulative GPA and carries minimum 12 credit hours per semester for letter grade. Awarded every year. Award may be used only at sponsoring institution.
Contact: Merit Scholarship Office, 211 Funkhouser Building, Lexington, KY 40506-0054, (606) 257-4198.

1633   Outstanding Achievement Scholarship

Valley Forge Christian College
1401 Charlestown Road
Phoenixville, PA 19460
(610) 935-0450, (610) 935-9353 (fax)
Average award: $4,000
Maximum award: $4,352
Minimum award: $1,000
Number of awards: 22
Deadline: May 1
College level: Freshman
Criteria: Applicant must demonstrate achievement in community involvement, ministry, and scholastics. Awarded every year. Award may be used only at sponsoring institution.
Contact: Tim Burns, Director of Admissions.

1634   Outstanding Scholars Awards

Waynesburg College
51 West College Street
Waynesburg, PA 15370
(800) 225-7393, (412) 627-6416 (fax)
admission@waynesburg.edu
http://waynesburg.edu
Average award: Full tuition
Number of awards: 2
Deadline: March 1
College level: Freshman
Criteria: Applicant must rank in top 5% of class. Selection is based upon class rank, on-campus interview, and personal recommendations. Recipient must participate in Honors Program. Minimum 3.2 GPA is required to retain scholarship. Awarded every year. Award may be used only at sponsoring institution.
Contact: Robin Moore, Dean of Admissions, (412) 852-3248.

1635   Outstanding Student Award

University of West Alabama
Station Four
Livingston, AL 35470
(205) 652-3400, (205) 652-3522 (fax)
http://www.westal.edu
Average award: $2,040
Number of awards: 10
Deadline: Early application is recommended.
College level: Transfers
Criteria: Renewable for up to two years. Awarded every year. Award may be used only at sponsoring institution.
Contact: Richard Hester, Director of Admissions, (205) 652-3400, extension 3578, rth@uwamail.westal.edu.

1636   Outstanding Transfer Scholarship

Rochester Institute of Technology
One Lomb Memorial Drive
Rochester, NY 14623
(716) 475-2186
Average award: $3,757
Maximum award: $6,262
Minimum award: $3,131
Number of awards: 50
Deadline: February 15
College level: Transfer student
Criteria: Applicant must have a minimum cumulative 3.2 GPA, have a two-year degree or equivalent, and compete in an on-campus scholarship competition. Minimum "B" grade average is required to retain scholarship. Awarded every year. Award may be used only at sponsoring institution.
Contact: Verna Hazen, Director of Financial Aid.

1637   Palmetto Fellows Scholarship

University of South Carolina
Office of Admissions
Columbia, SC 29208
(803) 777-4067
Maximum award: $5,000
Number of awards: 140
College level: Freshman
Criteria: Applicant must be named a Palmetto Fellows Scholar by the South Carolina Commission on Higher Education. Minimum 3.0 GPA and minimum 24 credit hours per year required to retain scholarship. Award may be used only at sponsoring institution.
Contact: Michael Jinnette, Scholarship Coordinator.

1638   Park Scholarship

North Carolina State University
P.O. Box 7009
Raleigh, NC 27695-7009
(919) 515-3794, (919) 515-8993 (fax)
park_scholars@ncsu.edu
Maximum award: $17,900
Number of awards: 50
College level: Freshman
Criteria: Students are nominated for award by their high school. Renewable if recipient maintains GPA requirement and participates in retreat and leadership course. Awarded every year. Award may be used only at sponsoring institution.
Contact: Laura L. Huntley, Associate Director, Campus Box 7009, Raleigh, NC 27695.

1639   Peer Mentor Scholarship

Portland State University
Financial Aid Department
P.O. Box 751
Portland, OR 97207-0751
(503) 725-5270
Average award: $2,800
Number of awards: 30
College level: Sophomore, Junior
Criteria: Applicant must have a minimum 3.0 GPA and be enrolled full time. Personal interview is required. Recipient must assist faculty teaching Freshman Inquiry courses to retain scholarship. Awarded every year. Award may be used only at sponsoring institution.
Contact: Scholarships, Office of University Studies, (503) 725-5890.

1640 Peggy Gordon Elliott Scholarship

Indiana University Northwest
3400 Broadway
Gary, IN 46408
(219) 980-6777, (219) 981-4219 (fax)
wlee@iunhawl.iun.indiana.edu
Maximum award: Full tuition, fees, books
Number of awards: 1
Deadline: March 15
College level: Freshman
Criteria: Selection is based upon academic achievement and potential for college success. Scholarship is renewable. Awarded every year. Award may be used only at sponsoring institution.
Contact: William D. Lee, Director of Admissions and Financial Aid, (219) 980-6991.

1641 Personal Accomplishment Scholarship

The Master's College
21726 Placerita Canyon Road
Santa Clarita, CA 91321-1200
(805) 259-3540, (805) 288-1037 (fax)
Average award: $3,000
Deadline: Early application is recommended
College level: Freshman
Criteria: Applicant must have a minimum 4.0 GPA for every semester of high school and have a minimum combined SAT I score of 1200 (composite ACT score of 26). Awarded every year. Award may be used only at sponsoring institution.
Contact: Timothy C. Wiegert, Associate Director of Enrollment, (800) 568-4268, extension 450.

1642 Personal Achievement Scholarship

The Master's College
21726 Placerita Canyon Road
Santa Clarita, CA 91321-1200
(805) 259-3540, (805) 288-1037 (fax)
Average award: $2,500
Deadline: Early application is recommended
College level: Freshman
Criteria: Applicant must have a minimum 3.5 GPA and a minimum combined SAT I score of 1110 (composite ACT score of 24), and have been significantly involved in one or more school clubs. Awarded every year. Award may be used only at sponsoring institution.
Contact: Timothy C. Wiegert, Associate Director of Enrollment, (800) 568-4268, extension 450.

1643 Phi Beta Kappa Scholarship

Birmingham-Southern College
Arkadelphia Road
Birmingham, AL 35254
(205) 226-4688
Average award: Full tuition
Number of awards: 7
Deadline: January 5
College level: Freshman
Criteria: Applicant should rank in top 5% of class, have a composite ACT score of 28-36 (combined SAT I score of 1150-1400), and have leadership ability. Selection is based upon academic qualifications. Minimum 3.0 GPA is required to retain scholarship. Awarded every year. Award may be used only at sponsoring institution.
Contact: Forrest Stuart, Interim Director of Financial Aid Services.

1644 Phi Beta Kappa Scholarship

Hofstra University
126 Memorial Hall
Hempstead, NY 11550
(516) 463-6677
Maximum award: $7,500
Deadline: February 15
College level: Freshman
Criteria: Applicant must graduate first in his or her high school class. Minimum 3.0 GPA by end of freshman year, 3.1 GPA by end of sophomore year, and 3.2 GPA by end of junior year are required to retain scholarship. Awarded every year. Award may be used only at sponsoring institution.
Contact: Joan Warren, Director of Financial and Academic Records.

1645 Phi Theta Kappa Directors Scholarship

Benedictine College
1020 North Second Street
Atchison, KS 66002
(913) 367-5340
Maximum award: $7,000
Number of awards: 10
Deadline: April 15
College level: Transfers
Criteria: Applicant must be an active Phi Theta Kappa member, have a minimum 3.5 GPA, submit letter of recommendation, and be accepted for admission. Renewable if recipient maintains 3.5 GPA and PTK membership. Awarded every year. Award may be used only at sponsoring institution.
Contact: Diane Adams, Associate Director of Admissions.

1646 Phi Theta Kappa Scholarship

Beaver College
450 South Easton Road
Glenside, PA 19038-3295
(215) 572-2910, (215) 572-4049 (fax)
admiss@beaver.edu
http://www.beaver.edu
Average award: $6,400
Maximum award: $8,000
Minimum award: $2,000
Number of awards: 15
Deadline: None
College level: Transfers
Criteria: Applicant must be a member of Phi Theta Kappa, be enrolled full time, have completed at least 30 credit hours, and have a minimum 3.5 GPA. Recipient must maintain good academic standing to retain scholarship. Awarded every year. Award may be used only at sponsoring institution.
Contact: Suzanne Allen, Transfer Coordinator.

1647 Phi Theta Kappa Scholarship

Cedar Crest College
100 College Drive
Allentown, PA 18104
(610) 740-3785, (610) 606-4647 (fax)
cccadmis@cedarcrest.edu
www.cedarcrest.edu
Average award: $4,000
Number of awards: 3
Deadline: Rolling
College level: Junior
Criteria: Applicant must have minimum 3.5 GPA, have completed 24 transferable credit hours, and enroll immediately following two-year college. Renewable if recipient maintains minimum 3.0 GPA and completes a minimum of 24 credit hours per year. Awarded every year. Award may be used only at sponsoring institution.
Contact: Judith Neyhart, Vice President for Enrollment Management, Financial Aid Office.

1648   Phi Theta Kappa Scholarship

Marquette University
P.O. Box 1881
Milwaukee, WI 53201-1881
(414) 288-7302, (414) 288-3764 (fax)
go2marquette@vms.csd.mu.edu
http://www.mu.edu
Average award: $3,000
Number of awards: 15
Deadline: May 15 (fall); November 15 (spring)
College level: Transfers from two-year college
Criteria: Selection is based upon academic qualifications, extracurricular activities, leadership, essay, and recommendation from applicant's Phi Theta Kappa advisor. Minimum 3.0 GPA and full-time enrollment are required to retain scholarship. Awarded every year. Award may be used only at sponsoring institution.
Contact: Carlos Garces, Senior Assistant Director of Admissions.

1649   Pickard Scholarship

Ripon College
300 Seward Street
P.O. Box 248
Ripon, WI 54971
(800) 94-RIPON, (414) 748-7243 (fax)
adminfo@mac.ripon.edu
http://www.ripon.edu
Maximum award: $17,000
Number of awards: 9
Deadline: December 1 (early decision), March 1
College level: Freshman
Criteria: Applicant must rank in top 5% of class, have a minimum composite ACT score of 30 (combined SAT I score of 1300), demonstrate strong leadership and community involvement, and be accepted for admission. Renewable if recipient maintains minimum 3.0 GPA in first year, minimum 3.2 GPA in subsequent years. Awarded every year. Award may be used only at sponsoring institution.
Contact: Paul J. Weeks, Vice President and Dean of Admission.

1650   Pillars for Excellence Scholarship

Culver-Stockton College
One College Hill
Canton, MO 63435-1299
(217) 231-6000
Average award: $8,000
Number of awards: 10
Deadline: January 10
College level: Freshman
Criteria: Applicant must have a minimum composite ACT score of 22 (combined SAT I score of 920), and two of the following: minimum 3.6 GPA, rank in top tenth of class, composite ACT score of 26 (combined SAT I score of 1090). Minimum 3.2 GPA is required to retain scholarship. Awarded every year. Award may be used only at sponsoring institution.
Contact: Diane Bozarth, Director of Student Financial Planning, (217) 231-6306.

1651   Pollard Turman Leadership Scholarship

Emory University
1380 Oxford Road, NE
Atlanta, GA 30322
(404) 727-6039
Average award: $2,040
Deadline: November 15
College level: Freshman
Criteria: Awarded to applicant with special leadership potential as demonstrated by sound academic achivement and commitment to excellence and service in civic, school, and other activities. Special consideration is given to residents of the Southeast. Nomination by school or Emory Admission Committee is required. Renewable for four years of undergraduate study. Awarded every year. Award may be used only at sponsoring institution.
Contact: Office of Admissions, 200 Boisfeuillet Jones Center, Atlanta, GA 30322-1950, (404) 727-6036, (800) 727-6036.

1652   President's Achievement Scholarship

Texas A&M University, College Station
College Station, TX 77843-4233
(409) 845-1957
Maximum award: $2,500
Number of awards: 135
Deadline: December 5
College level: Freshman
Criteria: Applicant must have a minimum combined SAT I score of 1050-1190 and rank in the top quarter of class. Academic achievement, rigor of curriculum, extracurricular activities, prizes and awards, leadership, and school recommendations are considered. Renewable if recipient maintains minimum 2.5 GPA. Awarded every year. Award may be used only at sponsoring institution.
Contact: Susanna Finnell, Executive Director of Honors Programs and Academic Scholarships.

1653   President's Award

University of West Alabama
Station Four
Livingston, AL 35470
(205) 652-3400, (205) 652-3522 (fax)
http://www.westal.edu
Average award: $2,040
Number of awards: 15
Deadline: Early application is recommended
College level: Transfers
Criteria: Applicant must have a minimum 3.75 GPA and have completed at least 60 credit hours. Renewable for up to two years. Awarded every year. Award may be used only at sponsoring institution.
Contact: Richard Hester, Director of Admissions, (205) 652-9661, extension 352.

1654   President's Endowed Scholarship

Texas A&M University, College Station
College Station, TX 77843-4233
(409) 845-1957
Average award: $3,000
Number of awards: 200
Deadline: December 5
College level: Freshman
Criteria: Applicant must have a minimum combined SAT I score of 1360 (composite ACT score of 31), or be a National Merit or National Achievement semifinalist. Academic achievement, rigor of curriculum, extracurricular activities, prizes and awards, leadership, and school recommendations are considered. Minimum 3.0 cumulative GPA is required to retain scholarship. Awarded every year. Award may be used only at sponsoring institution.
Contact: Susanna Finnell, Executive Director of Honors Programs and Academic Scholarships.

1655   President's Honor Award

John Carroll University
20700 North Park Boulevard
Cleveland, OH 44118
(216) 397-4248
Maximum award: $5,000
Deadline: March 1
College level: Freshman
Criteria: Applicant must have a minimum 3.5 GPA ("B+" grade average) and strong SAT I/ACT scores. Application is required; FAFSA is recommended. Selection is based upon academic merit. Minimum 3.0 GPA and full-time enrollment are required to retain scholarship. Awarded every year. Award may be used only at sponsoring institution.
Contact: Office of Admission.

1656 President's Leadership Award

Goshen College
1700 South Main Street
Goshen, IN 46526
(219) 535-7523
Average award: Half tuition
Number of awards: 10
Deadline: February 1
College level: Freshman
Criteria: Applicant must have a minimum 3.8 GPA, rank first in class, have a minimum combined SAT I score of 1200 (composite ACT score of 29), or be a National Merit finalist, and demonstrate leadership in church, extracurricular, and volunteer activities. Scholarship is renewable. Awarded every year. Award may be used only at sponsoring institution.
Contact: Walter Schmucker, Director of Student Financial Aid.

1657 President's Leadership Scholarship

University of Central Oklahoma
100 North University
Edmond, OK 73034
(405) 341-2980, extension 2631, (405) 341-7658 (fax)
Average award: $2,000
Maximum award: $3,000
Minimum award: $1,500
Number of awards: 20
Deadline: February 1
College level: Freshman
Criteria: Applicant must be active in three organizations, have a minimum 3.0 GPA, and be enrolled full time. Minimum 3.0 GPA, full-time enrollment, and participation in three campus organizations are required to retain scholarship. Awarded every year. Award may be used only at sponsoring institution.
Contact: Margaret Howell, Scholarship Coordinator.

1658 President's Leadership Scholarship

Marquette University
P.O. Box 1881
Milwaukee, WI 53201-1881
(414) 288-7302, (414) 288-3764 (fax)
go2marquette@vms.csd.mu.edu
http://www.mu.edu
Average award: $3,000
Deadline: February 1
College level: Freshman, Transfers
Criteria: Applicant must have demonstrated leadership ability and involvement in extracurricular activities. Academic achievement and SAT I or ACT scores are also considered. Minimum 2.0 GPA and full-time enrollment are required to retain scholarship. Awarded every year. Award may be used only at sponsoring institution.
Contact: Carlos Garces, Senior Assistant Director of Admissions.

1659 President's Merit Award

Bridgewater College
East College Street
Bridgewater, VA 22812
(540) 828-2501
Average award: $12,505
Number of awards: 17
Deadline: None
College level: Freshman
Criteria: Applicant must rank in top tenth of class. Selection is based upon class rank, standardized test scores, and academic quality of courses. Minimum 3.2 GPA is required to retain scholarship. Awarded every year. Award may be used only at sponsoring institution.
Contact: J. Vern Fairchilds, Jr., Director of Financial Aid, (540) 828-5376, vfairchi@bridgewater.edu.

1660 President's Meritorious Scholarship

Northern State University
1200 South Jay Street
Aberdeen, SD 57401
(605) 626-2640, (605) 626-3022 (fax)
kienows@wolf.northern.edu
http://www.northern.edu
Average award: Four-year full in-state tuition and fees
Number of awards: 4
Deadline: February 1
College level: Freshman
Criteria: Applicant must rank in top tenth of class or have a minimum composite ACT score of 28. Essay, letters of recommendation, and interview are required. Minimum 3.0 GPA required to retain scholarship. Awarded every year. Award may be used only at sponsoring institution.
Contact: Financial Assistance Office.

1661 President's Scholar Scholarship

Auburn University
Auburn University, AL 36849
(334) 844-4723
Average award: $2,100
Deadline: None
College level: Freshman
Criteria: Awarded to National Merit/National Achievement finalists who have received the National Merit/Achievement Award and have designated Auburn U as their first choice institution with National Merit Scholarship Corp. Minimum 3.0 GPA is required for renewal. Awarded every year. Award may be used only at sponsoring institution.
Contact: Mary Lynn Saidla, Assistant Director for Scholarships.

1662 President's Scholarship

Indiana State University
217 North Sixth Street
Terre Haute, IN 47809
(812) 237-2121, (812) 237-8023 (fax)
admisu@amber.indstate.edu
http://www.isu.indstate.edu
Average award: Comprehensive tuition
Number of awards: 15
Deadline: February 1
College level: Freshman
Criteria: Applicant must rank in the top tenth of graduating class. Satisfactory GPA and full-time status are required to retain scholarship. Awarded every year. Award may be used only at sponsoring institution.
Contact: Steve Manuel, Scholarships, Office of Admissions, Terre Haute, IN 47809, (800) 742-0891.

1663 President's Scholarship

Marietta College
Fifth Street
Marietta, OH 45750
(614) 376-4712
Average award: $7,000
Deadline: March 1
College level: Freshman
Criteria: Renewable if minimum 3.0 GPA and continuous full-time enrollment are maintained. Awarded every year. Award may be used only at sponsoring institution.
Contact: James M. Bauer, Associate Dean/Director of Financial Aid.

1664 President's Scholarship

Centre College
600 West Walnut Street
Danville, KY 40422
(606) 238-5350, (606) 238-5373 (fax)
admission@centre.edu
http://www.centre.edu
Average award: Full tuition
Number of awards: 10
Deadline: February 1
College level: Freshman
Criteria: Interview is required. Renewable if recipient maintains good academic standing and minimum 3.2 GPA (GPA requirement increases for subsequent years.) Awarded every year. Award may be used only at sponsoring institution.
Contact: Thomas B. Martin, Dean of Enrollment Management.

1665 President's Scholarship

Pacific Lutheran University
Tacoma, WA 98447
(206) 535-7161
Average award: $5,000
Number of awards: 25
Deadline: January 13
College level: Freshman
Criteria: Applicant must be a U.S. citizen, accepted for admission by January 13, have a minimum 3.8 GPA and a minimum combined SAT I score of 1200 (composite ACT score of 26), and demonstrate outstanding leadership and service. Financial need is not considered. Renewable for three years if minimum 3.3 GPA is maintained. Awarded every year. Award may be used only at sponsoring institution.
Contact: Office of Financial Aid and Scholarships.

1666 President's Scholarship

Philadelphia College of Bible
200 Manor Avenue
Langhorne, PA 19047-2992
(215) 752-5800
Average award: $2,400
Deadline: None
College level: Freshman
Criteria: Applicant must have a minimum 3.5 GPA, have a minimum combined SAT I score of 1100 (composite ACT score of 25), and be a first-time, full-time student. Minimum 3.4 GPA is required to retain scholarship. Awarded every year. Award may be used only at sponsoring institution.
Contact: Travis S. Roy, Financial Aid Administrator.

1667 President's Scholarship

Tri-State University
Angola, IN 46703-0307
(219) 665-4175
Maximum award: $8,000
Deadline: None
College level: Freshman
Criteria: Applicant must rank in top tenth of class and have a minimum combined SAT I score of 1200 (composite ACT score of 29). Minimum 3.2 GPA is required to retain scholarship. Awarded every year. Award may be used only at sponsoring institution.
Contact: Financial Aid Office.

1668 President's Scholarship

Trinity Bible College
50 Sixth Avenue South
Ellendale, ND 58436-7150
Average award: Full tuition
Number of awards: 3
Deadline: March 1
College level: Freshman
Criteria: Applicant must submit ACT scores, application, short essay, transcript, and three letters of reference. On-campus interview and FAFSA are required. Minimum 3.0 GPA is required to retain scholarship. Awarded every year. Award may be used only at sponsoring institution.
Contact: Financial Aid Office, (800) 523-1603.

1669 President's Scholarship

Taylor University
500 West Reade Avenue
Upland, IN 46989
(317) 998-5125, (317) 998-4910 (fax)
admissions@tayloru.edu
http://www.tayloru.edu
Maximum award: $3,000
Deadline: Early application is recommended
College level: Freshman
Criteria: Applicant must rank in top tenth of class and have a minimum combined SAT I score of 1300 (composite ACT score of 29). If high school does not have a ranking system, applicant must have minimum 3.8 GPA. Financial need is considered for maximum award. Transfers are not eligible for this award. Renewable for up to eight semesters if minimum 3.2 GPA is maintained. Awarded every year. Award may be used only at sponsoring institution.
Contact: Tim Nace, Financial Aid Office, (317) 998-5358, tmnace@tayloru.edu.

1670 President's Scholarship

Saint Martin's College
5300 Pacific Avenue, SE
Lacey, WA 98503
(360) 438-4397
Average award: $4,000
Number of awards: 29
Deadline: March 1
College level: Freshman, Sophomore, Junior, Senior
Criteria: Minimum 3.0 GPA is required to retain scholarship. Awarded every year. Award may be used only at sponsoring institution.
Contact: Ron Noborikawa, Director of Financial Aid.

1671 President's Scholarship

Southern Nazarene University
6729 N.W. 39th Expressway
Bethany, OK 73008
(405) 491-6310, (405) 491-6320 (fax)
dlee@snu.edu
Average award: $2,400
Deadline: None
College level: Freshman, Sophomore, Junior, Senior
Criteria: Freshman applicant must have a minimum composite ACT score of 29 (combined SAT I score of 1280) and be enrolled full time. Minimum 3.8 GPA is required to retain scholarship. Awarded every year. Award may be used only at sponsoring institution.
Contact: Diana Lee, Director of Financial Assistance.

1672 President's Scholarship

Holy Names College
3500 Mountain Boulevard
Oakland, CA 94619-1699
(510) 436-1327
Average award: Half tuition
Number of awards: 10
Deadline: March 2
College level: Freshman, Transfers
Criteria: Applicant must have a minimum 3.0 GPA and academic honors, demonstrate community service, and submit separate application and essay. Minimum 3.0 GPA required to retain scholarship. Awarded every year. Award may be used only at sponsoring institution.
Contact: Paula J. Lehrberger, Director of Financial Aid.

1673 Presidential Academic Scholarship

Johnson & Wales University
8 Abbott Park Place
Providence, RI 02903
(401) 598-1000, (401) 598-1040 (fax)
admissions@jwu.edu
http://jwu.edu
Maximum award: $10,000
Deadline: None
College level: Freshman
Criteria: Selection is based upon academic record/transcripts, class rank, and SAT I scores. Fi... ...ot considered. Minimum ... ...ademic progress are re... ...ry year. Award may be

...larship

...PA and minimum com... ...e of 29). Awarded ev... ...ing institution. ...for Scholarships.

...rship

...(priority)
College level: Freshman
Criteria: Applicant must have a minimum 3.5 GPA and minimum composite ACT score of 33 (combined SAT I score of 1350) and be a first-time, full-time freshman. FAFSA is required. Awarded every year. Award may be used only at sponsoring institution.
Contact: Director of Financial Aid.

1676 Presidential Honors Award

State University of New York at Buffalo
Buffalo, NY 14260
(716) 831-2000, (716) 829-2022 (fax)
Average award: $2,000
Maximum award: $3,000
Minimum award: $1,000
College level: Freshman, Sophomore, Junior, Senior
Criteria: Applicant must have a minimum combined SAT I score of 1300, rank in the top seven percent of class, and have an unweighted grade average of 93. Scholarship is renewable. Awarded every year. Award may be used only at sponsoring institution.
Contact: Josephine Capuana, Administrative Director, 214 Talbert Hall, Box 601700, Buffalo, NY 14260-1700, (716) 645-3020.

1677 Presidential Honors Award

Shawnee State University
940 Second Street
Portsmouth, OH 45662-4344
(614) 355-2237
Maximum award: $11,000
Deadline: July 15; early application is recommended
College level: Junior, Senior
Criteria: Applicant must have a minimum 3.25 GPA and have earned associate degree. Scholarship is renewable. Awarded every year. Award may be used only at sponsoring institution.
Contact: Financial Aid Office, (614) 355-2485.

1678 Presidential Honors Scholarship

Birmingham-Southern College
Arkadelphia Road
Birmingham, AL 35254
(205) 226-4688
Maximum award: $2,500
Number of awards: 200
Deadline: January 5
College level: Freshman
Criteria: Applicant should rank in top fifth of class, have a minimum composite ACT score of 26 (combined SAT I score of 1050), and have leadership ability. Selection is based upon academic qualifications. Satisfactory academic progress is required to retain scholarship. Awarded every year. Award may be used only at sponsoring institution.
Contact: Forrest Stuart, Interim Director of Financial Aid Services.

1679 Presidential Honors Scholarship

D'Youville College
320 Porter Avenue
Buffalo, NY 14201
(716) 881-7691
Average award: $3,250
Number of awards: 10
College level: Freshman
Criteria: Renewable if recipient maintains minimum 2.75 GPA. Renewable forup to four years. Awarded every year. Award may be used only at sponsoring institution.
Contact: R.H. Dannecker, Director of Admissions and Financial Aid, (716) 881-7600.

1680 Presidential Honors Scholarship

Texas A&M University–Kingsville
Scholarships
Box 116
Kingsville, TX 78363
(512) 593-3907, (512) 593-2991 (fax)
http://www.tamuk.edu
Maximum award: $5,000
Number of awards: No limit
Deadline: March 3
College level: Freshman
Criteria: Applicant must have a minimum 3.0 GPA, rank in the top quarter of graduating class, and have minimum combined SAT I score of 1280 (ACT score of 29). Renewable if recipient maintains a minimum 3.5 GPA. Award may be used only at sponsoring institution.
Contact: Laura Knipper, Counselor.

1681 Presidential Honor Scholarship

Waynesburg College
51 West College Street
Waynesburg, PA 15370
(800) 225-7393, (412) 627-6416 (fax)
admission@waynesburg.edu
http://waynesburg.edu
Average award: $4,000
Number of awards: No limit
Deadline: None
College level: Freshman
Criteria: Applicant must rank in top tenth of class and have a minimum combined SAT I score of 1180 (composite ACT score of 26) or be class valedictorian. Recipient must participate in Honors Program. Minimum 3.25 GPA is required to retain scholarship. Awarded every year. Award may be used only at sponsoring institution.
Contact: Robin Moord, Dean of Admissions, (412) 852-3248, 800 225-7393.

1682 Presidential Merit Scholarship

California Baptist College
8432 Magnolia Avenue
Riverside, CA 92504
(909) 689-5771
Maximum award: $7,000
Maximum number of awards: 20
Minimum number of awards: 12
Deadline: February 1
College level: Freshman
Criteria: Applicant must have a minimum 3.5 GPA and minimum combined SAT I score of 1000 (composite ACT score of 23). Scholarship is renewable. Awarded every year. Award may be used only at sponsoring institution.
Contact: Phillip Martinez, Director of Admissions/Financial Aid.

1683 Presidential Opportunity Scholarship

Auburn University
Auburn University, AL 36849
(334) 844-4723
Average award: $2,100
Deadline: December 15
College level: Freshman
Criteria: Applicant must have a minimum 3.5 GPA and minimum combined SAT I score of 1210 (composite ACT score of 29). Applicant must be a minority student. Scholarship is renewable. Awarded every year. Award may be used only at sponsoring institution.
Contact: Mary Lynn Saidla, Assistant Director for Scholarships.

1684 Presidential Scholar Award

Southern Illinois University at Carbondale
Carbondale, IL 62901
(618) 453-5351
Maximum award: $21,700
Minimum award: Tuition plus $1,000
Number of awards: 9
Deadline: February 1
College level: Freshman
Criteria: Applicant must rank in top two percent of class and have a composite ACT score in 98th percentile nationwide. Renewable for up to four years if minimum 3.5 GPA is maintained. Awarded every year. Award may be used only at sponsoring institution.
Contact: Tammy Cavaretta, Assistant Director, New Student Admission Services, Carbondale, IL 62901-4710, (618) 536-4405.

1685 Presidential Scholars Award

William Woods University
200 West 12th Street
Fulton, MO 65251-1098
(573) 592-4232, (573) 592-1146 (fax)
http://www.wmwoods.edu
Maximum award: $5,000
Deadline: February 1
College level: Freshman
Criteria: Applicant must rank in top 30% of graduating class, have a minimum composite ACT score of 26 (combined SAT I score of 1180), submit essay, and have on-campus interview. Finalists for the Amy Shelton McNutt Scholarship will be considered for this award. Recipient must reapply, be involved in campus activities, and maintain a minimum 3.5 GPA to retain scholarship. Awarded every year. Award may be used only at sponsoring institution.
Contact: Laura L. Archuleta, Director for Student Financial Aid, larchule@iris.wmwoods.edu.

1686 Presidential Scholars Award

Chapman University
333 North Glassell Street
Orange, CA 92866
(714) 997-6741, (714) 997-6743 (fax)
http://www.chapman.edu
Maximum award: $17,000
Number of awards: 40
Deadline: None
College level: Freshman
Criteria: Applicant must be an entering full-time freshman and have a minimum 3.7 GPA and a minimum combined SAT I score of 1200 (composite ACT score of 28). Renewable if recipient maintains a minimum 3.25 GPA. Awarded every year. Award may be used only at sponsoring institution.
Contact: Scholarships.

1687 Presidential Scholars' Program

University of Toledo
Financial Aid Office
Toledo, OH 43606-3390
(419) 537-2056
Average award: Comprehensive tuition
Number of awards: 4
Deadline: January 28
College level: Freshman
Criteria: Applicant must have a minimum 3.85 GPA or rank in top five percent of class, have a minimum composite ACT score of 30, and demonstrated leadership and citizenship. Essay and recommendations are required. Award is for four years. Awarded every year. Award may be used only at sponsoring institution.
Contact: Coordinator of Admissions Services for Scholars, Office of Admissions Services, Toledo, OH 43606, (419) 537-2073.

1688 Presidential Scholarship

DePaul University
1 East Jackson Boulevard
Chicago, IL 60604
(312) 362-8704, (312) 362-5749 (fax)
Average award: $4,000
Maximum award: $8,000
Minimum award: $2,000
Number of awards: 250
Deadline: None
College level: Freshman
Criteria: Applicant must rank in top tenth of class, have a minimum composite ACT score of 27 or minimum combined SAT I score of 1220, and demonstrate strong leadership and involvement in extracurricular activities. Minimum 3.3 cumulative GPA and full-time enrollment are required to retain scholarship. Awarded every year. Award may be used only at sponsoring institution.
Contact: Jennifer Sparrow, Scholarship Coordinator, jsparrow@wppost.depaul.edu.

1689 Presidential Scholarship

Grand Valley State University
Allendale, MI 49401
(616) 895-3234
Average award: $2,650
Maximum award: $2,858
Minimum award: $2,000
Number of awards: 25
Deadline: February 1
College level: Freshman
Criteria: Minimum 3.5 GPA is required to retain scholarship. Awarded every year. Award may be used only at sponsoring institution.
Contact: Ken Fridsma, Director of Financial Aid.

1690 Presidential Scholarship

Susquehanna University
Selinsgrove, PA 17870
(717) 372-4450
Maximum award: $7,500
Deadline: None
College level: Freshman
Criteria: Awarded to applicants who have demonstrated superior academic achievement and personal promise. Scholarship is renewable. Awarded every year. Award may be used only at sponsoring institution.
Contact: Office of Financial Aid.

1691 Presidential Scholarship

College of New Rochelle
29 Castle Place
New Rochelle, NY 10805
(914) 654-5224
Average award: $12,200
Number of awards: 5
Deadline: None
College level: Freshman
Criteria: Applicant must have a minimum 92 grade average, rank in top 5% of class, have a minimum combined SAT I score of 1300, and be accepted for admission. Scholarship is renewable. Awarded every year. Award may be used only at sponsoring institution.
Contact: Annette Gonzalez, Financial Aid Counselor.

1692 Presidential Scholarship

Roberts Wesleyan College
2301 Westside Drive
Rochester, NY 14624-1997
(716) 594-6422
Average award: $3,000
Deadline: None
College level: Freshman, Transfers
Criteria: Freshman applicant must rank in top 15% of class, have a minimum combined SAT I score of 1150 (composite ACT score of 25), and have character consistent with goals of college. Transfer applicant must have a minimum 3.6 GPA and character consisent with goals of college. Applicant must be a full-time student. Minimum 3.3 GPA is required to retain scholarship. Awarded every year. Award may be used only at sponsoring institution.
Contact: Brian P. Madden, Assistant Director of Financial Aid, (716) 594-6150.

1693 Presidential Scholarship

University of Iowa
208 Calvin Hall
Iowa City, IA 52242
(319) 335-1450, (319) 335-3060 (fax)
http://www.uiowa.edu/~finaid
Maximum award: Full tuition, room and board
Number of awards: 50
Deadline: Early December
College level: Freshman
Criteria: Applicant must rank in top five percent of high school class and have a minimum composite ACT score of 30. Minimum 3.0 cumulative GPA and full-time enrollment are required to retain scholarship. Awarded every year. Award may be used only at sponsoring institution.
Contact: Judith Carpenter, Assistant Director of Student Financial Aid, judith-carpenter@uiowa.edu.

1694 Presidential Scholarship

University of Indianapolis
1400 East Hanna Avenue
Indianapolis, IN 46227-3697
(317) 788-3217
Maximum award: $12,990
Number of awards: 12
Deadline: December 15
College level: Freshman
Criteria: Applicant must rank in top 5% of class, have a minimum combined SAT I score of 1270 (composite ACT score of 29), have academic record of college-preparatory courses, submit essay, and have on-campus interview. Recipient must maintain a minimum 3.3 GPA and full-time enrollment to retain scholarship. Awarded every year. Award may be used only at sponsoring institution.
Contact: Admissions Office, (317) 788-3216.

1695 Presidential Scholarship

George Mason University
4400 University Drive
Fairfax, VA 22030
(703) 993-2391
Average award: $3,372
Number of awards: 20
Deadline: March 1
College level: Freshman
Criteria: Minimum 3.0 GPA is required to retain scholarship. Awarded every year. Award may be used only at sponsoring institution.
Contact: Larry Beatty, Director of Client Services.

1696 Presidential Scholarship

Alfred University
Alumni Hall
26 North Main Street
Alfred, NY 14802
(607) 871-2159
Maximum award: $10,000
Deadline: Early application is recommended
College level: Freshman
Criteria: Applicant must have a minimum grade average of 90 and rank in top tenth of class. Standardized test scores, good citizenship, and extracurricular activities are considered. Interview recommended. Renewable for up to eight semesters if minimum 3.0 GPA and continuous full-time enrollment are maintained. Awarded every year. Award may be used only at sponsoring institution.
Contact: Scholarships.

1697 Presidential Scholarship

Northern Kentucky University
Administrative Center 416
Nunn Drive
Highland Heights, KY 41099-7101
(606) 572-5144
Average award: Full tuition
Deadline: February 1
College level: Freshman, community college graduate
Criteria: Freshman applicant must rank in the top tenth of class and have a minimum ACT composite score of 26. One valedictorian and one salutatorian from any high school and any National Merit finalist is automatically eligible. Community college applicant must have a minimum GPA of 3.25; one award for each college in the U of Kentucky community college system (Maysville Community Coll has one additional award). Minimum 3.25 GPA is required to retain scholarship. Awarded every year. Award may be used only at sponsoring institution.
Contact: Robert E. Sprague, Director of Financial Aid.

1698 Presidential Scholarship

Saint Joseph's College
Highway 231 South
P.O. Box 890
Rensselaer, IN 47978
(219) 866-6170, (219) 866-6100 (fax)
Maximum award: $17,400
Number of awards: 3
Deadline: December 15
College level: Freshman
Criteria: Selection is based upon academic achievements and leadership. Minimum GPA is required to retain scholarship. Awarded every year. Award may be used only at sponsoring institution.
Contact: Frank Bevec, Director of Admission, P.O. Box 890.

1699 Presidential Scholarship

Adelphi University
South Avenue
Garden City, NY 11530
(516) 877-3050
Average award: $12,600
Maximum award: $12,900
Minimum award: $12,000
Number of awards: 39
Deadline: None
College level: Freshman
Criteria: Renewable if recipient has minimum 3.3 GPA after freshman year, 3.4 GPA after sophomore year, and 3.5 GPA after junior year. Awarded every year. Award may be used only at sponsoring institution.
Contact: Scholarships.

1700 Presidential Scholarship

Villanova University
Villanova, PA 19085
(215) 645-4010
Average award: $13,499
Maximum award: $13,870
Minimum award: $13,200
Number of awards: 77
Deadline: December 15
College level: Freshman
Criteria: Applicant must have a minimum combined SAT I score of 1250 and rank in the top five percent of class. High school and community activities also considered. Minimum 3.5 GPA is required to retain scholarship. Awarded every year. Award may be used only at sponsoring institution.
Contact: George J. Walter, Director of Financial Aid.

1701 Presidential Scholarship

Wingate University
Wingate, NC 28174-0157
(800) 755-5550, (704) 233-8110 (fax)
admit@wingate.edu
http://www.wingate.edu
Average award: $2,434
Maximum award: $4,000
Minimum award: $2,000
Number of awards: 85
Deadline: April 15
College level: Freshman
Criteria: Renewable if recipient maintains a 2.8 GPA. Awarded every year. Award may be used only at sponsoring institution.
Contact: Walt Crutchfield, Dean of Admissions, Office of Admissions, Campus Box 3059, Wingate, NC 28174, admit@wingate.edu.

1702 Presidential Scholarship

Bradford College
320 South Main Street
Haverhill, MA 01835
(508) 372-7161, (508) 372-5240 (fax)
bradcoll@aol.com
http://bradford.edu
Average award: $4,000
Maximum award: $5,000
Minimum award: $1,000
Number of awards: 6
Deadline: None
College level: Freshman, Sophomore, Junior, Senior
Criteria: Selection is based upon academic achievements and special talents. Scholarship is renewable. Awarded every year. Award may be used only at sponsoring institution.
Contact: Scholarships.

1703 Presidential Scholarship

University of Northern Iowa
Financial Aid Office
Cedar Falls, IA 50613-0024
(319) 273-2700 or (800) 772-2736
Average award: Comprehensive tuition
Number of awards: 15
Deadline: October 1
College level: Freshman
Criteria: Applicant must receive an invitation to apply; university must receive ACT score prior to August 1 of junior year. Applicant must have a minimum composite ACT score of 29 and rank in the top tenth of class. Special program of study is required to retain scholarship. Awarded every year. Award may be used only at sponsoring institution.
Contact: Carol Geiger, Administrative Assistant, Office of the Vice President for Education and Student Services, Cedar Falls, IA 50614-2700, (319) 273-2331.

1704 Presidential Scholarship

Spalding University
851 South Fourth Street
Louisville, KY 40203
(502) 585-9911
Average award: Full tuition
Deadline: March 1 (priority)
College level: Freshman
Criteria: Applicant must have a minimum 3.0 GPA and minimum composite ACT score of 23 and be accepted for full-time enrollment. Selection is based upon campus interview, list of extracurricular activities, personal essay, and three letters of recommendation. Minimum 3.5 GPA is required to retain scholarship. Awarded every year. Award may be used only at sponsoring institution.
Contact: Janice White Russell, Assistant Director of Financial Aid and Scholarship Coordinator, (502) 585-9911, extension 242.

1705 Presidential Scholarship

Carnegie Mellon University
5000 Forbes Avenue
Pittsburgh, PA 15213
(412) 268-2068
Maximum award: $9,300
Number of awards: 150
Deadline: February 15
College level: Freshman
Criteria: Minimum 3.25 Quality Point Average (QPA) on a 4.00 scale is required to retain scholarship. Awarded every year. Award may be used only at sponsoring institution.
Contact: Linda M. Anderson, Director of Financial Aid.

1706 Presidential Scholarship

Seattle University
Broadway and Madison
Seattle, WA 98122
(206) 296-5840, (206) 296-5656 (fax)
admissions@seattleu.edu
http://www.seattleu.edu
Maximum award: $10,500
Number of awards: 34
Deadline: February 1
College level: Freshman
Criteria: Recipient must maintain a minimum 3.0 GPA and complete at least 45 credit hours to retain scholarship. Awarded every year. Award may be used only at sponsoring institution.
Contact: Undergraduate Admissions Office, 900 Broadway, Seattle, WA 98122-4340, (206) 296-5800, admissions@seattleu.edu.

1707 Presidential Scholarship

California State University, Dominguez Hills
1000 East Victoria Street
Carson, CA 90747
(310) 516-3647
Average award: Full fees
Maximum number of awards: 6
Minimum number of awards: 4
Deadline: March 10
College level: Freshman, community college transfers
Criteria: Applicant must have a minimum 3.4 GPA and minimum combined SAT I score of 1000 (composite ACT score of 25). Renewable for up to three years if high level of academic achievement is maintained. Awarded every year. Award may be used only at sponsoring institution.
Contact: Financial Aid Office.

1708 Presidential Scholarship

Ohio State University–Columbus
Third Floor Lincoln Tower
1800 Cannon Drive
Columbus, OH 43210-1200
(614) 292-3980
Average award: In-state tuition, room, board, book allowance, and miscellaneous expenses
Deadline: January 15
College level: Freshman
Criteria: Applicant must rank in the top three percent of class, have a minimum composite ACT score of 29 or combined SAT I score of 1250. Competitive selection process begins in March of applicant's senior year. Minimum 3.2 GPA and satisfactory academic progress are required to retain scholarship. Awarded every year. Award may be used only at sponsoring institution.
Contact: Mary Haldane, Director of Financial Aid.

1709 Presidential Scholarship

Wilson College
1015 Philadelphia Avenue
Chambersburg, PA 17201-1285
(717) 264-4141, (717) 264-1578 (fax)
http://www.wilson.edu
Average award: Half tuition
Number of awards: 10
Deadline: March 1
College level: Freshman, Transfers
Criteria: Applicant must be a woman, rank in top quarter of class, have a minimum combined SAT I score of 1100, and be enrolled full time. Transfer applicant must have a minimum 3.0 GPA in college work. Minimum 3.0 GPA is required to retain scholarship. Awarded every year. Award may be used only at sponsoring institution.
Contact: Jeffrey Stock, Associate Director of Admissions, (717) 262-2002.

1710 Presidential Scholarship

Benedictine College
1020 North Second Street
Atchison, KS 66002
(913) 367-5340
Average award: Full tuition
Number of awards: 5
Deadline: January 15
College level: Freshman
Criteria: Applicant must have a minimum 3.0 GPA and a minimum composite ACT score of 27 (combined SAT I score of 1060), or have a minimum 3.9 GPA. Applicant must have been accepted for admission as a first-time, full-time freshman. FAFSA is required. Renewable for up to four years if minimum 3.3 GPA is maintained. Awarded every year. Award may be used only at sponsoring institution.
Contact: Diane Adams, Associate Director of Admissions.

1711 Presidential Scholarship

The University of Alabama
Box 870162
Tuscaloosa, AL 35487-0162
(205) 348-6756
Average award: Tuition
Maximum award: $6,788
Number of awards: 100
Deadline: February 1
College level: Freshman
Criteria: Selection is based upon academic achievement and leadership. Applicant should have a minimum 3.8 GPA and minimum composite ACT score of 29 (combined SAT I score of 1210). Minimum 3.0 GPA is required to retain scholarship for four years. Awarded every year. Award may be used only at sponsoring institution.
Contact: Jeanetta Allen, Director of Financial Aid.

1712 Presidential Scholarship

Southern Arkansas University–Magnolia
SAU Box 9344
Magnolia, AR 71753
(501) 235-4023, (501) 235-5005 (fax)
Average award: $4,252
Number of awards: No limit
Deadline: March 15 (priority)
College level: Freshman
Criteria: Applicant must have a minimum composite ACT score of 30, be a National Merit Finalist, or be a National Achievement Finalist. Renewable for up to eight semesters if minimum 3.0 GPA and at least 15 credit hours per semester are maintained. Awarded every year. Award may be used only at sponsoring institution.
Contact: Bronwyn C. Sneed, Director of Student Aid.

1713 Presidential Scholarship

Ohio Wesleyan University
Office of Admissions
Delaware, OH 43015
(614) 368-3020, (614) 368-3314 (fax)
owuadmit@cc.owu.edu
http://www.owu.edu
Average award: $19,140
Number of awards: 30
Deadline: March 1
College level: Freshman
Criteria: Applicant must rank in top tenth of class, have a minimum composite ACT score of 32 (combined SAT I score of 1470), and submit essay and two teacher recommendations. Interview with faculty member is strongly recommended. Selection is based upon curriculum, extracurricular involvement, GPA, standardized test scores, and writing skills. Minimum 3.5 GPA by the end of sophmore year is required to retain scholarship. Awarded every year. Award may be used only at sponsoring institution.
Contact: Douglas C. Thompson, Dean of Admission.

1714 Presidential Scholarship

Ball State University
Muncie, IN 47306
(765) 285-5600
Maximum award: Out-of-state tuition
Minimum award: In-state tuition
Number of awards: 404
Deadline: March 1
College level: Freshman
Criteria: Applicant must rank in the top fifth of high school class and have a minimum combined SAT I score of 1120 or ACT composite score of 24. Minimum 3.0 GPA is required to retain scholarship. Awarded every year. Award may be used only at sponsoring institution.
Contact: Director of Admissions, Office of Admissions, Muncie, IN 47306, (765) 285-8300.

1715 Presidential Scholarship

Washington and Jefferson College
Washington, PA 15301
(412) 223-6019
Maximum award: $10,000
Number of awards: 150
Deadline: March 1
College level: Freshman
Criteria: Applicant must rank in top tenth of class and have a minimum combined SAT I score of 1200 (composite ACT score of 27). Minimum 3.33 GPA is required to retain scholarship. Awarded every year. Award may be used only at sponsoring institution.
Contact: Richard H. Soudan, Director of Financial Aid.

1716 Presidential Scholarship

Rhodes College
2000 North Parkway
Memphis, TN 38112
(901) 843-3700, (901) 843-3719 (fax)
adminfo@rhodes.edu
http://www.rhodes.edu
Average award: $5,000
Number of awards: 50
Deadline: February 1 (priority)
College level: Freshman
Criteria: Selection is based upon merit. Renewable if recipient maintains a minimum 2.5 GPA. Awarded every year. Award may be used only at sponsoring institution.
Contact: David J. Wottle, Dean of Admissions and Financial Aid, (901) 843-3700, (800) 844-5969.

1717 Presidential Scholarship

University of New Mexico
Mesa Vista Hall, 3rd Floor, Room 3020
Albuquerque, NM 87131
(505) 277-6090
Average award: $2,600
Number of awards: 200
Deadline: February 1
College level: Freshman
Criteria: Selection is based upon minimum 3.5 GPA, references, activities, class rank, minimum composite ACT score of 24 or SAT I equivalent, and leadership skills. Minimum 3.0 GPA with 30 hours per year is required to retain scholarship. Awarded every year. Award may be used only at sponsoring institution.
Contact: Rita M. Padilla, Associate Director for Scholarships and Financial Aid.

1718 Presidential Scholarship

Valparaiso University
Valparaiso, IN 46383-6493
(219) 464-5011, (219) 464-6898 (fax)
undergrad_admissions@valpo.edu
http:www.valpo.edu
Maximum award: $7,880
Deadline: May 1
College level: Freshman
Criteria: Selection is based upon academic accomplishments. Renewable for up to three years if minimum 3.0 GPA is maintained. Awarded every year. Award may be used only at sponsoring institution.
Contact: Office of Admissions and Financial Aid, Kretzman Hall, (888) GO VALPO.

1719 Presidential Scholarship

Kansas Wesleyan University
100 East Claflin
Salina, KS 67401
(913) 827-5541
Maximum award: $4,500
Number of awards: 20
Deadline: January 15
College level: Freshman
Criteria: Applicant must have a minimum 3.75 GPA, and minimum composite ACT score of 25 and demonstrate leadership qualities in interview. Recipient must maintain a minimum 3.3 GPA, complete 30 credit hours per year, and attend a leadership seminar. Awarded every year. Award may be used only at sponsoring institution.
Contact: Glenna Alexander, Director of Financial Assistance.

1720 Presidential Scholarship

Wheeling Jesuit University
316 Washington Avenue
Wheeling, WV 26003
(304) 243-2304
http://www.wju.edu/
Maximum award: $4,000
Deadline: None
College level: Freshman, Transfers.
Criteria: Selection is based upon GPA, class rank, and standardized test scores. FAFSA is required. Satisfactory academic progress is required to retain scholarship. Awarded every year. Award may be used only at sponsoring institution.
Contact: Admissions Office.

1721 **Presidential Scholarship**

Mount Union College
1972 Clark Avenue
Alliance, OH 44601
(216) 821-5320
Maximum award: Full tuition
Minimum award: Half tuition
Deadline: None
College level: Freshman
Criteria: Awarded to applicant who demonstrates outstanding academic achievement and aptitude for college. Financial need is not considered. Renewable for up to four years if minimum 3.0 GPA is maintained. Awarded every year. Award may be used only at sponsoring institution.
Contact: Office of Admissions.

1722 **Presidential Scholarship**

Western Baptist College
5000 Deer Park Drive, SE
Salem, OR 97301-9392
(503) 375-7006, (503) 585-4316 (fax)
http://www.wbc.edu
Average award: $3,500
Deadline: August 1
College level: Freshman
Criteria: Applicant must have a minimum 3.6 GPA, a minimum combined SAT I score of 1200 (composite ACT score of 27), and be an enrolled student. Minimum 3.3 GPA is required to retain scholarship. Awarded every year. Award may be used only at sponsoring institution.
Contact: Jason Derr, Senior Financial Aid Officer.

1723 **Presidential Scholarship**

Principia College
Elsah, IL 62028
(800) 277-4648, (800) 347-4000 (fax)
collegeadmissions@prin.edu
http://www.prin.edu
Average award: $7,500
Number of awards: 20
Deadline: January 15
College level: Freshman
Criteria: Recipient must maintain a minimum 3.6 GPA and support community standards to retain scholarship. Awarded every year. Award may be used only at sponsoring institution.
Contact: Martha Green Quirk, Director of Admissions and Enrollment, mgq@prin.edu.

1724 **Presidential Scholarship**

Wayne State College
1111 Main Street
Wayne, NE 68787
(402) 375-7230, (800) 228-9972
Average award: Full tuition
Deadline: March 15
College level: Freshman
Criteria: Applicant must rank in top quarter of class, have a minimum composite ACT score of 25, and be accepted for admission by March 15. Awarded every year. Award may be used only at sponsoring institution.
Contact: Financial Aid Office.

1725 **Presidential Scholarship**

Lee University
P.O. Box 3450
Cleveland, TN 37320-3450
(423) 614-8000
Average award: $5,232
Number of awards: 89
Deadline: September 1
College level: Freshman
Criteria: Applicant must have a composite ACT score of 27-30 (combined SAT I score of 1150-1340) and must enroll for academic year immediately following graduation. Award is equal to standard tuition. Awarded every year. Award may be used only at sponsoring institution.
Contact: Gary Ray, Director of Admissions, (423) 614-8500.

1726 **Presidential Scholarship**

Wilmington College
Pyle Center Box 1325
Wilmington, OH 45177
(800) 341-9318, (513) 382-7077 (fax)
admission@wilmington.edu
http://www.wilmington.edu
Average award: $6,500
Number of awards: 145
Deadline: May 1
College level: Freshman
Criteria: Applicant must have a minimum 3.0 GPA, rank in top fifth of class and have a minimum composite ACT score of 25 (combined SAT I score of 1040). Selection is based upon academic record. Renewable if recipient maintains a minimum 3.3 GPA. Awarded every year. Award may be used only at sponsoring institution.
Contact: Financial Aid Office.

1727 **Presidential Scholarship**

Northwest College
P.O. Box 579
Kirkland, WA 98083-0579
(800) 6-NWEST-1, (206) 827-0148 (fax)
admission@ncag.edu
http://www.nwcollege.edu
Maximum award: $8,250
Number of awards: 33
Deadline: March 1
College level: Freshman
Criteria: Minimum 3.4 GPA is required to retain scholarship. Awarded every year. Award may be used only at sponsoring institution.
Contact: Cal White, Director of Enrollment Services, (206) 889-5231, cal.white@ncag.edu.

1728 **Presidential Scholarship**

Piedmont College
165 Central Avenue
Demorest, GA 30535
(706) 778-3000
Average award: $4,000
Number of awards: 12
Deadline: February 15
College level: Freshman
Criteria: Applicant must have a minimum combined SAT I score of 1000. Recipient must participate in Piedmont Scholars Program and at least one other campus organization and live in college housing. Renewable for up to four years if minimum 3.0 GPA is maintained. Awarded every year. Award may be used only at sponsoring institution.
Contact: Kenneth L. Owen, Director of Financial Aid.

1729 Presidential Scholarship

High Point University
University Station
Montlieu Avenue
High Point, NC 27262-3598
(910) 841-9128, (910) 841-4599 (fax)
http://www.highpoint.edu
Average award: $4,500
Number of awards: 35
Deadline: February 1
College level: Freshman
Criteria: Applicant must be invited to attend Presidential Scholarship Interview Day. Competitive selection. Minimum 3.0 GPA is required to retain scholarship. Awarded every year. Award may be used only at sponsoring institution.
Contact: Jim Schlimmer, Dean of Admissions, Montlieu Avenue, High Point, NC 27262, (910) 841-9245.

1730 Presidential Scholarship

Northwestern College
101 College Lane
Orange City, IA 51041
(800) 747-4757, 712 737-7130, (712) 737-7164 (fax)
markb@nwciowa.edu
http://www.nwciowa.edu
Maximum award: $4,800
Deadline: None
College level: Freshman
Criteria: Applicant must rank in top 5% of class, have a minimum composite ACT score of 28, and submit recommendation and transcript. Minimum 3.0 GPA is required to retain scholarship. Awarded every year. Award may be used only at sponsoring institution.
Contact: Ron DeJong, Director of Admission, rondj@nwciowa.edu.

1731 Presidential Scholarship

Michigan Christian College
800 West Avon Road
Rochester Hills, MI 48307
(810) 650-6018, (810) 650-6060 (fax)
Maximum award: $9,691
Deadline: May 1 (priority)
College level: Freshman
Criteria: Applicant must have a minimum 3.5 GPA, a minimum composite ACT score of 30 (combined SAT I score of 1340), and a recommendation, and demonstrate leadership. Minimum 3.5 GPA is required to retain scholarship. Awarded every year. Award may be used only at sponsoring institution.
Contact: Admissions Office.

1732 Presidential Scholarship

Ohio Northern University
525 South Main Street
Ada, OH 45810
(419) 772-2272, (419) 772-2313 (fax)
admissions-ug@onu.edu
http://www.onu.edu
Average award: $18,000
Number of awards: 4
Deadline: December 15
College level: Freshman
Criteria: Selection is by invitation upon admission. Renewable if recipient maintains 3.30 GPA (freshman year), and 3.50 GPA thereafter. Awarded every year. Award may be used only at sponsoring institution.
Contact: Wendell A. Schick, Director of Financial Aid, admissions-ug@onu.edu.

1733 Presidential Scholarship

Lynn University
3601 North Military Trail
Boca Raton, FL 33431-5598
(561) 994-0770, (561) 247-3552 (fax)
admission@lynn.edu
http://www.lynn.edu
Maximum award: $16,300
Number of awards: 5
Deadline: February 15
College level: Freshman
Criteria: Applicant must be a U.S. citizen, and must meet at least two of the three of the criteria: minimum 3.75 GPA, rank in top tenth of class, minimum combined SAT I score of 1200. Essay may be required. Minimum 3.50 GPA is required to retain scholarship. Awarded every year. Award may be used only at sponsoring institution.
Contact: James Sullivan, Director of Admissions.

1734 Presidential Scholarship

Loyola Marymount University
7900 Loyola Boulevard
Los Angeles, CA 90045-8350
(310) 338-2753, (310) 338-2793 (fax)
http://www.lmu.edu
Average award: $7,500
Number of awards: 20
College level: Freshman
Criteria: Applicant must have a minimum 3.6 GPA and minimum SAT I math and verbal scores of 650 (combined SAT I score of 1300, composite ACT score of 29). Selection is based upon Academic Scholarship competition and interview. Renewable for four years. Awarded every year. Award may be used only at sponsoring institution.
Contact: Financial Aid Office.

1735 Presidential Scholarship

Eckerd College
4200 54th Avenue South
St. Petersburg, FL 33711
(813) 864-8331, 800 456-9009, (813) 866-2304 (fax)
admissions@eckerd.edu
http://www.eckerd.edu
Maximum award: $10,000
Number of awards: 25
Deadline: February 15
College level: Freshman
Criteria: Selection is based upon academic achievement and demonstrated leadership and service. Financial need is not considered. Renewable if recipient maintains a minimum 3.0 GPA. Awarded every year. Award may be used only at sponsoring institution.
Contact: Dr. Richard Hallin, Dean of Admissions.

1736 Presidential Scholarship

Eureka College
300 East College
Eureka, IL 61530
(309) 467-6310
Average award: $6,000
Deadline: February 1
College level: Freshman
Criteria: Applicant must have a minimum 3.5 GPA. Selection is based upon school project. Minimum 3.0 GPA is required for renewal. Awarded every year. Award may be used only at sponsoring institution.
Contact: Ellen M. Rigsby, Associate Director of Financial Aid.

1737 Presidential Scholarship

Hamline University
1536 Hewitt Avenue
St. Paul, MN 55104
(612) 641-2207
Maximum award: Full tuition
Number of awards: 20
Deadline: January 20
College level: Freshman
Criteria: Applicant must rank in top 5% of class and have high standardized test scores. Selection is based upon academic ability, motivation for independent scholarship, preparation for college, and sense of purpose as determined in interview with selection committee. Amount of award is determined by financial need. Renewable for up to three years if minimum 3.25 GPA is maintained. Awarded every year. Award may be used only at sponsoring institution.
Contact: Brian Peterson, Senior Associate Director of Undergraduate Admission.

1738 Presidential Scholarship

University of Nevada, Las Vegas
4505 South Maryland Parkway
Box 452016
Las Vegas, NV 89154-2016
(702) 739-3011
Average award: $2,500
Number of awards: 13
Deadline: February 1
College level: Freshman, Sophomore, Junior, Senior
Criteria: Applicant must be a National Merit finalist or semifinalist. Minimum 3.0 GPA is required. Class standing and class rank are considered. Scholarship is renewable. Awarded every year. Award may be used only at sponsoring institution.
Contact: Del Rae Dillard, Scholarship Coordinator.

1739 Presidential Scholarship

Georgia State University
P.O. Box 4040
Atlanta, GA 30302
(404) 651-2227, (404) 651-3418 (fax)
http://www.gsu.edu
Average award: $4,000
Maximum number of awards: 7
Minimum number of awards: 4
Deadline: None
College level: Freshman
Criteria: Selection is based upon academic qualifications. Minimum 3.0 cumulative GPA is required to retain scholarship. Awarded every year. Award may be used only at sponsoring institution.
Contact: Rob Sheinkopf, Director of Admissions, (404) 651-2365.

1740 Presidential Scholarship

Southwest Missouri State University
Student Financial Aid
901 South National Avenue
Springfield, MO 65804-0095
(417) 836-5000 or (800) 492-7900
Average award: Required student fees, on-campus room and board, and a $400 book allowance
Number of awards: 500
College level: Freshman
Criteria: Applicant must rank in the top three percent of class and have a minimum composite ACT score of 29 (combined SAT I score of 1200), rank in the top tenth of class and have a minimum composite ACT score of 31 (combined SAT I score of 1310), or be a National Merit Finalist. Minimum 3.5 GPA and completion of at least 30 credit hours per year are required to retain scholarship. Awarded every year. Award may be used only at sponsoring institution.
Contact: Scholarship Committee, (417) 836-5262.

1741 Presidential Scholarship

Western Kentucky University
Cravens Library 101
Bowling Green, KY 42101
(502) 745-2551
Average award: $4,354
Number of awards: 40
Deadline: February 15
College level: Freshman
Criteria: Selection is based upon standardized test scores, high school GPA, and class rank. Minimum 3.2 cumulative GPA and full-time enrollment are required to retain scholarship. Awarded every year. Award may be used only at sponsoring institution.
Contact: Dennis M. Smith, Assistant Director of Admissions.

1742 Presidential Scholarship

Hofstra University
126 Memorial Hall
Hempstead, NY 11550
(516) 463-6677
Maximum award: $6,500
Deadline: February 15
College level: Freshman
Criteria: Applicant must rank in the top fifth of his or her high school class and have a minimum combined SAT I score of 1270 or composite ACT score of 27. Minimum 3.0 GPA by end of freshman year, 3.1 GPA by end of sophomore year, and 3.2 GPA by end of junior year are required to retain scholarship. Awarded every year. Award may be used only at sponsoring institution.
Contact: Joan Warren, Director of Financial and Academic Records.

1743 Presidential Scholarship

Rochester Institute of Technology
One Lomb Memorial Drive
Rochester, NY 14623
(716) 475-2186
Maximum award: Half tuition
Minimum award: One-fourth tuition
Number of awards: 100
Deadline: January 1
College level: Freshman
Criteria: Applicant must compete in on-campus competition and meet one of the following criteria: minimum combined SAT I score of 1200, composite ACT score of 28, or rank in top tenth of class. Minimum "B" average is required to retain scholarship. Awarded every year. Award may be used only at sponsoring institution.
Contact: Verna Hazen, Director of Financial Aid.

1744 Presidential Scholarship

Eastern Michigan University
Office of Financial Aid
403 Pierce Hall
Ypsilanti, MI 48197
(313) 487-0455, (313) 487-1484 (fax)
financial.aid@mich.edu
http://www.emich.edu
Average award: $8,000
Number of awards: 10
Deadline: November 25
College level: Freshman
Criteria: Applicant must have a minimum high school GPA of 3.7 or a minimum composite ACT score of 25 or combined SAT I score of 1150. Applicant must attend the Presidential Scholarship competition held the first Saturday in December; this is a half-day comprehensive test, with the top 30 applicants being asked to return for an interview and write an essay. Minimum 3.5 GPA and 15 credit hours per semester are required to retain scholarship. Awarded every year. Award may be used only at sponsoring institution.
Contact: Cynthia Van Pelt, Assistant Director of Scholarships.

1745   Presidential Scholarship

Montana State University–Bozeman
Bozeman, MT 59717
(406) 994-2845
Maximum award: $7,335
Number of awards: 20
Deadline: January 8
College level: Freshman
Criteria: Applicant must demonstrate intellectual or creative distinction. Selection is not based solely upon academic achievements. Applicant should have a minimum cumulative GPA of 3.8 and a minimum composite ACT score of 30 (combined SAT I score of 1300). Minimum 3.5 GPA is required to retain scholarship. Awarded every year. Award may be used only at sponsoring institution.
Contact: Victoria O'Donnell, Director of Honors Program, Montana State University, Quad D, Bozeman, MT 59717, (406) 994-4110, iuhvo@montana.edu.

1746   Presidential Scholarship

Salem College
P.O. Box 10548
Winston-Salem, NC 27108
(910) 721-2808
Average award: $8,000
Maximum award: $9,000
Minimum award: $7,000
Maximum number of awards: 10
Minimum number of awards: 5
College level: Freshman
Criteria: Applicant must be a woman. Selection is based upon academic achievement, leadership, and service. Recipient must maintain a minimum 3.0 GPA and remain a full-time resident student to retain scholarship. Awarded every year. Award may be used only at sponsoring institution.
Contact: Bruce Blackman, Director of Financial Aid.

1747   Presidential Scholarship

Lawrence University
P.O. Box 599
Appleton, WI 54912-0599
(414) 832-6500, (414) 832-6782 (fax)
excel@lawrence.edu
http://www.lawrence.edu
Average award: $7,500
Number of awards: 40
Deadline: February 1
College level: Freshman
Criteria: Applicant must rank in top six percent of secondary school class and have a minimum 3.8 GPA; minimum combined SAT I score of 1240 (composite ACT score of 28) recommended. Scholarships are competitive. Renewable if recipient maintains minimum 3.0 GPA. Awarded every year. Award may be used only at sponsoring institution.
Contact: Director of Admissions, excel@lawrence.edu.

1748   Presidential Scholarship

Wisconsin Lutheran College
8800 West Bluemound Road
Milwaukee, WI 53226
(414) 443-8842, (414) 443-8514 (fax)
Average award: $6,000
Number of awards: 23
Deadline: May 1
College level: Freshman
Criteria: Applicant must have a minimum composite ACT score of 27 and either a minimum 3.7 GPA or rank in top tenth of class. Renewable if recipient maintains a minimum 3.4 GPA. Awarded every year. Award may be used only at sponsoring institution.
Contact: Donna Johnejack, Assistant Director of Financial Aid, (414) 443-8861.

1749   Presidential Scholarship

Elizabethtown College
One Alpha Drive
Elizabethtown, PA 17022
(717) 361-1404, (717) 361-1485 (fax)
Average award: $9,000
Number of awards: 12
Deadline: March 1
College level: Freshman, Sophomore, Junior, Senior
Criteria: Applicants must rank in top 2% of class and have a minimum combined SAT score of 1300. One award is given to a Hugh O'Brian seminar participant. Renewable if recipient has minimum 2.75 GPA at end of freshman year and minimum 3.0 GPA at end of sophomore and junior years. Award may be used only at sponsoring institution.
Contact: M. Clarke Paine, Director of Financial Aid, painemc@acad.etown.edu.

1750   Presidential Scholarship

West Virginia University
P.O. Box 6004
Morgantown, WV 26506-6004
(800) 344-9881, (304) 293-8763 (fax)
wvuinfo@wvu.edu
http://www.wvu.edu
Maximum award: $7,124
Deadline: January 15
Criteria: Applicant must have minimum 2.75 GPA. Renewable if recipient maintains 3.0 GPA. Awarded every year. Award may be used only at sponsoring institution.
Contact: Mary Ward, Scholars Program Coordinator.

1751   Presidential Scholarship

Ouachita Baptist University
410 Ouachita Street
Arkadelphia, AR 71998-0001
(501) 245-5570
Maximum award: $6,000
Number of awards: 7
Deadline: February 15
College level: Freshman
Majors/Fields: Business, education, humanities, music, natural science, religion, social science
Criteria: Applicant must have high GPA and standardized test scores. One award is given for each educational division. Minimum 3.0 GPA required to retain scholarship. Awarded every year. Award may be used only at sponsoring institution.
Contact: Susan Hurst, Director of Financial Aid.

1752   Presidential Scholarship

Kansas Newman College
3100 McCormick Avenue
Wichita, KS 67213
(316) 942-4291
Average award: $4,000
College level: Freshman, Transfers
Criteria: Applicant must have a minimum 3.6 GPA and minimum composite ACT score of 25 (combined SAT 1 score of 1200). Transfer applicant must have a minimum 3.6 GPA and at least 24 credit hours. Renewable if recipient maintains 3.25 GPA. Award may be used only at sponsoring institution.
Contact: Maria McClure, Director of Financial Aid, (316) 942-4291, extension 103, mcclurem@ksnewman.edu.

1753 **Presidential Scholarship**

Cedar Crest College
100 College Drive
Allentown, PA 18104
(610) 740-3785, (610) 606-4647 (fax)
cccadmis@cedarcrest.edu
www.cedarcrest.edu
Maximum award: $7,500
Number of awards: 41
Deadline: Rolling
College level: Freshman
Criteria: Applicant must have a minimum SAT score of 1150 and rank in top 10% of his or her class. Renewable if recipient maintains minimum 3.0 GPA. Awarded every year. Award may be used only at sponsoring institution.
Contact: Judith Neyhart, Vice President of Enrollment Management, Financial Aid Office.

1754 **Presidential Scholarship**

Seton Hill College
Greensburg, PA 15601
(412) 838-4293, (412) 830-4611 (fax)
Average award: $4,070
Maximum award: $6,104
Minimum award: $3,052
Maximum number of awards: 12
Minimum number of awards: 10
College level: Freshman
Criteria: Applicant must rank in top third of class. Renewable if recipient maintains 2.6 GPA. Awarded every year. Award may be used only at sponsoring institution.
Contact: Director of Financial Aid.

1755 **Presidential Scholarship**

Hope College
P.O. Box 9000
Holland, MI 49422-9000
(616) 395-7850, (616) 395-7130 (fax)
admissions@hope.edu
http://www.hope.edu
Average award: $8,000
Deadline: February 15
College level: Freshman, Sophomore, Junior, Senior
Criteria: Selection is based upon overall academic record and demonstrated leadership qualities in high school. Renewable if recipient maintains a minimum 3.0 GPA. Awarded every year. Award may be used only at sponsoring institution.
Contact: James R. Bekkering, Vice President for Admissions.

1756 **Presidential Scholarship**

Beloit College
700 College Street
Beloit, WI 53511
(608) 363-2663
Average award: $6,000
Number of awards: 53
Deadline: January 31
College level: Freshman
Criteria: Applicant must have a minimum 3.5 GPA, rank in top tenth of class, have a minimum composite ACT score of 25 (combined SAT I score of 1170), demonstrate leadership, and prove significant extracurricular activities. Selection is based upon exceptional academic preparation and performance. On-campus interview is required. Minimum 3.0 GPA is required to retain scholarship. Awarded every year. Award may be used only at sponsoring institution.
Contact: Thomas Kreiser, Coordinator of Freshman Financial Aid, (608) 363-2500.

1757 **Presidential Scholarship**

Dominican College of San Rafael
50 Acacia Avenue
San Rafael, CA 94901-2298
(415) 485-3204, (415) 485-3205 (fax)
enroll@dominican.edu
http://www.dominican.edu
Average award: $9,404
Maximum award: $10,685
Minimum award: $3,350
Number of awards: 29
Deadline: March 1
College level: Freshman, Transfers with fewer than 24 credit hours
Criteria: Applicant must have a minimum 3.5 GPA and strong SAT I scores, demonstrate leadership and service in community and school, and express commitment to liberal arts education. Application is required. Renewable for up to four years if recipient maintains a minimum 3.0 GPA. Awarded every year. Award may be used only at sponsoring institution.
Contact: Susan Gutierrez, Director of Financial Aid.

1758 **Presidential Scholarship**

Baylor University
P.O. Box 97028
Waco, TX 76798-7028
(817) 755-2611, (817) 755-2695 (fax)
financialaid_office@baylor.edu
http://www.baylor.edu
Average award: $1,500
Maximum award: $2,500
Number of awards: 50
Deadline: January 31
College level: Freshman
Criteria: Applicant must have a minimum combined SAT I score of 1350 (composite ACT score of 32). Renewable for up to four years if minimum 3.5 GPA is maintained. Awarded every year. Award may be used only at sponsoring institution.
Contact: Richard F. Nettles, Director of Scholarships, richard_nettles@baylor.edu.

1759 **Presidential Scholarship**

Gwynedd-Mercy College
Sumneytown Pike
Gwynedd Valley, PA 19437
(215) 641-5570
Average award: $5,700
Maximum award: Full tuition
Minimum award: Half tuition
Number of awards: 23
Deadline: January 15
College level: Freshman, Transfers
Criteria: Applicant must have a minimum 3.3 GPA (transfer applicant) or rank in top 15% of class and have a minimum combined SAT I score of 1100 (high school applicant). Minimum 3.5 GPA required to retain scholarship. Awarded every year. Award may be used only at sponsoring institution.
Contact: Kristine Weber, Associate Dean of Admissions, (215) 641-5510.

1760 **Presidential Scholarship**

Drury College
900 North Benton Avenue
Springfield, MO 65802
(417) 873-7319
Average award: $6,000
Number of awards: 13
Deadline: February 20
College level: Freshman
Criteria: Applicant must be accepted for full-time enrollment, have a minimum 3.5 GPA and minimum composite ACT score of 29 (combined SAT I score of 1210), submit essay, two letters of recommendation, and listing of leadership activities in church, community, and school, and attend an interview. Recipient will also receive $500 Leadership Award. Renewable for up to four years if recipient maintains a minimum 3.0 GPA. Awarded every year. Award may be used only at sponsoring institution.
Contact: Financial Aid Office.

1761   Presidential Scholarship

Elmira College
One Park Place
Elmira, NY 14901
(607) 735-1724, (607) 735-1718 (fax)
admissions@elmira.edu
www.elmira.edu
Average award: $7,500
Number of awards: 65
College level: Freshman
Criteria: Awarded to outstanding students with superior academic qualities. Applicant must be accepted for full-time enrollment. Selection is based upon academic record and standardized test scores. Minimum 3.2 GPA required for renewal. Awarded every year. Award may be used only at sponsoring institution.
Contact: Dean of Admissions.

1762   Presidential Scholarship

Emmanuel College
400 The Fenway
Boston, MA 02115
(617) 735-9725
Average award: Full tuition
Deadline: February 15
College level: Freshman
Criteria: Applicant must have a minimum 3.6 GPA and minimum combined SAT I score of 1200 (composite ACT score of 27) and be a woman. Application, recommendations, transcript, standardized test scores, essay/portfolio, interview, and FAFSA required. Recipient must live on campus. Minimum 3.4 GPA required to retain scholarship. Awarded every year. Award may be used only at sponsoring institution.
Contact: Patricia K. Harden, Director of Financial Aid.

1763   President's Scholarship

Brescia College
717 Frederica Street
Owensboro, KY 42301-3023
(502) 686-4290, (800) 264-1234, (502) 686-4266 (fax)
vpearson@brescia.edu
Average award: Comprehensive tuition
Deadline: March 1 (priority)
College level: Junior, Senior
Criteria: Applicant must have completed three semesters of full-time enrollment and must demonstrate leadership within an academic discipline, in co-curricular activities, and in social responsibility. Scholarship is renewable. Awarded every year. Award may be used only at sponsoring institution.
Contact: Scholarships.

1764   Presidential Scholarship

Queens College
1900 Selwyn Avenue
Charlotte, NC 28274
(704) 337-2212, 800 849-0202, (704) 337-2403 (fax)
cas@rex.queens.edu
http://www.queens.edu
Average award: Full tuition
Deadline: December 15
College level: Freshman
Criteria: Applicant must have a minimum combined SAT I score of 1200 and rank in top 5% of class. Selection is based upon superior academic and leadership achievement. Special application is required. Scholarship is renewable. Awarded every year. Award may be used only at sponsoring institution.
Contact: Eileen T. Dills, Director of Financial Aid.

1765   Presidential Scholarship

College of Notre Dame of Maryland
4701 North Charles Street
Baltimore, MD 21210
(410) 532-5369
Maximum award: Full tuition
Minimum award: Partial tuition
Deadline: December 31
College level: Freshman
Criteria: Applicant must be a woman, have a minimum 3.5 GPA and a minimum combined SAT I score of 1200, and demonstrate strong co-curricular involvement. Scholarship is renewable. Awarded every year. Award may be used only at sponsoring institution.
Contact: Financial Aid Office.

1766   Presidential Scholarship

Albany State University
504 College Drive
Albany, GA 31705
(912) 430-4650, (912) 430-3936 (fax)
kcaldwell@rams.alsnet.peachnet.edu
Maximum award: $5,200
Number of awards: 12
Deadline: February 1
College level: Freshman
Criteria: Applicant must have a minimum 3.5 GPA and minimum combined SAT I score of 1200. Letters of recommendation and essay required. Renewable if recipient maintains a minimum "B" grade average as a full-time student. Awarded every year. Award may be used only at sponsoring institution.
Contact: Kathleen J. Caldwell, Director of Admissions and Financial Aid, kcaldwell@rams.alsnet.peachnet.edu.

1767   Presidential Scholarship ($3,000)

University of South Alabama
260 Administration Building
Mobile, AL 36688-0002
(334) 460-6231
Average award: $3,000
Number of awards: 50
Deadline: Late November
College level: Freshman
Criteria: Applicant must have a minimum composite ACT score of 30 or SAT I equivalent and a minimum 3.5 GPA as computed by the Office of Admissions. Minimum 3.3 GPA is required to retain scholarship. Awarded every year. Award may be used only at sponsoring institution.
Contact: Catherine P. King, Director of Admissions.

1768   Presidential Scholarship ($5,000)

University of South Alabama
260 Administration Building
Mobile, AL 36688-0002
(334) 460-6231
Average award: $5,000
Number of awards: 15
Deadline: Late November
College level: Freshman
Criteria: Applicant must have a minimum composite ACT score of 33 or SAT I equivalent and a minimum 3.5 GPA as computed by the Office of Admissions. Minimum 3.5 GPA is required to retain scholarship. Awarded every year. Award may be used only at sponsoring institution.
Contact: Catherine P. King, Director of Admissions.

1769 Presidential Scholarship for Excellence

Iowa State University
314 Alumni Hall
Ames, IA 50011-2010
(515) 294-4111
Average award: $2,500
Number of awards: 15
Deadline: November 1
College level: Freshman
Criteria: Scholarship is renewable. Awarded every year. Award may be used only at sponsoring institution.
Contact: Earl Dowling, Director of Student Aid.

1770 Presidents' Scholarship

DeVry Institute of Technology (Addison)
1221 North Swift Road
Addison, IL 60101
(708) 953-1300
Average award: $1,800
Maximum award: $2,400
Minimum award: $1,200
Number of awards: 45
Deadline: March 24
College level: Sophomore
Criteria: Applicant must have completed 31 credit hours, and must maintain continuous enrollment, show commitment and excellence, and demonstrate financial need. Renewable if minimum 3.25 GPA is maintained. Awarded every year. Award may be used only at sponsoring institution.
Contact: William Edwards, Dean of Students.

1771 Project Advance Scholarship

Syracuse University
201 Administration Building
Syracuse, NY 13244
(315) 443-1870
orange@suadmin.syr.edu
http://ww.syr.edu
Average award: $6,000
College level: Freshman
Criteria: Selection is based upon academic credentials, standardized tests, class rank, extracurricular and community involvement, and overall citizenship and character. Renewable if recipient maintains a minimum 2.5 GPA. Award may be used only at sponsoring institution.
Contact: Scholarships.

1772 Provost Scholarship

Elizabethtown College
One Alpha Drive
Elizabethtown, PA 17022
(717) 361-1404, (717) 361-1485 (fax)
Average award: $5,500
Maximum award: $7,000
Minimum award: $3,000
Number of awards: 550
Deadline: March 1
College level: Freshman
Criteria: Applicant must rank in top tenth of class and have a minimum combined SAT I score of 1150. Recipient must have a minimum 2.75 GPA after freshman year and 3.0 GPA after sophomore and junior years to retain scholarship. Awarded every year. Award may be used only at sponsoring institution.
Contact: M. Clarke Paine, Director of Financial Aid, painemc@acad.etown.edu.

1773 Provost's Scholars Award

Chapman University
333 North Glassell Street
Orange, CA 92866
(714) 997-6741, (714) 997-6743 (fax)
http://www.chapman.edu
Maximum award: $9,000
Deadline: None
College level: Freshman, Transfers
Criteria: Applicant must be an entering full-time undergraduate with a minimum 3.5 GPA. Scholarship is renewable. Awarded every year. Award may be used only at sponsoring institution.
Contact: Scholarships.

1774 Queens Scholar Award

Queens College
1900 Selwyn Avenue
Charlotte, NC 28274
(704) 337-2212, 800 849-0202, (704) 337-2403 (fax)
cas@rex.queens.edu
http://www.queens.edu
Maximum award: $8,000
Deadline: None
College level: Freshman
Criteria: Awarded to applicant with outstanding academic and leadership records. Financial need is considered. Renewable for up to three years based upon academic performance. Awarded every year. Award may be used only at sponsoring institution.
Contact: Eileen T. Dills, Director of Financial Aid.

1775 Raven Recognition Scholarship

Benedictine College
1020 North Second Street
Atchison, KS 66002
(913) 367-5340
Maximum award: $2,750
Deadline: None
College level: Freshman
Criteria: Applicant must be a first-time, full-time freshman and meet one of the following criteria: composite ACT score of 20-23 (combined SAT I score of 780-930), rank in top 25th to 16th percentile of class and minimum composite ACT score of 18 (combined SAT I score of 780), or 3.00-3.49 GPA and minimum composite ACT score of 18 (combined SAT I score of 780). FAFSA is required. Recipients of the Presidential, Director's, Dean's, or Academic Scholarships are ineligible. Renewable for up to four years if a minimum 2.75 GPA is maintained. Awarded every year. Award may be used only at sponsoring institution.
Contact: Diane Adams, Associate Director of Admissions.

1776 R.C. Easley National Scholarship

National Academy of American Scholars (NAAS)
Department S
1249 South Diamond Bar Boulevard #325
Diamond Bar, CA 91765-4122
(909) 621-6856
staff@naas.org
http://www.naas.org
Maximum award: $6,000
Number of awards: 13
Deadline: February 1
College level: Freshman
Criteria: Applicant must be a U.S. citizen or permanent resident, be enrolled in public, private, or parochial secondary school and have been or anticipate being accepted into an accredited four-year institution, have a minimum "C" grade average, and have completed SAT I/ACT. Selection is based upon scholastic excellence and outstanding character. Send self-addressed stamped envelope (#10) with a $1.00 handling fee for application and information packet. Minimum 3.0 GPA or "B" grade average and full-time enrollment are required to retain scholarship. Awarded every year.
Contact: Scholarship Committee.

1777 Reagan Scholarship

Eureka College
300 East College
Eureka, IL 61530
(309) 467-6310
Average award: $13,066
Number of awards: 5
Deadline: January 1
College level: Freshman
Criteria: Selection is based upon academic record and student activities. Minimum 3.5 GPA is required for renewal. Awarded every year. Award may be used only at sponsoring institution.
Contact: Ellen Rigsby, Associate Director of Financial Aid.

1778 Recognition of Excellence Scholarship

Eastern Michigan University
Office of Financial Aid
403 Pierce Hall
Ypsilanti, MI 48197
(313) 487-0455, (313) 487-1484 (fax)
financial.aid@mich.edu
http://www.emich.edu
Average award: Half tuition
Maximum number of awards: 450
Minimum number of awards: 380
Deadline: February 15
College level: Freshman, Sophomore, Junior, Senior
Criteria: Applicant must have a minimum 3.3 GPA and composite ACT score of 21 or combined SAT I score of 1000. Minimum 3.30 GPA and completion of at least 12 credit hours per semester are required to retain scholarship. Awarded every year. Award may be used only at sponsoring institution.
Contact: Cynthia Van Pelt, Assistant Director of Scholarships.

1779 Redd Special Achievement Award

Queens College
1900 Selwyn Avenue
Charlotte, NC 28274
(704) 337-2212, 800 849-0202, (704) 337-2403 (fax)
cas@rex.queens.edu
http://www.queens.edu
Maximum award: $5,000
Deadline: None
College level: Freshman, Sophomore, Junior, Senior
Criteria: Awarded to applicants with demonstrated talent or ability in one of many fields. Financial need is considered. Awarded every year. Award may be used only at sponsoring institution.
Contact: Eileen T. Dills, Director of Financial Aid.

1780 Regents' Scholarship

Doane College
1014 Boswell Avenue
Crete, NE 68333
(800) 333-6263, (402) 826-8600 (fax)
http://www.doane.edu
Average award: $2,500
Number of awards: 51
Deadline: None
College level: Freshman
Criteria: Selection is based upon standardized test scores and/or class rank. Renewable for up to four years (eight semesters) if minimum 3.4 GPA is maintained. Awarded every year. Award may be used only at sponsoring institution.
Contact: Janet Dodson, Director of Financial Aid, (402) 826-8260, jdodson@doane.edu.

1781 Regents' Scholarship

Eastern Michigan University
Office of Financial Aid
403 Pierce Hall
Ypsilanti, MI 48197
(313) 487-0455, (313) 487-1484 (fax)
financial.aid@mich.edu
http://www.emich.edu
Maximum award: $3,000
Maximum number of awards: 350
Minimum number of awards: 350
Deadline: February 15
College level: Freshman, Sophomore, Junior, Senior
Criteria: Applicant must have a minimum 3.5 GPA and a composite ACT score of 25 or combined SAT I score of 1150. Minimum 3.5 GPA and 15 credit hours per semester are required to retain scholarship. Awarded every year. Award may be used only at sponsoring institution.
Contact: Cynthia Van Pelt, Assistant Director of Scholarships.

1782 Regents' Scholarship

University of Memphis
Scates Hall 204
Memphis, TN 38152
(901) 678-3213, (901) 678-5621 (fax)
katkinsn@cc.memphis.edu
http://www.memphis.edu/
Maximum award: $2,180
Deadline: March 1
College level: Freshman
Criteria: Applicant must have a minimum 3.0 GPA and minimum composite ACT score of 26 (combined SAT I score of 1170) and be a resident of Tennessee. Minimum 2.8 GPA and a service requirement of 30 hours per semester are required to retain scholarship. Awarded every year. Award may be used only at sponsoring institution.
Contact: Katherine Atkinson, Scholarship Coordinator.

1783 Regents' Scholarship

Holy Names College
3500 Mountain Boulevard
Oakland, CA 94619-1699
(510) 436-1327
Average award: $11,480
Minimum award: $6,230
Number of awards: 3
Deadline: March 2
College level: Freshman, Transfers
Criteria: Applicant must have a minimum 3.6 GPA and academic honors, demonstrate community service and extracurricular accomplishments, and submit separate application and essay. Minimum 3.0 GPA required to retain scholarship. Awarded every year. Award may be used only at sponsoring institution.
Contact: Paula J. Lehrberger, Director of Financial Aid.

1784 Regents' Scholarship

Pacific Lutheran University
Tacoma, WA 98447
(206) 535-7161
Number of awards: 3
Average award: Full tuition
Deadline: January 13
College level: Freshman
Criteria: Applicant must be a U.S. citizen, be accepted for admission by January 13, have a minimum 3.8 GPA, have a minimum combined SAT I score of 1200 (composite ACT score of 26), and demonstrate outstanding leadership and service. Financial need is not considered. Renewable for three years if minimum 3.3 GPA is maintained. Awarded every year. Award may be used only at sponsoring institution.
Contact: Office of Financial Aid and Scholarships.

1785 Regents' Scholarship

University of New Mexico
Mesa Vista Hall, 3rd Floor, Room 3020
Albuquerque, NM 87131
(505) 277-6090
Average award: $6,200
Maximum number of awards: 60
Minimum number of awards: 15
Deadline: December 1
College level: Freshman
Criteria: Applicant must meet at least one of the following qualifications: minimum GPA of 3.9, minimum composite ACT score of 31 or SAT I equivalent, class valedictorian, National Merit semifinalist, National Achievement scholar, National Hispanic scholar, extraordinary extracurricular activities, or excellent recommendations. Minimum 3.2 GPA after freshman year, (3.5 GPA thereafter), with 30 credit hours per year is required to retain scholarship. Awarded every year. Award may be used only at sponsoring institution.
Contact: Rita M. Padilla, Associate Director for Scholarships.

1786 Residential Leadership Grant

University of Missouri–Columbia
High School and Transfer Relations
219 Jesse Hall
Columbia, MO 65211
(800) 225-6075 (in-state), (314) 882-2456
http://www.missouri.edu
Maximum award: Full room and board
Maximum number of awards: 60
Number of awards: 111
College level: Freshman
Criteria: Applicant must have a minimum 2.5 GPA and live in a residence hall. Selection is based upon academic achievement and leadership. Award may be used only at sponsoring institution.
Contact: Grants.

1787 Residential Scholarship

D'Youville College
320 Porter Avenue
Buffalo, NY 14201
(716) 881-7691
Average award: $2,300
Number of awards: 45
College level: Freshman, Sophomore
Criteria: Renewable if recipient maintains minimum 2.5 GPA. Renewable up to two years. Award may be used only at sponsoring institution.
Contact: R.H. Dannecker, Director of Admissions and Financial Aid, (716) 881-7600.

1788 R.F. Poole Alumni Scholarship

Clemson University
G-01 Sikes Hall
Clemson, SC 29634-5123
(803) 656-2280
Maximum award: $5,000
Number of awards: 7
Deadline: None
College level: Freshman
Criteria: Awarded to outstanding applicants. Selection is based upon admissions application. Minimum 3.0 GPA and completion of at least 12 credits per semester are required to retain scholarship. Awarded every year. Award may be used only at sponsoring institution.
Contact: Marvin Carmichael, Director of Financial Aid.

1789 Rhodes Award

Rhodes College
2000 North Parkway
Memphis, TN 38112
(901) 843-3700, (901) 843-3719 (fax)
adminfo@rhodes.edu
http://www.rhodes.edu
Maximum award: $4,000
Number of awards: 35
Deadline: February 1 (priority)
College level: Freshman
Criteria: Selection is based upon merit. Renewable if recipient maintains a minimum 2.5 GPA. Awarded every year. Award may be used only at sponsoring institution.
Contact: David J. Wottle, Dean of Admissions and Financial Aid, (901) 843-3700, (800) 844-5969.

1790 Richard R. Green Memorial Scholarship

Susquehanna University
Selinsgrove, PA 17870
(717) 372-4450
Maximum award: $15,000
Deadline: None
College level: Freshman, Sophomore, Junior, Senior
Criteria: Selection is based upon academic ability and financial need. Scholarship is renewable. Awarded every year. Award may be used only at sponsoring institution.
Contact: Office of Financial Aid.

1791 Richardson Family Foundation Endowed Scholarship

Clemson University
G-01 Sikes Hall
Clemson, SC 29634-5123
(803) 656-2280
Average award: $2,500
Number of awards: 2
Deadline: None
College level: Freshman
Criteria: Selection is based upon admissions application. Renewable if recipient maintains minimum 3.0 GPA and completes at least 12 credits per semester. Award may be used only at sponsoring institution.
Contact: Scholarships.

1792 Robert C. Edwards Scholarship

Clemson University
G-01 Sikes Hall
Clemson, SC 29634-5123
(803) 656-2280
Maximum award: $3,000
Number of awards: 2
Deadline: December 31
College level: Freshman
Criteria: Selection is based upon admissions application. Minimum 2.5 GPA and completion of at least 12 credits per semester are required to retain scholarship. Awarded every year. Award may be used only at sponsoring institution.
Contact: Marvin Carmichael, Director of Financial Aid.

1793   Robert R. Neyland Scholarship

University of Tennessee, Knoxville
Financial Aid Office
115 Student Services Building
Knoxville, TN 37994
(615) 974-3131
Average award: $2,500
Number of awards: 4
Deadline: February 1
College level: Freshman
Criteria: Applicant must rank in top tenth of class and demonstrate leadership potential through church, community, and extracurricular activities. If other qualifications are equal, preference is given to applicants who participate in sports and demonstrate financial need. Applicant must be a Tennessee resident or the child of alumni regardless of the state of residence. Award is for four years. Awarded every year. Award may be used only at sponsoring institution.
Contact: University Honors Program, F-101 Melrose Hall, Knoxville, TN 37916, (615) 974-7875.

1794   Robert W. Woodruff Scholarship

Emory University
1380 Oxford Road, NE
Atlanta, GA 30322
(404) 727-6039
Average award: Full tuition, fees, room, and board
Deadline: November 15
College level: Freshman
Criteria: Awarded to applicant who demonstrates character, communication skills, intellectual and personal vigor, leadership and creativity in community or school, outstanding academic achievement, and potential for enriching lives. Nomination by school officials or Emory Admission Committee and interview are required. Awarded every year. Award may be used only at sponsoring institution.
Contact: Office of Admission, 200 Boisfeuillet Jones Center, Atlanta, GA 30322-1950, (404) 727-6036, (800) 727-6036.

1795   Roothbert Fund, Inc. Scholarship

Roothbert Fund
475 Riverside Drive
Suite 252
New York, NY 10115
(212) 870-3116
Average award: $2,000
Deadline: February 1
College level: Freshman, Sophomore, Junior, Senior, Graduate, Doctoral
Majors/Fields: Teaching
Criteria: Applicant must be primarily motivated by spiritual values. Applicants who are considering teaching as a vocation are given preference. Financial need is considered. More information is available upon request. Scholarship is renewable. Awarded every year.

1796   Russell Honors Scholarship

Texas A&M University–Kingsville
Scholarships
Box 116
Kingsville, TX 78363
(512) 593-3907, (512) 593-2991 (fax)
http://www.tamuk.edu
Maximum award: $5,000
Number of awards: No limit
Deadline: March 3
College level: Freshman
Criteria: Applicant must have a minimum 3.0 GPA, rank in the top quarter of graduating class, and have minimum combined SAT I score of 1280 (ACT score of 29). Renewable if recipient maintains a minimum 3.5 GPA. Award may be used only at sponsoring institution.
Contact: Laura Knipper, Counselor.

1797   Sacred Heart Scholarship

Kansas Newman College
3100 McCormick Avenue
Wichita, KS 67213
(316) 942-4291
Average award: $7,000
Number of awards: 4
Deadline: March 1
College level: Freshman
Criteria: Applicant must have a minimum 3.8 GPA (minimum combined SAT 1 score of 1370), and submit essay, evidence of community involvement, and letter of recommendation. Finalists must have on-campus interview. Renewable if recipient maintains 3.4 GPA. Awarded every year. Award may be used only at sponsoring institution.
Contact: Marla McClure, Director of Financial Aid, (316) 942-4291, extension 103, mcclurem@ksnewman.edu.

1798   Salutatorian Scholarship

Elmira College
One Park Place
Elmira, NY 14901
(607) 735-1724, (607) 735-1718 (fax)
admissions@elmira.edu
www.elmira.edu
Average award: Three-Fourths tuition
Number of awards: 10
College level: Freshman
Criteria: Applicant must be the salutatorian of graduating secondary or prep school class and be accepted for full-time enrollment. Recipient must live on campus. Renewable if recipient maintains minimum 3.4 GPA. Awarded every year. Award may be used only at sponsoring institution.
Contact: Dean of Admissions, admissions@elmira.edu.

1799   Salutatorian Scholarship

University of West Alabama
Station Four
Livingston, AL 35470
(205) 652-3400, (205) 652-3522 (fax)
http://www.westal.edu
Average award: Full tuition
Deadline: April 15
College level: Freshman
Criteria: Applicant must have been salutatorian of class. Renewable for up to four years if minimum 3.0 GPA is maintained. Awarded every year. Award may be used only at sponsoring institution.
Contact: Richard Hester, Director of Admission, (205) 652-9661, extension 352.

1800 Sam Hochberg Memorial Scholarship

Five Towns College
305 North Service Road
Dix Hills, NY 11746-6055
(516) 424-7000
Maximum award: Full tuition
Minimum award: Half tuition
Deadline: Early application is recommended
College level: Freshman
Majors/Fields: Business administration, liberal arts
Criteria: Applicant must be recommended by principal or guidance
counselor and be accepted for admission as a full-time student.
Selection is based upon academic potential. Awarded every year.
Award may be used only at sponsoring institution.
Contact: Financial Aid Office.

1801 Sarah Wilson Scholarship

Wilson College
1015 Philadelphia Avenue
Chambersburg, PA 17201-1285
(717) 264-4141, (717) 264-1578 (fax)
http://www.wilson.edu
Average award: Full tuition
Deadline: March 1
College level: Freshman, Transfers
Criteria: Applicant must be a woman, rank in top quarter of class,
have a minimum combined SAT I score of 1100, and be enrolled full
time. Transfer applicant must have a minimum 3.0 GPA in college
work. Minimum 3.4 GPA is required to retain scholarship. Awarded
every year. Award may be used only at sponsoring institution.
Contact: Jeffrey Stock, Associate Director of Admissions, (717)
262-2002.

1802 SAU Foundation Scholarship

Southern Arkansas University–Magnolia
SAU Box 9344
Magnolia, AR 71753
(501) 235-4023, (501) 235-5005 (fax)
Deadline: None
College level: Freshman
Criteria: Applicant must have a composite ACT score of 27-29. Re-
newable for up to eight semesters if recipient maintains minimum 3.0
GPA and completes at least 15 credit hours per semester. Awarded
every year. Award may be used only at sponsoring institution.
Contact: Bronwyn C. Sneed, Director of Student Aid.

1803 Schillig Leadership Scholarship

Mississippi State University
Department of Student Financial Aid
P.O. Box 6238
Mississippi State, MS 39762
(601) 325-7430
Average award: Comprehensive tuition
Deadline: February 1
College level: Freshman
Criteria: Applicant must demonstrate outstanding leadership, have a
minimum composite ACT score of 29 (combined SAT I score of
1200), and have an exceptional high school record. Minimum 3.0
GPA is required to retain scholarship. Awarded every year. Award
may be used only at sponsoring institution.
Contact: Audrey S. Lambert, Director of Student Financial Aid.

1804 Schillig-Baird and Presidential Scholarship

University of Southern Mississippi
Office of Recruitment and Orientation
Box 5166
Hattiesburg, MS 39406-5166
(601) 266-5000
Average award: Comprehensive tuition
Number of awards: 40
Deadline: February 1
College level: Freshman
Criteria: Applicant must be a National Merit finalist and have a mini-
mum composite ACT score of 32 or combined SAT I score of 1330.
Interview is required. Recipient must enroll in the Honors College.
Scholarship is renewable. Awarded every year. Award may be used
only at sponsoring institution.
Contact: Dr. Homer Wesley, Director of Recruitment and Orientation.

1805 Scholar's Scholarship

Messiah College
Grantham, PA 17027-0800
(717) 766-2511, (717) 691-6025 (fax)
http://www.messiah.edu
Maximum award: $11,800
Number of awards: 4
Deadline: None
College level: Freshman
Criteria: Applicant must be a full-time student of high academic
acheivement, Christian character, and leadership potential. Applicant must rank in the top tenth of his or her graduating class and have
a minimum combined SAT I score of 1260 (composite ACT score of
28). Renewable if recipient maintains a minimum 3.5 GPA and exhibits strong Christian character and a continuing leadership role.
Awarded every year. Award may be used only at sponsoring institution.
Contact: William G. Strausbaugh, Vice President for Enrollment,
(717) 691-6000, strausba@messiah.edu.

1806 Scholars Award

Drury College
900 North Benton Avenue
Springfield, MO 65802
(417) 873-7319
Average award: $5,000
Number of awards: 15
Deadline: February 20
College level: Freshman
Criteria: Applicant must be accepted for full-time enrollment, have a
minimum 3.5 GPA and minimum composite ACT score of 29 (combined SAT I score of 1210), submit essay, two letters of recommendation, and listing of leadership activities in church, community, and
school, and attend an interview. Recipient will also receive $500
Leadership Award. Renewable for up to four years if recipient maintains a minimum 3.0 GPA. Awarded every year. Award may be used
only at sponsoring institution.
Contact: Financial Aid Office.

1807 Scholars Award

Washington and Jefferson College
Washington, PA 15301
(412) 223-6019
Maximum award: $8,000
Number of awards: 125
Deadline: March 1
College level: Freshman
Criteria: Applicant must rank in top tenth of class and have a mini-
mum combined SAT I score of 1000 (composite ACT score of 23).
Minimum 3.10 GPA is required to retain scholarship. Awarded every
year. Award may be used only at sponsoring institution.
Contact: Ricahrd H. Soudan, Director of Financial Aid.

1808 Scholarship (Academic)

Brescia College
717 Frederica Street
Owensboro, KY 42301-3023
(502) 686-4290, (800) 264-1234, (502) 686-4266 (fax)
vpearson@brescia.edu
Average award: $3,500
Maximum award: Full tuition
Minimum award: Partial tuition
Number of awards: 130
Deadline: March 1 (priority)
College level: Freshman
Criteria: Selection is based upon application, letter of recommenda-
tion, and standardized test scores (ACT preferred). Recipient must
have a minimum 12 credit hours per semester and maintain specified
GPA to retain scholarship for up to three consecutive years. Awarded
every year. Award may be used only at sponsoring institution.
Contact: Sam McNair, Director of Admissions, (502) 686-4290.

1809 Scholarship for Academic Distinction

Marquette University
P.O. Box 1881
Milwaukee, WI 53201-1881
(414) 288-7302, (414) 288-3764 (fax)
go2marquette@vms.csd.mu.edu
http://www.mu.edu
Average award: $6,000
Deadline: February 1
College level: Freshman, Transfers
Criteria: Selection is based upon academic achievement, class rank,
standardized tests, and extracurricular activities. Minimum 3.0 GPA
and full-time enrollment are required to retain scholarship. Awarded
every year. Award may be used only at sponsoring institution.
Contact: Carlos Garces, Senior Assistant Director of Admissions.

1810 Scholarship for Academically Talented Out-of-State Student

Bowie State University
Bowie, MD 20715
(301) 464-6544
Average award: Tuition, fees, room, board, books
Deadline: February 1 (fall); November 1 (spring)
College level: Freshman
Criteria: Applicant must have a minimum 3.3 GPA, a minimum combined SAT I score of 1050 (composite ACT score of 26), be enrolled
full time, be a U.S. citizen or permanent resident, and have telephone
interview with at least two members of scholarship committee. Recipient must participate in Honors Program. Awarded every year. Award
may be used only at sponsoring institution.
Contact: Scholarship Committee, Career Services, Bowie, MD
20715-9465, (301)464-7110, (301) 464-7111.

1811 Scholarship for Honors

Adelphi University
South Avenue
Garden City, NY 11530
(516) 877-3050
Average award: $6,500
Maximum award: $10,000
Minimum award: $4,500
Number of awards: 160
Deadline: None
College level: Freshman
Criteria: Renewable for up to three years if recipient has minimum 3.2
GPA after freshman year and 3.3 GPA thereafter. Awarded every
year. Award may be used only at sponsoring institution.
Contact: Scholarships.

1812 Scholarship For Leaders

Wells College
Aurora, NY 13026
(315) 364-3264, (315) 364-3227 (fax)
admissions@wells.edu
http://www.wells.edu
Average award: $4,000
Maximum award: $7,500
Minimum award: $2,000
Maximum number of awards: 110
Minimum number of awards: 75
Deadline: February 15
College level: Freshman
Criteria: Applicant must have a minimum "B" grade average and lead-
ership ability as demonstrated in community and school activities.
Renewable if recipient maintains a minimum 3.0 GPA. Awarded ev-
ery year. Award may be used only at sponsoring institution.
Contact: Susan Raith Sloan, Director of Admissions.

1813 Scholarship for Student Leaders

Hamline University
1536 Hewitt Avenue
St. Paul, MN 55104
(612) 641-2207
Average award: $3,000
Number of awards: 30
Deadline: January 20
College level: Freshman
Criteria: Applicant must have a minimum 3.3 GPA ("B+" grade average) or rank in top 15% of class, a strong college-preparatory academic record, and have demonstrated leadership in community or
school. Selection is based upon interview with selection committee.
Renewable for up to three years based upon leadership and co-curricular involvement. Awarded every year. Award may be used only at
sponsoring institution.
Contact: Brian Peterson, Senior Associate Director of Undergraduate Admission.

1814 Scholarship for Transfer Students

Adelphi University
South Avenue
Garden City, NY 11530
(516) 877-3050
Average award: $3,200
Maximum award: $4,500
Minimum award: $2,000
Number of awards: 250
Deadline: None
College level: Sophomore, Junior, Senior
Criteria: Recipient must maintain minimum 3.0 GPA. Awarded every
year. Award may be used only at sponsoring institution.
Contact: Scholarships.

1815 Scholastic Distinction Scholarship

University of Alberta
Edmonton, Alberta, CN T6G 2M7
(403) 492-3111
Maximum award: $25,000 over 4 years
Number of awards: 40
Deadline: March 1
College level: Freshman, Transfers
Criteria: Applicant must have a minimum average of 95% and be
nominated by his or her school. Renewable of recipient continues to
excel in academics. Award may be used only at sponsoring institu-
tion.
Contact: Student Awards Office, 103 Administration Building, Ed-
monton, AB T6G 2M7, (403) 492-3221.

1816 Scholastic Excellence Scholarship

Ouachita Baptist University
410 Ouachita Street
Arkadelphia, AR 71998-0001
(501) 245-5570
Maximum award: $4,500
Number of awards: 315
Deadline: None
College level: Freshman
Criteria: Applicant must have a minimum composite ACT score of 24 (combined SAT I score of 980). Minimum 2.5 GPA for up to 58 credit hours (minimum 3.0 GPA for 59 and over) required to retain scholarship. Awarded every year. Award may be used only at sponsoring institution.
Contact: Susan Hurst, Director of Financial Aid.

1817 SCions Scholarship

University of Southern California
University Park
Los Angeles, CA 90089-5012
(213) 740-1111
Maximum award: $3,000
Maximum number of awards: 125
Minimum number of awards: 100
Deadline: December 15
College level: Freshman, Sophomore, Junior, Senior
Criteria: Applicant must be the child, grandchild, niece, nephew, or sibling of alumni/ae. (In the case of siblings, the other sibling must have already graduated.) Freshman applicant must have a minimum 3.6 GPA and minimum combined SAT I score of 1120 (composite ACT score of 27). Upperclass applicant must have a minimum 3.0 GPA. Interview is required. Awarded every year. Award may be used only at sponsoring institution.
Contact: Office of Admission, University Park Campus, Los Angeles, CA 90089-0911.

1818 Senior Class President Leadership Scholarship

University of West Alabama
Station Four
Livingston, AL 35470
(205) 652-3400, (205) 652-3522 (fax)
http://www.westal.edu
Average award: Full tuition
Deadline: April 15
College level: Freshman
Criteria: Applicant must have been senior class president while in high school. Renewable for up to four years if minimum 3.0 GPA is maintained. Awarded every year. Award may be used only at sponsoring institution.
Contact: Richard Hester, Director of Admissions, (205) 652-9661, extension 352.

1819 Shawnee State Academic Excellence for Ohio Scholarship

Shawnee State University
940 Second Street
Portsmouth, OH 45662-4344
(614) 355-2237
Average award: $2,750
Deadline: April 15
College level: Freshman
Criteria: Applicant must be valedictorian or salutatorian graduating the same year award is given, must attend full-time, and must maintain a minimum 3.0 GPA. Award covers tuition and fees for four years or 12 quarters. FAFSA is required. Early application is recommended. Awarded every year. Award may be used only at sponsoring institution.
Contact: Financial Aid Office, (614) 355-2485.

1820 Sophomore Excellence Scholarship

Northern Kentucky University
Administrative Center 416
Nunn Drive
Highland Heights, KY 41099-7101
(606) 572-5144
Average award: In-state tuition
Deadline: February 1
College level: Sophomore
Criteria: Applicant must have a minimum cumulative 3.25 GPA. Awarded every year. Award may be used only at sponsoring institution.
Contact: Robert E. Sprague, Director of Financial Aid.

1821 Southern Vermont College Scholarship

Southern Vermont College
Monument Avenue
Bennington, VT 05201
(802) 442-5427, (802) 447-4695 (fax)
admis@svc.edu
http://www.svc.edu
Average award: $3,939
Maximum award: $11,000
Minimum award: $100
Number of awards: 327
Deadline: May 1 (priority)
College level: Freshman, Sophomore, Junior, Senior
Criteria: Applicant must demonstrate satisfactory academic progress. Recipient must reapply and submit FAFSA for renewal. Awarded every year. Award may be used only at sponsoring institution.
Contact: Cathleen Seaton, Director of Financial Aid.

1822 Special Academic Scholarship

Indiana University Northwest
3400 Broadway
Gary, IN 46408
(219) 980-6777, (219) 981-4219 (fax)
wlee@iunhawl.iun.indiana.edu
Maximum award: Full tuition
Number of awards: 15
Deadline: March 15
College level: Freshman
Criteria: Selection is based upon academic achievement and potential for college succes. Scholarship is renewable. Awarded every year. Award may be used only at sponsoring institution.
Contact: William D. Lee, Director of Admissions and Financial Aids, (219) 980-6991.

1823 Special Talent Scholarship

Eckerd College
4200 54th Avenue South
St. Petersburg, FL 33711
(813) 864-8331, 800 456-9009, (813) 866-2304 (fax)
admissions@eckerd.edu
http://www.eckerd.edu
Average award: $5,000
Maximum award: $8,000
Minimum award: $1,000
Number of awards: 50
Deadline: None
College level: Freshman, Transfers
Criteria: Selection is based upon achievement in an academic area, special talent in the creative arts, demonstrated leadership and service in church, community, or school organizations, or athletic ability. Renewable if recipient maintains a minimum 2.0 GPA. Awarded every year. Award may be used only at sponsoring institution.
Contact: Dr. Richard Hallin, Dean of Admissions.

1824   Speck Farrar Scholarship

Clemson University
G-01 Sikes Hall
Clemson, SC 29634-5123
(803) 656-2280
Average award: $3,000
Number of awards: 5
Deadline: March 1
College level: Freshman, Sophomore, Junior, Senior
Criteria: Applicant must have a minimum 2.5 GPA and demonstrate financial need. Awarded every year. Award may be used only at sponsoring institution.
Contact: Marvin Carmichael, Director of Financial Aid.

1825   State Youth Organization Officer Leadership Scholarship

University of West Alabama
Station Four
Livingston, AL 35470
(205) 652-3400, (205) 652-3522 (fax)
http://www.westal.edu
Average award: Full tuition
Deadline: April 15
College level: Freshman
Criteria: Applicant must have been an officer of a state youth organization while in high school. Renewable for up to four years if minimum 3.0 GPA is maintained. Awarded every year. Award may be used only at sponsoring institution.
Contact: Richard Hester, Director of Admissions, (205) 652-9661, extension 352.

1826   Steven V. Mitchell Memorial Crimson Scholarship

The University of Alabama
Box 870162
Tuscaloosa, AL 35487-0162
(205) 348-6756
Average award: $2,470
Number of awards: 1
Deadline: December 3
College level: Freshman
Criteria: Applicant must have a minimum 3.9 GPA, rank in top 2% of class, and have a minimum composite ACT score of 32 (combined SAT I score of 1350). Preference is given to graduate of a Madison County, Ala., school who demonstrates financial need. Renewable for up to eight semesters if minimum 3.0 GPA is maintained. Award may be used only at sponsoring institution.
Contact: National Alumni Association, P.O. Box 1928, Tuscaloosa, AL 35486-1928.

1827   Storer Scholarship

The College of Wooster
Office of Admissions
Wooster, OH 44691
(330) 263-2270, (330) 263-2621 (fax)
admissions@acs.wooster.edu
http://www.wooster.edu
Average award: $10,000
Deadline: February 15
College level: Freshman
Majors/Fields: English, history
Criteria: Applicant must have a minimum 3.4 GPA and rank in top tenth of class. Recipient must maintain academic progress toward degree to retain scholarship. Renewable for four years. Award may be used only at sponsoring institution.
Contact: Office of Admissions.

1828   Student Council President Leadership Scholarship

University of West Alabama
Station Four
Livingston, AL 35470
(205) 652-3400, (205) 652-3522 (fax)
http://www.westal.edu
Average award: $3,040
Number of awards: 75
Deadline: Early application is recommended
College level: Freshman
Criteria: Applicant must have been student council president while in high school. Renewable for up to four years if minimum 3.0 GPA is maintained. Awarded every year. Award may be used only at sponsoring institution.
Contact: Richard Hester, Director of Admissions, (205) 652-3400, extension 3578, rth@uwamail.westal.edu.

1829   Student Tuition Assistance Recipient (STAR) Program

Wilson College
1015 Philadelphia Avenue
Chambersburg, PA 17201-1285
(717) 264-4141, (717) 264-1578 (fax)
http://www.wilson.edu
Maximum award: $3,500
Number of awards: 111
Deadline: None
College level: Freshman, Transfers
Criteria: Awarded automatically to entering students with a minimum combined SAT I score of 900 (composite ACT score of 22). Amount of award is based upon score. Recipients must enroll full time. Recipient must maintain minimum 2.5 GPA for renewal. Awarded every year. Award may be used only at sponsoring institution.
Contact: Jeffrey Stock, Associate Director of Admissions, (717) 262-2002.

1830   Study Grant

Long Island University, C.W. Post Campus
Route 25A
Brookville, NY 11548
(516) 299-2338, (516) 299-2137 (fax)
admissions@collegehall.liunet.edu
http://www.liunet.edu
Maximum award: $2,500
Deadline: May 15
College level: Freshman
Criteria: Applicant must be enrolled full time and have a minimum 2.5 GPA. Selection is based upon academic record and financial need. Awarded every year. Award may be used only at sponsoring institution.
Contact: Financial Aid Office, 720 Northern Boulevard, Brookville, NY 11548.

1831   Sturgis Fellowship

University of Arkansas, Fayetteville
Office of Scholarships and Financial Aid
114 Hunt Hall
Fayetteville, AR 72701
(501) 575-3806
Maximum award: $10,000
Deadline: February 1
College level: Freshman, Sophomore, Junior, Senior
Criteria: Applicant must have exceptional academic performance and major in the Fulbright College of Arts and Sciences. Outstanding academic performance is required to retain scholarship. Awarded every year. Award may be used only at sponsoring institution.
Contact: Director of Honors Studies, Old Main 517, Fayetteville, AR 72701.

1832 Sullivan Award

Seattle University
Broadway and Madison
Seattle, WA 98122
(206) 296-5840, (206) 296-5656 (fax)
admissions@seattleu.edu
http://www.seattleu.edu
Average award: $18,500
Number of awards: 5
Deadline: October 1
College level: Freshman
Criteria: Applicant must have demonstrated leadership skills. Minimum 3.0 GPA and completion of at least 45 credit hours per year are required to retain scholarship. Awarded every year. Award may be used only at sponsoring institution.
Contact: Undergraduate Admissions Office, 900 Broadway, Seattle, WA 98122-4340, (206) 296-5800, admissions@seattleu.edu.

1833 Summer Scholars Program in Biology & Biomedical Research

Washington University
One Brookings Drive
Campus Box 1089
St. Louis, MO 63130
(314) 935-6000 or (800) 638-0700
Average award: Full tuition and stipend for travel and living expenses
Number of awards: 30
Deadline: January 15
College level: Freshman
Majors/Fields: Natural sciences, mathematics, social sciences, humanities
Criteria: Selection is based upon academic merit without regard to financial need. Program lasts six weeks. Satisfactory academic performance is required to retain scholarship. Awarded every year. Award may be used only at sponsoring institution.
Contact: Office of Undergraduate Admissions.

1834 Sunshine Scholarship

Webber College
P.O. Box 96
Babson Park, FL 33827
(813) 638-1431
Average award: $4,000
College level: Freshman
Criteria: Applicant must have a minimum combined SAT I score of 950 (composite ACT score of 22). Minimum 3.0 GPA and continuous full-time enrollment are required to retain scholarship. Awarded every year. Award may be used only at sponsoring institution.
Contact: Kathleen Wilson, Financial Aid Director.

1835 Syd Garner Scholarship

Indiana University Northwest
3400 Broadway
Gary, IN 46408
(219) 980-6777, (219) 981-4219 (fax)
wlee@iunhawl.iun.indiana.edu
Maximum award: Full tuition, fees, books
Number of awards: 1
Deadline: March 15
College level: Freshman
Criteria: Selection is based upon academic achievement and potential for college succes. Scholarship is renewable. Awarded every year. Award may be used only at sponsoring institution.
Contact: William D. Lee, Director of Admissions and Financial Aids, (219) 980-6991.

1836 T. Brady Saunders Area Honor Scholarship

Lynchburg College
Lynchburg, VA 24501
(804) 522-8228
Average award: Half tuition
Deadline: February 15
College level: Freshman
Criteria: Applicant must have a minimum "B" grade average, rank in top tenth of class, and be recommended by school counselor. Awarded to graduates of specific central Virginia schools. Awarded every year. Award may be used only at sponsoring institution.
Contact: Scholarships.

1837 Technical Communication Scholarship

Milwaukee School of Engineering
1025 North Broadway
Milwaukee, WI 53202-3109
(800) 332-6763, (414) 277-7475 (fax)
goran@admin.msoe.edu
www.msoe.edu
Average award: Half tuition
Number of awards: 1
Deadline: February 1
College level: Freshman
Criteria: Applicant must have minimum 3.0 GPA. Recommendation is suggested. Renewable up to four years if recipient maintains minimum 3.0 GPA. Awarded every year. Award may be used only at sponsoring institution.
Contact: Sue Minzlaff, Financial Aid Office, (414) 277-7222, minzlaff@admin.msoe.edu.

1838 Tennessee Scholar

University of Tennessee, Knoxville
Financial Aid Office
115 Student Services Building
Knoxville, TN 37994
(615) 974-3131
Average award: $4,000
Number of awards: 25
Deadline: February 1
College level: Freshman
Criteria: Selection is based upon academic achievement. Creative abilities and involvement in school activities are considered. Award is for four years. Awarded every year. Award may be used only at sponsoring institution.
Contact: University Honors Program, F-101 Melrose Hall, Knoxville, TN 37916, (615) 974-7875.

1839 Texas Excellence Award

University of Texas at Austin
P.O. Box 7758, UT Station
Austin, TX 78713-7758
(512) 475-6200, (512) 475-6296 (fax)
finaid@www.utexas.edu
http://www.utexas.edu/student/finaid
Average award: $3,000
Maximum award: $7,000
Minimum award: $1,000
Maximum number of awards: 36
Minimum number of awards: 10
Deadline: December 1
College level: Freshman, Sophomore, Junior, Senior
Criteria: Applicant must rank in top five percent of class. Satisfactory academic progress is required to retain scholarship. Awarded every year. Award may be used only at sponsoring institution.
Contact: Eleanor Moore, Director of Scholarships, Ex-Students Association, Austin, TX 78713, (512) 471-8083.

1840   The Master's College (TMC) Grants

The Master's College
21726 Placerita Canyon Road
Santa Clarita, CA 91321-1200
(805) 259-3540, (805) 288-1037 (fax)
Maximum award: $3,000
College level: Freshman, Sophomore, Junior, Senior
Criteria: Selection is based upon academic achievement and financial need. Minimum 3.0 GPA required to retain scholarship. Awarded every year. Award may be used only at sponsoring institution.
Contact: Timothy C. Wiegert, Associate Director of Enrollment, (800) 568-6248 extension 450.

1841   Third Century Scholarship

Ohio University
Office of Student Financial Aid and Scholarships
Athens, OH 45701
(614) 593-4141, (614) 593-4140 (fax)
Average award: In-state tuition
Number of awards: 10
Deadline: February 15
College level: Freshman
Criteria: Selection is based upon academic qualifications. Minimum 3.3 GPA and 16 credit hours per quarter are required to retain scholarship. Awarded every year. Award may be used only at sponsoring institution.
Contact: Mrs. Yang-Hi Kim, Associate Director of Scholarships and Grants.

1842   Thurgood Marshall Scholarship Fund

Bowie State University
Bowie, MD 20715
(301) 464-6544
Average award: $4,000 plus fees, room, and board
Deadline: February 1
College level: Freshman
Criteria: Applicant must be a U.S. citizen, be enrolled full-time, be degree-seeking, have a minimum 3.0 GPA, have a minimum combined SAT I score of 1000 (composite ACT score of 24), and be recognized by school as an exceptional academic achiever or as having outstanding talent in creative and performing arts. Minimum 3.0 GPA is required to retain scholarship. Awarded every year. Award may be used only at sponsoring institution.
Contact: Scholarship Committee, Career Services, Bowie, MD 20715-9465, (301) 464-7110, (301) 464-7111.

1843   Top 10% Scholarship

Bradford College
320 South Main Street
Haverhill, MA 01835
(508) 372-7161, (508) 372-5240 (fax)
bradcoll@aol.com
http://bradford.edu
Average award: Half tuition
Number of awards: 20
Deadline: None
College level: Freshman, Sophomore, Junior, Senior
Criteria: Applicant must be in top tenth of class. Scholarship is renewable. Awarded every year. Award may be used only at sponsoring institution.
Contact: Scholarships.

1844   Tower Scholarship

Concordia College
800 North Columbia Avenue
Seward, NE 68434
(402) 643-7270
Maximum award: Full tuition
Deadline: None
College level: Transfers
Criteria: Applicant must be a full-time undergraduate and have a minimum 3.0 GPA and minimum composite ACT score of 24 (combined SAT I score of 1070) for minimum award. National Merit finalists may receive maximum award. Renewable for up to 10 consecutive semesters if minimum 3.0 GPA is maintained. Awarded every year. Award may be used only at sponsoring institution.
Contact: Scholarships.

1845   Tranfer Student Grand Mesa Scholarship

Mesa State College
Financial Aid Department
P.O. Box 2647
Grand Junction, CO 81502
(970) 248-1396
Maximum award: Full Tuition, fees, and $500
College level: Transfers with associate degree
Criteria: Applicant must have a minimum 3.5 GPA. Renewable for up to two years if recipient maintains a minimum 3.5 GPA, completes at least 15 credit hours per semester, and completes 50 hours of community service per year. Awarded every year. Award may be used only at sponsoring institution.
Contact: Office of Admission, (970) 248-1376.

1846   Transfer Award

William Woods University
200 West 12th Street
Fulton, MO 65251-1098
(573) 592-4232, (573) 592-1146 (fax)
http://www.wmwoods.edu
Average award: $3,000
Deadline: June 1
College level: Sophomore, Junior, Senior, Transfers
Criteria: Applicant must have a minimum 3.3 GPA and minimum 12 transfer credits. Recipient must reapply and maintain a minimum 3.3 GPA to retain scholarship. Awarded every year. Award may be used only at sponsoring institution.
Contact: Laura L. Archuleta, Director for Student Financial Aid, larchule@iris.wmwoods.edu.

1847   Transfer Chancellor Scholarship

Texas Christian University
2800 South University Drive
Fort Worth, TX 76129
(817) 921-7858, (817) 921-7462 (fax)
frogaid@tcu.edu
Average award: Full tuition
College level: Transfers
Criteria: Applicant must have a minimum 3.25 GPA and an Associate of Arts degree from a junior college or at least 64 transferable credit hours. Selection is based upon a student essay, teacher evaluation, and extracurricular activities or work experience. Renewable if recipient maintains a minimum 3.25 GPA and 27 credit hours per year. Awarded every year. Award may be used only at sponsoring institution.

1848 Transfer Deans Scholarship

Texas Christian University
2800 South University Drive
Fort Worth, TX 76129
(817) 921-7858, (817) 921-7462 (fax)
frogaid@tcu.edu
Average award: $3,000
Number of awards: 26
Deadline: May 30
College level: Transfers
Criteria: Applicant must have successfully completed at least 27 transferable semester hours with a minimum 3.25 GPA. Renewable for up to six semesters if recipient maintains a minimum 3.25 GPA and successfully completes at least 27 credit hours per year. Awarded every year. Award may be used only at sponsoring institution.
Contact: Office of Scholarships and Financial Aid, TCU Box 297012, Fort Worth, TX 76129.

1849 Transfer Excellence Award (TEA)

Long Island University, C.W. Post Campus
Route 25A
Brookville, NY 11548
(516) 299-2338, (516) 299-2137 (fax)
admissions@collegehall.liunet.edu
http://www.liunet.edu
Maximum award: $6,000
Deadline: July 1
College level: Transfers
Criteria: Applicant must have a minimum 3.75 GPA, have completed at least 32 credit hours before transferring, and be enrolled full time. Scholarship is renewable. Awarded every year. Award may be used only at sponsoring institution.
Contact: Admissions Office, 720 Northern Boulevard, Brookville, NY 11548, (516) 299-2413, admissions@collegehall.liunet.edu.

1850 Transfer Grant

Grand View College
1200 Grandview Avenue
Des Moines, IA 50316
(515) 263-2820
Average award: $2,450
Maximum award: $3,000
Minimum award: $2,000
Number of awards: 157
Deadline: None
College level: Transfers
Criteria: Applicant must be enrolled full time. Minimum 2.0 GPA is required to retain scholarship. Awarded every year. Award may be used only at sponsoring institution.
Contact: Lori S. Hanson, Director of Admissions, (515) 263-2800.

1851 Transfer Honor Scholarship

Wilmington College
Pyle Center Box 1325
Wilmington, OH 45177
(800) 341-9318, (513) 382-7077 (fax)
admission@wilmington.edu
http://www.wilmington.edu
Average award: $4,000
Number of awards: 30
Deadline: May 1
College level: Transfers
Criteria: Applicant must have a minimum 3.3 GPA after one year of college. Awarded every year. Award may be used only at sponsoring institution.
Contact: Financial Aid Office.

1852 Transfer Presidential Scholarship

Johnson & Wales University
8 Abbott Park Place
Providence, RI 02903
(401) 598-1000, (401) 598-1040 (fax)
admissions@jwu.edu
http://jwu.edu
Maximum award: $3,000
Deadline: April 15
College level: Transfers
Criteria: Applicant must have a minimum 3.0 GPA and have completed at least 30 credit hours at previous school. Minimum 2.75 GPA is required to retain scholarship. Awarded every year. Award may be used only at sponsoring institution.
Contact: Kristine McNamera/Licia Dwyer, Director of Admissions/Director of Culinary Admissions, (401) 598-2313, (401) 598-2370.

1853 Transfer Presidential Scholarship

Alfred University
Alumni Hall
26 North Main Street
Alfred, NY 14802
(607) 871-2159
Maximum award: $10,000
Deadline: None
College level: Students with associate degrees, Transfers from four-year school who have completed two years of study
Criteria: Renewable for up to four semesters if minimum 3.0 GPA and continuous full-time enrollment are maintained. Awarded every year. Award may be used only at sponsoring institution.
Contact: Scholarships.

1854 Transfer Scholars Award

Long Island University, C.W. Post Campus
Route 25A
Brookville, NY 11548
(516) 299-2338, (516) 299-2137 (fax)
admissions@collegehall.liunet.edu
http://www.liunet.edu
Average award: $10,000
Deadline: July 1
College level: Transfers
Criteria: Applicant must be a transferring with an associate degree directly from a community college. Applicant must be a full-time student with a minimum 3.9 GPA. Scholarship is renewable. Awarded every year. Award may be used only at sponsoring institution.
Contact: Admissions Office, 720 Northern Boulevard, Brookville, NY 11548-1300, (516) 299-2413, admissions@collegehall.liunet.edu.

1855 Transfer Scholarship

Grand View College
1200 Grandview Avenue
Des Moines, IA 50316
(515) 263-2820
Average award: $3,700
Maximum award: $4,000
Minimum award: $3,500
Number of awards: 14
Deadline: None
College level: Transfers
Criteria: Applicant must be enrolled full time. Minimum 3.0 GPA is required to retain scholarship. Awarded every year. Award may be used only at sponsoring institution.
Contact: Lori S. Hanson, Director of Admissions, (515) 263-2800.

1856 Transfer Scholarship

Cedar Crest College
100 College Drive
Allentown, PA 18104
(610) 740-3785, (610) 606-4647 (fax)
cccadmis@cedarcrest.edu
www.cedarcrest.edu
Average award: $3,000
Number of awards: 4
Deadline: Rolling
College level: Junior
Criteria: Renewable for up to two years if recipient maintains minimum 3.0 GPA. Awarded every year. Award may be used only at sponsoring institution.
Contact: Judith Neyhart, Vice President for Enrollment Management, Financial Aid Office, cccadmis@cedarcrest.edu.

1857 Transfer Scholarship

Salem College
P.O. Box 10548
Winston-Salem, NC 27108
(910) 721-2808
Maximum award: $6,000
Number of awards: 5
College level: Entering Transfers
Criteria: Selection is based upon academic achievement at previous school. Minimum 3.0 GPA required to retain scholarship. Awarded every year. Award may be used only at sponsoring institution.
Contact: Bruce Blackman, Director of Financial Aid.

1858 Transfer Scholarship

Elmira College
One Park Place
Elmira, NY 14901
(607) 735-1724, (607) 735-1718 (fax)
admissions@elmira.edu
www.elmira.edu
Maximum award: $3,500
Number of awards: 15
College level: Transfers with associate degree
Criteria: Applicant must be a full-time student transferring directly from community college. Graduates of Broome Comm Coll and Monroe Comm Coll receive minimum award; graduates of Corning Comm Coll receive $2,500 (commuting students) or $3,500 (dormitory students). Scholarship is renewable. Awarded every year. Award may be used only at sponsoring institution.
Contact: Dean of Admissions, admissions@elmira.edu.

1859 Transfer Scholarship

Lynn University
3601 North Military Trail
Boca Raton, FL 33431-5598
(561) 994-0770, (561) 247-3552 (fax)
admission@lynn.edu
http://www.lynn.edu
Maximum award: $6,000
Number of awards: 50
Deadline: None
College level: Sophomore, Junior
Criteria: Applicant must be a transfer student and have an associate degree or 15 credits completed. Applicant must have a minimum GPA of 2.0. Minimum 3.0 GPA is required to retain scholarship. Awarded every year. Award may be used only at sponsoring institution.
Contact: James Sullivan, Director of Admissions.

1860 Transfer Scholarship

College of New Rochelle
29 Castle Place
New Rochelle, NY 10805
(914) 654-5224
Average award: $2,500
Number of awards: 10
Deadline: None
College level: Sophomore, Junior
Criteria: Applicant must be a transfer student accepted for admission and have a minimum 3.3 GPA. Scholarship is renewable. Awarded every year. Award may be used only at sponsoring institution.
Contact: Annette Gonzalez, Financial Aid Counselor.

1861 Transfer Scholarship

Bradford College
320 South Main Street
Haverhill, MA 01835
(508) 372-7161, (508) 372-5240 (fax)
bradcoll@aol.com
http://bradford.edu
Average award: Half tuition
Number of awards: 15
College level: Sophomore, Junior, Senior, Transfers
Criteria: Applicant must have a minimum 3.2 GPA and an associate degree from one of the following institutions: Castle Coll, Bristol, Middlesex, North Shore and Bunker Hill, and Northern Essex Community Colleges. Renewable for up to two years of full-time enrollment. Awarded every year. Award may be used only at sponsoring institution.
Contact: Scholarships.

1862 Transfer Scholarship

Benedictine College
1020 North Second Street
Atchison, KS 66002
(913) 367-5340
Maximum range: $3,000-$5,000
Deadline: None
College level: Transfers
Criteria: Applicant must have completed a minimum of 24 credit hours. Applicant with 3.0-3.49 GPA is eligible for up to $3,000. Applicant with 3.5-4.0 GPA is eligible for up to $5,000. FAFSA is required. Renewable if GPA is maintained. Awarded every year. Award may be used only at sponsoring institution.
Contact: Diane Adams, Associate Director of Admissions.

1863 Transfer Scholarship

Wingate University
Wingate, NC 28174-0157
(800) 755-5550, (704) 233-8110 (fax)
admit@wingate.edu
http://www.wingate.edu
Average award: $1,407
Maximum award: $3,000
Minimum award: $500
Number of awards: 50
Deadline: August 15
College level: Sophomore, Junior, Senior
Criteria: Renewable if recipient maintains GPA. Awarded every year. Award may be used only at sponsoring institution.
Contact: Walt Crutchfield, Dean of Admissions, Office of Admissions Campus Box 3059, Wingate, NC 28174.

1864 Transfer Student Bookcliff Scholarship

Mesa State College
Financial Aid Department
P.O. Box 2647
Grand Junction, CO 81502
(970) 248-1396
Average award: Full tuition
Maximum award: Full tuition
College level: Transfers with associate degree
Criteria: Applicant must have a minimum 3.0 GPA and demonstrate a strong academic and/or leadership background. Renewable for up to two years if recipient maintains a minimum 3.0 GPA, completes at least 15 credit hours per semester, and completes 50 hours of community service per year. Awarded every year. Award may be used only at sponsoring institution.
Contact: Office of Admission, (970) 248-1376.

1865 Transfer Student Monument Scholarship

Mesa State College
Financial Aid Department
P.O. Box 2647
Grand Junction, CO 81502
(970) 248-1396
Maximum award: Tuition and Fees
College level: Transfers
Criteria: Applicant must have at least 30 transferable credits and a minimum 3.5 GPA. Selection is based upon academic background. Renewable for up to two years if recipient maintains a minimum 3.2 GPA, completes at least 15 credit hours per semester, and completes 500 hours of community service per year. Awarded every year. Award may be used only at sponsoring institution.
Contact: Office of Admission, (970) 248-1376.

1866 Transfer Student Scholarship

Susquehanna University
Selinsgrove, PA 17870
(717) 372-4450
Maximum award: $6,000
Deadline: None
College level: Transfers
Criteria: Selection is based upon academic achievement. Scholarship is renewable. Awarded every year. Award may be used only at sponsoring institution.
Contact: Office of Financial Aid.

1867 Transfer Student Tuition Award

Wilson College
1015 Philadelphia Avenue
Chambersburg, PA 17201-1285
(717) 264-4141, (717) 264-1578 (fax)
http://www.wilson.edu
Average award: One-quarter tuition discount
Number of awards: 2
Deadline: None
College level: Transfers
Criteria: Applicant must be a woman and hold an associate degree from one of the following schools: Central Penn Business Sch, Hagerstown Junior Coll, Harcum Junior Coll, Harrisburg Area Community Coll, Lehigh County Community Coll, Luzerne County Community Coll, Westmoreland County Community Coll. Renewable if satisfactory academic progress and at least half-time enrollment are maintained. Awarded every year. Award may be used only at sponsoring institution.
Contact: Ruth Cramer, Director of Financial Aid, (717) 262-2002.

1868 Trevecca Scholars Award

Trevecca Nazarene University
333 Murfreesboro Road
Nashville, TN 37210
(615) 248-1242
Maximum award: $3,000
Deadline: None
College level: Sophomore, Junior, Senior
Criteria: Applicant must be a full-time student with a 4.0 GPA. Scholarship is renewable. Awarded every year. Award may be used only at sponsoring institution.
Contact: Joanie Hall, Senior Counselor for Undergraduate Studies.

1869 Trustee Scholarship

Denison University
Box H
Granville, OH 43023
(614) 587-6276, 800-DENISON, (614) 587-6306 (fax)
admissions@denison.edu
http://www.denison.edu
Average award: Three-Quarters tuition
Number of awards: 59
Deadline: January 1
College level: Freshman
Criteria: Applicant must have rank of first or second in class and must meet criteria for Honors Program. Selection is based upon academic record, essay, extracurricular achievements, and counselor and teacher recommendations. Interview or campus visitation program is required. Finalist must submit special essay. Minimum GPA is required for renewal. Awarded every year. Award may be used only at sponsoring institution.
Contact: Janet Schultz, Scholarships, (614) 587-6625.

1870 Trustee Scholarship

Ouachita Baptist University
410 Ouachita Street
Arkadelphia, AR 71998-0001
(501) 245-5570
Maximum award: $9,970
Number of awards: 67
Deadline: None
College level: Freshman, Transfers
Criteria: Applicant must be an Arkansas Governor's Scholar or National Merit Finalist. Minimum 3.0 GPA required to retain scholarship. Awarded every year. Award may be used only at sponsoring institution.
Contact: Susan Hurst, Director of Financial Aid.

1871 Trustee Scholarship

Queens College
1900 Selwyn Avenue
Charlotte, NC 28274
(704) 337-2212, 800 849-0202, (704) 337-2403 (fax)
cas@rex.queens.edu
http://www.queens.edu
Maximum award: $7,000
Number of awards: 20
Deadline: December 15
College level: Freshman
Criteria: Applicants are taken from the Presidential Scholarship pool. Applicant must have a minimum combined SAT I score of 1200 and rank in top 5% of class. Selection is based upon superior academic and leadership achievement. Special application is required. Scholarship is renewable. Awarded every year. Award may be used only at sponsoring institution.
Contact: Scholarships.

1872 Trustee Scholarship

University of Southern California
University Park
Los Angeles, CA 90089-5012
(213) 740-1111
Average award: $19,500
Average award: Full tuition
Number of awards: 100
Deadline: December 15
College level: Freshman
Criteria: Selection is based upon academic performance and demonstrated leadership in school or community. Rank in top two percent of class and PSAT scores in the range for National Achievement, National Hispanic, and National Merit Scholar consideration are recommended. Application and interview are required. Scholarship is renewable. Awarded every year. Award may be used only at sponsoring institution.
Contact: Office of Admission, University Park Campus, Los Angeles, CA 90089-0911.

1873 Trustee Scholarship

Hope College
P.O. Box 9000
Holland, MI 49422-9000
(616) 395-7850, (616) 395-7130 (fax)
admissions@hope.edu
http://www.hope.edu
Average award: $12,000
Number of awards: 6
Deadline: January 20
College level: Freshman, Sophomore, Junior, Senior
Criteria: Selection is based upon academic record, demonstrated leadership abilities, involvement in school/community activities, essay, and campus interview with faculty. National Merit Scholarship recipients are not eligible. Renewable if recipient maintains a minimum 3.0 GPA. Awarded every year. Award may be used only at sponsoring institution.
Contact: James R. Bekkering, Vice President for Admissions and Student Life.

1874 Trustee Scholarship

Lawrence University
P.O. Box 599
Appleton, WI 54912-0599
(414) 832-6500, (414) 832-6782 (fax)
excel@lawrence.edu
http://www.lawrence.edu
Average award: $10,000
Number of awards: 33
Deadline: February 1
College level: Freshman
Criteria: Applicant must rank in top three percent of secondary school class, have a minimum 3.9 GPA, and a minimum combined SAT I score of 1250 (composite ACT score of 31) recommended. Scholarships are competitive. A minimum 3.0 GPA is required to retain scholarship. Awarded every year. Award may be used only at sponsoring institution.
Contact: Director of Admissions.

1875 Trustee Scholarship

Drury College
900 North Benton Avenue
Springfield, MO 65802
(417) 873-7319
Average award: Full tuition
Number of awards: 7
Deadline: February 20
College level: Freshman
Criteria: Applicant must be accepted for full-time enrollment, have a minimum 3.5 GPA and minimum composite ACT score of 29 (combined SAT I score of 1210), submit essay, two letters of recommendation, and listing of leadership activities in church, community, and school, and attend an interview. Renewable for up to four years if recipient maintains a minimum 3.0 GPA. Awarded every year. Award may be used only at sponsoring institution.
Contact: Financial Aid Office.

1876 Trustee Scholarship

Birmingham-Southern College
Arkadelphia Road
Birmingham, AL 35254
(205) 226-4688
Maximum award: $2,500
Number of awards: 10
Deadline: January 5
College level: Freshman
Criteria: Applicant should rank in top two-tenths of class, have a minimum composite ACT score of 26 (combined SAT I score of 1050), and have leadership ability. Extracurricular activities are considered. Selection is based upon academic qualifications. Satisfactory academic progress is required to retain scholarship. Awarded every year. Award may be used only at sponsoring institution.
Contact: Forrest Stuart, Interim Director of Financial Aid Services.

1877 Trustee Scholarship

Principia College
Elsah, IL 62028
(800) 277-4648, (800) 347-4000 (fax)
collegeadmissions@prin.edu
http://www.prin.edu
Average award: Full tuition
Number of awards: 22
Deadline: January 15
College level: Freshman
Criteria: Recipient must maintain a minimum 3.6 GPA and support community standards to retain scholarship. Awarded every year. Award may be used only at sponsoring institution.
Contact: Martha Green Quirk, Director of Admissions and Enrollment, (618) 374-5180, mgq@prin.edu.

1878 Trustee Scholarship

Wingate University
Wingate, NC 28174-0157
(800) 755-5550, (704) 233-8110 (fax)
admit@wingate.edu
http://www.wingate.edu
Average award: $3,911
Maximum award: $5,000
Minimum award: $3,000
Number of awards: 45
Deadline: April 15
College level: Freshman
Criteria: Minimum 3.0 GPA is required to retain scholarship. Awarded every year. Award may be used only at sponsoring institution.
Contact: Walt Crutchfield, Dean of Admissions, Office of Admissions Campus Box 3059, Wingate, NC 28174, admit@wingate.edu.

1879 Trustee Scholarship

Centre College
600 West Walnut Street
Danville, KY 40422
(606) 238-5350, (606) 238-5373 (fax)
admission@centre.edu
http://www.centre.edu
Average award: Comprehensive tuition
Number of awards: 2
Deadline: February 1
College level: Freshman
Criteria: Interview is required. Renewable if recipient maintains good academic standing and a minimum 3.4 GPA (GPA requirements increase for subsequent years). Awarded every year. Award may be used only at sponsoring institution.
Contact: Thomas B. Martin, Dean of Enrollment Management.

1880 Trustee Scholarship

Lawrence Technological University
21000 West Ten Mile Road
Southfield, MI 48075
(810) 204-2120
Average award: $2,000
Maximum award: $3,000
Minimum award: $1,000
Number of awards: 150
Deadline: March 1
College level: Freshman, Junior college transfers
*Criteria:*Applicant must have a minimum 3.0 GPA and minimum composite ACT score of 23. Minimum 2.7 GPA is required to retain scholarship. Awarded every year. Award may be used only at sponsoring institution.
Contact: Paul F. Kinder, Director of Financial Aid.

1881 Trustee Scholarship

Wilmington College
Pyle Center Box 1325
Wilmington, OH 45177
(800) 341-9318, (513) 382-7077 (fax)
admission@wilmington.edu
http://www.wilmington.edu
Average award: $5,000
Number of awards: 160
Deadline: May 1
College level: Freshman
Criteria: Applicant must have a minimum 3.0 GPA and either rank in top two-tenths of class or have a minimum composite ACT score of 25 (combined SAT I score of 1050). Selection is based upon academic record. Renewable if recipient maintains a minimum 3.3 GPA. Awarded every year. Award may be used only at sponsoring institution.
Contact: Financial Aid Office.

1882 Trustee Scholarship

Loyola Marymount University
7900 Loyola Boulevard
Los Angeles, CA 90045-8350
(310) 338-2753, (310) 338-2793 (fax)
http://www.lmu.edu
Average award: $16,000
Number of awards: 10
College level: Freshman
Criteria: Applicant must have a minimum 3.6 GPA and minimum SAT I math and verbal scores of 650 (combined SAT I score of 1300, composite ACT score of 29). Selection is based upon Academic Scholarship competition and interview. Renewable for four years. Awarded every year. Award may be used only at sponsoring institution.
Contact: Financial Aid Office.

1883 Trustee Scholarship

Ohio Wesleyan University
Office of Admissions
Delaware, OH 43015
(614) 368-3020, (614) 368-3314 (fax)
owuadmit@cc.owu.edu
http://www.owu.edu
Average award: $14,355
Number of awards: 45
Deadline: March 1
College level: Freshman, Sophomore, Junior, Senior
Criteria: Applicant must rank in top tenth of class, have a minimum composite ACT score of 30 (combined SAT I score of 1370), and submit essay and two teacher recommendations. Interview with faculty member is strongly recommended. Selection is based upon curriculum, extracurricular involvement, GPA, standardized test scores, and writing skills. Minimum 3.5 GPA by the end of sophomore year is required to retain scholarship. Awarded every year. Award may be used only at sponsoring institution.
Contact: Douglas C. Thompson, Dean of Admission.

1884 Trustee Scholarship

Boston University
Office of Financial Assistance
881 Commonwealth Avenue
Boston, MA 02215
(617) 353-4175
Average award: Full tuition
Maximum award: $22,398
Number of awards: 130
Deadline: December 15 (freshmen); March 15 (Transfers); May 15 (continuing students)
College level: Freshman, Sophomore, Junior, Senior, Transfers
*Criteria:*Applicant must be nominated by his or her high school, junior college, or community college. Selection is based upon academic performance and potential, leadership, and community involvement. Minimum 3.5 GPA and completion of at least 12 credit hours per semester are required to retain scholarship. Awarded every year. Award may be used only at sponsoring institution.
Contact: Maria B. DelSignore, Assistant Director for Special Programs.

1885 Trustee's Award for Outstanding Achievement

California State Polytechnic University, Pomona
3801 West Temple Avenue
Pomona, CA 917684019
(909) 869-3700
Average award: $2,500
Number of awards: 3
Criteria: Award may be used only at sponsoring institution.
Contact: Crystal Steele, Financial Aid Counselor.

1886 Trustee's Scholarship

Michigan Christian College
800 West Avon Road
Rochester Hills, MI 48307
(810) 650-6018, (810) 650-6060 (fax)
Average award: Three-Quarters tuition
Maximum award: Full tuition
Minimum award: Half tuition
Deadline: May 1 (priority)
College level: Freshman
*Criteria:*Applicant must have a minimum composite ACT score of 30 or combined SAT I score of 1300 to be considered for Level 3. Level 2 requires a composite ACT score of 28-29 or combined SAT I score of 1220-1299. Level 1 requires a composite ACT score of 26-28 or combined SAT I score of 1140-1219. Applicant must have a supportive GPA, be a full-time boarding student, and demonstrate leadership in church, community, and school. Selection is competitive. Renewable if minimum 3.6 GPA (Level I), 3.7 GPA (Level 2), or 3.8 GPA (Level 3) is maintained. Awarded every year. Award may be used only at sponsoring institution.
Contact: Admissions Office.

1887 Trustee's Scholarship

Piedmont College
165 Central Avenue
Demorest, GA 30535
(706) 778-3000
Average award: Tuition
Number of awards: 7
Deadline: February 15
College level: Freshman
Criteria: Applicant must have a minimum combined SAT I score of 1000. Recipient must participate in Piedmont Scholars Program and at least one other campus organization and live in college housing. Renewable for up to four years if minimum 3.0 GPA is maintained. Awarded every year. Award may be used only at sponsoring institution.
Contact: Kenneth L. Owen, Director of Financial Aid.

1888 Trustees Award

Heidelberg College
310 East Market Street
Tiffin, OH 44883
(419) 448-2293, (414) 448-2124 (fax)
jweing@mail.heidelberg.edu
Average award: $6,000
Maximum number of awards: 20
Minimum number of awards: 5
Deadline: December 15
College level: Freshman
Criteria: Selection is based upon an invitation-only competition held in February. Renewable if recipient maintains a minimum 3.0 GPA. Awarded every year. Award may be used only at sponsoring institution.
Contact: Juli Weninger, Director of Financial Aid.

1889 Trustees Scholarship

Seattle University
Broadway and Madison
Seattle, WA 98122
(206) 296-5840, (206) 296-5656 (fax)
admissions@seattleu.edu
http://www.seattleu.edu
Maximum award: $7,500
Number of awards: 130
Deadline: February 1
College level: Freshman, Transfers
Criteria: Recipient must maintain a minimum 3.0 GPA and complete at least 45 credit hours to retain scholarship. Awarded every year. Award may be used only at sponsoring institution.
Contact: Undergraduate Admissions Office, 900 Broadway, Seattle, WA 98122-4340, (206) 296-5800, admissions@seattleu.edu.

1890 Trustees' Award for Outstanding Achievement

California State University, Fullerton
P.O. Box 34080
Fullerton, CA 92634-9480
(714) 773-3128
Average award: $2,500
Number of awards: 33
Deadline: February 26
College level: Sophomore, Junior, Senior
Criteria: Applicant must be enrolled full-time. Selection is based upon superior academic performance, community service, and personal achievements. Awarded every year. Award may be used only at sponsoring institution.
Contact: Viceky Takeuchi, Scholarship Coordinator.

1891 Trustees' Endowment Scholarship

University of South Carolina (Columbia)
Office of Admissions
Columbia, SC 29208
(803) 777-4067
Average award: $3,500
Number of awards: 10
Deadline: Early November
College level: Freshman
Criteria: Selection is based upon extraordinary academic achievement. Consideration is also given to needy and minority students who meet the academic requirement. Minimum 3.0 GPA is required to retain scholarship. Awarded every year. Award may be used only at sponsoring institution.
Contact: Michael Jinnette, Scholarship Coordinator.

1892 Trustees' Scholarship

Marietta College
Fifth Street
Marietta, OH 45750
(614) 376-4712
Average award: $10,400
Deadline: March 1
College level: Freshman
Criteria: Renewable if minimum 3.0 GPA and continuous full-time enrollment are maintained. Awarded every year. Award may be used only at sponsoring institution.
Contact: James M. Bauer, Associate Dean/Director of Financial Aid.

1893 Tuition Equalization Program Scholarship

Bluffton College
280 West College Avenue
Bluffton, OH 45817
(419) 358-3257, (419) 358-3232 (fax)
admissions@bluffton.edu
http://www.bluffton.edu
Average award: $6,798
Number of awards: 100
Deadline: None
College level: Freshman
Criteria: Scholarship is renewable. Awarded every year. Award may be used only at sponsoring institution.
Contact: Dan Parent, Admissions Counselor, (419) 358-3250.

1894 Tuition Equalization Program Scholarship With Honors

Bluffton College
280 West College Avenue
Bluffton, OH 45817
(419) 358-3257, (419) 358-3232 (fax)
admissions@bluffton.edu
http://www.bluffton.edu
Average award: $7,298
Number of awards: 35
Deadline: None
College level: Freshman
Criteria: Scholarship is renewable. Awarded every year. Award may be used only at sponsoring institution.
Contact: Dan Parent, Admissions Counselor, (419) 358-3250.

1895 Tuition Scholarship

University of Iowa
208 Calvin Hall
Iowa City, IA 52242
(319) 335-1450, (319) 335-3060 (fax)
http://www.uiowa.edu/~finaid
Maximum award: $2,566
Number of awards: 1500
Deadline: Rolling
College level: Freshman, Sophomore, Junior, Senior
Criteria: Applicant must rank in the top tenth of class, have a minimum composite ACT score of 28, and demonstrate financial need. Minimum 3.0 cumulative GPA and financial need are required to retain scholarship. Awarded every year. Award may be used only at sponsoring institution.
Contact: Judith Carpenter, Assistant Director of Student Financial Aid, judith-carpenter@uiowa.edu.

1896 Tuition Scholarship

Daemen College
4380 Main Street
Amherst, NY 14226
(716) 839-8254, (716) 839-8516 (fax)
http:/www.daemen.edu
Average award: Tuition and fees
Number of awards: 36
Deadline: None
College level: Freshman, Sophomore, Junior, Senior, Graduate
Criteria: Minimum 3.5 GPA is required to retain scholarship. Awarded every year. Award may be used only at sponsoring institution.
Contact: Laura Worley, Director of Financial Aid.

1897 Tuition Waiver

University of Maine
Orono, ME 04469
(207) 581-1324
Average award: Full tuition
Number of awards: 58
Deadline: February 1
College level: Freshman
Criteria: Minimum 3.0 GPA and full-time enrollment are required to retain scholarship. Awarded every year. Award may be used only at sponsoring institution.
Contact: Office of Enrollment Management, 5713 Chadbourne Hall, Orono, ME 04469-5713, (207) 581-1826.

1898 2+2 Scholarship

Spalding University
851 South Fourth Street
Louisville, KY 40203
(502) 585-9911
Average award: Half tuition
Deadline: March 1 (priority)
College level: Freshman, Sophomore, Junior, Senior, Transfers
Criteria: Applicant must be accepted for full-time enrollment and submit personal essay and three letters of recommendation. Recipient must accumulate 60 credit hours with a minimum 3.5 GPA, including all earned credits. One award reserved for member of Phi Theta Kappa. Renewable for up to five semesters. Awarded every year. Award may be used only at sponsoring institution.
Contact: Janice White Russell, Assistant Director of Financial Aid and Scholarship Coordinator, (502) 585-9911, extension 242.

1899 Two-Year College Academic Scholarship

Alabama Commission on Higher Education
P.O. Box 302000
Montgomery, AL 36130-2000
(334) 242-1998, (334) 242-0268 (fax)
Average award: In-state tuition and books
College level: Freshman, Sophomore
Criteria: Applicant must be accepted for enrollment at a public, two-year, postsecondary educational institution in Alabama. Preference is given to Alabama residents. Selection is based upon academic merit. Financial need is not considered. Academic excellence is required to retain scholarship. Awarded every year.
Contact: Alabama Commission of Higher Education, (334) 242-2274.

1900 UC Davis Scholarship

University of California, Davis
Scholarship Office
Davis, CA 95616
(916) 752-2804, (916) 752-7339 (fax)
ugscholofc@ucdavis.edu
http://www.ucdavis.edu
Average award: $1,500
Maximum award: $13,000
Minimum award: $1,000
Number of awards: 1500
Deadline: November 30
College level: Freshman, Sophomore, Junior, Senior
Criteria: Awarded every year. Award may be used only at sponsoring institution.
Contact: John Dixon, Coordinator of Undergraduate Scholarships, ugscholofc@ucdavis.edu.

1901 Undergraduate Scholarship

University of California, Berkeley
210 Sproul Hall
Berkeley, CA 94720
(510) 642-0645
Average award: $1,233
Maximum award: $3,000
Minimum award: $300
Number of awards: 1900
Deadline: March 2
College level: Freshman, Sophomore, Junior, Senior
Criteria: Selection is based solely upon financial need for entering freshmen; $300 honorary scholarships are available to academically qualifying upperclass students with no financial need. Satisfactory academic progress, GPA, and academic level are required to retain scholarship. Awarded every year. Award may be used only at sponsoring institution.
Contact: Linda Popofsky, Assistant Director of Financial Aid for Scholarships, (510) 642-6449.

1902 Undergraduate Scholarship Program

Virginia Commonwealth University
821 West Franklin Street
Box 2526
Richmond, VA 23284
(804) 367-1190
Average award: $3,529
Maximum award: $7,673
Minimum award: $1,765
Number of awards: 185
Deadline: January 1
College level: Freshman, Transfers from Virginia community college system
Criteria: Selection is based upon academic qualifications and extracurricular activities. Minimum 3.3 GPA is required to retain scholarship. Awarded every year. Award may be used only at sponsoring institution.
Contact: Delores T. Taylor, Associate Director of Admissions.

1903 University Academic Scholarship

Alabama Agricultural and Mechanical University
P.O. Box 908
Normal, AL 35762
(205) 851-5245, (205) 851-5249 (fax)
jheyward@asnaam.edu
http://www.aamu.edu
Average award: $6,000
Maximum award: $7,500
Minimum award: $1,186
Number of awards: 25
Deadline: May 1
College level: Freshman, Sophomore, Junior, Senior
Criteria: Scholarship is renewable. Awarded every year. Award may be used only at sponsoring institution.
Contact: Director of Admissions.

1904   University Assistantship

Susquehanna University
Selinsgrove, PA 17870
(717) 372-4450
Average award: $9,000
Deadline: None
College level: Freshman
Criteria: Award includes creative work experience (about 10 hours per week) with a faculty or administrative staff member. Renewable for up to four years. Awarded every year. Award may be used only at sponsoring institution.
Contact: Office of Financial Aid.

1905   University Challenge Grant

Capital University
2199 East Main Street
Columbus, OH 43209-2394
(614) 236-6511
Maximum award: $4,500
Number of awards: 500
Deadline: August 1
College level: Freshman, Transfers
Criteria: Selection is based upon academic performance as measured by school record and standardized test scores. Renewable for up to eight semesters if minimum 2.0 GPA is maintained. Awarded every year. Award may be used only at sponsoring institution.
Contact: Beth Heiser, Director of Admission, (614) 236-6101.

1906   University Honors Tuition Scholarship

University of Pittsburgh, Pittsburgh Campus
4200 Fifth Avenue
Pittsburgh, PA 15260
(412) 624-4141
http://www.pitt.edu/-oafa/oafa.html
Maximum award: $7,974
Number of awards: 40-50
Deadline: January 15
College level: Freshman
Criteria: Selection is based upon high school performance, SAT I or ACT scores, essay, and interview. Minimum 3.0 GPA is required to retain scholarship. Awarded every year. Award may be used only at sponsoring institution.
Contact: Betsy Porter, Director of Admissions & Financial Aid, Office of Admissions & Financial Aid, Bruce Hall, Pittsburgh, PA 15260, (412) 624-7164.

1907   University Merit Scholarship

California State University, Dominguez Hills
1000 East Victoria Street
Carson, CA 90747
(310) 516-3647
Average award: Full fees
Number of awards: 5
Deadline: April 28
College level: Sophomore, Junior, Senior, Transfers
Criteria: Applicant must be a full-time undergraduate or be admitted as a transfer student, have a minimum 3.0 GPA, and demonstrate community/school involvement. Awarded every year. Award may be used only at sponsoring institution.
Contact: Scholarships.

1908   University of British Columbia Scholarship

University of British Columbia
Room 2016–1874 East Mall
Vancouver, British Columbia, CN V6T 1Z1
(604) 822-3014, (604) 822-3599 (fax)
registrar.records@ubc.ca
http://www.student-services.ubc.ca
Average award: $2,260
Minimum award: $250
Number of awards: 3670
Deadline: April 15 (entrance scholarship); May 15 (general and affiliation scholarships)
College level: Freshman, Sophomore, Junior, Senior, Graduate, Doctoral
Criteria: Scholarships are awarded on the basis of academic achievement primarily to undergraduate and professional degree applicants. Some awards are renewable, but most are not. Awarded every year. Award may be used only at sponsoring institution.
Contact: Ms. Carol Gibson, Director of Financial Aid, (604) 822-5111, awards.enquiry@ubc.ca.

1909   University of Calgary Senate Scholarship

University of Calgary
Department of Financial Aid
2500 University Drive, NW
Calgary, Alberta, CN T2N 1N4
(403) 220-7872, (403) 282-2999 (fax)
Average award: $2,500
Number of awards: 1
Deadline: June 15
College level: Sophomore, Junior, Senior
Criteria: Selection is based upon academic merit and involvement in campus and/or community activities. Awarded every year. Award may be used only at sponsoring institution.
Contact: J. Van Housen, Director of Student Awards/Financial Aid.

1910   University of Hawaii at Manoa Scholarship

University of Hawaii at Manoa
2600 Campus Road
Room #001
Honolulu, HI 96822
(808) 956-8975
Average award: $812
Maximum award: $2,500
Minimum award: $225
Number of awards: 166
Deadline: Varies
College level: Freshman, Sophomore, Junior, Senior, Graduate, Doctoral
Criteria: Many different scholarships are offered. Award may be used only at sponsoring institution.
Contact: Financial Aid Services, (808) 956-7251.

1911   University of Nebraska Regents Transfer Scholarship

University of Nebraska, Lincoln
14th and R Streets
Lincoln, NE 68588
(402) 472-2030, (402) 472-9826 (fax)
http://www.unl.edu/scholfa/cover.html
Average award: $2,250
Average award: Full tuition
Deadline: March 15
College level: Transfers
Criteria: Applicant must be a a transfer from a Nebraska community college with at least 45 credit hours and a minimum 3.0 GPA. Renewable for two years if recipient maintains 3.5 GPA and 24 credit hours per year. Awarded every year. Award may be used only at sponsoring institution.
Contact: Debra Augustyn, Assistant Director of Scholarship and Financial Aid.

1912 University Opportunity Scholarship

Auburn University
Auburn University, AL 36849
(334) 844-4723
Average award: $2,100
Deadline: December 15
College level: Freshman
Criteria: Applicant must have a minimum 3.5 GPA and minimum combined SAT I score of 1210 (composite ACT score of 29). Minimum "B" grade average is required for renewal. Awarded every year. Award may be used only at sponsoring institution.
Contact: Mary Lynn Saidla, Assistant Director for Scholarships.

1913 University President's Club Nonresident Scholarship

University of Utah
Financial Aid and Scholarships Office
105 Student Services Building
Salt Lake City, UT 84112
(801) 581-6211
Average award: Full nonresident tuition plus $1,800 cash award
Deadline: February 1
College level: Freshman
Criteria: Applicant must not be a resident of Utah. Selection is based upon GPA, test scores, leadership, extracurricular activities, and accomplishments. Minimum cumulative GPA of 3.7 and completion of 36 hours every three quarters are required to retain scholarship. Awarded every year. Award may be used only at sponsoring institution.
Contact: Financial Aid and Scholarships Office.

1914 University Professors Award

Bowling Green State University
Bowling Green, OH 43403
(419) 372-2531
Average award: Award covers instructional/general fees
Number of awards: 15
Deadline: None
College level: Freshman
Criteria: Applicant must have a minimum 3.8 GPA after junior year and a minimum composite ACT score of 30 (combined SAT I score of 1300). Renewable if recipient meets requirements. Awarded every year. Award may be used only at sponsoring institution.
Contact: Admissions Office.

1915 University Scholar Award

Central Missouri State University
Office of Admissions
Administration 104
Warrensburg, MO 64093
(816) 543-4541, (816) 543-8517 (fax)
Maximum award: Full fees
Number of awards: 47
Deadline: None
College level: Freshman
Criteria: Applicant must have a minimum composite ACT score of 28 and either rank in the top five percent of class or have a minimum cumulative GPA of 3.75 at the end of sixth or seventh semester in high school. Minimum 2.0 GPA after first semester, minimum 3.4 GPA at end of second semester, and minimum 3.6 GPA at end of fourth semester and thereafter at least 12 hours per semester are required to retain scholarship. Awarded every year. Award may be used only at sponsoring institution.
Contact: Scholarships and Awards Officer.

1916 University Scholar Award

Mississippi University for Women
Columbus, MS 39701
(601) 329-7114, (601) 241-7481 (fax)
admissions@muw.edu
http://www.muw.edu/admissions
Maximum award: $3,500
Maximum number of awards: 80
Minimum number of awards: 60
Deadline: December 1
College level: Freshman, Sophomore, Junior, Senior
Criteria: Applicant must have minimum 25 ACT score. Minimum 3.0 GPA is required to retain scholarship. Awarded every year. Award may be used only at sponsoring institution.
Contact: Melanie Freeman, Director of Admissions, (601) 329-7105.

1917 University Scholars Award

East Carolina University
East Fifth Street
Greenville, NC 27858
http://www.ecu.edu
Average award: $3,000
Number of awards: 20
Deadline: January 31
College level: Freshman
Criteria: Applicant must have a strong high school academic record and a record of extracurricular activities and leadership. Minimum 3.0 cumulative GPA and full-time enrollment are required to retain scholarship. Awarded every year. Award may be used only at sponsoring institution.
Contact: Scholarship Coordinator, Office of Admissions, (919) 328-6640, admis@ecuvm.cis.ecu.edu.

1918 University Scholars Award

Long Island University, C.W. Post Campus
Route 25A
Brookville, NY 11548
(516) 299-2338, (516) 299-2137 (fax)
admissions@collegehall.liunet.edu
http://www.liunet.edu
Maximum award: Full tuition
Deadline: March 1
College level: Freshman
Criteria: Applicant must be a first-time, full-time student, have a minimum grade average of 92, have a minimum SAT I verbal score of 550 and a minimum combined SAT I score of 1300. Applicant must participate in Honors Program and Merit Fellowship. Renewable for up to four years if minimum 3.5 GPA and full-time enrollment (at least 12 credit hours per semester) are maintained. Awarded every year. Award may be used only at sponsoring institution.
Contact: Admissions Office, 720 Northern Boulevard, Brookville, NY 11548, (516) 299-2413, admissions@collegehall.liunet.edu.

1919 University Scholars Award

Youngstown State University
One University Plaza
Youngstown, OH 44555-0001
(330) 742-3501, (330) 742-1659 (fax)
ysufinaid@ysu.edu
http://www.ysu.edu
Average award: $8,500
Number of awards: 150
Deadline: March 3
College level: Freshman
Criteria: Applicant must rank in top 15 percent of class. Minimum composite ACT score of 30 or combined SAT I score of 1340 is required for automatic award. Minimum composite ACT score of 28 or combined SAT I score of 1260 is required for competitive award. Minimum 3.5 cumulative GPA and 12 credit hours per quarter are required to retain scholarship. Awarded every year. Award may be used only at sponsoring institution.
Contact: Eileen Greaf, Director of Financial Aid.

1920   University Scholars Award

University of Richmond
Richmond, VA 23173
(804) 289-8438
Average award: Half tuition
Number of awards: 25
Deadline: None
College level: First-year students
Criteria: Awarded to applicants selected from admission applicant pool. Participation is by invitation. Award includes academic privileges. Reapplication is required for renewal. Awarded every year. Award may be used only at sponsoring institution.
Contact: Scholars Office, (804) 289-8916.

1921   University Scholarship

Our Lady of the Lake University
411 S.W. 24th Street
San Antonio, TX 78207-4666
(512) 434-6711
Maximum award: $5,250
Deadline: Early application is recommended
College level: Freshman
Criteria: Applicant must have a minimum 3.0 GPA and a minimum composite ACT score of 21 (combined SAT I score of 870). Amount of award is based upon GPA and standardized test scores. Renewable for up to seven semesters or completion of bachelor's degree (whichever comes first) if recipient maintains a minimum 3.0 GPA and completes at least 12 credit hours per semester. Awarded every year. Award may be used only at sponsoring institution.
Contact: Jeff R. Scofield, Director of Financial Aid.

1922   University Scholarship

Tri-State University
Angola, IN 46703-0307
(219) 665-4175
Average award: $2,400
Maximum award: $3,000
Minimum award: $1,500
Deadline: None
College level: Freshman
Criteria: Selection is based upon class rank and standardized test scores. Minimum 2.5 GPA is required to retain scholarship. Awarded every year. Award may be used only at sponsoring institution.
Contact: Financial Aid Office.

1923   University Scholarship

University of Pittsburgh, Pittsburgh Campus
4200 Fifth Avenue
Pittsburgh, PA 15260
(412) 624-4141
http://www.pitt.edu/-oafa/oafa.html
Average award: $2,000
Maximum award: $6,000
Minimum award: $1,000
Number of awards: 200
Deadline: January 15
College level: Freshman
Criteria: Selection is based upon high school performance and test scores. Minimum 3.0 GPA is required to retain scholarship. Awarded every year. Award may be used only at sponsoring institution.
Contact: Betsy A. Porter, Director of Admissions and Financial Aid, Bruce Hall, Pittsburgh, PA 15260, (412) 624-7164.

1924   University Scholarship

Rhodes College
2000 North Parkway
Memphis, TN 38112
(901) 843-3700, (901) 843-3719 (fax)
adminfo@rhodes.edu
http://www.rhodes.edu
Average award: $8,200
Number of awards: 48
Deadline: February 1 (priority)
College level: Freshman
Criteria: Selection is based upon merit. Renewable if recipient maintains a minimum 2.75 GPA. Awarded every year. Award may be used only at sponsoring institution.
Contact: David J. Wottle, Dean of Admissions and Financial Aid, (800) 844-5969.

1925   University Scholarship

University of Missouri–Rolla
Rolla, MO 65401
(314) 341-4282
Maximum award: $5,000
Deadline: February 1
College level: Freshman, Sophomore, Junior, Senior
Criteria: Requirements for renewal vary by award. Most awards are renewable. Awarded every year. Award may be used only at sponsoring institution.
Contact: Robert W. Whites, Associate Director of Admissions/Student Financial Aid, G-1 Parker Hall.

1926   University Scholarship

Capital University
2199 East Main Street
Columbus, OH 43209-2394
(614) 236-6511
Maximum award: $6,500
Number of awards: 225
Deadline: August 1
College level: Freshman, Transfers
Criteria: Selection is based upon academic performance as measured by school record and standardized test scores. Renewable for up to eight semesters if minimum 3.0 GPA is maintained. Awarded every year. Award may be used only at sponsoring institution.
Contact: Beth Heiser, Director of Admission.

1927   University Scholarship

California State University, Northridge
18111 Nordhoff Street
Northridge, CA 91330-8307
(818) 677-3000, (818) 677-7887 (fax)
financial.aid@csun.edu
http://www.csun.edu/finaid
Average award: $1,000
Maximum award: $2,500
Minimum award: $250
Number of awards: 300
Deadline: March 2
College level: Freshman, Sophomore, Junior, Senior, Graduate, Transfers
Criteria: Applicant must have a minimum 3.0 GPA. Financial need is considered. Awarded every year. Award may be used only at sponsoring institution.
Contact: Lili Vidal, Scholarship Administrator, (818) 677-4907.

1928 University Scholarship

Baker University
P.O. Box 61
Baldwin City, KS 66006
(913) 594-4595
Average award: $5,000
Number of awards: 12
Deadline: February 15
College level: Freshman
Criteria: Applicant must have a minimum 3.6 GPA and minimum composite ACT score of 28 (combined SAT I score of 1170). Letter of recommendation, resume, and transcript are required. Selection is based upon interview by faculty during Scholarship Days. Minimum 3.25 GPA is required for renewal. Award may be used only at sponsoring institution.
Contact: Scholarships.

1929 University Scholarship

Boston University
Office of Financial Assistance
881 Commonwealth Avenue
Boston, MA 02215
(617) 353-4175
Average award: $10,985
Average award: Half tuition
Number of awards: 240
Deadline: January 15 (freshman); May 15 (continuing student)
College level: Freshman, Sophomore, Junior, Senior
Criteria: Selection is by the Boston U Merit Scholarship Selection Committee on the basis of exceptionally strong high school academic record. Applicant does not have to apply for need-based aid. Minimum 3.2 GPA and completion of at least 12 credit hours per semester are required to retain scholarship. Awarded every year. Award may be used only at sponsoring institution.
Contact: Maria B. DelSignore, Assistant Director for Special Programs.

1930 University Scholarship

Brigham Young University
Scholarship Office, A-41 ASB
P.O. Box 21009
Provo, UT 84602-1009
(801) 378-4104
scholarships@byu.edu
http://adm5.byu.edu/ar/dept_scholarships/scholar.html
Average award: $1,690
Maximum award: $2,530
Minimum award: $1,265
Number of awards: 1600
Deadline: February 15
College level: Freshman, Transfers
Criteria: Selection is based upon high academic qualifications. Awarded every year. Award may be used only at sponsoring institution.
Contact: Duane L. Bartle, Associate Director of Scholarships.

1931 University Scholarship

Lawrence University
P.O. Box 599
Appleton, WI 54912-0599
(414) 832-6500, (414) 832-6782 (fax)
excel@lawrence.edu
http://www.lawrence.edu
Average award: $3,000
Maximum award: $5,000
Number of awards: 35
Deadline: February 1
College level: Freshman
Criteria: Selection is based upon academic performance. Rank in top tenth of class recommended. Minimum 3.0 GPA required to retain scholarship of $5,000 or more; minimum 2.5 GPA required to retain scholarship of less than $5,000. Awarded every year. Award may be used only at sponsoring institution.
Contact: Director of Admissions.

1932 University Scholarship for Merit

University of North Carolina at Charlotte
Highway 49
Charlotte, NC 28223
(704) 547-2000
Average award: $2,110
Maximum award: $5,000
Minimum award: $1,000
Number of awards: 27
Deadline: January 15
College level: Freshman
Criteria: Selection is based upon academic achievement and leadership. Minimum 3.0 GPA is required to retain scholarship. Awarded every year. Award may be used only at sponsoring institution.
Contact: Kathi M. Baucom, Director of Admissions, (704) 547-2214.

1933 University Scholarship for Transfer Student

Our Lady of the Lake University
411 S.W. 24th Street
San Antonio, TX 78207-4666
(512) 434-6711
Maximum award: $6,000
Deadline: Early application is recommended
College level: Transfers
Criteria: Applicant must have a minimum 3.0 GPA. Award ranges from $2,750-$5,250 for applicant with fewer than 30 transferable credit hours. Award ranges from $3,750-$6,000 for applicant with more than 30 transferable credit hours. Amount of award is based upon GPA. Renewable for up to seven semesters or completion of bachelor's degree (whichever comes first) if recipient maintains a minimum 3.0 GPA and completes at least 12 credit hours per semester. Awarded every year. Award may be used only at sponsoring institution.
Contact: Jeff R. Scofield, Director of Financial Aid.

1934 University Scholarship Program

Sonoma State University
Scholarship Office
1801 East Cotati Avenue
Rohnert Park, CA 94928
(707) 664-2261
Average award: $850
Maximum award: $2,500
Minimum award: $250
Number of awards: 350
Deadline: March 1
College level: Freshman, Sophomore, Junior, Senior, Graduate, Doctoral
Criteria: Selection is based upon career goal, ethnicity, major, merit, residence, or other factors. Awarded every year. Award may be used only at sponsoring institution.
Contact: Kay Ashbrook, Scholarship Coordinator, kay.ashbrook@sonoma.edu.

1935 University Scholarships

Alvernia College
400 St. Bernardine Street
Reading, PA 19607
(610) 796-8215
Average award: $3,800
Maximum award: $7,000
Minimum award: $1,000
Number of awards: 150
Deadline: April 1
College level: Freshman
Criteria: Selection is based upon GPA, standardized test scores, location of high school, ethnic background, and/or financial need. Scholarship is renewable. Awarded every year. Award may be used only at sponsoring institution.
Contact: Vali G. Heist, Director of Financial Aid.

1936   **UNM Scholars Scholarship**

University of New Mexico
Mesa Vista Hall
3rd Floor, Room 3020
Albuquerque, NM 87131
(505) 277-6090
Average award: Full tuition
Number of awards: 300
Deadline: February 1
College level: Freshman
Criteria: Applicant must rank in the top fifth of graduating class, have a minimum 3.0 GPA, and participate in activities. Minimum 3.0 GPA with 30 credit hours per year is required to retain scholarship. Awarded every year. Award may be used only at sponsoring institution.
Contact: Rita M. Padilla, Associate Director for Scholarships.

1937   **Upward Bound Scholarship**

Shawnee State University
940 Second Street
Portsmouth, OH 45662-4344
(614) 355-2237
Average award: $2,750
Deadline: April 15
College level: Freshman
Criteria: Applicant must be a participant in Upward Bound and have a minimum 2.5 GPA. Community involvement and extracurricular activities are considered. FAFSA is required. Early application is recommended. Awarded every year. Award may be used only at sponsoring institution.
Contact: Financial Aid Office, (614) 355-2485.

1938   **USA Today Scholarship**

USA Today
1000 Wilson Boulevard, 10th floor
Arlington, VA 22229
Average award: $2,500
Number of awards: 20
College level: Freshman
Criteria: Selection is based upon academic achievement, sports participation, extracurricular activities, and leadership.
Contact: Carol Sklaski.

1939   **USC Associates Scholarship**

University of Southern California
University Park
Los Angeles, CA 90089-5012
(213) 740-1111
Average award: $5,000
Number of awards: 20
Deadline: December 15
College level: Freshman, Transfers
Criteria: Applicant must have a minimum 3.5 GPA and demonstrate strong leadership in school and community service. Application is required. Awarded every year. Award may be used only at sponsoring institution.
Contact: Office of Admission, University Park Campus, Los Angeles, CA 90089-0911.

1940   **Vada B. Dow Term-In-Europe Scholarship**

Northwood University–Midland Campus
3225 Cook Road
Midland, MI 48640-2398
(515) 837-4160
Average award: $5,000
Number of awards: 2
Criteria: Applicant must be a U.S. student participating in the Term-In-Europe program. Selection is based upon academic merit and financial need. Award may be used only at sponsoring institution.
Contact: Dixie Dee Maxwell.

1941   **Valedictorian and Salutatorian Scholarship**

University of West Alabama
Station Four
Livingston, AL 35470
(205) 652-3400, (205) 652-3522 (fax)
http://www.westal.edu
Average award: $2,040
Number of awards: 75
Deadline: Early application is recommended.
College level: Freshman
Criteria: Applicant must have been valedictorian or salutatorian of class, have minimum 3.0 GPA, and minimum composite ACT score of 25. Renewable for up to four years if minimum 3.0 GPA is maintained. Awarded every year. Award may be used only at sponsoring institution.
Contact: Richard Hester, Director of Admissions, (205) 652-3400, extension 3578, rth@uwamail.westal.edu.

1942   **Valedictorian Scholarship**

Southwest Texas State University
J.C. Kellam Building
San Marcos, TX 78666
(512) 245-2340
Average award: Full tuition
Deadline: March 15
College level: Freshman
Criteria: Applicant must be the valedictorian of an accredited Texas high school graduating class. Awarded every year. Award may be used only at sponsoring institution.
Contact: Coordinator of Scholarships, Office of Student Financial Aid, 601 University Drive, San Marcos, TX 78666-4602, (512) 245-2315.

1943   **Valedictorian Scholarship**

Texas Christian University
2800 South University Drive
Fort Worth, TX 76129
(817) 921-7858, (817) 921-7462 (fax)
frogaid@tcu.edu
Average award: $3,000
Number of awards: 17
Deadline: January 15
College level: Freshman
Criteria: Applicant must be valedictorian of graduating class, rank in top 15% of class, and have a minimum combined SAT I score of 1180 (composite ACT score of 27). Renewable for up to eight semesters or 128 credit hours if recipient maintains a minimum 3.0 GPA after freshman year (3.25 GPA thereafter) and successfully completes at least 27 credit hours per year. Awarded every year. Award may be used only at sponsoring institution.
Contact: Office of Scholarships and Student Financial Aid, TCU Box 297012, Fort Worth, TX 76126.

1944 Valedictorian Scholarship

Lancaster Bible College
901 Eden Road
Lancaster, PA 17601
(717) 569-7071, (717) 569-7071 (fax)
Average award: $2,500
Number of awards: 5
Deadline: None
College level: Freshman
Criteria: Applicant must have been class valedictorian; class must have had a minimum of 25 students. Minimum GPA is required to retain scholarship. Awarded every year. Award may be used only at sponsoring institution.
Contact: Beth Kachel, Assistant Director of Financial Aid, (717) 569-7071, extension 352.

1945 Valedictorian Scholarship

Saint Martin's College
5300 Pacific Avenue, SE
Lacey, WA 98503
(360) 438-4397
Average award: $12,610
Number of awards: 2
Deadline: March 1
College level: Freshman
Criteria: Applicant must be class valedictorian. Minimum 3.5 GPA is required to retain scholarship. Awarded every year. Award may be used only at sponsoring institution.
Contact: Ron Noborikawa, Director of Financial Aid.

1946 Valedictorian Scholarship

Elmira College
One Park Place
Elmira, NY 14901
(607) 735-1724, (607) 735-1718 (fax)
admissions@elmira.edu
www.elmira.edu
Maximum award: Full tuition
Minimum award: Three-Quarters tuition
Number of awards: 20
College level: Freshman
Criteria: Applicant must be valedictorian of graduating secondary or prep school class and be accepted for full-time enrollment. Recipient must live on campus. Minimum 3.4 GPA required for renewal. Awarded every year. Award may be used only at sponsoring institution.
Contact: Dean of Admissions, admissions@elmira.edu.

1947 Valedictorian Scholarship

Ripon College
300 Seward Street
P.O. Box 248
Ripon, WI 54971
(800) 94-RIPON, (414) 748-7243 (fax)
adminfo@mac.ripon.edu
http://www.ripon.edu
Average award: $5,000
Number of awards: No limit
Deadline: December 1 (early decision) March 1
College level: Freshman
Criteria: Applicant must be accpted for admission to Ripon College and have been valedictorian of his or her class. Interview required. Renewable if recipient maintains minimum 2.5 GPA in first year, minimum 2.7 GPA thereafter. Awarded every year. Award may be used only at sponsoring institution.
Contact: Paul J. Weeks, Vice President & Dean of Admission.

1948 Valedictorian Scholarship

Hope College
P.O. Box 9000
Holland, MI 49422-9000
(616) 395-7850, (616) 395-7130 (fax)
admissions@hope.edu
http://www.hope.edu
Average award: $5,000
College level: Freshman, Sophomore, Junior, Senior
Criteria: Applicant must be a high school valedictorian who did not win any other Hope College-sponsored merit-based scholarships. Renewable if recipient maintains a minimum 2.75 GPA. Awarded every year. Award may be used only at sponsoring institution.
Contact: James R. Bekkering, Vice President for Admissions.

1949 Valedictorian/Salutatorian Scholarship

Cincinnati Bible College
2700 Glenway Avenue
Cincinnati, OH 45204-3200
(800) 949-4CBC, (513) 244-8141, (513) 244-8140 (fax)
admission@cincybible.edu
http://www.cincybible.edu/home.html.
Average award: $2,000
Number of awards: 8
Criteria: Applicant must be the valedictorian or salutatorian in class, have a minimum 3.5 GPA, and have a minimum composite ACT score of 28 (combined SAT 1 score of 1260). Renewable if recipient maintains 3.0 GPA. Awarded every year. Award may be used only at sponsoring institution.

1950 Valedictorian/Salutatorian Scholarship

Susquehanna University
Selinsgrove, PA 17870
(717) 372-4450
Maximum award: $7,500
Deadline: None
College level: Freshman
Criteria: Applicant must rank first or second in graduating class in a demanding academic program. Amount of award depends on academic credentials. Awarded every year. Award may be used only at sponsoring institution.
Contact: Office of Financial Aid.

1951 Vernon & Lucy Tobias Memorial Award

Bowling Green State University
Bowling Green, OH 43403
(419) 372-2531
Average award: $2,000
Maximum number of awards: 2
Minimum number of awards: 1
Deadline: None
College level: Freshman
Criteria: Applicant must be a graduate of Fremont High School in top quarter of class or with minimum "B" grade average. Awarded every year. Award may be used only at sponsoring institution.
Contact: Scholarships.

1952 Vickroy Scholarship

Lebanon Valley College
101 North College Avenue
Annville, PA 17003
(800) 445-6181, (717) 867-6026 (fax)
admiss@luc.edu
http://www.luc.edu
Maximum award: Half tuition
Number of awards: 100
Deadline: None
College level: Freshman
Criteria: Applicant must rank in top tenth of class. Minimum 3.0 GPA is required to retain scholarship. Awarded every year. Award may be used only at sponsoring institution.
Contact: Bill Brown, Dean of Admission/Financial Aid.

1953 Villanova Scholars Award

Villanova University
Villanova, PA 19085
(215) 645-4010
Average award: $8,000
Number of awards: 76
Deadline: January 15
College level: Freshman
Criteria: Applicant must have a minimum combined SAT I score of 1250, rank in the top tenth of class, and demonstrate leadership skills through high school and community involvement. Minimum 3.25 GPA is required to retain scholarship. Awarded every year. Award may be used only at sponsoring institution.
Contact: George J. Walter, Director of Financial Aid.

1954 Vulcan Materials Company Presidential Honors Scholarship

Auburn University
Auburn University, AL 36849
(334) 844-4723
Average award: $4,000
Number of awards: 1
Deadline: December 15
College level: Freshman
Criteria: Applicant must have a minimum 3.5 GPA and minimum combined SAT I score of 1210 (composite ACT score of 29). Applicant must demonstrate superior academic achievement and potential, outstanding character and integrity, leadership ability, and likelihood of significant achievement in his or her chosen field of endeavor. Renewable for up to three years if minimum "B" grade average is maintained. Awarded every year. Award may be used only at sponsoring institution.
Contact: Mary Lynn Saidla, Assistant Director for Scholarships.

1955 Vulcan Scholarship

The University of Alabama
Box 870162
Tuscaloosa, AL 35487-0162
(205) 348-6756
Average award: $7,000
Number of awards: 1
Deadline: February 1
College level: Freshman
Criteria: Applicant must have a minimum 3.8 GPA, a minimum composite ACT score of 32 (combined SAT I score of 1350), and demonstrate leadership. Essay and interview are required. An additional $2,000 is designated for special study related to major or minor. Minimum 3.0 GPA is required to retain scholarship for four years. Awarded every year. Award may be used only at sponsoring institution.
Contact: Jeanetta Allen, Director of Financial Aid.

1956 Wal-Mart Competitive Edge

Old Dominion University
Hampton Boulevard
Norfolk, VA 23529-0050
(804) 683-3683
Maximum award: $5,000
Number of awards: 1
Deadline: February 15
College level: Freshman
Majors/Fields: Technology-related area
Criteria: Applicant must have a minimum combined SAT I score of 1100 or composite ACT score of 27, a minimum 3.2 GPA, rank in top tenth of class, demonstrate community service and leadership ability, and apply for finanical aid. Scholarship is renewable. Awarded every year. Award may be used only at sponsoring institution.
Contact: Mary A. Schutz, Assistant Director of Scholarships.

1957 Walbro Scholarship

Northwood University–Midland Campus
3225 Cook Road
Midland, MI 48640-2398
(515) 837-4160
Average award: $2,275
Number of awards: 1
Criteria: Applicant must be a U.S. citizen with demonstrated academic merit and financial need. Award may be used only at sponsoring institution.
Contact: Dixie Dee Maxwell.

1958 Walter D. Bellingrath Scholarship

Rhodes College
2000 North Parkway
Memphis, TN 38112
(901) 843-3700, (901) 843-3719 (fax)
adminfo@rhodes.edu
http://www.rhodes.edu
Average award: $21,668
Number of awards: 2
Deadline: January 15
College level: Freshman
Criteria: Awarded to outstanding first-year student. Applicant must be nominated by counselor, principal, headmaster, minister of the Presbyterian Church (USA), or alumnus. Special nomination form is required. Renewable if recipient maintains a minimum 3.25 GPA. Awarded every year. Award may be used only at sponsoring institution.
Contact: David J. Wottle, Dean of Admissions and Financial Aid, (800) 844-5969.

1959 Walter T. Cox Presidential Scholarship

Clemson University
G-01 Sikes Hall
Clemson, SC 29634-5123
(803) 656-2280
Maximum award: $6,000
Number of awards: 1
Deadline: None
College level: Freshman
Criteria: Awarded to the most promising entering freshman. Minimum 3.0 GPA and completion of at least 12 credits per semester are required to retain scholarship. Awarded every year. Award may be used only at sponsoring institution.
Contact: Marvin Carmichael, Director of Financial Aid.

1960 Wesleyan Scholarship

Ohio Wesleyan University
Office of Admissions
Delaware, OH 43015
(614) 368-3020, (614) 368-3314 (fax)
owuadmit@cc.owu.edu
http://www.owu.edu
Average award: $4,500
Number of awards: 75
Deadline: March 1
College level: Freshman
Criteria: Applicant must rank in top tenth of class and have a minimum composite ACT score of 27 (combined SAT I score of 1150). Selection is based upon curriculum, extracurricular involvement, GPA, standardized test scores, and writing skills. Minimum 3.25 GPA is required to retain scholarship. Awarded every year. Award may be used only at sponsoring institution.
Contact: Lynn Kittel, Associate Director of Admission.

1961 Westover Honors Program

Lynchburg College
Lynchburg, VA 24501
(804) 522-8228
Average award: Half tuition
Deadline: February 15
College level: Freshman
Criteria: Applicant must have a minimum "A" grade average and minimum combined SAT I score of 1100 (composite ACT score of 24). Selection is competitive and is based upon merit. Scholarship is renewable. Awarded every year. Award may be used only at sponsoring institution.
Contact: Scholarships.

1962 Whitinger Scholarship

Ball State University
Muncie, IN 47306
(765) 285-5600
Maximum award: $12,498
Number of awards: 10
Deadline: April 1
College level: Freshman
Criteria: Applicant must rank in the top tenth of class and have a minimum combined SAT I score of 1270 or composite ACT score of 29. Scholarship is renewable. Awarded every year. Award may be used only at sponsoring institution.
Contact: Bruce Meyer, Dean of Honors College, (765) 285-1024.

1963 Whitman Merit Scholarship

Whitman College
345 Boyer Ave
Walla Walla, WA 99362
(509) 527-5178, (509) 527-4967 (fax)
http://www.whitman.edu
Average award: $4,800
Maximum award: $7,000
Minimum award: $2,000
Number of awards: 511
Deadline: February 1 (admissions)
College level: Freshman, Sophomore, Junior, Senior
Criteria: Applicant must have a minimum 3.7 GPA and have a minimum combined SAT I score of 1200. Selection is based upon academic credentials. Recipient must maintain good standing to retain scholarship. Awarded every year. Award may be used only at sponsoring institution.
Contact: Varga Fox, Manager of Financial Aid, fox@whitman.edu.

1964 Whittle Scholar Award

University of Tennessee, Knoxville
Financial Aid Office
115 Student Services Building
Knoxville, TN 37994
(615) 974-3131
Average award: Tuition plus $7,000
Number of awards: 20
Deadline: February 1; nomination is due by January 1.
College level: Freshman
Criteria: Selection is based upon academic performance and leadership qualities. Special consideration is given to applicants who demonstrate unusual or exceptional ways to pursue educational and leadership opportunities beyond the classroom setting. Award is for up to five years. Awarded every year. Award may be used only at sponsoring institution.
Contact: University Honors Program, F-101 Melrose Hall, Knoxville, TN 37916, (615) 974-7875.

1965 William A. Kenyon Scholarship

Clemson University
G-01 Sikes Hall
Clemson, SC 29634-5123
(803) 656-2280
Maximum award: $2,500
Number of awards: 4
Deadline: None
College level: Freshman
Criteria: Selection is based upon admissions application. Minimum 3.0 GPA and completion of at least 12 credits per semester are required to retain scholarship. Awarded every year. Award may be used only at sponsoring institution.
Contact: Marvin Carmichael, Director of Financial Aid.

1966 William James Erwin Scholarship

Clemson University
G-01 Sikes Hall
Clemson, SC 29634-5123
(803) 656-2280
Maximum award: $2,500
Number of awards: 2
Deadline: None
College level: Freshman
Criteria: Selection is based upon admissions application. Minimum 3.0 GPA and completion of at least 12 credits per semester are required to retain scholarship. Awarded every year. Award may be used only at sponsoring institution.
Contact: Marvin Carmichael, Director of Financial Aid.

1967 Wimmer Scholarship

Saint Vincent College
Admissions and Financial Aid
Latrobe, PA 15650-2690
(412) 537-4540, (412) 537-4554 (fax)
info@stvincent.edu
http://www.stvincent.edu
Maximum award: Full tuition, room, and board
Deadline: October 10
College level: Freshman
Criteria: Applicant must rank in top 5% of class and be nominated by principal. Selection is based upon competitive general knowledge exam held on campus in fall. Top finisher receives maximum award. Other awards go to second through fifth high scorers. All awards are for four years. Pre-registration is required. Renewable if recipient maintains a minimum 3.25 GPA as a full-time student. Awarded every year. Award may be used only at sponsoring institution.
Contact: Rev. Earl Henry, Dean of Admission and Financial Aid, 300 Fraser Purchase Road, Latrobe, PA 15650.

1968 WIU Foundation Honors Scholarship

Western Illinois University
One University Circle
Macomb, IL 61455
(309) 295-1414
Maximum award: $3,000
Number of awards: 4
Deadline: December 14
College level: Freshman
Criteria: Applicant must have a minimum composite ACT score of 30, rank in the top 15 percent of class, and reside on the Honors Floor. Minimum 3.5 GPA and participation in University Honors Program are required to retain scholarship. Awarded every year. Award may be used only at sponsoring institution.
Contact: Janice Owens, Scholarship Coordinator, (309) 298-2446.

1969   Wives of the Class of '34 Endowed Scholarship

Clemson University
G-01 Sikes Hall
Clemson, SC 29634-5123
(803) 656-2280
Maximum award: $4,500
Number of awards: 1
Deadline: None
College level: Freshman
Criteria: Selection is based upon admissions application. Minimum 3.0 GPA and completion of at least 12 credits per semester are required to retain scholarship. Awarded every year. Award may be used only at sponsoring institution.
Contact: Marvin Carmichael, Director of Financial Aid.

1970   Women in Education Scholarship

Emmanuel College
400 The Fenway
Boston, MA 02115
(617) 735-9725
Maximum award: $4,500
Deadline: February 15
College level: Freshman
Majors/Fields: Art, humanities/arts, math/natural science, social science/religious studies
Criteria: Applicant must have a minimum 3.0 GPA and minimum combined SAT I score of 900 (composite ACT score of 21), be a woman, demonstrate financial need, and select one of the following divisions of study: art, humanities/arts, math/natural science, social science/religious studies. Selection is based upon competition administered by faculty. Recipient must maintain a minimum 3.0 GPA, remain in chosen division, and reamin eligible for financial aid to retain scholarship. Awarded every year. Award may be used only at sponsoring institution.
Contact: Patricia K. Harden, Director of Financial Aid.

1971   Yoshiyama Award

Hitachi Foundation
P.O. Box 19247
Washington, DC 20036-9247
(202) 457-0588, (202) 296-1098 (fax)
Maximum award: $5,000
Maximum number of awards: 11
Minimum number of awards: 10
Deadline: April 1
College level: Freshman
Criteria: This is not an academic achievement scholarship. It is an award to recognize exemplary service, community involvement, leadership, and civic responsibility. Awarded every year.
Contact: Yoshiyama Award, rhron@hitachi-fndn.org.

Athletic Ability————————————

1972　Amateur Athletic Union/Mars Milky Way High School All-American Award

Amateur Athletic Union
P.O. Box 68207
Indianapolis, IN 46268-0207
(317) 872-2900
Average award: $1,000
Maximum award: $20,000
Number of awards: 102
Deadline: January 9
College level: Freshman
Criteria: Selection is based upon academics, athletics, and community service. Awarded every year.
Contact: Tom Leix, Director of Special Projects, Department CGP.

1973　Athletic Grant

Molloy College
1000 Hempstead Avenue
P.O. Box 5002
Rockville Centre, NY 11571-5002
(516) 678-5000
Maximum award: Full tuition
Deadline: late February (recommended); April 15
College level: Freshman, Sophomore, Junior, Senior
Criteria: Applicant must be a full-time student, demonstrate athletic ability, and file FAFSA. Recipient must maintain a minimum 2.0 GPA, complete at least 12 credit hours per semester, continue to participate in the sport for which the award was given, and reapply to retain scholarship. Awarded every year. Award may be used only at sponsoring institution.
Contact: Kathleen Bonnici, Director of Financial Aid.

1974　Athletic Grant

University of Indianapolis
1400 East Hanna Avenue
Indianapolis, IN 46227-3697
(317) 788-3217
Average award: $4,646
Maximum award: $15,200
Minimum award: $1,000
Number of awards: 269
Deadline: None
College level: Freshman, Sophomore, Junior, Senior
Criteria: Applicant must participate in athletics. Scholarship is renewable. Awarded every year. Award may be used only at sponsoring institution.
Contact: Athletic Office, (317) 788-3246.

1975　Athletic Grant-in-Aid

Piedmont College
165 Central Avenue
Demorest, GA 30535
(706) 778-3000
Average award: $1,700
Maximum award: $5,000
Minimum award: $500
Number of awards: 92
Deadline: None
College level: Freshman, Sophomore, Junior, Senior
Criteria: Awards given for baseball (M), basketball (M,W), cheerleading, cross-country, golf, soccer (M,W), softball (W), and tennis. Recipient must remain active in chosen sport and meet applicable NAIA standards to retain scholarship. Awarded every year. Award may be used only at sponsoring institution.
Contact: Kenneth L. Owen, Director of Financial Aid.

1976　Athletic Performance Scholarship

Houghton College
1 Willard Avenue
Houghton, NY 14744
(716) 567-9328
Average award: $2,500
Maximum award: $6,200
Minimum award: $500
Number of awards: 38
Deadline: March 15
College level: Freshman
Criteria: Applicant must participate in basketball, cross-country, field hockey, soccer, track, or volleyball. Recipient must continue to participate in sport to retain scholarship. Awarded every year. Award may be used only at sponsoring institution.
Contact: Troy Martin, Director of Financial Aid.

1977　Athletic Scholarship

Southern College of Technology
1100 South Marietta Parkway
Marietta, GA 30060-2896
(800) 869-1102, 404 528-7290
Maximum award: Full tuition, room and board, books
Deadline: None
College level: Freshman, Sophomore, Junior, Senior
Criteria: Applicant must demonstrate exceptional skill and ability in baseball, basketball, or tennis. Awarded every year. Award may be used only at sponsoring institution.
Contact: George Peridies, Athletic Director, (404) 528-7350.

1978　Athletic Scholarship

Emmanuel College
212 Spring Street
P.O. Box 129
Franklin Springs, GA 30639-0129
(706) 245-7226
Maximum award: $7,800
Number of awards: 24
Deadline: None
College level: Freshman, Sophomore, Junior, Senior
Criteria: Applicant must participate in intercollegiate competiton in baseball, basketball, softball, or tennis. Scholarship is renewable. Awarded every year. Award may be used only at sponsoring institution.
Contact: Glenn A. Bailey, Director of Financial Aid.

1979　Athletic Scholarship

Adelphi University
South Avenue
Garden City, NY 11530
(516) 877-3050
Average award: $9,000
Maximum award: $17,500
Minimum award: $1,000
Number of awards: 90
Deadline: None
College level: Freshman, Sophomore, Junior, Senior
Criteria: Recipient must maintain minimum 2.0 GPA. Awarded every year. Award may be used only at sponsoring institution.
Contact: Scholarships.

1980 Athletic Scholarship

Georgetown University
37th and O Streets, NW
Washington, DC 20057
(202) 687-4547, (202) 687-6542 (fax)
Average award: $14,183
Maximum award: $26,856
Minimum award: $200
Number of awards: 140
Deadline: None
College level: Freshman, Sophomore, Junior, Senior
Criteria: Applicant must participate in baseball, lacrosse, track, or other sport. Renewable if participation in athletics is continued. Awarded every year. Award may be used only at sponsoring institution.
Contact: Patricia McWade, Dean of Student Financial Services, G-19 Healy Hall.

1981 Athletic Scholarship

Mississippi Valley State University
14000 Highway 82 West
Itta Bena, MS 38941
(601) 254-3335, (601) 254-7900 (fax)
Maximum award: $7,270
Number of awards: 177
Deadline: None
College level: Freshman, Sophomore, Junior, Senior
Criteria: Applicant must demonstrate ability in one of the following sports: baseball, men's/women's basketball, football, men's/women's golf, women's softball, men's/women's tennis, men's/women's track, women's volleyball. Minimum 2.0 GPA required to retain scholarship. Awarded every year. Award may be used only at sponsoring institution.
Contact: Chuck Prophet, Athletic Director, (601) 254-3550.

1982 Athletic Scholarship

Colorado Christian University
180 South Garrison Street
Lakewood, CO 80226
(303) 202-0100, extension 117, (303) 274-7560 (fax)
drwilliams@ccu.edu
http://www.ccu.edu
Average award: $5,038
Maximum award: $14,000
Minimum award: $250
Number of awards: 118
Deadline: None
College level: Freshman, Sophomore, Junior, Senior
Criteria: Applicant must be enrolled full time. Awarded every year. Award may be used only at sponsoring institution.
Contact: Kent McGowan, Director of Financial Aid.

1983 Athletic Scholarship

Liberty University
1971 University Boulevard
Lynchburg, VA 24502-2269
(800) 543-5317
Average award: $5,314
Number of awards: 317
College level: Freshman, Sophomore, Junior, Senior, Graduate
Criteria: Applicant must demonstrate athletic talent and ability. Scholarship is renewable. Awarded every year. Award may be used only at sponsoring institution.
Contact: Athletic Department, (800) 522-6225 extension 2100.

1984 Athletic Scholarship

Dominican College of San Rafael
50 Acacia Avenue
San Rafael, CA 94901-2298
(415) 485-3204, (415) 485-3205 (fax)
enroll@dominican.edu
http://www.dominican.edu
Average award: $4,004
Maximum award: $9,343
Minimum award: $500
Number of awards: 76
Deadline: None
College level: Freshman, Sophomore, Junior, Senior
Criteria: Recipient must meet NAIA standards to retain scholarship. Awarded every year. Award may be used only at sponsoring institution.
Contact: Susan Gutierrez, Director of Financial Aid.

1985 AWSEF Scholarship

American Water Ski Education Foundation (AWSEF)
799 Overlook Drive, SE
Winter Haven, FL 33884-1671
(941) 324-2472, (941) 324-3996 (fax)
102726,2751@compuserve.com
Average award: $1,500
Number of awards: 6
Deadline: March 1
College level: Sophomore, Junior, Senior
Criteria: Applicant must be a U.S. citizen who is a current American Water Ski Association member. Selection is based upon academic qualifications, leadership, extracurricular involvement, recommendations, and financial need. Awarded every year.
Contact: Carole Lowe, Executive Director, P.O. Box 2957, Winter Haven, FL 33883-2957.

1986 Baseball Performance Grant

Campbellsville University
Office of Financial Aid
200 West College Street
Campbellsville, KY 42718
(502) 465-8158
Maximum award: $2,500
Number of awards: 15
Deadline: April 1 (priority)
College level: Freshman, Sophomore, Junior, Senior
Criteria: Applicant must be offered an athletic performance grant contract by the head coach, be approved by the athletic director, participate in the sport, have a minimum 2.0 GPA, and be a full-time student. FAFSA is required. Scholarship is renewable. Awarded every year. Award may be used only at sponsoring institution.
Contact: Athletic Department.

1987 Gloria Fecht Memorial Scholarship

Gloria Fecht Memorial Scholarship Fund
402 West Arrow Highway
Suite 10
San Dimas, CA 91773
(909) 592-1281, (909) 592-7542 (fax)
http://www.womensgolf.org
Average award: $3,000
Maximum award: $5,000
Minimum award: $2,000
Number of awards: 20
Deadline: March 1
College level: Freshman, Sophomore, Junior, Senior, Graduate, Doctoral
Criteria: Applicant must be a woman, have an active interest in golf, and be a Southern California resident or a resident of Northern California who attends school in Southern California. Minimum 3.0 GPA is required to retain scholarship. Awarded every year.
Contact: Mary Swingle, President.

1988 Junior and Community College Athletic Scholarship

Alabama Commission on Higher Education
P.O. Box 302000
Montgomery, AL 36130-2000
(334) 242-1998, (334) 242-0268 (fax)
Maximum award: Tuition and books
College level: Freshman, Sophomore
Criteria: Applicant must attend a public junior or community college in Alabama on a full-time basis. Selection is based upon demonstrated athletic ability determined through try-outs. Financial need is not considered. Continued participation in designated sport is required to retain scholarship. Awarded every year.
Contact: Dr. William H. Wall, Alabama Commission of Higher Education, (334) 242-2274.

1989 Men's/Women's Basketball Performance Grant

Campbellsville University
Office of Financial Aid
200 West College Street
Campbellsville, KY 42718
(502) 465-8158
Maximum award: Full tuition, room, and board
Number of awards: 20
Deadline: April 1 (priority)
College level: Freshman, Sophomore, Junior, Senior
Criteria: Applicant must be offered an athletic performance grant contract by the head coach, be approved by the athletic director, participate in the sport, have a minimum 2.0 GPA, and be a full-time student. FAFSA is required. Scholarship is renewable. Awarded every year. Award may be used only at sponsoring institution.
Contact: Athletic Department.

1990 NATA Scholarship

National Athletic Trainers Association (NATA)
Grants and Scholarships Committee
2952 Stemmons Freeway
Dallas, TX 75247
(214) 637-6282, (214) 637-2206 (fax)
Average award: $2,000
Deadline: February 1
College level: Senior, Graduate, Doctoral
Majors/Fields: Athletic training
Criteria: Applicant must have a minimum 3.0 GPA, be a NATA member, pursue athletic training as a career, and be recommended by a certified athletic trainer. Awarded every year.
Contact: Briana Ebmeier, Foundation Manager.

1991 Olympic Tuition Grant

U.S. Olympic Committee
One Olympic Plaza
Colorado Springs, CO 80909
(719) 578-4661
Average award: $1,400
Maximum award: $5,000
Minimum award: $500
Number of awards: 1000
Deadline: November 1; February 1; May 1; August 1
College level: Sophomore, Junior, Senior, Graduate, Doctoral
Criteria: Applicant must be a candidate for membership on the next U.S. Olympic or Pan American Games team and demonstrate financial need. Applicant must be a high-performance athlete endorsed by their sport's national governing body. Recipient must reapply for renewal. Awarded every year.
Contact: Curt Hamakawa, Director, Athlete Support Department.

1992 Peter A. McKernan Scholarship

Peter A. McKernan Scholarship Fund
P.O. Box 5601
Augusta, ME 04332-5601
(207) 582-2729
Average award: $2,000
Number of awards: 3
Deadline: April 15
College level: Freshman
Criteria: Applicant must be a Maine resident attending a Maine high school, have a minimum "C" grade average, have earned a varsity letter or its equivalent in a high school sport, submit an essay "What Friendship Means to Me," be nominated by high school, and demonstrate financial need. Each Maine high school may nominate two students, one who will be attending a four-year school and one for a vocational school. Applications available only through high school guidance office. Awarded every year.
Contact: Scholarship.

1993 United States Ski Team Foundation Scholarship Phase I

United States Ski Education Foundation
P.O. Box 100
Park City, UT 84060
Average award: $1,000
Maximum award: $2,000
Deadline: May 1
College level: Freshman, Sophomore, Junior, Senior, Graduate, Doctoral
Criteria: Applicant must be a current or retired member of the U.S. Ski Team. Recipient must reapply for renewal. Awarded every year.
Contact: Laurie Beck, Academic and Career Counselor.

1994 Varsity Scholarship

California Baptist College
8432 Magnolia Avenue
Riverside, CA 92504
(909) 689-5771
Maximum award: $8,100
Number of awards: 120
Deadline: None
College level: Freshman, Sophomore, Junior, Senior
Criteria: Selection is based upon merit and performance. Scholarship is renewable. Awarded every year. Award may be used only at sponsoring institution.
Contact: Phillip Martinez, Director of Admissions/Financial Aid.

1995 Wendy's High School Heisman Award

National Association of Secondary School Principals
1904 Association Drive
Reston, VA 22091
Average award: $3,000
Maximum award: $5,000
Number of awards: 12
Deadline: September 30
College level: Freshman
Criteria: Applicant must demonstrate athletic ability, scholarship, and citizenship. Schools may nominate two seniors (one male, one female). 12 national finalists will receive a trip to New York City for the Heisman Awards ceremony in December, and two of the finalists (one male, one female) will be named the Wendy's High School Heisman Award winners. Awarded every year.
Contact: Awards.

Automotive Studies

1996   Brouwer D. McIntyre Memorial Scholarship

Automotive Hall of Fame
3225 Cook Road
P.O. Box 1727
Midland, MI 48641-1727
(517) 631-5760
Maximum award: $2,000
Deadline: June 30
College level: Junior, Senior, Doctoral
Criteria: Applicant must show a sincere interest in an automotive career, be enrolled full-time at an accredited college or university, and maintain satisfactory academic progress. Financial need is considered.
Contact: Margaret Gifford, Director of Educational Services.

1997   Carlyle Fraser Fund Scholarship in Honor of Wilton D. Looney

Automotive Hall of Fame
3225 Cook Road
P.O. Box 1727
Midland, MI 48641-1727
(517) 631-5760
Maximum award: $2,000
Deadline: June 30
College level: Junior, Senior, Doctoral
Criteria: Applicant must demonstrate interest in automotive career, be enrolled full-time at an accredited college or university, and maintain satisfactory academic progress. Financial need is considered.
Contact: Margaret Gifford, Director of Educational Services.

1998   Harold D. Draper, Sr., Memorial Scholarship

Automotive Hall of Fame
3225 Cook Road
P.O. Box 1727
Midland, MI 48641-1727
(517) 631-5760
Maximum award: $2,000
Deadline: June 30
College level: Junior, Senior, Doctoral
Criteria: Applicant must demonstrate interest in automotive career, be enrolled full-time at an accredited college or university, and maintain satisfactory academic progress. Financial need is considered.
Contact: Margaret Gifford, Director of Educational Services.

1999   Jeanne S. Peck Memorial Endowed Scholarship

Northwood University–Midland Campus
3225 Cook Road
Midland, MI 48640-2398
(515) 837-4160
Average award: $2,675
Number of awards: 1
Majors/Fields: Automotive aftermarket
Criteria: Applicant must be a U.S. citizen and demonstrate financial need. First consideration will be given to the employees and/or dependents of the Federal Mogul Corportation. Award may be used only at sponsoring institution.
Contact: Dixie Dee Maxwell.

2000   Jesse J. Jones, Jr. Memorial Scholarship

Northwood University–Midland Campus
3225 Cook Road
Midland, MI 48640-2398
(515) 837-4160
Average award: $5,000
Number of awards: 4
Majors/Fields: Automotive marketing, automotive studies
Criteria: Applicant must be a minority student. Academic achievement, career interest, and financial need are considered. Award may be used only at sponsoring institution.
Contact: Dixie Dee Maxwell.

2001   John E. Echlin Memorial Scholarship

Automotive Hall of Fame
3225 Cook Road
P.O. Box 1727
Midland, MI 48641-1727
(517) 631-5760
Maximum award: $2,000
Maximum number of awards: 24
Minimum number of awards: 16
Deadline: June 30
College level: Junior, Senior, Doctoral
Criteria: Applicant must be a full-time student, have a sincere interest in pursuing an automotive career upon graduation, regardless of major, and demonstrate satisfactory academic performance. Financial need is considered but not necessary. Awarded every year.
Contact: Margaret Gifford, Director of Educational Services.

2002   John Goerlich Memorial Scholarship

Automotive Hall of Fame
3225 Cook Road
P.O. Box 1727
Midland, MI 48641-1727
(517) 631-5760
Maximum award: $2,000
Deadline: June 30
College level: Junior, Senior, Doctoral
Criteria: Applicant must demonstrate interest in automotive career, be enrolled full-time at an accredited college or university, and maintain satisfactory academic progress. Financial need is considered.
Contact: Margaret Gifford, Director of Educational Services.

2003   John W. Koons, Sr., Memorial Scholarship

Automotive Hall of Fame
3225 Cook Road
P.O. Box 1727
Midland, MI 48641-1727
(517) 631-5760
Maximum award: $2,000
Deadline: June 30
College level: Junior, Senior, Doctoral
Criteria: Applicant must demonstrate interest in automotive career, be enrolled full-time at an accredited college or university, and maintain satisfactory academic progress. Financial need is considered.
Contact: Margaret Gifford, Director of Educational Services.

2004   Larry H. Averill Memorial Scholarship

Automotive Hall of Fame
3225 Cook Road
P.O. Box 1727
Midland, MI 48641-1727
(517) 631-5760
Maximum award: $1,500
Maximum number of awards: 3
Minimum number of awards: 1
Deadline: June 30
College level: Junior, Senior, Doctoral
Majors/Fields: Automotive studies
Criteria: Applicant must show a sincere interest in an automotive career, be enrolled full-time at an accredited college or university, and maintain satisfactory academic progress. Financial need is considered. Awarded every year.
Contact: Margaret Gifford, Director of Educational Services.

2005 M.H. Yager Memorial Scholarship

Automotive Hall of Fame
3225 Cook Road
P.O. Box 1727
Midland, MI 48641-1727
(517) 631-5760
Maximum award: $2,000
Deadline: June 30
College level: Junior, Senior, Doctoral
Criteria: Applicant must show a sincere interest in an automotive career, be enrolled full-time at an accredited college or university, and maintain satisfactory academic progress. Financial need is considered. Award may be used only at Northwood U.
Contact: Margaret Gifford, Director of Educational Services.

2006 SEMA Scholarship Fund

Specialty Equipment Market Association (SEMA)
P.O. Box 4910
Diamond Bar, CA 91765-0910
(909) 396-0289
Maximum award: $2,500
Number of awards: 13
Deadline: April 15
College level: Sophomore, Junior, Senior, Graduate, Doctoral
Majors/Fields: Automotive
Criteria: Applicant must intend to enter the automotive aftermarket field. Awarded every year.
Contact: Foundation Director.

2007 Universal Underwriters Scholarship

Automotive Hall of Fame
3225 Cook Road
P.O. Box 1727
Midland, MI 48641-1727
(517) 631-5760
Maximum award: $2,000
Number of awards: 4
Deadline: June 30
College level: Junior, Senior
Majors/Fields: Automotive studies
Criteria: Applicant must show a sincere interest in an automotive career, be a full-time student, and maintain satisfactory academic progress. Financial need is considered. Awarded every year. Award may be used only at Northwood U.
Contact: Margaret Gifford, Director of Educational Services.

2008 Walter W. Stillman Scholarship

Automotive Hall of Fame
3225 Cook Road
P.O. Box 1727
Midland, MI 48641-1727
(517) 631-5760
Maximum award: $2,000
Maximum number of awards: 3
Minimum number of awards: 1
Deadline: June 30
College level: Junior, Senior
Majors/Fields: Automotive studies
Criteria: Applicant must show a sincere interest in an automotive career, be a full-time student, and maintain satisfactory academic progress. Financial need is considered. Preference is given to students from New Jersey. Awarded every year. Award may be used only at Northwood U.
Contact: Margaret Gifford, Director of Educational Services.

2009 Zenon C.R. Hansen Memorial Scholarship

Automotive Hall of Fame
3225 Cook Road
P.O. Box 1727
Midland, MI 48641-1727
(517) 631-5760
Maximum award: $2,000
Deadline: June 30
College level: Junior, Senior, Doctoral
Criteria: Applicant must demonstrate interest in automotive career, be enrolled full-time at an accredited college or university, and maintain satisfactory academic progress. Financial need is considered.
Contact: Margaret Gifford, Director of Educational Services.

Corporate Affiliation—————

2010 Aaron M. Aronov Endowed Tuition Scholarship

The University of Alabama
Box 870162
Tuscaloosa, AL 35487-0162
(205) 348-6756
Average award: $2,470
Number of awards: 1
Deadline: February 1
College level: Freshman
Criteria: First priority is given to children of Aronov Realty Co. employees, second priority to Montgomery area residents. Awarded every year. Award may be used only at sponsoring institution.
Contact: Helen Leathers, Scholarship Coordinator, Box 870132, Tuscaloosa, AL 35487-0132.

2011 A. D. Albright Staff Congress Scholarship

Northern Kentucky University
Administrative Center 416
Nunn Drive
Highland Heights, KY 41099-7101
(606) 572-5144
Average award: In-state tuition
Deadline: February 1
College level: Freshman, Sophomore, Junior, Senior
Criteria: Applicant must be the child of a Northern Kentucky U staff member. Awarded every year. Award may be used only at sponsoring institution.
Contact: Robert E. Sprague, Director of Financial Aid.

2012 Alvin G. and Sally M. Beaman Scholarship

University of Tennessee, Knoxville
Financial Aid Office
115 Student Services Building
Knoxville, TN 37994
(615) 974-3131
Average award: $2,500
Deadline: February 1
College level: Freshman, Sophomore, Junior, Senior
Criteria: Applicant must be the child or grandchild of an employee of Beaman Bottling Company, Inc., or Shelbyville Bottling Company, Inc., or have graduated from a high school in a county served by Beaman Bottling or Shelbyville Bottling as of January 1, 1990. Selection is based upon GPA, test scores, and financial need. Awarded every year. Award may be used only at sponsoring institution.
Contact: Financial Aid Office.

2013   American National Can Company Scholarship

American National Can Company
8770 West Bryn-Mawr
Chicago, IL 60631-3542
(312) 399-3476
Average award: $1,000
Maximum award: $4,000
Minimum award: $500
Maximum number of awards: 27
Minimum number of awards: 1
Deadline: March 1
College level: Freshman
Criteria: Applicant must be the child of an employee or retiree of American National Can Company or its U.S. subsidiaries. Selection is based upon PSAT/NMSQT scores, academic record, minimum 3.0 culmulative GPA, leadership and extracurricular activities. Program is administered by the National Merit Scholarship Corporation. Satisfactory academic progress is required to retain scholarship. Awarded every year.
Contact: J. Hatch, Director of Personnel.

2014   Biomet Foundation Scholarship

Biomet Foundation, Inc.
P.O. Box 587
Warsaw, IN 46581
Average award: $2,000
Number of awards: 10
Deadline: April 1
College level: Freshman, Sophomore, Junior, Senior
Criteria: Applicant must be the dependant child of an employee of Biomet, Inc. or its subsidiaries. Recipient must reapply and show satisfactory academic progress to retain scholarship. Awarded every year.
Contact: Scholarships.

2015   Butler Manufacturing Company Scholarship

Butler Manufacturing Company Foundation
BMA Tower, 31st and Southwest Trafficway
P.O. Box 419917
Kansas City, MO 64141-0917
(816) 968-3208
Average award: $2,000
Number of awards: 8
Deadline: February 19
College level: Freshman
Criteria: Applicant must be a U.S. citizen and the child of an employee of Butler Manufacturing Co. Financial need must be demonstrated. Minimum 2.0 GPA is required to retain scholarship. Awarded every year.
Contact: Barbara L. Fay, Foundation Administrator.

2016   Charles H. Hood Fund

Charles H. Hood Fund
500 Rutherford Avenue
Boston, MA 02129
(617) 242-0600, extension 2444
Average award: $4,000
Number of awards: 6
Deadline: January 15
College level: Freshman, Sophomore, Junior, Senior
Criteria: Applicant must be the child of a H.P. Hood, Inc. employee.
Contact: Awards.

2017   CMP Scholarship Fund

Maine Community Foundation
210 Main Street
P.O. Box 148
Ellsworth, ME 04605
(207) 667-9735
Average award: $1,500
Maximum award: $2,500
Number of awards: 6
Deadline: May 1
College level: Freshman
Criteria: Applicant must be a Maine resident and the dependent of a Central Maine Power employee or retiree, enrolled in an accredited two- or four-year undergraduate institution, and be a graduate of a Maine secondary school. Selection is based upon personal aspirations, academic achievement, financial need, and school and community activities. Awarded every year.
Contact: Scholarship Coordinator.

2018   Coca-Cola Scholars Program

Coca-Cola Scholars Foundation, Inc.
P.O. Box 442
Atlanta, GA 30301-0442
(404) 733-5420
Maximum award: $20,000
Number of awards: 150
Deadline: October 31
College level: Freshman
Criteria: Selection is based upon leadership, character, and merit. Applicant must attend a high school which is located in a participating bottler's territory. Contact high school guidance counselor for application information. Children and grandchildren of employees, officers, or owners of Coca-Cola bottling companies, divisions, or subsidiaries are not eligible. Scholarship is renewable. Awarded every year.
Contact: Scholarships, (800) 306-2653.

2019   Cochran-McDonald Scholarship

University of Tennessee, Knoxville
Financial Aid Office
115 Student Services Building
Knoxville, TN 37994
(615) 974-3131
Average award: In-state tuition
Maximum number of awards: 20
Minimum number of awards: 2
Deadline: February 1
College level: Freshman, Sophomore, Junior, Senior
Criteria: Applicant must be employed by a Cochran family operated McDonald's restaurant, with a good work record and recommendation from the manager. Financial need may be considered. Preference is given to freshmen and applicants demonstrating academic excellence. Awarded every year. Award may be used only at sponsoring institution.
Contact: Financial Aid Office, 115 Student Services Building, Knoxville, TN 37994.

2020   Cone Mills Corporation Four-Year or Vocational/Technical Scholarship

Cone Mills Corporation
3101 North Elm Street
Greensboro, NC 27415
(910) 379-6697
Maximum award: $2,500
Number of awards: 15
Deadline: November 30
College level: Freshman
Criteria: Applicant must be enrolled on a full-time basis and the child of an active, retired, or deceased employee of Cone Mills Corp. with one or more years of service. Children of corporate officers and divisional officers are not eligible. Renewal is based upon adherence to college's academic standards. Awarded every year.
Contact: H. Graham Dail, Manager, Employee Relations, (910) 379-6252.

2021 Connie M. Maynard Education Fund Program

Golden Corral Corporation
P.O. Box 29502
Raleigh, NC 27626
(919) 881-4487
Average award: $1,800
Maximum award: $2,000
Minimum award: $500
Maximum number of awards: 50
Minimum number of awards: 30
Deadline: March 15
College level: Freshman, Sophomore, Junior, Senior, Graduate, Doctoral, vocational/technical degree programs
Criteria: Applicant must have at least 870 hours of work in a Golden Corral Corp. restaurant and a minimum 2.5 GPA. Selection is based upon academic achievement, community involvement, potential to achieve education and career goals, and recommendation. Financial need is not considered. Applicant must maintain a minimum 2.0 GPA and have at least 200 hours of work in a Golden Corral Restaurant. Awarded every year.
Contact: Joanne Martin, HR Coordinator.

2022 CSX Transportation Corporation Scholarship

CSX Transportation Corporation
P.O. Box 5151
Richmond, VA 23220-8151
(800) 533-GRAD
Average award: $2,500
Number of awards: 115
Deadline: May 1
College level: Freshman, Sophomore, Junior, Senior
Criteria: Applicant must be a dependent of a CSX employee. Recipients are selected by the Richmond Area Scholarship Program. Awarded every year.
Contact: Mila Spaulding, Administrator.

2023 Daniel Ashley and Irene Houston Jewell Foundation Scholarship

Jewell Foundation
c/o Suntrust Bank
P.O. Box 1638
Chattanooga, TN 37401
(423) 757-3933
Maximum award: $3,000
Number of awards: 10
Deadline: None
College level: Freshman, Sophomore, Junior, Senior
Criteria: Applicant must reside in Dade, Catoosa, or Walker counties, Ga. Recipient must reapply and maintain minimum "B" average for renewal. Awarded every year.
Contact: Barbara J. Marter, Institutional Trust Officer.

2024 Dennison Manufacturing Company Scholarship

Dennison Manufacturing Company
Personnel Department, Room 208
300 Howard Street
Framingham, MA 01701
(508) 879-0511
Maximum award: $2,000
Maximum number of awards: 20
Minimum number of awards: 15
Deadline: March 15
College level: Freshman
Criteria: Applicant's parent must be an active employee of Dennison Manufacturing Company with at least three months of full-time employment. Award is based upon high school grades, SAT I scores, family need, interview, and extracurricular activities. Applicant must be attending a two- or four-year degree-granting institution or a three-year hospital school of nursing. Minimum 2.5 is required to maintain scholarship. Award is renewable for up to three additional years. Awarded every year.
Contact: John R. Alexander, Secretary of Scholarship Program.

2025 Dun and Bradstreet Merit Scholarship

Dun and Bradstreet Corporation
299 Park Avenue
New York, NY 10171
Maximum award: $2,000
Number of awards: 4
Deadline: October 1
Criteria: Applicant must be the child of an active or retired employee of Dun and Bradstreet Corp. and its subsidiaries. He or she must take the PSAT/NMSQT exam during October of junior year of high school. Qualification selection is automatic through the procedures of the National Merit Scholarship Corp. on the basis of PSAT/NMSQT scores, need, and high school grades. Contact high school guidance counselor for information on the PSAT/NMSQT exam. Awarded every year.
Contact: Scholarships.

2026 Eastman Kodak Scholarship

University of Tennessee, Knoxville
Financial Aid Office
115 Student Services Building
Knoxville, TN 37994
(615) 974-3131
Average award: Tuition and fees
Number of awards: 5
Deadline: February 1
College level: Sophomore, Junior, Senior
Majors/Fields: Chemical engineering, electrical engineering, industrial engineering, mechanical engineering
Criteria: Applicant must be the child of an Eastman Kodak employee, U.S. citizen, rank in top quarter of class, and be a National Merit scholar. Selection is based upon academic excellence without regard to financial need. Scholarship is renewable. Awarded every year. Award may be used only at sponsoring institution.
Contact: College of Engineering, 118 Perkins Hall, Knoxville, TN 37996, (615) 974-2454.

2027 EEOC Endowed Scholarship

General Motors Corporation (GMC)
3044 West Grand Boulevard
Detroit, MI 48202
Maximum award: $2,500
Number of awards: 462
College level: Sophomore, Junior, Senior
Criteria: Applicant must be an employee or the child of an employee of General Motors Corp. and be a member of one of the following minority groups: Alaskan Native, American Indian, Asian-American, African-American/Black, Mexican-American/Chicano, Hispanic, Puerto Rican. Contact the university to ask if it participates in the scholarship program.
Contact: L.J. Wicker, Manager, Education Relations, (313) 556-3509.

2028 Faculty Senate Scholarship

Northern Kentucky University
Administrative Center 416
Nunn Drive
Highland Heights, KY 41099-7101
(606) 572-5144
Average award: In-state tuition
Deadline: February 1
College level: Freshman, Sophomore, Junior, Senior
Criteria: Applicant must be the child or spouse of a Northern Kentucky U faculty member. Awarded every year. Award may be used only at sponsoring institution.
Contact: Robert E. Sprague, Director of Financial Aid.

2029   Faculty/Staff Tuition Benefits

Georgetown University
37th and O Streets, NW
Washington, DC 20057
(202) 687-4547, (202) 687-6542 (fax)
Average award: $14,780
Maximum award: $18,400
Minimum award: $1,830
Number of awards: 249
Deadline: Two months before registration
College level: Freshman, Sophomore, Junior, Senior, Graduate, Doctoral
Criteria: Applicant must be a dependent of or a full-time faculty or staff member. Scholarship is renewable. Awarded every year. Award may be used only at sponsoring institution.
Contact: Patricia McWade, Dean of Student Financial Services, G-19 Healy Hall.

2030   FEEA Scholarship Award

Federal Employee Education and Assistance Fund
8441 W. Bowles, Suite 200
Littleton, CO 80123-3245
(800) 323-4140, (303) 933-7587 (fax)
Maximum award: $2,000
Number of awards: 340
Deadline: Last Friday in May
College level: Freshman, Sophomore, Junior, Senior, Graduate, Doctoral
Criteria: Applicant must have been a civilian federal employee for at least three years or be the legal dependent of one. Selection is based upon merit. To receive an application, send SASE. Awarded every year.
Contact: Scholarships.

2031   Francis Ouimet Scholarship

Francis Ouimet Scholarship Fund
190 Park Road
Weston, MA 02193-3401
Average award: $1,700
Maximum award: $5,000
Minimum award: $500
Number of awards: 240
Deadline: December 1
College level: Freshman, Sophomore, Junior, Senior
Criteria: Applicant must have worked at least three years at a Massachusetts golf course as a caddie, proshop worker, or green's crew worker. Minimum 2.0 GPA is required for renewal. Awarded every year.
Contact: Victoria Prince, Scholarship Director.

2032   George A. Hormel and Company Scholarship

George A. Hormel and Company
P.O. Box 800
Austin, MN 55912
(507) 437-5611
Maximum award: $3,000
Number of awards: 5
Deadline: January 11
College level: Freshman
Criteria: Applicant must be a high school student who is the child of an employee of George A. Hormel and Co. or its subsidiaries. Selection is by the National Merit Scholarship Corp. upon the basis of test scores, academic records, leadership, and extracurricular accomplishments. Applicant must take the PSAT and NMSQT exams during junior year of high school and attend a regionally accredited U.S. college. Scholarship is renewable. Awarded every year.
Contact: V. Allen Krejci, Scholarship Program Director.

2033   Gerber Companies Foundation Scholarship

Gerber Companies Foundation
5 South Division Ave
Fremont, MI 49412
Maximum award: $1,500
Number of awards: 205
Deadline: March 31
College level: Freshman, Sophomore, Junior, Senior
Criteria: Applicant must be a dependent of an employee of Gerber Products Co. or its subsidiaries. Minimum 2.0 GPA is required to retain scholarship. Awarded every year.
Contact: Cynthia M. Ebert, Administrator, (616) 924-3175.

2034   Gibbs Scholarship

Gibbs Wire & Steel Company
Metals Drive
Southington, CT 06489
(203) 527-2027
Average award: $4,000
Number of awards: 4
Deadline: April 15
Criteria: Applicant must be the child of a Gibbs Wire & Steel employee. Scholarship is renewable. Awarded every year.
Contact: Robert B. Johnson, Vice President for Special Projects, (203) 621-0121.

2035   Halton Scholars

Halton Foundation
P.O. Box 3377
Portland, OR 97208
(503) 288-6411
Average award: $1,500
Maximum award: $3,390
Number of awards: 5
Deadline: January 31
College level: Freshman, Sophomore, Junior, Senior, Graduate, Doctoral
Criteria: Applicant must be less than 28 years of age and the child of a Halton Co. employee. Scholarship is renewable. Awarded every year.
Contact: Susan H. Findlay, Manager.

2036   Henry R. Towne Scholarship

Eaton Corporation
World Headquarters Eaton Center
Cleveland, OH 44114
(216) 523-5000
Maximum award: $3,000
Number of awards: 12
Deadline: December 31
College level: Unspecified undergraduate
Criteria: Applicants must be the child of an Eaton Corp. employee and be a high school senior who has taken the PSAT/NMSQT. Selection is based upon test scores, academic record, class rank (top fifth), leadership, extracurricular activities, and other factors as determined by the National Merit Scholarship Corp. Scholarship is renewable. Awarded every year.
Contact: Thomas R. Freyberg, Human Resource Manager.

2037 Jagannathan Scholarship

North Carolina State Education Assistance Authority
Box 2688
Chapel Hill, NC 27515-2688
(919) 549-8614, (919) 549-8481 (fax)
jdmartin@ga.unc.edu
Maximum award: $2,500
Deadline: April 16
College level: Freshman
Criteria: Applicant must enroll full time at one of the 16 U of North Carolina constituent institutions. First preference is given to the children of employees of Tolaram Polymers, Cookson Fibers, and related companies. Recipient must maintain satisfactory academic progress and demonstrate continued financial need for renewal. Awarded every year. U of North Carolina constituent institutions only.
Contact: Financial Aid Office at eligible school.

2038 James E. DeLong Foundation Scholarship

James E. DeLong Foundation, Inc.
1000 West Saint Paul Avenue
Waukesha, WI 53188
(414) 549-2773
Average award: $1,500
Number of awards: 2
Deadline: April 1
College level: Freshman
Criteria: Applicant must be the child of an employee of the Waukesha Engine Division, Waukesha, Wisc. Awarded every year.
Contact: Mr. Charles V. Zalewski, Secretary-Treasurer.

2039 Joseph and Virginia Altschuller Scholarship

University of Toledo
Financial Aid Office
Toledo, OH 43606-3390
(419) 537-2056
Average award: $2,500
Number of awards: 5
Deadline: March 1
College level: Freshman, Sophomore, Junior, Senior
Criteria: Applicant must be an employee or the dependent of an employee of Seaway Foodtown and enrolled full time. Award is for four years. Awarded every year. Award may be used only at sponsoring institution.

2040 Kellstadt Scholarship

DePaul University
1 East Jackson Boulevard
Chicago, IL 60604
(312) 362-8704, (312) 362-5749 (fax)
Maximum award: $4,000
Maximum number of awards: 4
Minimum number of awards: 2
College level: Freshman
Criteria: Applicant must be the child of a Sears employee (proof of employment required). Scholarship is renewable. Awarded every year. Award may be used only at sponsoring institution.
Contact: Jennifer Sparrow, Scholarship Coordinator, jsparrow@wppost.depaul.edu.

2041 Kohler Co. College Scholarship

Kohler Company
444 Highland Drive
Public Affairs Department
Kohler, WI 53044
(414) 457-4441, (414) 459-1656 (fax)
Average award: $1,550
Maximum award: $2,000
Minimum award: $500
Number of awards: 10
Deadline: February 15
College level: Freshman
Criteria: Applicant must be a U.S. citizen and an employee or the child of an employee of Kohler or its U.S. subsidiaries. Applicant should rank in the top tenth of class, have a near-perfect GPA, and have a minimum combined SAT I score of 1150. Good academic standing, full-time enrollment, and continuing employment are required to retain scholarship. Awarded every year.
Contact: Peter J. Fetterer, Manager of Media and Civic Services.

2042 Leland James Merit Scholarship

Consolidated Freightways Inc.
3240 Hillview Avenue
Palo Alto, CA 94304
(415) 326-1700
Maximum award: $2,000
Number of awards: 1
Deadline: August 1
College level: Unspecified undergraduate
Criteria: Applicant must be the child of an employee of Consolidated Freightways or a subsidiary who plans to enroll in a course of study leading to a bachelor's degree at an accredited college. Selection is based upon financial need, PSAT/NMSQT scores, high school grades, and recommendations. Minimum 2.8 GPA required. Renewable for four years. Awarded every year.
Contact: Lillian Maloney.

2043 Lewis Bear Scholarship

University of West Florida
11000 University Parkway
Pensacola, FL 32514-5750
(904) 474-2400
Average award: Full tuition, fees, and books.
Number of awards: 1
Deadline: None
College level: First-time undergraduate students
Criteria: Applicant must be employee or dependent of employee of Lewis Bear Company, Pensacola, Fla. Awarded every year. Award may be used only at sponsoring institution.
Contact: Georganne E. Major, Senior Financial Aid Officer.

2044 Luther A. Sizemore Foundation Scholarship

New Mexico State University
Box 30001
Department 5100
Las Cruces, NM 88003-0001
(505) 646-4105
Average award: Full tuition
Number of awards: 2
Deadline: March 1
College level: Freshman, Sophomore, Junior, Senior
Criteria: Preference is given to dependents of carpenters throughout New Mexico. Minimum 2.0 GPA and completion of at least 12 credit hours per semester are required to retain scholarship. Awarded every year. Award may be used only at sponsoring institution.
Contact: Greeley W. Myers, Director of Financial Aid.

2045   M.A. Hanna Company Scholarships

M.A. Hanna Company
200 Public Square
Suite 36-5000
Cleveland, OH 44114-2304
(216) 589-4000, (216) 589-4034 (fax)
Maximum award: $1,500
Number of awards: 50
Deadline: June 30
College level: Freshman, Sophomore, Junior, Senior
Criteria: Applicant must be the child or spouse of a full-time employee of M.A. Hanna Co. or a business unit of subsidiary which is majority-owned by M.A. Hanna. Recipient must submit grade transcript for renewal. Awarded every year.
Contact: John S. Pyke, Jr., Vice President, General Counsel, and Secretary.

2046   Maguire Educational Scholarships

PanEnergy Corporation
P.O. Box 1642
Houston, TX 77251-1642
(713) 627-4608
Average award: $2,500
Number of awards: 10
Deadline: October 1
College level: Freshman, Sophomore, Junior, Senior
Criteria: Applicant must be the child of an employee or retiree of the PanEnergy Corp. who has five years of service with the corporation. Children of officers and directors are not eligible. Recipient must maintain minimum 2.5 GPA per semester to retain scholarship. Awarded every year.
Contact: Dianne Wilson, Scholarship Coordinator.

2047   McDonnell Douglas Scholarship

McDonnell Douglas Scholarship Foundation
Mail Code 802-11
3855 Lakewood Boulevard
Long Beach, CA 90846
(310) 593-2612
Average award: $1,500
Maximum award: $4,000
Maximum number of awards: 56
Minimum number of awards: 30
Deadline: First Friday in March
College level: Freshman
Criteria: Applicant must be the dependent child, stepchild, or legally adopted child of an active, retired, disabled, or deceased employee of a McDonnell Douglas component company or subsidiary. Applicant must rank in the top third of class. Selection is based upon class standing, college entrance exams, leadership, lettering in varsity sports, extracurricular activities, community activity, and verifiable employment. Good academic standing is required to retain scholarship. Awarded every year.
Contact: Beverly A. Hoskinson, Administrator.

2048   Merit Gasoline Foundation Scholarship

Merit Gasoline Foundation Scholarship
551 West Lancaster Avenue
Haverford, PA 19041
Maximum award: $3,000
Number of awards: 4
Deadline: May 15
College level: Freshman, Sophomore, Junior, Senior
Criteria: Applicant must be the child or stepchild of a full-time employee of the Merit Oil Corp. and/or its affiliates for at least two consecutive years. Also eligible are dependents of employees who are retired under the company's pension plan, totally disabled due to an accident or illness under the wage continuation program, or deceased, but fully qualified prior to death. Selection is based upon financial need, academic achievement, SAT I scores, and evaluation of character, quality of leadership, work habits, and general interests. Satisfactory academic progress is required to retain scholarship. Awarded every year.
Contact: Executive Director.

2049   Miles Incorporated Foundation Scholarship

Miles Incorporated
1127 Myrtle Street
Elkhart, IN 46514
(219) 264-8225
Average award: $1,500
College level: Freshman
Criteria: Applicant must be the child of a Miles Incorporated U.S.A. employee. Award is paid over four years directly to the school.
Contact: Lem Beardsley, Chairman of Foundation.

2050   Minnesota Mining and Manufacturing Corporation Annual Program

Clemson University
G-01 Sikes Hall
Clemson, SC 29634-5123
(803) 656-2280
Average award: $3,000
Number of awards: 1
Deadline: March 1
College level: Freshman, Sophomore, Junior, Senior
Criteria: Applicant must have a minimum 2.5 GPA and be enrolled in the College of Engineering and Science. Award may be used only at sponsoring institution.
Contact: Scholarships.

2051   North Carolina Masonry Contractors Association Scholarship

North Carolina Department of Community Colleges
Caswell Building
200 West Jones Street
Raleigh, NC 27603-1337
(919) 733-7051 extension 319
Average award: $750
Number of awards: 1
Deadline: September 15
College level: Vocational/technical students
Criteria: Applicant must be an employee of a NCMCA member company and have a GPA at or above the level required for graduation. Selection is based upon academic acheivement, need, and extracurricular activities. North Carolina community colleges only.
Contact: Scholarships.

2052   Olivia Jackson McGee Endowed Scholarship

Clemson University
G-01 Sikes Hall
Clemson, SC 29634-5123
(803) 656-2280
Average award: $2,400
Number of awards: 1
Deadline: March 1
College level: Freshman, Sophomore, Junior, Senior
Majors/Fields: Architecture, English
Criteria: Applicant must be the child or grandchild of a Clemson U tenured professor and be studying architecture or English; if no eligible applicant meets the criteria, the scholarship will be awarded to a student in architecture or English. Renewable if recipient reapplies. Awarded every year. Award may be used only at sponsoring institution.
Contact: Marvin Carmichael, Director of Financial Aid.

2053 **Philip Morris Companies College Scholarship**

Philip Morris Companies
120 Park Avenue
New York, NY 10017-5592
(212) 880-5000
Maximum award: $5,000
Deadline: November 30
College level: Freshman, Sophomore, Junior, Senior
Criteria: Applicant must be the child of a full-time employee of Philip Morris Companies Inc. or any of its domestic subsidiaries and divisions, and be enrolled in a four-year, accredited college or university in the U.S., Canada, or Puerto Rico. Selection is based upon SAT I or ACT scores and class rank. Renewal report and transcript are required to retain scholarship. Awarded every year.
Contact: Phillip Morris Scholarship Program, College Scholarship Service/Sponsored Scholarship Programs, P.O. Box 6730, Princeton, NJ 08541.

2054 **Philip Morris Companies Vocational/Technical Scholarship**

Philip Morris Companies
120 Park Avenue
New York, NY 10017-5592
(212) 880-5000
Maximum award: $2,500
Deadline: November 30
College level: Freshman, Sophomore, High school graduates or GED holders
Majors/Fields: Vocational/technical
Criteria: Applicant must be the child of a full-time employee of Philip Morris Companies Inc. or any of its domestic subsidiaries and divisions, and plan to attend an accredited vocational or technical program of a maximum two-year duration. Renewal report and transcript are required to retain scholarship. Awarded every year.
Contact: Philip Morris Scholarship Program, College Scholarship Service/Sponsored Scholarship Programs, P.O. Box 6730, Princeton, NJ 08541.

2055 **Pitney-Bowes Scholarship**

Pitney-Bowes Inc.
One Elmcroft (52-11)
Stamford, CT 06926-0700
(203) 351-6203
Average award: $2,500
Number of awards: 30
Deadline: December 31
Criteria: Applicant must be a graduating high school senior, rank in top third of class, and be the dependent of a Pitney-Bowes employee. Selection is based upon high school class rank, SAT I scores, potential accomplishments, and financial need. Awarded every year.
Contact: Scholarships.

2056 **Prudential's Merit Scholarship**

Prudential Insurance Company
P.O. Box 388
Fort Washington, PA 19034
Maximum award: $3,000
Criteria: Applicant must be the child of an employee of the Prudential Insurance Co. who scored in the top percentile of the PSAT/NMSQT test given during the junior year of high school. Finalist's parent must be or have been a member of the home office or field staff (active or retired) on January 1st of the year in which the applicant will complete high school and be entering college. Awarded every year.
Contact: Scholarships.

2057 **Quaker Chemical Foundation Scholarship**

Quaker Chemical Foundation
P.O. Box 809
Elm and Lee Streets
Conshohocken, PA 19428-0809
(610) 832-4313
Average award: $2,750
Maximum award: $4,000
Minimum award: $1,500
Maximum number of awards: 3
Minimum number of awards: 1
Deadline: In December
College level: Freshman, Sophomore, Junior, Senior
Criteria: Applicant must be the child of a Quaker Chemical employee in a baccalaureate or nonbaccalaureate degree program. Scholarship is renewable. Awarded every year.
Contact: Kathleen A. Lasota, Secretary to the Foundation, (610) 832-4127.

2058 **Rahr Foundation Scholarship**

Rahr Malting Company
567 Grain Exchange Building
P.O. Box 15186
Minneapolis, MN 55414
(612) 332-5161, (612) 332-6841 (fax)
Average award: $3,000
Number of awards: 7
Deadline: March 15
College level: Freshman, Sophomore, Junior, Senior
Criteria: Applicant must be the child of a current Rahr Malting Co. employee. Satisfactory GPA and full-time status are required to retain scholarship. Awarded every year.
Contact: Mrs. Mary Gresham, Secretary and Director.

2059 **Sid Richardson Memorial Fund Scholarship**

Sid Richardson Memorial Fund
309 Main Street
Fort Worth, TX 76102
(817) 336-0494, (817) 332-2176 (fax)
Average award: $2,000
Number of awards: 45
Deadline: March 31
College level: Freshman, Sophomore, Junior, Senior, Graduate, Doctoral
Criteria: Applicant must be the child or grandchild of a current or retired employee (with at least three years of full-time service) of one of the following companies: Sid Richardson Carbon Co., Sid Richardson Gasoline Co., Richardson Products II Co., SRGC Aviation, Inc., Leapartners, L.P. (dba Sid Richardson Gasoline Co.-Jal), Bass Enterprises Production Co., Bass Brothers Enterprises, Inc., Richardson Oils, Inc., Perry R. Bass, Inc., Sid W. Richardson Foundation, San Jose Cattle Co., City Center Development Co., Richardson Aviation. Selection is competitive and is based upon academic achievement and financial need. Recipients may reapply if they maintain a minimum 2.0 GPA. Awarded every year.
Contact: Jo Helen Rosacker, Administrator.

2060 **Staff Congress Scholarship**

Northern Kentucky University
Administrative Center 416
Nunn Drive
Highland Heights, KY 41099-7101
(606) 572-5144
Average award: In-state tuition
Deadline: February 1
College level: Freshman, Sophomore, Junior, Senior
Criteria: Applicant must be the child or spouse of a Northern Kentucky U staff member. Awarded every year. Award may be used only at sponsoring institution.
Contact: Robert E. Sprague, Director of Financial Aid.

2061 **Stanadyne Inc. Educational Grant**

Stanadyne, Inc.
277 Woodland Avenue
Elyria, OH 44035
(216) 323-3341
Average award: $2,000
Number of awards: 12
Deadline: March 1
College level: Freshman
Criteria: Applicant must be the child of a full-time employee of Stanadyne, Inc. Awarded every year.
Contact: Scholarships.

2062 **State Farm Companies Foundation Scholarship**

State Farm Companies Foundation
One State Farm Plaza
Bloomington, IL 61710
(309) 766-2161
Maximum award: $8,000
Maximum number of awards: 75
Minimum number of awards: 75
Deadline: December 31
College level: Freshman
Criteria: Applicant must be the child of a full-time or retired State Farm Insurance employee or agent. Applicant must meet National Merit Scholarship Corp. requirements. Awarded every year.
Contact: Nancy Lynn, Program Coordinator, One State Farm Plaza, SC-3, Bloomington, IL 61710, (309) 766-2039.

2063 **Stone Foundation Scholarship**

Stone Foundation Scholarship
150 North Michigan Avenue
Chicago, IL 60601-7568
Average award: $2,000
Number of awards: 13
Deadline: April 1
College level: Freshman
Criteria: Applicant must be the child of a full-time Stone Container Corp. employee who has worked at the company for at least two years. Selection is based upon scholarship, character, community, and student activities. Financial need may be considered. Scholarship is renewable at the discretion of the scholarship committee. Recipient must maintain a minimum 2.0 GPA. Awarded every year.
Contact: Betsy Stetter, Personnel Supervisor, (312) 580-2291.

2064 **Texaco Foundation Employee Scholarship**

Texaco Foundation
2000 Westchester Avenue
White Plains, NY 10650
(914) 253-4049, (914) 253-4655 (fax)
Average award: $2,500
Number of awards: 100
Deadline: November 15
College level: Freshman
Criteria: Applicant must be the child of a Texaco employee or retiree who has been employed at least one year. Scholarship is renewable. Awarded every year.
Contact: Zenada Viray, (914) 253-7584, virayz@texaco.com.

2065 **Thomasville Furniture Industries Foundation Scholarship**

Thomasville Furniture Industries Foundation
Wachovia Bank and Trust Company
P.O. Box 3099
Winston-Salem, NC 27102
Maximum award: $1,500
Number of awards: 39
Criteria: Applicant must be the child of a regular employee of Thomasville Furniture Industries, Inc. Awarded every year.
Contact: Scholarships.

2066 **Washington Post Thomas Ewing Memorial Education Grant**

Washington Post
Thomas Ewing Memorial Carrier Scholarship
1150 15th Street, NW
Washington, DC 20079
(202) 334-6060, (202) 334-4319 (fax)
Average award: $1,000
Maximum award: $2,000
Number of awards: 35
Deadline: January 29
College level: Freshman, Sophomore, Junior, Senior, Graduate, Doctoral, technical or vocational school students
Criteria: Applicant must be a *Washington Post* carrier who has been on the route at least 18 months. Scholarship is renewable. Awarded every year.
Contact: Jay O'Hare or Terry Lyn Johnson, Sales Development Managers.

2067 **Weyerhaeuser Company Foundation College Scholarship Program**

Weyerhaeuser Company Foundation
CHIL32
Tacoma, WA 98477
(206) 924-2629, (206) 924-3658 (fax)
Maximum award: $4,000
Number of awards: 30
Deadline: January 15 of high school junior year
College level: Freshman
Criteria: Applicant must be the child of a Weyerhaeuser employee who has had one year of continuous service by December 1 of the child's junior year in high school and be in service on March 1 of child's senior year of high school. Children of retired or deceased employees who had one year of continuous service prior to their death or retirement are also eligible. Interested applicants should take the PSAT/NMSQT exam in October of their junior year in high school. Selection is based upon PSAT/NMSQT scores, academic record, qualities of leadership, and extracurricular accomplishments. Satisfactory academic standing is required to retain scholarship for up to four years. Awarded every year.
Contact: Penny Paul, Program Manager.

Culinary Arts/Baking

2068 **Baking Industry Scholarships**

American Institute of Baking (AIB)
1213 Bakers Way
Manhattan, KS 66502
(913) 537-4750
Average award: $2,500
Maximum award: $3,300
Minimum award: $500
Number of awards: 40
Majors/Fields: Baking, maintenance engineering
Criteria: Applicant must be planning to seek new employment in the baking industry. Experience in the industry or approved substitute is required. Selection is based upon educational background, work experience, recommendations, and financial need. Applicant must be attending or accepted for admission to AIB's maintenance engineering or baking science and technology courses. Awarded every year. Award may be used only at sponsoring institution.
Contact: Ken Embers.

2069 IACP Foundation Scholarships

**International Association of Culinary Professionals
Foundation (IACP)
304 West Liberty Street, Suite 201
Louisville, KY 40202
(502) 587-7953, (502) 589-3602 (fax)**
Average award: $3,000
Maximum award: $10,000
Minimum award: $500
Number of awards: 60
Deadline: December 1
College level: Freshman, Sophomore, Junior, Senior, Graduate, Doctoral
Majors/Fields: Culinary study
Criteria: Awarded every year.
Contact: Debbie Arnold, Director of Administration, (502) 581-9786.

2070 Recipe Contest Scholarship

**Johnson & Wales University
8 Abbott Park Place
Providence, RI 02903
(401) 598-1000, (401) 598-1040 (fax)
admissions@jwu.edu
http://jwu.edu**
Maximum award: $5,000
Deadline: None
College level: Freshman
Majors/Fields: Culinary arts, pastry arts
Criteria: Selection is based upon Recipe Contest. Recipient must maintain satisfactory academic progress to retain scholarship. Awarded every year. Award may be used only at sponsoring institution.
Contact: Licia Dwyer, Director of Culinary Admissions, (401) 598-2370.

City/County of Residence—

2071 50 Men and Women of Toledo, Inc. Scholarship

**University of Toledo
Financial Aid Office
Toledo, OH 43606-3390
(419) 537-2056**
Maximum award: $3,000
Number of awards: 1
Deadline: January 28
College level: Freshman
Criteria: Applicant must be an African-American graduate of a Toledo area high school. Award is for four years. Awarded every year. Award may be used only at sponsoring institution.
Contact: J.C. Caldwell, 50 Men and Women of Toledo, Inc., P.O. Box 3557, Toledo, OH 43608, (419) 729-4654.

2072 Alice Powers Scholarship

**The College of Wooster
Office of Admissions
Wooster, OH 44691
(330) 263-2270, (330) 263-2621 (fax)
admissions@acs.wooster.edu
http://www.wooster.edu**
Maximum award: $6,500
Deadline: February 15
College level: Freshman
Criteria: Applicant must be a resident of Mahoning or Trumbull County, Ohio and be nominated by a counselor or teacher. Selection is based upon academic achievement, extracurricular activities, and counselor and teacher recommendations. Recipient must maintain academic progress toward degree to retain scholarship. Renewable for four years. Awarded every year. Award may be used only at sponsoring institution.
Contact: Office of Admissions.

2073 Anna and Charles Stockwitz Children and Youth Fund

**Jewish Family and Children's Services (JFCS)
1600 Scott Street
San Francisco, CA 94115
(415) 561-1226, (415) 922-5938 (fax)**
Average award: $2,500
Maximum award: $5,000
Number of awards: 100
Deadline: None
College level: Freshman, Sophomore, Junior, Senior, Graduate, Doctoral, vocational students.
Criteria: Applicant must be Jewish, under age 26, demonstrate financial need, and be a resident of Marin, Mountain View, Palo Alto, San Francisco, San Mateo, or Sonoma County, Calif. Recipient must reapply for renewal. Awarded every year.
Contact: Ted Schreiber, Director of Loans and Grants Program.

2074 Anna F. Jones Scholarship

**State Scholarship Commission (Oregon)
1500 Valley River Drive
Suite 100
Eugene, OR 97401-2146
(541) 687-7400
http://www.teleport.com/~ossc/**
Average award: $2,100
Maximum award: $2,400
Minimum award: $1,800
Deadline: March 1
College level: Freshman, Sophomore, Junior, Senior
Criteria: Applicant must be a Lake County resident who completed all four years of secondary school at Paisley High School, be enrolled full time at an Oregon school, and demonstrate financial need. Scholarship is renewable. Awarded every year. Oregon public schools only.
Contact: Jim Beyer, Grant Program Director, (541) 687-7395.

2075 Aubrey Lee Brooks Scholarship

**North Carolina State Education Assistance Authority
Box 2688
Chapel Hill, NC 27515-2688
(919) 549-8614, (919) 549-8481 (fax)
jdmartin@ga.unc.edu**
Maximum award: $4,200
Average award: Half tuition
Number of awards: 17
Deadline: in February
College level: Freshman
Criteria: Applicant must be a resident of one of the following North Carolina counties: Alamance, Bertie, Caswell, Durham, Forsyth, Granville, Guilford, Orange, Person, Rockingham, Stokes, Surry, Swain, or Warren; or reside in the cities of Greensboro or High Point. One award is for a senior at the North Carolina Sch of Science and Mathematics. Applicant must attend North Carolina State U, U of North Carolina at Chapel Hill, or U of North Carolina at Greensboro. Selection is based upon academic standing, character, leadership, financial need, and applicant's willingness to prepare for a career as a well-informed citizen. Good academic standing, financial need, and full-time enrollment are required to retain scholarship. Awarded every year.
Contact: High school guidance counselor.

2076 Barrick Mercur Scholarship

**University of Utah
Financial Aid and Scholarships Office
105 Student Services Building
Salt Lake City, UT 84112
(801) 581-6211**
Maximum award: $2,400
Number of awards: 1
Deadline: February 1
College level: Freshman
Majors/Fields: Metallurgical engineering
Criteria: Applicant must be a resident of Tooele County, Utah. Awarded every year. Award may be used only at sponsoring institution.
Contact: Department of Metallurgical Engineering, 412 William C. Browning Building, Salt Lake City, UT 84112, (801) 581-5158.

2077 Battelle Scholarship

Capital University
2199 East Main Street
Columbus, OH 43209-2394
(614) 236-6511
Maximum award: One-Half tuition
Number of awards: 4
Deadline: March 1
College level: Freshman
Criteria: Applicant must be from Franklin county or surrounding area
and demonstrate potential for creativity, leadership, and motivation.
Renewable for up to eight semesters if minimum 2.5 GPA is main-
tained. Awarded every year. Award may be used only at sponsoring
institution.
Contact: Steve Crawford, Assistant Director of Admission.

2078 Battelle Scholarship

Denison University
Box H
Granville, OH 43023
(614) 587-6276, 800-DENISON, (614) 587-6306 (fax)
admissions@denison.edu
http://www.denison.edu
Average award: One-Half tuition
Maximum number of awards: 2
Minimum number of awards: 1
Deadline: January 1
College level: Freshman
Criteria: Applicant must be a resident of Central Ohio (Franklin and
contiguous counties). On-campus interview required. Minimum GPA
required for renewal. Awarded every year. Award may be used only
at sponsoring institution.
Contact: Janet Schultz, Scholarship, (614) 587-6625.

2079 Battelle Scholarship

WSU Tri-Cities
Battelle Scholarship
100 Sprout Road
Richland, WA 99352
(509) 372-7258, (509) 372-7354 (fax)
Average award: $2,000
Number of awards: 6
Deadline: March 15
College level: Freshman
Majors/Fields: Engineering or science
Criteria: Applicant must be a student at a high school in Benton or
Franklin County in Washington state. Renewable up to four years if
recipient submits proof of enrollment and transcript showing satisfac-
tory progress. Awarded every year.
Contact: Lori Williams, Assistant to the Dean, lwilliams@wsu.edu.

2080 Bernard Daly Educational Scholarship

Daly Educational Fund
620 North First Street
Lakeview, OR 97630
(503) 947-2196
Average award: $2,100
Number of awards: 60
Deadline: May 1
College level: Freshman
Criteria: Applicant must be a resident of Lake County, Ore., and a
graduate of a Lake County high school. Completion of a formal ap-
plication and an interview is required. Scholarship is renewable.
Awarded every year.
Contact: Scholarships.

2081 Betsy Norwood McLeod Endowed Scholarship

Clemson University
G-01 Sikes Hall
Clemson, SC 29634-5123
(803) 656-2280
Average award: $6,500
Minimum award: $5,000
Number of awards: 2
Deadline: March 1
College level: Freshman
Criteria: Applicant must have a minimum 2.5 GPA and demonstrate
financial need. The larger award goes to a resident of Chesterfield
County, S.C.; the other award is for a Chesterfield County resident
who is a graduate of one of the following schools: Chesterfield,
McBee, Cheraw, or Central High School (preference in that order).
Satisfactory GPA and completion of at least 12 credit hours per se-
mester are required to retain scholarship. Awarded every year.
Award may be used only at sponsoring institution.
Contact: Marvi Carmichael, Director of Financial Aid.

2082 Boston Youth Leadership Award

Northeastern University
360 Huntington Avenue
150 Richards Hall
Boston, MA 02115
(617) 373-2000
Average award: $6,500
Number of awards: 5
Deadline: March 1
College level: Freshman
Criteria: Applicant must attend a Boston public, private, or parochial
school, rank in the top quarter of class, and demonstrate outstanding
community leadership and service. Minimum 3.0 GPA is required to
retain scholarship. Awarded every year. Award may be used only at
sponsoring institution.
Contact: Alan Kines, Director of Admissions, (617) 373-2200.

2083 Burke Scholarship Program

Marquette University
P.O. Box 1881
Milwaukee, WI 53201-1881
(414) 288-7302, (414) 288-3764 (fax)
go2marquette@vms.csd.mu.edu
http://www.mu.edu
Average award: Full tuition plus a stipend
Number of awards: 5
Deadline: February 14
College level: Freshman
Criteria: Applicant must be a Wisconsin resident, rank in the top tenth
of his or her class, have a minimum combined SAT I score of 1200
(composite ACT score of 28), and have shown exceptional commit-
ment to others through community volunteer time and leadership.
FAFSA required. Minimum 3.0 GPA and full-time enrollment are required to retain scholarship. Awarded every year. Award may be
used only at sponsoring institution.
Contact: Carlos Garces, Senior Assistant Director of Admissions.

2084 Byron E. Morris Scholarship

The College of Wooster
Office of Admissions
Wooster, OH 44691
(330) 263-2270, (330) 263-2621 (fax)
admissions@acs.wooster.edu
http://www.wooster.edu
Maximum award: $6,000
Deadline: February 15
College level: Freshman
Criteria: Applicant must have a minimum 2.5 GPA and demonstrate
involvement in volunteer organizations, community service projects,
and/or positions of leadership in civic or educational programs. Recipient must maintain academic progress toward degree to retain
scholarship. Renewable for four years. Awarded every year. Award
may be used only at sponsoring institution.
Contact: Office of Admissions.

2085 Calhoun Math Tournament Scholarship

Jacksonville State University
Jacksonville, AL 36265-9982
(205) 782-5006
Average award: Full tuition
College level: Winner of Calhoun County Math Tournament
Criteria: Awarded every year. Award may be used only at sponsoring institution.
Contact: Student Financial Aid Office.

2086 Camp Foundation Scholarship

Camp Foundation
P.O. Box 813
Franklin, VA 23851
(804) 562-3439
Maximum award: $4,500
Number of awards: 7
Deadline: February 22
College level: Freshman
Criteria: Applicant must be a resident of the city of Franklin or the counties of Isle of Wight and Southampton, Va. Scholarship is renewable. Awarded every year.
Contact: Bobby Worrell, Executive Director.

2087 Cardinal Medeiros Scholarship

Emmanuel College
400 The Fenway
Boston, MA 02115
(617) 735-9725
Maximum award: $4,500
Deadline: February 15
College level: Freshman
Criteria: Applicant must have a minimum 3.0 GPA and minimum combined SAT I score of 900, be a woman, demonstrate financial need, and be a graduate of Catholic or public school in the Archdiocese of Boston or the Diocese of Fall River. Minimum 3.0 GPA required to retain scholarship. Awarded every year. Award may be used only at sponsoring institution.
Contact: Patricia K. Harden, Director of Financial Aid.

2088 Clark Foundation Scholarship

Clark Foundation Scholarship Program (Clark Estates)
30 Wall Street
New York, NY 10005
Average award: $2,000
Criteria: Scholarship is given to graduates of 11 secondary schools in and around Cooperstown, N.Y. Only these schools may recommend students for the award. Awards will be granted only if applicants have high credentials. Scholarship is renewable.
Contact: Edward W. Stack, Secretary of Clark Foundation.

2089 Collins–McDonald Trust Fund Scholarship

Collins–McDonald Trust Fund
P.O. Box 351
Lakeview, OR 97630
(503) 947-2196
Average award: $2,100
Number of awards: 25
Deadline: May 1
College level: Freshman
Criteria: Applicant must be a resident of Lake County, Oregon and a graduate of a Lake County high school. Completion of a formal application is required. Scholarship is renewable. Awarded every year.
Contact: Scholarships.

2090 Community College Achievement Award

Southern California Edison Company
1190 Durfee Avenue
Suite 200
South El Monte, CA 91733
(818) 302-0284
Maximum award: $6,000
Number of awards: 20
Deadline: March 1
College level: Community college students planning to attend a California four-year institution
Majors/Fields: Math or science (with secondary teaching credential)
Criteria: Applicant must be a member of an underrepresented ethnic or disadvantaged group, live in or attend a community college in the Southern California Edison service area, have a minimum 2.5 GPA, have sufficient transferrable units to enter a four-year college as a junior in the fall, and be a U.S. citizen or permanent resident. Dependents of Southern California Edison employees are not eligible. Selection is based upon career objectives and academic achievements. Applicant must submit an application to the Financial Aid Office by February 9. Recipients 18 years or older may be eligible for summer jobs with Edison Summer Employment Program. Awarded every year.
Contact: Scholarship Committee.

2091 Dain Bosworth, Inc. Scholarship

Mesa State College
Financial Aid Department
P.O. Box 2647
Grand Junction, CO 81502
(970) 248-1396
Maximum award: Tuition, fees, and $80 book allowance
College level: Sophomore
Majors/Fields: Vocational program
Criteria: Applicant must be a Mesa County, Colo., resident. Awarded every year. Award may be used only at sponsoring institution.
Contact: Unified Technical Education Center.

2092 Dane G. Hansen Foundation Leadership Scholarship

Dane G. Hansen Foundation
Logan, KS 67646
(913) 689-4832
Average award: $3,500
Number of awards: 6
Deadline: Fall of senior year in high school
College level: Freshman
Criteria: Applicant must be a graduating senior from a high school in the 26-county area of northwest Kansas and have a minimum 3.5 GPA. Renewable for up to three years if minimum "B" grade average is maintained. Awarded every year.
Contact: Raymond Lappin, Chairman of the Scholarship Committee.

2093 Dennis Wade Smith Memorial Scholarship

Southern Illinois University at Edwardsville
Box 1060
Edwardsville, IL 62026-1060
(618) 692-3880, (618) 692-3885 (fax)
finaid@siue.edu
http://www.finaid.siue.edu
Maximum award: $2,465
Maximum number of awards: 4
Minimum number of awards: 1
Deadline: March 1 (priority)
College level: Junior, Senior
Majors/Fields: Counseling, nursing, teaching
Criteria: Applicant must be a resident of Madison or St. Clair County, have a minimum 3.000 GPA, be age 25 or under, be enrolled full-time, be pursuing a degree program, and plan a career in the helping professions. Financial need is considered. FAFSA is required. Recipient must reapply for renewal. Awarded every year. Award may be used only at sponsoring institution.
Contact: Client Service Unit, Student Financial Aid.

2094   DuPage Medical Society Foundation Scholarship

DuPage Medical Society Foundation
498 Hillside Avenue #1
Glen Ellyn, IL 60137-4536
(630) 858-9603, (630) 858-9512 (fax)
dcmsdocs@aol.com
Average award: $1,000
Maximum award: $1,500
Minimum award: $500
Number of awards: 8
Deadline: April 30
College level: Sophomore, Junior, Senior, Graduate, Doctoral, Medical school
Majors/Fields: Medicine, medical technical, nursing, dentistry, pharmacy
Criteria: Awards are for residents of DuPage County, Ill., who are majoring in health-related fields. Applicant must be in a professional education or technical training program at the time of application. Selection is based upon academic ability and financial need. Awarded every year.
Contact: Anne O'Day, Communications Manager.

2095   Edmund J. Kricker Memorial Scholarship

Shawnee State University
940 Second Street
Portsmouth, OH 45662-4344
(614) 355-2237
Average award: $2,500
Deadline: April 15
College level: Freshman, Transfer
Majors/Fields: Business-related
Criteria: Applicant must be a resident of Scioto County, have a minimum 3.0 GPA, have a minimum composite ACT score of 20 (combined SAT I score of 1000), and be accepted for admission. Early application is recommended. Awarded every year. Award may be used only at sponsoring institution.
Contact: Financial Aid Office, (614) 355-2485.

2096   Elsie and Leonard Vosburgh Memorial Scholarship

University of Colorado at Boulder
Campus Box 106
Boulder, CO 80309-0106
(303) 492-5091
Average award: $2,500
Number of awards: 1
Deadline: March 3
College level: Freshman
Criteria: Applicant must be an African-American graduate of a Denver high school, have a minimum 3.0 GPA, and demonstrate financial need. Preference is given to applicants who intend to contribute to the Denver community during and after college. Essay required. Minimum 2.5 GPA and high level of motivation in academic work are required to retain scholarship. Awarded every year. Award may be used only at sponsoring institution.
Contact: Office of Financial Aid.

2097   Evelyn Abrahams Scholarship

Pamplin Foundation
Dinwiddie County Senior High School
P.O. Box 299
Dinwiddie, VA 23841
(804) 469-3711, (804) 469-3641 (fax)
Maximum award: $1,950
Number of awards: 21
Deadline: February 28
College level: Freshman
Criteria: Applicant must be a graduate of Dinwiddie County High School, Va. Good academic standing and letter requesting scholarship are required to retain scholarship. Awarded every year.
Contact: Carl Craig, Chairman of the Scholarship Committee.

2098   Fay T. Barnes Scholarship

Texas Commerce Bank, National Association
700 Lavaca
P.O. Box 550
Austin, TX 78789
(512) 479-2662, (512) 479-2656 (fax)
Maximum award: $3,000
Number of awards: 12
Deadline: January 31
College level: Freshman
Criteria: Applicant must be a resident of Travis or Williamson counties and plan to attend a college or university in Texas. Selection is based upon financial need and high school and community activities. Renewable if satisfactory GPA is maintained. Awarded twice per year. Award may be used at Texas schools only.
Contact: Sherry Wright, Assistant Administrator.

2099   Frank Roswell Fuller Scholarship

Fleet Bank, N.A.
300 Summit Street
Hartford, CT 06106
(860) 297-2046
Average award: $2,500
Maximum award: $5,000
Minimum award: $1,500
Number of awards: 12
Deadline: April 15
College level: Freshman
Criteria: Applicant must be a graduate of a Hartford County, Conn., high school, attend a four-year college, be a member of the Congregational Church, and demonstrate financial need. Satisfactory academic progress and financial need are required to retain scholarship. Awarded every year.
Contact: Manager.

2100   Franklin County Tuition Award

Wilson College
1015 Philadelphia Avenue
Chambersburg, PA 17201-1285
(717) 264-4141, (717) 264-1578 (fax)
http://www.wilson.edu
Average award: One-quarter tuition discount
Number of awards: 33
Deadline: None
College level: Freshman, Sophomore, Junior, Senior
Criteria: Applicant must be a resident of Franklin County, Pa. Renewable if satisfactory academic progress and at least half-time enrollment are maintained. Awarded every year. Award may be used only at sponsoring institution.
Contact: Ruth Cramer, Director of Financial Aid, (717) 262-2002.

2101   General Scholarship

The Van Wert County Foundation
138 East Main Street
Van Wert, OH 45891
(419) 238-1743, (419) 238-3374 (fax)
Average award: $1,000
Maximum award: $2,700
Minimum award: $250
Number of awards: 166
Deadline: June 1
College level: Sophomore, Junior, Senior
Criteria: Applicant must be a resident of Van Wert or Paulding counties, Ohio, with a minimum 3.0 GPA who can prove financial need. Renewable if recipient maintains a minimum 3.0 GPA and proves financial need. Awarded every year.
Contact: Larry L. Wendel, Executive Secretary.

2102 George E. Andrews Scholarship

Blackhawk State Bank
P.O. Box 719
Beloit, WI 53512-0719
(608) 364-8917
Average award: $3,000
Minimum award: $2,000
Number of awards: 1
Deadline: March 15
College level: Freshman
Criteria: In even-numbered years the award is made to a qualified senior at Beloit Memorial High School and in odd-numbered years to one at Beloit Catholic High School. Selection is based upon financial need, moral character, industriousness, and scholastic standing. Applicant must rank in top third of class. Scholarship is renewable. Awarded every year.
Contact: Dorothy L. Burton, Trust Officer.

2103 George J. Record School Foundation Scholarship

George J. Record School Foundation
P.O. Box 581
365 Main Street
Conneaut, OH 44030
(216) 599-8283
Average award: $2,500
Maximum award: $3,000
Minimum award: $500
Maximum number of awards: 82
Minimum number of awards: 64
Deadline: May 20 (freshmen); June 20 (others)
College level: Freshman, Sophomore, Junior, Senior
Criteria: Applicant must be a legal resident of Ashtabula County, Ohio, plan to attend on a full-time basis a private, Protestant-based college approved by the Foundation, and demonstrate financial need. Six semesters or nine quarters of religion over the four years of college are required to retain scholarship. Awarded every year.
Contact: Charles N. Lafferty, Executive Director.

2104 George T. Welch Scholarship

George T. Welch Trust
Baker Boyer National Bank
P.O. Box 1796
Walla Walla, WA 99362
Maximum award: $2,500
Number of awards: 60
College level: Freshman, Sophomore, Junior, Senior
Criteria: Applicant must be a resident of Walla Walla County, Wash., and demonstrate financial need. Scholarship is renewable. Awarded every year.
Contact: Holly T. Howard, Trust Officer.

2105 George W.F. and Martha Russell Myers Scholarship

Washington University
One Brookings Drive
Campus Box 1089
St. Louis, MO 63130
(314) 935-6000 or (800) 638-0700
Average award: Full tuition plus $1,000 stipend.
Number of awards: 1
Deadline: January 15
College level: Freshman
Criteria: Applicant must be a resident of St. Louis area. Selection is based upon academic merit without regard to financial need. Application is required. Renewable for up to three years based upon satisfactory academic performance. Awarded every year. Award may be used only at sponsoring institution.
Contact: Office of Undergraduate Admissions.

2106 Hatton Lovejoy Scholarship

Fuller E. Callaway Foundation
209 Broome Street
P.O. Box 790
LaGrange, GA 30241
(706) 884-7348, (706) 884-0201 (fax)
Average award: $3,600
Number of awards: 10
Deadline: February 15
College level: Freshman
Criteria: Applicant must have been a resident of Troup County, Ga., for at least two years, must graduate from an accredited high school, and must rank in the top quarter of graduating class. Applicant must rank in the top half of college class to retain scholarship. Awarded every year.
Contact: J. T. Gresham, General Manager.

2107 Hauss-Helms Foundation, Inc. Scholarship

Hauss-Helms Foundation, Inc.
P.O. Box 25
Wapakoneta, OH 45895
(419) 738-4911
Maximum award: $5,000
Number of awards: 600
Deadline: April 15
College level: Freshman, Sophomore, Junior, Senior, Graduate, Doctoral
Criteria: Applicant must be a resident of Allen County or Auglaize County, Ohio, demonstrate financial need, and rank in the top half of graduating class or have a minimum 2.0 GPA. Awarded every year.
Contact: James E. Weger, President.

2108 Herbert S. Walters Scholarship

University of Tennessee, Knoxville
Financial Aid Office
115 Student Services Building
Knoxville, TN 37994
(615) 974-3131
Average award: In-state tuition and fees
Number of awards: 25
Deadline: February 1
College level: Freshman
Criteria: Applicant must be a graduate of an East Tennessee high school, have a minimum 3.0 GPA, minimum composite ACT score of 24 or combined SAT I score of 940, demonstrate financial need, and show a desire to support education through employment. Award is for four years. Awarded every year. Award may be used only at sponsoring institution.
Contact: Financial Aid Office.

2109 Independent Colleges of Southern California Scholarship Program

Southern California Edison Company
1190 Durfee Avenue
Suite 200
South El Monte, CA 91733
(818) 302-0284
Average award: $20,000
Number of awards: 2
Deadline: March 6
College level: Freshman
Criteria: Applicant must reside in the Southern California Edison service area, be a member of an underrepresented ethnic group, be a U.S. citizen or permanent resident, demonstrate academic achievement and financial need, and plan to enter an ICSC school as a full-time undergraduate. Each member college selects applicants based upon academic performance, extracurricular activities, and demonstrated leadership. Applicant must be family's first generation to attend college. ICSC selects finalists. Dependents of Southern California Edison employees are not eligible. Awarded every year.
Contact: Scholarship Committee.

2110 India Lowry Shields Scholarship

University of West Alabama
Station Four
Livingston, AL 35470
(205) 652-3400, (205) 652-3522 (fax)
http://www.westal.edu
Average award: $2,500
Deadline: April 15
College level: Freshman
Criteria: Applicant must be an entering freshman from Marengo County. Scholarship is renewable. Awarded every year. Award may be used only at sponsoring institution.
Contact: Richard Hester, Director of Admissions, (205) 652-3400, extension 3578, rth@uwamail.westal.edu.

2111 Jacob Rassen Memorial Scholarship Fund

Jewish Family and Children's Services (JFCS)
1600 Scott Street
San Francisco, CA 94115
(415) 561-1226, (415) 922-5938 (fax)
Average award: $1,000
Maximum award: $2,000
Minimum award: $500
Number of awards: 4
College level: Freshman, Sophomore, Junior, Senior, Graduate
Criteria: Award is for a study trip to Israel for Jewish youth under age 22. Applicant must have demonstrated academic achievement, financial need, desire to enhance Jewish identity, and desire to increase knowledge of and connection to Israel. Applicant must be a resident of Marin County, San Francisco County, San Mateo County, Sonoma County, Palo Alto or Mountain View, Calif. Awarded every year.
Contact: Ted Schreiber, Director of Loans and Grants Program.

2112 James F. Martin Annual Scholarship

Clemson University
G-01 Sikes Hall
Clemson, SC 29634-5123
(803) 656-2280
Average award: $5,000
Number of awards: 1
Deadline: March 1
College level: Freshman, Sophomore, Junior, Senior
Criteria: Applicant must have a minimum 2.5 GPA and be a resident of Edgerfield County, S.C. Award may be used only at sponsoring institution.
Contact: Scholarships.

2113 Jan Walling Memorial Scholarship

Northern Kentucky University
Administrative Center 416
Nunn Drive
Highland Heights, KY 41099-7101
(606) 572-5144
Average award: In-state tuition
Deadline: February 1
College level: Freshman
Criteria: Applicant must be a graduate of Highlands, Ky., high school; priority is given to handicapped applicants. Awarded every year. Award may be used only at sponsoring institution.
Contact: Robert E. Sprague, Director of Financial Aid.

2114 Jewish Federation of Metropolitan Chicago Scholarship Program

Jewish Vocational Service
One South Franklin Street
Chicago, IL 60606
(312) 357-4500, (312) 855-3282 (fax)
jvschicago@jon.cjfny.org
Average award: $5,000
Minimum award: $1,000
Number of awards: 75
Deadline: March 1
College level: Junior, Senior, Graduate, Doctoral
Majors/Fields: Engineering, helping professions, mathematics, sciences
Criteria: Applicant must be Jewish, legally domiciled in either Cook County, Ill., or the Chicago metropolitan area, have a minimum "C" average, be a full-time student, demonstrate financial need, and show career promise. Preprofessional students are not eligible. Reapplication, academic excellence, and financial need are required to retain scholarship. Awarded every year.
Contact: Scholarship Secretary.

2115 John W. and Rose E. Watson Scholarship

John W. and Rose E. Watson Scholarship Foundation
5800 Weiss Street
Saginaw, MI 48603
(517) 797-6633
Average award: $1,200
Number of awards: 115
Deadline: April 1
College level: Freshman
Criteria: Applicant must be a graduate of a Saginaw, Mich., Catholic high school. Reapplication and satisfactory academic progress are required to retain scholarship. Awarded every year.
Contact: Jean Seman, Secretary.

2116 Jordaan Foundation Trust Scholarship

First State Bank and Trust Company
P.O. Box 360
Larned, KS 67550
(316) 285-3157
Average award: $1,500
Number of awards: 20
Deadline: April 15
Criteria: Applicant must be a resident of Pawnee County, Kan., who is planning to attend a college or university in Kansas. Awarded every year.
Contact: Scholarships.

2117 Joseph Walker Elliott Memorial Scholarship

Jacksonville State University
Jacksonville, AL 36265-9982
(205) 782-5006
Average award: Full tuition
Deadline: March 15
College level: Freshman, Sophomore, Junior, Senior
Criteria: Awarded every year. Award may be used only at sponsoring institution.
Contact: Student Financial Aid Office.

2118 Kimberly-Clark Honor Scholarship

Lawrence University
P.O. Box 599
Appleton, WI 54912-0599
(414) 832-6500, (414) 832-6782 (fax)
excel@lawrence.edu
http://www.lawrence.edu
Average award: $5,000
Number of awards: 10
Deadline: February 1
College level: Freshman
Criteria: Applicant must rank in the top tenth of high school graduating class, and reside or attend school in an area which has a major Kimberly-Clark Corp. facility. Eligible areas are determined each year by the company. Minimum 3.0 GPA required to retain scholarship. Awarded every year. Award may be used only at sponsoring institution.
Contact: Director of Admissions.

2119 Leora Y. Streeter Scholarship

Leora Y. Streeter Scholarship Fund
45 East Avenue
Sixth Floor
Rochester, NY 14638
(716) 546-9178
Average award: $1,600
Number of awards: 3
Deadline: In June
College level: Freshman
Criteria: Applicant must reside in the town of Arcadia, Galen, Lyons, Rose, or Sodus of Wayne County, N.Y., in Junius of Seneca County, N.Y., or in Phelps of Ontario County, N.Y. Satisfactory academic record is required to retain scholarship. Awarded when present recipients graduate or withdraw.
Contact: Norene S. Yount, Senior Client Service Administrator.

2120 Lions Club, Grand Junction Nontraditional Student Award

Mesa State College
Financial Aid Department
P.O. Box 2647
Grand Junction, CO 81502
(970) 248-1396
Maximum award: Tuition and fees
Number of awards: 1
College level: Sophomore, Junior, Senior
Criteria: Applicant must be enrolled full time, have a minimum 2.5 GPA, be degree-seeking, be age 25 or over, have been a Mesa County, Colo., resident for at least five years, and demonstrate financial need. Awarded every year. Award may be used only at sponsoring institution.
Contact: Office of Financial Aid, (970) 248-1376.

2121 Marcus and Theresa Levie Educational Fund

Jewish Vocational Service
One South Franklin Street
Chicago, IL 60606
(312) 357-4500, (312) 855-3282 (fax)
jvschicago@jon.cjfny.org
Average award: $5,000
Maximum number of awards: 40
Minimum number of awards: 35
Deadline: March 1
College level: Junior, Senior, Graduate, Doctoral
Majors/Fields: Helping professions
Criteria: Applicant must be a full-time Jewish student who is legally domiciled in Cook County, Ill. Applicant must be a superior student, demonstrate financial need, and show promise of significant contributions in a helping profession. Preprofessional students are not eligible. Reapplication is required to retain scholarship. Awarded every year.
Contact: Scholarship Secretary.

2122 Maurice and Catherine Sessel Alton Student Grant

Southern Illinois University at Edwardsville
Box 1060
Edwardsville, IL 62026-1060
(618) 692-3880, (618) 692-3885 (fax)
finaid@siue.edu
http://www.finaid.siue.edu
Maximum award: $2,465
Maximum number of awards: 4
Minimum number of awards: 1
Deadline: March 1 (priority)
College level: Freshman, Sophomore, Junior, Senior
Criteria: Applicant must be a graduate of an Alton school, have a minimum 2.500 GPA, be enrolled full-time, and be pursuing a degree program. FAFSA is required. Recipient must reapply for renewal. Awarded every year. Award may be used only at sponsoring institution.
Contact: Client Service Unit, Student Financial Aid, finaid@siue.edu.

2123 Mayor's Leadership 2000 Scholarship

DePaul University
1 East Jackson Boulevard
Chicago, IL 60604
(312) 362-8704, (312) 362-5749 (fax)
Average award: $5,000
Number of awards: 25
Deadline: April 1
College level: Freshman
Criteria: Applicant must demonstrate participation in community service, be a Chicago, Ill. resident, have strong academic ability, and demonstrate financial need. Scholarship is renewable. Awarded every year. Award may be used only at sponsoring institution.
Contact: Jennifer Sparrow, Scholarship Coordinator, jsparrow@wppost.depaul.edu.

2124 McKaig Foundation Scholarship

Pittsburgh National Bank
5th and Wood
Pittsburgh, PA 15265
(412) 355-3706
Maximum award: $2,500
Deadline: May 30
Criteria: Applicant must be a resident of Bedford County, Penn. Awarded every year.
Contact: Scholarships.

2125 Naomi Miller Memorial Award

Northern Kentucky University
Administrative Center 416
Nunn Drive
Highland Heights, KY 41099-7101
(606) 572-5144
Average award: In-state tuition and $400 book allowance
Deadline: February 1
College level: Freshman, Sophomore, Junior, Senior
Criteria: Applicant must be a graduate of a Harlan County high school and demonstrate financial need. Upperclass applicant must have completed at least 24 credit hours the previous year with a minimum cumulative GPA of 2.5. Awarded every year. Award may be used only at sponsoring institution.
Contact: Robert E. Sprague, Director of Financial Aid.

2126   Norman Topping Student Aid Fund

University of Southern California
University Park
Los Angeles, CA 90089-5012
(213) 740-1111
Maximum award: $4,000
Maximum number of awards: 30
Minimum number of awards: 25
Deadline: February 15
College level: Freshman, Transfer
Criteria: Priority is given to applicants from the University Park, Los Angeles area. Recipient must contribute at least 20 hours of community service per semester. Awarded every year. Award may be used only at sponsoring institution.
Contact: Norman Topping Student Aid Fund Office, Student Union 407, Los Angeles, CA 90089-4898, (213) 740-7575.

2127   Northern California Scholarship Foundations Undergraduate Scholarship

Northern California Scholarship Foundations
1547 Lakeside Drive
Oakland, CA 94612
(510) 451-1906
Maximum award: $3,000
Number of awards: 200
Deadline: March 17
College level: Freshman
Criteria: Applicant must be a senior in a public high school in northern or central California. Applicant is recommended by high school counselor or principal on the basis of high moral character, high GPA and test scores, financial need, and willingness to earn part of college expenses. Minimum 3.0 GPA, submission of reports to Trustees, demonstration of citizenship and leadership, and working for some portion of expenses are required to retain scholarship. Awarded every year.

2128   NOVA Urban League Scholarship Program for African-American Students

Northern Virginia Branch of Washington Urban League
908 King Street, #301
Alexandria, VA 22314
(703) 836-2858, (703) 836-8948 (fax)
Average award: $1,500
Minimum award: $700
Number of awards: 3
Deadline: January 5
College level: Freshman
Criteria: Competition is open to African-American students from Alexandria, Arlington, and Fairfax high schools, except the children of Urban League staff, Board of Directors, judging panel, and committee members. Selection is based upon the strong likelihood of a successful undergraduate school experience, high school academic performance, ability to communicate well both in written and verbal form, extracurricular activities, and documented leadership skills and participation in community activities. Awarded every year.
Contact: Pearl Turner, c/o Board of Directors, Scholarship Committee, Alexandria, VA 22314.

2129   Nursing Scholarship for Saint Scholastica Students

Ordean Foundation
501 Ordean Building
Duluth, MN 55802
(218) 726-4785
Maximum award: $2,000
Number of awards: 20
Deadline: April 1
College level: Junior, Senior
Majors/Fields: Nursing
Criteria: Applicant must demonstrate financial need and be a resident of the Duluth, Minn., area. Minimum 3.0 GPA is required to retain scholarship. Awarded every year.
Contact: Julie Ledermann, Financial Aid Coordinator, College of Saint Scholastica, 1200 Kenwood Avenue, Duluth, MN 55811, (218) 723-6656.

2130   Ordean Scholarship

Ordean Foundation
501 Ordean Building
Duluth, MN 55802
(218) 726-4785
Maximum award: $2,000
Number of awards: 150
Deadline: Rolling
College level: All students accepted into program of study
Majors/Fields: Health care occupations
Criteria: Applicant must be a resident of Duluth, Hermantown, Proctor, Canosia, Midway, or Rice Lake in St. Louis, Minn. Applicant must also demonstrate financial need. Scholarship is renewable. Awarded every year.
Contact: Bernie Moog, Financial Aid Administrator, Lake Superior College, Duluth, MN 55811, (218) 722-2801.

2131   Pacific Coca-Cola/Thriftway Stores Merit Award

Pacific Coca-Cola in Cooperation with Thriftway Stores
1150 124th Avenue, NE
P.O. Box C-93346
Bellevue, WA 98009-3346
(206) 455-2000
Average award: $1,500
Number of awards: 18
Deadline: Mid-April
College level: Freshman
Criteria: Applicant must be a high school senior in the western Washington, Yakima, and Wenatchee areas with a minimum 3.5 GPA and plan to enroll full time in a participating college or university. Selection is based upon academic achievement, leadership potential, school and/or community involvement, employment, and family responsibility. Awarded every year.
Contact: Terry Conner, Key Account Representative.

2132   Park National Bank

Denison University
Box H
Granville, OH 43023
(614) 587-6276, 800-DENISON, (614) 587-6306 (fax)
admissions@denison.edu
http://www.denison.edu
Maximum award: $6,000
Number of awards: 2
Deadline: January 1
College level: Freshman
Criteria: Applicant must be a resident of Central Ohio (preferably Licking County) who demonstrates superior academic performance or potential. Minimum GPA required to retain scholarship. Awarded every year. Award may be used only at sponsoring institution.
Contact: Scholarship.

2133   Philadelphia Collaborative Scholarship

Moore College of Art and Design
20th and the Parkway
Philadelphia, PA 19103
(215) 568-4515
Average award: $12,000
Maximum award: $14,097
Number of awards: 1
Deadline: April 1
College level: Freshman
Criteria: Applicant must be a graduate of a Philadelphia public school and be accepted for enrollment. Scholarship is renewable. Awarded every year. Award may be used only at sponsoring institution.
Contact: Karina Dayich, Associate Director of Admissions.

2134 Pickens County Scholars Program

Clemson University
G-01 Sikes Hall
Clemson, SC 29634-5123
(803) 656-2280
Maximum award: $7,500
Number of awards: 2
Deadline: None
College level: Freshman
Criteria: Applicant must be a graduate of a Pickens County, S.C., high school. Preference is given to graduates of Pickens and Easley High School. Minimum 3.0 GPA and completion of at least 12 credits per semester are required to retain scholarship. Awarded every year. Award may be used only at sponsoring institution.
Contact: Marvin Carmichael, Director of Financial Aid.

2135 Pinnacle Resources Ltd. Bursary

University of Calgary
Department of Financial Aid
2500 University Drive, NW
Calgary, Alberta, CN T2N 1N4
(403) 220-7872, (403) 282-2999 (fax)
Average award: $2,000 fellowship plus salary
Number of awards: 1
Deadline: July 15
College level: Freshman
Criteria: Applicant must be a graduate of an Athabasca, Provost, or Westlock area high school. Selection is based upon academic merit, finanical need, and extracurricular activities. Awarded every year. Award may be used only at sponsoring institution.
Contact: J. Van Housen, Director of Student Awards/ Financial Aid.

2136 Prince George's Chamber of Commerce Foundation Scholarship

Prince George's Chamber of Commerce Foundation, Inc.
4601 Presidents
Suite 230
Lanham, MD 20706
(301) 731-5000
Average award: $2,000
Maximum award: $2,760
Minimum award: $1,000
Number of awards: 16
Deadline: May 15
College level: Freshman, Sophomore, Junior, Senior
Criteria: Applicant must be a Prince George's County, Md., resident. Minimum 2.5 GPA is required to retain scholarship. Awarded every year.
Contact: Robert Zinsmeister, Administrator, 4640 Forbes Boulevard, Suite 200, Lanham, MD 20706.

2137 Prince George's Chamber of Commerce Scholarship

Bowie State University
Bowie, MD 20715
(301) 464-6544
Average award: Tuition and fees
Deadline: February 1 (fall); November 1 (spring)
College level: Freshman, Sophomore, Junior, Senior
Majors/Fields: Business, communications, computer science, engineering, fine arts, math
Criteria: Applicant must be a Prince George's County, Md., resident, be a commuter student enrolled full time, have a minimum 2.5 GPA, demonstrate financial need, and have high interest in and motivation for career in business and/or industry. Award is for four years. Awarded every year. Award may be used only at sponsoring institution.
Contact: Scholarship Committee, Career Services, Bowie, MD 20715-9465, (301) 464-7110, (301) 464-7111.

2138 Reeder-Siler Scholarship

University of Tennessee, Knoxville
Financial Aid Office
115 Student Services Building
Knoxville, TN 37994
(615) 974-3131
Average award: $2,500
Number of awards: 1
Deadline: February 1
College level: Freshman
Criteria: Applicant must be a graduate of a high school in Anderson, Blount, or Knox county, Tenn., have a minimum 3.0 GPA, a minimum composite ACT score of 27 or equivalent SAT I score, and demonstrate leadership through sports, academic organizations, or student activities. Financial need is considered if all other qualifications are equal. Award is for four years. Awarded every year. Award may be used only at sponsoring institution.
Contact: University Honors Program, F-101 Melrose Hall, Knoxville, TN 37916, (615) 974-7875.

2139 Robert A. Hine Memorial Scholarship

Southern California Edison Company
1190 Durfee Avenue
Suite 200
South El Monte, CA 91733
(818) 302-0284
Average award: $20,000
Number of awards: 1
Deadline: Take SAT I by first Saturday in December of senior year
College level: Freshman
Criteria: Applicant must reside in the Southern California Edison service area, be a member of an underrepresented ethnic group, be a U.S. citizen or permanent resident, demonstrate academic achievement, and plan to attend a four-year university as a full-time student. Preference is given to students with financial need. Dependents of Southern California Edison employees are not eligible. Top 100 applicants with the highest SAT I scores will be asked to complete an application for further evaluation. Awarded every year.
Contact: Scholarship Committee.

2140 Rosewood Family Scholarship

Florida Department of Education
Office of Student Financial Assistance
255 Collins
Tallahassee, FL 32399-0400
(904) 487-0049
Average award: $4,000
Number of awards: 25
Deadline: April 1
College level: Freshman, Sophomore, Junior, Senior
Criteria: Applicant must be African-American, Hispanic, Asian, Pacific Islander, American Indian, or Alaskan Native. Strong preference is given to African-Americans who are direct descendants of the Rosewood families affected by the incidents of January 1923. Minimum 2.0 with at least 12 credit hours per term is required to retain scholarship. Awarded every year.
Contact: Office of Student Financial Assistance.

2141 Russell Caldwell Neighborhood Scholarship

University of Southern California
University Park
Los Angeles, CA 90089-5012
(213) 740-1111
Average award: $3,000
Deadline: December 15
College level: Freshman
Criteria: Applicant must be nominated by high school prinicpal or college counselor and rank in the top of graduating class from one of the following Los Angeles high schools: Belmont, Crenshaw, Dorsey, Fremont, Huntington Park, Jefferson, Los Angeles, Manual Arts, Roosevelt. Priority is given to students majoring in the liberal arts. Awarded every year. Award may be used only at sponsoring institution.
Contact: Academic Relations, College of Letters, Arts, and Sciences, Los Angeles, CA 90089, (800) 722-3765.

2142   Santa Barbara Scholarship

Santa Barbara Scholarship Foundation
P.O. Box 1403
Santa Barbara, CA 93102
(805) 965-7212
Average award: $1,300
Maximum award: $2,500
Minimum award: $500
Number of awards: 800
Deadline: January 31
College level: Freshman, Sophomore, Junior, Senior
Criteria: Applicant must be a graduate of a Santa Barbara area high school and demonstrate financial need. Interview is required. Reapplication, demonstration of financial need, and a minimum 2.5 GPA are required to retain scholarship. Awarded every year.
Contact: Scholarships.

2143   Scidmore Scholarship

Lawrence University
P.O. Box 599
Appleton, WI 54912-0599
(414) 832-6500, (414) 832-6782 (fax)
excel@lawrence.edu
http://www.lawrence.edu
Maximum award: $2,500
Deadline: February 1
College level: Freshman
Criteria: Applicant must be a graduate of a Rock County, Wis., high school. Minimum 2.5 GPA required to retain scholarship. Awarded every year. Award may be used only at sponsoring institution.
Contact: Director of Admissions.

2144   Shackelford Scholarship

Denison University
Box H
Granville, OH 43023
(614) 587-6276, 800-DENISON, (614) 587-6306 (fax)
admissions@denison.edu
http://www.denison.edu
Average award: Full tuition
Number of awards: 1
Deadline: January 1
College level: Freshman
Criteria: Applicant must be a Columbus, Ohio public school graduate who is ranked first or second in their class. Selection is based upon academic record, essay, extracurricular achievements, and counselor and teacher recommendations. Minimum GPA is required for renewal. Awarded every year. Award may be used only at sponsoring institution.
Contact: Janet Schultz, Scholarship, (614) 587-6625.

2145   Skipper Scholarship

University of West Alabama
Station Four
Livingston, AL 35470
(205) 652-3400, (205) 652-3522 (fax)
http://www.westal.edu
Average award: Tuition, book allotment
Deadline: April 15
College level: Freshman, Sophomore, Junior, Senior
Criteria: Applicant must be from the Clarke-Washington County area and work for the local fire department. Scholarship is renewable. Awarded every year. Award may be used only at sponsoring institution.
Contact: Richard Hester, Director of Admissions, (205) 652-3400, extension 3578, rth@uwamail.westal.edu.

2146   Southern California Edison Company College Scholarship

Southern California Edison Company
1190 Durfee Avenue
Suite 200
South El Monte, CA 91733
(818) 302-0284
Average award: $20,000
Number of awards: 4
Deadline: Take SAT I by first Saturday in December of senior year
College level: Freshman
Criteria: Applicant must live in or attend school in the Southern California Edison service territory and be a U.S. citizen or permanent resident. Dependents of Southern California Edison employees are not eligible. Applicant must be a high school senior or have met high school requirements to enter college full time in the fall. Selection is by SAT I scores; the top candidates in each of Edison's seven regions will be asked to submit applications. Recipients 18 years or older may also be eligible to participate in the Edison Summer Employment Program. Award is for four years. Awarded every year.
Contact: Scholarship Committee.

2147   Southern Tier Scholarship

Alfred University
Alumni Hall
26 North Main Street
Alfred, NY 14802
(607) 871-2159
Maximum award: $10,000
Deadline: None
College level: Freshman
Criteria: Applicant must be a resident of Allegany, Cattaraugus, Chautauqua, Chemung, or Steuben county. Applicant must have a minimum grade average of 90 and rank in the top tenth of class. Extracurricular activities, good citizenship, and standardized test scores are considered. Renewable for up to eight semesters if minimum 3.0 GPA and continuous full-time enrollment are maintained. Awarded every year. Award may be used only at sponsoring institution.
Contact: Scholarships.

2148   Stanley Olson Youth Scholarship Fund

Jewish Family and Children's Services (JFCS)
1600 Scott Street
San Francisco, CA 94115
(415) 561-1226, (415) 922-5938 (fax)
Average award: $1,500
Maximum award: $2,500
Minimum award: $750
Number of awards: 3
Deadline: None
College level: Freshman, Sophomore, Junior, Senior, Graduate, Doctoral
Majors/Fields: Humanities
Criteria: Applicant must be a Jewish youth under age 26 with demonstrated academic achievement, have financial need, and be a resident of Marin County, San Francisco County, San Mateo County, Sonoma County, Palo Alto, or Mountain View, Calif. Scholarship is renewable. Awarded every year.
Contact: Ted Schreiber, Director of Loans and Grants Program.

2149   Steven V. Mitchell Memorial Endowed Scholarship

The University of Alabama
Box 870162
Tuscaloosa, AL 35487-0162
(205) 348-6756
Maximum award: $6,174
Number of awards: 1
Deadline: December 3
College level: Freshman
Criteria: Preference is given to graduate of a Madison County, Ala., school who demonstrates financial need. Minimum 3.0 GPA is required to retain scholarship. Awarded as funds are available. Award may be used only at sponsoring institution.
Contact: National Alumni Association, P.O. Box 1928, Tuscaloosa, AL 35486-1928.

2150 Sweetman Scholarship

Lawrence University
P.O. Box 599
Appleton, WI 54912-0599
(414) 832-6500, (414) 832-6782 (fax)
excel@lawrence.edu
http://www.lawrence.edu
Maximum award: $5,000
Number of awards: 2
Deadline: February 1
College level: Freshman
Criteria: Applicant must be a top-ranked graduate of a Green Bay, Wis., public high school who will be entering college in the year of award. Minimum 3.0 GPA required to retain scholarship. Awarded every year. Award may be used only at sponsoring institution.
Contact: Director of Admissions.

2151 Thelma and Harry Hair Scholarship

Clemson University
G-01 Sikes Hall
Clemson, SC 29634-5123
(803) 656-2280
Average award: $3,800
Number of awards: 1
Deadline: March 1
College level: Freshman, Sophomore, Junior, Senior
Criteria: Applicant must be a resident of Calhoun County, S.C. and have a minimum 2.5 GPA. Awarded every year. Award may be used only at sponsoring institution.
Contact: Marvin Carmichael, Director of Financial Aid.

2152 Thomas A. Folger Memorial Endowed Scholarship

Clemson University
G-01 Sikes Hall
Clemson, SC 29634-5123
(803) 656-2280
Average award: $2,400
Number of awards: 1
Deadline: March 1
College level: Freshman
Criteria: Applicant must be a resident of Pickens County and have a minimum 2.5 GPA. Minimum 3.0 GPA and completion of at least 12 credits per semester are required to retain scholarship for up to four years. Awarded every year. Award may be used only at sponsoring institution.
Contact: Marvin Carmichael, Director of Financial Aid.

2153 Thomas C. Sharpe Memorial Scholarship

Department of Planning and Community Development
City Hall
Roosevelt Square
Mount Vernon, NY 10550
(914) 699-7230, (914) 699-1435 (fax)
Average award: $800
Maximum award: $1,200
Minimum award: $300
Number of awards: 175
Deadline: first Friday in June
College level: Unspecified undergraduate
Criteria: Applicant must have a 2.0 GPA, be a resident of Mount Vernon, N.Y., and meet income guidelines. Scholarship is renewable. Awarded every year.
Contact: Donna Fulco, Scholarship Program Manager.

2154 Thomas E. Nott Annual Scholarship

Clemson University
G-01 Sikes Hall
Clemson, SC 29634-5123
(803) 656-2280
Average award: $5,000
Number of awards: 1
Deadline: March 1
College level: Freshman
Majors/Fields: Engineering
Criteria: Applicant must be a resident of Spartanburg County, S.C., or Mecklenburg County, N.C., and have a minimum 2.5 GPA. Awarded every year. Award may be used only at sponsoring institution.
Contact: Marvin Carmichael, Director of Financial Aid.

2155 Town and Gown Scholarship

University of Southern California
University Park
Los Angeles, CA 90089-5012
(213) 740-1111
Maximum award: $5,000
Maximum number of awards: 200
Minimum number of awards: 190
Deadline: December 15
College level: Freshman, Sophomore, Junior, Senior
Criteria: Applicant must be a resident of Southern California and demonstrate campus and community involvement. Freshman applicant must have a minimum 3.5 GPA and at least 1200 on SAT and 27 on ACT tests. Upperclass applicant must have a minimum 3.0 GPA. Personal interview is required. Selection is based upon achievement. Financial need is considered. Awarded every year. Award may be used only at sponsoring institution.
Contact: Office of Admission.

2156 Tuition Scholarship for Nonresidents

University of Missouri—Columbia
High School and Transfer Relations
219 Jesse Hall
Columbia, MO 65211
(800) 225-6075 (in-state), (314) 882-2456
http://www.missouri.edu
Average award: Full tuition
Number of awards: 293
College level: Freshman
Criteria: Applicant must be a resident of a county contiguous with Missouri, whose parents have accrued personal Missouri tax liability the year before the year in question. Renewable if recipient maintains a minimum 2.0 GPA. Award may be used only at sponsoring institution.
Contact: Residency Office, 230 Jesse Hall, Columbia, MO 25211, (800) 225-6075 (in-state), (314) 882-3852.

2157 Tuscaloosa County Public Safety Memorial Endowed Scholarship

The University of Alabama
Box 870162
Tuscaloosa, AL 35487-0162
(205) 348-6756
Average award: $2,470
Number of awards: 1
Deadline: March 1
College level: Freshman, Sophomore, Junior, Senior
Criteria: Applicant must be a dependent of a Tuscaloosa County fire or police official, a U of Alabama police officer, or an Alabama state trooper assigned to Tuscaloosa County who was disabled or killed in the line of duty or be a police officer disabled in the line of duty who wishes to continue education. Renewable for undergraduate study if minimum 3.0 GPA is maintained. Awarded every year. Award may be used only at sponsoring institution.
Contact: Paige Cooper, Scholarship Coordinator.

2158   Virginia and Anne Praytor Scholarship

Birmingham-Southern College
Arkadelphia Road
Birmingham, AL 35254
(205) 226-4688
Maximum award: $5,000
College level: Freshman
Criteria: Applicant must be a graduate of a Birmingham City School, should rank in top two-tenths of class, have a minimum composite ACT score of 26 (combined SAT I score of 1050), and have leadership ability. Financial need is considered. Minimum 2.5 GPA is required to retain scholarship. Awarded every year. Award may be used only at sponsoring institution.
Contact: Forrest Stuart, Interim Director of Financial Aid Services.

2159   Vivienne Camp College Scholarship

Jewish Family and Children's Services (JFCS)
1600 Scott Street
San Francisco, CA 94115
(415) 561-1226, (415) 922-5938 (fax)
Average award: $4,000
Maximum award: $5,000
Minimum award: $3,500
Number of awards: 4
Deadline: None
College level: Freshman, Sophomore, Junior, Senior
Criteria: Awarded to two young Jewish men and two young Jewish women for undergraduate or vocational studies. Applicant must reside in Marin County, San Francisco County, San Mateo County, Sonoma County, Palo Alto, or Mountain View, Calif. Applicant should have demonstrated academic achievement, financial need, broad-based extracurricular activities, in-depth community involvement, and be accepted to a school in California. Recipient must reapply to retain scholarship. Awarded every year.
Contact: Ted Schreiber, Director of Loans and Grants Program.

2160   Wallace Preston Greene Sr. Scholarship

Clemson University
G-01 Sikes Hall
Clemson, SC 29634-5123
(803) 656-2280
Average award: $2,100
Number of awards: 1
Deadline: March 1
College level: Freshman, Sophomore, Junior, Senior
Criteria: Applicant must be a resident of Oconee County, S.C., and demonstrate financial need. Minimum 3.0 GPA and completion of at least 12 credits per semester are required to retain scholarship. Awarded every year. Award may be used only at sponsoring institution.
Contact: Marvin Carmichael, Director of Financial Aid.

2161   Wayne County Scholarship

The College of Wooster
Office of Admissions
Wooster, OH 44691
(330) 263-2270, (330) 263-2621 (fax)
admissions@acs.wooster.edu
http://www.wooster.edu
Maximum award: $6,000
Deadline: February 15
College level: Freshman
Criteria: Applicant must be a resident of Wayne County, Ohio, have financial need, and be nominated by a school official on the basis of academic record. Recipient must maintain academic progress toward degree to retain scholarship. Renewable for four years. Awarded every year. Award may be used only at sponsoring institution.
Contact: Office of Admissions.

2162   West Crawford Jordan, Jr. Scholarship

University of Tennessee, Knoxville
Financial Aid Office
115 Student Services Building
Knoxville, TN 37994
(615) 974-3131
Average award: Fees, books, room and board
Deadline: February 1
College level: Freshman
Majors/Fields: Engineering
Criteria: Applicant must be a full-time engineering student who is a resident of Shelby County, Tenn., and demonstrates financial need. Award is for four years. Awarded every year. Award may be used only at sponsoring institution.
Contact: College of Engineering, 118 Perkins Hall, Knoxville, TN 37996, (615) 974-2454.

2163   William Simpson Scholarship

Waynesburg College
51 West College Street
Waynesburg, PA 15370
(800) 225-7393, (412) 627-6416 (fax)
admission@waynesburg.edu
http://waynesburg.edu
Maximum award: $3,500
Number of awards: 1
Deadline: March 1
College level: Freshman
Majors/Fields: Humanities, liberal arts
Criteria: First preference is for applicants from Laural Highlands High School in Fayette County, Pa. Second preference is from another Fayette County school. Renewable if recipient maintains minimum 3.0 GPA. Awarded every year. Award may be used only at sponsoring institution.
Contact: Robin Moore, Dean of Admissions, (412) 852-3248.

Club Affiliation

2164   Academic Year Ambassadorial Scholarship

Rotary Foundation of Rotary International
One Rotary Center
1560 Sherman Avenue
Evanston, IL 60201-3698
(847) 866-3000, (847) 328-8554 (fax)
Average award: $10,000
Maximum award: $22,000
College level: Junior, Senior, Graduate, Doctoral
Criteria: Applicant must apply for the scholarship through local Rotary club, and desire to study abroad for an academic year. Awarded every year.
Contact: Scholarships.

2165   Agnes Jones Jackson Scholarship

National Association for the Advancement of Colored People (NAACP)
4805 Mount Hope Drive
Baltimore, MD 21215-3297
(410) 358-8900
Average award: $1,500
Maximum award: $2,500
Deadline: April 30
College level: Freshman, Sophomore, Junior, Senior, Graduate, Doctoral
Criteria: Applicant must be a current, regular member of the NAACP for at least one year or a fully paid life member, and must not have reached age 25 by the April 30 deadline. Undergraduate applicant must have a minimum GPA of 2.5 and graduate applicant must have a minimum 3.0 GPA. Awarded every year.
Contact: Andrea E. Moss, Education Department.

2166 AKA Financial Assistance Scholarship

Alpha Kappa Alpha (AKA)
Educational Advancement Foundation
5656 South Stony Island Avenue
Chicago, IL 60637-1902
(312) 947-0026, (312) 947-0277 (fax)
Maximum award: $1,500
Deadline: February 15
College level: Sophomore, Junior, Senior
Criteria: Applicant must be currently enrolled in a course of study beyond the first year or in a Work in Process Program which may or may not be at a degree-granting institution.
Contact: Educational Advancement Foundation.

2167 AKA Merit Scholarship

Alpha Kappa Alpha (AKA)
Educational Advancement Foundation
5656 South Stony Island Avenue
Chicago, IL 60637-1902
(312) 947-0026, (312) 947-0277 (fax)
Average award: $1,000
Maximum award: $1,500
Minimum award: $500
Number of awards: 40
Deadline: February 15
College level: Sophomore, Junior, Senior, Graduate, Doctoral
Criteria: Applicant must have completed a minimum of one year in an accredited, degree-granting program and must demonstrate exceptional academic achievement. Awarded every year.
*Contact:*Scholarship Coordinator.

2168 Al Thompson Junior Bowlers Scholarship

Young American Bowling Alliance (YABA)
5301 South 76th Street
Greendale, WI 53129
(414) 421-4700, (414) 421-1301 (fax)
Maximum award: $1,500
Number of awards: 2
Deadline: June 15
College level: Freshman
Criteria: Applicant must be a member of YABA/ABC/WIBC. Send a self-addressed, stamped envelope (#10). Awarded every year.
Contact: Edward Gocha, Scholarship Administrator.

2169 Alberta E. Crowe Star of Tomorrow Scholarship

Young American Bowling Alliance (YABA)
5301 South 76th Street
Greendale, WI 53129
(414) 421-4700, (414) 421-1301 (fax)
Maximum award: $4,000
Number of awards: 1
College level: Freshman, Sophomore, Junior, Senior
Criteria: Applicant must be a member of YABA or WIBC and a woman age 21 or under. Send a self-addressed, stamped envelope (#10). No phone calls. Awarded every year.
Contact: Edward Gocha, Scholarship Administrator.

2170 American Humanics Scholarship

Missouri Valley College
500 East College
Marshall, MO 65340
(816) 886-6924
Average award: $6,500
Number of awards: 10
College level: Freshman
Criteria: Applicant must be a woman and a Girl Scout, be planning a career with youth/human service agency, have a minimum 2.5 GPA, and be able to document demonstrated leadership roles, community service involvement, and diverse activities in personal life. Renewable for up to four years if recipient maintains satisfactory academic progress. Awarded every year. Award may be used only at sponsoring institution.
Contact: Dr. Carl T. Gass, Dean of Human Services.

2171 ARAM Scholarship Award

Association of Railroad Advertising & Marketing (ARAM)
Scholarships
c/o Joe D. Singer, Secretary/Treasurer
3706 Palmerstown Road
Shaker Heights, OH 44122
(216) 751-9673
Average award: $1,500
Maximum number of awards: 2
Minimum number of awards: 2
Deadline: Mid-April
College level: Freshman, Sophomore, Junior, Senior, Graduate, Doctoral
Criteria: Applicant must be the child or grandchild of an ARAM member. Awarded every year.
Contact: Allen Basis, Scholarship Chairman, c/o K-III Directory Corp., 10 Lake Drive, Hightstown, NJ 08520, (609) 371-7866.

2172 Arby's/Big Brothers/Big Sisters of America Scholarship

Big Brothers/Big Sisters of America/Arby's
230 North 13th Street
Philadelphia, PA 19107
(215) 567-7000, (215) 567-0394 (fax)
Maximum award: $5,000
Number of awards: 2
Deadline: April 30
College level: Freshman, Sophomore, Junior, Senior
Criteria: Applicant must have participated in a Big Brother/Big Sister program as a "Little." 10 $1,000 nonrenewable awards are also available.Scholarship is renewable. Awarded every year.
Contact: Robert Kearney, Manager for National Partnerships.

2173 Beta Theta Pi Scholarships

Beta Theta Pi Foundation
P.O. Box 6277
Oxford, OH 45056
(513) 523-7591
Average award: $1,000
Maximum award: $1,500
Minimum award: $750
Number of awards: 46
Deadline: April 15
College level: Sophomore, Junior, Senior, Graduate, Doctoral
Criteria: Applicant must be a member of Beta Theta Pi. Selection is based upon academic achievement, undergraduate extracurricular activities, and financial need. Awarded every year.
Contact: Stephen B. Becker, Director of Advancement and Alumni Relations.

2174 Children and Youth Scholarship

American Legion–Washington
P.O. Box 3917
Lacey, WA 98509-3917
(360) 491-4373
Maximum award: $1,500
Number of awards: 2
Deadline: April 1
College level: Freshman
Criteria: Applicant must be the child of an American Legion member or its auxiliary. Awarded every year.
Contact: William Fortson, Department Adjutant.

2175 Chuck Hall Star of Tomorrow Scholarship

Young American Bowling Alliance (YABA)
5301 South 76th Street
Greendale, WI 53129
Maximum award: $4,000
Number of awards: 1
Deadline: January 15
College level: Freshman, Sophomore, Junior, Senior
Criteria: Applicant must be a member of YABA or WIBC and a man age 21 or under. Send a self-addressed, stamped envelope (#10). No phone calls. Awarded every year.
Contact: Edward Gocha, Scholarship Administrator.

2176   Creative and Performing Arts Award

Japanese American Citizens League (JACL)
National Headquarters
1765 Sutter Street
San Francisco, CA 94115
(415) 921-5225, (415) 931-4671 (fax)
jacl@hooked.net
Maximum award: $2,500
Number of awards: 2
Majors/Fields: Creative arts, performing arts
Criteria: Applicant must be a JACL member or child of a member and be currently enrolled in or planning to re-enter a creative or performing arts program. Applicant must submit additional materials (reviews, etc.) Request an application in writing and enclose a self-addressed, stamped envelope (#10). Applications are available in October. Awarded every year.
Contact: Scholarship Coordinator.

2177   Cultural Ambassadorial Scholarship

Rotary Foundation of Rotary International
One Rotary Center
1560 Sherman Avenue
Evanston, IL 60201-3698
Maximum award: $10,000 for three months; $17,000 for six months.
College level: Junior, Senior, Graduate, Doctoral
Criteria: Applicant must apply through local Rotary club, have completed at least one year of college level course work or its equivalent of the language they plan to study. Award is for intensive language training abroad for three or six months. Awarded every year.
Contact: Scholarships.

2178   DECA Scholarship

Distributive Education Clubs of America (DECA)
1908 Association Drive
Reston, VA 22091
(703) 860-5000
Average award: $1,000
Maximum award: $1,500
Minimum award: $500
Number of awards: 17
Deadline: Second Monday in March
College level: Freshman
Majors/Fields: Management, marketing, marketing education, merchandising
Criteria: Applicant must be an active member of DECA and rank in top third of class. Selection is based upon merit, club participation and accomplishments, leadership, responsibility, and character. Scholarship is renewable. Awarded every year.
Contact: Tim Coffey, Director of Corporate Marketing.

2179   Delta Gamma Foundation Fellowship

Delta Gamma Foundation
3250 Riverside Drive
P.O. Box 21397
Columbus, OH 43221-0397
(614) 481-8169
Average award: $2,500
Number of awards: 14
Deadline: April 1
Criteria: Applicant must be a member of Delta Gamma fraternity. Awarded every year.
Contact: Scholarships, Fellowships and Loans Chairman.

2180   Descendants of the Signers of the Declaration of Independence Scholarship

Descendants of the Signers of the Declaration of Independence, Inc. (DSDI)
P.O. Box 224
Suncook, NH 03275-0224
Average award: $1,500
Maximum number of awards: 6
Minimum number of awards: 5
Deadline: March 15
College level: Freshman, Sophomore, Junior, Senior, Graduate, Doctoral
Criteria: Applicant must be a proven lineal descendant of a signer of the Declaration of Independence as attested by the Registrar-General, and be a full-time student at a recognized U.S. college or university. Request must be made by January 15 in writing, with enclosed SASE, naming an ancestor signer to receive a reply. Recipient must reapply each year to retain scholarship. Awarded every year.
Contact: Mrs. Philip F. Kennedy, DSDI Scholarship Committee.

2181   Eagle Scout Scholarship

American Legion–Tennessee
State Headquarters
215 Eighth Avenue, North
Nashville, TN 37203
(615) 254-0568, (615) 255-1551 (fax)
Average award: $1,500
Number of awards: 1
Deadline: March 1
College level: Freshman
Criteria: Applicant must be the Tennessee American Legion Eagle Scout of the Year. Awarded every year.
Contact: A. Mike Hammer, Department Adjutant, 215 Eighth Avenue, North, Nashville, TN 37203.

2182   Eagle Scout Scholarship

National Society of the Sons of the American Revolution
Eagle Scout Scholarship
1000 South Fourth Street
Louisville, KY 40203
(502) 589-1776
Maximum award: $5,000
Number of awards: 2
Deadline: December 31
College level: Freshman
Criteria: Applicant must be in the current class of Eagle scouts (class year runs from July 1 to June 30 of each year). Awarded every year.
Contact: National Chairman, Eagle Scout Committee.

2183   Eagle Scout Scholarship

Birmingham-Southern College
Arkadelphia Road
Birmingham, AL 35254
(205) 226-4688
Average award: $2,500
Deadline: None
College level: Freshman
Criteria: Applicant must be an Eagle Scout member of the Boy Scouts. Selection is based upon academic record, standardized test scores, and recommendations. Scholarship is renewable. Awarded every year. Award may be used only at sponsoring institution.
Contact: Admissions Office, (800) 523-5793, extension 4696.

2184 "Eagle Scout of the Year" Scholarship

The American Legion
Education and Scholarships Program
P.O. Box 1055
Indianapolis, IN 46206
(317) 630-1212
http://www.legion.org
Maximum award: $8,000
Number of awards: 4
Deadline: March 1
College level: Freshman
Criteria: Applicant must be a registered active member of a Boy Scout troop or Varsity Scout team sponsored by an American Legion post or auxiliary unit, or a registered active member of a duly chartered Boy Scout troop or Varsity Scout team and the son or grandson of an American Legion or auxiliary member. Award must be used within four years of graduation date at an accredited post-secondary school in the continental U.S. or a U.S. possession. Awarded every year.
Contact: Mike Buss, National Americanism Commission.

2185 FBLA-PBL Scholarship

Future Business Leader Awards Phi Beta Lambda FBLA-PBL, Inc.
1912 Association Drive
Reston, VA 22091
(703) 860-3334, (703) 758-0749 (fax)
services@fbla.org
http://www.fbla-pbl.org
Maximum award: $5,000
College level: Freshman, Sophomore, Junior, Senior, Graduate
Criteria: Applicant must be a member of FBLA-PBL. Selection is based upon leadership, competitive event performances, and community service activities. Awarded every year.
Contact: Glenn Morris, Manager, Education & Programs.

2186 Fifth Marine Division Association Scholarship

Fifth Marine Division Association
Marine Corps Scholarship Foundation, Inc.
P.O. Box 3008
Princeton, NJ 08543-3008
(609) 921-3534
Average award: $2,000
Maximum award: $2,500
Minimum award: $500
Number of awards: 800
Deadline: April 1
College level: Freshman, Sophomore, Junior, Senior
Criteria: Applicant must be the child of Marine or Navy service member who served with the Fifth Marine Division and who has a current paid-up membership in the Fifth Marine Division Association. Inquiries must include sufficient data to establish parent's connection to the Fifth Marine Division Association and a self-addressed stamped envelope. Financial need is considered. Recipient must reapply and maintain a minimum 12 hours per semester with passing grades to retain scholarship. Awarded every year.
Contact: Scholarships.

2187 50 Men & Women of Toledo Scholarship

50 Men and Women of Toledo, Inc.
P.O. Box 3357
Toledo, OH 43608
(419) 729-4654, (419) 729-4004 (fax)
Average award: $1,500
Deadline: March 15
College level: Freshman
Criteria: Applicant must be a minority student from the Toledo, Ohio area. Recipient must maintain a minimum 3.0 GPA. Awarded every year.
Contact: James C. Caldwell, President, P.O. Box 80056, Toledo, OH 43608-0056.

2188 Fraternal College Scholarship

Modern Woodmen of America
1701 First Avenue
Rock Island, IL 61201
(309) 786-6481
Maximum award: $2,000
Number of awards: 36
Deadline: January 1
College level: Freshman
Criteria: Applicant must be a beneficial member of Modern Woodmen of America for at least two years and be in the top half of graduating class. Selection is based upon character, leadership, academic activities, extracurricular activities, and scholastic records. Renewable for up to four years. Awarded every year.
Contact: L. Michael Faulhaber, Fraternal Scholarship Administrator.

2189 Freshman Award

Japanese American Citizens League (JACL)
National Headquarters
1765 Sutter Street
San Francisco, CA 94115
(415) 921-5225, (415) 931-4671 (fax)
jacl@hooked.net
Average award: $1,000
Maximum award: $5,000
Number of awards: 8
Deadline: March 1
College level: Freshman
Criteria: Applicant must be a JACL member or child of a member, and be planning to attend a post-secondary institution in the fall of the award year. Some awards are restricted to California residents. Request an application in writing and enclose a self-addressed stamped envelope (#10). Applications are available in October. Awarded every year.
Contact: Scholarship Administrator.

2190 GCSAA Legacy Awards

Golf Course Superintendents Association of America (GSCAA) Foundation
1421 Research Park Drive
Lawrence, KS 66049
(913) 832-4445, (913) 832-4433 (fax)
fundmail@gcsaa.org
http://www.gcsaa.org
Average award: $1,500
Number of awards: 10
Deadline: April 15
College level: Freshman, Sophomore, Junior, Senior, Graduate, Doctoral
Majors/Fields: Golf course management
Criteria: Applicant must be the child or grandchild of a member of the Golf Course Superintendents Association of America. Selection is based upon academic excellence, extracurricular activities, and a brief essay. Awarded every year.
Contact: Jack Schwartz, Director of Development, (913) 841-2240.

2191 Girl Scout Gold Award

Birmingham-Southern College
Arkadelphia Road
Birmingham, AL 35254
(205) 226-4688
Average award: $2,500
Deadline: December 15
College level: Freshman
Criteria: Applicant must be a Gold Award member of the Girl Scouts, have a minimum 3.0 GPA and minimum composite ACT score of 26 (combined SAT I score of 1050), demonstrate academic strength and promise, and be accepted for admission as a freshman in the fall of the award year. Selection is based upon academic record, standardized test scores, and recommendations. Renewable for up to three additional years. Awarded every year. Award may be used only at sponsoring institution.
Contact: Office of Admissions, Box A-18, Birmingham, AL 35254, (205) 226-4686.

2192 Girl Scout Gold Scholarship

The College of St. Catherine
2004 Randolph Avenue
St. Paul, MN 55105
(612) 690-6540, (800) 945-4599
Average award: $2,500
Number of awards: 10
Deadline: February 1
College level: Freshman
Criteria: Applicant must be a woman and recipient of the Girl Scout Gold Award. To be considered for award, applicant must submit essay describing Gold Award work and letter requesting consideration by February 1 prior to enrollment. Renewable for up to four years if recipient maintains a minimum 3.0 GPA and completes at least 28 credit hours per year. Awarded every year. Award may be used only at sponsoring institution.
Contact: Susan Brady, Director of Financial Aid.

2193 Girl Scout Gold Scholarship

Cedar Crest College
100 College Drive
Allentown, PA 18104
(610) 740-3785, (610) 606-4647 (fax)
cccadmis@cedarcrest.edu
www.cedarcrest.edu
Maximum award: $2,500
College level: Freshman
Criteria: Applicant must be a woman and a recipient of the Girl Scout Gold Award. Award may be for up to four years. Awarded every year. Award may be used only at sponsoring institution.
Contact: Judith Neyhart, Financial Aid Office, 100 College Drive, Allentown, PA 18104, (215) 740-3785.

2194 Girl Scout Gold Scholarship

Lindenwood College
St. Charles, MO 63301
(514) 949-4949
Maximum award: $5,000
College level: Freshman
Criteria: Applicant must be a woman and recipient of the Girl Scout Gold Award. Scholarship amount includes $1,500 work-and-learn stipend. Renewable for up to four years if recipient maintains a minimum 2.0 GPA and good social standing. Awarded every year. Award may be used only at sponsoring institution.
Contact: Lise Keller, Assistant Director of Admissions.

2195 Girl Scout Gold Scholarship

Long Island University, Brooklyn Campus
One University Plaza
Brooklyn, NY 11201
(718) 488-1292
Average award: Full tuition
College level: Freshman
Criteria: Applicant must be a woman and recipient of the Girl Scout Gold Award, have a minimum 90 grade average, and have a minimum combined SAT I score of 1200. Award is for four years. Awarded every year. Award may be used only at sponsoring institution.
Contact: Alan Chavis, Dean of Admissions.

2196 Girl Scout Gold Scholarship

York College of Pennsylvania
Country Club Road
York, PA 17403
(717) 846-7788
Average award: One-Third tuition
College level: Freshman
Criteria: Applicant must be a woman and recipient of the Girl Scout Gold Award, rank in the top two-fifths of class, and have minimum SAT I scores of 460 verbal and 500 math. Minimum 3.5 GPA is required to retain scholarship. Awarded every year. Award may be used only at sponsoring institution.
Contact: Nancy Spataro, Director of Admissions.

2197 Girl Scout Gold Scholarship

University of Louisville
Brook Street
Louisville, KY 40292
(800) 334-8635
Average award: Full tuition
College level: Freshman
Criteria: Applicant must be a woman and a recipient of the Girl Scout Gold Award from the Kentuckiana Girl Scout Council, have a minimum "B" grade average and minimum composite ACT score of 20, and be a graduate of an accredited Kentucky school. Awarded every year. Award may be used only at sponsoring institution.
Contact: Financial Aid Advisor, Student Financial Aid Office, Louisville, KY 40292, (502) 588-6531.

2198 Girls Incorporated Scholars Program

Girls Incorporated
30 East 33rd Street, 7th Floor
New York, NY 10016-5394
(212) 689-3700, (212) 683-1253 (fax)
hn3581@handsnet.org
http://www.girlsinc.org
Maximum award: $10,000
Number of awards: 20
Deadline: December 15
College level: Freshman
Criteria: Applicant must be a member of a Girls Incorporated affiliate and submit application for local judging. Awarded every year.
Contact: Nettie Wolfe, Coordinator of Scholarships and Awards, hn3581@handsnet.org.

2199 International Essay Contest

Optimist International
Maximum award: $5,000 and a trip to the Optimist Convention
Deadline: In mid-January
College level: Freshman
Criteria: Applicant must be under 19 years of age as of December 31, in 10-12 grades (11-13 in Jamaica only), and be attending school in the U.S., Canada, or Jamaica.
Contact: local Optimist Club.

2200 James C. Caldwell Scholarship

50 Men and Women of Toledo, Inc.
P.O. Box 3357
Toledo, OH 43608
(419) 729-4654, (419) 729-4004 (fax)
Average award: $1,500
Deadline: March 15
College level: Freshman
Criteria: Applicant must be a minority student from the Toledo, Ohio area. Recipient must maintain a minimum 3.0 GPA. Awarded every year.
Contact: James C. Caldwell, President, P.O. Box 80056, Toledo, OH 43608.

2201 Jones-Laurence Award

Sigma Alpha Epsilon (SAE)
P.O. Box 1856
Evanston, IL 60204
(847) 475-1856
Maximum award: $3,500
Number of awards: 3
Deadline: May 1
College level: Senior, Graduate
Criteria: Applicant must be a member of SAE who displays the most outstanding academic achievement and genuine concern for the academic welfare and success of his fraternity brothers. Awarded every year.
Contact: Christopher Mundy, Director of Education Programs, (847) 475-1856, extension 235.

2202 Junior Girls Scholarship

Ladies Auxiliary to the Veterans of Foreign Wars
406 West 34th Street
Kansas City, MO 64111
(816) 561-8655, (816) 931-4753 (fax)
Maximum award: $5,000
Number of awards: 2
Deadline: April 15
College level: Freshman
Criteria: Applicant must have been an active member of the Ladies Auxiliary Junior Girls Unit for at least one year, have held an office in the unit, and be in grades 9-12. Selection is based upon participation in Junior Girls unit, community and school activities, and scholastic aptitude. Awarded every year.
Contact: Judy Millick, Administration of Programs.

2203 Kenneth Kendal King Leaders Scholarship

Sigma Chi Foundation
P.O. Box 469
Evanston, IL 60204
(847) 869-3655 extension 221, (847) 869-4906 (fax)
uncle_runkle@sigmachihq.org
Average award: $4,000
Number of awards: 6
Deadline: May 15
College level: Junior, Senior
Criteria: Applicant must be a full-time student and member of Sigma Chi fraternity. Selection is based upon GPA, leadership experience, and demonstrated financial need. Satisfactory GPA is required to retain scholarship. Awarded every year.
Contact: Assistant to the Director of Education, (847) 869-3655.

2204 Law Award

Japanese American Citizens League (JACL)
National Headquarters
1765 Sutter Street
San Francisco, CA 94115
(415) 921-5225, (415) 931-4671 (fax)
jacl@hooked.net
Maximum award: $2,500
Number of awards: 2
College level: Law school
Majors/Fields: Law
Criteria: Applicant must be a JACL member or child of a member, and be currently enrolled in or planning to re-enter a law school. Request an application in writing and enclose a self-addressed stamped envelope (#10). Applications are available in October. Awarded every year.
Contact: Scholarship Administrator.

2205 Lou Henry Hoover Scholarship

Temple University, Ambler Campus
580 Meetinghouse Road
Ambler, PA 19002-3994
(215) 283-1292
Maximum award: Full tuition
College level: Freshman
Criteria: Applicant must be a woman and have been active in Girl Scouts. Awarded every year. Award may be used only at sponsoring institution.
Contact: John R. Collins, FASLA, Professor and Chair.

2206 Marjorie Sells Carter Trust Boy Scout Scholarship

Marjorie Sells Carter Boy Scout Scholarship Trust
P.O. Box 527
West Chatham, MA 02669
(508) 945-1225
Average award: $1,500
Number of awards: 30
Deadline: April 15
College level: Freshman, Sophomore
Criteria: Applicant must be a Boy Scout from one of the six New England states who has been active in scouting for at least two years. Award is highly competitive. Selection is based upon demonstrated leadership ability and financial need. Letter requesting second year aid and minimum "C" grade average are required to retain scholarship. Awarded every year.
Contact: Mrs. B. J. Shaffer, Administrative Secretary.

2207 Most Worshipful Prince Hall Grand Lodge Scholarship

Prince Hall Grand Lodge
Masonic Temple
1000 U Street, N.W.
Washington, DC 20001
(202) 462-8878
Average award: $1,000
Maximum award: $2,000
Minimum award: $500
Number of awards: 37
Deadline: May 1
College level: Freshman
Criteria: Awarded every year.
Contact: Frank A. Porter, Chairman, P.O. Box 5111, Hyattsville, MD 20782, (301) 779-4827.

2208 Multi-Year Ambassadorial Scholarship

Rotary Foundation of Rotary International
One Rotary Center
1560 Sherman Avenue
Evanston, IL 60201-3698
(847) 866-3000, (847) 328-8554 (fax)
Average award: $22,000
Maximum award: $33,000
Minimum award: $11,000
College level: Junior, Senior, Graduate, Doctoral
Criteria: Applicant must apply through local Rotary club. Funding is for either two or three years and is intended to help supplement the costs of pursuing one degree at one study institution. Award is for two or three years. Awarded every year.
Contact: Scholarships.

2209 NAACP Willems Scholarship

National Association for the Advancement of Colored People (NAACP)
4805 Mount Hope Drive
Baltimore, MD 21215-3297
(410) 358-8900
Average award: $2,000
Maximum award: $3,000
Deadline: April 30
College level: Freshman, Sophomore, Junior, Senior, Graduate, Doctoral
Majors/Fields: Chemistry, computer science, engineering, mathematical science, physics
Criteria: Applicant must have a minimum 3.0 GPA and be a member of the NAACP. Undergraduate awards are for four years; graduate scholarships may be renewed. Awarded every year.
Contact: Andrea E. Moss, Education Department.

2210 National Association of Plumbing-Heating-Cooling Contractors Educational Foundation Scholarship

National Association of Plumbing-Heating-Cooling Contractors (NAPHCC)
Scholarship Program
P.O. Box 6808
Falls Church, VA 22046
(703) 237-8100, (703) 237-7442 (fax)
Average award: $2,500
Number of awards: 4
Deadline: April 1
College level: Freshman, Sophomore
Majors/Fields: Cooling, heating, plumbing
Criteria: Applicant must be sponsored by a NAPHCC member who is in good standing with the association for the entire term of the scholarship. Renewable if recipient continues original course of study indicated on application. Awarded every year.
Contact: Kelly Carson, Scholarship Liaison.

2211 National Beta Club Scholarship

National Beta Club
151 West Lee Street
Spartanburg, SC 29306
(864) 583-4553, (864) 542-9300 (fax)
betaclub@betaclub.org
http://www.betaclub.org
Maximum award: $2,500
Number of awards: 150
Deadline: December 10
College level: Freshman
Criteria: Applicant must be a member of National Beta Club and nominated by his or her school. Applicants should contact their school's Beta club for more information. Awarded every year. Award may be used only at Beta Club member institutions.
Contact: Joan Burnett, Information Resource Manager.

2212 National Student Organization Scholarship

Johnson & Wales University
8 Abbott Park Place
Providence, RI 02903
(401) 598-1000, (401) 598-1040 (fax)
admissions@jwu.edu
http://jwu.edu
Maximum award: $10,000
Deadline: April 15 and May 15
College level: Freshman
Criteria: Applicant must be a member of BPA, DECA, FFA, FHA, HERO, or VICA. Transcripts and recommendation from club advisor required. Recipient must maintain satisfactory academic progress and participation in organization to retain scholarship. Awarded every year. Award may be used only at sponsoring institution.
Contact: Maureen Dumas, Office of Admissions, (401) 598-2326.

2213 NCHA Scholarship

National Campers and Hikers Association (NCHA)
Scholarship Director
1960 Bounty Street
Aurora, CO 80011-4249
(315) 685-5223
Average award: $1,000
Maximum award: $2,000
Minimum award: $500
Deadline: April 15
College level: Freshman, Sophomore, Junior, Senior
Criteria: Applicant must have been a member or the child of a member of the National Campers and Hikers Association for at least one year prior to application. Membership must be maintained during the award. High school applicant must rank in the top two-fifths of class; college applicant must have a minimum "B" grade average. Selection is based upon maturity, leadership, activities, and goals. Special consideration is given to applicants majoring in fields related to conservation, ecology, or outdoor activities. Reapplication is required to retain scholarship. Awarded every year.
Contact: Barbara E. Harper, National Scholarship Director, 74 West Genesee Street, Skaneateles, NY 13152.

2214 Phi Kappa Theta Scholarship

Phi Kappa Theta
3901 West 86th Street
Suite 425
Indianapolis, IN 46268
Average award: $750
Maximum award: $1,500
Minimum award: $250
Number of awards: 6
Deadline: April 30
College level: Sophomore, Junior, Senior
Criteria: Applicant must be a member of Phi Kappa Theta National Fraternity. Scholarship is renewable. Awarded every year.
Contact: Scott Bora, Scholarships.

2215 Richard Heaney Scholarship

National Beverage Packaging Association
200 Daingerfield Road
Alexandria, VA 22314-2800
(703) 548-6563
Maximum award: $2,000
Number of awards: 6
Deadline: July 1
College level: Junior, Senior, Graduate, Doctoral, second-year student at two-year technical college
Majors/Fields: Packaging
Criteria: Awarded every year.
Contact: Gary Lile, President, (703) 684-1080, fpmsa@clark.net.

2216 Sagebrush Circuit–Lew & JoAnn Eklund Educational Scholarship

Appaloosa Youth Foundation
Appaloosa Horse Club, Inc.
P.O. Box 8403
Moscow, ID 83871
(208)-882-5578
Average award: $2,000
Number of awards: 1
Deadline: June 10
College level: Junior, Senior, Graduate, Doctoral
Majors/Fields: Equestrian
Criteria: Applicant must be a member of the Appaloosa Horse Club or be the son or daughter of an Appaloosa Horse Club member. Selection is based upon scholastic aptitude, leadership potential, sportsmanship, community and civic responsibilities, and accomplishments in horsemanship. Renewable if recipient maintains minimum 3.5 GPA. Recipient must reapply. Awarded every year.
Contact: Katie Williams, Youth Coordinator, (208) 882-5578.

2217 Scout of the Year

American Legion–Wisconsin
Department Headquarters
812 East State Street
Milwaukee, WI 53202
Maximum award: $8,000
Deadline: March 1
College level: Freshman
Criteria: Applicant must be an Eagle Scout. Awarded every year.
Contact: Scholarships.

2218 SIE Scholarships

Sigma Iota Epsilon (SIE) National Office
214 Westcott Boulevard
Florida State University
Tallahassee, FL 32306
(904) 644-6003
Average award: $775
Maximum award: $1,250
Minimum award: $500
Number of awards: 10
Deadline: May 10
College level: Junior, Senior, Graduate, Doctoral
Majors/Fields: Business administration, management
Criteria: Applicant must be an active SIE student member. Recipient must remain an active SIE student member to retain scholarship. Awarded every year.
Contact: Mike Hankin, Administrator.

2219 Stanley H. Stearman Scholarship Award

National Society of Public Accountants (NSPA)
Scholarship Foundation
1010 North Fairfax Street
Alexandria, VA 22314-1574
(703) 549-6400
Average award: $2,000
Number of awards: 1
Deadline: March 10
College level: Sophomore, Junior, Senior, Graduate, Doctoral
Majors/Fields: Accounting
Criteria: Applicant must be the child, grandchild, niece, nephew, son-in-law, or daughter-in-law of an active National Society of Public Accountants member or deceased member. Applicant must be a U.S. or Canadian citizen majoring in accounting with a minimum "B" grade average in a full-time degree program at an accredited college or university in the U.S. Accounting major is required to retain scholarship for a total of three years. Awarded every year.
Contact: Susan E. Noell, Foundation Director.

2220 Sutton Education Scholarship

National Association for the Advancement of Colored People (NAACP)
4805 Mount Hope Drive
Baltimore, MD 21215-3297
(410) 358-8900
Maximum award: $2,000
Deadline: April 30
College level: Freshman, Sophomore, Junior, Senior, Graduate, Doctoral
Majors/Fields: Education
Criteria: Applicant must be a NAACP member. Undergraduate applicant must have a minimum 2.5 GPA and graduate applicant must have a minimum 3.0 GPA. Renewable if satisfactory GPA is maintained. Awarded every year.
Contact: Andrea E. Moss, Education Department.

2221 Thomas Wood Baldridge Scholarship

U.S. Jaycee War Memorial Fund (JWMF)
Department 94922
Tulsa, OK 74194-0001
Maximum award: $2,500
Number of awards: 1
Deadline: February 1
College level: Freshman, Sophomore, Junior, Senior, Graduate, Doctoral
Criteria: Applicant must be a Jaycee or the immediate family member of a Jaycee, a U.S. citizen, possess academic potential and leadership qualities, and demonstrate financial need. Request application by February 1 with $5.00 application fee and self-addressed, business-sized stamped envelope to War Memorial Fund, 4 West 21st Street, Tulsa, OK 74114-1116. Check or money order must be made payable to the War Memorial Fund. Completed applications must be sent to applicants' respective state Junior Chamber organization by March 1. Awarded every year.
Contact: Scholarship Program Administrator, P.O. Box 7, Tulsa, OK 74102-0007, (918) 584-2481.

2222 Undergraduate Award

Japanese American Citizens League (JACL)
National Headquarters
1765 Sutter Street
San Francisco, CA 94115
(415) 921-5225, (415) 931-4671 (fax)
jacl@hooked.net
Maximum award: $5,000
Number of awards: 9
Deadline: April 1
College level: Sophomore, Junior, Senior
Criteria: Applicant must be a JACL member or child of a member, and be currently enrolled in or re-entering a college, trade school, junior college, or university. Request an application in writing and enclose a self-addressed stamped envelope (#10). Applications are available in October. Awarded every year.
Contact: Scholarship Administrator.

2223 Warren Poslusny Award for Outstanding Achievement

Sigma Alpha Epsilon (SAE)
P.O. Box 1856
Evanston, IL 60204
(847) 475-1856
Average award: $1,250
Maximum award: $3,000
Minimum award: $1,000
Number of awards: 7
Deadline: May 1
College level: Junior, Senior, Graduate, Doctoral
Criteria: Applicant must be a SAE brother demonstrating fraternity and community service. Academic record is considered. Awarded every year.
Contact: Christopher Mundy, Publications/Program Coordinator, (847) 475-1856, extension 235.

2224 Western Golf Association Evans Scholars Foundation Scholarship

Western Golf Association
Evans Scholars Foundation
1 Briar Road
Golf, IL 60029
(847) 724-4600
Average award: Full tuition and housing
Number of awards: 225
Deadline: November 1
College level: Freshman
Criteria: Applicant must have caddied for a minimum of two years at a Western Golf Association member club, rank in the top quarter of graduating class, have outstanding personal character, and demonstrate financial need. Renewable for four years. Awarded every year.
Contact: Scholarship Committee.

2225 Women's Board Scholarship

Boys and Girls Clubs of Chicago
625 West Jackson Boulevard
Suite 300
Chicago, IL 60661
(312) 627-2700, (312) 648-5628 (fax)
Average award: $1,000
Maximum award: $2,000
Minimum award: $200
Number of awards: 20
Deadline: May 1
College level: Freshman
Criteria: Applicant must be a member of the Boys and Girls Clubs of Chicago with a minimum 2.5 GPA. Application must be submitted by the club director. Selection is based upon financial need and grades. Renewable if satisfactory academic performance is maintained and letter of request is sent. Awarded every year.
Contact: Mary Ann Mahon-Huels, Vice President of Operations.

2226   YMCA Black Achievers Scholarship

Denison University
Box H
Granville, OH 43023
(614) 587-6276, 800-DENISON, (614) 587-6306 (fax)
admissions@denison.edu
http://www.denison.edu
Average award: Half tuition
Number of awards: No limit
Deadline: January 1
College level: Freshman
Criteria: Applicant must be an outstanding participant in the YMCA Black Achievers Program. Minimum 2.5 GPA is required for renewal. Awarded every year. Award may be used only at sponsoring institution.
Contact: Adele Brumfield, Scholarships, (614) 587-6703.

2227   Young American Bowling Alliance Coca-Cola Youth Bowling Championship Award

Young American Bowling Alliance (YABA)
5301 South 76th Street
Greendale, WI 53129
(414) 421-4700, (414) 421-1301 (fax)
Maximum award: $3,000
Number of awards: 900
Deadline: February 11
College level: Freshman, Sophomore, Junior, Senior
Criteria: Applicant must be a member of a YABA local league. Awarded every year.
Contact: Youth Coordinator, Local Bowling Center.

2228   Youth Scholarship Fund of IBHA, Inc.

International Buckskin Horse Association (IBHA)
P.O. Box 268
Shelby, IN 46377
(219) 552-1013
Maximum award: $1,500
Number of awards: 12
Deadline: March 1
College level: Freshman, Sophomore, Junior, Senior
Criteria: Applicant must hold membership in IBHA, participate in IBHA Youth events for at least two years, be age 22 or under with excellent test scores and strong recommendations, and participate in school and community activities. Minimum "C" grade average is required to maintain scholarship. Awarded every year.
Contact: Richard E. Kurzeja, Secretary, 3517 West 231st Avenue, Lowell, IN 46356.

2229   Zenon C.R. Hansen Leadership Scholarship

Doane College
1014 Boswell Avenue
Crete, NE 68333
(800) 333-6263, (402) 826-8600 (fax)
http://www.doane.edu
Average award: Tuition, fees, room, board, and books
Number of awards: 4
College level: Freshman
Criteria: Applicant must be a woman and recipient of the Girl Scout Gold Award. Scholarship is awarded on a competitive basis. Awarded every year. Award may be used only at sponsoring institution.
Contact: Dan Kunzman, Director of Admissions.

Ethnic/Race Specific——————

2230 Academic Excellence Scholarship

University of Houston
4800 Calhoun
Houston, TX 77204-2160
(713) 743-1010 extension 333, (713) 743-9098 (fax)
Average award: $1,500
Maximum award: $2,500
Minimum award: $1,000
Number of awards: 127
Deadline: April 1
College level: Freshman
Criteria: Minimum 2.0 GPA and 12 credit hours per semester are required to retain scholarship. Awarded every year. Award may be used only at sponsoring institution.
Contact: Robert Sheridan, Director of Scholarships and Financial Aid, 129 Ezekiel W. Cullen Building, Houston, TX 77204-2161.

2231 Afro-American Student Need Scholarship/ Afro-American Student Scholarship/Afro-American Adult Scholarship

Shawnee State University
940 Second Street
Portsmouth, OH 45662-4344
(614) 355-2237
Average award: $2,750
Deadline: April 15; early application is recommended
College level: Freshman, Entering student
Criteria: Applicant must be an Afro-American and demonstrate financial need. Applicant for Student Scholarship must rank in top third of class. Applicant for Adult Scholarship must have been out of high school at least one year. Selection is based upon academic record, creative endeavors, and school and community involvement. Awarded every year. Award may be used only at sponsoring institution.
Contact: Financial Aid Office, (614) 355-2485.

2232 Alex and Henry Recine Scholarship

National Italian American Foundation (NIAF)
Educational Scholarship Program
1860 19th Street, NW
Washington, DC 20009-5599
(202) 530-5315
Maximum award: $2,500
Deadline: May 31
College level: Freshman, Sophomore, Junior, Senior
Criteria: Applicant must be an Italian-American, demonstrate financial need, submit a transcript, and attend school in New York state.
Contact: Dr. Maria Lombardo, Education Director.

2233 Alyce M. Cafaro Scholarship

National Italian American Foundation (NIAF)
Educational Scholarship Program
1860 19th Street, NW
Washington, DC 20009-5599
(202) 530-5315
Average award: $5,000
Number of awards: 1
Deadline: May 31
College level: Freshman, Sophomore, Junior, Senior
Criteria: Applicant must be an Italian-American Ohio resident, demonstrate financial need, and submit transcript. Awarded every year.
Contact: Dr. Maria Lombardo, Education Director.

2234 Ambassadors for Diversity Award

William Woods University
200 West Twelfth Street
Fulton, MO 65251-1098
(573) 592-4232, (573) 592-1146 (fax)
http://www.wmwoods.edu
Average award: $5,000
Number of awards: 10
Deadline: June 1
College level: Freshman, Sophomore, Junior, Senior
Criteria: Applicant must be a minority student, under age 23, demonstrate leadership and service, submit two letters of recommendation, and have on-campus interview. Reapplication, a minimum 3.0 GPA, and participation in diversity programs are required to retain scholarship for up to four years. Awarded every year. Award may be used only at sponsoring institution.
Contact: Laura L. Archuleta, Director for Student Financial Aid, larchule@iris.wmwoods.edu.

2235 American Indian Tuition Waiver

University of Oklahoma
University Affairs
900 Asp Avenue, Room 236
Norman, OK 73019-0401
(405) 325-1701
Average award: $3,200
Number of awards: No limit
Deadline: June 1 (fall), November 1 (spring)
College level: Freshman, Sophomore, Junior, Senior
Criteria: Applicant must be a nonresident American Indian who is affiliated with one of the 34 federally recognized Indian tribes located within the Oklahoma state boundaries. Award is for a maximum of five years. Awarded every year. Award may be used only at sponsoring institution.
Contact: Prospective Student Services, (405) 325-2151.

2236 APS Corporate-Sponsored Scholarship for Minority Undergraduate Students

The American Physical Society (APS)
One Physics Ellipse
4th Floor
College Park, MD 20740
(301) 209-3200
Average award: $2,000
Number of awards: 26
Deadline: February 7
College level: Freshman, Sophomore, Junior
Majors/Fields: Physics
Criteria: Applicant must be a U.S. citizen of black, Hispanic, or Native American descent. Applicant must major in physics with satisfactory GPA to retain scholarship for one additional year. Awarded every year.
Contact: Arlene Modeste, Program Coordinator, (301) 209-3232, modeste@aps.org.

2237 Armenian Students' Association of America Scholarship

Armenian Students' Association of America, Inc.
395 Concord Avenue
Belmont, MA 02178
(617) 484-9548
Average award: $1,000
Maximum award: $2,500
Minimum award: $500
Number of awards: 30
Deadline: March 15
College level: Sophomore, Junior, Senior, Graduate, Doctoral
Criteria: Applicant must be of Armenian ancestry, be a full-time student attending a four-year, accredited college or university in the U.S., and have completed at least the first year of college. Selection is based upon financial need, academic performance, ability for self help, and participation in extracurricular activities. Request scholarship application by January 15. Awarded every year.
Contact: Christine Williamson, Scholarship Administrator.

2238   Asian/Pacific-American Support Group Scholarship

University of Southern California
University Park
Los Angeles, CA 90089-5012
(213) 740-1111
Maximum award: $2,500
Maximum number of awards: 20
Minimum number of awards: 10
College level: Freshman, Sophomore, Junior, Senior
Criteria: Applicant must be a U.S. citizen or permanent resident, have a strong sense of ethnic identity or commitment to Asian/Pacific-American community, have a minimum 3.0 GPA, and apply for institutional financial aid. Special application is required. Awarded every year. Award may be used only at sponsoring institution.
Contact: Asian/Pacific-American Student Services, Student Union 410, Los Angeles, CA 90089-4851, (213) 740-4999.

2239   A.T. Anderson Memorial Scholarship

American Indian Science and Engineering Society
Scholarship Coordinator
5661 Airport Boulevard
Boulder, CO 80301
(303) 939-0023, (303) 939-8150 (fax)
ascholar@spot.colorado.edu
http://www.colorado.edu/aises
Maximum award: $2,000
Deadline: June 15
College level: Freshman, Sophomore, Junior, Senior, Graduate, Doctoral
Majors/Fields: Business, health, natural resources, science, engineering, math secondary education, science secondary education
Criteria: Applicant must be one-quarter American Indian or be recognized as a member of a tribe, have a minimum 2.0 GPA, be a full-time student, and be a member of the American Indian Science and Engineering Society (membership information is included with the application). Recipient must reapply for renewal. Awarded every year.
Contact: Scholarship Coordinator.

2240   Bert Price Scholarship

Grand Valley State University
Allendale, MI 49401
(616) 895-3234
Average award: $2,658
Number of awards: 90
Deadline: February 1
College level: Freshman, Community college graduate
Criteria: Applicant must be a minority student with a disadvantaged background. Minimum 2.75 GPA is required to retain scholarship. Awarded every year. Award may be used only at sponsoring institution.
Contact: Ken Fridsma, Director of Financial Aid.

2241   Board of Governors Scholarship

Indiana University of Pennsylvania
308 Pratt Hall
Indiana, PA 15705
(412) 357-2218
Average award: Full tuition
Maximum number of awards: 90
Minimum number of awards: 61
Deadline: None
College level: Freshman, Sophomore, Junior, Senior
Criteria: Applicant must be black or Hispanic, demonstrate leadership, rank in the top quarter of class, and have a minimum combined SAT I score of 1000. Minimum 2.5 GPA after freshman year (2.75 GPA thereafter) is required to retain scholarship. Awarded every year. Award may be used only at sponsoring institution.
Contact: Patricia C. McCarthy, Assistant Director of Financial Aid.

2242   Bob and Nancy Good Scholarship

Denison University
Box H
Granville, OH 43023
(614) 587-6276, 800-DENISON, (614) 587-6306 (fax)
admissions@denison.edu
http://www.denison.edu
Average award: Half tuition
Number of awards: 2
Deadline: January 1
College level: Freshman
Criteria: Applicant must be an African-American with a strong academic background. Scholarship is renewable. Awarded every year. Award may be used only at sponsoring institution.
Contact: Scholarship.

2243   Burlington Northern Santa Fe Foundation Scholarship

American Indian Science and Engineering Society
Scholarship Coordinator
5661 Airport Boulevard
Boulder, CO 80301
(303) 939-0023, (303) 939-8150 (fax)
ascholar@spot.colorado.edu
http://www.colorado.edu/aises
Average award: $2,500
Number of awards: 5
Deadline: March 31
College level: Freshman
Majors/Fields: Business, Engineering, Health Administration, Education, Science
Criteria: Applicant must show proof of at least one-quarter American Indian blood, plan to attend a four-year, accredited educational institution full time, and live in one of the states served by the Burlington Northern, Atchison, Topeka, and Santa Fe Railway (Arizona, Colorado, Kansas, Minnesota, Montana, New Mexico, North Dakota, Oklahoma, Oregon, South Dakota, Washington, or San Bernardino County, Calif.). Scholarship is renewable. Awarded every year.
Contact: Scholarship Coordinator.

2244   Capital Scholars Award

Capital University
2199 East Main Street
Columbus, OH 43209-2394
(614) 236-6511
Maximum award: $5,000
Number of awards: 4
Deadline: February 21
College level: Freshman
Criteria: Applicant must be a minority student. Selection is based upon academic qualifications. Renewable for up to eight semesters if recipient maintains a minimum 2.5 GPA, lives on campus, and participates in two campus activities, one of which must be cultural. Awarded every year. Award may be used only at sponsoring institution.
Contact: Nancy Gibson, Assistant Director of Admission.

2245   Cardinal Bernadin Theology Scholarship

National Italian American Foundation (NIAF)
Educational Scholarship Program
1860 19th Street, NW
Washington, DC 20009-5599
(202) 530-5315
Maximum award: $2,500
Number of awards: 2
Deadline: May 31
College level: Second- and third-year theology students
Majors/Fields: Theology
Criteria: Applicant must be an Italian-American, demonstrate need, and submit a transcript. Award may be used only at Mundelein Seminary.
Contact: Dr. Maria Lombardo, Education Director, (202) 638-2137.

2246 Carmela Gagliardi Fellowships

National Italian American Foundation (NIAF)
Educational Scholarship Program
1860 19th Street, NW
Washington, DC 20009-5599
(202) 530-5315
Maximum award: $5,000
Number of awards: 4
Deadline: May 31
College level: Medical students
Majors/Fields: Medicine
Criteria: Applicant must be Italian-American, demonstrate financial need, rank in the top quarter of class, and submit transcript and essay entitled "A Comparison of the Italian and American Medical Systems."
Contact: Dr. Maria Lombardo, Education Director.

2247 Carnegie Mellon Scholarship

Carnegie Mellon University
5000 Forbes Avenue
Pittsburgh, PA 15213
(412) 268-2068
Average award: Full tuition
Number of awards: 20
Deadline: February 15
College level: Freshman
Criteria: Applicant must be a member of an underrepresented minority and have a "B+" grade average or rank in top tenth of class. Minimum 2.75 Quality Point Average (QPA) on a 4.00 scale is required to retain scholarship. Awarded every year. Award may be used only at sponsoring institution.
Contact: Linda M. Anderson, Director of Financial Aid.

2248 Central Virginia Black Teachers Scholarship

Lynchburg College
Lynchburg, VA 24501
(804) 522-8228
Award: Full tuition
Deadline: March 1
College level: Freshman
Majors/Fields: Education
Criteria: Awarded to black seniors at specific high schools who are committed to a career in public school teaching. Selection is competitive. Scholarship is renewable. Awarded every year. Award may be used only at sponsoring institution.
Contact: Scholarships.

2249 Challenge Scholarship

University of Pittsburgh, Pittsburgh Campus
4200 Fifth Avenue
Pittsburgh, PA 15260
(412) 624-4141
http://www.pitt.edu/-oafa/oafa.html
Average award: $4,000
Minimum award: $1,000
Number of awards: 30
Deadline: January 15
College level: Freshman
Majors/Fields: Arts/sciences
Criteria: Applicant must be a minority student enrolled in the College of Arts and Sciences. Selection is based upon high school performance and test scores. Scholarship is renewable. Awarded every year. Award may be used only at sponsoring institution.
Contact: Betsy A. Porter, Director of Admissions and Financial Aid, Office of Admissions & Financial Aid, Bruce Hall, Pittsburgh, PA 15260, (412) 624-7164.

2250 Charles Winter Wood Scholarship

Beloit College
700 College Street
Beloit, WI 53511
(608) 363-2663
Maximum award: $6,000
Deadline: February 15
College level: Freshman
Criteria: Applicant must be a person of color with a minimum 3.0 GPA, strong academic preparation, significant extracurricular activities, and the recommendation of a college counselor. Essay and on-campus interview required. Scholarship is renewable. Awarded every year. Award may be used only at sponsoring institution.
Contact: Thomas Kreiser, Director of Freshman Financial Aid, (608) 363-2500.

2251 Cheyenne-Arapaho Tribal Scholarship

Cheyenne-Arapaho Tribe
P.O. Box 38
Concho, OK 73022
(405) 262-0345, (405) 262-0745 (fax)
Maximum award: $2,000
Number of awards: 130
Deadline: June 1 (fall); November 1 (spring)
College level: Freshman, Sophomore, Junior, Senior, Graduate, Doctoral
Criteria: Applicant must be a member of the Cheyenne-Arapaho tribe, have a minimum 2.0 GPA, and demonstrate financial need. Renewable every semester if recipient maintains a minimum 2.0 GPA, completes 12 or more hours, and continues to demonstrate financial need. Awarded every year.
Contact: Teresa Dorsett, Director of Scholarships/Wanda Miller, Administrative Assistant of Scholarships.

2252 Cigna Corp. Scholarship

University of Richmond
Richmond, VA 23173
(804) 289-8438
Average award: Half tuition
Number of awards: 10
Deadline: January 15
College level: Freshman, Sophomore, Junior, Senior
Criteria: Applicant must be African-American and be nominated by high school. Award includes mentorship. Awarded every year. Award may be used only at sponsoring institution.
Contact: Scholars Office, (804) 289-8916.

2253 Clara B. Williams Scholarship

New Mexico State University
Box 30001, Department 5100
Las Cruces, NM 88003-0001
(505) 646-4105
Maximum award: Full tuition and fees
Deadline: March 1
College level: Freshman, Sophomore, Junior, Senior
Criteria: Applicant must be a black U.S. citizen with high academic merit. Awarded every year. Award may be used only at sponsoring institution.
Contact: Greeley W. Myers, Director of Financial Aid.

2254   Community College Minority Transfer Scholarship

University of Memphis
Scates Hall 204
Memphis, TN 38152
(901) 678-3213, (901) 678-5621 (fax)
katkinsn@cc.memphis.edu
http://www.memphis.edu/
Average award: $2,580
Deadline: April 1
College level: Junior
Criteria: Applicant must be African-American with an associates degree and a minimum 2.8 GPA. Minimum 2.8 GPA and a service requirement of 30 hours per year are required to retain scholarship. Awarded every year. Award may be used only at sponsoring institution.
Contact: Katherine Atkinson, Scholarship Coordinator.

2255   Council of Energy Resource Tribes Scholars Fund

Council of Energy Resource Tribes (CERT) Education Fund, Inc.
1999 Broadway, Suite 2600
Denver, CO 80202-5726
(303) 297-2378, (303) 296-5690 (fax)
Average award: $1,000
Minimum award: $500
Number of awards: 50
Deadline: January 30, July 15
College level: Freshman, Sophomore, Junior, Senior, Graduate, Doctoral
Majors/Fields: Business, engineering, environmental, natural resources, science
Criteria: Applicant must be a member of an American Indian tribe and must have successfully completed a high school summer transition program offered by CERT or a tribal internship program. Minimum 2.5 GPA is required to retain scholarship. Awarded every year.
Contact: Lesley Jackson, Education Director.

2256   Cultural Diversity Scholarship

The Evergreen State College
Olympia, WA 98505
(360) 866-6000
Average award: $2,256
Maximum number of awards: 28
Minimum number of awards: 20
Deadline: March 1
College level: Freshman, Sophomore, Junior, Senior
Criteria: Awarded to students enrolled at least half time who are from different ethnic backgrounds or diverse cultures. Reapplication is required for renewal. Awarded every year. Award may be used only at sponsoring institution.
Contact: Arnaldo Rodriguez, Dean of Enrollment Services, Library 1221, Olympia, WA 98505, (360) 866-6000 extension 6310.

2257   Davis Scholarship

University of Nebraska, Lincoln
14th and R Streets
Lincoln, NE 68588
(402) 472-2030, (402) 472-9826 (fax)
http://www.unl.edu/scholfa/cover.html
Average award: Comprehensive tuition
Number of awards: 10
Deadline: January 15
College level: Freshman
Criteria: Applicant must be an underrepresented minority from Nebraska. Scholarship is renewable. Awarded every year. Award may be used only at sponsoring institution.
Contact: Debra Augustyn, Assistant Director of Scholarships.

2258   Distinction Scholarship

Ohio State University–Columbus
Third Floor Lincoln Tower
1800 Cannon Drive
Columbus, OH 43210-1200
(614) 292-3980
Average award: Full in-state tuition, room, board, book allowance, and miscellaneous expenses
Deadline: December 4
College level: Freshman
Criteria: Applicant must graduate from a chartered Ohio high school, rank in the top 5% of class, have a minimum 3.75 GPA, and be African-American, Asian-American, Hispanic-American or Native American. If funding permits, out-of-state students will be considered. Scholarship is renewable. Awarded every year. Award may be used only at sponsoring institution.
Contact: Office of Minority Affairs, Columbus, OH 43210, (614) 292-0964.

2259   Diversity Award

Valparaiso University
Valparaiso, IN 46383-6493
(219) 464-5011, (219) 464-6898 (fax)
undergrad_admissions@valpo.edu
http:www.valpo.edu
Maximum award: $5,000
Deadline: May 1
College level: Freshman
Criteria: Applicant must be an American minority student with demonstrated academic promise and community contributions. Renewable for up to four years if minimum 3.0 GPA is maintained. Awarded every year. Award may be used only at sponsoring institution.
Contact: Office of Admissions and Financial Aid, Kretzman Hall, (888) GO VALPO.

2260   Diversity Scholarship

Oakland University
101 North Foundation Hall
Rochester, MI 48309-4401
(810) 370-3360, (810) 370-4462 (fax)
Average award: $2,500
Number of awards: 2
Deadline: February 1
College level: Freshman
Criteria: Minimum 2.5 GPA is required to retain scholarship. Awarded every year. Award may be used only at sponsoring institution.
Contact: Stacy M. Penkala, Assistant Director of Admissions.

2261   Ethnic Minority Continuing Student Scholarship/Ethnic Minority Scholarship

Shawnee State University
940 Second Street
Portsmouth, OH 45662-4344
(614) 355-2237
Average award: $2,750
Deadline: April 15
College level: Freshman, Sophomore, Junior, Senior
Criteria: Applicant must be a member of an ethnic minority. Selection is based upon creative endeavors (for freshmen), GPA, community and school/university involvement, and financial need. Awarded every year. Award may be used only at sponsoring institution.
Contact: Financial Aid Office, (614) 355-2485.

2262 Ethnic Student Scholarship

Taylor University
500 West Reade Avenue
Upland, IN 46989
(317) 998-5125, (317) 998-4910 (fax)
admissions@tayloru.edu
http://www.tayloru.edu
Maximum award: Half tuition
Minimum award: One-fourth tuition
Maximum number of awards: 10
Minimum number of awards: 5
Deadline: March 15
College level: Freshman, Sophomore, Junior, Senior
Criteria: Applicant must be either African-American, Hispanic, Asian-American, or Native American. Renewable for up to eight semesters if recipient maintains satisfactory academic progress. Awarded every year. Award may be used only at sponsoring institution.
Contact: Felicia Case, Ethnic Student Recruiter, (317) 998-5563, flcase@tayloru.edu.

2263 Excellence Scholarship

Ohio State University–Columbus
Third Floor Lincoln Tower
1800 Cannon Drive
Columbus, OH 43210-1200
(614) 292-3980
Average award: Full in-state tuition
Deadline: December 4
College level: Freshman
Criteria: Applicant must rank in the top fifth of class, graduate from a chartered Ohio high school, have a minimum 3.0 GPA, and be an African-American, Asian-American, Hispanic-American or Native American. If funding permits, out-of-state applicants will be considered. Scholarship is renewable. Awarded every year. Award may be used only at sponsoring institution.
Contact: Office of Minority Affairs, Columbus, OH 43210, (614) 292-0964.

2264 Finlandia Foundation Trust Scholarship Exchange Program and Grants

Finlandia Foundation Trust
P.O. Box 2590
Grand Central Station
New York, NY 10163
Maximum award: $5,000
Maximum number of awards: 40
Minimum number of awards: 40
Deadline: February 15
Majors/Fields: Finnish studies
Criteria: Applicant must be a U.S. or Finnish college student. Recipient must reapply to retain scholarship.
Contact: Grants.

2265 First People's Scholarship

The Evergreen State College
Olympia, WA 98505
(360) 866-6000
Average award: $2,256
Number of awards: 4
Deadline: March 1
College level: Freshman, Transfer
Criteria: Applicant must be a new, full-time, undergraduate student, demonstrate academic achievement, leadership in community service, or talent in a particular area, and be either African-American, Asian, Hispanic/Latino, or Native American. Awarded every year. Award may be used only at sponsoring institution.
Contact: Arnaldo Rodriguez, Dean of Enrollment Services, Library 1221, Olympia, WA 98505, (360) 866-6000, extension 6310.

2266 Fisher/Meredith Merit Scholarship

Denison University
Box H
Granville, OH 43023
(614) 587-6276, 800-DENISON, (614) 587-6306 (fax)
admissions@denison.edu
http://www.denison.edu
Average award: $6,000
Number of awards: 30
Deadline: January 1
College level: Freshman
Criteria: Applicant must be African-American and have a strong academic record. Minimum 2.5 GPA is required for renewal. Awarded every year. Award may be used only at sponsoring institution.
Contact: Scholarships.

2267 Frank De Pietro Memorial Scholarship

National Italian American Foundation (NIAF)
Educational Scholarship Program
1860 19th Street, NW
Washington, DC 20009-5599
(202) 530-5315
Maximum award: $14,000
Number of awards: 3
Deadline: May 31
College level: Freshman, Sophomore, Junior, Senior
Criteria: Applicant must demonstrate financial need, submit a transcript, and have a letter of acceptance from Harvey Mudd College of California. Preference given to Italian-American applicants. Awarded every year. Award may be used only at Harvey Mudd College.
Contact: Dr. Maria Lombardo, Education Director.

2268 George C. Brooks Scholarship

University of Missouri–Columbia
High School and Transfer Relations
219 Jesse Hall
Columbia, MO 65211
(800) 225-6075 (in-state), (314) 882-2456
http://www.missouri.edu
Maximum award: $8,500 plus out-of-state tuition
Number of awards: 136
Deadline: March 1
College level: Freshman
Criteria: Applicant must be a minority, have a high composite ACT score, and participate in the Minority Achievement Program. Minimum 2.5 GPA for 24 hours of graded course work is required to retain scholarship. Awarded every year. Award may be used only at sponsoring institution.
Contact: High School and Transfer Relations.

2269 George L. Graziadio Fellowship for Business

National Italian American Foundation (NIAF)
Educational Scholarship Program
1860 19th Street, NW
Washington, DC 20009-5599
(202) 530-5315
Average award: $2,500
Number of awards: 2
Deadline: May 31
College level: Freshman, Sophomore, Junior, Senior
Criteria: Applicant must be an Italian-American, demonstrate need, and submit a transcript. Applicant must have a letter of acceptance from the George L. Graziadio School of Business and Management at Pepperdine University. Awarded every year. Award may be used only at Pepperdine University.
Contact: Dr. Maria Lombardo, Education Director.

2270 **GTE Minority Traditional Student Scholarship/ GTE Minority Nontraditional Student Scholarship**

Shawnee State University
940 Second Street
Portsmouth, OH 45662-4344
(614) 355-2237
Average award: $2,750
Deadline: April 15; early application is recommended
College level: Freshman, Entering student
Criteria: Applicant must be a member of a minority and demonstrate financial need. Nontraditional applicant must have been out of school at least one year. Selection is based upon creative endeavors, grades, and school and community involvement (freshman applicant); upon potential for community and school involvement and creative endeavors (nontraditional applicant). Awarded every year. Award may be used only at sponsoring institution.
Contact: Financial Aid Office, (614) 355-2485.

2271 **Hanna and Brianna Yellowthunder Scholarship**

American Indian Studies Center
University of California–Los Angeles
Box 951548
Los Angeles, CA 90095-1548
(310) 825-7315, (310) 206-7060 (fax)
alsc@ucla.edu
http://www.sscnet.ucla.edu/indian
Average award: $2,000
Minimum award: $1,250
Number of awards: 3
Deadline: May 23
College level: Junior, Senior
Majors/Fields: Social sciences
Criteria: Applicant must be of American Indian decent. Recipient must reapply for renewal. Awarded every year. Award may be used only at U of California at Los Angeles.
Contact: Dwight Youpee, Student Affairs Officer, 3220 Campbell Hall, (310) 206-7511, dyoudee@ucla.edu.

2272 **Helen Faison Scholarship**

University of Pittsburgh, Pittsburgh Campus
4200 Fifth Avenue
Pittsburgh, PA 15260
(412) 624-4141
http://www.pitt.edu/~oafa/oafa.html
Maximum award: $19,558
Number of awards: 5
Deadline: January 15
College level: Freshman
Criteria: Applicant must be a minority student. Selection is based upon high school performance and test scores. Minimum 3.0 GPA is required to retain scholarship. Awarded every year. Award may be used only at sponsoring institution.
Contact: Betsy A. Porter, Director of Admissions and Financial Aid, Office of Admissions & Financial Aid, Bruce Hall, Pittsburgh, PA 15260, (412) 624-7164.

2273 **Herbert Lehman Scholarship**

Herbert Lehman Education Fund
99 Hudson Street
Suite 1600
New York, NY 10013
(212) 219-1900, extension 511
Maximum award: $1,400
Maximum number of awards: 60
Minimum number of awards: 50
Deadline: April 15
College level: Freshman
Criteria: Selection is based upon outstanding leadership potential and evidence of community service. Applicant must be an African-American U.S. citizen who is entering a college or university that has an enrollment of African-American undergraduates that is less than eight percent of the total undergraduate enrollment. Preference is given to students planning to attend a southern school that was at one time segregated. Good academic standing and full-time enrollment are required to retain scholarship. Awarded every year.
Contact: G. Michael Bagley, Executive Director.

2274 **Heritage Scholarship**

Centre College
600 West Walnut Street
Danville, KY 40422
(606) 238-5350, (606) 238-5373 (fax)
admission@centre.edu
http://www.centre.edu
Average award: $5,000
Maximum award: $7,500
Minimum award: $3,500
Deadline: February 1
College level: Freshman
Criteria: Applicant must be a minority student. Interview is required. Renewable if recipient maintains good academic standing and minimum 2.5 GPA. Awarded every year. Award may be used only at sponsoring institution.
Contact: Thomas B. Martin, Dean of Enrollment Management.

2275 **Heritage Scholarship**

Lawrence University
P.O. Box 599
Appleton, WI 54912-0599
(414) 832-6500, (414) 832-6782 (fax)
excel@lawrence.edu
http://www.lawrence.edu
Average award: $3,000
Maximum award: $5,000
Minimum award: $2,500
Deadline: February 1
College level: Freshman
Criteria: Applicant must be a member of an underrepresented population and demonstrate commitment to ethnic/cultural heritage. Recipient must maintain good academic standing to retain scholarship. Awarded every year. Award may be used only at sponsoring institution.
Contact: Director of Admissions.

2276 **Hispanic Alumni and Friends Scholarship**

California State University, Dominguez Hills
1000 East Victoria Street
Carson, CA 90747
(310) 516-3647
Maximum Award: Full fees
Number of awards: 3
Deadline: April 14
College level: Freshman, Sophomore, Junior, Senior, Graduate
Criteria: Applicant must have at least one natural parent of Central American, Chicano, Cuban, Puerto Rican, or South American heritage, be enrolled full time or accepted for admission, demonstrate community and school involvement, and have a minimum 2.7 GPA (high school/undergraduate) or 3.0 GPA (graduate student). Awarded every year. Award may be used only at sponsoring institution.
Contact: Financial Aid Office.

2277 **Hispanic Scholarship Program**

University of Central Florida
Undergraduate Admissions
P.O. Box 160111
Orlando, FL 32816-0111
(407) 823-3000, (407) 823-3419 (fax)
http://www.ucf.edu
Average award: $3,000
Maximum award: $4,000
Number of awards: 18
Deadline: March 15
College level: Freshman
Criteria: Applicant must be a finalist ($4,000 award) or semifinalist ($3,000 award) in the National Hispanic Scholarship Program. Minimum 3.0 GPA and full-time status required to retain scholarship. Awarded every year. Award may be used only at sponsoring institution.
Contact: Susan McKinnon, Assistant Director, Office of Recruitment, Orlando, FL 32816, (407) 823-5439.

2278 Hia Scholarship

Denison University
Box H
Granville, OH 43023
(614) 587-6276, 800-DENISON, (614) 587-6306 (fax)
admissions@denison.edu
http://www.denison.edu
Average award: $6,000
Number of awards: 30
Deadline: January 1
College level: Freshman
Criteria: Applicant must be of Asian, Hispanic, and/or Native American heritage and have a strong academic record. Minimum 2.5 GPA is required for renewal. Awarded every year. Award may be used only at sponsoring institution.
Contact: Scholarships.

2279 Ibero-PYRD Scholarship

Rochester Institute of Technology
One Lomb Memorial Drive
Rochester, NY 14623
(716) 475-2186
Average award: $2,500
Number of awards: 15
Deadline: February 15
College level: Freshman
Criteria: Applicant must be a Hispanic student. Selection is based upon academic qualifications, leadership ability, and demonstrated financial need. Satisfactory academic progress is required to retain scholarship. Awarded every year. Award may be used only at sponsoring institution.
Contact: Verna Hazen, Director of Financial Aid.

2280 Incentive Scholarship and Grant for Native Americans

University of North Carolina General Administration
Box 2688
Chapel Hill, NC 27515-2688
(919) 962-0008 (fax)
Maximum award: $5,000
Deadline: None
College level: Freshman, Sophomore, Junior, Senior, Graduate, Doctoral
Criteria: Applicant must be a North Carolina resident, a member of an Indian tribe recognized by the state or federal government, demonstrate financial need, and be enrolled at one of the U of North Carolina constituent institutions. Good academic standing and continued financial need are required to retain scholarship. Awarded every year. Award may be used only at sponsoring institution.
Contact: Financial Aid Office at Eligible School.

2281 Indian Scholarship

North Dakota State Board for Indian Scholarships
State Capitol Building
Bismark, ND 58505
(701) 328-2166, (701) 328-2961 (fax)
Average award: $700
Maximum award: $2,000
Maximum number of awards: 150
Minimum number of awards: 120
Deadline: July 15
College level: Freshman, Sophomore, Junior, Senior, Graduate, Doctoral
Criteria: Applicant must be a Native American North Dakota resident. Reapplication and submission of transcript and budget required to retain scholarship. Awarded every year. Award may be used only at North Dakota schools.
Contact: Rhonda Schauer, Coordinator.

2282 Ingolia Family Scholarship

National Italian American Foundation (NIAF)
Educational Scholarship Program
1860 19th Street, NW
Washington, DC 20009-5599
(202) 530-5315
Average award: $2,000
Number of awards: 1
Deadline: May 31
College level: Freshman, Sophomore, Junior, Senior, Graduate, Doctoral
Majors/Fields: Journalism, media
Criteria: Applicant must be Italian-American, demonstrate financial need, and submit transcript. Awarded every year.
Contact: Dr. Maria Lombardo, Education Director.

2283 Interco Scholarship

University of Missouri–St. Louis
8001 Natural Bridge Road
St. Louis, MO 63121
(314) 553-6396
Average award: $2,500
Number of awards: 9
Deadline: April 1
College level: Freshman
Criteria: Applicant must be a minority student, be enrolled full time for at least 12 credit hours per semester, and demonstrate high academic achievement in high school. Scholarship is renewable. Awarded when funds are available. Award may be used only at sponsoring institution.
Contact: James D. Reed, Financial Aid Advisor.

2284 James M. and Aune P. Nelson Minority Student Grant

Southern Illinois University at Edwardsville
Box 1060
Edwardsville, IL 62026-1060
(618) 692-3880, (618) 692-3885 (fax)
finaid@siue.edu
http://www.finaid.siue.edu
Maximum award: $2,465
Maximum number of awards: 6
Minimum number of awards: 1
Deadline: March 1 (priority)
College level: Freshman, Sophomore, Junior, Senior
Criteria: Applicant must be African-American, Native American, or Hispanic, a graduate of an Alton school, have a minimum 2.000 high school GPA and 2.500 college GPA, be enrolled full-time, and be pursuing a degree program. FAFSA is required. Recipient must reapply for renewal. Awarded every year. Award may be used only at sponsoring institution.
Contact: Client Service Unit, Student Financial Aid, finaid@siue.edu.

2285 JFCS Student Scholarship

Jewish Family and Children's Services (JFCS)
1600 Scott Street
San Francisco, CA 94115
(415) 561-1226, (415) 922-5938 (fax)
Average award: $2,500
Maximum award: $5,000
Minimum award: $500
Number of awards: 40
College level: Freshman, Sophomore, Junior, Senior, Graduate, Doctoral
Criteria: Applicant must be Jewish, be accepted for enrollment at a college, university, or vocational school, demonstrate academic achievement (usually a minimum 3.0 GPA) and financial need, and be a resident of San Francisco, the Peninsula, or Marin or Sonoma county, Calif. Awarded every year.
Contact: Ted Schreiber, Loans and Grants Director.

2286 Joe Tangaro Athletic Scholarship

National Italian American Foundation (NIAF)
Educational Scholarship Program
1860 19th Street, NW
Washington, DC 20009-5599
(202) 530-5315
Average award: $2,500
Number of awards: 1
Deadline: May 31
College level: Freshman
Criteria: Applicant must be an Italian-American, excel in athletics, demonstrate financial need, and submit a transcript. Applicant must attend a St. Louis, Mo. high school and submit a letter of recommendation form a school official along with a a personal letter of request. Awarded every year.
Contact: Dr. Maria Lombardo, Education Director.

2287 John B. Ervin Scholarship for Black Americans

Washington University
One Brookings Drive
Campus Box 1089
St. Louis, MO 63130
(314) 935-6000 or (800) 638-0700
Average award: Full tuition plus $2,500 stipend
Number of awards: 10
Deadline: January 15
College level: Freshman
Criteria: Applicant must be a black American. Selection is based upon academic merit without regard to financial need. Satisfactory academic performance is required to retain scholarship. Awarded every year. Award may be used only at sponsoring institution.
Contact: Office of Undergraduate Admissions.

2288 John D. Ishii Scholarship

Saint Martin's College
5300 Pacific Avenue, SE
Lacey, WA 98503
(360) 438-4397
Average award: $2,250
Number of awards: 7
Deadline: August 1
College level: Freshman, Sophomore, Junior, Senior
Criteria: Awarded to minority applicants with academic promise and financial need. Minimum 3.0 GPA is required to retain scholarship. Awarded every year. Award may be used only at sponsoring institution.
Contact: Ron Noborikawa, Director of Financial Aid.

2289 John Newton Templeton Scholarship

Ohio University
Office of Student Financial Aid and Scholarships
Athens, OH 45701
(614) 593-4141, (614) 593-4140 (fax)
Award: In-state tuition
Number of awards: 10
Deadline: February 15
College level: Freshman
Criteria: Applicant must be a minority student. Selection is based upon academic qualifications, talents, and leadership. Minimum 3.3 GPA and 16 credit hours per quarter are required to retain scholarship. Awarded every year. Award may be used only at sponsoring institution.
Contact: Mrs. Yang-Hi Kim, Associate Director of Scholarships and Grants.

2290 Johnetta Haley Scholarship

Southern Illinois University at Edwardsville
Box 1060
Edwardsville, IL 62026-1060
(618) 692-3880, (618) 692-3885 (fax)
finaid@siue.edu
http://www.finaid.siue.edu
Maximum award: $2,465
Number of awards: 100
Deadline: March 1 (priority)
College level: Freshman, Sophomore, Junior, Senior
Majors/Fields: Computer science, engineering, nursing, sciences, teaching
Criteria: Applicant must be African-American, Asian-American, Hispanic-American, or Native American. Recipient must reapply for renewal. Awarded every year. Award may be used only at sponsoring institution.
Contact: Client Service Unit, Student Financial Aid, finaid@siue.edu.

2291 Lancelot C. A. Thompson Minority Scholarship

University of Toledo
Financial Aid Office
Toledo, OH 43606-3390
(419) 537-2056
Average award: $3,000
Number of awards: 10
Deadline: January 28
College level: Freshman
Criteria: Applicant must be a minority student. Selection is based upon academic achievement, test scores, recommendations, essay, leadership, and citizenship. Award is for four years. Awarded every year. Award may be used only at sponsoring institution.
Contact: Coordinator of Minority Admissions, Office of Admissions Services, Toledo, OH 43606, (419) 537-2073.

2292 Lavelle Scholarship

University of Pittsburgh, Pittsburgh Campus
4200 Fifth Avenue
Pittsburgh, PA 15260
(412) 624-4141
http://www.pitt.edu/-oafa/oafa.html
Maximum award: $18,716
Number of awards: 1
Deadline: January 15
College level: Freshman
Majors/Fields: Business administration
Criteria: Applicant must be a minority student enrolled in the College of Business Administration. Selection is based upon high school performance and test scores. Minimum 3.0 GPA is required to retain scholarship. Awarded every year. Award may be used only at sponsoring institution.
Contact: Betsy A. Porter, Director of Admissions and Financial Aid, Office of Admissions & Financial Aid, Bruce Hall, Pittsburgh, PA 15260, (412) 624-7164.

2293 Lincoln Family Scholarship

California State University, Dominguez Hills
1000 East Victoria Street
Carson, CA 90747
(310) 516-3647
Award: Full fees for one semester
Number of awards: 1
Deadline: April 7
College level: Sophomore, Junior, Senior
Criteria: Applicant must have at least one biological parent of African-American heritage, be a full-time undergraduate, have a minimum 2.0 GPA, and demonstrate community and school involvement. Awarded every year. Award may be used only at sponsoring institution.
Contact: Scholarships.

2294 Mellon Fellow Minority Scholarship

City University of New York, Queens College
65-30 Kissena Boulevard
Flushing, NY 11367
(718) 997-5000
Average award: $4,000
Maximum award: $6,000
Minimum award: $3,000
Number of awards: 5
College level: Junior, Senior
Criteria: Applicant must be commited to apply for full-time Ph.D. study after graduation from college. Excellent academic record must be maintained to retain scholarship. Awarded every year. Award may be used only at sponsoring institution.
Contact: Elaine P. Maimon, Dean, (718) 520-7762.

2295 MESBEC Scholarships

Native American Scholarship Fund, Inc.
8200 Mountain Road, NE
Suite 203
Albuquerque, NM 87110
(505) 262-2351
nasfi@aol.com
Maximum award: $5,000
Maximum number of awards: 200
Minimum number of awards: 145
Deadline: September 15 (spring); March 15 (summer); April 15 (fall)
College level: Freshman, Sophomore, Junior, Senior, Graduate, Doctoral
Majors/Fields: Business, computers, education, engineering, fine arts, humanities, mathematics, science, social science
Criteria: Applicant must be at least one-quarter Native American and be an enrolled member of a U.S. tribe that is federally recognized, state recognized, or terminated. Applicant must have a high GPA and test scores and be enrolled in a college or university seeking a baccalaureate degree, master's degree, or doctoral degree. Renewable if student maintains respectable GPA. Awarded every year.
Contact: Lucille Kelley, Director of Recruitment.

2296 Mexican-American Alumni Association Scholarship

University of Southern California
University Park
Los Angeles, CA 90089-5012
(213) 740-1111
Maximum award: $4,500
Number of awards: 250
Deadline: June 30
College level: Freshman, Sophomore, Junior, Senior
Criteria: Applicant must be Hispanic. Selection is based upon academic achievement and eligibility for financial aid. Special application and financial aid application, including FAFSA, are required. Awarded every year. Award may be used only at sponsoring institution.
Contact: Mexican-American Programs Office, Student Union 203, Los Angeles, CA 90089-4890, (213) 740-4735.

2297 Minority Academically Talented Scholarship

University of Central Florida
Undergraduate Admissions
P.O. Box 160111
Orlando, FL 32816-0111
(407) 823-3000, (407) 823-3419 (fax)
http://www.ucf.edu
Maximum award: $3,000
Number of awards: 150
Deadline: March 15
College level: Freshman
Criteria: Applicant must be a minority student. Selection is based upon high school course work, weighted GPA, and SAT I or ACT scores. Minimum 2.5 GPA and full-time status are required to retain scholarship. Awarded every year. Award may be used only at sponsoring institution.
Contact: Susan McKinnon, Assistant Director, Office of Recruitment, Orlando, FL 323816, (407) 823-5439.

2298 Minority Achievement Award

Mount Union College
1972 Clark Avenue
Alliance, OH 44601
(216) 821-5320
Maximum award: Half tuition
Deadline: None
College level: Freshman
Criteria: Applicant must be African-American, American Indian, Asian-American, or Hispanic, a first-time, full-time student, and rank in top fifth of class. Selection is based upon essay competition and merit. Awarded every year. Award may be used only at sponsoring institution.
Contact: Office of Admissions.

2299 Minority Advertising Intern Program

American Association of Advertising Agencies
405 Lexington Avenue
18th Floor
New York, NY 10174-1801
(212) 850-0732, (212) 573-8968 (fax)
Average award: $3,000
Number of awards: 36
Deadline: January 30
Majors/Fields: Advertising, communications, liberal arts, marketing
Criteria: Applicant must be a minority U.S. citizen or permanent resident currently enrolled in an undergraduate or graduate program and have completed at least junior year. Minimum 3.0 GPA required. Selection is based upon application information, letters of recommendation, school transcripts, and supporting materials. Awarded every year.
Contact: Minority Advertising Intern Program.

2300 Minority Educational Achievement Award (MEAA)

Florida Atlantic University
500 N.W. 20th Street
P.O. Box 3091
Boca Raton, FL 334310991
(407) 367-3000
Average award: Full tuition
Deadline: None
College level: Incoming junior transfer
Criteria: Applicant must be a minority student, have a minimum 3.0 GPA, be a U.S. citizen or permanent resident alien, and be transferring from a community college. Renewable for up to five semesters if minimum 2.5 GPA and full-time enrollment are maintained. Awarded every year. Award may be used only at sponsoring institution.
Contact: Student Financial Aid Office.

2301 Minority Educational Opportunity Tuition Award

Northern Kentucky University
Administrative Center 416
Nunn Drive
Highland Heights, KY 41099-7101
(606) 572-5144
Average award: Full tuition
Deadline: February 1
College level: Freshman
Criteria: Applicant must be a minority U.S. citizen or permanent resident. Scholarship is renewable. Awarded every year. Award may be used only at sponsoring institution.
Contact: Robert E. Sprague, Director of Financial Aid.

2302   Minority Incentive Award

Kent State University
P.O. Box 5190
Kent, OH 44242-0001
(216) 672-2972
Maximum award: $3,000
Deadline: April 1
College level: Junior
Criteria: Applicant must be a minority transfer student admitted with junior status. Selection is based upon academic record. Satisfactory academic progress and full-time enrollment are required to retain scholarship for up to four semesters. Awarded every year. Award may be used only at sponsoring institution.
Contact: Theodore Hallenbeck, Director of Financial Aid, 103 Michael Schwartz Center.

2303   Minority Scholar Award

Washington State University
Office of Scholarship Services
Pullman, WA 99164-1728
(509) 335-1059
Average award: $2,000
Maximum award: $3,000
Minimum award: $1,500
Number of awards: 100
Deadline: February 15
College level: Freshman, Transfer
Criteria: Applicant must be a Native American, Alaskan Native, Asian or Pacific Islander, African-American, or Hispanic-American, a U.S. citizen or permanent resident, and have a minimum 3.0 GPA. Financial need is not considered. Scholarship is renewable. Awarded every year. Award may be used only at sponsoring institution.
Contact: Johanna H. Davis, Assistant Director.

2304   Minority Scholarship

University of Memphis
Scates Hall 204
Memphis, TN 38152
(901) 678-3213, (901) 678-5621 (fax)
katkinsn@cc.memphis.edu
http://www.memphis.edu/
Maximum award: $2,580
Deadline: March 1
College level: Freshman
Criteria: Applicant must be an African-American Tennessee resident. Selection is based upon test scores and high school record. Minimum composite ACT score of 20 (combined SAT I score of 930) and 3.0 GPA are recommended. Minimum 2.8 GPA and a service requirement of 30 hours per semester are required to retain scholarship. Awarded every year. Award may be used only at sponsoring institution.
Contact: Katherine Atkinson, Scholarship Coordinator.

2305   Minority Scholarship

Saint Vincent College
Admissions and Financial Aid
Latrobe, PA 15650-2690
(412) 537-4540, (412) 537-4554 (fax)
info@stvincent.edu
http://www.stvincent.edu
Average award: $5,000
Number of awards: 2
Deadline: March 1
College level: Freshman
Criteria: Applicant must be a minority student, have a minimum 3.0 high school GPA, and be accepted for admission. Letters of recommenation are encouraged. Renewable if recipient maintains GPA. Awarded every year. Award may be used only at sponsoring institution.
Contact: Rev. Earl Henry, O.S.B., Dean of Admission and Financial Aid, 300 Fraser Purchase Road, Latrobe, PA 15650.

2306   Minority Scholarship

Wilmington College
Pyle Center Box 1325
Wilmington, OH 45177
(800) 341-9318, (513) 382-7077 (fax)
admission@wilmington.edu
http://www.wilmington.edu
Average award: $5,000
Number of awards: 30
Deadline: May 1
College level: Freshman
Criteria: Applicant must be a member of a minority, have a minimum 2.5 GPA, rank in top half of class, and demonstrate financial need. Scholarship is renewable. Awarded every year. Award may be used only at sponsoring institution.
Contact: Financial Aid Office.

2307   Minority Student Scholarship

DePaul University
1 East Jackson Boulevard
Chicago, IL 60604
(312) 362-8704, (312) 362-5749 (fax)
Average award: $4,000
Maximum award: $8,000
Minimum award: $2,000
Number of awards: 40
Deadline: None
College level: Freshman
Criteria: Applicant must be African-American, Hispanic, Asian/Pacific Islander, or American Indian, have a minimum 3.0 GPA, rank in top quarter of class, and have a minimum composite ACT score of 24. Scholarship is renewable. Awarded every year. Award may be used only at sponsoring institution.
Contact: Jennifer Sparrow, Scholarship Coordinator, jsparrow@wppost.depaul.edu.

2308   Minority Students' Scholarship

Roberts Wesleyan College
2301 Westside Drive
Rochester, NY 14624-1997
(716) 594-6422
Maximum award: $2,500
Deadline: None
College level: Freshman
Criteria: Applicant must be a minority student, a U.S. citizen or permanent resident, be enrolled full-time, have a minimum 2.5 GPA, exhibit academic achievement and leadership qualities, and demonstrate financial need. Awarded every year. Award may be used only at sponsoring institution.
Contact: Brian P. Madden, Assistant Director of Financial Aid, (716) 594-6150.

2309   Minority Teachers of Illinois Scholarship

Illinois Student Assistance Commission/Client
Support Services
1755 Lake Cook Road
Deerfield, IL 60015-5209
(800) 899-ISAC, (708) 948-8500
Average award: $4,068
Maximum award: $5,000
Minimum award: $1,458
Number of awards: 38
Deadline: September 15
College level: Sophomore, Junior, Senior
Majors/Fields: Education
Criteria: Applicant must be a minority student of African-American, Hispanic, Asian-American or Native American origin. Applicant must be enrolled in a teacher education program or curriculum leading to initial teacher certification at a qualified Illinois institution of higher education. Recipient must sign a promissory note agreeing to fulfill teaching commitment or repay the scholarship with interest. Scholarship is renewable. Awarded every year.
Contact: Manager of Scholarships and Specialized Grants.

2310 Minority Teachers' Scholarship

Arkansas Department of Higher Education
114 East Capitol
Little Rock, AR 72201
(501) 324-9300
Maximum award: $5,000
Deadline: June 1
College level: Senior
Majors/Fields: Education
Criteria: Applicant must be an African-American resident of Arkansas and have a minimum 2.5 GPA. Applicants must be prepared to teach full-time in an Arkansas public school for 5 years following graduation or pay back the loan. Scholarship is renewable. Award may be used only at approved Arkansas schools.
Contact: Assistant Coordinator of Student Financial Aid.

2311 Minority Transfer Scholarship

Rochester Institute of Technology
One Lomb Memorial Drive
Rochester, NY 14623
(716) 475-2186
Average award: $2,500
Number of awards: 15
Deadline: February 15
College level: Transfer
Criteria: Applicant must be an African-American, Hispanic-American, or Native American student. Selection is based upon academic qualifications, leadership ability, and demonstrated financial need. Satisfactory academic progress is required to retain scholarship. Awarded every year. Award may be used only at sponsoring institution.
Contact: Verna Hazen, Director of Financial Aid.

2312 Missouri Minority Teacher Education Scholarship

Missouri Department of Elementary and Secondary Education
P.O. Box 480
Jefferson City, MO 65102
(573) 751-1668
Average award: $3,000
Number of awards: 30
Deadline: March 1
College level: Freshman, Sophomore, Junior, Senior, Graduate, Doctoral, nontraditional minority students
Majors/Fields: Education
Criteria: Applicant must be a Missouri resident, African-American, Asian-American, Hispanic-American or Native American, rank in the top quarter of high school class, score at or above the 75th percentile on the ACT or SAT, or have 30 college hours with a minimum 3.0 GPA. Applicant must agree to teach in the Missouri public schools (PreK-12) for five years after graduation. Recipient must remain in good standing with the college for renewal. Awarded every year.
Contact: Janet Goeller, Director of Teacher Recruitment & Retention.

2313 Morrison Center MSW Minority Scholarship

Portland State University
Financial Aid Department
P.O. Box 751
Portland, OR 97207-0751
(503) 725-5270
Average award: $6,000
Number of awards: 1
Majors/Fields: Social work
Criteria: Applicant must be a minority student entering the second year of MSW program. Scholarship is renewable. Awarded every year. Award may be used only at sponsoring institution.
Contact: Scholarships, Graduate School of Social Work, (503) 725-4712.

2314 Multicultural Merit Award

Ohio Wesleyan University
Office of Admissions
Delaware, OH 43015
(614) 368-3020, (614) 368-3314 (fax)
owuadmit@cc.owu.edu
http://www.owu.edu
Average award: $14,355
Maximum award: $19,140
Minimum award: $5,000
Number of awards: 30
Deadline: March 1
College level: Freshman, Sophomore, Junior, Senior, Transfer
Criteria: Applicant must be African-American, Asian-American, Hispanic/Latino, or Native American, have a minimum 3.5 GPA, and have a minimum composite ACT score of 19. U.S. permanent residents may be considered for award. Minimum 3.0 GPA is required to retain scholarships of $5,000-$10,000. Minimum 3.3 GPA is required to retain scholarships of $10,000-$19,140. Awarded every year. Award may be used only at sponsoring institution.
Contact: Karen M. Fasheun, Director of Multicultural Enrollment.

2315 National Hispanic Scholarship

University of Toledo
Financial Aid Office
Toledo, OH 43606-3390
(419) 537-2056
Average award: Comprehensive tuition
Deadline: January 28
College level: Freshman
Criteria: Applicant must be a National Hispanic finalist. Award is for four years. Awarded every year. Award may be used only at sponsoring institution.
Contact: Coordinator of Admissions Services for Scholars, Office of Admissions Services, Toledo, OH 43606, (419) 537-2073.

2316 NationsBank-Greenville Urban League Scholarship

Clemson University
G-01 Sikes Hall
Clemson, SC 29634-5123
(803) 656-2280
Average award: $2,500
Number of awards: 2
Deadline: March 1
College level: Freshman
Majors/Fields: Commerce/industry, computer science, liberal arts, mathematical sciences
Criteria: Applicant must be a minority student, a Greenville County, S.C., resident, have a minimum 2.0 GPA, enroll in College of Commerce and Industry, Liberal Arts, or Sciences, and demonstrate financial need. Minimum 2.7 GPA and completion of at least 12 credit hours per semester are required to retain scholarship. Awarded every year. Award may be used only at sponsoring institution.
Contact: Marvin Carmichael, Director of Financial Aid.

2317 NCR Annual Engineering Scholarship

Clemson University
G-01 Sikes Hall
Clemson, SC 29634-5123
(803) 656-2280
Average award: $2,500
Number of awards: 3
Deadline: March 1
College level: Freshman
Majors/Fields: Computer engineering, computer science, electrical engineering, engineering
Criteria: Applicant must be a black student with a minimum 3.0 GPA; preference is given to applicants intending to major in electrical engineering or computer engineering. Renewable for up to four years if recipient maintains a minimum 3.0 GPA. Awarded every year. Award may be used only at sponsoring institution.
Contact: Marvin Carmichael, Director of Financial Aid.

2318   NIAF/Pepperdine University Scholarship

National Italian American Foundation (NIAF)
Educational Scholarship Program
1860 19th Street, NW
Washington, DC 20009-5599
(202) 530-5315
Average award: $2,000
Number of awards: 1
Deadline: May 31
College level: Sophomore, Junior, Senior, Graduate
Criteria: Applicant must be an Italian-American, demonstrate financial need, and submit a transcript. Applicant must be accepted to the International Program at Pepperdine University. Awarded every year. Award may be used only at Pepperdine University.
Contact: Dr. Maria Lombardo, Education Director.

2319   NIAF/Sacred Heart University Matching Scholarship

National Italian American Foundation (NIAF)
Educational Scholarship Program
1860 19th Street, NW
Washington, DC 20009-5599
(202) 530-5315
Maximum award: $2,000
Deadline: May 31
College level: Freshman, Sophomore, Junior, Senior
Criteria: Applicant must be an Italian-American, demonstrate financial need, and submit a transcript. Award may be used only at Sacred Heart University.
Contact: Dr. Maria Lombardo, Education Director.

2320   Nicaraguan and Haitian Scholarship

Florida Department of Education
Office of Student Financial Assistance
255 Collins
Tallahassee, FL 32399-0400
(904) 487-0049
Average award: $4,000
Maximum award: $5,000
Number of awards: 2
Deadline: July 1
College level: Freshman, Sophomore, Junior, Senior, Graduate
Criteria: Applicant must be a Nicaraguan or Haitian citizen (or have been born there) now living in Florida, have a minimum 3.0 GPA ,and demonstrate community service. Applicant must enroll at a State University System institution for a minimum of 12 credit hours of undergraduate study or 9 credit hours of graduate study. Recipient must reapply for renewal. Awarded every year.
Contact: Office of Student Financial Assistance.

2321   Norman R. Peterson Scholarhip

National Italian American Foundation (NIAF)
Educational Scholarship Program
1860 19th Street, NW
Washington, DC 20009-5599
(202) 530-5315
Maximum award: $7,500
Number of awards: 2
Deadline: May 31
College level: Sophomore, Junior, Senior
Majors/Fields: Business
Criteria: Applicant must be Italian-American, demonstrate financial need, submit transcript, and be a U.S. citizen living in the midwest. First preference is for a resident of Michigan. Applicant also must attend the John Cabot University in Rome. Awarded every year. John Cabot University only.
Contact: Dr. Maria Lombardo, Education Director.

2322   NSA Undergraduate Training Program

National Security Agency (NSA)
M322 (UTP)
Ft. Meade, MD 20755-6000
(800) 962-9398
Average award: Full tuition
Deadline: November 10
College level: Freshman
Majors/Fields: Asian languages, computer science, computer engineering, electrical engineering, mathematics, Middle Eastern languages, Slavic languages
Criteria: Applicant must be a U.S. citizen, have a minimum combined SAT I score of 1000 (composite ACT score of 24), a minimum 3.0 GPA, and leadership abilities, and have participated in extracurricular activities. Minorities are encouraged to apply. Scholarship is renewable. Awarded every year.
Contact: NSA Training Program.

2323   O. Mike Marinelli Scholarship

National Italian American Foundation (NIAF)
Educational Scholarship Program
1860 19th Street, NW
Washington, DC 20009-5599
(202) 530-5315
Average award: $2,000
Number of awards: 1
Deadline: May 31
College level: Freshman, Sophomore, Junior, Senior
Criteria: Applicant must be Italian-American, demonstrate financial need, and submit transcript. Awarded every year. Award may be used only at NOVA University.
Contact: Dr. Maria Lombardo, Education Director.

2324   Opportunity at Iowa Scholarship

University of Iowa
208 Calvin Hall
Iowa City, IA 52242
(319) 335-1450, (319) 335-3060 (fax)
http://www.uiowa.edu/~finaid
Maximum award: $5,000
Number of awards: 50
College level: Freshman
Criteria: Applicant must be a minority student, rank in the top three-tenths of class, and have a minimum composite ACT score of 25. Minimum 3.0 cumulative GPA is required to retain scholarship. Awarded every year. Award may be used only at sponsoring institution.
Contact: Mark Warner, Director of Financial Aid, mark-warner@uiowa.edu.

2325   Oscar Ritchie Memorial Scholarship

Kent State University
P.O. Box 5190
Kent, OH 44242-0001
(216) 672-2972
Average award: Full tuition
Deadline: April 1
College level: Freshman
Criteria: Applicant must be an academically talented minority student. Selection is based upon academic record, competitive exam given in spring of applicant's junior year in high school, and high school recommendations. Minimum 2.0 GPA is required to retain scholarship. Awarded every year. Award may be used only at sponsoring institution.
Contact: Theodore Hallenbeck, Director of Financial Aid, 103 Michael Schwartz Center.

2326   Parajon Scholarship/Tyree Scholarship

Denison University
Box H
Granville, OH 43023
(614) 587-6276, 800-DENISON, (614) 587-6306 (fax)
admissions@denison.edu
http://www.denison.edu
Average award: Half tuition
Number of awards: 60
Deadline: January 1
College level: Freshman
Criteria: Applicant must be of African-American, Asian, Hispanic, and/or Native American heritage. Selection is based upon academic record, essay, extracurricular achievements, and counselor and teacher recommendations. Minimum 2.8 GPA is required for renewal. Awarded every year. Award may be used only at sponsoring institution.
Contact: Scholarships.

2327   Paul Phillips Scholarship

Grand Valley State University
Allendale, MI 49401
(616) 895-3234
Average award: $5,100
Maximum award: $6,638
Minimum award: $4,000
Number of awards: 3
Deadline: February 1
College level: Freshman
Criteria: Applicant must be a minority student. Minimum 3.0 GPA is required to retain scholarship. Awarded every year. Award may be used only at sponsoring institution.
Contact: Ken Fridsma, Director of Financial Aid.

2328   Phillip Morris Foundation Grant

Webster University
470 East Lockwood
St. Louis, MO 63119-3194
(314) 968-7004
www.websteruniv.edu
Maximum award: $3,000
Number of awards: 2
Deadline: May 1
College level: Sophomore, Junior, Senior, Graduate
Majors/Fields: Teacher certification program
Criteria: Applicant must be African-American, Hispanic, or Native American, be an undergraduate student with at least 30 credit hours completed or a graduate student seeking teacher certification, have a minimum "B" grade average, be competent in writing and math, must maintain enrollment status, and must submit application, autobiographical sketch, letter of recommendation from faculty member, and transcript. FAFSA is required. Renewable if recipient maintains full-time enrollment and good academic standing. Awarded every year. Award may be used only at sponsoring institution.
Contact: Shannon Frank, Coordinator of University Scholarships.

2329   Presidential Scholarship for African-Americans

Villanova University
Villanova, PA 19085
(215) 645-4010
Average award: $18,200
Maximum award: $19,640
Minimum award: $15,740
Number of awards: 13
Deadline: December 15
College level: Freshman
Criteria: Applicant must be an African-American student, have an outstanding high school record and class rank, and have a minimum combined SAT I score of 1200. Applicant must maintain high academic standards to retain scholarship. Award may be used only at sponsoring institution.
Contact: George J. Walter, Director of Financial Aid.

2330   Prestigious Scholarship

Ohio State University–Columbus
Third Floor Lincoln Tower
1800 Cannon Drive
Columbus, OH 43210-1200
(614) 292-3980
Average award: Full in-state tuition plus $500
Deadline: December 4
College level: Freshman
Criteria: Applicant must be a graduate of a chartered Ohio high school, rank in the top tenth of class, have a minimum 3.5 GPA, and be an African-American, Asian-American, Hispanic-American, or Native American. If funding permits out-of-state applicants will be considered. Scholarship is renewable. Awarded every year. Award may be used only at sponsoring institution.
Contact: Office of Minority Affairs, Columbus, OH 43210, (614) 292-0964.

2331   Purnell-Fort Scholarship

University of Akron
302 Buchtel Commons
Akron, OH 44325-6211
(216) 972-7032, (216) 972-7139 (fax)
Maximum award: $4,000
Deadline: February 1
College level: Freshman
Criteria: Applicant must be a minority student. Minimum 3.0 GPA is required to retain scholarship. Awarded every year. Award may be used only at sponsoring institution.
Contact: Doug McNutt, Director of Student Financial Aid.

2332   Ralph J. Bunche Scholarship

Northeastern University
360 Huntington Avenue
150 Richards Hall
Boston, MA 02115
(617) 373-2000
Maximum award: $23,895
Number of awards: 12
Deadline: March 1
College level: Freshman
Criteria: Applicant must be African-American, rank in the top tenth of class, and have a minimum combined SAT I score of 1150. Minimum 3.0 GPA is required to retain scholarship. Awarded every year. Award may be used only at sponsoring institution.
Contact: Alan Kines, Director of Admissions.

2333   Regent's Award

Seattle University
Broadway and Madison
Seattle, WA 98122
(206) 296-5840, (206) 296-5656 (fax)
admissions@seattleu.edu
http://www.seattleu.edu
Maximum award: $5,000
Number of awards: 30
Deadline: February 1
College level: Freshman, Transfer
Criteria: Applicant must be African-American, Hispanic, or Native American and be an entering student. Recipient must maintain a minimum 3.0 GPA and complete at least 45 credit hours to retain scholarship. Awarded every year. Award may be used only at sponsoring institution.
Contact: Undergraduate Admissions Office, 900 Broadway, Seattle, WA 98122-4340, (206) 296-5800, admissions@seattleu.edu.

2334   Reginaldo Howard Scholarship

Duke University
P.O. Box 90397
Durham, NC 27706
(919) 684-6225, (919) 660-9811 (fax)
Average award: $6,000
Number of awards: 7
Deadline: January 15
College level: Freshman
Criteria: Applicant must be African-American. Selection is based upon academic and extracurricular activities. A separate application is not required. Scholarship is renewable. Awarded every year. Award may be used only at sponsoring institution.
Contact: Christoph Guttentag, Director of Admissions, P.O. Box 90587, Durham, NC 27708-0587, (919) 684-3214.

2335   Richard and Jessie Barrington Educational Fund

Washoe Tribe of Nevada and California
Education Department
919 Highway 395 South
Gardnerville, NV 89410
(702) 265-4191, (702) 265-6240 (fax)
Average award: $1,000
Maximum award: $2,000
Minimum award: $800
Number of awards: 3
Deadline: August 15; December 15
College level: Freshman, Sophomore, Junior, Senior, Graduate
Criteria: Applicant must be an enrolled Washoe Tribe member with documented financial need. Awarded every year.
Contact: Sherry Smokey, Education Director.

2336   Richard Green Scholarship

St. Cloud State University
720 South 4th Avenue
St. Cloud, MN 56301
(320) 255-2244
Maximum award: $2,500
Maximum number of awards: 50
Minimum number of awards: 5
Deadline: April 1
College level: Freshman
Criteria: Awarded to applicant who will contribute to cultural diversity. Scholarship is renewable. Awarded every year. Award may be used only at sponsoring institution.
Contact: Susan Engel, Assistant Director of Admissions.

2337   Seneca Nation of Indians

Seneca Nation of Indians
Seneca Nation of Higher Education
Box 231
Salamanca, NY 14779
(716) 945-1790, (716) 945-7170 (fax)
Maximum award: $5,000
Deadline: July 15 (fall), December 31 (spring), May 20 (summer)
College level: Freshman, Sophomore, Junior, Senior, Graduate, Doctoral
Criteria: Applicant must be an enrolled member of the Seneca Nation of Indians. Selection is based upon financial need. Scholarship is renewable. Awarded every year.
Contact: Awards.

2338   Sons of Italy Foundation National Leadership Grant

Sons of Italy Foundation
219 East Street NE
Washington, DC 20002
(202) 547-2900
Average award: $4,000
Maximum award: $5,000
Number of awards: 12
Deadline: February 28
College level: Freshman, Sophomore, Junior, Senior, Graduate, Doctoral, Professional degree
Criteria: Applicant must be of Italian heritage and be a full-time student who has demonstrated exceptional leadership qualities and a distinguished level of scholastic achievement. Awarded every year.
Contact: Dayle Spinelli Lewis, Competition Coordinator.

2339   Undergraduate Diversity Scholarship

Southern California Institute of Architecture
5454 Beethoven Street
Los Angeles, CA 90066
(310) 574-1123
Average award: $5,000
Maximum award: $5,810
Number of awards: 4
Deadline: May
College level: Freshman, Transfer
Majors/Fields: Architecture
Criteria: Selection is based upon racial/ethnic background. Scholarship is renewable. Awarded every year. Award may be used only at sponsoring institution.
Contact: Director of Admissions.

2340   Undergraduate Scholarship for Full-time Students of Swiss Descent

Swiss Benevolent Society of Chicago
6440 North Bosworth Avenue
Chicago, IL 60626
Maximum award: $2,500
Number of awards: 30
Deadline: March 6
College level: Freshman, Sophomore, Junior, Senior
Criteria: Applicant must be of Swiss descent, live in Illinois or southern Wisconsin, and have a minimum 3.5 GPA. High school seniors must have a minimum composite ACT score of 26 or combined SAT I score of 1050. Application must be requested between November 15 and February 1. Recipient must reapply for renewal. Awarded every year.
Contact: Scholarships.

2341   Underrepresented Minority Achievement Scholarship

Portland State University
Financial Aid Department
P.O. Box 751
Portland, OR 97207-0751
(503) 725-5270
Average award: $3,060
Number of awards: 64
Deadline: March 1
College level: Freshman, Junior
Criteria: Applicant must be African-American, Hispanic-American, or Native American. Renewable if minimum 2.5 GPA (2.7 GPA in major) is maintained. Awarded every year. Award may be used only at sponsoring institution.
Contact: Scholarships, Admissions Office, (503) 725-3511.

2342 United Negro College Fund Scholarship

United Negro College Fund (UNCF)
8260 Willow Oaks Corporate Drive
P.O. Box 10444
Fairfax, VA 22031-4511
(703) 205-3400
Average award: $2,500
Maximum award: $7,500
Minimum award: $500
Number of awards: 1,500
Deadline: Rolling
College level: Unspecified undergraduate
Criteria: Applicant must attend one of 41 UNCF member institutions, have a minimum 2.5 GPA, demonstrate unmet financial need, and be nominated by the financial aid office of the UNCF institution student is attending. Renewal is based upon GPA, enrollment, and availability. Awarded every year. Award may be used only at UNCF-member schools.
Contact: The College Fund/UNCF.

2343 Urban League Scholarship

Rochester Institute of Technology
One Lomb Memorial Drive
Rochester, NY 14623
(716) 475-2186
Average award: $2,500
Number of awards: 15
Deadline: February 15
College level: Freshman
Criteria: Applicant must be an African-American, Hispanic-American or Native American. Selection is based upon academic qualifications, leadership potential, and demonstrated financial need. Satisfactory academic progress is required to retain scholarship. Awarded every year. Award may be used only at sponsoring institution.
Contact: Verna Hazen, Director of Financial Aid.

2344 Wasie Foundation Scholarship

Wasie Foundation
1st Bank Place, Suite 4700
601 Second Avenue South
Minneapolis, MN 55402-4319
(612) 332-3883
Maximum award: $15,000
Number of awards: 50
Deadline: April 15
College level: Freshman, Sophomore, Junior, Senior, Graduate, Doctoral
Criteria: Applicant must be a Christian, full-time student of Polish ancestry who intends to attend one of the following institutions in Minnesota: Coll of St. Benedict, Coll of St. Catherine, Coll of St. Scholastica, U of St. Thomas, Dunwoody Industrial Inst, Hamline U School of Law, St. John's U, St. Mary's Coll, U of Minnesota (Twin Cities), or William Mitchell Coll of Law. Selection is based upon academic ability, personal qualities, extracurricular activities, financial need, educational goals, and social conduct. Members of the Communist party are not eligible. Reapplication is required to retain scholarship. Awarded every year.
Contact: Ms. Lea M. Johnson, Scholarship Administrator, 909 Foshay Tower, Minneapolis, MN 55402.

2345 Westchester Community Scholarship

National Italian American Foundation (NIAF)
Educational Scholarship Program
1860 19th Street, NW
Washington, DC 20009-5599
(202) 530-5315
Average award: $2,000
Number of awards: 1
Deadline: May 31
College level: Freshman, Sophomore, Junior, Senior, Graduate, Doctoral
Criteria: Applicant must be Italian-American, a resident of the Westchester, N.Y., area, demonstrate financial need, and submit transcript. Awarded every year.
Contact: Dr. Maria Lombardo, Education Director.

2346 William Randolph Hearst Presidential Scholarship

Clemson University
G-01 Sikes Hall
Clemson, SC 29634-5123
(803) 656-2280
Maximum award: $5,000
Number of awards: 1
Deadline: March 1
College level: Freshman
Criteria: Awarded to the most outstanding black entering freshman. Awarded every year. Award may be used only at sponsoring institution.
Contact: Marvin Carmichael, Director of Financial Aid.

2347 Wisconsin HEAB Native American Student Grant

Wisconsin Higher Educational Aids Board (HEAB)
P.O. Box 7885
131 West Wilson Street
Madison, WI 53707-7885
(608) 266-0888, (608) 267-2808 (fax)
Maximum award: $2,200
College level: Freshman, Sophomore, Junior, Senior, Graduate, Doctoral
Criteria: Applicant must be a Wisconsin resident who is at least one-quarter Native American and must attend a Wisconsin institution (public, private, and proprietary schools are all eligible). HEAB has an informal matching arrangement with grant funds awarded by the Federal Bureau of Indian Affairs and Wisconsin Tribal governments. Renewable for up to 10 semesters. Awarded every year.
Contact: Joyce Apfel, Grants Coordinator.

Gender Specific——————————

2348 Alabama Junior Miss Scholarship

Birmingham-Southern College
Arkadelphia Road
Birmingham, AL 35254
(205) 226-4688
Maximum award: Full tuition
Number of awards: 13
Deadline: None
College level: Freshman
Criteria: Maximum award is given to Alabama's Junior Miss. Other awards go to top 10 finalists and two selected participants in talent competition. Scholarship is renewable. Awarded every year. Award may be used only at sponsoring institution.
Contact: Admissions Office, (800) 523-5793, extension 4696.

2349 Alumna Daughter Tuition Award

Wilson College
1015 Philadelphia Avenue
Chambersburg, PA 17201-1285
(717) 264-4141, (717) 264-1578 (fax)
http://www.wilson.edu
Award: One-fourth tuition discount
Deadline: None
College level: Daughters and granddaughters of alumnae of Wilson Coll, Penn Hall Junior Coll, and Tift Coll
Criteria: Renewable if satisfactory academic progress and at least half-time enrollment are maintained. Awarded every year. Award may be used only at sponsoring institution.
Contact: Ruth Cramer, Director of Financial Aid, (717) 262-2002.

2350   America's Junior Miss

America's Junior Miss
P.O. Box 2786
Mobile, AL 36652-2786
(205) 438-3621
Award: Full tuition, room, board and fees to each state winner
Number of awards: 51
College level: Freshman
Criteria: Applicant must be a U.S. citizen, a high school senior, have never been married, and be a legal resident of the district or state she represents. Applicants are chosen locally, then advance to state competitions, and the 50 state winners compete for the national title in Mobile, Ala. Selection is based upon panel evaluation (30%), scholastic achievement (20%), creative and performing arts (20%), fitness (15%), and poise (15%). Additionally, 215 colleges and universities throughout the U.S. give scholarship support to local, state, and national participants. Awarded every year.
Contact: America's Junior Miss.

2351   AWA Scholarships

Association for Women in Architecture
2550 Beverly Boulevard
Los Angeles, CA 90057
(213)-389-6490, (213) 389-7514 (fax)
Maximum award: $2,500
Number of awards: 3
Deadline: April 30
College level: Junior, Senior, Graduate
Majors/Fields: Architecture, landscape architecture, interior design, environmental design, urban and land planning, architectural rendering, civil, structural, mechanical, or electrical engineering as applied to architecture.
Criteria: Applicant must be a woman who has already completed one year (18 units) in major. If applicant is a non-California resident, she must attend a California school. Applicants who are California residents may attend school out-of-state. Finalists must attend interview in Los Angeles at their own expense and winners must be enrolled in ensuing term. Awarded every year.
Contact: Association for Women in Architecture Office.

2352   Bell Helicopter Whirly-Girls Scholarship

The Whirly-Girls, Inc.
Executive Towers 10-D
207 West Clarendon Avenue
Phoenix, AZ 85013
(602) 263-0190, (602) 264-5812 (fax)
Average award: Tuition for course (ground school and five hours of flight training)
Deadline: November 15
College level: Helicopter flight trainees
Majors/Fields: Aviation
Criteria: Applicant must be a woman, demonstrate financial need, and be a member in good standing of the Whirly-Girls. Award is to obtain Bell 206BIII Turbine training at the Customer Training Academy in Fort Worth, Tex. Awarded every year.
Contact: Charlotte Kelley, President.

2353   Betty Baum Hirschfield Scholarship

University of Oklahoma
University Affairs
900 Asp Avenue, Room 236
Norman, OK 73019-0401
(405) 325-1701
Average award: $3,500
Number of awards: 2
Deadline: March 1
College level: Returning student
Criteria: Applicant must be a single mother returning to school after an interruption at any stage of her education; equivalent of two semesters full-time work with a minimum "B" grade average must have been completed within the last five years. Selection is based upon academic potential and financial need. Awarded every year. Award may be used only at sponsoring institution.
Contact: Women's Studies Program, 530 PHSC, Norman, OK 73019, (405) 325-3481.

2354   Charlotte W. Newcombe Scholarship

Gwynedd-Mercy College
Sumneytown Pike
Gwynedd Valley, PA 19437
(215) 641-5570
Average award: $1,500
Maximum award: $2,750
Minimum award: $1,000
Number of awards: 9
Deadline: March 15
College level: Bachelor's degree candidates
Criteria: Applicant must be a woman, have earned at least 60 credits toward degree, and have serious career goals. Scholarship is renewable. Awarded every year. Award may be used only at sponsoring institution.
Contact: Sr. Barbara A. Kaufman, Director of Student Financial Aid.

2355   Curran Scholarship

Wilson College
1015 Philadelphia Avenue
Chambersburg, PA 17201-1285
(717) 264-4141, (717) 264-1578 (fax)
http://www.wilson.edu
Maximum award: Equivalent of total need-based aid
Number of awards: 6
Deadline: March 1
College level: Freshman, Transfers
Criteria: Applicant must be a woman, a strong student, and have a proven history of service to community and/or church. Recipient must maintain satisfactory academic progress, complete the annual volunteer service requirement, and take two classes in religion and/or philosophy. Awarded every year. Award may be used only at sponsoring institution.
Contact: Susan Olson, Chaplain, (717) 262-2002.

2356   Diocese of Pennsylvania Scholarship

Philadelphia Diocese
240 South Fourth Street
Philadelphia, PA 19106
Average award: $1,000
Maximum award: $3,000
Deadline: March 15
Criteria: Applicant must be a woman training for religious and benevolent work pertaining to the Episcopal Church.
Contact: Board of Managers.

2357   Doris Mullen Memorial Scholarship

The Whirly-Girls, Inc.
Executive Towers 10-D
207 West Clarendon Avenue
Phoenix, AZ 85013
(602) 263-0190, (602) 264-5812 (fax)
Average award: $4,500
Number of awards: 1
Deadline: November 15
College level: Helicopter flight trainees
Majors/Fields: Aviation
Criteria: Applicant must be a woman, demonstrate financial need, and be a member in good standing of the Whirly-Girls. Award is to receive an advanced certificate, rating, or specialized training. Awarded every year.
Contact: Charlotte Kelley, President.

2358 **Eleanor Roosevelt Teacher Fellowship**

American Association of University Women (AAUW)
Education Foundation
1111 16th Street, NW
Washington, DC 20036-4873
(202) 728-7700, (202) 872-1425 (fax)
http://www.aauw.org
Maximum award: $5,000
Deadline: December 1
College level: Teachers for specified educational advancement
Criteria: Applicant must be a woman, an elementary or secondary school teacher, a U.S. citizen, dedicated to improving educational opportunities for women of all ages, and presently employed with at least five years full-time teaching experience and plans to continue teaching for the next five years.
Contact: Fellowships, 2401 Virginia Avenue, NW, Washington, DC 20037, (202) 728-7603.

2359 **Elms College Catholic High School Scholarship**

Elms College (College of Our Lady of the Elms)
291 Springfield Street
Chicopee, MA 01013
(413) 592-3189, 800 255-ELMS, (413) 594-2781 (fax)
admissions@elms.edu
http://www.crocker.com/nelmscol/
Maximum award: $3,000
Number of awards: 10
Deadline: None
Criteria: Applicant must be a woman who has graduated from a Catholic high school and has completed the financial aid process. Renewable if recipient maintains good academic standing and full-time status. Awarded every year. Award may be used only at sponsoring institution.
Contact: Janet DaSilva, Director, Financial Aid, dasilvaj@elms.edu.

2360 **Elms Scholarship**

Elms College (College of Our Lady of the Elms)
291 Springfield Street
Chicopee, MA 01013
(413) 592-3189, 800 255-ELMS, (413) 594-2781 (fax)
admissions@elms.edu
http://www.crocker.com/nelmscol/
Maximum award: $5,000
Number of awards: 160
Deadline: None
College level: Freshman
Criteria: First priority is given to graduates of Catholic high schools in the Springfield Diocese. Second priority is given to graduates of Chicopee high schools. All applicants must be women. Applicant must complete financial aid process. Satisfactory academic progress and full-time status required for renewal. Awarded every year. Award may be used only at sponsoring institution.
Contact: Janet DaSilva, Director, Financial Aid, dasilva@elms.edu.

2361 **Frank McHale Memorial Scholarship**

American Legion—Indiana
Americanism Office
777 North Meridian Street
Indianapolis, IN 46204
(317) 630-1264, (317) 237-9891 (fax)
Average award: $2,300
Maximum award: $3,100
Minimum award: $2,100
Number of awards: 3
Deadline: in May
College level: High school junior
Criteria: Applicant must be a boy finishing his junior year at an Indiana high school and must be a participant in Hoosier Boys' State. Awarded every year.
Contact: Americanism Office.

2362 **Lettie Pate Whitehead Scholarship**

Florida Institute of Technology
150 West University Boulevard
Melbourne, FL 32901-6988
(800) 666-4348
Average award: $2,000
Maximum award: $2,500
Minimum award: $500
Number of awards: 27
Deadline: March 15
College level: Freshman, Sophomore, Junior, Senior
Criteria: Applicant must be a woman and a Christian, be a resident of Alabama, Florida, Georgia, Louisiana, Mississippi, North Carolina, South Carolina, Tennessee, or Virginia, have a minimum 3.0 GPA, be enrolled full time, and demonstrate financial need. Scholarship is renewable. Awarded every year. Award may be used only at sponsoring institution.
Contact: Elaine Grant, Scholarship Coordinator, (407) 768-8000, extension 8845.

2363 **Linda Riddle/SGMA Scholarship**

Women's Sports Foundation
Eisenhower Park
East Meadow, NY 11554
(800) 227-3988, (516) 542-4716 (fax)
wosport@aol.com
http://www.lifetimetv.com/wosport
Maximum award: $1,500
Number of awards: 1
Deadline: December 12
College level: Freshman
Criteria: Applicant must be a woman, have a minimim 2.5 GPA, have participated in girls' high school sports, and be interested in pursuing a career in a sports-related field. Awarded every year.
Contact: Dr. Marjorie Snyder, Associate Executive Director.

2364 **Mervyn's/Women's Sports Foundation College Scholarship**

Women's Sports Foundation
Eisenhower Park
East Meadow, NY 11554
(800) 227-3988, (516) 542-4716 (fax)
wosport@aol.com
http://www.lifetimetv.com/wosport
Maximum award: $1,000
Number of awards: 100
Deadline: May 30
College level: Freshman
Criteria: Applicant must be a woman, have a minimim 3.0 GPA, have participated in girls' high school sports and community, and be interested in pursuing a career in a sports-related field. Awarded every year.
Contact: Dr. Marjorie Snyder, Associate Executive Director.

2365 **Miss Alabama Pageant Scholarship**

Birmingham-Southern College
Arkadelphia Road
Birmingham, AL 35254
(205) 226-4688
Maximum award: Full tuition
Number of awards: 11
Deadline: None
College level: Freshman, Sophomore, Junior, Senior
Criteria: Maximum award is given to Miss Alabama. The next 10 finalists are eligible for a nonrenewable $3,000 award. Other contestants are eligible for a renewable $1,500 award. Scholarship is renewable. Awarded every year. Award may be used only at sponsoring institution.
Contact: Admissions Office, (800) 523-5793, extension 4696.

2366   Miss America Scholarship

Miss America Scholarship Foundation
Mrs. Karen E. Aarons, Executive Vice President
P.O. Box 119
Atlantic City, NJ 08404
(609) 345-7571, (609) 345-6565 (fax)
missamerica@ajerseycape.net
http://www.missamerica.org
Maximum award: $40,000
Number of awards: 50
Deadline: Rolling
College level: Freshman, Sophomore, Junior, Senior, Graduate, Doctoral
Criteria: Applicant must enter a local competition, advance to the state competition, and then enter national competition. Applicant must be a woman, a high school graduate, never have been married, of good moral character, and a U.S. citizen. Awarded every year.
Contact: Karen Aarons, Executive Vice President.

2367   Miss Teenage America Annual Competition

Miss Teenage America Pageant
6420 Wilshire Boulevard
Los Angeles, CA 90048-5515
(213) 782-2950, (213) 782-2660 (fax)
Maximum award: $10,000
Number of awards: 1
Deadline: September 15
College level: Freshman
Criteria: Selection is based upon applicant's scholastic achievement, individual accomplishment, community service, poise, appearance, and personality. Awarded every year.
Contact: Promotions Department, Miss Teenage America Pageant, P.O. Box 48994, Los Angeles, CA 90048-0994.

2368   Nancy Lorraine Jensen Memorial Scholarship

Sons of Norway Foundation
1455 West Lake Street
Minneapolis, MN 55408
(612) 827-3611, (612) 827-0658 (fax)
Maximum award: Full tuition for one year
Minimum award: Half tuition for one term
Number of awards: 1
Deadline: March 1
College level: Unspecified undergraduates
Majors/Fields: Chemical engineering, chemistry, electrical engineering, mechanical engineering, physics
Criteria: Applicant must be a woman between the ages of 17 and 35, a U.S. citizen, and a member, or daughter or granddaughter of a member, of Sons of Norway (membership must be for a minimum of three years). Employment at the NASA Goddard Space Flight Center, Greenbelt, Md. may be substituted. Applicant must be a full-time undergraduate who has completed at least one quarter or semester majoring in chemistry, chemical, electrical, or mechanical engineering, or physics. Applicant must have a minimum combined SAT I score of 1200 or minimum composite ACT score of 26. Renewable for up to three years of undergraduate study. Awarded every year.
Contact: Liv Dahl, Administrative Director.

2369   Nancy Ryles Scholarship

Portland State University
Financial Aid Department
P.O. Box 751
Portland, OR 97207-0751
(503) 725-5270
Average award: $5,000
Number of awards: 1
Deadline: April 10
College level: Sophomore, Junior, Senior, Graduate
Criteria: Applicant must be a woman returning to school after break in education due to family responsibilities. Selection is based upon financial need and potential for academic success. Scholarship is renewable. Awarded every year. Award may be used only at sponsoring institution.
Contact: Virginia McElroy, Scholarship Coordinator.

2370   Nevada Women's Fund Scholarship

Nevada Women's Fund
P.O. Box 50428
Reno, NV 89513
(702) 786-2335, (702) 786-8152 (fax)
Maximum award: $5,000
Maximum number of awards: 82
Minimum number of awards: 75
Deadline: February 28
College level: Freshman, Sophomore, Junior, Senior, Graduate, Doctoral
Criteria: Applicant must be a Nevada resident and a woman. Scholarship is renewable. Awarded every year.
Contact: Fritsi H. Ericson, President/CEO.

2371   Presbyterian Student Tuition Award

Wilson College
1015 Philadelphia Avenue
Chambersburg, PA 17201-1285
(717) 264-4141, (717) 264-1578 (fax)
http://www.wilson.edu
Average award: One-quarter tuition discount
Deadline: None
College level: Active members of the Presbyterian Church
Criteria: Applicant must be a woman and provide a letter from her minister on church letterhead to prove eligibility. Renewable if satisfactory academic progress and at least half-time enrollment are maintained. Awarded every year. Award may be used only at sponsoring institution.
Contact: Ruth Cramer, Director of Financial Aid, (717) 262-2002.

2372   Pritchard Corporate Air Service Inc. Lend a Hand Scholarship

The Whirly-Girls, Inc.
Executive Towers 10-D
207 West Clarendon Avenue
Phoenix, AZ 85013
(602) 263-0190, (602) 264-5812 (fax)
Average award: Tuition for course
Deadline: November 15
College level: Helicopter flight trainee/instructor
Majors/Fields: Aviation
Criteria: Applicant must be a woman, demonstrate financial need, and hold a pilot's license. Award is to obtain a Commercial Rotorcraft Helicopter Additional Rating and Certified Flight Instructor Rating. There is one year allotted to receive training and certificates, followed by six months employment as a Flight Instructor for Pritchard Air Service. Recipient must relocate to Navato, Calif. for the 18 month period.
Contact: Charlotte Kelley, President.

2373   Spence Reese Foundation

Spence Reese Foundation
Boys and Girls Clubs of San Diego
1761 Hotel Circle So., Suite 123
San Diego, CA 92108
(619) 298-3520, (619) 298-3615 (fax)
Average award: $2,000
Number of awards: 4
Deadline: May 15
College level: Freshman
Majors/Fields: Engineering, law, medicine, political science
Criteria: Applicant must be a boy and a graduating high school senior, preferably residing within a 250-mile radius of San Diego. Selection is based upon academic standing, academic ability, financial ability, and potential for good citizenship. To request an application, send a self-addressed, stamped envelope and pertinent information. Awarded for four years.
Contact: Tom Hazard, President.

2374 State Young Woman of the Year Scholarship

University of West Alabama
Station Four
Livingston, AL 35470
(205) 652-3400, (205) 652-3522 (fax)
http://www.westal.edu
Average award: $5,000
Maximum award: $5,400
Number of awards: 1
Deadline: Early application is recommended
College level: Freshman
Criteria: Applicant must have won the State Young Woman of the Year competiton. Renewable for up to four years if minimum 3.0 GPA is maintained. Awarded every year. Award may be used only at sponsoring institution.
Contact: Richard Hester, Director of Admissions, (205) 652-3400, extension 3578, rth@uwamail.westal.edu.

2375 Transfer Merit Scholarship

Elms College (College of Our Lady of the Elms)
291 Springfield Street
Chicopee, MA 01013
(413) 592-3189, 800 255-ELMS, (413) 594-2781 (fax)
admissions@elms.edu
http://www.crocker.com/nelmscol/
Maximum award: $6,000
Number of awards: 45
Deadline: None
College level: Transfer
Criteria: Applicant must be a woman, have attended previous school full-time for at least two consecutive semesters, and be a new applicant accepted as a full-time undergraduate. Financial aid transcript and application are required. Satisfactory academic progress and full-time status required for renewal. Awarded every year. Award may be used only at sponsoring institution.
Contact: Janet Dasilva, Director, Financial Aid, dasilvaj@elms.edu.

2376 Transfer Scholarship

Emmanuel College
400 The Fenway
Boston, MA 02115
(617) 735-9725
Maximum award: $4,500
Deadline: February 15
College level: Transfer
Criteria: Applicant must have a minimum 3.0 GPA, be a woman, and demonstrate financial need. Recipient must maintain a minimum 3.0 GPA and remain eligible for financial aid to retain scholarship. Awarded every year. Award may be used only at sponsoring institution.
Contact: Patricia K. Harden, Director of Financial Aid.

2377 Whirly-Girls Flight Training Scholarship

The Whirly-Girls, Inc.
Executive Towers 10-D
207 West Clarendon Avenue
Phoenix, AZ 85013
(602) 263-0190, (602) 264-5812 (fax)
Maximum award: $4,500
Deadline: November 15
College level: Helicopter flight trainee
Majors/Fields: Aviation
Criteria: Applicant must be a woman, demonstrate financial need, and possess a current airplane, glider, or balloon rating, and a current medical. Award is to obtain an additional Rotorcraft Helicopter Rating.
Contact: Charlotte Kelley, President.

2378 Women in Engineering Scholarship

Stevens Institute of Technology
Castle Point on Hudson
Hoboken, NJ 07030
(201) 216-5201, (201) 216-8348 (fax)
sheridan_d@stmisb.adm.stevens-tech.edu
http://www.stevens-tech.edu
Average award: $1,500
Maximum award: $2,500
Minimum award: $1,000
Number of awards: 35
College level: Freshman
Majors/Fields: Engineering
Criteria: Applicant must be a woman and a U.S. citizen or permanent resident. Minimum 2.0 GPA is required to retain scholarship. Awarded every year. Award may be used only at sponsoring institution.
Contact: David Sheridan, Director of Financial Aid.

2379 Women's Western Golf Foundation Scholarship

Women's Western Golf Foundation
Director of Scholarships
393 Ramsay Road
Deerfield, IL 60015
Average award: $2,000
Number of awards: 15
Deadline: April 5
College level: Freshman
Criteria: Applicant must be a woman and a U.S. citizen. Selection is based upon academic achievement, financial need, excellence of character, and involvement with the sport of golf. Skill or excellence in the sport of golf is not a criterion. Applicant must request application by March 1. Satisfactory GPA and financial need are required to retain scholarship. Awarded every year.
Contact: Mrs. Richard W. Willis, Director of Scholarships.

2380 Woodlake Fund Award

The Women's Foundation
340 Pine Street
Suite 302
San Francisco, CA 94104
(415) 837-1144, (412) 837-1144 (fax)
Average award: $1,500
Maximum award: $3,000
Minimum award: $500
Number of awards: 15
College level: Freshman
Criteria: Applicant must be a woman of color who lives in East Palo Alto, Calif. and has a minimum "C" grade average. Call in January for information package. Awarded every year.
Contact: Blandina Lansang-De Mesa, Program Officer, (415) 387-1113, extension 14.

Military Affiliation————————

2381 102nd Infantry Division Association Scholarship

102nd Infantry Division Association
1821 Shackleford Road
Nashville, TN 37215
(615) 292-2469
Maximum award: $1,200
Number of awards: 14
Deadline: May 15
Criteria: Applicant's father or grandfather must have been an active member of 102rd Infantry Division between August 1942 and March 1946 and must be a dues-paying member of the association. If deceased, must have been a dues-paying member at time of death.
Contact: Scholarships.

2382   Air Force Sergeants Association Scholarship

Air Force Sergeants Association (AFSA)
P.O. Box 50
Temple Hills, MD 20757-0050
(800) 638-0594
Average award: $2,000
Maximum award: $2,500
Number of awards: 12
Deadline: April 15
College level: Freshman, Sophomore, Junior, Senior
Criteria: Applicant must be an unmarried, dependent child, under age 23, of an AFSA member or AFSA Auxiliary member. Selection is based upon academic ability, character, leadership, writing ability, and potential for success. Financial need is not considered. Awarded every year.
Contact: Scholarship Administrator.

2383   Airmen Memorial Foundation CMSAF Richard D. Kisling Scholarship

Air Force Sergeants Association (AFSA)
P.O. Box 50
Temple Hills, MD 20757-0050
(800) 638-0594
Maximum award: $3,000
Number of awards: 7
Deadline: April 15
College level: Freshman, Sophomore, Junior, Senior
Criteria: Applicant must be an unmarried, dependent child, under age 25, of an enlisted member serving in the U.S. Air Force, Air National Guard, or Air Force Reserve, or in retired status. Selection is based upon academic ability, character, leadership, writing ability, and potential for success. SAT I required. Send self-addressed, stamped (78 cents) envelope (#10 business) for application. Awarded every year.
Contact: Scholarship Administrator, Airmen Memorial Building, 5211 Auth Road, Suitland, MD 20746.

2384   Alabama G.I. Dependents' Scholarship

Alabama GI and Dependents Educational Benefit Act
Alabama State Department of Veterans Affairs
P.O. Box 1509
Montgomery, AL 36102-1509
(334) 242-5077, (334) 242-5102 (fax)
Average award: $1,150
Maximum award: Tuition, books, and lab fees
Minimum award: $890
Number of awards: 854
Deadline: None
College level: Freshman, Sophomore, Junior, Senior, Graduate, Doctoral
Criteria: Applicant must be the dependent (under 26 years of age) of a disabled veteran [child, stepchild, spouse, or unremarried widow(er)]. The veteran must have honorably served at least 90 days of continuous active federal military service, be rated 20 percent or more disabled due to service-connected disabilities or have held the qualifying rating at the time of death, or be a former prisoner of war, declared missing in action, or have died as the result of a service-connected disability or in the line of duty while on active duty. The veteran must have been a permanent civilian resident of the state of Alabama for at least one year immediately prior to (a) initial entry into active military service or (b) any subsequent period of military service in which a break in service occurred and civilian residency was established. Dependents of permanently disabled service-connected veterans rated at 100 percent may also qualify after the veteran has established at least five years of permanent residency in Alabama. Renewable for 12 quarters or eight semesters. Awarded every year. Award may be used only at state-supported institutions in Alabama
Contact: Alabama G.I. Dependents' Scholarship Program.

2385   Army ROTC Scholarship

Portland State University
Financial Aid Department
P.O. Box 751
Portland, OR 97207-0751
(503) 725-5270
Average award: $4,500
Deadline: in January
College level: Sophomore, Junior, Senior
Criteria: Applicant must have a minimum 2.5 GPA, a minimum combined SAT I score of 850, and be physically and mentally sound. Half of awards are given on merit only; the other half include financial need. Scholarship is renewable. Award may be used only at sponsoring institution.
Contact: Scholarships, Department of Military Science, (503) 725-3212.

2386   Army ROTC Scholarship

Southwest Missouri State University
Student Financial Aid
901 South National Avenue
Springfield, MO 65804-0095
(417) 836-5000 or (800) 492-7900
Average award: Full fees, book allowance and $100 per month
Deadline: March 31
College level: Freshman, Sophomore, Junior, Senior
Criteria: Applicant must have a minimum 2.5 GPA and be a full-time student. Applicant must attend an interview, and pass a physical test, written exam, and free physical examination given by a local doctor. Recipient who accepts a two-, three-, or four-year scholarship will train to receive a commission as Second Lieutenant in the regular U.S. Army, Army Reserve, or Army National Guard. Scholarship is renewable. Awarded every year. Award may be used only at sponsoring institution.
Contact: Military Science Department, Southwest Missouri State University, Springfield, MO 65804, (417) 836-5262.

2387   Children of Prisoners of War or Persons Missing in Action Tuition Exemption

Texas Higher Education Coordinating Board
Student Financial Assistance
P.O. Box 12788, Capitol Station
Austin, TX 78711-2788
(512) 427-6340
Average award: $3,426
Number of awards: 2
College level: Freshman, Sophomore, Junior, Senior
Criteria: Applicant must be the dependent child of a Texas resident who is a POW or MIA; proof of parent's status from the Department of Defense is required. Applicant must attend a public college or university in Texas, and be under 21 years of age or under 25 years of age if majority of financial support is from parent. Scholarship is renewable. Awarded every year.
Contact: Sharon W. Cobb, Assistant Commissioner for Student Services.

2388   Claire Oliphant Memorial Scholarship

American Legion–New Jersey Auxiliary
Department Secretary
146 Route 130
Bordentown, NJ 08505-2226
(609) 291-9338
Average award: $1,800
Number of awards: 1
Deadline: March 15
College level: Freshman
Criteria: Applicant must be the son or daughter of an honorably discharged veteran of the U.S. Armed Forces, have been a resident of New Jersey for at least two years, and graduate from a New Jersey senior high school. Awarded every year.
Contact: Department Secretary.

2389 Daughters of the Cincinnati Scholarship

Daughters of the Cincinnati
122 East 58th Street
New York, NY 10022
Maximum award: $3,000
Deadline: March 15
College level: Freshman
Criteria: Applicant must be the daughter of a commissioned officer in the regular Army, Navy, Air Force, Coast Guard, or Marine Corps (active, retired or deceased). Send parent's rank and branch of service with request for application. Selection is based upon merit. Satisfactory academic performance is required to retain scholarship. Awarded every year.
Contact: Scholarship Administrator.

2390 Educational Benefits for Children of Deceased Veterans

Delaware Higher Education Commission
820 North French Street
Fourth Floor
Wilmington, DE 19801
(302) 577-3240, (302) 577-6765 (fax)
mlaffey@state.de.us
http://www.state.de.us/high-ed/commiss/webpage.htm
Maximum award: $8,500
Number of awards: 3
Deadline: three weeks prior to start of classes
College level: Freshman, Sophomore, Junior, Senior
Criteria: Applicant must be a Delaware resident between the ages of 16 and 24 who is the child of a deceased military veteran or state police officer who was a Delaware resident, and whose death was service related. Scholarship is renewable. Awarded every year.
Contact: Maureen Laffey, Associate Director.

2391 Edward T. Conroy Memorial Grant

Maryland Higher Education Commission
State Scholarship Administration
16 Francis Street
Annapolis, MD 21401-1781
(410) 974-5370, (410) 974-5994 (fax)
http://www.ubalt.edu/www/mhec
Average award: $1,925
Maximum award: $3,800
Number of awards: 71
Deadline: July 15
College level: Freshman, Sophomore, Junior, Senior, Graduate, Doctoral
Criteria: Award is available to children of Maryland residents who are deceased or 100-percent disabled, as a direct result of military service, U.S. Armed Forces personnel, to Maryland residents who were Vietnam-era P.O.W.s, and to Maryland state or local public safety personnel who, in the line of duty, became 100-percent disabled. Surviving spouses and children of safety personnel are also eligible. Renewable for up to 5 years full-time study or 8 years part-time study. Awarded every year. Award may be used only at Maryland schools.
Contact: Michael Smith, Program Administrator.

2392 Falcon Foundation Scholarships

Falcon Foundation
3116 Academy Drive #200
USAF Academy, CO 80840-4480
(719) 333-4096, (719) 333-3669 (fax)
Average award: $3,000
Maximum number of awards: 100
Minimum number of awards: 100
Deadline: April 30
Criteria: Applicant must have potential for U.S. Air Force Academy education and desire for Air Force career but need further academic preparation before cadet appointment. Applicant must be at least age 17 but not past 21st birthday on July 1 of year admitted, be a U.S. citizen, have good moral character, never have been married, have no dependent children, be in good physical condition, and range in height between 60 inches and 80 inches with proportionate weight. Awarded every year. Award may be used only at the U.S. Air Force Academy
Contact: Scholarships.

2393 Frank W. Garner Scholarship

Air Force Sergeants Association (AFSA)
P.O. Box 50
Temple Hills, MD 20757-0050
(800) 638-0594
Average award: $2,000
Number of awards: 12
Deadline: April 15
College level: Freshman, Sophomore, Junior, Senior
Criteria: Applicant must be an unmarried, dependent child, under age 23, of an Air Force Sergeants Association member or AFSA Auxiliary member. Selection is based upon academic ability, character, leadership, writing ability and potential for success. Financial need is not a consideration. Awarded every year.
Contact: Scholarship Administrator.

2394 Maine Vietnam Veterans Scholarship

Maine Community Foundation
210 Main Street
P.O. Box 148
Ellsworth, ME 04605
(207) 667-9735
Average award: $700
Maximum award: $1,000
Number of awards: 3
Deadline: May 1
College level: Freshman, Sophomore, Junior, Senior
Criteria: Applicant must be a Maine resident. First priority is given to armed services veterans who served in the Vietnam Theater and their dependents; second priority is children of other Maine veterans. Selection is based upon financial need, community service, and academic achievement. Application must include a $3.00 processing fee. Awarded every year.
Contact: Scholarship Coordinator.

2395 Marianas Officers' Wives' Club Scholarship

Marianas Naval Officers' Wives' Club (MNOWC)
Scholarship Chairwoman
PSC 489, Box 49 COMNAVMAR
FPO AP, 96536-0051
(671) 477-5405
Average award: $2,000
Number of awards: 11
Deadline: March 31
College level: Freshman, Sophomore, Junior, Senior, Graduate
Criteria: Applicant must be the dependent child or spouse of a regular or reserve Navy, Marine Corps, or Coast Guard member on active duty, retired with pay, deceased, or declared missing in action. Sponsor must have served on Guam for at least six consecutive months; current or past MNOWC members in good standing or their dependents are also eligible. Selection is based upon academic ability, community involvement, character, leadership ability, and financial need. Applicants must send a self-addressed, stamped envelope in order to receive an application. Reapplication is required to retain scholarship. Awarded every year.
Contact: Scholarship Chairwoman.

2396 Marine Corps Scholarship

Marine Corps Scholarship Foundation
P.O. Box 3008
Princeton, NJ 08543
(609) 921-3534
Maximum award: $2,500
Number of awards: 950
Deadline: April 1
College level: Sophomore, Junior, Senior, Graduate
Criteria: Applicant must be the child of a U.S. Marine on active duty, in the Reserve, or a former Marine or Reservist who has been honorably and/or medically discharged, is retired, or is deceased. Gross family income may not exceed $41,000 per year. Grants are for vocational, technical, or undergraduate college studies. A written request for an application is required. Reapplication is required for renewal. Awarded every year.
Contact: Scholarship Chairman.

2397   Montgomery GI Bill (MGIB)

U.S. Army
P.O. Box 3219
Warminster, PA 18974-9844
(800) USA Army
http://www.goarmy.com
Minimum award: $7,316
Maximum award: $15,403
Deadline: Continually accepting applicantions
College level: Freshman, Sophomore, Junior, Senior, Graduate, Doctoral
Criteria: Applicant must enlist in active Army (maximum award) or in Army Reserve for six years (minimum award). Individual must contribute $1,200, which is deducted from first year's pay. Awarded every year.
Contact: U.S. Army or U.S. Army Reserve.

2398   Montgomery GI Bill/Army College Fund

U.S. Army
P.O. Box 3219
Warminster, PA 18974-9844
(800) USA Army
http://www.goarmy.com
Maximum award: $30,000
Number of awards: No limit
Deadline: Continually accepting applications
College level: Freshman, Sophomore, Junior, Senior, Graduate, Doctoral
Criteria: Applicant must enlist in the active Army for specified critical military skills. Individual must contribute $1,200, which is deducted from first year's pay. Awarded every year.
Contact: U.S. Army.

2399   National President's Scholarship

American Legion Auxiliary (ALA), National Headquarters
777 North Meridian Street, Third Floor
Indianapolis, IN 46204
(317) 635-6291
Maximum award: $2,000
Number of awards: 10
Deadline: March 16
College level: Freshman
Criteria: Applicant must be the child of a veteran who served in the U.S. Armed Forces in World War I, World War II, or the Korean, Vietnam, Panama, Grenada, or Persian Gulf conflicts and have financial need. Selection is based upon character, Americanism, leadership, scholarship, and need.
Contact: National Secretary or National Treasurer.

2400   National President's Scholarship

American Legion–California Auxiliary
Auxiliary Department Headquarters
401 Van Ness #113
San Francisco, CA 94102-4586
Average award: $1,500
Maximum award: $2,000
Minimum award: $500
College level: Freshman
Criteria: State winner competes in the Western Division. Applicant must be the child of a veteran of World War I, World War II, or the Korean, Vietnam, Grenada/Lebanon, Panama, or Desert Storm conflicts. Applicant must have been a resident of California for at least five years; if less, veteran must have been reported missing by government or hopitalized in the state. Awarded every year.
Contact: Auxiliary Department Headquarters.

2401   Naval Academy Women's Club Scholarship

Naval Academy Women's Club (NAWC)
P.O. Box 826
Annapolis, MD 21404
Average award: $1,000
Number of awards: 20
Deadline: April 1
College level: Freshman, Sophomore, Junior, Senior
Criteria: Applicant must meet one of the following requirements: be the child of a Navy or Marine Corps officer on active duty, retired, or deceased, who is or has been stationed under permanent orders at the U.S. Naval Academy Complex; the child of a civilian faculty or senior staff member presently employed at or retired from the Naval Academy; the child of a Navy or Marine Corps enlisted person on active duty, retired, or deceased, who is or has been stationed under permanent orders at the Academy; the child of a NAWC member; or a current member of the Naval Academy Women's Club (member must be a full-time student). Reapplication and satisfactory GPA are required for renewal. Awarded every year.
Contact: Scholarship Chairman.

2402   Navy Nurse Corps NROTC

Naval Personnel Command
NMPC-602
Washington, DC 20370
Average award: Tuition, lab fees, books, and $100 per month stipend
College level: Freshman, Sophomore, Junior, Senior
Majors/Fields: Nursing
Criteria: Selection is based upon high school class rank, test scores, extracurricular activities, leadership qualities, and academic accomplishments. Applicant is commissioned as an ensign in the Navy Nurse Corps upon graduation. Awarded every year.
Contact: Local Navy recruiter, (800) 327-NAVY.

2403   Navy Supply Corps Foundation Scholarship

Navy Supply Corps Foundation, Inc.
Navy Supply Corps School
1425 Prince Avenue
Athens, GA 30606-2205
(706) 354-4111, (706) 354-0334 (fax)
Average award: $2,000
Number of awards: 50
Deadline: February 15
College level: Freshman, Sophomore, Junior, Senior
Criteria: Applicant must be the child of a Navy Supply Corps Officer (including Warrant) or Supply Corps service member on active duty, in reserve status, retired-with-pay, or deceased. Selection is based upon scholastic ability. Minimum 3.0 GPA is required. Awarded every year.
Contact: Kaye Morris, Adminstrative Budget Officer.

2404   Navy-Marine Corps Reserve Officer Training Corps (NROTC) College Scholarship

Naval Personnel Command
NMPC-602
Washington, DC 20370
Average award: Tuition, fees, books, and $100 per month stipend
College level: Freshman, Sophomore, Junior, Senior
Criteria: Applicant must attend a civilian college with an NROTC unit on campus or one that is affiliated with an NROTC institution. Upon graduation, applicant becomes an officer in the Navy or Marine Corps. Awards are for two, three, or four years. Awarded every year.
Contact: Local Navy recruiter, (800) 327-NAVY.

2405 **New Mexico Veterans Service Commission Scholarship Under Chapter 170**

New Mexico Veterans Service Commission
P.O. Box 2324
Santa Fe, NM 87503
(505) 827-6300
Average award: Tuition waiver and $300
Maximum number of awards: 15
Minimum number of awards: 12
Deadline: None
College level: Freshman, Sophomore, Junior, Senior
Criteria: Applicant must be the child of a deceased veteran who was a New Mexico resident at the time of entry into the service and who served during a period of armed conflict and was killed in action or died as the result of such service. Scholarship is also available for some children of deceased state policemen or deceased National Guard members. Reapplication is required to retain scholarship. Awarded every year.
Contact: Alan T. Martinez, State Benefits.

2406 **New York Council Navy League Scholarship**

New York Council Navy League Scholarship Fund
375 Park Avenue
Suite 3408
New York, NY 10152
(212) 355-4960, (212) 355-7922 (fax)
Average award: $2,500
Number of awards: 4
Deadline: June 15
College level: Freshman, Sophomore, Junior, Senior, college seniors
Criteria: Applicant must be the dependent of a regular/reserve Navy, Marine Corps, or Coast Guard service member who is serving on active duty, retired with pay, or died in the line of duty or after retirement. Applicant must also be a resident of Connecticut, New Jersey, or New York. Minimum "B-" grade average and transcripts are required to retain scholarship. Awarded every year.
Contact: Donald Sternberg, Executive Administrator.

2407 **NROTC Scholarship**

U.S. Naval Reserve Officers Training Corps (NROTC)
Navy Recruiting Command (Code 314)
801 North Randolph Street
Arlington, VA 22203-1991
(703) 696-4581, (703) 696-2086 (fax)
http://www.navyjobs.com
Average award: $10,000
Maximum award: $20,000
Number of awards: 1,000
Deadline: December 31
College level: Freshman
Criteria: Applicant must be a U.S. citizen, between 17 and 21 years of age, be physically qualified by Navy or Marine Corps standards, have no moral obligations or personal convictions that will prevent conscientious bearing of arms, and achieve qualifying scores on the SAT I or ACT. Applicant must maintain above-average grades to continue support. Awarded every year.
Contact: LCDR Doug Brazil, NROTC Program Manager.

2408 **Ohio War Orphans Scholarship**

Ohio Board of Regents, State Grants and Scholarships Department
309 South Fourth Street
P.O. Box 182452
Columbus, OH 43218-2452
(614) 466-1190, (614) 752-5903 (fax)
Average award: Full tuition
Number of awards: 400
Deadline: July 1
College level: Freshman, Sophomore, Junior, Senior
Criteria: Applicant must be the child of a veteran who served at least 90 days active duty during a period of war and must now be either disabled or deceased. Applicant must be an Ohio resident between the ages of 16 and 21 and attend a participating Ohio college or university. Satisfactory academic progress and full-time status are required to retain scholarship. Awarded every year. Award may be used only at participating Ohio schools.
Contact: Sue Minturn, Program Administrator.

2409 **President's Scholarship**

American Legion–Oregon Auxiliary
P.O. Box 1730
Wilsonville, OR 97070-1730
(503) 682-3162
Maximum award: $2,000
Number of awards: 10
Deadline: March 15
College level: Freshman
Criteria: Applicant must be the child of a veteran who served in the Armed Forces during the eligibility dates for membership in the American Legion and be recommended by an American Legion unit. Awarded every year.
Contact: Chairman of Education.

2410 **Richard D. Rousher Scholarship**

Air Force Sergeants Association (AFSA)
P.O. Box 50
Temple Hills, MD 20757-0050
(800) 638-0594
Average award: $2,000
Deadline: April 15
College level: Freshman, Sophomore, Junior, Senior
Criteria: Applicant must be an unmarried, dependent child, under age 23, of an Air Force Sergeants Association member or AFSA Auxiliary member. Selection is based upon academic ability, character, leadership, writing ability, and potential for success. Financial need is not considered. Awarded every year.
Contact: Scholarship Adminstrator.

2411 **Scholarship for Children of Disabled, Deceased, and POW/MIA Veterans**

North Carolina Division of Veterans Affairs
Albemarle Building, Suite #1065
325 North Salisbury Street
Raleigh, NC 27603
(919) 733-3851, (919) 733-2834 (fax)
Average award: $3,000
Maximum award: $4,500
Minimum award: $1,500
Maximum number of awards: 400
Minimum number of awards: 369
Deadline: May 31
College level: Freshman, Sophomore, Junior, Senior, Graduate, Doctoral
Criteria: Applicant must be the child of a desceased or disabled veteran or veteran listed as POW/MIA. The veteran must have been a legal resident of North Carolina at the time of entry into service, or the child must have been born in North Carolina and resided there continuously since birth. Award is for four years. Awarded every year.
Contact: Charles F. Smith, Assistant Secretary.

2412   Scholarships for Children of Deceased or Disabled Veterans or Children of Servicemen Classified as POW or MIA

Florida Department of Education
Office of Student Financial Assistance
255 Collins
Tallahassee, FL 32399-0400
(904) 487-0049
Average award: Tuition and fees
Deadline: April 1
College level: Freshman, Sophomore, Junior, Senior
Criteria: Applicant must be a Florida resident between age 16 and 22 who has not yet received a bachelor's degree and is enrolled full time in a Florida public university, community college, or public vocational-technical center. Applicant must be the dependent child of a deceased or disabled Florida veteran or serviceman, or of a Florida serviceman classifed as a POW or MIA. The parent(s) of a dependent student must have been a Florida resident for five years if the veteran parent served in World War I, World War II, the Korean Conflict, or the Vietnam Era. If the veteran parent served in more recent operations, one year of residency is required. Minimum 2.0 cumulative GPA with 12 credit hours per term is required to retain scholarship. Awarded every year.
Contact: Office of Student Financial Assistance.

2413   Seabee Memorial Scholarship Association Scholarship

Seabee Memorial Scholarship Association, Inc.
P.O. Box 6574
Silver Spring, MD 20916
(301) 871-3172
Average award: $1,750
Number of awards: 17
Deadline: April 15
College level: Freshman, Sophomore, Junior, Senior
Criteria: Applicant must be the child or grandchild of a regular, retired, reserve, or deceased officer or enlisted member of the Seabees. Selection is based upon financial need, citizenship, scholastic record, and good character. Fulfillment of scholarship contract is required to retain scholarship. Awarded every year.
Contact: Sheryl Chiogioji, Administrative Assistant, smsa@erols.com.

2414   Second Marine Division Association Memorial Scholarship

Second Marine Division Association
P.O. Box 8180
Camp LeJeune, NC 28547
(910) 451-3167, (910) 451-3167 (fax)
Average award: $800
Maximum award: $1,400
Number of awards: 30
Deadline: April 1
College level: Freshman, Sophomore, Junior, Senior
Criteria: Applicant must be the unmarried child of a parent who served in the Second Marine Division or a unit attached to the Second Marine Division. Parents' taxable income should not exceed $30,000. Minimum 2.5 GPA is required to retain scholarship. Awarded every year.
Contact: Chuck Van Horne, Executive Secretary.

2415   South Carolina Free Tuition for Children of Certain Veterans

South Carolina Governor's Office, Division of Veterans Affairs
1205 Pendleton Street
Columbia, SC 29201
(803) 765-5104, (803) 253-3180 (fax)
Average award: Full tuition
Deadline: None
College level: Freshman, Sophomore, Junior, Senior
Criteria: Applicant must be the child of a disabled or deceased American war veteran, POW, MIA, or Congressional Medal of Honor winner who was a South Carolina resident at the time of entry into the military or has been a resident of the state for at least one year. If deceased, veteran must have resided in South Carolina one year prior to death. Eligibility terminates upon the applicant's 26th birthday. Applicant must attend a South Carolina state-supported college, university, or post-high school technical educational institution. Scholarship is renewable. Awarded every year.
Contact: Stan Thornburgh, Field Office Supervisor.

2416   Southeast Asia POW/MIA Scholarship

Mississippi Board of Trustees of State Institutions of Higher Learning
Student Financial Aid Office
3825 Ridgewood Road
Jackson, MS 39211-6453
(601) 982-6663, (601) 982-6527 (fax)
Average award: Tuition, average cost of dorm room, and fees
College level: Freshman, Sophomore, Junior, Senior
Criteria: Applicant must be the child of a Mississippi veteran presently or formerly listed as MIA in Southeast Asia who has been a prisoner of a foreign government as a result of the military action against the U.S. naval vessel Pueblo. Applicant is eligible until age 23 and must be enrolled in a Mississippi public college or university. POW/MIA must have been a Mississippi resident at the time of induction into the armed forces and at the time he was officially listed as POW or MIA; spouse must have been a Mississippi resident for at least ten years during her minority and at the time of the child's enrollment. Award is for a maximum of eight semesters. Awarded every year.
Contact: Student Financial Aid Office.

2417   U.S. Coast Guard Academy Scholarship

United States Coast Guard Academy
15 Mohegan Avenue
New London, CT 06320-4195
(800) 883-8724, 203 444-8503 (fax)
UScgatr@dcseq.uscga.edu
Average award: Full tuition for four years
Number of awards: 240
Deadline: December 15
College level: Freshman
Majors/Fields: Coast Guard Academy program
Criteria: Applicant must be a U.S. citizen, a high school graduate, from age 17 to 22, unmarried, have no legal or moral responsibility to financially support children or a family, and have a genuine desire to serve in the Coast Guard. Selection is based upon annual nationwide competition. Recipient must maintain satisfactory academic and military performance to retain scholarship. Awarded every year. Award may be used only at sponsoring institution.
Contact: Director of Admissions.

2418 United States Naval Academy Class of 1963
Foundation Scholarship
United States Naval Academy Class of 1963 Foundation
3309 Parkside Terrace
Fairfax, VA 22031
Average award: $1,000
Maximum award: $4,000
Number of awards: 6
Deadline: None
College level: Freshman, Sophomore, Junior, Senior, Graduate,
Doctoral, vocational school students
Criteria: Applicant must be the son or daughter of a deceased member of the U.S. Naval Academy class of 1963. Satisfactory academic
progress is required to retain scholarship. Awarded every year.
Contact: Mr. J. Michael Lents, Chairman of Scholarship Committee,
lents@osg.saic.com.

2419 Veterans' Dependent Scholarship
Northern Kentucky University
Administrative Center 416
Nunn Drive
Highland Heights, KY 41099-7101
(606) 572-5144
Average award: Full tuition
Deadline: February 1
College level: Freshman, Sophomore, Junior, Senior
Criteria: Applicant must be a dependent of a permanently disabled
national guardsman, war veteran, prisoner of war, or serviceman
missing in action, or of a serviceman killed while in service or who
died as a result of a service-connected disability. Award is to age 23,
completion of degree or certification, or 36 months attendance,
whichever comes first. Scholarship is renewable. Awarded every
year. Award may be used only at sponsoring institution.
Contact: Robert E. Sprague, Director of Financial Aid.

2420 Vice Admiral E.P. Travers Scholarship
Navy-Marine Corps Relief Society
Education Division
801 North Randolph Street, Suite 1228
Arlington, VA 22203-1978
(703) 696-4960
Maximum award: $2,000
Number of awards: 500
Deadline: March 1
College level: Freshman, Sophomore, Junior, Senior
Criteria: Applicant must be the dependent child of an active duty or
retired Navy or Marine Corps servicemember, or the dependent
spouse of an active duty Navy or Marine Corps servicemember, and
demonstrate financial need. Reapplication, satisfactory academic
progress, and financial need are required to retain scholarship.
Awarded every year.
Contact: Education Specialist.

Multiple Majors—————

2421 Bodine Annual Scholarship
Clemson University
G-01 Sikes Hall
Clemson, SC 29634-5123
(803) 656-2280
Average award: $2,500
Number of awards: 1
Deadline: March 1
College level: Sophomore, Junior, Senior
Majors/Fields: Biological sciences, chemistry, microbiology, physics
Criteria: Applicant must have a minimum 2.7 GPA. Awarded every
year. Award may be used only at sponsoring institution.
Contact: Scholarships.

2422 Departmental Awards
Baker University
P.O. Box 61
Baldwin City, KS 66006
(913) 594-4595
Average award: $4,000
Number of awards: 40
Deadline: February 15
College level: Freshman, Transfer
Criteria: Award based upon faculty selection. Audition is required of
music and theater applicants. Portfolio is required of art applicants.
Minimum 3.0 GPA is required for renewal. Awarded every year.
Award may be used only at sponsoring institution.
Contact: Scholarships.

2423 Fund for American Scholarships
Fund for American Studies
1526 18th Street, NW
Washington, DC 20036
(202) 986-0384, (202) 986-0390 (fax)
http://www.dcinternships.org
Maximum award: $2,975
Deadline: In March
College level: Unspecified undergraduates.
Majors/Fields: Economics, politics, business/government affairs, or
journalism
Criteria: Applicants must plan to attend one of three seven-week
summer institutes. Fund for American Studies summer institutes
only.
Contact: Lisa Goldy, Director, Engalitcheff Institute, goldy@tfas.org.

2424 Henry I. and Thelma W. Sanders Endowed
Scholarship
Clemson University
G-01 Sikes Hall
Clemson, SC 29634-5123
(803) 656-2280
Average award: $3,500
Number of awards: 2
Deadline: March 1
College level: Freshman, Sophomore, Junior, Senior
Majors/Fields: Chemistry, electrical engineering
Criteria: Applicant must have a minimum 2.5 GPA. One award is for a
chemistry major, the other for an electrical engineering major. Satisfactory GPA and completion of at least 12 credit hours per semester
are required to retain scholarship. Awarded every year. Award may
be used only at sponsoring institution.
Contact: Marvin Carmichael, Director of Financial Aid.

2425 "Making Connections" Merit Aid Program
Bennington College
Bennington, VT 05201
(802) 442-5401
Maximum award: $10,000
Deadline: February 1
College level: Freshman
Majors/Fields: Environmental studies, multidisciplinary studies, performing arts, service and public issues, visual arts and new media,
writing
Criteria: Satisfactory academic performance is required to retain
scholarship. Awarded every year. Award may be used only at sponsoring institution.
Contact: Elena Ruocoo Bachrach, Dean of Admissions and the First
Year, (802) 442-5401, extension 161.

2426   Sumitomo Machinery Corporation of America

Old Dominion University
Hampton Boulevard
Norfolk, VA 23529-0050
(804) 683-3683
Maximum award: $2,500
Number of awards: 2
Deadline: February 15
College level: Freshman, Sophomore, Junior, Senior
Majors/Fields: Arts/letters, engineering, technology
Criteria: Preference is given to applicant planning to major in engineering and international studies. Recipient will be eligible for work-study in Japan during junior year with appropriate employment and renumeration by Sumitomo Machinery Corp. Minimum 3.0 GPA and approval of award committee are required to retain scholarship. Awarded every year. Award may be used only at sponsoring institution.
Contact: Dr. A. Sidney Roberts, Chair of Dual Degree Committee, College of Engineering, Norfolk, VA 23529, (804) 683-3720.

2427   Tyson Foundation Scholarship

Tyson Foundation
2210 West Oaklawn Drive
Springdale, AR 72762-6999
(501) 290-4955, (501) 290-7984 (fax)
Average award: $800
Maximum award: $1,500
Minimum award: $200
Deadline: April 20
College level: Freshman, Sophomore, Junior, Senior
Majors/Fields: Agriculture, business, computer science, engineering, nursing
Criteria: Applicant must be a U.S. citizen and a permanent resident in the vicinity of a Tyson operating facility. Applicant must be enrolled full time at an accredited institution, must demonstrate financial need, and must help fund award by semester or summer employment. Write for application by the last week in February. Scholarship continues as long as recipient maintains application criteria. Awarded every year.
Contact: Cheryl Tyson or Annetta Young.

National Merit

2428   Academic Achievement Award

The Master's College
21726 Placerita Canyon Road
Santa Clarita, CA 91321-1200
(805) 259-3540, (805) 288-1037 (fax)
Average award: Full tuition
College level: Freshman
Criteria: Applicant must be a National Merit Finalist. After first year, award is one-half tuition. Minimum 3.5 GPA required to retain scholarship. Awarded every year. Award may be used only at sponsoring institution.
Contact: Timothy C. Wiegert, Associate Director of Enrollment, (800) 568-6248 extension 450.

2429   Academic Achievement Scholarship

Wheeling Jesuit University
316 Washington Avenue
Wheeling, WV 26003
(304) 243-2304
http://www.wju.edu/
Average award: Half tuition
Deadline: None
College level: Freshman
Criteria: Applicant must be a National Merit semifinalist or finalist. Status must be verified by high school or by National Merit Scholarship Corp. FAFSA is required. Satisfactory academic progress is required to retain scholarship. Awarded every year. Award may be used only at sponsoring institution.
Contact: Admissions Office.

2430   Beatrice National Merit Scholarship

Beatrice Foundation
Two North LaSalle Street
Chicago, IL 60602
(312) 558-4000
Maximum award: $2,500
Number of awards: 10
Deadline: Take PSAT by fall of junior year
College level: Freshman
Criteria: Applicant must be the child of an employee of the Beatrice Co. Program is administered by the National Merit Scholarship Corp. Applicants must take the PSAT/NMSQT in the fall of their junior year in high school. Scholarship is for four years. Awarded every year.
Contact: Lynda Robbins, Scholarship Administrator.

2431   Discovery Scholarship

Ohio State University–Columbus
Third Floor Lincoln Tower
1800 Cannon Drive
Columbus, OH 43210-1200
(614) 292-3980
Average award: Full in-state tuition
Deadline: February 15
College level: Freshman
Criteria: Applicant must be a National Merit or National Achievement scholar not receiving the Distinguished Scholarship. First priority is given to finalists designating Ohio State U as their first choice institution. Minimum 3.2 GPA and satisfactory academic progress are required to retain scholarship. Awarded every year. Award may be used only at sponsoring institution.
Contact: Mary Haldane, Director of Financial Aid.

2432   Distinguished Scholar Award

Texas Christian University
2800 South University Drive
Fort Worth, TX 76129
(817) 921-7858, (817) 921-7462 (fax)
frogaid@tcu.edu
Maximum award: $10,048
Number of awards: 24
Deadline: None
College level: Freshman
Criteria: Applicant must be a National Merit or National Achievement finalist who listed Texas Christian U as a first choice college with the National Merit Corporation by February 1, or a National Hispanic finalist who listed Texas Christian U as a first choice college with The College Board. Renewable if recipient maintains a minimum 3.0 GPA (3.25 GPA after freshman year) and 27 credit hours per year. Awarded every year. Award may be used only at sponsoring institution.
Contact: Office of Scholarships and Financial Aid, TCU Box 297012, Fort Worth, TX 76129.

2433   Distinguished Scholarship

Ohio State University–Columbus
Third Floor Lincoln Tower
1800 Cannon Drive
Columbus, OH 43210-1200
(614) 292-3980
Average award: Full in-state tuition, room and board
Deadline: February 15
College level: Freshman
Criteria: Applicant must be a National Merit or National Achievement scholar. First priority is given to finalists designating Ohio State U as their first choice institution. Minimum 3.2 GPA and satisfactory academic progress are required to retain scholarship. Awarded every year. Award may be used only at sponsoring institution.
Contact: Mary Haldane, Director of Financial Aid.

2434 Foundation Merit Award

Southern Illinois University at Carbondale
Carbondale, IL 62901
(618) 453-5351
Average award: $3,150
Maximum award: $3,400
Minimum award: $2,900
Number of awards: 4
Deadline: February 1
College level: Freshman
Criteria: Selection is based upon National Merit status. Renewable for up to four years if minimum 3.5 GPA is maintained. Awarded every year. Award may be used only at sponsoring institution.
Contact: Tammy Cavaretta, Assistant Director, New Student Admission Services, Carbondale, IL 62901-4710, (618) 536-4405.

2435 Hallmark Scholarship

Western Kentucky University
Cravens Library 101
Bowling Green, KY 42101
(502) 745-2551
Average award: $3,104
Number of awards: 25
Deadline: February 15
College level: Freshman
Criteria: Applicant must be a National Merit, National Hispanic, or National Achievement semifinalist. Minimum 3.2 cumulative GPA is required to retain scholarship. Awarded every year. Award may be used only at sponsoring institution.
Contact: Dennis M. Smith, Assistant Director of Admissions.

2436 Mastin Scholarship in Natural Science and Mathematics

John Carroll University
20700 North Park Boulevard
Cleveland, OH 44118
(216) 397-4248
Average award: $10,000
Number of awards: 4
Deadline: April 1
College level: Freshman
Majors/Fields: Biology, chemistry, mathematics, physics
Criteria: Applicant must be a National Merit finalist or semifinalist, have a minimum composite ACT score of 27, and be committed to the fields of biology, chemistry, mathematics, or physics. Application with essay, recommendations, and high school course listing required; FAFSA recommended. Selection is based upon exceptional academic achievement. Recipient must major in mathematics or science and maintain a minimum 3.0 GPA and full-time enrollment to retain scholarship. Awarded every year. Award may be used only at sponsoring institution.
Contact: Office of Admission.

2437 Merit Award

William Woods University
200 West Twelfth Street
Fulton, MO 65251-1098
(573) 592-4232, (573) 592-1146 (fax)
http://www.wmwoods.edu
Average award: Full tuition
Number of awards: 2
Deadline: June 1
College level: Freshman
Criteria: Awarded to National Merit finalists and semifinalists. Written verification of status is required. Reapplication and a minimum 3.5 GPA are required for renewal. Awarded every year. Award may be used only at sponsoring institution.
Contact: Laura L. Archuleta, Director for Student Financial Aid, larchule@iris.wmwoods.edu.

2438 Merit Scholarship

St. Cloud State University
720 South 4th Avenue
St. Cloud, MN 56301
(320) 255-2244
Average award: $5,500
Number of awards: 3
Deadline: April 1
College level: Freshman
Criteria: Awarded to National Merit Finalists who designate St. Cloud St U as their first choice with National Merit Scholarship Corp. Minimum 3.0 GPA required to retain scholarship. Awarded every year. Award may be used only at sponsoring institution.
Contact: Susan Engel, Assistant Director of Admissions.

2439 National Achievement Scholarship

University of Central Florida
Undergraduate Admissions
P.O. Box 160111
Orlando, FL 32816-0111
(407) 823-3000, (407) 823-3419 (fax)
http://www.ucf.edu
Average award: $4,500
Maximum award: $5,000
Minimum award: $4,000
Number of awards: 10
Deadline: March 1
College level: Freshman
Criteria: Applicant must be a National Achievement finalist ($5,000 award) or semifinalist ($4,000 award). Minimum 3.0 GPA and full-time status are required to retain scholarship. Awarded every year. Award may be used only at sponsoring institution.
Contact: Susan McKinnon, Director.

2440 National Achievement Scholarship

University of Toledo
Financial Aid Office
Toledo, OH 43606-3390
(419) 537-2056
Average award: Comprehensive tuition
Deadline: January 28
College level: Freshman
Criteria: Applicant must be a minority National Achievement finalist. Award is for four years. Awarded every year. Award may be used only at sponsoring institution.
Contact: Coordinator of Admissions Services for Scholars, Office of Admissions Services, Toledo, OH 43606, (419) 537-2073.

2441 National Achievement/University Scholarship

University of Texas at Austin
P.O. Box 7758
UT Station
Austin, TX 78713-7758
(512) 475-6200, (512) 475-6296 (fax)
finaid@www.utexas.edu
http://www.utexas.edu/student/finaid
Average award: $1,250
Maximum award: $6,000
Minimum award: $750
Maximum number of awards: 200
Minimum number of awards: 50
Deadline: May 31
College level: Freshman
Criteria: Applicant must be a finalist in the National Achievement competition and must indicate U of Texas at Austin as first-choice institution. Renewable if recipient maintains a minimum 3.25 GPA. Awarded every year. Award may be used only at sponsoring institution.
Contact: Kathryn Cruz, National Merit Coordinator.

2442   National Merit Finalist Scholarship

Baylor University
P.O. Box 97028
Waco, TX 76798-7028
(817) 755-2611, (817) 755-2695 (fax)
financialaid_office@baylor.edu
http://www.baylor.edu
Average award: Full tuition
Deadline: None
College level: Freshman
Criteria: Applicant must be a National Merit Scholarship Finalist. Renewable if recipient maintains a minimum 3.5 GPA. Awarded every year. Award may be used only at sponsoring institution.
Contact: Richard F. Nettles, Director of Scholarships, richard_nettles@baylor.edu.

2443   National Merit Finalist Scholarship

University of Toledo
Financial Aid Office
Toledo, OH 43606-3390
(419) 537-2056
Average award: Comprehensive tuition
Deadline: January 28
College level: Freshman
Criteria: Applicant must be a National Merit finalist. Award is for four years. Awarded every year. Award may be used only at sponsoring institution.
Contact: Coordinator of Admissions Services for Scholars, Office of Admissions Services, Toledo, OH 43606, (419) 537-2073.

2444   National Merit Scholar Award

Florida Atlantic University
500 N.W. 20th Street
P.O. Box 3091
Boca Raton, FL 334310991
(407) 367-3000
Average award: $5,000
Deadline: None
College level: Freshman
Criteria: Awarded to National Merit scholars. Renewable for up to four years based upon academic achievement. Awarded every year. Award may be used only at sponsoring institution.
Contact: Office of Admissions.

2445   National Merit Scholarship

Alfred University
Alumni Hall
26 North Main Street
Alfred, NY 14802
(607) 871-2159
Maximum award: Full tuition, room and board
Minimum award: Full tuition
Number of awards: 25
Deadline: March 1
College level: Freshman
Criteria: Awarded to National Merit finalists who designate Alfred U as their first choice institution with National Merit Scholarship Corp. Renewable for up to eight semesters if minimum 3.3 GPA and continuous full-time enrollment are maintained. Awarded every year. Award may be used only at sponsoring institution.
Contact: Scholarships.

2446   National Merit Scholarship

University of Central Florida
Undergraduate Admissions
P.O. Box 160111
Orlando, FL 32816-0111
(407) 823-3000, (407) 823-3419 (fax)
http://www.ucf.edu
Average award: $4,000
Minimum award: $3,000
Number of awards: 25
Deadline: March 1
College level: Freshman
Criteria: Applicant must be a National Merit finalist ($5,000 award) or semifinalist ($4,000 award). Applicant will also be considered for an enhancement of $1000 for one year of involvement in the LEAD or Honors Program. Minimum 3.0 GPA and full-time enrollment are required to retain scholarship. Awarded every year. Award may be used only at sponsoring institution.
Contact: Susan McKinnon, Director.

2447   National Merit Scholarship

Denison University
Box H
Granville, OH 43023
(614) 587-6276, 800-DENISON, (614) 587-6306 (fax)
admissions@denison.edu
http://www.denison.edu
Maximum award: Half tuition
Deadline: January 1
College level: Freshman
Criteria: Applicant must be a National Merit Scholar (eligible for $500-$2,000), a National Merit Finalist, or a National Hispanic Scholar (both eligible for maximum Founders Award). Minimum 3.2 GPA is required for renewal. Awarded every year. Award may be used only at sponsoring institution.
Contact: Scholarships.

2448   National Merit Scholarship

Hope College
P.O. Box 9000
Holland, MI 49422-9000
(616) 395-7850, (616) 395-7130 (fax)
admissions@hope.edu
http://www.hope.edu
Average award: $12,000
College level: Freshman, Sophomore, Junior, Senior
Criteria: Awarded to National Merit Scholars who have designated Hope Coll as their first choice with National Merit Scholarship Corp. Renewable if recipient maintains a minimum 3.0 GPA. Awarded every year. Award may be used only at sponsoring institution.
Contact: James R. Bekkering, Vice President for Admissions.

2449   National Merit Scholarship

Liberty University
1971 University Boulevard
Lynchburg, VA 24502-2269
(800) 543-5317
Average award: $5,580
Number of awards: 14
Deadline: June 15; October 15
College level: Freshman
Criteria: Applicant is selected by the National Merit Foundation, have a minimum 3.9 GPA, and participate in the honors program. Renewable if recipient maintains eligibility for the Honors Program. Awarded every year. Award may be used only at sponsoring institution.
Contact: Dr. James Nutter, Director of Honors Program, (800) 522-6225, extension 2345.

2450 National Merit Scholarship

Northwestern College
101 College Lane
Orange City, IA 51041
(800) 747-4757, 712 737-7130, (712) 737-7164 (fax)
markb@nwciowa.edu
http://www.nwciowa.edu
Average award: $5,100
Deadline: None
College level: Freshman
Criteria: Applicant must be a National Merit finalist and submit recommendation and transcript. Minimum 3.0 GPA is required to retain scholarship. Awarded every year. Award may be used only at sponsoring institution.
Contact: Ron DeJong, Director of Admission, rondj@nwciowa.edu.

2451 National Merit Scholarship

Northwestern College
3003 North Snelling Avenue
St. Paul, MN 55113
(612) 631-5211
Average award: $8,750
Number of awards: 3
College level: Freshman
Criteria: Applicant must be a National Merit finalist, semi-finalist, or commended scholar. Renewable if recipient maintains 3.25 GPA. Awarded every year. Award may be used only at sponsoring institution.
Contact: Curtis Langemeier, Associate Dean of Admissions, (612) 631-5111.

2452 National Merit Scholarship

University of Richmond
Richmond, VA 23173
(804) 289-8438
Maximum award: Half tuition
Deadline: None
College level: Freshman
Criteria: Awarded to National Merit finalists who designate U of Richmond their first choice with National Merit Scholarship Corp. and who are not awarded a National Merit Scholarship from another sponsor. Awarded every year. Award may be used only at sponsoring institution.
Contact: Scholars Office, (804) 289-8916.

2453 National Merit Scholarship

Wichita State University
203 Jardine
Wichita, KS 67260-0024
(316) 978-3878
Average award: $3,000
Deadline: March 15
College level: Freshman
Criteria: Applicant must be a National Merit scholar. Minimum 3.2 GPA is required to retain scholarship. Awarded every year. Award may be used only at sponsoring institution.
Contact: Scholarship Coordinator.

2454 National Merit Supplemental Scholarship

University of Houston
4800 Calhoun
Houston, TX 77204-2160
(713) 743-1010 extension 333, (713) 743-9098 (fax)
Average award: $5,800
Maximum award: $6,700
Minimum award: $3,700
Number of awards: 76
Deadline: None
College level: Freshman
Criteria: Applicant must have National Merit status. Minimum 3.2 GPA and 15 hours per semester are required to retain scholarship. Awarded every year. Award may be used only at sponsoring institution.
Contact: Robert B. Sheridan, Director of Scholarships and Financial Aid, (713) 743-9090.

2455 National Merit Tuition Scholarship

Birmingham-Southern College
Arkadelphia Road
Birmingham, AL 35254
(205) 226-4688
Maximum award: $11,660
Deadline: January 5
College level: Freshman
Criteria: Awarded to National Merit or National Achievement finalists who list Birmingham-Southern Coll as their first choice. Minimum 3.0 GPA is required to retain scholarship. Awarded every year. Award may be used only at sponsoring institution.
Contact: Forrest Stuart, Interim Director of Financial Aid Services.

2456 National Merit/Achievement/Hispanic Scholarship Finalist Award and National Merit/Achievement/Hispanic Scholarship Semifinalist Award

Florida Atlantic University
500 N.W. 20th Street
P.O. Box 3091
Boca Raton, FL 334310991
(407) 367-3000
Average award: $3,000 (semifinalists), $4,000 (finalists)
Deadline: None
College level: Freshman
Criteria: Awarded to National Achievement, National Hispanic, and National Merit finalists. Renewable for up to four years based upon academic achievement. Awarded every year. Award may be used only at sponsoring institution.
Contact: Office of Admissions.

2457 National Scholarship

Wright State University
Coordinator of Scholarships
Dayton, OH 45435
(513) 873-5721
Average award: $6,672
Number of awards: 6
Deadline: March 1
College level: Freshman
Criteria: Applicant must be a National Merit finalist or National Achievement finalist. Minimum 3.0 cumulative GPA is required to retain scholarship. Awarded every year. Award may be used only at sponsoring institution.
Contact: Judy Rose, Assistant Director of Financial Aid, (513) 873-2321.

2458 Presidential Scholarship

Old Dominion University
Hampton Boulevard
Norfolk, VA 23529-0050
(804) 683-3683
Average award: Tuition, room, board, book allowance, and personal computer
Deadline: February 15
College level: Freshman
Criteria: Applicant must be a National Merit or National Achievement finalist who designates Old Dominion U as first choice. Minimum 3.25 GPA is required to retain scholarship for three additional years. Awarded every year. Award may be used only at sponsoring institution.
Contact: Mary A. Schutz, Assistant Director of Scholarships.

2459   Rock Island Securities Scholarship

Beloit College
700 College Street
Beloit, WI 53511
(608) 363-2663
Average award: $4,000
Deadline: January 31
College level: Freshman
Criteria: Applicant must be a National Merit Finalist who selected Beloit Coll as his or her first choice school. Scholarship is renewable. Awarded every year. Award may be used only at sponsoring institution.
Contact: Thorhas Kreiser, Director of Freshman Financial Aid.

2460   Special Honors Scholarship

Eckerd College
4200 54th Avenue South
St. Petersburg, FL 33711
(813) 864-8331, 800 456-9009, (813) 866-2304 (fax)
admissions@eckerd.edu
http://www.eckerd.edu
Average award: $16,450
Average award: Full tuition
Number of awards: 15
Deadline: February 15
College level: Freshman
Criteria: Applicant must be a finalist or semifinalist in the National Achievement, National Hispanic, or National Merit Scholarship programs. Financial need is not considered. Renewable if recipient maintains a minimum 3.0 GPA. Awarded every year. Award may be used only at sponsoring institution.
Contact: Dr. Richard Hallin, Dean of Admissions.

2461   Stanley Works National Merit Scholarship

Stanley Works Scholarship Program
1000 Stanley Drive
New Britain, CT 06053
Maximum award: $4,000
Number of awards: 4
Deadline: December 31
College level: Freshman
Criteria: Applicant must be a U.S. citizen and the child of a Stanley employee or retiree. Good academic and disciplinary standing required for renewal. Awarded every year.
Contact: Mona Zdun, Employee Relations Administrator, (203) 827-3872.

2462   Thomas Doane Scholarship

Doane College
1014 Boswell Avenue
Crete, NE 68333
(800) 333-6263, (402) 826-8600 (fax)
http://www.doane.edu
Average award: $12,610
Number of awards: 1
Deadline: None
College level: Freshman
Criteria: Applicant must be a National Merit finalist. Renewable for up to four years (eight semesters) if minimum 3.5 GPA is maintained. Awarded every year. Award may be used only at sponsoring institution.
Contact: Janet Dodson, Director of Financial Aid, (402) 826-8260, jdodson@doane.edu.

Physically Handicapped—

2463   ACB Scholarship

American Council of the Blind (ACB)
1155 Fifteenth Street, NW
Suite 720
Washington, DC 20005
(202) 467-5081 or (800) 424-8666, (202) 467-5085 (fax)
http://www.acb.org
Average award: $2,500
Maximum award: $4,000
Minimum award: $500
Number of awards: 25
Deadline: March 1
College level: Freshman, Sophomore, Junior, Senior, Graduate, Doctoral, vocational/technical school
Criteria: Applicant must be legally blind. Awarded every year.
Contact: Holly Fults, Scholarship Coordinator, hfults@erols.com.

2464   American Action Fund Scholarship

National Federation of the Blind (NFB)
805 Fifth Avenue
Grinnell, IA 50112
(515) 236-3366
Average award: $10,000
Number of awards: 1
Deadline: March 31
College level: Freshman, Sophomore, Junior, Senior, Graduate, Doctoral
Criteria: Applicant must be legally blind and pursuing a full-time course of study. Selection is based upon academic excellence, service to the community, and financial need. Awarded every year.
Contact: Peggy Elliott, Scholarship Committee Chairperson.

2465   Blind and Deaf Students Tuition Exemption

Texas Higher Education Coordinating Board
Student Financial Assistance
P.O. Box 12788, Capitol Station
Austin, TX 78711-2788
(512) 427-6340
Average award: $4,845
Number of awards: 1,954
College level: Freshman, Sophomore, Junior, Senior, Graduate, Doctoral
Criteria: Applicant must provide certification of deafness or blindness from the appropriate state vocational rehabilitation agency where applicant is a client. Applicant must have a high school diploma or its equivalent, demonstrate high moral character, and meet entrance requirements for public colleges or universities in Texas. Scholarship is renewable. Awarded every year.
Contact: Sharon Cobb, Assistant Commissioner for Student Services, Capitol Station, P.O. Box 12788, Austin, TX 78711-2788.

2466   Communication Contest for the Deaf and Hard of Hearing

Optimist International
Maximum award: $1,500
Maximum number of awards: 60
Minimum number of awards: 40
Deadline: varies
College level: Freshman
Criteria: Applicant must be attending secondary school in the U.S., Canada, or Jamaica and be identified by school as having hearing loss or impairment.
Contact: local Optimist Club.

2467 EIF Scholarship Fund

Electronic Industries Foundation (EIF)
919 18th Street, NW
Suite 900
Washington, DC 20006
(202) 955-5814, (202) 955-5836 (TDD), (202) 955-5837 (fax)
Average award: $5,000
Number of awards: 6
Deadline: February 1
College level: Freshman, Sophomore, Junior, Senior, Graduate, Doctoral
Majors/Fields: Electrical engineering, electromechanical technology, electronics, industrial engineering, industrial manufacturing, mechanical applied sciences, physics
Criteria: Applicant must be a disabled U.S. citizen. Selection is based upon career and academic goals, GPA, essay, and extracurricular activities. Awarded every year.
Contact: Scholarship Award Committee.

2468 E.U. Parker Scholarship

National Federation of the Blind (NFB)
805 Fifth Avenue
Grinnell, IA 50112
(515) 236-3366
Average award: $3,000
Number of awards: 1
Deadline: March 31
College level: Freshman, Sophomore, Junior, Senior, Graduate, Doctoral
Criteria: Applicant must be legally blind and pursuing a full-time course of study. Selection is based upon academic excellence, service to the community, and financial need. Awarded every year.
Contact: Peggy Elliott, Scholarship Committee Chairperson.

2469 Frank Walton Horn Memorial Scholarship

National Federation of the Blind (NFB)
805 Fifth Avenue
Grinnell, IA 50112
(515) 236-3366
Average award: $3,000
Number of awards: 1
Deadline: March 31
College level: Freshman, Sophomore, Junior, Senior, Graduate, Doctoral
Criteria: Applicant must be legally blind and pursing a full-time course of study. Preference is given to applicants studying architecture or engineering. Selection is based upon academic excellence, service to the community, and financial need. Awarded every year.
Contact: Peggy Elliott, Scholarship Commitee Chairperson.

2470 Frederick A. Downes Scholarship

American Foundation for the Blind (AFB)
11 Penn Plaza
Suite 300
New York, NY 10001
(212) 502-7600 (212) 502-7662 (TDD)
Average award: $2,500
Number of awards: 2
Deadline: April 1
College level: Freshman, Sophomore, Junior, Senior
Criteria: Applicant must be a U.S. citizen, legally blind, and age 22 or under. Selection is based upon transcript, three recommendations, and personal statement. Scholarship is renewable. Awarded every year.
Contact: Leslie Rosen, Director of Information Center/Scholarships, (212) 502-7600, (212) 502-7662 (TDD).

2471 Hermione Grant Calhoun Scholarship

National Federation of the Blind (NFB)
805 Fifth Avenue
Grinnell, IA 50112
(515) 236-3366
Average award: $3,000
Number of awards: 1
Deadline: March 31
College level: Freshman, Sophomore, Junior, Senior, Graduate, Doctoral
Criteria: Applicant must be a legally blind woman pursuing a full-time course of study. Selection is based upon academic excellence, service to the community, and financial need. Awarded every year.
Contact: Peggy Elliott, Scholarship Committee Chairperson.

2472 Howard Brown Rickard Scholarship/Kuchler-Killian Memorial Scholarship/Mozelle and Willard Gold Memorial Scholarship/National Federation of the Blind Computer Science Scholarship/NFB Educator of Tomorrow Award/NFB Humanities Scholarship

National Federation of the Blind (NFB)
805 Fifth Avenue
Grinnell, IA 50112
(515) 236-3366
Average award: $3,000
Number of awards: 1
Deadline: March 31
College level: Freshman, Sophomore, Junior, Senior, Graduate, Doctoral
Majors/Fields: Architecture, art, computer science, elementary teaching, engineering, English, foreign languages, history, humanities, law, medicine, natural sciences, philosophy, post-secondary teaching, religion, secondary teaching
Criteria: Applicant must be legally blind and pursuing a full-time course of study. Selection is based upon academic excellence, service to the community, and financial need. Awarded every year.
Contact: Peggy Elliott, Scholarship Committee Chairperson.

2473 Melva T. Owen Memorial Scholarship

National Federation of the Blind (NFB)
805 Fifth Avenue
Grinnell, IA 50112
(515) 236-3366
Average award: $4,000
Number of awards: 1
Deadline: March 31
College level: Freshman, Sophomore, Junior, Senior, Graduate, Doctoral
Criteria: Applicant must be legally blind and pursuing a full-time course of study. Specific major is not required, except that it be directed toward attaining financial independence and shall exclude religion and those seeking only to further general or cultural education. Selection is based upon academic excellence, service to the community, and financial need. Awarded every year.
Contact: Peggy Elliott, Chairperson.

2474 NFB Scholarship

National Federation of the Blind (NFB)
805 Fifth Avenue
Grinnell, IA 50112
(515) 236-3366
Maximum award: $4,000
Number of awards: 15
Deadline: March 31
College level: Freshman, Sophomore, Junior, Senior, Graduate, Doctoral
Criteria: Applicant must be legally blind and pursuing a full-time course of study. Selection is based upon academic excellence, service to the community, and financial need. Awarded every year.
Contact: Peggy Elliott, Scholarship Committee Chairperson.

2475   Nordstorm Scholarship

President's Committee on Employment of People with Disabilities
1331 F Street, NW
Washington, DC 20004-1107
(202) 376-6200
Average award: $2,000
Number of awards: 5
Deadline: January 14
College level: Freshman, Sophomore, Junior, Senior
Majors/Fields: Business
Criteria: Applicant must be disabled as defined in the Americans with Disabilities Act (ADA).
Contact: Ellen Daly, Coordinator, Awards/Scholarship Progam.

2476   Robert and Rosemary Low Memorial Scholarship

Portland State University
Financial Aid Department
P.O. Box 751
Portland, OR 97207-0751
(503) 725-5270
Average award: $3,633
Number of awards: 1
Deadline: April 15
College level: Doctoral, regularly admitted master's students
Criteria: Selection is based upon academic merit, statement of goals, faculty recommendations, and physical disability. Financial need is considered but not required. Reapplication with minimum of nine credits per term is required to retain scholarship. Awarded when funds are available. Award may be used only at sponsoring institution.
Contact: Scholarships, Office of Graduate Studies, 303 Cramer Hall, Portland, OR 97207-0751, (503) 725-3423.

2477   Rudolph Dillman Memorial Scholarship

American Foundation for the Blind (AFB)
11 Penn Plaza
Suite 300
New York, NY 10001
(212) 502-7600 (212) 502-7662 (TDD)
Average award: $2,500
Number of awards: 4
Deadline: April 1
College level: Sophomore, Junior, Senior, Graduate, Doctoral
Majors/Fields: Education of the blind/visually impaired, rehabilitation of the blind/visually impaired
Criteria: Applicant must be a U.S. citizen, be studying in the U.S., be legally blind, and be accepted into an accredited program. Selection is based upon transcript, three recommendations, and personal statement. One award is given to applicant who demonstrates financial need. Awarded every year.
Contact: Leslie Rosen, Director of Information Center/Scholarships.

2478   Wisconsin HEAB Visual and Hearing Impaired Program

Wisconsin Higher Educational Aids Board (HEAB)
P.O. Box 7885
131 West Wilson Street
Madison, WI 53707-7885
(608) 266-0888, (608) 267-2808 (fax)
Maximum award: $1,800
College level: Freshman, Sophomore, Junior, Senior
Criteria: Applicant must be a Wisconsin resident, legally deaf or blind, and demonstrate financial need. If the impairment prevents the student from studying in a Wisconsin institution, the grant can be used at an out-of-state institution that specializes in teaching the blind or deaf. Renewable for a maximum of ten semesters. Awarded every year.
Contact: Joyce Apfel, Grants Coordinator, 131 West Wilson Street, P.O. Box 7885, Madison, WI 53707-7885.

Religious Affiliation

2479   Beasley Foundation Grant

Texas Christian University
2800 South University Drive
Fort Worth, TX 76129
(817) 921-7858, (817) 921-7462 (fax)
frogaid@tcu.edu
Average award: $4,000
Number of awards: 125
Deadline: May 1
College level: Freshman, Transfer
Criteria: Applicant must be a member of the Christian Church (Disciples of Christ), have a minimum 3.0 high school GPA (2.5 transfer GPA), rank in top quarter of class, or have a minimum combined SAT I score of 950 (composite ACT score of 23). Selection is based upon academic achievement, leadership potential, and results of FAFSA. Minimum 2.5 GPA and successful completion of at least 24 credit hours per year are required for renewal. Awarded every year. Award may be used only at sponsoring institution.
Contact: Office of Scholarships and Financial Aid, TCU Box 297012, Fort Worth, TX 76129.

2480   Bishop's Award

Ohio Wesleyan University
Office of Admissions
Delaware, OH 43015
(614) 368-3020, (614) 368-3314 (fax)
owuadmit@cc.owu.edu
http://www.owu.edu
Average award: $4,000
Number of awards: 20
Deadline: None
College level: Freshman, Sophomore, Junior, Senior
Criteria: Applicant must be a member of the United Methodist Church who is recommended by his or her minister. Renewable if recipient maintains a minimum 2.75 GPA. Awarded every year. Award may be used only at sponsoring institution.
Contact: Douglas C. Thompson, Dean of Admission.

2481   Byzantine Rite Scholarship

Wheeling Jesuit University
316 Washington Avenue
Wheeling, WV 26003
(304) 243-2304
http://www.wju.edu/
Maximum award: $4,000
Deadline: early November
College level: Freshman
Criteria: Applicant must be from Byzantine parish in Ohio, Pennsylvania, or West Virginia and be nominated by pastor. Academic merit determines amount of award. Those interested should contact their pastors. FAFSA is required. Satisfactory academic progress is required to retain scholarship. Awarded every year. Award may be used only at sponsoring institution.
Contact: Admissions Office.

2482   Christian Church (Disciples of Christ) Award

Chapman University
333 North Glassell Street
Orange, CA 92866
(714) 997-6741, (714) 997-6743 (fax)
http://www.chapman.edu
Average award: Half tuition
Deadline: None
College level: Freshman, Sophomore, Junior, Senior
Criteria: Applicant must be a full-time undergraduate, a member of the Christian Church (Disciples of Christ), and be nominated by a minister. FAFSA is required. Scholarship is renewable. Awarded every year. Award may be used only at sponsoring institution.
Contact: Scholarships.

2483 Christian Leadership Scholarship

Taylor University
500 West Reade Avenue
Upland, IN 46989
(317) 998-5125, (317) 998-4910 (fax)
admissions@tayloru.edu
http://www.tayloru.edu
Maximum award: 80% tuition
Minimum award: One-tenth tuition
Number of awards: 30
Deadline: October 1
College level: Freshman
Criteria: Selection is based upon academic achievement, demonstrated leadership abilities, and scholarship competition held in fall prior to college entrance. Maximum award is given to three applicants; minimum award is given to 18 applicants for one year. Nine applicants receive 40% of tuition. Renewable for up to eight semesters if recipient maintains a minimum 3.0 GPA and involvement in specified leadership activities. Minimum award is not renewable. Awarded every year. Award may be used only at sponsoring institution.
Contact: Larry Mealy, Director of Career and Leadership Development, (317) 998-5384, lrmealy@tayloru.edu.

2484 Christian Worker Award

Philadelphia College of Bible
200 Manor Avenue
Langhorne, PA 19047-2992
(215) 752-5800
Maximum award: $3,000
Deadline: None
College level: Freshman, Sophomore, Junior, Senior
Criteria: Applicant must be the dependent child of a full-time Christian worker who is head of household. Financial need is considered. Award is divided between semesters. Scholarship is renewable. Awarded every year. Award may be used only at sponsoring institution.
Contact: Travis S. Roy, Financial Aid Administrator.

2485 Christian Youth Fellowship (CYF) Grant

Texas Christian University
2800 South University Drive
Fort Worth, TX 76129
(817) 921-7858, (817) 921-7462 (fax)
frogaid@tcu.edu
Average award: $4,400
Maximum award: Half tuition for up to 16 semester hours
Number of awards: 43
Deadline: May 1
College level: Freshman
Criteria: Applicant must be a regional officer of the Christian Youth Fellowship of the Christian Church (Disciples of Christ). Renewable for up to eight semesters if recipient maintains a minimum 2.5 GPA and meets academic criteria. Awarded every year. Award may be used only at sponsoring institution.
Contact: Office of Scholarships and Financial Aid, TCU Box 297012, Fort Worth, TX 76129.

2486 Church and Campus Scholarship

Eckerd College
4200 54th Avenue South
St. Petersburg, FL 33711
(813) 864-8331, 800 456-9009, (813) 866-2304 (fax)
admissions@eckerd.edu
http://www.eckerd.edu
Average award: $5,000
Maximum award: $7,000
Minimum award: $1,000
Number of awards: 30
Deadline: None
College level: Freshman, Transfer
Criteria: Applicant must be a Presbyterian student, have pastor's recommendation, and possess outstanding academic ability, character, and leadership. Financial need is considered. Renewable if recipient maintains a minimum 2.0 GPA. Awarded every year. Award may be used only at sponsoring institution.
Contact: Dr. Richard Hallin, Dean of Admissions.

2487 Clergy Dependent Scholarship

Drury College
900 North Benton Avenue
Springfield, MO 65802
(417) 873-7319
Average award: Half tuition
College level: Freshman
Criteria: Applicant must be accepted for full-time enrollment and be the dependent of clergy in the Christian Church (Disciples of Christ). When funds are available, dependents of clergy of the United Church of Christ may receive awards. This award may not be granted in addition to scholarships which exceed one-half tuition. Renewable for up to four years if recipient maintains a minimum 2.75 GPA after first year (3.0 GPA thereafter). Awarded every year. Award may be used only at sponsoring institution.
Contact: Financial Aid Office.

2488 Covenant Scholarship

The College of Wooster
Office of Admissions
Wooster, OH 44691
(330) 263-2270, (330) 263-2621 (fax)
admissions@acs.wooster.edu
http://www.wooster.edu
Maximum award: $10,000
Deadline: February 15
College level: Freshman
Criteria: Applicant must be a member of the Presbyterian Church (U.S.A.), have a minimum 3.0 GPA, and rank in top fifth of class. Selection is based upon academic achievement, competitive essay, financial need, leadership potential, and recommendation by minister or youth minister. Recipient must maintain academic progress toward degree to retain scholarship. Renewable for four years. Awarded every year. Award may be used only at sponsoring institution.
Contact: Office of Admissions.

2489 Dependent of Minister Scholarship

Trinity Bible College
50 Sixth Avenue South
Ellendale, ND 58436-7150
Average award: One-fourth tuition
Deadline: None
College level: Sophomore, Junior, Senior
Criteria: Applicant must be a full-time student, an unmarried dependent, age 23 or under, of an active ordained or licensed minister or appointed missionary and be claimed on parents' tax return. Verification letter from denomination's District Office is required. Minimum 2.5 GPA is required to retain scholarship. Awarded every year. Award may be used only at sponsoring institution.
Contact: Financial Aid Office, (800) 523-1063.

2490 Disciples Grant

William Woods University
200 West Twelfth Street
Fulton, MO 65251-1098
(573) 592-4232, (573) 592-1146 (fax)
http://www.wmwoods.edu
Average award: Half tuition
Deadline: June 1
College level: Freshman, Sophomore, Junior, Senior
Criteria: Applicant must be the child of an ordained Christian Church (Disciples of Christ) minister of good standing. Reapplication and a minimum 2.75 GPA are required for renewal. Awarded every year. Award may be used only at sponsoring institution.
Contact: Laura L. Archuleta, Director for Student Financial Aid, larchule@iris.wmwoods.edu.

2491   Disciples Leader Program

Lynchburg College
Lynchburg, VA 24501
(804) 522-8228
Average award: $5,000
Deadline: February 15
College level: Freshman
Criteria: Applicant must have served in an elected position on a regional or general youth ministry committee for the Christian Church (Disciples of Christ). Scholarship is renewable. Awarded every year. Award may be used only at sponsoring institution.
Contact: Scholarships.

2492   Elms College Transfer Diocesan/Chicopee Scholarship

Elms College (College of Our Lady of the Elms)
291 Springfield Street
Chicopee, MA 01013
(413) 592-3189, 800 255-ELMS, (413) 594-2781 (fax)
admissions@elms.edu
http://www.crocker.com/nelmscol/
Maximum award: $2,500
Number of awards: 19
Deadline: None
College level: Transfer
Criteria: First priority is given to graduates of a Catholic high school in the Springfield, Mass. diocese. Second priority is given to graduates of Chicopee high schools. All applicants must be women and complete the financial aid process. Satisfactory academic progress and full-time status are required for renewal. Awarded every year. Award may be used only at sponsoring institution.
Contact: Janet DaSilva, Director, Financial Aid, dasilverj@elms.edu.

2493   Jesuit Community Scholarship

Loyola Marymount University
7900 Loyola Boulevard
Los Angeles, CA 90045-8350
(310) 338-2753, (310) 338-2793 (fax)
http://www.lmu.edu
Average award: $4,000
Number of awards: 4
Deadline: February 14 (priority)
College level: Freshman
Criteria: Applicant must be a graduate of a Catholic school, have a good academic record, and be recommended by the school. Scholarship is renewable. Awarded every year. Award may be used only at sponsoring institution.
Contact: Financial Aid Office.

2494   Jesuit/Marymount High School Scholarship

Loyola Marymount University
7900 Loyola Boulevard
Los Angeles, CA 90045-8350
(310) 338-2753, (310) 338-2793 (fax)
http://www.lmu.edu
Average award: $7,500
College level: Freshman
Criteria: Applicant must be an outstanding student and have graduated from a Jesuit or Marymount secondary school. Scholarship is renewable. Awarded every year. Award may be used only at sponsoring institution.
Contact: Financial Aid Office.

2495   Martin Luther Award

Valparaiso University
Valparaiso, IN 46383-6493
(219) 464-5011, (219) 464-6898 (fax)
undergrad_admissions@valpo.edu
http:www.valpo.edu
Average award: $4,000
Deadline: May 1
College level: Freshman
Criteria: Applicant must be the child of a full-time professional Lutheran church worker. Available to transfer applicants on prorated basis. Renewable for up to three years if minimum 2.0 GPA is maintained. Awarded every year. Award may be used only at sponsoring institution.
Contact: Office of Admissions and Financial Aid, Kretzman Hall, (888) GO VALPO.

2496   Max and Emmy Dreyfuss Jewish Undergraduate Scholarship

Jewish Social Service Agency
6123 Montrose Road
Rockville, MD 20852
(301) 816-2676, (301) 770-8741 (fax)
Average award: $2,000
Maximum award: $3,500
Minimum award: $1,500
Deadline: May 30
College level: Freshman, Sophomore, Junior, Senior
Criteria: Applicant must be Jewish, under age 30, and a resident of the Washington Metropolitain area. Selection is based upon need. Special consideration will be given to refugees. Recipient must reapply for renewal.
Contact: Susan Hanenbaum, Scholarship and Loan Coordinator, (301) 881-3700.

2497   Methodist Clergy Scholarship

Boston University
Office of Financial Assistance
881 Commonwealth Avenue
Boston, MA 02215
(617) 353-4175
Average award: Half tuition
Number of awards: 25
Deadline: March 1 (freshmen); May 15 (continuing students)
College level: Freshman, Sophomore, Junior, Senior, Transfer
Criteria: Applicant must be the child of a Methodist minister and submit identification and request for consideration in writing. Applicant's Resident Bishop must provide written verification of parent's active status and church affiliation. Minimum 2.3 GPA and completion of at least 12 credit hours per semester are required to retain scholarship. Awarded every year. Award may be used only at sponsoring institution.
Contact: Maria B. DelSignore, Assistant Director, Special Programs.

2498   Methodist Ministerial Scholarship

Emory University
1380 Oxford Road, NE
Atlanta, GA 30322
(404) 727-6039
Average award: 45% tuition
Deadline: April 15
College level: Freshman
Criteria: Applicant must be the child of an active United Methodist minister or missionary. Awarded every year. Award may be used only at sponsoring institution.
Contact: Office of Financial Aid, 300 Boisfeuillet Jones Center, Atlanta, GA 30322-1960, (404) 727-6039, (800) 727-6039.

2499 Minister and Minister's Dependent Grant

Texas Christian University
2800 South University Drive
Fort Worth, TX 76129
(817) 921-7858, (817) 921-7462 (fax)
frogaid@tcu.edu
Average award: $4,348
Maximum award: Half tuition for up to 16 semester hours
Number of awards: 44
Deadline: May 1
College level: Full-time students
Criteria: Applicant must be one of the following: spouse of a full-time student at Brite Divinity School, the graduate seminary; unmarried, under age 23 dependent of full-time Christian Church ministers or missionaries; resident or employee of Juliette Fowler Home; spouse of a full-time Christian Church minister; full-time Christian Church minister who wishes to continue education part time in undergraduate program. Scholarship is renewable. Awarded every year. Award may be used only at sponsoring institution.
Contact: Office of Scholarships and Student Financial Aid, TCU Box 297012, Fort Worth, TX 76129.

2500 Minister's Dependent Scholarship

Piedmont College
165 Central Avenue
Demorest, GA 30535
(706) 778-3000
Average award: $5,000
Number of awards: 15
Deadline: None
College level: Freshman, Sophomore, Junior, Senior
Criteria: Applicant must be a dependent child of an ordained minister of National Association of Congregational Christian Churches or of an ordained minister serving a Congregational church that provides support to Piedmont Coll. Recipient must maintain a minimum 2.5 GPA and active participation in campus ministry to retain scholarship. Awarded every year. Award may be used only at sponsoring institution.
Contact: Kenneth L. Owen, Director of Financial Aid.

2501 Ministerial Grant

Mount Union College
1972 Clark Avenue
Alliance, OH 44601
(216) 821-5320
Average award: Half tuition
College level: Freshman, Sophomore, Junior, Senior
Criteria: Applicant must be the dependent child of a full-time ordained minister, be accepted for admission, and file FAFSA. Awarded every year. Award may be used only at sponsoring institution.
Contact: Office of Admissions.

2502 Ministerial Grant

University of Indianapolis
1400 East Hanna Avenue
Indianapolis, IN 46227-3697
(317) 788-3217
Maximum award: $3,336
Number of awards: 4
Deadline: None
College level: Freshman
Criteria: Applicant must apply for financial aid, demonstrate financial need, and be a child of a United Methodist Church minister who is under appointment by the Bishop within the connectional structure of church and is pursuing ministry as primary, full-time occupation. Scholarship is renewable. Awarded every year. Award may be used only at sponsoring institution.
Contact: Financial Aid Office.

2503 Missionary Award

Philadelphia College of Bible
200 Manor Avenue
Langhorne, PA 19047-2992
(215) 752-5800
Average award: $2,400
Deadline: None
College level: Sophomore, Junior, Senior
Criteria: Applicant must be a missionary currently serving under an approved board and having served at least four years. Award is divided between semesters. Scholarship is renewable. Awarded every year. Award may be used only at sponsoring institution.
Contact: Travis S. Roy, Financial Aid Administrator.

2504 Missionary Grant

Southeastern Bible College
3001 Highway 280 East
Birmingham, AL 35243
(205) 970-9215
Average award: $3,400
Number of awards: 4
Deadline: May 1
College level: Freshman, Sophomore, Junior, Senior, Graduate
Criteria: Applicant must be a dependent of a missionary. Recipient must remain a dependent of a missionary to retain scholarship. Awarded every year. Award may be used only at sponsoring institution.
Contact: Joanne Belin, Financial Aid Administrator.

2505 Missionary Kids' Scholarship

Campbellsville University
Office of Financial Aid
200 West College Street
Campbellsville, KY 42718
(502) 465-8158
Maximum award: Full tuition
Deadline: April 1 (priority)
College level: Freshman, Sophomore, Junior, Senior
Criteria: Applicant must be the child of missionaries serving with the Southern Baptist Foreign Mission Board, have a minimum 2.0 GPA, and be a full-time student. FAFSA is required. Awarded every year. Award may be used only at sponsoring institution.
Contact: Director of Financial Aid.

2506 Morton A. Gibson Memorial Scholarship

Jewish Social Service Agency
6123 Montrose Road
Rockville, MD 20852
(301) 816-2676, (301) 770-8741 (fax)
Maximum award: $2,500
Number of awards: 2
Deadline: May 30
College level: Freshman
Criteria: Applicant must be a Jewish resident of the Washington metropolitan area who has performed significant volunteer service to the local Jewish community or under the auspices of a Jewish organization. Selection is based upon volunteer service, academics, and need.
Contact: Susan Hanenbaum, Scholarship and Loan Coordinator, (301) 881-3700.

2507   National Presbyterian College Scholarship

Presbyterian Church USA
Office of Financial Aid for Studies
100 Witherspoon Street
Louisville, KY 40202-1396
(502) 569-5776, (502) 569-8766 (fax)
Maximum award: $1,400
Deadline: December 1
College level: Freshman
Criteria: Applicant must be preparing full-time entrance to one of the participating colleges related to the Presbyterian Church USA. Applicant must be a U.S. citizen or permanent resident, a member of the Presbyterian Church, and take the SAT I or ACT no later than December 15 of senior year. Selection is based upon financial need. Scholarship is renewable. Awarded every year. Award may be used only at participating Presbyterian schools.
Contact: Scholarships.

2508   Native American Education Grant

Presbyterian Church USA
Office of Financial Aid for Studies
100 Witherspoon Street
Louisville, KY 40202-1396
(502) 569-5776, (502) 569-8766 (fax)
Maximum award: $1,500
Deadline: June 1
College level: Sophomore
Criteria: Applicant must be an Alaskan Native or Native American, a member of the Presbyterian Church USA, a U.S. citizen or permanent resident, have completed at least one semester of work at an accredited institution, and demonstrated financial need. Scholarship is renewable. Awarded every year.
Contact: Scholarships.

2509   Nazarene Missionary's Dependent Scholarship

Southern Nazarene University
6729 N.W. 39th Expressway
Bethany, OK 73008
(405) 491-6310, (405) 491-6320 (fax)
dlee@snu.edu
Average award: Half tuition
Deadline: None
College level: Freshman, Sophomore, Junior, Senior
Criteria: Applicant must be the dependent of a Nazarene missionary. Renewable if parents of recipient continue to be a Nazarene missionaries. Awarded every year. Award may be used only at sponsoring institution.
Contact: Diana Lee, Director of Financial Assistance.

2510   Pastors' Scholarship

Wheeling Jesuit University
316 Washington Avenue
Wheeling, WV 26003
(304) 243-2304
http://www.wju.edu/
Maximum award: $4,000
Deadline: early November
College level: Freshman
Criteria: Applicant must be from the Diocese of Wheeling-Charleston and be nominated by pastor. Academic merit determines amount of award. Those interested should contact their pastors. FAFSA is required. Satisfactory academic progress is required to retain scholarship. Awarded every year. Award may be used only at sponsoring institution.
Contact: Admissions Office.

2511   Pro Deo and Pro Patria Scholarships

Knights of Columbus
P.O. Box 1670
Department of Scholarships
New Haven, CT 06507-0901
(203) 772-2130, extension 332, (203) 777-0114 (fax)
Average award: $1,500
Number of awards: 50
Deadline: March 1
College level: Freshman
Criteria: Applicant must be a member or the child of a member of the Knights of Columbus and must be attending a Catholic college. Selection is based upon academic excellence. Satisfactory academic performance required to retain scholarship. Awarded every year.
Contact: Father Donald Barry, S.J., Director of Scholarship Aid.

2512   Quaker Leader Scholarship

Wilmington College
Pyle Center Box 1325
Wilmington, OH 45177
(800) 341-9318, (513) 382-7077 (fax)
admission@wilmington.edu
http://www.wilmington.edu
Average award: $7,000
Maximum number of awards: 10
Minimum number of awards: 8
Deadline: May 1
College level: Freshman, Sophomore, Junior, Senior
Criteria: Applicant must be a Quaker. Selection is based upon academic ability, leadership in weekly meeting, and on-campus testing. Awarded every year. Award may be used only at sponsoring institution.
Contact: Financial Aid Office, Pyle Center Box 1184.

2513   Shannon Scholarship

Trinity Episcopal Church
Second Street and Howard Avenue
Pottsville, PA 17901
(717) 622-8720
Average award: $2,500
Number of awards: 16
College level: Freshman
Criteria: Available to daughters of Episcopal priests residing in one of the five dioceses of Pennsylvania. Recipient may pursue field of choice at a two- or four-year institution. Awarded every year.
Contact: Scholarships.

2514   Sikh Education Aid Fund

Sikh Education Aid Fund
P.O. Box 140
Hopewell, VA 23860
(804) 541-9290, (804) 452-1270 (fax)
Average award: $1,400
Maximum award: $3,000
Minimum award: $400
Number of awards: 14
Deadline: June 20
College level: Freshman, Sophomore, Junior, Senior, Graduate, Doctoral
Criteria: Applicant must be of the Sikh faith or studying the Sikh faith with a minimum 3.0 GPA. Financial need is required. Recipient must maintain acceptable performance in academic programs to retain scholarship/loan. Awarded every year.
Contact: Dr. G.S. Bhuller, Coordinator.

2515 Student Opportunity Scholarship

Presbyterian Church USA
Office of Financial Aid for Studies
100 Witherspoon Street
Louisville, KY 40202-1396
(502) 569-5776, (502) 569-8766 (fax)
Maximum award: $1,400
Deadline: April 1
College level: Freshman
Criteria: Applicant must be African-American, Alaskan Native, Asian-American, Hispanic-American, or Native American, a member of the Presbyterian Church USA, a U.S. citizen or permanent resident, and demonstrate financial need. Scholarship is renewable. Awarded every year.
Contact: Scholarships.

2516 United Methodist Award

University of Indianapolis
1400 East Hanna Avenue
Indianapolis, IN 46227-3697
(317) 788-3217
Maximum award: $2,500
Number of awards: 106
Deadline: None
College level: Freshman
Criteria: Applicant must be a member of the United Methodist Church. Minimum "C" grade average is required to retain scholarship. Awarded every year. Award may be used only at sponsoring institution.
Contact: Admissions Office, (317) 788-3216.

2517 Virginia Baptist Scholars Award

University of Richmond
Richmond, VA 23173
(804) 289-8438
Maximum award: Full tuition, room and board
Number of awards: 5
Deadline: January 15
College level: Freshman
Criteria: Awarded to applicants who are nominated by pastors of churches affiliated with Baptist General Association of Virginia. Two Scholars are given the maximum award; three receive the minimum. Awarded every year. Award may be used only at sponsoring institution.
Contact: Scholars Office, (804) 289-8916.

2518 Women of the Evangelical Lutheran Church in America Scholarship

Women of the Evangelical Lutheran Church in America
8765 West Higgins Road
Chicago, IL 60631
(800) 638-3522
Maximum award: $2,000
Number of awards: 6
Deadline: March 1
College level: Unspecified graduate, unspecified undergraduate
Criteria: All scholarships are for mature, Evangelical Lutheran Church in America women who for a number of years have been out of school, in the work force, or homemakers and are returning to school for vocational, academic training, or degrees. Cronk, Mehring, and Piero/Wade scholarships are for undergraduate, graduate, professional, or vocational courses of study. Kahler/Vickers/Raup scholarship is for medical school study. Kemp scholarship is for minority laywomen in graduate courses of study. Knudstrup scholarship is for occupation of service through graduate study. Awarded every year.
Contact: Scholarships.

2519 Zolp Scholarship

Loyola University, Chicago
380 Granada Centre
Chicago, IL 60626
(312) 508-3164
Average award: Full tuition
Deadline: None
College level: Freshman, Sophomore, Junior, Senior, Graduate, Doctoral
Criteria: Applicant must be Roman Catholic and have a last name spelled "Zolp." Scholarship is renewable. Award may be used only at sponsoring institution.
Contact: James G. Dwyer, Director of Financial Aid.

State/Country of Residence

2520   A.W. Bodine–Sunkist Memorial Scholarship

A.W. Bodine–Sunkist Memorial Scholarship
P.O. Box 7888
Van Nuys, CA 91409
(818) 379-7510
Average award: $3,000
Number of awards: 30
Deadline: April 30
College level: Freshman, Sophomore, Junior, Senior
Criteria: Applicant must have a background in Arizona or California agriculture, a minimum 3.0 GPA, and demonstrate financial need. Selection is based upon a combination of grades, ACT or SAT I scores, an essay, and references. Renewable if minimum 2.7 GPA is maintained, 12 units of study are taken, and financial need is demonstrated. Awarded every year.
Contact: Claire Peters, Scholarship Administrator.

2521   Abney Foundation Endowed Scholarship Fund

Clemson University
G-01 Sikes Hall
Clemson, SC 29634-5123
(803) 656-2280
Average award: $2,500
Number of awards: 2
Deadline: None
College level: Freshman, Sophomore, Junior, Senior
Criteria: Applicant must be a resident of South Carolina. Renewable for up to three years if recipient maintains minimum 3.0 GPA and completes at least 12 credits per semester. Awarded every year. Award may be used only at sponsoring institution.
Contact: Scholarships.

2522   Academic Scholars Program

Oklahoma State Regents for Higher Education
500 Education Building
State Capitol Complex
Oklahoma City, OK 73105
(405) 524-9100
Average award: $3,500
Maximum award: $5,000
Minimum award: $3,100
Number of awards: 350
Deadline: Mid-August
College level: Freshman
Criteria: Applicant must be an Oklahoma resident at or above the 99.5 percentile on ACT or SAT I, or be a resident or nonresident that is one of the following: National Merit scholar or finalist, National Achievement scholar or finalist, National Hispanic scholar or honorable mention awardee, or Presidential scholar. Minimum 3.25 GPA and full-time enrollment are required to retain scholarship. Awarded every year.
Contact: Dawn Scott, Research Analyst, (405) 524-9153, dscott@osrhe.edu.

2523   Admissions Academic Scholarships–Non-Resident

University of Central Florida
Undergraduate Admissions
P.O. Box 160111
Orlando, FL 32816-0111
(407) 823-3000, (407) 823-3419 (fax)
http://www.ucf.edu
Average award: $3,000
Maximum award: $3,500
Number of awards: 60
Deadline: March 1
College level: Freshman
Criteria: Applicant must not be a Florida resident. Minimum 3.0 GPA, full-time enrollment, and nonresident status are required to retain scholarship. Awarded every year. Award may be used only at sponsoring institution.
Contact: Susan McKinnon, Director.

2524   Alabama Scholarship for Dependents of Blind Parents

Alabama Department of Education
Administrative and Financial Services Division
Gordon Persons Building, 50 North Ripley
Montgomery, AL 36130
(334) 242-9755, (334) 353-4497 (fax)
Average award: Tuition and instructional fees
College level: Freshman, Sophomore, Junior, Senior
Criteria: Applicant must be an Alabama resident, attend an Alabama postsecondary institit<ion, and come from a family in which the head of the family is blind and whose family income is insufficient to provide educational benefits. Applicant must apply within two years of high school graduation. Scholarship is renewable. Awarded every year.
Contact: Barry Buford, Department of Alabama, (334) 242-8228.

2525   Alaska State Educational Incentive Grants (SEIG)

Alaska Commission on Postsecondary Education
Division of Student Financial Aid
3030 Vintage Boulevard
Juneau, AK 99801-7109
(907) 465-6741, (907) 465-5316 (fax)
ftolbert@acpe.educ.state.ak.us
Average award: $1,500
Minimum award: $100
Number of awards: 300
Deadline: May 31
College level: Freshman, Sophomore, Junior, Senior
Criteria: Awarded every year.
Contact: Program Coordinator.

2526   Alberta Heritage Louise McKinney Scholarship

University of Calgary
Department of Financial Aid
2500 University Drive, NW
Calgary, Alberta, CN T2N 1N4
(403) 220-7872, (403) 282-2999 (fax)
Maximum award: $4,000
Deadline: June 15
College level: Sophomore, Junior, Senior
Criteria: Applicant must be an Alberta resident with outstanding academic ability. Awarded every year. Award may be used only at sponsoring institution.
Contact: J. Van Housen, Director of Student Awards/ Financial Aid.

2527 Alumnae Scholarship

University of Southern California
University Park
Los Angeles, CA 90089-5012
(213) 740-1111
Maximum award: $5,000
Maximum number of awards: 60
Minimum number of awards: 50
Deadline: December 15
College level: Freshman, Transfer
Criteria: Minimum GPA: freshman: 3.6 (must score at least 1200 on SAT and 27 on ACT); transfer students: 3.0. Personal interview is required. Selection is based upon academic performance and leadership. Priority is given to California residents. Scholarship is renewable. Awarded every year. Award may be used only at sponsoring institution.
Contact: Office of Admission, University Park Campus, Los Angeles, CA 90089-0911.

2528 Alumni Past Presidents Scholarship

Clemson University
G-01 Sikes Hall
Clemson, SC 29634-5123
(803) 656-2280
Maximum award: $3,500
Number of awards: 1
Deadline: None
College level: Freshman
Criteria: Applicant must be a South Carolina resident. Selection is based upon admissions application. Minimum 3.0 GPA and completion of at least 12 credits per semester are required to retain scholarship. Awarded every year. Award may be used only at sponsoring institution.
Contact: Marvin Carmichael, Director of Financial Aid.

2529 Alumni Scholarship

University of California, Los Angeles
A129 Murphy Hall
Box 951435
Los Angeles, CA 90095-1435
(310) 206-0404
Maximum award: $10,000
Number of awards: 355
College level: Freshman, Transfer
Criteria: Freshman applicant must graduate from a California high school with a minimum 3.85 GPA and a minimum combined SAT I score of 1200. Transfer applicant must have at least 84 transferable quarter units from a California community college and have a minimum 3.5 GPA. Awarded every year. Award may be used only at sponsoring institution.
Contact: Beverly LeMay, Assistant Director of Scholarships, (310) 206-0417.

2530 Alumni Valedictorian Scholarship

University of Memphis
Scates Hall 204
Memphis, TN 38152
(901) 678-3213, (901) 678-5621 (fax)
katkinsn@cc.memphis.edu
http://www.memphis.edu/
Average award: $2,180
Deadline: March 1
College level: Freshman
Criteria: Applicant must be the top graduating student from any accredited or state-approved high school in Tennessee. Minimum 3.0 GPA is required to retain scholarship. Awarded every year. Award may be used only at sponsoring institution.
Contact: Katherine Atkinson, Scholarship Coordinator.

2531 American Legion-Maryland Auxiliary Scholarships

American Legion–Maryland Auxiliary
5205 East Drive
Suite R
Baltimore, MD 21227
(301) 242-9519
Maximum award: $2,000
Number of awards: 2
Deadline: May 1
Majors/Fields: Arts, business, education, home economics, nursing, public administration, sciences
Criteria: Applicant must be a Maryland resident and the daughter of a veteran. One award is for an applicant planning to study arts, sciences, business, public administration, education, or home economics at a college or university in Maryland. One award is for an applicant age 16-22 training to be an R.N. who demonstrates financial need and has resided in Maryland for at least five years. Awarded every year.
Contact: Department Secretary.

2532 American Legion-Utah Auxiliary Scholarship

American Legion–Utah Auxiliary
Girls State Chairman
B-61 State Capitol Building
Salt Lake City, UT 84114
(801) 538-1014
Average award: Full tuition
Number of awards: 4
College level: Freshman
Criteria: Applicant must attend Utah Girls State and demonstrate good citizenship. Scholarship must be used at Southern Utah State Coll. Awarded every year.
Contact: Girls State Chairman.

2533 Amick Farms Scholarship

Clemson University
G-01 Sikes Hall
Clemson, SC 29634-5123
(803) 656-2280
Maximum award: $4,000
Number of awards: 1
Deadline: December 31
College level: Freshman
Criteria: Applicant must have a minimum 2.0 GPA and be a South Carolina resident. Preference is given (in descending order) to entering freshmen who are residents of Saluda County, Lexington County, Edgefield County, or Newberry County. Satisfactory GPA and completion of at least 12 credits per semester are required to retain scholarship. Awarded every year. Award may be used only at sponsoring institution.
Contact: Marvin Carmichael, Director of Financial Aid.

2534 Arcade Guindon Scholarship

University of Ottawa
85 University Private, Room 123
P.O. Box 450, Station "A"
Ottawa, Ontario, CN K1N 6N5
(613) 562-5810, (613) 562-5155 (fax)
Average award: $4,000
Number of awards: 1
Deadline: End of February
College level: Sophomore, Junior, Senior
Criteria: Selection is based upon academic excellence, involvement in community and university life, and understanding of bilingualism and biculturalism. Applicant must be Canadian or a permanent resident. Awarded every year. Award may be used only at sponsoring institution.
Contact: Mrs. Diane Pelletier, Awards Administrator.

2535 Arkansas Academic Challenge Scholarship

Arkansas Department of Higher Education
114 East Capitol
Little Rock, AR 72201
(501) 324-9300
Average award: $1,500
Number of awards: 2,516
Deadline: October 1
College level: Freshman
Criteria: Applicant must have completed the precollegiate core curriculum recommended by the Arkansas Boards of Higher Education and Education, have a minimum composite ACT score of 19, and have a minimum 2.5 GPA in the core curriculum. Applicant must be an Arkansas resident, a U.S. citizen, and demonstrate financial need. Renewable if minimum 2.5 GPA is maintained and 24 credit hours per year are taken. Awarded every year. Award may be used at approved Arkansas schools only.
Contact: Tammy Lynne Smith, Assistant Coordinator of Student Financial Aid.

2536 Arkansas Governor's Scholars Award

Arkansas Department of Higher Education
114 East Capitol
Little Rock, AR 72201
(501) 324-9300
Maximum award: $4,000
Number of awards: 100
Deadline: March 1
College level: Freshman
Criteria: Applicant must be an Arkansas resident, have a minimum 1100 SAT score (27 composite ACT score) or a minimum 3.6 GPA, and demonstrate leadership abilities. One scholarship is awarded in each county in Arkansas and 25 at large. Each recipient must attend an approved Arkansas institution. Renewable if minimum 3.0 GPA is maintained and 24 credit hours per year are taken. Awarded every year. Award may be used at approved Arkansas schools only.
Contact: Ellen Avers, Assistant Coordinator of Student Financial Aid.

2537 Associate Degree Transfer Scholarship

DePaul University
1 East Jackson Boulevard
Chicago, IL 60604
(312) 362-8704, (312) 362-5749 (fax)
Average award: $2,750
Maximum award: $4,000
Minimum award: $1,500
Number of awards: 36
Deadline: None
College level: Transfer students
Criteria: Applicant must have completed an associate degree at an Illinois community college with a minimum 3.5 GPA. Scholarship is renewable. Awarded every year. Award may be used only at sponsoring institution.
Contact: Jennifer Sparrow, Scholarship Coordinator, jsparrow@wppost.depaul.edu.

2538 Bill Hudson Family Endowment Scholarship

Clemson University
G-01 Sikes Hall
Clemson, SC 29634-5123
(803) 656-2280
Average award: $5,300
Number of awards: 1
Deadline: March 1
College level: Freshman, Sophomore, Junior, Senior
Criteria: Applicant must be a South Carolina resident, have a minimum 2.5 GPA, and demonstrate financial need. Satisfactory GPA and completion of at least 12 credit hours per semester are required to retain scholarship. Awarded every year. Award may be used only at sponsoring institution.
Contact: Marvin Carmichael, Director of Financial Aid.

2539 Blount Scholarship

The University of Alabama
Box 870162
Tuscaloosa, AL 35487-0162
(205) 348-6756
Average award: $6,000
Number of awards: 1
Deadline: February 1
College level: Freshman
Majors/Fields: Arts, business administration, commerce, engineering, sciences
Criteria: Applicant must be an Alabama resident, have a minimum 3.8 GPA, a minimum composite ACT score of 32 (combined SAT I score of 1350), and demonstrate broad leadership experience. Minimum 3.0 GPA is required to retain scholarship for four years. Awarded every year. Award may be used only at sponsoring institution.
Contact: Jeanetta Allen, Director of Financial Aid.

2540 Board of Trustees' Scholarship

Wayne State College
1111 Main Street
Wayne, NE 68787
(402) 375-7230, (800) 228-9972
Average award: Full tuition
Deadline: January 13
College level: Freshman
Criteria: Applicant must be a Nebraska resident, rank in top quarter of class, and have a minimum composite ACT score of 25. Award is for four years. Scholarship is renewable. Awarded every year. Award may be used only at sponsoring institution.
Contact: Financial Aid Office.

2541 C.G. Fuller Foundation Scholarship

C.G. Fuller Foundation
c/o NationsBank, N.A.
P.O. Box 448
Columbia, SC 29202
(803) 929-5879
Average award: $2,000
Number of awards: 15
Deadline: March 31
College level: Freshman
Criteria: Applicant must be a South Carolina resident attending a South Carolina college or university and demonstrate financial need. Renewable if minimum 3.0 GPA is maintained. Awarded every year.
Contact: Pamela S. Postal, Vice President, NationsBank, N.A.

2542 Cal Grant

University of San Diego
Alcala Park
San Diego, CA 92110-2492
(619) 260-4514
Maximum award: $6,660
College level: Freshman
Criteria: Applicant must be a legal resident of California and demonstrate academic achievement and financial need. FAFSA is required. Academic/financial verification may be required. Awarded every year. Award may be used only at sponsoring institution.
Contact: Office of Financial Aid.

2543 Cal Grant A

California Student Aid Commission
P.O.Box 510845
Sacramento, CA 94245-0845
(916) 445-0880, (916) 327-6599 (fax)
custsvcs@csac.ca.gov
http://www.csac.ca.gov
Average award: $2,448
Maximum award: $7,164
Minimum award: $700
Number of awards: 36,500
Deadline: March 2
College level: Freshman, Sophomore, Junior, Senior, mandatory fifth year undergraduate degree program or teaching credential program
Criteria: Applicant must be a California resident attending a California educational institution, demonstrate financial need, and have satisfactory academic qualifications. Renewable if academic progress is satisfactory and financial need is demonstrated. Awarded every year.
Contact: Grant Services Branch.

2544 Cal Grant B

California Student Aid Commission
P.O.Box 510845
Sacramento, CA 94245-0845
(916) 445-0880, (916) 327-6599 (fax)
custsvcs@csac.ca.gov
http://www.csac.ca.gov
Average award: $1,662
Maximum award: $7,164
Minimum award: $1,410
Number of awards: 21520
Deadline: March 2
College level: Freshman, Sophomore, Junior, Senior, mandatory fifth year undergraduate degree program or teaching credential program
Criteria: Applicant must be a California resident attending a California educational institution. Selection is based upon financial need and academic qualifications; disadvantaged background increases likelihood of receiving award. Renewable if academic progress is satisfactory and financial need is demonstrated. Awarded every year.
Contact: Grant Services Branch, (916) 322-5112.

2545 Cal Grant C

California Student Aid Commission
P.O.Box 510845
Sacramento, CA 94245-0845
(916) 445-0880, (916) 327-6599 (fax)
custsvcs@csac.ca.gov
http://www.csac.ca.gov
Average award: $1,075
Maximum award: $2,450
Minimum award: $594
Number of awards: 2534
Deadline: March 2
College level: Freshman, Sophomore, Vocational schools /courses
Criteria: Applicant must be a California resident pursuing a vocationally oriented course of study at a two-year community college, two-year program within a college, or vocational school in California. Selection is based upon financial need, academic qualifications, and aptitude, interest, and experience in chosen vocational field. Award is for completion of a two-year curriculum. Awarded every year.
Contact: Grant Services Branch.

2546 California–Hawaii Elks Major Project, Inc. Scholarships

California–Hawaii Elks Major Project, Inc.
5450 East Lamona
Fresno, CA 93727
(209) 255-4531
Average award: $1,000
Maximum award: $2,000
Deadline: March 15
College level: Freshman, High school graduate with GED
Criteria: Applicant must be a disabled U.S. citizen and resident of California or Hawaii. Scholarships are for undergraduate work at an accredited community college, university, or licensed vocational school only. Applicant must be sponsored by an Elks lodge member.
Contact: Jennifer Samarin, Administrative Services.

2547 California Masonic Foundation Scholarship

California Masonic Foundation
1111 California Street
San Francisco, CA 94108
(415) 292-9196
Average award: $2,000
Maximum award: $10,000
Number of awards: 175
Deadline: February 28
College level: Freshman
Criteria: Applicant must be a U.S. citizen, a California resident for at least one year, demonstrate financial need, and have a minimum 3.0 GPA. Renewable if recipient maintains minimum 3.0 GPA. Awarded every year.
Contact: Judy Liang, Coordination, (415) 776-7000.

2548 Carolina Scholars Award

University of South Carolina (Columbia)
Office of Admissions
Columbia, SC 29208
(803) 777-4067
Average award: $7,000
Number of awards: 20
Deadline: Early November
College level: Freshman
Criteria: Applicant must be a South Carolina resident and demonstrate extraordinary academic achievement, leadership, and character. Minimum 3.0 GPA is required to retain scholarship. Awarded every year. Award may be used only at sponsoring institution.
Contact: Michael Jinnette, Scholarship Coordinator, (803) 777-4062.

2549 Carolina Scholars Finalist Award

University of South Carolina
Office of Admissions
Columbia, SC 29208
(803) 777-4067
Average award: $4,000
Number of awards: 30
Deadline: Early November
College level: Freshman
Criteria: Applicant must be a South Carolina resident and demonstrate extraordinary academic achievement, leadership, and character. Minimum 3.0 GPA is required to retain scholarship. Awarded every year. Award may be used only at sponsoring institution.
Contact: Michael Jinnette, Scholarship Coordinator, (803) 777-4062.

2550   Carver Scholarship

University of Northern Iowa
Financial Aid Office
Cedar Falls, IA 50613-0024
(319) 273-2700 or (800) 772-2736
Average award: $3,600
Number of awards: 19
Deadline: March 16
College level: Junior
Criteria: Applicant must have a minimum 2.8 GPA, be a graduate of an Iowa high school, be a U.S. citizen, and have overcome some personal obstacle to have come this far in a college career (physical, financial, emotional, etc.). Applicant must have a minimum 2.8 GPA and socio-emotional situation must remain the same to retain scholarship. Awarded every year. Award may be used only at sponsoring institution.
Contact: Evelyn Waack, Scholarship Coordinator, Financial Aid.

2551   Catholic College Tuition Waiver

Kansas Newman College
3100 McCormick Avenue
Wichita, KS 67213
(316) 942-4291
Average award: Full tuition
Criteria: Applicant must be a dependent of a full-time Kansas Catholic college employee. Renewable if recipient maintains full-time enrollment and good academic standing. Award may be used only at sponsoring institution.
Contact: Marla McClure, Director of Financial Aid, (316) 942-4291, extension 103, mcclurem@ksnewman.edu.

2552   Chancellor's Club Scholarship

University of Calgary
Department of Financial Aid
2500 University Drive, NW
Calgary, Alberta, CN T2N 1N4
(403) 220-7872, (403) 282-2999 (fax)
Average award: $6,000
Number of awards: 10
Deadline: March 15
College level: Freshman
Criteria: Applicant must be a Canadian citizen or permanent resident. Selection is based upon academic merit, contribution to school and community life, and academic promise. Minimum 3.0 GPA and full course load are required to retain scholarship. Awarded every year. Award may be used only at sponsoring institution.
Contact: J. Van Housen, Director of Student Awards/Financial Aid.

2553   Children of Disabled Firemen and Peace Officers Tuition Exemption

Texas Higher Education Coordinating Board
Student Financial Assistance
P.O. Box 12788, Capitol Station
Austin, TX 78711-2788
(512) 427-6340
Average award: $1,295
Number of awards: 63
College level: Freshman, Sophomore, Junior, Senior
Criteria: Applicant must be the child of a deceased or disabled fireman, peace officer, custodial employee of the Department of Conservation, or game warden who died or was disabled in the line of duty while serving Texas. Applicant must apply prior to 21st birthday and attend a public college or university in Texas. Scholarship is renewable. Awarded every year.
Contact: Sharon W. Cobb, Assistant Commissioner for Student Services.

2554   Christian A. Herter Memorial Scholarship

Massachusetts Higher Education Coordinator Council
1 Ashburton Place
McCormack Building, Rm 1401
Boston, MA 02108
(617) 727-7785
Average award: $9,721
Number of awards: 24
Deadline: March 31
College level: Freshman
Criteria: Applicant must be a permanent Massachusetts resident and have exhibited severe personal or family difficulties, medical problems, or have overcome a personal obstacle or hardship. Recipient must continue to demonstrate financial need and file a FAFSA to retain scholarship. Awarded every year.
Contact: Cynthia M. Gray, Scholarship Officer, Office of Student Financial Assistance, 330 Stuart Street, Boston, MA 02116, (617) 727-9420.

2555   Clemson Alumni Past Presidents Scholarship

Clemson University
G-01 Sikes Hall
Clemson, SC 29634-5123
(803) 656-2280
Average award: $3,500
Number of awards: 1
College level: Freshman
Criteria: Applicant must be a South Carolina resident. Renewable for up to three years if recipient maintains minimum 3.0 GPA and completes minimum of 12 credits each semester. Award may be used only at sponsoring institution.
Contact: Scholarships.

2556   Clemson Scholars Program

Clemson University
G-01 Sikes Hall
Clemson, SC 29634-5123
(803) 656-2280
Average award: $2,500
Deadline: December 31
College level: Freshman
Criteria: Awarded to the top-ranked minority and non-minority student in each South Carolina public high school. Award is based upon GPA at the end of junior year in high school. Minimum 2.5 GPA and completion of at least 12 credits per semester are required to retain scholarship. Awarded every year. Award may be used only at sponsoring institution.
Contact: Marvin Carmichael, Director of Financial Aid.

2557   Colorado Undergraduate Merit Award

Colorado Commission on Higher Education
1300 Broadway, 2nd Floor
Denver, CO 80203
(303) 866-2723, (303) 860-9750 (fax)
http://www.co.us/cche_dir/hecche.html
Average award: $1,500
Maximum award: $2,000
Minimum award: $1,000
Number of awards: 9000
College level: Freshman, Sophomore, Junior, Senior
Criteria: Individual institutions administer the program, determining eligibility and awards. Scholarship is renewable. Awarded every year.
Contact: John Ceru, Adminstrator of Colorado Student Aid Programs, john.ceru@state.co.us.

2558 **Community College Presidential Scholarship**
Wayne State University
Office of Admissions
HNJ Student Services 3 East
Detroit, MI 48202
(313) 577-2424 (General), 313 577-3577 (Admissions), (313) 577-7536 (fax)
Average award: $4,112
Number of awards: 125
Deadline: April 28
College level: Michigan Community College graduates with associate degree
Criteria: Applicant must have a minimum cumulative 3.5 GPA, have an associate degree from a Michigan community college, and be a resident of Michigan. Maximum 16 semester/24 quarter hours earned at a four-year institution is allowed toward eligibility. Minimum 3.0 cumulative GPA and 24 semester credits per year are required to retain scholarship. Awarded every year. Award may be used only at sponsoring institution.
Contact: Dorothy J. Papajohn, Assistant Director of Admissions, (313) 577-4935.

2559 **Copp Family Scholarship**
University of Calgary
Department of Financial Aid
2500 University Drive, NW
Calgary, Alberta, CN T2N 1N4
(403) 220-7872, (403) 282-2999 (fax)
Average award: $3,000
Number of awards: 6
Deadline: March 15
College level: Freshman
Criteria: Selection is based upon academic merit, contribution to school and community life, and academic promise. Applicant must be a Canadian citizen or permanent resident. Awarded every year. Award may be used only at sponsoring institution.
Contact: J. Van Housen, Director of Student Awards/Financial Aid.

2560 **Curator's Scholarship**
University of Missouri–St. Louis
8001 Natural Bridge Road
St. Louis, MO 63121
(314) 553-6396
Average award: Full tuition
Number of awards: 24
Deadline: April 1
College level: Freshman
Criteria: Applicant must be a Missouri resident, rank in the top three percent of class, score in at least the 90th percentile on a college entrance test, and be recommended by high school counselor. Minimum 3.5 cumulative GPA is required to retain scholarship. Awarded every year. Award may be used only at sponsoring institution.
Contact: James D. Reed, Financial Aid Advisor.

2561 **Curators Scholar Award**
University of Missouri–Columbia
High School and Transfer Relations
219 Jesse Hall
Columbia, MO 65211
(800) 225-6075 (in-state), (314) 882-2456
http://www.missouri.edu
Average award: $3,500
Average award: Full tuition
Number of awards: 1113
Deadline: August 15
College level: Freshman
Criteria: Applicant must be a Missouri resident, rank in the top 5% of class, and have a minimum composite ACT score of 28 (combined SAT I score of 1240). Minimum 3.25 GPA is required to retain scholarship. Awarded every year. Award may be used only at sponsoring institution.
Contact: Office of the Curators Scholars Program, 306 Clark Hall, Columbia, MO 65211, (314) 882-6292.

2562 **Curators Scholarship**
University of Missouri–Rolla
Rolla, MO 65401
(314) 341-4282
Average award: $3,500
Number of awards: 120
Deadline: None
College level: Freshman, Sophomore, Junior, Senior
Criteria: Applicant must be a resident of Missouri, rank in top 5% of class, and have a minimum composite ACT score of 28. Minimum 3.20 GPA is required to retain scholarship. Awarded every year. Award may be used only at sponsoring institution.
Contact: Robert W. Whites, Associate Director of Admissions/Student Financial Aid, G-1 Parker Hall.

2563 **Delegate Scholarship**
Maryland Higher Education Commission
State Scholarship Administration
16 Francis Street
Annapolis, MD 21401-1781
(410) 974-5370, (410) 974-5994 (fax)
http://www.ubalt.edu/www/mhec
Maximum award: In-state tuition and fees
Number of awards: 2,600
Deadline: Varies
College level: Freshman, Sophomore, Junior, Senior, Graduate, Doctoral
Criteria: Applicant must be a Maryland resident, a full- or part-time student, and must contact all three delegates in their state legislative district for application instructions. Reapplication is required to retain scholarship. Awarded every year. Maryland schools prefered.
Contact: Gail Fisher, Program Administrator.

2564 **Department President's Scholarship**
American Legion–Ohio Auxiliary
P.O. Box 2279
Zanesville, OH 43702-2279
(614) 452-8245
Maximum award: $1,500
Number of awards: 2
Deadline: March 15
College level: Freshman
Criteria: Applicant must be the child or grandchild of a living or deceased veteran who served in World War I, World War II, Korean, Vietnam, Lebanon, or Desert Storm conflicts. Applicant must be an Ohio resident and be sponsored by an American Legion Auxiliary unit. Awarded every year.
Contact: Scholarships.

2565 **Distinguished Scholar Award**
Maryland Higher Education Commission
State Scholarship Administration
16 Francis Street
Annapolis, MD 21401-1781
(410) 974-5370, (410) 974-5994 (fax)
http://www.ubalt.edu/www/mhec
Maximum award: $3,000
Number of awards: 1449
Deadline: Varies
College level: Freshman
Criteria: Applicant must be a Maryland resident, and be a National Merit finalist, National Achievement finalist, demonstrate superior academic achievement (3.7 GPA), or demonstrate superior talent in the arts. Applicant must be nominated by high school during second semester of junior year. Minimum 3.0 GPA is required to retain scholarship. Awarded every year. Award may be used at Maryland Schools only.
Contact: Margaret Riley, Program Administrator.

2566   Distinguished Scholarship

University of Missouri–Rolla
Rolla, MO 65401
(314) 341-4282
Maximum award: $4,000
Number of awards: 200
Deadline: February 1
College level: Freshman, Sophomore, Junior, Senior, Graduate
Criteria: Applicant must be a non-Missouri resident. Selection is based upon class rank and standardized test scores. Minimum 2.5 GPA is required to retain scholarship. Awarded every year. Award may be used only at sponsoring institution.
Contact: Robert W. Whites, Associate Director of Admissions/Student Financial Aid, G-1 Parker Hall.

2567   District of Columbia Public Schools Scholarships

District of Columbia Public Schools
Student Affairs Branch
4501 Lee Street, NE
Washington, DC 20019
(202) 724-4934
Average award: $10,780
Maximum award: $25,000
Minimum award: $100
Number of awards: 2098
Deadline: Variable
College level: Freshman
Criteria: The public schools have an application that covers a wide variety of private scholarship funds; selection criteria varies with each award. Applicant must be a District of Columbia resident and graduate from a District of Columbia high school. Most awards are renewable. Awarded every year.
Contact: Annabelle F. Strayhorn, Director of Student Affairs Branch.

2568   Diversity Scholarship

Alabama Agricultural and Mechanical University
P.O. Box 908
Normal, AL 35762
(205) 851-5245, (205) 851-5249 (fax)
jheyward@asnaam.edu
http://www.aamu.edu
Average award: $6,000
Maximum award: $7,500
Minimum award: $1,186
Number of awards: 76
College level: Freshman, Sophomore, Junior, Senior, Graduate
Criteria: Applicant must be a white graduate of an Alabama high school, and must have at least one parent or guardian residing in Alabama. Award may be used only at sponsoring institution.
Contact: Director of Admissions.

2569   Dominion Merit Scholarship

Old Dominion University
Hampton Boulevard
Norfolk, VA 23529-0050
(804) 683-3683
Maximum award: Tuition and $500 books
Number of awards: 5
Deadline: February 15
College level: Freshman
Criteria: Applicant must be a Virginia resident, rank in the top tenth of class, have a minimum combined SAT I score of 1200, and demonstrate potential for leadership. Minimum 3.25 GPA is required to retain scholarship for three additional years. Awarded every year. Award may be used only at sponsoring institution.
Contact: Mary A. Schutz, Assistant Director of Scholarships.

2570   Donovan Senior Citizen Scholarship

Northern Kentucky University
Administrative Center 416
Nunn Drive
Highland Heights, KY 41099-7101
(606) 572-5144
Average award: Full tuition
Deadline: February 1
College level: Students age 65 or older
Criteria: Applicant must be a Kentucky resident age 65 years or older. Scholarship is renewable. Awarded every year. Award may be used only at sponsoring institution.
Contact: Robert E. Sprague, Director of Financial Aid.

2571   Dr. Claudia Hampton Scholarship

California State University, Dominguez Hills
1000 East Victoria Street
Carson, CA 90747
(310) 516-3647
Average award: $3,000
Number of awards: 1
Deadline: April 28
College level: Freshman
Criteria: Applicant must be a California resident and have graduated from a school in an inner-city area with low college attendance rate. Applicant must be an entering freshman eligible for financial aid, enroll full time, and demonstrate motivation and enthusiasm for a university education. Awarded every year. Award may be used only at sponsoring institution.
Contact: Scholarships.

2572   East West Partners Annual Scholarship

Clemson University
G-01 Sikes Hall
Clemson, SC 29634-5123
(803) 656-2280
Average award: $3,000
Number of awards: 1
Deadline: December 31
College level: Freshman
Majors/Fields: Construction science/management, design, fine arts, landscape architecture
Criteria: Applicant must be a South Carolina resident. Satisfactory GPA and completion of at least 12 credits per semester are required to retain scholarship. Awarded every year. Award may be used only at sponsoring institution.
Contact: Marvin Carmichael, Director of Financial Aid.

2573   Educational Assistance Grant

Maryland Higher Education Commission
State Scholarship Administration
16 Francis Street
Annapolis, MD 21401-1781
(410) 974-5370, (410) 974-5994 (fax)
http://www.ubalt.edu/www/mhec
Average award: $1,260
Maximum award: $3,000
Minimum award: $200
Number of awards: 18893
Deadline: March 1
College level: Freshman, Sophomore, Junior, Senior
Criteria: Applicant must be a Maryland resident, a full-time student, and demonstrate financial need. Selection is based upon satisfactory academic progress. Minimum 2.0 GPA, reapplication, and financial need are required to retain scholarship. Awarded every year. Award may be used at Maryland schools only.
Contact: Marya Dennis, Program Manager.

2574 Educational Opportunity Fund Grant

New Jersey Department of Higher Education
4 Quakerbridge Plaza
CN 540
Trenton, NJ 08625
(609) 588-3230
Maximum award: $1,950
Deadline: October 1; March 1 (spring)
College level: Freshman, Sophomore, Junior, Senior
Criteria: Applicant must be from an educationally disadvantaged background and demonstrate financial need. Applicant must be a full-time, matriculated student at a New Jersey college or university and be a resident of New Jersey for at least 12 consecutive months. Satisfactory academic progress and financial need are required to retain scholarship. Awarded every year.
Contact: Leah Fletcher, Assistant Director, Office of Grants and Scholarships.

2575 Elizabeth and James MacKenzie Andrews Bursary

University of Calgary
Department of Financial Aid
2500 University Drive, NW
Calgary, Alberta, CN T2N 1N4
(403) 220-7872, (403) 282-2999 (fax)
Maximum award: $3,500
Number of awards: 4
Deadline: July 15
College level: Freshman
Majors/Fields: Education
Criteria: Applicant must have graduated from a high school in the province of Alberta. Selection is based upon financial need and academic merit. Minimum 2.6 GPA in the Faculty of Education is required to retain scholarship. Awarded every year. Award may be used only at sponsoring institution.
Contact: J. Van Housen, Director of Student Awards/Financial Aid.

2576 Faculty Scholars Award

Jacksonville State University
Jacksonville, AL 36265-9982
(205) 782-5006
Average award: Full tuition
Deadline: March 15
College level: Freshman
Criteria: Applicant must be an Alabama resident and have a minimum composite ACT score of 28 (combined SAT I score of 1230). Scholarship is renewable. Awarded every year. Award may be used only at sponsoring institution.
Contact: Student Financial Aid Office.

2577 Fireman's Dependent Scholarship

Northern Kentucky University
Administrative Center 416
Nunn Drive
Highland Heights, KY 41099-7101
(606) 572-5144
Average award: In-state tuition
Deadline: February 1
College level: Freshman, Sophomore, Junior, Senior
Criteria: Applicant must be a dependent or spouse of a permanently disabled or deceased Kentucky resident fire fighter. Award is to age 23, completion of degree or certification, or 36 months attendance, whichever comes first. Awarded every year. Award may be used only at sponsoring institution.
Contact: Robert E. Sprague, Director of Financial Aid.

2578 First Generation Award

Colorado State University
Financial Aid Office
103 Administration Annex Building
Fort Collins, CO 80523-8024
(970) 491-6321, (970) 491-5010 (fax)
Average award: Full tuition and fees
Number of awards: 68
Deadline: April 1
College level: Freshman, Transfer
Criteria: Applicant must be a Colorado resident, a first-generation college student, and demonstrate financial need. Emphasis given to students who demonstrate the ability to contribute to the diversity of Colorado State University. Reapplication, minimum 2.0 cumulative GPA, and satisfactory progress are required to retain scholarship. Awarded every year. Award may be used only at sponsoring institution.
Contact: Eileen Griego, Financial Aid Counselor.

2579 Florida Resident Academic Incentive Scholarship

Lynn University
3601 North Military Trail
Boca Raton, FL 33431-5598
(561) 994-0770, (561) 247-3552 (fax)
admission@lynn.edu
http://www.lynn.edu
Maximum award: $8,300
Number of awards: 25
Deadline: None
College level: Freshman
Criteria: Applicant must be a resident of Florida, and must meet two out three of the following critera: Have a minimum 3.0 GPA, rank in top third of class, and have a minimum combined SAT I score of 1000. Minimum 3.0 GPA is required to retain scholarship. Awarded every year. Award may be used only at sponsoring institution.
Contact: James Sullivan, Director of Admissions.

2580 Florida Resident Access Grant

Florida Department of Education
Office of Student Financial Assistance
255 Collins
Tallahassee, FL 32399-0400
(904) 487-0049
Average award: Full tuition
Deadline: Varies by institution
College level: Sophomore, Junior, Senior
Criteria: Applicant must be a Florida resident for a minimum of twelve months prior to the start of classes, have not earned a bachelor's degree, meet the requirements of the Selective Service System, have participated in the college-level communication and computation skills testing (CLAST) program, and enroll at a regionally-accredited non-profit Florida institution. Renewable up to nine semesters or fourteen quarters, if recipient maintains a minimum 2.0 GPA, demonstrates satisfactory progress, and earns a minimum 12 credit hours per term. Awarded every year.
Contact: Office of Student Financial Assistance.

2581 Florida Student Assistance Grant

Florida Department of Education
Office of Student Financial Assistance
255 Collins
Tallahassee, FL 32399-0400
(904) 487-0049
Maximum award: $1,500
Deadline: April 15
College level: Sophomore, Junior, Senior
Criteria: Applicant must be a Florida resident for a minimum of twelve months prior to the start of classes, have not earned a bachelor's degree, meet the requirements of the Selective Service System, and have participated in the college-level communication and computation skills testing (CLAST) program. Financial need is considered. Renewable up to six years, nine semesters, 14 quarters, or until recipient earns a bachelor's degree, if a minimum 2.0 GPA is maintained and a minimum 12 credit hours are earned each term. Awarded every year.
Contact: Office of Student Financial Assistance.

2582 Florida Teacher Scholarship

Florida Department of Education
Office of Student Financial Assistance
255 Collins
Tallahassee, FL 32399-0400
(904) 487-0049
Maximum award: $1,500
Deadline: March 1
College level: Freshman
Criteria: Applicant must have attended a Florida high school, have a minimum 3.0 GPA, rank in the top quarter of senior class, be an active member of a future teacher's organization (if feasible), have taken the SAT or ACT, enroll in an eligible Florida public institution for a minimum of 12 credit hours each term, meet the registration requirements of the Selective Service System, have participated in the college-level communication and computation skills testing (CLAST) program, and express an intent to teach in Florida public schools. Renewable for an additional year if recipient maintains a minimum 2.0 GPA and earns a minimum 12 credit hours per term. Awarded every year.
Contact: Office of Student Financial Assistance, 255 Collins, Tallahassee, FL 32399-0400.

2583 Florida Undergraduate Scholars' Fund

Florida Department of Education
Office of Student Financial Assistance
255 Collins
Tallahassee, FL 32399-0400
(904) 487-0049
Average award: $2,500
Maximum award: $4,000
Deadline: April 1
College level: Freshman, Sophomore, Junior, Senior
Criteria: Applicant must either (1) be a finalist in the National Merit or National Achievement Scholarship Program, (2) have a minimum 3.5 GPA and a minimum combined SAT I score of 1200 (1270 if recentered) or composite ACT score of 29, (3) be designated by the State Board of Education as a Florida Academic Scholar, (4) have been awarded an International Baccalaureate Diploma from the International Baccalaureate Office, or (5) have participated in state-approved home education and have a minimum combined SAT I score of 1250 (1310 if recentered) or composite ACT score of 30. Applicant must have a Florida high school diploma or its equivalent, be a Florida resident, and be enrolled at an eligible Florida institution. Minimum 3.2 GPA with 12 credit hours per term is required to retain scholarship. Awarded every year.
Contact: Office of Student Financial Assistance.

2584 Ford Family Foundation Scholarship

State Scholarship Commission (Oregon)
1500 Valley River Drive
Suite 100
Eugene, OR 97401-2146
(541) 687-7400
http://www.teleport.com/~ossc/
Average award: $5,500
Maximum award: $10,000
Minimum award: $1,000
Deadline: March 1
College level: Freshman, Junior
Criteria: Applicant must be an Oregon resident, have a minimum 3.0 GPA, be enrolled full time at a two- or four-year Oregon school, and demonstrate financial need. Scholarship is renewable. Awarded every year. Award may be used at Oregon schools only.
Contact: Jim Beyer, Grant Program Director.

2585 Georgia Military Scholarship

Georgia Student Finance Commission
2082 East Exchange Place
Suite 200
Tucker, GA 30084
(770) 414-3000, (912) 757-3626, (800) 776-6878
Average award: Full tuition
College level: Freshman, Sophomore, Junior, Senior
Majors/Fields: Military
Criteria: Applicant must be a Georgia resident and be nominated by a Georgia State Legislator for the scholarship. Recipients are obligated to serve in the Georgia Army National Guard after graduation. Award may be used only at Georgia Military Coll or North Georgia Coll.
Contact: Scholarships.

2586 Good Neighbor Scholarship

Texas Higher Education Coordinating Board
Student Financial Assistance
P.O. Box 12788, Capitol Station
Austin, TX 78711-2788
(512) 427-6340
Average award: $4,427
Maximum award: Tuition at public colleges and universities in Texas
Number of awards: 321
Deadline: March 15
College level: Freshman, Sophomore, Junior, Senior, Graduate, Doctoral
Criteria: Applicant must be a native-born citizen and resident from another nation of the American hemisphere, certified by native country, and scholastically qualified for admission to a public college or university in Texas. Scholarship is renewable. Awarded every year.
Contact: Gustavo O. DeLeon, Assistant Director of Grant Programs

2587 Good Neighbor Scholarship

Southwest Texas State University
J.C. Kellam Building
San Marcos, TX 78666
(512) 245-2340
Average award: Full tuition
Deadline: March 1 (fall/spring); February 15 (summer)
College level: Freshman, Sophomore, Junior, Senior
Criteria: Applicant must be an academically talented student from a country in the American hemisphere. Awarded every year. Award may be used only at sponsoring institution.
Contact: Coordinator of Scholarships, Office of Student Financial Aid, 601 University Drive, San Marcos, TX 78666-4602, (512) 245-2315.

2588 Gordon Edward Wright Scholarship

University of Calgary
Department of Financial Aid
2500 University Drive, NW
Calgary, Alberta, CN T2N 1N4
(403) 220-7872, (403) 282-2999 (fax)
Average award: $3,000
Number of awards: 1
Deadline: March 15
College level: Freshman
Criteria: Applicant must be a Canadian citizen or permanent resident. Selection is based upon academic merit, contribution to school and community, and academic promise. Awarded every year. Award may be used only at sponsoring institution.
Contact: J. Van Housen, Director of Student Awards/Financial Aid.

2589 Governor's Scholarship

Idaho State Board of Education
Len B. Jordan Building, Room 307
P.O. Box 83720
Boise, ID 83720-0037
(208) 334-2270, (208) 334-2632 (fax)
csmith@osbe.state.id.us
Average award: $3,000
Number of awards: 20
Deadline: January 31
College level: Freshman
Majors/Fields: Vocational/technical
Criteria: Applicant must be a Idaho resident interested in pursuing a vocational/technical program in Idaho. Selection is based upon personal essay, transcripts, and letters of recommendation. Scholarship is renewable. Awarded every year.
Contact: Caryl Smith, Scholarship Assistant.

2590 Governor's Scholarship

Georgia Student Finance Commission
2082 East Exchange Place, Suite 200
Tucker, GA 30084
(770) 414-3000, (912) 757-3626, (800) 776-6878
Maximum award: $1,575
College level: Freshman
Criteria: Applicant must be a Georgia resident. Awarded to students selected as Georgia Scholars, STAR Students, valedictorians, and salutatorians. Financial need is not considered. Scholarship is renewable. Awarded every year. Award may be used at Georgia schools only.
Contact: Scholarships.

2591 Guaranteed Access Grant

Maryland Higher Education Commission
State Scholarship Administration
16 Francis Street
Annapolis, MD 21401-1781
(410) 974-5370, (410) 974-5994 (fax)
http://www.ubalt.edu/www/mhec
Average award: $4,435
Maximum award: $8,000
Number of awards: 401
Deadline: March 1 (FAFSA & SSA)
College level: Freshman
Criteria: Applicant must be a Maryland resident, be a full-time student, have a minimum 2.5 GPA, and have a total annual family income which qualifies for the federal Free Lunch Program. Minimum 2.0 GPA is required to maintain grant. Awarded every year. Award may be used at Maryland schools only.
Contact: Judy Colgan, Program Administrator.

2592 H. and N. Morgan Foundation Inc. Annual Scholarship

Clemson University
G-01 Sikes Hall
Clemson, SC 29634-5123
(803) 656-2280
Maximum award: $3,000
Number of awards: 2
Deadline: None
College level: Freshman
Criteria: Applicant must be designated as a Palmetto Fellow by the South Carolina Commission on Higher Education. Minimum 3.0 GPA and completion of at least 12 credits per semester are required to retain scholarship. Awarded every year. Award may be used only at sponsoring institution.
Contact: Marvin Carmichael, Director of Financial Aid.

2593 Harbert Memorial Scholarship

Southern Illinois University at Edwardsville
Box 1060
Edwardsville, IL 62026-1060
(618) 692-3880, (618) 692-3885 (fax)
finaid@siue.edu
http://www.finaid.siue.edu
Maximum award: $2,465
Deadline: March 1 (priority)
College level: Freshman, Sophomore, Junior, Senior
Criteria: Applicant must be a graduate of Centralia High School in Illinois. Renewable if recipient maintains a minimum 3.0 GPA and if funds are available. Awarded every year. Award may be used only at sponsoring institution.
Contact: Client Service Unit, Student Financial Aid, Box 1078, Edwardsville, IL 62040, finaid@siue.edu.

2594 Harry S Truman Scholarship

University of Texas at San Antonio
Office of Student Financial Aid
6900 North Loop 1604 West
San Antonio, TX 78249-0687
(210) 691-44855
Average award: Tuition, books, fees, and $100 per month allowance
Deadline: October 14
College level: Junior, Senior
Criteria: Applicant must be a Texas resident, a U.S. citizen or U.S. national, have a minimum 3.0 GPA, aspire to a career in public service, and be nominated by his or her college. Minimum 3.0 GPA is required to retain scholarship. Awarded every year. Award may be used only at sponsoring institution.
Contact: Office of Student Financial Aid, (512) 691-4011.

2595 Harvey B. Gantt Scholarship Endowment Fund

Clemson University
G-01 Sikes Hall
Clemson, SC 29634-5123
(803) 656-2280
Average award: $2,500
Number of awards: 2
Deadline: December 31
College level: Freshman
Criteria: Applicant must be a resident of South Carolina. Renewable if recipient maintains minimum 2.5 GPA and completes at least 12 credits per semester. Award may be used only at sponsoring institution.
Contact: Scholarships.

2596 Henry Sachs Foundation Scholarship

Henry Sachs Foundation
90 South Cascade Avenue, Suite 1410
Colorado Springs, CO 80903
(719) 633-2353
Average award: $3,500
Maximum award: $6,500
Minimum award: $1,500
Number of awards: 50
Deadline: March 1
College level: Freshman
Criteria: Applicant must be a black Colorado resident and demonstrate financial need. Minimum 3.4 GPA recommended. Minimum 2.5 GPA and at least 12 credit hours per term are required to retain scholarship. Awarded every year.
Contact: Scholarships.

2597 Herman M. Holloway Sr. Memorial Scholarship

Delaware Higher Education Commission
820 North French Street
Fourth Floor
Wilmington, DE 19801
(302) 577-3240, (302) 577-6765 (fax)
mlaffey@state.de.us
http://www.state.de.us/high-ed/commiss/webpage.htm
Maximum award: $7,400
Number of awards: 1
Deadline: March 14
College level: Freshman
Criteria: Applicant must be a Delaware resident with a minimum 3.25 GPA. Renewable if recipient maintains a minimum 3.0 GPA. Awarded every year. Award may be used at Delaware St U only.
Contact: Maureen Laffey, Associate Director.

2598 High School Public Speaking Scholarship Contest

National Sons of the Golden West
414 Mason Street
San Francisco, CA 94102
(415) 392-1223
Maximum award: $2,000
Number of awards: 5
College level: Freshman
Criteria: Applicant must be a California high school student. Applicant must be prepared to give a speech, seven to nine minutes long, on any subject related to past or present history, geography, or the cultural development of California.
Contact: Ralph Cordero, State Chairman, 160 Everglade Drive, San Francisco, CA 94132, (415) 566-4117.

2599 Hodson Achievement Scholarship

The Johns Hopkins University
3400 North Charles Street
Baltimore, MD 21218
(410) 516-8028
Average award: Grant to meet need
Number of awards: 15
Deadline: January 1
College level: Freshman
Criteria: Applicant must be an underrepresented minority student from Delaware, the District of Columbia, or Maryland. Renewable for up to four years. Awarded every year. Award may be used only at sponsoring institution.
Contact: Paula Abernethy, Assistant Director of Financial Aid.

2600 Honors at Entrance Scholarship

University of Utah
Financial Aid and Scholarships Office
105 Student Services Building
Salt Lake City, UT 84112
(801) 581-6211
Average award: Resident tuition
Number of awards: 250
Deadline: February 1
College level: Freshman
Criteria: Applicant must be a Utah resident, National Merit finalist, have a minimum composite ACT score of 28 or equivalent SAT I score, have a minimum 3.9 GPA, and have an admissions index of at least 126. Minimum cumulative GPA of 3.7 and 36 hours of course work every three quarters are required to retain scholarship. Awarded every year. Award may be used only at sponsoring institution.
Contact: Financial Aid and Scholarship Office.

2601 Houston International Fund

School for International Training (SIT)
P.O. Box 676
Kipling Road
Brattleboro, VT 05302
(802) 257-7751, (802) 258-3500 (fax)
admissions.sit@worldlearning.org
http://www.worldlearning/sit.html
Average award: $3,333
Maximum award: $5,000
Minimum award: $2,000
Number of awards: 2
Deadline: April 30 (fall semester); October 15 (spring semester)
College level: Undergraduate
Criteria: Applicant must be an undergraduate student from Houston, Tex., who is participating in the semester-abroad program. Financial need is considered. Minorities are strongly encouraged to apply. Awarded every year. Award may be used only at sponsoring institution.
Contact: Mary Henderson, Financial Aid Officer, (802) 258-3280.

2602 Incentive Scholarship

University of North Carolina General Administration
Box 2688
Chapel Hill, NC 27515-2688
(919) 962-0008 (fax)
Maximum award: $3,000
Deadline: None
College level: Freshman, Sophomore, Junior, Senior
Criteria: Applicant must be a resident of North carolina, meet specified admission standards, and participate in required public service activities. Applicant must be a highly qualified student planning to attend one of the eligible schools. Scholarship is renewable. Awarded every year. Award may be used only at sponsoring institution.
Contact: Financial Aid Office at Eligible School.

2603 International Student Award

Lynchburg College
Lynchburg, VA 24501
(804) 522-8228
Maximum award: $4,000
Deadline: February 15
College level: Freshman, Sophomore, Junior, Senior
Criteria: Applicant must be an international student on a student visa, have a minimum TOEFEL score of 500, and have an exceptional academic record. Scholarship is renewable. Awarded every year. Award may be used only at sponsoring institution.
Contact: Scholarships.

2604 International Student Essay Competition

International Group Services
10530 Rosehaven Street, Suite 350
Fairfax, VA 22030
(703) 591-9800, (703) 691-7500 (fax)
Maximum award: $2,000
Number of awards: 4
Deadline: December 1
Criteria: Applicant must be an international student or scholar studying in the U.S. Awarded every year.
Contact: Mr. Chris Foster, Regional Marketing Manager.

2605 International Student Fee Remission Scholarship

Portland State University
Financial Aid Department
P.O. Box 751
Portland, OR 97207-0751
(503) 725-5270
Maximum award: $9,000
College level: Freshman, Sophomore, Junior, Senior, Graduate, Doctoral
Criteria: Applicant must hold legal, non-immigrant status and be an international student. Applicant must have a minimum 3.0 GPA, clearly defined degree goals, and meet all regular admissions requirements. Outstanding academic performance will be recognized. Renewable if minimum 3.0 GPA is maintained. Awarded every year. Award may be used only at sponsoring institution.
Contact: International Student Admissions Officer, (503) 725-3511.

2606 International Student Scholarship

Alfred University
Alumni Hall
26 North Main Street
Alfred, NY 14802
(607) 871-2159
Maximum award: $10,000
Deadline: None
College level: Non-U.S. residents
Criteria: Applicant must be a non-U.S. resident with a student visa. Renewable for up to eight semesters if minimum 3.0 GPA and full-time enrolllment are maintained. Awarded every year. Award may be used only at sponsoring institution.
Contact: Scholarships.

2607 International Student Scholarship

Lawrence University
P.O. Box 599
Appleton, WI 54912-0599
(414) 832-6500, (414) 832-6782 (fax)
excel@lawrence.edu
http://www.lawrence.edu
Average award: $10,000
Maximum award: Three-Quarters tuition
Minimum award: One-Quarter tuition
Number of awards: 25
Deadline: February 1
College level: Freshman, Sophomore, Junior
Criteria: Applicant must be a resident of a country other than the U.S. Recipient must maintain good academic standing to retain scholarship. Awarded every year. Award may be used only at sponsoring institution.
Contact: Director of Admissions.

2608 Iowa Federation of Labor AFL-CIO High School Scholarship

Iowa Federation of Labor AFL-CIO
2000 Walker Street, Suite A
Des Moines, IA 50317
(515) 262-9571
Average award: $1,500
Number of awards: 1
Deadline: March 30
College level: Freshman
Criteria: Competition is open to all seniors attending an Iowa high school who successfully complete an essay. Awarded every year.
Contact: Mark Smith, Secretary-Treasurer.

2609 Iowa Tuition Grant

Iowa College Aid Commission
200 Tenth Street, Fourth Floor
Des Moines, IA 50309-3609
(515) 281-3501
Maximum award: $3,150
Deadline: April 21 (priority)
College level: Freshman, Sophomore, Junior, Senior
Criteria: Applicant must be an Iowa resident and a U.S. citizen, permanent resident, or refugee. FAFSA required. Renewable up to four years. Award may be used at eligible Iowa schools only.
Contact: Grants.

2610 Iris Carmack-Atlanta, Georgia, Alumni Chapter Endowed Scholarship

The University of Alabama
Box 870162
Tuscaloosa, AL 35487-0162
(205) 348-6756
Average award: $3,334
Average award: Half tuition
Number of awards: 1
Deadline: None
College level: Freshman
Criteria: Applicant must be a Georgia resident and graduate of a Georgia school. Preference is given to applicant from Atlanta area. Awarded as funds are available. Award may be used only at sponsoring institution.
Contact: National Alumni Association, P.O. Box 1928, Tuscaloosa, AL 35486-1928.

2611 Jack F. Tolbert Memorial Grant

Maryland Higher Education Commission
State Scholarship Administration
16 Francis Street
Annapolis, MD 21401-1781
(410) 974-5370, (410) 974-5994 (fax)
http://www.ubalt.edu/www/mhec
Maximum award: $1,500
Number of awards: 912
Deadline: March 1
College level: Private career school student
Majors/Fields: Vocational
Criteria: Applicant must be a Maryland resident, a full-time student, and demonstrate financial need. Apply to financial aid office at institution. FAFSA must be submitted by March 1. Awarded every year. Award may be used at Maryland private career schools only.
Contact: Gail Fisher, Program Administrator.

2612   Jack T. Wood Bursary

University of Calgary
Department of Financial Aid
2500 University Drive, NW
Calgary, Alberta, CN T2N 1N4
(403) 220-7872, (403) 282-2999 (fax)
Average award: $2,500
Number of awards: 1
Deadline: June 15
College level: Junior, Senior
Majors/Fields: Management
Criteria: Applicant must be a Canadian citizen, province of Alberta resident, and have made a contribution to a Faculty of Management student organization or other university activity. Selection is based upon outstanding academic merit, demonstrated leadership ability, and financial need. Awarded every year. Award may be used only at sponsoring institution.
Contact: J. Van Housen, Director of Student Awards/Financial Aid.

2613   James B. Black Scholarship

Pacific Gas and Electric Company
77 Beale Street, Room 2825-F
San Francisco, CA 94106
(415) 973-1338
Maximum award: $4,000
Number of awards: 36
Deadline: November 15
College level: Freshman
Criteria: Applicant must be a California resident and must reside in or attend school in the Pacific Gas and Electric Company service area. Applications may be obtained from high school guidance counselors. Selection is based upon SAT scores, class rank, community involvement, and outside work experience. Awarded every year.
Contact: Scholarships.

2614   James Lee Love Scholarship

North Carolina State Education Assistance Authority
Box 2688
Chapel Hill, NC 27515-2688
(919) 549-8614, (919) 549-8481 (fax)
jdmartin@ga.unc.edu
Maximum award: $2,600
Number of awards: 16
College level: Freshman, Sophomore, Junior, Senior
Criteria: Applicant must be a North Carolina resident enrolled full-time at one of the 16 constituent institutions of the U of North Carolina, and demonstrate financial need approximately the same amount as the fixed stipend. Awarded every year.
Contact: Financial aid office at eligible school.

2615   James Roy Carter Jr. Endowed Presidential Scholarship

Clemson University
G-01 Sikes Hall
Clemson, SC 29634-5123
(803) 656-2280
Maximum award: $3,700
Number of awards: 2
Deadline: March 1
College level: Freshman, Sophomore, Junior, Senior
Criteria: Applicant must be a South Carolina resident and have a minimum 2.5 GPA. Preference is given to residents of Chester, York, or Lancaster County majoring in agricultural education, agricultural engineering, agricultural/ applied economics, agricultural mechanization/business, agronomy, animal industries, engineering, or forestry. Awarded every year. Award may be used only at sponsoring institution.
Contact: Marvin Carmichael, Director of Financial Aid.

2616   Jeff Smith Memorial Scholarship

New Mexico State University
Box 30001, Department 5100
Las Cruces, NM 88003-0001
(505) 646-4105
Average award: Full tuition and fees
Number of awards: 1
Deadline: March 1
College level: Students who have been out of school for at least one year
Criteria: Applicant must be a New Mexico resident and have been out of high school for at least one year and working, or out of college for at least one year, or have been in the military and be planning to re-enter college. Minimum 2.0 GPA the first year (minimum 2.5 GPA thereafter) is required to retain scholarship. Awarded every year. Award may be used only at sponsoring institution.
Contact: Greeley W. Myers, Director of Financial Aid.

2617   Johanna Fisher Scholarship

Bowie State University
Bowie, MD 20715
(301) 464-6544
Average award: Tuition waiver
Deadline: February 1
College level: Freshman, Sophomore, Junior, Senior, Graduate
Criteria: Applicant must be a Maryland resident, have a physical or learning disability, be degree-seeking, have a minimum 2.5 GPA, submit two letters of recommendation from non-relatives, demonstrate financial need, and present written reasons for award. Diagnostic evaluation required if disability is invisible. Awarded every year. Award may be used only at sponsoring institution.
Contact: Scholarship Committee, Career Services, Bowie, MD 20715-9465, (301) 464-7110, (301) 464-7111.

2618   Jose Marti Scholarship Challenge Grant

Florida Department of Education
Office of Student Financial Assistance
255 Collins
Tallahassee, FL 32399-0400
(904) 487-0049
Average award: $2,000
Deadline: April 1
College level: Freshman, Sophomore, Junior, Senior, Graduate, Doctoral
Criteria: Applicant must be a Florida resident, a U.S. citizen or eligible noncitizen, be enrolled full-time at an eligible Florida college or university, demonstrate financial need, have a minimum 3.0 GPA, and be an Hispanic-American or a person of Spanish culture with origins in the Caribbean, Central America, Mexico, South America, or Spain, regardless of race. Minimum 3.0 cumulative GPA with at least 12 credit hours per term is required to retain scholarship. Awarded every year.
Contact: Office of Student Financial Assistance.

2619   Joseph Collie Scholarship

Beloit College
700 College Street
Beloit, WI 53511
(608) 363-2663
Average award: $3,000
Number of awards: 22
Deadline: February 28
College level: Freshman
Criteria: Applicant must be a Wisconsin resident with a minimum 3.0 GPA, strong academic preparation, leadership qualities, extracurricular activities, and counselor recommendation. On-campus interview is required. Minimum 2.5 GPA is required to retain scholarship. Awarded every year. Award may be used only at sponsoring institution.
Contact: Thomas Kreiser, Coordinator of Freshman Financial Aid, (608) 363-2500.

2620 Joyce Margaret Wright Scholarship

University of Calgary
Department of Financial Aid
2500 University Drive, NW
Calgary, Alberta, CN T2N 1N4
(403) 220-7872, (403) 282-2999 (fax)
Average award: $3,000
Number of awards: 1
Deadline: March 15
College level: Freshman
Criteria: Applicant must be a Canadian citizen or permanent resident. Selection is based upon academic merit, contribution to school and community, and academic promise. Awarded every year. Award may be used only at sponsoring institution.
Contact: J. Van Housen, Director of Student Awards/Financial Aid.

2621 Judge William C. Hooker Scholarship

Beloit College
700 College Street
Beloit, WI 53511
(608) 363-2663
Average award: $3,000
Number of awards: 20
Deadline: February 28
College level: Freshman
Criteria: Applicant must be an Illinois resident with a minimum 3.0 GPA, strong academic preparation, leadership qualities, extracurricular activities, and counselor recommendation. On-campus interview is required. Minimum 2.5 GPA is required to retain scholarship. Awarded every year. Award may be used only at sponsoring institution.
Contact: Thomas Kreiser, Coordinator of Freshman Financial Aid.

2622 Junior College Transfer Scholarship

University of Central Oklahoma
100 North University
Edmond, OK 73034
(405) 341-2980, extension 2631, (405) 341-7658 (fax)
Average award: Full tuition and fees
Number of awards: 28
Deadline: April 1
College level: Junior, Senior, Graduate
Criteria: Applicant must be an Oklahoma resident enrolled for a minimum of six hours, have 50 transferrable hours, and a minimum 3.6 GPA. Student activities are also considered. Minimum 3.6 GPA is required to retain scholarship. Awarded every year. Award may be used only at sponsoring institution.
Contact: Margaret Howell, Scholarship Coordinator.

2623 Kansas Minority Scholarship

Kansas Board of Regents
700 S.W. Harrison, Suite 1410
Topeka, KS 66603-3760
(913) 296-3517, (913) 296-0983 (fax)
christy@kbor.state.ks.us
http://www.ukans.edu/~kbor/
Maximum award: $1,500
Number of awards: 200
Deadline: April 1
College level: Freshman, Sophomore, Junior, Senior
Criteria: Applicant must be an ethnic minority, Kansas resident, and demonstrate financial need. Selection is based upon academic performance, ethnic category, and financial need. Minimum 2.0 GPA, demonstrated financial need, and reapplication are required to retain scholarship. Awarded every year. Award may be used at eligible Kansas schools only.
Contact: Scholarships.

2624 Kansas Nursing Scholarship

Kansas Board of Regents
700 S.W. Harrison, Suite 1410
Topeka, KS 66603-3760
(913) 296-3517, (913) 296-0983 (fax)
christy@kbor.state.ks.us
http://www.ukans.edu/~kbor/
Maximum award: $3,500
Number of awards: 300
Deadline: April 1
College level: Freshman, Sophomore, Junior, Senior
Majors/Fields: Licensed practical nursing, registered nursing
Criteria: Applicant must be a Kansas resident, attend an eligible Kansas institution full-time, and secure sponsorship with a health care agency. After passing the licensing exam, applicant must be employed by sponsor for one year for each year of funding or repay the funds at 15% interest. Minimum award is for L.P.N. program; maximum award is for R.N. program. Good academic standing and reapplication are required to retain scholarship. Awarded every year.
Contact: Scholarships.

2625 Kansas Teacher Scholarship

Kansas Board of Regents
700 S.W. Harrison, Suite 1410
Topeka, KS 66603-3760
(913) 296-3517, (913) 296-0983 (fax)
christy@kbor.state.ks.us
http://www.ukans.edu/~kbor/
Average award: $5,000
Number of awards: 100
Deadline: April 1
College level: Freshman, Sophomore, Junior, Senior
Majors/Fields: Education
Criteria: Applicant must be a Kansas resident with high academic credentials and be a full-time student in a program leading to teacher certification in hard to fill discipline. Applicant must agree to teach in Kansas one year for each year of funding or repay the funds with 15 percent interest. Good academic standing, enrollment in selected teacher certification program, and completion of renewal contract are required to retain scholarship. Awarded every year. Award may be used at Kansas schools only.
Contact: Scholarships.

2626 Kansas Tuition Grant

Kansas Board of Regents
700 S.W. Harrison, Suite 1410
Topeka, KS 66603-3760
(913) 296-3517, (913) 296-0983 (fax)
christy@kbor.state.ks.us
http://www.ukans.edu/~kbor/
Maximum award: $2,000
Number of awards: 3,500
Deadline: April 1
College level: Freshman, Sophomore, Junior, Senior
Criteria: Applicant must be a Kansas resident, be a full time student, and demonstrate financial need. Need-based grant assists students who choose Kansas independent or private institutions. Demonstrated financial need and reapplication are required to retain grant. Awarded every year. Award may be used at eligible Kansas schools only.
Contact: Grants.

2627   Kennecott Scholarship

University of Utah
Financial Aid and Scholarships Office
105 Student Services Building
Salt Lake City, UT 84112
(801) 581-6211
Average award: $2,500
Number of awards: 40
Deadline: February 15
College level: Freshman, Sophomore, Junior, Senior
Criteria: Applicant must be an outstanding student selected by a committee of deans and a Utah resident. Recipients become members of the Honor Society of Kennecott Scholars. Awarded every year. Award may be used only at sponsoring institution.
Contact: Financial Aid and Scholarships Office.

2628   Law Enforcement Officers and Fireman Scholarship Program

Mississippi Board of Trustees of State Institutions of Higher Learning
Student Financial Aid Office
3825 Ridgewood Road
Jackson, MS 39211-6453
(601) 982-6663, (601) 982-6527 (fax)
Average award: Tuition, required fees, and room
College level: Freshman, Sophomore, Junior, Senior
Criteria: Applicant must be the spouse or child of a full-time Mississippi law enforcement officer or firefighter who was fatally injured or totally disabled from injuries that occured in the line of duty. Applicant must attend a Mississippi public college or university. Children are eligible until age 23. Awarded for a maximum of eight semesters. Awarded every year.
Contact: Student Financial Aid Office.

2629   Law Enforcement Personnel Dependents Grant

Georgia Student Finance Commission
2082 East Exchange Place
Suite 200
Tucker, GA 30084
(770) 414-3000, (912) 757-3626, (800) 776-6878
Average award: $2,000
College level: Freshman, Sophomore, Junior, Senior
Criteria: Applicant must be a Georgia resident and the child of a law enforcement officer, firefighter, or prison guard in Georgia who has been permanently disabled or killed in the line of duty. Scholarship is renewable. Awarded every year. Award may be used at eligible post-secondary schools in Georgia only.
Contact: Scholarships.

2630   Law Enforcement Personnel Dependents Scholarship

California Student Aid Commission
P.O. Box 510845
Sacramento, CA 94245-0845
(916) 445-0880, (916) 327-6599 (fax)
custsvcs@csac.ca.gov
http://www.csac.ca.gov
Maximum award: $1,500
Deadline: None
College level: Freshman, Sophomore, Junior, Senior, Graduate, Doctoral
Criteria: Applicant must be a dependent or spouse of a California peace officer, Department of Corrections employee, Youth Authority employee, or full-time firefighter who has been killed or totally disabled in the line of duty. Award is not to exceed $6,000 in a six-year period at a four-year college or $2,000 total at a community college. Awarded every year.
Contact: Scholarships, P.O. Box 510624, Sacramento, CA 94245-0624.

2631   Lawrence V. Starkey Scholarship

Clemson University
G-01 Sikes Hall
Clemson, SC 29634-5123
(803) 656-2280
Average award: $2,500
Number of awards: 1
Deadline: March 1
College level: Freshman, Sophomore, Junior, Senior
Criteria: Applicant must have a minimum 2.5 GPA and be a resident of north Georgia. Awarded every year. Award may be used only at sponsoring institution.
Contact: Scholarships.

2632   Leadership Scholarship

University of Utah
Financial Aid and Scholarships Office
105 Student Services Building
Salt Lake City, UT 84112
(801) 581-6211
Average award: Resident tuition
Number of awards: 50
Deadline: February 1 (entering freshman); April 1 (transfer)
College level: Freshman, transfer student
Criteria: Applicant must be a Utah resident, have a minimum 3.0 GPA, and demonstrate outstanding leadership through activities and achievements. Transfer applicant must have an associate degree or at least 90 hours from a Utah two-year college. Awarded every year. Award may be used only at sponsoring institution.
Contact: Financial Aid and Scholarships Office.

2633   Louise Bryant Tate Memorial Endowed Scholarship

The University of Alabama
Box 870162
Tuscaloosa, AL 35487-0162
(205) 348-6756
Average award: $2,500
Number of awards: 1
Deadline: None
College level: Freshman, Sophomore, Junior, Senior
Criteria: Applicant must be a resident of the Washington, D.C., area, including Maryland and Virginia, and have proven academic excellence and leadership skills. Preference is given to student seeking degree in American studies. Awarded every year. Award may be used only at sponsoring institution.
Contact: National Alumni Association, P.O. Box 1928, Tuscaloosa, AL 35486-1928.

2634 Louisiana Honors Scholarship

Louisiana Office of Student Financial Assistance
P.O. Box 91202
Baton Rouge, LA 70821-9202
(504) 922-1012, (504) 922-1089 (fax)
Average award: Full tuition
Number of awards: 23613
Deadline: none
College level: Freshman
Criteria: Applicant must be a Louisiana resident, graduate in the top five percent of a Louisiana high school class, and enroll full-time in a Louisiana college or university. Recipient must maintain minimum 3.0 GPA and earn 24 hours for renewal. Awarded every year.
Contact: Winona Kahao, Director of Scholarship/Grant Division, (504) 922-1038.

2635 Louisiana Tuition Assistance Plan

Louisiana Office of Student Financial Assistance
P.O. Box 91202
Baton Rouge, LA 70821-9202
(504) 922-1012, (504) 922-1089 (fax)
Maximum award: Full tuition
Deadline: March 15
College level: Freshman
Criteria: Applicant must have resided in Louisiana for at least two years prior to enrollment, have a parent/guardian who is a resident of Louisiana, have graduated from high school within two years, have no criminal record other than misdemeanor traffic violations, enroll at a Louisiana two- or four-year public institution of higher education as a first-time, full-time undergraduate student, demonstrate specific financial need, and have a minimum 2.5 GPA, a minimum composite ACT score of 20, and complete 17.5 units of a specified curriculum. FAFSA must be by postmarked by March 15, or received by the federal processor by April 1. Minimum 2.1 GPA after completion of less than 48 hours, minimum 2.3 GPA after completion of 48 hours, or 2.5 minimum GPA after completion of 72 hours required to renew scholarship. Awarded every year.
Contact: Winona Kahao, Director of Scholarship/Grant Division, (504) 922-1038.

2636 Louisiana Tuition Assistance Plan

State of Louisiana Office of Student Financial Assistance
P.O. Box 91202
Baton Rouge, LA 70821-9202
(504) 922-1012, 800 259-5626, (504) 922-1089 (fax)
Average award: Full tuition and mandatory fees
Deadline: April 1
College level: Entering students
Criteria: Applicant must be a U.S. citizen, parent/guardian must be a resident of Louisiana, be a resident of Louisiana for at least 24 months before college enrollment, must not have a criminal record, show financial need, and be within two years of high school graduation. Applicant must have a minimum 2.5 GPA, have a minimum composite ACT score of 20, and have competed 17.5 units of a core curriculum. Renewable if recipient maintains minimum 2.3 GPA after 48 credit hours completed. Awarded every year. Award may be used only at Louisiana public two or four year post-secondary institutions.
Contact: Scholarship & Grant Division.

2637 Major Rudolf Anderson Jr. Scholarship Fund

Clemson University
G-01 Sikes Hall
Clemson, SC 29634-5123
(803) 656-2280
Average award: $2,500
Number of awards: 4
Deadline: March 1
College level: Freshman, Sophomore, Junior, Senior
Criteria: Applicant must have a minimum 2.5 GPA and be a resident of South Carolina. Financial need is considered. Awarded every year. Award may be used only at sponsoring institution.
Contact: Scholarships.

2638 Marguerite Ross Barnett Memorial Scholarship

Missouri Coordinating Board of Higher Education
P.O. Box 6730
Jefferson City, MO 65102
(573) 751-3940, (573) 751-6635 (fax)
http://www.mocbhe.gov
Maximum award: $2,202
Deadline: July 31
College level: Sophomore, Junior, Senior
Criteria: Applicant must attend school part time and be compensated for a minimum of 20 hours per week. Reapplication is required to retain scholarship. Awarded every year.
Contact: Information Service Center, (800) 473-6757.

2639 Mary McLeod Bethune Scholarship

Florida Department of Education
Office of Student Financial Assistance
255 Collins
Tallahassee, FL 32399-0400
(904) 487-0049
Average award: $3,000
Deadline: Varies by institution
College level: Freshman
Criteria: Applicant must be a Florida resident, demonstrate financial need, have a minimum 3.0 GPA, and be enrolled for at least 12 hours per term at Bethune-Cookman Coll, Edward Waters Coll, Florida A&M U, or Florida Memorial Coll. Minimum 3.0 GPA with at least 12 credit hours per term is required to retain scholarship. Awarded every year. Award may be used only at the following schools: Bethune-Cookman Coll, Edward Waters Coll, Florida A&M U, Florida Memorial Coll.
Contact: Office of Student of Financial Assistance.

2640 Mason Scholarship

George Mason University
4400 University Drive
Fairfax, VA 22030
(703) 993-2391
Average award: $9,100
Average award: Comprehensive tuition
Number of awards: 11
Deadline: February 1
College level: Freshman
Criteria: Applicant must be a Virginia resident attending a Virginia high school, have a minimum 3.5 GPA, have a minimum combined SAT I score of 1150, and demonstrate community service and leadership. One recipient is chosen from each of the 11 Virginia Congressional Districts. Minimum 3.0 GPA is required to retain scholarship. Awarded every year. Award may be used only at sponsoring institution.
Contact: Larry Beatty, Director of Enrollment Services.

2641 Massachusetts State General Scholarship

Massachusetts State Scholarship
330 Stuart Street
Boston, MA 02116
(617) 727-9420
Average award: $1,400
Maximum award: $3,800
Minimum award: $200
Deadline: May 1
College level: Sophomore, Junior, Senior, Graduate, Doctoral
Criteria: Applicant must be a resident of Massachusetts, enrolled full-time, and in good academic standing. Recipient must file Massachusetts financial aid form for renewal. Awarded every year.
Contact: Elizabeth K. Fontaine, Director.

2642 Massachusetts State Scholarship Program

Massachusetts Higher Education Coordinator Council
1 Ashburton Place
McCormack Building, Rm 1401
Boston, MA 02108
(617) 727-7785
Average award: $1,100
Maximum award: $2,500
Minimum award: $250
Deadline: May 1
College level: Freshman, Sophomore, Junior, Senior
Criteria: Applicant must be a resident of Massachusetts, be enrolled as a full-time student, and demonstrate financial need. Recipient must demonstrate financial need and submit FAFSA to retain scholarship. Awarded every year.
Contact: Clantha Carrigan McCurdy, Director of Student Financial Assisstance, Office of Student Financial Assistance, 330 Stuart Street, Boston, MA 02116, (617) 727-9420.

2643 Memorial Scholarship for Children and Spouses of Deceased Police Officers and Firefighters

Higher Education Services Corporation
99 Washington Avenue
Albany, NY 12255
(518) 473-7087, (518) 474-2839 (fax)
http://www.hesc.com
Average award: Full tuition
Deadline: May 1
College level: Freshman, Sophomore, Junior, Senior
Criteria: Applicant must be the child or spouse of a police officer, firefighter, or volunteer firefighter and a New York resident attending a New York school at the start of the term for which payment is requested. Parent must have died as a result of injury sustained in the line of duty. Renewable for up to five years. Awarded every year. New York schools only.
Contact: New York State Higher Education Services Corporation.

2644 Michigan Competitive Scholarship Program

Michigan Higher Education Assistance Authority
Office of Scholarships and Grants
P.O. Box 30462
Lansing, MI 48909-7962
(517) 373-3394
Maximum award: $1,200
Number of awards: 27,200
Deadline: February 21 (high school seniors); March 21 (college students)
College level: Freshman, Sophomore, Junior, Senior
Criteria: Applicant must receive a qualifying ACT score prior to attending college, attend a Michigan college (public or private), be a Michigan resident, complete FAFSA, and demonstrate need. Applicant cannot major in religious education. Minimum 2.0 GPA is required to maintain scholarship. Awarded every year.

2645 Michigan Tuition Grant Program

Michigan Higher Education Assistance Authority
Office of Scholarships and Grants
P.O. Box 30462
Lansing, MI 48909-7962
(517) 373-3394
Maximum award: $1,975
Number of awards: 34,000
Deadline: September 1
College level: Freshman, Sophomore, Junior, Senior, Graduate, Doctoral
Criteria: Applicant must be a Michigan resident attending a private, independent, degree-granting, Michigan college, demonstrate financial need, and complete FAFSA. Applicant cannot major in religious education. Applicant must maintain satisfactory academic progress. Awarded every year.

2646 Minnesota State Grant

Minnesota Higher Education Services Office Division of Student Financial Aid
Suite 400, Capitol Square
550 Cedar Street
St. Paul, MN 55101
(800) 657-3866, (612) 296-3974
http://www.heso.state.mn.us
Average award: $1,300
Maximum award: $5,932
Minimum award: $300
Number of awards: 60,000
Deadline: May 31
College level: Freshman, Sophomore, Junior, Senior
Criteria: Applicant must show need, be a U.S. citizen or permanent resident, meet state residency requirements, be in first four years of postsecondary education, not be in default on a student loan, and be current in child support obligation. Applicant must reapply and demonstrate need for renewal. Awarded every year.
Contact: Grants Staff.

2647 Minority Achievement Scholarship

University of Central Oklahoma
100 North University
Edmond, OK 73034
(405) 341-2980, extension 2631, (405) 341-7658 (fax)
Average award: $1,500
Maximum award: Full tuition and fees up to 18 hours
Number of awards: 15
Deadline: April 1
College level: Freshman
Criteria: Applicant must be a minority Oklahoma resident enrolled for at least 12 credit hours, have a minimum composite ACT score of 24, and have a minimum 3.0 GPA. Minimum 3.0 GPA and full-time enrollment are required to retain scholarship. Awarded every year. Award may be used only at sponsoring institution.
Contact: Margaret Howell, Scholarship Coordinator.

2648 Missouri Higher Education Academic Scholarship

Missouri Coordinating Board of Higher Education
P.O. Box 6730
Jefferson City, MO 65102
(573) 751-3940, (573) 751-6635 (fax)
http://www.mocbhe.gov
Average award: $2,000
Deadline: July 31
College level: Freshman
Criteria: Applicant must score in the top three percent on the ACT or SAT I while in high school and attend an eligible Missouri college. Applicant must maintain satisfactory academic progress for renewal. Awarded every year.
Contact: Information Service Center, (800) 473-6757.

2649 Missouri Student Grant Program

Missouri Coordinating Board of Higher Education
P.O. Box 6730
Jefferson City, MO 65102
(573) 751-3940, (573) 751-6635 (fax)
http://www.mocbhe.gov
Maximum award: $1,500
Deadline: April 1
College level: Unspecified undergraduate
Criteria: Applicant must demonstrate financial need, be a U.S. citizen and legal Missouri resident, and be working toward his or her first undergraduate degree as a full-time student attending an approved non-profit Missouri institution. Students majoring in theology or divinity are not eligible. FAFSA required. Renewable if financial need is continued. Awarded every year.
Contact: Missouri Student Grant Program, (800) 473-6757.

2650 Mrs. Yuen Leung Mo-Tak Scholarship

University of Tennessee, Knoxville
Financial Aid Office
115 Student Services Building
Knoxville, TN 37994
(615) 974-3131
Average award: Full tuition
Deadline: February 1
College level: Sophomore, Junior, Senior, Graduate, Doctoral
Criteria: Applicant must be a currently enrolled student from Hong Kong with a minimum 3.0 GPA for undergraduates and 3.5 GPA for graduate students. Selection is based upon faculty recommendations and financial need. Scholarship is renewable. Awarded every year. Award may be used only at sponsoring institution.
Contact: Center for International Education, 201 Aconda Court, Knoxville, TN 37996, (615) 974-3177.

2651 National Association of Water Companies-New Jersey Chapter Scholarship

National Association of Water Companies-New Jersey Chapter
600 South Avenue
Westfield, NJ 07090
(908) 654-9122, (908) 232-2719 (fax)
Maximum award: $2,500
Number of awards: 2
Deadline: April 1
College level: Freshman, Doctoral
Majors/Fields: Biology, business, chemistry, communication, computer science, engineering, environmental sciences, law, natural resource management
Criteria: Applicant must be a U.S. citizen, a New Jersey resident for at least five years, and pursuing a degree at a New Jersey college or university. Applicant must have a minimum 3.0 GPA and be pursuing a professional career in the water utility industry or any field related to it. Awarded every year.
Contact: Gail P. Brady, NAWC-NJ Scholarship Committee Chairman, Elizabethtown Water Company, 600 South Avenue, Westfield, NJ 07090.

2652 NationsBank-Greenville Urban League Scholarship

Clemson University
G-01 Sikes Hall
Clemson, SC 29634-5123
(803) 656-2280
Average award: $2,500
Number of awards: 2
Deadline: None
College level: Freshman
Criteria: Applicant must be a resident of Greenville County. Renewable if recipient maintians minimum 3.0 GPA, Awarded every year. Award may be used only at sponsoring institution.
Contact: Marvin Carmichael, Director of Financial Aid.

2653 Ned McWherter Scholars Program

Tennessee Student Assistance Corporation
Parkway Towers, Suite 1950
404 James Robertson Parkway
Nashville, TN 37243-0820
(615) 741-1346, (615) 741-6101 (fax)
Average award: $6,000
Number of awards: 55
Deadline: February 15
College level: Freshman
Criteria: Applicant must be a U.S. citizen, attend a participating college or university in Tennessee, be a Tennessee resident, have graduated from a Tennessee high school with a minimum 3.5 GPA, and rank in the top five percent nationally on the ACT or SAT I. High school grades, standardized test scores, leadership roles in high school, and difficulty of high school program are all considered; recipient is selected competitively. Minimum 3.2 GPA and full-time status are required to retain scholarship. Awarded every year. Award may be used at Tennessee schools only.
Contact: Michael C. Roberts, Program Administrator.

2654 Nelson Mandela Scholarship

Saint Paul's College
406 Windsor Avenue
Lawrenceville, VA 23868
(804) 848-4505
Average award: $4,000
Maximum number of awards: 2
Minimum number of awards: 1
Deadline: None
College level: Freshman, Sophomore, Junior, Senior, Graduate
Criteria: Applicant must be a South African citizen and pass the college's certificate exam. Minimum 3.0 GPA is required to retain scholarship. Awarded every year. Award may be used only at sponsoring institution.
Contact: Samuel L. Wade, J.D., Director of Financial Aid.

2655 New Hampshire Charitable Foundation Statewide Student Aid Program

New Hampshire Charitable Foundation
1 South Street
Concord, NH 03301-4005
(603) 225-6641
Average award: $1,200
Maximum award: $2,500
Minimum award: $100
Number of awards: 667
Deadline: April 21
College level: Freshman, Sophomore, Junior, Senior, Graduate, Doctoral, non-traditional students
Criteria: Applicant must be a New Hampshire resident. Some funds have specific eligibility requirements such as field of study or residential area. Selection is made through a statewide competition and is based upon merit and financial need. Some awards are renewable. To retain aid, applicant must maintain a satisfactory GPA and financial situation must remain substantially unchanged. Awarded every year.
Contact: Judith T. Burrows, Director of Student Aid Programs, 37 Pleasant Street, Concord, NH 03301-4005.

2656 New Mexico Scholars Program

New Mexico State University
Box 30001, Department 5100
Las Cruces, NM 88003-0001
(505) 646-4105
Average award: Tuition, fees, book stipend
Deadline: March 1
College level: Freshman
Criteria: Applicant must be a New Mexico resident, graduate from a New Mexico high school in the year of the award, plan to enroll full time, and meet family income guidelines. Applicant must have a minimum composite ACT score of 25 (combined SAT I score of 1050) or rank in the top five percent of class. Minimum 3.0 GPA is required to retain scholarship. Awarded every year. Award may be used only at sponsoring institution.
Contact: Greeley W. Myers, Director of Financial Aid.

2657   New Mexico Scholars Scholarship

University of New Mexico
Mesa Vista Hall, 3rd Floor, Room 3020
Albuquerque, NM 87131
(505) 277-6090
Average award: Full tuition and books
Number of awards: 75
Deadline: February 1
College level: Freshman
Criteria: Applicant must be a New Mexico resident, have a minimum composite ACT score of 25 (combined SAT I score of 1020) and rank in top five percent of class, and have a family adjusted gross income of $30,000 ($40,000 if two members are in college). Minimum 3.0 GPA and 24 credit hours per year are required to retain scholarship. Awarded every year. Award may be used only at sponsoring institution.
Contact: Rita M. Padillo, Associate Director for Scholarships.

2658   Non-AFDC Child Care Grant

Minnesota Higher Education Services Office Division of Student Financial Aid
Suite 400, Capitol Square
550 Cedar Street
St. Paul, MN 55101
(800) 657-3866, (612) 296-3974
http://www.heso.state.mn.us
Maximum award: $1,700
Number of awards: 1,669
College level: Freshman, Sophomore, Junior, Senior
Criteria: Applicant must be pursuing a nonsectarian program, be a U.S. citizen or permanent resident, meet state residency requirements, be enrolled at least half-time, be in the first four years of post-secondary education, must not be in default on a student loan, must not receive AFDC, must have a child 12 years or younger, and must meet eligible income guidelines. Applicant must reapply for renewal. Awarded every year.
Contact: Financial Aid Division Staff, larter@heso.state.mn.us.

2659   Non-Resident Fee Waiver

Louisiana State University and Agricultural and Mechanical College
Baton Rouge, LA 70803-2750
(504) 388-3103
Average award: $3,300
Number of awards: 150
Deadline: February 1
College level: Freshman, Sophomore, Junior, Senior
Criteria: Applicant must have a commendable academic record. Minimum 3.0 cumulative GPA and full-time enrollment are required to retain scholarship. Awarded every year. Award may be used only at sponsoring institution.
Contact: Kathleen Sciacchetano, Director of Financial Aid.

2660   Non-Resident Incentive Tuition Waiver

Oklahoma State University
260 Student Union
Stillwater, OK 74078
(405) 744-7541
Average award: $3,500
Maximum award: $4,000
Minimum award: $3,000
Number of awards: 300
Deadline: February 1 (priority)
College level: Freshman, Transfer
Criteria: Applicant must be a nonresident of Oklahoma, have high GPA and ACT scores, and be the child or grandchild of OSU alumni/ae. Satisfactory GPA and minimum credit hours are required to retain scholarship. Awarded every year. Award may be used only at sponsoring institution.
Contact: Bob Graalman, Director.

2661   Non-Resident Scholar Award

University of Missouri–Columbia
High School and Transfer Relations
219 Jesse Hall
Columbia, MO 65211
(800) 225-6075 (in-state), (314) 882-2456
http://www.missouri.edu
Maximum award: $5,000
Number of awards: 235
Deadline: August 15
College level: Freshman
Criteria: Applicant must rank in top quarter of class, have a minimum composite ACT score of 26 (combined SAT I score of 1170), and be a resident of any state except Missouri. Minimum 2.5 GPA and a minimum 24 credit hours per year are required to retain scholarship. Awarded every year. Award may be used only at sponsoring institution.
Contact: Kathryn E. Bass, Assistant Director, 11 Jesse Hall, Columbia, MO 65211.

2662   Non-Resident Tuition Exemption

Louisiana State University and Agricultural and Mechanical College
Baton Rouge, LA 70803-2750
(504) 388-3103
Average award: $7,245
Number of awards: 159
Deadline: February 1
College level: Freshman, Sophomore, Junior, Senior
Criteria: Applicant must be a resident of a state other than Louisiana, have high standardized test scores, and an excellent academic record, especially in English and math. Minimum 3.0 GPA and full-time enrollment are required to retain scholarship subject to availability of funds. Awarded every year. Award may be used only at sponsoring institution.
Contact: Kathleen Sciacchetano, Director of Financial Aid, LSU, Baton Rouge, LA 70803-2750.

2663   Nonresident Academic Full Tuition Scholarship

University of Utah
Financial Aid and Scholarships Office
105 Student Services Building
Salt Lake City, UT 84112
(801) 581-6211
Average award: Full nonresident tuition
Deadline: February 1
College level: Freshman
Criteria: Applicant must be a nonresident of Utah. Selection is based upon GPA, test scores, leadership, activities, and accomplishments. Awarded every year. Nonresident leadership scholarship is also available. Award may be used only at sponsoring institution.
Contact: Financial Aid and Scholarships Office.

2664   Nonresident Academic Partial Tuition Scholarship

University of Utah
Financial Aid and Scholarships Office
105 Student Services Building
Salt Lake City, UT 84112
(801) 581-6211
Average award: In-state tuition
Number of awards: 50
Deadline: February 1
College level: Freshman
Criteria: Applicant must be a nonresident of Utah. Selection is based upon scholastic ability. Awarded every year. Nonresident transfer student scholarship is also available. Award may be used only at sponsoring institution.
Contact: Financial Aid and Scholarships Office.

2665 North Carolina Bar Association Scholarship

North Carolina Bar Association
P.O. Box 3688
Cary, NC 27519
(919) 677-0561, (919) 677-0761 (fax)
Maximum award: $2,000
Deadline: April 1
College level: Freshman, Sophomore, Junior, Senior, Graduate, Doctoral
Criteria: Applicant must be the child of a North Carolina law enforcement officer who was killed or permanently disabled in the line of duty and must apply prior to age 27. Selection is based upon financial need and merit. Renewable up to a maximum of $8,000 over 4 years. Awarded every year.
Contact: Jacquelyn Terrell-Fountain, Assistant Director of Sections and Divisions.

2666 North Carolina Teaching Fellows Scholarship

North Carolina Teaching Fellows Commission
3739 National Drive, Suite 210
Raleigh, NC 27612
(919) 781-6833, (919) 781-6527 (fax)
http://www.ncforum.org
Maximum award: $5,000
Number of awards: 400
College level: Freshman
Majors/Fields: Education
Criteria: Applicant must be a North Carolina resident planning to attend Appalachian St U, East Carolina U, Elon College, Meredith College, North Carolina A&T St U, North Carolina Central U, North Carolina St U, UNC Asheville, UNC Chapel Hill, UNC Charlotte, UNC Greensboro, UNC Wilmington, UNC Pembroke, or Western Carolina U. Selection is based upon GPA, class rank, SAT I scores, writing samples, community service, extracurricular activities, interview, and references. Applicant must agree to teach in a North Carolina public school one year for each year of scholarship assistance (or for three years in a system designated by the State Board of Education as "low performing") or repay the amount with 10 percent interest. Award is for four years. Awarded every year. Award may be used only at Appalachian St U, East Carolina U, Elon Coll, Meredith Coll, North Carolina A&T St U, North Carolina Central U, North Carolina St U, UNC Asheville, UNC Chapel Hill, UNC Charlotte, UNC Greensboro, UNC Wilmington, UNC Pembroke, or Western Carolina U.
Contact: Public Schools Forum, North Carolina Teaching Fellows Commission, Koger Center, Cumberland Building, 3739 National Drive, Suite 210, Raleigh, NC 27612.

2667 North Georgia College ROTC Grant

Georgia Student Finance Commission
2082 East Exchange Place, Suite 200
Tucker, GA 30084
(770) 414-3000, (912) 757-3626, (800) 776-6878
Average award: $1,500
College level: Freshman, Sophomore, Junior, Senior
Criteria: Applicant must be a Georgia resident enrolled in the Army ROTC program. Financial need is not considered. Award may be used at North Georgia Coll only.
Contact: Grants.

2668 Ohio Academic Scholarship

Ohio Board of Regents, State Grants and Scholarships Department
309 South Fourth Street, P.O. Box 182452
Columbus, OH 43218-2452
(614) 466-1190, (614) 752-5903 (fax)
Average award: $2,000
Number of awards: 1000
Deadline: February 23
College level: Freshman
Criteria: Applicant must be an Ohio resident, graduate from an Ohio chartered high school, and have full-time status in a participating Ohio college or university. Selection is based upon academic excellence in high school and ACT scores. Satisfactory academic progress and full-time enrollment are required to retain scholarship. Awarded every year. Participating Ohio schools only.
Contact: Sue Minturn, Program Administrator.

2669 Ohio Academic Scholarship and Matching Program

University of Toledo
Financial Aid Office
Toledo, OH 43606-3390
(419) 537-2056
Average award: $2,500
Deadline: January 28
College level: Freshman
Criteria: Applicant must be an Ohio resident who has been awarded the Ohio Academic Scholarship from the Ohio Board of Regents. Selection is based upon academic achievement. Applicant must be enrolled full-time with a minimum 3.0 GPA for university funding and minimum 2.0 GPA for Ohio Academic Scholarship. Awarded every year. Award may be used only at sponsoring institution.

2670 Ohio Honors Scholarship

Waynesburg College
51 West College Street
Waynesburg, PA 15370
(800) 225-7393, (412) 627-6416 (fax)
admission@waynesburg.edu
http://waynesburg.edu
Average award: Full tuition, room and board
Number of awards: 2
Deadline: March 1
College level: Freshman
Majors/Fields: Mathematics, sciences
Criteria: Applicant must be from an Ohio school, have a minimum 3.0 GPA, be planning a career in math or science, and demonstrate financial need. Minimum 3.0 GPA is required to retain scholarship. Awarded every year. Award may be used only at sponsoring institution.
Contact: Robin Moore, Dean of Admissions, (412) 852-3248.

2671 Ohio Instructional Grant

Ohio Board of Regents, State Grants and Scholarships Department
309 South Fourth Street, P.O. Box 182452
Columbus, OH 43218-2452
(614) 466-1190, (614) 752-5903 (fax)
Maximum award: $3,750
Deadline: October 1
College level: Freshman, Sophomore, Junior, Senior
Criteria: Applicant must be a U.S. citizen, an Ohio resident attending full-time at an Ohio or Pennsylvania postsecondary school, complete the FAFSA, and have a household income of less than $29,000. Awarded every year. Ohio and Pennsylvania schools only.
Contact: Barbara Metheney, Administrator.

2672 Oregon AFL-CIO May Darling-Asat. Williams-Northwest Labor Press Scholarship

Oregon AFL-CIO
2110 State Street
Salem, OR 97301
(503) 585-6320
Maximum award: $3,000
Number of awards: 6
Deadline: February 15
Criteria: Applicant must be a graduating senior from an accredited Oregon high school in the year that the written scholarship exam is given. Selection is based upon superior performance on the written labor history exam, financial need, high school GPA, and an interview by a panel of professionals. Applicant must plan to attend a certified trade school. Awarded every year.
Contact: Amy Klare, Research and Education Director, 1900 Hines Street, SE, Salem, OR 97302.

2673 Oregon Need Grant

State Scholarship Commission (Oregon)
1500 Valley River Drive, Suite 100
Eugene, OR 97401-2146
(541) 687-7400
http://www.teleport.com/~ossc/
Average award: $1,104
Maximum award: $1,584
Minimum award: $906
Deadline: as soon as possible after January 1
College level: Freshman, Sophomore, Junior, Senior
Criteria: Applicant must be an Oregon resident, be enrolled full time at an Oregon school, and demonstrate financial need. Scholarship is renewable. Awarded every year.
Contact: Jim Beyer, Grant Program Director.

2674 Out-of-State Tuition Waivers

University of Idaho
Moscow, ID 83843
(208) 885-6312, (208) 885-5592 (fax)
finaid@uidaho.edu
http://www.uidaho/edu
Average award: $3,500
Maximum award: $5,800
Minimum award: $2,900
Number of awards: 95
Deadline: February 15
College level: Freshman, Sophomore, Junior, Senior
Criteria: Applicant must not be a resident of Idaho and must show academic ability. Awarded every year. Award may be used only at sponsoring institution.
Contact: Shawna Lindquist, Scholarship Advisor, Financial Aid Office, University of Idaho, Moscow, ID 83844, finaid@uidaho.edu.

2675 Outstanding Citizen of Boys State

American Legion–Iowa
Department Headquarters
720 Lyon Street
Des Moines, IA 50309
Average award: $1,500
Number of awards: 1
College level: Freshman
Criteria: Applicant must demonstrate outstanding citizenship while attending Iowa American Legion Boys State. Applicant must attend a college or university in Iowa. Selection is based upon the recommendation of Boys State Counselors. Awarded every year.
Contact: Boys State, 720 Lyon Street, Des Moines, IA 50309.

2676 Outstanding Citizen of Girls State

American Legion–Iowa
Department Headquarters
720 Lyon Street
Des Moines, IA 50309
Average award: $1,500
Number of awards: 1
College level: Freshman
Criteria: Applicant must demonstrate outstanding leadership while attending Iowa American Legion Auxiliary Girls State. Applicant must attend a college or university in Iowa. Selection is based upon the recommendation of Girls State Counselors. Awarded every year.
Contact: Girls State, 720 Lyon Street, Des Moines, IA 50309.

2677 Palmetto Fellows Scholarship

Clemson University
G-01 Sikes Hall
Clemson, SC 29634-5123
(803) 656-2280
Maximum award: $2,500
Deadline: None
College level: Freshman
Criteria: Award is for the most outstanding entering freshman from South Carolina. Minimum 3.0 GPA and completion of at least 12 credits per semester are required to retain scholarship. Awarded every year. Award may be used only at sponsoring institution.
Contact: Marvin Carmichael, Director of Financial Aid.

2678 Part-Time Student Instructional Grant Program

Ohio Board of Regents, State Grants and Scholarships Department
309 South Fourth Street, P.O. Box 182452
Columbus, OH 43218-2452
(614) 466-1190, (614) 752-5903 (fax)
Maximum award: $3,180
College level: Freshman, Sophomore, Junior, Senior
Criteria: Applicant must be an Ohio resident attending part-time at an Ohio postsecondary school and complete the FAFSA. Special consideration given to single heads of household or displaced homemakers. Awarded every year. Ohio schools only.
Contact: Barbara Metheney, Administrator, (614) 752-9535.

2679 Patrick H. Johnson Memorial Scholarship

Marianas Naval Officers' Wives' Club
Scholarship Chairwoman
PSC 489, Box 49 COMNAVMAR
FPO AP, 96536-0051
(671) 477-5405
Average award: $3,000
Number of awards: 1
Deadline: March 31
College level: Freshman
Criteria: Applicant must be a graduating senior from a Guam high school; no military affiliation is required. Selection is based upon academic ability, character, leadership ability, community involvement, financial need, and the cost of the school. Applicant must send a self-addressed, double-stamped envelope in order to receive a application. Awarded every year.
Contact: Scholarship Chairwoman, PSC 489, Box 49 COMNAVMAR, FPO AP, 96536-0051.

2680 Paul L. Fowler Memorial Scholarship

Idaho State Board of Education
Len B. Jordan Building, Room 307
P.O. Box 83720
Boise, ID 83720-0037
(208) 334-2270, (208) 334-2632 (fax)
csmith@osbe.state.id.us
Average award: $3,000
Number of awards: 2
Deadline: January 31
College level: Freshman
Criteria: Applicant must be an Idaho resident who has demonstrated outstanding ability and willingness to work for a higher education. Selection is based upon class rank and ACT scores. Applicant must enroll as a full-time student in an academic program. Awarded every year.
Contact: Caryl Smith, Scholarship Assistant, csmith@osbe.state.id.us.

2681 Police Officers and Firefighters Survivor's Educational Assistance Program

Alabama Commission on Higher Education
P.O. Box 302000
Montgomery, AL 36130-2000
(334) 242-1998, (334) 242-0268 (fax)
Average award: Tuition, fees, books, and supplies
College level: Freshman, Sophomore, Junior, Senior
Criteria: Applicant must be the dependent or spouse of a police officer or firefighter killed in the line of duty in Alabama, and be enrolled at a public postsecondary educational institution in Alabama. Scholarship is renewable. Awarded every year.
Contact: Mrs. Jan B. Hilyer, Assistant Director of Grants and Scholarships, (334) 242-2273.

2682 Policeman's Dependent Scholarship

Northern Kentucky University
Administrative Center 416
Nunn Drive
Highland Heights, KY 41099-7101
(606) 572-5144
Average award: In-state tuition
Deadline: February 1
College level: Freshman, Sophomore, Junior, Senior
Criteria: Applicant must be a dependent or spouse of a permanently disabled or deceased Kentucky resident police officer. Award is to age 23, completion of degree or certification, or 36 months attendance, whichever comes first. Awarded every year. Award may be used only at sponsoring institution.
Contact: Robert E. Sprague, Director of Financial Aid.

2683 Potlatch Foundation for Higher Education Scholarship

Potlatch Foundation for Higher Education
P.O. Box 193591
San Francisco, CA 94119-3591
(415) 576-8829, (415) 576-8832 (fax)
Average award: $1,400
Number of awards: 80
Deadline: February 15
College level: Freshman, Sophomore, Junior, Senior
Criteria: Applicant must reside within 30 miles of a major Potlatch Corp. facility in Arkansas, California, Idaho, Minnesota, or Nevada or attend high school in such an area. Selection is based upon character, personality, leadership qualities, scholastic achievement and ability, and financial need. Application must be requested by December 15. Minimum 2.1 GPA is required to retain scholarship. Awarded every year.
Contact: Rita Bodlak.

2684 President's Achievement Scholarship—Tier 1

University of Texas at Austin
P.O. Box 7758
UT Station
Austin, TX 78713-7758
(512) 475-6200, (512) 475-6296 (fax)
finaid@www.utexas.edu
http://www.utexas.edu/student/finaid
Average award: $5,000
Deadline: December 1
College level: Freshman
Criteria: Applicant must be a Texas resident, graduate from a Texas high school, and demonstrate the ability to overcome academic and socioeconomic adversity. Minimum 3.0 GPA is required to retain scholarship. Awarded every year. Award may be used only at sponsoring institution.
Contact: Gloria DeLeon, Special Programs Coordinator, (512) 475-6282, faged@utxdp.dp.utexas.edu.

2685 President's Associates Honors Scholarship

New Mexico State University
Box 30001, Department 5100
Las Cruces, NM 88003-0001
(505) 646-4105
Average award: $3,000 plus tuition and fees
Number of awards: 5
Deadline: March 1
College level: Freshman
Criteria: Applicant must have a minimum 3.5 GPA and minimum composite ACT score of 26 (combined SAT I score of 1090) or a minimum 3.0 GPA and a minimum composite ACT score of 28 (combined SAT I score of 1170). Applicant must be a graduate of a New Mexico high school. Selection is based upon academic achievement. Minimum 3.5 GPA is required to retain scholarship for up to four years. Awarded every year. Award may be used only at sponsoring institution.
Contact: Greeley W. Myers, Director of Financial Aid.

2686 President's Scholarship

University of Utah
Financial Aid and Scholarships Office
105 Student Services Building
Salt Lake City, UT 84112
(801) 581-6211
Average award: Resident tuition plus a cash award
Number of awards: 50
Deadline: February 1
College level: Freshman
Criteria: Applicant must be a Utah resident, have a minimum composite ACT score of 28 or equivalent SAT I score, be a National Merit finalist, have a minimum 3.9 GPA, and have an Admissions Index of at least 126. Selection is based upon academic excellence, leadership, and civic activities. Awarded for a maximum of 12 quarters or until baccalaureate degree is obtained, whichever comes first. Minimum 3.7 GPA and 36 hours every three quarters are required to retain scholarship. Awarded every year. Award may be used only at sponsoring institution.
Contact: Financial Aid and Scholarships Office.

2687 Presidental Scholarship

University of Oregon
1242 University of Oregon
Eugene, OR 97403-1242
(541) 346-3044, (541) 346-2537 (fax)
http://www.uoregon.edu/
Maximum award: $2,400
Number of awards: 50
Deadline: February 1
College level: Freshman
Criteria: Applicant must be an Oregon resident. Renewable for four years if a minimum 3.25 GPA is maintained. Awarded every year. Award may be used only at sponsoring institution.
Contact: Jim Gilmour, Associate Director of Financial Aid, (541) 346-1187.

2688 Presidential Scholarship

Wayne State University
Office of Admissions
HNJ Student Services 3 East
Detroit, MI 48202
(313) 577-2424 (General), 313 577-3577 (Admissions), (313) 577-7536 (fax)
Average award: $3,504
Maximum number of awards: 320
Minimum number of awards: 300
Deadline: February 14
College level: Freshman
Criteria: Applicant must have a minimum 3.5 cumulative GPA, minimum composite ACT score of 22 or combined SAT I score of 1010, be a Michigan resident, and graduate from a Michigan accredited high school. Minimum 3.0 cumulative GPA and completion of 24 semester credits per year are required to retain scholarship. Awarded every year. Award may be used only at sponsoring institution.
Contact: Dorothy J. Papajohn, Assistant Director of Admissions, dpapajoh@cms.cc.wayne.edu.

2689 Presidential Scholarship

Bowie State University
Bowie, MD 20715
(301) 464-6544
Average award: Tuition and fees
Deadline: February 1 (fall); November 1 (spring)
College level: Freshman, Transfer
Criteria: Applicant must be a Maryland resident, enrolled full time, have a minimum combined SAT I score of 1000, submit essay and three letters of recommendation, and schedule on-campus interview. Freshman applicant must have a minimum 3.0 GPA; transfer student applicant must have a minimum 3.25 GPA with at least 30 transferable credit hours and submit resume. Awarded every year. Award may be used only at sponsoring institution.
Contact: Scholarship Committee, Career Services, Bowie, MD 20715-9465, (301) 464-7110, (301) 464-7111.

2690 Profile in Courage Essay Contest

John F. Kennedy Library Foundation
Columbia Point
Boston, MA 02125
(617) 436-9986, (617) 436-3395 (fax)
Maximum award: $2,000
Number of awards: 1
College level: High school students
Criteria: Applicants must be residents of New England, New Jersey, or New York. Awarded every year.
Contact: Shelley Sommer, Director, Profile in Courage Award.

2691 Public Safety Officers Survivor Grant

Minnesota Higher Education Services Office Division of Student Financial Aid
Suite 400, Capitol Square
550 Cedar Street
St. Paul, MN 55101
(800) 657-3866, (612) 296-3974
http://www.heso.state.mn.us
Average award: $3,377
Maximum award: $4,244
Number of awards: 9
Deadline: Last day of classes.
College level: Freshman, Sophomore, Junior, Senior
Criteria: Applicant must be the dependent child under age 23 or the surviving spouse of a public safety officer who was killed in the line of duty on or after January 1, 1973. Applicant must also be a U.S. citizen or permanent resident, meet state residency requirements, be enrolled at least half time, be in the first four years of postsecondary education, and must not be in default on a student loan. Reapplication is required for renewal for each academic term. Awarded every year.
Contact: Brenda Larter, Program Assistant, (612) 296-3974, larter@heso.state.mn.us.

2692 Rector's Scholarship

University of Ottawa
85 University Private, Room 123
P.O. Box 450, Station "A"
Ottawa, Ontario, CN K1N 6N5
(613) 562-5810, (613) 562-5155 (fax)
Average award: $4,000
Number of awards: 6
Deadline: January 30
College level: Freshman
Majors/Fields: Administration, arts, engineering, health sciences, social sciences, science
Criteria: Applicant must be a bilingual Canadian citizen or permanent resident, with a minimum 92.0 admission average including six OACs or equivalent, and must meet extracurricular or community excellence criteria. Renewable if recipient maintains a minimum GPA of 9.0 (on a 12.0 scale) and full-time status. Awarded every year. Award may be used only at sponsoring institution.
Contact: Mrs. Diane Pelletier, Awards Administrator.

2693 Regents Professional Opportunity Scholarship

New York State Education Department
Bureau HEOP/DATEA/Scholarships
Cultural Education Center
Albany, NY 12230
(518) 486-1319
Maximum award: $5,000
Number of awards: 220
Deadline: April 1
College level: Freshman, Sophomore, Junior, Senior, Graduate, Doctoral
Majors/Fields: Accounting, architecture, audiology, chiropractic, dental hygiene, engineering, landscape architecture, law, nursing, occupational therapy, occupational therapy assistant, ophthalmic dispensing, optometry, pharmacy, physical therapy, physical therapy assistant, physician assistant, psychology, social work, speech-language pathology, veterinary medicine
Criteria: Applicant must attend or plan to attend an approved licensure-qualifying program in New York state, be a legal resident of New York state for one year prior to September 1, be a U.S. citizen or permanent resident, and be economically disadvantaged or a member of a minority group underrepresented in one of the designated licensed professions. Applicant must agree to practice in New York state in chosen profession for 12 months for each annual payment received. Scholarship is renewable. Awarded when funding is available.
Contact: Office of Equity and Access, (518) 474-5705.

2694 Regents Scholarship

University of Nebraska, Lincoln
14th and R Streets
Lincoln, NE 68588
(402) 472-2030, (402) 472-9826 (fax)
http://www.unl.edu/scholfa/cover.html
Average award: $2,250
Maximum award: Full tuition
Minimum award: In-state tuition
Number of awards: 322
Deadline: January 15
College level: Freshman
Criteria: Applicant must be a graduate of a Nebraska high school. Minimum 3.5 GPA and 24 credit hours per year are required to retain scholarship. Awarded every year. Award may be used only at sponsoring institution.
Contact: Debra Augustyn, Assistant Director of Scholarships.

2695 Regents' Scholarship

New Mexico State University
Box 30001, Department 5100
Las Cruces, NM 88003-0001
(505) 646-4105
Average award: Full tuition
Deadline: March 1
College level: Freshman
Criteria: Applicant must have a minimum 3.0 GPA, minimum composite ACT score of 23 (combined SAT I score of 970), and rank in top tenth of class, or have a minimum composite ACT score of 26 (combined SAT I score of 1090). Minimum 3.2 GPA at end of first semester (minimum 3.5 GPA thereafter) is required to retain scholarship. Awarded every year. Award may be used only at sponsoring institution.
Contact: Greeley W. Myers, Director of Financial Aid.

2696 Regional Grant

Ohio Wesleyan University
Office of Admissions
Delaware, OH 43015
(614) 368-3020, (614) 368-3314 (fax)
owuadmit@cc.owu.edu
http://www.owu.edu
Average award: $4,000
Number of awards: 200
Deadline: None
College level: Freshman, Sophomore, Junior, Senior
Criteria: Applicant must be a resident of Alaska, Ariz., Calif., Colo., Conn., D.C., Fla., Ga., Hawaii, Idaho, Maine, Md., Mass., Mont., Nev., N.H., N.J., N.Mex., N.Y., N.C., Okla., Oreg., R.I., S.C., Tex., Utah, Vt., Va., Wash., or Wyo., or be a U.S. citizen or permanent resident studying abroad. Scholarship is renewable. Awarded every year. Award may be used only at sponsoring institution.
Contact: Douglas C. Thompson, Dean of Admission.

2697 Robert C. Byrd Honors Scholarship

Higher Education Services Corporation
99 Washington Avenue
Albany, NY 12255
(518) 473-7087, (518) 474-2839 (fax)
http://www.hesc.com
Maximum award: $1,121
College level: Freshman
Criteria: Applicant must be a New York resident planning to attend college. At least 10 scholarships will be awarded from each of the state's 34 congressional districts. Selection is based upon academic record and standardized test scores. Awarded when sufficient funds are available, renewable for up to four years. Awarded every year.
Contact: New York State Education Department, Bureau of College, School, and Community Collaboration,, Cultural Education Center, Room 5C64, Albany, NY 12230, (518) 486-5202.

2698 Robert C. Byrd Honors Scholarship

North Carolina Department of Public Instruction
301 North Wilmington Street
Raleigh, NC 27601-2825
(919) 715-1000, (919) 715-1094 (fax)
Maximum award: $1,110
Number of awards: 160
Deadline: in February
College level: Freshman
Criteria: Applicant must be a North Carolina resident who graduated from a North Carolina public or private secondary school. Selection is based upon outstanding academic achievement. Financial need is not considered. Renewable for up to four years. Awarded every year.
Contact: Department of Public Instruction.

2699 Robert C. Byrd Honors Scholarship

California Student Aid Commission
P.O.Box 510845
Sacramento, CA 94245-0845
(916) 445-0880, (916) 327-6599 (fax)
custsvcs@csac.ca.gov
http://www.csac.ca.gov
Average award: $1,500
Number of awards: 450
Deadline: April 1
College level: Freshman
Criteria: Applicant must be a legal resident of California; approximately 10 applicants from each of the 45 California Congressional Districts will be selected. Applicant must have graduated from high school during the previous year, plan to enroll in a U.S. public or private nonprofit postsecondary institution, and plan to file a Selective Service Registration Status statement. Selection is based solely on merit. Awarded every year.
Contact: High School Robert C. Byrd Scholarship Coordinator.

2700 Robert C. Byrd Honors Scholarship

Ohio Board of Regents, State Grants and Scholarships Department
309 South Fourth Street, P.O. Box 182452
Columbus, OH 43218-2452
(614) 466-1190, (614) 752-5903 (fax)
Average award: $1,500
Number of awards: 270
Deadline: March 10
College level: Freshman, GED recipient
Criteria: Applicant must be an Ohio resident and graduating high school senior or GED recipient. Selection is based upon leadership activities and outstanding achievement indicated by test scores and GPA. Renewable for up to three years. Awarded every year.
Contact: Barbara Wilson, Administrator, (614) 752-9137.

2701 Robert C. Byrd Honors Scholarship

Missouri Department of Elementary and Secondary Education
P.O. Box 480
Jefferson City, MO 65102
(573) 751-1668
Average award: $1,121
Number of awards: 126
Deadline: April 15
College level: Freshman
Criteria: Applicant must be a resident of Missouri, rank in the top tenth of class, score in the top 10 percent on the ACT, and file with the school a statement certifying registration with the Selective Service. Recipient must remain in good standing with the college for scholarship to be renewed. Awarded every year.
Contact: Janet Goeller, Director of Teacher Recruitment & Retention.

2702 Robert C. Byrd Honors Scholarship

Texas Higher Education Coordinating Board
Student Financial Assistance
P.O. Box 12788, Capitol Station
Austin, TX 78711-2788
(512) 427-6340
Average award: $1,471
Maximum award: $1,500
Number of awards: 1199
Deadline: March 15
College level: Freshman
Criteria: Selection is based upon GPA, class rank, and test scores. Financial need is not considered. Each Texas high school is allowed to nominate three candidates. Renewable when funds are available. Awarded every year.
Contact: Gustavo DeLeon, Assistant Director of Grant Programs.

2703   Robert C. Byrd Honors Scholarship

District of Columbia Public Schools
Student Affairs Branch
4501 Lee Street, NE
Washington, DC 20019
(202) 724-4934
Average award: $1,500
Deadline: May 14
College level: Freshman
Criteria: Applicant must be a District of Columbia resident, a U.S. citizen, demonstrate outstanding academic achievment, have a minimum 3.2 GPA, graduate from a District of Columbia high school, and be accepted at an institution of higher education. Male applicant must provide proof of registration with Selective Services. Awarded every year.
Contact: Annabelle F. Strayhorn, Director of Student Affairs Branch.

2704   Robert C. Byrd Honors Scholarship Program

New York State Education Department
Bureau HEOP/DATEA/Scholarships
Cultural Education Center
Albany, NY 12230
(518) 486-1319
Maximum award: $1,100
Number of awards: 416
College level: Freshman
Criteria: Applicant must be a legal resident of New York state and a senior in high school or a student earning a GED diploma by the end of February. Scholarship is renewable. Awarded every year.
Contact: Office of Equity and Access.

2705   Robert C. Byrd Scholarship

Georgia Student Finance Commission
2082 East Exchange Place, Suite 200
Tucker, GA 30084
(770) 414-3000, (912) 757-3626, (800) 776-6878
Average award: $1,121
College level: Freshman, Sophomore, Junior, Senior
Criteria: Awarded to Georgia residents for academic excellence. Financial need is not considered. Renewable awards are made to entering freshman. Awarded every year.
Contact: Scholarships, (800) 776-6878.

2706   S.C. Poultry Federation Poultry Science Freshman Scholarship

Clemson University
G-01 Sikes Hall
Clemson, SC 29634-5123
(803) 656-2280
Average award: $2,500
Number of awards: 1
Deadline: None
College level: Freshman
Majors/Fields: Poultry science
Criteria: Applicant must be a resident of South Carolina. Renewable for one year if recipient maintains minimum 2.5 GPA. Award may be used only at sponsoring institution.
Contact: Scholarships.

2707   Sachs Foundation Scholarship

Sachs Foundation
90 South Cascade Avenue, Suite 1410
Colorado Springs, CO 80903
(719) 633-2353
Average award: $3,000
Maximum award: $6,000
Minimum award: $1,500
Number of awards: 50
Deadline: March 1
College level: Freshman
Criteria: Applicant must be African-American, a Colorado resident for at least five years, a high school senior and have a minimum 3.5 GPA. Minimum 2.5 GPA for 12 credit hours with no failures or incompletes is required to retain scholarship. Awarded every year.
Contact: Lisa Harris, Secretary/Treasurer.

2708   Salutatorian Scholarship

University of Central Florida
Undergraduate Admissions
P.O. Box 160111
Orlando, FL 32816-0111
(407) 823-3000, (407) 823-3419 (fax)
http://www.ucf.edu
Average award: $1,500
Number of awards: 20
Deadline: March 15
College level: Freshman
Criteria: Applicant must be a salutatorian from a Florida high school. Minimum 3.0 GPA and full-time status are required to retain scholarship. Awarded every year. Award may be used only at sponsoring institution.
Contact: Susan McKinnon, Assistant Director, Office of Recruitment, Orlando, FL 32816, (407) 823-5439.

2709   Scholarship for Commonwealth Scholars

Northern Kentucky University
Administrative Center 416
Nunn Drive
Highland Heights, KY 41099-7101
(606) 572-5144
Average award: In-state tuition
Deadline: February 1
College level: Freshman
Criteria: Applicant must be a Kentucky resident with a minimum ACT composite score of 23. Renewable for one additional year. Awarded every year. Award may be used only at sponsoring institution.
Contact: Robert E. Sprague, Director of Financial Aid.

2710   Scholarship for New Nebraskans

University of Nebraska, Lincoln
14th and R Streets
Lincoln, NE 68588
(402) 472-2030, (402) 472-9826 (fax)
http://www.unl.edu/scholfa/cover.html
Average award: Full tuition
Deadline: Beginning of fall semester
College level: Freshman, Transfer
Criteria: Applicant must not be a resident of Nebraska. Satisfactory academic progress is required to retain scholarship. Awarded every year. Award may be used only at sponsoring institution.
Contact: Debra Augustyn, Assistant Director of Scholarships and Financial Aid.

2711   Scholarship for Rural Professional or Vocational Nursing Students

Texas Higher Education Coordinating Board
Student Financial Assistance
P.O. Box 12788, Capitol Station
Austin, TX 78711-2788
(512) 427-6340
Maximum award: $2,500
Number of awards: 36
Deadline: July 15
College level: Freshman, Sophomore, Junior, Senior, Graduate, Doctoral
Majors/Fields: Nursing
Criteria: Applicant must be a Texas resident from a rural county, enrolled at least half time in a program leading to licensure as an L.V.N. or in an associate, bachelor, or graduate degree program in professional nursing. Applicant must attend a public or independent nonprofit institution in a nonmetropolitan county in Texas. Recipient must reapply each year. No preference is given to renewals. Awarded every year.
Contact: Jane Caldwell, Director of Grants and Special Programs, (512) 427-6455.

2712 Scholarship for Winners of the "Concours provincial de francais" of the Alumni Association

University of Ottawa
85 University Private, Room 123
P.O. Box 450, Station "A"
Ottawa, Ontario, CN K1N 6N5
(613) 562-5810, (613) 562-5155 (fax)
Average award: $2,500
Number of awards: 2
College level: Freshman
Criteria: Applicant must attend an Ontario secondary school and compete in the "Concours provincial de francais," and be enrolled in one of the direct-access faculties. Awarded every year. Award may be used only at sponsoring institution.
Contact: Mrs. Diane Pelletier, Awards Administrator.

2713 Scholarship Incentive Program

Delaware Higher Education Commission
820 North French Street, Fourth Floor
Wilmington, DE 19801
(302) 577-3240, (302) 577-6765 (fax)
mlaffey@state.de.us
http://www.state.de.us/high-ed/commiss/webpage.htm
Average award: $1,200
Maximum award: $2,200
Minimum award: $600
Number of awards: 1,200
Deadline: April 15
College level: Freshman, Sophomore, Junior, Senior, Graduate, Doctoral
Criteria: Applicant must be a Delaware resident enrolled full time with a minimum 2.5 GPA and be able to demonstrate financial need. Preference is given to applicants attending Delaware or Pennsylvania schools. Awarded every year.
Contact: Maureen Laffey, Associate Director.

2714 Scholastic Achievement Grant

Connecticut Department of Higher Education
Office of Student Financial Aid
61 Woodland Street
Hartford, CT 06105
(203) 566-2618
Average award: $1,100
Maximum award: $2,000
Minimum award: $500
Deadline: February 15
College level: Freshman
Criteria: Applicant must be a Connecticut resident, a U.S. citizen or national, rank in top fifth of high school class or have a minimum combined SAT I score of 1200, and attend a Connecticut college or a college in a state that has reciprocity agreements with Connecticut. Scholarship is renewable. Awarded every year.
Contact: Office of Student Financial Aid, 61 Woodland Street, Hartford, CT 06105.

2715 Seminole and Miccosukee Indian Scholarship

Florida Department of Education
Office of Student Financial Assistance
255 Collins
Tallahassee, FL 32399-0400
(904) 487-0049
Maximum award: Annual cost of education
Deadline: Varies by tribal office
College level: Freshman, Sophomore, Junior, Senior, Graduate, Doctoral
Criteria: Applicant must be a Seminole or Miccosukee Indian, a Florida resident, have a high school diploma or equivalent, be enrolled at an eligible Florida college or university, and demonstrate financial need. Applicant can contact the tribal offices listed below: Miccosukee Tribe of Florida, c/o Higher Education Committee, P.O. Box 440021, Tamiami Station, Miami, FL 33144 or Seminole Tribe of Florida, c/o Higher Education Committee, 6073 Sterling Road, Hollywood, FL 33024. Minimum 2.0 GPA with at least 12 credit hours per term is required to retain scholarship. Awarded every year.
Contact: Office of Student Financial Assistance, 255 Collins, Tallahassee, FL 32399-0400.

2716 Senator George J. Mitchell Scholarship Fund

Maine Community Foundation
210 Main Street, P.O. Box 148
Ellsworth, ME 04605
(207) 667-9735
Average award: $2,500
Number of awards: 20
Deadline: April 26
College level: Freshman, Sophomore, Junior, Senior
Criteria: Applicant must be a Maine resident and a graduate of a Maine High school. Selection is based upon academic achievement, financial need, and community spirit/public service. Awarded every year. Award may be used at Maine schools only.
Contact: Scholarship Coordinator.

2717 Senatorial Scholarship

Maryland Higher Education Commission
State Scholarship Administration
16 Francis Street
Annapolis, MD 21401-1781
(410) 974-5370, (410) 974-5994 (fax)
http://www.ubalt.edu/www/mhec
Average award: $803
Maximum award: $2,000
Minimum award: $200
Number of awards: 7088
Deadline: March 1
College level: Freshman, Sophomore, Junior, Senior, Graduate, Doctoral
Criteria: Applicant must be a Maryland resident who is a full-time or part-time student. Applicant should contact his or her state senator for additional information. Automatically renewed for three years. Awarded every year. Maryland schools preferred.
Contact: Marya Dennis, Program Manager.

2718 South Carolina Tuition Grants Program

South Carolina Higher Education Tuition Grants Commission
1310 Lady Street, Suite 811
Columbia, SC 29211
(803) 734-1200, (803) 734-1426 (fax)
earl@scsn.net
Average award: $2,100
Maximum award: $3,420
Minimum award: $1,900
Number of awards: 9000
Deadline: June 30
College level: Freshman, Sophomore, Junior, Senior
Criteria: Applicant must be a South Carolina resident attending a South Carolina independent college full-time and must demonstrate financial need. Recipient must complete 24 semester hours, submit the FAFSA, and meet institutional satisfactory progress requirements to retain scholarship. Awarded every year.
Contact: Earl Mayo, Deputy Director, earl@scsn.net.

2719 Southwest Scholarship

St. John's College
1160 Camino Cruz Blanca
Santa Fe, NM 87501
(505) 984-6058
Average award: $2,625
Maximum award: $5,000
Minimum award: $2,500
Number of awards: 4
Deadline: March 1
College level: Freshman
Criteria: Applicant must be a resident of Arizona, Colorado, New Mexico, Oklahoma, Texas, or Utah, and demonstrate academic promise, community involvement, and financial need. Essay, application, and financial aid forms are required. Academic progress and continued enrollment are required to retain award. Awarded every year. Award may be used only at sponsoring institution.
Contact: Larry Clendenin, Director of Admission, (505) 984-6090.

2720   Special Department Scholarship

University of Utah
Financial Aid and Scholarships Office
105 Student Services Building
Salt Lake City, UT 84112
(801) 581-6211
Average award: Full tuition
Deadline: February 1 (freshman); April 1 (transfer)
College level: Freshman, Transfer
Criteria: Applicant must be an outstanding Utah resident who has declared a major. Minimum 3.5 GPA and completion of 36 hours every three quarters are required to retain scholarship. Recipient must continue studies in the department from which the scholarship originated. Awarded every year. Award may be used only at sponsoring institution.
Contact: Financial Aid and Scholarships Office.

2721   State Need Grant

Washington Higher Education Coordinating Board
917 Lakeridge Way
P.O. Box 43430
Olympia, WA 98504-3430
(360) 753-7850
Average award: $1,350
Number of awards: 40,000
Deadline: None
College level: Freshman, Sophomore, Junior, Senior
Criteria: Awards are for Washington state residents with a low family income, planning to attend an eligible Washington state institution. Students are designated for the grant by their school's financial aid office. Awarded every year.
Contact: Barbara Theiss, Program Administrator.

2722   State of Idaho Scholarship

Idaho State Board of Education
Len B. Jordan Building, Room 307
P.O. Box 83720
Boise, ID 83720-0037
(208) 334-2270, (208) 334-2632 (fax)
csmith@osbe.state.id.us
Average award: $2,700
Number of awards: 32
Deadline: January 31
College level: Freshman
Criteria: Applicant must take the ACT and be an Idaho resident planning to enroll full time in an academic or vocational program at an Idaho college or university. Selection is based upon academic merit; 25 percent of initial awards are given to vocational students. Award is automatically renewed if recipient maintains a satisfactory GPA. Awarded every year.
Contact: Caryl Smith, Scholarship Assistant,
  csmith@osbe.state.id.us.

2723   State Scholarship for Ethnic Minorities in Professional/Vocational Nursing

Texas Higher Education Coordinating Board
Student Financial Assistance
P.O. Box 12788, Capitol Station
Austin, TX 78711-2788
(512) 427-6340
Maximum award: $3,000
Number of awards: 62
Deadline: July 15
College level: Freshman, Sophomore, Junior, Senior, Graduate, Doctoral
Majors/Fields: Nursing
Criteria: Applicant must be a member of an ethnic minority and a Texas resident enrolled at least half time in a program leading to licensure as an L.V.N. or in an associate, bachelor, or graduate degree program in professional nursing at an accredited Texas institution. Recipient must reapply each year. No preference is given to renewals. Awarded every year.
Contact: Jane Caldwell, Director of Grants and Special Programs, (512) 427-6455.

2724   State Waiver of Tuition

Kentucky Department for Veterans Affairs
545 South Third Street, Room 123
Louisville, KY 40202
(502) 595-4447, (502) 595-4448 (fax)
Average award: Waiver of tuition
Deadline: Apply at least three months before entering college
College level: State vocational/technical students
Criteria: Applicant must be the dependent of a veteran who served during a wartime period, must be rated 100 percent disabled service connected or 100 percent permanently and totally disabled non-service connected, and resident of Kentucky. Awarded every year. Award may be used at state-supported schools only.
Contact: Larry Garrett, Coordinator.

2725   State Student Incentive Grant

Louisiana Office of Student Financial Assistance
P.O. Box 91202
Baton Rouge, LA 70821-9202
(504) 922-1012, (504) 922-1089 (fax)
Maximum award: $2,000
Number of awards: 3000
Deadline: March 15
College level: Freshman, unspecified undergraduate
Criteria: Applicant must be a Louisiana resident, have a minimum 2.0 GPA, and attend a Louisiana institution full-time. Selection is based upon academics and financial need. File FAFSA by March 15 to apply. Scholarship is renewable. Awarded every year.
Contact: Winona Kahao, Director of Scholarship/Grant Division, (504) 922-1038.

2726   Student Incentive Grant

Georgia Student Finance Commission
2082 East Exchange Place, Suite 200
Tucker, GA 30084
(770) 414-3000, (912) 757-3626, (800) 776-6878
Maximum award: $5,000
College level: Freshman, Sophomore, Junior, Senior
Criteria: Applicant must be a Georgia resident, and demonstrate financial need. Awarded every year. Award may be used at eligible Georgia schools only.
Contact: (800) 776-6878.

2727   Talent Scholarship

University of Missouri–St. Louis
8001 Natural Bridge Road
St. Louis, MO 63121
(314) 553-6396
Average award: Full tuition
Number of awards: 14
Deadline: April 1
College level: Freshman
Criteria: Applicant must be a Missouri resident with ACT or SAT I scores in the top three percent of Missouri students. Minimum cumulative GPA of 3.2 and 24 hours per year are required to retain scholarship. Awarded every year. Award may be used only at sponsoring institution.
Contact: James D. Reed, Financial Aid Advisor.

2728   Tennessee Academic Scholars Program

Rhodes College
2000 North Parkway
Memphis, TN 38112
(901) 843-3700, (901) 843-3719 (fax)
adminfo@rhodes.edu
http://www.rhodes.edu
Maximum award: $5,000
Deadline: January 31
College level: Freshman
Criteria: Applicant must have a minimum 3.5 GPA and standardized test scores in at least the 95th percentile nationally and be a Tennessee resident. Scholarship is renewable. Awarded every year. Award may be used only at sponsoring institution.
Contact: Tennessee Student Assistance Corporation.

2729 Terry Foundation Scholarship

University of Texas at Austin
P.O. Box 7758
UT Station
Austin, TX 78713-7758
(512) 475-6200, (512) 475-6296 (fax)
finaid@www.utexas.edu
http://www.utexas.edu/student/finaid
Average award: $5,000
Maximum award: $7,000
Minimum award: $1,000
Number of awards: 50
Deadline: December 1
College level: Freshman
Criteria: Applicant must be a Texas resident, demonstrate leadership, and have high SAT I or ACT scores. Financial need is considered. Satisfactory academic progress is required to retain scholarship. Awarded every year. Award may be used only at sponsoring institution.
Contact: Joe Wilcox, Scholarship Coordinator, (512) 475-6282.

2730 Thomas C. Lynch Jr. Scholarship

Clemson University
G-01 Sikes Hall
Clemson, SC 29634-5123
(803) 656-2280
Average award: $2,500
Number of awards: 2
Deadline: March 1
College level: Freshman
Criteria: Applicant must be a South Carolina resident. Renewable for up to three years if recipient maintains minimum 3.0 GPA and completes at least 12 credits per semester. Awarded every year. Award may be used only at sponsoring institution.
Contact: Marvin Carmichael, Director of Financial Aid.

2731 Transfer Tuition Scholarship

New Mexico State University
Box 30001, Department 5100
Las Cruces, NM 88003-0001
(505) 646-4105
Average award: Tuition and fees
Deadline: March 1
College level: Transfer students
Criteria: Applicant must be a New Mexico resident, have a minimum 3.5 GPA, and have at least 30 transferable credit hours from a branch, community, or junior college. Minimum 3.5 GPA and full-time enrollment are required to retain scholarship. Awarded every year. Award may be used only at sponsoring institution.
Contact: Greely W. Myers, Director of Financial Aid.

2732 Truman Leadership Scholarship

Truman State University
Office of Admission
McClain Hall 205
Kirksville, MO 63501
(816) 785-4114, (816) 785-7456 (fax)
admissions@truman.edu
http://www.truman.edu
Average award: Comprehensive tuition
Number of awards: 50
College level: Freshman
Criteria: Applicant must be a Missouri resident and have exceptional academic and leadership records from high school. Renewable if recipient maintains 3.25 GPA. Awarded every year. Award may be used only at sponsoring institution.
Contact: Brad Chambers, Co-Director of Admission.

2733 Tuition Aid Grant

New Jersey Department of Higher Education
4 Quakerbridge Plaza, CN 540
Trenton, NJ 08625
(609) 588-3230
Maximum award: $4,500
Deadline: October 1
College level: Freshman, Sophomore, Junior, Senior
Criteria: Applicant must be or intend to be a full-time undergraduate at a New Jersey college or university, demonstrate financial need, and must have lived in New Jersey for at least 12 consecutive months. Grant amount is based upon applicant's need and college choice. Satisfactory academic progress and financial need are required to retain scholarship. Awarded every year.
Contact: Leah Fletcher, Assistant Director, Office of Grants and Scholarships.

2734 Ty Cobb Scholarship

Ty Cobb Foundation
P.O. Box 725
Forest Park, GA 30051
Average award: $2,500
Maximum award: $3,000
Minimum award: $2,000
Number of awards: 100
Deadline: June 15
College level: Sophomore, Junior, Senior, medical and dental professional degrees
Criteria: Applicant must demonstrate financial need and be a resident of Georgia. Applicant must submit application, reason for requesting financial assistance, recommendation, and transcript. Minimum "B" grade average for 45 quarter or 30 semester hours is required to retain scholarship. Satisfactory academic progress is required for professional degree students to retain scholarship. Awarded every year.
Contact: Rosie C. Atkins, Secretary.

2735 UI Scholars Scholarship

University of Idaho
Moscow, ID 83843
(208) 885-6312, (208) 885-5592 (fax)
finaid@uidaho.edu
http://www.uidaho/edu
Average award: $2,800
Maximum award: $3,000
Minimum award: $2,000
Number of awards: 20
Deadline: February 15
College level: Freshman, Sophomore, Junior, Senior
Criteria: Applicant must be a resident of Idaho direct from high school with a minimum composite ACT score of 32 (combined SAT I score of 1430). Scholarship is renewable. Awarded every year. Award may be used only at sponsoring institution.
Contact: Shawna Lindquist, Scholarship Advisor.

2736 University of Maryland System Alumni Association-International Inc. Scholarship

Bowie State University
Bowie, MD 20715
(301) 464-6544
Average award: Tuition and fees
Deadline: March 15
College level: Freshman, Sophomore, Junior, Senior, Transfer
Criteria: Applicant must be a Maryland resident, be enrolled full time as an undergraduate student, demonstrate leadership ability through community and school involvement, and maintain a minimum 3.25 GPA. New applicant must have a minimum 3.5 GPA in academic work and a minimum combined SAT I score of 1000 (1200 preferred). Transfer applicant must be accepted for admission and have a minimum 3.5 GPA. Continuing student must have a minimum 3.25 GPA. Awarded every year. Award may be used only at sponsoring institution.
Contact: Scholarship Committee, Career Services, Bowie, MD 20715-9465, (301) 464-7110, (301) 464-7111.

2737   University Scholar Award

Northern Illinois University
Swen Parson Hall 245
DeKalb, IL 60115
(815) 753-1000
Average award: $7,300
Maximum award: $7,500
Minimum award: $6,530
Number of awards: 6
Deadline: February 1
College level: Freshman, Transfers entering as juniors
Criteria: Applicant must be an Illinois resident, rank in top five percent of class, have a minimum composite ACT score of 27, and be admitted by application deadline. Transfer applicant must be entering from a two-year junior college and have at least 45 transferrable credit hours. Minimum 3.3 GPA and completion of at least 12 credit hours per semester required to retain scholarship. Awarded every year. Award may be used only at sponsoring institution.
Contact: Joanne Ganshirt, Program Secretary, Campus Life Center, (815) 753-9398.

2738   University Scholarship

University of Arkansas, Fayetteville
Office of Scholarships and Financial Aid
114 Hunt Hall
Fayetteville, AR 72701
(501) 575-3806
Maximum award: $2,228
Deadline: February 15
College level: Freshman
Criteria: Applicant must have a minimum cumulative GPA of 3.25, minimum composite ACT score of 27 or combined SAT I score of 1130, be an Arkansas resident, and have not enrolled in any other postsecondary institution. Minimum 3.0 GPA and 27 hours by end of freshman year, and minimum 3.2 GPA and 30 hours per year, thereafter, are required to retain scholarship. Awarded every year. Award may be used only at sponsoring institution.
Contact: Office of Admissions, 200 Silas H. Hunt Hall, Fayetteville, AR 72701.

2739   Valedictorian Scholarship

University of South Carolina
Office of Admissions
Columbia, SC 29208
(803) 777-4067
Average award: $3,000
Number of awards: 35
Deadline: None
College level: Freshman
Criteria: Applicant must be a valedictorian, South Carolina resident or a graduate of a South Carolina high school, and have a minimum combined SAT I score of 1100. Minimum 3.0 GPA is required to retain scholarship. Awarded every year. Award may be used only at sponsoring institution.
Contact: Michael Jinnette, Scholarship Coordinator.

2740   Vermont Incentive Grant

Vermont Student Assistance Corporation (VSAC)
Champlain Mill
P.O. Box 2000
Winooski, VT 05404
(800) 642-3177 (in-state), (802) 655-9602, (802) 654-3765 (fax)
Average award: $1,183
Maximum award: $5,200
Minimum award: $500
Number of awards: 8834
Deadline: March 1 (priority)
College level: Unspecified undergraduate, unspecified graduate
Criteria: Applicant must be a Vermont resident, be enrolled full-time at an approved postsecondary institution, and demonstrate financial need. Graduate applicants must be enrolled at the U of Vermont Medical School or at an approved school of veterinary medicine. Applicant should complete the ACT aid form or CSS financial aid form and have it sent to VSAC. Recipient must reapply for renewal. Awarded every year.
Contact: Grant Department, (800) 642-3177, (802) 655-9602.

2741   Vocational Gold Seal Endorsement Scholarship

Florida Department of Education
Office of Student Financial Assistance
255 Collins
Tallahassee, FL 32399-0400
(904) 487-0049
Maximum award: $4,000
Deadline: April 1
College level: Freshman
Criteria: Applicant must receive a standard high school diploma with a Florida Gold Seal Endorsement from a Florida public high school, be a Florida resident for at least 12 months, and enroll in a degree or certificate program at an eligible Florida public or private, postsecondary vocational, technical, trade, or business school, or college or university for a minimum of 12 hours per term. Minimum 3.0 GPA with at least 12 credit hours per term is required to retain scholarship. Awarded every year.
Contact: Office of Student Financial Assistance.

2742   Waiver of Tuition for Meritorious Undergraduate Students

Bowie State University
Bowie, MD 20715
(301) 464-6544
Average award: Tuition waiver
Deadline: February 1 (fall); November 1 (spring)
College level: Freshman, Transfer from community college
Criteria: Applicant must be a Maryland resident and have one of the following: a minimum 3.5 GPA (transfer students must have associate of arts degree or have completed 56 credit hours), rank in top tenth of class, a minimum combined SAT I score of 1200 (composite ACT score of 24), academic leadership qualities, or demonstrated ability in visual or performing arts. Awarded every year. Award may be used only at sponsoring institution.
Contact: Scholarship Committee, Career Services, Bowie, MD 20715-9465, (301) 464-7110, (301) 464-7111.

2743   Walter International Student Scholarship

Piedmont College
165 Central Avenue
Demorest, GA 30535
(706) 778-3000
Average award: $3,000
Maximum award: $9,000
Minimum award: $1,000
Number of awards: 8
Deadline: None
College level: Freshman, Sophomore, Junior, Senior
Criteria: Applicant must be a non-U.S. resident, meet all INS requirements for attending college in U.S., and prove financial support for need not covered by award. Renewable if satisfactory academic progress is maintained. Awarded every year. Award may be used only at sponsoring institution.
Contact: Kenneth L. Owen, Director of Financial Aid.

2744   Washington Crossing Foundation Scholarship

Washington Crossing Foundation
P.O. Box 17
Washington Crossing, PA 18977
(215) 493-6577
Maximum award: $10,000
Number of awards: 6
Deadline: January 15
College level: Freshman, Sophomore, Junior, Senior
Majors/Fields: Government service
Criteria: Applicant must be a U.S. citizen with a career interest in government service. Recipient must maintain career goals and meet school's requirements to retain scholarship. Awarded every year.
Contact: Eugene C. Fish, Esq., Vice Chairman of the Board.

2745 Washington Scholars

Washington Higher Education Coordinating Board
917 Lakeridge Way
P.O. Box 43430
Olympia, WA 98504-3430
(360) 753-7850
Average award: Full tuition and fee waiver
College level: Freshman
Criteria: Award is intended to recognize and honor the accomplishments of three high school seniors from each legislative district. High school principals nominate the top one percent of the graduating senior class based upon academic accomplishment, leadership, and community service. Minimum 3.3 GPA is required for renewal. Awarded every year.
Contact: Elizabeth A. Gebhardt, Assistant Director of Student Financial Aid, (206) 753-4592.

2746 Washington State Educational Opportunity Grant

Washington Higher Education Coordinating Board
917 Lakeridge Way
P.O. Box 43430
Olympia, WA 98504-3430
(360) 753-7850
Average award: $2,500
Number of awards: 425
Deadline: June 1
College level: Junior transfer
Criteria: Applicant must be an eligible placebound student, demonstrate financial need, and have an associate degree or its equivalent from a community college. Award is for upper-division study at an eligible Washington institution. Applicant must be a resident in one of 14 designated counties in Washington State. Renewable for two years if recipient demonstrates continued financial need and satisfactory progress. Awarded every year.
Contact: Barbara Theiss, Program Administrator.

2747 West Virginia Higher Education Grant

State College and University Systems of West Virginia
Central Office
1018 Kanawha Boulevard, Suite 700
Charleston, WV 25301-2827
(304) 558-4618, (304) 558-4622 (fax)
crocket@scusco.wvnet.edu
http://www.scusco.wvnet.edu/
Average award: $1,431
Maximum award: $2,216
Minimum award: $350
Maximum number of awards: 7,600
Minimum number of awards: 7,300
Deadline: March 1
College level: Freshman, Sophomore, Junior, Senior
Criteria: Applicant must demonstrate financial need, meet academic qualifications, be a U.S. citizen, have been a resident of the state of West Virginia for at least one year, and enroll as a full-time undergraduate student at an approved educational institution. Reapplication, financial need, and satisfactory academic performance are required for renewal. Awarded every year.
Contact: Robert E. Long, Grant Program Coordinator, (304) 558-4614, long@scusco.wvnet.edu.

2748 William P. Willis Scholarship

Oklahoma State Regents for Higher Education
500 Education Building
State Capitol Complex
Oklahoma City, OK 73105
(405) 524-9100
Average award: $1,800
Maximum award: $2,600
Minimum award: $1,700
Number of awards: 26
Deadline: Late May
College level: Freshman, Sophomore, Junior, Senior
Criteria: Applicant must be an Oklahoma resident and demonstrate financial need. Only one award is available per state institution. Applicant must obtain university president's nomination to retain scholarship. Awarded every year.
Contact: Dawn Scott, Research Analyst, (405) 524-9153, dscott@osrhe.edu.

2749 William Randolph Hearst Endowed BioPrep Scholarship

The University of Alabama
Box 870162
Tuscaloosa, AL 35487-0162
(205) 348-6756
Average award: $2,470
Number of awards: 1
Deadline: March 1
College level: Freshman
Majors/Fields: Pre-health professions program
Criteria: Applicant must be a graduate of rural Alabama school participating in the BioPrep Academic Honors Program. Selection is based upon academic record entrance exam scores, and character. Renewable for years of undergraduate study if minimum 3.0 GPA is maintained. Awarded every year. Award may be used only at sponsoring institution.
Contact: Paige Cooper, Scholarship Coordinator.

2750 Wisconsin Native American Student Assistance Program

Higher Education Aids Board
P.O. Box 7885
Madison, WI 53707
(608) 266-1954
Average award: $1,800
Deadline: Early application is recommended
Criteria: Applicant must be at least 25% Native American and attend a Wisconsin institution, either public, independent, or proprietary, as an undergraduate or graduate student. Application is made through use of a joint Board-BIA-Tribal form in addition to needs analysis forms. Renewable for up to five years. Awarded every year.
Contact: Awards.

Textile Science ——————

2751 CIBA/Geigy Prestige Scholarship

Clemson University
G-01 Sikes Hall
Clemson, SC 29634-5123
(803) 656-2280
Maximum award: $5,000
Number of awards: 1
Deadline: March 1
College level: Freshman
Majors/Fields: Textile chemistry
Criteria: Applicant must have a minimum 2.5 GPA. Selection is based upon admissions application. Awarded every year. Award may be used only at sponsoring institution.
Contact: Marvin Carmichael, Director of Financial Aid.

2752   Comer Foundation Scholarship in Fashion and Design

The University of Alabama
Box 870162
Tuscaloosa, AL 35487-0162
(205) 348-6756
Average award: $2,500
Number of awards: 1
Deadline: March 15
College level: Freshman
Majors/Fields: Clothing, design, textiles
Criteria: Minimum 3.0 GPA is required to retain scholarship. Awarded as funds are available. Award may be used only at sponsoring institution.
Contact: Dean, College of Human Environmental Sciences, Box 870158, Tuscaloosa, AL 35487-0158, (205) 348-6250.

2753   David Jennings Memorial Fund Scholarship

Clemson University
G-01 Sikes Hall
Clemson, SC 29634-5123
(803) 656-2280
Average award: $5,000
Number of awards: 1
Deadline: March 1
College level: Freshman
Majors/Fields: Textiles
Criteria: Applicant must have a minimum 2.0 GPA and demonstrate financial need. Awarded every year. Award may be used only at sponsoring institution.
Contact: Marvin Carmichael, Director of Financial Aid.

2754   Fieldcrest Foundation Scholarship

Clemson University
G-01 Sikes Hall
Clemson, SC 29634-5123
(803) 656-2280
Maximum award: $2,500
Number of awards: 2
Deadline: March 1
College level: Junior, Senior
Majors/Fields: Textiles, industrial management
Criteria: Applicant must have a minimum 2.5 GPA. Minimum 2.5 GPA and completion of at least 12 credit hours per semester are required to retain scholarship. Awarded every year. Award may be used only at sponsoring institution.
Contact: Marvin Carmichael, Director of Financial Aid.

Union Affiliation

2755   Air Line Pilots Association Scholarship

Air Line Pilots Association
1625 Massachusetts Avenue, NW
Washington, DC 20036
(202) 797-4050, (202) 797-4052 (fax)
Average award: $3,000
Number of awards: 1
Deadline: April 1
College level: Freshman, Sophomore, Junior, Senior
Criteria: Applicant must be the child of a medically retired or deceased pilot member of the Air Line Pilots Association. Academic capability and financial need are considered. Renewable for up to four years if minimum 3.0 GPA is maintained. Awarded every year.
Contact: Jan Redden, Scholarship Program Monitor.

2756   Ashby B. Carter Memorial Scholarship

National Alliance of Postal and Federal Employees (NAPFE)
1628 11th Street, NW
Washington, DC 20001
(202) 939-6325, (202) 939-6389 (fax)
Maximum award: $5,000
Number of awards: 6
Deadline: April 1
College level: Freshman
Criteria: Applicant must be the child of a NAPFE member. Awarded every year.
Contact: Wilbur Duncan, Secretary.

2757   ATU Scholarships

Amalgamated Transit Union
5025 Wisconsin Avenue, NW
Washington, DC 20016
(202) 537-1645
Average award: $2,000
Number of awards: 5
Deadline: January 31
College level: Freshman, first-year vocational/technical students
Criteria: Applicant must be an ATU member in good standing or the child or stepchild of a deceased member who was in good standing at the time of death, and be planning to enter their first year of postsecondary education for the first time. One Canadian and four U.S. scholarships will be awarded each year. Awarded every year.
Contact: Oliver W. Green, International Secretary/Treasurer.

2758   BC&T Power Union MasterCard Scholarship

Bakery, Confectionery, and Tobacco Workers International Union (BC&TWIU)
10401 Connecticut Avenue
Kensington, MD 20895-3961
(301) 933-8600, (301) 946-8452 (fax)
Maximum award: $4,000
Deadline: February 28
College level: Freshman, Sophomore, Junior, Senior
Criteria: Applicant must be a member in good standing for at least one year or be the spouse or child of a member of the BC&T International Union, and be accepted into or attending an accredited school. Application should be sent to: Union MasterCard Scholarship, P.O. Box 9389, Minneapolis, MN 55440-9389. Awarded every year.
Contact: Sally P. Payne, BC&T Scholarship Administrator.

2759   BC&TWIU Scholarship

Bakery, Confectionery, and Tobacco Workers International Union (BC&TWIU)
10401 Connecticut Avenue
Kensington, MD 20895-3961
(301) 933-8600, (301) 946-8452 (fax)
Average award: $1,000
Maximum award: $3,000
Number of awards: 8
Deadline: December 31
College level: Freshman, first-time students
Criteria: Applicant must be a member or the child of a member of the Bakery, Confectionery, and Tobacco Workers International Union. One scholarship is is designated for a Canadian applicant. Additional one-time awards of $2,000 and $1,500 are given to the most outstanding and second most outstanding applicants, respectively. The American Income Life Insurance Company awards a one-time $2,000 scholarship in cooperation with the BC&T. Academic record, essay, and personal profile are required. Renewable for up to four years if satisfactory academic progress is maintained. Awarded every year.
Contact: Scholarships.

2760 Charlie Logan Scholarship for Seamen

Seafarers International Union
5201 Auth Way
Camp Springs, MD 20746
(301) 899-0675
Maximum award: $3,750
Number of awards: 3
Deadline: April 15
College level: Freshman
Criteria: Available to active seamen who are high school graduates (or equivalent) and have credit for two years (730 days) of employment with an employer who is obligated to make contributions to the Seafarers' Welfare Plan on the employee's behalf. Recipient may attend any institution (college or trade school) in the U.S. Renewal is based upon good scholastic standing. Awarded every year.
Contact: Lou Delma, Assistant Administrator, (301) 702-4405.

2761 College Vocational/Technical Scholarship

Loyal Christian Benefit Association (LCBA)
700 Peach Street, P.O. Box 13005
Erie, PA 16514-1305
(814) 453-4331, (814) 453-3211 (fax)
Average award: $1,000
Maximum number of awards: 10
Minimum number of awards: 5
Deadline: in October
College level: Freshman
Criteria: Applicant must be a member in good standing of the Loyal Christian Benefit Association and be enrolled in a permanent LCBA insurance plan for one year prior to application with a minimum of $1,000 permanent insurance or have a term insurance certificate in force for three years. Minimum 3.0 GPA and financial need are required. Five college scholarships and five vocational/technical awards are offered. A LCBA certificate must remain in force during the entire scholarship period. Evidence of satisfactory progress must be submitted to Scholarship Committee for renewal. Awarded every year.
Contact: Eileen Jefferys, Branch Development Coordinator.

2762 CTA Scholarship for Dependent Children

California Teachers Association (CTA)
1705 Murchison Drive, P.O. Box 921
Burlingame, CA 94011-0921
(415) 697-1400
Average award: $2,000
Number of awards: 17
Deadline: February 15
College level: Freshman, Sophomore, Junior, Senior, Graduate, Doctoral
Criteria: Applicant must be an active member, the dependent child of an active member, or the dependent child of a deceased or retired member of the CTA. Scholarship is renewable. Awarded every year.
Contact: Human Rights Department.

2763 David J. Fitzmaurice Scholarship

International Union of Electronic, Electrical, Salaried, Machine and Furniture Workers (IUE)
1126 16th Street, NW
Department of Social Action
Washington, DC 20036-4866
Average award: $2,000
Number of awards: 1
Deadline: April 15
College level: Freshman, Sophomore, Junior, Senior
Majors/Fields: Engineering
Criteria: Applicant must be the child of an IUE member and submit class rank, GPA, SAT I or ACT scores, copy of W-2 form, short statement of interest and goals, and three recommendations. Selection is based upon academic record, character, leadership ability, and a desire to improve and move ahead. Awarded every year.
Contact: Gloria T. Johnson, Director, Department of Social Action, 1126 16th Street, NW, Washington, DC 20036-4866.

2764 Gordon M. Freeman Memorial Scholarship

Shawnee State University
940 Second Street
Portsmouth, OH 45662-4344
(614) 355-2237
Average award: One-Third tuition and fees
Deadline: April 15
College level: Entering students
Criteria: Applicant must be a member (or immediate family of a member) of IBEW Local 575, a high school graduate or GED recipient, have a minimum 3.0 GPA, and be pursuing a bachelor's degree. Early application is recommended. Award is for four years. Awarded every year. Award may be used only at sponsoring institution.
Contact: Financial Aid Office, (614) 355-2485.

2765 Harry C. Bates Merit Scholarship

International Union of Bricklayers and Allied Craftsmen (BAC)
Education Department
815 15th Street, NW
Washington, DC 20005
(202) 783-3788
Maximum award: $2,000
Number of awards: 3
Deadline: June 1 (Canada); mid-October (U.S.)
College level: Freshman
Criteria: Applicant must be the natural or legally adopted child of a current, retired, or deceased International Union of Bricklayers and Allied Craftsmen member. U.S. applicant must take PSAT/NMSQT during junior year of high school. If test results qualify applicant as a semifinalist, this information must be reported to the International Union by mid-October. Canadian applicant does not have to take a qualifying test. One U.S. award and two Canadian awards are given. Selection is based upon test scores (U.S. only), grades, leadership qualities, and extracurricular achievements. Canadian students can obtain an application from Mr. Brian Strickland, BAC Vice President, 161 Markwood Drive, Kitchener, ON N2M 2H3. Scholarship is renewable. Awarded every year.
Contact: Scholarships, (202) 783-3788.

2766 IAM Scholarship

International Association of Machinists and Aerospace Workers (IAM)
9000 Machinists Place, Room 117
Upper Marlboro, MD 20772-2687
(301) 967-4708
Maximum award: $2,000
Number of awards: 12
Deadline: February 27
College level: Freshman
Criteria: Applicant must be either an IAM member with two years of continuous good-standing membership who is working full-time in a company under contract with the IAM, or be the son, daughter, stepchild, or legally adopted child of an IAM member. Child of IAM member must be a high school senior when applying. Scholarship is renewable. Awarded every year.
Contact: IAM Scholarship Program.

2767 International Brotherhood of Teamsters Scholarship

International Brotherhood of Teamsters
25 Louisiana Avenue, NW
Washington, DC 20001
(202) 624-8735
Maximum award: $1,500
Number of awards: 15
Deadline: December 15
College level: Freshman
Criteria: Applicant must be the child of a Teamsters member, rank in top 15 percent of class, have or expect to have excellent SAT I or ACT scores, and be able to demonstrate financial need. Application may be obtained from all Teamsters offices, from the scholarship fund, or by mailing the order form found in the summer and fall issues of the International Teamsters magazine. Applicant should complete the first part of the application and then forward it to the appropriate local union. Some awards are renewable. Awarded every year.
Contact: Denise D. McLeod, Scholarship Administrator.

2768 IUOE/MasterCard Scholarship

International Union of Operating Engineers (IUOE)
1125 17th Street, NW
Washington, DC 20036
(202) 429-9100, (202) 778-2618 (fax)
Maximum award: $4,000
Number of awards: 15
Deadline: January 31
College level: Freshman, Sophomore, Junior, Senior
Criteria: Applicant must be a IUOE member or the spouse or child of a member. Awarded every year.
Contact: Joe Brady, Director of Communications.

2769 John H. Lyons Sr. Scholarship

International Association of Bridge, Structural, Ornamental, and Reinforcing Ironworkers Union (IABSOIU)
1750 New York Avenue, NW, Suite 400
Washington, DC 20006
(202) 383-4830, (202) 638-4856 (fax)
Maximum award: $2,500
Number of awards: 2
Deadline: March 31
College level: Freshman
Criteria: Applicant must be the child, stepchild, or adopted child of an IABSOIU member who has five or more years of continuous membership or of a deceased member who was in good standing at the time of his or her death. Applicant must rank in the top half of class. Selection is based upon academic standing, SAT I or ACT scores, extracurricular activities, leadership, character reference, and citizenship. Satisfactory scholastic record and conduct, and IABSOIU affiliation are required to retain scholarship. Awarded every year.
Contact: Scholarship Committee.

2770 Joseph Tauber Scholarship

National Benefit Fund for Hospital and Health Care Employees
310 West 43rd Street
Attn: Scholarship Department
New York, NY 10036
(212) 465-4861
Maximum award: $6,000
Number of awards: 1,000
Deadline: March 15
College level: Freshman, Sophomore, Junior, Senior
Criteria: Applicant must be a high school graduate, a post-secondary school student, or previous awardee whose parent is a member of 1199 National Benefit Fund and in wage class one for at least one year at the time of the application. Selection is based upon financial need, the member's seniority in the Benefit Fund, and scholastic standing. Request for official application forms must be made from December 1 through January 31. Scholarship is renewable. Awarded every year.
Contact: Scholarship Representative.

2771 Joseph W. Childs Memorial Scholarship

United Rubber, Cork, Linoleum, and Plastic Workers of America (URW)
URW Fair Practices Department
570 White Pond Drive
Akron, OH 44320-1156
(216) 869-0320
Average award: $2,000
Number of awards: 4
Deadline: February 1
College level: Freshman
Criteria: Applicant's parent or guardian must be an URW member. Selection is based upon academic excellence, community involvement, and commitment to serve humanity. Awarded every year.
Contact: Lyle D. Skinner, Fair Practices Director, URW Scholarships.

2772 Maine State Employees Association Scholarship

Maine State Employees Association (MSEA) Local 1989, SEIU
65 State Street
P.O. Box 1072
Augusta, ME 04332-1072
(207) 622-3151 or (800) 452-8794 (in-state), (207) 623-4961 (fax)
Maximum award: $1,500
Number of awards: 17
Deadline: In mid-April
College level: Freshman, MSEA members returning to school
Criteria: Applicant must be the child of a MSEA member who is enrolling in a postsecondary academic or vocational institution for the first time or be a MSEA member who is continuing his or her education on a part-time basis or full-time with an educational leave of absence. Selection is based upon character, leadership, financial need, and academic achievement. Renewable for MSEA members only. Awarded every year.
Contact: Joan C. Towle, Director of Finance and Administration.

2773 Memorial Foundation Education Grant

Eagles Memorial Foundation
4710 14th Street, West
Bradenton, FL 34207
Maximum award: $4,000
College level: Freshman, Sophomore, Junior, Senior
Criteria: Applicant must be the child of a member of the Fraternal Order of Eagles or its Ladies Auxiliary who died from injuries or diseases incurred or aggravated in the line of duty while serving in the armed forces (U.S., Canada, Philippines, Mexico, United Kingdom), as a law enforcement officer, or as a full-time or volunteer firefighter or EMS officer. Applicant must attend college or vocational school, be unmarried, and be under 25 years of age. Award is not to exceed $20,000, payable until applicant reaches 25 years of age unless married and/or self-supporting before then. Awarded every year.
Contact: Grants.

2774 Michael J. Quill Scholarship

Transport Workers Union of America, AFL-CIO (TWU)
80 West End Avenue
New York, NY 10023
(212) 873-6000
Average award: $1,200
Number of awards: 15
Deadline: May 1
College level: Freshman
Criteria: Applicant must be a high school senior who is entering college the following fall. Applicant must be the child of a TWU member, deceased member, pensioner, deceased pensioner, or disabled member. All union members must be in good standing or have been in good standing when deceased, disabled, or retired. Dependent siblings, under 21 years of age of TWU members in good standing are also eligible. Selection is made from eligible applicants by a public drawing. Scholarship is renewable. Awarded every year.
Contact: Frank McCann, International Vice President.

2775 National Office Products Association Scholarship

National Office Products Association
301 North Fairfax Street
Alexandria, VA 22314-2696
(703) 549-9040
Average award: $2,000
Number of awards: 80
Deadline: March 15
College level: Unspecified undergraduate
Criteria: Applicant must be an employee or related to an employee of an NOPA member firm. Selection is based upon academic success, interests, special abilities, and financial need. Awarded every year.
Contact: Bruce McLellan, Coordinator, NOPA Scholarship Fund.

2776 Student CTA Scholarship

California Teachers Association (CTA)
1705 Murchison Drive, P.O. Box 921
Burlingame, CA 94011-0921
(415) 697-1400
Average award: $2,000
Number of awards: 3
Deadline: February 15
College level: Freshman, Sophomore, Junior, Senior, Graduate, Doctoral
Majors/Fields: Education
Criteria: Applicant must be an active student CTA member enrolled in a teacher credential program. Awarded every year.
Contact: Human Rights Department.

2777 Two/Ten International Footwear Foundation College Scholarship

Two/Ten International Footwear Foundation
56 Main Street
Watertown, MA 02172
(800) 346-3210
Average award: $900
Maximum award: $2,000
Minimum award: $200
Number of awards: 600
Deadline: January 15
College level: Freshman, Sophomore, Junior, Senior
Criteria: Applicant's parent must have worked in the footwear, leather, or allied industries for at least one year, or the student must have worked for a minimum of 500 hours in those industries in the year before the scholarship will be used. Selection is based upon academic achievement, personal promise, and financial need. Satisfactory academic progress and financial need are required to retain scholarship. Awarded every year.
Contact: Catherine M. Nelson, Scholarship Coordinator.

2778 URW American Income Scholarship

United Rubber, Cork, Linoleum, and Plastic Workers of America (URW)
URW Fair Practices Department
570 White Pond Drive
Akron, OH 44320-1156
(216) 869-0320
Average award: $1,250
Number of awards: 4
Deadline: February 1
College level: Freshman
Criteria: Applicant's parent or guardian must be a URW member. Selection is based upon academic excellence, community involvement, and commitment to serve humanity. Awarded every year.
Contact: Lyle D. Skinner, Fair Practices Director, URW Scholarships.

2779 Utility Workers Union of America Merit Scholarships

Utility Workers Union of America
815 16th Street, NW, Suite 605
Washington, DC 20006
(202) 347-8105, (202) 347-4872 (fax)
Average award: $1,500
Maximum award: $2,000
Minimum award: $500
Number of awards: 2
Deadline: January 1 of junior year
College level: Freshman
Criteria: Applicant's parent must be a member of the Utility Workers Union of America. Selection is made by the National Merit Scholarship Corp. Satisfactory academic progress is required to retain scholarship. Awarded every year.
Contact: Donald E. Wightman, National President.

2780 William H. Bywater Scholarship

International Union of Electronic, Electrical, Salaried, Machine and Furniture Workers (IUE)
1126 16th Street, NW
Department of Social Action
Washington, DC 20036-4866
Average award: $3,000
Number of awards: 1
Deadline: April 15
College level: Freshman, Sophomore, Junior, Senior
Criteria: Applicant must be the child of a IUE local union elected official and submit class rank, GPA, SAT I or ACT scores, copy of W-2 form, short statement of interest and goals, and three recommendations. Selection is based upon academic record, character, leadership ability, and a desire to improve and move ahead. Awarded every year.
Contact: Gloria T. Johnson, Department of Social Action.

Vocational/Technical——

2781 AFSA Financial Aid Scholarship

American Foreign Service Association (AFSA)
2101 E Street, NW
Washington, DC 20037
(202) 338-4045, (202) 338-6820 (fax)
scholar@afsa.org
http://www.afsa.org
Average award: $1,800
Maximum award: $2,500
Minimum award: $500
Number of awards: 55
Deadline: February 15
College level: Freshman, Sophomore, Junior, Senior
Criteria: Applicant must be a dependent of a U.S. government foreign service employee and must complete at least 12 credit hours per semester. Applicant must attend a college in the U.S. Renewable if recipient maintains minimum 2.0 GPA. Awarded every year.
Contact: Lori Dee, Scholarship Administrator, scholar@afsa.edu.

2782 Alumni Family Scholarship

Northern Kentucky University
Administrative Center 416
Nunn Drive
Highland Heights, KY 41099-7101
(606) 572-5144
Average award: In-state tuition and $150 for books and supplies
Deadline: February 1
College level: Freshman, Sophomore, Junior, Senior, Graduate, Doctoral
Criteria: Applicant must be the child or spouse of a Northern Kentucky U graduate. Awarded every year. Award may be used only at sponsoring institution.
Contact: Robert E. Sprague, Director of Financial Aid.

2783 Annual/Endowed Scholarship

Milwaukee School of Engineering
1025 North Broadway
Milwaukee, WI 53202-3109
(800) 332-6763, (414) 277-7475 (fax)
goran@admin.msoe.edu
www.msoe.edu
Maximum award: $5,000
Deadline: February 1
College level: Freshman
Criteria: Recommendation and interview recommended. Awarded every year. Award may be used only at sponsoring institution.
Contact: Sue Minzlaff, Financial Aid Office, (414) 277-7222, minzlaff@admin.msoe.edu.

2784 Arc Welded Design, Engineering, and Fabrication Awards

James F. Lincoln Arc Welding Foundation
P.O Box 17035
Cleveland, OH 44117-0035
(216)-481-4300
Maximum award: $2,000
Number of awards: 35
Deadline: June 16
College level: Sophomore, Junior, Senior, Graduate, Doctoral
Criteria: Applicants must submit a paper or report representing their work on design, engineering, or fabrication problems relating to any type of building, bridge, or other generally stationary structure, any type of machine, product, or mechanical apparatus, or arc welding research, testing, procedure, or process development. Send SASE for application. Awarded every year.

2785 Arthur F. Schulz Jr. Scholarship

Principia College
Elsah, IL 62028
(800) 277-4648, (800) 347-4000 (fax)
collegeadmissions@prin.edu
http://www.prin.edu
Average award: $2,500
Number of awards: 6
Deadline: January 15
College level: Freshman
Criteria: Applicant must be a child or grandchild of alumni/ae. Recipient must maintain a minimum 3.2 GPA and support community standards to retain scholarship. Awarded every year. Award may be used only at sponsoring institution.
Contact: Martha Green Quirk, Director of Admissions and Enrollment, (618) 374-5180, mgq@prin.edu.

2786 Beneficial-Hodson Scholarship

The Johns Hopkins University
3400 North Charles Street
Baltimore, MD 21218
(410) 516-8028
Average award: $12,000
Number of awards: 17
Deadline: January 1
College level: Freshman
Criteria: Minimum 3.0 GPA is required to retain scholarship. Awarded every year. Award may be used only at sponsoring institution.
Contact: Paula Abernethy, Assistant Director of Financial Aid.

2787 Centennial Scholarship

University of North Carolina at Greensboro
1000 Spring Garden Street
Greensboro, NC 27412
(910) 334-5702
Average award: $7,500
Maximum award: $12,000
Minimum award: $5,000
Number of awards: 4
Deadline: January 15
College level: Freshman
Criteria: Minimum 3.0 GPA is required to retain scholarship. Awarded every year. Award may be used only at sponsoring institution.
Contact: Tolly D. Nagy, Director of Financial Aid.

2788 Chapman Grant

Chapman University
333 North Glassell Street
Orange, CA 92866
(714) 997-6741, (714) 997-6743 (fax)
http://www.chapman.edu
Maximum award: $11,600
Deadline: None
College level: Freshman, Sophomore, Junior, Senior
Criteria: Applicant must be a full-time student. Selection is based upon financial need. FAFSA required. Scholarship is renewable. Awarded every year. Award may be used only at sponsoring institution.
Contact: Scholarships.

2789 Clara Abbott Foundation Educational Grant Program

The Clara Abbott Foundation
200 Abbott Park Road
Abbott Park, IL 60064-3537
(847) 937-1090, (847) 938-6511 (fax)
Average award: $2,400
Maximum award: $9,900
Minimum award: $500
Number of awards: 3000
Deadline: March 17
College level: Freshman, Sophomore, Junior, Senior
Criteria: Applicant must be a child of an Abbott Laboratories employee or retiree. Selection is based upon financial need. Scholarship is renewable. Awarded every year.
Contact: Barry Wojtak, Executive Director, (847) 937-1091.

2790 College Scholarship Competitions

Marquette University
P.O. Box 1881
Milwaukee, WI 53201-1881
(414) 288-7302, (414) 288-3764 (fax)
go2marquette@vms.csd.mu.edu
http://www.mu.edu
Average award: $7,500
Deadline: End of January or beginning of February
College level: Freshman
Criteria: Competitions are held by colleges of Arts and Sciences, Business, Communication, Engineering, Health Sciences, and Nursing. Minimum 3.0 GPA and full-time enrollment are required to retain scholarship. Awarded every year. Award may be used only at sponsoring institution.
Contact: Carlos Garces, Senior Assistant Director of Admissions.

2791 Colorado Christian University Grant

Colorado Christian University
180 South Garrison Street
Lakewood, CO 80226
(303) 202-0100, extension 117, (303) 274-7560 (fax)
drwilliams@ccu.edu
http://www.ccu.edu
Average award: $974
Maximum award: $2,750
Minimum award: $200
Number of awards: 263
Deadline: None
College level: Freshman, Sophomore, Junior, Senior
Criteria: Applicant must be enrolled full time and apply for federal financial aid. Awarded every year. Award may be used only at sponsoring institution.
Contact: Kent McGowan, Director of Financial Aid.

2792 Community Service Award

Ohio Wesleyan University
Office of Admissions
Delaware, OH 43015
(614) 368-3020, (614) 368-3314 (fax)
owuadmit@cc.owu.edu
http://www.owu.edu
Average award: $3,000
Maximum award: $5,000
Minimum award: $1,500
Number of awards: 30
Deadline: March 1
College level: Freshman, Sophomore, Junior, Senior
Criteria: Applicant must submit letter of recommendation with application. Selection is based upon number of hours in community service, breadth of experience, leadership, and commitment to community service. Scholarship is renewable. Awarded every year. Award may be used only at sponsoring institution.
Contact: Doug Thompson, Dean of Admission.

2793 Departmental Endowed Scholarships

Eastern Michigan University
Office of Financial Aid
403 Pierce Hall
Ypsilanti, MI 48197
(313) 487-0455, (313) 487-1484 (fax)
financial.aid@mich.edu
http://www.emich.edu
Average award: $1,000
Maximum award: $3,000
Minimum award: $150
Number of awards: 500
Deadline: February 15
College level: Freshman, Sophomore, Junior, Senior, Graduate
Criteria: Each scholarship has its own specifications. Awarded every year. Award may be used only at sponsoring institution.
Contact: Cynthia Van Pelt, Assistant Director, Scholarships.

2794 Diversity Scholarship

Ripon College
300 Seward Street
P.O. Box 248
Ripon, WI 54971
(800) 94-RIPON, (414) 748-7243 (fax)
adminfo@mac.ripon.edu
http://www.ripon.edu
Maximum award: $15,000
Maximum number of awards: 3
Minimum number of awards: 1
College level: Freshman
Criteria: Applicant must demonstrate financial need and ability to contribute to the cultural, ethnic, geographical, and socio-economic diversity of Ripon College student body. Interview required. Renewable if recipient maintains minimum 2.5 GPA in first year, minimum 2.7 GPA subsequent years. Awarded every year. Award may be used only at sponsoring institution.
Contact: Paul J. Weeks, Vice President & Dean of Admission.

2795 Division Scholarship

D'Youville College
320 Porter Avenue
Buffalo, NY 14201
(716) 881-7691
Average award: $1,750
Maximum award: $2,500
Minimum award: $1,000
Number of awards: 30
Deadline: None
College level: Freshman, Sophomore, Junior
Criteria: Scholarship is renewable. Awarded every year. Award may be used only at sponsoring institution.
Contact: R.H. Dannecker, Director of Admission and Financial Aid.

2796 Endowed Scholarships

Ohio University
Office of Student Financial Aid and Scholarships
Athens, OH 45701
(614) 593-4141, (614) 593-4140 (fax)
Average award: $750
Maximum award: Full tuition
Minimum award: $250
Number of awards: 800
Deadline: February 15 (freshman); March 1 (upperclass applicant)
College level: Freshman, Sophomore, Junior, Senior
Criteria: Each scholarship has its own criteria, including parent's employment, organizational affiliation, financial need, religion, gender, academic qualifications, place of residence, or academic major. Reapplication is required to retain scholarship. Awarded every year. Award may be used only at sponsoring institution.
Contact: Mrs. Yang-Hi Kim, Associate Director of Scholarships and Grants.

2797 Entering Freshman Scholarship

University of Arkansas at Little Rock
Office of Admissions
2801 South University
Little Rock, AR 72204
(501) 569-3130
Average award: Full tuition and standard fees
Number of awards: 230
Deadline: March 15
College level: Freshman
Criteria: Minimum 3.25 cumulative GPA and 24 semester hours are required to retain scholarship. Awarded every year. Award may be used only at sponsoring institution.
Contact: Office of Admissions, 2801 South University, Little Rock, AR 72204, (501) 569-3127.

2798 Entrepreneurship Contest Scholarship

Johnson & Wales University
8 Abbott Park Place
Providence, RI 02903
(401) 598-1000, (401) 598-1040 (fax)
admissions@jwu.edu
http://jwu.edu
Maximum award: $5,000
Deadline: January
College level: Freshman
Criteria: Selection is based upon Entrepreneurship Contest. Minimum 2.75 GPA is required to retain scholarship. Awarded every year. Award may be used only at sponsoring institution.
Contact: Kristine McNamara, Director of Admissions, (401) 598-1050.

2799 FFTA Scholarship Competition

Foundation of Flexographic Technical Association (FFTA)
Scholarship Committee
900 Marconi Avenue
Ronkonkoma, NY 11779
(516) 737-6020, (516) 737-6813 (fax)
Average award: $1,000
Maximum award: $1,200
Minimum award: $500
Deadline: Varies
College level: Freshman, Sophomore, Junior, Senior
Majors/Fields: Flexography
Criteria: Recipient must reapply for renewal. Awarded every year.
Contact: Jennifer Leonovich, Educational Coordinator.

2800   Financial Grant

Long Island University, C.W. Post Campus
Route 25A
Brookville, NY 11548
(516) 299-2338, (516) 299-2137 (fax)
admissions@collegehall.liunet.edu
http://www.liunet.edu
Maximum award: $2,500
Deadline: May 15
College level: Freshman
Criteria: Applicant must be enrolled full time. Financial need is considered. Awarded every year. Award may be used only at sponsoring institution.
Contact: Financial Aid Office, 720 Northern Boulevard, Brookville, NY 11548.

2801   Half Hollow Hills Central School District Scholarship

Five Towns College
305 North Service Road
Dix Hills, NY 11746-6055
(516) 424-7000
Maximum award: $6,000
Number of awards: 2
Deadline: Early application is recommended
College level: Freshman
Criteria: Applicant must be a recent graduate of the Half Hollow Hills Central School District, have a recommendation from the superintendent, and be accepted for admission as a full-time student. Awarded every year. Award may be used only at sponsoring institution.
Contact: Financial Aid Office.

2802   Half Spouse Tuition Grant

Colorado Christian University
180 South Garrison Street
Lakewood, CO 80226
(303) 202-0100, extension 117, (303) 274-7560 (fax)
drwilliams@ccu.edu
http://www.ccu.edu
Average award: $3,165
Maximum award: $4,760
Minimum award: $510
Number of awards: 13
Deadline: None
College level: Freshman, Sophomore, Junior, Senior
Criteria: Applicant and spouse both must be enrolled full time. Awarded every year. Award may be used only at sponsoring institution.
Contact: Kent McGowan, Director of Financial Aid.

2803   John E. Godwin Flight Training Scholarship

National Air Transportation Foundation
4226 King Street
Alexandria, VA 22302
(703) 845-9000, (703) 845-8176 (fax)
Average award: $2,500
Number of awards: 1
Deadline: November 15
College level: Flight trainee
Majors/Fields: Aviation
Criteria: Awarded every year.
Contact: Tracy Thompson, Manager, Administration.

2804   Law Enforcement Officers Dependents' Scholarship

Arkansas Department of Higher Education
114 East Capitol
Little Rock, AR 72201
(501) 324-9300
Average award: Comprehensive tuition
Deadline: August 1
College level: Sophomore, Junior, Senior
Criteria: Applicant must be a resident of Arkansas who is the dependent child or spouse of a person who was killed or permanently disabled in the line of duty as a law enforcement officer in the State of Arkansas or of certain Highway and Transportation Department employees. Applicant must be under age 23.
Contact: Assistant Coordinator of Student Financial Aid.

2805   Legacy Scholarship

Milwaukee School of Engineering
1025 North Broadway
Milwaukee, WI 53202-3109
(800) 332-6763, (414) 277-7475 (fax)
goran@admin.msoe.edu
www.msoe.edu
Average award: $2,500
Number of awards: 1
Deadline: February 1
College level: Freshman
Criteria: Applicant must be the daughter, son, granddaughter, or grandson or an alumnus and have a minimum 2.5 GPA. Recommendation is suggested. Interview is required. Awarded every year. Award may be used only at sponsoring institution.
Contact: Sue Minzlaff, Financial Aid Office, (414) 277-7222, minzlaff@admin.msoe.edu.

2806   Liberty Assistance Grant

Liberty University
1971 University Boulevard
Lynchburg, VA 24502-2269
(800) 543-5317
Average award: $3,000
Maximum award: $4,000
Minimum award: $1,000
Number of awards: 900
Deadline: August 1 and January 1
College level: Freshman
Criteria: Applicant must demonstrate Christian character and have substantial financial need. Satisfactory academic progress and financial need are required to retain scholarship. Awarded every year. Award may be used only at sponsoring institution.
Contact: Admissions Representative.

2807   Lillie Hawkins Floyd Trust Scholarship

Clemson University
G-01 Sikes Hall
Clemson, SC 29634-5123
(803) 656-2280
Average award: $2,500
Number of awards: 3
Deadline: March 1
College level: Freshman, Sophomore, Junior, Senior
Criteria: Applicant must have a minimum 2.5 GPA, be a single student, and demonstrate financial need. Recipient must remain unmarried to retain scholarship. Awarded every year. Award may be used only at sponsoring institution.
Contact: Marvin Carmichael, Director of Financial Aid.

2808 Lincoln Technical Institute Scholarship

Boys and Girls Clubs of Chicago
625 West Jackson Boulevard, Suite 300
Chicago, IL 60661
(312) 627-2700, (312) 648-5628 (fax)
Average award: $14,000
Number of awards: 2
College level: Freshman
Majors/Fields: Auto/diesel, automotive technician, diesel technician
Criteria: Applicant must be a current or former member of the Boys & Girls Clubs of Chicago. Applicant must submit application, a copy of high school diploma or GED certificate, and recommendation. Award may be used only at Lincoln Technical Institute.
Contact: Mary Ann Mahon-Huels, Vice President of Operations.

2809 Lippincott & Margulies Summer Internship

Smithsonian Institution Cooper-Hewitt Museum Internships
2 East 91st Street
New York, NY 10128
Average award: $2,500
Number of awards: 1
Deadline: March 31
College level: Freshman, Sophomore, Junior, Senior, Graduate
Majors/Fields: Design, design history/criticism
Criteria: Internship encourages promising young students to explore careers in the museum profession. Internship runs annually from the second week of June through the second week of August. Housing is not provided.
Contact: Intern Coordinator, Cooper-Hewitt, National Design Museum.

2810 Maryland Association of Private Career Schools Scholarship

Maryland Association of Private Career Schools
584 Bellerive Drive, Suite 3D
Annapolis, MD 21401
(410) 974-4473, (410) 757-3809 (fax)
mapcs@mdassn.com
Average award: $1,000
Maximum award: $5,000
Minimum award: $500
Number of awards: 30
Deadline: March 31
College level: Freshman
Majors/Fields: Vocational/technical
Criteria: Applicant must be a Maryland high school graduate planning to attend a private career school in Maryland. Selection is based upon academic qualifications. Awarded every year. Award may be used only at trade schools in Maryland.
Contact: Karen Koyne, Scholarship Coordinator.

2811 Merit Awards Program

University of North Carolina at Greensboro
1000 Spring Garden Street
Greensboro, NC 27412
(910) 334-5702
Average award: $3,500
Maximum award: $12,000
Minimum award: $2,500
Number of awards: 40
Deadline: January 15
College level: Freshman
Criteria: Some awards are for performing arts and business; others are for all majors. Minimum 3.0 GPA is required to retain scholarship. Awarded every year. Award may be used only at sponsoring institution.
Contact: Tolly D. Nagy, Director of Financial Aid.

2812 Mother Mary Raymond Scholarship

Dominican College of San Rafael
50 Acacia Avenue
San Rafael, CA 94901-2298
(415) 485-3204, (415) 485-3205 (fax)
enroll@dominican.edu
http://www.dominican.edu
Average award: $1,192
Maximum award: $3,109
Minimum award: $200
Number of awards: 44
Deadline: None
College level: Relatives of alumni/ae at any grade level
Criteria: Scholarship is renewable. Awarded every year. Award may be used only at sponsoring institution.
Contact: Susan Gutierrez, Director of Financial Aid.

2813 Need-Based Scholarship

Tulane University
6823 St. Charles Avenue
New Orleans, LA 70118
(504) 865-5723
Average award: $12,000
Maximum award: $18,000
Minimum award: $100
Number of awards: 500
Deadline: March 1
College level: Freshman, Sophomore, Junior, Senior
Criteria: Applicant must demonstrate financial need. Minimum 2.3 GPA, full-time enrollment, and financial need are required to retain scholarship. Awarded every year. Award may be used only at sponsoring institution.
Contact: Thomas P. Lovett, Director of Financial Aid.

2814 Need-Based Scholarships

Lafayette College
Easton, PA 18042-1770
(610) 250-5055, (610) 250-5355 (fax)
mccartyb@lafayette.edu
http://www.lafayette.edu/info/finaid
Average award: $8,621
Maximum award: $28,560
Minimum award: $500
Number of awards: 306
Deadline: January 1 (admissions); February 15 (financial aid)
College level: Freshman, Sophomore, Junior, Senior
Criteria: Scholarship is renewable. Award may be used only at sponsoring institution.
Contact: Barry W. McCarty, Director of Student Financial Aid, 107 Markle Hall, Easton, PA 18042-1777, mccartyb@lafayette.edu.

2815 P.A.L. Scholarship

Piedmont College
165 Central Avenue
Demorest, GA 30535
(706) 778-3000
Average award: $1,000
Maximum award: $2,500
Minimum award: $500
Number of awards: 25
Deadline: None
College level: Freshman, Sophomore, Junior, Senior
Criteria: Applicant must be a nontraditional student enrolled in Program for Adult Learners. Selection is based upon financial need. Renewal is based upon need. Awarded every year. Award may be used only at sponsoring institution.
Contact: Kenneth L. Owen, Director of Financial Aid.

2816   Pioneers of Flight Scholarship

National Air Transportation Foundation
4226 King Street
Alexandria, VA 22302
(703) 845-9000, (703) 845-8176 (fax)
Average award: $2,500
Number of awards: 4
Deadline: November 15
College level: Sophomore, Junior
Majors/Fields: Aviation
Criteria: Renewable is recipient maintains satisfactory academic performance. Awarded every year.
Contact: Tracy Thompson, Manager, Administration.

2817   Presidential Scholarship

Oakland University
101 North Foundation Hall
Rochester, MI 48309-4401
(810) 370-3360, (810) 370-4462 (fax)
Average award: $6,000
Number of awards: 2
Deadline: February 1
College level: Freshman
Criteria: Applicant must live in the residence halls on campus. Minimum 3.3 GPA is required to retain scholarship. Awarded every year. Award may be used only at sponsoring institution.
Contact: Stacy M. Penkala, Assistant Director of Admissions.

2818   Presidential Tuition Scholarship

National University
4025 Camino del Rio South
San Diego, CA 92108-4194
(619) 563-7175
Maximum award: $2,500
Number of awards: 40
Deadline: None
College level: Junior, Senior
Criteria: Applicant must be a U.S. citizen or eligible noncitizen, be an undergraduate working toward first bachelor's degree, have completed at least 56 credit hours at an accredited institution, have a minimum 2.3 GPA, be eligible for financial aid with an annual family income of $18,000 or less or annual single income of $11,000 or less, and be one of the following: educationally and economically disadvantaged and member of a minority that has been historically underrepresented in colleges, a single parent with demonstrated financial need, or certifiably handicapped with demonstrated financial need. Scholarship is renewable. Awarded every year. Award may be used only at sponsoring institution.
Contact: George S. Ford, Director of Scholarship Office.

2819   Raymond H. Kiefer Scholarship

University of Toledo
Financial Aid Office
Toledo, OH 43606-3390
(419) 537-2056
Average award: $2,500
Deadline: January 28
College level: Freshman
Criteria: Applicant must enroll full time and demonstrate financial need. Awarded every year. Award may be used only at sponsoring institution.
Contact: Scholarships.

2820   Regents Registration Fee Scholarship

Arizona State University
Tempe, AZ 85287-0412
(602) 965-4045
Average award: $1,528
Number of awards: 3,150
Deadline: March 15
College level: Freshman, Sophomore, Junior, Senior, Graduate, Doctoral
Criteria: Selection is based upon a combination of financial need, racial or ethnic background, gender, academic qualifications, field of interest, physical disability, and organizational affiliation. Scholarship is renewable. Awarded every year. Award may be used only at sponsoring institution.
Contact: Frank Granillo, Scholarship Director.

2821   Regents Scholarship

University of California, San Diego
Department of Financial Aid
9500 Gilman Drive
La Jolla, CA 92093
(619) 534-3263
Average award: $3,474
Maximum award: $7,462
Minimum award: $3,013
Number of awards: 51
Deadline: November 30
College level: Freshman, Junior
Criteria: Minimum 3.0 GPA and 36 units per academic year are required to retain scholarship. Awarded every year. Award may be used only at sponsoring institution.
Contact: Debi Fidler, Scholarship Coordinator.

2822   Regents Tuition Scholarship

Arizona State University
Tempe, AZ 85287-0412
(602) 965-4045
Average award: $5,406
Number of awards: 830
Deadline: March 15
College level: Freshman, Sophomore, Junior, Senior, Graduate, Doctoral
Criteria: Selection is based upon a combination of financial need, academic merit, racial or ethnic background, gender, field of interest, and organizational affiliation. Scholarship is renewable. Awarded every year. Award may be used only at sponsoring institution.
Contact: Frank Granillo, Scholarship Director.

2823   Scholarship

St. Mary's College of Maryland
St. Mary's City, MD 20686
(301) 862-0300
Maximum award: $6,000
Number of awards: 30
Deadline: March 1
College level: Freshman
Criteria: Scholarship is renewable. Awarded when available. Award may be used only at sponsoring institution.
Contact: Financial Aid Office.

2824   Service Award

University of Indianapolis
1400 East Hanna Avenue
Indianapolis, IN 46227-3697
(317) 788-3217
Maximum award: $2,500
Number of awards: 109
Deadline: None
College level: Freshman
Criteria: Applicant must demonstrate commitment to community service. Minimum "C" grade average is required to retain scholarship. Awarded every year. Award may be used only at sponsoring institution.
Contact: Admissions Office, (317) 788-3216.

2825 Southern California Strawberry Growers Scholarship

California State Polytechnic University, Pomona
3801 West Temple Avenue
Pomona, CA 91768-4019
(909) 869-3700
Average award: $2,500
Number of awards: 1
Criteria: Award may be used only at sponsoring institution.
Contact: Crystal Steele, Financial Aid Counselor.

2826 Talent Scholarship

Adelphi University
South Avenue
Garden City, NY 11530
(516) 877-3050
Average award: $2,000
Maximum award: $5,000
Minimum award: $1,000
Number of awards: 30
Deadline: None
College level: Freshman, Sophomore, Junior, Senior
Criteria: Recipient must major in the field in which the scholarship is given. Awarded every year. Award may be used only at sponsoring institution.
Contact: Scholarships.

2827 Trustee Scholarship

Five Towns College
305 North Service Road
Dix Hills, NY 11746-6055
(516) 424-7000
Average award: Full tuition
Deadline: Early application is recommended
College level: Freshman
Criteria: Applicant must be an economically disadvantaged student from a school participating in the Five Towns College Partnership Project and be recommended by school principal. Awarded every year. Award may be used only at sponsoring institution.
Contact: Financial Aid Office.

2828 University of Nevada-Reno General Scholarship

University of Nevada–Reno
Scholarship Office (076)
Reno, NV 89557
(702) 784-4661
Average award: $1,000
Maximum award: $2,500
Minimum award: $250
Number of awards: 1800
Deadline: March 1
College level: Freshman, Sophomore, Junior, Senior
Criteria: Some awards are renewable. Awarded every year. Award may be used only at sponsoring institution.
Contact: Thomas Reed, Director of Scholarships.

2829 Volunteer Service Scholarship

John Carroll University
20700 North Park Boulevard
Cleveland, OH 44118
(216) 397-4248
Average award: $3,000
Number of awards: 10
Deadline: April 1
College level: Freshman
Criteria: Applicant must demonstrate commitment to volunteerism and community service. Application with essay and recommendation required; FAFSA recommended. Renewal is based upon recommendation of renewal committee. Awarded every year. Award may be used only at sponsoring institution.
Contact: Office of Admission.

2830 Young Women of America Award

Columbia College
1001 Rogers Street
Columbia, MO 65216
(800) 231-2391
Maximum award: $5,500
Number of awards: No limit
Deadline: None
College level: Freshman
Criteria: Applicant must be a local Young Woman contestant in Missouri ($2,000), a local Young Woman winner in Missouri ($2,500), a runner-up in a state pageant ($2,500), a State's Young Woman ($3,500), or America's Young Woman ($5,500). Awarded every year. Award may be used only at sponsoring institution.
Contact: Financial Aid Office, (800) 231-2391, extension 7361.

2831 Xerox Technical Minority Scholarship Fund

Xerox Corporation
800 Phillips Road
Building 205-99E
Webster, NY 14580
(716) 422-7689, (716) 422-7726 (fax)
cheryl_l_williams@wb.xerox.com
Average award: $1,400
Maximum award: $4,000
Minimum award: $500
Number of awards: 70
Deadline: September 15
College level: Freshman, Sophomore, Junior, Senior, Graduate, Doctoral
Majors/Fields: Technology
Criteria: Applicant must be a minority student enrolled in a technical degree program. Award is not open to Xerox Corporation employees, or their spouses and children. Recipient must reapply for renewal.
Contact: Cheryl L. Williams, Human Resources Assistant.

Index of Majors

Index of Criteria

Business/Corporate Affiliation

State Farm Insurance, 2062
Stone Container Corporation, 2063
Teaching, 554
Texaco, 2064
Thomasville Furniture Industries Inc., 2065
Tolaram Polymers, 2037
Travel Industry, 191
Washington Post, 2066
Waukeska Engine Division, 2038
Weyerhaeuser Company, 2067
Youth Authority, 2630

City/County of Residence

Club Affiliation

Gender/Marital Status

Handicapped Student

Military Affiliation

National Merit Status

Race/Ethnicity

Religious Affiliation

Sports

State/Country of Residence

Union Affiliation

Index of Scholarships

C

E

F

K

L

O

P

U

X

Y

Z